WEST'S
INTERMEDIATE
ACCOUNTING

WEST'S
INTERMEDIATE
ACCOUNTING

General Editor
VINCENT C. BRENNER
Louisiana State University

Contributing Authors

VINCENT C. BRENNER
Louisiana State University

JONATHAN DAVIES
Coopers & Lybrand

MICHAEL A. DIAMOND
California State University, Los Angeles

BART P. HARTMAN
Louisiana State University

M. HERSCHEL MANN
Texas Tech University

THOMAS A. RATCLIFFE
Texas Tech University

JAMES H. SCHEINER
University of Tennessee, Knoxville

RICHARD E. ZIEGLER
University of Illinois at Urbana-Champaign

West Publishing Company
St. Paul   New York   Los Angeles   San Francisco

A study guide has been developed to assist you in mastering concepts presented in this text. The study guide reinforces concepts by presenting them in condensed concise form. Additional illustrations and examples are also included. The study guide is available from your local bookstore under the title, *Study Guide to Accompany West's Intermediate Accounting*, prepared by J. David Spiceland.

Cover design: Taly Design Group, Minneapolis
Interior design: Parallelogram/Marsha Cohen, New York
Composition: York Graphic Services, Inc.

Credits

Material from Uniform CPA Examination Questions and Unofficial Answers, copyright © 1957, 1967–1981 by the American Institute of Certified Public Accountants, Inc., is reprinted or adapted with permission.
pages 60–61 Exhibit 3-2 Courtesy of Puritan Fashions Corporation
pages 202–203 Exhibit 6-10 Courtesy of General Motors Corporation; Eastern Airlines, Inc.; and Ford Motor Company
page 249 Exhibit 7-9 Warner Communications, Inc. Annual Report 1980
page 250 Exhibit 7-10 Courtesy of Rockwell International Corporation
page 288 Exhibit 8-11 Courtesy of Ogden Corporation
page 289 Exhibit 8-12 Courtesy of Champion International Corporation

(continued following Index)

Copyright © 1983 By WEST PUBLISHING CO.

50 West Kellogg Boulevard
P.O. Box 3526
St. Paul, Minnesota 55165

Library of Congress Cataloging in Publication Data

Main entry under title:
West's intermediate accounting.
  Includes index.
  1. Accounting. I. Brenner, Vincent C.
HF5635.W5225 1983   657'.044   82-21797
ISBN 0-314-63307-3

To our all too often neglected families

Contents

Preface   **xxi**

1. The Development of Generally Accepted Accounting Principles   1

Historical Development of Accounting   2
Primary Uses of Accounting Information   3
The Need for Generally Accepted Accounting Principles   5
Developing Promulgated GAAP   6
   Profession Promulgated GAAP   *6*
   Government Promulgated GAAP   *13*
Developing Unpromulgated GAAP   15
   American Institute of Certified Public Accountants
   (AICPA)   *15*
   American Accounting Association (AAA)   *16*
   Other Sources of Unpromulgated GAAP   *16*

2. Underlying Theory of Financial Accounting   21

Qualitative Objectives   22
   Decision Maker Characteristics   *23*
   Benefits vs. Costs   *23*
   Understandable Information   *24*
   Useful Information   *24*
   Comparability   *26*
   Materiality   *26*
Quantitative Objectives   27
   Wealth Measurement   *27*
   Income Measurement   *27*
Assumptions Made to Simplify Problems   28
   Unit of Measure Assumption   *28*
   Going Concern Assumption   *29*
   Separate Entity Assumption   *30*
   Time Period Assumption   *30*
   User Needs Assumption   *31*
Principles Based Upon Simplifying Assumptions   31
   Historical Cost Principle   *31*
   Revenue Realization Principle   *32*
   Matching Principle   *34*
   Comparability Principle   *36*

Full Disclosure Principle   *37*
Principle of Substance Over Form   *37*
Modifying Conventions   38
Materiality   *38*
Conservatism   *38*

3. Income Determination and Reporting   49

Nature of Income Reporting   50
Emphasis on Income   *50*
Estimation of Income   *52*
Realization vs. Recognition of Revenues   *54*
Realization Principle   *54*
Current Operating vs. All-Inclusive Income   *57*
Disclosure of Unusual Items   58
Extraordinary Items   *59*
Prior Period Adjustments   *61*
Discontinued Operations   *62*
Alternative Concepts of Income   62
Cash Concept   *62*
Discounted Present Value   *63*
Market Value Concepts   *63*

4. The Accounting Process and Basic Financial Statements   74

The Accounting Model   75
The Accounting Cycle   78
Collecting Data   *78*
Recording Data   *78*
Posting Data   *81*
Adjusting Data   *87*
Closing the Books   *94*
Computerized Accounting Systems   97
The Basic Financial Statements   97
The Balance Sheet   *98*
The Income Statement   *103*
Statement of Changes in Financial Position   *105*
Statement of Retained Earnings   *107*
Supplementary Financial Information   *108*
Appendix: The Worksheet System   111

5. Present Value Concepts   132

Time Value of Money   133
Interest   135
Future Value of a Single Sum   137

Present Value of a Single Sum   139
Future Value of an Annuity   141
    Ordinary Annuity   *141*
    Annuity Due   *143*
Present Value of an Annuity   144
    Ordinary Annuity   *145*
    Annuity Due   *146*
Deferred Annuities   148
Interpolation   149
Other Time Value of Money Considerations   149
Summary of Accounting Applications   151
List of Symbols Used in Chapter   152

6. Cash and Receivables   169

Nature and Composition of Cash   170
    Cash in Bank Accounts   *170*
    Cash on Hand   *171*
    Restricted Cash   *173*
Control of Cash   173
    Internal Control   *173*
    Elements of Internal Control   *174*
Bank Reconciliations   176
    Standard Bank Reconciliations   *177*
    Four-Column Bank Reconciliations   *181*
Imprest Cash Systems   181
Nature and Types of Receivables   183
Trade Accounts Receivable   184
    Trade Discounts   *185*
    Cash Discounts   *186*
    Other Deductions   *187*
Accounting for Uncollectible Accounts   188
    Percentage of Sales Method   *189*
    Percentage of Receivables Method   *190*
    Comparison of the Sales and Receivables Methods   *193*
Notes Receivable   194
    Valuation   *194*
    Disclosure   *196*
Using Receivables to Generate Cash   196
    Pledging of Receivables   *196*
    Assignment of Trade Receivables   *197*
    Sale of Trade Receivables   *198*
    Factoring Trade Receivables   *198*
    Accepting Credit Cards   *199*
    Discounting Notes Receivable   *199*
    Other Receivables   *201*
Financial Statement Disclosures   201
Appendix: Four-Column Bank Reconciliations   206

7. Investments in Stock   223

Determining the Appropriate Accounting Method   224
  Controlling Interest   *224*
  Significant Influence   *226*
  Lack of Significant Influence   *227*
Recording the Investment at the Date of Acquisition   227
Accounting for Equity Investments Subsequent to Acquisition   228
  The Cost Method   *229*
  The Market Method   *229*
  The Lower of Cost or Market Method   *230*
  The Equity Method   *237*
Financial Statement Disclosures   247
  Lower of Cost or Market Method   *247*
  Equity Method   *251*

8. Inventories—General Issues   264

Classifications of Inventory   266
  Raw Materials Inventories   *266*
  Work-in-Process Inventories   *266*
  Finished Goods Inventory   *267*
  Supplies Inventory   *267*
  Merchandise Inventory   *267*
The Physical Composition of the Inventory—What to Include   269
  Merchandise in Transit   *269*
  Merchandise on Consignment   *270*
  Installment Sales   *270*
Periodic and Perpetual Inventory Systems   270
Valuation of Inventories—General Principles   273
  Purchase Discounts   *275*
  Trade Discounts   *276*
  Interest Costs   *276*
  Effects of Inventory Errors   *276*
Valuation of Inventories—Exceptions to the Cost Principle   279
  Lower of Cost or Market   *279*
  Long-Term Construction Contracts   *286*
  Relative Sales Value Method   *286*
  Purchase Commitments   *287*
Disclosure Requirements for Inventories   287
Appendix: Accounting for Long-Term Construction Contracts   292

9. Inventories—Cost Flow Methods   314

Physical Flow and Cost Flow   315
The Basic Cost Flow Methods   316
  Specific Identification   *316*
  First-In, First-Out (FIFO)   *317*

Last-In, First-Out (LIFO)   *319*
Average Cost Method   *323*
Comparison of Basic Cost Flow Methods   *325*
Other Valuation Methods   328
Base Stock Method   *328*
Standard Cost System   *329*
Variable or Direct Costing   *330*
LIFO Complexities   330
Dollar-Value LIFO   *330*
Price Index Used   *334*
Other LIFO Problems   *336*
Disclosure   338

10. Inventories—Cost Estimation Methods   354

The Gross Profit Method   355
Assumptions Underlying the Gross Profit Method   *356*
Application of the Gross Profit Method   *356*
Calculation of Gross Profit Percentages   *359*
Comprehensive Example of Gross Profit Method   *361*
Evaluation of the Gross Profit Method   *361*
Retail Inventory Method   362
Assumptions of Retail Method   *362*
Basic Illustration and Terminology   *362*
Application of the Retail Inventory Method   *365*
Dollar-Value Retail LIFO Method   370
Computing Inventory Cost Using Retail LIFO   *372*
Computing Inventory Cost Using Dollar-Value Retail
LIFO Method   *373*
Disclosure   383

11. Plant Assets—Acquisition, Use, and Disposition   397

Valuation of Property, Plant, and Equipment   398
Initial Acquisition Cost   399
Cost of Land   *399*
Cost of Buildings   *400*
Cost of Equipment   *401*
Cost of Self-Constructed Assets   *401*
Interest Costs   *402*
Method of Asset Acquisition   405
Acquisition for Cash   *405*
Acquisition under Deferred Payment Plans   *405*
Acquisition with Equity Securities   *407*
Acquisition through Exchanges   *408*
Lump Sum Purchases   *412*

Donated Assets 413
Costs Incurred after Acquisition 414
   Maintenance and Repairs 415
   Improvements and Replacements 416
   Reinstallments and Rearrangements 418
   Additions 418
Asset Dispositions 419
   Sale of Plant Assets 419
   Exchanges 420
   Involuntary Conversion 420
   Abandonment 420
Discovery Value and Asset Impairment 420
   Discovery Value 421
   Asset Impairment 421
General Disclosure Requirements 421

12. Plant Assets—Depreciation and Depletion   443

Nature of Depreciation 444
Elements of Depreciation 445
   Cost of the Asset 445
   Salvage Value 445
   Useful Life 445
   Selection of Depreciation Methods 446
Methods of Depreciation 448
   Units of Production Method 448
   Straight-Line Method 449
   Accelerated Methods 449
   Special Depreciation Methods 454
Other Aspects of Depreciation 458
   Depreciation and Replacement Funds 458
   Partial Year Depreciation 458
   Revision of Estimates 460
Investment Credit 461
Depletion 463
Financial Statement Disclosures 465
Appendix: Oil and Gas Accounting 470

13. Intangible Assets   486

Accounting for Intangible Assets 487
   Valuation at Acquisition 487
   Accounting Subsequent to Acquisition 489
Specifically Identifiable Intangible Assets 490
   Patents 490
   Copyrights 492
   Trademarks and Tradenames 492
   Leases 492

Franchises   *493*
Organization Costs   *493*
Deferred Charges   *493*
Research and Development Costs   493
GAAP Relating to Research and Development   *494*
Definition of Research and Development   *494*
Costs Associated with R & D Activities   *496*
Costs Outside the Scope of Statement No. 2   *497*
Goodwill   497
Accounting for Goodwill   *500*
Negative Goodwill   *502*
Financial Management   *503*
Disclosure of Intangibles   505

14. Current Liabilities   527

Definition of Liabilities   528
Classification of Liabilities   529
Valuation of Current Liabilities   529
Determination and Measurement of Current Liabilities   530
Liabilities Definitely Determinable in Amount   530
Accounts Payable   *530*
Trade Notes Payable   *531*
Short-Term Notes Payable   *531*
Current Maturities of Long-Term Debt   *532*
Short-Term Obligations to Be Refinanced   *533*
Dividends Payable   *535*
Collections for Third Parties and Payrolls   535
Sales Taxes   *536*
Payroll Taxes and Employee Withholding Taxes   *536*
Compensated Absences   *538*
Liabilities Conditional on Operations   539
Income Taxes Payable   *539*
Property Taxes Payable   *540*
Bonus Agreements   *542*
Other Conditional Payments   *543*
Contingent Liabilities   543
Accounting for Contingencies   *543*
Contingent Liabilities That Are Accrued   *545*
Contingent Liabilities That Are Not Accrued   *550*
Deposits and Advances from Customers   552
Obligations Arising from Executory Agreement   552
Financial Statement Disclosure Current Liabilities   555

15. Long-Term Liabilities   575

Valuation of Long-Term Liabilities   576
Notes Issued Solely for Cash   *578*
Notes Issued with Unstated Rights or Privileges   *579*

Notes Exchanged for Property, Goods, or Services   *581*
Bonds Payable   584
Accounting for Bonds by the Borrower   588
   Determination of Bond Prices—Premium and Discount   *588*
   Subsequent Entries after Bond Issue Date   *592*
   Issuance of Bonds between Interest Dates   *596*
   Expenses Incurred When Issuing Bonds   *601*
   Bond Sinking Fund Provisions   *602*
Early Extinguishment of Debt   602
   Accounting for Early Extinguishment of Debt   *603*
   The Period in Which the Gain or Loss Is Recognized   *603*
   The Nature of the Gain or Loss   *604*
Accounting for Bonds by the Investor   605
   Accounting for the Acquisition of Bonds   *605*
   Discount and Premium Amortization   *607*
   Sale of Bonds Before the Maturity Date   *609*
Other Forms of Long-Term Debt   609
   Dilutive Debt Securities   *610*
   Mortgages Payable   *610*
   Short-Term Debt Expected to Be Refinanced   *610*
Troubled Debt Restructurings   610
   What Is a Troubled Debt Restructuring?   *611*
   Accounting for Troubled Debt Restructurings   *612*
   Summary of Troubled Debt Transactions   *616*
Financial Statement Presentation of Long-Term Liabilities   618
Appendix: Accounting for Serial Bonds   627

16. Accounting for Income Taxes   **646**

Differences between Pretax Accounting Income and
Taxable Income   647
   Permanent Differences   *648*
   Timing Differences   *649*
The Need for Interperiod Income Tax Allocation   650
   Procedures for Applying Income Tax Allocation   *654*
   Partial Versus Comprehensive Allocation   *655*
   Differing Methods of Income Tax Allocation   *658*
Applications of the Deferred Method of Comprehensive
Income Tax Allocation in Practice   661
   Individual Item Basis   *662*
   Group-of-Similar-Items-Basis   *662*
   The With and Without Method   *666*
Accounting for Net Operating Losses   668
   Accounting for Loss Carrybacks   *669*
   Accounting for Loss Carryforwards   *670*
   The Effect of Timing Differences   *673*
Financial Statement Disclosures Related to Interperiod
Income Tax Allocation   675
   APB Opinion No. 11 Disclosures   *675*
   SEC Required Disclosure—ASR No. 149   *678*

17. Accounting for Pension Costs   **701**

Nature of Pension Plans   702
Historical Development of Pension GAAP   704
Pension Accounting   705
   Accounting for Defined Contribution Plans   *706*
   Accounting for Defined Benefit Plans   *706*
Actuarial Gains and Losses   717
Accounting and Reporting by Defined Benefit Plans   718
Disclosure   719

18. Accounting for Leases   **733**

The Development of Authoritative Lease Accounting Literature   734
Lease Classification Criteria   735
Lessee Accounting and Reporting   737
   Capital Leases   *737*
   Operating Leases   *738*
Lessor Accounting and Reporting   741
   Capital Leases—Sales-Type   *741*
   Capital Leases—Direct Financing Type   *743*
   Operating Leases   *746*
Accounting for Initial Direct Costs   746
Accounting for Subleases   747
   Accounting by the Original Lessor   *748*
   Accounting by the Original Lessee (Sublessor)   *748*
Real Estate Leases   749
   Leases Involving Land Only   *750*
   Leases Involving Land and Building   *750*
   Leases Involving Equipment and Real Estate   *752*
   Leases Involving Only Part of a Building   *753*
   Profit Recognition of Sales-Type Leases of Real Estate   *753*
Accounting for Sales with Leasebacks   754
Financial Statement Disclosures   757
Appendix: Accounting for Leveraged Leases   765

19. Stockholders' Equity—Issuance and Reacquisition   **783**

Forms of Business Organization   784
   Advantages of the Corporate Form   *784*
   Forming a Corporation   *785*
   Nature of the Capital Stock   *786*
   Par and No-Par Stocks   *787*
Common Stock   787
Preferred Stock   788
   Rights of Preferred Stock   *788*
   Limitations of Preferred Stock   *792*
Accounting for Contributed Capital   793

Accounting for Capital Stock   794
Stock Subscriptions   798
Costs of Issuing Stock   801
Reacquisition of Stock—Treasury Stock   801
Cost Method   802
Par Value Method   805
Donated Treasury Stock   808
Retirement of Treasury Stock   809
Restriction of Retained Earnings for Treasury Stock   810
Other Retirements of Stock   811
Financial Statement Disclosures of Contributed Capital   812

20. Stockholders' Equity—Retained Earnings and Dividends

831

Functions of Retained Earnings   832
Factors Affecting Dividend Decisions   833
Legality of the Dividend   833
Availability of Cash   833
Contractual Restrictions   834
Dividend Policy   834
Accounting for Dividends   835
Kinds of Dividends   836
Dividends on Treasury Stock   842
Liquidating Dividends   842
Stock Split   843
Ordinary Stock Split   843
Alternative Form of Stock Split   844
Reverse Stock Split   845
Appropriations of Retained Earnings   846
Legal Restriction   846
Contractual Restriction   846
Voluntary Restriction   848
Quasi Reorganizations   849
Disclosure   852

21. Dilutive Securities and Earnings Per Share

871

Dilutive Securities   872
Convertible Debt   872
Debt Issued with Stock Warrants   876
Pervasive Concepts   878
Convertible Preferred Stock   878
Stock Options   879
Disclosure Requirements   883
Earnings Per Share   883
Simple vs. Complex Capital Structures   884

Weighted Average Common Shares   *885*
Simple Capital Structure   *887*
Complex Capital Structure—Introduction   *887*
Primary Earnings Per Share and Common Stock
Equivalents   *889*
Fully Diluted Earnings Per Share   *889*
Convertible Securities   *890*
Stock Options and Warrants   *893*
Contingent Issuances   *901*
Financial Statement Disclosure of EPS   903
Appendix: Comprehensive Earnings Per Share Illustration   907

22. Accounting Changes and Correction of Errors   923

Change in an Accounting Principle   925
General Rules for Accounting Principle Changes   *926*
Exceptions to the General Rules   *932*
Change in an Accounting Estimate   934
Single-Period Estimate Changes   *935*
Multi-Period Estimate Changes   *935*
Combined Estimate-Principle Change   937
Change in a Reporting Entity   939
Correcting Accounting Errors   940
Errors Made and Discovered in the Same Period   *941*
Errors Made and Discovered in Different Periods   *942*
Computational Analysis for Cumulative and Retroactive
Restatement   949
Journal Entry Approach   *949*
Worksheet Approach   *952*
Financial Statement Disclosures   955

23. Reporting Income and Retained Earnings   985

Concept of Income   986
Income Statement Format   989
Single-Step Format   *989*
Multiple-Step Format   *990*
Comparative Income Statements   *992*
Sections of the Income Statement   992
Discontinued Operations   *995*
Extraordinary Items—Overview   *1002*
Accounting Changes—Overview   *1004*
Income Taxes—Overview   *1007*
Earnings Per Share—Overview   *1007*
Prior Period Adjustments—Overview   *1008*
Statement of Retained Earnings   1008
Comprehensive Illustration   1010

24. Balance Sheet Presentations   1029

The Balance Sheet   1030
    Purpose and Usefulness of the Balance Sheet   1031
    Limitations of the Balance Sheet   1031
    Classifications in the Balance Sheet   1031
Disclosure of Financial Information   1036
    Note 1. Summary of Significant Accounting Policies   1036
    Note 2. Accounts Receivable   1039
    Note 3. Inventories   1039
    Notes 4 and 5. Short- and Long-Term Debt   1039
    Note 6. Federal and Foreign Income Taxes   1042
    Note 7. Retirement Plans   1042
    Notes 8, 9, 10. Equity Financing   1042
    Notes 11 and 12. Interest Capitalized and Foreign Exchange   1043
    Other Footnotes   1043
Segment Reporting   1043
    Identification of a Reportable Segment   1049
    Disclosure   1055
    Evaluation   1055
Interim Reporting   1056
    Requirements of APB Opinion No. 28   1057
    Requirements of FASB Statement No. 3   1060
    Requirements of FASB Interpretation No. 18   1061
    Evaluation   1061
Appendix: Ogden Corporation and Subsidiaries Financial
Statements   1064

25. Statement of Changes in Financial Position   1087

Evolution of the Statement of Changes in Financial Position   1088
Measuring Changes in Financial Position   1089
Preparing the Statement of Changes in Financial Position   1091
Worksheet Approach—Working Capital Basis   1100
    Worksheet Approach—Underlying Foundation   1100
    Worksheet Approach—Format and Procedures   1101
    Special Problem Areas   1108
Comprehensive Illustration: Worksheet Approach—Working
Capital Basis   1119
Statement of Changes in Financial Position—Cash Basis   1126
    Comparison of Procedures for Cash and Working Capital   1126
    Computing Cash Flows   1127
Financial Statement Disclosures   1130
Appendix: The T-Account Approach   1135

26. Financial Reporting and Changing Prices   1171

Types of Price Changes   1172
    General Price-Level versus Specific Price-Level Changes   1172

*The Relationship Between General Price Changes and
Specific Price Changes*   1173
Problems with Financial Statements Not Adjusted for
Price Changes   1175
*Limitations of Financial Statements Not Adjusted for
General Price Changes*   1176
*Limitations of Financial Statements Not Adjusted for
Specific Price Changes*   1176
*Limitations of Financial Statements Not Adjusted for
Both General and Specific Prices*   1177
Official Pronouncements Concerning Accounting for
Price Changes   1177
Developments Since the 1960s   1178
Development of Current Value Accounting   1178
The Constant Dollar Accounting Model   1179
Monetary and Nonmonetary Items   1180
Purchasing Power Gains and Losses on Net Monetary Items   1180
Restating Nonmonetary Assets and Liabilities   1181
Restating Nonmonetary Items   1182
Restating Income Statement Items   1182
Constant Dollar Restatement Procedures—Comprehensive
Illustration   1183
Monetary Assets and Liabilities   1183
Nonmonetary Items   1185
Restated Balance Sheet   1191
*Restatements of the Income and Retained Earnings
Statements*   1191
Calculation of Purchasing Power Gain or Losses   1191
The Income Statement and Retained Earnings Statement   1195
The Constant Dollar Accounting Model: A Retrospective   1197
The Current Value Model   1198
Present Value of Future Cash Flows   1198
Net Realizable Value   1199
Replacement Cost   1199
Current Cost   1200
The Current Cost Model   1200
The Current Cost Model—A Complete Illustration   1202
Balance Sheet Items   1202
Income Statement Items   1203
The Current Cost/Constant Dollar Model   1210
Balance Sheet   1210
Income Statement Items   1211
Realized Holding Gains and Losses   1212
Unrealized Gains and Losses   1212
FASB *Statement No. 33*—Financial Reporting and
Changing Prices   1216
Application of FASB Statement No. 33   1216
Differences in FASB Procedures   1217
Restatement Procedures Required by FASB Statement No. 33 1218

FASB Disclosures for the Stout Corporation   *1222*

The Future   1223

Appendix: Calculation of Current Cost Depreciation   1233

27. Analysis and Disclosure of Financial Information   **1263**

Ratio Analysis   1264

    Liquidity Measures   *1267*

    Activity Measures   *1268*

    Profitability Measures   *1270*

    Measures of Financial Stability   *1275*

Trend and Percentage Analysis   1277

    Horizontal Analysis   *1277*

    Vertical Analysis   *1280*

Evaluation of Financial Statement Analysis   1282

Glossary   1307

Index   1323

Preface

This text is intended for a full-year course in intermediate accounting. Our goal in writing the text was to provide an up-to-date comprehensive treatment of traditional as well as evolving financial accounting topics. Since we believe it is very important for students to have a text that is up-to-date, we have committed ourselves to biennial editions. We believe the rapidly changing nature of Generally Accepted Accounting Principles necessitates a new edition every other year.

Throughout the text we have tried to present the basic theory underlying each topic as well as acceptable accounting procedures. Because of the increasing emphasis on financial statement disclosures we have set forth separate chapter sections on disclosures where applicable. These sections provide a description of the required disclosures as well as examples from actual annual reports.

We have tried to show how each chapter's material relates to the "real world" so that students can appreciate the relevance of the topic to actual business operations. As an introduction to each chapter, there is a section called "Accounting in the News." This section includes an excerpt from a recent magazine or newspaper article which discusses a current practical problem relating to a topic discussed in the chapter. In addition, some of the chapters include a discussion of the political and socioeconomic pressures that have led to changes in specific accounting principles. Finally, the use of excerpts from actual annual reports helps to relate the chapter material to actual accounting practice and reporting.

The text organization differs from other texts on the market. Other texts provide three to four chapters early in the text that review the accounting process and basic financial statements. Most texts do not again provide an in-depth coverage of the income statement and balance sheet at, or near, the end of the text. We believe that this results in the student completing intermediate accounting with a grasp of the specifics of each topic without an appreciation for how these fit together into a set of meaningful financial statements. In other words, the student sees the trees and not the forest. In this text, we use a single chapter (Chapter 4) to review the accounting process and basic financial statements. The last five chapters in the text give a view of the forest by examining (1) the purpose and content of the various financial statements as well as related disclosures (Chapters 23 through 26), and (2) the usefulness of financial statements in analyzing a company's performance and current financial condition (Chapter 27).

Concept Summaries

This text is unique in that it is the only intermediate text that provides concept summaries. These summaries, which appear at the end of each chapter, provide the student with a concise summary of the major concepts covered in the chapter. The summaries will aid students in their initial comprehension and understanding of the chapter material as well as provide them with a quick reference for review.

Glossary

The text also includes a glossary at the end of the text. The glossary sets forth, in one place, the terms used in the text along with their definitions. The glossary will aid the student in studying the text material and will provide a quick reference to text terms when studying for homework or exams.

Assignment Material

We have provided a comprehensive set of assignment material at the end of each chapter. The material is designed to aid in the student's comprehension of the theoretical as well as the procedural aspects of each topic. Four types of assignment material are provided: questions, discussion problems and cases, exercises, and problems. The questions and discussion material relate mostly to theoretical considerations. The exercises generally involve procedures relating to a single topic in the chapter. The problem material is more complex and comprehensive; this material may relate to theoretical as well as procedural issues for one or more topics presented in the text.

The discussion questions, exercises, and problems include a sampling of items taken from past CPA and CMA exams. These are included to give the student an appreciation for the type and complexity of problem material used in these professional certification exams.

Supplementary Materials

This text is accompanied by a package of supplements intended to aid the student and the instructor. For the student there is a *Study Guide* (prepared by J. David Spiceland of Memphis State University) and a set of *Working Papers*. The *Study Guide* provides the student with a review of the chapter material and problem-type material with solutions to aid in the student's comprehension of the text material. The *Working Papers* provide partially filled-in pages for problem solutions. These are intended to reduce the amount of busy work for the student as well as provide an organized format for problem solutions.

Instructor materials include a *Solutions Manual* (edited by Michael A. Diamond), an *Instructor's Manual* (edited by William K. Carter and Kenneth Peacock, both of the University of Virginia), and overhead projector transparencies for selected problems. The *Solutions Manual* contains solutions to all end-of-chapter assignment material. The *Instructor's Manual* includes lecture outlines for each chapter, a recommended syllabus including chapter problem assignments, a listing of end-of-chapter material by topic, and test and examination questions (including solutions) for each chapter.

Acknowledgments

We would like to express special thanks to our colleagues who have read portions of the book and made numerous valuable suggestions. They are:

Name	*School*
Wayne C. Alderman	*Auburn University*
Terry L. Arndt	*Ball State University*
Robert L. Baker	*University of South Carolina*

David B. Byrd	Southwest Missouri State University
Benny R. Copeland	North Texas State University
Gary M. Cunningham	Virginia Polytechnic Institute
Kent T. Fields	Louisiana State University
James F. Gaertner	University of Notre Dame
Donald E. Garner	Kent State University
Joseph F. Guy	Georgia State University
Jack O. Hall, Jr.	Western Kentucky University
Orville R. Keister, Jr.	University of Akron
Dennis L. Knutson	University of Wisconsin at Eau Claire
Park E. Leathers	Bowling Green State University
Lynn W. Marples	Northeastern University
Charles L. McDonald	University of Florida
Lyle H. McIff	University of Arizona
Arthur C. Nieminsky	California State—Northridge
Russell J. Peterson	University of Iowa
William Max Rexroad	Illinois State University
Rudolph W. Schattke	University of Colorado
J. David Spiceland	Memphis State University
James F. Volkert	Northeastern University
Arnold M. Wright	University of Nevada at Reno
Roland M. Wright	Southern Illinois University

We would also like to express our sincere gratitude to Mary Francois Rockcastle, our copy editor, and to the following individuals at West for their support and dedication to this project: Richard T. Fenton, Sherry H. James, Esther W. Craig, and Marjorie A. Johnson. We also thank the various individuals who typed the manuscript.

Our thanks go also to the numerous graduate students who assisted the authors in preparing their respective chapters, especially Mark Ashley, Matthew Bettenhausen, John Brydels, Allan Chow, Bobby Densford, Caroline Der, Mike Dorman, Rick Goncher, Bruce Hahn, Bill Henry, Craig Holmes, Judi Hora, Randy Humphreys, Mark Lansford, Cheryl Medema, Anne Neilson, Neena Rane, Wayne Rodrigs, Gary Ross, Marlane Rossman, Solmoon Shin, Robert Smith, Alan Swaringen, and Jordan Zoot.

We appreciate the permissions granted by the FASB, the American Institute of CPAs, and the American Accounting Association to quote from their pronouncements and other publications. We also thank the American Institute of CPAs and the Institute of Management Accountants for their permission to make liberal use of materials from their professional certification exams. We appreciate the permission from numerous corporations to use excerpts from their annual reports.

We would also like to thank David Spiceland for preparation of the Study Guide, William K. Carter and Kenneth Peacock for preparation of the Instructor's Manual, and Michael A. Diamond for preparation of the Solutions Manual and Working Papers.

Suggestions and comments from the users of this book are invited.

Baton Rouge, Louisiana
January, 1983

Vincent C. Brenner, Editor

1

The Development of Generally Accepted Accounting Principles

Accounting in the News

Accounting principles in the United States currently are set primarily by the Financial Accounting Standards Board and the Securities and Exchange Commission. The approach to establishing accounting standards varies throughout the world. Worldwide, there are at least 20 national standard-setting organizations or boards, with very little synchronization of activities among them.

From a political perspective, national financial accounting standard setting throughout the world takes four different approaches:

1. The *purely political approach*, as found predominantly in France and West Germany. Here national legislative action decrees accounting standards.
2. The *private, professional approach*, exemplified by Australia, Canada and the United Kingdom. In these cases, financial accounting standards are set and enforced by private professional actions only.
3. The *public/private mixed approach*, for which the U.S. is the leading example and which countries like Japan appear to be emulating. Here standards are basically set by private sector bodies which behave as though they were public agencies and whose standards are enforced through governmental actions.
4. The *broadly mixed system*, like that in the Netherlands, where not only accounting professionals and governmental agencies but also labor unions, industry and trade associations take an active direct hand in setting and enforcing accounting standards.*

*Lane A. Daley and Gerhard G. Mueller, "Accounting in the Arena of World Politics," *Journal of Accountancy*, February 1982, pp. 40 and 41. Copyright © 1982 by the American Institute of Certified Public Accountants, Inc.

This chapter includes a description of the evolution of the accounting standards process in the United States. The process started in the late 1920s and has gone through some major changes since that time.

Over the years the accounting function has been described in a number of different ways. While the image of the accountant has changed greatly, the definition of the accounting process has remained relatively stable. Accounting is defined traditionally as an organized system of gathering and communicating relevant economic information to the users of financial statements.

The theoretical intricacies of this definition will be explored in more detail in Chapter 2. Even after a theoretical analysis of the accounting function is conducted, **generally accepted accounting principles** (GAAP) will be deemed the fundamental body of practical accounting knowledge. The remainder of this chapter discusses the development of the accounting function and the GAAP that define its parameters.

Historical Development of Accounting

Accounting as it is practiced today developed over a period of more than 600 years. Although the developmental process was gradual and evolutionary, there are at least four important stages in the history of accounting that warrant further discussion.

Before the fifteenth century there is an abundance of evidence indicating that some type of formal accounting was practiced. During this time period acounting seems to have been practiced primarily at a personal level; that is, the accounting systems that were in use were aimed at keeping records of personal transactions. The principal exception to the personal nature of early accounting consists of the tax collection records that were maintained for governmental purposes.

There is little evidence of accounting systems oriented toward the production of financial reports for business enterprises during this period. More important, there is little evidence of any consistency in accounting systems. The systems that seem to have been used during this period were as individual as the persons who developed and used them.

In 1494 a book written by a Franciscan monk, Luca Pacioli, was published in Italy. Although Pacioli was a mathematician and the book was concerned principally with mathematics, the work did contain a section on bookkeeping. The Pacioli text was not the first manuscript on bookkeeping, but it generally is recognized as the first printed book on the subject and the first book that attempted to show the interrelationship between mathematics and bookkeeping. In other words, the Pacioli text is viewed as the first comprehensive description of a consistent and broadly applicable system of double-entry bookkeeping. More important, since the Pacioli text became generally available through the print media, its double-entry system became the first system of bookkeeping available for application in general business situations.

After the printing of the Pacioli work, accounting continued to develop toward a greater degree of formalization. During this time there are many examples of formalized accounting systems designed to aid businesses in the management of their activities.

The next major period of accounting development began in 1776 with the publication of Adam Smith's *Wealth of Nations*. This work had a significant impact on the world and helped lead to the Industrial Revolution. Although the effects of the Industrial Revolution on the development of accounting were not felt for a number of years, the effects were substantial.

The Industrial Revolution forced businessmen who had organized their affairs previously as sole-proprietorships and joint ventures to seek means of acquiring massive amounts of capital. Although the proprietors and joint venturers possessed first-hand information about their businesses, the providers of the needed capital, the absentee owners of corporations and stock companies, did not. This new degree of absentee ownership created an enormous need for accountability by management, and an even larger need for accountants to insure that accountability.

The accounting profession in both the United States and England developed as a result of this need for corporate accountability. As the distinction between the managers and the owners of business grew, so did the need for an objective and independent third party, capable of communicating in the language of business. More important, as individuals possessing large amounts of capital were confronted with more potential investment opportunities, the need for consistent and comparable financial information increased. Again, accountants, and the formalized system of financial reporting that they were capable of applying, represented the best available answer to these needs.

In the nineteenth and twentieth centuries, the accounting profession began to receive formal sanction. In the late 1800s and early 1900s, governments in both England and the United States passed statutes that formally recognized the existence of practicing public accountants. Accountants sought to introduce further formalization into their profession by forming societies of practicing public accountants. These formal statutes and societal organizations represented a further attempt on the part of the profession and government to insure that practitioners of public accounting would be capable of providing an economic society with consistent, comparable, and needed financial information.

Primary Uses of Accounting Information

Since accounting is primarily a service function, accountants must be concerned with meeting the needs of those whom they serve. Accounting information must be developed and presented in such a way that it is compatible with the communicative skills and financial sophistication of those who use it. The development of such a system of financial reporting requires that accountants first identify those who will make use of the financial information. The Financial Accounting Standards Board (FASB) has undertaken the task of promulgating a broad set of conceptual statements. More specifically, the *Statement of Financial Accounting*

Concepts No. 1 dealt with the process of identifying the uses to which published financial statement information is put.[1]

Accountants generally assume that financial statements will be used by investors and creditors. Although the individuals who make up these two groups may possess unique skills and information needs, there seems to be a common factor that binds all of them. Each individual who may be classified as either an investor in or creditor of a particular entity is interested in the ability of that entity to generate a cash flow. The investor is interested in whether the entity will be able to pay dividends. These dividends represent part of the investor's *return* for investing his or her resources in the entity, and therefore have a direct effect on the value of the interest that s/he holds in the firm. Likewise, the creditor is interested in the ability of the entity to make cash payments in repayment of resources previously lent to it. If the entity is able to make the required cash payments, the creditor will feel that his or her loan of resources is safe and has retained its value. Conversely, if the entity cannot produce an adequate cash flow, creditors may feel insecure about their extension of credit, and therefore may seek other means of financial protection (e.g., the placement of liens on the firm's property).

Although investors and creditors are the primary users of accounting information, there are others, such as federal, state, and local governments, who make substantial use of financial statements. Since government is charged by society with the responsibility of administering desired regulations, government often turns to accounting for the information needed to apply those regulations to particular institutions. For example, when a regulated public utility asks for a rate increase, the authorized government agency turns to accounting for information concerning the need for such an increase. When government seeks to determine whether a particular transaction is in violation of antitrust laws, the government seeks accounting information regarding the effect of that transaction on the market. When a legislature considers the adoption of a new law, accounting information is used to evaluate the desirability and impact of that new law.

In addition to investors, creditors, and governments, there are other groups that make constant use of accounting information. Labor unions use financial information in the process of negotiating a new contract for their members. Environmental and consumer groups use accounting information in evaluating whether a particular entity has met perceived social obligations. For example, such groups often use accounting information to determine how much an entity has spent on charitable contributions, pollution abatement, and worker safety.

There are virtually endless uses to which accounting information can be put. Yet, it is important to note that accountants rely upon a single system of information gathering and communication to meet all of these needs. Therefore, accountants have been very concerned with the success of that particular system. The system must be capable of gathering all relevant information regarding a particular entity; however, the system also must be able to communicate the important parts of that information set to all divergent users of accounting data. If the system should begin to fail individual groups of data users, the value of accounting would decline substantially.

---

[1] "Objectives of Financial Reporting by Business Enterprises," *Statement of Financial Accounting Concepts No. 1* (Stamford, Conn.: FASB, 1978).

The Need for Generally
Accepted Accounting Principles

Given the fact that accounting is a process of communication, it is subject to the imperfections inherent in all languages. In other words, unless every party to the communicative process assigns exactly the same meaning to each of the symbols used to implement that process, the messages are likely to be miscommunicated and/or misunderstood.

Generally accepted accounting principles are designed to serve as a standardized language of accounting. These principles define how certain events are to be interpreted, how those events are to be expressed in the terminology of accounting, and how a user of the product of accounting—published financial statements—is to interpret the messages contained therein. GAAP—a body of rules concerning how the accounting function is to be applied to specific fact situations—are absolutely necessary if economic society is to avoid the mass confusion that would result from a communication system in which each transmitter and receiver of data were left to devise their own set of rules of interpretation.

A simple example can demonstrate easily both the need for and purpose of GAAP. In 1983 Jackson acquires a building from Pickett. Under the conditions of the contract, Jackson is to have exclusive use of the building for a period of 40 years in exchange for annual payments of $45,000. At the end of the 40-year period, the building is to be returned to Pickett unless Jackson elects to pay Pickett an additional $120,000. If Jackson elects to make the additional payment, Pickett will surrender to Jackson absolute and perpetual title to the building.

There are several possible approaches in interpreting the facts presented above. One approach would be to treat the transaction as a sale of the building from Pickett to Jackson. In this case Jackson's financial statements would show that he owns the building and has a future obligation to Pickett. A second approach would be to treat the transaction as a lease of the building from Pickett to Jackson. In this case Jackson's financial statements would show neither the building nor the obligation. Instead, Pickett's financial statements would report his continued ownership of the building.

If users of financial statements were confronted with each of these varying interpretations of the same fact situation, they would become confused easily. Generally accepted accounting principles are intended to avoid this potential confusion by prescribing the proper method of reporting such situations. In this way GAAP introduce a degree of standardization into financial statements, and thus make those statements more useful to those who need them.

Generally accepted accounting principles can come from two separate sets of sources. The first set of sources produces what can be called **promulgated GAAP,** which consists of the generally accepted accounting principles that have been developed by authoritative bodies, and therefore are binding upon practicing members of the accounting profession.

The second set of sources produces what could be called **unpromulgated GAAP,** which are the generally accepted accounting principles that have been developed by respected bodies and/or individuals, or that have evolved over time. Since the producers of unpromulgated GAAP do not have specific powers delegated to them, practicing accountants are not required to abide by their pronouncements. Instead, unpromulgated GAAP exist, and are applied to fact situations, because they have been applied traditionally, or because they are logical and emanate from recognized experts in the field of financial accounting. A discussion of the process by which each of these forms of GAAP is developed follows.

Developing Promulgated GAAP

As said previously, promulgated GAAP represent the body of generally accepted accounting principles that has been established by organizations with the power to set standards for financial accounting. The key element of promulgated GAAP lies in the authority that has been granted to the particular organization. In general, that authority consists of the power to choose among alternative accounting procedures and to mandate that the selected alternative is the one that should be used.

At present, there are two different types of bodies that promulgate GAAP: profession promulgated GAAP and government promulgated GAAP.

Profession Promulgated GAAP

Since its initial organization, the accounting profession traditionally has established a professional board or committee to supervise the promulgation of GAAP. A discussion of each of the professional organizations that has promulgated GAAP, and the type of statements that have been issued, follows.

American Institute of Certified Public Accountants' Committees.   Almost immediately after the stock market crash of 1929, the accounting profession—through the American Institute of Certified Public Accountants (AICPA)—and the New York Stock Exchange formed a special committee to investigate matters of interest to investors, the accounting profession, and the Exchange. The activities of this special committee were undertaken later by several committees administered by the AICPA.

The Committee on Accounting Procedure (CAP) was organized originally by the AICPA to narrow the areas of differences and inconsistencies in accounting practice, and thus eliminate many of the less than desirable practices that were highlighted by the market crash. During the 20-year period of the Committee's existence, 51 *Accounting Research Bulletins* (ARBs) were issued. These Bulletins recommended improvements that should be made in accounting practice; however, the conclusions expressed in the ARBs were not binding upon members of the profession.

Another AICPA committee, the Committee on Terminology, issued a series of pronouncements that were combined in 1953 into *Accounting Terminology Bulletin No. 1*. This Bulletin consists of AICPA-sanctioned recommendations on improvements in accounting terminology. Again, it should be noted that the conclusions reached in the *Terminology Bulletin* constituted recommendations of the AICPA, and thus were not binding on practicing members of the profession.

Accounting Principles Board (APB).   In 1959 the AICPA undertook a major reorganization of its research function. The purpose of this reorganization was twofold: (1) to provide a means for the development of postulates, principles, and rules of accounting practice; (2) to establish a mechanism for the development of written statements concerning these postulates, principles, and rules.

One part of the reorganization process consisted of the formation of the Accounting Principles Board. The APB, which operated as a direct arm of the AICPA, existed from 1959 until 1973. During its period of operation, the APB issued two types of pronouncements. *Opinions of the Accounting Principles Board* were statements of the Board's position on various issues. *Statements of the Accounting Principles Board* constituted recommendations of the Board that it hoped would be implemented.

Before 1964 the pronouncements of authoritative professional bodies (i.e., the AICPA Committee on Accounting Procedure, the AICPA Committee on Terminology, and the Accounting Principles Board) did not mandate compliance on the part of individual accounting practitioners. Instead, these organizations relied upon the belief that their promulgations would gain general acceptance, and therefore would be used by members of the profession. Obviously, all accountants did not comply with the pronouncements of professional bodies.

Finally, in October, 1964, the AICPA adopted rules requiring that departures from GAAP, as defined by the promulgations of authorized professional bodies, be disclosed in footnotes to the financial statements. This decision had the effect of giving professional pronouncements the authority not present previously. As a result, APB Opinions and CAP Bulletins were deemed to be GAAP and had to be followed whenever an applicable fact situation arose. It should be noted that *Accounting Terminology Bulletin No. 1* and APB Statements were never deemed to be procedural statements requiring mandatory compliance from practitioners.

In 1973 the APB was supplanted by the Financial Accounting Standards Board. The APB was replaced because of certain problems that were inherent in its structure. First, the APB often was considered to be too large a body—with 18 members the Board frequently encountered difficulties that were a direct function of its size. Second, the APB was criticized often because its members were merely part-time employees. Many argued that the job of setting accounting principles should be carried out on a full-time basis. Third, critics said the APB lacked the independence needed by a rule-making body. Since most members of the APB maintained other jobs, it was argued that they often made decisions based upon the effect of the decision on their primary employer. Finally, critics also suggested that the APB represented the accounting profession and not both the profession and the users of financial statements. Since membership on the APB was limited to members of the AICPA (i.e., practicing CPAs), many segments of the business world were not afforded representation in the process of developing accounting principles.

Although these problems resulted in the dissolution of the APB, the Board did issue 31 Opinions. The Opinions continue to constitute GAAP, and thus are binding upon practicing accountants. Exhibit 1-1 provides a list of these Opinions.

Financial Accounting Standards Board (FASB). In July, 1973, the FASB was formed in response to the criticism directed at the prior standards-setting bodies. As currently structured, the FASB is a seven-member body charged with supervising the development of GAAP. The members of the FASB are appointed to full-time positions by the nine-member Financial Accounting Foundation—a body

---

Exhibit 1-1
Opinions of the Accounting Principles Board

Number 1	New Depreciation Guidelines and Rules
Number 2	Accounting for the Investment Credit
Number 3	The Statement of Source and Application of Funds
Number 4	Accounting for the Investment Credit (amending No. 2)
Number 5	Reporting of Leases in Financial Statements of Lessee
Number 6	Status of Accounting Research Bulletins
Number 7	Accounting for Leases in Financial Statements of Lessors
Number 8	Accounting for the Cost of Pension Plans
Number 9	Reporting the Results of Operations
Number 10	Omnibus Opinion—1966
Number 11	Accounting for Income Taxes
Number 12	Omnibus Opinion—1967
Number 13	Amending Paragraph 6 of APB Opinion No. 9, Application to Commercial Banks
Number 14	Accounting for Convertible Debt Issued with Stock Purchase Warrants
Number 15	Earnings Per Share
Number 16	Business Combinations
Number 17	Intangible Assets
Number 18	The Equity Method of Accounting for Investments in Common Stock
Number 19	Reporting Changes in Financial Position
Number 20	Accounting Changes
Number 21	Interest on Receivables and Payables
Number 22	Disclosure of Accounting Policies
Number 23	Accounting for Income Taxes—Special Areas
Number 24	Accounting for Income Taxes—Equity Method Investments
Number 25	Accounting for Stock Issued to Employees
Number 26	Early Extinguishment of Debt
Number 27	Accounting for Lease Transactions by Manufacturer or Dealer Lessors
Number 28	Interim Financial Reporting
Number 29	Accounting for Nonmonetary Transactions
Number 30	Reporting the Results of Operations
Number 31	Disclosure of Lease Commitments by Lessees

---

independent of other professional organizations and responsible for procuring the funds needed for FASB operations. Although the FASB is free to consider any significant financial accounting matter, the Financial Accounting Standards Advisory Council—an organization with approximately 20 members—exists to advise the FASB whenever necessary. At present there are no membership prerequisites that would preclude any of these organizations from having members with diverse backgrounds.

Since its inception the FASB has produced four distinct types of authoritative documents. The first type, *Statements of Financial Accounting Standards* (Standards), represents the final decision of the Board on certain aspects of GAAP. In most cases FASB Standards constitute conclusions on broad-based accounting issues. To date, the FASB has issued over 60 *Statements of Financial Accounting Standards*. These Standards are listed in Exhibit 1-2.

The second type of document produced by the FASB is *Interpretations* of Standards. In many instances a Standard that has been designed to deal with a particular financial issue produces problems when applied to a specific fact situation. In those cases the FASB will issue an Interpretation of how the given Standard should be applied to the fact situation. Interpretations, then, serve to apply Standards to a limited number of specific fact situations.

Statements of Financial Accounting Concepts (Concepts) is the third type of document produced by the FASB. When the FASB was first formed, it was envisioned as an organization that would not only deal with the day-to-day problems of accounting practice, but also investigate the underlying nature of accounting theory. In trying to achieve the second half of this objective, the FASB has promulgated *Statements of Financial Accounting Concepts*. These Concepts deal with the underlying theory of financial accounting. Although the Concepts seldom provide direct solutions to practical problems, they do offer explanations and interpretations of the principles and assumptions that underlie the financial accounting process. Therefore, FASB *Statements of Accounting Concepts* in the future may provide a foundation for the development of solutions to practical problems.

The last type of document derived from the FASB is *Technical Bulletins*. These Bulletins are produced by the FASB staff and are intended to provide practitioners with timely guidance on certain financial accounting and reporting problems. Although Board members are provided with copies of the Bulletins before their issuance, the Board does not expressly approve the positions taken in these Bulletins.

In producing documents the FASB generally uses a due process system. As a first step the FASB identifies a problem area and establishes a task force of experts to study and propose solutions to this problem. After a substantial amount of research has been conducted, the Board issues a *Discussion Memorandum* that outlines the fundamental issues inherent in the topic addressed by the Board and invites input from any individual or organization interested in the topic.

A period of time after the issuance of the *Discussion Memorandum*, the Board will put forth an *Exposure Draft* of a Standard. The *Exposure Draft* summarizes the Board's initial position on the issue in question and invites further comment with respect to this position.

Once the *Exposure Draft* is issued, the FASB schedules hearings on the subject. At these hearings individuals are allowed to give testimony and present evidence concerning the issue involved. Only after consideration of the information obtained at all stages of the process does the Board issue a Standard. Exhibit 1-3 provides an example of the due process procedure that is followed by the Board.

Although the process above exemplifies the FASB's commitment to obtaining complete input, the process is not always followed in detail. In some pressing

Exhibit 1-2
Statements of Financial Accounting Standards

Number 1	Disclosure of Foreign Currency Translation Information
Number 2	Accounting for Research and Development Costs
Number 3	Reporting Accounting Changes in Interim Financial Statements
Number 4	Reporting Gains and Losses from Extinguishment of Debt
Number 5	Accounting for Contingencies
Number 6	Classification of Short-Term Obligations Expected to be Refinanced
Number 7	Accounting and Reporting by Development Stage Enterprises
Number 8	Accounting for the Translation of Foreign Currency Transactions and Foreign Financial Statements
Number 9	Accounting for Income Taxes—Oil and Gas Producing Companies
Number 10	Extension of "Grandfather" Provisions for Business Combinations
Number 11	Accounting for Contingencies—Transition Method
Number 12	Accounting for Certain Marketable Securities
Number 13	Accounting for Leases
Number 14	Financial Reporting for Segments of a Business Enterprise
Number 15	Accounting by Debtors and Creditors for Troubled Debt Restructurings
Number 16	Prior Period Adjustments
Number 17	Accounting for Leases—Initial Direct Costs
Number 18	Financial Reporting for Segments of a Business Enterprise—Interim Financial Statements
Number 19	Financial Accounting and Reporting by Oil and Gas Producing Companies
Number 20	Accounting for Forward Exchange Contracts
Number 21	Suspension of the Reporting of Earnings per Share and Segment Information by Nonpublic Enterprises
Number 22	Changes in the Provisions of Lease Agreements Resulting from Refundings of Tax-Exempt Debt
Number 23	Inception of the Lease
Number 24	Reporting Segment Information in Financial Statements That Are Presented in Another Enterprise's Financial Report
Number 25	Suspension of Certain Accounting Requirements for Oil and Gas Producing Companies
Number 26	Profit Recognition on Sales-Type Leases of Real Estate
Number 27	Classification of Renewals or Extensions of Existing Sales-Type or Direct Financing Leases
Number 28	Accounting for Sales with Leasebacks
Number 29	Determining Contingent Rentals
Number 30	Disclosure of Information About Major Customers

Exhibit 1-2 (continued)
Statements of Financial Accounting Standards

Number 31	Accounting for Tax Benefits Related to U.K. Tax Legislation Concerning Stock Relief
Number 32	Specialized Accounting and Reporting Principles and Practices in AICPA Statements of Position and Guides on Accounting and Auditing Matters
Number 33	Financial Reporting and Changing Prices
Number 34	Capitalization of Interest Cost
Number 35	Accounting and Reporting by Defined Benefit Pension Plans
Number 36	Disclosure of Pension Information
Number 37	Balance Sheet Classification of Deferred Income Taxes
Number 38	Accounting for Preacquisition Contingencies of Purchased Enterprises
Number 39	Financial Reporting and Changing Prices: Specialized Assets—Mining and Oil and Gas
Number 40	Financial Reporting and Changing Prices: Specialized Assets—Timberlands and Growing Timber
Number 41	Financial Reporting and Changing Prices: Specialized Assets—Income-Producing Real Estate
Number 42	Determining Materiality for Capitalization of Interest Cost
Number 43	Accounting for Compensated Absences
Number 44	Accounting for Intangible Assets of Motor Carriers
Number 45	Accounting for Franchise Fee Revenue
Number 46	Financial Reporting and Changing Prices: Motion Picture Films
Number 47	Disclosure of Long-Term Obligations
Number 48	Revenue Recognition When Right of Return Exists
Number 49	Accounting for Product Financing Arrangements
Number 50	Financial Reporting in the Record and Music Industry
Number 51	Financial Reporting by Cable Television Companies
Number 52	Foreign Currency Translation
Number 53	Financial Reporting by Producers and Distributors of Motion Picture Films
Number 54	Financial Reporting and Changing Prices: Investment Companies
Number 55	Determining whether a Convertible Security is a Common Stock Equivalent
Number 56	Designation of AICPA Guide and Statement of Position (SOP) 81-1 on Contractor Accounting and SOP 81-2 Concerning Hospital-Related Organizations as Preferable for Purposes of Applying APB Opinion 20
Number 57	Related Party Disclosures

Exhibit 1-2 (continued)
Statements of Financial Accounting Standards

Number 58	Capitalization of Interest Cost in Financial Statements That Include Investments Accounted for by the Equity Method (an amendment of FASB Statement No. 34)
Number 59	Deferral of the Effective Date of Certain Accounting Requirements for Pension Plans of State and Local Governmental Units (an amendment of Statement No. 35)
Number 60	Accounting and Reporting by Insurance Enterprises
Number 61	Accounting for Title Plant
Number 62	Capitalization of Interest Cost in Situations Involving Certain Tax Exempt Borrowing and Certain Gifts and Grants
Number 63	Financial Reporting by Broadcasters
Number 64	Extinguishment of Debt Made to Satisfy Sinking Fund Requirements
Number 65	Accounting For Certain Mortgage Banking Activities

situations, like that involving the treatment of payments for the transfer of tax benefits, the Board is forced by events to act in a more rapid manner than due process would allow. Yet, even in such urgent situations the Board seeks to obtain as much outside input as possible.

Given the fact that the accounting profession has delegated to the FASB the power to establish and interpret GAAP, all promulgations of the Board have a

Exhibit 1-3
Financial Accounting Standards Board
Due Process Procedures—Implementation of
Statement of Financial Accounting Standards No. 52

Date	Step Toward Implementation
August 28, 1980	Issued Exposure Draft: "Foreign Currency Translation"
August 28, 1980—December 1, 1980	Public Comment Period
December 17, 1980— December 19, 1980	Public Hearings
June 30, 1981	Issued Revised Exposure Draft: "Foreign Currency Translation"
June 30, 1981—September 20, 1981	Public Comment Period
September 28, 1981	Public Hearings
December 1981	Final Statement Issued: "Foreign Currency Translation"

mandatory impact upon the status of accounting principles. Thus, the FASB serves as the primary professional organization charged with the promulgation of GAAP.

Government Promulgated GAAP

Since many government agencies have been authorized by statute to require financial reports from certain private entities, these agencies often have the power to prescribe the accounting methods to be used in preparing the reports. Although it would seem that the methods prescribed by these agencies would be used only in preparing reports for submission to the government, the principles developed often spill over into financial statements prepared for the general public.

Many government agencies have the power to require private entities to file financial reports. The Federal Trade Commission, the Federal Power Commission, the Interstate Commerce Commission, and numerous state and local agencies are empowered to determine the accounting principles that should be used in preparing required filings. Yet, two other arms of government seem to have had the most pronounced effect on promulgated GAAP: The Securities and Exchange Commission and Congress.

Securities and Exchange Commission (SEC). The SEC was established when Congress passed the Securities Exchange Act of 1934. The Act specifically charged the SEC with the duty of supervising the operation of the interstate securities markets. Inherent in this delegated duty was the power to require firms that offer securities in those markets to file certain information with the Commission. More specifically, the SEC was granted the power to prescribe the rules and procedures to be used in the preparation of that information.

Since its formation the SEC has promulgated accounting principles in three separate forms. The first is Regulation S-X, which constitutes the original set of SEC rules regarding the form and content of filed financial statements.

The second form used by the SEC to promulgate accounting principles is *Accounting Series Releases* (ASR), which are amendments to and/or explanations of Regulation S-X. The SEC, then, uses the ASRs as a means of keeping accounting principles up-to-date.

Staff Accounting Bulletins (SABs) are the third form of promulgating accounting principles. *Staff Bulletins* are advisory opinions issued by the SEC professional staff. Since SABs are not issued by the SEC itself, they are not binding on accounting practice. However, the position taken by the staff in a SAB clearly indicates the position the SEC might take at a later date.

The SEC implements the accounting principles it promulgates by means of available enforcement proceedings. An accountant who fails to comply with the rules and regulations established by the SEC may be subject to discipline in an administrative action. For example, the accountant may be precluded from performing work for SEC clients. In addition, an accountant who violates a provision of federal securities law may be subject to SEC-initiated judicial action that could result in a fine and/or prison sentence. Thus, the means by which the SEC enforces its promulgated rules of accounting practice are potentially severe in result.

Technically, the SEC has the power to establish all accounting principles for companies required to file financial data. Fortunately, the Commission and the profession generally have worked well together; therefore, the SEC often has accepted the conclusions of professional bodies on the best form of GAAP. It would seem that the Commission traditionally has preferred to allow the accounting profession to develop GAAP, unless the profession clearly fails to react to an obvious need.

One example of the Commission's willingness to defer to the accounting profession, if positive action is taken, has to do with the reporting of current value information. For many years accounting theorists, investors, market analysts, and securities regulators complained that traditional historical cost financial statements failed to provide users with complete information in periods when prices were changing rapidly. After a substantial period of professional inaction, the SEC issued *ASR No. 190,* which required certain corporations to provide statement users with information concerning the replacement cost of assets. After this action by the SEC, the profession undertook a major study of alternative means of accounting for changing prices. This study resulted in the promulgation of *Statement of Financial Accounting Standards No. 33.* Although this Standard did not require the reporting of replacement cost data, it did require accountants to prepare certain supplemental current value information. As the profession's required current value information began to enter the economic system, the SEC removed its replacement cost requirement. Thus, when the profession failed to act, the SEC took steps it deemed necessary to protect financial statement users. As the profession finally took action to fill the void, the SEC removed itself from the position of a professional rule-making body.

Congress. In addition to authorizing administrative bodies such as the SEC to promulgate GAAP, Congress has acted on its own to force the adoption of particular accounting methods. In the past Congress has virtually mandated that the flow-through method of accounting for investment tax credits and the deferred method of accounting for the tax expense of a regulated public utility be allowed.

Congress also has instituted major studies of the accounting profession. In 1976 Congressman John Moss chaired a committee that issued a report on the FASB. In particular, the report criticized the FASB for not acting more rapidly to eliminate the availability of alternative accounting practices. The report concluded that steps should be taken to develop uniform accounting principles and suggested that a government organization, such as the SEC, would be in the best position to promulgate such principles.

One year later Senator Lee Metcalf chaired a committee that concluded that the current structure of the accounting profession was untenable. The Metcalf committee suggested that the profession was incapable of self-regulation, and therefore should be subject to some more direct form of government regulation.

The suggestion that the accounting profession should forego self-regulation in favor of government regulation produced a great deal of concern among practicing accountants. In response to the Metcalf committee's conclusions, the profession undertook a major study of the methods by which it functions. The Commission on Auditor's Responsibilities soon was established to carry out this study. The Commission made several recommendations concerning the audit process.

A second step taken by the AICPA in response to the Metcalf committee's conclusions was a major reorganization. Today, the AICPA is divided into two groups: (1) the SEC Practice Section, consisting of accounting firms that audit SEC registrants, and (2) the Private Companies Section, consisting of accounting firms that do not audit SEC-registered companies. Members of both sections are subject to a high degree of quality control. In particular, members of the SEC Practice Section are required to submit to periodic **peer review.** In a peer review one firm reviews another firm's work and evaluates its quality. In addition, the entire SEC Practice Section is subject to the scrutiny of the AICPA's Public Oversight Board, which consists of nonaccountants who are free to inquire about accounting practices and to report to the general public.

After the AICPA took these actions, the SEC issued a report on the accounting profession. The report concluded that the responsibility for standard setting did not lie in the public sector and that the professional standard-setting process had performed adequately. Thus, while Congress has encouraged the accounting profession to do a better job of self-regulation, it appears that direct congressional intervention into the standard-setting process is not needed currently.

Developing Unpromulgated GAAP

Although the authoritative bodies just described do provide some answers to a substantial number of questions concerning generally accepted accounting principles, there are many questions that would go unanswered if promulgated GAAP were the only source of information on practical accounting problems. To deal with these unanswered problems, the accountant must look to a number of other accounting sources. Although these other sources, sometimes referred to as unpromulgated GAAP, cannot be enforced, they often are followed by members of the profession.

American Institute of Certified Public Accountants (AICPA)

The AICPA is a national organization of CPAs who have elected to become members. With over 160,000 members, the AICPA is by far the largest organization of CPAs in the world.

The AICPA influences the development of accounting principles in several different ways. First, the AICPA maintains a number of committees charged with monitoring the development of accounting principles. These committees constantly discuss and evaluate practical problems, propose solutions, and issue statements that express the AICPA's position on the best approach available. Although these opinions do not have the weight of FASB Standards or SEC Releases, they are regarded highly by practicing members of the profession. Therefore, in the absence of a related promulgated GAAP, the statements issued by AICPA committees have a major impact on the practices employed by accountants confronted with practice problems. In fact, many of the opinions of AICPA committees are used later as the basis for Standards promulgated by the FASB.

The AICPA also contributes to the development of accounting principles by sponsoring scholarly research. If a particular problem arises, the AICPA often will commission a recognized expert in the field to study the problem in detail and prepare a written report. In the past these written reports have been published in the form of *Accounting Research Studies.* In addition, the AICPA maintains continuing doctoral research grants, which are intended to help doctoral students complete their dissertation research—research that helps to refine and develop new accounting principles.

The third way in which the AICPA contributes to the development of accounting principles is by publishing the *Journal of Accountancy* on a monthly basis. A professional publication with an extremely large circulation, the *Journal* provides a forum for the discussion of the issues confronting the profession.

Another way in which the AICPA contributes to the development of accounting principles is by maintaining an extensive continuing education program. The courses taught through the Continuing Professional Education Division of the Institute cover a broad range of topics and are designed to keep accounting practitioners abreast of new developments in their field. By keeping practicing members of the profession up-to-date, the courses offered by the AICPA promote a basic interchange of ideas, and thus contribute to the further development of accounting principles.

American Accounting Association (AAA)

The American Accounting Association is another voluntary organization that is closely aligned with the academic community. Since AAA membership is primarily for professors, the Association's main contributions are in the area of research. The Association prides itself on the production and publication of material that lies on the leading edge of accounting theory development.

The AAA facilitates this process of theory development in three ways. First, the AAA sponsors research conducted by recognized scholars in particular areas of accounting. The results of research are published in *Statements* and *Research Monographs*.

The Association also publishes quarterly *The Accounting Review*, a professional journal with wide circulation. The articles contained in the *Review* are primarily theoretical and represent a summary of the research findings of those engaged in significant investigations into the foundation of accounting theory.

Finally, the Association provides a number of research grants for graduate students in accounting. These grants are intended to allow students to have the time necessary to design and implement scholarly projects in the field of accounting.

Although the efforts of the AAA are not designed to provide immediate answers to the day-to-day problems encountered by practitioners of accounting, they are designed to create a better understanding of the theoretical foundation that underlies the entire discipline. Therefore, the current efforts of the AAA may not have an immediate impact upon GAAP, but they will have an effect on the long-term development of accounting principles.

Other Sources of Unpromulgated GAAP

Although the AICPA and the AAA are the major organizations contributing to the body of unpromulgated GAAP, there are many other sources of significant input. The National Association of Accountants (NAA), the Financial Executives Institute (FEI), the Municipal Finance Officers Association (MFOA), and many other groups have made significant contributions. In addition, hundreds of individuals are engaged constantly in the production of scholarly works involving the development of generally accepted accounting principles. The results of the work produced by these organizations and individuals generally are limited in scope, but when the input is viewed in the aggregate, it certainly constitutes a major contribution to the body of accounting knowledge.

Concept Summary

DEVELOPMENT OF ACCOUNTING PRINCIPLES

OBJECTIVE OF ACCOUNTING—to provide information that is useful in making business and economic decisions.

GENERALLY ACCEPTED ACCOUNTING PRINCIPLES (GAAP)—the set of established accounting principles that provide a common basis for the preparation of financial statements. GAAP help provide comparability between reports and provide the basic framework for understanding financial statements.

DEVELOPMENT OF PROMULGATED GAAP

Organization	Pronouncements	Description
AICPA		
Committee on Accounting Procedure	Accounting Research Bulletins	Recommended procedures for accounting practice
Committee on Terminology	Accounting Terminology Bulletins	Set forth desired terminology for financial statements
Accounting Principles Board (APB)	APB Opinions	Established GAAP to be used in preparing financial statements
	APB Statements	Set forth nonbinding recommendations concerning external financial reporting
	Accounting Interpretations of ABP Opinions	Provide guidance in application of Opinions to specific problem areas or industries

Financial Accounting Standards Board (FASB)	Statements of Financial Accounting Standards	Establish GAAP to be used in preparing financial statements
	FASB Interpretations	Provide guidance in application of Standards to specific problem areas
	Statement of Financial Accounting Concepts	Statements concerning the underlying theory of financial accounting and reporting
	FASB Staff Technical Bulletins	Bulletins intended to provide practitioners with timely guidance on certain financial accounting and reporting problems
Securities and Exchange Commission (SEC)	Regulation S-X	Original set of SEC rules regarding the form and content of filed financial statements
	Accounting Series Releases	Provide amendments to and/or explanations of regulations
	Staff Accounting Bulletins	Nonbinding advisory opinions issued by the SEC professional staff
Congress	Various laws	Have allowed legal use of accounting methods in certain accounting areas or industries

Questions

Q-1-1   Explain the effect that the introduction of absentee ownership had on the development of the accounting function?

Q-1-2   Explain the relationship that exists between the availability of a number of potential investment opportunities and the need for consistency and comparability in accounting information?

Q-1-3   What effect did governmental recognition of the accounting profession have on the development of the accounting function?

Q-1-4   Why is it important for accountants to understand who the users of financial information are? Does the accounting profession attempt to meet the needs of specific groups of financial statement users?

Q–1–5 Discuss the type of information that would be used most often by each of the following groups of financial statement users:

a) Investors.

b) Creditors.

c) Governments.

d) Public interest groups.

e) Labor unions.

Q–1–6 Why has the accounting profession sought to develop generally accepted accounting principles?

Q–1–7 Distinguish promulgated GAAP from unpromulgated GAAP. Is there a difference in the effect that each of these bodies has on the practice of accounting?

Q–1–8 Identify each of the following professional organizations:

a) Financial Accounting Standards Board.

b) Accounting Principles Board.

c) Committee on Accounting Procedure.

d) American Institute of Certified Public Accountants.

e) American Accounting Association.

Q–1–9 Describe the process used by the FASB in promulgating Financial Accounting Standards.

Q–1–10 Distinguish each of the following types of FASB pronouncements:

a) Statements of Financial Accounting Standards.

b) Interpretations of Financial Accounting Standards.

c) Statements of Financial Accounting Concepts.

Q–1–11 Explain the effect that each of the following governmental organizations has had on the development of GAAP:

a) Securities and Exchange Commission.

b) Congress.

Q–1–12 Explain the function of each of the following "arms" of the AICPA:

a) Private Companies Practice Section.

b) SEC Practice Section.

c) Public Oversight Board.

Q–1–13 Discuss how a practicing accountant should approach the finding of a solution to a problem encountered in his or her work.

Discussion Questions and Cases

D–1–1 While conducting their first examination of the financial statements of Sheridan Corporation, Meade & Co., CPAs, discovered a unique situation regarding the inventory accounting practices of Sheridan. Specifically, the accountants discovered that Sheridan used a rather unique method of identifying the goods on hand at the end of the year. This method of identification had a significant effect on the balances shown in both the ending inventory and cost of goods sold accounts.

After obtaining a complete understanding of the specific practice used by Sheridan, the accountant in charge of the job assigned a staff accountant to do some research into the matter. After conducting a significant amount of primary research, the staff accountant reported the following:

a) Although there were several *Accounting Research Bulletins*, APB *Opinions* and *Statements of Financial Accounting Standards* that dealt with the inventory issue, none of these promulgations dealt with the specific systems being used by Sheridan. More important, none of the promulgations specifically stated that inventory systems not specifically approved in an authoritative pronouncement were unacceptable.

b)   The American Accounting Association sponsored a research study concerning the specific inventory system being used by Sheridan. The study concluded that this particular system produced results that were significantly different from those produced by the more traditional inventory systems. The study concluded, however, that there was at least some theoretical basis for the use of such an inventory system.

c)   An article in the *Journal of Accountancy* discussed the inventory system in detail and concluded that the adoption of the system, particularly for purposes of federal taxation, could be quite beneficial for the entity.

d)   A research study conducted by a doctoral student, who was funded by an AICPA grant, concluded that financial statements that relied upon this inventory system substantially distorted investors' projections of the future value of the firm's securities.

Required:

Based upon the information above, would you conclude that the Sheridan accounting system represents generally accepted accounting principles?

D–1–2   Assume you are the controller of a medium-sized company and that a problem has come up concerning the proper accounting treatment of a particular transaction. You have never before encountered this type of problem.

Required:

What process would you go through to determine the current GAAP relating to the transaction?

D–1–3   You are an accountant with a small publicly held company. The company has just started leasing equipment rather than buying it. The company president is unfamiliar with the proper accounting treatment of leases, and the company must issue financial statements. The president has asked you to get him a list of promulgated GAAP pronouncements related to leases.

Required:

Go to the library and get a list of all pronouncements relating to leases. Indicate which ones are no longer in effect.

2

Underlying Theory of Financial Accounting

Accounting in the News

The accounting profession is striving constantly to improve the financial reports it prepares. Accounting principles and disclosure requirements change continually. When making such changes, the accounting profession must keep in mind the objectives of financial reporting, defined as follows:

> *Objectives of Financial Reporting by Business Enterprises*, issued by the Financial Accounting Standards Board in 1978, and *Qualitative Characteristics of Accounting Information*, issued in 1980, could be termed "flagship" Concepts Statements. This is because they deal with fundamentals of what financial executives, as preparers, practitioners, and attestors, should be trying to do. That is, we should be making our financial statements useful, relevant, and reliable for decision-making. All these concepts are succinctly captured in the exhortation—Tell It Like It Is—not as it might have been, not as it once used to be, and not as it perhaps could be.*

These concepts guide the profession in its attempt to make financial statements more useful to statement readers.

*Joseph E. Connor, "Telling It Like It Is," *Financial Executive*, July 1982, p. 10.

The discussion in Chapter 1 indicated that generally accepted accounting principles (GAAP) constitute a body of rules developed by the accounting profession for purposes of obtaining some degree of consistency in financial statements. Since the development of GAAP cannot be based upon pure scientific process (that is, the development of GAAP cannot be based upon testing in a controlled laboratory environment), accountants often have referred to goals, or objectives, as the quantitative and qualitative standards against which the adequacy of a particular principle should be judged.

The first section of this chapter presents a discussion of the qualitative and quantitative objectives that accountants seek most often in the development of

GAAP. The second section of this chapter discusses the major assumptions and principles that accountants have developed in an attempt to produce the most useful set of financial statement disclosures.

In Chapter 1 the accounting function was described as a process of gathering and communicating information that could be used in the making of economic decisions. Two of the problems encountered most often in implementing this process are deciding what information should be gathered and how that information should be presented for purposes of communication. In an effort to deal with these problems, accountants have developed both qualitative and quantitative objectives for data. A discussion of these objectives follows.

Qualitative Objectives

When the Financial Accounting Standards Board (FASB) was formed, it was assigned the task of enunciating concepts of financial accounting that could be used as a foundation for the further development of GAAP. To accomplish its task the FASB embarked upon a substantial, and continuous, research program, which has resulted in the issuance of Statements of Financial Accounting Concepts (SFAC). These Statements represent the FASB's synthesis of what it perceives to be the foundation of financial accounting theory.

In *SFAC No. 1* the FASB attempted to lay a theoretical foundation for the contents of financial statements. In general, the FASB concluded that the accounting profession should strive to develop general purpose financial statements—financial statements that a broad class of decision makers could use in predicting the ability of an enterprise to generate future cash flows.[1] The FASB also concluded that such general purpose financial statements should provide users with information concerning the following:

1. Changes in financial position resulting from the income-producing efforts of the entity.
2. Earnings of an enterprise, presented in a manner that emphasizes both sources of earnings and trends.
3. Economic resources and obligations of a firm.
4. Changes in net financial resources that result from financing and investing activities of a firm.
5. Additional information that is relevant to statement users in predicting a particular firm's future prospects.

Although the contents of *SFAC No. 1* did give accountants an idea about the types of disclosures to be made in published financial statements, it did not describe specifically the characteristics of the information to be included. In *SFAC No. 2* the FASB attempted to become more specific about the qualitative characteristics of the data to be used to produce the desired disclosures.

The FASB concluded in *SFAC No. 2* that a "hierarchy" of accounting qualities exists.[2] This hierarchy, as depicted in Exhibit 2-1, delineates the basic factors

---

[1]"Objectives of Financial Reporting by Business Enterprises," *Statement of Financial Accounting Concepts No. 1* (Stamford, Conn.: FASB, 1978), par. 28.

[2]"Qualitative Characteristics of Accounting Information," *Statement of Financial Accounting Concepts No. 2.* (Stamford, Conn.: FASB, 1980), Figure 1.

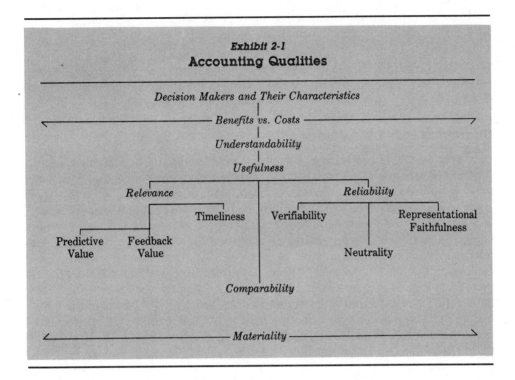

Exhibit 2-1
Accounting Qualities

Decision Makers and Their Characteristics

Benefits vs. Costs

Understandability

Usefulness

Relevance   *Reliability*

Timeliness   Verifiability   Representational Faithfulness

Predictive Value   Feedback Value   Neutrality

Comparability

Materiality

that accountants should consider in evaluating information for inclusion in published financial statements.

Decision Maker Characteristics

At the top of the hierarchy is the decision maker. Most all financial statement users are decision makers in one capacity or another. For example, they may make loan decisions or investment decisions. If the decision maker cannot use the information provided, the accounting function has failed to accomplish its objective. Therefore, in performing their task accountants always must begin with a consideration of the characteristics of the individuals who will use the information.

In considering the decision maker's characteristics, the accountant must take into account the degree of accounting sophistication possessed by the majority of potential users. A sophisticated financial statement user can make more efficient use of complex information than can an unsophisticated user. Yet, accountants seek to produce a single set of financial statements that can serve the general purpose needs of a large number of potential users. Accountants cannot gear their product to either the most sophisticated or the least sophisticated of users. Instead, financial statements must be structured to serve the broadest class of potential users, without neglecting the needs of any particular class.

Benefits vs. Costs

The hierarchy developed by the FASB recognizes that accountants constantly must acknowledge the existence of a **cost/benefit** constraint. In other words, while some particular information may be of great value to a particular user, the total cost of gathering that information—expressed in terms of both dollar cost and the cost of its effect on other users—must be compared with the benefit to be derived from its dissemination. The particular piece of information should be gathered and communicated to users only if the total benefits exceed the total costs.

Understandable Information

Once accountants have identified the characteristics of financial statement users, determined the type of information that should be gathered, and gathered it, they must communicate the information to financial statement users.

The key to the process of communication is the concept of **understandability.** If the users of the financial statements are unable to understand the message being communicated, there almost certainly will be one of two results. If the information confuses the user (that is, if the user simply is unable to identify any message contained in the information), the user will reject the financial statements and seek other sources of financial information. On the other hand, if the information communicates an incorrect message (that is, if the user of the information perceives the data to contain a message that it was not intended to contain), the user will be misled and a poor economic decision may result. In either of these cases, the financial statements will have failed to serve their basic purpose.

Useful Information

In addition to being understandable, the information communicated by the accountant must be **useful** with respect to the economic decisions being made. Therefore, accountants must maintain a constant awareness of the types of decisions being made. In determining whether information is useful with respect to decisions, accountants generally consider two other qualitative characteristics of accounting information: relevance and reliability. *FSAC No. 2* covered these concepts in detail.[3]

Relevance. Accountants must consider the relevance of the data in deciding whether data are useful in making decisions. Information is considered **relevant** if it constitutes significant input into the decision making process. For example, if a decision maker has decided that historical trends are important factors to consider in making current decisions, information concerning these historical trends will be deemed relevant to the decision making process.

It should be noted that a major element in the relevance of information is its predictive nature. Information that merely confirms a result that the decision maker was already aware of is of little or no relevance. Conversely, data that assist the decision maker in predicting the occurrence of a result are highly relevant.

The FASB recognized that **timeliness** is a second major determinant of the relevance of information. Even if a given piece of information is capable of producing a perfect prediction of future events, that information is irrelevant if it is

---

[3] Ibid., pars. 46–97.

not received by the decision maker within the proper time frame. For information to be relevant, it must represent timely assistance in predicting the course of future events that are of interest to the decision maker.

Reliability.   Even if information is relevant, it is of no use to the decision maker unless it is also **reliable.** In other words, unless the user can believe in the accuracy of the data supplied, the information is of little use in the decision making process. The FASB noted three factors that should be considered in evaluating the reliability of a given piece of information.

The first of these factors is **verifiability.** Information is verifiable when it is possible for independent parties, using essentially the same measurement technique, to measure the same event and reach the same conclusion. In accounting, a measure is considered verifiable if another accountant could apply GAAP to the same transaction and produce essentially the same financial reporting result.

The second factor identified by the FASB is termed **representational faithfulness.** Representational faithfulness exists when the data are free from bias— that is, the accountant who gathered and communicated the information introduced no bias into the measurement.

Bias exists when the information communicated in the financial statements differs from the event subject to accounting measurement. Since it is impossible to structure financial statements so that a perfect communication network results (that is, words are simply not capable of producing a description of the real world), accountants must strive to reduce the amount of bias present in information. As this amount of bias is reduced, the representational faithfulness of the reported information increases.

The third factor of reliability identified by the FASB is **neutrality.** Accounting information is neutral when the format of the information's presentation has no effect on the decision being made. Economic decisions should be based upon the substantive content of information communicated to decision makers. Decisions should not be influenced by the form in which a particular piece of information is communicated. Accountants should seek to present the information in such a way that the form of presentation does not have an input into the decision making process.

At this point it should be noted that it is impossible for accountants to produce financial statements that are both completely relevant and completely reliable. The very nature of these qualitative characteristics dictates that some trade-offs must be made.

As accountants seek to increase the relevance of information, they also must seek to increase the speed at which information is delivered to users. As the speed of the information-gathering process is increased, however, the reliability of the information produced must decrease. Conversely, as accountants seek to increase the reliability of data, they must forgo the communication of certain risky information. Yet, some of the more risky information (e.g., predictions of future events) is what is the most relevant to ultimate users. Financial statement users would be happy to receive information made up of accurate forecasts of future events; unfortunately such information must be based upon a set of assumptions and predictions, and thus does not possess a high degree of reliability. In preparing financial statements, accountants must balance all of the needs of users to produce an optimum benefit for all.

Comparability

Economic decisions generally do not represent simple yes or no decisions. Instead, they involve the making of choices from a virtually infinite number of possibilities. When a production manager decides to manufacture product A, he also has decided to forgo the production of products B, C, and D. In addition, that manager has made a decision to manufacture goods rather than invest his capital in income-producing assets. Thus, every economic decision represents the selection of one or more alternatives from a larger number of potential alternatives.

Given the number of alternatives, accounting must supply the information that will be useful to the decision maker in selecting among these alternatives. By necessity, this information must be comparative in nature; that is, the information must allow the decision maker to compare one of the available alternatives to all of the other available alternatives.

In its most simplistic form, **comparability** of financial information means three things. First, comparability means that the users of financial statements should be able to view comfortably a firm's financial statements for a number of years without fearing that changes in the accounting process have made interperiod comparison impossible. Second, comparability means that financial statement users can conduct an economic analysis of two or more firms without fear that varying accounting practices have made the comparison impractical. Finally, comparability means that financial statement users can analyze the economic impact of different types of transactions without concern over the effect of the accounting methods employed on the results of their comparisons. Comparability, then, means that accounting constitutes a common language for the conduct of general purpose economic analyses.

Materiality

Like the cost/benefit analysis discussed previously, **materiality** permeates the entire hierarchy of accounting qualities. Even if the accountant were to provide information that was reliable and relevant, that information would be useless to decision makers unless it is material. For example, an individual interested in investing in a particular security generally is quite interested in information regarding the price at which the security will sell at some future date. If the accountant could provide the information user with reliable information that can be used to develop accurate projections of future prices, the user would be pleased. Yet, if the accountant were to provide information regarding only an insignificant number of transactions, or if the accountant were to provide information relating to a single transaction that was atypical of the market as a whole, the decision maker would be unwilling to rely upon this information as the basis of his projection. Such information would be deemed to be immaterial to the decision the user was attempting to make.

Given the fact that large quantities of immaterial information easily could disrupt accounting's process of communication, it is important that accountants constantly consider the materiality of the information being included in financial statements. Since accountants must segregate what is material from what is not, they must have a firm grasp of both the economic environment and the needs of the users they serve. In addition, accountants must exercise a great degree of judgment in establishing the threshold of materiality.

It is important to note that the accountant must use subjective judgment in establishing this threshold. It is impossible to establish an arbitrary dollar amount as the level at which transactions become material. Instead, the accountant must consider each transaction in light of how that transaction relates to all of the other reported information, and how users of financial statements will react to information regarding that transaction. In many cases an item of small economic value may be quite important to the users of financial statements, and thus will be deemed material. In other cases, items of relatively large economic value may be of little significance to financial statement users, and thus will be deemed immaterial. Accountants must use their professional judgment in determining the materiality of a given transaction.

Quantitative Objectives

Although accountants constantly strive to achieve certain qualitative objectives, the financial statements they produce are designed primarily to achieve two quantitative objectives. A brief discussion of each of these quantitative objectives follows.

Wealth Measurement

As was discussed previously, the FASB concluded that general purpose financial statements should provide users with five types of information. A substantial number of these relate to the wealth possessed by the entity at a given point in time.

Wealth consists of the value of all of the rights and possessions owned by the firm at a point in time, less all of the obligations the firm is required to pay. In other words, wealth represents a measure of the unencumbered stock of assets possessed by a firm at a particular point in time.

Since the firm will use this wealth to carry out its activities in the future, the size and content are important to financial statement users. By carefully analyzing the wealth possessed by a firm at a point in time, a financial statement user can obtain important insight into the firm's future prospects.

Income Measurement

The remainder of the information types deemed important by the FASB relate to the income of the firm. **Income** is the value of the net inflow of resources earned by a firm over a period of time. While wealth represents a stock of items that physically exists, income is an activity measure. Income represents the success the firm has had in using the wealth it possesses.

Since income is a measure of firm success, many financial statement users seek information that assists them in projecting the future income of the firm. By doing so, these financial statement users hope to be able to estimate future dividends and stock prices.

Although some financial statement users attempt to place primary emphasis on either wealth or income measures, the two measures are interrelated. Given that income is a net inflow of resources into the firm, any income that is earned represents an increase in the resources owned. Such increases are really nothing more than increases in wealth. Income measures the change in wealth resulting from the operation of a business.

Assumptions Made to Simplify Problems

Since there are fundamental problems inherent in the implementation of the accounting process, accountants are forced to make certain simplifying assumptions about the environment in which they operate. The making of these assumptions should not be viewed as an unwillingness on the part of accountants to recognize the complex nature of the environment. On the contrary, accounting fully recognizes that the nature of the economic environment precludes the application of perfect measurement techniques. Instead, accounting uses simplifying assumptions as a form of compromise; that is, assumptions are made as a means of producing valuable, but less than perfect, information about a complex system. By making these simplifying assumptions, accountants can produce a general purpose set of financial statements that provides the degree of comparability demanded by users. An explanation of each of the five major accounting assumptions follows.

Unit of Measure Assumption

Before an accountant can report to financial statement users about the wealth and income of an entity, s/he must assign values to the individual pieces of data that make up those measures. To guarantee that the individual pieces of information can be aggregated in a meaningful way, accountants must make assumptions about the **unit of measure** that will be adopted to facilitate the aggregation.

In general, accountants assume that all economically useful information can be expressed in terms of a monetary unit. The reason for the use of a standard measurement unit is quite simple—in this way accountants avoid the many problems inherent in attempting to report certain "qualitative" data. For example, information concerning the capabilities and qualifications of a firm's management team—commonly referred to as human resource information—generally is deemed to be unquantifiable, and therefore accountants do not attempt to integrate this information into published financial statements. Likewise, information concerning a firm's access to clean air and water generally cannot be expressed in monetary terms. Hence, accountants do not attempt to include such information in any of the standard financial statements.

In addition to assuming that economically significant information may be expressed in terms of a monetary unit, most accountants assume that that monetary unit is of a **constant value.** In other words, most accountants assume that there is no problem created by comparing monetary information prepared in 1952 with monetary information prepared in 1982—accountants simply assume that the monetary unit has remained constant in value, and therefore is comparable.

The problems inherent in the unit of measure assumption should be apparent. First, information that is material to financial statement users exists that generally cannot be stated in terms of a monetary unit. The two types of information mentioned above—information concerning management capabilities and access to clean air and water—can be of substantial economic significance. Yet, because these items are not subject to monetary measurement, accountants ignore their existence when preparing financial statements. Although the loss of material information may be significant, the accounting profession has decided that the difficulty inherent in measuring and communicating most nonmonetary information simply outweighs the benefits to be derived from its presentation.

Second, the assumption that the monetary unit is constant in value has not proven to be true. Even in those nations with the soundest of currencies, changes in the value of the monetary unit have been constant and significant in recent years. In recognition of this fact, the accounting profession has begun to present supplemental information designed to compensate for changes in the value of the monetary unit. The accounting profession's experiment with current value accounting will be discussed in detail in Chapter 26.

Going Concern Assumption

The **going concern assumption** states that, in the absence of clear evidence to the contrary, accountants assume that all entities are going concerns. In other words, when there is no clear evidence indicating that an entity will not survive in the short run, accountants assume that the entity will survive and continue to pursue its business purpose.

There are at least two reasons for the presence of the going concern assumption in modern accounting. First, the going concern assumption is needed to supplement the unit of measure assumption. Even after assuming that significant economic events can be measured in terms of a relatively stable monetary unit, accountants are confronted with fundamental problems of valuation. In determining the monetary value to be assigned to a particular item, should the accountant consider the historical cost of that item, the current market value of that item, the current use value of that item, or some other measure of the item's economic value?

The going concern assumption indicates that historical cost is the best of the alternative measures. Since accounting assumes that the entity will continue to operate, there is no need to consider the alternative values that are present in the market place. Instead, the entity probably will continue to use its assets in the manner in which it originally intended. Given the presence of a stable monetary unit, the value of this continued use can be measured most objectively in terms of historical cost.

A second reason for the going concern assumption is that it is a means of freeing the accountant from the need to be concerned with the possibility of a firm's future liquidation. Complex disclosures would be necessary if the possibility of future liquidation were considered significant. By assuming that there is no need for such disclosures in all but a limited number of situations, the going concern assumption helps to simplify the published financial statements.

Separate Entity Assumption

The **separate entity assumption** is based on the belief that accountants will treat every economic entity as an independent unit for purposes of measurement. In other words, no matter what degree of relationship exists between two firms, or between a firm and a set of individuals, the activities of each firm, or each individual, will be accounted for separately.

The value of the separate entity assumption is the fact that it allows accountants to ignore economic interdependencies. Without the separate entity assumption, accountants would be forced constantly to evaluate the effects of one firm's activity on that of other firms. For example, without the separate entity assumption the accountant for a major steel manufacturer constantly would have to consider events that affect the auto industry and the financial markets. Although such consideration would produce an undue degree of accounting complexity, it would be difficult for anyone to deny that events that affect the auto industry and financial markets eventually have a major effect on steel producers.

In addition, the separate entity assumption allows accountants to draw boundaries around any unit of economic activity. It should be noted that in identifying these units of activity, accountants are not constrained by the traditional legal boundaries. If information is needed about a particular department of a firm, accountants can assume that that department is a separate entity, even though the department is an interrelated segment of a much larger legal entity. Thus, the separate entity assumption also provides accountants with an opportunity to report on several activity centers (such as departments) within one accounting system.

Time Period Assumption

As was mentioned previously, accounting information is only of value to financial statement users if it is presented in a timely manner. Yet, perfectly accurate measures of a firm's income and wealth can be made only at two points in time: the date on which the firm is formed and the date on which the firm is liquidated. At all other points in time the wealth and income of a firm are subject to constant and immediate change.

The **time period assumption** (also called **periodicity**) implies that all relevant economic data can be segregated into separate, distinct, and identifiable time periods. In other words, the continuous flow of economic activity may be divided into arbitrary time periods without affecting the quality of the reported information.

The purpose of the time period assumption is to allow accountants to report the economic effects of the activities engaged in by a firm during a particular period of time. Although accountants recognize that the information reported at the end of an arbitrary period of entity activity may lack some degree of accuracy, they also recognize that without a time period assumption, information communicated to financial statement users would lack a substantial degree of relevance. With the time period assumption in place, accountants may ignore the timing problem, and instead may concentrate on the quality of the information contained in the periodic financial reports.

User Needs Assumption

The **user needs assumption** is that the users of financial statements are investors and creditors interested in general purpose financial information that enables them to predict the future cash flows of the entity. By its very nature, the user needs assumption is based upon two hypotheses.

The first hypothesis is that financial statements should be aimed at current and potential investors and creditors. This aspect of the user needs assumption means that accountants may ignore the special purpose needs of groups such as federal and state taxing authorities when preparing general financial statements.

The second hypothesis is that the financial statements prepared for investors and creditors should be general in nature. In other words, financial statements should not be designed to meet desires for specifically detailed information. Instead, the user needs assumption is that financial statements should consist of broad sets of general purpose financial information.

Principles Based Upon Simplifying Assumptions

When the objectives of financial accounting are viewed in light of the simplifying assumptions that have to be made in order to make the achievement of those objectives possible, the foundation upon which a theory of financial accounting may be built begins to emerge. Based upon this foundation, the accounting profession has developed several underlying principles. A discussion of each of these six principles follows.

Historical Cost Principle

At any point in time the value of a particular item or service can be established by finding the price at which a buyer and seller, neither under any compulsion to act, would enter into a transaction. Obviously, at the date on which an actual arms-length transaction takes place (i.e., the date of a purchase/sale), the cost incurred by the buyer, the price received by the seller, constitutes the most reliable measure of the item's value that is the subject of the transaction.

Unfortunately, accountants must perform the measurement process without the aid of a constant series of arms-length transactions. In many cases accountants cannot isolate a comparable arms-length transaction for the particular items they are trying to value for financial statement purposes. Therefore, the accountant must seek alternative means of valuation.

In considering alternate valuation techniques, accountants must take into account all of the information available to them. At any point in time, information exists concerning the market value, replacement cost, and historical cost of particular items. More perplexing is the fact that at any point in time each of the available valuation techniques may produce a different value for the same item.

In an attempt to deal with this complex valuation problem, accountants have adopted the **historical cost principle.** Simply stated, the historical cost principle is that historical cost, once measured in an arms-length market transaction, is the best continuing measure of the economic value derived from a given transaction.

In other words, the price at which a willing seller and willing buyer once transacted business is the best measure of the continuing value of the item that was the subject of that transaction.

The historical cost principle flows directly from two of the assumptions previously discussed: the unit of measure assumption and the going concern assumption. Since accountants assume that significant economic events can be stated in terms of a monetary unit of stable value, it is reasonable to assume that historical cost, once accurately measured, is a continually accurate measure of value. Also, since it is reasonable to assume that an entity will continue to operate over a long period of time, it must be reasonable as well to assume that the entity will not attempt to sell a large portion of its assets in the market. Therefore, measures of current market price and current replacement cost can be ignored in favor of historical cost measures.

More important, the historical cost principle ensures that accounting measurement will consist of objective and verifiable information. Given that the historical cost of an item is established in a transaction involving adverse parties, the historical cost measure has been established objectively in the market place. In addition, the fact that historical cost was established in the market clearly indicates the presence of an objective measure—the adverse nature of the dealing parties made it impossible for bias to be introduced into the measurement system.

Although the historical cost principle may seem to solve many of the valuation problems that confront accountants, it is not a panacea. There are many transactions that are not the result of arms-length bargaining. It is not unusual for entities to receive property as gifts or contributions in exchange for the issuance of capital stock. In addition, accountants often have difficulty in defining what is meant by cost. The cost of introducing an asset into the operations of a manufacturing facility may be far greater than the price paid to the supplier of the asset. The costs of transportation and installation also must be considered in identifying the total cost incurred in acquiring the asset. Thus, while the historical cost principle may solve many of the accountant's valuation problems, it still must be viewed as only a principle—a general precept that can be applied only by individuals using trained judgment in individual fact situations.

Revenue Realization Principle

As was stated previously, the activity of an entity may be segregated into separate time periods for purposes of financial reporting. If the time period assumption is to be implemented properly, accountants must develop principles for determining the economic period in which the results of activity should be reported.

For example, a public accounting firm that performs audits of major companies may provide services over an extended period of time. However, the firm must identify a single point in time at which the revenue from the performance of those services should be recognized for financial statement purposes. Should that point be the time at which the individual services are rendered, the time at which the audit is completed, or the time at which payment is received from the client?

The **revenue realization principle** is accounting's recognition of the fact that a going concern earns revenue continuously but periodically must report to financial statement users. Revenue should not be considered earned for financial statement purposes (i.e., should not be recognized) until (1) the earnings process is complete or essentially complete and (2) an exchange has taken place.

Given this definition of revenue realization, it appears that three conditions must be met before an item of income will be recognized on the financial statements. First, the items of revenue must be subject to measurement. If the item of revenue is of contingent value (that is, if the item's value is indeterminate, or if it is subject to some contingency), it will not be considered realized for financial statement purposes.

The second condition is that the measurement must be unbiased (i.e., the product of an arms-length exchange transaction). For example, accountants certainly would consider realized the purchase price paid for an item in an irrevocable transaction between two unrelated parties. If the transaction were between related parties, however, or if the agreement gave the buyer the right to force the seller to repurchase the item at the same price at a later date, the transaction might not be considered arms-length, and revenue recognition might be deferred.

Finally, a crucial event that represents the end, or virtual end, of the earnings process must occur. Accountants generally look for a transaction or event that evidences a clear termination in the earnings process. An exchange of items of material economic value or the signing of an enforceable contract constitute events that illustrate the conclusion of the earnings process. Since each of these three conditions must be met, the timing of revenue recognition becomes a most difficult, although important, task.

The description of the revenue realization process presented above may seem to indicate that accountants forgo judgment in favor of absolute rules in determining when to report revenue. In fact, accountants must use their judgment in many cases to determine whether to modify the dictates of the revenue realization principle. Accountants have recognized at least two other methods, applicable to specific and limited fact situations, of determining when to recognize revenues.

Long-Term Contract Accounting. In the construction industry, companies often enter into transactions that take a number of years to complete. A contract to build a major highway, or a contract to construct a large commercial building, may provide for cash payments to the contractor during the term of construction, but the project is not complete, and the contractor is not relieved of his duty, until the construction process is completed.

If the realization principle were applied to the construction industry, financial statements would display great variances in the income patterns of firms. Entities that report zero revenue over a number of periods later would report huge revenues in a single period. The financial statements that would result from the application of a pure realization principle would be of very little benefit to the users of financial statements. Therefore, accountants have developed special accounting systems for those entities that enter into long-term contracts.

One such system is the **percentage-of-completion method** of accounting. Under this method of accounting, the revenues that will be derived from the eventual completion of a project, and the costs that eventually will be incurred, are recognized as the project is completed. Therefore, if 75% of a project is finished at the end of a particular reporting period, 75% of the revenues, expenses, and profits to be derived from the project will have been reported on the financial statements. Thus, the financial statements more accurately will reflect the continuing economic activity and the continuing earnings process inherent in industries that enter long-term contracts.

Installment Accounting.   In many situations a firm will enter into a transaction in which the cash exchanged for its product will not be received until sometime in the future. In most cases the fact that the cash is not to be received until a future date is of no significance in determining whether the revenue has been realized. Yet, isn't there a problem if there is some doubt as to whether the cash payments actually will be received?

If there were some doubt as to whether the purchaser actually will pay the debt, or if the contract specified some future event that could result in a novation of the debt, accountants would be less willing to recognize the full amount of the revenue in the current period. In these cases accountants often resort to installment accounting.

Under the **installment accounting method,** the revenues, costs, and profits inherent in a given transaction are recognized only as cash payments actually are received. Therefore, if there is some doubt about a deferred payment contract, the installment method provides the accountant an opportunity to defer the recognition of revenue and profit until the doubt is replaced by an actual cash payment. Although accountants do not particularly favor this method of recording transactions, the profession does recognize that it is valid and useful in certain limited situations.

The problems inherent in the process of revenue recognition are complex. Hence, accountants must use both existent theory and trained judgment in dealing with specific fact situations. A more detailed discussion is presented in Chapter 3.

Matching Principle

If all entities used the cash method of accounting, revenues would be recognized as cash is received, and expenses would be recognized as cash is paid. However, accounting has determined that the cash method is inappropriate for most entities. Instead, accountants opt for the **accrual method** of accounting. Under the accrual method, revenues are recognized as realized (whether or not cash has been received), and expenses are deducted from these revenues to determine net income.

The revenue realization principle represents the basic foundation of the accrual method of accounting, but it provides the practicing accountant with very little guidance on when expense should be reported for financial statement purposes. Without some theoretical guidance on this matter, accountants would be forced to apply varied judgment, and the comparability of published financial statements would be impaired substantially.

To deal with the problem of expense recognition, accountants have relied upon the matching principle. The **matching principle** dictates that expenses associated with the process of producing revenues should be reported in the period in which those revenues are recognized. In its most simplistic form, the matching principle requires that the cost of goods sold in the market place be reported on the same periodic financial statements (i.e., matched with) as the revenues realized from the sale of those goods.

Essentially, the matching principle is the mirror-image of the revenue realization principle. If revenues are recorded when an unbiased measure of an economic event exists, the expenses associated with that revenue should be recorded simultaneously. If revenue is recognized on a percentage-of-completion or installment basis, the expense of producing that revenue should be recorded simultaneously.

Unfortunately, the matching principle, and its impact upon expense recognition, becomes much more complicated when you realize that all expenditures made by a firm are not related directly to an identifiable source of revenue. Also, all expenditures made by a firm do not constitute expenses that should be recognized immediately. More specifically, accountants cannot always identify a revenue measure that will indicate when an expense should be recognized, and accountants are not free to assume that all costs incurred can be recorded as expenses of the current period.

To deal with these problems, accountants divide all incurred costs into three groups. First, there are costs that are incurred to acquire a future benefit for the firm. Certainly, when a firm purchases manufacturing equipment, that firm expects its expenditure to produce benefits over a number of future periods. Therefore, the cost incurred in acquiring that manufacturing equipment should not be matched solely against the revenue earned in the current period. That cost will help to produce revenue in the current period and in a number of future periods.

Capital expenditures

Costs incurred to acquire future benefits should be recorded as assets. The cost of these assets should be matched with the revenues earned during the periods in which the asset is of economic benefit. In other words, the cost of an asset should be spread over the periods during which the asset is of benefit to the firm. When the asset's economic benefit has been consumed fully, its cost will have been allocated fully, and the expense will have been matched properly to the revenues that were produced as a result of the consumption of the economic value inherent in the asset.

The second group of costs produces no benefit other than that realized in the current period. When an entity purchases electricity for use in the manufacturing process, the benefit derived from incurring that cost is limited to that obtained from the immediate operation of the manufacturing facility: the goods and services that are produced during the period of operation. If you assume that those goods and services are sold immediately, the entity will realize revenue. More important, the benefit derived from paying the cost of electricity will be transferred to the buyer of the goods or services in exchange for his payment of the agreed-upon price. Therefore, the cost incurred will be of no future benefit to the firm. That cost should be recognized as a current expense and matched with the revenue it helped to produce.

Revenue expenditures

Finally, there are costs incurred that produce no economic benefit at all. Such costs, generally referred to as losses, are recognized as reductions of income in the period in which the loss is actually incurred. These losses are recognized regardless of whether they can be matched against any specific revenue stream.

losses

Exhibit 2-2 summarizes the distinction that accountants draw between different types of costs. The net result of all of the expenditure/cost classifications is

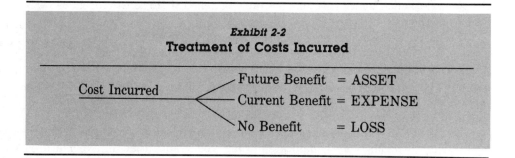

Exhibit 2-2
Treatment of Costs Incurred

Cost Incurred
- Future Benefit = ASSET
- Current Benefit = EXPENSE
- No Benefit   = LOSS

that financial statements are prepared on the basis of proper matching of inflows and outflows of resources. Only if such a matching of revenue and expense is accomplished properly can accountants be sure that financial statements reflect a reasonable measure of the income earned by an entity in a particular period of time.

Comparability Principle

Since economic decisions are primarily a selection of one of a number of available alternatives, financial statements must facilitate the comparison of the various alternatives. The implementation of the **comparability principle** basically is dependent upon the consistency of financial statement data.

In particular, accountants are interested in three levels of comparability or consistency. First, accountants are interested in achieving **intrafirm comparability**—comparability of the annual financial statements of a single entity. Intrafirm comparability requires that financial statements be prepared from year to year in a consistent manner. Second, accountants are interested in achieving **interfirm comparability**—comparability of the financial statements of different entities in the same industry. The accounting principles used in the preparation of the financial statements of different firms engaged in the *same* activities should be relatively consistent. Finally, accountants are interested in achieving **interindustry comparability**—comparability of the financial statements of firms in different industries. In this case the accounting principles used by different firms engaged in *different* activities should be relatively consistent.

Obviously, the achievement of perfect comparability would require one set of accounting principles for all firms in all industries. Although such a set of rigid accounting rules might promote consistent and comparable financial reporting, such rules also might have a negative impact on the overall quality of disseminated financial information. As was discussed previously, the rigid application of the realization principle does not result in fair financial presentation in all cases. In some limited instances accountants must use their judgment to develop methods of accounting that are appropriate in specific circumstances. An accounting principle that works well in one situation may not work as well in another situation.

Therefore, in seeking to achieve comparability and consistency, accountants tend to opt for a compromise based upon clear financial reporting combined with disclosure rather than rigid rules. This compromise approach not only provides the financial statement user with the information needed to make comparisons but also guarantees the relative accuracy of the data upon which this final decision will be based.

Full Disclosure Principle

The **full disclosure principle** requires that financial statements be designed to give users relevant and understandable information about the economic transactions in which the entity has engaged. As currently implemented, the full disclosure principle mandates two distinct types of financial information. The first type of information consists of the financial statements themselves: the balance sheet, the income statement, the statement of changes in financial position, and the statement of retained earnings. These financial statements represent the primary means by which relevant economic information is communicated to those who wish to make decisions.

In communicating their financial message, the statements do not rely upon numbers alone. The face of the financial statements communicates information through parenthetical notations and account titles. In addition, the format and organization of the financial statements often provide the user with valuable information.

The second type of information provided to the users of financial statements are the footnotes to the financial statements. These footnotes explain what cannot be communicated fully on the face of the statements. When footnotes accompany the information on the face of the statements, accountants are able to give users a complete picture of what they deem to be relevant.

Principle of Substance Over Form

When an individual first encounters the theoretical foundations of accounting, s/he generally sees a set of rules that should be applied in given fact situations. If practicing accountants are to produce the greatest benefit for the users of financial statements, they always must remember that the rules of accounting have been established to serve a purpose—the communication of useful economic information to the makers of decisions. Accountants can best serve this purpose by adhering to the principle of **substance over form:** the accountant should be more concerned with reporting the economic substance of a transaction than with reporting the form of the transaction.

If accountants allow the application of the rules of accounting to outweigh their overall objective, they will be guilty of allowing the form of a transaction, or the form of the financial accounting system, to distort the substantive message that should be communicated. As a result, the economic message will not be understood properly by the user of financial statements. More important, users of financial statements soon will find that their reliance on the accountant's information results in poor decisions. Thus, these users soon will seek other sources of relevant information.

Accountants, then, must not tie themselves to the mechanical application of rules, but instead should be constantly aware of their primary objective—the production of relevant and reliable information. If accountants continually seek to achieve this objective, the substantive content of the communication will control the preparation of financial statements.

Modifying Conventions

As was stated previously, accountants cannot use rigid rules in the practice of their profession. Instead, accountants must use their judgment in following and modifying basic theoretical principles. In applying professional judgment, accountants often rely upon two basic conventions.

Materiality

If accountants were to try to disclose all of the economic information about a firm, financial statements would become so tedious they would be of little value. The communication process would be destroyed by an information overload. Therefore, accountants use their judgment to determine what information should be reported. In exercising this judgment accountants consider the **materiality,** or significance, of the information.

The obvious problem for accountants is to determine what is significant. Traditionally, the accounting profession has argued that the determination of significance should be made on a case-by-case basis; that is, the individual practitioner, considering all of the facts and circumstances present in a given situation, is best able to decide if an event or piece of information is significant. Over the years there have been attempts to quantify materiality. Various professional promulgations use a fixed percentage analysis in determining materiality with respect to a particular practical problem. The Securities and Exchange Commission suggests that 10% is the benchmark of materiality. Yet, on the whole the question of materiality remains one that is answered by individual accountants exercising individual judgment.

Conservatism

The **conservatism** convention dictates that given two alternative methods of presenting an economic event, each being of equal theoretical and logical validity, the one that results in the lowest reported levels of net income and/or net assets should be selected. In other words, when there is a question as to whether revenue should be recognized or postponed, it should be postponed. Similarly, when there is a question as to whether an expenditure should be capitalized or expensed, conservatism dictates that the item be expensed.

The key to conservatism is that before it can be used to control a decision, there should be equal authoritative and logical support for at least two alternative methods of treating the same situation. If any of the available alternatives is superior to the others, that superior alternative should be selected for financial statement purposes, regardless of its impact upon net income and/or net assets. Thus, conservatism can be viewed as a type of tie-breaker, to be used only when all other alternatives are equal.

Concept Summary

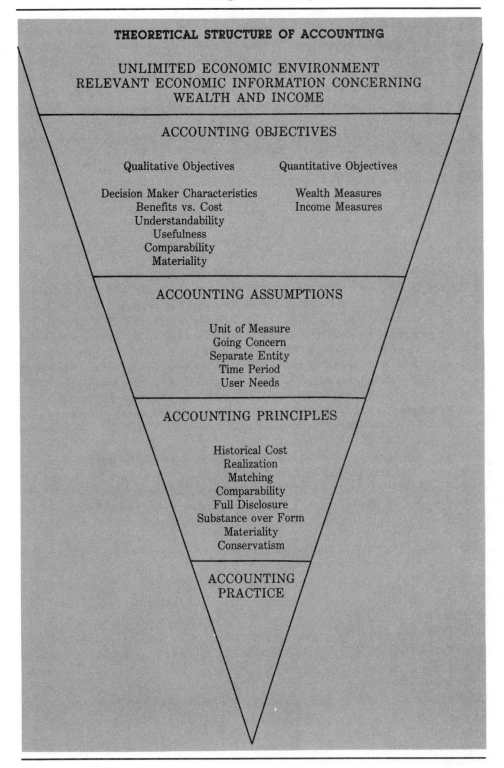

THEORETICAL STRUCTURE OF ACCOUNTING

UNLIMITED ECONOMIC ENVIRONMENT
RELEVANT ECONOMIC INFORMATION CONCERNING
WEALTH AND INCOME

ACCOUNTING OBJECTIVES

Qualitative Objectives   Quantitative Objectives

Decision Maker Characteristics   Wealth Measures
Benefits vs. Cost   Income Measures
Understandability
Usefulness
Comparability
Materiality

ACCOUNTING ASSUMPTIONS

Unit of Measure
Going Concern
Separate Entity
Time Period
User Needs

ACCOUNTING PRINCIPLES

Historical Cost
Realization
Matching
Comparability
Full Disclosure
Substance over Form
Materiality
Conservatism

ACCOUNTING
PRACTICE

Questions

Q–2–1 Distinguish between the qualitative characteristics of usefulness and understandability. Why must accounting information possess both of these characteristics?

Q–2–2 Distinguish between the characteristics of relevance and reliability. Why do accountants often refer to a trade-off that must be made between these two characteristics?

Q–2–3 Explain some of the different uses that may be made of information regarding firm wealth.

Q–2–4 Explain some of the different uses that may be made of information regarding firm income.

Q–2–5 Explain the basic relationship that exists between income and wealth.

Q–2–6 Explain the effect that the choice of a particular method of valuation would have on the content of published financial statements.

Q–2–7 Why is the timing of the release of financial data important to users of financial statements?

Q–2–8 Why must accountants select an arbitrary cutoff date in preparing financial statements?

Q–2–9 Why do accountants attempt to meet the needs of all users with a single set of financial statements?

Q–2–10 Explain three uses to which financial statement information may be put. Explain the difference in the information that would be used for each of these purposes.

Q–2–11 Why must accountants make assumptions?

Q–2–12 Briefly explain each of the following assumptions:
- **a)** Unit of measure assumption.
- **b)** Going concern assumption.
- **c)** Separate entity assumption.
- **d)** Time period assumption.
- **e)** User needs assumption.

Q–2–13 What is the relationship between accounting assumptions and accounting principles?

Q–2–14 Why do accountants search for an arms-length transaction as evidence of a significant economic event?

Q–2–15 What do accountants mean when they say that information is "free from bias"?

Q–2–16 Why is it important that financial information be presented in an objective manner?

Q–2–17 What is required before the earnings process is considered complete?

Q–2–18 What is the purpose of matching revenues and expenses?

Q–2–19 Explain the difference between a cost, an expenditure, and a loss.

Q–2–20 Why are financial statements designed to be comparable?

Q–2–21 What is meant by full disclosure?

Q–2–22 Explain the balance that must be achieved between full disclosure and materiality.

Q–2–23 Why do accountants adhere to the conservatism principle?

Q–2–24 What is the difference between form and substance? Why are accountants concerned with the substance of transactions rather than their form?

Discussion Questions and Cases

D–2–1 For the past seven months, Sheridan Corporation has been negotiating with Grant Corporation concerning a loan. At present, the corporations have agreed upon the following terms: Sheridan would lend Grant $2,000,000 at an annual rate of interest of 12%. Interest would be paid semiannually, and 10% of the original principal amount would be paid each December 31, until the loan was repaid fully.

The officers of Sheridan have some doubts about whether they should go through with the transaction. Although the parties have agreed to the terms of the loan, Sheridan has not made a final commitment to transfer the funds.

Before making a final decision, the officers of Sheridan requested a set of audited financial statements from Grant. Grant provided Sheridan with an income statement, balance sheet, and statement of changes in financial position that had been audited by a reputable firm of certified public accountants. The auditor's opinion indicated that there were no deficiencies in the financial statements.

The officers have disagreed about their analysis of the financial statements. The president of Sheridan has argued that primary emphasis should be placed on the Grant Corporation balance sheet. It is the president's position that if Grant were to default on the loan, Sheridan would have to claim the assets owned by Grant in an effort to recover its funds.

The treasurer of Sheridan has argued that primary emphasis should be placed on the Grant Corporation income statement. It is the treasurer's position that if Grant is to repay the loan, the funds for repayment will have to be earned by the firm in the future. Therefore, Sheridan should be concerned with Grant's ability to produce income in future years.

Required:

You have been asked to help reconcile the disagreement between the officers and to complete the analysis prerequisite to making a decision on the loan. Prepare a brief statement explaining the type of financial information that Sheridan should rely upon in deciding about the loan. Be sure to explain both the objectives you seek to achieve in your analysis and the method you intend to use in achieving these objectives.

D–2–2 During the last three years Smith Corporation, a manufacturer of small parts used in the automotive industry, has lost money. The officers of Smith consistently have explained that their close tie to the automotive industry, particularly their close tie to the manufacturers of large, inefficient engines, has been the reason for the repeated losses.

As of the end of the year, Smith Corporation was in dire need of outside funds. Smith approached several banks about loans, and at one point company officers actually considered selling controlling interest in the corporation to a foreign competitor. Although the problems encountered at year-end were overcome, Smith Corporation is in a financially vulnerable position. Smith's balance sheet shows assets with a book value of $22,000,000. Yet, if these assets were offered on the open market, Smith would receive only about $5,000,000. In fact, if Smith Corporation were to be sold in its entirety, the estimated market price would be only about $6,500,000.

Smith Corporation recently approached another bank concerning additional financing. The bank responded that it would be willing to consider additional financing, but that an audited set of financial statements would be required. The officers of Smith Corporation have approached you with regard to the preparation of these statements and the necessary opinion.

The Smith Corporation executives have admitted that there may be a going concern problem present in this situation. Yet, they have explained that if Smith is able to get the loan, the company will be able to diversify and continue to operate. Although your examination of the Smith Corporation records confirms the conclusion of the officers (i.e., if the loan is made, the company will be able to continue in business), you also are convinced that if the loan is not made, Smith Corporation will soon cease to operate. More important, your

discussions with the bank have indicated that if your opinion does not assume Smith to be a going concern, the loan will not be made.
Required:
Draft a brief memo explaining the position you should take in your audit opinion. Are there any alternative actions that you should consider taking with respect to this situation?

D–2–3 Robert Lee, an individual, is the sole owner of three distinct corporations: Lee Enterprises, Inc., Lee Land Development, Inc., and Lee Real Property Investments, Inc. Although the corporations have separate management, they often are forced to transact business (at arms-length) with each other. More important, Mr. Lee often has lent money to and borrowed money from the corporations.

Last week Mr. Lee approached a local bank about a loan. When asked to list the value of the property that he owned, Mr. Lee listed his stock holdings in each of the three corporations and assigned them a total value of approximately $4,000,000. The bank officer in charge of Mr. Lee's request soon discovered that Mr. Lee's only assets consisted of his corporate stock. Therefore, the officer refused to make the loan to Mr. Lee before examining financial statements of each of the corporations.

Mr. Lee objected to the bank officer's request and asked for a meeting with the bank's board of directors. At this meeting Mr. Lee explained that he and his corporations were separate entities. Mr. Lee further explained that none of the money obtained from the loan would be invested in the companies. More important, Mr. Lee explained that personal funds, and not corporate funds, would be used to repay the loan.

After Mr. Lee's presentation, the bank officers and directors discussed the separate entity assumption as it applied to this situation. One of the officers argued that Mr. Lee should be viewed as an entity separate from his corporations, and therefore the financial status of the corporations was of no significance. The loan officer who originally handled Mr. Lee's application objected to this position. The loan officer argued that since the stock in the corporations was Mr. Lee's only substantial asset, the bank should consider the financial status of the companies in arriving at the value of the stock, and thus the value of Mr. Lee.
Required:
Prepare a brief memo explaining the applicability of the separate entity assumption to this situation. Be sure to explain whether the bank should consider the financial status of the Lee corporations in deciding whether to make the requested loan.

D–2–4 Your accounting firm has been engaged to perform an audit on a local bank. In the past few months there have been rumors that one of the bank's largest customers is in financial trouble. Your examination has revealed that this customer owes the bank a substantial sum of money that must be repaid within the next 30 days.

You have been assigned the task of auditing the "loan loss reserve" (i.e., the allowance for loans that will not be paid by customers). In the course of your examination, you discover that the bank has assumed that the loan made to the large customer will be paid in full at the due date. Although the rumors about the large customer have come from reliable sources, there is no certainty that the loan will not be repaid. The customer has been financially weak for a number of years, but traditionally has been able to pay his debts.

You have suggested that the publication of the bank's financial statements be delayed until the financial condition of this customer becomes clear. You have discussed this matter with the financial vice-president of the bank, and although he objects to delaying the publication of the statements, he has agreed to abide by your decision.
Required:
Prepare a brief memo discussing the issues present in this case and the factors that should be considered in reaching a final decision. Be sure to indicate any alternatives available for solving this problem.

D–2–5 The R. J. Walters Company has been in the retail sales business for the last 15 years. Before the current year, Walters had a firm-wide policy that merchandise purchased for purposes of resale was not to be used by company personnel in the performance of corporate functions.

The "credit crunch" that industry has experienced during the last few years has had a serious effect on the affairs of R. J. Walters. During the last year the company modified the policy on company use of merchandise held for resale in an effort to reduce the need to borrow short-term funds. During the past year company personnel used merchandise that had cost $25,000 in the performance of R. J. Walters business. Although the merchandise was removed physically from the warehouse where inventory usually is stored, it was understood that if a shortage of the particular item(s) were to develop, the merchandise would be returned to the warehouse and be sold to customers. The new company policy severely reduced the need of R. J. Walters to borrow funds, and thus produced great savings in the form of unincurred interest expense.

At the end of the year R. J. Walters executives began to consider the impact of the inventory use on the current year's balance sheet. Several executives proposed that the inventory that had been used for company purposes should be treated as follows:

a) The corporate president argued that there should be no change in the balance sheet classification or valuation of the merchandise. The president argued that the company's use of the inventory had no effect on its historical cost, and the fact that the merchandise was always available for resale meant that the merchandise always should have been classified as inventory.

b) The corporate vice-president agreed that the merchandise should continue to be presented as inventory, but argued that the value of the inventory should be lowered. The vice-president argued that since the company had used the merchandise, it could no longer be sold as new. Therefore, it was unlikely that the company could sell the merchandise for an amount equal to its cost. The vice-president believed that the inventory should be shown at its fair market value less any expense that would be incurred before the merchandise could be sold. In addition, the vice-president thought that the difference between the new balance sheet value and the merchandise's historical cost should be reported as an expense of operations.

c) The corporate treasurer believes that the merchandise should no longer be classified as inventory. Instead, the treasurer believes that the merchandise should be reclassified as "assets held for use in operations" and should be valued at the lower of the fair market value or historical cost of the assets. Furthermore, the treasurer thinks that as the assets continue to decline in value, the amount of the decline should be recognized as an annual expense of operations.

d) The corporate bookkeeper believes that the executives are worrying about nothing. The bookkeeper argues that $25,000 is no more than a "fistful of change" and should be forgotten.

Required:

Analyze each of the arguments presented above in terms of their use of accounting assumptions and accounting principles. Suggest the proper accounting treatment of the merchandise held for intrafirm use.

D–2–6 Cynamide Company is in the business of producing industrial chemicals. The company sells the chemicals to other industrial firms, and therefore deals on an advance contract basis only. On January 1, 1981, Cynamide Company and R. T. Howling Company entered into a contract for the provision of industrial chemicals. The contract specifically provided that Cynamide was to supply Howling with 1,000 tons of a specified chemical at a price of $450 per ton. The contract required that Cynamide make delivery of the chemicals on or after January 1, 1982.

During 1981 Cynamide acquired all of the materials needed to manufacture the chemicals called for in the Howling contract. By December 31, 1981, Cynamide had completed the manufacture of the chemicals at a cost of $325 per ton. All that remained to be done was to deliver the chemicals to the Howling plant. The delivery of the chemicals was provided for in a contract with the local railroad and was to cost Cynamide $25 per ton.

At the board of directors' meeting on December 31, 1981, the members entered into a discussion of the effect of the Cynamide-Howling contract on 1981 income. The executives were unsure as to whether the profit of $100 per ton should be recognized in 1981 or 1982.

Required:

Prepare a memo to Cynamide management explaining the basic theory that governs the accounting treatment of the profit derived from the Cynamide-Howling contract.

Exercises

E–2–1 Answer the following multiple choice questions.

a) Which of the following is considered a pervasive constraint by *Statement of Financial Accounting Concepts No. 2?*

   (1) Benefits/costs.
   (2) Conservatism.
   (3) Timeliness.
   (4) Verifiability.

b) Uncertainty and risks inherent in business situations should be considered adequately in financial reporting. This statement is an example of which of the following concepts?

   (1) Conservatism.
   (2) Completeness.
   (3) Neutrality.
   (4) Representational faithfulness.

c) According to *Statement of Financial Accounting Concepts No. 2*, relevance and reliability are the two primary qualities that make accounting information useful for decision making. Predictive value is an ingredient of

	Relevance	*Reliability*
(1)	No	No
(2)	No	Yes
(3)	Yes	Yes
(4)	Yes	No

d) Which of the following is one of the basic features of financial accounting?

   (1) Direct measurement of economic resources and obligations, and changes in them in terms of money and sociological and psychological impact.
   (2) Direct measurement of economic resources and obligations, and changes in them in terms of money.
   (3) Direct measurement of economic resources and obligations, and changes in them in terms of money and sociological impact.
   (4) Direct measurement of economic resources and obligations, and changes in them in terms of money and psychological impact.

(AICPA adapted)

E–2–2 Answer the following multiple choice questions.

a) The premium on a three-year insurance policy that expires in 1984 was paid in advance in 1980. What is the effect of this transaction on the 1980 financial statements for each of the following?

	Prepaid Assets	*Expenses*
(1)	Increase	No effect
(2)	Increase	Increase

(3) No effect   Increase
(4) No effect   No effect

b) The valuation of a promise to receive cash in the future as present value on the financial statements of a business entity is valid because of the accounting concept of
(1) Entity.
(2) Materiality.
(3) Going concern.
(4) Neutrality.

c) Which of the following is an example of the expense recognition principle of associating cause and effect?
(1) Allocation of insurance cost.
(2) Sales commissions.
(3) Depreciation of fixed assets.
(4) Officers' salaries.

d) Accruing net losses on firm purchase commitments for inventory is an example of which accounting concept?
(1) Conservatism.
(2) Realization.
(3) Consistency.
(4) Materiality.

e) When a specific customer's account receivable is written off as uncollectible, what will be the effect on net income under each of the following methods of recognizing bad debt expense?

	Allowance	*Direct Write-Off*
(1)	None	Decreased
(2)	Decreased	None
(3)	Decreased	Decreased
(4)	None	None

(AICPA adapted)

E–2–3 Answer the following multiple choice questions.

a) A patent, purchased in 1978 and being amortized over a 10-year life, was determined to be worthless in 1981. The write-off of the asset in 1981 is an example of which of the following principles?
(1) Associating cause and effect.
(2) Immediate recognition.
(3) Systematic and rational allocation.
(4) Objectivity.

b) What accounting concept justifies the use of accruals and deferrals?
(1) Going concern.
(2) Materiality.
(3) Consistency.
(4) Stable monetary unit.

c) Which of the following is *not* a basis for the immediate recognition of a cost during a period?
(1) The cost provides no discernible future benefit.
(2) The cost recorded in a prior period no longer produces discernible benefits.
(3) The federal income tax savings using the immediate write-off method exceed the savings obtained by allocating the cost to several periods.
(4) Allocation of the cost on the basis of association with revenue or among several accounting periods is considered to serve no useful purpose.

d) The information provided by financial reporting pertains to which of the following?
(1) Individual business enterprises, rather than to industries or to an economy as a whole or to members of society as consumers.

(2) Individual business enterprises and industries, rather than to an economy as a whole or to members of society as consumers.

(3) Individual business enterprises and an economy as a whole, rather than to industries or to members of society as consumers.

(4) Individual business enterprises, industries, and an economy as a whole, rather than to members of society as consumers.

e) Under what condition is it proper to recognize revenues before the sale of merchandise?

(1) When the ultimate sale of the goods is at an assured sales price.

(2) When the revenue is to be reported as an installment sale.

(3) When the concept of internal consistency (of amounts of revenue) must be complied with.

(4) When management has a long-established policy to do so.

(AICPA adapted)

E–2–4 Answer the following multiple choice questions.

a) When bad debt expense is estimated on the basis of the percentage of past actual losses from bad debts to past net credit sales, and when this percentage is adjusted for anticipated conditions, the accounting concept of

(1) Matching is being followed.

(2) Matching is *not* being followed.

(3) Substance over form is being followed.

(4) Going concern is *not* being followed.

b) The principle of objectivity includes which accounting concept?

(1) Summarization.

(2) Classification.

(3) Conservatism.

(4) Verifiability.

c) The accrued balance in a revenue account represents an amount that is

	Earned	*Collected*
(1)	Yes	Yes
(2)	Yes	No
(3)	No	Yes
(4)	No	No

(AICPA adapted)

Problems

P–2–1 The Financial Accounting Standards Board (FASB) has been working on a conceptual framework for financial accounting and reporting. The FASB has issued four Statements of Financial Accounting Concepts. These Statements are intended to set forth objectives and fundamentals that will be the basis for developing financial accounting and reporting standards. The objectives identify the goals and purposes of financial reporting. The fundamentals are the underlying concepts of financial accounting—concepts that guide the selection of transactions, events, and circumstances to be accounted for; their recognition and measurement; and the means of summarizing and communicating them to interested parties.

The purpose of *Statement of Financial Accounting Concepts No. 2*, "Qualitative Characteristics of Accounting Information," is to examine the characteristics that make accounting information useful. The characteristics or qualities of information discussed in *SFAC No. 2* are the ingredients that make information useful and are the qualities to be sought when accounting choices are made.

Required:
1.   Identify and discuss the benefits which can be expected to be derived from the FASB's conceptual framework study.
2.   What is the most important quality for accounting information as identified in *SFAC No. 2* and explain why it is the most important.
3.   *SFAC No. 2* describes a number of key characteristics or qualities for accounting information. Briefly discuss the importance of any three of these qualities for financial reporting purposes.

(AICPA adapted)

P–2–2   The concept of the accounting entity often is considered to be the most fundamental of accounting concepts, one that pervades all of accounting.

Required:
1.   What is an accounting entity? Explain.
2.   Explain why the accounting entity concept is so fundamental that it pervades all of accounting.
3.   For each of the following indicate whether an accounting concept of entity is applicable; discuss and give illustrations.

    a)   A unit created by or under law.
    b)   The product-line segment of an enterprise.
    c)   A combination of legal units and /or product-line segments.
    d)   All of the activities of an owner or a group of owners.
    e)   An industry.
    f)   The economy of the United States.

(AICPA adapted)

P–2–3   Three independent, unrelated statements follow regarding financial accounting. Each statement contains some unsound reasoning.

Statement I: One function of financial accounting is to measure a company's net earnings for a given period of time. An earnings statement will measure a company's true net earnings if it is prepared in accordance with generally accepted accounting principles. Other financial statements are basically unrelated to the earnings statement. Net earnings would be measured as the difference between revenues and expenses. Revenues are an inflow of cash to the enterprise and should be realized when recognized. This may be accomplished by using the sales basis or the production basis. Expenses should be matched with revenues to measure net earnings. Usually, variable expenses are assigned to the product, and fixed expenses are assigned to the period.

Statement II: One function of financial accounting is to accurately present a company's financial position at a given point in time. This is done with a statement of financial position, which is prepared using historical-cost valuations for all assets and liabilities except inventories. Inventories are stated at first-in, first-out (FIFO), last-in, first-out (LIFO), or average valuations. The statement of financial position must be prepared on a consistent basis with prior years' statements.

In addition to reflecting assets, liabilities, and stockholders' equity, a statement of financial position, in a separate section, should reflect a company's reserves. The section should include three different types of reserves: depreciation reserves, product warranty reserves, and retained earnings reserves. All three of these types of reserves are established by a credit to the reserve account.

Statement III: Financial statement analysis involves using ratios to test past performance of a given company. Past performance is compared to a predetermined standard, and the company is evaluated accordingly. One such ratio is the current ratio, which is computed as current assets divided by current liabilities, or as monetary assets divided by monetary liabilities. A current ratio of two to one is considered good for companies; but the higher the ratio, the better the company's financial position is assumed to be. The current ratio is dynamic because it helps to measure fund flows.

Required:
Identify the areas that are not in accordance with generally accepted accounting principles or are untrue with respect to the financial statement analysis discussed in each of the statements and explain why the reasoning is incorrect. Complete your identification and explanation of each statement before proceeding to the next statement.

(AICPA adapted)

3

Income Determination and Reporting

In many areas of practice, determination of revenues is not an easy task. Frequently revenue measurement involves estimates. Measuring revenue for a "Mom and Pop" grocery is easy, particularly if sales are on a cash basis. On the other hand, measuring the annual revenues earned by a shipbuilder or building contractor is heavily dependent upon estimates.

One industry in which revenue measurement initially seems to be fairly simple is the airline industry. The airlines usually collect fares in cash or through customer credit cards. There appears to be no problem in determining the dollar amount of revenues. But what happens when the fares are prepaid, or when part of the airfare collected goes to other airlines? The following excerpts from a recent article point out the problem:

> Perhaps the most peculiar aspect of airline accounting is how much revenue to record and when . . . .
>
> Obviously, it wouldn't be fair for an airline to record revenue from your ticket before it has given you the service you paid for. So once a year, each airline opens an account called Air Traffic Liability or Unearned Transportation Revenue (you can look it up under the current liabilities in the balance sheet). When you pay for your ticket, that is where your money goes. Then, when you use the ticket, the airline moves those dollars from ATL into revenue.
>
> Of course, with 300 million people flying every year and with up to 40 different types of fares on any given route, things get a lot more complicated. As one airline man puts it, "It's a real paper mill." You might think the airline would simply bundle together all the tickets it collects each day, add up the fares and make the proper adjustments to ATL and revenue. But only very small carriers that don't have many tickets to keep track of, and very large ones like United and American, can afford to do so.
>
> Instead, most airlines—Eastern, Delta, and Braniff among them—use statistics to figure out how much money they have made—that is, how much they *think* they have made. Every day, they take a random sample of tickets and figure out an average revenue per passenger-mile. Then they assume all their tickets had that average revenue, and they multiply by total passenger-miles

flown. This will get them within 1% or 2% of the real number. When the ATL account for the year is closed, months after the year is up, whatever remains is lumped into the current year's revenue. All the real dollars do get to the bottom line—it just takes time.*

Problems exist in the measurement of revenues in many industries. In addition to APB Opinions, FASB Standards, and SEC Releases, the AICPA issues industry guides that help the practicing accountant in the measurement of revenues for companies in certain specialized industries.

*Jane Carmichael, "The Wild Blue Yonder," *Forbes*, November 9, 1981, p. 94.

It can be said that all businesses exist to generate revenues. The revenue-generating process requires that the company incur costs or expenses. As discussed in the previous chapter, these revenues and expenses are matched to determine the income from the company's operations. The process of determining income appears very simple, and in many cases it is simple. However, accountants face numerous situations when the process is not as easy as it first appears. The purpose of this chapter is to look at the basic theory underlying the measurement of income. The chapter presents the basic concepts underlying current GAAP for revenue recognition and also looks at some alternative income measurement concepts.

Revenues have been defined as "inflows or other enhancements of assets of an entity or settlements of its liabilities (or a combination of both) during a period from delivering or producing goods, rendering services, or other activities that constitute the entity's ongoing major or central operations."[1] Generally, the inflow of assets represents actual or expected cash inflows.

Nature of Income Reporting

Five aspects of income reporting are considered in this section: (1) emphasis on income, (2) estimation of income, (3) realization vs. recognition of revenues, (4) the realization principle, and (5) current operating vs. all-inclusive income.

Emphasis on Income

Accountants prepare two, basic, related statements—the income or earnings statement and the statement of financial position (also referred to as the balance sheet). Often accountants must make decisions concerning the choice of alternative accounting practices. One choice may be better for measuring income but not for portraying current financial position. For example, the last-in first-out (LIFO) inventory method may be considered better for income measurement because it matches current costs with current revenues, and thereby gives a measure of current operating efficiency. The use of LIFO, however, has a detrimental impact on the statement of financial position. LIFO shows inventory at old

[1] "Elements of Financial Statements of Business Enterprises," *Statement of Financial Accounting Concepts No. 3* (Stamford, Conn.: FASB, 1980), par. 63.

values that generally are not indicative of the inventory's current value. Thus, while LIFO is good for measuring income, it is not desirable for measuring current financial position. Accountants need some guidelines to help them determine whether the income statement or the statement of financial position is more important.

An emphasis on financial position would indicate that perhaps those accounting alternatives that most closely reflected the current value of assets should be used. In the early part of the century the emphasis was on the statement of financial position. At that time few guidelines existed for preparing the statements. Some companies wrote up assets, others depreciated them on a liberal basis, and still others took very conservative depreciation. The income statement was viewed as a link between the annual statements of financial position or balance sheets.

During the 1920s and 1930s the income statement began to evolve as the primary statement. Financial statement users became more concerned with current and future operating results than with current liquidity and financial position. Under today's GAAP the primary emphasis is placed on the income statement. The FASB recently expressed this position as follows: "The primary focus of financial reporting is information about an enterprise's performance provided by measures of earnings and its components."[2] The focus on earnings is tied to the objectives of financial reporting; the FASB defines some of these objectives as follows:

> Financial reporting should provide information that is useful to present and potential investors and creditors and other users in making rational investment, credit, and similar decisions.[3]

> Financial reporting should provide information to help present and potential . . . users in assessing the amounts, timing, and uncertainty of prospective cash receipts from dividends or interest and the proceeds from the sale, redemption or maturity of securities or loans.[4]

The FASB believes that financial information is useful if it aids statement users in projecting their future cash flows. Information that would help in assessing the enterprise's future cash flows would be most useful to statement users in trying to predict their personal future cash flows.

> . . . since an enterprise's ability to generate favorable cash flows affects both its ability to pay dividends and interest and the market prices of its securities, expected cash flows to investors and creditors are related to expected cash flows to the enterprise in which they have invested or to which they have loaned funds.[5]

Thus, the profession has taken the position that the measurement of income is more important than the measurement of financial position.

[2]"Objectives of Financial Reporting by Business Enterprises," *Statement of Financial Accounting Concepts No. 1* (Stamford, Conn.: FASB, 1978), par. 43.

[3]Ibid., par. 34.

[4]Ibid., par. 37.

[5]Ibid., par. 39.

Estimation of Income

It is important to realize that income measurement is not an exact science; rather, it is a process of estimation. Although accountants may determine a net income figure down to the penny, it is not the precise measurement it appears to be. To understand why accountants' income measurements are only estimates, you must take into account those circumstances that must exist in order to have a precise measurement.

Consider the following simple situation. Mr. Chip invests $10,000 cash into a business. He does not invest any additional funds nor withdraw any funds during the five-year life of the business. At the end of these five years, Mr. Chip takes $60,000 cash out of the business as complete payment of his equity. This situation can be depicted as follows:

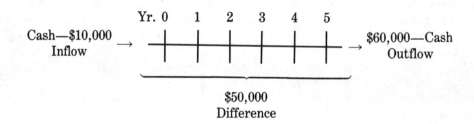

It is obvious that in this simple situation Mr. Chip's business earned a $50,000 net income over its five-year life. There are no measurement problems because only cash was invested and withdrawn from the business. The business started and ended in a purely cash position. If the dollar invested in year 0 is equal in purchasing power to the dollar withdrawn in year 5, there is no fluctuation in the value of the unit of measure used to determine the net income. In this situation it could be said that there is an accurate measurement of income. There are two basic conditions essential to an accurate measurement of income:

1. Only cash is invested and withdrawn from the business.
2. There is no change in the purchasing power of the unit of measurement being used.

The first condition is essential because it eliminates the measurement problems inherent in investing or withdrawing a noncash asset. Consider the following illustration, which shows cash and land being invested:

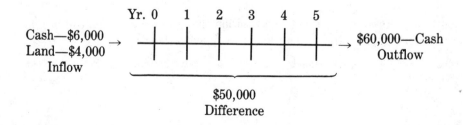

Is the $50,000 difference an accurate measurement of income for the life of the business? The answer is perhaps, but most probably not; the cash value placed on the land is probably not accurate. How can you be sure that the value of the land is precisely $4,000 and not $3,900 or $4,100 or some other figure? To the extent that the measurement of the cash value of land is incorrect, income is also incorrect. When noncash assets are invested or withdrawn from a business, the measurement of income can be correct only by chance. If the noncash assets were valued accurately, income would be accurate. It is highly unlikely, however, that the valuation of noncash assets is precise or accurate. Therefore, income measurement cannot be accurate.

The second condition (no change in purchasing power) is also essential to the accurate measurement of income. If the value of the monetary unit of measure changes, the beginning dollars are not equivalent to the ending dollars. If this change in purchasing power could be measured accurately, income could also be measured accurately. The federal government has attempted to measure changes in the purchasing power of the dollar through indices such as the GNP Implicit Price Deflator, the Producer's Price Index, and the Consumer Price Index. These indices are very imprecise; they provide an indication of the direction and general magnitude of changes in purchasing power but are not intended to reflect precise measurements. Too many assumptions must be made in calculating these indices to consider them precise or accurate. Therefore, since the purchasing power of the dollar fluctuates, and since there is no accurate measurement of purchasing power changes, income measurement cannot be accurate.

In normal business operations there are few, if any, instances in which only cash is invested and withdrawn from a business while at the same time there is no change in the purchasing power of the monetary unit; hence, precise or accurate measurement of income is impossible. If accurate income measurement is impossible for the whole life of the business, imagine the problems encountered in trying to determine income for a part of the life of the business. Annual income measurement is imprecise because it violates both prerequisites for accurate income measurement. In normal situations annual determination of income would involve noncash assets at both the beginning and end of the period and purchasing power changes during the year. As a result, it is impossible to have an accurate measurement of annual income.

You might argue that since GAAP emphasize the income statement, income should be measured and reported only when it can be done accurately, or as near accurately as possible. Income measurement is most accurate when done for the whole life of the firm, assuming no change in price levels. Therefore, why not report income only when the firm ceases operations? To do so would violate several accounting principles. One is the time period assumption (discussed in the previous chapter), which requires that firms prepare periodic financial statements. Two other principles are timeliness and relevance. GAAP require that periodic (annual) financial statements be prepared because they will provide timely and relevant information to statement users. Accounting measurements and reports should be timely and relevant for their intended use. An investor in Exxon could not be expected to have to wait until Exxon ceased to exist to be informed as to its profitability. In all probability the investor would cease to exist before Exxon.

Financial information must also be reliable.

Relevance and reliability are the two primary qualities that make accounting information useful for decision making. Subject to constraints imposed by cost and materiality, increased relevance and increased reliability are the characteristics that make information a more desirable commodity—that is, one useful in making decisions. If either of these qualities is completely missing, the information will not be useful.[6]

The profession realizes that there is a trade-off between reliability (accuracy) and the timeliness and relevance of information. In the case of periodic reports, what is given up in terms of the accuracy of accounting measurements is more than offset by the provision of relevant accounting information when needed.

Realization vs. Recognition of Revenues

A distinction must be made between revenue realization (earning revenue) and revenue recognition (reporting revenue). **Revenue realization** refers to the time and activities involved in generating revenue; it usually entails a continuous process of production and sale of goods. The process of measuring and reporting revenue is called **revenue recognition.** Recognition refers to the selection of the time period for reporting the revenues as earned. While the earning process may be continuous, the reporting of revenue is periodic—that is, quarterly or annually.

Since the earning process is generally continuous, accountants need to have some guidelines to help them determine the point in time when the revenues should be reported as having been earned.

Realization Principle

As discussed in the previous chapter, the realization principle provides a guideline to be used in determining when to report revenues as having been earned. The principle basically indicates that revenue should be recognized (reported) when substantially all of the earning process is complete.

There are several possible points at which revenue can be recognized. Exhibit 3-1 depicts the normal process of earning revenue. Included in this process are production, sale of the goods, and a period of cash collection. The seven possible times when revenue could be recognized are as follows:

1. When an order is received or production scheduled.
2. During the production process.
3. When production is complete.
4. When the sale takes place.
5. As cash is collected.
6. After the whole earning process is complete.
7. Throughout the whole process.

A distinction was made earlier between earning revenue and revenue recognition. Look at Exhibit 3-1 and ask yourself when revenue actually is *earned*. Is it

[6]"Qualitative Characteristics of Accounting Information," *Statement of Financial Accounting Concepts No. 2* (Stamford, Conn.: FASB, 1980), quoted from the "Summary of Principal Conclusions."

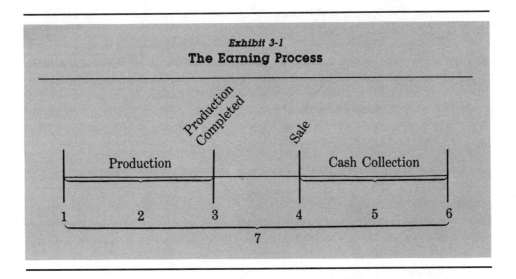

Exhibit 3-1
The Earning Process

Production Completed

Sale

Production

Cash Collection

1   2   3   4   5   6

7

at point "3"? Is revenue earned if items are produced but unsold? Consider point "4." Is revenue earned if you have produced and sold the item but have no cash collections? Is the process of cash collection part of the earning process? The answer most definitely is "yes," since collection is essential to the earning process.

Revenue is *earned* under "7"—throughout the whole process of production, sale, and cash collection. Each step in the scale contributes to the earning process. If income were to be recognized as it is earned, accountants would have to adopt number seven. Although it might be theoretically desirable to recognize revenue as it is earned, it is impossible because of the insurmountable measurement problems involved in such an approach. For example, a company manufactures desks at a cost of $100 and sells them for $150. The gross profit on the sale is $50. If a desk were half-complete at year-end, how much of the sales price or gross profit should be recognized? If a desk were completed but unsold, how much revenue should be recognized? The production process definitely contributes to the revenue-earning process, but it is impossible to tell exactly how much revenue is generated at each stage of production or how much of the $150 sale price is attributable to the selling or cash collection functions. All that is known for sure is that the whole process generates $150 of revenues. It is impossible to determine how much of the $150 is attributable to each separate step within the earning process. Thus, while number "seven" may be the most desirable from a theoretical point of view—that is, recognizing revenue as it is earned—it is impossible to apply in practice.

Since revenue cannot be recognized during the earning process, accountants have adopted the realization principle to determine the point in time when revenue will be recognized. As noted earlier, the realization principle indicates that the earning process must be substantially complete before revenue can be recognized. Point "1" cannot be used for recognizing revenues because little, if any, activity has taken place.

At "2" revenue would be recognized as production takes place. For example, if an item were one-half complete at the end of the year, half of the revenue would be recognized. Recognizing revenue at "2" violates the realization principle since the earning process is not substantially complete.

Point "3" recognizes revenue when production is complete. In most instances the earning process is not substantially complete at this point because a selling and cash collection effort are needed still. However, in those cases when selling and cash collection efforts are negligible, it can be argued that revenue should be recognized when production is completed because the earning process is substantially complete. To record revenue at this point, you would assume that the production costs, selling price, and selling costs are known. Generally point "3" is used for revenue recognition only when the revenue is from mining precious metals, such as gold and silver, and from farm products. In these cases there must be a stable selling price, no significant marketing efforts or costs are involved, and the seller cannot sell enough of the product to affect the market price. When these conditions exist, the critical part of the earning process is the mining of the metal, or planting and harvesting the crop. Once production is complete and the product is ready for sale, the earning process is substantially complete and revenue can be recognized.

Point "4," the point of sale, is when revenue recognition takes place for most companies. Usually the effort and costs of collection are minimal, and the earning process is substantially complete at the point of sale. In most instances all costs of production are known at this point; the sales price is known, and collection costs are negligible or may be estimated with reasonable accuracy. Revenue would not be recognized at this point if there were a significant doubt about future collection or if there were an inability to estimate future collection costs, if material.

Item "5" recognizes revenue as cash is collected. This method, referred to as the installment method, is used widely for tax purpose but may not be used for financial reporting unless the collection of the sale price is not reasonably assured.[7] In the rare situations when this method is used for financial reporting, each cash sales dollar collected is considered to be part recovery of cost and part gross profit. For example, if a company's gross profit rate were 40%, and it collected $1,000 during the year, $400 ($1,000 × 0.4) would be included in gross profit.

Point "6" recognizes revenue when production, sale, and cash collection are complete. This method is extremely conservative and frequently will result in revenue being recognized in a period when no substantial earning activity took place—for example, collection of cash from a sale that took place in an earlier period. The method is not generally accepted.

Consider "2" again. It was indicated previously that this method is unacceptable because the earning process is not substantially complete. This view causes problems in financial reporting for companies that have a long production process. For example, it may take a shipbuilder four years to build a large ship. Under the realization principle no revenue would be reported until the fourth year, when production is completed. Recognition of revenues in this manner is referred to as the **completed-contract method.**

There is an inconsistency between the time period assumption (periodic financial statements) and the realization principle. The time period assumption

[7]"Omnibus Opinion—1966," *Opinions of the Accounting Principles Board No. 10* (New York: AICPA, 1966), par. 12.

requires that the life of the firm be broken down into time segments and that financial statements be prepared for each time period. Recall that the reason for this is to present timely and relevant information to the statement reader. The purpose of the realization principle is to ensure that revenue is recognized only when it has been substantially earned. The peculiar nature of the construction industry requires that the realization principle be ignored or violated if timely and relevant periodic reports are to be prepared. The position of current GAAP in this regard is that timely and relevant financial reports are more important than limiting revenue recognition to when the earning process is substantially complete. Current GAAP prefer that income from construction contracts be recognized during each period of construction rather than at the completion of the contract.

Recognition of construction revenue during each year of the construction period is referred to as the **percentage-of-completion method.** (The completed-contract and percentage-of-completion methods are illustrated in the Appendix to Chapter 8.) Under the percentage-of-completion method the expected gross profit on the contract is recognized in the proportion that the current year's construction costs have to the total expected production cost. In other words, if one-fourth of the total expected construction costs were incurred in the current year, one-fourth of the expected gross profit on the project would be recognized. Current GAAP prefer the percentage-of-completion method except in those cases in which dependable estimates cannot be made.

Current Operating vs. All-Inclusive Income

There have been basically two schools of thought regarding what should be included in the disclosure of the determination of net income. The two schools have been referred to as the current operating and all-inclusive approaches.

The **current operating approach** holds that reported income should reflect only the results of normal recurring operations. Items that do not relate directly to normal operations are disclosed in the statement of retained earnings. The purpose of this approach is to provide the statement reader with a picture of operations as they might be expected to continue in the future. The underlying belief is that statement users should be better able to understand and predict future results of operations if yearly income figures are not biased up or down by items that are not expected to recur.

The **all-inclusive approach,** as its name implies, requires that reported income should include all items occurring during the year, whether or not they are part of normal and recurring operations. The proponents of this approach believe that placing unusual items in the statement of retained earnings will mislead the income statement reader because it will not include items that may have had a significant effect on the year's operations.

Although both approaches had logical reasoning, the controversy between them existed for many years. The controversy was settled in practice by the issuance of APB *Opinion No. 9,* which adopted a compromise position in concluding that "net income should reflect all items of profit and loss recognized during the period with the sole exception of the prior period adjustments . . . . Extraordinary items should, however, be segregated from the results of ordinary operations and shown separately in the income statement, with disclosure of the nature and amounts thereof."[8] The Board essentially adopted the all-inclusive approach. The requirement of separate disclosure for extraordinary items means that the current operating income is reflected also in the statement. The statement reader can determine both the results of normal recurring operations as well as a total picture of all items affecting income during the year.

Part of the FASB's conceptual framework project is concerned with the issues relating to reporting earnings. In a discussion memorandum the FASB essentially retained the all-inclusive approach:

> The concept of earnings used in this project is the increase in net assets or owners' equity from all transactions and other events and circumstances affecting the enterprise during the period . . .[9]

However, it appears that the FASB may propose an additional breakdown of items in the income statement.

> The main focus of this project is to consider which particular categories of revenue, expense, gain, and loss should be disclosed separately to assist the assessment of future cash flows. In studying that question, it seems helpful to consider whether a distinction between regular revenues and expenses and irregular items can be workable and useful.[10]

The FASB apparently believes that significant improvements can be made to improve the usefulness of the income statement in projecting cash flows. In the *Discussion Memorandum* the FASB retitled the term earnings and now refers to it as comprehensive income.

> . . . the reason for using comprehensive income rather than earnings . . . is that the Board has decided to reserve earnings for possible use to designate a different concept that is a component part of—that is, a narrower than or less than—comprehensive income. . . . [11]

The earnings portion of the conceptual framework project has not been completed yet.

Disclosure of Unusual Items

Frequently the reporting of income includes items that are unusual or that will not be a part of the future operations of the company. These items are discussed under the following three areas: (1) extraordinary items, (2) prior period adjustments, and (3) discontinued operations.

---

[8]"Reporting the Results of Operations," *Opinions of the Accounting Principles Board No. 9* (New York: AICPA, 1966), par. 17.

[9]"An Analysis of the Issues Related to Reporting Earnings," *FASB Discussion Memorandum* (Stamford, Conn.: FASB, 1979), par. 11.

[10]Ibid., par. 15.

[11]"Elements of Financial Statements," par. 58.

Extraordinary Items

An **extraordinary item** is essentially an unusual gain or loss that is not a recurring part of normal business operations. Disclosure of extraordinary items was addressed first by the APB in *Opinion No. 9*. The Opinion states that extraordinary items are "events and transactions of material effect which would not be expected to recur frequently and which would not be considered as recurring factors in any evaluation of the ordinary operating processes of the business."[12] Examples included such items as gains and losses from sale or abandonment of a plant or significant segment of the business. Certain items were excluded specifically from being considered extraordinary items because they were "of a character typical of the customary business activities of the entity."[13] Such items as a write-down of receivables or inventory, even though significant in amount, could not be considered extraordinary for a business that had receivables and owned inventory.

The Opinion was subjected to varying interpretations in practice. Often there was an inconsistency among companies in the application of the Opinion. The Board became particularly concerned with interpretations relating to disposal of a segment of the business. As a result of the problems in interpreting *Opinion No. 9*, the Board issued *Opinion No. 30*, which provides additional guidelines to be used in determining if an item is extraordinary. According to this Opinion there were basically two criteria that should be used: the item should be unusual in nature and infrequent in occurence.

> Unusual nature—the underlying event or transaction should possess a high degree of abnormality and be of a type clearly unrelated to, or only incidentally related to, the ordinary and typical activities of the entity, taking into account the environment in which the entity operates.

> Infrequency of occurrence—the underlying event or transaction should be of a type that would not reasonably be expected to recur in the foreseeable future, taking into account the environment in which the entity operates.[14]

An extraordinary item can be defined currently as an item that is unusual in nature and infrequent in occurrence given the environment in which the entity operates. The emphasis is on the environment in which the entity operates. A flood loss may be extraordinary to a company with operations in a mountainous area, while it would not necessarily be extraordinary to a company whose operations are next to a river. The Opinion again included a list of items that could not be considered extraordinary items:

1. Write-down or write-off of receivables, inventories, equipment leased to others, deferred research and development costs, or other intangible assets.
2. Gains or losses from exchange or translation of foreign currencies, including those relating to major devaluations and revaluations.

---

[12] "Results of Operations," *Opinion No. 9*, par. 21.

[13] Ibid., par. 22.

[14] "Reporting the Results of Operations," *Opinions of the Accounting Principles Board No. 30.* (New York: AICPA, 1973), par. 20.

3. Gains or losses on disposal of a segment of a business.
4. Other gains or losses from sale or abandonment of property, plant, or equipment used in the business.
5. Effects of a strike, including those against competitors and major suppliers.
6. Adjustments for accruals on long-term contracts. [15]

Extraordinary items should be disclosed separately, net of their income tax impact, in both total dollars and in per share amounts on the face of the income statement. If an item meets one of the criteria but not the other, it should be disclosed as a separate component of operating income (income before extraordinary items).

An example of the disclosures for extraordinary items appears in Exhibit 3-2. The disclosure was taken from a recent annual report of Puritan Fashions Corporation, the maker of Calvin Klein jeans. Notice that the extraordinary item is shown as a separate item net of tax. The footnote provides information relating to the nature of the extraordinary item.

[15] Ibid., par. 23.

Exhibit 3-2
PURITAN FASHIONS CORPORATION
Disclosures for Extraordinary Items
(In Thousands of Dollars, Except for Per Share Data)

For the Years Ended	December 29, 1979	December 30, 1978
Net Sales	$ 160,335	$ 147,221
Cost and Expenses:		
Cost of sales	110,776	113,197
Selling, warehouse, general and administrative	32,408	27,090
Royalties	5,471	1,498
Interest	4,650	3,476
Total Cost and Expenses	153,305	145,261
Operating Income	7,030	**1,960**
Nonrecurring Losses (Note 1)		(6,911)
Income (Loss) Before Federal Income Tax, Minority Interest and Extraordinary Item	7,030	(4,951)
Provision for Federal Income Tax (Notes 1 and 9):		
Current	1,881	437
Deferred	8	268
	1,889	705

Exhibit 3-2 (continued)
PURITAN FASHIONS CORPORATION
Disclosures for Extraordinary Items
(In Thousands of Dollars, Except for Per Share Data)

For the Years Ended	December 29, 1979	December 30, 1978
Income (Loss) Before Minority Interest and Extraordinary Item	5,141	(5,656)
Minority Interest in Net Income of Subsidiaries	40	44
Income (Loss) Before Extraordinary Item	**5,101**	**(5,700)**
Extraordinary Item—equity in partially-owned company (Note 5)	797	
Net Income (Loss)	**$ 5,898**	**($ 5,700)**
Per share data (Note 1):		
Primary:		
Income (loss) before extraordinary item	**$ 1.42**	**($ 1.59)**
Extraordinary item	.22	
Net income (loss)	**$ 1.64**	**($ 1.59)**
Weighted average number of shares	3,589,580	3,575,077
Fully diluted:		
Income (loss) before extraordinary item	**$ 1.37**	**($ 1.59)**
Extraordinary item	.21	
Net income (loss)	**$ 1.58**	**($ 1.59)**
Weighted average number of shares	3,737,450	3,575,077

NOTE 5. Investment in Unconsolidated Companies—At Equity
The Company had written off its investment in Winston Mills, Inc., ("Winston") a previously majority-owned subsidiary (now 34% owned) prior to Winston's filing a petition for an arrangement under Chapter XI of the Federal Bankruptcy Act on May 22, 1978. A plan of arrangement was confirmed with its creditors on December 5, 1979. Confirmation of the plan enabled Winston to continue its operations as a going concern. The Company's extraordinary item of $797,000 arose from Winston's extraordinary credit representing the forgiveness of indebtedness under the plan and is included in investment in unconsolidated companies at December 29, 1979.

Prior Period Adjustments

As indicated previously, APB *Opinion No. 9* took the position that all items should be reported in the income statement except prior period adjustments. The Opinion provided guidelines for determining if an item were a prior period adjustment. These guidelines were dropped in FASB *Statement No. 16*, which set forth a very restrictive definition of prior period adjustments. The classification currently is limited to two items:

1. Correction of an error in the financial statements of a prior period.
2. Adjustments that result from realization of income tax benefits of preacquisition operating loss carryforwards of purchased subsidiaries.[16]

These items are to be reported in the statement of retained earnings and not in the income statement. A more detailed discussion is presented in Chapter 22.

Discontinued Operations

One type of unusual item that occurs frequently is discontinuing the operations of a segment of the business or product line. Two basic problems are encountered in accounting for discontinued operations: (1) the treatment of current earnings or loss before the disposal decision and (2) the treatment of any gain or loss on disposal. Current GAAP relating to these items are presented in APB *Opinion No. 30*, and are discussed in detail in Chapter 23. The position taken by the APB was that "the results of continuing operations should be reported separately from discontinued operations . . ."[17] and should not be considered an extraordinary item.

Alternative Concepts of Income

Under current GAAP income is calculated using the historical cost (accrual) concept of income. Under this method revenues are recognized when realized, and expenses are recognized when incurred. The previous chapter and preceding sections of this chapter discussed the concepts used in the measurement of historical cost income.

Other methods of income determination exist but are not generally accepted. These concepts are (1) cash, (2) discounted present values, and (3) market value concepts.

Cash Concept

Under the **cash concept** of income, revenues and expenses are measured when cash is received and paid. Income is the difference between the cash receipts from revenues and the cash disbursements for expenses. Individuals use the cash concept most frequently; for income tax purposes it is used most by individuals and small businesses.

The cash concept is not accepted for external reporting because it can distort income and is subject to manipulation. It distorts income in that revenues are

---

[16]"Prior Period Adjustments," *Statement of Financial Accounting Standards No. 16* (Stamford, Conn.: FASB, 1977), par. 11.

[17]"Results of Operations," *Opinion No. 30*, par. 8.

reported in the period collected, not in the period in which the substantial earning process took place. Expenses are reported in the period paid, not in the period in which benefits were received from the costs incurred. The cash basis income figure is subject to manipulation through the timing of cash receipts and disbursements. This is why the method is favored for tax purposes. A small business that wants to minimize income need only delay collection of receipts and accelerate payment or prepay expenses.

Discounted Present Value

The **discounted present value concept** of income measures income as the difference between the present value of the company at the beginning and end of the year. The approach involves estimating all future net cash receipts as of the beginning and end of the year and discounting these expected receipts, at an appropriate interest rate, to the date of measurement. This method has merit from a conceptual point of view because the value of a firm is essentially the discounted value of all future receipts. If measurements were accurate, all financial statement users probably would prefer this method since it looks into the future.

Although this method is desirable from a conceptual point of view, it is impossible to apply realistically in practice. The method requires estimates of net receipts for the foreseeable future. It is impossible to make reasonably accurate forecasts 20, 30, or 40 years into the future. Even if these estimates could be made, what interest rate should be used to discount the future stream of revenues back to the present? Some of the possibilities include current cost of capital, incremental cost of capital, desired rate of return, and current rate of return. If an interest rate or cost of capital figure is to be used, it would be very hard to determine the specific rate. Ten to fifteen years ago, interest rates were constant and at a low level. Today, interest rates fluctuate widely. In recent years the prime rate has gone from 8% to 22% and has started to decline again. The measurement of income under the net present value method is a very rough "guesstimate" at best. It is not a figure on which financial statement users could rely.

Another problem with the approach is that it results in one value for the firm—the discounted net present value. Individual assets do not have specific recorded values. The reason for this is the same as why revenue is not realized as earned (at "7" in Exhibit 3-1) under the historical cost concept. Although each step is part of the earning process, it is impossible to tell exactly how much of the revenue or income is earned at each particular stage in the process. In the net present value concept each asset contributes to the total future cash flows, but it is impossible to determine the specific cash flows that relate to each individual asset. All that is known is that the total group of assets is expected to generate the total future cash flows.

Market Value Concepts

The **market value methods** measure income as the difference in the market value of the firm at the beginning and end of the year, adjusted for additional investments and withdrawals. Under this method the assets are valued at market value at the beginning and end of the year. If the value of the firm's net assets increases during the year, the increase is considered to be the income for the year, assuming no additional investment or withdrawal.

The assets can be valued using essentially two concepts of value: replacement cost and net realizable value.

Replacement Cost. **Replacement cost** is an entry value, or the cost to buy or manufacture the asset in question. In other words, if the company wanted another of the assets in question, it is the cost of acquiring that asset.

Some problems arise in determining the replacement cost. Should the replacement cost be the cost to replace the asset with an exact duplicate, or should replacement consider technological change and replace the asset with similar production capability? For example, suppose the company owns a Model 100 machine that produces 10,000 units a month, and a Model 200 is available that can produce the same quantity but at a lower cost. The question is whether replacement cost should be determined using Model 100 or 200. Generally Model 200 would be used. Replacement cost is considered by the Securities and Exchange Commission (SEC) to be the cost of replacing equivalent production capacity rather than the exact replacement of the asset. The SEC took this approach when it required supplemental footnote disclosure of certain replacement cost data. This approach is similar to that recently taken by the FASB in its requirement of current cost disclosures, which are discussed in detail in Chapter 26.

One other problem with replacement value is whether or not to make an adjustment for the age of the asset. Assume that an asset would cost $10,000 to replace and that half of its useful life has passed. Should its replacement cost be $10,000 or $5,000 (replacement adjusted for the age of the asset)? The preference has been for the $5,000. This, again, was the position taken by the SEC and the FASB. Many theorists consider replacement cost useful. They believe it gives a better measure of current operating efficiency because it matches current costs with current revenues.

Net Realizable Value. **Net realizable value** is an exit value, or what a company could get for an asset if it sold the asset. Usually it is considered to be the sale price in a normal, orderly disposal, not a forced liquidation sale.

Proponents of this method believe it is preferable to replacement cost or historical cost because it informs management and the statement readers of the exit value of the firm's assets. They contend that, from a stewardship point of view, this is the current dollar value of assets entrusted to management. Proponents also contend that this value must be known if intelligent decisions are to be made about continuing or discontinuing the use of an asset or group of assets. Only if this amount is known can management know what amount would be available for investment in alternative investments. For example, if a plant currently is producing a $50,000 a year income on assets with a book value (historical cost) of $250,000, it has a 20% return on historical cost. If the plant has a net realizable value of $350,000, the return is approximately 14% on net realizable value. If the company could invest these funds in another investment that would provide a long-run return in excess of 14%, it should do so, even if the return is below the 20% return on historical cost. An 18% return on net realizable value would provide more revenues to the company than its current 20% return on historical cost. The relevant rate of return is the return on net realizable value, not the return on historical cost.

Critics have argued against net realizable value because it does not use a going-concern approach. They contend that businesses invest in assets to use them in the business, not to liquidate them. The key figure is the asset's value in use, not its resale value. As will be seen in Chapter 26, the FASB recommends use of net realizable value for supplemental disclosures only when the asset in question is to be sold.

Concept Summary

INCOME MEASUREMENT

REVENUE

Definition	Recognized	Earned
Inflow of assets or settlement of liabilities from delivering or producing goods, rendering services, or carrying on other activities that constitute the entity's ongoing major or central operations.	According to the realization rule, revenue should be recognized (reported) when the earning process is substantially complete.	Revenue is actually earned throughout the whole revenue generating process, not just at the point of recognition.

CONCEPTS OF INCOME

Concept	Basis for Measurement
Cash	The difference between the cash inflows and outflows resulting from operations.
Historical Cost	The difference between realized revenues and their related expenses.
Discounted Present Value	The difference between the present value of the company at the beginning and end of the period. The present values are measured by discounting back future cash flows.
Market Value Concepts	The difference between the market value of the firm at the beginning and end of the

year, adjusted for additional investments and withdrawals. (Also measured as operating income plus or minus changes in market value of assets.) Market values may be measured as:
1. Replacement cost—what it would cost to replace the asset
2. Realizable value—what the asset could be sold for

UNUSUAL ITEMS

Item	Definition	Accounting Treatment
Extraordinary Gain or Loss	An item that is unusual in nature and infrequent in occurrence given the environment of the entity.	Disclose as a separate item, net of tax, in the income statement.
Prior Period Adjustments	Adjustment resulting from an error in a prior period or realization of tax benefits of preacquisition operating loss carryforwards of purchased subsidiaries.	Disclose as an adjustment to the beginning balance of the retained earnings account.
Discontinued Operations	Gains or losses resulting from final operations and from sale of a segment of the business.	Disclose in the income statement as a separate item before extraordinary items.

Questions

Q–3–1 Define the term *revenue*.

Q–3–2 Do current financial statements have an emphasis on income or on current financial condition? What is the reason for this emphasis?

Q–3–3 Under what conditions can income be measured accurately?

Q–3–4 What problems in income measurement are caused by the periodicity principal?

Q-3-5 Distinguish between earning revenue and recognizing revenue. When is revenue earned?

Q-3-6 From a theoretical point of view, what are the different points at which revenue could be recognized?

Q-3-7 What problems are encountered in recognizing revenue throughout each phase of the earning process?

Q-3-8 Under current GAAP, when should revenue be recognized?

Q-3-9 Briefly describe each of the following concepts of income:
  a) Cash concept.
  b) Discounted present value concept.
  c) Market value concepts.

Q-3-10 Jobe Co. has a machine that is five years old. The machine originally had a 10-year useful life. It would currently cost $50,000 to buy a new machine exactly like the old one. A new improved machine, capable of the same production capacity as the old machine, can be purchased for $46,000. What are the possible replacement cost values for the machine? Which is preferred and why?

Q-3-11 Netter Co. has a truck that has been used in the business for six years. The truck originally had an eight-year useful life and cost $60,000. The company estimates that it could sell the truck currently for $10,000. It would incur the following selling costs: advertising, $200; selling commission, $500. In addition, the transmission would have to be repaired at a cost of $800. What is the truck's net realizable value?

Q-3-12 What are the criteria used in determining if an item is an extraordinary item?

Q-3-13 Indicate whether or not the following items are extraordinary items:
  a) Write-off of a very large receivable from a customer who went bankrupt.
  b) Gain on the sale of machinery used in the business.
  c) Loss from a fire in a manufacturing plant.
  d) A write-off of computer equipment held for lease to others. The equipment has become obsolete.
  e) A loss resulting from hurricane damage to a plant located on the eastern coast of Florida.
  f) A wholly owned subsidiary has had liquidity problems. An arrangement with creditors, under Chapter XI of the Federal Bankruptcy Act, resulted in forgiveness of a significant portion of the subsidiary's debt. The debt forgiveness resulted in a significant gain.

Q-3-14 What two items qualify as a prior period adjustment? How are prior period adjustments presented in the financial statements?

Q-3-15 Briefly describe the GAAP for accounting for discontinued operations.

Discussion Questions and Cases

D-3-1 Jason Co. is preparing financial statements to present to its banker to secure a loan. The company's accountant prepared a set of financial statements under GAAP. Mr. Jason, president of the company, complained that the financial statements did not fairly present the financial position of the company. Some of his comments to the company accountant were as follows:
  a) "You show inventory at a dollar amount that incorrectly states the value of our inventory. It would cost us $80,000 to replace the inventory, and you show it at only $40,000."

b) "I can't believe you are showing our land at $60,000; that's what we paid for it 10 years ago. It probably is worth $500,000 today."

c) "This $25,000 figure for investment in securities is also out of line. Check your *Wall Street Journal* . . . these are selling for close to $60,000. Why don't you show its market value and include the increase in income?"

Required:

Develop a reply to Mr. Jason explaining the proper theoretical treatment of the items above.

D-3-2   Grace Co. had financial statements prepared by an independent CPA. The company president was confused when he read the completed statements. Several unusual things occurred during the year. The company wrote off a sizable receivable from a very large customer who went into bankruptcy. The company also sold an old building that had been owned by the company for a number of years. The sale was at a significant loss. In addition, the company incurred a loss as a result of a fire in one of its warehouses.

The president is confused because only the fire loss was listed as an extraordinary item in the income statement. He thought that since the large receivable write-off was the only substantial one ever to occur in the life of the company, it also should be considered extraordinary. The president contends that the loss on the building should be extraordinary as well since the company very infrequently sells one of its plant, property, and equipment type assets.

Required:

The president has asked you, his company accountant, to explain why these items were included in income before extraordinary items rather than as part of extraordinary items. Describe the nature of an extraordinary item and explain why the CPA did not consider the items in question extraordinary.

D-3-3   Generally accepted accounting principles require the use of accruals and deferrals in the determination of income.

Required:

1.   How does accrual accounting affect the determination of income? Include in your discussion what constitutes an accrual and a deferral, and give appropriate examples of each.

2.   Contrast accrual accounting with cash accounting.

(AICPA adapted)

D-3-4   Assume you are the new accountant for Midnight Supply, a large supply company. You have just prepared the year-end financial statements and submitted them to Mr. Day, the owner and president of Midnight Supply. Mr. Day is concerned because you prepared the statements rounding calculations to the nearest $1,000. Mr. Day commented, "I know the effect of rounding is immaterial, but I don't want our bankers thinking we can't measure income or balance sheet values accurately. I want to show them we know how much we earned down to the last penny."

Required:

Draft a reply to Mr. Day concerning the accuracy of income measurement.

Exercises

E-3-1   Answer the following multiple choice questions.

a)   During the lifetime of an entity accountants produce financial statements at arbitrary points in time in accordance with which basic accounting concept?

    (1)   Objectivity.

    (2)   Periodicity.

    (3)   Conservatism.

    (4)   Matching.

b) Generally revenues should be recognized at a point when
    (1) Management decides it is appropriate to do so.
    (2) The product is available for sale to the ultimate consumer.
    (3) An exchange has taken place, and the earnings process is virtually complete.
    (4) An order for a definite amount of merchandise has been received for shipment, fob destination.

c) How should rent revenue collected one month in advance be accounted for?
    (1) As revenue in the month collected.
    (2) As a current liability.
    (3) As a separate item in stockholders' equity.
    (4) As an accrued liability.

(AICPA adapted)

E–3–2 Answer the following multiple choice questions.

a) How should an unusual event not meeting the current criteria for an extraordinary item be disclosed in the financial statements?
    (1) Shown as a separate item in operating revenues or expenses and supplemented by a footnote if deemed appropriate.
    (2) Shown in operating revenues or expenses but not shown as a separate item.
    (3) Shown after ordinary net earnings but before extraordinary items.
    (4) Shown after extraordinary items net of income tax but before net earnings.

b) When a segment of a business has been discontinued during the year, the gain or loss on disposal should
    (1) Be an extraordinary item.
    (2) Exclude operating losses during the phase-out period.
    (3) Include operating losses of the current period up to the measurement date.
    (4) Be net of applicable income taxes.

c) In order to be classified as an extraordinary item in the income statement, an event or transaction should be which of the following?
    (1) Infrequent and material, but it need not be unusual in nature.
    (2) Unusual in nature and material, but it need not be infrequent.
    (3) Unusual in nature, infrequent, and material.
    (4) Unusual in nature and infrequent, but it need not be material.

(AICPA adapted)

E–3–3 The earning of revenue by a business enterprise is recognized for accounting purposes when the transaction is recorded. In some situations revenue is recognized approximately as it is earned in the economic sense. In other situations, however, accountants have developed guidelines for recognizing revenue by other criteria, such as, at the point of sale.

Required (ignore income taxes):

1. Explain and justify why revenue often is recognized as earned at the time of sale.
2. Explain in what situations it would be appropriate to recognize revenue as the productive activity takes place.
3. At what times, other than those included in 1. and 2. above, may it be appropriate to recognize revenue? Explain.

(AICPA adapted)

E–3–4 Indicate whether or not each of the following items should be included in the income of Patten Co. for 1982.

a) Received an order for $1,000 of merchandise on December 30, 1982. The merchandise was not shipped until 1983.
b) On December 31, 1982, sold a large item for 10% of the sales price down, with the remainder to be paid off over the next two years.
c) Completed production of 500 widgets whose sale value is $5,000. The widgets were put into finished goods inventory.

d) Collected cash from customers for payment on their prior years' installment purchases.

e) In late December, 1982, sold a customer a large appliance and collected the total sale price. The appliance will be picked up by the customer early in January, 1983.

f) Collected $1,000 in late December, 1982, for services to be rendered in January and February, 1983.

E–3–5 A review of the December 31, 1978, financial statements of Rhur Corporation revealed that under the caption "extraordinary losses," Rhur reported a total of $260,000. Further analysis revealed that the $260,000 in losses was comprised of the following items:

a) Rhur recorded a loss of $50,000 incurred in the abandonment of equipment formerly used in the business.

b) In an unusual and infrequent occurrence, a loss of $75,000 was sustained as a result of hurricane damage to a warehouse.

c) In 1978 several factories were shut down during a major strike by employees. Shutdown expenses totaled $120,000.

d) Uncollectible accounts receivable of $15,000 were written off as uncollectible. If you ignore income taxes, what amount of loss should Rhur report as extraordinary on its 1978 statement of income?

E–3–6 Answer the following multiple choice questions.

a) Which of the following items, if material in amount, normally would be considered an extraordinary item for reporting the results of operations?

    (1) Utilization of a net operating loss carryforward.

    (2) Gains or losses on disposal of a segment of a business.

    (3) Adjustments of accruals on long-term contracts.

    (4) Gains or losses from a fire.

b) When a company discontinues an operation and disposes of the discontinued operation (segment), the transaction should be included in the earnings statement as a gain or loss on disposal reported as

    (1) A prior period adjustment.

    (2) An extraordinary item.

    (3) An amount after continuing operations and before extraordinary items.

    (4) A bulk sale of fixed assets included in earnings from continuing operations.

(AICPA adapted)

E–3–7 For each of the following independent cases indicate when revenue should be recognized in the income statement.

a) On December 15, 1981, sold $1,000 of merchandise, receiving $100 down and agreeing to accept payments of $50 per month plus interest until fully paid.

b) Sold merchandise for cash on December 20, 1982. The goods are to be delivered on January 10, 1983.

c) Planted a soybean crop in April, 1982, which was harvested and stored in the barn in July, 1982. The harvest amounted to 3,000 bushels. Assume that there is a government price support program for $2 a bushel. The grain is sold in February, 1983, for $2.25 a bushel.

d) Sold merchandise on December 1, 1982, for $2,000. Payment was not received until January, 1983.

E–3–8 E. Phillips Co. has a truck on its books that was purchased in 1978 at a cost of $20,000 and is estimated to have a useful life of six years. The company uses straight-line depreciation. In 1981 it was determined that it would cost $12,000 to buy the same truck in a similar used condition. A new truck would cost $24,000. The old truck has an estimated resale value of $11,000.

Required:

What are the truck's net realizable value and replacement cost? State any assumptions made in determining these values.

E–3–9   H. H. Publishing Company has been recognizing revenue as its monthly magazine is published and mailed to subscribers and newsstands. The company president, Mr.
Hold, has expressed a desire to record revenue on subscriptions when they are received.
He indicates that the majority of the magazine's sales are through subscriptions. Since
getting the subscriptions is the critical event for this source of revenue, Mr. Hold wants
revenue to be reported when the cash is received.
Required:
1. How would you reply to Mr. Hold?
2. If Mr. Hold's suggestion were adopted, what measurement problems would the accountant encounter?

E–3–10   Assume that in 1982 Goncher Company had a net income from operations before
tax of $180,000. The company's income tax rate is 30%. The following events occurred
during the year that are not reflected in the income figure above.

   a)   On June 15, 1982, Goncher wrote off a very large receivable in the amount of
   $50,000. This was by far the largest receivable write-off the company has ever experi-
   enced. The write-off resulted from an uninsured explosion and fire in the customer's
   plant. The loss was total and was the only significant asset of the customer.
   b)   During 1982 Goncher sold land that it purchased in the 1940s. The land was
   purchased originally for $10,000 and sold for $900,000. This was the first time Goncher
   has ever sold any of its land.
   c)   Goncher had a fire in its warehouse during the year that destroyed $80,000 of
   inventory. Insurance proceeds amounted to $50,000.
Required:
Prepare a partial income statement for Goncher Co. for 1982.

Problems

P–3–1   Curt Company reported an income before gains and losses and extraordinary
items of $185,000. During the current year the following events occurred:
   a) $50,000 of inventories were written off as obsolete when a new, competing, much
   superior product was introduced.
   b) $75,000 loss occurred from fire damage to the company's plant.
   c)   The president of the company died. The company had a $100,000 life insurance
   policy on the president and collected the insured amount.
   d)   The company sold some old machinery at a $40,000 gain.
   e)   The company wrote off a $30,000 receivable from a large customer who filed for
   bankruptcy.
The company currently has 100,000 shares of common stock outstanding.
Required:
Prepare a partial income statement to show how the items above would be disclosed.
(Ignore income taxes.)

P–3–2   Chip Chocolate Co. had the following income statement for 1982.

Revenues		
Sales		$360,000
Expenses		
Cost of goods sold	$200,000	
Salaries expense	50,000	
Pension expense	4,000	
Utilities expense	3,000	

Depreciation expense	15,000	
Patent amortization	2,000	274,000
Net income before tax		$ 86,000
Income tax (40%)		34,400
Net income after tax		$ 51,600

Required:

For each of the revenues and expenses in the income statement indicate whether they are estimates or precise measurements. If they are estimates indicate why they are estimates.

P–3–3 For each of the following transactions indicate the amount of revenue that Jake Co. should report in 1981 and 1982. (Ignore the time value of money consideration.)

a) On December 20, 1981, Jake sold merchandise for $8,000. Jake received $1,000 down and agreed to take monthly installment payments of $200 plus interest.

b) Jake's publishing division received subscriptions totaling $80,000 during June, 1981. The subscriptions were for a one-year period starting July 1, 1981.

c) Jake's agricultural subsidiary harvested 10,000 bushels of corn during 1981. The corn was stored in Jake's grain storage elevators. Assume the federal government has established a support price of $2 a bushel and will buy all corn produced at that price. Jake sold the corn to a cereal company in April, 1982, for $2.50 a bushel.

d) Jake's manufacturing division received an order on November 10, 1981, to build a machine to customer specification. The order was received with a check for $340,000 to prepay the contract price.

e) Jake's manufacturing division has a backlog of noncancelable orders received in 1981 which total $940,000. The gross profit on these orders averages 30%.

f) On December 10, 1981, Jake sold merchandise to Skate Co. for $40,000. Skate Co. asked Jake to store the merchandise in its warehouse until January, 1982, when delivery will be made. The sale was put on a 30-day account.

P–3–4 Dickens Co. reported a pretax operating income of $840,000 for 1982. The following events also occurred during 1982.

a) A flood destroyed merchandise stored in one of Dickens's warehouses. The cost of the merchandise was $80,000. The warehouse is located next to the river that has flooded four times in the last 20 years.

b) Dickens sold a building it has owned for 30 years for $100,000 above book value. This is the first time since Dickens started business that it has sold a building.

c) A small plane crashed into one of Dickens's warehouses causing $25,000 of uninsured damage.

d) Dickens Co. received $50,000 from a life insurance policy it held on one of its executives. The executive was killed when his plane crashed into one of Dickens's warehouses.

e) A new product came on the market during 1982 that made one of Dickens's products obsolete. As a result, Dickens wrote down inventory by $110,000.

f) Dickens's bookkeeper made an error in 1979 recording $125,000 of revenue twice. The error was discovered and corrected in 1982.

Required:

Prepare a partial income statement for Dickens Co. for 1982.

P–3–5 For each of the following items, indicate whether it should be reported as an extraordinary item. Explain your choice.

a) Curatola Co. sold one of its divisions at a $250,000 loss. The division operations in the year of sale reported a $300,000 loss to the point of sale.

b) Harper Co. is a very large company. It is the company's policy to carry a million-dollar life insurance policy on each of its top 50 executives. The company is the beneficiary of these policies. During the current year, the company collected $2,000,000 from the policies as a result of the death of two executives.

c) Freidberg & Son, Inc. is a small department store. Several years ago the elder Mr. Friedberg had the company take out a $100,000 insurance policy on his life, with the company as the beneficiary. During the current year the elder Mr. Friedberg died and the company collected the insurance.

d) Vicknair Trucking Company owns 50 trucks. During the year one of the trucks with a book value of $45,000 was destroyed in an accident. This was the first major accident since the company began operations eight years ago.

e) Strawser Produce Co. suffered a loss of $250,000 during the current year when a truckers' strike halted shipments of the fresh produce.

f) Spiceland Dock Co. facilities located on the Mississippi River in Memphis, Tennessee, sustained $150,000 in damage when a runaway barge loaded with grain rammed into the facility. The loss was not insured.

P–3–6 Knoblett Co. of Lexington, Kentucky, has been operating a merchandising concern for some time. Mr. Jim, the owner of the company, is considering the use of market value statements for internal use. He is considering the following three methods:

a) Replacement cost.

b) Net realizable value.

c) Discounted present value.

Required:

Indicate how the information provided by each method would be useful to the manager of a business.

P–3–7 Referring back to Problem 3–6, assume Mr. Jim wants his accountant to prepare a set of financial statements under each of the three methods. What are the major problems the accountant would encounter in trying to develop these statements?

P–3–8 In each of the following independent cases indicate under current GAAP the point at which revenue should be recognized and why.

a) Black Jack Distillery produces an expensive and highly regarded bourbon. The company uses an old secret recipe and ages its bourbon for 12 years. In 1981 Black Jack puts $500,000 of bourbon in casks to age for 12 years. It is expected that the bourbon will increase in value at a compound annual rate of 20%. The bourbon will be bottled and sold in 12 years.

b) Dollar Bill Mining Co. mines gold. During the current year it mined, and put into ingots, 2,000 ounces of gold. Dollar Bill has a firm purchase order from Short Cake Minerals to buy, at market, all the gold Dollar Bill can produce. During the year Dollar Bill delivered 1,800 ounces to Short Cake. At year-end, 200 ounces were held to be delivered. Assume the price was stable throughout the year at $350 per ounce.

c) Time Was Publishing Co. sells special-interest magazines by subscription only. During the year, $100,000 of subscriptions were received which covered one-year subscriptions. By year-end it was estimated that $40,000 of the subscriptions collected related to future magazine publications.

d) Noah Ship Yards builds large ocean-going freighters. Each freighter usually takes three to four years to complete and is built to customer specification. Noah usually is entitled to receive progress payments as various stages of completion are reached.

4

The Accounting Process and Basic Financial Statements

The basic purpose of the bookkeeping and accounting process is to provide financial statements to various user groups. As the following article excerpt indicates, the company's annual report may be the most important document it issues each year:

> Possibly the most important document a company issues during the year— and perhaps the most valuable—is the annual report to shareholders. Not only is it the single most effective way to communicate with shareholders, but it is in fact a marketing tool aimed at showing a company off in its best possible light to a whole list of audiences. The company's image is portrayed and conveyed not only to its shareholders, but to security analysts who are in a position to recommend its stock, customers or clients; potential shareholders, customers or clients, and the press. It can also be helpful in attracting employees and in finding acquisition prospects.*

Since the annual report is so important, it is essential that the company's basic accounting system provide information that is as accurate and up-to-date as possible. This chapter describes the basic accounting process and the resulting financial statements that are included as part of a company's annual report.

*Ellen Gartner, "Beyond the Look: Current Trends in Annual Reports," *Financial Executive*, January 1981, p. 26.

In the last three chapters the function of accountants—the gathering and communicating of relevant economic data—has been discussed in some detail. Given the fact that an abundance of such data may exist with respect to any particular entity, it becomes important for accountants to develop an organized system of data collection. Without such a system, the accountant and the information user would be overwhelmed with both useful and useless information, and the quality of the communication would suffer significantly.

To avoid the problems inherent in an unorganized communication process, the accounting profession has developed a basic model to control the information-gathering process. This model, which contains several steps, is applied to individual entities. The result is an organized information system that can be applied to virtually any economic entity. A discussion of this system, and the methods through which it is applied, follows.

The Accounting Model

In their attempt to measure and communicate information, accountants have developed two, general purpose financial statements: the balance sheet and the income statement. The balance sheet represents an attempt to communicate information about the wealth possessed by a firm and the existing claims against that wealth at a particular point in time. The underlying foundation of the balance sheet is that at any particular point in time, assets (A) must equal liabilities (L) plus stockholders' equity (SE) (owner's equity for a proprietorship or partnership form of organization).

$$A = L + SE$$

The fundamental equation of the balance sheet, then, is that all assets (resources) of an entity must be subject to the claims of either the creditors or stockholders of the firm. If the total assets of a firm were to increase (decrease), there must be an equal increase (decrease) in the liabilities and/or stockholders' equity of the firm. That is, all of the properties possessed by a firm at a point in time must be subject to the claims of someone.

The income statement represents the accounting profession's attempt to communicate information concerning the earnings of an entity over a period of time. The underlying foundation of the income statement is the premise that over a period of time income (I) is equal to revenues (R) minus expenses (E).

$$I = R - E$$

The true virtue of these two general purpose financial statements lies in a concept called **articulation,** which is the use of a single accounting model to produce two sets of financial statements. As a result of articulation, the income statement and the balance sheet are joined into a unified reporting system.

The articulation of the balance sheet and income statement is accomplished through the stockholders' equity accounts. Since stockholders' equity represents the claims of the firm's owners against the assets of the firm, stockholders' equity should be increased by any income the firm earns during the period, if that income is not actually distributed to the stockholders in the form of dividends. More precisely, stockholders' equity at the end of any period (SEend) is equal to stockholders' equity at the beginning of the period (SEbeg) plus income (I) and less any dividends (D) paid during the period.

$$SEend = SEbeg + I - D$$

Another explanation of this equation is that stockholders' equity at the end of a period is equal to stockholders' equity at the beginning of the period plus revenues minus expenses minus dividends.

$$SEend = SEbeg + R - E - D$$

If this reformulation then is introduced into the balance sheet equation, a comprehensive accounting model is derived: assets at the end of the period (Aend) equal liabilities at the end of the period (Lend) plus stockholders' equity at the beginning of the period plus revenues minus expenses minus dividends.

$$Aend = Lend + SEbeg + R - E - D$$

A little simplification and reorganization yield the following expression of the accounting equation:

$$A + E + D = L + SE + R$$

Any transaction a firm enters into, when recorded through the financial accounting process, must result in a balanced accounting equation. A few simple examples will serve to demonstrate the functioning of the accounting equation.

1. A firm receives $1,000 cash as investments by its stockholders. The result of this transaction is that both assets and stockholders' equity increase by $1,000. The accounting equation remains in balance.
2. A firm pays $300 for office equipment. This transaction results in both an increase and a decrease in assets—an increase of $300 in office equipment, a decrease of $300 in cash. The accounting equation remains in balance.
3. A firm purchases $500 of supplies on account. This transaction results in a $500 increase in assets and a $500 increase in liabilities. The accounting equation remains in balance.
4. A firm renders services to its customers in exchange for $1,200 cash. The workers who perform the services receive wages of $400. This transaction results in an increase in assets of $800 ($1,200 − $400). In addition, the transaction results in a $400 increase in expenses and a $1,200 increase in revenues. Again, the accounting equation remains in balance.

Exhibit 4-1 summarizes the effect that each of the above transactions has on the accounting equation.

The accounting equation not only provides for articulation of the financial statements, but also simplifies the accounting process. Within the accounting

Exhibit 4-1
Summary of Transactions

Trans. #	A	+	E	+ D	=	L	+	R	+	SE
1.	+$1,000									+$1,000
2.	+ 300									
	− 300									
3.	+ 500					+500				
4.	+ 800		+400					+$1,200		

equation accountants have developed a common method to record and aggregate economic transactions that are vastly different.

Accountants arbitrarily define all positive effects on the left side of the accounting equation (i.e., increases in assets, expenses, and dividends) to be **debits.** All positive effects on the right side of the accounting equation (i.e., increases in liabilities, stockholders' equity, and revenues) are defined as **credits.** Conversely, negative effects on the left side of the equation (i.e., decreases in assets, expenses, and dividends) are called credits, while negative effects on the right side of the equation (i.e., decreases in liabilities, revenues, and stockholders' equity) are called debits.

The value of the debit/credit system does not lie in the terminology used; the words "debit" and "credit" are derived from ancient Latin and have no current accounting significance. Instead, the significance of the debit/credit terminology is that it helps to simplify the accounting system. As previously stated, the accounting equation has six distinct elements—assets, expenses, dividends, liabilities, stockholders' equity, and revenues. If restated in accounting terminology, the equation has only two elements—debits and credits.

$$A + E + D = L + SE + R$$

$$\left.\begin{array}{c} + \text{ Debits} \\ - \text{ Credits} \end{array}\right\} = \left\{\begin{array}{c} + \text{ Credits} \\ - \text{ Debits} \end{array}\right.$$

Since debits always must equal credits (by definition), the shift to the debit/credit terminology will have no effect on the continued balance of the accounting equation. More important, since the debit/credit terminology represents a good surrogate for the accounting equation, and since it allows accountants to state all economic transactions in a common format, the terminology facilitates both the aggregation and articulation needed in published financial statements. The following represents a restatement in debit/credit format of the illustrative transactions presented previously.

1. A firm receives $1,000 cash as investments by its stockholders. The increase in an asset can be expressed as a debit. The increase in stockholders' equity can be expressed as a credit. Overall, the transaction produces $1,000 of debits and $1,000 of credits.

Exhibit 4-2
Summary of Debit and Credit Transactions

Trans. #	Debits		Credits	
1.	Assets	$1,000	Stockholders' equity	$1,000
2.	Assets	300	Assets	300
3.	Assets	500	Liabilities	500
4.	Assets	800	Revenues	1,200
	Expenses	400		

---

2. A firm pays $300 for office equipment. The increase in assets can be expressed as a debit. The decrease in assets can be expressed as a credit. The net result of the transaction is $300 of both debits and credits.
3. A firm purchases $500 of supplies on account. The increase in assets may be expressed as a debit. The increase in liabilities may be expressed as a credit. Debits and credits remain equal, and the accounting equation remains in balance.
4. A firm renders services to its customers in exchange for $1,200 cash. The workers who perform the services receive wages of $400. The increase in assets and the increase in expenses may be expressed as debits. The increase in revenues may be expressed as a credit. Again, debits and credits remain equal.

   Exhibit 4-2 summarizes the debit/credit effect of each of the above transactions. The model represents the mechanical device that is used to convert raw economic data into a format that can be used to prepare general purpose financial statements.

The Accounting Cycle

The accounting model described in the previous section is used to convert raw economic data into finished financial statements. However, the overall process of financial accounting is not so simple. Five distinct steps are required before the accounting model produces published financial reports: (1) collecting data, (2) recording data, (3) posting data, (4) adjusting data, and (5) closing the books.

Collecting Data

Before the accounting model can be applied to produce published financial statements, someone must collect all of the relevant economic data. This data collection process consists of two distinct steps. The first step is to identify those economic events that are deemed to be material. If an event is deemed immaterial, there is no need to gather any further information about its particulars; the materiality principle dictates that the event be considered insignificant.

The second step is to collect economic data about material events. There are several ways in which this data can be collected. If the economic event is an **exchange transaction** (i.e., if the event is an exchange of value between two or more individuals), the internal control system used by the firm probably will generate some permanent evidence of the transaction. A purchase order, an invoice, a delivery report, a check received or sent in payment, or even a computer file may contain all of the information needed to introduce the relevant aspects of the transaction into the firm's financial accounting system.

On the other hand, if the economic event is not an exchange transaction, but instead is a physical state of being, such as a fire loss, trained observation may suffice as a data collection process. When the economic significance of the end-of-the-period inventory is to be judged, or when the effects of an unforeseen casualty are to be evaluated, physical observation may constitute the most efficient means of collecting the data needed for the financial accounting system.

Recording Data

Once the presence of an economic transaction is identified and relevant data collected, the effects of that transaction must be integrated into the financial accounting system. It is at this point in the process that the accounting model begins to play a significant role.

Raw economic data are introduced into the financial accounting system by means of a journal entry. The **journal**—actually, there are several types of journals—is a chronological record of all the economic transactions in which the firm has engaged. Each time an economic event takes place, that event is recorded in the form of a journal entry.

Each journal entry has five parts. First, every journal entry is dated. The date assigned to an entry is the date on which the transaction occurred. Second, every journal entry shows the accounts affected. In most firms, there is a well-established list and description of accounts. In recording a particular transaction, the accountant chooses those account titles the particular event best fits. By custom, the accounts to be debited are listed first and usually begin at the left margin of the journal. The accounts to be credited are listed after those to be debited and generally are indented to the right. Third, every journal entry must specify the amounts involved. Each account affected by the transaction must be debited or credited for a specific sum. The dollar amounts generally appear in two columns of the journal, with the debited amounts on the left and the credited amounts on the right. Fourth, the journal entry may require a written explanation. The explanation usually appears just below the entry and is designed to provide later users of the journal with a more detailed description of the transaction. Finally, all journal entries are cross referenced to other affected parts of the accounting records. This cross referencing will be discussed in more detail later in this chapter.

The following examples serve to demonstrate the use of a general journal when a "hand" bookkeeping system is in use.

1. A firm receives $1,000 cash as investments by its shareholders. The investment is received on January 2, 1983. See Exhibit 4-3.
2. The firm pays $300 cash for office equipment. The payment is made on January 26, 1983. See Exhibit 4-4.

Exhibit 4-3
Journal Entry

	Date		Accounts	Cross Ref.	DR	CR
1	1/2	83	Cash	(Led. Act. 1)	1000	
2			Stockholders' equity	(Led. Act. 38)		1000
3			To record initial investment by owners			
4			of firm.			
5						
6						
7						
8						
9						
10						
11						
12						
13						
14						
15						
16						
17						
18						
19						
20						
21						
22						
23						
24						
25						
26						
27						
28						
29						
30						

B7112 BUFF • WB7112 'WYRING BOUND' • G7112 GREEN • 7012 WHITE

3. On February 28, 1983, the firm purchases $500 of supplies on account. See Exhibit 4-5.

4. The firm renders services to its customers in exchange for $1,200 cash. The workers who perform the services receive wages of $400 cash. The services are paid for on March 31, 1983, and the workers are paid on April 4, 1983. See Exhibit 4-6.

Exhibit 4-4
Journal Entry

	Date	Accounts	Cross Ref.	DR	CR
1	1/26 83	Office equipment	(Led. Act, 12)	300	
2		Cash	(Led. Act, 1)		300
3		To record the purchase of office			
4		equipment for cash.			
5					
6					
7					
8					
9					
10					
11					
12					
13					
14					
15					
16					
17					
18					
19					
20					
21					
22					
23					
24					
25					
26					
27					
28					
29					
30					

WILSON JONES MADE IN USA

B7112 BUFF • WB7112 "WYRING BOUND" • G7112 GREEN • 7012 WHITE

Posting Data

Although the journal will contain all the information necessary for financial statement preparation, the data are not in a form suitable for efficient aggregation.
The chronological format present in the journal makes it virtually impossible for
the accountant to determine the balance in a particular account after a large

Exhibit 4-5
Journal Entry

	Date	Accounts	Cross Ref.	DR	CR
1	2/21 83	Supplies	(Led. Act. 6)	500	
2		Accounts payable	(Led. Act. 22)		500
3		To record the purchase of supplies			
4		on account.			
5					
6					
7					
8					
9					
10					
11					
12					
13					
14					
15					
16					
17					
18					
19					
20					
21					
22					
23					
24					
25					
26					
27					
28					
29					
30					

WILSON JONES MADE IN USA

B7112 BUFF • WB7112 WYRING BOUND • G7112 GREEN • 7012 WHITE

number of transactions have been recorded. Therefore, another step in the accounting cycle is needed to facilitate the summarization of recorded financial data.

This additional step in the accounting cycle consists of **posting.** The posting process transfers the journalized information to the ledger and is implemented at

Exhibit 4-6
Journal Entry

	Date		Accounts	Cross Ref.		DR		CR
1	3/31	83	Cash	(Led. Act. 1)		1200		
2			Service revenue	(Led. Act. 34)				1200
3			To record receipt of cash from					
4			Customers for services rendered.					
5								
6	4/4	83	Wage expense	(Led. Act. 21)		400		
7			Cash	(Led. Act. 1)				400
8			To record payment of wages to					
9			workers.					
10								
11								
12								
13								
14								
15								
16								
17								
18								
19								
20								
21								
22								
23								
24								
25								
26								
27								
28								
29								
30								

WILSON JONES MADE IN USA

B7112 BUFF • WB7112 "WYRING BOUND" • G7112 GREEN • 7012 WHITE

regular intervals—daily, weekly, or monthly, depending upon the number of transactions recorded in the general journal.

At the end of each predetermined interval, information is transferred from the journal to the ledger. The **ledger** constitutes the master set of accounts used by the firm; therefore, when information is transferred from the journal to the ledger, it is transferred from a transaction format to an account format. In the account format all of the events that affect a single account are summarized in a single place. Thus, the single account summary of prior transactions can be relied upon in the preparation of published financial statements.

The typical ledger entry consists of three parts. The first of these parts is a

---

Exhibit 4-7
Ledger Accounts

Account Number 1   CASH   2   3

Date	Cross Ref.	DR	CR	Balance
1/1 83	Balance			500
1/2 83	Gen. Journal Pg. 1	1000		1500
1/26 83	Gen. Journal Pg. 5		300	1200
3/31 83	Gen. Journal Pg. 25	1200		2400
4/4 83	Gen. Journal Pg. 31		400	2000

Account Number 38   STOCKHOLDERS' EQUITY

Date	Cross Ref	DR	CR	Balance
1/1 83	Balance			2500
1/2 83	Gen. Journal Pg. 1		1000	3500

Account Number 12   OFFICE EQUIPMENT

Date	Cross Ref	DR	CR	Balance
1/1 83	Balance			-0-
1/26 83	Gen. Journal Pg. 5	300		300

Account Number 6   SUPPLIES

Date	Cross Ref	DR	CR	Balance
1/1 83	Balance			-0-
2/21 83	Gen. Journal Pg. 16	500		500

Account Number 22   ACCOUNTS PAYABLE

Date	Cross Ref.	DR	CR	Balance
1/1 83	Balance			-0-
2/21 83	Gen. Journal Pg. 16		500	500

B7112 BUFF • WB7112 WYRING BOUND • G7112 GREEN • 7012 WHITE

date. Again, the date of the recorded transaction, not the date of posting, is used. The second part of a ledger entry consists of the amount. The amount recorded in the journal is transferred into the ledger as either a debit or a credit. After each amount is posted, a new balance is determined for the ledger account. The final part of each ledger entry is a cross reference. Each ledger entry is tied to the

Exhibit 4-7 (continued)
Ledger Accounts

	Date	Cross Ref.		DR	CR	Balance
		Account Number 21 WAGES EXPENSE 3				
1	1/1 83	Balance				-0-
2	4/4 83	Gen. Journal Pg. 31		400		400
3						
4						
5		Account Number 34 SERVICE REVENUE				
6	Date	Cross Ref.		DR	CR	Balance
7	1/1 83	Balance				-0-
8	3/31 83	Gen. Journal Pg. 25			1200	1200
9						
10						
11						
12						
13						
14						
15						
16						
17						
18						
19						
20						
21						
22						
23						
24						
25						
26						
27						
28						
29						
30						

B7112 BUFF • WB7112 "WYRING BOUND" • G7112 GREEN • 7012 WHITE

journal entry from which it came by way of an alphabetic and/or numeric cross reference. In a like manner, each journal entry is tied to its posting in the ledger by means of a cross reference. The cross references provide a handy "road map" in case a later party needs to trace a particular piece of information through the financial records. Exhibit 4-7 shows how the previously illustrated journal entries are posted to the ledger accounts.

In some cases, when record keeping formality is not required (such as for instructional purposes), a T-account may be substituted for the ledger. The **T-account** contains all of the same information, works in the same manner, and accomplishes the same purposes as the ledger, but is less formal. For example, if the first two transactions from the previous example were posted to T-accounts, they would appear as follows:

1. A firm receives $1,000 cash as investments by its shareholders. The investment is received on January 2, 1983.

Act. #1		CASH	Act. #38		STOCK-HOLDERS' EQUITY
DR		CR	DR		CR
Bal.	$ 500			Bal.	$2,500
1/2/83	1,000			1/2/83	1000

2. The firm pays $300 cash for office equipment. The payment is made on January 26, 1983.

Act. #1		CASH		Act. #12		OFFICE EQUIPMENT
DR		CR		DR		CR
Bal.	$ 500	1/26/83	$300	Bal.	$ 0	
1/2/83	1,000			1/26/83	300	

In some instances a single ledger account may be affected by a large number of relatively repetitive transactions (e.g., repeated transactions with the same customer). In such cases the use of control and subsidiary ledger accounts may be desirable.

Control accounts and **subsidiary accounts** are employed when a single account (termed a control account) summarizes a substantial amount of activity that requires segregation into smaller units (termed subsidiary accounts). Accounts receivable generally is segregated into separate accounts for each customer. However, an accounts receivable control account includes the amounts owed by all customers. Control and subsidiary accounts are used also in such areas as accounts payable and merchandise inventory. The following example demonstrates the use of control and subsidiary ledger accounts.

Sheridan Corporation maintains an inventory consisting of three different items, as shown in the following illustration.

INVENTORY—
CONTROL

Act. #14

DR		CR	
Bal.	$2,400	2/1/83	$225
1/7/83	200		
2/2/83	300		

Act. #14A   Item 1

DR		CR
Bal.	$750	
1/7/83	200	

Act. #14B   Item 2

DR		CR
Bal.	$800	
2/2/83	300	

Act. #14C   Item 3

DR		CR	
Bal.	$850	2/1/83	$225

This example demonstrates three points about the control-subsidiary account system. First, subsidiary ledger accounts are simply breakdowns of information contained in the control account. The opening balance in the inventory-control account ($2,400) is exactly equal to the opening balances in the three subsidiary accounts ($750 + $800 + $850). In addition, each of the inventory additions or subtractions reflected in the control account is reflected also in some combination of the subsidiary accounts. Second, since subsidiary accounts are only detailed analyses of the control accounts, the total of the subsidiary account balances at all times must equal the balance in the control account. Finally, when a control-subsidiary format is used, each journal entry must be posted twice—once to the control account and once to the subsidiary account. This double posting is the only way to guarantee that parity between the two sets of accounts will be maintained.

Adjusting Data

At the end of each economic period, after all transactions have been recorded and posted, the accountant should prepare a trial balance of all of the firm's accounts. An example of such a trial balance is shown in Exhibit 4-8.

A **trial balance** is a listing of all account balances as of a specific date. The trial balance serves two purposes. First, it allows the accountant to test the simple mechanics of the accounting system. If the total of the accounts with debit balances equals that of the accounts with credit balances, the accounting system is assumed to have operated correctly. It should be noted that this equivalence of debits and credits does not mean that the accounting data are correct—errors could have found their way into the accounting system. For example, entries could have been omitted or recorded twice; incorrect dollar amounts could have been entered as both debits and credits, or an improper account could have been affected. The equivalence of debits and credits means only that the mechanical processes of recording and posting transactions have been carried out efficiently,

Exhibit 4-8
GRANT CORPORATION
Unadjusted Trial Balance
December 31, Year 1

Account	DR	CR
Cash	$ 17,000	
Short-term investments	10,000	
Accounts receivable	14,000	
Inventory	12,000	
Land	105,000	
Machinery	50,000	
Accumulated depreciation—machinery		$ –0–
Accounts payable		8,000
Rent received in advance		12,000
Notes payable		20,000
Common stock		100,000
Contributed capital in excess of par		50,000
Retained earnings		52,600
Sales revenue		50,000
Subscriptions revenue		1,800
Purchases	75,000	
Freight-in	5,000	
Purchase returns		1,000
Purchase discounts		5,000
Subscriptions expense	2,400	
Dividends declared	5,000	
Prepaid insurance	5,000	
Totals	$300,400	$300,400

and therefore any error that does exist must have had an equal effect on both debits and credits.

The second purpose of trial balance preparation is that it allows the accountant to review all of the ledger accounts at the end of the accounting period. This review of the accounts may reveal the need for certain adjustments to the financial records. These adjustments will be implemented by **adjusting journal entries** that are posted to the ledger accounts.

For the most part, adjusting journal entries are made necessary by the passage of time. Certain significant economic data are not evidenced by the occurrence of a particular event on a particular date but rather by a process that takes place over time. The depreciation of assets, the amortization of patents, and the accrual of interest are all examples of this process of continuous occurrence.

Therefore, if accountants are to make sure that financial statements properly reflect the economic status of an entity, adjusting journal entries must be made. These adjusting entries are designed to insure that all revenues earned and all expenses incurred are reported in the proper period—regardless of the date on which a tangible transaction evidencing these events occurs.

Even though a large number of financially significant events occurs over time, and thus requires adjusting entries, all adjusting entries may be categorized into one of three basic groups: accruals, prepaids, and cost allocations.

Accruals. An **accrual** is the recognition of revenues and expenses before a transaction is recorded. Accruals record revenues that have been earned and expenses that have been incurred but not recorded previously. The accrual of a revenue (expense) produces a receivable (payable) that is to be settled in a future period. The accrual of the revenue or expense is designed to insure that the financial statements properly reflect all items that have arisen as a result of the activity during the current period, whether or not they have been recorded previously. In general, accruals can be divided into two groups.

The first of these two groups consists of revenues that have been earned but not received. In many instances an entity engages in continuous economic activity that only periodically results in a definite transaction in which revenue is received. A prime example of such a transaction is when a firm agrees to provide continuous services for an individual in exchange for a promise from the individual to make periodic payments, such as a public utility providing electricity.

An agreement like this does result in the periodic receipt of revenues—a definite transaction that will result in the making of a journal entry. However, unless the periodic payment is made at exactly the end of the period, the revenues recorded will not include all of the revenues earned during the period. For example, if payment is received for services rendered through the 15th of the month, revenues will not be reported for the last half of the month even though they have been earned. The reporting of these revenues requires an adjusting entry that reflects an increase in assets in the form of a receivable and an increase in revenues. An example of such an adjusting entry follows.

On July 1, 1983, Grant placed $10,000 cash in an 8% savings account that paid interest each June 30. As of December 31, 1983, Grant Corporation should be entitled to interest for six months. The entry to record Grant Corporation's right to this interest would appear as follows:

Dec. 31, 1983	Interest receivable	400	
	Interest revenue		400
	To record six months of interest earned on $10,000 placed in an 8% savings account ($10,000 × 0.08 × 6/12).		

The second group of accruals consists of expenses incurred but not paid. In many instances a firm enters into agreements in which the firm is to receive and consume certain continuous benefits in exchange for a later payment. If the payment for benefits consumed does not coincide with the firm's year-end, an adjusting entry is needed to record the expense actually incurred and the liability owed. For example, on February 1, 1983, Grant Corporation borrowed $20,000 from a local bank. Grant Corporation agreed to pay 18% interest each January 31 until the loan was repaid. On December 31, 1983, Grant Corporation had used the bank's money for 11 months, but had recorded neither interest expense nor interest payable. Therefore, the following adjusting entry is needed:

Dec. 31, 1983	Interest expense	3,300	
	Interest payable		3,300
	To record 11 months of accrued but unpaid interest ($20,000 × 0.18 × 11/12).		

Prepaids. A **prepaid** item results whenever one party to a transaction transfers assets to another party to a transaction before the performance required of the receiving party is completed. More simply stated, a prepaid item is the result of an advance payment. Like accruals, prepaids generally can be grouped into two basic categories.

The first of these categories consists of revenues received but not yet earned. In some cases a customer will make an advance payment for services to be rendered continuously over a future period. If, at the end of the period the firm that has agreed to render services has not completed its task, it should not recognize revenue to the full extent of the prepayment. Instead, a liability should be recognized for the unearned portion of the prepayment. The actual adjusting entry to be made depends on the manner in which the original prepayment was recorded. The following example will demonstrate the process of adjusting for revenues received but not yet earned.

On July 1, 1983, Grant Corporation received $12,000 as a prepayment of one year's rent by one of its tenants. At that date of receipt Grant made the following journal entry:

July 1, 1983	Cash	12,000	
	Rent received in advance		12,000
	To record $12,000 received as one year's rent paid in advance.		

Since the rent received in advance account is a liability, Grant Corporation's financial statements would show an obligation to the tenant of $12,000 and no revenue if no adjusting entry were made. Yet, on December 31, 1983, Grant has only a $6,000 obligation to its tenant and has earned $6,000 of revenue. Therefore, the following adjusting entry is required:

Dec. 31, 1983	Rent received in advance	6,000	
	Rent revenue		6,000
	To adjust accounts to		
	reflect the six months		
	of rent revenue earned.		

The effect of this adjusting entry is to increase rent revenue and to decrease the rent received in advance liability.

As an alternative, Grant Corporation could have recorded the initial receipt of cash by using the rent revenue account as follows:

July 1, 1983	Cash	12,000	
	Rent revenue		12,000
	To record the		
	receipt of one		
	year's rent		
	revenue paid in		
	advance.		

If the books are not adjusted, Grant Corporation's financial statements will show revenues of $12,000 when only $6,000 has been earned. In addition, without an adjusting entry, Grant's financial statements will fail to reflect the $6,000 liability for services that must be rendered in the future. To correct these inaccuracies, Grant must make the following adjusting entry:

Dec. 31, 1983	Rent revenue	6,000	
	Rent received in advance		6,000
	To record obligations to		
	tenants for the future use		
	of property.		

The form of the revenue received but not earned adjusting entry can be summarized in two simple rules. If the original receipt were recognized as a liability, the necessary adjusting entry must reduce the liability and recognize a revenue. If the original receipt were recorded as a revenue, the necessary adjusting entry must reduce the revenue and recognize a liability. To determine how the initial receipt was recorded, the accountant need only look at the trial balance. A simple examination of the accounts will reveal whether a revenue or liability was recorded initially.

The second group of prepaid items consists of expenses paid but not incurred. In many cases a firm makes expenditures that are intended to benefit more than one period. When such an expenditure is made, adjusting entries are needed to record the portion of the purchased benefit that was consumed in the current period and the portion that will be carried forward to future periods. The following examples will demonstrate the different methods of making such needed adjusting entries.

On January 1, 1983, Grant Corporation purchased a five-year insurance policy for $5,000. The cost of the policy was recorded initially as an asset—prepaid insurance. On December 31, 1983, one year of the policy benefits had been consumed. Therefore, the following adjusting entry is needed:

Dec. 31, 1983	Insurance expense	1,000	
	Prepaid insurance		1,000
	To record the expiration of one year of insurance benefits.		

Alternatively, Grant Corporation could have recorded the original purchase as an expense—insurance expense. In that case an adjustment is necessary to remove the amount related to future periods from the expense account and to put it into a prepaid account. The entry would be recorded as follows:

Dec. 31, 1983	Prepaid insurance	1,600	
	Insurance expense		1,600
	To adjust the insurance accounts to reflect the remaining coverage available under the existent policy.		

Again, the treatment of adjusting entries for expenses paid but not incurred can be summarized in two simple rules. If the original transaction recognized an expense, an asset must be established by the adjusting entry. If the original transaction recognized the existence of an asset, an expense must be recorded through the adjusting entry. Information concerning the initial entry can be obtained simply by examining the contents of the unadjusted trial balance.

Cost Allocations. **A cost allocation** is required whenever a cost incurred produces benefits that will be realized over a number of future periods. In most cases the cost is recorded initially as an asset, and a portion of the cost of the asset is allocated as an expense to each of the future periods in which benefits are expected. Although accountants encounter many different types of cost allocations, a discussion of two of them should provide the foundation needed to deal with any adjusting entry that may be required.

One type of cost allocation that often confronts accountants is the determination of the cost of goods sold when a periodic inventory system is in use. Since the periodic inventory system actually measures inventory only at the beginning and end of each year, an adjusting entry is needed to establish the cost of goods sold incurred during any particular period. This adjusting entry represents an attempt to allocate the cost of inventory items between separate periods and can be accomplished in five simple steps.

First, the beginning inventory balance should be removed from the books by crediting the inventory account for this amount. Second, all of the periodic inventory accounts with a debit balance (e.g., purchases, freight-in, and so forth) should be credited for the full amount of their balance. Next, all of the periodic inventory accounts with a credit balance (e.g., purchase returns and allowances, purchase discounts, and so forth) should be debited for the full amount of their balance. Fourth, the ending inventory balance should be recorded by debiting the inventory account. Finally, the cost of goods sold should be recorded as the difference between all of the above debits and credits.

It should be noted that this procedure conforms with the standard formula for the calculation of the cost of goods sold:

+ Beginning inventory	(Credit)
+ Purchases	(Credit)
+ Freight-in	(Credit)
− Purchase returns & allowances	(Debit)
− Purchase discounts	(Debit)
− Ending inventory	(Debit)
= COST OF GOODS SOLD	(Credits − Debits)

The following example will demonstrate the use of this adjusting entry system.

On December 31, 1983, a physical count of Grant Corporation's inventory reveals that $48,000 of merchandise is on hand. The other account balances are as presented in the trial balance in Exhibit 4-8. The following journal entry is needed to record the cost of goods sold:

Dec. 31, 1983	Inventory (ending)	48,000	
	Purchase returns	1,000	
	Purchase discounts	5,000	
	Cost of goods sold	38,000	
	Purchases		75,000
	Freight-in		5,000
	Inventory (beginning)		12,000
	To record the cost of goods sold and establish ending inventory.		

A second type of cost allocation consists of allocating the cost of a single item to a number of future periods. In many cases a firm expends funds on long-lived assets. When those assets are acquired, they are recorded on the books at their acquisition cost. Thus, at the time of acquisition no expense is recognized with respect to the assets.

As the asset is used, its inherent value is consumed. Hence, the expense associated with an asset's use should be recognized over the period of the asset's usefulness—its useful life. This expense recognition is accomplished by amortizing or depreciating the cost of the asset over its useful life. The following example demonstrates the necessary adjusting entry.

On January 1, 1983, Gardner Corporation purchased machinery for $50,000. The machinery was estimated to have a useful life of ten years. On December 31, 1983, one year of that life had expired. Therefore, the following adjusting entry is needed:

Dec. 31, 1983	Depreciation expense	5,000	
	Accumulated depreciation		5,000
	To record depreciation expense for 1983 ($50,000/10).		

The entry above allocates one-tenth of the cost of the machinery to 1983—the period in which the benefit of the asset's use was realized.

Closing the Books

Once all of the necessary adjusting entries are made and posted to the ledger, the accountant should prepare an adjusted trial balance. Like the unadjusted trial balance, the adjusted trial balance represents a simple device that can be used to test the mechanical accuracy of the accounting system. An adjusted trial balance for Burke Corporation is presented in Exhibit 4-9.

The adjusted trial balance includes all of the information that will be presented on the balance sheet and income statement. Therefore, once the adjusted trial balance is prepared, the financial statements of the entity may be constructed.

After financial statements have been prepared, two required accounting tasks remain to be performed. The first task consists of transferring the undistributed earnings of the firm from the revenue, expense, and dividend accounts to the stockholders' equity accounts. As was noted previously, income not actually distributed to the owners of a company serves to increase the claims of those owners (stockholders' equity) against the firm's assets.

The second of the remaining tasks is to get the nominal accounts—those accounts that measure an activity undertaken over a period of time rather than a real asset or equity at a point in time—ready for a new year. Since nominal accounts measure activity on an annual basis, they should begin each period with a zero balance. Therefore, at the end of each period the accountant must take steps to make sure that the revenue, expense, and dividend accounts (i.e., nomi-

Exhibit 4-9
BURKE CORPORATION
Adjusted Trial Balance
December 31, Year 1

Account	DR	CR
Cash	$ 17,000	
Short-term investments	10,000	
Accounts receivable	14,000	
Inventory	48,000	
Machinery	50,000	
Land	105,000	
Accumulated depreciation		$ 2,000
Accounts payable		8,000
Rent received in advance		6,000
Notes payable		20,000
Common stock		100,000
Contributed capital in excess of par		50,000
Retained earnings		52,600
Sales revenue		50,000
Subscriptions revenue		1,350
Rent revenue		6,000
Interest revenue		400
Cost of goods sold	38,000	
Insurance expense	1,000	
Subscriptions expense	800	
Depreciation expense	2,000	
Interest expense	3,300	
Dividends declared	5,000	
Interest payable		3,300
Subscriptions received in advance		450
Prepaid insurance	4,000	
Prepaid subscriptions	1,600	
Interest receivable	400	
Totals	$300,100	$300,100

nal accounts) show a zero balance, and thus are ready to measure activity in a new economic period.

Fortunately, both of these required accounting functions can be accomplished in the simple process of **closing the books.** The closing process consists of a set of four standard steps that, in a single operation, transfer undistributed income to the stockholders' equity accounts and establish a zero balance in all nominal accounts.

The first step in the process is to close all revenue accounts. Since these accounts have a credit balance, closing is accomplished by debiting each account for its full balance. The total of all of these balances is transferred by means of a corresponding credit to an account called "income summary," which is a temporary nominal account used to facilitate the closing process.

Closing all expense accounts is the second step in the process. Since these accounts have a debit balance, closing is accomplished by crediting each account for its full balance. The total of all of these balances is transferred by means of a corresponding credit to the income summary account.

At this point the income summary account contains credits equal to all of the revenues earned during the period and debits equal to all of the expenses incurred during the period. Thus, the net balance in the income summary account is equal to the net income (credit) or net loss (debit) earned by the firm during the period.

The third step in the closing process consists of transferring the balance in the income summary account to stockholders' equity. This task is accomplished by debiting (crediting) the income summary account for its full balance—the amount of the firm's net income (loss). The corresponding credit (debit) is to retained earnings. Thus, the net income (loss) of the entity is transferred to the stockholders' equity accounts.

The final step in the closing process consists of reducing the retained earnings account by the portion of earnings that has been distributed to owners in the form of dividends. A credit to the dividends account for its balance and an equal debit to the retained earnings account accomplish this reduction. The following entries demonstrate the application of the closing process to the accounts shown in the Burke Corporation adjusted trial balance in Exhibit 4-9.

Dec. 31, 1983	Sales revenue	50,000	
	Subscription revenue	1,350	
	Interest revenue	400	
	Rent revenue	6,000	
	Income summary		57,750
	To close all revenue		
	accounts.		
Dec. 31, 1983	Income summary	45,100	
	Depreciation expense		2,000
	Cost of goods sold		38,000
	Subscription expense		800
	Insurance expense		1,000
	Interest expense		3,300
	To close all expense		
	accounts.		
Dec. 31, 1983	Income summary	12,650	
	Retained earnings		12,650
	To close the income		
	summary account.		
Dec. 31, 1983	Retained earnings	5,000	
	Dividends declared		5,000
	To close the dividends		
	declared account.		

Once the closing entries are made, all nominal accounts have balances of zero. In addition, the stockholders' equity accounts reflect the contributions of investors plus all undistributed income earned over the life of the firm. Thus, the closing process accomplishes the last two required tasks of the annual accounting cycle.

Computerized Accounting Systems

For the most part, the preceding discussion has concerned the functioning of a bookkeeping system kept by hand. Although such systems are still used by smaller businesses, in the last few years computerized accounting systems have been introduced into many business environments. The fact that computerized systems will replace (probably) all handwritten bookkeeping systems should not deter the student of accounting from obtaining a sound understanding of the functional elements of the handwritten system. The mechanical application of the accounting function will remain virtually unchanged.

Before a computer can record relevant economic data, an individual must analyze the available data and select that data to be recorded. When the selected data are entered into the computer system, the debit/credit format of accounting is used.

The advantages of computerization become most apparent after the information has been gathered, analyzed, and placed in a machine-usable form. The first of these advantages is the computer's ability to carry out mechanical functions in a rapid and accurate manner. Since the processes of posting the ledger and preparing the unadjusted trial balance are essentially mechanical, they are highly subject to being programmed in a fashion that can be carried out by a computer. The second advantage of a computer is its ability to selectively analyze data in the memory system. Although the computer cannot undertake data analysis, it can produce underlying information that is needed to carry out data analysis processes.

The introduction of computers into accounting represents the only way that accountants will be able to deal with the information explosion that is confronting business. However, the accountant should not view the computer as his or her replacement. Instead, accountants should view the computer as an additional tool—a tool that will relieve them of the mechanical chores that have plagued accountants. More important, accountants should realize that the accounting function is essentially one of transaction analysis and communication. A computer can accomplish very little with respect to either of these elements of the accounting function. Therefore, the need for individual accountants will continue after computerization if the accountant is willing to recognize and take advantage of this mechanical device.

The Basic Financial Statements

The end-product of the accounting cycle is a set of financial statements that provide users with the information needed to make economic decisions. Accountants generally produce four financial statements—balance sheet, income statement,

statement of changes in financial position, and statement of retained earnings. The remainder of this chapter presents a basic explanation of the contents of these statements. A more detailed discussion of financial statement preparation will be undertaken in Chapters 23, 24, and 25.

The Balance Sheet

The **balance sheet** generally is referred to as a statement of financial position; that is, the balance sheet is a representation of the status of the firm at a given point in time—it shows the wealth owned by the firm and the different claims that exist with respect to that wealth. In portraying this financial position, the balance sheet generally is divided into three major sections: assets, liabilities, and stockholders' equity.

Assets. The first major section of the balance sheet consists of **assets,** which include all of the rights and possessions of the firm at the point of balance sheet preparation. Although there are some instances in which all of the firm's assets can be grouped into a single category, most balance sheets are classified further. In establishing asset classifications, accountants usually take into consideration the physical and legal attributes of the rights and possessions owned by the particular firm in question. Generally, this process of specific identification results in the development of at least five asset classifications.

Current assets consist of cash and other assets that will be converted to cash or consumed within one year or one operating cycle, whichever is longer. Although few individuals have problems with the concept of a measurement period equal to a year, the idea of an operating cycle sometimes introduces a degree of confusion. The **operating cycle** of a firm is the period it takes to acquire raw materials, convert the raw material into a salable product, sell the product, and receive cash for it. In other words, the operating cycle is the period between the time that cash is spent to begin the process of production and the time that cash is received from those who purchase the items produced. Usually the operating cycle is substantially shorter than one year, but in some cases—situations when the production process is long and drawn out—the operating cycle will serve as the proper measurement period for purposes of current asset identification.

Current assets most often consist of cash, accounts receivable, short-term investments, inventory, and prepaid items. In general, these assets are readily identifiable as being current in nature. However, certain assets present classification problems.

When the accountant discovers the firm holding marketable securities, a question arises as to whether it is reasonable to assume that the firm will dispose of these securities in the coming period. This question can only be answered by consulting management about the firm's intention. Thus, in determining the proper classification of current assets, the accountant must consider not only physical and legal attributes, but also the intent of those in control of the firm with respect to the disposition of those assets.

Assets will be classified as **long-term investments** if they are not used in the operation of the firm and if they will be held over a long term—a period of more than the current year or operating cycle—for the purpose of income realization. In general, marketable securities, such as stocks and bonds, are the most common long-term investments. However, assets that are held for use in the future operations of the business and special funds that are being accumulated for future use should be reported also in the long-term investment section of the balance sheet. The key to the long-term investment classification is the fact that the holding of these assets is expected to result in the realization of income by the firm, but that this income will not result (currently) from the use of the assets in the firm's operations.

Since long-term investments are classified, at least partially, on the basis of the intended holding period, it is important for accountants to have a proper grasp of management's intent with respect to the future disposition of these assets. If management makes the assets available for current disposition, classification as a long-term investment would be improper. An asset should be listed in the long-term investment category only if management expresses a direct intent to maintain ownership of the asset over a long-term period.

The **property, plant, and equipment** category includes all of the entity's long-lived tangible assets that are used to maintain the firm's operations. Thus, the three keys to classification in the property, plant, and equipment category are long life, use in operations, and physical substance.

An asset will be classified as property, plant, and equipment only if it has a useful life at the time of its acquisition of more than one year. An asset that has all of the attributes of property, plant, and equipment except long life generally would be expensed in the period of acquisition or classified as a current asset.

In addition to having a life of more than one year, assets included in the property, plant, and equipment category must be used in the normal operations of the firm. An asset that is held for resale in the ordinary course of business, or an asset that is being held for purposes of realizing future appreciation, is not being used in operations, and therefore should not be classified in the property, plant, and equipment section of the balance sheet. Such assets should be shown in either the long-term investments or other assets section of the balance sheet.

Physical existence is the final attribute of the property, plant, and equipment category. Certainly, assets such as land and buildings have physical substance and would be included in the property, plant, and equipment class. However, certain long-lived assets that are used in the operations of the firm do not have tangible substance. A patent or a copyright that is important to firm operation has a long life that is protected generally by law. Yet, the fact that these assets have no physical substance means that they will not be included in the property, plant, and equipment category.

Since the assets included in the property, plant, and equipment category do not always have infinite lives, they must be reported net of any previous cost allocations. Therefore, **accumulated depreciation**—the total of all prior allocations of the cost of tangible assets—is reported with respect to the assets included in the property, plant, and equipment category. The result of reporting accumulated depreciation is that the property, plant, and equipment classification includes only the unexpensed cost of long-lived operating assets.

A long-lived asset that is held for use in the operations of the entity and that does not possess the characteristics of tangible physical substance will be classified as an **intangible asset.** Intangible assets generally are made up of rights of the firm that relate to the operations conducted by it. Such assets have a legal or economic life that is greater than one year.

Examples of intangibles are patents, copyrights, franchises, trademarks, and tradenames. Although the right of an entity to these assets is established by law, intangible assets are not limited necessarily to legal rights. Other intangibles, such as goodwill (recorded only after the acquisition of a business) or trade secrets, are not protected directly by legislation.

In some cases an accountant will encounter an asset that does not fit into any of the four categories presented above. When such an asset is encountered, it generally is shown on the balance sheet under the heading of **other assets.** One example of an asset that does not fit into any of the categories above is a deferred cost. A **deferred cost** is a cost that is both incurred and paid in the current period but in some way relates to future periods—for example, the cost incurred in issuing a group of long-term bonds, or the costs incurred in organizing a business.

Since such costs do not fall into any of the other asset classifications, they generally are placed in the other asset section of the balance sheet. Thus, the other asset classification becomes a catch-all that may contain a number of totally dissimilar types of assets.

Liabilities. The second major section of the balance sheet consists of liabilities. A **liability** is a claim of a creditor against the assets of the firm. In an effort to give the financial statement user a more detailed description of the obligations to which the firm is subject, accountants generally report liabilities in two separate classifications.

Current liabilities are those obligations whose settlement will require the use of existing current assets or the creation of another current liability. In most cases if the obligation to the creditor will have to be settled during the next year, the liability will be reported as a current liability.

The one general exception to the rule above concerns liabilities that will be paid with the proceeds derived from the sale of a long-lived asset. Even though such a liability will be paid within the next year, the payment of that liability will not require the use of current assets. Therefore, such a liability generally is not included in the current liability classification.

Accounts payable, taxes currently payable, and advances from customers are common examples of current liabilities. Each of these accounts represents an obligation (debt) to a third party that will be settled by surrendering current assets (e.g., accounts and taxes payable are generally settled with cash; advances from customers are settled by delivering inventory).

Although the term **long-term liabilities** would seem to refer to any obligation that will not require payment during the next period, this balance sheet classification is somewhat broader. In general, the long-term liabilities category includes all obligations of the firm to outside creditors that are not reported in the current liabilities section of the balance sheet.

Thus, the long-term liabilities section of the balance sheet becomes a catch-all for those obligations that are not properly reported as current liabilities. Regardless of when a particular obligation is to become due, if that obligation does not require the use of assets reported in the current assets section of the balance sheet, that obligation will be classified as a long-term liability.

Long-term liabilities may be either secured or unsecured. **Secured** liabilities are those obligations whose payment is secured by a creditor's lien on specific property owned by the firm. A mortgage payable represents a long-term liability that is secured by the property subject to the mortgage. If the firm were to fail to pay its obligation, the mortgagee could settle the obligation by repossessing the property that serves as security. **Unsecured** liabilities are those obligations whose payment is secured only by the general creditworthiness of the borrowing entity. A long-term note payable generally represents an unsecured obligation of the borrowing entity. If the entity fails to make payment, the creditor has a general right to take legal action but does not have a favored position with respect to any specific property of the borrower.

Stockholders' Equity. The third major section of the balance sheet consists of **stockholders' equity,** which represents the claims of the owners of the firm against the firm's assets. In general, the owners of the firm are entitled to whatever portion of the firm's assets remains after the claims of the creditors have been satisfied.

Since stockholders' equity represents a residuary claim, it would seem that all of the relevant information could be reported on a single line of the balance sheet. However, stockholders' equity is derived from two distinct sources—contributions and earnings. Therefore, in reporting stockholders' equity, accountants generally use two separate classifications.

Contributed capital represents the total assets contributed (paid-in) to the firm by its owners. In the case of a corporation, stock is issued to the owners in exchange for their capital contributions. Therefore, the contributed capital accounts generally report the amount paid by the owners for their stock. In some cases capital is contributed to the corporation, and no stock is issued to the donor. Even in such a case, the amount given to the firm is reported on the balance sheet as contributed capital.

The contributed capital section of the balance sheet generally is divided into two types of accounts. **Capital stock** accounts report the amount of legal value, usually referred to as **par value,** that is paid for the stock issued. This legal or par value is generally a nominal amount and has no economic significance. Any capital contributed in excess of the legal or par value of the stock issued by the firm is classified as **paid-in** or **contributed capital in excess of par.** Therefore, if a stockholder pays the firm $25 for a share of $5 par value common stock, $5 would be reported in the capital stock account and $20 would be reported as paid-in or contributed capital in excess of par.

If a single entity issues more than one class of stock, separate capital stock accounts will be used for each. Therefore, if a single entity were to issue both common and preferred stock, the stockholders' equity section of the balance sheet would report both preferred and common stock accounts.

Retained earnings is the total of all of the prior earnings of the firm that have not been distributed to stockholders. Thus, the retained earnings account represents the total amount of capital earned and retained by the firm.

As mentioned previously in the section on closing entries, the retained earnings account is adjusted each year for the revenues, expenses, and dividends recorded. In addition, the retained earnings account may be affected by prior period adjustments (discussed in Chapter 22) and quasi reorganizations (discussed in Chapter 20). Although there are a number of accounting entries that

Exhibit 4-10
SHERMAN CORPORATION
Balance Sheet
December 31, 1983

ASSETS
Current assets
Cash		$20,000	
Accounts receivable		13,000	
Merchandise inventory		2,000	
			$ 35,000

Long-term investments
Long-term bonds		12,000	
Land held for future use		5,000	
			17,000

Property, plant, and equipment
Land		15,000	
Buildings	$86,000		
Accumulated depreciation	(29,000)		
		57,000	
Machinery	44,000		
Accumulated depreciation	(8,000)		
		36,000	
			108,000

Intangibles
Patents (net of amortization)		12,000	
Trademarks		15,000	
			27,000

Other assets
Bond issue costs		4,000	
			4,000
Total Assets			$191,000

LIABILITIES
Current liabilities
Accounts payable		37,000	
Wages payable		9,000	
Taxes currently payable		3,000	
Advances from customers		2,000	
			$ 51,000

Long-term liabilities
Mortgage payable		22,000	
Long-term notes payable		12,000	
			34,000
Total Liabilities			$ 85,000

STOCKHOLDERS' EQUITY		
Contributed capital		
Common stock—Class A	5,000	
Common stock—Class B	8,000	
Contributed capital in excess		
of par	<u>22,000</u>	
		35,000
Retained earnings		<u>71,000</u>
Total Stockholders' Equity		<u>$106,000</u>
Total Liabilities and		
Stockholders' Equity		<u>$191,000</u>

have a direct effect on the retained earnings balance, few of the transactions encountered in the everyday operation of the business will result directly in journal entries that use the retained earnings account.

The system of balance sheet classification discussed above is exemplified by the detailed financial statement presented in Exhibit 4-10.

The Income Statement

The **income statement** generally is referred to as a statement of operations; that is, the income statement is a representation of the results of the firm's operations over a period of time. Since the income statement is a report on the entity's operations, it is, by necessity, an activity statement.

The information contained in the income statement can be segregated into two basic categories. The first of these categories is **revenues,** which are inflows of resources—assets—resulting from business operations. To the extent that an entity is capable of increasing revenues without affecting any other activity measure, the firm is better off. The second category of income statement information is **expenses,** which are outflows of resources from the firm for the purpose of generating revenues. To the extent that an entity incurs additional expenses without receiving increased revenue, the firm is worse off.

Although there are only two basic categories of income statement information, accountants have proposed a multitude of formats for the presentation of this information. Most of these formats can be classified as either a single-step or multistep approach.

Single-Step Income Statement.   The **single-step income statement** makes no attempt to distinguish between different types of revenues and expenses. Instead, it groups all revenues and all expenses into two, all-encompassing categories. The great virtue of the single-step format is its simplicity. The single-step income statement presents the financial statement user with information regarding firm activity, and, more important, presents that information in the simplest available form.

The format shows total revenues and deducts total expenses. The term single-step refers to the single subtraction in the statement to arrive at the net

Exhibit 4-11
SHERIDAN CORPORATION
Income Statement
For the year ended December 31, 1983

Revenues		
Sales revenue	$75,000	
Interest revenue	27,000	
Extraordinary gain	61,000	
		$163,000
Expenses		
Cost of goods sold	41,000	
Interest expense	25,000	
Advertising expense	3,000	
Salaries expense	13,000	
Depreciation expense	8,000	
Repairs and maintenance	3,000	
Property taxes	2,000	
		95,000
Income before taxes		$ 68,000
Income tax expense (50% of income from operations plus 20% of extraordinary gain)		15,700
Net income		$ 52,300

income figure. There is, however, usually a second subtraction for income taxes. The single-step income statement is illustrated in Exhibit 4-11.

Multistep Income Statement. The **multistep income statement** format presents the same information as the single-step format. Under the multistep format, however, revenues and expenses are classified into several different categories. A brief explanation of each of the major categories follows.

The first section of the multistep income statement relates to **operating revenue**—revenue derived from the sale of the firm's products or services.

In many multistep income statements, detailed information relating to the computation of the **cost of goods sold** (i.e., beginning and ending inventory balances, purchases, freight-in, purchase returns and allowances, and purchase discounts) is presented as a separate step in the income computation process.

The difference between sales revenue and the cost of goods sold is reported as **gross profit** or **gross margin,** which are the terms used to refer to the mark-up the entity has been able to earn. In other words, gross profit refers to the amount of revenues remaining after payment for the goods or products that were sold.

Operating expenses, which consist of selling and general and administrative expenses, are deducted next. Selling expenses include the cost of marketing the company's product. It comprises such costs as advertising, sales salaries and commissions, and travel. General and administrative expenses include costs related to the administration of the company, such as salaries, depreciation on office space and equipment, property taxes, and so forth.

When the operating expenses are deducted, the resulting figure is net income from operations before taxes. This represents the income, before tax, that was earned by the primary, recurring, revenue-generating activity of the firm.

Frequently firms have secondary or minor revenues or expenses, such as interest income or expense or rental income. These items are reflected in the **other revenue and expense** section of the income statement, which immediately follows the net income from operations before tax. The net addition or deduction from other revenue and expense results in net income before extraordinary items and taxes. This figure includes the net of all revenue and expense (other than tax) that relate to normal recurring operations, whether they are primary or secondary operations.

The next step in the income statement is to deduct the **income tax expense,** which is the amount of taxes that relates to the income from the normal recurring activities of the firm. If there are taxes that relate to unusual and nonrecurring items, these taxes will be shown separately in a multiple-step income statement. When this income tax expense is subtracted from net income before extraordinary items and taxes, the result is net income before extraordinary items.

Sometimes a firm will experience an unusual and infrequent event that affects the income statement. In such a case, that item is reported, net of its tax effect, as an **extraordinary item.** When the net effect of such extraordinary items is added to net income before extraordinary items, the result is net income.

An example of a multistep income statement, based upon the same information used to construct the single-step income statement shown in Exhibit 4-11, is presented in Exhibit 4-12.

The basic theory behind the multistep income statement is the premise that the users of income statements are interested in predicting how well the firm will perform in future periods. Since these users are interested in predictive information concerning the firm's primary activities, they would be confused if information relating to nonrecurring events—information related to items such as extraordinary gains—were combined with information relating to the firm's recurring activity. To satisfy the demands of these financial statements users, the multistep income statement categorizes revenue and expense data on the basis of the nature of the underlying transaction that resulted in the revenue or expense.

Statement of Changes in Financial Position

The **statement of changes in financial position,** the most recent addition to the set of basic financial statements, presents an analysis of the sources and uses of funds available to the firm. For this reason the statement of changes in financial position often is referred to as a funds-flow statement.

With regard to the statement of changes in financial position, the term funds is defined in either of two ways. In many cases funds is defined as **cash funds.** When the cash definition of funds is used, the statement of changes in financial position becomes a statement of sources and uses of cash. In other cases the term funds is defined as **working capital funds,** which is the excess of current assets over current liabilities.

In either case, the statement of changes in financial position is intended to

Exhibit 4-12
SHERIDAN CORPORATION
Income Statement
For the year ended December 31, 1983

Sales revenue	$75,000	
Cost of goods sold	41,000	
Gross margin		$34,000
Selling expenses		
Advertising expense	3,000	
General and administrative expense		
Salaries expense	13,000	
Depreciation expense	8,000	
Property taxes	2,000	
Repairs and maintenance	3,000	
		29,000
Net income from operations before taxes		$ 5,000
Other revenue and expense		
Interest revenue	27,000	
Interest expense	25,000	
		2,000
Net income before extraordinary items and income taxes		$ 7,000
Income tax expense		3,500
		$ 3,500
Extraordinary gain	61,000	
Tax effect of gain	12,200	
		48,800
Net income		$52,300

provide users with information that may assist them in an analysis of the flow of funds in and out of the business. Such information is useful in evaluating the company's ability to generate funds for future use. The statement of changes in financial position is divided into two sections: sources of funds and uses of funds.

Sources of Funds. The first section of the statement of changes in financial position concerns sources of funds—where the firm obtained liquid assets during the last period. In general, an entity may obtain funds from four sources: (1) from profitable operations, (2) from creditors, (3) from equity investors, and (4) from the sale of other, less liquid, assets. In most cases the sources of funds section of the statement of changes in financial position will provide information on each of these four potential sources.

Exhibit 4-13
PICKETT CORPORATION
Statement of Changes in Financial Position
Cash Basis
For the year ended December 31, 1983

Sources of cash	
From operations	$10,000
From borrowings	25,000
From issuance of common stock	22,000
From sale of land	3,000
Total sources of cash	$60,000
Uses of cash	
To repay debt	$42,000
To pay stockholder dividends	21,000
To purchase assets	6,000
Total uses of cash	$69,000
Net Use of Cash	$ 9,000

Uses of Funds. The second section of the statement of changes in financial position concerns uses or applications of funds—what the firm did with the funds it obtained. An entity may use funds in any of four ways: (1) to cover losses suffered due to unprofitable operations, (2) to acquire nonliquid assets, (3) to repay debts owed to creditors, and (4) to make distributions to equity owners. The difference between the total sources of funds and the total uses of funds is reported as a net change in funds. This net change in funds should be exactly equal to the change that is reflected in the funds accounts (i.e., cash or working capital accounts) on the two most recent balance sheets.

An example of a statement of changes in financial position is presented in Exhibit 4-13.

Statement of Retained Earnings

The **statement of retained earnings** presents the financial statement user with a reconciliation of the retained earnings balances presented on the two most recent balance sheets. In its most simplistic form the statement shows the retained earnings balance as of the beginning of the current period (i.e., the end of the immediately preceding period), the transactions that have affected retained earnings during the current period, and the current balance in the retained earnings account (i.e., the balance in the retained earnings account as of the end of the current period). The main items that affect retained earnings are net income (loss) and dividends declared.

An example of a statement of retained earnings is presented in Exhibit 4-14.

Exhibit 4-14

MEADE CORPORATION
Statement of Retained Earnings
December 31, 1983

Retained earnings—January 1, 1983	$122,000
Net income for the year 1983	32,000
Dividends declared in 1983	(11,000)
Prior period adjustment	7,000
Retained earnings—~~January 1,~~ December 31, 1983	$150,000

Supplementary Financial Information

In addition to the information presented on the face of the basic financial statements, the user of accounting information should be aware of the fact that financial statements contain an abundance of supplemental disclosures. The footnotes to financial statements explain much of the information presented on the face of the statements. In most cases footnotes to the financial statements will provide the user with information concerning the accounting policies used in preparing the financial statements, the valuation techniques used in assigning dollar amounts to certain of the items presented on the financial statements (e.g., inventory, marketable securities, and so forth), and the contingent liabilities and commitments of the firm that are not reported directly on the face of the financial statements. In some cases footnotes will contain supplemental information, such as the effect that changes in the general price level have had on the reported financial information.

Therefore, if the financial statement user is to gain a full understanding of the financial status of an entity, the balance sheet, income statement, statement of changes in financial position, and statement of retained earnings must be read in conjunction with the available supplemental data. More important, if accountants are to communicate fully with the users of financial statements, they must make sure that all necessary supplemental data are properly included in the package delivered to the financial community.

Concept Summary

ACCOUNTING PROCESS AND
FINANCIAL STATEMENTS

ACCOUNTING RECORDS

Type	Purpose
Journal	To provide a chronological record of *transactions*
Ledger	To provide a record of *accounts*

ACCOUNTING PROCESS

Process	Description	Purpose
Journalizing	Recording the enterprise's transactions in a chronological record—the journal	To provide a record of transactions
Posting	Recording transaction data from the journal into account data in the ledger	To provide a summary record of the effect of transactions in individual accounts
Adjusting	A process of recording entries to properly reflect all revenues earned and expenses incurred in the period	To properly reflect the period's earned revenues and incurred expenses so that income can be properly determined
Closing	A process of entering zero balances in all nominal accounts (revenue, expenses, and dividends)	To provide a fresh start for the accumulation of revenues and expenses for the new year

FINANCIAL STATEMENTS

Statement	Equation	Purpose
Balance Sheet	Assets = Liabilities + Stockholders' Equity	To show, as of a specific date, the resources of the enterprise and the claims against those resources
Income Statement	Income = Revenues − Expenses	To reflect the results of operations for a specific period of time

Statement of Changes in Financial Position	Change in Funds = Source of Funds − Uses of Funds	To reflect the major sources and uses of funds during the period
Statement of Retained Earnings	Ending Retained Earnings = Beginning Retained Earnings + Income − Dividends + or − Prior Period Adjustment	To reflect the increase in undistributed earnings for the year and the total earnings that have been retained in the enterprise since its inception

Appendix

The Worksheet System

In many instances the accountant would like to map out the financial statement preparation process before entering the actual elements of that process into the primary financial records. In such a case the worksheet represents a means by which the accountant may obtain an overview of the information that will appear on the financial statements.

Worksheets, such as the one for Grant Corporation presented in Exhibit 4-15, are prepared in five simple steps. First, the accountant assembles the unadjusted trial balance of the entity accounts by taking information directly from the ledger. In the Grant Corporation example, the unadjusted trial balance is shown in column number one. It should be noted that the accountant must make sure that the total debits and credits shown in the trial balance are equal before proceeding to any other worksheet step.

After the accountant is satisfied with the raw data contained in the unadjusted trial balance, s/he may proceed to the second step in the worksheet process—analyzing the unadjusted trial balance for needed adjustments. The adjustments that the accountant feels are necessary are entered onto the worksheet in debit/credit format. In the Grant Corporation worksheet, the adjustments are shown in column two and are cross-referenced (by means of parenthetical numbers) to the examples of adjusting entries discussed earlier in this chapter. Again, before proceeding to the next step, the accountant should make sure that the total debits and credits recorded in the adjustment columns are equal.

The third step in the worksheet process is to develop an adjusted trial balance. The adjusted trial balance simply consists of the unadjusted trial balance data as modified by the adjustments. In the Grant Corporation example, the adjusted trial balance is shown in column three.

Developing the income statement is the fourth worksheet step. This is done by transferring the income information in the adjusted trial balance to a new column. In the Grant Corporation example, the income statement information has been transferred to column four.

The income statement column is the first place on the worksheet where total debits and credits are not equal. If the total credits exceed the total debits, the difference is net income that has been earned by the firm. This difference generally is entered at the bottom of the debit column to make the two column totals equal. If the total debits are greater than the total credits, the difference is equal to a net loss incurred by the firm. This difference will be entered at the bottom of the credit column.

The final step in the worksheet process consists of developing the balance sheet. This is done by taking all balance sheet information contained in the adjusted trial balance and transferring it to a separate column. In the Grant Corporation example, all balance sheet information has been transferred to column five.

Exhibit 4-15
GRANT CORPORATION
Worksheet
December 31, Year 1

Account Name	Unadj. Trial Bal. DR	CR	Adjusting Entries DR	CR
Cash	$ 17,000			
Short-term investments	10,000			
Accounts receivable	14,000			
Inventory	12,000		(28) $48,000	(28) $12,000
Land	105,000			
Machinery	50,000			
Accumulated depreciation		$ —0—		(29) 2,000
Accounts payable		8,000		
Rent received in advance		12,000	(23) 6,000	
Notes payable		20,000		
Common stock		100,000		
Contributed cap. in excess		50,000		
Retained earnings		52,600		
Sales revenue		50,000		
Subscriptions revenues (Sub. rev.)		1,800	(24) 450	
Purchases	75,000			( ) 75,000
Freight-in	5,000			( ) 5,000
Purchase returns		1,000	( ) 1,000	
Purchase discounts		5,000	(28) 5,000	
Subscriptions expense (Sub. exp.)	2,400			(27) 1,600
Dividends declared	5,000			
Prepaid insurance	5,000			(26) 1,000
Interest receivable	—0—		(22) 400	
Interest revenue	—0—			(22) 400
Rent revenue		—0—		(23) 6,000
Sub. rec. in advance		—0—		(24) 450
Interest expense	—0—		(25) 3,300	
Interest payable		—0—		(25) 3,300
Insurance expense	—0—		(26) 1,000	
Prepaid subscription	—0—		(27) 1,600	
Cost of goods sold	—0—		( ) 38,000	
Depreciation expense	—0—		( ) 2,000	
SUBTOTALS	$300,400	$300,400	$106,750	$106,750
NET INCOME				
TOTALS	$300,400	$300,400	$106,750	$106,750

	Adj. Trial Bal.		Income Statement		Balance Sheet		
	6 DR	7 CR	8 DR	9 CR	10 DR	11 CR	12
	$17,000				$17,000		
	10,000				10,000		
	14,000				14,000		
	48,000				48,000		
	105,000				105,000		
	50,000				50,000		
		$2,000				$2,000	
		8,000				8,000	
		6,000				6,000	
		20,000				20,000	
		100,000				100,000	
		50,000				50,000	
		52,600				52,600	
		50,000		$50,000			
		1,350		1,350			
	-0-						
	-0-						
			-0-				
			-0-				
	800		$800				
	5,000				5,000		
	4,000				4,000		
	400				400		
		400		400			
		6,000		6,000			
		450				450	
	3,300		3,300				
		3,300				3,300	
	1,000		1,000				
	1,600				1,600		
	38,000		38,000				
	2,000		2,000				
	$300,100	$300,100	$95,100	$57,750	$255,000	$242,350	
				12,650		12,650	
	$300,100	$300,100	$57,750	$57,750	$255,000	$255,000	

As with the income statement, the total debits and credits shown in the balance sheet column are not equal. This difference is explained by the fact that the worksheet process does not allow for the closing of the books. Therefore, the retained earnings account has not been adjusted to reflect the income earned by the firm in the current year.

To account for this difference in debits and credits, the accountant transfers the net income (loss) figure computed in preparing the income statement information to the balance sheet column. If the firm earned income (i.e., if there were an excess of credits over debits in the income statement column), this income is transferred to the balance sheet column by means of an additional credit shown at the bottom of the balance sheet column. If the firm incurred a net loss (i.e., if there were an excess of debits over credits in the income statement column), this loss is transferred to the balance sheet column by means of an additional debit shown at the bottom of that column.

The advantage of the worksheet is the degree of organization it introduces into the accounting process. When a particular firm uses hundreds of accounts in the everyday accounting process, it is difficult for the accountant to analyze each of those accounts individually, prepare the necessary adjustments, segregate the information needed for the different financial statements, and prepare the required closing entries. The worksheet provides the accountant with a single document in which the entire accounting process is summarized. In addition, the worksheet offers a simple and systematic approach to the more complicated analytical processes inherent in the accounting function. Although this approach is not capable of producing financial statements in final form, it constitutes an invaluable tool during the final stages of the accounting cycle.

Questions

Q–4–1   What are the three elements of the balance sheet equation?

Q–4–2   What are the three elements of the income statement equation?

Q–4–3   What is meant by the concept of articulation?

Q–4–4   How is the stockholders' equity account used to accomplish financial statement articulation?

Q–4–5   In financial accounting, what is the significance of the terms debit and credit?

Q–4–6   What is the accounting equation?

Q–4–7   Why is the principle of materiality significant with respect to the process of data collection?

Q–4–8   Explain two ways in which the accountant can collect data for financial accounting purposes.

Q–4–9   What is the purpose of a journal?

Q–4–10   What are the major parts of a journal entry?

Q–4–11   Why is it necessary to post data that have been recorded in the general journal?

Q–4–12   What is a general ledger?

Q–4–13   What are subsidiary ledgers and control accounts? Why are they used?

Q–4–14   Why do accountants have to make adjusting entries?

Q–4–15 Explain the five basic types of adjusting entries.

Q–4–16 Why, with respect to some of the types of adjusting entries, are there alternative methods of recording the necessary data?

Q–4–17 What are the two purposes of closing entries?

Q–4–18 What is the difference between a real account and a nominal account?

Q–4–19 Why is it desirable to prepare trial balances at various points in the accounting cycle?

Q–4–20 What is the major benefit to be achieved from computerized accounting systems?

Q–4–21 What are the basic balance sheet classifications?

Q–4–22 What is the difference between a single-step and a multistep income statement?

Q–4–23 What information is contained in the balance sheet?

Q–4–24 What information is contained in the income statement?

Q–4–25 To what extent is the accountant forced to rely upon the representations of management in the preparation of detailed financial statements?

Q–4–26 What is the role of supplemental financial information?

Q–4–27 What is the purpose of preparing a worksheet?

Discussion Questions and Cases

D–4–1 In 1975 Jackson Corporation acquired a $5,000,000 loan from a local bank. The original terms of the loan required annual interest payments at a rate of 12% with the principal of the loan to be due 20 years after origination. In addition, the loan agreement stipulated that at all times during the term of the loan, current assets of Jackson Corporation would be at least two times as great as current liabilities.

Before the current year, Jackson Corporation has had no trouble with respect to this loan. Unfortunately, a preliminary computation of current assets and current liabilities indicates that the loan requirements will not be met in the current period. If the loan agreement is violated, the principal amount of the loan will be due immediately. At present, Jackson is unable to pay the $5,000,000 principal amount; therefore, an acceleration of the loan almost certainly would force Jackson into bankruptcy.

The president of Jackson has approached you with a possible way of dealing with this problem. For the past 10 years, Jackson has owned a substantial portfolio of stocks and bonds. The current value of the securities in the portfolio is about $800,000. Since management always has expressed an intent to hold these securities for long-term investment purposes, the portfolio has been reported as a part of the long-term investments section of the balance sheet. The president of Jackson has suggested that the $800,000 of stocks and bonds be reclassified as marketable securities—a current asset. If the portfolio is reclassified into the current asset section of the balance sheet, the loan agreement will be met.

The president argues that the securities that make up the investment portfolio are traded actively on the market and could be sold quite easily. In addition, the president has indicated that Jackson's management always has had the power to dispose of the securities. Finally, the president has hinted that if you, the current accountant, do not allow the reclassification, he will seek another accountant more willing to comply with his wishes.

Required:
Prepare a brief memo explaining the position that you should take on this matter.

D–4–2 On December 1, 1982, Davis Corporation began negotiating with Sherman Corporation concerning the sale of significant assets owned by Davis. After initial negotiations were complete, it became apparent that Davis would recognize a substantial gain upon the sale of the assets. On December 21, 1982, Davis and Sherman reached agreement with regard to the terms of the sale. In fact, the parties signed a letter of intent on December 27, 1982. The letter of intent recognized, assuming that neither party was guilty of a misrepresentation of fact, that each party was bound to execute the contract.

The actual closing of the transaction was to take place on January 6, 1983. The reason for the delay in the actual transfer of the assets was to facilitate the preparation of the necessary legal documents and to allow each party an opportunity to conduct the investigation necessary to determine whether the other had misrepresented a fact.

At the time of preparing the Davis Corporation 1982 financial statements, management recognizes that it has incurred a substantial loss in the past few years and would like to show a profit as soon as possible. The president of Davis Corporation has argued that the gain from the sale of the assets should be reported on the 1982 financial statements. It is the president's position that all of the elements of the sale, including the execution of a legally binding agreement, were completed in 1982.

Required:
Prepare a brief memo explaining your position with regard to the timing of the recognition of the gain from the Davis asset sale.

D–4–3 On April 15, 1982, a customer who was shopping in a store owned by Meade Corporation slipped and fell on an ice patch in the freezer area. Several witnesses claimed that the ice patch had been there for hours and had been reported to management. The manager on duty indicated that he was not aware of the ice patch and that the patch probably had resulted from a power failure that had occurred less than 30 minutes before the accident.

After being treated by a local physician, the customer was hospitalized for several months. Although there is no hard evidence that indicates that the customer was injured in the fall, the customer has threatened to sue Meade Corporation for damages, but as of December 31, 1982, no legal action has been taken. Company management is aware of the fact that there is a substantial possibility that legal action will result. In fact, the president of Meade Corporation has indicated that the company has made preparations for any financial loss that might result from litigation.

Although company management is prepared for the loss that may result from this accident, no one is sure how the accident should be reflected on the current year's financial statements. Some executives have argued that the company should recognize an estimate of the future liability on the current year's financial statements. Other executives have suggested that a mere footnote would be more than adequate. Still others have suggested that the situation need not be disclosed.

Required:
Prepare a brief memo indicating how this situation should be reflected on the Meade Corporation financial statements. Be sure to recognize the fact that the case at hand is not likely to be resolved in the near future. Therefore, your memo should address the factors that should be used to determine whether a change in your initial position should be implemented in future years.

D–4–4 Lee Corporation has been engaged in the business of leasing films to local theatres for the last eight years. Essentially, the business is conducted by purchasing prints of films from other companies, or by manufacturing films internally, and then renting the films to local users. Since entering this business, Lee Corporation has manufactured 12 films. Over the last eight years the manufactured films have represented a significant part of Lee's leasing operations. Yet, in December of this year, Lee Corporation sold all rights to its manufactured films to another company that wished to enter the leasing business. Lee realized a substantial profit on the sale. The fact that Lee sold all of its manufactured films does not mean that Lee intends to remove itself from the leasing business. On the contrary, Lee fully intends to continue to both manufacture and purchase films for leasing purposes.

While preparing the Lee Corporation multistep income statement, the president advanced the position that the gain from the sale of the manufactured films should be reported as income from the operations of the company. The president has explained that while the sale of the films did involve the permanent transfer of all rights to the films—as opposed to the temporary transfer of a limited set of rights that is involved in leasing—the transaction was not substantially different from those entered into by Lee in the ordinary course of business.

Required:
Prepare a brief memo explaining how the gain from the sale of the film rights should be treated on the Lee Corporation multistep income statement.

Exercises

E–4–1   During January, 1983, Sheridan Corporation entered into the following transactions:

January   3: Sold merchandise to customers for a total cash price of $1,800. The merchandise originally cost the company $600.

5: Purchased office furniture from a local supplier for a total cost of $3,400.

8: Paid employees' salaries of $2,300.

10: Sold merchandise to customers for a total of $3,600. The customers agreed to pay for the merchandise within 30 days. The merchandise originally cost the company $1,100.

12: Sold 27 shares of common stock in the company to new stockholders for a total cash price of $21,000.

14: Purchased merchandise from suppliers for a total price of $1,800. The merchandise was to be paid for in 60 days.

20: Paid a cash dividend to stockholders of $2 per share. The total cost of the dividend was $3,200.

29: Received $2,000 from customers who had purchased merchandise on a 30-day credit basis in December.

31: Paid suppliers $2,400 for merchandise that had been purchased on a 60-day credit basis in November.

Required:
Prepare a workpaper that includes columns for each of the major categories of the accounting equation (see below).

Assets + Expenses + Dividends = Liabilities + Revenues + Stockholders' Equity

Record each of the transactions above in the proper columns. Prove that your entries have maintained the equality of the accounting equation by determining a total for each of the columns.

E–4–2   Using the information that was given in Exercise 4–1, classify each of the entries that you made as a debit or a credit.

E–4–3   Two years ago Pickett Repair Corporation accepted the position of maintenance engineers for a major office building. Upon accepting the position, Pickett received $27,000 cash. The cash represented payment for services to be rendered over a four-year period.

Required:
Prepare the two possible adjusting entries that could be made at the end of the first year.

E–4–4 The 1983 income statement of Sherman Corporation is shown below:

SHERMAN CORPORATION
Income Statement
1/1/83—12/31/83

Sales revenue	$39,000
Interest revenue	14,000
Gain on sale of investments	9,000
	$62,000
Cost of goods sold	31,000
Depreciation on office eq.	3,000
Employee salaries	3,000
Interest expense	11,000
Loss on sale of investments	8,000
Income tax expense	2,700
	$58,700
Net income	$ 3,300

Required:
Using the information presented above, prepare a multistep income statement for Sherman Corporation. You may assume that operating income and net interest income are taxed at a 50% rate.

E–4–5 The following information relates to the 1/1/83—12/31/83 year of Pickett Corporation.

Sales revenue	$100,000
Cost of goods sold	35,000
Interest revenue	15,000
Advertising expense	4,500
Depreciation expense	6,500
Gain on sale of assets	12,000
Interest expense	14,000
Bad debt expense	2,000
Sales returns	3,500
Investment gains	4,000
Extraordinary gains	8,000

Pickett corporation pays taxes on extraordinary gains at a rate of 25%. All other income is taxed at a rate of 45%.

Required:
Based upon the information above, prepare a multistep income statement for Pickett Corporation.

E–4–6 The following information was taken from the financial records of Lee Corporation.

	1/1/81	*12/31/83*
Merchandise inventory	$20,000	$25,000
Accounts payable	35,000	18,000

	1/1/83—12/31/83
Purchases	$67,000
Purchase returns & allowances	8,000
Freight-in	4,000

Required:
1. Assuming that Lee Corporation uses the periodic inventory system, reconstruct the entries made during the year with respect to the following accounts:
   a) Accounts payable.
   b) Purchases.
   c) Purchase returns & allowances.
   d) Freight-in.
2. Prepare the adjusting entry needed to recognize the cost of goods sold.

E–4–7   The following information was taken from the financial records of Grant Corporation.

	1/1/83	12/31/83
Accounts receivable	$35,000	$42,000
Allowance for doubtful accounts	(3,500)	(4,800)

	1/1/83—12/31/83
Sales revenue	$145,000

Required:
1. Assuming that Grant Corporation wrote off $3,000 of bad accounts receivable in 1983, reconstruct the adjusting entry that was made on 12/31/83.
2. Assuming that all Grant Corporation sales are made on credit terms, reconstruct the entries that were used to record transactions that affected the following:
   a) Sales revenue
   b) Accounts receivable

E–4–8   The following information was obtained from the records of Sheridan Corporation.

Account	Debit	Credit
Notes payable		$25,000
Accounts receivable	$28,000	
Land held for investment	32,000	
Land—plant site	48,000	
Land—prior plant site being held for disposition	8,000	
Bonds payable		35,000
Deferred bond issue costs	12,000	
Prepaid rent	5,000	
Prepaid insurance (three years)	1,800	
Buildings	97,000	
Sales revenue		156,000
Cost of goods sold	38,000	
Accumulated depreciation—buildings		46,000
Machinery & equipment	81,000	
Common stock		72,000
Accumulated depreciation—machinery		12,000

Allowance for doubtful accounts		8,000
Marketable securities	52,000	
Patents (net of amortization)	13,000	
Allowance for reduction in market value of securities		2,000

Required:

Using the information above, prepare the assets section of the Sheridan Corporation balance sheet.

E–4–9 On April 1, 1983, Sherman Corporation received $30,000 cash from a customer. The payment was an advance on a service contract that required Sherman to provide maintenance services for the customer over a period of 12 months.

Required:

1. Prepare general journal entries showing the two possible ways that Sherman could have recorded the receipt of the $30,000 cash payment.

2. Prepare adjusting entries, as of December 31, 1983, with respect to each of the journal entries prepared in part 1.

E–4–10 The following information was obtained from the records of Jackson Corporation as of December 31, 1983.

Account	Debit	Credit
Cash	$12,000	
Sales revenue		$49,000
Income tax expense	8,000	
Accounts receivable	42,000	
Administrative expense	19,000	
Interest revenue		56,000
Extraordinary gains		51,000
Interest expense	16,000	
Accumulated depreciation—buildings		25,000
Cost of goods sold	25,000	
Advertising expense	23,000	
Dividends payable		16,000
Depreciation expense	38,000	
Dividends declared	28,000	
Notes payable		31,000
Common stock		42,000
Retained earnings	13,000	

Required:

Prepare the closing entries required for Jackson Corporation.

Problems

P–4–1 The Sherman Corporation was formed on January 1, 1981. During the month of January, 1981, the company entered into the following transactions.

Jan. 2   Stockholders invested $200,000 cash in exchange for 100 shares of $150 par value common stock.

    4   The company purchased $5,000 of raw materials from suppliers. The suppliers agreed to accept final payment at any time before February 3, 1981.

5   The company paid wages to the workers of $3,500 cash.

6   The company sold $10,000 of merchandise to customers for cash. The materials used to produce the merchandise cost the company $2,200.

7   The company received a shipment of office supplies from a local vendor. The supplies cost $3,000. Payment is required at any time before February 10, 1981.

11   The company sold $5,000 of merchandise to customers. The materials used to produce the merchandise cost the company $1,200. The customers agreed to pay for their purchases before February 12, 1981.

12   The company purchased a six-month certificate of deposit for $10,000 cash.

18   The company paid for $5,000 of raw materials that it purchased on January 4, 1981.

19   The company borrowed $250,000 from a local bank. The loan was for a period of 10 years with interest (annually) at a rate of 11%. The funds from the loan were to be used to purchase land and a building.

22   The company purchased land and a building to be used for company operations. The total purchase price was $230,000. At the time of purchase, the land had a fair market value of $22,500, while the building had a fair market value of $223,500.

25   The company paid $8,000 cash as rent for the facility that was used during January for company operations.

31   The company paid executive salaries of $25,000.

Required:
Prepare general journal entries to record each of the transactions above.

P–4–2 On December 31, 1982, the accountant for Sheridan Corporation conducted an analysis of the unadjusted trial balance of the company. His analysis revealed the following information.

a) As of December 31, the company owned the following assets subject to depreciation or amortization:

Asset	Cost	Acquisition Date	Life
Building	$250,000	1/1/81	20 years
Machinery	100,000	1/1/81	5 years
Automobiles	80,000	1/1/82	3 years
Office equip.	15,000	7/1/82	5 years
Patents	75,000	9/1/82	17 years

Based on the analysis conducted, none of the properties was estimated to have a material salvage value.

b) On July 1, 1981, the company purchased an insurance policy for $8,000. The policy provided coverage for a period of four years. Company accounting policy dictates that such policies should be shown as an expense before making adjusting entries.

c) On December 1, 1982, the company paid rent on some office space. The $6,000 payment that was made represented rent for three months. The bookkeeper recorded the payment as an asset—prepaid rent.

d) On July 1, 1982, the company received a security deposit of $14,000 from a customer. The deposit initially was recorded as a liability. When the company delivered the customer's merchandise in December, 1982, the customer paid the difference between the total price of the merchandise and the amount previously deposited. The amount paid was recorded as sales revenue at the time of the sale, but no adjustment was made to the deposit liability.

e) A physical count of inventory on December 31, 1982, revealed that merchandise costing $28,000 was present. The inventory account (based upon a periodic record-keeping system) showed a balance of $21,000. In addition, the unadjusted trial balance showed purchases of $48,000, freight-in of $500, purchase discounts of $800, and purchase returns of $900.

Required:

Prepare, in general journal format, the adjusting entries required by the information above.

P–4–3 On January 1, 1982, the trial balance of Smith Corporation showed the following information.

	Debit	Credit
Cash	$ 5,000	
Accounts receivable	8,000	
Land	10,000	
Buildings	28,000	
Accumulated depreciation—buildings		$ 3,000
Goodwill	8,000	
Accounts payable		5,000
Long-term notes payable		38,000
Capital stock		8,000
Capital in excess of par		2,000
Retained earnings		3,000
Totals	$59,000	$59,000

During the month of January, 1982, the company entered into the following transactions:

Jan. 2   The company received $7,000 in payment on various accounts of customers.

5   The company paid vendors $3,000 on its accounts payable.

8   The company purchased raw materials from vendors for $12,000. The materials were to be paid for at any time prior to February 8, 1982.

12   The company sold $18,000 of merchandise to customers. The customers agreed to pay for the merchandise within 30 days. The merchandise sold cost the company $8,500.

18   The company paid rent of $3,200 for equipment that is used in its operations.

22   The company paid wages to its employees of $4,200.

28   The company purchased a delivery truck for $8,900. Of the total price of $8,900, $300 was paid in cash. The remainder was paid in the form of a three-year note payable at 18% interest.

29   The company purchased office supplies for $1,200 cash.

30   The company borrowed $8,000 by issuing a 30-day note at 14% interest.

31   The company paid executive salaries of $5,000. In addition, the company reimbursed executives for $500 of expenses that they incurred on behalf of the firm.

Required:

1. Prepare general journal entries to record each of the transactions above.
2. Prepare T-accounts for each account listed in the trial balance and each additional account used in recording the transactions.
3. Post the general journal entries to the T-accounts.
4. Prepare an unadjusted trial balance as of January 31, 1982.

P–4–4 Below is the December 31, 1982, unadjusted trial balance of McGee Manufacturing Corporation. (Continued on next page.)

	Debit	Credit
Cash	$40,500	
Accounts receivable	38,000	
Allowance for doubtful accounts		$ 4,700
Inventory	36,000	
Prepaid rent	6,000	
Investment in bonds (at face value)	20,000	
Land	25,000	
Buildings	75,000	
Accumulated depreciation—buildings		1,500
Patents (net of amortization)	15,000	
Accounts payable		25,000
Rent received in advance		3,500
Wages payable		28,000
Taxes currently payable		32,000
Long-term notes payable		48,000
Common stock		1,000
Contributed capital in excess of par		20,000
Retained earnings		124,600
Sales revenue		130,000
Purchases	85,000	
Purchase returns		5,000
Purchase discounts		3,000
Purchase allowances		2,000
Freight-in	4,000	
Wage expense	42,000	
General and administrative expense	18,000	
Tax expense	33,000	
Dividends	5,000	
Service revenue		16,000
Subscriptions expense	300	
Supplies expense	1,500	
	$444,300	$444,300

A thorough examination of the trial balance on December 31, 1982, revealed the following additional information:

a) A count of inventory on hand at year-end revealed inventory at a cost of $31,000.

b) A review of the company's insurance policies revealed that the company purchased a three-year fire policy on July 1, 1982. The policy cost the company $3,600.

c) A review of the company's leases revealed that the company rented equipment from a local supplier. The lease on the equipment was for a term of one year, beginning September 1, 1982. The entire year's rent, $6,000, was paid upon entering into the lease.

d) The bonds purchased by the company pay interest annually. The bonds were purchased in 1980 and pay interest at a rate of 12%. The next interest payment is due on April 1, 1983.

e) On June 1, 1982, the company leased a small space in its building to another manufacturer. The lease was for a period of ten months at a rate of $350 per month. Rent for the entire 10-month period was collected in advance.

f) During the year the company entered into contracts to provide service to several customers. Under the contracts, customers are to receive free service for a period of one year. The contracts require an annual fee of $300 to be paid in advance. As of

December 31, 1982, the company has eight contracts in force. Two of these contracts were entered on February 1, 1982; six were entered on August 1, 1982.

g) The company purchases subscriptions to several trade magazines. Most of these subscriptions are paid for in advance and run for a period of two years. Company executives in charge of the subscriptions estimate that as of December 31, 1982, one-half of the subscriptions purchased during the year have expired.

h) A physical count revealed that $200 of office supplies were on hand as of December 31.

Required:

1. Prepare the adjusting entries needed as of December 31, 1982.
2. Prepare an adjusted trial balance as of December 31, 1982.

P–4–5 Shown below is the adjusted trial balance of Sheridan Corporation as of December 31, 1983.

Account	Debit	Credit
Cash	$ 92,000	
Allowance for doubtful accounts		$ 4,500
Accounts receivable	27,000	
Marketable securities	15,000	
Prepaid rent	26,000	
Long-term investments	12,000	
Land	228,000	
Building	197,000	
Accumulated depreciation—buildings		32,000
Equipment	51,000	
Accumulated depreciation—equipment		16,000
Patents (net of amortization)	118,000	
Goodwill (net of amortization)	53,000	
Land held for future plant site	14,000	
Deferred bond issue costs	5,000	
Accounts payable		13,000
Wages payable		16,000
Taxes currently payable		15,000
Long-term notes payable		18,000
Bonds payable		101,000
Preferred stock		50,000
Contributed capital in excess of par—preferred		30,000
Common stock		20,000
Contributed capital in excess of par—common		35,000
Retained earnings		172,500
Sales revenue		956,000
Interest revenue		9,000
Gain on sale of marketable securities		3,000
Gain on sale of operating assets		4,000
Cost of goods sold	295,000	
Depreciation expense	18,000	
Salaries expense	116,000	
General and administrative expense	117,000	
Tax expense	42,000	
Loss on sale of operating assets	41,000	
Interest expense	28,000	
Dividends declared	36,000	
Dividends payable		36,000
Totals	$1,531,000	$1,531,000

Required:
1. Prepare the closing entries justified by the adjusted trial balance above.
2. Prepare a classified balance sheet for Sheridan Corporation.
3. Prepare a single-step income statement for Sheridan Corporation.

P–4–6 On January 1, 1983, Meade Corporation was organized to enter the construction business. During the month of January, 1983, the corporation entered into the following transactions.

Jan. 1   Received $10,000 cash from investors in exchange for 1,000 shares of $5 par value common stock.

1   Received $950,000 cash from investors in exchange for bonds payable with a face value of $1,000,000.

4   Paid $400,000 cash for two acres of land, a five-year-old building and several pieces of large equipment. At the time of the transaction, an appraiser estimated that the land was worth $200,000, the building was worth $220,000, and the equipment was worth $35,000.

6   Exchanged the equipment purchased above and $5,000 cash for a new truck. The list price on the truck was $41,500, but the dealer normally would sell the truck at a slight discount.

7   Entered into a contract with a customer. The contract called for the construction of a small warehouse by January 31, 1983. The total price to be received under the contract was $35,000.

8   Rented equipment that was needed to perform the construction contract. The equipment lessor required a prepayment of $12,000. The $12,000 cash payment secured use of the rental equipment for a period of 45 days. If the equipment were returned early, a pro rata refund would be received.

9   Purchased the materials that would be needed for the construction of the warehouse. The materials cost $18,000, but the vendor extended credit for a period of 30 days.

29   Paid employee wages for construction of the warehouse. Total cash payments of $8,000 were made.

30   Paid executive salaries of $5,000 for the month of January.

31   The warehouse was completed, and title was transferred to the owner. Payment under the contract was to be made within 10 days.

31   Returned rented equipment to the lessor. In addition, the company recorded depreciation of $1,050 on its building for the month of January, paid a monthly interest payment of $10,000 to the holders of the bonds, and amortized $800 of the bond discount.

Required:
1. Record the transactions that are described above in general journal form.
2. Prepare any adjusting entries that you feel are required as of January 31.
3. Establish T-accounts as needed and post the journalized transactions to the proper accounts.
4. Prepare an adjusted trial balance for Meade Corporation as of January 31, 1983.
5. Prepare a single-step income statement as of January 31, 1983. You may assume that the income of Meade Corporation is subject to taxation at a rate of 40%.

(Problems continued on next page.)

P–4–7   Below is the multistep income statement of Pickett Corporation as of December 31, 1983.

PICKETT CORPORATION
Income Statement
January 1, 1983–December 31, 1983

Sales revenue	$935,000	
Sales returns	(27,000)	$908,000
Cost of goods sold		501,000
Gross margin		$407,000
Executive salaries expense	75,000	
Depreciation expense	82,000	
General expense	18,000	
Administrative expense	31,000	206,000
Income from operations before taxes		$201,000
Income tax expense		96,000
Net income from recurring operations		$105,000
Interest revenue (net of income tax effect)	12,000	
Interest expense (net of income tax effect)	(15,000)	
Amortization expense—bond issue cost (net of income tax effect)	(6,000)	(9,000)
Net income before extraordinary items		$ 96,000
Extraordinary loss (net of income tax effect)		(38,000)
Net income		$ 58,000
Earnings per share		
Earnings per share—income from recurring operations		$1.05
Earnings per share—income from nonoperating/nonextraordinary items		(0.09)
Earnings per share—income from extraordinary items		(0.38)
Earnings per share—net income		$0.58

Required:
Prepare the closing entries needed for Pickett Corporation assuming that during the year, $18,000 of dividends were declared.

P–4–8 Below is the adjusted trial balance of Jackson Corporation as of January 1, 1983.

Account	Debit	Credit
Cash	$ 5,000	
Accounts receivable	25,000	
Allowance for doubtful accounts		$ 1,500
Inventory	38,000	
Marketable securities	9,000	
Land held for investment	42,000	
Land—plant site	61,000	
Buildings	95,000	
Accumulated depreciation—buildings		15,000
Equipment	85,000	
Accumulated depreciation—equipment		12,000
Copyrights (net of amortization)	15,000	
Tradenames (net of amortization)	8,000	
Equipment held for disposition	6,000	
Accounts payable		21,000
Wages payable		19,000
Taxes currently payable		13,000
Long-term notes payable		35,000
Common stock		10,000
Contributed capital in excess of par		15,000
Retained earnings		247,500
Totals	$389,000	$389,000

On December 31, 1983, Jackson Corporation distributed the following financial statements to its shareholders.

JACKSON CORPORATION
Income Statement
January 1, 1983–December 31, 1983

Sales revenue		$235,000
Cost of goods sold		81,000
Gross margin		$154,000
Depreciation expense	$38,000	
Wage expense	71,000	
Amortization expense	5,000	114,000
Income from operations before income taxes		$ 40,000
Income tax expense		20,000
Net operating income		$ 20,000
Interest revenue (net of $10,000 tax effect)		10,000
Interest expense (net of $3,000 tax effect)		(3,000)
Gain on asset disposition (net of $2,000 tax effect)		8,000
Net income		$ 35,000

JACKSON CORPORATION
Balance Sheet
December 31, 1983

ASSETS

Cash		$ 74,000	
Accounts receivable	$32,000		
Allowance for doubtful accounts	(500)	31,500	
Inventory		46,000	
Marketable securities		12,000	
Total current assets			$163,500
Land held for investment		42,000	
Total long-term investments			42,000
Land—plant site		61,000	
Buildings	95,000		
Acc. depreciation—buildings	(23,000)	72,000	
Equipment	$97,000		
Acc. depreciation—equipment	(42,000)	55,000	
Total plant, property, & equipment			188,000
Copyrights (net of amortization)		13,000	
Tradenames (net of amortization)		10,000	
Total intangible assets			23,000
Equipment held for disposition		3,000	
Total other assets			3,000
Total assets			$419,500

LIABILITIES

Accounts payable		$ 42,000	
Taxes currently payable		35,000	
Wages payable		8,000	
Total current liabilities			$ 85,000
Long-term notes payable		40,000	
Total long-term liabilities			40,000
Total liabilities			$125,000

STOCKHOLDERS' EQUITY

Common stock		12,000	
Contributed capital in excess of par		32,000	
Total contributed capital			$ 44,000
Retained earnings		250,500	
Total retained earnings			$250,500
Total stockholders' equity			$294,500
Total liabilities and stockholders' equity			$419,500

Required:

1. Prepare the closing entries that are needed by Jackson Corporation as of December 31, 1983.

2. Using general journal entry format, reconstruct the entries made by Jackson Corporation during 1983. Assume that financial statements are prepared only at year-end.

P–4–9 On December 31, 1983, the following unadjusted trial balance was prepared from the books of Shelby Corporation.

Account	Debit	Credit
Interest receivable	*600*	
Cash	$ 10,000	
Accounts receivable	52,000	
Allowance for doubtful accounts		$ 2,700
Inventory	28,000 *28000*	
Prepaid rent	*1200* 2,800	
Long-term bonds (held for investment)	50,000	
Land—plant site	40,000	
Buildings	275,000	
Accumulated depreciation—buildings		*41,000* ~~27,500~~
Machinery & equipment	150,000	
Accumulated depreciation—machinery		*45000* ~~30,000~~
Transportation equipment	80,000	
Accumulated depreciation—trans. eq.		*40,000* ~~24,000~~
Patents (net of $5,000 amortization)	*15000* ~~21,000~~	
Deferred bond issue costs	10,000 *8000*	
Interest payable		*8000*
Accounts payable		24,000
Wages payable		~~36,000~~ *39,500*
Utilities payable		37,000
Taxes currently payable—state & local		42,000
Bonds payable		150,000
Preferred stock		15,000
Common stock		10,000
Contributed capital in excess of par—preferred		35,000
Contributed capital in excess of par—common		105,000
Sales revenue		395,000
Sales returns & allowances	18,000	
Purchases	195,000	
Purchase returns & allowances		5,000
Freight-in	8,000	
Wage expense	*65,500* ~~62,000~~	
General & administrative expense	*23000* 15,000	
Advertising expense	35,000	
Interest revenue	*24000*	6,000 *6600*
Interest expense	16,000	
Rent expense *depreciation expense*	*3000* 1,400 *44,500*	
Extraordinary gain		32,000
Loss on sale of machinery & equipment	15,000	
Dividends declared	13,000	
Retained earnings		121,000
Totals	$1,097,200	$1,097,200

(Problems continued on next page.)

A detailed analysis of the information above reveals the following additional information.

a) On September 1, 1983, the company paid $2,800 to rent some needed equipment for a period of seven months. As of the end of the year, the company intended to continue to use the equipment until the end of the lease term.

b) The long-term bonds (held for investment) call for the receipt of interest at a rate of 14% on each December 1. The December 1 interest payment was received and recorded.

c) The property, plant, and equipment, and the intangible assets owned by the firm have not been adjusted for depreciation or amortization. Proper recognition of these expenses would reflect the following:

	Depreciation	Amortization
Buildings	$13,500	
Machinery	15,000	
Transportation eq.	16,000	
Patents		$6,000

d) The bonds payable require interest payments at a rate of 16% each September 1. The required payment was made on September 1, 1983. In addition, the deferred bond issue costs are being amortized at a rate of $2,000 per year.

e) Although state & local taxes have been accrued, no entry has been made to record federal taxes. The company is subject to a 40% rate of tax on income from operations and interest income. Interest expense may be used to reduce interest income and income from operations subject to tax. Extraordinary gains are subject to tax at a rate of 20%.

f) As of December 31, 1983, the company had not paid employees for two days of labor. The cost of two days' labor is $3,500.

g) A count of inventory revealed that merchandise costing $32,000 was on hand on December 31, 1983.

Required:
1. Prepare the adjusting entries necessitated by the information above.
2. Prepare an adjusted trial balance for Shelby Corporation.
3. Prepare a multi-step income statement and a classified balance sheet for Shelby Corporation.
4. Prepare the closing entries needed by Shelby Corporation.

*P–4–10
Required:
Using the information supplied in Problem 4–4, prepare a worksheet for McGee Corporation that includes the following columns:
   a) Unadjusted trial balance.
   b) Adjustments.
   c) Adjusted trial balance.
   d) Income statement accounts.
   e) Balance sheet accounts.

*P–4–11   Using the information supplied in Problem 4–9, prepare a worksheet for Shelby
Corporation that includes the following columns:

  a)   Unadjusted trial balance.
  b)   Adjusting entries.
  c)   Adjusted trial balance.
  d)   Income statement accounts.
  e)   Balance sheet accounts.

Note: Items with an *asterisk* relate to material contained in the appendix.

5

Present Value Concepts

Accounting in the News

Given the choice of receiving $1,000 in cash today or $1,000 in cash a year from now, we would all prefer the cash today. If we get the cash today, it can be invested and earn interest so that it will be worth more than $1,000 a year from now. This is referred to as the time value of money. This basic concept applies to personal as well as business investment decisions, as illustrated by the following excerpt:

It's strictly a buyer's market for homes these days—if you have a lot of cash. But with the new alphabet soup of mortgages and the new awareness among sellers of the need to take back mortgages, to compromise on price or to offer to arrange other attractive terms, it can be hard to choose the right deal.

Probably the most common choice offered to buyers, however, is to pay less than the seller's asking price—but to make payment in full, using a big down payment and conventional financing from a bank. Or, if you can pay the full asking price—but with the proviso that the seller take back a mortgage at a below-market rate. It's a dilemma many buyers face.

Which is the better deal? Barry R. Goodman, a certified financial planner with Leopold & Linowers, CPAs in Washington, D.C., cautions that there is no simple answer for all situations. . . .

Let's say you want to buy a house that the owner prices at $200,000. You have about $50,000 in cash that you are willing to put down. You bargain with the seller, and he agrees to accept $185,000—if he can get all the money now. To do that would require that you put up $45,000 in cash and take a 30-year, $140,000 mortgage at 17% (if you are lucky and can get such a mortgage).

On the other hand, the seller also agrees to take back a mortgage of $150,000 at only 12%, provided you put up $50,000 in cash—meaning you are then paying the full asking price. Which is the better deal? Paying $185,000 and carrying the 30-year $140,000 mortgage at 17% interest or paying the full $200,000 and carrying a 30-year, $150,000 mortgage at 12% interest?

Goodman assumes that you would sell the house after ten years, and that you are currently in the 50% income tax bracket. . . .

All things considered, according to Goodman, the latter deal would net you about $9,504 more than the former. So, in this case at least, the lower interest rate on the mortgage more than offsets the higher price actually paid for the property.*

Various time value of money techniques are discussed in this chapter.

*"Homing Pigeons," *Forbes*, November 9, 1981, p. 214.

All businesses at times enter into transactions that involve a delayed receipt or disbursement of cash. Frequently such transactions will involve a stipulated interest charge. Occasionally, however, no interest will be specified. The accountant must be aware of the time value of money and related interest to be able to account properly for these transactions.

Time Value of Money

When making a loan, the lender expects to earn income for allowing the borrower to use his funds. The difference between the amount borrowed and the amount repaid is interest. This amount represents both a cost to the borrower for using the funds (principal) and income for the lender. The interest represents the **time value of money,** or the compensation for the use of money over time. Given the choice between receiving $1,000 today or one year from now, we probably would choose today. We realize that the $1,000 is more valuable today because it could be invested to earn interest, thus making it worth more than $1,000 in a year from now.

Time value of money is important in financial decision making and accounting for transactions. For example, current GAAP require that interest be considered explicitly when the accountant values a long-lived asset obtained by exchanging a note that has no stated interest rate. The topics discussed in this chapter are also relevant to other accounting valuation situations, such as the valuation of bonds and leases.

Differences in the amount of return from alternative business (and personal) investment decisions, or differential payback requirements in alternative borrowing decisions require that the alternatives be considered from a common base. For example, on January 1, 1981, an individual considers the following:

Alternative A—An investment that, if purchased on 1/1/81, would result in the receipt of a single lump sum of $1,220 on 12/31/84.

Alternative B—An investment that, if purchased on 1/1/81, would result in the receipt of four equal payments of $450 each at the end of each year, beginning on 12/31/81.

In order to decide which investment to make, individuals must consider the value of the investment to them. Since each alternative has different cash flows in each year, a common point in time is needed to make the evaluation. Given these two alternatives, the best time to evaluate them is at the present. This chapter discusses how to accomplish this evaluation. The alternatives are presented in Exhibit 5-1.

Exhibit 5-1
Comparison of Alternative Cash Flows

Alternative A:
1/1/81	12/31/81	12/31/82	12/31/83	12/31/84
				Return of $1,220

Present Value ‹--‹
?

Alternative B:
1/1/81	12/31/81	12/31/82	12/31/83	12/31/84
	Return of $450	Return of $450	Return of $450	Return of $450

Present Value ‹---------‹---------‹---------‹---------‹
?

One concept of the time value of money, the **present value of a single sum,** is illustrated by Alternative A. In order to determine how much Alternative A is worth on January 1, 1981, you must use an appropriate interest rate to compute the current (or present) value of the investment. In other words, how much would you have to invest today at a specified interest rate to have $1,220 four years from now? Alternative B illustrates another time value of money concept, the **present value of an annuity,** which represents the present value of a recurring receipt (or payment) of the same amount.

Other business and personal decisions may involve the need for having a specific amount of funds available at a future date. One alternative is to invest an equal amount each year to have the needed future amount. This is illustrated by Alternative C in Exhibit 5-2. Given a specified interest rate, you can determine the future value of the series of equal payments of $10,000. This is called determining the **future value of an annuity,** which is another time value of money concept.

As another alternative, a one-time investment of a single sum could be made and its worth five years from now determined. Alternative D in Exhibit 5-2 illustrates this time value of money concept, the **future value of a single sum.** This concept answers a question such as if I invest $1,000 today at 12% interest, how much will I have at the end of five years?

These four concepts of the time value of money are discussed in this chapter. Because inflows or outflows do not necessarily include only one of the four concepts, more complex situations are examined later in the chapter. The use of the time value of money in valuation and reporting in financial statements also is discussed later in the chapter.

Exhibit 5-2
Annuity vs. Single-Sum Investments

Alternative C: 1/1/81	12/31/81	12/31/82	12/31/83	12/31/84	12/31/85
	Invest $10,000	Invest $10,000	Invest $10,000	Invest $10,000	Invest $10,000

→Value of Investment ?

Alternative D: 1/1/81	12/31/81	12/31/82	12/31/83	12/31/84	12/31/85
	Invest $39,000				

→Value of Investment ?

Interest

Interest is considered to be the cost for (or income from) the use of funds over time. In order to compute interest you must determine the following:

1. The amount of principal.
2. The interest per time period.
3. The type of interest computation used.
4. The number of time periods.

The **principal** represents the amount of funds borrowed or loaned. Interest usually is stated as a rate (percentage) for a specific time period. If no time period is stated, an annual rate is assumed. There are two types of interest computations—simple and compound.

With **simple interest,** interest is computed on the principal amount only. Since the rate is stated on a yearly basis, the time periods used to compute interest are based upon a year: a fraction of a year, a single year, or multiple years. Simple interest is computed by multiplying principal by rate by time. For example, if Bo Corporation receives a $1,000 note from So Corporation, for one year, at 10% interest, Bo Corporation will receive $100 in interest. (Since Principal ($1,000) × Rate (10%) × Time (1) = $100). If Bo also received a $1,000 note from Si Corporation, for six months, at 8% interest, Bo will receive $40 in interest ($1,000 × 0.08 × $\frac{6 \text{ months}}{12 \text{ months}}$ = $40). If Bo also had a $1,000 note from Sue Corpo-

---

Exhibit 5-3
Semiannual Compounding of Interest

1/1/81   7/1/81   12/31/81
|--- $1,000 × 5% × $50 ---|--- $1,050 × 5% × $52.50 ---|

$1,000 $1,050 $1,102.50

---

ration, for 60 days, at 8% interest, Bo will receive $13.33 in interest ($1,000 ×

$0.08 \times \dfrac{60 \text{ days}}{360 \text{ days}} = \$13.33$). Notice that 360 days is used instead of 365 days. For ease in computations, 360 days usually is considered a year. By convention, using 360 days is called the **Merchants Rule** and using 365 days is called the **Bankers Rule.** This change does increase interest slightly. For example, on this note the difference is $\$0.18 \left[\$13.33 - \left(\$1,000 \times 0.08 \times \dfrac{60 \text{ days}}{365 \text{ days}} = \$13.15 \right) \right]$. In some business transactions, the term **add on** is used instead of stating simple interest. Thus, a $2,000, 8% add on note, for two years, would pay $320 in interest ($2,000 × 0.08 × 2).

Compound interest includes any unpaid principal and unpaid previously accrued interest in computing interest. In addition to knowing the interest rate and its stated period, you also must know when interest is computed. The interest rate and compounding period are used to determine an interest rate per compounding period. For example, on a note paying 10% interest compounded quarterly, the interest rate per compounding period is 2½% every three months. Finally, the number of time periods must be a multiple of the period used in compounding. For example, if Bo Corporation receives a $1,000 note for one year, at 10% interest compounded semiannually, Bo would earn 5% interest on the unpaid principal and unpaid interest for two six-month periods as indicated in Exhibit 5-3. At the end of the year, Bo will receive $1,102.50. If the note had provided for quarterly compounding, 2½% would be earned on the unpaid principal and interest each quarter. As Exhibit 5-4 indicates, compounding quarterly pays $1.32 more than compounding semiannually. If Bo had received a one-year

---

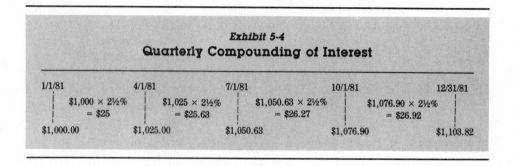

Exhibit 5-4
Quarterly Compounding of Interest

1/1/81   4/1/81   7/1/81   10/1/81   12/31/81
| $1,000 × 2½% | $1,025 × 2½% | $1,050.63 × 2½% | $1,076.90 × 2½% |
| = $25 | = $25.63 | = $26.27 | = $26.92 |
$1,000.00 $1,025.00 $1,050.63 $1,076.90 $1,103.82

note earning *simple* interest, the note would have had to pay 10.25% interest for Bo to receive the equivalent of 10% interest compounded semiannually. The note would have to pay 10.38% simple interest for Bo to receive the equivalent of 10% interest compounded quarterly. Compound interest is used in the four time-value-of-money calculations that are presented in this chapter.

Future Value of a Single Sum

Specific time value of money concepts will be discussed now. Future value of a single sum is the easiest to examine conceptually because of its relationship to the amount in savings accounts. For example, consider an investor who deposits $10,000 in a certificate account paying 12% interest compounded annually. The investor wants to know how much money he will have at the end of three years if the $10,000 and any interest received are kept on deposit. Alternatively, he may want to know how much he will have at the end of five years.

The computations in Exhibit 5-5 indicate that the amount at the end of each year is equal to 1.12 times the beginning-of-the-year balance. In fact, the balance at the end of the second year is equal to [($10,000 × 1.12) × 1.12] or ($10,000 × 1.12^2). The balance at the end of the third year is equal to [($10,000 × 1.12^2) × 1.12] or ($10,000 × 1.12^3). The balance at the end of the fifth year is ($10,000 × 1.12^5). Notice that 1.12 is determined by taking 1 + the interest rate. The 1 represents the amount of principal. Hence, you can use the following formula to compute future value: $a = p \times (1 + i)^n$, in which a is the future value (amount), p is the amount of principal, i is the interest rate, and n is the number of periods. The formula can be solved easily on most electronic calculators. The value of the certificate of deposit using the formula at the end of three years is $10,000 × $(1 + 0.12)^3 = \$14,049.30$. The value at the end of five years is $10,000 × $(1 + 0.12)^5 = \$17,623.40$. The value at the end of five years could have been determined also by using the principal at the end of the third year and by computing interest for the next two years, $14,049.30 × $(1 + 0.12)^2 = \$17,623.40$.

Before the development of inexpensive electronic calculators, tables were constructed to aid in computing the time value of money. Table 5-1 presents a table for the computation of the **future value of a single sum** (also called the **amount of a single sum**). The table provides the value of $(1 + i)^n$ for various i and n. The factor for a three-year note at 12% interest can be found by reading across to $i = 12\%$ and down to $n = 3$. The factor is 1.40493. If you read further

---

Exhibit 5-5
Determining the Future Value of a Single-Sum Investment

1/1/81	12/31/81	12/31/82	12/31/83	12/31/84	12/31/85
	$10,000 × 12% = $1,200	$11,200 × 12% = $1,344	$12,544 × 12% = $1,505.30	$14,049.30 × 12% = $1,685.90	$15,735.20 × 12% = $1,888.20
$10,000.00	$11,200.00	$12,544.00	$14,049.30	$15,735.20	$17,623.40

down the $i = 12$ column to $n = 5$, the factor for five years (1.76234) is found. Thus, the future value of a $10,000 investment at 12% for three years is $14,049.30 ($10,000 × 1.40493); for five years it is $17,623.40 ($10,000 × 1.76234). Since tables have been used extensively, $(1 + i)^n$ has been abbreviated traditionally as $a_{\overline{n}|i}$. Hence, the equation for the future value of an amount traditionally has been written as:

$$a = p \times a_{\overline{n}|i}$$

The title of the table, **Future Value of $1**, is based upon the fact that if the principal is $1, the future value is equal to the table value because $a = 1$.

As with compound interest, care must be taken when using the formula or tables to make sure that the proper number of time periods and the proper interest rate are used. Remember that i is based upon the stated rate and its compounding frequency. The rate per period *(i)* is determined by dividing the stated rate by the compounding frequency on a per-year basis. The number of periods *(n)* must be the number of compounding periods in the length of the note (investment). For example, if the value of a $1,000, two-year note at 16% interest (compounded semiannually) is needed, the interest rate would be 8% (16%/2) per period, and there would be four periods (2 years × 2 periods per year). The factor from Table 5-1, for $a_{\overline{n=4}|i=8\%}$ is 1.36049. The note would have a future value of $1,360.49 ($1,000 × 1.36049). If the note were compounded quarterly instead, the factor from Table 5-1 for $a_{\overline{n=8}|i=4\%}$ is 1.3686. The value of this note at the end of two years would be $1,368.60.

The example illustrates that the more frequently interest is compounded, the higher is the future value. If the $1,000 note at 16% interest is compounded daily, the value of the note in two years can be computed by formula as $1,000 × (1 + 16%/360)^{720} = $1,377.02.

In some cases the principal (present value), future value, and number of periods are stated. The unknown is the interest rate. The equation, $a = p \times a_{\overline{n}|i}$, can be solved for $a_{\overline{n}|i}$:

$$\frac{a}{p} = a_{\overline{n}|i}$$

Table 5-1 is used also to solve these types of problems. Read down to the number of periods and then across until the value a/p is found. The interest rate is equal to the rate at the top of the column in which the value a/p is found. For example, the rate of return earned by a homeowner who buys a house for $40,000 and sells it two years later for $50,176 is calculated as follows:

$$\frac{\$50,176}{\$40,000} = a_{\overline{n=2}|i=?}$$

$$1.2544 = a_{\overline{n=2}|i=?}$$

Using Table 5-1, if you read across the row for $n = 2$, the a/p value of 1.25440 can be found. Since the value is in the 12% column, the rate of return is 12%. If tables are not available, the formula $a = (1 + i)^n$ can be solved by trial and error.

In other cases the present value, future value, and interest rate are stated; the unknown is the number of periods. The formula $a/p = a_{\overline{n}|i}$ is used also to solve this problem. In Table 5-1, you read down the appropriate interest rate column until the value a/p is found. The number of periods is then determined by reading across the row to determine the number of periods. For example, an investor may want to know how long it will take for the investment to double if the investment earns 15% interest compounded annually. This can be solved as follows:

$$\frac{a}{p} = \frac{2}{1} = a_{\overline{n=?}|i=15\%}$$

From Table 5-1, you read down the 15% column to the value of 2.01136. Since this is the closest value to 2 (double), reading across the row gives the answer of 5 years.

Present Value of a Single Sum

In some business and personal decisions, a future value is known and the present value of the future amount is needed. For example, an investor may want to determine the value today of a promise to pay $2,000 in four years if an 8% interest rate compounded semiannually is used. As Exhibit 5-6 indicates, the objective is to find the present value of the future amount of $2,000. This sometimes is referred to as **discounting the future sum.** The formulas developed in the previous section (Future Value of a Single Sum) can be used also for this type of problem. The equation, $a = (1 + i)^n \times p$, can be solved for p, the new unknown:

$$p = \frac{1}{(1 + i)^n} \times a$$

In this example,

$$p = \frac{1}{(1 + .04)^8} \times \$2,000$$

Exhibit 5-6
Present Value of a Single-Sum Payment

1/1/81	12/31/81	12/31/82	12/31/83	12/31/84
				$2,000

Present Value ? ←---

$n = 8, i = 4\%$

The present value of the promise to pay $2,000 four years from now is $1,461.38. Thus, if $1,461.38 were invested today at 8% compounded semiannually, its value at the end of four years would be $2,000 [$1,461.38 × (1.04)^8].

Given that $(1 + i)^n$ was abbreviated as $a_{\overline{n}|i}$, the present value formula could be written as follows:

$$p = \frac{1}{a_{\overline{n}|i}} \times a$$

The future value tables could be used to solve the present value problems by taking the reciprocal of the appropriate factor. In the previous example, the factor from Table 5-1 $a_{\overline{n}|i}$ was 1.3686. The present value can be determined by applying the reciprocal as follows:

$$p = \frac{1}{1.3686} \times \$2,000 = \$1,461.38$$

In order to aid in computations, present value tables, such as Table 5-2 are used. The values in the table are as follows:

$$\frac{1}{(1 + i)^n} = (1 + i)^{-n} = 1/a_{\overline{n}|i}$$

which is abbreviated $p_{\overline{n}|i}$. Hence, using the previous example,

$$p_{\overline{n=8}|i=4\%} = 0.73069$$
$$p = (0.73069) \times \$2,000 = \$1,461.38$$

The present value equation and table can be used to solve for an unknown interest rate or number of periods when the present and future values are known. For both situations, the formula is solved for $p_{\overline{n}|i}$:

$$\frac{p}{a} = p_{\overline{n}|i}$$

For example, if a $35,000 investment is sold for $61,680 five years after the investment, what is the rate of return (interest rate) for this investment? The present value factor is determined as follows:

$$0.5674 = \$35,000/\$61,680 = p_{\overline{n=5}|i=?}$$

If you look in the body of Table 5-2, in the $n = 5$ row the factor 0.56743 is found in the 12% column. Hence, the investment earned 12% interest compounded annually.

The number of periods can be found in a similar manner. For example, how many years must $20,000 be on deposit to accumulate to $28,000 at 10% interest compounded semiannually?

$$\$20,000/\$28,000 = p_{\overline{n=?}|i=5\%}$$
$$0.7143 = p_{\overline{n=?}|i=5\%}$$

From Table 5-2, $p_{\overline{n=7}|i=5\%} = 0.71068$; hence, $\$20,000$ will take approximately 7 periods or 3½ years to increase to $\$28,000$.

Future Value of an Annuity

Some business decisions may require knowledge of the amount of a future annuity. For example, assume a local businessman wants to know how much he would have available for the purchase of a new machine if he invested $\$600$ every six months for four years into an account that pays 12% interest. There are two possibilities regarding the $\$600$ investment for each six-month period. The payments could be made at the beginning or at the end of each six-month period. When the payment is made at the end of the period, it is referred to as an **ordinary annuity**. However, if the payments are to be made at the beginning of each period, it is an **annuity due**. Both types of annuities are discussed below.

Ordinary Annuity

The determination of the future amount of an ordinary annuity can be made by summing the individual future values of each payment as illustrated in Exhibit 5-7. Alternatively, and more simply, it can be calculated by using the following formula:

$$A = \frac{(1 + i)^n - 1)}{i} \times r$$

A is the future value of an ordinary annuity

r is the period payment (receipt)

If you apply the formula to the example presented above, the calculations are as follows:

$$A = \frac{(1 + 0.06)^8 - 1}{0.06} \times \$600 = \$5,938.50$$

The formula $\dfrac{(1 + i)^n - 1}{i}$ can be abbreviated as $A_{\overline{n}|i}$. Values of A for various i and n are presented in Table 5-3. From Table 5-3, $A_{\overline{n=8}|i=6\%} = 9.89747$. Hence, the future value of the annuity is $\$5,938.50$ ($9.89747 \times \$600$).

In computing the present value of an annuity, you must be careful to assure that the interest rate and number of periods correspond as discussed with the present value or future value of a single sum computations. With annuities, an annuity payment must be made in each time period.

The future value of an annuity formula can be used to compute (1) the amount of the annuity payment (r), (2) the interest rate (i), or (3) the number of periods (n), if all other information is available. For example, the Hott family plans to buy a new car every 48 months. If the family expects to pay $7,000 for their next car and wants to have that amount by making equal payments to a savings account paying 9% interest compounded monthly, how much must they deposit at the end of each month? For this example:

$$A = A_{\overline{n=48}|i=0.75\%} \times r$$
$$\$7{,}000 = 57.52071 \times r$$
$$\$7{,}000/57.52071 = r$$
$$\$121.70 = r$$

They would have to invest $121.70 at the end of each month for the next 48 months to save $7,000.

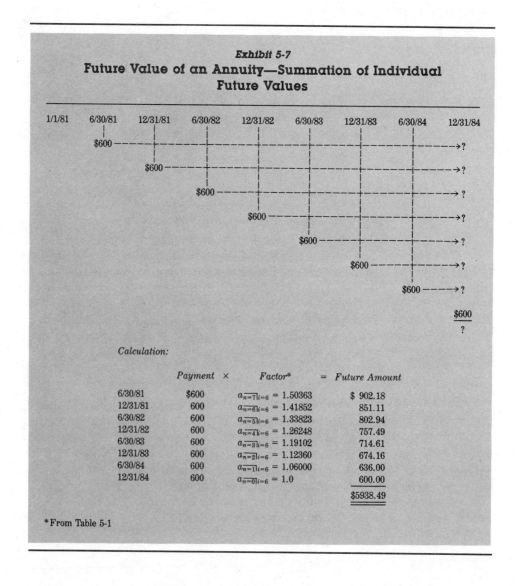

Exhibit 5-7
Future Value of an Annuity—Summation of Individual Future Values

Calculation:

	Payment	×	Factor*	=	Future Amount
6/30/81	$600		$a_{\overline{n=7}|i=6} = 1.50363$		$ 902.18
12/31/81	600		$a_{\overline{n=6}|i=6} = 1.41852$		851.11
6/30/82	600		$a_{\overline{n=5}|i=6} = 1.33823$		802.94
12/31/82	600		$a_{\overline{n=4}|i=6} = 1.26248$		757.49
6/30/83	600		$a_{\overline{n=3}|i=6} = 1.19102$		714.61
12/31/83	600		$a_{\overline{n=2}|i=6} = 1.12360$		674.16
6/30/84	600		$a_{\overline{n=1}|i=6} = 1.06000$		636.00
12/31/84	600		$a_{\overline{n=0}|i=6} = 1.0$		600.00
					$5938.49

*From Table 5-1

The Cherry family is planning an addition to their home that is expected to cost $12,000. They plan to put $180 at the end of each month in a savings account paying 9% interest compounded monthly. How long will it take to accumulate the needed funds? Using the formula:

$$A = A_{\overline{n=?}|i=0.75\%} \times r$$
$$\$12,000 = A_{\overline{n=?}|i=0.75\%} \times \$180$$
$$\$12,000/\$180 = A_{\overline{n=?}|i=0.75\%}$$
$$66.66667 = A_{\overline{n=?}|i=0.75\%}$$

Since $A_{\overline{n=55}|i=0.75\%} = 67.76883$, 55 months will be needed to accumulate the $12,000.

Annuity Due

In an annuity due, the payments (receipts) occur at the beginning of the time period rather than at the end. Exhibit 5-8 illustrates the difference between an annuity due and an ordinary annuity for an annuity of $600 every three months for two years. Notice that an annuity due involves the payment (receipt) of funds sooner than an ordinary annuity. The deposits (payments) are made at the beginning of the period, and thus the first and last months' deposits (payments) each earn an additional period's interest as indicated in Exhibit 5-8. Notice that the ordinary annuity earns interest in only seven periods whereas the annuity due earns interest in all eight periods. Hence, for this illustration, ordinary annuity tables, such as Table 5-3, reflect seven interest payment periods and eight princi-

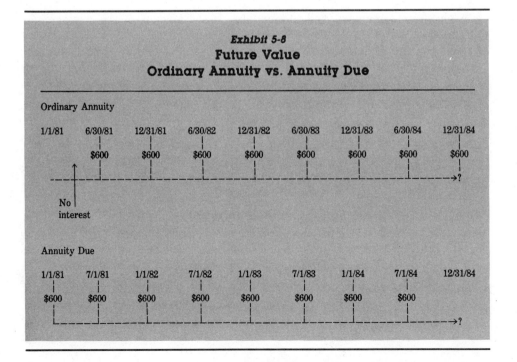

Exhibit 5-8
Future Value
Ordinary Annuity vs. Annuity Due

pal payments (investments). The annuity due includes eight interest payment periods and eight principal payments. If we were to use Table 5-3 without adjustment to calculate an annuity due, the figure would be in error because it is short one interest period as follows:

Ordinary annuity table	7 interest periods, 8 payments
Annuity due	8 interest periods, 8 payments

A simple adjustment can be made, however, which allows the use of an ordinary annuity table for annuity due calculations. Using the example above, if we found the future value factor for $n = 9$, it would reflect eight interest payment periods (the amount needed for the annuity due) and nine principal payments. Now the interest periods are correct, but there is one too many principal payments. This is corrected easily by subtracting one payment (1.0) from the factor found in the table. Thus, the formula for determining the future value of an annuity due using an ordinary annuity table is as follows:

$$A_D = (A_{\overline{n+1}|i} - 1.0) \times r$$

A_D equals the future amount of an annuity due

This formula is applied to the annuity due indicated in Exhibit 5-8 as follows:

$$A_D = (A_{\overline{n=9}|i=1.5\%} - 1) \times \$600$$
$$A_D = (9.55933 - 1.) \times \$600$$
$$A_D = \$5,135.60$$

The formula can be used to compute (1) the amount of the payment *(r)*, (2) the interest rate *(i)*, or (3) the number of periods *(n)*, if all other information is known. Since the computations are similar to the ones discussed previously, no examples are provided.

Present Value of an Annuity

It is frequently necessary in business decisions to compute the present value of a stream of future annuity payments or receipts. For example, a business has purchased an asset under a deferred payment plan in which payments of $10,000 are to be made at the end of each year for the next three years. No interest rate was stipulated. The asset should not be recorded at $30,000, the total of the three payments, because these payments include an inherent interest charge called **implicit interest.** Presumably if the business had paid cash on the date of purchase, it could have acquired the asset for less than the $30,000 total payments. In such situations the future payments must be discounted to the present value (removing the implicit interest) and the asset recorded at the present value.

Like future values, the calculation of present values for annuities may involve either ordinary annuities or annuities due.

Ordinary Annuity

The formula for the calculation of the present value of an ordinary annuity is:

$$P = \frac{1 - \dfrac{1}{(1 + i)^n}}{i} \times r$$

P is the present value of an ordinary annuity where r is the periodic payment.

The calculations can be illustrated by the following simple example. O'Neal, Inc. must make payments of $1,000 to a former employee at the end of each year for the next three years. The company can invest its money in an account that pays 15% interest compounded annually. O'Neal would like to know how much it would have to invest now in order to make the future payments. One approach is to determine the present value of each individual payment as illustrated in Exhibit 5-9. This method must be used when the amount of the payments varies from year to year.

When the payments remain constant, as in this example, it is simpler to use present value tables that are based on the formula presented above. The illustra-

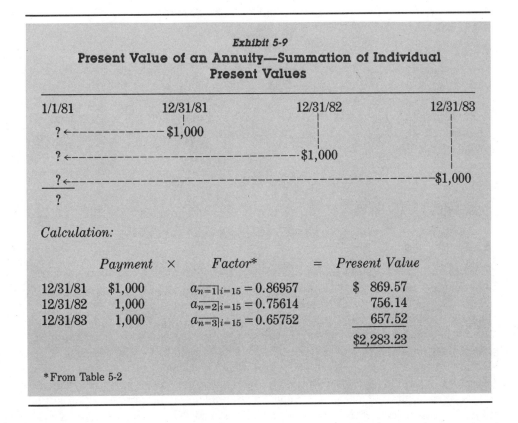

Exhibit 5-9
Present Value of an Annuity—Summation of Individual Present Values

1/1/81	12/31/81	12/31/82	12/31/83
? ←-------------	$1,000		
? ←------------------------------------		-$1,000	
? ←---			-$1,000
?			

Calculation:

	Payment	×	Factor*	=	Present Value
12/31/81	$1,000		$a_{\overline{n=1}|i=15} = 0.86957$		$ 869.57
12/31/82	1,000		$a_{\overline{n=2}|i=15} = 0.75614$		756.14
12/31/83	1,000		$a_{\overline{n=3}|i=15} = 0.65752$		657.52
					$2,283.23

*From Table 5-2

tion problem can be solved with the formula as follows:

$$\frac{1 - \dfrac{1}{(1 + 0.15)^3}}{0.15} \times \$1{,}000 = \$2{,}283.23$$

The formula $\dfrac{1 - \dfrac{1}{(1 + i)^n}}{i}$ can be abbreviated as $P_{\overline{n}|i}$. Values of $P_{\overline{n}|i}$ for various n and i are presented in Table 5-4. For $P_{\overline{n=3}|i=15\%}$ the factor 2.28323 can be found in Table 5-4. The present value of the future obligation is \$2,283.23 (\$1,000 × 2.28323).

The present value of an annuity table (and formula) can be used also to compute (1) the amount of the periodic payment (r), (2) the interest rate (i), or (3) the number of periods (n), if all other information is available. For example, the Jones family purchases a \$6,000 car for \$1,000 down and a \$5,000 note. The bank is charging 12% interest compounded monthly for a four-year loan with payments at the end of each month. The Jones's monthly payment is computed as follows: $P = \$5{,}000$, $r = ?$; and from the tables, $P_{\overline{n=48}|i=1\%} = 37.97396$. If you solve the formula $P = P_{\overline{n}|i} \times r$ for the unknown:

$$r = \frac{P}{P_{\overline{n=48}|i=1\%}} = \$5{,}000/37.97396 = \$131.67$$

The monthly payment will be \$131.67.

In some cases the present value, the amount of the rent, and the number of periods are known, but the interest rate is unknown. For example, Sham Corporation is considering the purchase of a \$5,000 machine by signing a note that requires monthly payments of \$131.67 at the end of each of the next 48 months. The formula $P = P_{\overline{n}|i} \times r$ may be used to determine the applicable interest rate by solving for the $P_{\overline{n}|i}$ factor:

$$P_{\overline{n=48}|i=?} = \$5{,}000/\$131.67 = 37.973$$

Using Table 5-3, you find the factor in the 1% per period interest rate column.

Annuity Due

As with the future values discussed earlier, the present value ordinary annuity table can be used to calculate the present value of an annuity due. Exhibit 5-10 illustrates the timing of a \$300 quarterly annuity payment over a two-year period. The top half of the exhibit shows the ordinary annuity, while the bottom half shows the annuity due. In comparing the two, notice that since ordinary annuities aren't paid until the end of the period, the total amount of money deposited on January 1 gets to earn interest before the first \$300 payment is made on March 31. However, for the annuity due, \$300 of the original deposit (investment) does not earn interest because it must be paid out immediately. A similar situation exists at the end of the two-year period. The last \$300 payment will be able to

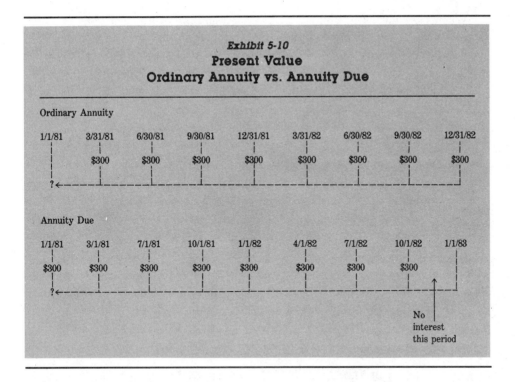

Exhibit 5-10
Present Value
Ordinary Annuity vs. Annuity Due

earn interest in the last quarter under an ordinary annuity since payment isn't made until the end of the quarter. This same $300 will not earn interest in the last quarter under the annuity due since it must be paid at the beginning of the quarter. In this situation the two annuities reflect the following:

Ordinary annuity   8 interest periods, 8 payments
Annuity due   7 interest periods, 8 payments

Since Table 5-4 reflects an ordinary annuity, the present value factors in the body of the table contain one interest period more than is needed for an annuity due. However, if you look at the factor for seven quarterly periods instead of eight, the factor will reflect seven interest periods (the correct amount for the annuity due) and seven payments (one less than the amount needed.) Thus, when using an ordinary annuity present value table to compute an annuity due, you must deduct one from the number of periods and add 1.0 (one payment) to the factor obtained from the table. The following formula is used to determine the present value of an annuity due:

$$P_D = (P_{\overline{n-1}|i} + 1.0) \times r$$

P_D = the present value of an annuity due

Hence, the present value of the annuity due indicated in Exhibit 5-10 is as follows:

$$P_D = (P_{\overline{n=7}|i=3\%} + 1.0) \times \$300, \text{ or } P_D = (6.23028 + 1.0) \times \$300 = \$2,169.08$$

When payments are required at the beginning of each period, annuity due computations can be used to compute (1) the amount of the periodic payment (r), (2) the interest rate (i), or (3) the number of periods (n), if all other information is available. Since the computations are similar to the ones discussed previously, no additional examples are provided.

Deferred Annuities

Another type of annuity is a **deferred annuity,** in which a series of equal payments starts after a specified time period. For example, ACE Corporation wants to determine the present value of an agreement to pay $100 at the end of each month for four years, starting a year from now, if an interest rate of 12% compounded monthly is used. Exhibit 5-11 illustrates this situation.

One approach to solving this problem is as follows: (1) find the present value of the annuity at January 1, 1982 using $P_{\overline{n}|i}$ (Table 5-4), and (2) then find the present value at January 1, 1981 by finding the present value of the January 1, 1982, present value calculated in (1) using $p_{\overline{n}|i}$ (Table 5-2). This also is illustrated in Exhibit 5-11 and is calculated as follows:

$$P \text{ at } 1/1/82 = P_{\overline{n=48}|i=\%} \times \$100$$
$$P \text{ at } 1/1/82 = 37.97396 \times \$100 = \$3,797.40$$
$$p \text{ at } 1/1/81 = p_{\overline{n=12}|i=1\%} \times a$$
$$p \text{ at } 1/1/81 = 0.88745 \times \$3,797.40 = \$3,370.00$$

Another approach is to treat the annuity ACE will receive as the difference between two annuities—a five-year annuity less a one-year annuity.

$$P \text{ at } 1/1/81 = (P_{\overline{n=60}|i=1\%} \times \$100) - (P_{\overline{n=12}|i=1\%} \times \$100)$$
$$P \text{ at } 1/1/81 = (44.95504 \times \$100) - (11.25508 \times \$100)$$
$$p \text{ at } 1/1/81 = (\$4,495.50 - \$1,125.50)$$
$$p \text{ at } 1/1/81 = \$3,370.00$$

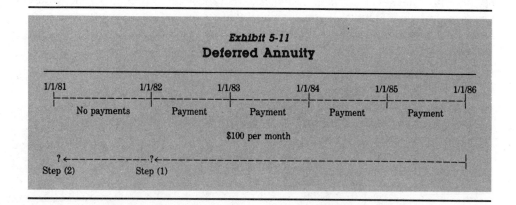

Exhibit 5-11
Deferred Annuity

Interpolation

All of the examples presented in this chapter have produced factors that can be found in the tables. In this section, interpolation will be used to determine an interest rate when the exact factor cannot be found in the tables. Interpolation can be used with any table. The present value of a single sum table will be used to illustrate interpolation.

If the Lacy family purchased a home in 1965 for $22,000 and sold it in 1980 for $160,000, what is their return (interest rate compounded annually) on the investment? Using the present value formula:

$$p = p_{\overline{n=15}|i=?} \times a$$
$$0.1375 = \$22,000/\$160,000 = p_{\overline{n=15}|i=?}$$

Using Table 5-2 and looking across the 15-year row, you find no specific value of 0.1375. The value for 12% (0.18270) is too high, and the value for 15% (0.2289) is too low. If we assume a linear relationship, we can interpolate as follows:

$$0.03 \begin{bmatrix} \Delta \begin{bmatrix} 0.12 & = & 0.18270 \\ ? & & 0.13750 \end{bmatrix} 0.0452 \\ \\ 0.15 = 0.12289 \end{bmatrix} 0.05981$$

where:

$$\frac{\Delta}{0.03} = \frac{0.0452}{0.05981} = \frac{0.0452}{0.05981} \times (0.03) = 0.02267$$

and therefore:

$$i = 0.12 + 0.02267 = 0.14267$$

Hence, the interpolated interest rate is 0.14267. Although the calculations above assume that the change between any two values in the table is linear, it in fact is not. If the ranges between the interest rates are small, however, the amount of error will be insignificant.

Other Time Value of Money Considerations

In many instances the time value of money may involve combinations of annuities and single payments. For example, you may need to know the present value of a $100 payment for each of the next five years and the present value of an additional payment of $1,000 at the end of the fifth year at 12% interest compounded annually. Actually, this is the same as a $1,000, five-year bond with a stated interest rate of 10%. In this situation, illustrated by Exhibit 5-12, the present value of the annuity and the present value of the single payment must be computed. The purchase of the bond basically is purchasing two flows: (1) an annuity of $100 per year and (2) a lump-sum payment at the end of five years. The present values of these two flows are added to determine the present value of the total payments. Since the present value of the single sum is $p_{\overline{n}|i} \times \$1,000 = \$567.43$ ($0.56743 \times$ $1,000), and since the present value of the annuity is $P_{\overline{n}|i} \times \$100 = \$360.49$

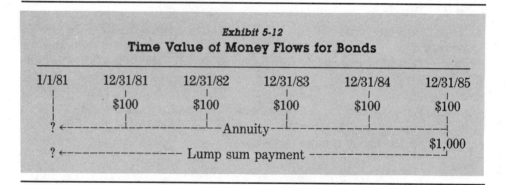

Exhibit 5-12
Time Value of Money Flows for Bonds

1/1/81	12/31/81	12/31/82	12/31/83	12/31/84	12/31/85
	$100	$100	$100	$100	$100

? ←————————————Annuity——————————————

? ←——————————— Lump sum payment ——————————— $1,000

(3.60478 × $100), the present value of the payments is $927.92 ($567.43 + $360.49). Thus, if the bond is to yield a 12% return, it will sell for $927.92.

In certain computations you may need to use both present and future values. For example, Mr. Rich desires to retire at age 65 and to have a semiannual income of $10,000 until he dies. How much does he need to deposit at the end of each six months if he is 20 years away from retirement and anticipates earning 6% interest each semiannual period on the funds invested? He will withdraw the $10,000 at the end of each six-month period and expects to live for ten years after his 65th birthday.

In order to ascertain the necessary monthly investment, you must follow a two-step process as illustrated in Exhibit 5-13. First, the future $10,000 semiannual retirement annuity must be discounted back to the retirement date. This procedure determines the amount of money that must be on hand on the retirement date if the desired monthly retirement income is to be met. The second step is to find out which unknown semiannual investment will accumulate to a future value at retirement date that is equal to the present value calculated in Step 1.

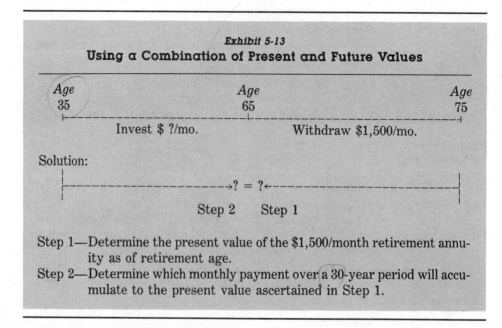

Exhibit 5-13
Using a Combination of Present and Future Values

Age	*Age*	*Age*
35	65	75

Invest $?/mo.   Withdraw $1,500/mo.

Solution:

? = ?←

Step 2   Step 1

Step 1—Determine the present value of the $1,500/month retirement annuity as of retirement age.
Step 2—Determine which monthly payment over a 30-year period will accumulate to the present value ascertained in Step 1.

If you apply the procedure to the Mr. Rich example, the calculations are as follows:

$$\text{Step 1: } P_{\overline{n=20}|i=6\%} \times r$$

or:

$$11.46992 \times \$10,000 = \$114,699$$

Hence, Mr. Rich must have \$114,699 available on his retirement date to meet his retirement objective.

$$\text{Step 2: } \$114,699 = A_{\overline{n=40}|i=6} \times r$$
$$\$114,699 = 154.762 \times r$$
$$\frac{\$114,699}{154.762} = r$$
$$\$741.13 = r$$

Thus, if Mr. Rich deposits semiannual payments of \$741.13 into an account paying 6% interest per semiannual period for 20 years, he will be able to retire with a semiannual income of \$10,000 up to age 75.

Summary of Accounting Applications

Present value not only aids in managerial decisions but is relevant to a number of financial accounting topics discussed in this text. These topics include accounting for the following:

1. Notes and bonds payable (including sinking funds) and receivables (and related income and expense).
2. Plant assets (including depreciation).
3. Leases (including the related expense).
4. Pensions.

Present value is also important for certain types of business combinations discussed in advanced accounting texts, as well as for accounting and reporting for defined benefit pension plans. Present values are discussed in numerous APB Opinions and FASB Statements, which are presented throughout the remainder of the text.

List of Symbols
Used in Chapter

a = Future value

$a_{\overline{n}|i}$ = Future value factor of a single sum for n periods at i interest rate

$A_{\overline{n}|i}$ = Future value factor of an annuity for n periods at i interest rate

$A_D = (A_{\overline{n+1}|i-1.0})$ = Future value factor of an annuity due for n periods at i interest rate

i = Interest rate

n = Number of periods

p = Principal (present value)

$p_{\overline{n}|i}$ = Present value factor of a single sum for n periods at i interest rate

$P_{\overline{n}|i}$ = Present value factor of an annuity for n periods at i interest rate

$P_D(P_{\overline{n-1}|i} + 1.0)$ = Present value factor of an annuity due for n periods at i interest rate

r = Rent, period payment (receipt)

Δ = Change

Concept Summary

TIME VALUE OF MONEY FORMULAS

Type of Payment	Time	Formula	Table	Remarks
Single Sum	Present Value	$p = a \times \dfrac{1}{(1 + i)^n}$	5-2	
	Future Value	$a = p \times (1 + i)^n$	5-1	
Ordinary Annuity	Present Value	$P = \left(\dfrac{1 - \dfrac{1}{(1 + i)^n}}{i} \right) \times r$	5-3	
	Future Value	$A = \left(\dfrac{((1 + i)^n - 1)}{i} \right) \times r$	5-4	

Annuity Due	Present Value	5-3	Subtract one from the number of periods and add 1 to the table value.
	Future Value	5-4	Take one more period and deduct 1 from the table value.
Deferred Annuity	Present Value		Use either 1. Ordinary annuity and a single sum 2. Difference between two ordinary annuities
	Future Value		Use either 1. Ordinary annuity and a single sum 2. Difference between two ordinary annuities

Table 5-1
Future Value of $1
$$a = (1 + i)^n$$

Interest

Periods	½%	¾%	1%	1½%	2%	2½%	3%	4%	5%
1	1.00500	1.00750	1.01000	1.01500	1.02000	1.02500	1.03000	1.04000	1.05000
2	1.01002	1.01506	1.02010	1.03022	1.04040	1.05062	1.06090	1.08160	1.10250
3	1.01508	1.02267	1.03030	1.04568	1.06121	1.07689	1.09273	1.12486	1.15762
4	1.02015	1.03034	1.04060	1.06136	1.08243	1.10381	1.12551	1.16986	1.21551
5	1.02525	1.03807	1.05101	1.07728	1.10408	1.13141	1.15927	1.21665	1.27628
6	1.03038	1.04585	1.06152	1.09344	1.12616	1.15969	1.19405	1.26532	1.34010
7	1.03553	1.05370	1.07214	1.10984	1.14869	1.18869	1.22987	1.31593	1.40710
8	1.04071	1.06160	1.08286	1.12649	1.17166	1.21840	1.26677	1.36857	1.47746
9	1.04591	1.06956	1.09369	1.14339	1.19509	1.24886	1.30477	1.42331	1.55133
10	1.05114	1.07758	1.10462	1.16054	1.21899	1.28008	1.34392	1.48024	1.62889
11	1.05640	1.08566	1.11567	1.17795	1.24337	1.31209	1.38423	1.53945	1.71034
12	1.06168	1.09381	1.12683	1.19562	1.26824	1.34489	1.42576	1.60103	1.79586
13	1.06699	1.10201	1.13809	1.21355	1.29361	1.37851	1.46853	1.66507	1.88565
14	1.07232	1.11028	1.14947	1.23176	1.31948	1.41297	1.51259	1.73168	1.97993
15	1.07768	1.11860	1.16097	1.25023	1.34587	1.44830	1.55797	1.80094	2.07893
16	1.08307	1.12699	1.17258	1.26899	1.37279	1.48451	1.60471	1.87298	2.18287
17	1.08849	1.13544	1.18430	1.28802	1.40024	1.52162	1.65285	1.94790	2.29202
18	1.09393	1.14396	1.19615	1.30734	1.42825	1.55966	1.70243	2.02582	2.40662
19	1.09940	1.15254	1.20811	1.32695	1.45681	1.59865	1.75351	2.10685	2.52695
20	1.10490	1.16118	1.22019	1.34686	1.48595	1.63862	1.80611	2.19112	2.65330
21	1.11042	1.16989	1.23239	1.36706	1.51567	1.67958	1.86029	2.27877	2.78596
22	1.11597	1.17867	1.24472	1.38756	1.54598	1.72157	1.91610	2.36992	2.92526
23	1.12155	1.18751	1.25716	1.40838	1.57690	1.76461	1.97359	2.46472	3.07152
24	1.12716	1.19641	1.26973	1.42950	1.60844	1.80873	2.03279	2.56330	3.22510
25	1.13280	1.20539	1.28243	1.45095	1.64061	1.85394	2.09378	2.66584	3.38635
26	1.13846	1.21443	1.29526	1.47271	1.67342	1.90029	2.15659	2.77247	3.55567
27	1.14415	1.22354	1.30821	1.49480	1.70689	1.94780	2.22129	2.88337	3.73346
28	1.14987	1.23271	1.32129	1.51722	1.74102	1.99650	2.28793	2.99870	3.92013
29	1.15562	1.24196	1.33450	1.53998	1.77584	2.04641	2.35657	3.11865	4.11614
30	1.16140	1.25127	1.34785	1.56308	1.81136	2.09757	2.42726	3.24340	4.32194
31	1.16721	1.26066	1.36133	1.58653	1.84759	2.15001	2.50008	3.37313	4.53804
32	1.17304	1.27011	1.37494	1.61032	1.88454	2.20376	2.57508	3.50806	4.76494
33	1.17891	1.27964	1.38869	1.63448	1.92223	2.25885	2.65234	3.64838	5.00319
34	1.18480	1.28923	1.40258	1.65900	1.96068	2.31532	2.73191	3.79432	5.25335
35	1.19073	1.29890	1.41660	1.68388	1.99989	2.37321	2.81386	3.94609	5.51602
36	1.19668	1.30865	1.43077	1.70914	2.03989	2.43254	2.89828	4.10393	5.79182
37	1.20266	1.31846	1.44508	1.73478	2.08069	2.49335	2.98523	4.26809	6.08141
38	1.20868	1.32835	1.45953	1.76080	2.12230	2.55568	3.07478	4.43881	6.38548
39	1.21472	1.33831	1.47412	1.78721	2.16474	2.61957	3.16703	4.61637	6.70475
40	1.22079	1.34835	1.48886	1.81402	2.20804	2.68506	3.26204	4.80102	7.03999
41	1.22690	1.35846	1.50375	1.84123	2.25220	2.75219	3.35990	4.99306	7.39199
42	1.23303	1.36865	1.51879	1.86885	2.29724	2.82100	3.46070	5.19278	7.76159
43	1.23920	1.37891	1.53398	1.89688	2.34319	2.89152	3.56452	5.40050	8.14967
44	1.24539	1.38926	1.54932	1.92533	2.39005	2.96381	3.67145	5.61652	8.55715
45	1.25162	1.39968	1.56481	1.95421	2.43785	3.03790	3.78160	5.84118	8.98501
46	1.25788	1.41017	1.58046	1.98353	2.48661	3.11385	3.89504	6.07482	9.43426
47	1.26417	1.42075	1.59626	2.01328	2.53634	3.19170	4.01190	6.31782	9.90597
48	1.27049	1.43141	1.61223	2.04348	2.58707	3.27149	4.13225	6.57053	10.40127
49	1.27684	1.44214	1.62835	2.07413	2.63881	3.35328	4.25622	6.83335	10.92133
50	1.28323	1.45296	1.64463	2.10524	2.69159	3.43711	4.38391	7.10668	11.46740
51	1.28964	1.46385	1.66108	2.13682	2.74542	3.52304	4.51542	7.39095	12.04077
52	1.29609	1.47483	1.67769	2.16887	2.80033	3.61111	4.65089	7.68659	12.64281
53	1.30257	1.48589	1.69447	2.20141	2.85633	3.70139	4.79041	7.99405	13.27495
54	1.30908	1.49704	1.71141	2.23443	2.91346	3.79392	4.93412	8.31381	13.93870
55	1.31563	1.50827	1.72852	2.26794	2.97173	3.88877	5.08215	8.64637	14.63563
56	1.32221	1.51958	1.74581	2.30196	3.03117	3.98599	5.23461	8.99222	15.36741
57	1.32882	1.53098	1.76327	2.33649	3.09179	4.08564	5.39165	9.35191	16.13578
58	1.33546	1.54246	1.78090	2.37154	3.15362	4.18778	5.55340	9.72599	16.94257
59	1.34214	1.55403	1.79871	2.40711	3.21670	4.29248	5.72000	10.11503	17.78970
60	1.34885	1.56568	1.81670	2.44322	3.28103	4.39979	5.89160	10.51963	18.67919

					Interest				
Periods	6%	8%	10%	11%	12%	15%	18%	20%	25%
1	1.06000	1.08000	1.10000	1.11000	1.12000	1.15000	1.18000	1.20000	1.250
2	1.12360	1.16640	1.21000	1.23210	1.25440	1.32250	1.39240	1.44000	1.562
3	1.19102	1.25971	1.33100	1.36763	1.40493	1.52087	1.64303	1.72800	1.958
4	1.26248	1.36049	1.46410	1.51807	1.57352	1.74901	1.93878	2.07360	2.441
5	1.33823	1.46933	1.61051	1.68506	1.76234	2.01136	2.28776	2.48832	3.051
6	1.41852	1.58687	1.77156	1.87041	1.97382	2.31306	2.69955	2.98598	3.814
7	1.50363	1.71382	1.94872	2.07616	2.21068	2.66002	3.18547	3.58318	4.768
8	1.59385	1.85093	2.14359	2.30454	2.47596	3.05902	3.75886	4.29982	5.960
9	1.68948	1.99900	2.35795	2.55804	2.77308	3.51788	4.43545	5.15978	7.450
10	1.79085	2.15892	2.59374	2.83942	3.10585	4.04556	5.23384	6.19174	9.313
11	1.89830	2.33164	2.85312	3.15176	3.47855	4.65239	6.17593	7.43008	11.641
12	2.01220	2.51817	3.13843	3.49845	3.89598	5.35025	7.28759	8.91610	14.551
13	2.13293	2.71962	3.45227	3.88328	4.36349	6.15279	8.59936	10.69932	18.189
14	2.26090	2.93719	3.79750	4.31044	4.88711	7.07571	10.14724	12.83918	22.737
15	2.39656	3.17217	4.17725	4.78459	5.47357	8.13706	11.97375	15.40702	28.421
16	2.54035	3.42594	4.59497	5.31089	6.13039	9.35762	14.12902	18.48843	35.527
17	2.69277	3.70002	5.05447	5.89509	6.86604	10.76126	16.67225	22.18611	44.408
18	2.85434	3.99602	5.55992	6.54355	7.68997	12.37545	19.67325	26.62333	55.511
19	3.02560	4.31570	6.11591	7.26334	8.61276	14.23177	23.21444	31.94800	69.388
20	3.20714	4.66096	6.72750	8.06231	9.64629	16.36654	27.39303	38.33760	86.736
21	3.39956	5.03383	7.40025	8.94917	10.80385	18.82152	32.32378	46.00512	108.420
22	3.60354	5.43654	8.14027	9.93357	12.10031	21.64475	38.14206	55.20614	135.525
23	3.81975	5.87146	8.95430	11.02627	13.55235	24.89146	45.00763	66.24737	169.406
24	4.04893	6.34118	9.84973	12.23916	15.17863	28.62518	53.10901	79.49685	211.758
25	4.29187	6.84848	10.83471	13.58546	17.00006	32.91895	62.66863	95.39622	264.697
26	4.54938	7.39635	11.91818	15.07986	19.04007	37.85680	73.94898	114.47546	330.872
27	4.82235	7.98806	13.10999	16.73865	21.32488	43.53531	87.25980	137.37055	413.590
28	5.11169	8.62711	14.42099	18.57990	23.83387	50.06561	102.96656	164.84466	516.987
29	5.41839	9.31727	15.86309	20.62369	26.74993	57.57545	121.50054	197.81359	646.234
30	5.74349	10.06266	17.44940	22.89230	29.95992	66.21177	143.37064	237.37631	807.793
31	6.08810	10.86767	19.19434	25.41045	33.55511	76.14354	169.17735	284.85158	1009.741
32	6.45339	11.73708	21.11378	28.20560	37.58173	87.56507	199.62928	341.82189	1262.177
33	6.84059	12.67605	23.22515	31.30821	42.09153	100.69983	235.56255	410.18627	1577.721
34	7.25103	13.69013	25.54767	34.75212	47.14252	115.80480	277.96381	492.22352	1972.152
35	7.68609	14.78534	28.10244	38.57485	52.79962	133.17552	327.99729	590.66823	2465.190
36	8.14725	15.96817	30.91268	42.81808	59.13557	153.15185	387.03680	708.80187	3081.487
37	8.63609	17.24563	34.00395	47.52807	66.23184	176.12463	456.70343	850.56225	3851.859
38	9.15425	18.62528	37.40434	52.75616	74.17966	202.54332	538.91004	1020.67470	4814.824
39	9.70351	20.11530	41.14478	58.55934	83.08122	232.92482	635.91385	1224.80964	6018.531
40	10.28572	21.72452	45.25926	65.00087	93.05097	267.86355	750.37834	1469.77157	7523.163
41	10.90286	23.46248	49.78518	72.15096	104.21709	308.04308	885.44645	1763.72588	9403.954
42	11.55703	25.33948	54.76370	80.08757	116.72314	354.24954	1044.82681	2116.47106	11754.943
43	12.25045	27.36664	60.24007	88.89720	130.72991	407.38697	1232.89563	2539.76527	14693.679
44	12.98548	29.55597	66.26408	98.67589	146.41750	468.49502	1454.81685	3047.71832	18367.099
45	13.76461	31.92045	72.89048	109.53024	163.98760	538.76927	1716.68388	3657.26199	22958.874
46	14.59049	34.47409	80.17953	121.57857	183.66612	619.58466	2025.68698	4388.71439	28698.592
47	15.46592	37.23201	88.19749	134.95221	205.70605	712.52236	2390.31063	5266.45726	35873.240
48	16.39387	40.21057	97.01723	149.79695	230.39078	819.40071	2820.56655	6319.74872	44841.550
49	17.37750	43.42742	106.71896	166.27462	258.03767	942.31082	3328.26853	7583.69846	56051.938
50	18.42015	46.90161	117.39085	184.56483	289.00219	1083.65744	3927.35686	9100.43815	70064.923
51	19.52536	50.65374	129.12994	204.86696	323.68245	1246.20606	4634.28109	10920.52578	87581.154
52	20.69689	54.70604	142.04293	227.40232	362.52435	1433.13697	5468.45169	13104.63094	109476.442
53	21.93870	59.08252	156.24723	252.41658	406.02727	1648.10751	6452.77300	15725.55712	136845.553
54	23.25502	63.80913	171.87195	280.18240	454.75054	1895.32364	7614.27214	18870.66855	171056.941
55	24.65032	68.91386	189.05914	311.00247	509.32061	2179.62218	8984.84112	22644.80226	213821.176
56	26.12934	74.42696	207.96506	345.21274	570.43908	2506.56551	10602.11252	27173.76271	267276.471
57	27.69710	80.38112	228.76156	383.18614	638.89177	2882.55034	12510.49278	32608.51525	334095.588
58	29.35893	86.81161	251.63772	425.33661	715.55878	3314.93289	14762.38148	39130.21830	417619.485
59	31.12046	93.75654	276.80149	472.12364	801.42583	3812.17282	17419.61014	46956.26196	522024.357
60	32.98769	101.25706	304.48164	524.05724	897.59693	4383.99875	20555.13997	56347.51435	652530.446

Table 5-2
Present Value of $1

$$p = \frac{1}{(1 + i)^n}$$

					Interest				
Periods	½%	¾%	1%	1½%	2%	2½%	3%	4%	5%
1	0.99502	0.99256	0.99010	0.98522	0.98039	0.97561	0.97087	0.96154	0.95238
2	0.99007	0.98517	0.98030	0.97066	0.96117	0.95181	0.94260	0.92456	0.90703
3	0.98515	0.97783	0.97059	0.95632	0.94232	0.92860	0.91514	0.88900	0.86384
4	0.98025	0.97055	0.96098	0.94218	0.92385	0.90595	0.88849	0.85480	0.82270
5	0.97537	0.96333	0.95147	0.92826	0.90573	0.88385	0.86261	0.82193	0.78353
6	0.97052	0.95616	0.94205	0.91454	0.88797	0.86230	0.83748	0.79031	0.74622
7	0.96569	0.94904	0.93272	0.90103	0.87056	0.84127	0.81309	0.75992	0.71068
8	0.96089	0.94198	0.92348	0.88771	0.85349	0.82075	0.78941	0.73069	0.67684
9	0.95610	0.93496	0.91434	0.87459	0.83676	0.80073	0.76642	0.70259	0.64461
10	0.95135	0.92800	0.90529	0.86167	0.82035	0.78120	0.74409	0.67556	0.61391
11	0.94661	0.92109	0.89632	0.84893	0.80426	0.76214	0.72242	0.64958	0.58468
12	0.94191	0.91424	0.88745	0.83639	0.78849	0.74356	0.70138	0.62460	0.55684
13	0.93722	0.90743	0.87866	0.82403	0.77303	0.72542	0.68095	0.60057	0.53032
14	0.93256	0.90068	0.86996	0.81185	0.75788	0.70773	0.66112	0.57748	0.50507
15	0.92792	0.89397	0.86135	0.79985	0.74301	0.69047	0.64186	0.55526	0.48102
16	0.92330	0.88732	0.85282	0.78803	0.72845	0.67362	0.62317	0.53391	0.45811
17	0.91871	0.88071	0.84438	0.77639	0.71416	0.65720	0.60502	0.51337	0.43630
18	0.91414	0.87416	0.83602	0.76491	0.70016	0.64117	0.58739	0.49363	0.41552
19	0.90959	0.86765	0.82774	0.75361	0.68643	0.62553	0.57029	0.47464	0.39573
20	0.90506	0.86119	0.81954	0.74247	0.67297	0.61027	0.55368	0.45639	0.37689
21	0.90056	0.85478	0.81143	0.73150	0.65978	0.59539	0.53755	0.43883	0.35894
22	0.89608	0.84842	0.80340	0.72069	0.64684	0.58086	0.52189	0.42196	0.34185
23	0.89162	0.84210	0.79544	0.71004	0.63416	0.56670	0.50669	0.40573	0.32557
24	0.88719	0.83583	0.78757	0.69954	0.62172	0.55288	0.49193	0.39012	0.31007
25	0.88277	0.82961	0.77977	0.68921	0.60953	0.53939	0.47761	0.37512	0.29530
26	0.87838	0.82343	0.77205	0.67902	0.59758	0.52623	0.46369	0.36069	0.28124
27	0.87401	0.81730	0.76440	0.66899	0.58586	0.51340	0.45019	0.34682	0.26785
28	0.86966	0.81122	0.75684	0.65910	0.57437	0.50088	0.43708	0.33348	0.25509
29	0.86533	0.80518	0.74934	0.64936	0.56311	0.48866	0.42435	0.32065	0.24295
30	0.86103	0.79919	0.74192	0.63976	0.55207	0.47674	0.41199	0.30832	0.23138
31	0.85675	0.79324	0.73458	0.63031	0.54125	0.46511	0.39999	0.29646	0.22036
32	0.85248	0.78733	0.72730	0.62099	0.53063	0.45377	0.38834	0.28506	0.20987
33	0.84824	0.78147	0.72010	0.61182	0.52023	0.44270	0.37703	0.27409	0.19987
34	0.84402	0.77565	0.71297	0.60277	0.51003	0.43191	0.36604	0.26355	0.19035
35	0.83982	0.76988	0.70591	0.59387	0.50003	0.42137	0.35538	0.25342	0.18129
36	0.83564	0.76415	0.69892	0.58509	0.49022	0.41109	0.34503	0.24367	0.17266
37	0.83149	0.75846	0.69200	0.57644	0.48061	0.40107	0.33498	0.23430	0.16444
38	0.82735	0.75281	0.68515	0.56792	0.47119	0.39128	0.32523	0.22529	0.15661
39	0.82323	0.74721	0.67837	0.55953	0.46195	0.38174	0.31575	0.21662	0.14915
40	0.81914	0.74165	0.67165	0.55126	0.45289	0.37243	0.30656	0.20829	0.14205
41	0.81506	0.73613	0.66500	0.54312	0.44401	0.36335	0.29763	0.20028	0.13528
42	0.81101	0.73065	0.65842	0.53509	0.43530	0.35448	0.28896	0.19257	0.12884
43	0.80697	0.72521	0.65190	0.52718	0.42677	0.34584	0.28054	0.18517	0.12270
44	0.80296	0.71981	0.64545	0.51939	0.41840	0.33740	0.27237	0.17805	0.11686
45	0.79896	0.71445	0.63905	0.51171	0.41020	0.32917	0.26444	0.17120	0.11130
46	0.79499	0.70913	0.63273	0.50415	0.40215	0.32115	0.25674	0.16461	0.10600
47	0.79103	0.70385	0.62646	0.49670	0.39427	0.31331	0.24926	0.15828	0.10095
48	0.78710	0.69861	0.62026	0.48936	0.38654	0.30567	0.24200	0.15219	0.09614
49	0.78318	0.69341	0.61412	0.48213	0.37896	0.29822	0.23495	0.14634	0.09156
50	0.77929	0.68825	0.60804	0.47500	0.37153	0.29094	0.22811	0.14071	0.08720
51	0.77541	0.68313	0.60202	0.46798	0.36424	0.28385	0.22146	0.13530	0.08305
52	0.77155	0.67804	0.59606	0.46107	0.35710	0.27692	0.21501	0.13010	0.07910
53	0.76771	0.67300	0.59016	0.45426	0.35010	0.27017	0.20875	0.12509	0.07533
54	0.76389	0.66799	0.58431	0.44754	0.34323	0.26358	0.20267	0.12028	0.07174
55	0.76009	0.66301	0.57853	0.44093	0.33650	0.25715	0.19677	0.11566	0.06833
56	0.75631	0.65808	0.57280	0.43441	0.32991	0.25088	0.19104	0.11121	0.06507
57	0.75255	0.65318	0.56713	0.42799	0.32344	0.24476	0.18547	0.10693	0.06197
58	0.74880	0.64832	0.56151	0.42167	0.31710	0.23879	0.18007	0.10282	0.05902
59	0.74508	0.64349	0.55595	0.41544	0.31088	0.23297	0.17483	0.09886	0.05621
60	0.74137	0.63870	0.55045	0.40930	0.30478	0.22728	0.16973	0.09506	0.05354

				Interest					
Periods	6%	8%	10%	11%	12%	15%	18%	20%	25%
1	0.94340	0.92593	0.90909	0.90090	0.89286	0.86957	0.84746	0.83333	0.80000
2	0.89000	0.85734	0.82645	0.81162	0.79719	0.75614	0.71818	0.69444	0.64000
3	0.83962	0.79383	0.75131	0.73119	0.71178	0.65752	0.60863	0.57870	0.51200
4	0.79209	0.73503	0.68301	0.65873	0.63552	0.57175	0.51579	0.48225	0.40960
5	0.74726	0.68058	0.62092	0.59345	0.56743	0.49718	0.43711	0.40188	0.32768
6	0.70496	0.63017	0.56447	0.53464	0.50663	0.43233	0.37043	0.33490	0.26214
7	0.66506	0.58349	0.51316	0.48166	0.45235	0.37594	0.31393	0.27908	0.20972
8	0.62741	0.54027	0.46651	0.43393	0.40388	0.32690	0.26604	0.23257	0.16777
9	0.59190	0.50025	0.42410	0.39092	0.36061	0.28426	0.22546	0.19381	0.13422
10	0.55839	0.46319	0.38554	0.35218	0.32197	0.24718	0.19106	0.16151	0.10737
11	0.52679	0.42888	0.35049	0.31728	0.28748	0.21494	0.16192	0.13459	0.08590
12	0.49697	0.39711	0.31863	0.28584	0.25668	0.18691	0.13722	0.11216	0.06872
13	0.46884	0.36770	0.28966	0.25751	0.22917	0.16253	0.11629	0.09346	0.05498
14	0.44230	0.34046	0.26333	0.23199	0.20462	0.14133	0.09855	0.07789	0.04398
15	0.41727	0.31524	0.23939	0.20900	0.18270	0.12289	0.08352	0.06491	0.03518
16	0.39365	0.29189	0.21763	0.18829	0.16312	0.10686	0.07078	0.05409	0.02815
17	0.37136	0.27027	0.19784	0.16963	0.14564	0.09293	0.05998	0.04507	0.02252
18	0.35034	0.25025	0.17986	0.15282	0.13004	0.08081	0.05083	0.03756	0.01801
19	0.33051	0.23171	0.16351	0.13768	0.11611	0.07027	0.04308	0.03130	0.01441
20	0.31180	0.21455	0.14864	0.12403	0.10367	0.06110	0.03651	0.02608	0.01153
21	0.29416	0.19866	0.13513	0.11174	0.09256	0.05313	0.03094	0.02174	0.00922
22	0.27751	0.18394	0.12285	0.10067	0.08264	0.04620	0.02622	0.01811	0.00738
23	0.26180	0.17032	0.11168	0.09069	0.07379	0.04017	0.02222	0.01509	0.00590
24	0.24698	0.15770	0.10153	0.08170	0.06588	0.03493	0.01883	0.01258	0.00472
25	0.23300	0.14602	0.09230	0.07361	0.05882	0.03038	0.01596	0.01048	0.00378
26	0.21981	0.13520	0.08391	0.06631	0.05252	0.02642	0.01352	0.00874	0.00302
27	0.20737	0.12519	0.07628	0.05974	0.04689	0.02297	0.01146	0.00728	0.00242
28	0.19563	0.11591	0.06934	0.05382	0.04187	0.01997	0.00971	0.00607	0.00193
29	0.18456	0.10733	0.06304	0.04849	0.03738	0.01737	0.00823	0.00506	0.00155
30	0.17411	0.09938	0.05731	0.04368	0.03338	0.01510	0.00697	0.00421	0.00124
31	0.16425	0.09202	0.05210	0.03935	0.02980	0.01313	0.00591	0.00351	0.00099
32	0.15496	0.08520	0.04736	0.03545	0.02661	0.01142	0.00501	0.00293	0.00079
33	0.14619	0.07889	0.04306	0.03194	0.02376	0.00993	0.00425	0.00244	0.00063
34	0.13791	0.07305	0.03914	0.02878	0.02121	0.00864	0.00360	0.00203	0.00051
35	0.13011	0.06763	0.03558	0.02592	0.01894	0.00751	0.00305	0.00169	0.00041
36	0.12274	0.06262	0.03235	0.02335	0.01691	0.00653	0.00258	0.00141	0.00032
37	0.11579	0.05799	0.02941	0.02104	0.01510	0.00568	0.00219	0.00118	0.00026
38	0.10924	0.05369	0.02673	0.01896	0.01348	0.00494	0.00186	0.00098	0.00021
39	0.10306	0.04971	0.02430	0.01708	0.01204	0.00429	0.00157	0.00082	0.00017
40	0.09722	0.04603	0.02209	0.01538	0.01075	0.00373	0.00133	0.00068	0.00013
41	0.09172	0.04262	0.02009	0.01386	0.00960	0.00325	0.00113	0.00057	0.00011
42	0.08653	0.03946	0.01826	0.01249	0.00857	0.00282	0.00096	0.00047	0.00009
43	0.08163	0.03654	0.01660	0.01125	0.00765	0.00245	0.00081	0.00039	0.00007
44	0.07701	0.03383	0.01509	0.01013	0.00683	0.00213	0.00069	0.00033	0.00005
45	0.07265	0.03133	0.01372	0.00913	0.00610	0.00186	0.00058	0.00027	0.00004
46	0.06854	0.02901	0.01247	0.00823	0.00544	0.00161	0.00049	0.00023	0.00003
47	0.06466	0.02686	0.01134	0.00741	0.00486	0.00140	0.00042	0.00019	0.00003
48	0.06100	0.02487	0.01031	0.00668	0.00434	0.00122	0.00035	0.00016	0.00002
49	0.05755	0.02303	0.00937	0.00601	0.00388	0.00106	0.00030	0.00013	0.00002
50	0.05429	0.02132	0.00852	0.00542	0.00346	0.00092	0.00025	0.00011	0.00001
51	0.05122	0.01974	0.00774	0.00488	0.00309	0.00080	0.00022	0.00009	0.00001
52	0.04832	0.01828	0.00704	0.00440	0.00276	0.00070	0.00018	0.00008	0.00001
53	0.04558	0.01693	0.00640	0.00396	0.00246	0.00061	0.00015	0.00006	0.00001
54	0.04300	0.01567	0.00582	0.00357	0.00220	0.00053	0.00013	0.00005	0.00001
55	0.04057	0.01451	0.00529	0.00322	0.00196	0.00046	0.00011	0.00004	0.00000
56	0.03827	0.01344	0.00481	0.00290	0.00175	0.00040	0.00009	0.00004	0.00000
57	0.03610	0.01244	0.00437	0.00261	0.00157	0.00035	0.00008	0.00003	0.00000
58	0.03406	0.01152	0.00397	0.00235	0.00140	0.00030	0.00007	0.00003	0.00000
59	0.03213	0.01067	0.00361	0.00212	0.00125	0.00026	0.00006	0.00002	0.00000
60	0.03031	0.00988	0.00328	0.00191	0.00111	0.00023	0.00005	0.00002	0.00000

Table 5-3
Future Value of Annuity of $1 in Arrears

$$A = \frac{(1 + i)^n - 1}{i}$$

Interest

Periods	1/2%	3/4%	1%	1½%	2%	2½%	3%	4%	5%
1	1.00000	1.00000	1.00000	1.00000	1.00000	1.00000	1.00000	1.00000	1.00000
2	2.00500	2.00750	2.01000	2.01500	2.02000	2.02500	2.03000	2.04000	2.05000
3	3.01502	3.02256	3.03010	3.04522	3.06040	3.07562	3.09090	3.12160	3.15250
4	4.03010	4.04523	4.06040	4.09090	4.12161	4.15252	4.18363	4.24646	4.31012
5	5.05025	5.07556	5.10101	5.15227	5.20404	5.25633	5.30914	5.41632	5.52563
6	6.07550	6.11363	6.15202	6.22955	6.30812	6.38774	6.46841	6.63298	6.80191
7	7.10588	7.15948	7.21354	7.32299	7.43428	7.54743	7.66246	7.89829	8.14201
8	8.14141	8.21318	8.28567	8.43284	8.58297	8.73612	8.89234	9.21423	9.54911
9	9.18212	9.27478	9.36853	9.55933	9.75463	9.95452	10.15911	10.58280	11.02656
10	10.22803	10.34434	10.46221	10.70272	10.94972	11.20338	11.46388	12.00611	12.57789
11	11.27917	11.42192	11.56683	11.86326	12.16872	12.48347	12.80780	13.48635	14.20679
12	12.33556	12.50759	12.68250	13.04121	13.41209	13.79555	14.19203	15.02581	15.91713
13	13.39724	13.60139	13.80933	14.23683	14.68033	15.14044	15.61779	16.62684	17.71298
14	14.46423	14.70340	14.94742	15.45038	15.97394	16.51895	17.08632	18.29191	19.59863
15	15.53655	15.81368	16.09690	16.68214	17.29342	17.93193	18.59891	20.02359	21.57856
16	16.61423	16.93228	17.25786	17.93237	18.63929	19.38022	20.15688	21.82453	23.65749
17	17.69730	18.05927	18.43044	19.20136	20.01207	20.86473	21.76159	23.69751	25.84037
18	18.78579	19.19472	19.61475	20.48938	21.41231	22.38635	23.41444	25.64541	28.13238
19	19.87972	20.33868	20.81090	21.79672	22.84056	23.94601	25.11687	27.67123	30.53900
20	20.97912	21.49122	22.01900	23.12367	24.29737	25.54466	26.87037	29.77808	33.06595
21	22.08401	22.65240	23.23919	24.47052	25.78332	27.18327	28.67649	31.96920	35.71925
22	23.19443	23.82230	24.47159	25.83758	27.29898	28.86286	30.53678	34.24797	38.50521
23	24.31040	25.00096	25.71630	27.22514	28.84496	30.58443	32.45288	36.61789	41.43048
24	25.43196	26.18847	26.97346	28.63352	30.42186	32.34904	34.42647	39.08260	44.50200
25	26.55912	27.38488	28.24320	30.06302	32.03030	34.15776	36.45926	41.64591	47.72710
26	27.69191	28.59027	29.52563	31.51397	33.67091	36.01171	38.55304	44.31174	51.11345
27	28.83037	29.80470	30.82089	32.98668	35.34432	37.91200	40.70963	47.08421	54.66913
28	29.97452	31.02823	32.12910	34.48148	37.05121	39.85980	42.93092	49.96758	58.40258
29	31.12439	32.26094	33.45039	35.99870	38.79223	41.85630	45.21885	52.96629	62.32271
30	32.28002	33.50290	34.78489	37.53868	40.56808	43.90270	47.57542	56.08494	66.43885
31	33.44142	34.75417	36.13274	39.10176	42.37944	46.00027	50.00268	59.32834	70.76079
32	34.60862	36.01483	37.49407	40.68829	44.22703	48.15028	52.50276	62.70147	75.29883
33	35.78167	37.28494	38.86901	42.29861	46.11157	50.35403	55.07784	66.20953	80.06377
34	36.96058	38.56458	40.25770	43.93309	48.03380	52.61289	57.73018	69.85791	85.06696
35	38.14538	39.85381	41.66028	45.59209	49.99448	54.92821	60.46208	73.65222	90.32031
36	39.33610	41.15272	43.07688	47.27597	51.99437	57.30141	63.27594	77.59831	95.83632
37	40.53279	42.46136	44.50765	48.98511	54.03425	59.73395	66.17422	81.70225	101.62814
38	41.73545	43.77982	45.95272	50.71989	56.11494	62.22730	69.15945	85.97034	107.70955
39	42.94413	45.10817	47.41225	52.48068	58.23724	64.78298	72.23423	90.40915	114.09502
40	44.15885	46.44648	48.88637	54.26789	60.40198	67.40255	75.40126	95.02552	120.79977
41	45.37964	47.79483	50.37524	56.08191	62.61002	70.08762	78.66330	99.82654	127.83976
42	46.60654	49.15329	51.87899	57.92314	64.86222	72.83981	82.02320	104.81960	135.23175
43	47.83957	50.52194	53.39778	59.79199	67.15947	75.66080	85.48389	110.01238	142.99334
44	49.07877	51.90086	54.93176	61.68887	69.50266	78.55232	89.04841	115.41288	151.14301
45	50.32416	53.29011	56.48107	63.61420	71.89271	81.51613	92.71986	121.02939	159.70016
46	51.57578	54.68979	58.04589	65.56841	74.33056	84.55403	96.50146	126.87057	168.68516
47	52.83366	56.09996	59.62634	67.55194	76.81718	87.66789	100.39650	132.94539	178.11942
48	54.09783	57.52071	61.22261	69.56522	79.35352	90.85958	104.40840	139.26321	188.02539
49	55.36832	58.95212	62.83483	71.60870	81.94059	94.13107	108.54065	145.83373	198.42666
50	56.64516	60.39426	64.46318	73.68283	84.57940	97.48435	112.79687	152.66708	209.34800
51	57.92839	61.84721	66.10781	75.78807	87.27099	100.92146	117.18077	159.77377	220.81540
52	59.21803	63.31107	67.76889	77.92489	90.01641	104.44449	121.69620	167.16472	232.85617
53	60.51412	64.78590	69.44658	80.09376	92.81674	108.05561	126.34708	174.85131	245.49897
54	61.81669	66.27180	71.14105	82.29517	95.67307	111.75700	131.13749	182.84536	258.77392
55	63.12577	67.76883	72.85246	84.52960	98.58653	115.55092	136.07162	191.15917	272.71262
56	64.44140	69.27710	74.58098	86.79754	101.55826	119.43969	141.15377	199.80554	287.34825
57	65.76361	70.79668	76.32679	89.09951	104.58943	123.42569	146.38838	208.79776	302.71566
58	67.09243	72.32765	78.09006	91.43600	107.68122	127.51133	151.78003	218.14967	318.85144
59	68.42789	73.87011	79.87096	93.80754	110.83484	131.69911	157.33343	227.87566	335.79402
60	69.77003	75.42414	81.66967	96.21465	114.05154	135.99159	163.05344	237.99069	353.58372

NOTE: To convert this table to Annuity Due, take one more period and subtract 1.0.

					Interest				
Periods	6%	8%	10%	11%	12%	15%	18%	20%	25%
1	1.00000	1.00000	1.00000	1.00000	1.00000	1.00000	1.00000	1.00000	1.00000
2	2.06000	2.08000	2.10000	2.11000	2.12000	2.15000	2.18000	2.20000	2.25000
3	3.18360	3.24640	3.31000	3.34210	3.37440	3.47250	3.57240	3.64000	3.81250
4	4.37462	4.50611	4.64100	4.70973	4.77933	4.99337	5.21543	5.36800	5.76562
5	5.63709	5.86660	6.10510	6.22780	6.35285	6.74238	7.15421	7.44160	8.20703
6	6.97532	7.33593	7.71561	7.91286	8.11519	8.75374	9.44197	9.92992	11.25879
7	8.39384	8.92280	9.48717	9.78327	10.08901	11.06680	12.14152	12.91590	15.07349
8	9.89747	10.63663	11.43589	11.85943	12.29969	13.72682	15.32700	16.49908	19.84186
9	11.49132	12.48756	13.57948	14.16397	14.77566	16.78584	19.08585	20.79890	25.80232
10	13.18079	14.48656	15.93742	16.72201	17.54874	20.30372	23.52131	25.95868	33.25290
11	14.97164	16.64549	18.53117	19.56143	20.65458	24.34928	28.75514	32.15042	42.56613
12	16.86994	18.97713	21.38428	22.71319	24.13313	29.00167	34.93107	39.58050	54.20766
13	18.88214	21.49530	24.52271	26.21164	28.02911	34.35192	42.21866	48.49660	68.75958
14	21.01507	24.21492	27.97498	30.09492	32.39260	40.50471	50.81802	59.19592	86.94947
15	23.27597	27.15211	31.77248	34.40536	37.27971	47.58041	60.96527	72.03511	109.68684
16	25.67253	30.32428	35.94973	39.18995	42.74328	55.71747	72.93901	87.44213	138.10855
17	28.21288	33.75023	40.54470	44.50084	48.88367	65.07509	87.06804	105.93056	173.63568
18	30.90565	37.45024	45.59917	50.39594	55.74971	75.83636	103.74028	128.11667	218.04460
19	33.75999	41.44626	51.15909	56.93949	63.43968	88.21181	123.41353	154.74000	273.55576
20	36.78559	45.76196	57.27500	64.20283	72.05244	102.44358	146.62797	186.68800	342.94470
21	39.99273	50.42292	64.00250	72.26514	81.69874	118.81012	174.02100	225.02560	429.68087
22	43.39229	55.45676	71.40275	81.21431	92.50258	137.63164	206.34479	271.03072	538.10109
23	46.99583	60.89330	79.54302	91.14788	104.60289	159.27638	244.48685	326.23686	673.62636
24	50.81558	66.76476	88.49733	102.17415	118.15524	184.16784	289.49448	392.48424	843.03295
25	54.86451	73.10594	98.34706	114.41331	133.33387	212.79302	342.60349	471.98108	1054.79118
26	59.15638	79.95442	109.18177	127.99877	150.33393	245.71197	405.27211	567.37730	1319.48898
27	63.70577	87.35077	121.09994	143.07864	169.37401	283.56877	479.22109	681.85276	1650.36123
28	68.52811	95.33883	134.20994	159.81729	190.69889	327.10408	566.48089	819.22331	2063.95153
29	73.63980	103.96594	148.63093	178.39719	214.58275	377.16969	669.44745	984.06797	2580.93941
30	79.05819	113.28321	164.49402	199.02088	241.33268	434.74515	790.94799	1181.88157	3227.17427
31	84.80168	123.34587	181.94342	221.91317	271.29261	500.95692	934.31863	1419.25788	4034.96783
32	90.88978	134.21354	201.13777	247.32362	304.84772	577.10046	1103.49598	1704.10946	5044.70979
33	97.34316	145.95062	222.25154	275.52922	342.42945	664.66552	1303.12526	2045.93135	6306.88724
34	104.18375	158.62667	245.47670	306.83744	384.52098	765.36535	1538.68781	2456.11762	7884.60905
35	111.43478	172.31680	271.02437	341.58955	431.66350	881.17016	1816.65161	2948.34115	9856.76132
36	119.12087	187.10215	299.12681	380.16441	484.46312	1014.34568	2144.64890	3539.00937	12321.95164
37	127.26812	203.07032	330.03949	422.98249	543.59869	1167.49753	2531.68570	4247.81125	15403.43956
38	135.90421	220.31595	364.04343	470.51056	609.83053	1343.62216	2988.38913	5098.37350	19255.29944
39	145.05846	238.94122	401.44778	523.26673	684.01020	1546.16549	3527.29918	6119.04820	24070.12430
40	154.76197	259.05652	442.59256	581.82607	767.09142	1779.09031	4163.21303	7343.85784	30088.65538
41	165.04768	280.78104	487.85181	646.82693	860.14239	2046.95385	4913.59137	8813.62941	37611.81923
42	175.95054	304.24352	537.63699	718.97790	964.35948	2354.99693	5799.03782	10577.35529	47015.77403
43	187.50758	329.58301	592.40069	799.06547	1081.08262	2709.24647	6843.86463	12693.82635	58770.71754
44	199.75803	356.94965	652.64076	887.96267	1211.81253	3116.63344	8076.76026	15233.59162	73464.39693
45	212.74351	386.50562	718.90484	986.63856	1358.23003	3585.12846	9531.57711	18281.30994	91831.49616
46	226.50812	418.42607	791.79532	1096.16880	1522.21764	4123.89773	11248.26098	21938.57193	114790.37020
47	241.09861	452.90015	871.97485	1217.74737	1705.88375	4743.48239	13273.94796	26327.28631	143488.96275
48	256.56453	490.13216	960.17234	1352.69958	1911.58980	5456.00475	15664.25859	31593.74358	179362.20343
49	272.95840	530.34274	1057.18957	1502.49653	2141.98058	6275.40546	18484.82514	37913.49229	224203.75429
50	290.33590	573.77016	1163.90853	1668.77115	2400.01825	7217.71628	21813.09367	45497.19075	280255.69286
51	308.75606	620.67177	1281.29938	1853.33598	2689.02044	8301.37372	25740.45053	54597.62890	350320.61608
52	328.28142	671.32551	1410.42932	2058.20294	3012.70289	9547.57978	30374.73162	65518.15468	437901.77010
53	348.97831	726.03155	1552.47225	2285.60526	3375.22724	10980.71674	35843.18331	78622.78562	547378.21263
54	370.91701	785.11408	1708.71948	2538.02184	3781.25451	12628.82425	42295.95631	94348.34274	684223.76578
55	394.17203	848.92320	1880.59142	2818.20424	4236.00505	14524.14789	49910.22844	113219.01129	855280.70723
56	418.82235	917.83706	2069.65057	3129.20671	4745.32565	16703.77008	58895.06957	135863.81354	1069101.88404
57	444.95169	992.26402	2277.61562	3474.41944	5315.76473	19210.33559	69497.18209	163037.57625	1336378.35505
58	472.64879	1072.64514	2506.37719	3857.60558	5954.65650	22092.88593	82007.67486	195646.09150	1670473.94381
59	502.00772	1159.45676	2758.01490	4282.94220	6670.21528	25407.81882	96770.05634	234776.30980	2088093.42976
60	533.12818	1253.21330	3034.81640	4755.06584	7471.64111	29219.99164	114189.66648	281732.57177	2610117.78720

NOTE: To convert this table to Annuity Due, take one more period and subtract 1.0.

Table 5-4
Present Value of an Annuity of $1 in Arrears

$$P = \frac{1 - \dfrac{1}{(1+i)^n}}{i}$$

					Interest				
Periods	½%	¾%	1%	1½%	2%	2½%	3%	4%	5%
1	0.99502	0.99256	0.99010	0.98522	0.98039	0.97561	0.97087	0.96154	0.95238
2	1.98510	1.97772	1.97040	1.95588	1.94156	1.92742	1.91347	1.88609	1.85941
3	2.97025	2.95556	2.94099	2.91220	2.88388	2.85602	2.82861	2.77509	2.72325
4	3.95050	3.92611	3.90197	3.85438	3.80773	3.76197	3.71710	3.62990	3.54595
5	4.92587	4.88944	4.85343	4.78264	4.71346	4.64583	4.57971	4.45182	4.32948
6	5.89638	5.84560	5.79548	5.69719	5.60143	5.50813	5.41719	5.24214	5.07569
7	6.86207	6.79464	6.72819	6.59821	6.47199	6.34939	6.23028	6.00205	5.78637
8	7.82296	7.73661	7.65168	7.48593	7.32548	7.17014	7.01969	6.73274	6.46321
9	8.77906	8.67158	8.56602	8.36052	8.16224	7.97087	7.78611	7.43533	7.10782
10	9.73041	9.59958	9.47130	9.22218	8.98259	8.75206	8.53020	8.11090	7.72173
11	10.67703	10.52067	10.36763	10.07112	9.78685	9.51421	9.25262	8.76048	8.30641
12	11.61893	11.43491	11.25508	10.90751	10.57534	10.25776	9.95400	9.38507	8.86325
13	12.55615	12.34235	12.13374	11.73153	11.34837	10.98318	10.63496	9.98565	9.39357
14	13.48871	13.24302	13.00370	12.54338	12.10625	11.69091	11.29607	10.56312	9.89864
15	14.41662	14.13699	13.86505	13.34323	12.84926	12.38138	11.93794	11.11839	10.37966
16	15.33993	15.02431	14.71787	14.13126	13.57771	13.05500	12.56110	11.65230	10.83777
17	16.25863	15.90502	15.56225	14.90765	14.29187	13.71220	13.16612	12.16567	11.27407
18	17.17277	16.77918	16.39827	15.67256	14.99203	14.35336	13.75351	12.65930	11.68959
19	18.08236	17.64683	17.22601	16.42617	15.67846	14.97889	14.32380	13.13394	12.08532
20	18.98742	18.50802	18.04555	17.16864	16.35143	15.58916	14.87747	13.59033	12.46221
21	19.88798	19.36280	18.85698	17.90014	17.01121	16.18455	15.41502	14.02916	12.82115
22	20.78406	20.21121	19.66038	18.62082	17.65805	16.76541	15.93692	14.45112	13.16300
23	21.67568	21.05331	20.45582	19.33086	18.29220	17.33211	16.44361	14.85684	13.48857
24	22.56287	21.88915	21.24339	20.03041	18.91393	17.88499	16.93554	15.24696	13.79864
25	23.44564	22.71876	22.02316	20.71961	19.52346	18.42438	17.41315	15.62208	14.09394
26	24.32402	23.54219	22.79520	21.39863	20.12104	18.95061	17.87684	15.98277	14.37519
27	25.19803	24.35949	23.55961	22.06762	20.70690	19.46401	18.32703	16.32959	14.64303
28	26.06769	25.17071	24.31644	22.72672	21.28127	19.96489	18.76411	16.66306	14.89813
29	26.93302	25.97589	25.06579	23.37608	21.84438	20.45355	19.18845	16.98371	15.14107
30	27.79405	26.77508	25.80771	24.01584	22.39646	20.93029	19.60044	17.29203	15.37245
31	28.65080	27.56832	26.54229	24.64615	22.93770	21.39541	20.00043	17.58849	15.59281
32	29.50328	28.35565	27.26959	25.26714	23.46833	21.84918	20.38877	17.87355	15.80268
33	30.35153	29.13712	27.98969	25.87895	23.98856	22.29188	20.76579	18.14765	16.00255
34	31.19555	29.91278	28.70267	26.48173	24.49859	22.72379	21.13184	18.41120	16.19290
35	32.03537	30.68266	29.40858	27.07559	24.99862	23.14516	21.48722	18.66461	16.37419
36	32.87102	31.44681	30.10751	27.66068	25.48884	23.55625	21.83225	18.90828	16.54685
37	33.70250	32.20527	30.79951	28.23713	25.96945	23.95732	22.16724	19.14258	16.71129
38	34.52985	32.95808	31.48466	28.80505	26.44064	24.34860	22.49246	19.36786	16.86789
39	35.35309	33.70529	32.16303	29.36458	26.90259	24.73034	22.80822	19.58448	17.01704
40	36.17223	34.44694	32.83469	29.91585	27.35548	25.10278	23.11477	19.79277	17.15909
41	36.98729	35.18307	33.49969	30.45896	27.79949	25.46612	23.41240	19.99305	17.29437
42	37.79830	35.91371	34.15811	30.99405	28.23479	25.82061	23.70136	20.18563	17.42321
43	38.60527	36.63892	34.81001	31.52123	28.66156	26.16645	23.98190	20.37079	17.54591
44	39.40823	37.35873	35.45545	32.04062	29.07996	26.50385	24.25427	20.54884	17.66277
45	40.20720	38.07318	36.09451	32.55234	29.49016	26.83302	24.51871	20.72004	17.77407
46	41.00219	38.78231	36.72724	33.05649	29.89231	27.15417	24.77545	20.88465	17.88007
47	41.79322	39.48617	37.35370	33.55319	30.28658	27.46748	25.02471	21.04294	17.98102
48	42.58032	40.18478	37.97396	34.04255	30.67312	27.77315	25.26671	21.19513	18.07716
49	43.36350	40.87820	38.58808	34.52468	31.05208	28.07137	25.50166	21.34147	18.16872
50	44.14279	41.56645	39.19612	34.99969	31.42361	28.36231	25.72976	21.48218	18.25593
51	44.91820	42.24958	39.79814	35.46767	31.78785	28.64616	25.95123	21.61749	18.33898
52	45.68975	42.92762	40.39419	35.92874	32.14495	28.92308	26.16624	21.74758	18.41807
53	46.45746	43.60061	40.98435	36.38300	32.49505	29.19325	26.37499	21.87267	18.49340
54	47.22135	44.26860	41.56866	36.83054	32.83828	29.45683	26.57766	21.99296	18.56515
55	47.98145	44.93161	42.14719	37.27147	33.17479	29.71398	26.77443	22.10861	18.63347
56	48.73776	45.58969	42.71999	37.70588	33.50469	29.96486	26.96546	22.21982	18.69854
57	49.49031	46.24287	43.28712	38.13387	33.82813	30.20962	27.15094	22.32675	18.76052
58	50.23911	46.89118	43.84863	38.55554	34.14523	30.44841	27.33101	22.42957	18.81954
59	50.98419	47.53467	44.40459	38.97097	34.45610	30.68137	27.50583	22.52843	18.87575
60	51.72556	48.17337	44.95504	39.38027	34.76089	30.90866	27.67556	22.62349	18.92929

NOTE: To convert this table to annuity due take one less period and add 1.0.

	Interest								
Periods	6%	8%	10%	11%	12%	15%	18%	20%	25%
1	0.94340	0.92593	0.90909	0.90090	0.89286	0.86957	0.84746	0.83333	0.80000
2	1.83339	1.78326	1.73554	1.71252	1.69005	1.62571	1.56564	1.52778	1.44000
3	2.67301	2.57710	2.48685	2.44371	2.40183	2.28323	2.17427	2.10648	1.95200
4	3.46511	3.31213	3.16987	3.10245	3.03735	2.85498	2.69006	2.58873	2.36160
5	4.21236	3.99271	3.79079	3.69590	3.60478	3.35216	3.12717	2.99061	2.68928
6	4.91732	4.62288	4.35526	4.23054	4.11141	3.78448	3.49760	3.32551	2.95142
7	5.58238	5.20637	4.86842	4.71220	4.56376	4.16042	3.81153	3.60459	3.16114
8	6.20979	5.74664	5.33493	5.14612	4.96764	4.48732	4.07757	3.83716	3.32891
9	6.80169	6.24689	5.75902	5.53705	5.32825	4.77158	4.30302	4.03097	3.46313
10	7.36009	6.71008	6.14457	5.88923	5.65022	5.01877	4.49409	4.19247	3.57050
11	7.88687	7.13896	6.49506	6.20652	5.93770	5.23371	4.65601	4.32706	3.65640
12	8.38384	7.53608	6.81369	6.49236	6.19437	5.42062	4.79322	4.43922	3.72512
13	8.85268	7.90378	7.10336	6.74987	6.42355	5.58315	4.90951	4.53268	3.78010
14	9.29498	8.24424	7.36669	6.98187	6.62817	5.72448	5.00806	4.61057	3.82408
15	9.71225	8.55948	7.60608	7.19087	6.81086	5.84737	5.09158	4.67547	3.85926
16	10.10590	8.85137	7.82371	7.37916	6.97399	5.95423	5.16235	4.72956	3.88741
17	10.47726	9.12164	8.02155	7.54879	7.11963	6.04716	5.22233	4.77463	3.90993
18	10.82760	9.37189	8.20141	7.70162	7.24967	6.12797	5.27316	4.81219	3.92794
19	11.15812	9.60360	8.36492	7.83929	7.36578	6.19823	5.31624	4.84350	3.94235
20	11.46992	9.81815	8.51356	7.96333	7.46944	6.25933	5.35275	4.86958	3.95388
21	11.76408	10.01680	8.64869	8.07507	7.56200	6.31246	5.38368	4.89132	3.96311
22	12.04158	10.20074	8.77154	8.17574	7.64465	6.35866	5.40990	4.90943	3.97049
23	12.30338	10.37106	8.88322	8.26643	7.71843	6.39884	5.43212	4.92453	3.97639
24	12.55036	10.52876	8.98474	8.34814	7.78432	6.43377	5.45095	4.93710	3.98111
25	12.78336	10.67478	9.07704	8.42174	7.84314	6.46415	5.46691	4.94759	3.98489
26	13.00317	10.80998	9.16095	8.48806	7.89566	6.49056	5.48043	4.95632	3.98791
27	13.21053	10.93516	9.23722	8.54780	7.94255	6.51353	5.49189	4.96360	3.99033
28	13.40616	11.05108	9.30657	8.60162	7.98442	6.53351	5.50160	4.96967	3.99226
29	13.59072	11.15841	9.36961	8.65011	8.02181	6.55088	5.50983	4.97472	3.99381
30	13.76483	11.25778	9.42691	8.69379	8.05518	6.56598	5.51681	4.97894	3.99505
31	13.92909	11.34980	9.47901	8.73315	8.08499	6.57911	5.52272	4.98245	3.99604
32	14.08404	11.43500	9.52638	8.76860	8.11159	6.59053	5.52773	4.98537	3.99683
33	14.23023	11.51389	9.56943	8.80054	8.13535	6.60046	5.53197	4.98781	3.99746
34	14.36814	11.58693	9.60857	8.82932	8.15656	6.60910	5.53557	4.98984	3.99797
35	14.49825	11.65457	9.64416	8.85524	8.17550	6.61661	5.53862	4.99154	3.99838
36	14.62099	11.71719	9.67651	8.87859	8.19241	6.62314	5.54120	4.99295	3.99870
37	14.73678	11.77518	9.70592	8.89963	8.20751	6.62881	5.54339	4.99412	3.99896
38	14.84602	11.82887	9.73265	8.91859	8.22099	6.63375	5.54525	4.99510	3.99917
39	14.94907	11.87858	9.75696	8.93567	8.23303	6.63805	5.54682	4.99592	3.99934
40	15.04630	11.92461	9.77905	8.95105	8.24378	6.64178	5.54815	4.99660	3.99947
41	15.13802	11.96723	9.79914	8.96491	8.25337	6.64502	5.54928	4.99717	3.99957
42	15.22454	12.00670	9.81740	8.97740	8.26194	6.64785	5.55024	4.99764	3.99966
43	15.30617	12.04324	9.83400	8.98865	8.26959	6.65030	5.55105	4.99803	3.99973
44	15.38318	12.07707	9.84909	8.99878	8.27642	6.65244	5.55174	4.99836	3.99978
45	15.45583	12.10840	9.86281	9.00791	8.28252	6.65429	5.55232	4.99863	3.99983
46	15.52437	12.13741	9.87528	9.01614	8.28796	6.65591	5.55281	4.99886	3.99986
47	15.58903	12.16427	9.88662	9.02355	8.29282	6.65731	5.55323	4.99905	3.99989
48	15.65003	12.18914	9.89693	9.03022	8.29716	6.65853	5.55359	4.99921	3.99991
49	15.70757	12.21216	9.90630	9.03624	8.30104	6.65959	5.55389	4.99934	3.99993
50	15.76186	12.23348	9.91481	9.04165	8.30450	6.66051	5.55414	4.99945	3.99994
51	15.81308	12.25323	9.92256	9.04653	8.30759	6.66132	5.55436	4.99954	3.99995
52	15.86139	12.27151	9.92960	9.05093	8.31035	6.66201	5.55454	4.99962	3.99996
53	15.90697	12.28843	9.93600	9.05489	8.31281	6.66262	5.55469	4.99968	3.99997
54	15.94998	12.30410	9.94182	9.05846	8.31501	6.66315	5.55483	4.99974	3.99998
55	15.99054	12.31861	9.94711	9.06168	8.31697	6.66361	5.55494	4.99978	3.99998
56	16.02881	12.33205	9.95191	9.06457	8.31872	6.66401	5.55503	4.99982	3.99999
57	16.06492	12.34449	9.95629	9.06718	8.32029	6.66435	5.55511	4.99985	3.99999
58	16.09898	12.35601	9.96026	9.06954	8.32169	6.66466	5.55518	4.99987	3.99999
59	16.13111	12.36668	9.96387	9.07165	8.32294	6.66492	5.55524	4.99989	3.99999
60	16.16143	12.37655	9.96716	9.07356	8.32405	6.66515	5.55529	4.99991	3.99999

NOTE: To convert this table to annuity due, take one less period and add 1.0.

Questions

Q–5–1 How do the following differ?
  a) Future value of $1.
  b) Future value of $1 per period.
  c) Present value of $1.
  d) Present value of $1 per period.

Q–5–2 How do simple interest and compound interest differ?

Q–5–3 How are present value and discounting related?

Q–5–4 How does an ordinary annuity differ from an annuity due?

Q–5–5 What is a deferred annuity?

Q–5–6 When you compute the present value of a single sum, what relationship between the number of time periods and the interest rate must be made?

Q–5–7 For a given amount placed on deposit for a given time period, what happens to the future value of the amount as the frequency of compounding increases?

Q–5–8 What variables must be determined in order to find a specific factor in a specific table?

Q–5–9 Given the proper information, what other variables besides the present or future value of an amount can be determined?

Q–5–10 How are the values in the present value of $1 table related to the present value of $1 per period?

Q–5–11 When you compute the present value of an annuity, what relationship must be made between (a) the number of time periods, (b) interest rates, and (c) the payments (receipts)?

Q–5–12 Explain how you convert the present value and future value table values for an ordinary annuity into an annuity due.

Q–5–13 What does the term *time value of money* mean?

Discussion Questions and Cases

D–5–1 An alumni association of a large midwestern state university offers life membership in the alumni association for $300 payable in three yearly installments of $100 each. The first installment is due at the time of application for life membership. The association also offers yearly membrships at $15.
Required:
If your interest rate for the first three years is 18% compounded semiannually and 12% computed annually thereafter, and you expect to live for 45 years, which alternative should you take? (For the yearly alternative you may assume an interest rate of 18% compounded annually for the first three payments only.)

D–5–2 A student is trying to decide whether to complete an MBA program. This student's grades and test scores are so high that scholarship money is available to pay all costs of the additional two years required for the program. Following are the projected salaries for the student with and without an MBA.

| | Projected Salaries | |
| | Without MBA | With MBA |
Years	Salary/Year	Salary/Year
1 & 2	$15,000	–0–
2–5	17,000	$22,500
6–15	20,000	25,500
16–30	45,000	54,500
31–40	60,000	69,500

Required:

If you use a 12% discount rate, should the individual go on for an MBA? To ease the computations, assume that all salaries are paid at the end of the year.

D–5–3   Mike Company is trying to decide between two alternative methods of financing a truck. One is to lease the truck for four years at $700/month payable at the beginning of each month. At the end of the four years the truck is returned to the leasing company. The other alternative is to purchase the truck by signing a 48-month note requiring a $1,000 a month payment at the beginning of each month. At the end of the fourth year, the company could sell the truck for $11,000.

Required:

Compute the present value of these two alternatives at 18% interest compounded monthly. Ignoring tax considerations and all other factors not discussed, which alternative should Mike select? Why?

D–5–4   A friend owns an auto parts store. Two years ago he considered installing a computer system that would cost approximately $20,000 initially and $3,000 a year to operate. He believed the system would save him $9,000 a year over the five-year life of the system. At the time his interest rate was 12% compounded annually.

Now, given inflation, the savings from the system still would be projected at $9,000 a year, but his interest rate has risen to 15% compounded annually. Technology has caused the initial price to drop to $19,000 and subsequent yearly costs of the computer to remain constant.

Required:

If you ignore income tax and all other factors, should he have made the investment two years ago? Should he make it now?

D–5–5   John Smith is considering a job in another city. One of his concerns is the increased home payments that will be incurred because of increased mortgage rates. John currently has a $50,000, 10%, 30-year home loan on a home he just moved into. If he moves, his new house will require a $50,000 mortgage. The current rate in the new city for a 30-year loan is 15%.

Required:

1.   Assuming that John makes yearly mortgage payments, how much will his yearly payments increase if he takes the new job?

2.   John's potential employer is willing to make a lump sum payment to reduce John's monthly payments. Assuming that John makes yearly mortgage payments and that the interest rate of 15% is a permanent one and should be used by John in his discounting, how much will the lump sum payment have to be to keep John's yearly payment in the new city the same as the old? (Ignore tax considerations.)

E–5–1 What is the present value of the promise to pay $800 at the end of each of the next 20 years at 15% interest compounded annually?

E–5–2 What is the present value of an investment that will return $5,000 five years from today at 20% interest compounded annually?

E–5–3 What is the present value of the promise to pay $900 at the beginning of each of the next 15 years at 12% interest compounded annually?

E–5–4 If $100 is invested at the end of each month for four years in a savings account paying 9% interest compounded monthly, how much will the account be worth at the end of the fourth year?

E–5–5 If $10,000 is invested today in a savings account paying 12% interest compounded monthly, how much will the account balance be at the end of five years?

E–5–6 If $200 is invested at the beginning of each six-month period for the next ten years, how much will the account be worth at the end of the tenth year at 10% interest compounded semiannually?

E–5–7 How long will it take an amount to triple at 10% interest compounded annually?

E–5–8 If a $2,000 investment will accumulate to $2,800 in six years, what interest rate (compounded annually) is being paid on the investment?

E–5–9 How much more will an individual earn if s/he places $10,000 in a savings account for one year paying 8% interest compounded annually rather than a savings account paying 8% simple interest?

E–5–10 The telephone company requires a deposit of $50, which by law must pay interest at 6% compounded annually. If the deposit is held for two years, how much will the telephone company return?

E–5–11 What is the present value of an annuity that will pay $200 at the end of each month for 48 months starting one year from now if 12% interest compounded monthly is an appropriate interest rate?

E–5–12 You have decided to undertake an investment that requires an initial investment of $1,000 and $50 a month at the end of the quarter for the next 10 years. The investment will pay 12% interest compounded quarterly. How much will the investment be worth at the end of the payment period?

E–5–13 Happy Company is considering making a $100,000 investment that will return $12,500 at the end of each of the next 17 years. What interest rate (compounded on an annual basis) will Happy earn on this investment?

E–5–14 **a)** If $30,000 is deposited on January 1, 1981, in an investment paying 12% interest compounded yearly, what will its future value be on January 1, 1986?
b) If instead of the investment paying 12% compounded yearly, the investment paid 12% interest compounded semiannually, how much would the $30,000 investment be worth on January 1, 1986?

E–5–15 Mr. Jones is considering whether to borrow $3,000. The money is to be repaid in 36 equal payments to be made at the end of each month, including 1½% interest per month on the unpaid balance. What will his monthly payment be?

E–5–16 Ms. Jones has been offered the opportunity to invest in a company that will pay her $100,000 ten years from now. At 15% interest compounded annually, how much should Ms. Jones pay for the investment?

E–5–17 **a)** What is the value on January 1, 1981, of the promise to pay $25,000 on January 1, 1989, discounted at 10% interest compounded annually?
b) What is the value on January 1, 1981, of the promise to pay $25,000 on January 1, 1989, discounted at 10% interest compounded semiannually?

E-5-18 Answer the following five multiple choice questions.

a) If an individual put $3,000 in a savings account today, what amount of cash would be available two years from today?

(1) $3,000 × 0.857

(2) $3,000 × 0.857 × 2

(3) $\dfrac{\$3,000}{0.857}$

(4) $\dfrac{\$3,000}{0.926} \times 2$

b) What is the present value today of $4,000 to be received six years from today?

(1) $4,000 × 0.926 × 6

(2) $4,000 × 0.794 × 2

(3) $4,000 × 0.681 × 0.926

(4) Cannot be determined from the information given.

c) Calculation of the amount of the equal periodic payments which would be equivalent to a year 0 outlay of $1,000 is affected most readily by reference to a table that shows the

(1) Amount of 1.

(2) Present value of 1.

(3) Amount of an annuity of 1.

(4) Present value of an annuity of 1.

d) What amount should be deposited in a bank today to accumulate to $1,000 three years from today?

(1) $\dfrac{\$1,000}{0.794}$

(2) $1,000 × 0.926 × 3

(3) ($1,000 × 0.926) + ($1,000 × 0.857) + ($1,000 × 0.794)

(4) $1,000 × 0.794

e) What amount should an individual have in his bank account today before withdrawal if he needs $2,000 each year for four years, with the first withdrawal to be made today and each subsequent withdrawal to be made at one-year intervals? (He is to have exactly a zero balance in his bank account after the fourth withdrawal.)

(1) $2,000 + ($2,000 × 0.926) × ($2,000 × 0.857) + ($2,000 × 0.794)

(2) $\dfrac{\$2,000}{0.735} \times 4$

(3) ($2,000 × 0.926) + ($2,000 × 0.857) + ($2,000 × 0.794) + ($2,000 × 0.735)

(4) $\dfrac{\$2,000}{0.926} \times 4$

(AICPA adapted)

E-5-19 Answer the following six multiple-choice questions.

a) At the beginning of 1973, Garmar Company received a three-year, non-interest--bearing, $1,000 trade note. The market rate for equivalent notes was 8% at that time. Garmar reported this note as $1,000 trade notes receivable on its 1973 year-end statement of financial position and $1,000 as sales revenue for 1973. What effect did this accounting for the note have on Garmar's net earnings for 1973, 1974, and 1975, and on its retained earnings at the end of 1975, respectively.

(1) Overstate, understate, understate, zero.

(2) Overstate, understate, understate, understate.

(3) Overstate, overstate, understate, zero.

(4) No effect on any of these.

(b) The figure 0.9423 is taken from the column marked 2% and the row marked three periods in what interest table?

(1) Amount of $1.

(2) Amount of annuity of $1.

(3) Present value of $1.

(4) Present value of annuity of $1.

c) A businessman wants to withdraw $3,000 (including principal) from an investment fund at the end of each year for five years. How should he compute his required initial investment at the beginning of the first year if the fund earns 6% interest compounded annually?

(1) $3,000 times the amount of an annuity of $1 at 6% interest at the end of each year for five years.

(2) $3,000 divided by the amount of an annuity of $1 at 6% interest at the end of each year for five years.

(3) $3,000 times the present value of an annuity of $1 at 6% interest at the end of each year for five years.

(4) $3,000 divided by the present value of an annuity of $1 at 6% interest at the end of each year for five years.

d) Glen, Inc. purchased certain plant assets under a deferred payment contract on December 31, 1980. The agreement was to pay $10,000 at the time of purchase and $10,000 at the end of each of the next five years. The plant assets should be valued at

(1) The present value of a $10,000 ordinary annuity for five years.

(2) $60,000.

(3) $60,000 plus imputed interest.

(4) $60,000 less imputed interest.

e) Which of the following transactions would require the use of the present value of an annuity due concept in order to calculate the present value of the asset obtained or liability owed at the date of incurrence?

(1) A capital lease is entered into with the initial lease payment due upon the signing of the lease agreement.

(2) A capital lease is entered into with the initial lease payment due one month after the signing of the lease agreement.

(3) A ten-year, 8% bond is issued on January 2 with interest payable semiannually on July 1 and January 1, yielding 7%.

(4) A ten-year, 8% bond is issued on January 2 with interest payable semiannually on July 1 and January 1, yielding 9%.

f) On May 1, 1980, a company purchased a new machine that it does not have to pay for until May 1, 1982. The total payment on May 1, 1982, will include both principal and interest. If you assume interest at a 10% rate, the cost of the machine would be the total payment multiplied by what time value of money concept?

(1) Future amount of annuity of 1.

(2) Future amount of 1.

(3) Present value of annuity of 1.

(4) Present value of 1.

(AICPA adapted)

Problems

P–5–1 Mr. Smith is considering an investment that will pay 8% interest compounded annually for five years, 10% interest compounded annually for the next three years, and 15% interest compounded annually for the last two years. If Mr. Smith invests $50,000, how much will his investment be worth at the end of the 10 years? What is the average annual interest rate that he will receive on this investment?

P–5–2 Harold Worker has decided to start a retirement program. He believes that after retirement, $20,000 a year will be needed at the beginning of each year. Harold believes that his life expectancy is 15 years after retirement. Harold plans to deposit the needed amount semiannually until retirement (over the next 25 years) starting six months from now. Harold believes the amounts will earn 10% interest compounded semiannually until retirement and 10% interest compounded annually after retirement.

Required:

What amount will Harold need to deposit each six months?

P–5–3   The Viggers desire to have necessary funds available to send their two children to college 10 years from now. They believe that $80,000 will be needed 10 years from now. How much must they deposit quarterly (at the end of each quarter) in a savings account paying 12% interest compounded quarterly to have the needed $80,000?

P–5–4   How much would you pay for an investment which promises to pay you $20,000

   a)   10 years from now at 8% interest compounded annually?

   b)   9 years from now at 8% interest compounded annually?

P–5–5   Mr. Smith bought an investment that promised to return $500 at the end of each of the next five years and $5,000 at the end of the fifth year.

   a)   If the investment were purchased to return 11% interest compounded annually, how much did Mr. Smith pay for the investment?

   b)   If Mr. Smith sold the investment one year later (after receiving the first of the $500 payments) to Mr. Jones at 8% interest compounded annually, how much did Mr. Smith receive?

P–5–6   What is the present value of the promise to pay you $2,500 at the end of each of the next 10 years and an additional payment of $25,000 at the end of the tenth year:

   a)   At 10% interest compounded annually?

   b)   At 8% interest compounded annually?

   c)   At 12% interest compounded annually?

P–5–7   What is the present value of the promise to pay $2,400 at the end of each of the first five years; $1,200 at the end of each of the next five years; and two $15,000 payments, one at the end of the fifth year and the other at the end of the tenth year:

   a)   At 10% interest compounded annually?

   b)   At 15% interest compounded annually?

P–5–8   What is the present value of the promise to pay $2,000 at the end of each of the next

   a)   20 years at 12% interest compounded annually?

   b)   21 years at 12% interest compounded annually?

   c)   Using your answer to Part a), compute the answer to Part b) without using the Future Value of an Annuity Table. (Table 5-3)

P–5–9   Joe Glutz decided to buy a $12,000 list price car. The best deal he could find was for $10,200.

   a)   At 12% interest compounded monthly for a 48-month auto loan, how much will his monthly payment be?

   b)   If the auto manufacturer offers a 10% cash rebate off list price that Joe uses to reduce the amount financed, how much will his monthly payment be?

P–5–10   The Normans decided that they could afford a $150 monthly payment to purchase a new car. What price car could they purchase if the current interest rate is 18% compounded monthly for

   a)   48 months?

   b)   60 months?

P–5–11   The Smith family decided that they could afford a $175 monthly payment to purchase a new car. What price car could they purchase if

   a)   The going interest rate on auto loans was 12% compounded monthly for 48 months?

   b)   The going interest rate on auto loans was 18% compounded monthly for 48 months?

P–5–12   The Kusmus family is considering the purchase of a home that will be financed with a $60,000, 30-year mortgage at 12% interest compounded annually. They have arranged to make yearly payments. How much will their yearly payments be if
   a)   The payments are made at the beginning of each year?
   b)   The payments are made at the end of each year?
   c)   If payments are made at the end of each year, how much interest expense will the family pay in the first year? The second year?

P–5–13   The Schneider family is considering the purchase of a home that will be financed by a $70,000, 30-year mortgage. The Schneiders have arranged to make payments at the end of each of the next 30 years. What will their yearly payments be at the following interest rates?
   a)   10% compounded annually?
   b)   11% compounded annually?
   c)   12% compounded annually?

P–5–14   In five years, Mr. Ed desires to purchase some new equipment for his farm. The equipment will cost approximately $38,000. How much will Mr. Ed have to deposit at the end of each quarter in a savings account paying 8% compounded quarterly to have the needed funds?

P–5–15   Mr. Thompson desires to place $50 a month in an investment so that at the end of five years he will have $3,750. What is the minimum interest rate that the investment can pay so that Mr. Thompson will have $3,750?

P–5–16   Tracy Corporation is considering a $50,000 investment that has several possible returns.
Required:
Compute the rate of return (interest rate) compounded annually for the following alternatives:
   a) $9,960 a year for 10 years.
   b) $8,550 a year for 15 years.

P–5–17   The Smith family purchased a car for $5,000 by signing a 48-month note requiring 1% per month on the unpaid balance. The note payments start 30 days after the car is purchased.
   a)   What is the monthly payment?
   b)   How much is owed on the note after the first payment is made? (Compute your answer in two ways.)
   c)   How much is owed on the note after the second payment is made?

P–5–18   Using the appropriate interest table, compute the present value of the following amounts due at the beginning of the designated periods.
   a) $20,000 due at the beginning of each period for 5 periods at 12% interest.
   b) $10,000 due at the beginning of each period for 10 periods at 15% interest.
   c) $25,000 payable at the beginning of the eighth, ninth, and tenth periods at 15% interest.

P–5–19   Using the appropriate interest table, compute the future amount of the following payments made at the beginning of the designated periods.
   a) $20,000 each period for 20 periods at 12%.
   b) $10,000 each six-month period for 10 years at 14% interest per year compounded semiannually.
   c) $10,000 each period for 5 periods at 12% interest and for another 10 periods at 15% interest.

6

Cash and
Receivables

Accounting in the News

In recessionary times companies are frequently short of cash and need to do whatever is necessary to raise it. As the following article excerpt indicates, companies occasionally come up with novel ways of getting cash without adverse effects on their financial statements.

> When it comes to opportunities for shrewd financing, J. C. Penney rarely misses a trick. Last October the giant retailer bought back $260 million worth of its accounts receivable, which it had sold to Citicorp for $287 million in February 1980.
>
> In so doing, Penney got a quick infusion of cash when it needed it. Now it is earning handsome rates of up to 21% again on the receivables. What's more, none of these maneuvers ever showed up on the balance sheet. That's a neat way to borrow.
>
> Penney is just one of a growing number of companies that are selling their receivables off balance sheet. It's estimated that something like $60 billion worth of accounts receivable were sold last year. . . .
>
> The companies refer to these transactions as sales, but to many eyes they are not sales at all, but merely a form of collateralized borrowing that has the effect of making a balance sheet look sounder than it is.*

This chapter discusses cash and receivables, including several ways that receivables can be used to generate cash.

*Barbara Rudolph, "The Invisible Debt," *Forbes*, March 1, 1982, p. 102.

Cash, receivables, and temporary investments are the primary liquid assets for most companies. There are few problems in accounting for cash. The main problems in accounting for receivables and investments involve their classification and valuation for financial statement purposes. Accounting for cash and receivables is discussed in this chapter, and accounting for investments is discussed in Chapter 7.

Nature and Composition of Cash

Cash consists of coin, currency, and unrestricted funds on deposit with a bank. Cash also is considered to include negotiable instruments on hand, such as certified checks, money orders, cashier's checks, and personal checks.

To be included as part of cash in the current asset section of a statement of financial position, an item must meet two criteria: (1) it must be cash or "near cash" and (2) it must have no restrictions on its use. Various types of cash accounts maintained at banks usually meet both criteria. Cash and checks on hand awaiting deposit, deposits in transit, and change and petty cash funds are considered part of cash. If an item meets the first criterion but not the second, the item is considered restricted cash. For example, cash held in a checking account to meet long-term debt payments would be considered restricted cash. The classification of restricted cash depends upon the specific restrictions involved.

Cash in Bank Accounts

To improve the management or the control of cash, a company may have several bank accounts. These accounts generally can be divided into four different types: (1) general cash accounts, (2) payroll accounts, (3) branch (division) accounts, and (4) depository (cash clearing) accounts.

The **general cash account** ultimately handles most cash receipts and disbursements. It is the only bank checking account maintained by most smaller companies.

Companies establish **payroll accounts,** which are separate bank accounts for payroll transactions, in order to handle the numerous routine transactions involved. Usually these are **imprest accounts** that have a fixed minimum balance. In an imprest account a specific sum of money is deposited for a specific purpose. Before each payday a check is drawn on the general cash account for the total net pay for the period. This check is deposited in the imprest payroll account. At this time the balance in the imprest payroll account at the bank is equal to the fixed minimum balance plus the net pay for the period. After the payroll checks, which are drawn on the payroll account, are distributed to and cashed by employees, the balance in the payroll account at the bank once again will equal its fixed minimum balance.

A company operating in multiple geographical locations may establish separate accounts, called **branch** (division) **accounts,** at each location. Several types of branch accounts are possible. One is a general cash account established by some companies to handle all cash receipts and disbursements at the branch (division) level. Excess funds are forwarded routinely to the company's main general cash account. The other type of branch (division) account involves separate accounts for receipts and disbursements. All branch receipts are deposited in the account designated for receipts. This type of account is called a **depository** or **cash clearing account.** The disbursement account is usually an imprest account.

In accordance with company policy, branch personnel make disbursements on the disbursement account to pay for expenditures incurred. When the account has been depleted, the branch makes an accounting to the home office, which then reimburses the account for the expenditures. This type of imprest account differs from an imprest payroll account. The actual balance on the company's books for the payroll account is the fixed minimum sum. The bank will show as a balance, however, the minimum fixed sum plus any payroll checks that have not cleared. The balance on the company's ledger for the disbursement account also is the imprest amount. But the balance in the account as maintained at the branch is the fixed sum less any expenses paid by the branch but not yet reimbursed by the home office.

The depository account is only for the deposit of receipts. On a regular basis funds are forwarded from the depository account to the general cash account. Depository accounts usually are established in different geographical regions to obtain payments from customers quickly. For example, a business located in New York might establish a depository account in Los Angeles so that California customers' payments will not have to be sent by mail to New York. Hence, the business is able to use the funds sooner than if it waited for the mail to deliver the actual check. In some cases these customer payments may not even be handled by company personnel. The payments may be sent to cities where the company has no offices; the company rents post office boxes to which customers send their payments. For a fee banks or other companies will pick up the mail, open it, verify the amount of the checks with the amount indicated as paid on the returned portion of the statements, endorse the checks, and deposit them to the appropriate bank account. The returned portion of the statement then is forwarded for processing to the company. Receipts without the returned portion of the statement, and other correspondence are forwarded to the company. The term **lockbox service** is used to describe this service.

When a company maintains multiple checking accounts, **interaccount transfers** must be recorded carefully. The complexity of these transfers can be seen in Exhibit 6-1. Procedures must be established to insure that the disbursement from one account and the deposit to another account are recorded on a timely basis. Cash understatements or overstatements can result if both the deposit and disbursement of an interaccount transfer are not recorded properly.

In addition to various checking accounts, a business may have **savings accounts** for short-term excess funds. A savings account presents potential question about whether such funds should be considered as cash. Savings and loan associations and banks have the legal right to require advance notice of a withdrawal from a savings account. This raises the question of whether the savings account is available to meet current company obligations. Since this legal right is exercised seldom, savings accounts are considered part of cash. Other types of interest-bearing accounts are considered temporary investments. These include certificates of deposit, which are generally available without penalty only on specific dates.

Cash on Hand

In addition to funds on deposit, various other items in the company's possession are included in cash. Negotiable instruments (whether personal or business checks), bank drafts, certified checks, and cashier's checks are considered part of cash. Usually these items will be deposited soon in a company bank account. Customers' postdated checks, which are checks with a future date, should not be treated as part of cash. Neither should customers' checks held by the company under an agreement not to deposit before a certain date be considered part of

Exhibit 6-1

InterAccount Transfers

General Cash Account
Maintained at Third National
Bank of This City

Receipts from
Local Customers

As Needed
InterAccount
Transfers

Disbursements to
Creditors

InterAccount
Transfers

Receipts
from Customers

Division A Account
Maintained at First
National Bank of a
Distant City

Branch B—Deposit Account
Maintained at First
National Bank of a Third
Distant City

Disbursement

Disbursement

Branch B Disbursement Account
Maintained in
Second National Bank
of Another Distant
City—Deposit
Account

Receipts from
Customers

Disbursements
Interaccount
Transfers
Total
Net Payroll

Receipts

Payroll Account
Maintained at Third
National Bank of Third
City

Disbursements

To Employees

Receipt

Branch B Account
Maintained at
Second National Bank
of Another Distant
City—Disbursement
Account

Disbursements

cash. In both of these cases the amount represented by the checks should be considered a receivable. If a company is holding its own checks, the checks may be included as disbursements but these obligations still should be considered as payables. This is particularly important if a company is holding its checks because of a poor liquidity position.

A company may have petty cash funds and change funds. A **petty cash account** is an imprest fund used to pay for small expense items that a company incurs. **Change funds** are given to cashiers or placed in change machines or cash registers in order to provide change to customers. Normally both are considered part of cash.

Restricted Cash

Cash that is restricted as to purpose should be segregated and disclosed separately in the financial statements. The restricted cash should be classified as a current asset if the payment will extinguish debts classified as current liabilities or if it will be used within a year or one operating cycle, whichever is longer.

Restricted cash not meeting the above criteria generally should be classified as a noncurrent asset. Funds designated for construction of long-lived assets or for the liquidation of long-term debts should be classified as noncurrent. Funds do not have to be set aside in special accounts to meet the noncurrent criteria.[1]

One type of cash restriction is a minimum balance requirement of a loan agreement. This minimum balance, called a **compensating balance,** may be required to be maintained in checking accounts, in savings accounts, or in certificates of deposit. Financial statement disclosure of these arrangements usually is required.

Control of Cash

The control of cash is important for two reasons: first, without adequate controls cash can be stolen easily; second, a large volume of transactions involves cash. The receipt or disbursement of cash occurs in many business transactions, including (1) sales, (2) the collection of accounts receivable, (3) the acquisition of goods and services, and (4) the payment of goods and services.

Internal Control

To safeguard cash and other assets, a company establishes a system of **internal control** which

> comprises the plan of organization and all of the coordinate methods and measures adopted within a business to safeguard its assets, check the accuracy and reliability of its accounting data, promote operational efficiency, and encourage adherence to prescribed managerial policies.[2]

---

[1]"Restatement and Revision of Accounting Research Bulletins," *Accounting Research Bulletin No. 43* (New York: AICPA, 1953), Chapter 3, par. 3.

[2]*AICPA Professional Standards—Auditing, Management Advisory Services, Tax Practice* (New York: AICPA, 1980), par. AU320.26.

Internal control can be divided into two broad categories: administrative control and accounting control. **Administrative control** is concerned primarily with the decision making processes leading to management's authorization of transactions.[3] **Accounting control,** on the other hand, includes

the plan of organization and the procedures and records that are concerned with the safeguarding of assets and the reliability of financial records and consequently are designed to provide reasonable assurance that:

a. Transactions are executed in accordance with management's general or specific authorization.
b. Transactions are recorded as necessary to permit preparation of financial statements in conformity with generally accepted accounting principles . . . and to maintain accountability for assets.
c. Access to assets is permitted only in accordance with management's authorization.
d. The recorded accountability for assets is compared with existing assets at reasonable intervals and appropriate action is taken with respect to any differences.[4]

The accounting control objectives can be made more specific for transactions involving the receipt or disbursement of cash. A company's internal control system for cash should be designed to provide reasonable assurance that

1. Recorded cash transactions are valid. The system should not allow payment to a fictitious vendor for fictitious goods.
2. Existing cash transactions are recorded. The system should not allow an employee to divert payments from customers to his/her own pocket.
3. Cash transactions are authorized properly. Without proper authorization, fictitious transactions could be recorded. Proper authorization also helps to ensure that existing transactions are recorded and that transactions not in the best interest of the company are not executed.
4. Cash transactions are
   a) Properly valued.
   b) Properly classified.
   c) Properly included in subsidiary records.
   d) Recorded at the proper time.

These four objectives are designed to ensure that valid transactions are recorded properly in a company's books in the correct accounting period.

Elements of Internal Control

Certain characteristics of an internal accounting control system help to meet the four objectives just discussed. These characteristics, sometimes called **elements of internal control,** are as follows:

1. Competent, trustworthy personnel who work under clear lines of authority and responsibility.

[3] Ibid., par. AU320.26.
[4] Ibid., par. AU320.28.

2. Segregation of functions (duties).
3. Proper procedures for authorization of transactions.
4. Adequate documents and records.
5. Restriction of access to assets, documents, and records.
6. Independent comparison of recorded accountability with assets.

Personnel. Competent, trustworthy personnel should be employed, and a company should provide clear lines of authority and responsibility. In addition, a company should have mandatory vacation policy that requires personnel to take earned vacations. In most cases this policy will require collusion among employees to conceal an embezzlement because some other employee will have to perform the vacationing employee's duties. The company also should purchase insurance, called a **bond,** for losses incurred as a result of employee theft. Most insurance companies will not bond an employee for substantial amounts without a background investigation. Of course, a bond on employees does not eliminate the need for the other elements of internal control.

Written documentation is needed to establish clear lines of authority and personnel responsibilities. This written documentation should include an organization chart, a job description manual, and a procedures manual.

Segregation of Functions. Four types of segregation of functions should be considered. First, the custody of assets should be separated from accounting for the assets. If a person receives cash and also has access to the cash receipts journal and accounts receivable subsidiary ledger, s/he can steal cash and cover up the theft by failing to record the cash received and by recording a fictitious credit to the account. Second, custody of assets should be separated from the authorization of transactions. If someone who authorizes the write-off of uncollectible accounts also has access to incoming cash receipts, that individual can steal cash and cover up the theft by writing off the amount of the payment as a bad debt. Third, operational responsibility should be separated from record keeping responsibility. This is designed to help ensure unbiased reporting of performance. Finally, duties should be separated within the accounting function. This helps to prevent errors from being undetected.

In most larger businesses, segregation of duties results in three important divisions in the organization structure:

1. The controller and his/her staff have sole record keeping responsibility. They should have no custody of assets, nor should they be allowed to authorize transactions.
2. The treasurer and his/her staff should be responsible for the custody of cash.
3. The internal audit department should report directly to the board of directors, the audit committee (a subcommittee of the board of directors), or the president.

Proper Authorization Procedures. Proper authorization procedures can involve general or specific authorizations. Employees who are granted general authorization authority receive specific instructions from their superiors on what constitutes an acceptable transaction. For example, general authority may be given for approval of disbursements when the amount is less than $10,000. Specific authorization authority generally is reserved for upper-level management, and each situation is considered on a case-by-case basis. For example, disbursements of $10,000 and over might have to be approved by the vice-president for finance.

Adequate Documents and Records.   Adequate documents and records are important for recording the transaction and for checking the transaction at a later date. Documents and records include purchase orders, invoices, packing slips, bills of lading, and other documents generated by a transaction; also included are the books in which transactions are recorded—the sales journal, cash receipts journal, and accounts receivable subsidiary ledger. Documents should be simple to use, prenumbered, and designed for multiple uses. They also should be prepared on a timely basis. In addition to the documents and records, adequate instructions must be provided. These normally include a chart of accounts and a procedures manual. Also important is the preparation of adequate reports at reasonable times to meet management's needs. This includes preparation and review of budgets. Further, policies must be established to retain documents, records, and reports to meet various legal requirements.

Physical Control.   Physical control must be established to protect assets and records. For example, cash should be kept in a safe or locked drawer. There should be controlled access to records; for example, computer tapes should be maintained in a controlled library. Backup records also must be established.

Independent Comparisons.   Independent checks on performance help to ensure that the internal control system is functioning as planned. There are two types of independent checks: (1) those accomplished by separation of duties and (2) those accomplished by internal auditors. Independent checks accomplished by separation of duties are usually the less expensive. In some cases verification is effected by having someone check the procedures done by another person. In others, instead of having someone who has similar duties accomplish a specific procedure, an uninvolved individual is assigned to accomplish the procedure. For example, an independent person preparing the bank reconciliation should provide verification of receipts, disbursements, and cash balances.

   Internal audit departments typically are more expensive to operate because they involve salary costs for internal auditors who must be independent of the functions they audit. In addition, substantial amounts may have to be expended for travel costs and out-of-town lodging costs. The recent growth of internal audit departments may be an indication that most companies feel that the benefits obtained from independent checks by internal auditors greatly exceed their costs.

   Although the internal control objectives and characteristics have been discussed with respect to cash, you should remember that they apply throughout the company.

Bank Reconciliations

Two general types of reconciliations of bank balances and book balances are used commonly: a standard bank reconciliation, usually called a **bank reconciliation,** and a four-column bank reconciliation, also called a **proof of cash.** The four-column bank reconciliation involves more independent checks than does the standard bank reconciliation. One of two formats generally is used for each type of reconciliation: (1) reconciliation of bank and book balances to the corrected balance and (2) reconciliation of the bank balance to the book balance.

Detailed bank reconciliations are necessary because of timing differences between the company and the bank in recording items. The receipt and recording of a deposit by the company usually precedes the bank's recording of the deposit. Most companies follow the procedure of depositing cash and checks received on a daily basis. To provide better control, companies commonly require that cash and checks be deposited intact as received. Banks may end their day for posting purposes early, such as at 1:00 p.m. Any deposits received (or checks cashed) after 1:00 p.m. are credited (or charged) on the next business day. This can mean a lag in recording by the bank for as long as three days for a deposit made after 1:00 p.m. on Friday.

Sometimes the recording of a deposit on the bank statement precedes its recording on the company books. For example, when a bank collects funds for a customer, the collection department prepares a multiple-copy credit memo. One copy is used for posting to the customer's account, and another copy usually is sent by mail to inform the company of the collection. The copy received by the company should be used for posting purposes, but this might occur several days later.

A company records a disbursement in the cash disbursements journal when a check is sent to the payee. Hence, most disbursements are recorded by a company before they are recorded by a bank. However, charges against an account for returned checks and bank service charges typically are made by a bank before they are recorded on a company's books. In fact, a company usually doesn't know about bank service charges until the bank statement is received.

In addition to these timing differences, errors may occur that must be corrected on the company's books or brought to the attention of the bank for correction. For example, a check for $65 may have been recorded in the cash disbursements journal for $56. This transposition error must be corrected through an adjusted entry of $9. As another example, a bank may have charged another company's check to the wrong account. No adjustment on the company's books is necessary. However, the bank must be informed of the error so that the account can be credited. With the advent of machine readable account codes and greater computer processing of checks, bank errors tend to occur infrequently.

A summary of these adjustments, using the reconciliation format that determines the correct ending cash balance, is shown in Exhibit 6-2.

Standard Bank Reconciliation

A standard bank reconciliation requires certain procedures regardless of the form of the reconciliation itself. These procedures are as follows:

1. Comparing the amounts on canceled checks and other charges with the bank statement and placing the canceled checks in numerical order.
2. Comparing date, payee, and amount on the canceled checks with the cash disbursements journal (and last month's bank reconciliation for those checks that were outstanding at that time).

Exhibit 6-2
Basic Bank Reconciliation Adjustments

Balance per bank statement	Balance per books
Add:	Add:
Deposits in transit	Unrecorded collections by bank
Bank errors understating the account	Book errors understating the account
Deduct:	Deduct:
Outstanding checks	Bank service charges
Bank errors overstating the account	Nonsufficient Fund (NSF) checks
	Book errors overstating the account
Corrected cash balance	Corrected cash balance

---

3. Reviewing canceled checks for proper signature of authorized check signer and for proper endorsement of payee.
4. Investigating any checks that have been outstanding for long periods of time and charges on the bank statement not recorded on the books (and making any appropriate adjustments).
5. Comparing recorded amount and date of deposits on the bank statement with those contained in the cash receipts journal (and in last month's bank reconciliation).
6. Investigating any deposits outstanding for longer than expected or credits on the bank statements not recorded on the books (and making any appropriate adjustments).

The information obtained from completing steps one through six, the ending balance contained on the bank statement, and the balance in the cash account on the books are used in the reconciliation.

The first format to be discussed is the reconciliation of bank and book balances to a corrected balance. This format, illustrated in Exhibits 6-2 and 6-3, contains two sections. One section begins with the balance per bank statement, adds deposits recorded on the books but not yet credited by the bank[5] (determined in Step 5), and deducts any outstanding checks (determined in Step 2). Any errors made by the bank, which it will have to correct, are also included in this section (determined in Steps 3 and 6). The result is the corrected balance per bank statement at the end of the month.

---

[5]Deposits recorded on the books but not yet credited by the bank represent deposits in transit and receipts that have been posted but not prepared for deposit. On bank reconciliations, "deposits in transit" is usually used in place of "deposits recorded on the books but not yet credited by the bank."

Exhibit 6-3
VOLUNTEER COMPANY
Bank Reconciliation—Buckeye National Bank Account
December 31, 1983

Balance per bank statement, 12/31/83		$36,500.50
Add: Cash recorded on books and not yet		
recorded by bank		2,600.25
		$39,100.75
Less: Outstanding checks:		
#10200	$750.00	
# 01	470.60	
# 02	825.00	
# 04	25.40	2,071.00
		$37,029.75
Add: Check drawn on Volunteer Company		
charged to Volunteer account by error		185.00
Corrected balance per bank statement, 12/31/83		$37,214.75
Balance per books, 12/31/83		$35,311.25
Add: Collection of note receivable from Blue		
Company by bank on 12/31/83 not yet		
recorded on books		2,000.00
Less: Bank service charge for December not		
yet recorded on books		6.50
Error in recordings of check #10023.		
Recorded as $230.00 in cash		
disbursements journal. The check was		
written for the amount owed, $320.00		90.00
Corrected balance per books, 12/31/83		$37,214.75

The other section starts with the balance per books at the end of the current month and adds (deducts) any errors made by the company or items not yet recorded on the books (determined in Steps 3 and 6). Items not recorded on the books usually include collections by the bank, service charges, and NSF checks. The result of this section is the corrected balance per books at the end of the month. When the corrected balance per bank and the corrected balance per books agree, the reconciliation is completed.

The second format, the reconciliation of bank balance to book balance, illustrated in Exhibit 6-4, has only one section. This section starts with the balance per bank statement at the end of the month. Additions and deductions are made to obtain agreement with the balance per books at the end of the month. Deposits not yet credited by the bank and outstanding checks are treated as additions and deductions respectively. This is the same treatment as in the previous format.

Exhibit 6-4
VOLUNTEER COMPANY
Bank Reconciliation—Buckeye National Bank Account
December 31, 1983

Balance per bank statement, 12/31/83		$36,500.50
Add: Cash recorded on books and not yet recorded by bank		2,600.25
Bank service charge for December not yet recorded on books		6.50
Error in recording of check #10023; recorded as $230.00 in cash disbursements journal; the check was written for the amount owed, $320.00		90.00
Check drawn on Volunteer Company charged to Volunteer account in error		185.00
		$39,382.25
Less: Outstanding checks:		
#10200	$750.00	
01	470.60	
02	825.00	
04	25.40	
	$2,071.00	
Collection of note receivable from Blue Company by bank on 12/31/83 not yet recorded on books	2,000.00	4,071.00
Balance per books, 12/31/83		$35,311.25

The differences that occur when using this format are as follows:

1. Appropriate charges made by the bank and not recorded on the books, and inappropriate charges made by the bank are treated as additions.
2. Collections made by the bank and not recorded on the books, and inappropriate credits made by the bank are treated as deductions.

By examining the two formats, you'll see the following similarities and differences:

1. Both itemize any differences between the bank and book balances.
2. The first format places items requiring adjusting journal entries in the section that reconciles the book balance to the correct balance.
3. The first format places items requiring action by the bank because of bank errors in the section that reconciles the bank balance to the correct balance.

For the Volunteer Company, both reconciliations indicate that journal entries are required to (1) record the bank service charge, (2) correct the error in recording check #10023, and (3) record the collection of the $2,000 note from Blue Company by the bank.

These are recorded in the following entry:

Cash	1,903.50	
Bank service charge	6.50	
Purchases	90.00	
Notes receivable		2,000.00
To record adjustments for December, 1981.		

In addition, both reconciliations indicate that the check charged to the wrong account must be brought to the bank's attention. The reconciliation to the correct ending cash balance is used frequently because it provides the ending cash balance for preparation of the balance sheet.

Four-Column Bank Reconciliations

To provide additional verification, a company may require the preparation of a four-column bank reconciliation on a routine or nonroutine basis. In addition, an auditor may perform a four-column bank reconciliation if s/he believes control over cash is not adequate. The four-column reconciliation is illustrated in the Appendix.

Imprest Cash Systems

Most companies incur small expenses on a routine basis that must be paid on receipt of the goods or services because the company has concluded that it is not worth establishing a charge account with all vendors. Indeed, certain vendors may not accept charge accounts; examples include postage due, freight charges, minor office supplies, and occasional lunches. In addition, the costs of processing purchase orders, receiving reports, and ultimately of preparing a company check make the processing of small expenses relatively costly. In order to provide payment quickly, to reduce processing costs, and to maintain control, companies often use an imprest petty cash fund. The fund is placed under the control of a responsible individual, called a custodian. Instead of cash a custodian sometimes receives a bank account that contains a fixed dollar amount. Only the custodian is authorized to sign checks or to disburse funds. S/he also is given appropriate instructions regarding the safekeeping of the fund, categories of expenses that can be paid with the fund, the documentation for expenses needed to be paid with the fund, and reimbursement procedures. These instructions emphasize physical security, the importance of the amount contained in the fund balancing at all times with the imprest amount less paid expenses, and the importance of not allowing anyone to borrow from the fund. To ensure that instructions are being followed, an independent person performs surprise reconciliations.[6] The independent person determines that all expenses paid by the fund are valid and that the amount of cash actually on hand is equal to the amount that should be on hand (the imprest amount less the expenses paid).

When the custodian requests reimbursement, appropriate officials should examine the documentation for expenses paid from the fund to verify their propriety. If the total expenses paid plus cash on hand do not equal the imprest amount, **cash over or short account** may be debited in case of a shortage or credited in case of an overage. If the custodian is doing a good job, however, this should seldom occur. A cash over or short account is more likely to be used with change funds. In either case, consistent shortages or overages need to be investigated.

For example, Azod Company instituted a $250 petty cash fund, which is the responsibility of Ron Slaglen. When the fund was established, the following entry was made:

Petty cash	250	
Cash		250
To establish		
a petty cash		
fund.		

As Ron paid bills, no entries were made on Azod's books. In accordance with company policy, Ron prepared petty cash vouchers and obtained receipts for all funds disbursed. At the end of November, Ron summarized the petty cash transactions as follows:

Postage	$ 35
Freight	100
Office supplies	65
	$200
Cash remaining	50
Total	$250

The summary and the underlying support for the expenditures were forwarded for reimbursement. The documents were approved for payment and a check was drawn. The entry to record the check was as follows:

---

[6]Surprise counts are also appropriate for change funds.

Postage expense	35	
Freight expense	100	
Office supplies	65	
Cash		200
To record November petty cash expenditures.		

The reimbursement check for the amount of the expenses is drawn to cash (or petty cash) when the fund is maintained in cash or to the specific name of the bank account if a petty cash bank account is maintained. As with other disbursements, supporting documents should be marked paid to prevent their resubmission as support for later disbursements.

The accounting for an imprest petty cash fund and a branch (division) disbursement account are similar. During the fiscal year journal entries to the imprest account are made only when the account is established or when the imprest amount is changed. When the custodian disburses funds, no entry is made on the company's books. The entry made to reimburse the fund for expenses paid is to debit the specific expenses incurred and to credit the general account cash. Since the recording of the expenses lags the actual payment, at year-end the account either should be reimbursed or an accrual should be made to recognize the expenses paid since the last reimbursement. If an accrual is made, the debits are to the appropriate expense accounts and the credit is to the fund itself.

Nature and Types of Receivables

Amounts due from others generally can be classified into three distinct types: trade receivables, nontrade receivables, and notes receivables. **Notes receivable** are distinguished from the other receivables by having a formal, written promise (a note, which frequently includes interest) to document the receivable. **Trade receivables** are amounts owed to the company that arise from the sale of goods and services to customers and usually are evidenced by sales invoices and statements. **Nontrade receivables** arise from transactions with employees, officers, or affiliates. A receivable can be classified as current if collection is expected within a year or within the normal operating cycle, whichever is longer; otherwise, the receivable is classified as noncurrent. A statement of financial position or a balance sheet may contain eight types of receivables:

Current:
    Trade accounts receivable
    Nontrade receivables
    Trade notes receivable
    Nontrade notes receivable

Noncurrent:
    Trade accounts receivable
    Nontrade receivables
    Trade notes receivable
    Nontrade notes receivable

Trade, nontrade, and notes receivable are discussed in subsequent sections of this chapter.

Like cash, receivables could be valued at their present realizable value (the discounted value of expected future receipts). This would require that the time value of money be considered. With most trade receivables, accountants exclude time value of money considerations.[7] When the APB considered interest on payables and receivables, it specifically excluded "receivables and payables arising from transactions with customers or suppliers in the normal course of business which are due in customary trade terms not exceeding approximately one year."[8] Hence, most trade receivables are valued at their **cash realizable value** (sometimes called **net realizable value**). *APB Opinion No. 6*, "Status of Accounting Research Bulletins," indicates that when finance, interest, and similar charges are included in the stated amount of the trade receivable, they should be shown as a deduction from the receivable.[9] These charges would be included in income as earned, and the net value of the receivable would be adjusted accordingly.

Notes receivable and all other receivables, unless specifically excluded by *APB Opinion No. 21*, should be carried at their present value. In addition to the trade receivables discussed previously, the *Opinion* excludes receivables from (1) lending activities of financial institutions and (2) parents and subsidiaries or related subsidiaries.[10]

In order to value receivables, an accountant must determine the following:

1. The stated value of the receivables.
2. The amount that ultimately will be realized.
3. Whether any receivables have been pledged, assigned, factored, or discounted.
4. The present value of nontrade accounts and notes receivable.

Trade Accounts Receivable

Trade accounts receivable arise from the sale of goods and services to customers on credit in the ordinary course of business. For merchandising or manufacturing companies, ordinary course of business usually means the sale of inventory or custom-made goods to customers. For service companies, ordinary course of busi-

---

[7]"Interest on Receivables and Payables," *Opinions of the Accounting Principles Board No. 21* (New York: AICPA, 1971), par. 3.

[8]Ibid., par. 3.

[9]"Status of Accounting Research Bulletins," *Opinions of the Accounting Principles Board No. 6* (New York: AICPA, 1965), par. 14.

[10]"Interest on Receivables and Payables," par. 3.

ness usually means providing its services to customers. Trade receivables may be evidenced by written or oral promises to pay amounts at certain due dates, which tend to be within 10 to 60 days after the sale date, depending upon the company's credit terms. Usually trade receivables are indicated by sales invoices. Typically, a sales invoice shows the total amount due, any discounts allowed for early payment (called a cash discount), the time period considered for early payment, the period after which a specified interest rate is added for late payment, and any additional deductions allowed. The period of early payment and any cash discounts for early payment frequently are indicated by abbreviations. These abbreviations include 2/10, net 30 (a 2% discount is applicable if paid in 10 days, or the total amount is due in 30 days); and 2/10th, net EOM (a 2% discount is applicable if paid by the 10th of the next month; otherwise, the total is due by the end of the next month).

Both trade and cash discounts can affect the stated value of trade receivables. In addition, other deductions allowed customers can affect the net realizable value of receivables.

Trade Discounts

Depending on industry practices, companies may quote prices to customers either as a dollar amount called a net price, or as a percentage discount off list price. The percentage off list price frequently is referred to as a **trade discount, distributor's discount,** or **quantity discount.** The use of trade discounts rather than dollar amounts allows a company to offer more easily different prices to different types of customers or different prices based upon different quantities purchased. Also, as long as a company does not change list prices, selling prices can be changed by changing trade discounts offered without reprinting price sheets or catalogs. An important benefit of pricing based upon trade discounts is that the customer, or the company itself, can determine more easily its gross profit from selling goods.

Occasionally **multiple (or chain) trade discounts** are given, such as "20 + 10." In this case, 20% is given off the list price and 10% is given off the price determined after the 20% is deducted. For example, assume Molly Manufacturing sells merchandise with a $1,000 retail value to Daisey Distributors and gives a "20 + 10" discount. The sale price is determined as follows:

Retail	$1,000
Less 20%	200
	$800
Less 10%	80
	$720

The net sale price is $720. Such multiple discounts may be given to provide compensation to those involved in the distribution of the product. In the case above, Daisey may sell the merchandise at a 20% discount and may keep the 10% discount as its distributors' commission. Care must be taken not to confuse part of the multiple trade discounts with part of a cash discount. As long as a discount is allowed without regard to when payment is made, it is considered a trade discount.

With trade discounts, the list price (sometimes called retail price) is for reference purposes only. Distributors, wholesalers, or manufacturers rarely, if ever, sell the goods for the list price. Hence, it is appropriate to consider the stated value of a trade receivable to be the value of the invoice net of trade discounts.

Cash Discounts

Cash discounts, sometimes called sales discounts, are offered to encourage customers to pay their obligations promptly. Although cash discounts are usually between 1% and 2%, the short time period between the last day on which the discount is allowed and the last day on which the net amount is due makes the discount attractive. For example, cash discount terms of 1/10, net 30, and 2/10, net 30, are equivalent to 18% ($1\% \times {}^{360}/_{20}$) and 36% ($2\% \times {}^{360}/_{20}$) interest per annum (the interest is 1% and 2% for delaying payment for 20 days). Given borrowing costs, most firms would find it advantageous to take cash discounts. In fact, a firm's inability to pay within the discount period may be a sign of severe liquidity problems.

Net Method.   Because of the high interest cost of not taking cash discounts, you would expect most firms to take them. Hence, if the objective is to record trade receivables at their net realizable value, these receivables should be recorded net of cash discounts. This approach normally is called the **net method.** The sale and corresponding trade receivable are recorded net of cash discounts. If payment is made within the discount period, the credit to trade receivables is for the amount of the cash payment. If payment is made after the discount period, the difference between the gross and net amounts is credited to discounts forfeited. The net method is illustrated in Exhibit 6-5.

When sales are reported net of cash discounts the sales discounts forfeited are reported as other income on the income statement. When a company records

Exhibit 6-5
Sales Entries Under the Net and Gross Methods

Net Method		*Gross Method*	
Sold $1,000 of merchandise under terms 2/10, net 30:			
Accounts receivable 980		Accounts receivable 1,000	
Sales 980		Sales 1,000	
Collection of $600 within the discount period:			
Cash 588		Cash 588	
Accounts receivable 588		Sales discounts 12	
		Accounts receivable 600	
Collection of $400 after the discount period:			
Cash 400		Cash 400	
Sales discounts forfeited 8		Accounts receivable 400	
Accounts receivable 392			

sales net of discount, it is usually necessary to make a year-end adjusting entry to reflect the sales discounts that will not be taken because the discount period has passed. Some estimate also should be made of the remaining discounts that will not be taken. The net method is seldom used for sales because of the additional analysis and bookkeeping required.

Gross Method.   Whereas the net method is consistent with the net realizable value principle, in practice, more firms use the **gross method.** Under the gross method (also illustrated in Exhibit 6-5), sales are recorded without considering cash discounts. If payments are made within the discount period, the cash discount is recorded as a debit to the sales discounts account. On the income statement, sales discounts are deducted from sales to determine net sales. For most larger companies, however, sales are shown net of sales discounts. If payments are made after the discount period, the amount of the payment is credited to trade receivables.

   If all customers take their cash discounts, the amount of net sales on the income statement is the same as the sales amount under the net method. However, if all customers take their discounts, a potential problem of using the gross method is that at year-end trade receivables are not stated at their net realizable value. To solve this problem, you can make an adjusting entry to reduce trade receivables and increase cash discounts earned. The difference in value of trade receivables under the gross and net methods typically is immaterial, so no adjustment usually is made.

   On the other hand, if all customers don't pay within the discount period, trade receivables are stated at their realizable value. In this situation the net method understates trade receivables. However, this amount also will usually be immaterial. A potential problem of using the gross method occurs on the income statement because the discounts forfeited are included in sales under the net method. The difference, which in all likelihood would be considered immaterial, does not affect net income.

   Since the differences in the two extreme cases are immaterial, the gross method and the net method will produce immaterial differences in all other cases. Given that many view the gross method as easier, its greater usage in practice is understandable.

Other Deductions

In some industries, companies allow customers deductions in addition to cash and trade discounts. Examples include deductions for freight charges incurred in delivering the goods from the company to the customer and deductions for authorized advertising expenditures. To minimize bookkeeping procedures, the accountant usually records these costs when the customer remits payment and indicates the actual amount deducted. In some industries, recording receivables at invoice price overstates their realizable value because of returned goods and/or substantial costs incurred in collecting the receivables. At year-end an estimate of these amounts should be made, and allowance accounts should be established to record receivables at their net realizable value and to match costs with revenues. In practice, the amounts tend to be immaterial, and no estimate normally is recorded.

Accounting for Uncollectible Accounts

The stricter a company's credit policy is, the more limited are its credit customers. Generally, a strict credit policy will result in reduced total sales. In order to increase its sales, a company usually sells to firms that may have some potential credit problems. As long as the incremental benefit of selling to these firms does not exceed the incremental costs, including losses from bad debts, a company is making an appropriate decision. Hence, companies establish credit departments to evaluate potential and current customers. Some companies set up sophisticated decision making rules using quantitative techniques to assist them in granting credit.

Given that a company may establish credit policies that recognize the possibility of some accounts being ultimately uncollectible, receivables may be overstated. General economic conditions and specific firm conditions occurring after the date of sale may cause receivables to be uncollectible.

Two approaches are used to account for uncollectible accounts (bad debts). One approach, called the **direct write-off method** or specific charge-off method, makes no adjustment until a receivable proves to be uncollectible. When a specific receivable is determined to be uncollectible, trade receivables are reduced (credited) and bad debts (uncollectible accounts) expense is increased (debited) for the appropriate amount. The other approach, called the **allowance method,** makes an estimate of uncollectibles at each balance sheet date. Since the amount determined is an estimate, a contra receivables account, called **allowance for uncollectible accounts,** is increased (credited) and bad debts expense is debited. Those who advocate the use of the direct write-off method claim that it is more objective than the allowance method for several reasons: (1) estimates of uncollectibles are not used and (2) the primary causes of uncollectible accounts are general economic and specific firm conditions occurring after the sale.

Those who advocate the use of the allowance method claim that uncollectible accounts are an expense that must be matched with sales. Since sales of the current period actually may not prove to be uncollectible until subsequent periods, an estimate is needed to match period costs and period revenues properly. For most companies a reasonable estimate can be obtained by considering past experience and current conditions. Furthermore, advocates emphasize that by matching costs and revenues properly, receivables are included at their net realizable value.

FASB Statement No. 5, "Accounting for Contingencies," adopted the allowance method by including uncollectible accounts as a loss contingency. Hence, an expense should be accrued if information available at year-end indicates that a loss is likely to occur and that the loss can be estimated reasonably.[11] If no material differences exist between the allowance and direct write-off methods, a company still can use the direct write-off method. However, the materiality of the differences in expense recognition and asset valuation must be reevaluated each year.

Two approaches are commonly used to estimate the potential amount of uncollectibles. The first method, which is based upon sales, uses a percentage of

---

[11]"Accounting for Contingencies," *Statement of Financial Accounting Standards No. 5* (Stanford, Conn.: FASB, 1975), par. 8.

sales to determine the uncollectible accounts expense for the period. The other method, which is based upon the ending receivables, uses a percentage of trade receivables to determine the balance in the allowance account.

Percentage of Sales Method

With the percentage of sales method, a firm is attempting to match current costs with current revenues by estimating the amount of this year's sales that will prove uncollectible. The estimate is made by taking a percentage of sales to determine uncollectible accounts expense. The estimate is based upon past experience and is modified to provide for changing conditions. Usually firms consider only credit sales in establishing their percentage. However, when cash sales are immaterial or when the sales mix between cash and credit sales is expected to remain constant, some firms use total sales in establishing the percentage.

This method establishes uncollectible accounts expense based only on sales for the current period. For example, assume that Curatola Co. has $800,000 of sales during the period and that past uncollectibles have averaged 1% of sales. The entry to record the estimated uncollectibles is as follows:

Bad debts expense	8,000	
Allowance for uncollectible accounts		8,000
To establish uncollectible accounts		
expense (1% of the $800,000 sales).		

The credit part of the journal is made to the allowance for uncollectible accounts account. The allowance is credited because it is impossible to know which specific customer accounts will prove uncollectible. When a specific account proves uncollectible, the allowance is debited and trade receivables are credited for the amount of the uncollectible. The write-off of an uncollectible has no impact on total assets, net trade receivables, or income. For example, assume Curatola Co. wrote off a $500 receivable from Red Company. The entry is as follows:

Allowance for uncollectible accounts	500	
Accounts receivable		500
To write off receivable from		
Red Company.		

Occasionally an account that previously has been written off is collected in whole or in part. In this case, the write-off entry is reversed (trade receivables are debited and allowance for uncollectible accounts is credited for the amount of the collection). The reversing entry reinstates the specific customer's receivable in the subsidiary ledger. The collection then is recorded as a normal collection of the receivable.[12] Recording the reinstatement and subsequent collection is necessary so that the subsidiary ledger reflects all of the events related to the account. If this procedure is not followed, the last entry in the customer's account would be a write-off as a bad debt even though the customer has made partial or complete payment of the account.

If one half of the receivable from Red Company is paid eventually, the following journal entries would be made:

Accounts Receivable	250	
Allowance for uncollectible accounts		250
To reverse the portion of the receivable collected from Red Company.		
Cash	250	
Accounts receivable		250
To record payment by Red Company.		

Percentage of Receivables Method

Instead of estimating uncollectible accounts based upon sales, some firms estimate uncollectibles based upon outstanding trade receivables. This approach determines the appropriate ending balance in the allowance account rather than the amount of the adjustment, as under the percentage of sales method. The difference between the current balance and the appropriate ending balance establishes the uncollectible accounts expense for the period. The write-off of uncollectibles and the collection of previously written-off receivables are treated in the same way as with the percentage of sales method.

Two approaches are used to establish the rates for the percentage of receivables method. One approach is to base the estimate on total receivables. This approach ignores the fact that the length of time receivables have been outstanding, commonly called the **age of receivables,** may have an impact on their ultimate collection. For example, a firm selling 1/10, net 30, would have a higher probability of collecting a 10-day-old receivable than collecting a 120-day-old receivable. Basing the estimate on total receivables is acceptable as long as the relative mix of the age of receivables and their relative collectibility remains fairly constant.

As an illustration, assume Jacobs Co. has been experiencing a bad debt rate equal to 6% of ending receivables and that the current ending receivables are $60,000. Also assume that the allowance for uncollectible accounts has a credit

---

[12] If the direct write-off method is used, and if a previously written-off account is collected, an account titled "recovery of uncollectible accounts" is credited, and cash is debited for the amount collected.

balance of $200. In this situation the following year-end adjustment would be made for bad debts:

Bad debts expense	3,400	
Allowance for uncollectible accounts		3,400
To record estimated bad debts.		
($60,000 × 0.06 = $3,600 − $200 = $3,400)		

The other approach, called the aging approach, establishes the balance in uncollectible accounts by using past experience to determine the likelihood of not collecting receivables in different age categories. Under this approach, a company prepares an **aging schedule,** which includes all trade receivables outstanding as of a specific date. Each specific receivable is broken down by reference to the accounts receivable subsidiary ledger. Typically the breakdown is in 30- to 60-day intervals, with an "over category" for the oldest receivables. Exhibit 6-6 presents an aging schedule for Buckeye Corporation. Buckeye uses 30-day increments and its oldest category is over 120 days. The aging schedule is self-balancing. The total of the individual aging columns agrees with the receivables balance at December 31; the balance at December 31 also agrees with the accounts receivable balance per books at December 31.

The actual aging of receivables can present some problems. The general rule is to identify payments as pertaining to specific receivable amounts. For example, Exhibit 6-7 presents the subsidiary accounts receivable for Alou Company, the first customer listed on Buckeye's aging schedule. Notice that the first three payments can be identified with specific receivable amounts. The payments are

Exhibit 6-6
BUCKEYE CORPORATION
Aging Schedule
December 31, 1983

Name of Customer	Balance December 31	Aging				
		Under 30 Days	31–60 Days	61–90 Days	91–120 Days	Over 120 Days
Alou Company	$275,000	$261,000	$14,000			
Big Ben Corp.	330,000	330,000				
City Cloth Company	2,000					$2,000
Ville Corporation	28,000	10,000	15,000	$3,000		
Zend Co.	68,000	35,000	33,000			
	$703,000	$636,000	$62,000	$3,000		$2,000

Exhibit 6-7
BUCKEYE CORPORATION
Subsidiary Account Receivable

Customer: ALOU COMPANY

Box 604

Columbus, TN 43210

Date 1983	Reference	Charges	Credits	Balance
7 10	Balance Forward			$ 780
7 12	CRJ #12		$ 780	–0–
8 10	#82565	$ 1,000		1,000
20	#83635	1,500		2,500
9 10	CRJ #15		2,500	–0–
10 2	#89215	4,000		4,000
10 15	#93621	185,000		189,000
11 10	CRJ #23 (on 93621)		185,000	4,000
11 25	#94651	260,000		264,000
12 2	CRJ #29 Payment on Account		250,000	14,000
12 10	#98254	261,000		275,000

Exhibit 6-8
BUCKEYE CORPORATION
Estimate of Allowance for Uncollectible Accounts
December 31, 1983

Age of Receivables	Amount of Receivables	Uncollectible Percentage	Amount of Estimated Uncollectibles
Under 30 Days	$636,000	2%	$12,720
31–60 Days	62,000	10%	6,200
61–90 Days	3,000	40%	1,200
Over 120 Days	2,000	60%	1,200
Total	$703,000		$21,320

considered to be offsets to these specific receivables. Frequently companies receive payments that are not identifiable with any specific receivable amount; for example, the $25,000 payment on account received on December 2. When this occurs, aging receivables is difficult unless some assumption is made concerning such payments. Generally, when payments are received that are not specifically identifiable with a particular receivable amount, a FIFO application of payments is assumed. For example, the $250,000 payment on account in Exhibit 6-7 is considered to be a payment of the $4,000 balance from October 2 and a $246,000 partial payment of the November 25 receivable.

Once an aging schedule is prepared, the percentages can be applied to each age group to determine the appropriate balance for the allowance account. (The percentages for Buckeye are listed in Exhibit 6-8.) At December 31, 1983, Buckeye should have an allowance account balance of $21,320. The difference between the current balance in the allowance account and the $21,320 would be the uncollectible accounts expense. For example, if Buckeye's allowance account had a debit balance of $6,000 before adjustment, an adjustment of $27,320 would be needed as illustrated in the following T-account.

Allowance for Uncollectible Accounts

Balance	$6,000		
		Adjustment needed to get desired ending balance	$27,320
	$6,000		$27,320
		Ending balance per Exhibit 6-8	$21,320

The entry to record the adjustment would be as follows:

Bad debts expense	27,320	
Allowance for uncollectible accounts		27,320
To record estimated bad debts.		

Write-offs of bad debts and collections of previously written-off accounts are treated the same as with the percentage of sales method.

Comparison of the Sales and Receivables Methods

Both the sales and the receivables approaches to estimating bad debts attempt to match costs with related revenues and to value receivables at their net realizable value. The sales approach emphasizes the matching of revenues and expenses more than the valuation of receivables, whereas the receivables approach emphasizes the valuation of receivables.

Note that the sales approach does not consider the percent balance in the allowance account, as does the receivables approach. Thus, if the estimated percentage of sales is incorrect, the discrepancy will accumulate from year to year in the allowance account. Care must be taken each year to make sure that the percentage estimate is reasonable. If a significant difference should occur, an additional adjustment may be necessary to adjust the allowance balance to a reasonable figure.

Of the methods discussed (sales, and receivables using both total receivables and an aging schedule), the aging method provides the most accurate measure of estimated bad debts because it involves the most detailed analysis of the receivables. In practice, most companies use the sales or total receivable methods because they are easier to apply. Auditors frequently use an aging schedule to test the reasonableness of the allowance balance.

Notes Receivable

Notes receivable can be generated by a variety of sources, including sales of goods or services, loans to other companies, or loans to officers and employees. Some companies require customers to give notes in exchange for goods and services. Others require customers who have old trade receivables outstanding to issue notes to settle them. The purpose is to obtain a formal recognition of the receivable.

Valuation

Notes receivable should be recorded at their present value. At the time of receipt of the note, the present value would be the amount of consideration given in exchange for the note. When cash is the consideration given, the cash proceeds represent the present value of the note. When the consideration is other than cash, the valuation is not as simple. *APB Opinion No. 21* concluded that unless evidence to the contrary exists, the stated interest rate provided in the note should be considered an appropriate borrowing rate. In this case the present value and the fair market value of the note are approximately equal, and the note is valued at its face value. If the interest rate is not reasonable, alternate valuation of the note is necessary. The interest rate is not considered to be fair and adequate compensation when (1) no interest rate is stated, (2) the stated rate is unreasonable, or (3) the face value of the note is materially different from the market value of the property exchanged or from the market value of the note.[13]

When evidence indicates that the stated interest rate doesn't approximate an appropriate borrowing rate, the note should be valued at the fair market value of the goods or services given in the transaction. If the fair market value of the consideration given is not readily determinable, the fair market value of the note should be used. If a market value for the note cannot be determined, it should be recorded at its present value, which is determined by using an appropriate interest rate. This rate is called the **imputed interest rate.** Specifically, *APB Opinion No. 21* states that

[13]"Interest on Receivables and Payables," par. 12.

The objective is to approximate the rate which would have resulted if an independent borrower and an independent lender had negotiated a similar transaction under comparable terms and conditions with the option to pay the cash price upon purchase or to give a note for the amount of the purchase which bears the prevailing rate of interest to maturity.[14]

Once the note is recorded at its present value, interest expense should be recognized using the effective yield method. This method recognizes interest at a constant rate, the rate used to discount the note.[15]

For example, on January 1, 1981, Site Corporation purchased an unimproved parcel of real estate by providing a two-year, $90,000 note to Former Corporation, the previous owners. The two-year note contained no provision for interest. According to *Opinion No. 21*, this is a situation in which the fair market value of the consideration received or given must be determined. Assume that a fair market value cannot be determined for either the land or the note but that the purchaser's incremental borrowing interest rate is 15%. Exhibit 6-9 presents the

[14]Ibid., par. 13.

[15]Ibid., par. 15.

Exhibit 6-9

1981

January 1

Land	68,049*	
Discount on note payable	21,951	
Note payable		90,000

To record purchase of land at its present value.

*$90,000 × $p_{\overline{n=2}|i=15\%}$

$90,000 × 0.7561 = $68,049

December 31

Interest expense	10,207*	
Discount on note payable		10,207

To record interest on note.

*$68,049 × 15% = $10,207

1982

December 31

Interest expense	11,744*	
Discount on note payable		11,744

To record interest on note.

*(90,000 − ($21,951 − $10,207))

= $78,256 × 15% = $11,744

1983

January 1

Note payable	90,000	
Cash		90,000

To record payment on note.

journal entries to account for the purchase. In the first entry the acquired land is recorded at the present value of the note. The present value is determined by discounting the $90,000 note for two years at 15% interest. The face value of the note is recorded, and a discount on note payable account is set up.

The interest each December 31 is determined by multiplying the interest rate times the book value (i.e., face value minus the balance in the discount account) of the note. A straight-line amortization of the discount is acceptable when it would not result in an interest expense that is materially different from those that result from the effective interest method.

Notice that if Site Corporation had failed to recognize the imputed interest, the land account would be overstated and interest expense over the years would be understated by the $21,951 discount.

Disclosure

If an imputed rate is used, either a premium (when the stated rate is greater than the imputed rate) or a discount (when the imputed rate is greater than the stated rate) will result. The premium or discount should be an addition to (or deduction from) the face value of the note receivable. The note can be shown in the statement of financial position as a net amount (with appropriate disclosure of the face amount and premium or discount) or at its face value, with the premium or discount shown to determine the net amount. In either case, the effective yield must be disclosed. Notes receivable are segregated into current and noncurrent (long-term) receivables, following the same year or operating cycle rule discussed for trade receivables. Trade and nontrade notes receivable also are segregated.

Using Receivables to Generate Cash

Some companies find it desirable to convert their receivables into cash at a faster rate than could be expected from normal collection. In this situation, a company can pledge, assign, factor, or sell trade receivables to generate immediate cash. A company also can accept credit cards as payments instead of having its own trade receivables. To generate immediate cash from notes receivable, a company typically can pledge or discount the notes.

Pledging of Receivables

In negotiating a loan, a company may have to provide some collateral in case of default on the loan. **Pledging** of accounts or notes receivable may provide the needed collateral. When accounts are pledged, the borrower continues to bill and to collect the pledged accounts. Usually the borrower is required to make payments on the loan or to provide additional receivables as collateral. In this case the loan would be recorded on the books the same as any other loan. The pledging must be disclosed in the financial statements.

Assignment of Trade Receivables

In order to obtain a loan, a borrower may have to assign specific receivables to the lender—usually a financial institution. In an **assignment** the borrower (the assignor) transfers receivable rights under a contract to the lender (the assignee). The borrower typically collects the receivables and remits collections to the lender, although in some cases the lender may collect the receivables.

In most cases the borrower must guarantee the collection of the receivables. If a receivable becomes delinquent or uncollectible, or is extinguished because goods are returned, the borrower either must repay the loan or must replace it with other receivables. This is referred to as an **assignment with recourse.**

The amount of cash received by the borrower is less than the total amount of receivables pledged. The percentage of the total receivables pledged in relation to the cash received and the interest rate charged depends on the lender's perceptions of the risks involved. In general, the more risk, the lower the percentage of cash received to the total receivables pledged, and the higher the interest rate. In addition to interest on the unpaid balance, lenders typically will charge a fixed fee for the loan.

When a company assigns receivables, the new liability and the assignment of the receivables must be recognized. For illustration purposes, assume that on December 31, 1982, Step Company assigns $50,000 of its total accounts receivable of $140,000 to its bank in exchange for a loan, at a 15% interest rate, on 80% of the pledged receivables. The entries Step would make are as follows:

Cash	40,000	
Notes payable		40,000
To record receipt of loan proceeds.		
Accounts receivable assigned	50,000	
Accounts receivable		50,000
To record assignment of receivables.		

Since December 31 is Step's year-end, the current assets section of the balance sheet at December 31, 1982, would include the unassigned receivables and the equity in assigned accounts receivable, shown as follows:

Accounts receivable		$ 90,000
Accounts receivable assigned	$50,000	
Less: Note payable	40,000	
Equity in assigned accounts receivable		10,000
Total accounts receivable		$100,000

The liability is offset against the asset because the receivables are assigned to liquidate the debt.

When a collection is made on an assigned account, the entry is similar to an unassigned collection except that instead of crediting accounts receivable, the accounts receivable assigned account is credited. The amount of collections and the interest are remitted to the lender. This entry is treated the same as any other note payment. When the note is paid in full, any uncollected pledged receivables are transferred back to accounts receivable.

Sale of Trade Receivables

Sometimes receivables are sold to another company. Since the purchasing company has to receive compensation for interest and for bearing the complete risk that accounts will prove uncollectible, high discount rates are usually common. When accounts receivable are sold, cash is increased, accounts receivable and related allowance accounts are reduced, and **finance expense** is increased for the difference.[16] For example, when Norr Company decided to sell $20,000 of its accounts receivable for $15,000, the journal entry to record this transaction was as follows:

Cash	15,000	
Finance expense	5,000	
Accounts receivable		20,000
To record the sale of		
receivables to another		
company.		

Factoring Trade Receivables

The previous arrangements involved existing receivables. **Factoring** is a more formal, ongoing relationship between a company and a purchaser of receivables called a factor. Factors are generally banks or finance companies that buy receivables from businesses for a fee and usually collect directly from the customer. Factoring tends to be used by companies in the textile and the furniture industries. Companies that use factors typically will submit a customer's order to the factor for credit review. After approval, the company executes the transaction. The sales invoice is given to the factor who bills the customer and receives the payment. The company is allowed to draw on the net price less a predetermined factor's charge (usually called factor's commission) and a reserve to cover expected returns. If the company doesn't draw until the invoice due date, no additional interest is charged. If the company draws before the invoice due date, interest is charged from the date of draw until the invoice due date. Accounting for this transaction is similar to the accounting for the sale of accounts receivable.

[16] If receivables are sold *with recourse*, including the guarantee of a specific yield, the Accounting Standards Division of the AICPA concluded that the transaction is a "financing transaction." The effective yield method should be used to recognize interest expense and revenue, and allowance for uncollectibles should be accounted for. "Recognition of Profit on Sales of Receivables with Recourse," *AICPA Technical Practice Aids* (New York: AICPA, 1980), Section 10,010.

The difference between the cash received from the factor and the net invoice price is charged to factoring expense for the factor's commission and to a special receivable account for the factor's reserve.

Accepting Credit Cards

Instead of selling to a customer on credit and carrying the receivable, a company may decide to accept certain credit cards, including bank cards, as payment. As long as company personnel carry out the procedures required by the credit card agreement to process the transaction, payment will be made by the credit card company or financial institution. The specific procedures required depend upon the agreement and the amount of transaction. After the transaction the company submits copies of the charge slips for payment. Later, the company receives payment for the amount of the sales less a discount, which ranges from 1% to 6%, depending upon the agreement. There are two types of remittance procedures. In the first, the company submits charge slips for payment and later a check is received or the amount is credited to the company's bank account. In this case a receivable net of the discount and credit card expense should be recognized at the time the sale is made. In the second, the company treats the charge slips like customer checks and deposits them to its bank account. In this case the amount of the charge slips less the discount is credited immediately to the company's cash account. The recording of this sale should include recognition of the credit card expense and an increase in cash.

Discounting Notes Receivable

Notes can be **discounted** (sold) to a third party either with or without recourse. In the case of endorsement without recourse, the payee, who becomes the endorser, has no further obligation on the note. Endorsement with recourse requires the payee to make the payment if the maker of the note does not. This results in a contingent liability.

  Whether the note is endorsed with or without recourse, the proceeds from the discounting must be determined. The proceeds are the difference between the maturity value (face value plus interest to maturity) of the note less the discount. The discount is based upon the maturity value of the note, the discount rate, and the number of days remaining before the note matures (as a percentage of a year). For example, Finer Company decided to sell a note receivable from Darby Company. The 120-day, 15%, $1,000 note was discounted with a bank at 18% interest when the note had 60 days remaining. The cash proceeds to Finer were as follows:

Face value of note	$1,000.00
Interest at 15% for 120 days	50.00
Maturity value of note	$1,050.00
Discount on maturity value for 60 days at 18%	31.50
Net proceeds	$1,018.50

  Two approaches to recording the interest are available: (1) the interest revenue and interest expense are recorded separately and (2) interest revenue and interest expense on the note are netted.

If Finer Company sold the note without recourse and followed the policy of recording interest only when the note is sold, the entry using the net method would be as follows:

Cash	1,018.50	
Interest revenue ($50.00 − $31.50)		18.50
Notes receivable		1,000.00
To record sale of note.		

If the note were sold with recourse, two approaches could be used. The first is the same as that used if the note were sold without recourse; the financial statement notes would disclose the contingency. If Darby Company paid the note when due, no further entry would be needed. If Darby did not pay the note, Finer would be required to pay it and to record an asset, notes receivable past due.

The other approach uses a **notes receivable discounted** account as a contra-account to notes receivable. The entry for the Finer Company using this approach is below:

Cash	1,018.50	
Interest revenue		18.50
Notes receivable discounted		1,000.50
To record sale of note.		

If Darby paid the note at maturity, Finer would record the payment by debiting notes receivable discounted and by crediting notes receivable for $1,000. If Darby failed to pay the note, the note is said to be dishonored. To recognize this, Finer would make the following journal entries:

Notes receivable past due	1,050	
Cash		1,050
To record payment of the dishonored note.		
Notes receivable discounted	1,000	
Notes receivable		1,000
To remove the contingent liability on the discounted note.		

Note that the new receivable (notes receivable past due) and the cash payment were for the maturity value of the note since this was the amount owed.

Past due notes should be disclosed separately. If notes are uncollectible or if they meet the criteria for recognition of a loss contingency, they should be written off.

Other Receivables

Nontrade accounts and notes receivable are classified as other receivables. They result from transactions between the company and its employees, officers, stockholders, affiliated companies, or other companies. Other receivables also can result from tax refunds due.

Receivables between the company and its employees, officers, or stockholders can arise from advances or loans, the sale of common stock, or the sale of goods (including long-lived assets) and services. Receivables between the company and affiliated companies generally result from loans, the sale of goods (including long-lived assets) and services, or dividends or interest. Receivables between the company and other companies arise from loans, the sale of goods (including long-lived assets) and services, dividends or interest, claims, or deposits.

Care must be taken in recording claims and deposits receivable. Claims receivable must be valid and must be recognized by all parties involved. Gain contingencies should not be recorded as receivables. Deposits receivable must be differentiated carefully from prepaid items. For example, the payment of last month's rent at the beginning of a lease should be treated as a prepaid item, not as a deposit receivable, since the payment will not be returned.

As with trade receivables, other receivables should be segregated between current and noncurrent. Time value of money and potential uncollectible accounts also should be considered. However, *APB Opinion No. 21* does not apply to receivables resulting from the following:

1. Amounts intended to provide security for one party to an agreement.
2. The customary cash-lending activities and demand or the savings deposit activities of financial institutions whose primary business is lending money.
3. Transactions in which interest rates are affected by tax attributes or by legal restrictions prescribed by a government agency.
4. Transactions between parent and subsidiary companies and between subsidiaries of a common parent.[17]

Financial Statement Disclosures

There are very few specific disclosure requirements relating to receivables. *ARB No. 43* indicates that the "concept of the nature of current assets contemplates the exclusion from that classification of such resources as . . . receivables arising from unusual transaction (such as the sale of capital assets, or loans or advances to affiliates, officers, or employees) which are not expected to be collected within twelve months."[18]

[17]"Interest on Receivables and Payables," par. 3.

[18]"Restatement and Revision of Accounting Research Bulletins," Chapter 3, par. 6.

Exhibit 6-10
Financial Statement Disclosures of Receivables

General Motors
Consolidated Balance Sheet
December 31, 1980 and 1979
(Dollars in Millions)

Assets	1980	1979
Current Assets		
Cash	$ 157.2	$ 247.1
United States Government and other marketable securities and time deposits—at cost, which approximates market of $3,541.4 and $2,721.5	3,558.0	2,789.3
Accounts and notes receivable (including GMAC and its subsidiaries—$704.9 and $2,274.0)—less allowances	3,768.4	5,030.4
Inventories (less allowances) (Note 1)	7,231.2	8,076.3
Prepaid expenses	706.5	463.4
Total Current Assets	15,421.3	16,556.5

Eastern Airlines

The 8-1/4% A300 Notes, the Airbus Senior Obligations, the 9-1/4% Airbus Subordinated debt and the 9-1/4% General Electric Subordinated Notes have been created under credit arrangements established for the purpose of providing financing to meet a portion of the purchase price of 19 A300-B4 aircraft covered by a purchase agreement entered into in 1978. Under these credit arrangements, the Company has unused availability of approximately $92 million to cover a portion of the purchase price of the six undelivered aircraft scheduled for 1981 and 1982 deliveries. Of the $92 million, $25 million will be in the form of 8-1/4% ten-year senior notes, $9 million will be 15-year subordinated debt from the manufacturers, and $58 million will be a four-year open account senior credit arrangement with Airbus Industrie.

The 8-3/4% 1979 Airbus Notes due 1981–1990 were issued pursuant to a financing arrangement entered into in 1979 by the Company and a group of European banks. The financing is guaranteed by governmental export credit agencies and covers 70 percent of the purchase price of two used A300-B2 aircraft acquired by the Company in January 1980.

In accordance with customary and normal practices, the Company maintains compensating balances on certain bank borrowings. Such balances amounted to approximately $2 million as of December 31, 1980 and $9 million as of December 31, 1979. Compensating balances are maintained under informal and unwritten arrangements, and their withdrawal is not generally subject to any legally binding restrictions.

Exhibit 6-10 (continued)
Financial Statement Disclosures of Receivables

Ford Motor Company
Note 8. Receivables
Included in receivables at December 31 were the following:

	1980	1979
	(in millions)	
Accounts and notes............................	$2,275.9	$2,346.3
U.S. Federal income taxes......................	591.3	205.9
Unconsolidated subsidiaries.....................	144.9	189.7
Total...	3,012.1	2,741.9
Less allowance for doubtful accounts	14.0	18.2
Total...	$2,998.1	$2,723.7

Opinion No. 21 indicates that any unamortized discount resulting from recording receivables at their present value should be shown as a reduction in the receivable on the balance sheet. It should not be classified as a deferred credit.[19]

APB Op. #21

Samples of disclosures relating to receivables are shown in Exhibit 6-10.

Concept Summary

ACCOUNTING FOR CASH AND RECEIVABLES

TYPES OF ACCOUNTS

Account	Characteristic
Cash	Includes cash and near cash that are not restricted for use.
Accounts Receivable	Receivables from customers arising from revenue-generating activity of the firm.

[19]"Interest on Receivables and Payables," par. 16.

Note Receivable	Receivable, generally from customers. It is a formal, signed legal document.
	Due date, amount, and interest rate are stated on the document.

BANK RECONCILIATION FORMAT

Bank Balance—Ending

Book Balance—Ending

Add:
  Deposits in transit
  Bank errors understating
    account
Deduct:
  Outstanding checks
  Bank errors overstating
    account
Correct ending balance

Add:
  Collections by bank
  Book errors understating
    account
Deduct:
  Service Charges
  NSF checks
  Bank errors overstating
    account
Correct ending balance

ACCOUNTING FOR ACCOUNTS RECEIVABLE

Objective—Value Receivables at Their Net Realizable Value

Methods of Accounting for Bad Debts

Method	Acceptibility	Description
Direct Write-Off	Not acceptable because it violates the matching concept	Receivable written off in the period it is determined uncollectible
Allowance	Acceptable because it attempts to match estimated expenses with revenues	Uses past ratios to estimate expense in the year of sale

Methods of Applying Allowance Approach

Method	Basis for Estimate	Resulting Estimate Represents
Sales	Percent of credit sales	Actual adjustment to bad debt expense
Accounts Receivable	Percent of ending receivables	Ending balance in the allowance account
Aging of Receivables	Percent of ending receivables by age categories	Ending balance in the allowance account

USING RECEIVABLES TO GENERATE CASH

Method	Description
Pledging	Receivables are used as collateral for a loan.
Assignment	Receivables are used as collateral for a loan and the right to cash receipts from specific receivables is turned over to the lender.
Sale	Receivables are sold for cash.
Factor	The sale of receivables in an ongoing relationship—typically the factor approves a customer's order before the receivable is factored.

Appendix

Four-Column Bank Reconciliations

Another form of bank reconciliation is the four-column reconciliation. The fourth column of a four-column bank reconciliation provides a reconciliation of the balance per bank statement with the balance per books. The four-column bank reconciliation can be done using either a bank and book balance to a corrected balance format or a bank balance format. The reconciliation to a corrected balance will be discussed first.

A sample of the reconciliation of bank and book balances to a corrected balance appears in Exhibit A6-1. The first section starts with the beginning-of-the-month balances, total receipts (credits), total disbursements (charges), and the end-of-the-month balance as contained on the bank statement. The first and fourth columns present computations similiar to those used in the standard bank reconciliation. In completing the reconciliation of receipts and disbursements, you should remember that the goal is to approach the corrected receipts and disbursements for the *current* month. Hence, deposits recorded on the books but not yet credited by the bank at the end of the previous month are deducted from the current month's receipts because they are included in the current month's receipts but actually were a part of the previous month's corrected total receipts. Following a similar logic, outstanding checks from the previous month are deducted from the current month's disbursements. Notice that the check charged in error is deducted from disbursements and added to the ending balance.

Deposits recorded on the books but not yet recorded by the bank at the end of the current month are added to receipts and to the ending bank balance. Outstanding checks at the end of the current month are added to disbursements and are deducted from the ending bank balance.

The second section starts with the following: the previous month's ending balance per books, total receipts for the current month from the cash receipts journal, total disbursements for the current month from the cash disbursements journal, and the current month's ending balance per books. Unrecorded items and other adjustments required to be made on the books are included appropriately. Notice the adjustment of $100 for a customer's check deposited. In this case Volunteer Company does not record returned checks as a charge in the disbursements journal and their redeposit as a receipt in the cash receipts journal. Since the check was returned and redeposited in the same month, no adjustment to the bank balance is necessary. However, the disbursements and receipts recorded on the books are each understated by $100. The inclusion of this $100 item is necessary to reconcile total receipts and total disbursements. The reconciliation is complete when the corrected balances agree and the end of the prior month's balance plus total receipts and minus total disbursements equals the current month's ending balance.

Exhibit A6-1

VOLUNTEER COMPANY

Four-Column Bank Reconciliation—Buckeye National Bank Account

December 31, 1983

	Balance November 30	December Receipts	December Disbursements	Balance December 31
Per bank statement, December 31, 1983	$32,765.00	$28,750.25	$25,014.75	$36,500.50
Cash recorded on books and not yet recorded by bank				
At November 30	2,800.65	(2,800.65)		
At December 31		2,600.25		2,600.25
Outstanding checks				
At November 30	(3,400.50)		(3,400.50)	
At December 31			2,071.00	(2,071.00)
Check drawn on Volunteer Company charged to Volunteer account by bank in error			(185.00)	185.00
Corrected balance per bank statement, December 31	$32,165.15	$28,549.85	$23,500.25	$37,214.75

	Balance November 30	December Receipts	December Disbursements	Balance December 31
Balance per books, December 31, 1983	$32,165.15	$26,449.85	$23,303.75	$35,311.25
Collection of note receivable from Blue Company by bank on December 31, 1983, not yet recorded on company books		2,000.00		2,000.00
Bank service charge for December not yet recorded			6.50	(6.50)
Error in Recording of Check #10023. Recorded as $230 in cash disbursements journal. The check was written for amount owed, $320.			90.00	(90.00)
Check returned for Not Sufficient Funds (NSF) by bank on December 12 and redeposited on December 13, not recorded on company books		100.00	100.00	
Corrected balance per books, December 31, 1983	$32,165.15	$28,549.85	$23,500.25	$37,214.75

The use of a four-column reconciling format for the Volunteer Company appears in Exhibit A6-2. The deposits recorded on the books but not yet recorded by the bank, and outstanding checks are treated as they are in the other format. Charges and credits appearing on the bank statement that need to be posted to the books are deducted from the appropriate disbursement or receipt column and are included also in the ending balance column. Overstatements in the cash disbursement or receipts must be deducted from the appropriate disbursement or receipt column and included in the ending balance column.

Exhibit A6-2
VOLUNTEER COMPANY
Four-Column Bank Reconciliation—Buckeye National Bank Account
December 31, 1983

	Balance November 30	December		Balance December 31
		Receipts	Disbursements	
Balance per bank statement, December 31, 1983	$32,765.00	$28,750.25	$25,014.75	$36,500.50
Cash recorded on books and not yet recorded by bank				
At November 30	2,800.65	(2,800.65)		
At December 31		2,600.25		2,600.25
Outstanding checks				
At November 30	(3,400.50)		(3,400.50)	
At December 31			2,071.00	(2,071.00)
Check drawn on Volunteer Company charged to Volunteer account by bank in error.			(185.00)	185.00
Bank service charge for December not recorded on company books.			(6.50)	6.50
Error in recording of check #10023. Recorded as $230 in cash disbursements journal. The check was written for the amount owed, $320			(90.00)	90.00
Collection of note receivable from Blue Company by bank on December 31, 1983, not yet recorded on company books		(2,000.00)		(2,000.00)
Check returned for Not Sufficient Funds (NSF) by bank on December 12 and redeposited on December 13, not recorded on company books		(100.00)	(100.00)	
	$32,165.15	$26,449.85	$23,303.75	$35,311.25

Questions

Q-6-1 How does an accountant determine whether an item should be included in "cash" on a client's balance sheet?

Q-6-2 How do trade receivables differ from nontrade receivables?

Q-6-3 What is a *compensating balance?* How is it reported in financial statements?

Q-6-4 Why are cash discounts offered?

Q-6-5 How do cash and trade discounts differ?

Q-6-6 What are the differences between the direct write-off and the allowance method of accounting for bad debts?

Q-6-7 How do the percentage of sales and percentage of receivables methods differ? How are they similar?

Q-6-8 How do factoring, pledging, and assignment of receivables differ? How are they similar?

Q–6–9   What is *net realizable value?* How is it applied to receivables?

Q–6–10   How do notes receivable differ from accounts receivable?

Q–6–11   What types of allowance accounts may be used with accounts receivable?

Q–6–12   Miss Jones is the office manager/bookkeeper for a physician. In this position Miss Jones posts charges to accounts receivable, collects and deposits payments, and posts credits to accounts receivable. In what ways could Miss Jones take funds?

Q–6–13   What is an imprest petty cash acount?

Q–6–14   What types of bank accounts could a company have?

Q–6–15   What are interaccount transfers?

Q–6–16   What are the elements of internal control?

Q–6–17   How does assignment with recourse differ from assignment without recourse?

Q–6–18   In what ways can the assignment of receivables be disclosed?

*Q–6–19   What additional information will a proof of cash provide over a standard bank reconciliation?

Q–6–20   What will be the net cost of a piece of equipment listing for $100 if the following trade discounts are offered:

    a)   60% & 20%.

    b)   70% & 10%.

    c)   73%.

Note: Items with an *asterisk* relate to material contained in the appendix.

Discussion Questions and Cases

D–6–1   One of your corporate clients operates a full-line department store that is dominant in its market area, is easily accessible to public and private transportation, has adequate parking facilities, and is near a large, permanent military base. The president of the company seeks your advice on a recently received proposal.

A local bank in which your client has an account recently affiliated with a popular national credit card plan and has extended an invitation to your client to participate in the plan. Under the plan, affiliated banks mail credit card applications to persons in the community who have good credit ratings regardless of whether they are bank customers. If the recipient wishes to receive a credit card, he completes, signs, and returns the application and installment credit agreement. Holders of the cards thus activated may charge merchandise or services at any participating establishment throughout the nation.

The bank guarantees payment to all participating merchants on all presented invoices that have been properly completed, signed, and validated with the impression of credit cards that have not expired, been reported stolen, or otherwise canceled. Local merchants, including your client, may turn in all card-validated sales tickets or invoices to their affiliated local bank at any time and receive immediate credits to their checking accounts of 96.5% of the face value of the invoices. If card users pay the bank in full within 30 days for amounts billed, the bank levies no added charges against them. If they elect to make their payments under a deferred payment plan, the bank adds a service charge, which amounts to an effective interest rate of 18% per annum on unpaid balances. Only the local affiliated banks and the franchiser of the credit card plan share in these revenues. The 18% service charge approximates what your client has been billing customers who pay their accounts over an extended period on a schedule similar to that offered under the credit card plans. Participation in the plan does not prevent your client from continuing to carry on its credit business as in the past.

Required:

1. What are (a) the positive and (b) the negative financial—and accounting—related factors that your client should consider in deciding whether to participate in the described credit card plan? Explain.

2. If your client does participate in the plan, which income statement and balance sheet accounts may change materially as the plan becomes fully operative? (Such factors as market position, sales mix, prices, markup, and so forth are expected to remain about the same as in the past.) Explain.

(AICPA adapted)

D–6–2 In order to obtain needed cash, Smithit is considering several alternative financing methods involving its accounts receivable. What alternatives could Smithit use? What are some of the positive and negative features of the methods suggested?

D–6–3 Bray Company uses the allowance method to estimate uncollectibles. Bray consistently records bad debts expense using 5% of net sales. The auditors check this percentage using an aging of receivables with the following percentages:

Receivables	Percentage
Under 60 days	2%
61–120 days	5
121–180 days	20
Over 180–days	50

The following are relevant balances for 1980 and 1981.

	1980	1981
Sales	$500,000	$600,000
Accounts receivable	48,000	60,000
Under 60 days	30,000	30,000
61 to 120 days	10,000	15,000
121 to 180 days	5,000	10,000
Over 180 days	3,000	5,000
Allowance for uncollectibles		
(after write-off of bad debts)	1,100	1,300

Required:

Evaluate the appropriateness of the percentage of sales used by Bray.

D–6–4 You have been asked by the board of trustees of a local church to review their accounting procedures. As part of your review, you prepared the following comments:

a) The church's board of trustees has delegated responsibility for financial management and audit of the financial records to the finance committee. This group prepares the annual budget and approves major disbursements but is not involved in collections or record keeping. No audit has been considered necessary in recent years because the same trusted employee has kept church records and served as financial secretary for 15 years.

b) The collection at the weekly service is taken by a team of ushers. The head usher counts the collection in the church office following each service. He then places the collection and a notation of the amount counted in the church safe. Next morning the financial secretary opens the safe and recounts the collection. He withholds about $100 to meet cash expenditures during the coming week and deposits the remainder of the collection intact. In order to facilitate the deposit, members who contribute by check are asked to draw their checks to "cash."

c) At their request a few members are furnished prenumbered, predated envelopes in which to insert their weekly contributions. The head usher removes the cash from the envelopes, to be counted with the loose cash included in the collection, and discards the envelopes. No record is maintained of issuance or return of the envelopes, and the envelope system is not encouraged.

d) Each member is asked to prepare a contribution pledge card annually. The pledge is regarded as a moral commitment by the member to contribute a stated weekly amount. Based upon the amounts shown on the pledge cards, the financial secretary furnishes a letter to requesting members to support the tax deductibility of their contributions.

Required:

Describe the weaknesses in the procedures for collections made at weekly services and in the record keeping for members' pledges and contributions.

(AICPA adapted)

Exercises

E–6–1 John Corporation sells widgets to dealers around the country. Sales for the year ended November 30, 1981, were $1,500,000. John uses the allowance method for uncollectibles. The balance in the allowance account at the beginning of the year was $10,000. Based upon past experience, an expense of 2% of sales should be established. During 1981 the bookkeeper improperly recorded $5,000 of write-offs by debiting sales and crediting accounts receivable. At year-end you determine that an additional $20,000 should be written off.

Required:

1. Record all necessary entries for uncollectibles for the year ending November 30, 1981, including any needed to correct the bookkeeper's error.
2. What are the balances after adjustments in sales, bad debts expense, and allowance for uncollectibles?
3. If the additional amount that should be written off were $40,000 instead of $20,000, what would be the balances in part 2? What additional considerations, if any, need to be addressed by increasing write-offs to $40,000?

E–6–2 Karen Corporation uses the allowance method to record uncollectibles. During 1981 the following occurred:

May 15	Wrote off uncollectible account of D Beet Company—$300
June 25	Collected $50 from the bankruptcy trustee of Long Gone Company. The $50 represents a final (and only) distribution to creditors of the bankrupt company. The sale of $800 took place in early 1980, and the account was written off fully when the bankruptcy was announced in December, 1980.
Sept. 15	Collected the full amount owed by D Beet Company that was written off on May 15.
Oct. 25	Wrote off uncollectible account of Cheat Company—$1,000

Required:

Prepare journal entries to record these events.

E–6–3 Alpha Company has several bank accounts. Alpha's accountant has reconciled each bank account. Based upon the reconciliations, the total cash balance in all accounts is $125,000.50. You instruct your assistant to examine interbank transfers. Your assistant uncovers the following potential problems:

a) A $30,000 check to the company drawn on its first Beta bank account was not recorded as a disbursement but was included as a cash receipt and as a deposit in transit on the first Gamma bank account.

b) A $25,000 check to the company drawn on its first Sigma bank account was properly recorded as a disbursement and included as an outstanding check. The check was not included as a receipt on the Gamma bank account.

Required:

What is the correct cash balance?

E–6–4 The November bank statement of Jay Company contains the following information:

Balance Nov. 1, 1981	$125,635.82
Credits	525,285.51
Charges	−522,273.52
Balance Nov. 30 1981	$128,647.81

Jay Company books contain the following information:

Cash Balance Nov. 30, 1981 $130,550.25

An examination of the bank statement and company books indicates the following:

Deposit in transit	$5,255.00
Service charges included in the bank statement—not included in cash disbursements	45.00
Outstanding checks	$3,297.56

Required:

1. Prepare a bank reconciliation for Jay Company.

2. If this is the only cash account maintained by Jay Company, what will be the amount of cash reported in the November 30, 1981, balance sheet?

3. Prepare any necessary journal entries.

E–6–5 The Gloria Corporation established a petty cash fund of $200 on March 30, 1981. During April the following expenses were paid:

Postage	$22.50
Office supplies	65.80
Delivery expense	85.40

Gloria's fiscal year ends on April 30. These expenses were reimbursed on May 1, 1981, by Gloria Corporation (check number 76543).

Required:

1. What should be the actual balance in petty cash on March 30? April 30?

2. What journal entries dealing with petty cash transactions would you expect to find on Gloria's books?

E–6–6 The following is part of the trial balance of Richard Corporation as of March 31, 1982:

Account Number	Description	DR (CR)
101	Cash in bank—Mercantile Bank	$15,682.50
102	Cash in bank—Mercantile Bank— general payroll account	4,000.00
103	Cash in bank—Security Bank	7,650.00

104	Cash in bank—Mutual Bank—	
	disbursement account	500.00
105	Petty cash fund	200.00
106	Change fund	800.00
107	Certificate of deposit	20,000.00
108	Employee travel advances	400.00

Required:
Which items should be included in cash on Richard's March 31, 1982, balance sheet?

E–6–7   B. Swindle Co. sold $15,000 of merchandise to Mr. Ken Peacock on account. After 30 days Mr. Peacock made a payment of $5,000 on the account and gave Swindle Co. a 90-day, 18% interest note for the remaining $10,000. After Swindle Co. had held the note for 45 days, it took the note to the bank and discounted it. The bank charged 20% interest.

Required:
Prepare the journal entries necessary to record the transactions above.

E–6–8   On January 1, 1980, the credit balance in the allowance for uncollectible accounts of Master Company was $400,000. For 1980 the doubtful accounts expense is based on 0.7% of net credit sales. Net credit sales were $50,000,000. During 1980 uncollectible accounts amounting to $410,000 were written off.

Required:
Compute the balance in Master's allowance for uncollectible accounts at December 31, 1980.

(AICPA adapted)

E–6–9   The Guise Company needs additional cash to operate. To raise additional funds, Guise assigned $200,000 of accounts receivable to High Risk Finance Company. Guise received an advance from High Risk of 85% of the assigned receivables less a commission of 3% on the advance. Before year-end Guise collected $150,000 on the assigned receivables and remitted $160,000 to High Risk. The additional $10,000 represented interest on the advance. The balance in accounts receivable not including assigned accounts at year-end, is $350,000.

Required:
1. Prepare the appropriate journal entries to record the transaction above.
2. Determine the financial statement balances in accounts receivable at year end.

(AICPA adapted)

E–6–10   Scrapped Company entered into the following transactions to obtain additional cash:

On November 1, 1980, $300,000 of net accounts receivable were sold to Factor Corporation for $260,000. The receivables were sold outright on a nonrecourse basis.

On December 31, 1980, Scrapped obtained an advance of $100,000 from the bank by pledging $120,000 of accounts receivable. Fifteen percent interest is to be charged, and the first payment is due on January 31, 1980.

Required:
1. Prepare the appropriate journal entries to record the transactions above.
2. Determine the financial statement balances and/or disclosures at December 31, 1980, that relate to the two transactions.

(AICPA adapted)

E–6–11   On May 1, 1983, Bossetta Co. sold Watts Co. merchandise with a list price of $20,000. The terms of the sale were 20%, 10% trade discount and 2/10, net 30. On May 31 Bossetta Co. accepted a 60-day, 12% interest note in settlement of the Watts receivable. On June 20 Bossetta Co. discounted the Watts note at the Second National Bank. The bank charged 18% interest.

Required:
Give the journal entries necessary to record the transactions above.

E–6–12 Systems Corporation uses the allowance method to account for uncollectibles. Its estimate of uncollectibles is based upon ending receivables balances. At June 30, 1981, Systems' aging of receivables indicates the following:

Accounts	Amount
0–90 days	$25,000
91–180 days	10,000
181–365 days	5,000

All accounts over one year old are written off. The balance in the allowance account after writing off appropriate accounts is $4,000. Systems historically has used the following to estimate uncollectibles:

Accounts	Percentage
0–90 days	1%
91–180 days	20%
181–365 days	80%

Required:
What journal entries relating to receivables must be made for the year ended June 30, 1981.

E–6–13 Avid is considering the purchase of some new office furniture having a list price of $2,000. One company has indicated that it will sell the furniture at 50% and 10% off list with a 5% cash discount if paid in 10 days. Another company has indicated it will sell at 57% off list with a 1% cash discount if paid at the end of 10 days.
Required:
What is the net cost of each to Avid if (a) Avid takes advantage of the cash discounts, and (b) Avid does not take advantage of the cash discounts.

E–6–14 Mindfull Company bought some equipment in exchange for a note promising to pay $30,000 at the end of two years. The note provided for no interest.
Required:
If 15% is an appropriate interest rate, prepare the journal entry to record the purchase of the equipment.

*****E–6–15** Spunk Corporation's November 30, 1981, bank statement contained the following information:

Beginning balance	$24,000
Credits	80,000
Charges	92,000
Ending balance	12,000

Spunk's books contained the following information for November:

Beginning bank balance	$22,000
Receipts	80,000
Disbursements	94,000
Ending bank balance	8,000

After comparing the November bank statement to the October bank reconcilation and November receipts and disbursements, Spunk's accountant determined that there were no deposits in transit and only $4,000 in outstanding checks. At October 31 there were no deposits in transit and only $2,000 in outstanding checks.

Required:
Prepare a four-column bank reconcilation.

Note: Items with an *asterisk* relate to material contained in the appendix.

Problems

P-6-1 Provided below is relevant information for Store Company during 1981:

Cash sales	$ 85,000
Credit sales	265,000
Accounts receivable, 1/1	35,000
Accounts receivable, 12/31	38,500

When accounts prove uncollectible, the bookkeeper debits accounts receivable—uncollectible and credits accounts receivable. When accounts previously considered to be uncollectible are collected, cash is debited and recovered accounts is credited. At Dec. 31, the balances in these accounts are as follows:

Accounts receivable—uncollectible	$9,000
Recovered accounts	750

Only 1981 transactions are included in these two accounts.

Required:
1. If Store Company uses the direct write-off method:
    a) Prepare any necessary adjusting journal entries.
    b) What are the relevant financial statement account balances at Dec. 31?
2. If Store Company estimates bad debt expense based upon 3% of credit sales and if the beginning and current ending balance in the allowance account is $10,000:
    a) Prepare any necessary adjusting journal entries.
    b) What are the relevant financial statement account balances at Dec. 31?
3. What differences would result in the financial statements if using the allowance method instead of the direct write-off method?

P-6-2 Goldfish Enterprises, Inc. uses the allowance method to account for uncollectibles. Historically, Goldfish has used the following percentages to estimate the allowance account:

Receivables under 30 days	2%
Receivables between 31 and 90 days old	5%
Receivables between 91 and 180 days old	10%
Receivables between 181 and 300 days old	30%
Receivables over 301 days old	100%

Receivables at year-end included the following amounts and uncollectibles:

	Total Amount	Amount Uncollectible
Under 30 days	$110,000	–0–
31 to 90 days	80,000	$2,000
91 to 180 days	40,000	5,000
181 to 300 days	8,000	2,000
Over 300	9,000	9,000

No entries have been made to the allowance or bad debts expense accounts during the year. The current balance in the allowance account (carried over from last year) is $20,000 (debit).

Required:

1. Prepare any necessary journal entries relating to bad debts.
2. What are the appropriate year-end balances in the allowance and bad debts expense accounts?

P–6–3 People, Inc. uses the allowance method to record bad debts expense. The company estimates uncollectibles based upon the age of receivables. Specifically, the company uses the following rule: accounts under 90 days old—1%, accounts between 91 and 180 days old—5%, accounts between 181 and 360 days old—50%, and accounts over one year old—95%. At June 30, 1981, the aging indicated the following:

Accounts	Amount
Under 90 days old	$250,000
Between 91 and 180 days	120,010
Between 181 and 360 days	25,625
Over 1 year	3,255
Total accounts receivable (per general ledger)	$398,890

All uncollectibles have been written off.

Required:

1. If the balance in the allowance account before adjustment is a credit of $6,250, prepare any necessary journal entries for uncollectibles.
2. If the balance in the allowance account before adjustment is a debit balance of $6,250, prepare any necessary journal entries for uncollectibles.
3. If the balance in the allowance account before adjustment is $28,000, prepare any necessary journal entries for uncollectibles.

P–6–4 Lin Company routinely transfers funds by check among several bank accounts. Listed below are four interbank transfers made near December 31, 1981.

	First National Bank		Last National Bank	
	Disbursing Date		Receiving Date	
Transfer Number	Books	Bank Statement	Books	Bank Statement
A-202	12/30/81	12/31/81	12/30/81	12/31/81
A-203	12/30/81	1/2/82	12/31/81	1/2/82
A-204	12/31/81	1/3/82	1/2/82	1/2/82
A-205	12/31/81	1/3/82	12/31/81	1/2/82

Required:
1. Which of the cash transfers would appear as a deposit in transit on the December 31, 1981, bank reconciliation?
2. Which of the cash transfers would appear as outstanding checks on the December 31, 1981, bank reconciliation?
3. Which of the cash transfers would require an adjusting entry on December 31, 1981?

(AICPA adapted)

P–6–5 Each month Ace Counter reconciles the bank statement of his employer, Apple Company. You have been assigned to review Ace's work. The bank reconciliation for January 31, 1981, appears below:

APPLE COMPANY
Bank Reconciliation
January 31, 1981

Balance per bank statement 1/31/81		$26,050.00
Deposits in transit (2)		8,255.50
		$34,305.50

Outstanding checks:

Number	Amount	
2051	$ 88.00	
22635	2,500.00	
36	1,875.25	
37	225.00	
38	1,625.00	
39	7,552.20	15,865.45
Balance per bank 1/31/81		$18,440.05

In examining the receipts and disbursements books, you note the following:
   a) Check number 2051 was issued over a year ago.
   b) Check number 22636 was issued for $3,875.25.
   c) The two deposits in transit appear to be composed of a deposit on 2/1 of $6,255.50 and a deposit on 2/4 of $2,000.00.

Required:
What questions/problems are raised by your review?

P–6–6 The June bank statement of Lucas Company showed an ending balance of $187,387. Deposits in transit were $20,400. Outstanding checks on June 30 were $60,645. The bank statement revealed a $2,300 item that was charged to Lucas on June 15 which should have been charged to another company. The bank statement also indicated that the bank collected certain foreign accounts receivable amounting to $8,684. For collecting these items the bank charged Lucas's account a $19 service charge. Neither the $8,684 nor the $19 had been recorded on Lucas's books.

The June 30 cash balance per books (before any adjustments) was $140,777.

Required:
1 Prepare a bank reconciliation for Lucas Company at June 30.
2 Prepare any necessary adjusting journal entries.

(AICPA adapted)

P–6–7 Sam Company maintains an imprest petty cash fund of $300 at each of its 15 branches. On March 15, you go to the Smithfield Branch to do a surprise reconciliation of the petty cash fund. In the petty cash fund box you find the following:

Cash	$55.00
Change	10.00

Stamps	15.00
5 checks from the bookkeeper	85.00
5 Petty cash receipts (made out in pencil)	30.00

Required:

What concerns do you have about the handling of the petty cash fund?

P–6–8 Your client, Deb Corporation, has an account called cash on hand. For the year ended September 30, 1981, the only entry to the account is from an adjusting entry of $900 at year-end. The client provides you with the following schedule of the items making up the $900.

Check from AAAA Corporation dated November 15, 1981, in payment of an invoice	$300
Check from Skip Company dated September 1, 1980, in payment of an invoice. This check has been returned three times for NSF.	250
Employee IOUs	100
3 Deb Company payroll checks being held until employees return from vacation	250
Check from Glutz Company dated September 29, 1981	100
	$900

Required:

1. Which items should be included in cash on hand?
2. What is the appropriate disposition of those items that should not be included in cash on hand?

P–6–9 Abeles Stores, Inc., a chain of retail men's stores, honors two bank credit cards and makes daily deposits of credit card sales in two credit card bank accounts (Security Bank and Mercantile Bank). Each day the stores batch their credit card sales slips, bank deposit slips, and authorized sales return documents and send them to the appropriate bank. Store copies of these items are sent to the company's accounting office for posting. Each week detailed reports of the general ledger credit-card cash accounts are prepared.

The banks provide weekly statements for the credit card accounts. The banks have been instructed to make an automatic weekly transfer to the general cash account. The banks charge the accounts for invalid transactions (sales on stolen or expired cards) and return the documents for these transactions to the accounting office.

Below are copies of the detailed general ledger accounts and a summary of the bank statements for the week ended December 31, 1981.

SUMMARY OF THE BANK STATEMENTS
For the Week Ended December 31, 1981

	Security Bank	Mercantile Bank
	(Charges) or Credits	
Beginning balance		
December 24, 1981	$10,000	$ 0
Deposits dated		
December 24, 1981	2,100	4,200
27, 1981	2,500	5,000
28, 1981	3,000	7,000
29, 1981	2,000	5,500
30, 1981	1,900	4,000
Cash transfers to general bank account		
December 27, 1981	(10,700)	0
31, 1981	0	(22,600)

Chargebacks		
Stolen cards	(100)	0
Expired cards	(300)	(1,600)
Invalid deposits	(1,400)	(1,000)
Bank service charges	(400)	(500)
Ending balance		
December 31, 1981	$ 8,600	$ 0

DETAILED GENERAL LEDGER CREDIT CARD
CASH ACCOUNT PRINTOUTS
For the Week Ended December 31, 1981

	Security Bank Dr. or (Cr.)	Mercantile Bank Dr. or (Cr.)
Beginning balance		
December 24, 1981	$12,100	$4,200
Deposits		
December 27, 1981	2,500	5,000
28, 1981	3,000	7,000
29, 1981	0	5,400
30, 1981	1,900	4,000
31, 1981	2,200	6,000
Cash transfer		
December 27, 1981	(10,700)	0
Chargebacks		
Expired cards	(300)	(1,600)
Invalid deposits (physically deposited in wrong account)	(1,400)	(1,000)
Redeposit of invalid deposits	1,000	1,400
Sales returns for week ending		
December 31, 1981	(600)	(1,200)
Ending balance		
December 31, 1981	$ 9,700	$29,200

Required:
Prepare a reconciliation for the two bank accounts at December 31, 1981.

(AICPA adapted)

P–6–10 You are examining Bum Corporation's financial statements for the year ended December 31, 1981. Your analysis of the 1981 entries in the trade notes receivable account was as follows:

BUM CORPORATION
Analysis of Trade Notes Receivable
For the Year Ended December 31, 1981

Date 1981		Folio	Trade Notes Receivable Debit	Credit
Jan. 1	Balance forward		$118,000	
Feb. 29	Received $25,000, 6% note due on 10/29/81 from Daley whose trade account was past due	MEMO		

29	Discounted Daley note at 6%	CR		$ 24,960
Mar. 20	Received non-interest-bearing demand note from Edge, the corporation's treasurer for a loan	CD	6,200	
Aug. 30	Received principal and interest due from Allen and, in accordance with agreement, two principal payments in advance	CR		34,200
Sept. 4	Paid protest fee on note dishonored by Charnes	CD	5	
Nov. 1	Received check dated 2/1/82 in settlement of Bailey note. The check was included in cash on hand 12/31/81	CR		8,120
4	Paid protest fee and maturity value of Daley note to bank. Note discounted 2/29/81 was dishonored	CD	26,031	
Dec. 27	Accepted furniture and fixtures with a fair market value of $24,000 in full settlement from Daley	GJ		24,000
31	Received check dated 1/3/82 from Edge in payment of 3/29/81 note. (The check was included in petty cash until 1/2/82 when it was returned to Edge in exchange for a new demand note of the same amount.)	CR		6,200
31	Received principal and interest on Charnes note	CR		42,437
31	Accrued interest on Allen note	GJ	1,200	
	Totals		$151,436	$139,917

The following information is also available:

a) Balances at January 1, 1981, were a debit of $1,400 in the accrued interest receivable account and a credit of $400 in the unearned interest income account. The $118,000 debit balance in the trade notes receivable account consisted of the following three notes:

Allen note dated 8/31/77, payable in annual installments of $10,000 principal plus accrued interest at 6% each August 31	$70,000
Bailey note discounted to Bum at 6% interest on 11/1/80 due on 11/1/81	8,000
Charnes note for $40,000 plus 6% interest dated 12/31/80 due on 9/1/81	40,000

b) No entries were made during 1981 to the accrued interest receivable account or the unearned interest income account, and only one entry for a credit of $1,200 on December 31 appeared in the interest income account.

c) All notes were from trade customers unless otherwise indicated.

d) Debits and credits offsetting trade notes receivable debit and credit entries were recorded correctly unless the facts indicate otherwise.

Required:

Prepare a worksheet to adjust each entry to correct or properly reclassify it, if necessary. Enter your adjustments in the proper columns to correspond with the date of each entry. Do not combine related entries for different dates. Your completed worksheet will provide the basis for one compound journal entry to correct all entries to trade notes receivable and related accounts for 1981. Formal journal entries are not required. In addition to the information shown in the analysis above, the following column headings are suggested for your worksheet:

Adjustment or Reclassification Required

	Trade Notes Receivable	Trade Accounts Receivable	Interest Income	Other Accounts		
					Amount	
Item	Debit-(Credit)	Debit-(Credit)	Debit-(Credit)	Account Title	Debit	Credit

(AICPA adapted)

P–6–11 ABC Company, a calendar-year corporation, purchased a building from DEF Company on January 2 by providing a five-year, $100,000 note payable in five equal install-ments ($20,000) at the end of each year. The note provided for no interest. ABC accounted for the purchase by posting the following journal entry:

Building	$80,000	
Land	20,000	
Notes payable		100,000

The building is to be depreciated, using the straight-line method, over 20 years. At the time of sale an imputed interest rate of 18% per year was appropriate, and the value of a similar piece of land next to the property bought was $20,000.
Required:
1. If the books have not yet been closed for the year of the purchase, what adjusting journal entries should be prepared to properly account for the purchase?
2. What are the balances in the financial statement accounts that relate to the building, land, and note at the end of the year of purchase?
3. What impact will applying APB *Opinion No. 21* have on ABC's financial statements at the end of the year of purchase?

P–6–12 Hap Corporation, a calendar-year corporation, purchased equipment on January 2, 1979, for a $250,000 non-interest-bearing note providing payment of $25,000 on Decem-ber 31 of each of the next 10 years. The equipment was assumed to have a 25-year life and is being depreciated using the straight-line method.
Required:
You have been asked to make any needed adjusting entries for the year ended December 31, 1982. All necessary note payments have been made. The appropriate imputed interest rate for Hap on January 2, 1979, was 12% compounded annually. You may assume that the books have not been closed for 1982.

*P–6–13 You have been instructed to prepare a four-column bank reconciliation (proof of cash) for Step Products Co. for October, 1981. You obtain the following information:

| | Bank Statement Dated | |
	September 30, 1981	*October 31, 1981*
Beginning balance	$18,750.25	$16,178.75
Credits	16,253.80	21,750.30

Charges	(18,825.30)	(18,930.20)
Ending balance	$16,178.75	$18,998.85

Per books	September	October
Beginning balance	$18,750.25	$18,250.30
Receipts	19,753.55	22,283.50
Disbursements	(20,253.50)	(21,583.30)
Ending balance	$18,250.30	$18,950.50

	September	October
Outstanding checks	$ 1,428.20	$ 4,081.30
Deposits in transit	3,499.75	4,032.95

Required:

Prepare a four-column bank reconciliation (proof of cash) for October, 1981.

*P-6-14 On the audit of Ruth Company you are asked to prepare a proof of cash (four-column bank reconciliation) for April, 1981.

Information obtained from bank statement:

Balance, 4/1	$ 85,265 ✓
Credits	175,422 ✓
Charges	(157,735) ✓
Balance, 4/30	$102,952 ✓

Information obtained from company books:

Cash balance, 4/1/81	$ 82,516 ✓
Receipts—April	177,956 ✓
Disbursements—April	(153,454) ✓
Cash balance, 4/30/81	$107,018 ✓

Information obtained from March bank reconciliation:

Balance per bank statement, 3/31	$ 85,265 ✓
Deposits in transit	15,625 ✓
Outstanding checks	(18,374) ✓
Balance per bank, 3/31	$ 82,516

Additional information:

Outstanding checks, 4/30/81	$ 15,293 ✓
Deposits in transit, 4/30/81	18,259 ✓

Included as a charge was a $1,000 check drawn on Fran Company that should have been charged to another account.

The bank charged Ruth $100 for printing checks. This amount had not been recorded on Ruth's books.

A $100 check from a Ruth customer was returned by the bank because of NSF. The check was redeposited on April 15 and was *not* returned. Ruth follows the practice of not recording returned checks or its subsequent redeposit.

Required:

1. Prepare a proof of cash.
2. Prepare any needed adjusting journal entries.
3. What amount will be included for this checking account as part of cash if financial statements are prepared at April 30, 1981?

Note: Items with an *asterisk* relate to material contained in the appendix.

7

Investments in Stock

Accounting in the News

It is not uncommon for enterprises to invest in the stock of other enterprises for a variety of reasons: to get a good return on investment, to influence the financial and operating policies of investees, or to control (own) another entity. Authoritative rule-making bodies in the accounting profession have devoted extensive amounts of time and literature in attempts to explain generally accepted accounting principles applicable to those investments.

Almost daily, business journals and magazines report the efforts of large companies attempting to acquire the stock of other companies. One of the largest takeover attempts ever to occur is described in the following excerpts from a recent article:

> The pursuit of Marathon Oil Co. may well end in the costliest takeover in corporate history—and it has already broken the record for confusion. If the complexities involving possible new bidders, government actions and court rulings continue to grow as they did last week, the implications may become unfathomable for all but MBAs with law degrees who study economics as a hobby.
>
> So far the major players are United States Steel Corp., Marathon's choice as a marriage partner, and Mobil Corp., which started the race and whose current bid of $6.5 billion is slightly higher than its rival's. But other bidders may soon join the chase; Allied Corp., the chemicals giant turned conglomerate, has already made a verbal offer for Marathon. And in an ingenious takeover try, Mobil may ask another oil company to join it as a partner. That would gain the way for other oil companies large and small to enter the race. And the outcome is not solely in the hands of acquisition-happy executives: no company can win Marathon without antitrust clearance from the Federal Trade Commission, and three separate Federal courts have already snarled the bidders in frustrating legal tangles. . . .
>
> Mobil said it would try to overcome antitrust objectives by making a highly unusual deal: another unnamed oil company that does not now compete heavily with Marathon would buy Marathon's refining and marketing operations, leaving Mobil with Marathon's prized crude-oil reserves, especially those in the prolific Yates Field in West Texas. . . .*

> While not all business combinations are this extensive, there exist accounting problems associated with all investments in corporate stock. This chapter presents the proper accounting for investments in other companies.
>
> *"Marathon's Marathon," *Newsweek*, December 14, 1981, p. 127. Copyright 1981, by Newsweek, Inc. All Rights Reserved. Reprinted by Permission.

There are many reasons that might prompt a corporation to invest in the stock of another corporation, but the primary motive is normally the same—to enhance the investor's own income. A corporation can derive economic benefits directly through the receipt of dividends or interest or through appreciation in the market value of the securities. Indirect benefits also can be realized through the creation of desirable operating relationships between the investor company and the investee company. These indirect benefits are derived from the influence or control that may be exercised over a major supplier, customer, or otherwise related company.

The terms investor and investee will be used frequently in this chapter and are defined as follows: **investor** refers to a business entity that holds an investment in *voting stock* of another company; **investee** refers to a corporation that issued *voting stock* held by an investor.

Voting stock allows the investor to exercise influence or control over the operating and financial policies of the investee company. The degree of influence generally is based on the proportion of voting shares owned to the total outstanding voting shares. Other relevant factors considered in the determination of the degree of influence will be discussed in the following sections.

This chapter is divided into three sections; the first deals with the factors that need to be considered when determining which accounting method to apply to account for marketable equity securities; the second discusses the initial recording of an investment in equity securities; and the third section addresses accounting for the investment subsequent to acquisition.

Determining the Appropriate Accounting Method

The amount of influence an investor corporation can exert on an investee corporation determines the accounting procedures that need to be followed (see Exhibit 7-1). The investor will account for his or her investment in one of three ways:

1. Present consolidated financial statements.
2. Use the equity method.
3. Use the lower of cost or market method.

Controlling Interest

The objective behind reporting the results of operations and the financial position of an entity is to communicate meaningful and useful financial information to the users of financial statements.[1] In accordance with this objective, consolidated

[1] "Objectives of Financial Reporting by Business Enterprises," *Statement of Financial Accounting Concepts No. 1* (Stamford, Conn.: FASB, 1978), par. 9.

Exhibit 7-1

Relationship between Consolidated Financial Statements, Equity Method Investees, and Cost Method Investees

Controlling interest (more than 50% ownership of outstanding voting shares) } Consolidated financial statements are appropriate.

Significant influence
1. Ownership of 20% or more of outstanding voting shares.
2. Personnel interrelationships.
3. Technological dependency.
4. Material intercompany transactions.
5. Participation in policy decisions.
6. Represented on board of directors.

Equity method of accounting is appropriate.

Lack of significant influence (See tests above for significant influence) } Lower of cost or market method of accounting is appropriate.

financial statements have evolved to present information in a concise and informative manner for two or more commonly controlled entities. The presentation of consolidated financial statements is justified if one of the companies included in the consolidation has, either directly or indirectly, a controlling interest. With the exception of certain factors, **controlling interest** is deemed to exist when an investor company (the **parent**) owns more than 50% of the outstanding voting stock of an investee company (the **subsidiary**). If you follow the principle of substance over form, the parent and subsidiary are considered as one entity, but from a legal perspective each retains its separate corporate identity. As a result, both the parent and subsidiary may prepare separate financial statements in addition to consolidated statements.

There are exceptions to the general rule concerning the existence of a controlling interest. A corporation should not consolidate a subsidiary in the following cases:

1. Control of the subsidiary is likely to be temporary (e.g., management intends to dispose of the securities within one year or one operating cycle, whichever is greater).
2. Control does not rest with the majority shareholders (e.g., the subsidiary is in legal reorganization or in bankruptcy).
3. Minority interest in the subsidiary is so large in relation to the equity of the parent shareholders in the consolidated net assets that presentation of separate statements would be more meaningful and useful (e.g., a 50-50 joint venture between two separate corporations).

APB #51

4. A subsidiary is so different in operations from the parent that it would be best to present separate statements (e.g., a bank and a manufacturing company).

5. A subsidiary may be in a foreign country where there are restrictions on transfers of funds to the parent company.[2]   ARB #51

Accountants do realize that effective managerial control can exist with less than 50% ownership interest. However, since continuous control is not assured, accountants believe it is unwise to include in consolidated financial statements investee companies when less than 50% of the outstanding voting shares are owned.[3]

Consolidated statements basically combine the balance sheets and income statements of the parent and subsidiary into one statement. While this process may sound simple, it is in reality very complex. For example, there may be transactions between the parent and subsidiary that must be adjusted or eliminated. When individual company statements are combined into a consolidated statement, the intercompany loan transactions must be eliminated since an entity cannot loan money to itself.

Because of the complexity involved in the preparation of consolidated statements, they are not covered in this text. A detailed discussion of the topic may be found in any advanced accounting text.

Significant Influence

In APB *Opinion No. 18* the APB concluded that the equity method of accounting for an investment in common stock should be used by investors who exercise a **significant influence** over the operating and financial policies of an investee company, even though the investor owns 50% or less of the outstanding voting shares of the investee.[4] The ability to exercise significant influence over an investee could be evidenced in several ways:

APB Opinion #18

1. Interchange of managerial personnel.
2. Technological dependency.
3. Material intercompany transactions.
4. Participation in policy decisions.
5. Representation on board of directors.[5]

All these items are considered to determine if the investor has significant influence over the financial and operating policies of the investee.

The APB distinguishes another factor that should be considered in assessing the degree of influence: the extent of other concentrations of shareholdings in relation to those shares held by the investor. Even though substantial ownership

---

[2]"Consolidated Financial Statements," *Accounting Research Bulletin No. 51* (New York: AICPA, 1959), pars. 2 and 3.

[3]SEC regulations prohibit a registrant from consolidating any investee company that is not majority-owned in filings with the Commission.

[4]"The Equity Method of Accounting For Investments in Common Stock," *Opinions of the Accounting Principles Board No. 18* (New York: AICPA, 1971), par. 14.

[5]Ibid., par. 17.

by another investor may exist, the investee is still accounted for by using the equity method on the books of the investor, who has significant influence. The APB recognizes that determining the investor's ability to exercise such influence is not always clear, and professional judgment is necessary when making this determination.

In an attempt to achieve uniformity, the APB concluded that an investment, direct or indirect, of 20% or more of the voting stock of an investee should lead to the presumption that, in the absence of evidence to the contrary, the investor exercises significant influence over the investee. Conversely, an investment of less than 20% of the outstanding voting stock of an investee should lead to a presumption that an investor does not have the ability to exercise significant influence unless such ability can be demonstrated.[6]

Lack of Significant Influence

When the investor lacks significant influence over the investee, the investment is accounted for using the lower of cost or market method, except for certain circumstances when the cost method or the market method is acceptable.

Before the issuance of FASB *Statement No. 12*, "Accounting for Certain Marketable Securities," accounting varied significantly with respect to investments in marketable securities when significant influence or controlling interest could not be demonstrated. Some enterprises were carrying marketable securities at cost, some at market, and some at the lower of cost or market. This lack of definitive guidance in authoritative accounting literature prompted the FASB to issue *Statement No. 12*, which requires the use of the **lower of aggregate cost or market** method by all companies that do not have specialized accounting practices in accounting for marketable equity securities.[7] The FASB concludes that nonprofit organizations, mutual life insurance companies, employee benefit plans, and nonmarketable securities are excluded from the valuation procedures outlined in *Statement No. 12*.

Recording the Investment at the Date of Acquisition

Before discussing the various accounting methods, there are a few general rules applicable to the initial recording of all investments in stock that need to be explained.

At the date of acquisition of an investment in stock, the investment account is debited for the total cost of the investment. The total cost includes the basic cost of the security (e.g., the fair market value) plus brokerage fees and other transfer costs incurred in the purchase. Stock normally is purchased for cash, on margin, or on a subscription basis. When stock is acquired on margin or on a subscription basis, only part of the purchase price is paid initially, and the remainder is borrowed. The stock still is recorded at cost, and the liability is recognized. Interest

---

[6] Ibid.

[7] "Accounting For Certain Marketable Securities," *Statement of Financial Accounting Standards No. 12* (Stamford, Conn.: FASB, 1975).

paid on a subscription contract or on funds borrowed is expensed; the interest is not capitalized as part of the cost of the investment.

When property or services are exchanged for the investment, the cost assigned to the investment should be the fair market value of the consideration surrendered or the fair market value of the consideration received, whichever is more reasonably determinable. If neither market value can be determined, an estimate or appraisal should be used.

When two or more classes of securities are purchased in a single transaction, the total purchase price is allocated to the securities based on their relative fair market values. For example, if a block of Security C purchased alone is worth $1,000, and a block of Security H purchased alone is worth $3,000, one-fourth of the total lump-sum cost would be allocated to Security C and three-fourths to Security H, whether the total cost is $4,000 or some other amount. If one security has a known market value and the other does not, the known market value is used for that security, and the remainder of the cost is allocated to the other. If neither market value is known, it is better to wait until at least one market value is established before any allocation is made.

Accounting for numerous purchases of securities requires that the cost of the individual purchases and the dates of the purchases and sales be established. If specific identification is not possible, an average cost may be used for multiple purchases in the same class of stock. The first-in, first-out method (FIFO) of assigning costs to investments at the time of sale also is acceptable and is used most commonly.

Accounting for Equity Investments Subsequent to Acquisition

In *Statement No. 12*, the FASB established the guidelines for investments in marketable equity securitites. Generally, a **marketable equity security** is a share of stock (preferred or common), or a stock option or warrant on which a market price can be determined.

The FASB defines marketable equity securities as follows:

> An equity security is any instrument representing ownership shares (e.g., common, preferred, and other capital stock) or the right to acquire (e.g., warrants, rights, and call options) or dispose of (e.g., put options) ownership shares in an enterprise at fixed or determinable prices. The term does not encompass preferred stock that by its terms either must be redeemed by the issuing enterprise or is redeemable at the option of the investor, nor does it include treasury stock or convertible bonds.

> Marketable, as applied to an equity security, means an equity security as to which sales prices or bid and ask prices are currently available on a national securities exchange (i.e., those registered with the Securities and Exchange Commission) or in the over-the-counter market.[8]

FASB #12

---

[8]Ibid., par. 7. In the over-the-counter market a security shall be considered marketable when a quotation is reported publicly by the National Association of Securities Dealers Automatic Quotations System or by the National Quotations Bureau, Inc. (provided in the latter case that quotations are available from at least three dealers).

Stock for which sale is restricted by a government or contractual requirement is not marketable.[9]

The determination of marketability is made at the balance sheet date. A temporary lack of a market (no listings for the security) does not necessarily preclude an equity security from being marketable, as long as a market did exist at a date closely preceding the balance sheet date. Also, if the balance sheet date falls on a day when the markets are closed, the valuation is made when the market subsequently is reopened.

There are basically four methods that are used, depending on the circumstances, in accounting for investments in stock subsequent to the acquisition of an investment when control of the investee does not exist. These methods are (1) the cost method, (2) the market value method, (3) the lower of cost or market method, and (4) the equity method. The cost and market value methods are used in specialized industries. The lower of cost or market method is used when the investor does not have significant influence over the investee. The equity method is used when the investor has significant influence over the investee.

The Cost Method

Under the **cost method** of valuation, the securities are recorded at cost and are carried in the balance sheet at that amount. If the market value becomes less than cost by a substantial amount and if the decline in market is not due to a mere temporary condition, then the securities are written down to the market value. Under the cost method this valuation would be treated as the new cost basis for the security, and subsequent recoveries in market value would never be recognized. When the security is sold, the amount of the gain or loss recognized is equal to the difference between the cost of the investment as represented on the balance sheet and the fair value of the consideration received.

The major objection to the cost method is that an investment is overstated in the balance sheet when a temporary market decline has occurred. Under the cost method identical assets are represented by different amounts on the balance sheet simply because they were acquired at different times. Income can be manipulated by selecting which units are to be sold if there is more than one lot of the same security. The cost method does have its advantages, however. It is the same valuation used for most other assets and is acceptable to the IRS for income tax determination. It is also the most objective valuation alternative.

The cost method is used most commonly in practice when accounting for nonmarketable or nonequity securities. The cost method is used also by investors reporting under the equity method—that is, accountants will account for their investments at cost between reporting dates and will convert to the equity method at the end of the period.

The Market Method

Under the **market method** of valuing marketable equity securities, the securities should be classified into current and noncurrent portfolios.

---

[9] If it can be reasonably expected that a restricted security can qualify for sale within one year of the balance sheet date, and a market price quotation is available as of the balance sheet date, that security is deemed marketable (FASB *Interpretation No. 16*).

The **current portfolio** is a list of all of the marketable equity securities that are classified as current assets. the **noncurrent portfolio** is a list of all the marketable equity securities that are classified as noncurrent assets.

In theory, these groups of investments, or investment portfolios, are considered and accounted for as a single asset. Both the current and the noncurrent portfolios are valued at the aggregate market value of the securities at the end of each accounting period. Any difference in carrying amount from one period to the next results in a **holding gain** or **loss**, depending on the direction of the net change in market value. Once the holding gains or losses are determined, they can be accounted for in one of two ways:

1. They can be recognized in the period as adjustments to the income statement. These gains (or losses) would be treated as nonoperating items and come before "income from continuing operations."
2. The holding gains are treated as unrecognized capital and are recognized only when actually disposed of. These gains would be classified on the balance sheet under owners' equity as "unrealized capital." (Losses would be written off immediately as in "1" above).

Both of these methods are observed in practice.

Reporting investments at market informs the reader of the real value of the portfolio. Also, because investments are assets that management has chosen to substitute for cash, it would seem that the cash value of the asset should be reported in the financial statements. Unfortunately, the recognition of unrealized gains contradicts the revenue realization principle of accounting, and therefore is not considered GAAP, except in certain industry exceptions.

The Lower of Cost or Market Method

When an investor purchases marketable equity securities, the investment initially is recorded at the total acquisition cost by a debit to marketable equity securities and a credit to cash or to a liability account. However, FASB *Statement No. 12* requires that after acquisition the investment should be reflected in the accounts at the lower of aggregate cost or market when there is no significant influence. The first step in applying *Statement No. 12* is to divide all of the marketable equity securities into a current and a noncurrent portfolio. If the financial statements of an enterprise include a classified balance sheet (one in which current assets and noncurrent assets are separated), then marketable equity securities should be classified as either current or noncurrent assets. If a classified balance sheet is not prepared, all marketable equity securities are considered to be noncurrent. The determination of the current or noncurrent classification is related to marketability and the intent of management. If the securities have a ready market and if management intends to dispose of a security within one year or the normal operating cycle, whichever is longer, the security should be classified as current and placed in the current portfolio. If the security does not have a ready market or if management intends to hold a security for a period longer than one year or the normal operating cycle, the security should be classified as noncurrent and placed in the noncurrent portfolio. The current and noncurrent portfolios will be discussed separately in order to illustrate the basic accounting differences between them.

Equity Securities—Current Portfolio. As stated previously, if the financial statements of an enterprise include a classified balance sheet, then the short-term investments in marketable equity securities are classified as current assets. To determine lower of cost or market, the accountant places the securities in a current portfolio to compare their aggregate cost and aggregate market value. The FASB concluded in *Statement No. 12* that the carrying amount of a marketable equity securities portfolio shall be the lower of its *aggregate* cost or *aggregate* market value, determined at the balance sheet date. The aggregate cost of the portfolio is determined easily because it is the sum of the individual security costs. To determine the aggregate market value, you multiply the market price of each individual security by the number of shares of that security owned by the investor. The resulting amount is referred to as the aggregate market price or market value of the security. The sum of these individual market values is the aggregate market value for the entire portfolio.

If the aggregate market value is less than the aggregate cost at the balance sheet date, an allowance account is established to reduce the portfolio from cost to market.[10] This amount also is recognized as an unrealized loss and is included in the determination of net income for the period. Once the portfolio has been written down to market, it may be written up as a result of a subsequent recovery in the market value of the securities in the portfolio. However, this write-up can never exceed the amount required to restore the portfolio to its cost basis.

If the aggregate market value is greater than the aggregate cost at the balance sheet date, the portfolio is carried in the accounts at cost. If a balance exists in the valuation allowance account, it should be eliminated. This balance also will be recognized as a recovery of a loss and will be included in the determination of net income for the period.

The following example will illustrate the application of the lower of cost or market method to the current portfolio. A series of transactions and entries for Lee Corporation, a calendar-year corporation, are presented below:

January 10, 1981—Purchased 10,000 shares of Security A at a market price of $5 per share (total cost = $50,000).

February 27, 1981—Purchased 3,000 shares of Security B at a market price of $10 per share (total cost = $30,000).

June 19, 1981—Purchased 2,000 shares of Security C at a market price of $11 per share (total cost = $22,000).

In each case above, the number of shares purchased was less than 20% of the outstanding shares of the investee corporation. Each of the purchases is recorded initially at the total acquisition cost by a debit to "marketable equity securities—current."

---

[10] Any valuation allowance that was established before the application of *Statement No. 12* must be eliminated by a credit to income. This restores the marketable equity securities to their original cost basis.

On December 31, 1981, Lee Corporation determined the carrying amount of its current portfolio to be as follows:

| | | December 31, 1981 | |
	Cost	Market	Unrealized Gain (Loss)
Marketable equity securities—current			
Security A	$ 50,000	$45,000	$(5,000)
Security B	30,000	32,000	2,000
Security C	22,000	20,000	(2,000)
Total—current portfolio	$102,000	$97,000	$(5,000)
Balance—valuation allowance			$(5,000)

For 1981 the aggregate market value is $5,000 less than the aggregate cost. The difference between cost and market for individual securities is not considered. The $5,000 decline in the current portfolio is recognized as an *unrealized* loss because the securities have not been sold to an outside party. The journal entry to record the unrealized loss is as follows:

Net unrealized loss on current marketable equity securities	5,000	
Valuation allowance for net unrealized loss on current marketable equity securities		5,000

The net unrealized loss will be reflected on the income statement in 1981 as an item of "other expense" included in income from continuing operations. The valuation allowance is a contra-asset account and will be shown on the balance sheet as a reduction of the current marketable equity securities account.

During 1982 Lee Corporation did not sell or purchase any marketable equity securities. On December 31, 1982 Lee determined the carrying amount of its current portfolio to be as follows:

| | | December 31, 1982 | |
	Cost	Market	Unrealized Gain (Loss)
Marketable equity securities—current			
Security A	$ 50,000	$49,000	$(1,000)
Security B	30,000	28,000	(2,000)
Security C	22,000	22,000	–0–
Total—current portfolio	$102,000	$99,000	$(3,000)
Balance—valuation allowance			$(3,000)

As can be seen, in 1982 there was a market recovery in the current portfolio ($97,000 to $99,000). However, on December 31, 1982 the aggregate market value was still less than the aggregate cost by $3,000. Therefore, the balance in the valuation allowance account must be reduced from the prior 1981 balance of $5,000 to the required balance of $3,000 (i.e., a reduction of $2,000). The following journal entry would be necessary:

Valuation allowance for net unrealized loss on current marketable equity securities	2,000	
Recovery of unrealized loss on current marketable equity securities		2,000

The recovery of the unrealized loss is reported as an item of "other income" included in income from continuing operations. The valuation allowance, with a current balance of $3,000, would reduce the cost basis of the securities from $102,000 to the market value of $99,000.

During 1983 Lee Corporation did not sell or purchase any marketable equity securities. Lee determined the carrying amount of its current portfolio on December 31, 1983, to be as follows:

	Cost	*Market*	*Unrealized Gain (Loss)*
		December 31, 1983	
Marketable equity securities—current			
Security A	$ 50,000	$51,000	$1,000
Security B	30,000	30,000	–0–
Security C	22,000	25,000	3,000
Total—current portfolio	$102,000	$106,000	$4,000
Balance—valuation allowance			–0–

On December 31, 1983, the market value of the current portfolio is greater than cost. A write-up is allowed only to the original cost basis; therefore, the amount is limited to $3,000. This is the amount needed to eliminate the valuation allowance account so that the securities will be reported on the financial statements at cost. The entry to adjust the current portfolio would be as follows:

Valuation allowance for net unrealized loss on current marketable equity securities	3,000	
Recovery of unrealized loss on current marketable equity securities		3,000

The valuation allowance account has been reduced now to zero. Therefore, the current marketable equity security portfolio will be carried at cost ($102,000) on the balance sheet. The recovery of the unrealized loss will be included in income from continuing operations as an item of other income. Under no circumstances can the cumulative recoveries of unrealized losses recorded exceed the cumulative unrealized losses.

The FASB does not think the reversal of a write-down represents recognition of an unrealized gain. The unrealized gain is the excess of the market value over cost, or the $4,000 net difference between the aggregate cost and the aggregate market value of Lee's portfolio on December 31, 1983. The FASB views the write-down as establishing a valuation allowance that represents the estimated reduction in the realizable value of the portfolio. A subsequent market increase reduces or eliminates the requirement for such an allowance. In the FASB's view, the reversal of the write-down represents a change in an accounting estimate of an unrealized loss.[11]

Sales of securities in the current portfolio are treated the same as they are under the noncurrent portfolio. These are illustrated next.

Equity Securities—Noncurrent Portfolio. Investments in marketable equity securities that management intends to hold longer than one year, or the normal operating cycle, are classified as noncurrent assets. A long-term investment in equity securities is recorded initially in the accounts at total acquisition cost. Subsequently, it is reflected in the accounts at lower of cost or market. Accounting for noncurrent marketable equity securities is basically the same as accounting for marketable equity securities classified as current assets. However, for the noncurrent portfolio it is necessary first to evaluate each security at the balance sheet date to determine if there has been a permanent decline in the value of the security. The accounting treatment applicable to a permanent decline will be discussed later in this section. Another important difference between accounting for noncurrent and current assets is the accounting treatment of unrealized losses. The net unrealized loss that relates to the noncurrent portfolio is *not* included in income, as it is in the current portfolio. Instead, the loss is included in the stockholders' equity section of the balance sheet as a contra-equity account. It should be placed below retained earnings but before treasury stock.

For example, assume that Lee Corporation has the following carrying amount for its noncurrent portfolio on December 31, 1982. All declines in market value are determined to be temporary.

	Cost	*Market*	*Unrealized Gain (Loss)*
		December 31, 1982	
Marketable equity securities—noncurrent			
Security D	$ 40,000	$ 35,000	$(5,000)
Security E	70,000	68,000	(2,000)
Total—noncurrent portfolio	$110,000	$103,000	$(7,000)
Balance—valuation allowance			$(7,000)

The net unrealized loss for 1982 is $7,000 ($110,000 − $103,000). The required journal entry appears at the top of page 235.

---

[11] "Certain Marketable Securities," par. 29 (c).

Net unrealized loss on noncurrent marketable equity securities	7,000	
Valuation allowance for unrealized loss on noncurrent marketable equity securities		7,000

The valuation allowance account is a contra-asset account and will be shown as a reduction from the noncurrent marketable equity securities account (just as the current valuation allowance was shown as a reduction from the current portfolio). The net unrealized loss will be included in the stockholders' equity as a contra-equity account.

On February 6, 1983, Lee sold one-half of Security E for net proceeds of $25,000. The difference between the net proceeds received from the sale and the original cost of the security represents a *realized* loss. At the date of sale, the *realized* loss is determined without considering previously recorded unrealized losses, recoveries, or the amount accumulated in the valuation allowance account. The allowance account is ignored because it relates to the total portfolio, not to the individual securities in the portfolio. The individual securities do not have a book value other than their original cost. Hence, the allowance account is ignored, and the realized gain or loss is defined as the difference between the individual security's selling price and its original cost.

The journal entry required to record this sale would be as follows:

Cash	25,000	
Realized loss on sale of marketable equity securities	10,000	
Marketable equity securities—noncurrent (at cost)		35,000

If the net proceeds had been greater than $35,000, Lee Corporation would have incurred a *realized* gain on the sale. No adjustment is made to the valuation allowance on the date of sale. At the balance sheet date, however, the effects of the sale will be reflected in the carrying amount of the noncurrent portfolio.

On December 31, 1983, Lee Corporation determined the carrying amount of its noncurrent portfolio to be as follows:

		December 31, 1983	
	Cost	*Market*	*Unrealized Gain (Loss)*
Marketable equity securities—noncurrent			
Security D	$40,000	$38,000	$(2,000)
Security E	35,000	34,500	(500)
Total—noncurrent portfolio	$75,000	$72,500	$(2,500)
Balance—valuation allowance			$ 2,500)

The necessary entry to reduce the valuation allowance account to $2,500 is below:

Valuation allowance for unrealized loss on noncurrent marketable equity securities	4,500	
Net unrealized loss on noncurrent marketable equity securities		4,500

Remember that the unrealized loss in 1982 of $7,000 was shown on the balance sheet. Therefore, the entry in 1983 is an adjustment to this existing unrealized loss account, rather than a recovery of a loss. In effect, the entry for the noncurrent portfolio is merely a reversal of the entry used to record the initial decline. The subsequent write-up cannot cause the portfolio to exceed its original cost basis.

Permanent Declines in Value. For marketable equity securities in the noncurrent portfolio, the FASB refers to declines in value that are "other than temporary."[12] These declines will be referred to as **permanent declines** in value. If a permanent decline exists at the balance sheet date, the individual security is written down to its market value, which then becomes the new cost basis for subsequent periods. The amount of this write-down is accounted for as a realized loss and is reported on the current income statement, even though there has been no transaction with an outside party. The new cost basis will be used for all future comparisons of cost and market.

For example, assume first that Raider Company has the following securities included in its noncurrent portfolio on December 31, 1981:

		December 31, 1981	
	Cost	Market	Unrealized Gain (Loss)
Marketable equity securities—noncurrent			
IBM, Inc.	$25,000	$21,000	$(4,000)
Southland Farms Co.	45,000	40,000	(5,000)
Total—noncurrent portfolio	$70,000	$61,000	$(9,000)

Then, assume that the decline in value of the Southland stock ($5,000) is determined to be permanent. Below is the journal entry to record the decline:

Realized loss on noncurrent marketable equity securities	5,000	
Marketable equity securities—Southland Farms Co.		5,000

---

[12] Ibid., par. 21.

The realized loss would be shown on the income statement as an item of other expense included in income from continuing operations. The new cost basis for the Southland security is $40,000 ($45,000 − $5,000 write-down). This new cost basis will be carried forward to 1982 and will be used in future comparisons of cost and market.

Transfers Between Portfolios. If there is a change in the classification of an individual security between current and noncurrent, the security must be transferred at the lower of its cost or market value at the date of transfer. If market value is less than cost, the market value becomes the new cost basis, and the difference is treated as a realized loss in determining income for the period.

For example, assume that Raider Company transferred the IBM stock from its noncurrent portfolio to its current portfolio on June 18, 1982. On this date the market value of the security was $22,000. The change in classification would be recorded as follows:

Marketable equity securities—current	22,000	
Realized loss on transfer between noncurrent and current portfolios	3,000	
Marketable equity securities—noncurrent		25,000

The realized loss would be included in the income statement as an item of other expense. The IBM stock will have a new cost basis of $22,000 and will be carried at that amount in the current portfolio. If the market value of the IBM stock had been above $25,000 on the date of transfer, the security would have been transferred at cost, and no loss would have been recognized. The following journal entry would have been made:

Marketable equity securities—current	25,000	
Marketable equity securities—noncurrent		25,000

The Equity Method

In *Opinion No. 18* the APB concluded that the **equity method** best enables investors in corporate joint ventures to reflect the underlying nature of their investment in those ventures. Therefore, investors should use the equity method to account for investments in the common stock of corporate joint ventures, both in consolidated financial statements and in parent company financial statements.

The equity method is conceptually different from the cost, market, and lower of cost or market methods. Under the equity method the investor recognizes investment income based on his or her proportionate share of the investee's earnings, whereas under the other methods the investor recognizes income based on the receipt of investee dividends. The equity method is based on the presumption that the investor has the ability to exert significant influence over the operating and financial policies of the investee company. This significant influence may be demonstrated in any of the ways discussed earlier. Remember, without evidence to the contrary, an investor with a 20% or greater interest in the voting common stock is deemed to exert significant influence over the operating and financing policies of the investee.

Under the equity method an investor initially records an investment in the stock of an investee at cost. The carrying amount of this investment subsequently is adjusted to recognize the investor's proportionate share of the earnings of the investee. The investor also must compute the goodwill purchased from the investee, as well as any difference between the book value and market value of other investee assets. The APB established the following guidelines for applying the equity method. The investment carrying amount is adjusted as follows:

1. Increase (decrease) to reflect the investor's proportionate share of investee earnings (losses) (intercompany profits and losses should be eliminated until realized by the investor or investee).
2. Decrease by the investor's proportionate share of cash dividends paid by the investee.
3. Increase or decrease by amortizing any difference between the investor's initial cost and the investor's proportionate share of the underlying equity in the net assets of the investee at the date of acquisition (this difference between the actual cost and the book value at the acquisition date is amortized over the life of the assets involved).[13]

The combined effects of these adjustments are included in the determination of the investor's reported net income. This reported net income also must reflect the investor's proportionate share of the investee's extraordinary items and prior period adjustments when these amounts are material to the investor's net income.

Finally, a situation may arise indicating that a decrease, which is other than temporary, has occurred in the value of the investment. In this circumstance, the decline in value should be recognized even though recognition reduces the carrying amount of the investment below the equity method valuation.

Purchase Price Greater Than Book Value. In most cases the investor will pay a price that is in excess of the book value of the assets he has acquired because book values do not reflect the current value of the assets.

As an illustration of the equity method when the purchase price is in excess of the book value, assume the following:

1. Tom, Inc. purchased 25,000 shares of Grad, Inc.'s 100,000 shares of outstanding common stock for $10,000,000 on January 1, 1982.
2. The book value of Grad, Inc. was $36,000,000 at the date of acquisition.
3. Any excess purchase price over the book value is attributed to undervalued depreciable assets of Grad, Inc. that have a remaining useful life of eight

---

[13] "The Equity Method," par. 19.

years and to Grad, Inc.'s goodwill, which Tom, Inc. would amortize over a 40-year period.

4. For the year 1982, Grad, Inc. reports net income of $4,000,000 and pays cash dividends of $1,000,000 on June 30 and December 31.

To apply the equity method, Tom, Inc. must compute the goodwill purchased and must identify assets of the investee that have a market value different from their book value at the acquisition date.

Purchase price (for 25% interest)	$10,000,000
Book value of net assets purchased (25% × $36,000,000)	9,000,000
Excess cost over book value	$ 1,000,000

This excess is to be allocated to the following:
1. To specific undervalued depreciable assets of Grad, Inc.
2. The unallocated excess is attributed to goodwill.

The relevant values of Grad, Inc. at the acquisition date are shown in Exhibit 7-2. The data indicate that the fair value of the depreciable assets is $3,200,000 greater than their book value. Since Tom, Inc. purchased 25% of Grad, Inc., $800,000 of the excess of the purchase price over the book value of the assets is attributable to a difference between the book value and fair value of depreciable assets. The remaining $200,000 is goodwill.

Exhibit 7-2
GRAD, INC.
Partial Values

	Book Value	Fair Value
Nondepreciable assets	$30,000,000	$30,000,000
Depreciable assets (8-year life, straight-line deprec.)	6,000,000	9,200,000
Total	$36,000,000	$39,200,000
Liabilities	$15,000,000	$15,000,000
Stockholders' equity	21,000,000	
Total	$36,000,000	

The allocation would be made as follows:

Excess of cost over book value	$1,000,000
Allocated to depreciable assets ($9,200,000 − $6,000,000 = $3,200,000 × 25%)	800,000
Unallocated excess = goodwill	$ 200,000

Exhibit 7-3

TOM, INC.
Entries to Apply Equity Method to Investment in Tom, Inc.

Jan. 1, 1981	Investment in Grad, Inc. stock	10,000,000	
	Cash		10,000,000
	To record the investment at cost.		
June 30, 1982	Cash	250,000	
	Investment in Grad, Inc. stock		250,000
	To recognize as a return of capital Tom, Inc.'s proportionate share (25% × $1,000,000 of Grad, Inc.'s cash dividend).		
Dec. 31, 1982	Cash	250,000	
	Investment in Grad, Inc. stock		250,000
	Same as June 30.		
	Investment in Grad, Inc. stock	1,000,000	
	Equity in Grad, Inc. earnings		1,000,000
	To recognize Tom, Inc.'s proportionate share (25% × $4,000,000) of Grad, Inc.'s net income. The equity account will be shown on Tom, Inc.'s income statement.		
	Equity in Grad, Inc. earnings	105,000	
	Investment in Grad, Inc. stock		105,000
	To recognize the depreciation of the undervalued assets and to amortize the goodwill of Grad, Inc.		

Assets:

$800,000 ÷ 8 years = $100,000

Goodwill:

$200,000 ÷ 40 years = $5,000

$105,000

Tom, Inc. would record the entries in Exhibit 7-3 to reflect its investment in Grad, Inc.

The December 31, 1982, carrying amount of investment in Grad, Inc. stock is computed as follows:

Purchase Price (1–1–82)	$10,000,000	
Add: Share of 1981 income	1,000,000	$11,000,000
Deduct:		
June 30 dividend	250,000	
December 31 dividend	250,000	
Depreciation of undervalued assets	100,000	
Amortization of goodwill	5,000	605,000
Carrying amount (12–31–82)		$10,395,000

Tom, Inc. will present the $10,395,000 carrying amount in its balance sheet in the long-term investments section. The net equity in Grad, Inc. earnings ($1,000,000 − $105,000) of $895,000 will be presented in Tom, Inc.'s income statement.

Frequently, part of the difference between the purchase price and the book value is from nondepreciable assets having a market value in excess of their book value. When this occurs, there must be an adjustment to the equity in earnings account when the investee realizes the increased market value. For example, assume the same information as before for Grad, Inc. (Exhibit 7-2) except that now the market value of the nondepreciable assets is $30,100,000. The goodwill will be $100,000, as illustrated in Exhibit 7-4. The excess of cost over book value that is attributable to depreciable assets and goodwill will be treated in the same manner as in the previous illustration except that the goodwill amortization is now cut in half.

The treatment of the excess of cost over book value of the amount attributable to the *nondepreciable* assets is dependent upon the asset or assets to which it relates. For example, assume that the excess is related to investments in securities whose market value was $100,000 more than their cost at the date of Tom's

---

Exhibit 7-4
Goodwill Determination
Market Value of Depreciable and Nondepreciable Assets in Excess of Cost

Excess of cost over book value (as determined previously)		$1,000,000
Less: Allocations to		
Nondepreciable assets	$100,000	
Depreciable assets	800,000	900,000
Goodwill		$ 100,000

purchase of Grad's stock. Also assume that these securities were sold at a $120,000 gain in 1982 after Tom's investment in Grad, Inc.'s stock. In this situation Grad's income of $4,000,000 would include a gain of $120,000 on the sale of investments. Since Tom, Inc. purchased Grad, Inc. stock when Grad's investment in securities had a market value of $100,000 in excess of book value, Tom's $10,000,000 purchase price already reflected $100,000 of the $120,000 gain. Therefore, as far as Tom is concerned in applying the equity method, only the unrecognized portion of the gain ($20,000) should be included in its equity in earnings account. In the previous illustration (Exhibit 7-3) Tom recognized $1,000,000 (25%) of Grad's income on December 31, 1982. This includes 25% of Grad's gain of $120,000 on the sale of investments. Since $100,000 of this was recognized previously in Tom's purchase price of Grad's shares, Tom should have recognized only 25% of $20,000 ($120,000 − $100,000) as an increase in equity and earnings. Therefore, the following adjustment would be necessary:

Equity in Grad, Inc. earnings	25,000*	
Investment in Grad, Inc. stock		25,000

*($100,000 × 0.25)
  To adjust the earnings from
  the investment in Grad, Inc.
  to eliminate the portion of the
  gain on nondepreciable assets
  that was recognized in the
  acquisition price of Grad, Inc.

This is a one-time adjustment in the year in which the investee company disposes of the nondepreciable asset in question. If Grad, Inc. did not sell the securities until 1983, the entry above would not be made until 1983.

Frequently the excess over cost relating to nondepreciable assets is attributable to inventory, particularly when the LIFO inventory method is used. As long as inventory levels remain constant or increase, no adjustment is needed. If inventories decrease, an adjustment will be necessary to recognize the fact that part of the difference between book value and market value that existed on the date of the investor's acquisition has been realized by the investee and is included in the investee's reported income. Therefore, the investor will have to remove its portion of the difference from its investment and income account in an entry similar to that above.

Purchase Price Less Than Book Value. In the preceding illustrations the purchase price exceeded the underlying book value. An investor may acquire an investment at a cost less than the underlying book value. When this occurs, the investor's proportionate share of the investee's noncurrent assets (except for marketable equity securities) will be reduced proportionately, based on their fair value, to reflect the investor's cost of the investment. If noncurrent assets are reduced to zero and unallocated excess book value still exists, then the excess book value is assigned to a deferred credit account titled "negative goodwill."

Negative goodwill will be amortized as an increment to investment income for a period not to exceed 40 years.

When the book value of depreciable assets is reduced, an amount equal to the excess depreciation based on the difference between the investee's depreciation expense and the investor's depreciation expense (based on the investor's cost) is an increment to income. For example, assume that in the previous example Tom, Inc. paid only $8,000,000 for a 25% investment in Grad, Inc. The cost is less than the investor's proportionate book value of $9,000,000. Now, assume this difference is due solely to specific depreciable assets with an eight-year life that Grad, Inc. has overvalued. Tom's 25% of the $4,000,000 difference between book value and fair value must be amortized as an adjustment to earnings from Grad, Inc. over the eight-year useful life of the assets as follows:

Grad, Inc. Asset Valuation

	Book Value	*Fair Value*
Depreciable Assets	$6,000,000	$2,000,000

The entry at December 31, 1982, to reflect this circumstance is as follows:

Investment in Grad, Inc. stock	125,000	
Equity in Grad, Inc. earnings		125,000
To allocate excess depreciation		
to Grad, Inc. investment		
income ($1,000,000 ÷ 8 years		
= $125,000).		

Losses Exceed Carrying Amount.   A situation may arise in which the investor's proportionate share of investee losses exceeds the investor's carrying amount of the investment. Ordinarily, the investor should discontinue applying the equity method when the investment carrying amount is reduced to zero and should not provide for additional losses. However, when the investor's potential loss is not limited to the amount of the original investment (by guarantee of investee obligations or other commitments to provide future financial support), or when imminent return to profitable operations by the investee is assured, it is appropriate for the investor to provide for additional losses.[14] When the carrying amount of the investment is written down to zero and the equity method has been discontinued, the investor should resume applying the equity method only when the investor's proportionate share of investee earnings has equaled the investor's proportionate share of investee losses not recognized during the period in which the equity method was suspended.

Change from the Equity Method.   When an investor's level of influence over an investee falls below the level required for continued use of the equity method, a

[14] An imminent return to profitable operations could be assured when the investee suffers an extraordinary loss in the current period but expects to return to normal profits in all succeeding periods.

change to the appropriate method of accounting for the investment is required. No adjustment should be made to the current carrying amount of the investment. All earnings, losses, dividends, and amortizations previously affecting the carrying amount of the investment should remain the same. Again, when a change from the equity method is made, the cost basis for future accounting purposes is the carrying amount of the investment at the date the level of investor influence over the investee is reduced. As an illustration of a change from the equity method, assume the following:

1. Bum, Inc. currently owns 20% of the common stock of Saints, Inc. Bum, Inc. uses the equity method to account for this investment.
2. On January 1, 1982, Bum, Inc. sells 50% of its investment in Saints, Inc. for $250,000. Bum, Inc.'s total investment has a carrying amount of $426,000 on this date.
3. Saints, Inc. pays $50,000 cash dividend to its common shareholders on June 20, 1981. Saints, Inc. reports a $100,000 net income for the year ended December 31, 1981.

Bum, Inc. would record the following entries for 1982:

Jan. 1, 1982	Cash	250,000	
	Gain on sale of investments		37,000
	Investment in Saints, Inc. stock		213,000
	To record sale of investment. Ownership is now 10%. The equity method is no longer applied.		
June 30, 1982	Cash	5,000	
	Dividend income		5,000
	To record cash dividends received (1/10 × $50,000).		
Dec. 31, 1982	No entry		

Change to the Equity Method. An investment in the common stock of an investee that was accounted for previously under a method other than the equity method may qualify for the use of the equity method. A change in the level of the investor's ownership or any event that allows the investor to exert significant influence over the investee can qualify that investor for use of the equity method. When the requirements have been met, the investor should adopt the equity method. A change to the equity method requires retroactive adjustment of the carrying amount of the investment, results of operations, and retained earnings of the investor in a step-by-step acquisition manner as if the equity method had been in effect during all previous periods in which the investment was held. For example, assume the following:

1. On January 2, 1981, Bama, Inc. purchased, for $100,000 cash, 10% of the outstanding shares of Jam, Inc. common stock. On that date the net assets of

Exhibit 7-5
BAMA COMPANY
Entries for Change to Equity Method

Jan. 2, 1981	Investment in Jam, Inc. stock	100,000	
	Cash		100,000
	To record purchase of 10%		
	of Jam, Inc. common stock.		
Dec. 31, 1981	Cash	8,000	
	Dividend income		8,000
	To record receipt of Jam,		
	Inc. cash dividend (10% ×		
	$80,000).		
Dec. 31, 1982	Cash	10,000	
	Dividend income		10,000
	To record receipt of Jam,		
	Inc. cash dividend (10% ×		
	$100,000).		
Jan. 2, 1983	Investment in Jam, Inc. stock	280,000	
	Cash		250,000
	Retained earnings		30,000
	To record the purchase of		
	an additional 20% interest		
	in Jam, Inc. and to reflect		
	a retroactive change from		
	the lower of cost or market		
	method to the equity		
	method of accounting for		
	the investment. The $30,000		
	adjustment is computed in		
	Exhibit 7-6.		
Dec. 31, 1983	Investment in Jam, Inc. stock	120,000	
	Equity in Jam, Inc. earnings		120,000
	To record Bama, Inc.		
	proportionate share of		
	Jam, Inc. earnings (30% ×		
	$400,000		
	Cash	45,000	
	Investment in Jam, Inc. stock		45,000
	To record as a return of		
	capital Bama, Inc.'s		
	proportionate share of		
	Jam, Inc. dividends		
	(30% × $150,000).		

Exhibit 7-5 (continued)
BAMA COMPANY
Entries for Change to Equity Method

Equity in Jam, Inc. earnings	2,250	
Investment in Jam, Inc. stock		2,250
To record amortization		
of excess cost over book value		
to goodwill		
1981 purchase: [$100,000 −		
(10% × $600,000)] ÷		
40 years = $1,000		
1983 purchase: [$250,000 −		
(20% × $1,000,000)] ÷		
40 years =	1,250	
Total	$2,250	

Jam, Inc. had a book value of $600,000. The excess of cost over the underlying equity in net assets is attributed to goodwill, which is amortized over 40 years.

common stock for $250,000. The book value of Jam, Inc.'s net assets is now $1,000,000. (Bama, Inc. now owns 30% of Jam, Inc. and must use the equity method.)

3. Jam, Inc.'s net income and cash dividends for 1981 through 1983 are as follows:

Exhibit 7-6
BAMA, INC.
Calculation of Retroactive Adjustment
For Change to Equity Method

	1981	1982	Total
1. Bama, Inc. equity in Jam, Inc. earnings (10%)	$20,000	$30,000	$50,000
2. Amortization of excess cost over book value to goodwill [$100,000 − (10% × $600,000)] ÷ 40 years = $1,000 per year	(1,000)	(1,000)	(2,000)
3. Dividends received	(8,000)	(10,000)	(18,000)
Retroactive adjustment	$11,000	$19,000	$30,000

Year	Net Income	Cash Dividends to Common Shareholders
1981	$200,000	$ 80,000
1982	300,000	100,000
1983	400,000	150,000

The entries in Exhibit 7-5 would be made by Bama, Inc. to record its investment in Jam, Inc. and to record Bama, Inc.'s subsequent change to the equity method. Included in these adjustments is one to retroactively account for the change from the lower of cost or market method of recording the investment to the equity method. The calculations for this retroactive adjustment are presented in Exhibit 7-6.

A change to the equity method is accomplished by placing the accounts related to the investment and affected by it on the same basis as if the equity method always had been the basis of accounting for that investment.

Financial Statement Disclosures

The disclosure requirements for investments in securities carried under both the lower of cost or market method and the equity method are presented below. In each case the requirements are set forth first, followed by an illustration of the required disclosures.

Lower of Cost or Market Method

FASB *Statement No. 12* requires the following disclosures for the lower of cost or market method of accounting:

1. As of the date of each balance sheet presented, the total cost and the total market value should be disclosed either in the body of the financial statements or in the accompanying notes. When a classified balance sheet is pre-

FASB 12

Exhibit 7-7
LEE CORPORATION
Partial Income Statement

	Year Ended December 31	
	1983	1982
Other income:		
Recovery of unrealized loss on current marketable equity securities	$ 3,000	$2,000
Other expense:		
Realized loss on sale of marketable equity securities	(10,000)	

sented, this information should be segregated between the current and noncurrent portfolios.

2. For the latest balance sheet presented, gross unrealized gains and gross unrealized losses must be presented. They also should be divided between the current and noncurrent portfolios.

3. For each period for which an income statement is presented, the following items must be disclosed:

    a. The net realized gains and losses included in the determination of net income.

    b. The basis on which cost was determined in computing the gains and losses.

Exhibit 7-8
LEE CORPORATION
Balance Sheet

	Year Ended December 31	
	1983	*1982*
Current assets		
Short-term investments:		
Marketable equity securities—current (carried at cost in 1983 and at market in 1982 (Note 1)	$102,000	$ 99,000
Noncurrent assets		
Long-term investments:		
Marketable equity securities—noncurrent (carried at market) (Note 1)	72,500	103,000
Stockholders' equity		
Unrealized capital:		
Net unrealized loss on noncurrent marketable equity securities (Note 1)	(2,500)	(7,000)

NOTE 1. Marketable equity securities are carried at the lower of cost or market method at the balance sheet date. Marketable equity securities included in current assets had an aggregate cost at December 31, 1982, of $102,000 and an aggregate market value at December 31, 1983, of $106,000. The aggregate cost of the marketable equity securities included in noncurrent assets was $110,000 at December 31, 1982, and $75,000 at December 31, 1983.

At December 31, 1983, there were gross unrealized gains of $4,000 pertaining to the current portfolio and gross unrealized losses of $2,500 pertaining to the noncurrent portfolio.

A net realized loss of $10,000 on the sale of marketable equity securities was included in the determination of net income for 1983. The cost of the securities sold was based on the first-in, first-out method. Reductions in the valuation allowance for net unrealized losses of $2,000 and $3,000 were included in income during 1982 and 1983, respectively.

The carrying amount of the long-term marketable equity securities portfolio was reduced to market at December 31, 1982 by establishing a valuation allowance in the amount of $7,000. The allowance was established by a charge to stockholder's equity. A reduction of this allowance of $4,500 was used in determining the net unrealized loss charged to stockholder's equity at December 31, 1983.

WARNER COMMUNICATIONS, INC.
Disclosure of Investment in
Marketable Equity Securities

Assets *As of December 31 (Dollars in thousands)*	*1980*	*1979*
Current assets:		
Cash and short-term investments	$226,304	$ 212,020
Accounts and notes receivable, less allowances		
for doubtful receivables and returns		
(1980—$204,280; 1979—$152,289)	445,868	333,052
Inventories	228,705	214,714
Advance royalties	53,217	53,237
Other current assets	32,127	24,192
Total current assets	986,221	837,215
Marketable equity securities, carried at lower		
of cost or market	37,175	44,143
Accounts and notes receivable due after one year	133,254	126,510
Non-current inventories	136,253	159,154
Investments—other	130,464	99,802
Property, plant and equipment, net	271,053	201,541
Other assets:		
License agreements, music copyrights and		
distribution rights, at cost, less accumulated		
amortization	25,799	32,931
Excess of cost over net assets of businesses		
acquired, less accumulated amortization	28,429	26,624
Deferred charges and other assets	20,127	17,847
	$1,768,775	$1,545,767

See accompanying notes to consolidated financial statements and summary of significant accounting policies.

Marketable Equity Securities

At December 31, 1980, the portfolio of marketable equity securities is carried at its aggregate cost of $37,175,000 (market $49,302,000) and at December 31, 1979, at its aggregate quoted market value of $44,143,000 (cost $48,030,000).

Gross unrealized gains and gross unrealized losses pertaining to the marketable equity securities were $15,921,000 and $3,794,000, respectively, at December 31, 1980, and $6,895,000 and $10,782,000, respectively, at December 31, 1979. Realized gains and losses during 1980, 1979 and 1978 were not material.

It is management's present intention to maintain a portfolio of marketable equity securities as a source of capital for long-term investments. Accordingly, the investment in these marketable equity securities has been classified as a noncurrent asset.

   c. The changes in the valuation allowances which have occurred during the period.[15]

The data from Lee Corporation's December 31, 1982, and December 31, 1983, portfolio valuations will be used to illustrate these requirements. These

[15]"Certain Marketable Securities," par. 12.

Exhibit 7-10
ROCKWELL INTERNATIONAL
Disclosure of Investment in
Marketable Equity Securities

Consolidated Balance Sheet

Assets (In millions)	September 30	
	1980	1979
Current assets		
Cash (including time deposits and certificates of deposit: 1980, $660.8 million; 1979, $584.2 million)	$ 741.7	$ 633.6
Receivables	1,046.2	1,060.1
Inventories	1,175.4	1,092.6
Prepaid expenses and other current assets	33.5	31.8
Total current assets	2,996.8	2,818.1
Investments	130.9	156.9

4. Investments

Investments at September 30 are summarized as follows (in millions):

	1980	1979
Investments in and long-term advances to:		
Unconsolidated finance subsidiary (Note 5)	$ 40.0	$ 75.4
Other unconsolidated subsidiaries	15.3	17.7
Affiliates	53.1	49.2
Other investments	22.5	14.6
Investments	$130.9	$156.9

Investments in unconsolidated subsidiaries are accounted for on the equity method. Investments in affiliates (companies owned 20% to 50%) in which the Company has the ability to exercise significant influence (within the meaning of the Accounting Principles Board's opinion on accounting for investments in common stock) are accounted for on the equity method. Other investments are accounted for at the lower of cost or market.

portfolios were presented earlier in the chapter in the section, "Equity Securities—Current Portfolio." Lee's investments in marketable equity securities might be presented in the financial statements and in the accompanying notes as shown in Exhibits 7-7 and 7-8.

An actual example of a disclosure concerning an investment in securities carried under the lower of cost or market method appears in Exhibit 7-9. The disclosures were taken from a recent annual report of Warner Communications, Inc.

Equity Method

The following disclosures are applicable to the equity method of accounting:

1. The name of the investee and the percentage of ownership.
2. The difference, if any, between the amount in the investment account and the amount of underlying equity in the net assets of the investee.
3. The aggregate value of each identified investment based on quoted market prices.
4. When the investment is material in relation to the financial position of the investor, summarized information concerning assets, liabilities, and results of operations of the investee is also appropriate.
5. Finally, the investor should disclose reasons for not using the equity method in cases of a 20% or greater ownership interest and the reasons for using the equity method in cases of less than 20% ownership interest in the investee.[16]

The materiality of the investment should be considered when disclosing information regarding the investment and the investee company. A sample disclosure appears in Exhibit 7-10. The information was taken from a recent annual report of Rockwell International.

Concept Summary,

INVESTMENTS IN STOCK

INVESTMENTS IN STOCK—BALANCE SHEET AND INCOME STATEMENT EFFECTS

Investment	Balance Sheet Impact	Income Statement Impact
Short-Term Investment in Marketable Securities	Value at lower of aggregate cost or market and classify as current asset.	Recognize realized and unrealized losses in income; recognize dividend income as declared by investee.

[16] "The Equity Method," par. 20.

Long-Term Investment— No Significant Influence	Value at lower of aggregate cost or market and classify as noncurrent asset; accumulated unrealized losses disclosed as contra-equity account.	Recognize realized losses and declines in value deemed other than temporary in income; recognize dividend income as declared by investee.
Long-Term Investment— Equity Method Investee	Value at acquisition cost plus (minus) proportionate share of investee earnings (losses) and classify as noncurrent asset; dividends constitute return of investment.	Recognize proportionate share of investee earnings (losses) in income as generated (incurred) by investee; investee dividend declarations have no impact on income.
Long-Term Investments— Controlling Interest	Prepare consolidated financial statements for parent and subsidiaries as if separate entities were one.	Prepare consolidated financial statements for parent and subsidiaries as if separate entities were one.

Questions

Q-7-1 Distinguish between short-term investments and long-term investments in marketable equity securities.

Q-7-2 What accounting principle is applicable to recording the acquisition of an investment? Explain its application.

Q-7-3 How are marketable equity securities classified in the case of a classified balance sheet? If the balance sheet is not classified, how should they be classified?

Q-7-4 Explain the accounting treatment of the current and noncurrent portfolios of marketable equity securities.

Q-7-5 What disclosures should be made with respect to marketable equity securities in the financial statements?

Q-7-6 Explain when an investor should apply the LCM method for investments in marketable equity securities.

Q-7-7 Explain when an investor should apply the equity method for long-term investments.

Q-7-8 Contrast the LCM and equity methods of accounting for long-term investments subsequent to acquisition.

Q-7-9 Under what circumstances will an investor recognize additional losses when the carrying amount of an investment, under the equity method, is reduced to zero?

Q-7-10 What is the basic difference between the consolidation and equity methods of accounting for long-term investments?

Q–7–11 Define a marketable equity security for purposes of applying *SFAS No. 12*.

Q–7–12 If you apply the equity method of accounting for an investment in stock, is goodwill accounted for? If so, how?

Q–7–13 If you apply the equity method, what type of securities are used to determine the percentage amount of voting shares held by an investor?

Q–7–14 When is restricted stock considered marketable for purposes of applying *SFAS No. 12?*

Q–7–15 A net unrealized loss on a company's long-term portfolio of marketable equity securities should be reflected in the current financial statements as

    a) An extraordinary item shown as a direct reduction from retained earnings.

    b) A current loss resulting from holding marketable equity securities.

    c) A footnote or parenthetical disclosure only.

    d) A valuation allowance and included in the equity section of the statement of financial position.

                                (AICPA adapted)

Q–7–16 A net unrealized gain on a company's long-term portfolio of marketable equity securities should be reflected in the current financial statements as

    a) An extraordinary item shown as a direct increase to retained earnings.

    b) A current gain resulting from holding marketable equity securities.

    c) A footnote or parenthetical disclosure only.

    d) A valuation allowance and included in the equity section of the statement of financial position.

                                (AICPA adapted)

Q–7–17 Which of the following conditions generally exists before market value can be used as the basis for valuation of a company's marketable equity securities?

    a) Market value must approximate historical cost.

    b) Management's intention must be to dispose of the security within one year.

    c) Market value must be less than the cost for each security held in the company's marketable equity security portfolio.

    d) The aggregate valuation of a company's marketable equity security portfolio must be less than the aggregate cost of the portfolio.

                                (AICPA adapted)

Q–7–18 A marketable equity security must have a ready market in order to be classified as current, and must

    a) Be available to management for use in short-run operations.

    b) Be traded on a recognized national exchange.

    c) Have a current market value in excess of original cost.

    d) Have been owned less than one year.

                                (AICPA adapted)

Discussion Questions and Cases

D–7–1 The most common method of accounting for unconsolidated subsidiaries is the equity method.

Required:

Answer the questions shown below with respect to the equity method.

    a) Under what circumstances should the equity method be applied?

    b) At what amount should the initial investment be recorded, and what events subsequent to the initial investment (if any) would change this amount?

c) How are investment earnings recognized under the equity method, and how is the amount determined?

(AICPA adapted)

D–7–2 For the past five years Herbert has maintained an investment (properly accounted for and reported upon) in Broome, amounting to a 10% interest in the voting common stock of Broome. The purchase price was $700,000, and the underlying net equity in Broome at the date of purchase was $620,000. On January 2 of the current year, Herbert purchased an additional 15% of the voting common stock of Broome for $1,200,000; the underlying net equity of the additional investment at January 2 was $1,000,000. Broome has been profitable and has paid dividends annually since Herbert's initial acquisition.
Required:
Discuss how this increase in ownership affects the accounting for and reporting upon the investment in Broome. Include in your discussion adjustments, if any, to the amount shown before the increase in investment to bring the amount into conformity with generally accepted accounting principles. Also include how current and subsequent periods would be reported upon.

(AICPA adapted)

D–7–3 The Financial Accounting Standards Board issued *Statement No. 12* to clarify accounting methods and procedures with respect to certain marketable securities. An important part of the Statement concerns the distinction between noncurrent and current classification of marketable securities.
Required:
1. Why does a company maintain an investment portfolio of current and noncurrent securities?
2. What factors should be considered in determining whether investments in marketable equity securities should be classified as current or noncurrent, and how do these factors affect the accounting treatment for unrealized losses?

(AICPA adapted)

D–7–4 Presented below are four unrelated situations involving marketable equity securities:
a) A noncurrent portfolio with an aggregate market value in excess of cost includes one particular security whose market value has declined to less than one half of the original cost. The decline in value is considered to be other than temporary.
b) The statement of financial position of a company does not classify assets and liabilities as current and noncurrent. The portfolio of marketable equity securities includes securities normally considered current that have a net cost in excess of market value of $2,000. The remainder of the portfolio has a net market value in excess of cost of $5,000.
c) A marketable equity security, whose market value is currently less than cost, is classified as noncurrent but is to be reclassified as current.
d) A company's noncurrent portfolio of marketable equity securities consists of the common stock of one company. At the end of the prior year the market value of the security was 50% of original cost, and this effect was properly reflected in a valuation allowance account. However, at the end of the current year the market value of the security had appreciated to twice the original cost. The security is still considered noncurrent at year-end.
Required:
What is the effect upon classification, carrying value, and earnings for each of the situations above? Complete your response to each situation before proceeding to the next situation.

(AICPA adapted)

Exercises

E-7-1   On January 1, 1979, Barton Corporation acquired as a long-term investment for $500,000, a 30% common stock interest in Buffer Company. On that date Buffer had net assets with a book value and current market value of $1,600,000. During 1979 Buffer reported net income of $180,000 and declared and paid cash dividends of $40,000.

Required:

1. What is the maximum amount of income that Barton should report from this investment for 1979?

2. Prepare all of the journal entries required of Barton Corporation during 1979 as relates to the investment in Buffer Company.

(AICPA adapted)

E-7-2   On January 1, 1976, Brevity Corporation acquired as a long-term investment for $130,000, a 40% common stock interest in Astute Company. On that date Astute had net assets of $300,000. During 1976 Astute reported net income of $60,000 and declared and paid cash dividends of $15,000.

Required:

1. What is the maximum amount of income that Brevity can report from this investment for the calendar year 1976?

2. Prepare all of the journal entries required of Brevity Corporation during 1976 relating to the investment in Astute Company.

(AICPA adapted)

E-7-3   The Carson Company's marketable equity securities portfolio, which is appropriately included in current assets, is as follows:

December 31, 1977

	Cost	Market	Unrealized Gain (Loss)
Archer, Inc.	$100,000	$100,000	$ —
Kelly Co.	200,000	150,000	(50,000)
Pelt Company	250,000	260,000	10,000
	$550,000	$510,000	$(40,000)

Required:

1. If you ignore income taxes, what amount should be reported as a charge against income in Carson's 1977 income statement?

2. Prepare any required journal entry(ies) to reflect the data above.

(AICPA adapted)

E-7-4   On January 1, 1977, the Robohn Company purchased 40% of the 300,000 shares of voting common stock of the Lowell Company for $1,800,000 cash when 40% of the underlying equity in the net assets of Lowell was $1,400,000. Robohn amortizes goodwill over a 40-year period, with a full year's amortization taken in the year of the purchase. The amortization is not deductible for income tax reporting. As a result of this transaction, Robohn has the ability to exercise significant influence over Lowell's operating and financial policies. Lowell's net income for the year ended December 31, 1977, was $600,000. During 1977 Lowell paid $325,000 in dividends to its stockholders. What income should be reported by Robohn for its investment in Lowell?

(AICPA adapted)

E-7-5   On January 1, 1977, the Pint Corporation paid $400,000 for 10,000 shares of Quart Company's common stock, which represents a 10% investment in Quart. Pint received dividends of $1.00 per share from Quart in 1977. Quart reported net income of $150,000 for the year ended December 31, 1977. The market value of Quart's common stock on December 31, 1977, was $42 per share. If you ignore income taxes, what should be the amount reported in Pint's 1977 income statement as a result of Pint's investment in Quart should be what amount?

(AICPA adapted)

E–7–6   On January 1, 1978, Avow, Inc. purchased 30% of the outstanding common stock of Depot Corporation for $129,000 cash. Avow is accounting for this investment on the equity method. On the date of acquisition the fair value of Depot's net assets was $310,000. Avow has determined that the excess of the cost of the investment over its share of Depot's net assets has an indeterminate life. Depot's net income for the year ended December 31, 1978, was $90,000. During 1978 Depot declared and paid cash dividends of $10,000. There were no other transactions between the two companies.
Required:
1. On January 1, 1978, the investment in Depot should have been recorded at what amount?
2. If you ignore income taxes, Avow's statement of income for the year ended December 31, 1978, should include "equity in net income of Depot Corporation" in what amount?

(AICPA adapted)

E–7–7   On January 1, 1978, Grade Company paid $300,000 for 20,000 shares of Medium Company's common stock, which represents a 15% investment in Medium. Grade does not have the ability to exercise significant influence over Medium. Medium declared and paid a dividend of $1 a share to its stockholders during 1978. Medium reported net income of $260,000 for the year ended December 31, 1978.
Required:
1. What amount should be the balance in Grade's balance sheet account "investment in Medium Company" at December 31, 1978?
2. Prepare all required journal entries applicable to Grade Corporation's investment in Medium's common stock for 1978.

(AICPA adapted)

E–7–8   On January 1, 1977, Barley Corp. paid $600,000 for 60,000 shares of Oat Company's common stock, which represents a 25% investment in Oat. Barley has the ability to exercise significant influence over Oat. Barley received a dividend of $1 per share from Oat in 1977. Oat reported net income of $320,000 for the year ended December 31, 1977.
Required:
1. What amount should be the balance in Barley's balance sheet account "investment in Oat Company" at December 31, 1977?
2. Prepare all required journal entries applicable to Barley Corporation's investment in Oat for 1977.

(AICPA adapted)

E–7–9   On January 1, 1976, Tom Kat, Inc. purchased 25% of the outstanding shares of stock of Carmel for $115,000 cash. The investment will be accounted for by the equity method. On that date Carmel's net assets (book and fair value) were $300,000. Tom Kat has determined that the excess of the cost of its investment in Carmel over its share of Carmel's net assets has an undeterminate life.
Carmel's net income for the year ended December 31, 1976, was $50,000. During 1976 Tom Kat received $5,000 cash dividends from Carmel. There were no other transactions between the two companies.
Required:
1. On January 1, 1976, the investment in Carmel would be recorded on Tom Kat's books at what amount?
2. If you ignore income taxes, Tom Kat's income statement for the year ended December 31, 1976, should include "equity in 1976 net income of Carmel Co." in what amount?

(AICPA adapted)

E-7-10 On its December 31, 1977, balance sheet, the Noble Corporation reported the following as investments in long-term marketable equity securities:

Investment in long-term marketable equity securities at cost	$300,000
Less: Allowance to reduce long-term equity securities to market	28,000
	$272,000

At December 31, 1978, the market valuation of the portfolio was $298,000. What should Noble report on its 1978 statement of income as a result of the market value of the investments in 1978?

E-7-11 In January, 1975, the Harold Corporation acquired 20% of the outstanding common stock of Otis Company for $400,000. This investment gave Harold the ability to exercise significant influence over Otis. The book value of these shares was $300,000. The excess of cost over book value was attributed to an identifiable intangible asset that was undervalued on Otis' balance sheet and that had a remaining useful life of 10 years.

For the year ended December 31, 1975, Otis reported net income of $90,000 and paid cash dividends of $20,000 on its common stock. What is the carrying value of Harold's investment in Otis Company at December 31, 1975?

E-7-12 The summarized balance sheets of Sweets Candy Company and Honey Wrapper Company as of December 31, 1968, are as follows:

SWEETS CANDY COMPANY
Balance Sheet
December 31, 1968

Assets	$600,000
Liabilities	$150,000
Capital stock	300,000
Retained earnings	150,000
Total equities	$600,000

HONEY WRAPPER COMPANY
Balance Sheet
December 31, 1968

Assets	$400,000
Liabilities	$100,000
Capital Stock	250,000
Retained earnings	50,000
Total equities	$400,000

Required:
1. If Sweets Candy Company acquired a 90% interest in Honey Wrapper Company on December 31, 1968, for $290,000 and the cost (or legal basis) method of accounting for the investment was used, what would have been the amount of the debit to investment in stock of Honey Wrapper Company?

2. If Sweets Candy Company acquired an 80% interest in Honey Wrapper Company on December 31, 1968, for $210,000 and the equity (or accrual) method of accounting for the investment was used, what would have been the amount of the debit to investment in stock of Honey Wrapper Company?

E–7–13 On April 1, 1980, Miller Corporation acquired a 20% interest in the voting common stock of Johnson Company for $280,000. On April 1 the Johnson Company balance sheet reflected net assets of $1,400,000. During 1980 Johnson Company reported net income of $90,000 and declared and paid cash dividends of $18,000. The market value of Miller's investment in Johnson at December 31, 1980, was $260,000, but the decline in value was expected to be temporary. Both Miller and Johnson report on a calendar-year basis.

Required:
1. Assuming that Miller's investment in Johnson allows the exercise of significant influence, prepare all journal entries required by Miller during 1980 applicable to the investment in Johnson.
2. Assuming that Miller's investment in Johnson does not allow the exercise of significant influence, prepare all journal entries required by Miller during 1980 applicable to the investment in Johnson.

E–7–14 Caldwell Corporation had the following portfolio of long-term marketable equity securities at December 31, 1980:

Security	Quantity	Percent Ownership	Cost	Market
			Per Share	
Alpha, Inc.	2,000 shares	8%	$20	$30
Beta, Inc.	6,000 shares	14%	44	32
Gamma, Inc.	4,000 shares	2%	60	50

At December 31, 1981, Caldwell's portfolio of long-term marketable equity securities consisted of the following common stocks:

Security	Quantity	Percent Ownership	Cost	Market
			Per Share	
Beta, Inc.	6,000 shares	14%	$44	$58
Gamma, Inc.	4,000 shares	2%	60	48
Gamma, Inc.	2,000 shares	1%	48	48

During 1981 Caldwell Corporation changed its investment intent relative to the Alpha, Inc. stock and on April 6, 1981, sold one-half of the Alpha, Inc. shares in the open market for $19 per share and, at the same time, reclassified the remaining Alpha, Inc. shares as current assets. The decline in value of the Gamma, Inc. shares is deemed to be permanent.

Required:
1. What amounts relative to the long-term investments portfolio in Caldwell's December 31, 1980, balance sheet should be classified as (a) long-term investments and (b) stockholder's equity?
2. What amounts relative to the long-term investments portfolio in Caldwell's December 31, 1981, balance sheet should be classified as (a) long-term investments and (b) stockholder's equity?
3. What amounts relative to the long-term investments portfolio should be reflected in Caldwell's 1981 income statement? (Continued on next page.)

4. Prepare all journal entries required of Caldwell applicable to the long-term investments portfolio during 1981.

E–7–15 On January 1, 1979, Jimbo Company paid $1,200,000 for 40,000 shares of Crane Corporation's common stock, which represents a 25% investment interest in the net assets of Crane. Jimbo has the ability to exercise significant influence over Crane. Jimbo received a dividend of $3 per share from Crane in 1979. Crane reported net income of $640,000 for the year ended December 31, 1979.

Required:
Compute the balance in Jimbo's balance sheet account "investment in Crane Corporation."

E–7–16 On January 1, 1975, the Swing Company purchased at book value 100,000 shares (20%) of the voting common stock of Harpo Instruments, Inc. for $1,200,000. Direct costs associated with the purchase were $50,000. On December 1, 1975, the board of directors of Harpo declared a dividend of $2 per share payable to holders of record on December 28, 1975. The net income of Harpo for the year ended December 31, 1975, was $1,600,000.

Required:
Compute the balance in Swing's "investment in Harpo Instruments, Inc.," account at December 31, 1975.

Problems

P–7–1 B & B Company has the following portfolio of short-term marketable equity securities at December 31, 1979:

		Per Share	
Security	Quantity	Cost	Market
Jackson, Inc.	500 shares	50	52
Wells, Inc.	1,000 shares	20	18
Canon Company	2,000 shares	30	20

On December 31, 1980, B & B Company's portfolio of short-term marketable equity securities consisted of the following:

		Per Share	
Security	Quantity	Cost	Market
Wells, Inc.	1,000 shares	20	25
Canon Company	2,000 shares	30	29

Required:
1. What amounts should be reported on the face of B & B Company's December 31, 1979, balance sheet relative to short-term investment?
2. What amounts should be reported on the face of B & B Company's December 31, 1980, balance sheet? What amounts should be reported to reflect the transactions above in B & B Company's 1980 income statement?

P-7-2 The following table shows Smith Company's current portfolio for marketable equity securities at December 31, 1978, 1979, and 1980:

| | | | | Market Value at December 31 | | |
| | | | | 1978 | 1979 | 1980 |
Stock	Cost	Sales Proceeds	Sale Date			
AAA	$20,000	$24,000	Jan. 3, 1980	$16,000	$14,000	
BBB	10,000	not sold		12,000	14,000	$16,000
CCC	40,000	not sold		30,000		

Assume that all stocks were purchased on January 2, 1978. On January 2, 1980, the CCC stock was transferred from the current portfolio to the noncurrent portfolio. The market value of the CCC stock on Jan. 2, 1980 was still $30,000.
Required:
1. Prepare the entry needed to properly adjust the current marketable equity securities account and its related allowance account for Smith Company on December 31, 1978.
2. Prepare the entry needed to properly adjust the current marketable equity securities account and its related allowance account for Smith Company on December 31, 1979.
3. Prepare the entry to transfer the CCC stock from the current portfolio to the noncurrent portfolio.
4. Prepare the entry to record the sale of the AAA stock.
5. Prepare the entry needed to properly adjust the current marketable equity securities account and its related allowance account for Smith Company on December 31, 1980.

P-7-3 SM Company purchased 2,000 shares (a 30% interest) of the common stock of Baker Company at $20 per share on January 2, 1979. During 1979 Baker Company reported net income of $40,000 and paid dividends of $10,000. On January 2, 1980, SM received 1,000 shares of common stock as a result of a stock dividend by Baker Company.
Required:
1. Prepare the journal entries necessary to record the transactions listed above on the SM Company's books, applying the cost method in accounting for the investment (due to lack of significant influence).
2. Prepare the journal entries necessary to record the transactions listed above on the SM Company's books, applying the equity method in accounting for the investment.

P-7-4 On January 2, 1979, Harrison Company purchased 2,000 shares of Lone Star Company common stock at $18 per share. At that time, Lone Star Company's balance sheet showed total assets of $180,000, liabilities of $30,000, common stock ($10 par value) of $100,000, and retained earnings of $50,000. The book values of assets and liabilities of Lone Star Company are equal to the fair values.

At the end of 1979, Lone Star Company reported net income of $30,000 and paid cash dividends of $10,000 on December 31, 1979. The market value of Lone Star Company common stock was $15 per share at December 31, 1979.

Required:
1. Prepare the journal entries necessary to record the transactions above, assuming that Harrison Company does not have the ability to exercise significant influence over Lone Star Copany.
2. Prepare the journal entries necessary to record the transactions above, applying the equity method.

P–7–5   On December 31, 1978, David Company acquired 20,000 shares of Small Company common stock at a cost of $25 a share; the purchase represented 25% of Small Company's outstanding stock.

On July 1, 1979, Small Company paid a cash dividend of $1.20 a common share. For the year 1979, Small Company reported net income of $20,000; the market value of Small Company common stock was $23 at December 31, 1979.

On July 1, 1980, Small Company paid a dividend of $1 a common share. For the year 1980, Small Company reported a net income of $40,000; the market value of Small Company common stock was $24 at December 31, 1980.

Required:

1.   Prepare the journal entries necessary to record the transactions listed above on David Company's books, assuming that David Company does not have the ability to exercise significant influence over Small Company.

2.   Prepare the journal entries necessary to record the transactions listed above on David Company's books, assuming that David Company has the ability to exercise significant influence over Small Company.

P–7–6   On January 2, 1977, Evans Company purchased for $500,000 cash a 10% investment in Winston Company. On that date the net assets of Winston Company had a book value of $450,000. The difference between the book value acquired and the purchase price is attributable to depreciable assets having a remaining life of 20 years. During 1977 Winston Company reported net income of $300,000 and paid cash dividends of $100,000.

On January 2, 1978, Evans Company purchased an additional 30% of Winston Company stock for $1,950,000. Due to increases in ownership interest, Evans Company has the ability to exercise significant influence over Winston Company.

Required:

Prepare all journal entries on the books of Evans Company, reflecting a change from the cost method to the equity method.

P–7–7   On January 2, 1979, Sunny Company purchased 40% of Conners Company for $80,000. At the time of the investment, the book values of Conners Company's assets and liabilities were equal to their fair values. Conners Company's balance sheet on January 2, 1979, was as follows:

CONNERS COMPANY
Balance Sheet

Cash	$ 10,000
Accounts receivable	5,000
Inventory	50,000
Plant and equipment (net)	65,000
Land	60,000
	$190,000
Accounts payable	$ 15,000
Notes payable	25,000
Capital stock	50,000
Retained earnings	100,000
	$190,000

Required:

1.   Assuming the equity method is appropriate, show the computation of goodwill purchased at acquisition.

2. Assuming that all other facts are the same as Part 1, except that the fair value of land was $80,000, show the computation of goodwill purchased at acquisition.

P–7–8   On January 2, 1979, A Company purchased 1,000 shares (25%) of the 4,000 shares of B Company for $40,000 cash. At that date the following data were available:

B COMPANY

	Book Value	Fair Value
Nondepreciable assets	$ 40,000	$ 60,000
Depreciable asset		
(10-year remaining life)	90,000	150,000
Total	$130,000	$210,000
Liabilities	$ 50,000	$ 50,000
Stockholders' equity	80,000	
Total	$130,000	

At the end of 1979, B Company reported net income of $20,000 and paid cash dividends of $8,000.
Required:
Prepare the journal entries necessary to record the transactions listed above.

P–7–9   Hawkes System, Inc., a chemical processing company, has been operating profitably for many years. On March 1, 1977, Hawkes purchased 50,000 shares of Diversified Insurance Company stock for $2,000,000. The 50,000 shares represented 25% of Diversified's outstanding stock. Both Hawkes and Diversified operate on a fiscal year ending August 31.

For the fiscal year ended August 31, 1977, Diversified reported net income of $800,000 earned ratably throughout the year. During November, 1976, and February, May, and August of 1977, Diversified paid its regular quarterly cash dividend of $100,000.
Required:
1. What criteria should Hawkes consider in determining whether its investment in Diversified should be classified as (a) a current asset (marketable security) or (b) a noncurrent asset (investment) in Hawkes' August 31, 1977, balance sheet? Confine your discussion to the decision criteria for determining the balance sheet classification of the investment.
2. Assume that the investment should be classified as a long-term investment in the noncurrent asset section of Hawkes' balance sheet. The cost of Hawkes' investment equaled its equity in the recorded values of Diversified's net assets: recorded values were not materially different from fair values (individually or collectively). For the fiscal year ended August 31, 1977, how did the net income reported and the dividends paid by Diversified affect the accounts of Hawkes (including Hawkes' income tax accounts)? Indicate each account effected, whether it increased or decreased, and explain the reason for the change in the account balance (such as cash, investment in diversified, etc.). Organize your answer in the following format:

Account Name	Increase or Decrease	Reason for Change in Account Balance

(AICPA adapted)

P–7–10 First Company made the following investments in marketable securities during the current year:

	Cost	Market
Current portfolio:		
A Stock	$10,000	$11,000
B Stock	7,000	5,000
Noncurrent portfolio:		
C Stock	$10,000	$10,000
D Stock	10,000	2,000

Required:
Present the balance sheet and the income statement disclosure that would be necessary relative to the investments above.

P–7–11 The Rocky Company purchased 4,000 shares of common stock of the Friend Company at $15 per share on February 1, 1981. The 4,000 shares represented a 30% interest in the Friend Company. During 1981 the Friend Company had a net income of 100,000 and paid dividends of $20,000. On February 1, 1982, Rocky Company received 2,000 shares in a stock split by the Friend Company.

Required:
1. Prepare the entry to record the transactions occurring in 1981 and 1982 using the equity method of accounting.
2. Prepare the entry to record the sale of 1,000 shares of Friend Company Stock at $12 per share on February 1, 1983. Use the equity method in accounting for the investment.

P–7–12 On January 1, 1981, Investor Company acquired a 60% interest in Investee Company for $226,000. On this date Investee Company had capital stock of $40,000 and retained earnings of $80,000.

An examination of Investee Company's assets and liabilities revealed that book values were equal to fair values for all except plant and equipment (net), which have a book value of $200,000 and a fair value of $300,000, and inventory, which has a book value of $50,000 and a fair value of $60,000. Plant and equipment have an expected remaining life of five years, and the inventory will be sold during 1981. Investor Company planned to amortize any goodwill acquired in the combination over 40 years.

Investor Company's income from its own operations was $100,000 during 1981 and $80,000 during 1982. Investee Company's income was $70,000 during 1981 and $60,000 during 1982. Investee Company paid cash dividends of $20,000 each year.

Required:
Prepare all of the journal entries required of Investor Company applicable to its investment in Investee Company during 1982.

8
Inventories— General Issues

Accounting in the News

Inventory management is one of the most difficult, and most important, functions of business management. Control of inventories is a critical factor in company profitability. Excessive inventories result in waste and high costs of overhead, whereas inadequate inventories can result in production delays or lost sales opportunities. On a macro-basis, the level of inventories is watched very closely because it is one of the indicators of economic activity. The following excerpts from a recent article illustrate the impact of inventories on the economy.

One of the most closely watched signs of business activity is the level of company inventories. As sales slump during a recession and stockpiles of unsold goods swell, businessmen begin dumping their inventories and cutting back on orders from suppliers. In the process, layoffs surge throughout industry, and inventories grow skimpy. Then, when sales hungry businessmen detect the first signs of an improving economy, they begin to rehire workers and restock warehouses. The level of inventories, thus, is usually a telltale signal of a recession or recovery. . . .

With interest rates high and sales projections dismal throughout virtually all of American industry, few businessmen seem eager to start hastily rebuilding their stock to former levels. Instead, more firms are studying ways to hold down costs and operate with leaner inventories.

No inventory problems are bigger than those of the U.S. auto industry. To produce a car or truck requires thousands of parts supplied by dozens of subcontractors scattered across the U.S. Running short of even one crucial component can force the shutdown of an entire assembly or production line at a plant. On the other hand, the costs of buildings and guards for equipment that is not needed can be staggering. For example, at Ford Motor Co., which lost $1.06 billion in 1981 on sales of $38.2 billion, every $1 worth of inventory costs the company an additional 26¢ a year in overhead expenses. Sums up William J. Harahan, Ford's director of technical planning: "Substantial inventories are just no longer an affordable luxury."*

*Christopher Byron, "Getting Control of Inventories," *Time*, May 10, 1982, p. 93. Copyright 1982 Time Inc. All rights reserved. Reprinted by permission from *Time*.

Inventory management and control, which is discussed in this chapter, is an important part of the general economy and important to individual companies.

The purpose of this chapter is to introduce the topic of inventories. Some general issues related to inventory classification, composition, and valuation will be discussed; more detailed discussions of inventory valuation and estimation methods are presented in Chapters 9 and 10.

Inventories can be defined as assets held by the business either for future sale in the ordinary course of business, or for use in the production of goods or services for future sale. Not included as inventory are any assets that are not sold in the ordinary course of business or not used in the manufacture of goods or services for future sale. For example, a company often will hold investments in the form of marketable securities or even fixed assets for the purpose of resale. These types of assets are not considered inventory; instead, they are considered investments. Inventory would include only those assets that are sold in the ordinary course of business or are used in the production of goods or providing of services.

Because inventories often comprise a significant portion of a company's assets, management is very concerned with inventory procedures and valuation. It is extremely important to maintain the proper levels of inventory because customers may be lost if a company is temporarily out of stock. On the other hand, since it is very expensive to carry inventory, management would like to maintain the minimum levels necessary to service customers. There is also the danger that an overstock of inventory will become obsolete. Therefore, management must insist on good inventory record keeping procedures and must monitor them frequently.

The valuation of inventories is crucial for companies such as merchandising or retailing concerns. Typically, the inventory of these companies (such as supermarket chains, catalog showroom stores, and retailers) comprises a major portion of their assets on the balance sheet. Thus, the inventory valuation can affect the working capital, the working capital ratio, and many of the other standard ratios used by financial analysts for credit purposes. On the other hand, there are some companies whose inventories are negligible. For example, an electric utility or railroad has a very limited amount of inventory. The valuation of inventory for these kinds of companies is important, but not as crucial as it is in a merchandising concern.

For companies engaged in manufacturing, the acquisition, manufacture, and sale of inventories often represents the only, or major, revenue-generating activity of the business. Accounting for these inventories can be particularly important because the financial statements can be affected dramatically. The use of one method of valuation over another can have a potential impact of millions of dollars on the balance sheet and income statements. A highly profitable company may use a valuation method that reduces its income and thereby its income tax liability. Conversely, a marginally profitable company, or one losing money, may be using a method that improves its reported profit.

Classifications of Inventory

The classifications of inventories in individual businesses are dependent on the nature of the business. A manufacturing entity will classify inventories as *raw materials*, *work-in-process*, and *finished goods*. These three classes of inventory represent the various stages of completion of the product being manufactured for sale. Conversely, a company that purchases a completed product for the purpose of resale (e.g., a trading or merchandising company), usually uses a single *merchandise inventory* account. Both types of company may have other minor inventory accounts, such as a supplies account.

Raw Materials Inventories

The **raw materials inventories** include the cost of the basic materials used in the manufacture of the product. Raw materials consist of natural resources such as wood, oil, coal, iron ore, or cotton that become a part of the final product. The raw materials inventory account also would include the cost of merchandise, such as subassemblies or components, purchased from other manufacturing firms and used in the final product. For example, a company that makes electric fans might purchase the electric motors (or parts of the motors) from someone else.

Work-In-Process Inventories

The cost of merchandise that is only partially complete at the end of the accounting period constitutes the **work-in-process inventories**. In the manufacturing process raw materials are combined with direct labor and factory overhead to make finished products. If the goods are not completed at the end of the accounting period, an inventory account showing work-in-process, including the related costs of raw materials, labor, and overhead, is necessary.

Direct labor and factory overhead usually are referred to as **conversion costs**, or the cost of converting the raw materials to finished products in the manufacturing process. These costs are added to the raw material costs and accumulated in the work-in-process account. **Direct labor** is the cost of the labor used to make the product; this refers only to labor working on the product itself. For example, the costs incurred by a carpenter in the furniture factory or by a sewing machine operator in a clothing factory are considered direct labor costs. However, supervisory costs in those factories would be considered indirect labor and a part of overhead instead of direct labor costs. Direct labor costs usually are traceable to the products directly. The sewing machine operator may produce five shirts in one hour and be paid at the rate of $7.50 per hour. Each shirt then would have a direct labor cost of $1.50.

Factory overhead consists of all the factory costs incurred except the costs of direct material and direct labor. This includes such costs as indirect labor, indirect materials or supplies used, factory power and utility costs, factory insurance costs, property taxes paid on the factory buildings, repair and maintenance expenses, depreciation or rental charges, or any other cost of manufacturing the finished product. Some overhead costs may be incurred only once a year (i.e., insurance and property taxes), whereas others (i.e., utility costs) may be incurred continuously. Because some overhead costs occur sporadically, overhead is charged to units produced using a predetermined overhead rate. The overhead costs are *applied to the work-in-process account by multiplying a predetermined overhead rate by some measure of production activity.* The predetermined overhead rate is calculated in the following manner:

$$\text{Predetermined rate} = \frac{\text{estimated overhead cost for period}}{\text{estimated activity for period}}$$

The numerator would include all of the overhead costs expected for the time period. The activity in the denominator refers to some measure of productivity in the factory and could be units of output or some measure of input such as direct labor hours or direct machine hours. Once the predetermined rate is established, it is multiplied by the actual amount of activity for the job to obtain the overhead applied to work-in-process. When the products are completed, their manufacturing costs are transferred to the finished goods inventory account.

The upper portion of Exhibit 8-1 depicts inventory systems for manufacturing companies; merchandising companies are illustrated in the lower section of the exhibit. The raw materials account is similar to any inventory account. The purchases plus the beginning inventory provide the materials available for use in the manufacturing process. The materials used are removed from the raw materials account and transferred to the work-in-process account. Direct labor and factory overhead also are accumulated in this account. The work-in-process account includes current manufacturing costs, materials, labor, overhead, and the beginning inventory cost. As the products are completed, the costs are transferred to finished goods. The amount transferred from work-in-process to finished goods is referred to as the **cost of goods manufactured.** The cost of the products that are not yet completed will remain in the work-in-process account as the ending inventory.

Finished Goods Inventory

The **finished goods inventory** includes the cost of completed products that have not been sold. When the finished goods are sold, the cost is transferred from the finished goods account to the cost of goods sold account.

Supplies Inventory

A **supplies inventory** account is also generally necessary in manufacturing operations. Supplies include items that are necessary to keep the factory functioning but that do not become a part of the final product. They become part of the factory overhead and are accounted for in the same manner as overhead. As the supplies are used, they are charged to the factory overhead account.

Merchandise Inventory

Merchandising companies use the **merchandise inventory** account, which includes the cost of goods held for sale. When goods are acquired, their cost is put into the merchandise inventory account. When the goods are sold, their cost is transferred from the merchandise inventory account to the cost of goods sold account.

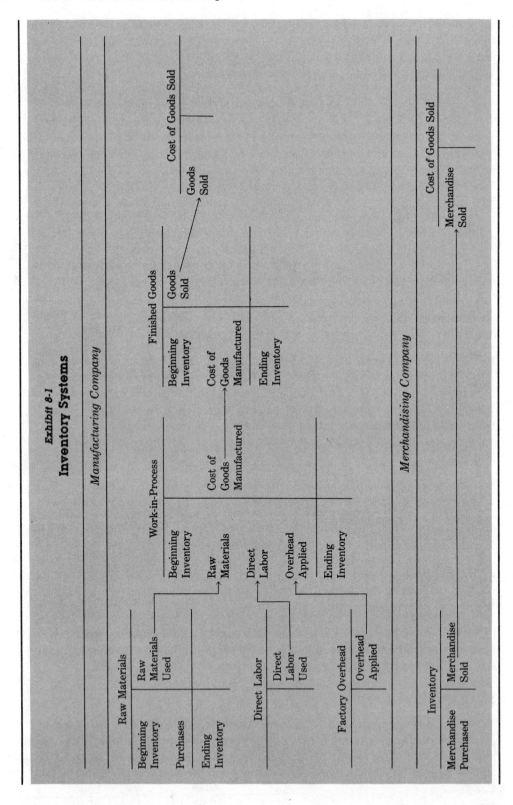

Exhibit 8-1
Inventory Systems

Manufacturing Company

Merchandising Company

The Physical Composition
of the Inventory—What to Include

As a general rule a company should include as inventory all the goods and merchandise to which it possesses legal title. Physical possession is not relevant; only legal title to the goods is relevant. The exceptions to this general rule are for certain items whose title is retained by the company but which should not be included as inventory; for example, certain leased merchandise (see Chapter 18) or goods sold on installment sales contracts (discussed in a later section of this chapter).

The problems associated with determination of whether to include certain merchandise as inventory generally stem from two factors—ownership and possession. Ownership, or who holds legal title, is particularly difficult to determine when merchandise is in transit from the seller to the buyer. Merchandise that is on consignment also can create inventory problems at times because title has not transferred but possession has. The holder of the consigned merchandise tends to include that merchandise as inventory whereas the owner can overlook it easily. A similar type of problem exists in installment sales. These three problem areas are discussed below.

Merchandise in Transit

Merchandise in transit can create a problem in inventory determination at the end of the accounting period. The inventory should include all merchandise to which the company has legal title. Merchandise in transit usually is shipped either f.o.b. (free on board) shipping point or f.o.b. destination. In a transaction that is made **f.o.b. shipping point,** title passes to the buyer at the time the goods are delivered to the common carrier (the transportation company). The buyer then assumes title and the risk of loss. In this case the goods in transit should be included as part of the inventory of the buyer. If the transaction takes place **f.o.b. destination,** title passes to the buyer when the buyer receives the goods from the common carrier. In this instance, the goods in transit should not be included as part of the inventory of the buyer since they are the seller's legal property. Sometimes the "shipping point" or "destination" is designated by a particular place, the seller's city, the buyer's city, or a city between the buyer and seller. Title, ownership, and risk of loss pass at the designated place.

Other situations can occur also with merchandise in transit. Sometimes the merchandise is delivered to a warehouse instead of to the buyer. Title passes when the warehouseman notifies the buyer that s/he is holding the merchandise for the buyer. After the warehouseman acknowledges the buyer's ownership of the merchandise, the buyer should include it as a part of the buyer's inventory. In another situation a buyer may request "special order" merchandise from the seller. Special order merchandise usually is considered the buyer's property at the time it is segregated and identified with the contract. In addition, there are special legal complications when the buyer or seller is insolvent or in bankruptcy. The general principle followed is that the right of ownership belongs to the party that has paid for the merchandise. For example, if the seller has not received payment from a bankrupt buyer, but has delivered the goods, the seller is entitled to retrieve the merchandise. Conversely, if a buyer receives merchandise from an insolvent seller, the buyer is entitled to the merchandise if s/he has paid for it.

Merchandise on Consignment

Consignment of merchandise is a marketing arrangement in which one company (e.g., Company A) delivers goods to another company (e.g., Company B) to be sold to a third party. Company A, which is the *consignor*, retains title to the goods. The *consignee*, Company B, acts as the sales agent; B receives the selling price from the buyer, retains an agreed percentage or sales commission, and remits the remainder to Company A, the consignor. If the goods are not sold, they are returned to the consignor.

The merchandise remains the property of the consignor; therefore, the consignor must include the merchandise as part of its inventory. The consignee's obligation is to exercise due care and protection of the goods until sold. The consignee does not include them as part of its inventory.

Installment Sales

Installment sales are transactions in which payment for the merchandise is made in regular installments over an extended period of time. In this kind of transaction the seller normally retains title to the merchandise until all of the installment payments have been made. Even though title remains with the seller, however, a sale has taken place and the risk of loss passes to the buyer. Therefore, the seller does not include the merchandise as part of the seller's inventory. The substance of the transaction is that a sale has been made upon delivery of the merchandise, and the purchaser presumably will make payment in the normal course of business.

Periodic and Perpetual Inventory Systems

Periodic and **perpetual inventory systems** refer to the inventory record keeping procedures employed by businesses. Under the periodic method, inventory quantities and values are determined only periodically (as the name implies), usually when financial statements are prepared. The perpetual method, on the other hand, keeps a running balance of inventory. Although the record keeping necessary in a periodic system is less than what is required in a perpetual system, a perpetual system will allow a greater degree of control over the inventory. The basic differences between the two methods are as follows: (1) purchases are charged (debited) to a purchases account in a periodic system and to the inventory account in a perpetual system; (2) when a sale is made, no entry for cost is made in the periodic system, but the inventory account is credited for the cost in the perpetual system; (3) the value of the ending inventory in a periodic system is found by taking a physical inventory, whereas in a perpetual system the inventory account will maintain a continuous record of the inventory value. Even though the accounting procedures are different in the two systems, the cost of goods sold and the net income will be the same.

Following is an example of the differences between a perpetual and periodic inventory system. Assume that the Trap Company had these transactions during the current accounting period:

Inventory, June 1— 50 units @ $5 $ 250

Purchase, June 2—100 units @ 5   500
Sale,   June 5—120 units @ 8   960
Purchase, June 15—150 units @ 5   750
Sale,   June 20—140 units @ 8   1120
Inventory, June 30— 40 units @ $5   200

The journal entries to record the transactions are illustrated in Exhibit 8-2. This exhibit assumes that there are no price changes; hence, there is no need to be concerned with cost flow assumptions, which will be discussed in Chapter 9.

In Exhibit 8-2 the journal entries to record the purchases require a debit to the purchases account in the periodic inventory system and to the inventory account in the perpetual system. When the sales are made, the periodic method requires a single entry to record the sale. However, the perpetual method re-

Exhibit 8-2
Journal Entries for
Periodic and Perpetual Inventory Systems

	Periodic Inventory System			*Perpetual Inventory System*		
June 2 (Purchase)	Purchases	500		Inventory	500	
	Accounts payable		500	Accounts payable		500
	(100 @ $5)					
June 5 (Sale)	Accounts receivable	960		Accounts receivable	960	
	Sales		960	Sales		960
	(120 @ $8)					
	No entry necessary to record cost of goods sold.			Cost of goods sold	600	
				Inventory		600
				(120 @ $5)		
June 15 (Purchases)	Purchases	750		Inventory	750	
	Accounts payable		750	Accounts payable		750
	(150 @ $5)					
June 20 (Sales)	Accounts receivable	1,120		Accounts receivable	1,120	
	Sales		1,120	Sales		1,120
	(140 @ $8)					
	No entry necessary.			Cost of goods sold	700	
				Inventory		700
				(140 @ $5)		
June 30 (Adjusting)	Cost of goods sold	1,250		No adjusting entries required.		
	Purchases		1,250			
	(250 @ $5)					
	Cost of goods sold	250				
	Inventory		250			
	(50 @ $5)					
	Inventory (June 30)	200				
	Cost of goods sold		200			
	(40 @ $5)					

quires an entry to record the sale and another entry to charge the cost of goods sold account for the cost of the merchandise removed from the inventory. At the end of the month the periodic method requires three adjusting entries: (1) the first entry transfers the accumulated amount in the purchases account to the cost of goods sold; (2) the second entry removes the beginning inventory from the books; and (3) the third entry records the ending inventory on the books. For the perpetual method no similar adjusting entries are required because the cost of goods sold and the inventory accounts are already current. By referring to Exhibit 8-3, you can see that the cost of goods sold and the gross profit for the two methods are the same.

Companies use periodic inventory systems for inventory items that are relatively inexpensive and that have a high turnover rate—for example, small, inexpensive parts needed in the manufacturing or assembly process. A periodic inventory system does not maintain a continuous record of the items on hand so is not suitable for expensive components. A periodic system has the advantage of being a relatively simple system without a need for detailed record keeping. The disadvantage, of course, is the lack of detailed records and the consequent lessening of control over the inventory.

Exhibit 8-3 illustrates the gross profit calculations involved in a periodic inventory system. The merchandise inventory account will carry only the beginning inventory balance throughout the period and it is not debited or credited during the period. At the end of the period the physical inventory is counted, and the value of the merchandise on hand is determined by using one of the cost flow

---

Exhibit 8-3
Gross Profit Calculations

Periodic System

Sales ($960 & $1,120)		$2,080
Cost of goods sold		
Inventory, June 1	$ 250	
Purchases ($500 & $750)	1,250	
Merchandise available for sale	$1,500	
Inventory June 30	(200)	
Cost of goods sold		(1,300)
Gross profit		$ 780

Perpetual System

Sales	$2,080
Cost of goods sold ($600 & $700)	(1,300)
Gross profit	$ 780

assumptions.[1] The ending inventory value is subtracted from the sum of the beginning inventory plus the purchases to obtain the cost of goods sold for the period.

In a perpetual inventory system, a continuous record of all purchases and sales is maintained in the merchandise inventory account. All purchases are debited to this account, and all withdrawals are credited to it. With this system of record keeping, the merchandise inventory account theoretically should reflect at all times the actual quantities of merchandise on hand. A perpetual inventory system is used for merchandise with relatively high unit values and in most manufacturing companies.

Even in companies that use perpetual inventory systems, periodic physical counts of the merchandise on hand are still necessary. Usually physical counts are taken of the entire inventory at least once a year. Any discrepancies between the book figures and the physical count figures are adjusted at that time. Many companies count randomly selected items during the year. The purpose of the test counts is to insure that the record keeping is being maintained properly. Periodic verification of inventories by physical count is necessary because of such factors as waste, breakage, theft, or improper record keeping.

Perpetual inventory systems afford the company much better control over its merchandise than does a periodic system. Because cost information is included in the records in the perpetual system, financial statement preparation is facilitated also. As the cost of computer technology decreases, these kinds of detailed information are becoming more accessible to many more companies and are no longer a barrier to adoption of a perpetual system.

Valuation of Inventories—General Principles

Inventory valuation encompasses (1) the accumulation of costs assigned to the merchandise available for sale and (2) allocation of these costs to the ending inventory and cost of goods sold. The accumulation of costs assigned to the merchandise inventory will be discussed in this section; the cost flow assumptions for the ending inventory and cost of goods sold will be deferred until the next chapter.

The accumulation of costs assigned to merchandise includes all inventoriable costs—that is, all direct and indirect costs necessary to bring an inventory item to the point of sale. The AICPA defines cost as follows:

> The primary basis of accounting for inventories is cost, which has been defined generally as the price paid or consideration given to acquire an asset. As applied to inventories, cost means in principle the sum of the applicable expenditures and charges directly or indirectly incurred in bringing an article to its existing condition and location.[2]

AR B#43

---

[1] The cost flow assumptions (FIFO, LIFO, average cost, specific identification) refer to the movement of cost through the inventory accounts as opposed to the physical flow of physical units. The cost flows will be discussed in Chapter 10.

[2] "Restatement and Revision of Accounting Bulletins," *Accounting Research Bulletin No. 43* (New York: AICPA, 1953), Chapter 4, par. 4.

Under this definition, inventoriable costs would include the manufacturing costs (both direct and indirect) and the other costs required to get the merchandise ready for sale. Indirect costs include factory overhead costs but not selling, general, or administrative expenses, which are treated more properly as period costs and not as product or inventoriable costs. The AICPA made the distinction between period costs and inventoriable costs in *Accounting Research Bulletin No. 43* in which they concluded that inventoriable costs included manufacturing overhead but that ". . . general and administrative expenses should be included as period charges . . . (and) . . . selling expenses constitute no part of inventory costs."[3]

ARB#43

In summary, the cost of the inventory would include all of the charges related to obtaining and transporting merchandise or materials to the buyer's place of business, and converting the merchandise or materials to a product ready for sale. These charges include the purchase price, freight and handling charges of materials, and other manufacturing costs, such as direct labor and factory overhead.

A manufacturing company usually maintains at least three and sometimes four inventory accounts: raw materials, work-in-process, finished goods, and supplies. The balance sheet of a typical manufacturing company would show the three or four categories of inventories as follows:

Inventories
Raw materials and supplies	$40,000
Work-in-process	70,000
Finished goods	90,000

The income statement of a manufacturing company would be slightly different from that of a trading company. The principal difference would be found in the cost of goods sold section. A manufacturing company's cost of goods sold would include the cost of goods manufactured and would appear as follows:

Cost of goods sold
Finished goods, Jan. 1	$ 90,000
Cost of goods manufactured	500,000
Cost of goods available for sale	$590,000
Finished goods, Dec. 31	(75,000)
Cost of goods sold	$515,000

The cost of goods manufactured is equivalent to the purchases for a merchandising company. The $500,000 cost of goods manufactured should be detailed in a supporting schedule (shown in Exhibit 8-4) and would indicate the materials, labor, and overhead consumed in the production of the finished goods. In the example $190,000 worth of materials and $175,000 of direct labor are used, and $155,000 of factory costs are consumed in the current period. By adding the cost of the beginning inventory ($25,000) and by subtracting the value of the ending inventory ($45,000), you can find the cost of goods manufactured ($500,000).

[3] Ibid.

Exhibit 8-4
Statement of Cost of Goods Manufactured

Direct materials used		
Direct materials, Jan. 1		$ 10,000
Purchases of direct materials	$200,000	
Less: Purchase discounts	4,000	196,000
Direct materials available for use		$206,000
Direct materials, Dec. 31		16,000
Direct materials used		$190,000
Direct labor		175,000
Factory overhead		
Indirect material	$ 10,000	
Indirect labor	80,000	
Depreciation—building	4,000	
Depreciation—machine & equipment	3,000	
Factory insurance	13,000	
Property tax paid	20,000	
Utilities expense	25,000	
Total factory overhead		155,000
Total current manufacturing costs		$520,000
Work-in-process, Jan. 1		25,000
		$545,000
Work-in-process, December 31		45,000
Cost of goods manufactured		$500,000

Purchase Discounts

Purchase discounts are cash discounts offered by sellers of merchandise for early payment of purchases and are reductions in the price of the purchases. Cash discounts were discussed previously in Chapter 6. They are usually quoted as 2/10, net 20, or other similar terms.

Accounting for purchase discounts by the buyers traditionally has been on either a gross basis or a net basis. Under the **gross price method** the buyer records the purchases at full cost, and the discount appears in the accounting records only when it is taken. The purchase discounts are deducted from the purchases. In the **net price method** the purchases are recorded at the net price, and the discount appears in the accounting records only when it is not taken. The purchase discounts lost are treated as a financing expense and show up as a period cost on the income statement.

Under the gross price method the purchase discounts account is shown in the cost of goods sold section of the income statement where it appears as a reduction (or offset) to the purchases account. Treating the discount in this manner reduces purchases and the cost of goods sold by the amount of the discounts taken. In the net price method the purchase discounts lost account is treated as a financing expense. The discounts lost are shown on the income statement as "other expense," and purchases and cost of goods sold are stated at the price less the discounts. There would be a similar effect on the balance sheet for the inventories. The gross price method would value the inventory at the gross price whereas the net method would reflect the net price.

There is more theoretical support for the net price method. The bargained purchase price of the merchandise is clearly the net amount, and the discount is merely interest expense. The cost principle would indicate that cost is the net cash payment after discounts are deducted. Under the net method the discounts lost are treated as financial costs, and the inventory values are reported properly at cost. In the gross price method the inventory value is overstated by the amount of the discount. In practice, the discounts taken are treated either as a reduction of cost of goods sold or as revenue. A discount taken should not be considered revenue, however, since it originates from the purchase and not from the sale of the merchandise.

Trade Discounts

Trade discounts, which were discussed in Chapter 6, are used frequently when quoting prices in a catalog. Usually the listed price in the catalog is subject to a discount if various quantities of the item are purchased. Trade discounts are not recorded on the books. Purchases are recorded at their net purchase price.

Interest Costs

Interest costs associated with inventories traditionally have been expensed as incurred. This practice is justified on the basis that interest costs are financing charges, and are not a part of the cost of the asset. The counter argument to this position is that interest charges associated with readying the asset for sale are similar to the charges for materials, labor, and overhead, and therefore should be treated as part of the cost of the asset and capitalized.

In *Statement No. 34* the FASB indicated that some interest costs properly should be capitalized. Interest charges associated with assets constructed for a company's own use, or assets produced as discrete projects for sale or lease (i.e., a real estate development project) should be capitalized.[4] Emphasis was placed on discrete projects, such as ship building, that would take a long period of time and would involve a significant number of dollars. Interest costs for products that are manufactured routinely should not be capitalized.

Effects of Inventory Errors

There are several kinds of inventory errors: (1) items that should be included are omitted; (2) items that should be omitted are included instead; and (3) errors in quantities or costs. The results of these and similar errors will affect both the income statement and the balance sheet. The nature of each error must be analyzed carefully to make the proper corrections.

[4]"Capitalization of Interest Cost." *Statement of Financial Accounting Standards No. 34* (Stamford, Conn.: FASB, 1979).

Suppose, for example, that merchandise out on consignment that had a cost of $1,000 was omitted from the inventory. This very easily could be an oversight by the owner of the merchandise. The effect of this error would be to understate the ending inventory, which consequently would overstate the cost of goods sold, understate net income, and understate the inventory value on the balance sheet, all by $1,000. In addition, the working capital and the gross profit percentages would be understated because the inventory was understated. Working capital and gross profit percentages are important tools for analytical purposes as will be explained in Chapter 27. On the other hand, suppose that merchandise on consignment to a company from another vendor was mistakenly included in the company's inventory. The effects would be just the opposite of the previous example; everything would be overstated on the financial statements except the cost of

---

Exhibit 8-5
JOHNSON COMPANY
Comparative Income Statements
For the Years 1981 and 1982

	$100 Error		Correct	
1981:				
Sales		$2,000		$2,000
Cost of sales				
Beginning inventory	$ 450		$ 450	
Purchases	1,800		1,900	
Available for sale	$2,250		$2,350	
Ending inventory	(550)		(650)	
Cost of sales		1,700		1,700
Gross profit		$ 300		$ 300
Operating expense		(150)		(150)
Income before tax		$ 150		$ 150
1982:				
Sales		$2,300		$2,300
Cost of sales				
Beginning inventory	$ 550		$ 650	
Purchases	2,100		2,000	
Available for sale	$2,650		$2,650	
Ending inventory	(800)		(800)	
Cost of sales		1,850		1,850
Gross profit		$ 450		$ 450
Operating expenses		(200)		(200)
Income before tax		$ 250		$ 250

goods sold, which would be understated because the ending inventory was too large.

Another common inventory error is the failure to record a purchase at or near the end of an accounting period and the omission of the merchandise from the ending inventory. For example, assume that the Johnson Company failed to record a $100 purchase in 1981, and the merchandise was omitted from the ending inventory. The net income for 1981 would be correct because the purchases and inventory both would be understated and would cancel each other.

Understating purchases understates the cost of goods sold and overstates income. Understating inventory overstates the cost of goods sold and understates income. The income in 1982 would be correct also, but for exactly the opposite reasons. The purchases would be offset by the understated beginning inventory; therefore, the cost of goods sold and income both would be correct. These errors are illustrated in Exhibit 8-5.

A related situation occurs if a purchase at or near the end of the accounting period is not recorded, but the merchandise has been received and is included in the ending inventory. The liabilities would be understated because of the failure to recognize an account payable. Income would be overstated because purchases (and therefore the cost of goods sold) are understated. In the following year purchases would be overstated and income understated. Note that the total income for the two years combined would be correct.

Another common inventory error arises from quantity and/or costing errors. If the ending inventory is overstated, income will be overstated also in the first

---

Exhibit 8-6
Effects of Common Inventory Errors

Nature of Errors	First Year Effects	Second Year Effects
1. Merchandise excluded from inventory	Understate ending inventory	Understate beginning inventory
	Understate net income	Overstate net income
2. Merchandise improperly included	Overstate ending inventory	Overstate beginning inventory
	Overstate income	Understate income
3. Purchase not recorded; merchandise excluded from inventory	Understate ending inventory	Understate beginning inventory
	Understate purchases	Overstate purchases
	Income correct	Income correct
4. Purchase not recorded; merchandise included in ending inventory	Understate purchases and accounts payable	Overstate purchases
	Overstate income	Understate income
5. Quantity or cost overstated	Overstate ending inventory	Overstate beginning inventory
	Overstate income	Understate income
6. Quantity or cost understated	Understate ending inventory	Understate beginning inventory
	Understate income	Overstate income

year but understated in the second year. If the ending inventory is understated, income will be understated also the first year, but overstated the second year.

Exhibit 8-6 summarizes the effects of common inventory errors for the first and second years. Note that for both years combined, the total income of both years always will be correct. For example, in error number one merchandise was excluded from the inventory. The income would be understated the first year and overstated by an equal amount in the second year. The same thing is true for every error listed with the exception of the third one in which the purchase was not recorded and the merchandise was excluded from the inventory count. As a result of this error, income is correct in both years. All the other errors illustrate that inventory errors are self-correcting. After two years, assuming the books have been closed; the total income is correct and will be unaffected thereafter. Accounting errors are discussed in more detail in Chapter 22.

Valuation of Inventories— Exceptions to the Cost Principle

As emphasized in the preceding sections, the general principle followed in valuation of inventories is that of historical cost. There are several methods (more precisely, cost flow methods) of determining the historical cost of inventories, and these will be discussed in the next chapter. Exceptions to the valuation of inventories at historical cost are the lower of cost or market (LCM) method, accounting for long-term construction projects, the relative sales value method, and purchase commitments.

Lower of Cost or Market

If the market value of the inventory declines below the historical cost, the generally accepted principle of historical cost valuation is modified. In this case (due to such factors as obsolescence, changing price levels, damaged merchandise, and so forth) a loss in utility has occurred in the accounting period and properly should be recognized as a loss in that period. The inventory value should be written down to reflect the loss by applying the lower of cost or market rule. The **lower of cost or market rule** states that inventory should be valued at the lower of its cost or current market value. Writing down the value of the asset when a decline occurs is consistent with the conservatism principle, which dictates that if an economic event (the decline in value) has taken place during the accounting period, there should be a lower value in the financial statements of that period.

Theoretical justification for use of the lower of cost or market method is found in *Accounting Research Bulletin No. 43:*

> . . . a departure from the cost basis is required when the utility of the goods is no longer as great as its cost. Where there is evidence that the utility of goods, in their disposal in the ordinary course of business, will be less than cost, . . . the difference should be recognized as a loss of the current period. This is generally accomplished by stating such goods at a lower level, commonly designated as market.[5]

ARB # 43

---

[5] *Accounting Research Bulletin No. 43*, par. 7.

The term **market** means the current replacement cost of the item, not the resale market price or value. **Current replacement cost** means replacement either by purchase or manufacture—in other words, what it would cost to either purchase or manufacture another unit of inventory. Market is limited by upper and lower bounds; the upper bound is the **"ceiling"** and the lower bound is the **"floor."** The "ceiling" limitation means that the market value may not exceed the net realizable value (the estimated selling price in the ordinary course of business, less reasonably predictable costs of completion and disposal). The "floor" limitation is the net realizable value reduced by an allowance for a normal profit margin.

The reason for a floor and a ceiling on the market value used is to prevent over or understatement of the inventory value. For example, assume the replacement cost of an item was $100, but the net realizable value was only $90. If the item were valued at $100 for inventory purposes, the value would be overstated by $10. It is unreasonable to value an item at more than its known sale value. Therefore, the ceiling of net realizable value should be used. In the same manner, if the replacement cost were again $100, but this time the net realizable value was $135 and the normal profit was $20, the proper market valuation would be $115. In this case it is again unreasonable to use the $100 replacement cost because the company is certain it could get at least $115 for the item. The market value should not be less than the absolute minimum expected selling price. If the $100 replacement cost figure were used, the inventory value would be understated by $15; hence, the floor valuation is used.

The concept of market value (replacement cost), and the boundaries of ceiling and floor are illustrated in the following example:

Inventory—sales value		$100
Less: Packaging costs	$ 8	
Transportation costs	10	(18)
Net realizable value (ceiling)		$ 82
Less: Normal profit margin (15%)		(15)
Floor		$ 67

In the example the ceiling for the market value is $82 and the floor is $67. If the replacement cost falls between the two, it will be used as the "market" value and compared to cost. If the replacement cost falls outside the range, the ceiling or floor will be used as "market" value. It is important to note that the ceiling and floor are tests of the reasonableness of the replacement cost figure. These tests are separate from and occur before the comparison of the market with cost to determine which is lower.

Exhibit 8-7 shows that the market used can be the replacement cost, ceiling, or floor. In cases 1, 2, and 5 the replacement cost is used as the market price. The net realizable value (ceiling) is used in case 3, and in case 4 the net realizable value less a normal markup (floor) is used. In each case the market value is determined first, and then it is compared to the original cost figure. The lesser of the original cost and the designated market value becomes the inventory valuation figure. In summary, the replacement cost must lie between the ceiling and the floor to be considered "market." If the replacement cost is above the ceiling, the ceiling is used as "market." If the replacement cost is below the floor, the floor is used as

Exhibit 8-7
Illustration of Lower of Cost or Market

Case	Cost	Replacement Cost	Net Realizable Value	Net Realizable Value Less Normal Markup	Market	Inventory Value
1	$5.00	$5.50	$6.00	$5.40	$5.50	$5.00
2	5.00	4.50	5.10	4.45	4.50	4.50
3	5.00	4.90	4.80	4.30	4.80	4.80
4	5.00	4.50	5.20	4.75	4.75	4.75
5	5.00	5.30	5.50	5.20	5.30	5.00

Case 1: Cost is used because it is lower than market.

Case 2: Replacement cost is market because it falls between ceiling and floor. Market is used because it is lower than cost.

Case 3: Net realizable value (ceiling) is market because replacement cost is above the ceiling. Market is used because it is lower than cost.

Case 4: Net realizable value less normal markup (floor) is market because replacement cost is below floor. Market is used because it is lower than cost.

Case 5: Replacement cost is market because it falls between ceiling and floor. Cost is used because it is lower than market.

"market." After "market" is determined, it is compared to cost for inventory valuation purposes.

Methods of Applying Lower of Cost or Market.   The lower of cost or market rule may be applied ". . . to each item or to the total of the inventory (or, in some cases, to the total of the components of each major category). The method should be the one that most clearly reflects periodic income."[6] The method that usually approximates cost most closely is application of the lower of cost or market to the total of the inventory. The next closest approximation is usually the total of the components of major categories, and the furthest from cost is the individual item method. The reason for this order is that in the total inventory and major categories methods, increases and decreases in individual items are netted against each other. On an individual item basis, however, all decreases are used, but increases in values are not used to offset these decreases.

Exhibit 8-8 illustrates the three alternative methods of applying the lower of cost or market rule. The valuation for the individual items is $25,900, compared to $26,600 for the categories and $27,000 for the total inventory.

Note that in Exhibit 8-8 each of the individual items with a market valuation less than cost was extended and used in the valuation. These were items C, D,

ARB 43

[6] Ibid., par. 10.

Exhibit 8-8
Alternative Methods of Applying Lower of Cost or Market

Units	Cost	Market	Individual Items	Major Categories	Inventory Total
Category 1					
Item A	$ 5,000	$ 6,000	$ 5,000		
Item B	5,500	7,000	5,500		
Item C	6,000	5,500	5,500		
Total	$16,500	$18,500		$16,500	
Category 2					
Item D	$ 3,000	$ 2,800	2,800		
Item E	3,500	3,100	3,100		
Item F	4,000	4,200	4,000		
Total	$10,500	$10,100		10,100	
Total Inventory	$27,000	$28,600	$25,900	$26,600	$27,000

and E, which differed from cost by $500, $200, and $400 respectively, a total of $1,100 less than the cost total. In the major categories, cost ($16,500) is used in category 1, and market ($10,100) is used in category 2. The total difference from cost is only $400, which results from combining a minus $200 from D, a minus $400 from E, and a plus $200 from E. The net change is only $400. For the inventory as a whole, the cost figure is used since it is less than market. Thus, the order of methods that approximate cost most closely is applying LCM to the inventory as a whole, then to the major categories, and last to individual items.

Most companies use the individual item method, which is the method required by the IRS when practical. Regardless of which method is used, it must be used consistently from one period to the next.

Recording Reductions of Inventory Cost to Market. Either the direct method or the allowance method may be used to write down inventory cost to market value. In the **direct method** the loss is recorded directly in the inventory and cost of goods sold accounts. In the **allowance method** the loss is recorded in a separate loss account and a contra-asset allowance account. The two methods have the same effect on net income. However, the allowance method provides more information because the loss from decline in market value of the inventory is identified clearly and shown as a separate item. The journal entries for both methods are illustrated in Exhibit 8-9. The entries are based on the following data:

	Cost	Market	Amount Required in Allowance Account
Jan. 1, 1981	$10,000	$10,000	–0–
Dec. 31, 1981	15,000	14,000	$1,000
Dec. 31, 1982	13,000	12,500	500

Exhibit 8-9

Journal Entries Required for Lower of Cost or Market

	Direct Method		Allowance Method	
Dec. 31, 1981				
Income summary	10,000		10,000	
Inventory		10,000		10,000
To close beginning inventory.				
Inventory	14,000		15,000	
Income summary		14,000		15,000
To record ending inventory.				
Loss in inventory market value	None required		1,000	
Allowance to reduce inventory to market				1,000
To reduce inventory to market value.				
Dec. 31, 1982				
Income summary	14,000		14,000	
Allowance to reduce inventory to market			1,000	
Inventory		14,000		15,000
To close beginning inventory. (and the allowance account)				
Inventory	12,500		13,000	
Income summary		12,500		13,000
To record ending inventory.				
Loss in inventory market value	None required		500	
Allowance to reduce inventory to market				500
To reduce ending inventory to market value.				

Under the direct method the $1,000 decline in inventory value below cost in the first year is buried in the closing entry at year-end. The ending inventory is recorded simply at the $14,000 market value. Consequently, the ending inventory is $1,000 below cost, and the cost of goods sold will be correspondingly $1,000 greater. The $1,000 loss is not shown separately. However, the allowance method clearly shows the loss as a separate item. A separate entry is made with a debit to the loss account and a credit to the allowance account. The loss then is shown as a separate item in the income statement; this has the added advantage of not distorting the cost of goods sold or the gross profit percentage for the year. Partial income statements and balance sheets are shown in Exhibit 8-10.

Exhibit 8-10
Partial Financial Statements for Lower of Cost or Market

Income Statements—Direct Method	1981	1982
Beginning inventory	$10,000	$14,000
Purchases (assumed)	75,000	75,000
Available for sale	$85,000	$89,000
Ending inventory (LCM)	(14,000)	(12,500)
Cost of goods sold	$71,000	$76,500

Income Statements—Allowance Method		
Beginning inventory	$10,000	$14,000
Purchases	75,000	75,000
Available for sale	$85,000	$89,000
Ending inventory	(15,000)	(13,000)
Cost of goods sold	$70,000	$76,000
Loss in inventory market value	1,000	500
Adjusted cost of goods sold	$71,000	$76,500

Balance Sheets—Direct Method	12–31–81	12–31–82
Inventory (LCM)	$14,000	$12,500

Balance Sheets—Allowance Method	12–31–81	12–31–82
Inventory (cost)	$15,000	$13,000
Less: Allowance to reduce inventory to market	(1,000)	(500)
Inventory (LCM)	$14,000	$12,500

In the second year the market value of the inventory is $500 less than cost. The journal entries in the direct method are comparable to those in the first year. In the allowance method the beginning allowance account is closed with the beginning inventory. The ending balance in the allowance is established the same way as done above for 1981. Again, the advantage of the allowance method is that it clearly identifies the losses in the income statements and the balance sheets. Note in Exhibit 8-10 that the cost of goods sold is the same ($71,000 and $76,500) for the two methods. The $1,000 loss in 1981 is added to the cost of goods sold of $70,000 to obtain the adjusted figure of $71,000. In 1982, the $500 adjustment is treated in the same way. Note also that in the direct method the $1,000 and $500 adjustments are simply buried in the cost of goods sold, but in the allowance method they are shown clearly and separately.

Exhibit 8-10 also illustrates the balance sheet presentation of the two methods. The inventory value is the same for both methods in both years. However, the allowance method provides both the cost and the lower of cost or market values.

Evaluation of Lower of Cost or Market.   The lower of cost or market rule serves to reduce the asset value in the balance sheet when a decline in value has occurred. The rule also serves to recognize the loss in the income statement in the period in which it occurs. Reduction of the asset value and recognition of the loss can be justified by the conservatism principle. If the asset value has declined to less than its cost, an overstatement of the asset would result if the decline were not recognized. The principle of conservatism requires the recognition of all reasonably anticipated losses; hence, if the inventory value has declined, the loss would be recognized in the period in which it takes place.

The revenue realization principle requires that gains be recognized when a transaction (sale) has occurred and is completed. Under the LCM rule, losses are recognized before the period of sale. If losses are recognized before the sale, it would seem to follow that gains also should be recognized in the period in which they occur instead of waiting for the period of sale. But the LCM rule does not recognize increases in the inventory value, only decreases. In other words, the rule is applied only in one direction—the downside. This again is justified by reference to the conservatism principle, which precludes the anticipation of possible gains. The contradiction between the principles of conservatism and revenue realization has been resolved in favor of conservatism.

If the loss is recognized in the period before sale, income will be greater in the period of sale. In effect, the loss is shifted from the period of sale to the prior period when the decline in value occurs. The total income for the two periods, however, will remain the same.

There also has been some criticism of the market values used in LCM. Three different market values potentially could be used: replacement cost, net realizable value (ceiling), or net realizable value less a normal markup (floor). Replacement cost was chosen as the basis for LCM because it was assumed that replacement cost moved in the same direction as selling prices. This means that increases in replacement costs indicate increases in selling prices, and decreases in replacement costs indicate decreases in selling prices. The ceiling and floor limits were imposed to prevent gross misstatements of the replacement costs.

Long-Term Construction Contracts

Long-term construction contracts for major projects such as buildings, dams, large bridges, or ships pose a different set of circumstances to the accountant. The valuation of inventory and income recognition for a contractor can vary significantly depending on the choice of accounting methods employed. The two alternative accounting methods for long-term construction contracts, the **percentage-of-completion method** and the **completed-contract method,** are discussed in detail in the Appendix to this chapter. The accounting profession recommends the use of the percentage-of-completion method if the contractor is able to provide reasonable and dependable estimates of the future costs of completing the contract and reasonable estimates of the extent of work completed.[7] In the percentage-of-completion method, income is recognized over the life of the project, and inventory is valued at the accumulated cost plus the profit recognized and less the billings to-date. In the completed-contract method, the inventory is valued at the accumulated cost, and profit is not recognized until the project is completed. The percentage-of-completion method represents a departure from the cost method of inventory valuation. A complete discussion of the relative differences between these two methods is presented in the Appendix.

Relative Sales Value Method

Another exception to the cost principle for pricing inventory is the **relative sales value method** of apportioning the cost of a joint purchase. This problem occurs when a group of varying products (i.e., varying in grade or quality) is purchased at a single, lump sum price. Assume, for example, that the Alligator Shirt Company purchases a batch of fabric for a total cost of $1,000. There are three different types or grades of fabric included in the purchase: 100 yards of Type A, 150 yards of Type B, and 250 yards of Type C. As the fabric is used to make shirts, the purchase cost must be apportioned between the fabric used and the fabric remaining in inventory.

One method of allocating the cost might be simply to divide the total cost ($1,000) by the total yards of fabric (500) to obtain the cost per yard ($2). This does not seem reasonable, however, because the different types of fabric have a different value and grade; therefore, each type should be allocated a different portion of the total cost.

A very common and logical method of dealing with this problem is to allocate the cost based on the relative sales value of each type of fabric. The total sales value of each grade is used as the basis for the allocation as follows:

Fabric Type	Yards	Sales Price Per Yard	Total Sales Value	Allocation Proportion	Cost Allocated	Cost Per Yard
A	100	$6.50	$ 650	650/2,000	$ 325	$3.25
B	150	4.00	600	600/2,000	300	2.00
C	250	3.00	750	750/2,000	375	1.50
			$2,000		$1,000	

[7]"Long-Term Construction-Type Contracts," *Accounting Research Bulletin No. 45* (New York: AICPA, 1955), par. 15.

Purchase Commitments

Frequently a company will enter into a noncancelable contract to buy materials or merchandise at a firm price. These arrangements are known as **purchase commitments.** If they have been made at a definite price, they should be disclosed in a footnote to the financial statements as follows:

Note 5. The company has contracted for the purchase of materials in the amount of $1,500,000 during 1983. The market price of these materials at December 31, 1982, is $1,200,000.

Because the company has a noncancelable contract to purchase these materials at the stated price, it is proper for the company to recognize the loss in 1982, the period in which it occurred. Recognition of the loss in the current period is the same as if the company had owned the inventory already. The following journal entry illustrates recognition of the loss:

Loss on purchase commitments	300,000	
Accrued loss on purchase commitments		300,000

The loss on purchase commitments account is closed at the end of the period, and the accrued loss account is shown as a liability on the balance sheet.

In 1983, when the actual purchases are made, the accrued loss will be written off as follows:

Purchases	1,200,000	
Accrued loss on purchase commitments	300,000	
Accounts payable		1,500,000

If the price were to go up sufficiently to recover a portion or all of the loss before delivery of the merchandise, a gain would result and be charged against the accrued loss.

This procedure is a departure from the cost principle and is to be used only for firm or noncancelable orders. Proponents of this procedure justify it on the basis that the loss should be recognized in the period in which it occurs.

Disclosure Requirements for Inventories

Disclosure requirements for inventories fall into five categories: composition, financing, cost flow assumption, consistency, and price-level information. The price-level information has been required only recently and only for very large companies.

The inventory composition refers to the manufacturer's inventories of raw materials, work-in-process, and finished goods that were discussed early in this

---

Exhibit 8-11
OGDEN CORPORATION
Notes to Financial Statements

---

3. Inventories

Inventories (expressed in thousands of dollars) consist, of the following:

	1980	1979
Finished goods	$ 99,200	$102,172
Raw materials, supplies and products in progress	84,772	75,286
Scrap metals, etc.	10,144	11,486
Total	$194,116	$188,944

Certain inventories were valued at LIFO. If such inventories were shown at current cost (determined by the average cost method) inventories would have been $5,588,000 and $6,443,000 higher than reported at December 31, 1980 and 1979, respectively.

Inventory and Cost of Goods Sold: Current costs of raw material and ferrous and nonferrous scrap inventories were calculated by the direct pricing method for approximately 80% of dollar value of the items. Year end costs were determined by reference to vendors' invoices, catalog prices, suppliers' and vendors' price quotes, and published market prices. The remaining items were adjusted to year end current cost using an estimated composite rate.

Work in process and finished goods inventories were adjusted to current cost by determining the average inventory turnover rate for the various inventories and restating historical recorded costs of such inventories giving effect to the current price changes during the period of material, labor, and overhead components of such inventories.

Cost of goods sold was restated to current cost at time of sales by calculating the material, labor, and overhead components and determining inventory turnover rates mentioned above by component for applicable inventories.

The current cost of sales using the LIFO method of inventory valuation approximates the historical cost of sales. Inventories of such operations have been adjusted to current year end cost.

For long-term contracts of operations where materials are purchased and costs incurred or committed specifically for identifiable contracts with a determinable sales price, the cost of sales and work in process inventory were measured for constant dollar (general inflation) and current cost (specific) at date of commitment. Accordingly, current cost, both general and specific, is the same as historical cost in such operations. However, depreciation of assets used in such operations was adjusted to current cost and is reflected in the restatements.

chapter. The manufacturer is required to provide information about the relative mix of the three inventory accounts.

Any unusual financing arrangements related to inventories also require disclosure. Some examples of these would be involuntary liquidation of LIFO inventories (discussed in Chapter 10), pledging inventories as collateral, or inventory transactions involving related parties. The cost flow assumption used to value inventories must be disclosed also. Cost flow assumptions will be discussed in Chapter 9.

Consistency refers to year-to-year consistency in valuation methods as opposed to consistency within the entire inventory. A change in valuation method from one year to the next is a consistency change and also a change in accounting principle. This is a required disclosure and is discussed more fully in Chapter 22.

Accounting Series Release 190 (ASR 190), which was issued by the SEC in 1976, required that certain companies disclose the estimated replacement of inventories and property, plant, and equipment. Approximately 1,000 of the largest manufacturing companies were affected. *ASR 190* was very controversial in that compliance was extremely costly for the affected companies. In addition, the companies contended that the disclosure provided no significant new information.

In 1979 the FASB issued *Statement No. 33*, "Financial Reporting and Changing Prices," requiring certain large companies to disclose supplementary information on both a constant-dollar basis and a current-cost basis. The companies affected are required to report the current cost of inventories (i.e., replacement cost) and the cost of goods sold. In addition, the companies are required to compute and disclose increases or decreases arising from the difference between

---

Exhibit 8-12
CHAMPION INTERNATIONAL CORPORATION
Notes To Financial Statements

B. Inventories

Inventories, which include material, labor and factory overhead, are generally stated at the lower of average cost or market (approximates net realizable values), except for certain inventories of the paper and packaging segments which are stated on the last-in, first-out (LIFO) method. (See Note 2.)

Note 2. Inventories:

At December 31, 1980 and 1979, inventories stated on the last-in, first-out (LIFO) method, representing 22% and 19% of total inventories, were $106,832,000 and $88,835,000, respectively. If the lower of an average cost or market method (which approximates current cost) had been utilized for inventories carried at LIFO, it would have had the effect of increasing inventory balances by $95,928,000 and $78,884,000 at December 31, 1980 and 1979, respectively.

the current cost of inventory and the price-level adjusted cost of inventory. Chapter 26 provides an in-depth discussion of the requirements of FASB *Statement No. 33.*

Exhibits 8-11 and 8-12 provide examples of inventory disclosures by two different companies. Exhibit 8-11 contains inventory data for Ogden Corporation, whose inventories consist of three categories and are valued at LIFO. Ogden also indicates the impact on the value of the inventory by using LIFO instead of average cost. Exhibit 8-12 presents the data for Champion International Corporation. Two notes related to the inventories provide details on how they were valued.

Concept Summary

INVENTORIES—GENERAL CONCEPTS

BASIC CONCEPTS

Term	Description	Explanation
Inventory	Assets held for future sale or for use in production of goods and services.	Inventory includes the raw material, the work-in-process and the finished products awaiting sale.
Classifications of Inventory	Raw material, work-in-process, finished goods, supplies.	The various classes of inventory are reported separately for manufacturing companies.
Periodic Inventory System	Ending inventory units determined by count at end of period.	Useful when companies have large quantities of low unit value products, such as, supermarkets.
Perpetual Inventory System	Continuous record of purchases and sales maintained.	Useful for companies with high value products.
Inventory Valuation	ARB *No. 43*—inventory value includes sum of all direct and indirect costs incurred to bring an item to the point of sale.	The cost of inventory includes all the costs incurred in the manufacturing process to make the product ready for sale.

INVENTORY METHODS—DEPARTURES FROM COST

Term	Description	Explanation
Lower of Cost or Market	Current replacement cost (as limited by the ceiling and the floor) is compared to historical cost.	Inventory valuation for reporting purposes will be at the lower of cost or market value, where market value is the replacement cost limited by the ceiling and the floor.
Percentage-of-Completion	ARB *No. 45* recommends this method for long-term construction when reasonable estimates of costs can be made. Inventory is valued at accumulated cost plus recognized profit and less the billings to-date.	This method is used for long-term construction contracts, those that will extend over several years. The purpose is to recognize revenue over the life of the project.
Completed-Contract	ARB *No. 45* recommends this method for long-term construction when reasonable estimates of costs cannot be made. Inventory valued at accumulated cost.	If the amount of revenue or the completion period cannot be reasonably estimated, the completed-contract method must be used. In this method all income is recognized at the end of the project.

Appendix

Accounting for Long-Term Construction Contracts

There are two methods used in accounting for long-term construction contracts: the completed-contract method and the percentage-of-completion method. The completed-contract method recognizes all profit on the contract in the year of completion, while the percentage-of-completion method recognizes a proportionate share of the profit each year during construction. According to current GAAP, the percentage-of-completion method should be used except when reasonable estimates cannot be made. The theory behind the two methods was discussed in the chapter. An illustration of the methods is presented in this Appendix.

Assume that Swindle Construction Co. has a contract starting April 1, 1980, to construct an office building for Peacock Enterprises. The expected date of completion is June, 1982. The contract price is $10,000,000, and the expected cost of construction is $9,000,000. The following information relates to the construction period:

	1980	1981	1982
Costs to-date	$2,500,000	$6,500,000	$ 9,300,000
Estimated costs to complete	6,500,000	2,750,000	0
Progress billings to-date	1,000,000	6,000,000	10,000,000
Cash collection to-date	800,000	5,400,000	10,000,000

Percentage-of-Completion Method

Various methods can be used under the percentage-of-completion method to recognize profit on the contract. Under each method the objective is to measure the proportion of the contract that is completed and to recognize that proportion of the gross profit in the year in which that partial completion took place. Estimates can be based on inputs or outputs. When based on inputs, the following are some of the measures that could be used: (1) costs incurred, (2) labor hours incurred, and (3) raw material costs incurred. Output measures include (1) engineering estimate of percent completed or (2) unit measures, such as miles of road completed. The method most used is the one based on construction costs incurred to-date. This method is applied in the illustration.

Exhibit 8-13 shows how the annual profit recognition is determined. Profit is recognized in the proportion that costs incurred to-date bear to total estimated

Exhibit 8-13
Percentage-of-Completion Method

	1980	1981	1982
Contract price	$10,000,000	$10,000,000	$10,000,000
Less: Costs			
Cost incurred to-date	$ 2,500,000	$ 6,500,000	$ 9,300,000
Estimated future costs	6,500,000	2,750,000	—
Total estimated cost	$ 9,000,000	$ 9,250,000	$ 9,300,000
Estimated gross profit	$ 1,000,000	$ 750,000	$ 700,000

Gross Profit Recognized

1980: $\dfrac{\$2,500,000}{\$9,000,000} \times \$1,000,000 =$ $ 277,778

1981: $\dfrac{\$6,500,000}{\$9,250,000} \times \$750,000 =$ $ 527,027

Less: Gross profit recognized
in prior years   277,778

$ 249,249

1982 total gross profit $ 700,000
Less: Gross profit recognized
in prior years   527,027

$ 172,973

costs. In 1980 the costs incurred to-date were $2,500,000 of a total estimated cost of $9,000,000. This fraction is multiplied by the estimated gross profit to determine the portion of the profit that should have been recognized to-date. In 1980 this was $277,778; in 1981 it was $527,027. Notice also that in 1981 the $527,027 represents the *total* gross profit that should be recognized through 1981. To find the amount to be recognized as 1981 gross profit, you must deduct the $277,778 already recognized in 1980 from the total. Thus, $249,249 is recognized in 1981 ($527,027–$277,778).

Another aspect of Exhibit 8-13 that should be noticed is the treatment of changes in estimated costs and gross profit. The 1980 gross profit recognition was based on an expected gross profit of $1,000,000. The expected gross profit decreased to $750,000 in 1981. There is no retroactive adjustment of prior years' profits for a change in estimates (this is discussed in detail in Chapter 22). Calculations for the current year are based on the new estimates of total cost and gross profit.

When a loss or a gross profit less than that already recognized is estimated, a loss should be recorded in the year in which the determination is made. For example, assume that in 1981 it was estimated that the total cost of the project would be $10,100,000. Thus, a $100,000 loss is anticipated. In this situation the anticipated loss, plus the previously recognized gross profit, would be recorded as a loss in 1981. If a total net loss of $100,000 were expected on the project, the 1981 income statement would show a $377,778 loss on the project. This is the anticipated loss of $100,000 plus the previously recognized profit of $277,778. Note that when a loss is anticipated, it is recognized in the year in which it is determined, not throughout the term of the project as is done with an anticipated profit.

If projected profit falls below the amount already recognized, the difference is written off as a loss in the year in which the decrease is determined. Assume that in 1981 the total anticipated profit fell to $200,000. Since $277,778 has been recognized already in 1980, a $77,778 loss would have to be recognized in 1981.

The journal entries to be made regarding the contract (using original data) appear in Exhibit 8-14. When costs are incurred, they are charged to a construction in-progress account. This account is essentially a work in-process inventory account. When the customer is billed, the entry records the receivable and credits the billings on construction in-progress account (entry #2). The billings account is basically a contra-construction in-progress account. The billings account reflects the customers' equity in the inventory. If you subtract billings from the inventory account, the balance reflects the contractor's equity in the inventory. For example, at the end of 1980 the customer has $1,000,000 equity in the construction in-progress account, and the contractor has $1,500,000 equity. The third entry records the receipt of the receivable and is a typical entry for collection of receivables. The fourth entry recognizes the annual gross profit on the contract and adds it to the construction in-progress account. When the contract is complete, the construction in-progress account and the billings on construction in-progress are equal to the total contract price. At the completion date the fifth entry is made to close out the inventory and billings account. This is done because at this point the customer has total equity in the inventory.

Disclosure in the statement of financial position would include the receivable, inventory, and billings accounts. For example, the 1981 statement would show the following:

December 31, 1981

Current assets
    Receivables from construction in-progress $ 600,000
    Inventories—construction in-progress totalling
      $7,027,027*, less progress billings of
      $6,000.000   1,022,027
   *($2,500,000 + $277,778 + $4,000,000 + $249,249)

Occasionally, the terms of the contract may allow billings early in the contract at amounts greater than the construction in-progress. When this occurs, the billings are in excess of the inventory account, and the net credit amount would be disclosed as a current liability. In this case the excess billings are in essence an unearned revenue.

The contractor's financial statements also will include footnote disclosures, such as the method of revenue recognition, the basis for classifying assets and liabilities (that is, the nature of the operating cycle), the effects of revisions in estimates, and details concerning the receivables on construction in-progress.

Exhibit 8-14

SWINDLE CONSTRUCTION COMPANY
Journal Entries

	1980		1981		1982	
Construction in progress	2,500,000		4,000,000		2,800,000	
Materials, cash, payables, etc.		2,500,000		4,000,000		2,800,000
To record construction costs.						
Accounts receivable—construction in-progress	1,000,000		5,000,000		4,000,000	
Billings on construction in-progress		1,000,000		5,000,000		4,000,000
To record the progress billings.						
Cash	800,000		4,600,000		5,600,000	
Accounts receivable—construction in-progress		800,000		4,600,000		5,600,000
To record collections.						
Construction in-progress	277,778		249,249		172,973	
Gross profit on construction contracts		277,778		249,249		172,973
To recognize gross profit (per Exhibit 8-14).						
Billings on construction in-progress					10,000,000	
Construction in-progress						10,000,000
To record completion of the contract.						

Completed-Contract Method

Under the completed-contract method, profit on the contract would not be recognized until the year of completion. In the Swindle Construction Company example, the following is the revenue recognition under the completed-contract method:

Year	Profit Recognized
1980	0
1981	0
1982	$700,000

As indicated in the chapter, this is not a desirable method of reporting profit on construction contracts because it recognizes all of the profit in one period even though substantial earning activities took place over a number of years. The method should be used only when it is not possible to make reasonable estimates of future costs or percent of completion.

Journal entries under the completed-contract method would be the same as in Exhibit 8-14 except for entries 4 and 5. No entries would be made to recognize income during the life of the project. Instead of the entries under 4 and 5, the following entry would be made in 1982:

Billings on construction in-progress	10,000,000	
Construction in-progress		9,300,000
Gross profit on construction contracts		700,000

Financial statement disclosures under the completed-contract method are similar to those under the percentage-of-completion method.

Questions

Q-8-1 Define inventories.

Q-8-2 Do inventories include any asset that is not sold in the ordinary course of business?

Q-8-3 What inventory account(s) does a trading company normally need?

Q-8-4 Partially completed merchandise or goods at the end of the accounting period are included in which inventory account?

Q-8-5 Differentiate between the supplies inventory and the raw materials inventory.

Q-8-6 Indicate whether the following would be included in the inventory of the buyer or the seller:

   a) Transaction, f.o.b. destination.
   b) Transaction, f.o.b. shipping point.
   c) Goods delivered to a warehouseman who notifies buyer of arrival of the goods.

Q-8-7 Who holds title to goods on consignment?

Q–8–8   Companies that use perpetual inventory systems still must take physical counts of inventory at least once a year. Why?

Q–8–9   What items comprise manufacturing costs? Are these manufacturing costs period or product costs?

Q–8–10   Which of the following are product or inventoriable costs?
  a)   Depreciation on factory equipment.
  b)   Depreciation on a delivery van.
  c)   Cost of a calculator used by the accountant.
  d)   Plant supervisor's salary.
  e)   Insurance on the factory.
  f)   Machine repairs in the machine shop.

Q–8–11   What two methods exist for accounting for purchase discounts? How are purchases treated under each of those methods?

Q–8–12   Of the two methods of accounting for purchase discounts, which is conceptually superior? Why?

Q–8–13   What would be the effect of a failure to include merchandise on consignment as part of the inventory?

Q–8–14   What is the effect on the cost of goods sold and on net income if the ending inventory is overstated?

Q–8–15   What accounting principle(s) justifies the writing down of an asset when a decline in value occurs?

Q–8–16   What does *floor* mean under the lower of cost or market rule?

Q–8–17   What two methods exist to write down inventory cost to market value? How are these methods recorded?

Q–8–18   Which of the two methods referred to in Question 8-17 clearly identifies gains and losses in the income statements and balance sheets? How?

Q–8–19   Answer the following multiple choice questions.
  a)   Which of the following is an example of an inventory accounting policy that should be disclosed?
    (1)   Effect of inventory profits caused by inflation.
    (2)   Composition of inventory into the various types of raw materials.
    (3)   Identification of major suppliers.
    (4)   Method used for inventory pricing.
  b)   When valuing raw materials inventory at lower of cost or market, what is the meaning of the term *market?*
    (1)   Net realizable value.
    (2)   Net realizable value less a normal profit margin.
    (3)   Current replacement cost.
    (4)   Discounted present value.

(AICPA adapted)

*Q–8–20   Answer the following multiple choice questions.
  a)   How should the balances of progress billings and construction in-progress be shown at reporting dates before the completion of a long-term contract?
    (1)   Progress billings as deferred income, construction in-progress as a deferred expense.
    (2)   Progress billings as income, construction in-progress as inventory.
    (3)   Net, as a current asset if debit balance, and current liability if credit balance.
    (4)   Net, as income from construction if credit balance, and loss from construction if debit balance.
  b)   The calculation of the income recognized in the second year of a four-year con-

struction contract that is accounted for using the percentage-of-completion method is based on which one of the following?

(1) Cumulative actual costs incurred only.

(2) Incremental cost for the second year only.

(3) Estimated costs at the inception of the contract.

(4) Latest available estimated costs.

c) How should earned but unbilled revenues at the balance sheet date on a long-term construction contract be disclosed if the percentage-of-completion method of revenue recognition is used?

(1) As construction in-progress in the current asset section of the balance sheet.

(2) As construction in-progress in the noncurrent asset section of the balance sheet.

(3) As a receivable in the noncurrent asset section of the balance sheet.

(4) In a footnote to the financial statements until the customer is billed formally for the portion of work completed.

(AICPA adapted)

*Q–8–21 Answer the following multiple choice questions.

a) When is the percentage-of-completion method of accounting for long-term construction-type contracts preferable?

(1) When estimates of cost to complete and extent of progress toward completion are reasonably dependable.

(2) When the collectibility of progress billings from the customer is reasonably assured.

(3) When contractor is involved in numerous projects.

(4) When the contracts are of a relatively short duration.

b) When you account for a long-term construction-type contract using the percentage-of-completion method, the gross profit recognized during the first year would be the estimated total gross profit from the contract multiplied by the percentage of the costs incurred during the year to the

(1) Total costs incurred to-date.

(2) Total estimated cost.

(3) Unbilled portion of the contract price.

(4) Total contract price.

(AICPA adapted)

Note: Items with an *asterisk* relate to material contained in the appendix.

Discussion Questions and Cases

D–8–1 Habitat Corporation manufactures and sells a variety of equipment that is useful for camping and other outdoor recreational activities. Habitat maintains its own retail outlets, but also sells its merchandise through other outlets it does not own. The merchandise sold through the nonowned outlets is sold on a consignment basis. The merchandise is shipped to the other retailer; the other retailer then sells the merchandise, extracts a seller's commission, and remits the remaining proceeds to Habitat.

Habitat uses a periodic FIFO inventory system. The ending inventory is counted and only the merchandise on hand is included. The merchandise on consignment consistently has been excluded from the ending inventory of Habitat.

Required:

1. What is the proper accounting treatment for goods on consignment?

2. What is the effect of excluding the merchandise on consignment from the ending inventory?

D–8–2 Jones Company has been in business for several years and always follows good accounting procedures. It is only very seldom that a mistake occurs, and Jones immediately rectifies it as soon as it is brought to the attention of management. Jones uses a periodic inventory system and neglected to record a purchase of merchandise on account at year-end. This merchandise also was omitted from the physical count. How will these errors affect assets, liabilities, and stockholders' equity at year-end and how will they affect net earnings for the year?

D–8–3 Rosemound Corporation started in business on March 15, 1979. The company was established for the purpose of selling maintenance equipment to oil drilling rigs along the Gulf coast. A fairly large variety of products was maintained and sold to the drilling companies. Rosemound always has followed the periodic inventory system. When the company was established originally, the owner was able to track the individual products handled by the company very easily. As business has grown and become more complex, however, the owner is considering switching to a perpetual system. Rosemound uses the FIFO cost flow method for valuation purposes.

Required:
1. What is the difference between a perpetual and a periodic inventory system?
2. If Rosemound changes from periodic to perpetual and continues to use FIFO, what will be the impact on inventory valuation and on income?
3. If Rosemound switches from FIFO to LIFO, what would be the impact of changing from periodic to perpetual?

D–8–4 *Accounting Research Bulletin No. 43* justifies and supports the use of lower of cost or market for inventory valuation purposes by stating in paragraph 7, "Where there is evidence that the utility of goods, in their disposal in the ordinary course of business, will be less than cost, . . . the difference should be recognized as a loss of the current period. This is generally accomplished by stating such goods at a lower level, commonly designated as market." *ARB No. 43* takes the position that the economic event (the decline in value) should be recognized in the period in which it occurs.

Required:
What is the meaning of the term *market* as used by *ARB No. 43?* Explain fully.

*D–8–5 In accounting for long-term contracts (those taking longer than one year to complete), the two methods commonly followed are the percentage-of-completion method and the completed-contract method.

Required:
1. Discuss how earnings on long-term contracts are recognized and computed under these two methods.
2. Under what circumstances is it preferable to use one method over the other?
3. Why is earnings recognition as measured by interim billings not generally accepted for long-term contracts?
4. How are job costs and interim billings reflected on the balance sheet under the percentage-of-completion method and the completed-contract method?

(AICPA adapted)

*D–8–6 Income determination for long-term construction contracts presents special problems because the construction work often extends over two or more accounting periods. The two methods commonly followed are the percentage-of-completion method and the completed-contract method.

Required:
Evaluate the use of the percentage-of-completion method for income determination purposes for long-term construction contracts. Discuss only theoretical arguments.

(AICPA adapted)

*D–8–7 ABC Construction Company began business operations on May 12, 1983. ABC is a small company that builds residential houses, duplexes, and fourplexes. The company has a fairly large credit line from one of the local banks and has made preliminary arrangements with a local CPA firm to have its accounting work done. The CPA firm has given the owner the option of choosing either the completed-contract or the percentage-of-completion method for revenue recognition. The CPA firm also has recommended the use of the percentage-of-completion method.

Required:

1. Briefly describe the two methods of accounting for long-term construction contracts. Under what circumstances should each be used?

2. Why is the percentage-of-completion method preferred over the completed-contract method?

3. In practice, what are some of the methods that can be used to determine the extent of completion?

Note: Items with an *asterisk* relate to material contained in the appendix.

Exercises

E–8–1 On July 1, Y Corporation buys $20,000 in merchandise from M Company on account. Terms granted Y Corporation are 2/10, net 30. On July 10, Y Corporation makes payment.

Required:

1. Prepare all necessary entries under the net price method.

2. Assuming payment was not made until after the discount period expired, prepare all necessary entries under the net price method. Also indicate how the purchase discount lost would be recorded on the income statement.

E–8–2 Lewis Corporation manufactures shirts, pants, sweaters, jeans, and other items of men's clothing. Lewis has received an order for 1,000 pairs of jeans from a major retail outlet. The company finishes the order on December 30 and plans to ship it on January 5. Lewis' fiscal year ends on December 31. Lewis incurred the following direct material and direct labor costs in the manufacture of the jeans:

Raw materials	$5,500
Direct labor (1,500 hours @ $5 per hour)	7,500

Lewis follows the practice of applying factory overhead at the rate of $3 per direct labor hour.

Required:

1. Calculate the total cost of the order for inventory purposes on December 31.

2. What is the unit cost of each pair of jeans?

E–8–3 The value of the inventory on the books of K Company at December 31, 1982, was $25,600. The company uses the perpetual inventory system. Subsequently, the following items related to the inventory are discovered:

a) Merchandise in transit shipped f.o.b. destination worth $2,200 had been excluded from the inventory value. K had recorded the sale for $3,000.

b) Merchandise in transit shipped f.o.b. destination had been received by a warehouseman who had notified the buyer that he was holding $1,400 worth of merchandise for the buyer. This merchandise had been excluded from inventory. K had recorded the sale.

c) Purchases of raw material from a new supplier had been shipped f.o.b. shipping point on December 30, 1982. These materials had a cost of $3,700, had not been received or recorded, and had been excluded from the inventory value.

d) Consigned merchandise held by K company for R company had been excluded from the inventory of K.

Required:

1. Determine the proper value of K inventory.
2. Prepare any necessary adjusting entries at December 31, 1982.

E–8–4 The following transactions of M Company have not been recorded at year-end.

a) A purchase of $4,000 in transit shipped f.o.b. shipping point.

b) A sale of merchandise out on consignment with a cost of $1,500 and sales price of $2,500.

c) A purchase of $800 currently being held by a warehouseman who has notified M of its arrival.

d) A special order by Zip Company for $3,000 has been completed by M at the cost of $2,000. The merchandise is on the shipping dock awaiting pick-up by Zip.

e) Merchandise that has been shipped f.o.b. shipping point was stopped in transit and recalled because of bankruptcy on the part of the buyer. The merchandise had a cost of $1,000 and was sold for $1,800. It had been properly recorded at the time of the shipment.

Required:

Assume that M company uses a perpetual inventory system and record the adjustments necessary at year-end.

E–8–5 Assume the same facts as in Exercise 8–4 except that M company uses a periodic inventory system. Record the adjustment necessary at year-end.

E–8–6 Paton Corporation has the following transactions during the month of October:

Date	Transaction	Qty	Price Per Unit
October 2	Purchase	100	$5
4	Purchase	250	5
7	Sale	120	7
10	Purchase	80	5
14	Sale	200	7

Required:

1. Record the transactions assuming use of the perpetual inventory system.
2. Record the transactions assuming use of the periodic inventory system.

E–8–7 The following transactions take place for Bee Company:

May 1	Purchased on account 100 units at $5 per unit, terms 2/15, net 30.
5	Purchased on account 10 units at $60 per unit, terms 3/10, net 40.
6	Returned 10 units from the May 1 purchase because they were defective, and paid for the rest.
10	Purchased 25 units for a total cash price of $125, which was equivalent to a 20% trade discount.
15	Paid for one-half of the units in the May 5 transaction.
25	Paid for the remaining units in the May 6 transaction.

Required:

Prepare the journal entries to record these transactions assuming the use of the net price method and a periodic inventory system.

E–8–8 Refer to the transactions in Exercise 8–7. Prepare the journal entries to record these transactions using the gross price method and a periodic inventory system.

E–8–9 Jorgenson Company makes the following purchases on the stated terms:

Purchase 1   100 units at $15 per unit subject to trade discounts of 10% and 10%.
Purchase 2   300 units at $10 per unit subject to a purchase discount of 2/10, net 30.
Purchase 3   200 units at $20 per unit subject to trade discounts of 20% and 10% and a purchase discount of 2/10, net 30.

Required:
Calculate the total value of the purchases assuming that all discounts are taken and that Jorgenson uses the following:
   a) The gross price method of recording purchase discounts.
   b) The net price method of recording purchase discounts.

E–8–10 The inventory account of Benson Company at December 31, 1976, included the following items:

	Inventory Amount
Merchandise out on consignment at sales price (including markup of 40% on selling price)	$7,000
Goods purchased, in transit (shipped f.o.b. shipping point)	6,000
Goods held on consignment by Benson	4,000
Goods out on approval (sales price $2,500, cost $2,000)	2,500

Based on the information above, the inventory account at December 31, 1976, should be reduced by what amount?

(AICPA adapted)

E–8–11 The following errors in the ending inventory were discovered for the years indicated.

	Income Per Books	Error
1982	$70,000	$ 4,000 overstated
1981	81,000	11,000 understated
1980	78,000	3,000 understated
1979	67,000	2,000 overstated
1978	72,000	5,000 understated
1977	60,000	correct

Required:
Prepare a schedule to show the adjusted net income for each of the years.

E–8–12 James Co. values its inventory according to the lower of cost or market rule. The following data relate to inventory.

Item	Units	Cost	Replacement Cost	Selling and Disposal Costs	Sales Price	Normal Profit
A	100	$ 6.00	$6.80	$0.50	$7.00	$0.65
B	100	10.00	9.50	1.00	9.00	0.80
C	100	8.00	6.00	0.50	8.00	1.00
D	100	7.50	7.25	0.75	8.50	0.75

Required:

Calculate the inventory value on an item-by-item basis using lower of cost or market.

E–8–13 Use the information below to calculate lower of cost or market inventory values under the following assumptions:

a) Individual item basis.
b) Major category basis.
c) Total inventory basis.

	Total Cost	Total Market
Category 1		
Item A	$20,000	$21,000
Item B	5,000	4,500
Item C	11,000	13,000
Category 2		
Item D	$ 7,500	$ 6,000
Item E	9,500	10,000
Item F	11,000	8,500

E–8–14 C & H Company began operations on January 1, 1981, and provides the following data with respect to the cost and the market value of the inventory:

	Cost	Market
Jan. 1, 1981	$50,000	$50,000
Dec. 31, 1981	80,000	76,000
Dec. 31, 1982	75,000	73,500

Assume that C & H uses the allowance method to reduce inventory cost to market.

Required:

Prepare the journal entries for 1981 and 1982 to record the data.

E–8–15 R. Welton Co. has the following year-end account balances:

Beginning inventory	$ 20,000
Purchases	260,000
Accounts receivable	30,000
Freight-in	5,000
Sales	390,000
Purchase discounts	4,000
Transportation out	3,500
Sales commissions	39,000
Purchase returns and allowances	2,500

A year-end inventory indicated $32,000 of inventory on hand.

Required:

1. Prepare the adjusting entry(ies) necessary to determine the cost of goods sold.
2. Prepare a formal income statement through the calculation of gross profit.

E–8–16 D. Humphrey, Inc. is a merchandising concern dealing in precious metals and gems. It had the following year-end account balances:

Beginning inventory	$ 290,000
Loss on purchase committments	20,000
Purchase discounts lost	2,000
Freight-in	5,000

Purchases	1,450,000
Purchase returns and allowances	18,000
Insurance on goods purchased (covered goods while in transit)	11,000

The year-end inventory amounted to $320,000.

Required:

Prepare a formal cost of goods sold section for an income statement.

E–8–17 The Oregon Corporation has contracted for the purchase of materials in the amount of $2,500,000 in 1983. After Oregon signed the contract, the market price dropped to $1,800,000. Oregon has a noncancelable contract.

Required:

1. Prepare the journal entry required in 1982 to reflect the accrued loss.

2. Prepare the journal entry to record the purchase in 1983 assuming no further price changes.

3. Prepare the journal entry to record the purchase in 1983 assuming the market price goes up to $2,100,000.

*E–8–18 The Kirby Construction Company consistently has used the percentage-of-completion method of recognizing income. In 1978 it began a construction project to erect a building for $3,000,000. The project was completed during 1979. Under this method the accounting records disclosed the following:

	1978	1979
Progress billings during year	$1,110,000	$1,900,000
Cost incurred during year	900,000	1,800,000
Collections on billings during year	700,000	2,300,000
Estimated cost to complete	1,800,000	—

Required:

Determine the amount of income Kirby should have recognized in 1978.

(AICPA adapted)

*E–8–19 Buildit Construction Corporation contracted to construct a building for $400,000. Construction began in 1976 and was completed in 1978. Data relating to the contract are summarized below:

	Year Ended December 31,	
	1976	1977
Cost incurred	$200,000	$110,000
Estimated costs to complete	100,000	—

Buildit uses the percentage-of-completion method as the basis for income recognition.

Required:

For the years ended December 31, 1976, and 1977, respectively, Buildit should report how much income?

(AICPA adapted)

*E–8–20 In 1974 Long Corporation began construction work under a three-year contract. The contract price is $800,000. Long uses the percentage-of-cost-completion method for financial accounting purposes. The income to be recognized each year is based on the proportion of cost incurred to the total estimated cost for completing the contract. The

financial statement presentations relating to this contract at December 31, 1974, are as follows:

Balance Sheet

Accounts receivable—construction		
contract billings		$15,000
Construction in-progress	$50,000	
Less contract billings	47,000	
Cost of uncompleted contract in		
excess of billings		3,000

Income Statement

Income (before tax) on the contract		
recognized in 1974		$10,000

Required:

1. How much cash was collected in 1974 on this contract?
2. What was the initial estimated total income before tax on this contract?

(AICPA adapted)

*E–8–21   Mercer Construction Company recognizes income under the percentage-of-completion method of reporting income from long-term construction contracts. During 1978 Mercer entered into a fixed-price contract to construct a bridge for $15,000,000. Contract costs incurred and estimated costs to complete the bridge were as follows:

	Cumulative Contract Costs incurred	Estimated Costs To Complete
At December 31, 1978	$ 1,000,000	$8,000,000
At December 31, 1979	5,500,000	5,500,000
At December 31, 1980	10,000,000	2,000,000

How much income should Mercer recognize on the contract above for the year ended December 31, 1980?

(AICPA adapted)

*E–8–22   Flint Construction signed a contract to build an office building at a cost of $500,000. Flint estimated that its cost of construction would be $450,000. The following yearly costs were incurred:

1982	$ 90,000
1983	250,000
1984	110,000

Required:

1. What amount of gross profit should Flint record each year under the percentage-of-completion method?
2. What amount of profit should be reported each year under the completed contract method?

Note: Items with an *asterisk* relate to material contained in the appendix.

Problems

P–8–1 ACME Corporation commences operations this year on a calendar-year basis. ACME's inventory operations are as follows:

Purchases of raw materials	$250,000
Purchase discounts	5,000
Raw materials used	212,500
Direct labor applied	150,000
Factory overhead applied	112,500
Ending balance, work in process	125,000
Cost of goods sold	240,000

Required:
1. Compute the cost of goods manufactured.
2. Compute the ending balance in finished goods.

P–8–2 Adam Company uses a June 30 fiscal year-end. Its related inventory balances are presented below:

Beginning balance, raw materials	$140,000
Purchases (net)	285,000
Direct labor	162,000
Factory overhead:	
Indirect labor	35,000
Indirect supplies	40,000
Depreciation	8,000
Factory insurance	2,000
Utilities	10,000
Beginning balance, work in process	93,000
Beginning balance, finished goods	39,000
Ending balance, raw materials inventory	45,000
Ending balance, work in process	104,000
Ending balance, finished goods	48,000

Required:
1. Prepare a cost-of-goods-manufactured statement.
2. Determine the goods available for sale and the cost of goods sold.

P–8–3 Scott Company is a manufacturer of specialty products and merchandise. All of its business is "special order" business. A physical inventory taken on December 31, 1982, indicated inventory with a total cost of $21,700. Subsequently, you find the following:

   a) Merchandise in transit with a value of $2,200 was omitted from the count. This merchandise was shipped f.o.b. shipping point.

   b) Merchandise out on consignment valued at $800 was omitted from the inventory.

   c) Merchandise in transit worth $1,200 shipped f.o.b. shipping point was included as part of the inventory.

   d) A special order costing $4,500, which had been set aside but not yet shipped, was included as part of the inventory.

   e) Merchandise worth $2,200 was being shipped to a warehouse and was excluded from the inventory. The goods had not yet reached the warehouse.

   f) Mechandise worth $4,000 had been sold on an installment basis and excluded from the inventory. Only 15% of the sales price has been received.

   g) A special order of $1,400 has been shipped to the buyer f.o.b. shipping point on December 26. On December 27 the buyer received the merchandise, declared bankruptcy, and did not pay Scott. The merchandise was excluded from the inventory.

Required:

1. Indicate whether each of the items above should be included as inventory and state why.

2. What is the ending inventory value as corrected?

P–8–4 A corporation has no accounts payable as of January 31. During February it has the following transactions:

February	2	Bought merchandise costing $30,000 from West Company. Terms 2/10, net 30.
	5	Bought merchandise costing $12,500 from East Company. Terms 2/15, net 30.
	8	Paid West Company the money owed on account.
	12	Purchased merchandise costing $5,000 from South Company. Terms net 30.
	14	Sold the merchandise bought from West Company for $42,000 in cash.
	14	Paid East Company for 80% of the merchandise purchased.
	21	Paid South Company for the goods bought on account.
	22	Sold half of the merchandise acquired from East Company for $7,500 cash.
	24	Paid East Company the remainder of the money owed.

Required:

1. Make the appropriate journal entries assuming the net price method was used.

2. Compute the sales, cost of goods sold, and ending inventory balance for February. Assume there was no beginning inventory balance and it is a merchandising company.

P–8–5 Wrong Company has decided it will go public. It engages a noted CPA firm to handle all the essential accounting work. The CPAs notice the following inventory problems:

a) December 31, 1977: Inventory of $40,000 included twice
b) 31, 1977: Inventory cost was understated by $14,500 for a particular item
c) December 31, 1978: Merchandise costing $30,000 was excluded from inventory
d) December 31, 1979: The company actually had 15,200 units on hand. Through a transposition error, it was recorded as 12,500. Cost per item was $8.50.

There was no problem with ending inventory at 12/31/1980.

Wrong Company's reported net earnings for each year were as follows:

1977	$27,900
1978	40,300
1979	36,000
1980	45,000

Required:

What are the correct earnings for 1977, 1978, 1979, and 1980?

P–8–6 The following information relates to Crittenden Co.'s ending inventory.

Item	Quantity	Cost	Unit Replacement Cost	Unit Realizable Value	Unit Net Realizable Value less Mark-Up
A	20,000	$6.25	$6.00	$5.80	$5.40
B	12,000	6.25	7.75–	8.00	6.50
C	12,500	5.00	4.80	5.40	4.85
D	10,000	4.00	3.50	4.20	3.60

Required:
1. For each item, indicate what market price should be used and why.
2. Apply the lower of cost or market to each item, then total the individual items.
3. Apply the lower of cost or market on a total basis.
4. Apply the allowance method to the total computed in Part 3.

P-8-7 The Paul Company values its inventories at lower of cost or market. Paul has three major categories of inventory: A, B, and C. It has used this classification system to facilitate planning and control of the inventories. A consists of high-cost, low-volume items, B consists of medium-cost items, and C includes low-cost items with a high turnover rate. At the end of the year the following information is available.

Item	Units	Unit Cost	Replacement Cost	Sales Price	Disposal Costs	Normal Profit
A1	50	$20.00	$19.00	$40.00	$10.00	$15.00
A2	60	25.00	30.00	50.00	5.00	10.00
A3	40	21.00	18.00	35.00	8.00	10.00
B1	120	6.00	6.50	10.00	2.00	1.00
B2	100	8.00	7.00	11.00	4.50	1.00
B3	130	7.50	7.75	11.50	2.50	1.25
B4	90	6.50	6.00	10.50	3.00	2.00
C1	500	2.50	2.00	4.00	0.50	1.00
C2	550	1.70	2.00	3.50	0.50	0.75

Required:
Calculate the lower of cost or market inventory value under the following assumptions:
   a) Individual items basis.
   b) Category by category basis.
   c) Inventory as a whole basis.

P-8-8 Land Lubber Company failed to maintain a complete accounting system. However, you believe that the following account balances are correct at the stated dates.

	September 30	
	1979	1980
Cash	$ 8,250	$16,500
Accounts receivable	28,500	21,000
Merchandise inventory	50,000	62,500
Land	17,250	17,250
Accounts payable	32,500	39,500

Land Lubber's checkbook reveals the following:
   a) Payments to vendors for merchandise purchased: $130,500. The remainder of the cash disbursements were for expenses incurred during the fiscal year. All of these expenses were paid for by cash.
   b) Cash receipts from customers (the only cash receipts): $205,000.

Required:
Compute the amount of sales, cost of goods sold, purchases, gross margin, operational expenses, and net earnings for the fiscal year ended September 30, 1980.

P-8-9 On August 1, 1980, Maverick has merchandise inventory of $27,900, cash of $25,000, and accounts payable of $16,000. Among its balances of the accounts payable, $12,000 involved purchases from White Company on July 31, 1980, terms 2/10, net 30; and

$4,000 from Orange Corporation on July 31, terms net 15. In addition, the following transactions occurred:

August 2:   Purchased merchandise for $10,000, terms 3/10, net 30.
        6:     Sold merchandise with a cost of $17,500 for $25,000 cash.
        9:     Paid White Company the amount owed.
        12:    Purchased merchandise from Blue Company with a list price of $60,000. Blue Company allows trade discounts of 10% and 5%, credit terms 3/10, net 45.
        13:    Paid Orange Corporation the amount owed.
        15:    Sold the remaining $10,400 in merchandise on hand at August 1, 1980, for $16,000. Of that, 25% was received in cash, and the remainder is on account.
        15:    Paid selling and administrative expenses of $7,000.
        15:    Maverick Company discovers that 33-1/3% of the goods purchased from Blue Corporation are defective. Maverick requests and receives a credit memorandum from Blue.
        19:    Sold merchandise costing $12,000 to Black Corporation for $19,600 cash.
        20:    Sold merchandise costing $15,000 to several customers for $24,000. Of that amount, one third was received in cash, and the remainder is on account. Terms are net 20.
        21:    Collected 75% of the account receivable from August 15 sale.
        24:    Paid Blue Corporation in full.
        25:    Purchased $25,000 in merchandise on account from Yellow Corporation, terms 3/15, net 30.

Maverick uses the gross price method.

Required:
1. Prepare all necessary journal entries to record these transactions. (Assume the perpetual inventory method.)
2. Compute the gross margin for the month.

P–8–10 Thurston Company purchased merchandise X with a list price of $36,000, and terms of 2/10, net 30. The company also purchased merchandise Y with a list price of $30,000 and terms of 3/10, net 30. During the discount period, payments of $24,500 and $25,000 were made for X and Y, respectively. The remainder of the price was paid for each after the discount period had expired.

Required:
Prepare the appropriate journal entries to record the purchase of the merchandise and the payments using the following methods:
  a) The net price method.
  b) The gross price method.

P–8–11 You are the auditor for XYZ, Inc. for the year ended December 31, 1980. As part of your examination, you discover the following transactions near the closing dates:
  a) Merchandise costing $2,325 was received on January 2, 1981, and the related purchase invoice was recorded on January 6, 1981. The invoice indicated that the shipment was made on December 30, 1980, f.o.b. shipping point.
  b) Merchandise received on January 3, 1981, costing $1,011 was recorded on the purchase register on January 6, 1981. The invoice indicated that shipment was made f.o.b. destination on December 30, 1980.
  c) Merchandise costing $1,225 was received on December 29, 1980. The invoice was not recorded. On closer examination, you notice it was marked on consignment.
  d) Items received on December 31, 1980, but rejected and to be returned for credit, have a cost of $300.

e) Items held by agents on December 31, 1980, amounted to $1,395.

f) Merchandise under contract for sale costing $2,100, but which the company has not yet segregated and applied to the contract.

Each transaction is material.

Required:

1. Indicate for each item whether or not it should be included in the inventory.

2. Briefly indicate your reason for your decision on each item in Part 1.

P–8–12 Pearl Boutique Company purchased merchandise on open account for $30,000, terms 2/10, net 30. Pearl paid one-half of the amount owed within the discount period, and the other one-half was paid after the discount period. Pearl uses a periodic inventory system.

Required:

Provide the journal entries needed to record the purchase and payments under each of the following assumptions:

a) The net method is used when recording purchases.

b) The gross method is used when recording purchases.

Which method do you prefer? Why?

P–8–13 During 1981 the Louisiana Oil Company entered into a series of long-term contracts for the purchase of crude oil in 1982 and 1983. The terms of the contracts were as follows:

| | | | Price | |
Company	Qty. in 1982	Qty. in 1983	1982	1983
A	1,000,000 bbls.	2,000,000 bbls.	$40	$45
B	2,000,000 bbls.	3,000,000 bbls.	35	40
C	2,500,000 bbls.	4,000,000 bbls.	32	35

Louisiana entered into these contracts expecting the price of crude oil to increase. The price of crude oil at 12/31/81 was quoted at $33 per barrel. This price held throughout 1982. During 1983 the average price of crude was $42 per barrel.

Required:

1. Prepare the footnotes required to reflect this information in 1981, and in 1982.

2. Prepare all the journal entries necessary in 1981, 1982, and 1983.

P–8–14 A disgruntled employee of Rubble Bubble Company, upon learning that he would be terminated, mischievously damaged or destroyed some of the company's records. You are assigned the task of reconstructing the records so that the company can prepare its income statements for the month.

From the badly torn general ledger, you discover the following:

Cash		
Beginning	$24,000	
Ending	$30,000	

Accounts Receivable		
Beginning	$ 48,000	
Credit		
sales	100,000	

Raw Materials		
Beginning	$24,000	
Ending	$22,000	

Work in Process		
Beginning	$ 9,000	

Finished Goods		
Ending	$60,000	

Accounts Payable		
		Ending	$16,000

Through your diligence, you learn the following:
a) All accounts receivable are collected in the month following sale.
b) 40% of the sales are credit sales.
c) Accounts payable are used only for raw material purchases. The A/P clerk is willing to swear that the beginning balance was $12,000. Through the canceled checks you learn that payments on account were $80,000 this month.
d) Cash is disbursed only for labor, manufacturing overhead, accounts payable, and selling and administrative expenses.
e) The production superintendent's records show that only one job remains in process at the end of the month. Materials of $5,200 had been added. There had been 400 hours of labor expended on the job at $9 an hour. Furthermore, total direct labor hours for the month amounted to 6,933-1/3 hours. Each employee is paid the same rate.
f) Overhead is applied on the basis of direct labor hours at $4.50 an hour.
g) Your investigation uncovers records indicating the beginning balance in finished goods totaled $22,000. Also, the beginning balance in work in process amounted to $9,000.
The cost of goods manufactured for the month amounted to $178,000.
Required:
1. Compute the following:
   a) Cash disbursements.
   b) Cash receipts.
   c) Purchases.
   d) Raw materials used.
   e) Direct labor.
   f) Applied overhead.
   g) Operating expenses.
   h) Sales.
2. Prepare a cost-of-goods-manufactured statement for the month.
3. Prepare a cost-of-goods-sold statement for the month.

*P–8–15 Peggy Construction Co. entered into a contract with Anderson Investments to build an office building at a contract price of $1,500,000. The following data relate to the contract:

	1981	1982	1983
Costs to-date	$400,000	$1,000,000	$1,300,000
Estimated cost to complete	800,000	300,000	–0–
Progress billings to-date	300,000	850,000	1,500,000
Cash collection to-date	200,000	600,000	1,500,000

The contract was completed in 1983, and Anderson Investment accepted the building and made final payment.
Required:
1. Calculate the profit to be reported each year under the percentage-of-completion method.
2. Prepare the journal entries necessary in each of the three years.

*P–8–16 Curtis Construction Company, Inc. entered into a firm fixed-price contract with Axelrod Associates on July 1, 1977, to construct a four-story office building. At that time Curtis estimated that it would take between two and three years to complete the project. The total contract price for construction of the building is $4,000,000. Curtis appropriately accounts for this contract under the completed-contract method in its financial statements and for income tax reporting. The building was deemed substantially completed on December 31, 1979. Estimated percentage-of-completion, accumulated contract costs incurred, estimated costs to complete the contract, and accumulated billings to Axelrod under the contract were as follows:

	At December 31, 1977	At December 31, 1978	At December 31, 1979
Percentage of completion	10%	60%	100%
Contract costs incurred	$ 350,000	$2,500,000	$4,250,000
Estimated costs to complete the contract	3,150,000	1,700,000	–0–
Billings to Axelrod	720,000	2,160,000	3,600,000

Required:
1. Prepare schedules to compute the amount to be shown as "cost of uncompleted contract in excess of related billings" or "billings on uncompleted contract in excess of related costs" at December 31, 1977, 1978, and 1979. Ignore income taxes. Show supporting computations in good form.
2. Prepare schedules to compute the profit or loss to be recognized as a result of this contract for the years ended December 31, 1977, 1978, and 1979. Ignore income taxes. Show supporting computations in good form.

(AICPA adapted)

*P–8–17   Alan Construction Co. contracted to build a plant for Stave Co. The contract price was $5,000,000. The following are data relating to the construction project:

	1980	1981	1982
Cost incurred to-date	$1,300,000	$2,850,000	$4,300,000
Estimated cost to complete the contract	2,700,000	1,350,000	–0–
Progress billings to-date	900,000	2,500,000	5,000,000
Cash collection to-date	820,000	2,300,000	5,000,000

Required:
1. Determine the amount of profit that should be recognized each year under the percentage-of-completion method.
2. Give the appropriate journal entries for the three years.
3. Assume that the estimated cost to complete in 1981 was $2,100,000 and that the total cost incurred through 1982 was $5,050,000. How much profit should be reported in each of the years during construction?
4. Assume that the estimated cost to complete in 1981 was $1,700,000 and total construction cost incurred on the project through 1982 was $4,550,000. What amount of profit should be reported each year?

*P–8–18   There are two construction companies operating in the same town. One uses the percentage-of-completion method while the other uses the completed-contract method. Both were awarded three-year projects with estimated costs of $90,000, an estimated profit of $150,000, and a firm contract price of $1,050,000.
      Each project has the following applicable data:

	1979	1980	1981
To-date construction costs	$243,000	$567,000	$ 950,000
Estimated cost to complete	657,000	378,000	—

Progress billing to-date	200,000	525,000	1,050,000
Collections	175,000	495,000	1,050,000

Required:

1. Prepare the journal entries for the percentage-of-completion method.
2. Prepare the journal entries necessary for the completed-contract method.
3. Prepare partial balance sheets for the percentage-of-completion method for each of the years.

Note: Items with an *asterisk* relate to material contained in the appendix.

9

Inventories—
Cost Flow Methods

Accounting in the News

The method used to value inventories can have a significant impact on a company's operating results. During the first quarter of 1982, the prices for gas and oil decreased slightly. According to the following article from the *Wall Street Journal*, the use of FIFO combined with falling prices resulted in a 25% decrease in net income in spite of a 20% increase in sales for the Royal Dutch/Shell Oil Company.

> The Royal Dutch/Shell Group posted a 25% drop in net income for the first quarter despite a 20% revenue gain. . . .
>
> The group said that the drop was the result of its use of the first-in first-out, or FIFO, method of inventory accounting. Under FIFO, the cost of goods sold is based on the oldest prices of raw materials.
>
> Stripped of the effects of FIFO, net income would have jumped 56%, to $819.7 million from $526.8 million.
>
> First quarter overall results were depressed by the continued drop in demand and the decrease of high industry inventories "coupled with surplus crude oil supply," Shell said.*

The method of accounting used for inventory valuation can have a dramatic impact on income during periods of falling and rising prices. This chapter discusses the various inventory costing methods that may be used and looks at how these affect income measurement and asset values.

*Wall Street Journal, 20 May 1982, p. 35. Reprinted by permission of The Wall Street Journal, © Dow Jones & Company, Inc. 1982. All Rights Reserved.

The purpose of this chapter is to identify and compare the various cost flow methods of valuation of inventories. Cost flow refers to the dollar values that flow through the inventory and cost of goods sold accounts and should be distinguished from the physical flow, which refers to the movement of the physical units through the system. The cost flow method chosen for inventory valuation will have a significant impact on income determination and asset valuation for the balance sheet.

Physical Flow and Cost Flow

A distinction between the physical flow and the cost flow must be made at the outset of the discussion. The **physical flow** of the merchandise refers to the orderly movement of the goods through the company. For example, in a petroleum refinery operation, the raw material input, crude oil, is started into the refining or manufacturing process at the beginning of that process. The material (oil) flows through the refining operation, which is analogous to work-in-process, until it reaches the end of the processing. By that time it has been turned into gasoline, diesel oil, home heating oil, and any number of other end products. These products then are transferred to tank farms and other storage places and held as finished goods inventory until they are sold. The point to be made here is that the physical units progress through the process in a systematic and orderly fashion. Even in a retailing business the flow of merchandise is systematic and orderly. A grocer puts the new boxes of cereal behind the old boxes so that the oldest merchandise is sold first.

The cost flow does not necessarily have to coincide with the physical flow. Indeed, in most large business organizations, tracing the physical flow is very difficult, if not actually impossible. If there are large quantities of the same items that come in and go out of the business, it is extremely difficult to keep track of individual units.

The **cost flow** assumption chosen refers to the movement of costs through the system rather than the movement of physical units. According to *ARB No. 43*, the major objective of choosing a cost flow method is to choose one that most clearly reflects periodic income.[1] The emphasis is on income determination as opposed to asset valuation. Because the various cost flow assumptions can have a significant impact on income, the income determination problem is critical. The cost flow method used affects directly the cost of goods sold for income statement purposes. Consider the data in the following T account:

ARB# 43

Inventory

Beginning inventory:				Cost of goods sold:
	1,000 @ $6.00 =	$ 6,000		18,000 @ $?
Add:				
Purchase 14,000 @ $7.00 =		98,000		
Purchase 5,000 @ $8.00 =		40,000		
Available 20,000		$144,000		
Ending inventory: 2,000 @ $?				

Of the $144,000 associated with the 20,000 units, some of it will be expensed through the cost of goods sold, and some of the cost will appear as inventory. The amount expensed and the amount of the asset are dependent on the cost flow assumption chosen by the company. Based on the data above, if we choose a cost flow method in which the earliest cost elements are transferred to the cost of

---

[1] *Accounting Research Bulletin No. 43* "Restatement and Revision of Accounting Research Bulletins," (New York: AICPA, 1953), Statement 4.

goods sold, and the later cost elements are placed in ending inventory, the effect will be to increase income because the lowest (earliest) costs are transferred to the cost of goods sold. On the other hand, if we were to choose a cost method that transferred the most recent cost elements to the cost of goods sold, and placed the earliest cost elements in inventory, the effect would be to decrease income because the latest (highest) costs are expensed and the earliest (lowest) costs are inventoried.

The basic cost flow methods will be discussed in the following section. Pay particular attention to the impact of each method on income and asset valuation as well as to the computational aspects of each method.

The Basic Cost Flow Methods

The basic cost flow methods include specific identification, FIFO, LIFO, and average cost. The choice of method for a particular company to use depends on a number of factors within the individual company, including profitability, financial position, economic conditions, and tax factors. For example, a highly profitable company in an expanding and growth economy may have as its objective the minimization of income tax payments. Often, this is the most important consideration for inventory valuation. The impact of income tax will be discussed in a later section of this chapter. Each company will choose the inventory method most suited to its particular needs and objectives. It is important to point out that the inventory method chosen cannot be changed on a yearly basis but must be used consistently from year to year.

Specific Identification

The **specific identification** method of inventory valuation requires that the actual cost of each unit of merchandise sold be included in the cost of goods sold, and that the actual cost of each unit unsold be included in the ending inventory. In this inventory method the cost flow and the physical flow are exactly the same. It is most useful when the inventory consists of a small number of units, each of which has a relatively high cost. An appliance store that sells such major items as refrigerators, freezers, washers, dryers, and microwave ovens may choose the specific identification method because of the relatively small number of units and the high cost of each.

There are, however, some drawbacks associated with this cost flow assumption. In a situation in which a large volume of business is done, it becomes very difficult (and costly) to track individual units for costing purposes. In addition, some acquisition costs, such as freight or storage charges, may have to be allocated on an arbitrary basis rather than be assigned to individual units. For example, if a retailer receives a truckload of merchandise, the freight charge will apply to all the merchandise on the truck. Suppose that particular shipment contains a large variety of products that are of differing sizes and prices. Each unit will have some freight cost assigned, but it will be difficult to determine the amount charged to each unit.

Another problem arises in that specific identification can allow manipulation of the income. If the appliance dealer has several refrigerators to sell at different costs, the dealer's income may be manipulated by selecting a high or low cost unit to ship to the customer. For example, suppose the retailer has four identical refrigerators in the model ordered by the customer, two of which cost $400, one $450, and one $500. If the retailer wanted to decrease income, the $500 refrigerator would be shipped; if the retailer wanted to increase income, one of the $400 units would be shipped.

The specific identification method can be used with either a perpetual or periodic system; the results (i.e., impact on income and asset valuation) will be identical because the costs and units are matched exactly and move through the system together.

First-In, First-Out (FIFO)

The **FIFO** system of inventory valuation is based on the assumption that the earliest cost elements (first ones) introduced to the system will be the first costs expensed or charged to the cost of goods sold. The cost of the merchandise purchased will be allocated to the ending inventory and to the cost of goods sold based on that same assumption: the costs associated with the first purchases will be the first expensed, and the latest costs will be inventoried. Thus, in every period the cost of goods sold would include the cost carried over from the prior period as beginning inventory and the costs of the earliest purchases during the current period. The ending inventory value would consist of the costs associated with the most recent purchases.

FIFO can be used with either a perpetual or a periodic system, and the results will be identical. The results are the same because you will always end up with the most recent costs in the inventory and the earliest costs expensed in the cost of goods sold account.

If prices were stable and did not change, it would not matter which method of inventory valuation was used. The results would be exactly the same under each method. Unfortunately, the real world is not so simple and prices fluctuate. The predominant price change since the 1930s has been upward, although prices for specific items have decreased in some instances. Downward trends in prices (when they have existed) usually have resulted from technological advances. A good example is the price of hand-held calculators throughout the 1970s. The first calculators introduced in the market place could perform the basic four functions and sold for $60—$100. By the late 1970s those same calculators could be purchased for as little as $7—$10. However, for most merchandise the long-term price trend has been upward. Changing prices have made the choice of an inventory valuation method crucial because of the impact it will have on reported income and the balance sheet values of the inventory.

In periods of rising prices, FIFO will result in a reduced or lower cost of goods sold figure because the earliest (or lower) costs will be charged to the cost of goods sold. The ending inventory will contain the highest or most recent costs, and thus will have a higher value. In periods of rising prices, use of the FIFO inventory method will result in higher reported profit. For example, examine the data in Exhibit 9-1. Assume that the Johnson Company's beginning inventory in August consisted of 3,000 units with a cost of $5.00 each, and that Johnson's transactions during August were as listed in Exhibit 9-1.

Application of the FIFO method to the Johnson Company data is illustrated

---

Exhibit 9-1
JOHNSON COMPANY Transactions
Month of August

	Units	Cost Per Unit
Beginning inventory	3,000	$5.00
8-3 Purchase	9,000	5.20
8-6 Sale	6,000	
8-10 Sale	4,000	
8-15 Purchase	5,000	5.40
8-20 Purchase	5,000	5.60
8-28 Sale	5,000	
Ending inventory	7,000	

---

in Exhibit 9-2. The illustration includes both the perpetual and the periodic systems. The exhibit shows a beginning inventory of 3,000 units, total purchases of 19,000 units, total sales of 15,000 units, and an ending inventory of 7,000 units. For both the perpetual and the periodic systems, the ending inventory values are $38,800, which consists of 2,000 units at $5.40 and 5,000 units at $5.60. For both systems the cost of goods sold is $78,000, which is the sum of the five different batches of sales. If we assume that Johnson sold this merchandise at a total sales price of $150,000, the gross profit would be $72,000.

Sales (assumed)		$150,000
Cost of goods sold		
Beginning inventory	$ 15,000	
Purchases	101,800	
Merchandise available for sale	$116,800	
Ending inventory	(38,800)	
Cost of goods sold		78,000
Gross profit		$ 72,000

Johnson's ending inventory contains the most recent costs ($5.40 and $5.60 per unit), and the cost of goods sold contains the earliest costs ($5.00, $5.20, and $5.40 per unit). The gross profit ($72,000) is the same for both periodic and perpetual systems.

An advantage associated with FIFO is that in many cases the physical flow is on a FIFO basis, and therefore the dollar flow matches the physical flow. When the inventory turnover is very rapid, the ending inventory cost will be relatively current and will tend to approximate the replacement cost. For balance sheet purposes FIFO will provide fairly good asset valuation data for the inventory, assuming it is desirable to have an inventory value that approximates replacement cost.

Exhibit 9-2
JOHNSON COMPANY
FIFO Inventory System

(Perpetual)

Date	Inventory/Purchases	Cost of Goods Sold	Balance	Total
8–1	3,000 @ $5.00		3,000 @ $5.00	$15,000
8–3	9,000 @ 5.20		3,000 @ 5.00	
			9,000 @ 5.20	61,800
8–6		3,000 @ $5.00		
		3,000 @ 5.20	6,000 @ 5.20	31,200
8–10		4,000 @ 5.20	2,000 @ 5.20	10,400
8–15	5,000 @ 5.40		2,000 @ 5.20	
			5,000 @ 5.40	37,400
8–20	5,000 @ 5.60		2,000 @ 5.20	
			5,000 @ 5.40	
			5,000 @ 5.60	65,400
8–28		2,000 @ 5.20	2,000 @ 5.40	
		3,000 @ 5.40	5,000 @ 5.60	38,800
8–31			2,000 @ 5.40	
			5,000 @ 5.60	38,800
Totals	$116,800	$78,000		$38,800

(Periodic)

Date	Inventory/Purchases	Cost of Goods Sold	Balance	Total
8–31	Balance 3,000 units Purchases 19,000 units	15,000 units	2,000 @ $5.40	
			5,000 @ 5.60	$38,800
Totals	$116,800	$78,000		$38,800

FIFO does not provide the best income statement data, however. The oldest costs are expensed or transferred to the cost of goods sold; therefore, the most current costs are not matched against current revenues. Because there may be a situation in which prior period costs are matched against current period revenue, you will end up with a slight distortion of income. If you assume that the purpose of the income statement is to match current revenue with current costs, there will be a mismatch of cost and revenue. In summary, FIFO provides current asset valuation data for the inventory on the balance sheet, but it can result in a distortion of income.

Last-In, First-Out (LIFO)

The **LIFO** method of inventory valuation is based on the assumption that the cost elements that entered the system most recently will be the first ones expensed or transferred to the cost of goods sold. Under this assumption the cost of the merchandise purchased will be allocated to the cost of goods sold and to the ending inventory; the most recent purchase costs will be expensed, and the earliest or oldest costs will be inventoried.

For purposes of income determination, LIFO offers a close matching of current revenues with current costs since the most recent costs are the first expensed. Hence, LIFO provides a better income statement measurement of current operating efficiency. This meets the criterion of income determination as the primary objective of inventory valuation set forth in *ARB No. 43*. However, the balance sheet valuation of the inventory will not contain the current costs; instead, it will contain the oldest costs, which may not even approximate the current prices for the inventory items. This is particularly a problem with companies that have been in existence for some time and have the same type of items in inventory. For example, a steel pipe fabricator would have a raw inventory of steel. Assume that the company has been in existence for 20 years and has a policy of maintaining at least enough steel on hand to meet one month's production needs. In this case the company could have an inventory of steel that is priced, under LIFO, at prices that existed 20 years ago.

In periods of rising prices, the lowest (oldest) costs remain in inventory while the highest (most recent) costs are expensed. In periods of falling prices, the opposite would be true. In either rising or falling price situations, the current costs are expensed and the oldest costs are inventoried.

As an illustration of the LIFO method, the Johnson Company data for the month of August from Exhibit 9-1 will be used again. With the LIFO method, use of the perpetual or periodic inventory system will have an impact on both the asset valuation and the income determination. Use of LIFO under the periodic inventory system is illustrated in Exhibit 9-3, and LIFO under the perpetual is illustrated in Exhibit 9-4.

Exhibit 9-3
JOHNSON COMPANY
LIFO—Periodic Inventory

Date	Transaction	Units	Unit Cost	Total Cost
8–1	Balance	3,000	$5.00	$ 15,000
8–3	Purchase	9,000	5.20	46,800
8–15	Purchase	5,000	5.40	27,000
8–20	Purchase	5,000	5.60	28,000
	Total available	22,000		$116,800
	Ending inventory:			
	(7,000 units)	3,000	5.00	15,000
		4,000	5.20	20,800
8–31	Total ending inventory	(7,000)		($35,800)
	Cost of goods sold	15,000		$ 81,000

LIFO—Periodic. In Exhibit 9-3 the total merchandise available for sale is 22,000 units with a total cost of $116,800. When Johnson Company counts the physical inventory at the end of the period, there are 7,000 units on hand. The costs assigned to those units are the earliest costs, $5.00 and $5.20 per unit; therefore, the ending inventory is valued at $35,800. The cost of goods sold would contain the most recent costs, which would include the following:

$$
\begin{array}{rcl}
5{,}000 \times \$5.60 & = & \$28{,}000 \\
5{,}000 \times 5.40 & = & 27{,}000 \\
\underline{5{,}000} \times 5.20 & = & \underline{26{,}000} \\
15{,}000 & & \$81{,}000
\end{array}
$$

If you again assume that Johnson Company has net sales of $150,000, the calculation of gross profit would be as follows:

Sales (assumed)		$150,000
Cost of goods sold		
Beginning inventory	$ 15,000	
Purchases	101,800	
Merchandise available for sale	$116,800	
Less: Ending inventory	(35,800)	
Cost of goods sold		81,000
Gross profit		$ 69,000

Note that this gross profit ($69,000) is $3,000 less than the gross profit calculated under the FIFO method ($72,000). The difference arises because the most recent prices are higher than the earlier prices and are the ones assigned to the cost of goods sold.

LIFO—Perpetual. Exhibit 9-4 illustrates LIFO in a perpetual inventory system. The value of the ending inventory is now $37,000 and is composed of 2,000 units of the beginning inventory at $5.00 per unit and 5,000 units of the August 15 purchase at $5.40 per unit. Note the difference between the perpetual and periodic values for the inventory. In the periodic method the units are assigned the very earliest costs at the end of the period, whereas in the perpetual method some of those earlier costs had to be sold. The entire purchase of August 3 and 1,000 units of the beginning inventory were sold on August 6 and 10.

If you again assume that Johnson Company has net sales of $150,000, the calculation of gross profit would be as follows:

Sales (assumed)		$150,000
Cost of goods sold		
Beginning inventory	$ 15,000	
Purchases	101,800	
Merchandise available for sale	$116,800	
Less: Ending inventory	(37,000)	
Cost of goods sold		79,800
Gross profit		$ 70,200

Exhibit 9-4
JOHNSON COMPANY
LIFO—Perpetual Inventory

Date	Purchases	Sales	Balance	
8–1			3,000 @ $5.00	$15,000
8–3	9,000 @ $5.20		3,000 @ 5.00	15,000
			9,000 @ 5.20	46,800
8–6		6,000 @ $5.20	3,000 @ 5.00	15,000
			3,000 @ 5.20	15,600
8–10		3,000 @ 5.20		
		1,000 @ 5.00	2,000 @ 5.00	10,000
8–15	5,000 @ 5.40		2,000 @ 5.00	10,000
			5,000 @ 5.40	27,000
8–20	5,000 @ 5.60		2,000 @ 5.00	10,000
			5,000 @ 5.40	27,000
			5,000 @ 5.60	28,000
8–28		5,000 @ 5.60	2,000 @ 5.00	10,000
			5,000 @ 5.40	27,000
8–31			2,000 @ 5.00	10,000
			5,000 @ 5.40	27,000
				$37,000

The gross profit here ($70,200) is greater than the gross profit in LIFO under the periodic system but is still less than that in the FIFO methods. LIFO always will result in a lower net income than FIFO during periods of rising prices because the most recent (higher) costs are charged to the cost of goods sold. In periods of falling prices, the opposite will occur.

A company may sometimes use a LIFO perpetual system but will cost the merchandise issued as of the end of the period instead of currently throughout the period. In this situation the results will be exactly the same as using LIFO under a periodic system for inventory valuation.

During periods of rising prices, LIFO with a periodic system will give an income before tax that is equal to or below that of LIFO under a perpetual system costed currently. Therefore, if the company is using LIFO for tax reasons, it will minimize the tax burden by using LIFO and periodic or perpetual costed at the end of the period. The primary problem with using LIFO under the perpetual system and costing it currently concerns what happens when significant reductions in inventory or stockouts occur during the year. We previously discussed a situation with a steel pipe fabricator in which the inventory was priced at 20-year-old prices under the LIFO method. Suppose that during the year there was a rail strike or a steel mill strike and that steel could not be purchased for a month. If the fabricator were forced to use its entire stock of inventory, it could have been in a stockout position as of a monthly or quarterly financial statement date. If this occurred and if inventory were costed currently, the cost of goods produced and sold would include steel at prices that are 20 years old. Such a situation could have a drastic effect on net income and could increase income taxes significantly. Costing inventory at year-end rather than currently assumes that as long as inventory levels are maintained from the beginning to the end of the year, the financial statements should not be affected by temporary inventory fluctuations that may have occurred during the year.

Average Cost Method

The **average cost method** of inventory valuation follows a procedure in which the cost of all the merchandise on hand is averaged, and that average cost is applied to the units sold. If a periodic inventory system is used, the cost of the beginning inventory is added to the cost of all the purchases during the period and divided by the total units to obtain a weighted average cost per unit. This weighted average cost per unit is multiplied by the number of units sold to obtain the cost of goods sold, and by the number of units in the ending inventory to obtain the value of the ending inventory. If a perpetual inventory system is used, a new average cost must be calculated after each purchase, and thus the cost becomes a moving average.

Average Cost—Periodic. The average cost under the periodic inventory system is illustrated in Exhibit 9-5. The data for Exhibit 9-5 are again the Johnson Company data from Exhibit 9-1. The beginning inventory is combined with the total purchases to obtain the total value of the merchandise available for sale. Dividing the total cost ($116,800) by the number of units available (22,000) results in the

---

Exhibit 9-5
JOHNSON COMPANY
Weighted Average—Periodic Inventory

Date	Transaction	Units	Cost	Total Cost
8–1	Balance	3,000	$5.00	$ 15,000
8–3	Purchase	9,000	5.20	46,800
8–15	Purchase	5,000	5.40	27,000
8–20	Purchase	5,000	5.60	28,000
Totals		22,000	$5.30909*	$116,800.00
Cost of goods sold =		(15,000) ×	$5.30909 =	(79,636.36)
Ending inventory =		7,000 ×	5.30909 =	$ 37,163.64

$* \dfrac{\$116,800}{22,000} = \$5.30909$

average cost per unit of $5.30909. The cost of goods sold and the ending inventory values are obtained by multiplying the cost per unit by the number of units as follows:

$$\text{Cost of goods sold} = 15{,}000 \times \$5.30909 = \$79{,}636.36$$
$$\text{Ending inventory} \; = \; 7{,}000 \times \$5.30909 = \$37{,}163.64$$

If we again assume a sales figure of $150,000, the gross profit calculation is as follows:

Sales (assumed)		$150,000
Cost of goods sold		
Beginning inventory	$ 15,000	
Purchases	101,800	
Merchandise available for sale	$116,800	
Ending inventory	(37,164)	
Cost of goods sold		79,636
Gross Profit		$ 70,364

The gross profit calculated using this method is greater than either of the LIFO gross profit figures but less than the FIFO figures. The reason is that the averaging effect results in a gross profit figure between the two extremes.

Average Cost—Perpetual. The average cost under a perpetual system is illustrated in Exhibit 9-6, which also is based on the Johnson Company data from Exhibit 9-1. The procedure used in a perpetual system is to calculate a new average cost after each purchase is made, thus creating a moving average. The moving average cost is applied to the units when they are sold. In Exhibit 9-6 the average cost after the first purchase is $5.15, which is the amount applied to the sales on August 6 and 10. After the purchase on August 15, the average cost

Exhibit 9-6
JOHNSON COMPANY
Moving Average—Perpetual Inventory

		Transaction			Balance		
Date		Units	Unit Cost	Total Cost	Units	Total Cost	Unit Cost
8–1	Balance				3,000	$15,000	$5.00
8–3	Purchase	9,000	$5.20	$46,800	12,000	61,800	5.15
8–6	Sales	6,000	5.15	30,900	6,000	30,900	5.15
8–10	Sales	4,000	5.15	20,600	2,000	10,300	5.15
8–15	Purchase	5,000	5.40	27,000	7,000	37,300	5.329
8–20	Purchase	5,000	5.60	28,000	12,000	65,300	5.442
8–28	Sales	5,000	5.442	27,208	7,000	38,092	5.442
8–31	Balance				7,000	38,092	5.442

becomes $5.329 per unit. The cost changes again after the purchase on August 20; it now becomes $5.442, which is the amount applied to the final sale on August 28 and also to the ending inventory units.

The ending inventory contains 7,000 units at a cost of $5.442 per unit, or a total value of $38,092. The cost of goods sold can be calculated by subtracting the ending inventory from purchases:

Beginning inventory	$ 15,000
Purchases	101,800
Available for sale	$116,800
Ending inventory	38,092
Cost of goods sold	$ 78,708

The cost of goods sold also could be calculated by adding all of the sales.

$$8\text{-}6 \quad 6,000 \times \$5.150 = \$30,900$$
$$8\text{-}10 \quad 4,000 \times \;\;5.150 = \;\;20,600$$
$$8\text{-}28 \quad 5,000 \times \;\;5.442 = \;\;27,208$$

Total cost of goods sold $78,708

Under this method and with a sales figure of $150,000, the gross profit would be as follows:

Sales (assumed)	$150,000
Cost of goods sold (see above)	78,708
Gross profit	$ 71,292

This gross profit figure is closest to the FIFO gross profit.

Comparison of Basic Cost Flow Methods

The different cost flow methods result in different values for the cost of goods sold and the ending inventory. Assume that Johnson Company has net sales of $150,000 for the period, has other expenses totalling $15,000, and pays income tax at a rate of 40%. A comparison of the different cost flow assumptions and their effect on gross profit, income tax, and net income are presented in Exhibit 9-7. You can analyze the impact of the cost flow assumption used by looking at the ending inventory value, the income tax, and the income after tax. Remember that the assumed data reflect an inflationary period.

Ending Inventory Value. The ending inventory value is a critical figure because it is the asset valuation figure that will appear on the balance sheet. The inventory value is used in many of the analytical ratios that are so important to the users of financial statements. For example, the inventory is part of current assets, which are used as part of the working capital and the working capital ratio. In addition, the inventory is used in the inventory turnover ratio and in percent-

Exhibit 9-7

JOHNSON COMPANY

Inventory Cost Flow Assumptions

	FIFO		LIFO		Average Cost	
	Periodic	*Perpetual*	*Periodic*	*Perpetual*	*Periodic*	*Perpetual*
Net sales	$150,000	$150,000	$150,000	$150,000	$150,000	$150,000
Cost of goods sold						
Beginning inventory	$ 15,000	$ 15,000	$ 15,000	$ 15,000	$ 15,000	$ 15,000
Purchases	101,800	101,800	101,800	101,800	101,800	101,800
Available for sale	$116,800	$116,800	$116,800	$116,800	$116,800	$116,800
Ending inventory	38,800	38,800	35,800	37,000	37,164	38,092
Cost of goods sold	$ 78,000	$ 78,000	$ 81,000	$ 79,800	$ 79,636	$ 78,708
Gross profit	72,000	72,000	69,000	70,200	70,364	71,292
Other expenses	15,000	15,000	15,000	15,000	15,000	15,000
Income before tax	$ 57,000	$ 57,000	$ 54,000	$ 55,200	$ 55,364	$ 56,292
Income tax (0.40)	22,800	22,800	21,600	22,080	22,146	22,517
Income after tax	$ 34,200	$ 34,200	$ 32,400	$ 33,120	$ 33,218	$ 33,775

age analysis. Chapter 27 provides an extensive discussion of financial statement analysis and the emphasis placed on the inventory valuation figure.

Because the inventory value is so critical to the analysis of financial statements, the importance of the cost flow assumption used cannot be overemphasized. Most financial analysts would prefer that the ending inventory value reflect the most recent costs of the merchandise on hand, or use of the FIFO method. From their point of view FIFO will state the inventory at closest to the current market value, thus providing the best data for the various analytical techniques. On the other hand, LIFO will provide an inventory value that is not based on the most current costs and thus is not as useful for analytical purposes.

Income Tax.   The income tax is also a key figure because it represents an actual cash outlay, and most businesses (and individuals) would prefer to minimize their tax payments. Exhibit 9-7 indicates that the use of LIFO minimizes income tax whereas the use of FIFO maximizes it. The difference arises, of course, from the income differences in the methods.

The Internal Revenue Service has sanctioned the use of LIFO for tax purposes only if it is used also for financial reporting purposes. This is the reason most companies use LIFO for reporting purposes. There is no difference in cash flows for any of the methods *except in the amount of the tax payment.* For example, assume that Johnson Company made all its sales for cash, and paid cash for its purchases and for all other expenses. The company's income before tax (on a cash basis) would be as follows:

Sales (all cash)		$150,000
Purchases (all in cash)	$101,800	
Other expenses (all cash)	15,000	
		116,800
Cash flow before tax		$ 33,200

The $33,200 represents the net cash flow to Johnson before income tax regardless of the inventory valuation method chosen. By using LIFO periodic, rather than the FIFO method, Johnson can save $1,200 in cash (tax payments) and can save lesser amounts compared to the other methods.

Income after Tax.   The use of FIFO will maximize income in periods of rising prices whereas LIFO tends to minimize income. These differences are seen clearly in Exhibit 9-7. The LIFO methods reflect a matching of current cost with current revenue—the best method for measuring current operating efficiency.

Arguments related to which cost flow method should be used always include income measurement as well as asset valuation. There are two views of income measurement: one view holds that it is (or should be) a measure of operating efficiency, whereas the other view is that it is a matching process. Those who believe that the purpose of income measurement should be to measure operating efficiency would favor the use of LIFO. Proponents of the matching process contend that income measurement should be the result of matching costs with revenues. They believe that since FIFO costing more closely approximates the physical flow, FIFO results in a better matching of revenues and expenses.

Exhibit 9-8
Inventory Cost Flow Assumptions
Rankings of Results

	Rising Prices					
	FIFO		LIFO		Average	
	Periodic	Perpetual	Periodic	Perpetual	Periodic	Perpetual
Ending inventory value	1	1	5	4	3	2
Income tax	1	1	5	4	3	2
Income after tax	1	1	5	4	3	2
	Falling Prices					
Ending inventory value	5	5	1	2	3	4
Income tax	5	5	1	2	3	4
Income after tax	5	5	1	2	3	4

1 = highest or greatest amount.
5 = lowest or least amount.

Rising and Falling Prices. Exhibit 9-8 presents a summary of the rankings of the inventory cost flow assumptions during periods of rising prices and falling prices. The rankings refer to the highest or lowest amounts. In periods of rising prices, FIFO gives the highest inventory values, tax payments, and income after tax; therefore, it has a ranking of 1 in each category. LIFO periodic is lowest in each category, so has a rank of 5.

During periods of falling prices, the rankings reverse themselves. FIFO will result in the lowest values and LIFO periodic will result in the highest values. The average periodic method retains the third rank with both rising and falling prices.

Other Valuation Methods

Companies frequently will use another method of inventory valuation for internal or management purposes but not for external reporting purposes. Some of these other methods include the base stock method, the standard cost method, and the variable or direct cost method. Management may use these methods internally for purposes of planning or for better cost control.

Base Stock Method

The **base stock method** assumes that a portion of the inventory (a *normal* or base stock of goods) should be maintained at all times. The normal or base stock of goods should be valued at a long-run, "normal" price, which usually is regarded as the lowest cost experienced by the company, or the original cost. The lowest cost is used to avoid "unrealized" inventory profits—that is, price increases for inventory items. The base stock of inventory is considered to be similar to a fixed asset and should not be affected by price fluctuations. The costs of maintaining and replenishing the "normal" stock are charged to operations. The cost of the extra stock is viewed as a temporary increment and is priced at current costs using LIFO, FIFO, or average cost. A shortage in base stock also is viewed as a temporary decrement and is charged against revenue at the current replacement cost.

Critics of the base stock method contend that it represents a departure from the cost principle. The "normal" cost of the base stock bears no relationship to the units currently held in inventory; it may represent the cost of several years ago. Another problem associated with this method is the determination of "normal" quantities that are set arbitrarily. The base stock method is similar in effect to LIFO in that it approximately matches current cost with current revenue; however, it is not acceptable for income tax purposes.

Standard Cost System

Manufacturing companies often will use a **standard cost system** for internal purposes in conjunction with FIFO, LIFO, or average cost methods for pricing inventories of raw material, work-in-process, and finished goods. In a standard cost system the material costs, labor costs, and factory overhead costs are based on standard rates that are carefully predetermined amounts. The material quantity standards and the labor time standards generally are based on engineering estimates and specifications. The material price standards usually are based on current market conditions while labor rates are set by union contract or company policy. Factory overhead is applied at a standard rate which is related to some measure of activity such as labor hours or machine hours. The differences between the standard costs and the actual costs are called **variances;** investigation of these variances allows management to achieve a greater degree of control over the manufacturing costs.

Planning and control are two major reasons for using a standard cost system internally. Because the costs are predetermined, and because management knows what the costs *should be* at the beginning of the budgetary period, management is better able to plan the fund flows and cash requirements. In addition, if the actual costs are significantly different from the standards, management will investigate these variances to determine the underlying cause. This investigative process allows a much greater degree of control than would a system in which no standards were used.

Generally accepted accounting principles permit the pricing of inventories at standard cost as long as there is not a significant difference between the actual and the standard cost. If there is a significant difference, the inventories must be adjusted to actual costs. The AICPA deems the use of standard cost to be acceptable if the standards are adjusted at reasonable intervals to reflect current conditions.[2] A complete discussion of standard cost systems can be found in any cost accounting text.

---

[2] *Accounting Research and Terminology Bulletins,* Final Edition (New York: AICPA, 1961), Chapter 4, p. 30.

Variable or Direct Costing

Variable or direct costing is used also for internal management purposes by manufacturing companies. It is not, however, an alternative to FIFO, LIFO, average cost, or specific identification. In a variable cost system the fixed overhead charges are treated as period costs instead of product costs. Fixed overhead charges are items such as supervisory salaries, factory insurance, depreciation of buildings and equipment, or any other fixed factory cost. Instead of charging these fixed costs to the units produced, a company expenses them during the period.

In the traditional or absorption method of accounting for fixed overhead, these costs are charged to work-in-process and become part of the product cost. Any unfinished or unsold product at the end of the period (ending inventories) would include a portion of the fixed overhead charge and would be inventoried until the next period. The only fixed overhead charge expensed would be that portion included in the costs of goods sold. In the direct or variable cost method, the entire fixed overhead charge is expensed in the period in which it occurs.

Inventories stated at direct or variable cost will be less than those stated at absorption cost due to the exclusion of the fixed overhead. If production is greater than sales, absorption income will be greater because a portion of the fixed overhead is stored in inventory instead of being expensed currently. However, if production is less than sales, absorption income is less because the fixed cost expensed currently includes the entire amount from the current period plus the stored portion from the beginning inventory.

Direct costing is used only for internal management purposes. It is not acceptable for external reporting nor for income tax purposes.

LIFO Complexities

The LIFO method illustrated earlier is very appealing to business for several reasons. First, it matches current cost with currrent revenue and therefore is a good measure to use for income determination. Second, there can be major tax benefits with LIFO. In periods of rising prices, reported income is less that it is with other inventory methods; thus, the tax liability is also less. Finally, because of the reduced tax liability, net cash flow will be increased.

However, the LIFO method does possess some inherent difficulties that limit its usefulness and application. The dollar-value method of LIFO has been developed to overcome the difficulties associated with the simple LIFO approach.

Dollar-Value LIFO

One of the problems with the simple LIFO approach is that it requires a large amount of very detailed clerical work and bookkeeping. Complete records for each item are necessary, including the physical quantities and unit costs in the beginning inventory and each purchase during the period. The value of each item in the ending inventory must be calculated separately, and this can be an enormous task for any company with sizable inventories.

Technological changes may cause another serious problem. As new parts and materials replace older ones, a new LIFO base should be started for the replacement parts. Again, the LIFO advantage is lost as current costs used for the replacement parts are added to the inventory in place of the older ones.

Dollar-value LIFO, with its use of price indexes and inventory "pools," was developed to overcome these problems. Under dollar-value LIFO, the inventory is grouped into pools that need not be identical units as in the traditional LIFO method. Instead, the pools contain inventory items that are similar in purpose or use, and that are substitutes for the original inventory items. The entire inventory could be considered as a single pool, but most companies use several pools for their inventory.

The underlying concept of the dollar-value LIFO method of inventory valuation is that price fluctuations and quantity fluctuations are separated in the computations. Changes in inventory value from year to year are due to either changes in price or changes in quantity. The dollar-value method eliminates the price change, isolating the quantity change without actually keeping track of quantities.

Although the computations necessary for the dollar-value LIFO method appear to be complex, they are not as difficult as they seem. The computations can be broken down into a series of five steps, which simplifies the procedure a great deal. The five steps are as follows:

1. Determine ending inventory value at current prices.
2. Convert the ending inventory to base-year prices to eliminate the price change effect.
3. Subtract the ending inventory at base-year prices from the beginning inventory at base-year prices to isolate the quantity change.
4. Value any increase in inventory quantities at current-year prices. Any decreases in inventory quantity should be valued at prices of most recent LIFO layers.
5. Add or subtract results from #4 to the beginning inventory value for the period to obtain the ending inventory value for the balance sheet.

Base year means the year in which LIFO was adopted. The ending inventory value is stated in terms of the base-year prices by dividing by the appropriate price index. This allows the price fluctuation to be eliminated from the ending inventory. In step three the base-year inventory layer is removed from the ending inventory leaving the added quantity at the base-year price. This added quantity becomes a new LIFO layer, which is then priced at the appropriate current cost level. If there is a decrease in quantity, it is subtracted from the most recently added LIFO layers.

The dollar-value LIFO method can be illustrated using the data for the Murphy Company in Exhibit 9-9. The 1981 ending inventory has a cost of $150,000, and you may assume that this is considered the base-year layer with a price index of 100. Exhibit 9-9 also presents the ending inventory data for each year through 1985 and the price index for each year. The **price index** is the amount of price change in comparison to the base year. The 1981 inventory of $150,000 is assumed to be the original inventory, and all subsequent years' ending inventories will be stated in terms of the base year's price. The ending inventory

Exhibit 9-9
MURPHY COMPANY
Inventory and Price Index Data

Date	Ending Inventory End-of-Year Cost	Price Index
12–31–81	$150,000	100
12–31–82	184,000	115
12–31–83	237,500	125
12–31–84	238,000	140
12–31–85	292,500	150

Exhibit 9-10
MURPHY COMPANY
Dollar-Value LIFO Computations

Year	Inventory EOY Cost	÷ Price Index =	Inventory Base Year	Layers	× Price Index =	LIFO Inventory
1981	$150,000	100	$150,000	$150,000	100	$150,000
1982	184,000	115	160,000	150,000	100	$150,000
				10,000	115	11,500
						$161,500
1983	237,500	125	190,000	150,000	100	$150,000
				10,000	115	11,500
				30,000	125	37,500
						$199,000
1984	238,000	140	170,000	150,000	100	$150,000
				10,000	115	11,500
				10,000	125	12,500
						$174,000
1985	292,500	150	195,000	150,000	100	$150,000
				10,000	115	11,500
				10,000	125	12,500
				25,000	150	31,500
						$205,500

values can be divided by the price index for the year, which will restate the inventory to the base-year price and will remove the price fluctuations.

After the total year-end inventory is restated in base-year prices, the base-year layer ($150,000) is removed, leaving the added layers at base-year prices. The added layers then are multiplied by the price index from the year in which the layer was added. Next, the layers are summed to find the dollar-value LIFO value at the end of the year. Exhibit 9-10 illustrates the calculation of the inventory values for the Murphy Company.

Murphy's base-year layer for 1981 is $150,000. The end-of-year cost is $150,000 and the price index is 100%. In the following year the 1982 inventory has an end-of-year cost of $184,000. Here is how to state this in terms of LIFO cost. First, you state the $184,000 in terms of base-year cost by dividing it by the price index of 115%, which gives the 1982 inventory at a base-year price of $160,000. The $160,000 is composed of two layers; the base-year layer of $150,000 and the 1982 layer of $10,000. Then, you multiply the 1982 layer by the 1982 price index of 115% and add it to the base layer. Thus, the 1982 LIFO inventory contains the base-year (1981) layer of $150,000 plus the current-year (1982) layer of $11,500. This is illustrated below:

Inventory at Base-Year Price	Layers	Price Index	LIFO Inventory
$160,000	$150,000	100	$150,000
	10,000	115	11,500
			$161,500

At the end of 1983 the current cost of the inventory is $237,500. Dividing by the price index of 125% gives an inventory value of $190,000 at base-year prices. The $190,000 is comprised of the original $150,000 layer from 1981, the $10,000 layer from 1982, and an added layer of $30,000 from 1983. Each of the layers is multiplied by the appropriate index and summed to arrive at the total LIFO value of $199,000, as shown below:

Inventory at Base-Year Price	Layers	Price Index	LIFO Inventory
$190,000	$150,000	100	$150,000
	10,000	115	11,500
	30,000	125	37,500
			$199,000

In 1984 the inventory value at year-end prices is $238,000. Dividing by the price index of 140% yields a value of $170,000 at base-year prices. Comparing the ending inventory at base-year prices ($170,000) with the beginning inventory at base-year prices ($190,000) indicates a $20,000 decrease in physical inventory at base-year prices. Since LIFO is being used, this decrease must have come from the 1983 layer. With a 1983 index of 125%, there is a $25,000 decrease in inventory from the beginning of the year. Inventory is now composed of the following:

Inventory at Base-Year Price	Layers	Price Index	LIFO Inventory
$170,000	$150,000	100	$150,000
	10,000	115	11,500
	10,000	125	12,500
			$174,000

In 1985 the ending inventory value at year-end prices was $292,500; since the index is 150, its value at base-year prices is $195,000, or $21,000 more than the beginning inventory at base-year prices. The ending inventory is composed of the following:

Inventory at Base-Year Prices	Layers	Price Index	LIFO Inventory
$195,000	$150,000	100	$150,000
	10,000	115	11,500
	10,000	125	12,500
	21,000	150	31,500
			$205,500

Note that the $20,000 decrease in the prior year's layer (1984) cannot be restored in subsequent years. In 1985 a new $21,000 layer is added.

Application of the dollar-value LIFO method as illustrated in Exhibit 9-10 indicates that it is really a simple procedure. By grouping the inventory items into pools of similar items or items with similar functions, you can eliminate much of the mechanical bookkeeping aspects of tracking individual units, and computation of the added layers (or decreases in existing layers) each year is simplified. In actual practice the most difficult aspect of applying dollar-value LIFO probably is finding the proper *price index* to use. This is discussed in the following section.

Price Index Used

The preceding discussion of dollar-value LIFO has referred to the use of a price index, which also could be referred to as a *cost* index. The price index generally is computed by taking the cost of the most recently purchased merchandise and applying that cost to the entire inventory pool at year-end. The formula for the index is calculated as follows:

$$\frac{\text{Ending inventory @ current-year cost}}{\text{Ending inventory @ base-year-cost}} = \text{price index}$$

The index is computed on the entire inventory pool and uses current-year and base-year costs. This is known as the *double-extension* method. Assume that the Murphy Company inventory at the end of 1981 was composed of the following:

Items	Quantity	Unit Cost	Total Cost
A1 Pumps	50	$1,000	$ 50,000
A2 Pumps	50	1,200	60,000
A3 Pumps	10	4,000	40,000
	Inventory 1981 base year		$150,000

This is also the beginning inventory of 1982. By the end of 1982 the inventory contains 52 units of A1 pumps, 50 units of A2 pumps, and 12 units of A3 pumps. The most recent purchase prices of these pumps were as follows:

Item	Unit Cost
A1	$1,050
A2	1,388
A3	5,000

The price index for 1982 is found by dividing the ending inventory at the current-year prices by the ending inventory at the base-year prices. The computations required are illustrated in Exhibit 9-11.

The $160,000 represents the 1982 ending inventory priced at the base-year (1981) unit costs. The $184,000 represents the 1982 ending inventory priced at the 1982 year-end costs. The price index of 115% is calculated by dividing the $184,000 by the $160,000. Then the price index of 115% is applied to the inventory layer of $10,000 added in 1982. (This was illustrated in Exhibit 9-10. The same process is used in the following years to calculate the index.

In this example the most recent costs of the purchases were used. Murphy Company also could use any other cost flow assumption, such as FIFO or average, as long as it is applied consistently from one period to the next.

Exhibit 9-11
MURPHY COMPANY
1982 Price Index Computations

Items	Quantity	Base Year Unit Cost	Base Year Total Cost	Current Year Unit Cost	Current Year Total Cost
A1 Pumps	52	$1,000	$ 52,000	$1,050	$ 54,600
A2 Pumps	50	1,200	60,000	1,388	69,400
A3 Pumps	12	4,000	48,000	5,000	60,000
			$160,000		$184,000

$$\text{1982 Price index} = \frac{\$184,000}{\$160,000} = 1.15 \text{ or } 115\%$$

Other LIFO Problems

In addition to the problems and complexities associated with LIFO that we have discussed already, there are several other special problems that need to be identified. One is the LIFO valuation problem, which is an adjustment that must be made to the inventory account. A second problem occurs with interim reports for companies that use LIFO. A third problem associated with LIFO occurs with the initial adoption of the method.

LIFO Valuations.   Companies frequently will use LIFO for tax and financial statement purposes, and will use some other method (FIFO, average, or special identification) for internal purposes. The difference between the LIFO value and the internal value is recorded in an account called "allowance to reduce inventory to LIFO" or some other appropriate title. The change in the account balance from one period to the next is the amount of the adjustment necessary in the year. For example, assume that the balance in the allowance account at 12-31-81 was $16,000. At 12-31-82, the required balance is $22,000 (i.e., the difference between the LIFO and the internal value was $22,000). The following adjusting entry would be made at the end of 1982:

Cost of goods sold	6,000	
Allowance to reduce inventory to LIFO		6,000

The allowance account then is deducted from inventory at year-end.

Interim Reporting of LIFO.   Companies that use LIFO for annual reporting purposes also must use LIFO for interim reporting purposes. APB *Opinion No. 28* requires consistency in the application of accounting principles between interim periods and year-end.[3] Dollar-value LIFO is based on year-end quantities and prices; therefore, some problems can arise in interim reporting. For example, in the second quarter of the fiscal year, the year-end quantities and prices are unknown. The accountant must estimate the total year-end change in the "allowance to reduce inventory to LIFO" account (discussed in the previous section), and must allocate that estimated change over the four quarters in some reasonable manner. The allocation could be based on estimated quarterly production or sales, an equal amount each quarter, or some other rational manner.

A special problem occurs in interim periods when a LIFO layer is liquidated partially or wholly. If the liquidation is *temporary* and is expected to be replaced by the end of the year, the effects of the liquidation should be removed from the interim statements. This means that the inventory value should be decreased and the cost of goods sold increased by the difference between the replacement cost and the LIFO cost of the liquidated goods. For example, suppose Murphy Company has a temporary liquidation of five units in the third quarter at a LIFO cost

[3]"Interim Financial Reporting," *Opinions of the Accounting Principles Board No. 28* (New York: AICPA, 1973).

of $1,000. Murphy will replenish these units in the fourth quarter at a cost of $1,050. The journal entries in the third and fourth quarters would be as follows:

Third quarter:		
Cost of goods sold (5 × $1,050)	5,250	
Inventory (5 × $1,000)		5,000
Temporary LIFO liquidation		250
Fourth quarter:		
Inventory (5 × $1,000)	5,000	
Temporary LIFO liquidation	250	
Accounts payable or cash		5,250

The effect of the third quarter entry is to remove the inventory from the books charge the cost of goods sold for the current cost, and place the difference between the LIFO and current cost ($250) in the temporary LIFO liquidation account. This is a temporary account that shows up only in interim reports. The entry in the fourth quarter replenishes the LIFO layer at the LIFO cost, removes the temporary liquidation account, and records the amount paid (or owed) for the replacement merchandise.

If the forecast in the interim period indicates that the LIFO layer liquidation will be *permanent*, those permanent reductions should be reflected in the interim reports, In addition, the year-end report must disclose any permanent reduction and liquidation of the LIFO base.

Initial Adoption of LIFO. Changing from any other method of inventory accounting to LIFO is considered a change in accounting principle, the rules for which are governed by APB *Opinion No. 20*.[4] In general, *Opinion No. 20* requires that changes in accounting principle be accounted for by the *cumulative effect method* with certain specific exceptions. The initial adoption of LIFO is one of those exceptions.

Determination of the cumulative effect of the initial adoption of LIFO is generally not possible because the records necessary to reflect the impact of LIFO are not available. To determine the impact of LIFO, you would need records of the costs of the layers added or reduced in the prior years, and these records are usually not available.

Because the cumulative effect is not determinable, *Opinion No. 20* requires that the beginning inventory in the year in which LIFO is adopted be treated as the base-year inventory for all future LIFO computations. Further, the *Opinion* requires disclosure of the effect of the change on the current year's results (the year the change to LIFO takes place). Finally, an explanation must be included as to why the computation of the cumulative effect and pro forma amounts for prior years has been omitted. A complete discussion of accounting changes will be found in Chapter 22.

---

[4]"Accounting Changes," *Opinions of the Accounting Principles Board No. 20* (New York: AICPA, 1971), par. 26.

Disclosure

Chapter 8 discussed the general disclosure requirements for inventories, which included information relative to inventory composition, financing, cost flow assumption used for valuation, consistency from one period to the next, and price-level. Some examples of inventory disclosures relative to composition and the use of lower of cost or market were presented.

The cost flow assumption used to value the inventories must be disclosed also. Most companies disclose the pertinent information about inventories in the notes to the financial statements. Following are several examples of the disclosure of inventory policies taken from the annual reports of the companies.

Examine the inventory data for Jostens Inc. in Exhibit 9-12. Jostens shows three categories of inventories and two notes pertaining to them. The first note indicates that certain of the inventories were valued by using LIFO, and others

Exhibit 9-12
JOSTENS, INC.
Inventory Disclosure and Notes to Financial Statements
Partial Consolidated Balance Sheet

June 30	1980	1979
Assets		
Current Assets		
Cash	$ 6,178,233	$ 4,243,342
Marketable securities—at cost		
(approximates market)	33,822,777	27,106,122
Accounts receivable, less allowances		
(1980—$910,000; 1979—$610,000)	48,782,739	41,585,168
Inventories—Notes A and B		
Finished products	5,976,143	5,974,838
Work-in-process	19,685,270	18,400,592
Materials and supplies	25,664,841	22,118,583
	$ 51,326,254	$ 46,494,013
Prepaid expenses	320,880	303,771
Total Current Assets	$140,430,883	$119,732,416

B. Inventories
Gold and certain other inventories aggregating $4,211,000 at June 30, 1980, and $4,638,000 at June 30, 1979, are stated at cost determined by the last-in, first-out method, and are $29,622,000 and $17,362,000 lower in the respective years than such inventories determined under the first-in, first-out cost method.

were valued by using lower of FIFO cost or market. This exemplifies the fact that a company may use different valuation methods for different parts of its inventories, as long as the methods are applied consistently. Note B for Jostens indicates the amount of the inventories stated at LIFO and the difference between what the LIFO valuation is and what the valuations *would have been* on a FIFO basis.

Keystone Consolidated Industries inventory disclosures are presented in Exhibit 9-13. In Note C to the financial statements, Keystone provides data about four categories of inventories—raw materials, semifinished products, finished products, and supplies. These inventories are valued at the lower of LIFO cost or market with the exception of supplies, which are valued at average cost. The impact of using LIFO instead of current cost to value the inventories is given also. Finally, Keystone provides an illustration of a partial liquidation of a LIFO base. During 1979 Keystone reduced inventories, which partially liquidated a

---

Exhibit 9-13
KEYSTONE CONSOLIDATED INDUSTRIES
Notes To Financial Statements

C. INVENTORIES
Inventories at June 30, 1979, and 1978 are valued at the lower of last-in, first-out (LIFO) cost or market, except for supplies, and consist of the following:

	(In Thousands)	
	1979	1978
Raw materials	$22,119	$22,058
Semifinished products	28,374	26,302
Finished products	23,856	24,205
Supplies (average cost)	9,575	10,092
	$83,924	$82,657

Cost of goods sold would have been approximately $11,490,000 and $3,464,000 lower, and net earnings would have been $6,698,000 ($3.57 per share) and $1,746,000 ($.93 per share) higher for the years ended June 30, 1979, and 1978, respectively, if LIFO inventories had been valued at current cost.

LIFO inventories at current cost would have been $21,611,000 and $10,121,000 higher at June 30, 1979, and 1978, respectively.

During 1979 the company reduced inventory quantities. This resulted in a partial liquidation of the LIFO base, which had the effect of decreasing the cost of goods sold by approximately $1,089,000 and increasing net earnings by approximately $544,000 or $.29 per share.

Exhibit 9-14
LAMSON AND SESSIONS CO.
Notes To Financial Statements

Note C—Inventories
Inventories in the consolidated statement of financial position are comprised of the following:

	December 31,	
	1979	1978
(Thousands of dollars)		
Finished goods and work-in process	$60,548	$26,227
Raw materials and supplies	21,552	17,435
	$82,100	$43,662

Inventories valued using the LIFO method amounted to approximately $53,300,000 and $30,500,000 at December 31, 1979, and 1978, after deducting LIFO reserves of $13,638,000 and $10,525,000, respectively. As a result of business acquisitions, certain acquired inventories have a federal income tax basis which is approximately $8,500,000 lower than the amount included in the financial statements at December 31, 1979, and taxable income for 1979 was approximately $4,000 greater than financial earnings.

During 1978 a reduction of inventory quantities resulted in a liquidation of LIFO inventory carried at lower costs prevailing in prior years as compared with the cost of 1978 purchases, the effect of which increased net earnings by $679,000, or $.17 per share.

LIFO base layer. The impact to Keystone was to decrease the cost of goods sold and to increase earnings.

Exhibit 9-14 presents inventory disclosures for Lamson and Sessions Company. The note indicates that Lamson used LIFO, had a LIFO reserve in 1979 of $13,638,000, and also partially liquidated a LIFO layer.

Concept Summary

INVENTORIES—COST FLOW METHOD

INVENTORY COSTING METHODS

Method	Description	Explanation
Specific Identification	Unit flow and cost flow are exactly the same.	Used when inventory units have very high cost.

First-in, First-out	Earliest cost elements are first ones charged to cost of goods sold.	Provides the most current ending inventory value, and charges the oldest costs against revenues.
Last-in, First-out	Latest cost elements are charged first to cost of goods sold.	Provides the oldest value for the ending inventory, but charges most recent costs against revenues.
Average Cost	The cost of all merchandise on hand is averaged, and the average cost per unit is expensed at the time of sale or inventoried at the end of the period.	Falls between FIFO and LIFO; it is very useful for companies that use process cost accounting.
Base stock	A portion of the inventory is maintained at all times as a normal or base stock of goods, and is valued at the normal or original cost.	Similar to LIFO in that the base layer remains at original cost.
Standard Cost	A carefully predetermined cost, used by manufacturing companies for planning and control purposes.	Used for internal purposes only; may not be used for external reporting.
Dollar-Value LIFO	A system based on inventory pools and the separation of price and quantity fluctuations in the computations.	Used mainly for income tax purposes.

FIFO vs. LIFO—EFFECT ON INCOME AND BALANCE SHEET

Method	General Economic Condition	Income Statement	Balance Sheet
FIFO	Inflation	Higher income than LIFO	Higher inventory value than LIFO

	Deflation	Lower income figure than LIFO	Lower inventory value than LIFO
LIFO	Inflation	Lower income than FIFO	Lower inventory value than FIFO
	Deflation	Higher income than FIFO	Higher inventory value than FIFO

Questions

Q-9-1 What are the four most commonly used cost flow methods of inventory valuation that follow the cost principle?

Q-9-2 What is the major objective involved in choosing a cost flow method for inventory valuation?

Q-9-3 When is the use of the specific identification method most beneficial and most proper?

Q-9-4 Is FIFO more appropriate for asset valuation purposes or for income measurement purposes? Why?

Q-9-5 In periods of falling prices, which method of inventory valuation will reflect the largest income? Why?

Q-9-6 For purposes of income measurement, which inventory valuation method is best—LIFO or FIFO?

Q-9-7 What is the major assumption underlying the base stock method of inventory valuation?

Q-9-8 Under a standard cost system, what is the meaning of a "favorable expense variance"?

Q-9-9 Under what circumstances does the AICPA permit the use of a standard cost system?

Q-9-10 What is the essential difference between variable and absorption costing?

Q-9-11 Indicate some of the problems that exist with regard to the simple LIFO method of inventory valuation.

Q-9-12 What is the underlying concept of dollar-value LIFO?

Q-9-13 How is the price index for dollar-value LIFO computed?

Q-9-14 When you use dollar-value LIFO for interim reporting purposes, the inventory at the interim date is based on year-end quantities and prices. How are those quantities and prices estimated?

Q-9-15 If a LIFO layer is partially or wholly liquidated at an interim reporting period, and if the liquidation is expected to be temporary, how is the liquidation effect handled? If the liquidation is expected to be permanent, how is it handled?

Q-9-16 Which of the following statements is *not* valid as it applies to inventory costing methods?

    a) If inventory quantities are to be maintained, part of the earnings must be invested (plowed back) in inventories when FIFO is used during a period of rising prices.

b)   LIFO tends to smooth out the net income pattern since it matches the current cost of goods sold with current revenue, when inventories remain at constant quantities.

c)   When a firm using the LIFO method fails to maintain its usual inventory position (that is, stock on hand is reduced below customary levels), there may be a matching of old costs with current revenue.

d)   The use of FIFO permits some control by management over the amount of net income for a period through controlled purchases, which is not true with LIFO.

(AICPA adapted)

Q–9–17   If you assume no beginning inventory, what can be said about the trend of inventory prices if the cost of goods sold computed when inventory is valued using the FIFO method exceeds the cost of goods sold when inventory is valued using the LIFO method?

(AICPA adapted)

Discussion Questions and Cases

D–9–1   Following are descriptions of two different situations related to inventory valuation and price movements. For each of these situations, assume that we are comparing LIFO and FIFO and that there are no beginning inventories.
Required:
1.   Assume that the cost of the ending inventory was lower using FIFO than if LIFO were used. In which direction were prices moving during the period? Explain.
2.   Assume that the cost of the ending inventory was lower using LIFO than if FIFO were used. In which direction were prices moving during the period? Explain.

D–9–2   Franz Corporation is a manufacturer of specialty products used in the oil field supply business. Franz has become very successful and profitable in a short period of time and now could be classed as a medium-sized company with total revenues approaching $35,000,000. The company was started in 1975; at that time the prices of gas and oil increased and led to an increased amount of exploration and development.

Franz has been using LIFO to value its inventories. As the business has grown, however, records have become exceedingly complex. Franz has been required to keep detailed and complete records for each item of inventory, including the physical quantities and unit costs in the beginning inventory and for each purchase during the period. Each item in the ending inventory must be valued separately. Franz management is becoming frustrated with the bookkeeping and clerical requirements of the inventory system but wishes to maintain the LIFO system because of the tax advantages.
Required:
Explain how the use of dollar-value LIFO can overcome the problems described above.

D–9–3   In most manufacturing situations the FIFO cost flow method approximates the actual flow of costs and units. Give an example of a manufacturing situation in which the following cost flow methods are more closely aligned to physical flow than FIFO.
   a)   Average cost
   b)   LIFO
   c)   Specific identification

(AICPA adapted)

D–9–4   Inventory may be computed under one of various cost flow assumptions, including FIFO and LIFO. In the past some companies have changed from FIFO to LIFO for computing portions or all of their inventory.

Required:
1. If you ignore income tax, what effect does a change from FIFO to LIFO have on net earnings and working capital? Explain.
2. Explain the difference between the FIFO assumption of earnings and operating cycle and the LIFO assumption of earnings and operating cycle.

(AICPA adapted)

D–9–5

a) Companies using LIFO inventory sometimes establish a "reserve for the replacement of LIFO inventory" account. Explain why and how this reserve account is established and where it should be shown on the statement of financial position.

b) Which of the inventory cost flow valuation methods requires estimates of price-level changes for specific inventories?

(AICPA adapted)

D–9–6 Changing from one inventory method of valuation to another is considered a change in accounting principle, the rules for which are governed by APB *Opinion No. 20* (par. 26). In general, *Opinion No. 20* requires that changes in accounting principle be accounted for by the cumulative effect method with certain specific exceptions. The initial adoption of LIFO is one of those exceptions. Determination of the cumulative effect of the initial adoption of LIFO is not generally possible. Therefore, *Opinion No. 20* contains special provisions and rules governing the initial adoption of LIFO.
Required:
1. Why is the cumulative effect of the change to LIFO usually not possible to determine?
2. What are the provisions of APB *Opinion No. 20* that apply to LIFO?

Exercises

E–9–1 More Corporation provides the following information relative to its inventory:

Purchases

January	1, 1982	Balance 100 @ $15
	5, 1982	Purchase 150 @ $16
	10, 1982	Purchase 200 @ $17
	20, 1982	Purchase 200 @ $18

Sales

January	3, 1982	80 units
	8, 1982	100 units
	15, 1982	210 units
	21, 1982	130 units

Required:
Calculate the ending inventory value assuming a periodic inventory system using the following methods:
a) FIFO.
b) LIFO.
c) Weighted average.

E–9–2 Repeat Exercise 9–1 assuming the use of a perpetual inventory system.

E–9–3 The following information was available from the inventory records of the Alexander Company for January, 1977:

	Units	Unit Cost	Total Cost
Balance at January 1, 1977	2,000	$ 9.775	$19,550

Purchases			
January 6, 1977	1,500	10.300	15,450
26, 1977	3,400	10.750	36,550
Sales			
January 7, 1977	1,800		
31, 1977	3,200		
Balance at January 31, 1977	1,900		

If you assume that Alexander maintains perpetual inventory records, what should be the inventory at January 31, 1977, using the weighted moving average inventory method, rounded to the nearest dollar?

(AICPA adapted)

E–9–4   Assume the same facts as in Exercise 9–3 except that Alexander maintains periodic inventory records. What should the inventory value be at January 31, 1977, using the weighted average method?

E–9–5   Assume the same facts as in Exercise 9–3, and assume that Alexander uses a perpetual LIFO system. What should the ending inventory value be assuming the units are costed currently?

E–9–6   Assume the following purchases and sales are made for Zales Company. What is the value of the ending inventory if Zales uses LIFO periodic?

Beginning inventory: 1,000 @ $10.00

Purchases	Sales (at Various Dates)
2,000 @ $ 9.50	500
1,500 @ $10.20	1,400
1,600 @ $10.40	3,000

E–9–7   Assume the same facts as in Exercise 9–6. What is the value of the ending inventory using FIFO perpetual? FIFO periodic?

E–9–8   The following information is available from the records of the Gonzalez Company:

Date	Purchases	Sales	Balance
Jan. 1			100 @ $20
15	200 @ $25		300 units
20		120 units	180 units
25		50 units	130 units
26	150 @ $30		280 units
29		130 units	150 units

Required:
From the information above, determine the cost of goods sold for the month of January assuming Gonzalez uses a perpetual inventory system and each of the following:
   a)   FIFO.
   b)   LIFO.
   c)   Average cost.

E–9–9   The Hastings Company began operations on January 1, 1976, and uses the FIFO method in costing its raw material inventory. Management is contemplating a change to the LIFO method and is interested in determining what effect such a change will have on net income. Accordingly, the following information has been developed:

Final Inventory	*1976*	*1977*
FIFO	$240,000	$270,000
LIFO	200,000	210,000
Net Income		
(Computed under the FIFO method)	120,000	170,000

Based upon the information above, a change to the LIFO method in 1977 would result in how much net income for 1977?

(AICPA adapted)

E–9–10 The Frate Company was formed on December 31, 1978. The following information is available from Frate's inventory records for Product Ply:

	Units	*Unit Cost*
January 1, 1979 (beginning inventory)	800	$ 9.00
Purchases		
January 5, 1979	1,500	10.00
25, 1979	1,200	10.50
February 16, 1979	600	11.00
March 26, 1979	900	11.50

A physical inventory on March 31, 1979, shows 1,600 units on hand.
Required:
Prepare schedules to compute the ending inventory at March 31, 1979, under each of the following inventory methods (assume a periodic inventory system).
Show supporting computatons in good form.

a) FIFO.

b) LIFO.

c) Weighted average.

(AICPA adapted)

E–9–11 The Michael Company uses the dollar-value LIFO method for valuation of inventories. The company provides the following information:

Date	*Ending Inventory*	*Price Index*
Dec. 31, 1980	8,000	100
Dec. 31, 1981	15,000	110
Dec. 31, 1982	26,000	120

Assume 1980 is the base year.
Required:
Calculate the dollar-value LIFO inventory values at the end of each year.

E–9–12 Assume that the Jay Company uses dollar-value LIFO for reporting purposes. Further, assume that Jay has a temporary layer liquidation in the third quarter of 10 units at a LIFO cost of $50 per unit. Jay replenishes these units in the fourth quarter at a cost of $55 per unit. What journal entries are necessary in the third and the fourth quarters?

E–9–13 You are given the following information about the inventory of Trey Company:

Item	*Qty*	*Unit Cost Base Year*	*Unit Cost Current Year, 1982*
X	10	$150	$175
Y	40	200	210
Z	50	300	350

Required:
Calculate the price index for the 1982 current year.

E-9-14 The Johnstone Company uses the dollar-value LIFO method to determine inventory values. The company provides the following data, and you ascertain that 1980 is the base year.

Date	Ending Inventory Value	Price Index
1980	$31,000	100
1981	44,000	110
1982	45,000	120
1983	56,000	125

Required:
Determine the value of the ending inventories for each of the years using dollar-value LIFO.

E-9-15 Assume that the base-year index is 100 for a company that uses dollar-value LIFO for inventory reporting. The other data are presented below:

Year	Ending Inventory Value	Price Index
1	$42,000	100
2	49,000	118
3	58,000	125

Assume Year 1 to be the base year.
Required:
Determine the value of the ending inventories using dollar-value LIFO.

E-9-16 M & M Company uses dollar-value LIFO for inventory valuation. The company is constructing the price index for the current year and has the following data available:

Product	Quantity	Unit Cost Base Year	Unit Cost Current Year
A	600	$ 5.00	$ 8.00
B	1,000	9.00	9.50
C	800	10.00	12.00
D	900	7.00	8.00

Required:
Calculate the current year's price index using the double extension method.

Problems

P-9-1 Integer Computer Company was organized in 1974. Integer uses the FIFO inventory method and reports the following amounts for net income:

	Income
1978	$ 12,000
1979	170,000
1980	163,500
1981	168,250

Integer has calculated the values of its year-end inventories for this period on both the FIFO and LIFO basis as follows:

Dec. 31	FIFO	LIFO
1978	$37,500	$35,000
1979	43,000	39,500
1980	42,000	39,000
1981	45,750	41,750

Assume the following data as well:

	1979	1980	1981
Purchases	$ 73,000	$ 73,000	$ 73,000
Selling & administrative	12,500	12,500	12,500
Sales	250,000	250,000	250,000

Required:
Compute the net income that would have been reported in 1979, 1980, and 1981 if Integer had used LIFO instead of FIFO.

P–9–2 Primary Enterprises has the following purchases and sales of a particular product for 1980 and 1981. Primary had 20,000 units of this product on hand at January 1, 1980, with a cost of $6.00 per unit.

1980				1981			
Purchases		Sales		Purchases		Sales	
Units	Cost	Units	Price	Units	Cost	Units	Price
4,000	$6.00	6,000	$9.00	6,000	$5.85	5,000	$7.50
10,000	5.85	8,000	7.50	10,000	6.00	5,000	7.80
10,000	5.70	8,000	7.20	6,000	6.30	3,000	7.80
8,000	5.76	7,000	7.35	8,000	6.60	5,000	7.80
						9,000	8.25

Primary uses periodic inventory procedures.
Required:
1. Compute the cost of goods sold and the ending inventory value for 1980 and 1981 using LIFO.
2. Repeat Part 1 using FIFO.

P–9–3 Secondary Company has procrastinated on selecting its inventory method. July, the first month of operations, has just ended. Secondary's president wants you to determine the ending inventory and the cost of goods sold using FIFO, LIFO, and the average cost methods. He then will select the method which he deems most appropriate. The following data are available:

Purchases			Sales		
July	1	4,000 @ $5.00	July	3	2,400 @ $7.75
	8	3,200 @ 5.20		11	2,000 @ 7.80
	15	6,400 @ 4.60		16	2,000 @ 7.50
	24	3,600 @ 4.80		23	1,600 @ 7.75
		17,200		25	600 @ 7.90
				29	1,800 @ 7.25
					10,400

Required:
Assume a periodic inventory system and compute the cost of goods sold and the ending inventory values for the month of July using the following:
- **a)** FIFO.
- **b)** LIFO.
- **c)** Average cost.

P–9–4 Assume the same facts as in Problem 9-3, except that Secondary Company would like to use a perpetual inventory system instead of a periodic system.

Required:
Compute the cost of goods sold and the ending inventory values using the following:
- **a)** FIFO.
- **b)** LIFO.
- **c)** Average cost.

P–9–5 Peach Company is a southern manufacturing company which has been in business for several years. Peach uses the dollar-value LIFO method for determining ending inventory values. They provide you with the following data for a three-year period:

1980	Item	Qty.	Base Year Unit Cost	Current Year Unit Cost
	A	1,000	$20	$30
	B	1,100	18	24
	C	800	45	36
	D	600	50	52
1981	A	800	20	32
	B	1,300	18	25
	C	600	45	34
	D	700	50	55
1982	A	900	20	35
	B	1,200	18	28
	C	500	45	25
	D	800	50	60

Required:
Calculate the price index for each year using the double extension method.

P–9–6 Macker Company presents you, its new CPA, with the following data:

Net income: 1981 $250,000; 1980 $150,000
Inventory method, LIFO
Sales: 1981 $775,000; 1980 $640,000
Purchases: 1981 $300,000; 1980 $280,000
Ending inventory values:

	LIFO	FIFO
12/31/81	$84,000	$97,000
12/31/80	75,000	81,000
12/31/79	93,000	99,000

Required:
Macker requests you to compute (for internal purposes only) the gross profit and net income for 1980 and 1981 as if FIFO has been used instead of LIFO and to present those in income statement form. (Ignore income taxes.)

P–9–7 Windchimes Incorporated was established in 1980 as a specialty goods retailer. In

1983, Windchimes has asked for assistance in preparation of its financial statements. You are in the process of determining the value of the ending inventory. Windchimes uses dollar-value LIFO with the base year being 1980. The following information is available:

Year	Ending Inventory Value	Price Index
1980	$55,000	100
1981	63,000	110
1982	69,000	120
1983	78,000	130

Required:
Calculate the dollar-value LIFO inventory value for the end of the year 1983.

P–9–8 Mantle Corporation is preparing its third-quarter interim report. You are the accountant. You discover that there is a temporary reduction in the LIFO inventory of 775 units that cost $52 per unit. Mantle fully anticipates to replace those units in the fourth quarter at $59 per unit.

Required:
1. Make the necessary journal entry or entries, if any, to write the inventory down for the temporary reduction.
2. If Mantle does procure those 775 units at $59 per unit in the fourth quarter, make the appropriate entry.

P–9–9 Dixie Digits Widgets uses specific identification for Product D3PAL. Data for the month of January follow:

Purchases

January	5:	100 units @ $69.75 =	$6,975
	12:	30 units @ $77.50 =	2,325
	18:	20 units @ $80.00 =	1,600
	23:	15 units @ $75.00 =	1,125
Available:		165 units	$12,025

Sales

January	10:	30 units from January 5 purchase—sales price $85 unit
	11:	25 units from January 5 purchase—sales price $88 unit
	17:	20 units from January 5 purchase—sales price $90 unit
	18:	30 units from January 12 purchase—sales price $93 unit
	24:	10 units from January 5 purchase—sales price $90 unit
	25:	20 units from January 18 purchase—sales price $95 unit
	30:	10 units from January 23 purchase—sales price $100 unit

Required:
1. Assuming there was no beginning inventory, compute the ending inventory under specific identification.
2. Same as Part 1 but use FIFO periodic inventory method.

P–9–10 X. Smith Company's data for August are as follows:

Date	Inventory			Purchases		
	Units	Cost	Total	Units	Cost	Sales Units
August 1	775	$9	$6,975			
5						200

7			300	$ 9.75	
10			200	9.50	
11					250
12					150
16			250	10.00	
17					375
22					100
25			225	10.40	
28					350
Totals	775	$6,975	975		1,425

Required:

1. Compute the cost assigned to the ending inventory using the following, (assume the periodic method),

    a) LIFO.

    b) FIFO.

2. Compute the cost assigned to the ending inventory under LIFO but with the perpetual inventory method used.

P-9-11 Add 'N Subtract Company started operations on January 1, 1982. The quarterly data for the first quarter of 1982 are presented below.

Purchases

Date		Unit	Unit Cost	Total Cost
January	4	300	$ 8.50	$ 2,550
	12	250	9.30	2,325
	27	100	9.50	950
February	3	125	9.60	1,200
	10	200	9.30	1,860
	26	100	9.25	925
March	5	150	10.20	1,530
	25	200	10.10	2,020
Totals		1,425		$12,360

Sales

Date		Unit	Unit Price	Total Sales Price
January	11	225	$12.40	$ 2,790
	26	200	12.75	2,550
February	11	300	13.20	3,960
	23	100	13.00	1,300
March	12	150	13.50	2,025
	23	100	14.00	1,400
		1,075		$14,025

Required:

1. Compute the ending inventory and gross margin under FIFO, assuming the periodic inventory system is used.

2. Same as part 1. but assume that LIFO inventory system is used instead.

3. If there were any differences between parts 1. and 2., why did they occur?

P-9-12 The BPH Company manufactures a single product. On December 31, 1979, BPH adopted the dollar-value LIFO method of inventory valuation. The inventory on that date using dollar-value LIFO was $45,000. The inventory in the following years was as follows (all at their respective year-end prices):

1980	56,000
1981	77,000
1982	65,000

The price indexes were as listed below:

1980	110
1981	120
1982	130

Required:
Compute the value of the inventory using dollar-value LIFO at December 31, 1980, 1981, and 1982. (Round answers to nearest whole dollars.)

P–9–13 Presented below is information pertaining to Green Company for the last four years:

Item	Quantities in Ending Inventory	Base Year Cost		Current Year Cost	
		Unit Cost	Amount	Unit Cost	Amount
X_1	20,000	$ 2.00	$40,000	$ 2.20	$ 44,000
X_2	4,000	4.00	16,000	5.00	20,000
X_3	2,000	10.00	20,000	13.60	27,200
December 31, 1980			$76,000		$ 91,200
X_1	18,400	$ 2.00	$36,800	$ 2.40	$ 44,160
X_2	6,000	4.00	24,000	5.00	30,000
X_3	1,600	10.00	16,000	13.65	21,840
December 31, 1981			$76,800		$ 96,000
X_1	16,000	$ 2.00	$32,000	$ 2.60	$ 41,600
X_2	4,800	4.00	19,200	5.80	27,840
X_3	3,200	10.00	32,000	14.70	47,040
December 31, 1982			$83,200		$116,480
X_1	16,000	$ 2.00	$32,000	$ 3.00	$ 48,000
X_2	5,000	4.00	20,000	6.40	32,000
X_3	3,200	10.00	32,000	17.00	54,400
December 31, 1983			$84,000		$134,400

Required:
Compute the value of the ending inventories under the dollar-value LIFO method. These items are substantially similar. The base period is January 1, 1980. The beginning inventory cost at that date was $76,000.

P–9–14 The 1981 inventory records of Pop's Pipe Shop show the following data regarding its most popular style pipe:

Date		Transaction	Units	Unit Cost
January	1	Inventory	3,000	$3.00
April	15	Purchase	20,000	3.50

June	11	Sale (at $12 per unit)	8,000	
August	12	Purchase	5,000	3.75
October	15	Sale (at $12.75 per unit)	13,000	
November 11		Purchase	7,000	4.00
December 3		Sale (at $13 per unit)	6,000	

Required:

For each of the following inventory flow methods, compute the ending inventory, cost of goods sold, and gross margin. Round unit costs to cents and totals to dollars.

    a) FIFO (periodic system).

    b) Weighted average.

    c) LIFO (unit basis, periodic system, 3,000 units in base layer).

    d) LIFO (unit basis, perpetual system, 3,000 units in base layer).

    e) Moving average.

P–9–15 The records of BCD Retailer Co. show the following amounts relative to the movement of merchandise Item G:

Jan.	1	Beginning inventory	4,020 units @ $2.40 unit cost
	3	Purchase	3,000 units @ 2.60 unit cost
	5	Sale	6,000 units
	17	Purchase	3,580 units @ 2.80 unit cost
	26	Sale	2,500 units
	30	Purchase	340 units @ 3.00 unit cost

Required:

1. Compute the ending inventory and the cost of issues for January assuming the following:

    a) Weighted average.

    b) Moving average.

    c) FIFO (assume periodic system).

    d) LIFO (assume periodic system).

2. State the conditions under which each method would be preferable.

10

Inventories—
Cost Estimation
Methods

Accounting in the News

Inventory valuation is often a problem to companies during the year as well as at the end of the year. Because companies must issue financial reports at interim periods, estimates of the value of inventories must be made at these interim dates. APB *Opinion No. 28* prescribes the interim reporting requirements:

> An enterprise shall generally use the same inventory pricing methods and make provisions for write-downs to market at interim dates on the same basis as used at annual inventory dates with the following exceptions, as appropriate, at interim reporting dates:
>
> a. Some enterprises use estimated gross profit rates to determine the costs of goods sold during interim periods or use other methods different from those used at annual inventory dates. Those enterprises shall disclose the method used at the interim date and any significant adjustments that result from reconciliation with the annual physical inventory.

Estimation of inventories at interim dates is a recurring and continuing problem for the accountant. Use of inventory estimation methods at interim dates is a common practice among many companies because of the expense of taking a physical inventory. This chapter presents various methods of estimating inventory.

*"Interim Financial Reporting," *Opinions of the Accounting Principles Board No. 28* (New York: AICPA, 1973), par. 14. Copyright © 1973 by the American Institute of Certified Public Accountants, Inc.

In many situations an accountant may wish (or may have) to estimate the amount of inventory on hand. For example, an auditor may wish to determine if the reported inventory is *reasonable,* or if it is in line with inventory amounts from other periods. At an interim reporting date, an auditor may wish to estimate the inventory rather than take a physical inventory, which is quite costly. Also, in case of a fire or other form of casualty loss, taking a physical inventory would be impossible because the inventory may be destroyed partially or totally, but the amount of the loss still must be determined. Because of the cost and inconvenience involved in taking a physical inventory, most businesses prefer to count their inventory only once a year. A retailer, for example, may be forced to close operations for a day to take inventory, or at best, may have to do it in the late evening or on a Sunday. This is not only inconvenient, but costly as well.

Two popular methods have become widely accepted for making estimates of inventory value—the gross profit method and the retail method. The **gross profit method** may be used in a situation in which it is desirable to test the *reasonableness* of the reported value; it is based on the assumption that the rate of gross profit is constant from one period to the next. It assumes that the gross profit percentage in the period of estimation is the same as in prior periods, or if different, that it can be adjusted to reflect the current rate.

The **retail method** is used by retailers to estimate inventory; like the gross profit method, it allows estimates of the inventory to be made at interim dates without resorting to a physical inventory. The retail method is based on the assumption that there is a consistent spread, or difference, between the selling price and the cost of the merchandise. This implies that the relationship between cost and retail prices remains fairly stable from one period to the next. In this chapter the gross profit method and the retail method will be discussed in detail.

The Gross Profit Method

Remember that gross profit is the difference between the amount of sales and the cost of goods sold. For a trading company, the cost of goods sold includes the net purchases for the period plus the beginning inventory minus the ending inventory. This is illustrated below.

Trading Company

Sales		$1,000
Cost of goods sold		
Beginning inventory	$ 75	
Net purchases	900	
Total available for sale	975	
Ending inventory	130	
Cost of goods sold		845
Gross profit		$ 155

$$\text{Gross Profit \%} = \frac{155}{1,000} = 15.5\%$$

In this example the net purchases are adjusted for inventories (add the beginning and subtract the ending) to obtain the $845 cost of goods sold figure. If there were no inventories, or if there were *no change* in the inventories, the cost of goods sold would have been $900, which is the amount of net purchases.

Recall that in Chapter 8 the inventory system and the cost of goods sold calculations for manufacturing companies were explained. The gross profit for a manufacturing company is calculated by subtracting the cost of goods sold from the sales. The gross profit percentage again will be the gross profit divided by the sales. The relationship between the cost of goods sold and the sales is very important in using the gross profit method of estimating inventory values.

Assumptions Underlying Gross Profit Method

The gross profit method of estimating inventory is based on the assumption that the **rate of gross profit** is constant, or unchanged, from one period to the next. By rate of gross profit is meant the **gross profit percentage,** calculated by dividing the total gross profit by the total sales. By assuming a constant rate of gross profit, we are saying that the relationship between the cost of goods sold and sales has not changed. This implies that (1) the relationship between costs and selling prices (in the aggregate) has been constant, and (2) the product mix sold has not changed.

The first implication means that as costs fluctuate up and down, selling prices will also fluctuate up and down and that the net result will be no change in the aggregate ratio of cost to selling price. For example, if the cost ratio in the prior year was 70%, all the increases and decreases in the costs and selling prices of the various products will result again in a cost ratio of 70% in the current year.

The implication that the product mix has not changed means that the proportions of each product sold remain the same. For example, if a company's sales in the prior year consisted of 30% of Product A, 20% of Product B, and 50% of Product C, the company would sell the same proportions of A, B, and C in the current year. If either the cost relationship or the mix relationship changes, the rate of gross profit also will change.

A test of the reasonableness of the gross profit rate can be made by comparing the calculated rate to the industry rate. Care must be exercised, however, to be certain the proper comparison is made. For example, the rate of gross profit for a discount store is likely to be significantly different from the rate of gross profit for a specialty goods store or for a regular department store. The gross profit rate is, in reality, a composite rate for the various products of the company. Although each product may have a different rate, the composite rate is used in the computation of the estimated inventory value.

Application of the Gross Profit Method

The general procedure used to apply the gross profit method is simple. The beginning inventory is added to the amount of purchases for the period to obtain the cost of goods available for sale. Next, the composite gross profit percentage (rate) is multiplied by the sales to obtain the total gross profit. The gross profit subtracted from sales results in the cost of goods sold. Finally, the ending inventory is found by subtracting the cost of goods sold from the goods available for sale. The format for the calculations would be the following:

Beginning inventory	XX
Purchases	XX
Goods available for sale	XX

Sales	XX	
Gross profit % (Sales × GP%)	(XX)	
Cost of goods sold		(XX)
Estimated ending inventory		XX

The gross profit percentage is the complement of the **cost of goods sold percentage.** That is, if sales are 100%, and if the gross profit percentage is 40%, the cost of goods sold must be 60%. The ending inventory could be estimated just as easily by using the cost percentage instead of using the gross profit percentage as is illustrated below.

Beginning inventory	XX
Purchases	XX
Goods available for sale	XX
Cost of goods sold (Cost % × sales)	(XX)
Estimated ending inventory	XX

Both of the above methods (cost % and gross profit %) give the same results so it does not matter which is used.

Following is an example of the application of the gross profit method of estimating inventories. Assume that the following information is known for the Johnson Company.

Beginning inventory	$ 25,000
Purchases	350,000
Sales	600,000
Composite gross profit rate	45%

The value of the ending inventory for Johnson can be estimated as follows:

Beginning inventory		$ 25,000
Purchases		350,000
Cost of goods available for sale		$375,000
Sales	$600,000	
Gross profit ($600,000 × 0.45)	(270,000)	
Cost of goods sold		(330,000)
Ending inventory (at cost)		$ 45,000

In this example the cost of the beginning inventory is added to the cost of the purchases to obtain the cost of goods available for sale ($375,000). The cost of goods sold is obtained by multiplying the gross profit rate (45%) by the sales ($600,000) to obtain the total gross profit ($270,000), and then subtracting the gross profit from the sales. Instead, we could multiply the cost percentage (55%) by the sales to obtain the cost of goods sold directly:

$$55\% \times \$600,000 = \$330,000$$

In either case, the cost of goods sold ($330,000) is subtracted from the goods available for sale to obtain the estimated value of the ending inventory.

The critical factor in this method is the ability to determine the gross profit rate. For the Johnson Company the rate was assumed to be 45%. The 45% is a *composite* rate because it represents a weighted average gross profit rate from all the Johnson Company products. Suppose Johnson Co. sells three different products—Alpha, Beta, and Gamma—and that the respective rates of gross profit are 40%, 34%, and 55%. The composite rate of 45% is a weighted average of all three, and is based on the proportion of total gross profit that each product contributes.

For example, assume Johnson Co. has the following sales of each product:

	Unit Sales	Unit Price	Sales
Alpha	15,000	$ 8	$120,000
Beta	20,000	10	200,000
Gamma	20,000	14	280,000
Totals	55,000		$600,000

The composite gross profit rate of 45% is determined in the following manner:

	Sales	% Gross Profit	$ Gross Profit
Alpha	$120,000	0.40	$ 48,000
Beta	200,000	0.34	68,000
Gamma	280,000	0.55	154,000
Total	$600,000		$270,000

$$\text{Composite rate} = \frac{\$270,000}{\$600,000} = 45\%$$

The composite rate of 45% represents a weighted average of the individual gross profit rates. It assumes that the gross profit rates of the individual products are the same in the current year as in the prior year. If the rate on any individual product changes, the composite rate also would have to change. For example, if Gamma's rate dropped from 55% to 40%, the composite rate would drop to 38%.

	Sales	% Gross Profit	$ Gross Profit
Alpha	$120,000	0.40	$ 48,000
Beta	200,000	0.34	68,000
Gamma	280,000	0.40	112,000
Total	$600,000		$228,000

$$\text{Composite rate} = \frac{\$228,000}{\$600,000} = 38\%$$

This composite rate also assumes that the sales mix proportion for the individual products does not change. When the sales mix changes, a new composite rate must be determined. Suppose, for example, that the sales of Beta doubled whereas the sales of Alpha and Gamma remained constant. A new composite rate would be necessary.

	Sales	% Gross Profit	% Gross Profit
Alpha	$120,000	0.40	$ 48,000
Beta	400,000	0.34	136,000
Gamma	280,000	0.55	154,000
Total	$800,000		$338,000

$$\text{Composite rate} = \frac{\$338,000}{\$800,000} = 42.25\%$$

The new composite rate would be 42.25%.

It is entirely possible that the changes in the individual rates will offset each other, or that changes in the sales mix will offset each other. The point is that if a change in any of these factors is suspected, a new rate should be calculated.

Calculation of Gross Profit Percentages

The gross profit usually is stated as a percentage of the selling price; that is, the selling price, which is equal to 100%, is comprised of a cost percentage plus a profit percentage.

Sales	100%
Cost of sales	60%
Gross profit	40%

The cost of sales (60%) plus the gross profit (40%) equals the sales (100%).

Markups by retailers can be stated either in terms of selling price or in terms of cost. Therefore, the gross profit can be stated as a percent of sales price or a percent of cost. For example, assume the following data for a product:

Selling price	$40
Cost	24
Gross profit	$16

The gross profit percentage is 40% of the sales price.

$$16/40 = 40\%$$

This is also the *markup based on selling price.*

If the markup were based on cost, it would be 67% of cost.

$$16/24 = 67\%$$

The amount of the profit ($16) is the same, but the stated percentage markup differs. Retailers most often will state markup in terms of selling price because the percentage is smaller. The accountant should be familiar with both and also should understand the relationship between the two.

The relationship between the gross profit based on selling price and the gross profit based on cost can be expressed in the following formula:

$$\text{Gross Profit \% Based on Sales Price} = \frac{\text{Gross Profit \% Based on Cost}}{1 + \text{Gross Profit \% Based on Cost}}$$

If you use the earlier data of a $40 selling price, a $24 cost, and a gross profit of $16, the gross profit percentage based on cost is:

$$\text{Cost \%} = 16/24 = 67\%$$

The formula above may be used to convert this markup to a percent of sales rather than cost as follows:

$$\text{GP \% sales} = \frac{67\%}{1 + 67\%}$$

$$40\% = \frac{67\%}{167\%}$$

Or, as another example, assume a markup on cost of 25%. The markup on selling price would be calculated as follows:

$$20\% = \frac{25\%}{100\% + 25\%}$$

Suppose, instead, that we wanted to calculate the gross profit percentage based on cost. The following formula would be used:

$$\text{Gross Profit \% Based on Cost} = \frac{\text{Gross Profit \% Based on Sales Price}}{1 - \text{Gross Profit \% Based on Sales Price}}$$

For example, assume a gross profit percentage based on sales price of 25%. The gross profit percentage based on cost would be:

$$33\tfrac{1}{3}\% = \frac{25\%}{100\% - 25\%}$$

The dollar amount of the gross profit will be the same regardless of how the retailer states the percentage markup. However, it is necessary for the accountant to understand the terminology and the relationship between these two methods.

Comprehensive Example of Gross Profit Method

As an illustration of the application of the gross profit method, assume that the Smith Company had a fire on February 14th, and has requested its accountant to determine the amount of merchandise inventory that was destroyed by the fire. The accountant is able to ascertain the following information from the records:

Inventory, January 1	$ 47,500
Purchases (net of discounts)	420,000
Purchase returns and allowances	14,000
Sales (January 1 to Feb. 14)	560,000
Merchandise in transit (FOB Shipping Pt.)	10,000

Smith follows the practice of marking up its merchandise 67% on the cost price. Smith has had an offer of $30,000 from a salvage company for all the damaged merchandise, not including the merchandise in transit.

The value of the merchandise destroyed by the fire can be estimated as follows, using the gross profit method:

Beginning inventory		$ 47,500
Purchases	$420,000	
Less: returns & allowances	(14,000)	406,000
Merchandise available for sale		$453,500
Less: Cost of goods sold (60% × $560,000)		(336,000)

Sales price = 167% of cost

$$\therefore \text{Cost} = \frac{100\%}{167\%} = 60\% \text{ sales}$$

Ending inventory		$117,500
Less: merchandise in transit	$10,000	
salvage value	30,000	(40,000)
Value of inventory destroyed		$ 67,500

The cost of goods sold percentage of 60% is found by dividing the cost by the sales price. In this example, the sales price was 67% above cost; therefore

Sales price	=	167%
Cost	=	100%
Gross profit	=	67%

The cost percentage is 100%/167%, or 60%. The merchandise in transit must be deducted since it was not destroyed but was included in purchases. We must assume that it is included in purchases because it was shipped FOB Shipping Point, and not FOB Destination. The salvage value of $30,000 must be deducted also to arrive at the amount of the fire loss, which is $67,500.

Evaluation of the Gross Profit Method

The gross profit method is a useful method of estimating the value of the ending inventory. It is, however, based on the composite gross profit rate, which is a weighted average of the gross profit rates of all the individual products. The composite rate incorporates several limiting assumptions that must be recognized when this method is used. First, it assumes that the gross profit rates on the individual products are constant from one period to the next. Second, it assumes that the product mix sold is constant from one period to the next. Third, it assumes that if changes in individual rates or product mix sold did occur, they would be offset by each other so that the composite rate would not change. If any of these three assumptions are violated, a new composite rate should be calculated.

Using the gross profit method to estimate the ending inventory is not a substitute for taking a physical inventory. The estimating procedure is done for convenience only; the physical inventory should be taken at least once per year.

Retail Inventory Method

The retail inventory method is used mainly by retailers to estimate their inventory and is preferred by many businesses because it can save the merchant a great deal of time. When the purchases are received, the merchant immediately marks them at the selling price. The goods are placed for sale in the store and stocked on the shelves with the selling prices already marked on them. Under this method, when the retailer takes the physical inventory, the goods are valued originally at the retail price. The retail method then is applied to estimate the cost of the merchandise on hand by converting the retail valuation back to cost. This eliminates the need to find the original cost of each item in the inventory, which would be a tedious and time-consuming process of going back to the original invoices for each unit of product.

Assumptions of Retail Method

The retail method and the gross profit method are based on similar assumptions. There are two fundamental assumptions underlying the retail method: (1) the relationship between the costs and selling prices has been stable for all the goods in the inventory and (2) the mixture of goods in the ending inventory is the same as the mix in the purchases. The first assumption, stability between costs and selling prices, means that there is a consistent spread, or difference, between the selling prices and costs of the merchandise. For most retailers the spread is a consistent markup throughout the company as a whole, or a consistent markup within departments. The second assumption, a similar mix of goods in both purchases and inventory, means that the ending inventory contains the same kinds of merchandise in the same proportions as the purchases.

Basic Illustration and Terminology

The retail method of inventory can be used in conjunction with the FIFO, average, or LIFO cost flow assumptions. Lower of Cost or Market can be used with the FIFO and with the average cost flow assumptions. The IRS and the accounting profession have approved the retail method for use.

The retail inventory method is based on a cost-to-retail ratio, which is computed using the cost-to-retail relationship for goods available for sale. The goods available for sale at cost are divided by the goods available for sale at retail to obtain the cost-to-retail ratio. The sales are deducted from the merchandise available for sale at retail to find the ending inventory at retail. The cost-to-retail ratio applied to the inventory at retail results in the inventory at cost figure. This is illustrated in Exhibit 10-1, which contains data for the Johnson Company.

The cost-to-retail ratio in Exhibit 10-1 is 60%, which is calculated using the goods available for sale. The ending inventory at retail ($90,000) is multiplied by the cost percentage (60%) to obtain the cost of the ending inventory. Note that the cost of goods sold at retail is actually net sales. The retail method is similar to the gross profit method in that in both of them the cost of goods sold is subtracted from the goods available for sale to estimate the ending inventory. In the retail method, the cost of goods sold and the goods available for sale are both stated at retail, so the ending inventory will be stated at retail. The ending inventory then is multiplied by the cost percentage to find the estimated cost.

Advantages of Retail Method. Use of the retail method has several advantages. First, it allows estimates of the inventory values to be made without having to take a physical count. This is helpful for interim reporting purposes and also for insurance purposes in the event of casualty losses. Second, the bookkeeping is simplified because the costs associated with individual items are unnecessary. The cost ratio is based on the total goods available for sale, and not on individual units. Therefore, cost information for individual units need not be kept. Third, taking a physical inventory at the end of the year is expedited because only the retail prices need to be checked. There is no need to refer back to invoices for the costs of individual items.

Retail Method Terminology. The Johnson Company illustration in Exhibit 10-1 assumed that there were no changes in the retail prices after they were established. This is an unrealistic assumption because most retail stores will change

---

Exhibit 10-1
JOHNSON COMPANY
Retail Inventory Method

	Cost	Retail
Beginning inventory	$ 60,000	$100,000
Purchases	420,000	700,000
Goods available for sale	$480,000	$800,000
Cost-to-retail ratio = $\dfrac{\$480,000}{\$800,000} = 60\%$		
Less: sales		(710,000)
Ending inventory at retail		$ 90,000
Ending inventory at cost ($90,000 × 0.6)	$ 54,000	

prices, often several times on individual items. The terms used in the retail method are defined below:

MARKUP—The amount by which the original sales price exceeds the cost. This is referred to sometimes as MARK-ON.

MARKDOWN—A decrease in the sales price below the original sales price.

ADDITIONAL MARKUP—An increase above the original selling price.

MARKUP CANCELLATION—The cancellation of part or all of the additional markup. The amount of the markup cancellation cannot exceed the amount of the additional markup.

NET MARKUP—The difference between the total additional markups and the total markup cancellations.

MARKDOWN CANCELLATION—Cancellation of part or all of the markdown. The amount of the markdown cancellation cannot exceed the amount of the markdown.

NET MARKDOWN—The difference between the total markdowns and the total markdown cancellations.

Here is an example of the terminology usage. Assume that a pair of gloves is purchased at a cost of $10. The original price is set at $15, a markup of $5. Subsequently, the price is increased to $18, an additional markup of $3. The gloves do not sell, and the gloves are later sale-priced at $16, a markup cancellation of $2. The gloves still do not sell and are reduced further to $12, a markup cancellation of $1 and a markdown of $3. The gloves still do not sell, and are priced at $16 for the new season, a markdown cancellation of $3 and an additional markup of $1. At this point the activity would be summarized as follows:

Cost	$10
Markup	5
Original sales price	$15
Additional markup	3
Sales price	$18
Markup cancellation	(2)
Sales price	$16
Markup cancellation	(1)
Markdown	(3)
Sales price	$12
Markdown cancellation	3
Additional markup	1
Sales price for new season	$16

Net markup = $3 − $2 − $1 + $1 = $1

Net markdown = −$3 + $3 = 0

The net markups and the net markdowns are added and subtracted in the retail column to obtain the ending inventory at retail.

Application of the Retail Inventory Method

The retail inventory method can be combined with the inventory methods discussed in Chapter 9—FIFO, average cost, and LIFO. The retail FIFO and retail average cost also can be used in conjunction with the lower of cost or market (LCM) method discussed in Chapter 8. Thus, there are five possible alternatives in the application of the retail method: retail FIFO, retail average cost, retail FIFO-LCM, retail average cost-LCM, and retail LIFO. The basic differences among these methods are in the computations of the cost-to-retail ratios. The computations can be summarized as follows:

RETAIL FIFO—Exclude the beginning inventory value from the calculation of the cost-to-retail ratio; include the net markups and net markdowns.

RETAIL AVERAGE COST—Include the beginning inventory value in the calculation of the cost-to-retail ratio; also include the net markups and the net markdowns.

RETAIL FIFO-LCM—Exclude the beginning inventory value from the calculation of the cost-to-retail ratio; include the net markups but EXCLUDE the net markdowns.

RETAIL AVERAGE COST-LCM—Include the beginning inventory value in the calculation of the cost-to-retail ratio; also include the net markups but EXCLUDE the net markdowns.

RETAIL LIFO—Calculate separate cost-to-retail ratios for the beginning inventory and the current period purchases. The beginning inventory would include the layers of inventory at the beginning of the year; if the size of the inventory is increased, the added layer is valued at the current cost-to-retail ratio. If the size of the inventory is decreased, the cost-to-retail ratios existing in the layers of the opening inventory are used to reduce those layers.

The first four methods are similar in their computations; the LIFO method is different and will be discussed later in this chapter.

Exhibit 10-2 summarizes the similarities and the differences in the first four methods. The lower of cost or market methods for FIFO and average cost exclude the net markdowns from the cost-to-retail ratio calculations, but otherwise they are exactly the same as the retail FIFO and retail average cost methods. In both retail FIFO and retail FIFO-LCM, the beginning inventory is *excluded* from the cost-to-retail computation, whereas it is *included* in both the retail average cost and the retail average cost-LCM methods.

The beginning inventories are excluded from the cost-to-retail ratio computation in both FIFO methods because FIFO assumes that the earliest cost elements introduced to the system are the first ones expensed to cost of goods sold. Therefore, the ending inventory would contain no cost elements from the beginning inventory; those costs would be entirely expensed to cost of goods sold. The ending inventory would contain only those cost elements from the most recent purchases.

The cost of the beginning inventories would be included in the cost-to-retail ratios for the average cost methods because average cost assumes that the costs associated with inventories and all purchases are averaged to find the average cost per unit. This average cost per unit then is multiplied by the number of units

Exhibit 10-2
Calculation of Cost-to-Retail Ratio
Comparison of Four Retail Inventory Methods

| | | | Lower of Cost or Market | |
	Retail FIFO	Retail Average Cost	Retail FIFO	Retail Average Cost
Beginning inventory	exclude	include	exclude	include
Purchases	include	include	include	include
Net markups	include	include	include	include
Net markdowns	include	include	exclude	exclude

sold to find the cost of goods sold, and is multiplied by the number of units in ending inventory to find the cost of the ending inventory.

The net markdowns are excluded from the cost-to-retail ratio computation for both the LCM methods. This lowers the cost-to-retail ratio because the denominator is larger. Consider the following example:

	Cost	Retail
Purchases	$100,000	$150,000
Net markups		20,000
Net markdowns		(30,000)

Assume there is zero beginning inventory. We may calculate the cost-to-retail ratios including the markdowns and then excluding the markdowns. If we include the markdown (as in the *non*-LCM methods), we would have the following:

$$\frac{\$100,000}{\$150,000 + \$20,000 - \$30,000} = \frac{\$100,000}{\$140,000} = 71.43\%$$

However, if we exclude the markdowns, the computation would be:

$$\frac{\$100,000}{\$150,000 + \$20,000} = \frac{\$100,000}{\$170,000} = 58.82\%$$

Now, if we assume the ending inventory at retail is $10,000, the appropriate costs would be as follows:

$$\$10,000 \times 71.43\% = \$7,143$$
or
$$\$10,000 \times 58.82\% = \$5,882$$

We can see that excluding the markdowns in the LCM methods results in a lower cost for the inventory. The lower cost of the ending inventory approximates the lower of cost or market value.

Each of the four methods—retail FIFO, retail average cost, retail FIFO-LCM, and retail average cost-LCM—will be illustrated using the data from Exhibit 10-3 for the Bryce Company.

Retail FIFO. The retail FIFO method requires the exclusion of the beginning inventory from the calculation of the cost-to-retail ratio. The net markups and net markdowns are included in the calculation of the cost-to-retail ratio. The retail FIFO method calculations for the Bryce Company are shown in Exhibit 10-4.

The cost-to-retail ratio of 71.43% is calculated by dividing the purchases of $150,000 at cost by the purchases at retail adjusted for the markups and markdowns. The beginning inventory is excluded from the computation. Thus, the cost-to-retail ratio is as follows:

$$\frac{\$150,000}{\$200,000 + \$20,000 - \$10,000} = 71.43\%$$

The cost ratio then is multiplied by the retail value of the ending inventory to obtain the cost of the ending inventory:

$$(\$25,000 \times 71.43\%) = \$17,857.50$$

This procedure follows the FIFO cost flow assumption; therefore, it assumes that the entire beginning inventory is sold during the period and that the ending inventory is composed of purchases made during the current period.

Retail Average Cost. The retail average cost method includes the beginning inventory, net markups, and net markdowns in the calculation of the cost-to-retail

---

Exhibit 10-3
BRYCE COMPANY
Cost and Retail Inventory Data

	Cost	Retail
Beginning inventory	$ 10,000	$ 15,000
Net purchases	150,000	200,000
Net markups		20,000
Net markdowns		(10,000)
Goods available for sale		$225,000
Sales		(200,000)
Ending inventory		$ 25,000

Exhibit 10-4
BRYCE COMPANY
Retail FIFO Inventory

	Cost	Retail
Beginning inventory	$ 10,000	$ 15,000
Net purchases	$150,000	$200,000
Net markups		20,000
Net markdowns		(10,000)
Total excluding beginning inventory	$150,000	$210,000

Cost-to-retail ratio:
$$\frac{\$150,000}{\$210,000} = 71.43\%$$

	Cost	Retail
Goods available for sale	$160,000	$225,000
Sales		(200,000)
Ending inventory at retail		$ 25,000
Ending inventory at cost ($25,000 × 0.7143)	$ 17,857.50	
Cost of goods sold:		
Beginning inventory	$ 10,000	$ 15,000
Current purchases		
At retail ($200,000 − $15,000)		185,000
At cost $160,000 − ($10,000 + $17,857.50)	132,142.50	
Cost of goods sold	$142,142.50	$200,000

ratio. Exhibit 10-5 illustrates the retail average cost method for the Bryce Company.

The cost-to-retail ratio of 71.11% is calculated based on the goods available for sale. The beginning inventory cost and the purchases from the current period are combined, or averaged, in this method. The goods available for sale are apportioned to the cost of goods sold and the ending inventory at the average cost percentage of 71.11%.

Retail FIFO-Lower of Cost or Market. The lower of cost or market (LCM) method can be used in conjunction with either the retail FIFO or the retail average cost method. In the LCM method, the net markdowns are excluded from the computation of the cost-to-retail ratio. Exhibit 10-6 illustrates the retail FIFO-LCM method for the Bryce Company.

The cost-to-retail ratio of 68.18% is based on the net purchases of $200,000 plus the net markups of $20,000 divided into the net purchases at cost of $150,000. The beginning inventory and the net markdowns both are excluded from the cost-to-retail ratio. Exclusion of the beginning inventory from the ratio assumes that the entire amount of beginning inventory was sold during the period, and that the ending inventory consists of merchandise purchased during the current period. Exclusion of the net markdowns from the computation of the cost ratio has the effect of lowering that ratio. Excluding the markdowns recognizes that the current purchase price or the replacement cost has decreased for some reason, perhaps as a result of obsolescence or decline in the utility of the merchandise.

Retail Average Cost-Lower of Cost or Market.   Exhibit 10-7 illustrates the use of the retail average cost-LCM method. The beginning inventory is included in the cost-to-retail ratio computation because the average cost method assumes a commingling of prior period and current period costs. However, the net markdowns again are excluded for the same reasons as in the retail FIFO-LCM method. The cost-to-retail ratio of 68.09% is applied to the ending inventory ($25,000) to obtain the cost of the ending inventory ($17,022.50).

Most companies that use the retail method combined with lower of cost or market choose the average cost method instead of FIFO. The average cost

---

Exhibit 10-5
BRYCE COMPANY
Retail Average Cost Inventory

	Cost	Retail
Beginning inventory	$ 10,000	$ 15,000
Net purchases	150,000	200,000
Net markups		20,000
Net markdowns		(10,000)
Goods available for sale	$160,000	$225,000
Cost-to-retail ratio: $\frac{\$160,000}{\$225,000} = 71.11\%$		
Sales		(200,000)
Ending inventory at retail		$ 25,000
Ending inventory at cost ($25,000 × 0.7111)	$ 17,778	
Cost of goods sold ($160,000 − $17,778)	$142,222	

Exhibit 10-6
BRYCE COMPANY
Retail FIFO-LCM

		Cost	Retail
1.	Beginning inventory	$ 10,000	$ 15,000
	Net purchases	$150,000	$200,000
	Net markups		20,000
2.	Total excluding beginning inventory	$150,000	$220,000
	Cost-to-retail ratio:		
	$\dfrac{\$150,000}{\$220,000} = 68.18\%$		
3.	Net markdowns		(10,000)
	Goods available for sale (1 + 2 + 3)	$160,000	$225,000
	Sales		(200,000)
	Ending inventory at retail		$ 25,000
	Ending inventory at cost ($25,000 × 68.18%)	$ 17,045	
	Cost of goods sold: ($160,000 − $17,045)	$142,955	

method is somewhat easier to apply. Both LCM methods are more conservative than the conventional methods.

Comparison of the Methods. Exhibit 10-8 compares the results obtained for the four methods discussed above. The cost-to-retail ratios, the ending inventory values, and the cost of goods sold are presented.

The average cost-LCM method has the lowest cost-to-retail ratio. Thus, this method results in the lowest inventory value and the highest cost of goods sold figure. Both of the LCM methods have lower cost-to-retail ratios than do the other two methods; therefore, both LCM methods provide lower values for the ending inventory. The LCM methods are a more conservative approach to inventory valuation.

Dollar-Value Retail LIFO Method

The **dollar-value retail LIFO method** combines the dollar value LIFO method discussed in Chapter 9 and the retail method discussed in the previous section of this chapter. Many retail establishments have adopted the dollar-value retail

Exhibit 10-7
BRYCE COMPANY
Retail Average Cost-LCM

	Cost	Retail
Beginning inventory	$ 10,000	$ 15,000
Net purchases	150,000	200,000
Net markups		20,000
Total	$160,000	$235,000

Cost-to-retail ratio:

$$\frac{\$160,000}{\$235,000} = 68.09\%$$

	Cost	Retail
Net markdowns		(10,000)
Goods available for sale	$160,000	$225,000
Sales		(200,000)
Ending inventory at retail		$ 25,000
Ending inventory at cost (0.6809 × $25,000)	$ 17,022.50	
Cost of goods sold: ($160,000 − $17,022.50)	$142,977.50	

LIFO method. One of the reasons for its popularity is that it matches current costs with current revenues for income determination. Another reason is that in periods of rising prices, LIFO results in lower income and therefore, a lower tax liability. When LIFO was approved for use by the IRS, many businesses adopted it to take advantage of the lowered tax liability.

Exhibit 10-8
BRYCE COMPANY
Comparison of Retail Inventory Methods

	Retail FIFO	Retail Average Cost	LCM Retail FIFO	LCM Retail Average Cost
Cost-to-retail ratio	71.43%	71.11%	68.18%	68.09%
Ending inventory	$ 17,857.50	$ 17,778.00	$ 17,045.00	$17,022.50
Cost of goods sold	142,142.50	142,222.00	142,955.00	142,977.50

Computing Inventory Cost Using Retail LIFO

The computations involved in determining the value of the ending inventory under this approach are conceptually quite simple. Each year, any change in the quantity of the inventory is assumed to be from the purchases of the most recent period. Thus, increases in the quantity are assumed to be from the purchases of the current period and result in the newest layer added to the inventory. Any decreases in quantity are subtracted from the layers that have been added most recently. In determining the costs of the layers added, you use only the net purchases in calculating the cost-to-retail ratio. The beginning inventory is not used since it is a cost associated with a previous layer. Each year, any additions to the inventory quantities are assumed to be at current prices. Also, both the markups and the markdowns are used to find the proper cost-to-retail percentage. The markups and markdowns apply to the current period purchases only and not to the beginning inventory.

Exhibit 10-9 illustrates a case in which the retail LIFO method is used. The beginning inventory has a cost of $300 and a retail value of $500. The cost-to-retail ratio for the beginning inventory is 60% (300/500 = 60%). During the current period, purchases are made that cost $1,000 and have a retail value of $1,500. There are net markups of $150 and net markdowns of $50. The net markups and net markdowns both are used in the calculation of the cost-to-retail ratio of 62½%. This ratio applies to current period purchases only; the beginning inventory is excluded.

Exhibit 10-9
Retail LIFO Inventory Method

	Cost	Retail
Beginning inventory	$ 300	$ 500
Net purchases	$1,000	$1,500
Net markups		150
Net markdowns		(50)
Total current purchases	$1,000	$1,600
Cost-to-retail-ratio $\dfrac{\$1,000}{\$1,600} = 62\frac{1}{2}\%$		
Merchandise available for sale	$1,300	$2,100
Sales		(1,500)
Ending inventory at retail		$ 600
Ending inventory at cost:		
Beginning inventory	$ 300	$ 500
Current layer		
$100 = 0.625	62.50	100
Total ending inventory	$ 362.50	$ 600

To find the cost of the ending inventory, you carry forward the beginning inventory cost and add the new layer from the current period. The ending inventory has a retail value of $600, composed of $500 from the beginning inventory and a new layer of $100 from the current period. The cost of the ending inventory is found by carrying forward the beginning inventory cost of $300, and adding the cost of the new layer, $62.50.

The example in Exhibit 10-9 illustrates the layering concept and the separation of the beginning inventory from the current period activities. The cost-to-retail ratio from the current period (62½%) is calculated using the purchases, markups, and markdowns, but excluding the beginning inventory.

Two simplifying assumptions were made in Exhibit 10-9. First, there were only two layers of inventory, the beginning and the current year. More likely, the beginning inventory will be composed of several layers that have been added over a number of years. Second, there was an implicit assumption that prices were stable over the periods involved. In most cases, prices are changing, usually increasing. The changing prices are the reason for the layering effect in LIFO. Prices changing over several time periods necessitate the use of the dollar-value retail LIFO method.

Computing Inventory Cost Using Dollar-Value Retail LIFO Method

When prices are changing, the dollar-value method illustrated in Chapter 9 is combined with the retail method. In order to apply the dollar-value retail LIFO method, you should follow a six-step procedure:

Step 1. Calculate the retail value of the ending inventory.
Step 2. Calculate the retail value of the ending inventory at base year prices.
Step 3. Calculate the inventory change (increase or decrease) at base year prices.
Step 4. Calculate the inventory change (increase or decrease) at current period prices.
Step 5. Calculate the cost-to-retail ratio for the current period's purchases (including markups and markdowns, but excluding beginning inventory).
Step 6. Calculate the cost of the ending inventory by adding the cost of the current period's layer to the beginning inventory (or subtracting the decrease from the most recent layer).

The relatively complex computations required for the dollar-value retail LIFO method will be simplified following this six-step procedure.

The data in Exhibit 10-10 for the Smythe Company will be used to illustrate the six-step procedure for the dollar-value retail LIFO method. Three years of data are provided for Smythe Company—1981, 1982, and 1983. The base year price index of 100 is assumed for January 1, 1981. The current price indexes are assumed to be 112 for 1981, 125 for 1982, and 140 for 1983.

Exhibit 10-11 illustrates the six-step procedure for the year 1981. The first step is to calculate the ending inventory at retail value; this is done in the conventional manner and is $38,080.

The second step is to calculate the retail value of the ending inventory using the base year's prices. To do this you divide the ending inventory by the current

Exhibit 10-10

SMYTHE COMPANY
Basic Data

	1981		1982		1983	
	Cost	Retail	Cost	Retail	Cost	Retail
Inventory, January 1	$20,000	$ 28,000	$120,000	$195,000	$145,000	$226,000
Purchases	92,748	150,000				12,000
Net markups		11,000		14,000		
Net markdowns		(6,420)		(4,000)		(8,000)
Sales		(144,500)		(172,000)		(190,000)
Current price index (January 1, 1981 = 100)		112		125		140

Exhibit 10-11
SMYTHE COMPANY
Dollar-Value Retail LIFO Method—1981

	Cost		Retail
Step 1: *Retail value of ending inventory*			
Inventory, January 1	$ 20,000		$ 28,000
Purchases	92,748	$150,000	
Net markups		11,000	
Net markdowns		(6,420)	154,580
Goods available for sale	$112,748		$182,580
Sales			(144,500)
Ending inventory at retail			$ 38,080
Step 2: *Retail value of ending inventory*			
at base year prices			
Ending inventory ÷ current			
year index			
$38,080 ÷ 1.12			$ 34,000
Step 3: *Inventory change at base year*			
prices			
Ending inventory—beginning			
inventory			
$34,000 − $28,000			$ 6,000
Step 4: *Inventory change at current year*			
prices			
$6,000 × 1.12			$ 6,720
Step 5: *Cost-to-retail ratio for current*			
period			
$92,748 ÷ $154,580 = 60%			
Step 6: *Cost of ending inventory*			
at LIFO			
January 1, 1981, layer	$ 20,000		$ 28,000
1981 layer added			
$6,720 × 60%	4,032		6,720
Ending inventory at LIFO	$ 24,032		$ 34,720

year's price index of 112%. The value of the ending inventory at base year prices is then

$$\$38,080 \div 112\% = \$34,000$$

This means that the ending inventory for 1981 has a value of $34,000 at base year prices. We can divide the ending inventory by the current year's index of 112% in this step because the base year index is 100%. If the base year index were anything other than 100%, the ending inventory would have to be divided by a ratio of the current year's index to the base year's index. For example, if the base year's index for Smythe were 104% instead of 100%, the calculation in Step 2 would be as follows:

$$\$38,080 \div \frac{112\%}{104\%}$$

In this second step, we are trying to calculate the retail value of the ending inventory at *base year prices;* therefore, the current year prices (index) must be divided by the base year prices (index). In the original Smythe Company example, we actually are dividing by the ratio 112%/100%, and the computation for the ending inventory is

$$\$38,080 \div \frac{112\%}{100\%}$$

The third step is to determine the quantity change in inventory by subtracting the beginning inventory at base year prices from the ending inventory at base year prices.

$$\$34,000 - \$28,000 = \$6,000$$

The $6,000 represents the quantity increase in inventory with no price differences; that is, if prices had not changed, we would have increased the inventory by $6,000.

The fourth step is to isolate the inventory change at current year prices by multiplying the $6,000 quantity change by the current year's index of 112%. The result ($6,720) represents the retail value of the layer added to the inventory in 1981. We now have two layers of inventory at retail prices:

Beginning inventory	$28,000
1981 layer added	6,720
Ending inventory at retail LIFO	$34,720

Now we must convert the retail layers of the inventory to cost.

The fifth step is the calculation of the cost-to-retail ratio for the current year. The ratio (60%) includes net purchases, net markups, and net markdowns, but excludes the beginning inventory.

The sixth and final step is to calculate the value of the ending inventory using the dollar-value retail LIFO method. This is done now easily; simply add the cost of the new layer to the cost of the beginning inventory.

	Cost	*Retail*
Beginning inventory	$20,000	$28,000
1981 layer ($6,720 × 60%)	4,032	6,720
	$24,032	$34,720

These inventory values become the beginning inventory for the next period, 1982.

Exhibits 10-12 and 10-13 illustrate the six-step procedure for the years 1982 and 1983. The computations, which are quite mechanical, are understood easily if the six-step procedure is followed. The computations for the six steps are the same each year. Step 1 is the calculation of the ending inventory value at the retail price. This is done in the conventional manner, and includes both markups

---

Exhibit 10-12
SMYTHE COMPANY
Dollar-Value Retail LIFO Method—1982

	Cost		Retail
Step 1: *Retail value of ending inventory*			
Inventory, January 1	$ 24,032		$ 34,720
.Purchases	120,000	$195,000	
Net markups		14,000	
Net markdowns		(4,000)	205,000
Goods available for sale	$144,032		$239,720
Sales			(172,000)
Ending inventory at retail			$ 67,720
Step 2: *Retail value of ending inventory at base year prices*			
Ending inventory ÷ current index			
($67,720 ÷ 1.25)			$ 54,176
Step 3: *Inventory change at base year prices*			
Ending inventory—beginning inventory			
$54,176 − $34,000			$ 20,176
Step 4: *Inventory change at current year prices*			
$20,176 × 1.25			$ 25,220
Step 5: *Cost-to-retail ratio for current period*			
$120,000 ÷ $205,000 = 58.54%			
Step 6: *Cost of ending inventory at LIFO*			
Beginning inventory:			
Base layer, January 1, 1981	$ 20,000		$ 28,000
1981 layer (Exhibit 10-11)	4,032		6,720
Total inventory, Jan. 1, 1982	$ 24,032		$ 34,720
1982 layer added			
$25,220 × 58.54%	14,764		25,220
Inventory, 12–31–82	$ 38,796		$ 59,940

Exhibit 10-13
SMYTHE COMPANY
Dollar-Value Retail LIFO Method—1983

	Cost		Retail
Step 1: *Retail Value of Ending Inventory*			
Inventory, January 1	$ 38,796		$ 59,940
Net purchases	145,000	$226,000	
Net markups		12,000	
Net markdowns		(8,000)	230,000
Goods available for sale	$183,796		$289,940
Sales			(190,000)
Ending inventory at retail			$ 99,940
Step 2: *Retail value of ending inventory at base year prices*			
Ending inventory ÷ current index			
$99,940 ÷ 1.40			$ 71,386
Step 3: *Inventory change at base year prices*			
Ending inventory—beginning inventory			
$71,386 − $54,176			$ 17,210
Step 4: *Inventory change at current year prices*			
$17,210 × 1.40			$ 24,094
Step 5: *Cost-to-retail ratio for current period*			
$145,000 ÷ $230,000 = 63%			
Step 6: *Cost of ending inventory at LIFO*			
Beginning inventory:			
Base layer, January 1, 1981	$ 20,000		$ 28,000
1981 layer (Exhibit 10-11)	4,032		6,720
1982 layer (Exhibit 10-12)	14,764		25,220
Total beginning inventory	$ 38,796		$ 59,940
1983 layer added			
$24,094 × 63%	15,179		24,094
Inventory, 12–31–83	$ 53,975		$ 84,034

and markdowns. Step 2 converts the retail value of the ending inventory into the base year prices. This is done by dividing the ending inventory by the current price index. In Step 3, the inventory quantity change is isolated by subtracting the beginning inventory (at base year prices) from the ending inventory (also at base year prices). By using the base year values for both the inventories, you remove all the price fluctuations, and the physical quantity change is isolated. This physical quantity change is the new layer (at base year prices) that will be added to (or subtracted from) the beginning inventory.

In Step 4, the quantity change is converted to current year prices by multiplying it by the current year price index. This results in the retail value of the layer added in the current year. In Exhibits 10-12 and 10-13, the amounts are $25,220 and $24,094 respectively.

Step 5 is the calculation of the cost-to-retail ratio for the current year. For 1982, it is 58.54%; and for 1983, it is 63%. The ratio is calculated by dividing the net purchases at cost by the retail value of the net purchases, plus the net markups and minus the net markdowns. Below is an illustration of these calculations as presented in Exhibits 10-12 and 10-13:

| | 1982 | | 1983 | |
	Cost	Retail	Cost	Retail
Net purchases	$120,000	$195,000	$145,000	$226,000
Net markups		14,000		12,000
Net markdowns		(4,000)		(8,000)
Totals	$120,000 ÷ $205,000		$145,000 ÷ $230,000	
Ratio	58.54%		63%	

Finally, in Step 6, the ending inventory at cost is calculated. The beginning inventory is carried forward, and the current year's layer is added. The cost of the current year's layer is found by multiplying the cost percentage (from Step 5) times the inventory change at current year prices (from Step 4). Note that the beginning inventory is comprised of the base year layer (from January 1, 1981) plus the following year's layers. Thus, for 1982 and 1983, the amounts are as follows:

| | 1982 | | 1983 | |
	Cost	Retail	Cost	Retail
Beginning inventory:				
Base layer, 1–1–80	$20,000	$28,000	$20,000	$28,000
1981 layer, (Ex. 10-11)	4,032	6,720	4,032	6,720
Inventory, 1–1–82	$24,032	$34,720		
1982 layer, (Ex. 10-12)	14,764	25,220	14,764	25,220
Inventory, 12–31–82	$38,796	$59,940	$38,796	$59,940
1983 layer, (Ex. 10-13)			15,179	24,094
Inventory, 12–31–83			$53,975	$84,034

Each year the new layer is added to the beginning inventory layers from the previous years. If, in some year, a quantity decrease were calculated in the fourth step, the decrease would be treated as a liquidation (or partial liquidation) of a LIFO layer that would be lost forever and could not be replaced (see discussion in Chapter 9). In the Smythe Company example, new layers were added each year.

Exhibit 10-14

SMYTHE COMPANY
Dollar-Value Retail LIFO Method—Three Years

	1981		1982		1983	
	Cost	*Retail*	*Cost*	*Retail*	*Cost*	*Retail*
Step 1: Retail value of ending inventory						
Inventory, January 1	$ 20,000	$ 28,000	$ 24,032	$ 34,720	$ 38,796	$ 59,940
Purchases	92,748	$150,000	120,000	$195,000	145,000	$226,000
Net markups		11,000		14,000		12,000
Net markdowns		(6,420)		(4,000)		(8,000)
		154,580		205,000		230,000
Goods available for sale	$112,748	$182,580	$144,032	$239,720	$183,796	$289,940
Sales		(144,500)		(172,000)		(190,000)
Ending inventory at retail		$ 38,080		$ 67,720		$ 99,940
Step 2: Retail value of ending inventory						
at base year prices						
$38,080 ÷ 1.12		$ 34,000				
67,720 ÷ 1.25				$ 54,176		
99,940 ÷ 1.40						$ 71,386

Step 3: *Inventory change at base year prices*

$34,000 − $28,000	$ 6,000			
54,176 − 34,000			$ 20,176	
71,386 − 54,176				$ 17,210

Step 4: *Inventory change at current year prices*

$6,000 × 1.12	$ 6,720			
20,176 × 1.25			$ 25,220	
17,210 × 1.40				$ 24,094

Step 5: *Cost to retail ratio for current period*

1981, $92,748 ÷ $154,580	60%			
1982, 120,000 ÷ 205,000		58.54%		
1983, 145,000 ÷ 230,000			63%	

Step 6: *Inventory, December 31 at LIFO*

January 1, 1980, Layer	$ 20,000	$ 28,000	$ 28,000	$ 20,000	$ 28,000
1981 layer, $6,720 × 60%	4,032	6,720	6,720	4,032	6,720
1982 layer, 25,220 × 58.54%		14,764	25,220	14,764	25,220
1983 layer, 24,094 × 63%				15,179	24,094
Ending inventory	$ 24,032	$ 38,796	$ 59,940	$ 53,975	$ 84,034

Exhibit 10-15
WINN-DIXIE Inventory Disclosure

WINN-DIXIE STORES, INC.
Consolidated Balance Sheets

June 24, 1981 and June 25, 1980

Assets	1981	1980
	(Amounts in thousands)	
CURRENT ASSETS:		
Cash and marketable securities	$160,019	165,136
Receivables, less allowance for doubtful items of $563,000 ($512,000 in 1980)	28,966	33,549
Merchandise inventories at lower of cost or market less LIFO reserve of $114,683,000 ($85,686,000 in 1980)	352,862	342,324
Prepaid expenses	17,551	16,380
Total current assets	559,398	557,389

WINN-DIXIE STORES, INC.
Notes to Consolidated Financial Statements

(1) Summary of Significant Accounting Policies.

Inventories: Inventories are stated at the lower of cost or market. The last-in, first-out (LIFO) method is used to determine the cost of inventories consisting primarily of merchandise in stores and distribution warehouses. As of June 24, 1981, manufacturing and produce inventories are valued at the lower of first-in, first-out (FIFO) cost or market.

(2) Inventories.

At June 24, 1981, inventories valued by the LIFO method would have been $114,683,000 higher ($85,686,000 at June 25, 1980) if they were stated at the lower of FIFO cost or market. Under the LIFO method it is assumed that the most recent additions to inventory are sold first. In times of rising costs, this method of inventory valuation tends to present a conservative statement of earnings in that the "last-in" item is frequently more expensive, and therefore generates a lower profit, than like items purchased in earlier periods. Accordingly, the Company's inventories are valued at approximately 75% of current costs for financial and income tax purposes. If the FIFO method of inventory valuation had been used for the year ended June 24, 1981, reported net earnings would have been $15,078,000 or $.58 per share higher ($12,989,000 or $.48 per share higher and $8,505,000 or $.30 per share higher for fiscal 1980 and 1979, respectively).

Exhibit 10-14 combines all three years for the Smythe Company. Note that the computational procedure each year is exactly the same. In each of the three years, a new layer is added to the ending inventory.

Retail businesses have two principal reasons for using the dollar-value retail LIFO method. One, there are potential tax savings with this method. Since current costs are matched against current revenues, reported income (and taxes) will be less in periods of inflation. Second, due to the increase in clerical efficiency associated with this method, there are some clerical cost savings.

Disclosure

Exhibit 10-15 is a reproduction of the current asset and footnote disclosure for Winn-Dixie, a large supermarket chain. Winn-Dixie uses LIFO to value its inventories and indicates in the footnotes that there would be a $114,683,000 difference in income at June 24, 1981, if it had used FIFO. Exhibit 10-16 illustrates the disclosure for Carter Hawley Hale Stores, Inc., and indicates in the summary of significant accounting policies that it used retail LIFO for its department store inventories.

Exhibit 10-16
CARTER HAWLEY HALE STORES, INC.

Balance Sheet		
(In thousands)	February 2, 1980	February 3, 1979
Assets		
Current assets		
Cash	$ 29,656	$ 25,819
Reimbursable property costs under sale and leaseback agreements	13,391	
Merchandise inventories	410,632	378,034
Other current assets	28,752	25,516

Summary of Significant Accounting Policies

Inventories
Merchandise inventories are valued at the lower of cost or market as determined by the retail method applied on the last-in, first-out basis for department store inventories and on the first-in, first-out basis for all other inventories.

Concept Summary

INVENTORIES—COST ESTIMATION METHODS

UNDERLYING ASSUMPTIONS OF THE GROSS PROFIT AND THE RETAIL METHODS OF INVENTORY

The relationship between costs and selling prices remains constant from period to period.

The mix of products in the ending inventory reflects the mix of products purchased.

The composite rate of gross profit is a weighted average of the rate of gross profit from several different product lines.

The cost-to-retail ratio is the goods available for sale at cost divided by the goods available for sale at retail.

BASIC CALCULATIONS IN ESTIMATION OF INVENTORY

Gross Profit Method

Beginning inventory		XX
Add: Purchases		XX
Goods available for sale		XX
Less: Sales	XX	
Less: Gross profit	XX	XX
Estimated ending inventory		XX

Retail Method

	Cost	Retail
Beginning inventory	XX	XX
Add: Purchases	XX	XX
Goods available for sale	XX	XX
Less sales		XX
Estimated ending inventory at retail		XX
Cost/retail ratio		X%
At cost		XX

RETAIL METHOD—CALCULATION OF COST-TO-RETAIL RATIO

Inventory Method	Calculation Includes
Retail FIFO	Purchases + net markups − net markdowns

Retail average	Beginning inventory + purchases
	+ net markups − net markdowns
Retail FIFO—LCM	Purchases + net markups
Retail average—LCM	Beginning inventory + purchases + net markups

Questions

Q–10–1 When would the gross profit method of inventory valuation be used? Cite some examples

Q–10–2 When the gross profit method is used by a company that has several products, what, in reality, is the gross profit rate?

Q–10–3 May the gross profit method be used as a substitute for taking an annual physical inventory?

Q–10–4 What are some advantages of the retail method of inventory valuation?

Q–10–5 What is meant by *markup?*

Q–10–6 The retail valuation method may be used with which inventory methods?

Q–10–7 What is the difference between retail average cost and retail average cost-LCM?

Q–10–8 Will the retail average cost-LCM have a higher, lower, or the same ending inventory value as retail average cost? Explain.

Q–10–9 What is meant by *net markdowns?*

Q–10–10 What steps are involved in the calculation of the dollar-value LIFO retail method?

Q–10–11 Why is the dollar-value LIFO Retail method used?

Q–10–12 What are the assumptions underlying the gross profit method?

Q–10–13 Explain the general procedure used to apply the gross profit method.

Q–10–14 How is the composite rate of gross profit found?

Q–10–15 Which of the following inventory cost flow methods could use dollar-value pools?

    a) Conventional (lower of cost or market) retail.

    b) Weighted average.

    c) FIFO.

    d) LIFO.

(AICPA adapted)

Q–10–16 If the conventional (lower of cost or market) retail inventory method is used, which of the following calculations would include (exclude) net markdowns?

	Cost Ratio (Percentage)	Ending Inventory at Retail
a)	Include	Include
b)	Include	Exclude
c)	Exclude	Include
d)	Exclude	Exclude

(AICPA adapted)

Discussion Questions and Cases

D–10–1 Johnson Foods is a food processing company. Johnson owns several farms in the west and in the southeast sections of the country. On these farms Johnson grows many different kinds of vegetables and some fruit, including corn, peas, asparagus, tomatoes, green beans, pears, apples, and peaches. Although other crops are grown, they usually are sold to outside purchasers.

Johnson processes these main crops for sale itself; some of the vegetables are frozen and the remainder are canned. All the fruit is canned. Johnson's costs of production and its selling prices have been consistent for several years. Johnson follows the practice of estimating and reporting inventories using the retail FIFO method.

Required:
1. What are the underlying assumptions of the retail method of estimating inventories?
2. How is Johnson able to justify the use of this method?

D–10–2 If the conventional (lower of cost or market) retail inventory method is used, the net markdowns are excluded in calculating the percentage cost ratio and included for the ending inventory at retail. Why?

(AICPA adapted)

D–10–3 Pixie Company is a large retailer of fashion merchandise. Pixie has outlets (stores) in several cities across the country, but is located primarily in the Midwest. Pixie sells a complete line of all types of clothing and stocks only very expensive fashion merchandise. Twice a year Pixie has a moderate sale to clean out its stock and to get ready for the next season. Pixie uses the retail method of inventory estimation.

Required:
1. What are the underlying assumptions of the retail method?
2. What are the advantages associated with using the retail method of inventory estimations?

D–10–4 Jackson Company is a discount retailing chain that sells a variety of products through its discount department stores. The volume of merchandise that a typical store handles is very large. Jackson depends on a very high turnover rate to generate its profits because the profit margins are very low. Jackson averages only about a 20% markup on the cost of its merchandise. The company is considering changing from the FIFO method of inventory to the dollar value LIFO retail method. Explain why Jackson would want to make the change.

D–10–5 Alpha Company has been in the manufacturing business for over 50 years. The company makes small electrical components for motors, pumps, switches, and so forth. Alpha has had a long standing relationship with both its customers and suppliers. It has maintained its prices at reasonable levels over the years, and its suppliers have also. Alpha has used the FIFO method of inventory valuation for both year-end and interim reporting. Management has inquired about using the gross profit method.

Required:
The president has asked you to answer the following questions:
1. What are the assumptions and implications of the gross profit method?
2. Evaluate the usefulness of the gross profit method of estimating inventories.

Exercises

E–10–1 Assume the following information is given for Trey Company:

Product	Unit Sales	Selling Price	% Gross Profit
A	10,000	$20.00	0.50

| B | 12,000 | 18.00 | 0.40 |
| C | 20,000 | 15.00 | 0.30 |

Required:
Calculate the composite gross profit rate.

E–10–2 Q Company prepares monthly income statements. A physical inventory is taken only at year-end; hence, month-end inventories must be estimated. All sales are made on account. The rate of mark-up on cost is 50%. The following information relates to the month of June, 1973:

Accounts receivable, June 1, 1973	$10,000
Accounts receivable, June 30, 1973	15,000
Collection of accounts receivable during June, 1973	25,000
Inventory, June 1, 1973	18,000
Purchases of inventory during June	16,000

What is the estimated cost of the June 30, 1973, inventory?

(AICPA adapted)

E–10–3 For the year 1975 the gross profit of Dumas Company was $96,000; the cost of goods manufactured was $340,000; the beginning inventories of goods in process and finished goods were $28,000 and $45,000, respectively; and the ending inventories of goods in process and finished goods were $38,000 and $52,000, respectively. What would have been the sales of Dumas Company for 1975?

(AICPA adapted)

E–10–4 The following data were available from the records of the Bricker Department Store for the year ended December 31, 1980:

	At Cost	At Retail
Merchandise inventory, January 1, 1980	$180,000	$260,000
Purchases	660,000	920,000
Markups		20,000
Markdowns		80,000
Sales		960,000

If you use the retail method, what would be an estimate of the merchandise inventory at December 31, 1980, valued at the lower of average cost or market?

(AICPA adapted)

E–10–5 Hestor Company's records indicate the following information:

Merchandise inventory, January 1, 1980	$ 550,000
Purchases, January 1 through December 31, 1980	2,250,000
Sales, January 1 through December 31, 1980	3,000,000

On December 31, 1980, a physical inventory determined that an ending inventory of $600,000 was in the warehouse. Hestor's gross profit on sales has remained constant at 30%. Hestor suspects some of the inventory may have been taken by some new employees. At December 31, 1980, what is the estimated cost of the missing inventory?

(AICPA adapted)

E–10–6 On November 21, 1978, a fire at Hodge Company's warehouse caused severe damage to its entire inventory of Product Tex. Hodge estimates that all usable damaged goods can be sold for $10,000. The following information was available from Hodge's accounting records for Product Tex:

Inventory at November 1, 1978	$100,000
Purchases from November 1, 1978, to date of fire	140,000
Net sales from November 1, 1978, to date of fire	220,000

Based on recent history, Hodge had a gross margin (profit) on Product Tex of 30% of net sales.

Required:

Prepare a schedule to calculate the estimated loss on the inventory in the fire, using the gross margin (profit) method. Show supporting computations in good form.

(AICPA adapted)

E–10–7 The following information is available for the Silver Company for the three months ended March 31, 1979:

Merchandise inventory, January 1, 1979	$ 900,000
Purchases	3,400,000
Freight-in	200,000
Sales	4,800,000

The gross margin recorded was 25% of sales. What should be the merchandise inventory at March 31, 1979?

(AICPA adapted)

E–10–8 The Good Trader Company values its inventory by using the retail method (FIFO basis, lower of cost or market). The following information is available for the year 1978.

	Cost	*Retail*
Beginning inventory	$ 80,000	$140,000
Purchases	297,000	420,000
Freight-in	4,000	
Shortages	—	8,000
Markups (net)	—	10,000
Markdowns (net)	—	2,000
Sales	—	400,000

At what amount would the Good Trader Company report its ending inventory?

(AICPA adapted)

E–10–9 On May 2, 1975, a fire destroyed the entire merchandise inventory on hand of Sanchez Wholesale Corporation. The following information is available:

Sales, January 1 through May 2, 1975	$360,000
Inventory, January 1, 1975	80,000
Merchandise purchases, January 1 through May 2, 1975 (including $40,000 of goods in transit on May 2, 1975, shipped f.o.b. shipping point)	330,000
Markup percentage on cost	20%

What is the estimated inventory on May 2, 1975, immediately before the fire?

(AICPA adapted)

E–10–10 The following information is available for the Gant Company for 1976:

Freight-in	$ 20,000
Purchase returns	80,000
Selling expenses	200,000
Ending inventory	90,000

The cost of goods sold is equal to 700% of selling expenses. What is the cost of goods available for sale?

(AICPA adapted)

E–10–11 Goldstein Co., a specialty clothing store, uses the retail inventory method. The following information relates to 1973 operations:

Inventory, January 1, 1973, at cost	$14,200
Inventory, January 1, 1973, at sales price	20,100
Purchases in 1973 at cost	32,600
Purchases in 1973 at sales price	50,000
Additional markups on normal sales price	1,900
Sales (including $4,200 of items that were marked down from $6,400)	60,000

What is the cost of the December 31, 1973, inventory determined by the retail inventory method? The company uses average inventory costing (LCM).

(AICPA adapted)

E–10–12 The Quick Sales Company uses the retail inventory method (average cost) to value its merchandise inventory. The following information is available:

	Cost	Retail
Beginning inventory	$ 40,000	$ 70,000
Purchases	290,000	400,000
Freight-in	2,000	—
Markups (net)	—	3,000
Markdowns (net)	—	5,000
Employee discounts	—	1,000
Sales		390,000

Required:
1. What is the ending inventory at retail?
2. If the ending inventory is to be valued at the lower of cost or market, what is the cost-to-retail ratio?
3. If Quick Sales used the retail FIFO lower of cost or market to value the inventory, what is the cost-to-retail ratio and the value of the ending inventory at cost?

(AICPA adapted)

E–10–13 The Red Department Store uses the retail inventory method. Information relating to the computation of the inventory at December 31, 1978, is as follows:

	Cost	Retail
Inventory at January 1, 1978	$ 32,000	$ 80,000
Sales		600,000
Purchases	270,000	590,000
Freight-in	7,600	
Markups		60,000
Markup cancellations		10,000

Markdowns	25,000
Markdown cancellations	5,000
Estimated normal shrinkage is 2% of sales	

Required:
1. Prepare a schedule to calculate the estimated ending inventory at the lower of average cost or market at December 31, 1978, using the retail inventory method. Show supporting computations in good form.
2. Calculate the estimated ending inventory at December 31, 1978, using the retail FIFO, lower of cost or market method.

(AICPA adapted)

E–10–14 The Barometer Company manufactures one product. On December 31, 1972, Barometer adopted the dollar-value LIFO inventory method. The inventory on that date using the dollar-value LIFO inventory method was $200,000.

Inventory data are as follows:

Year	Inventory at Respective Year-End Prices	Price Index (Base Year 1972)
1973	$231,000	1.05
1974	299,000	1.15
1975	300,000	1.20

Required:
Compute the inventory at December 31, 1973, 1974, and 1975, using the dollar-value LIFO method for each year.

(AICPA adapted)

E–10–15 The Jericho Variety Store uses the LIFO retail inventory method. Information relating to the computation of the inventory at December 31, 1975, is as follows:

	Cost	Retail
Inventory, January 1, 1975	$ 29,000	$ 45,000
Purchases	120,000	172,000
Freight-in	20,000	
Sales		190,000
Net markups		40,000
Net markdowns		12,000

Required:
Assuming that there was no change in the price index during the year, compute the inventory at December 31, 1975, using the LIFO retail inventory method.

(AICPA adapted)

E–10–16 The Computer Company adopted the dollar-value LIFO inventory method on December 31, 1980. The inventory on that date using dollar-value LIFO was $350,000. The applicable price index (the base-year index) used by the company was 126. Inventory data follow:

Year	Inventory at Year-End Prices	Price Index (1980 Base Year)
1980	$350,000	126
1981	379,000	135
1982	412,000	142

Required:

Compute the inventory at December 31, 1981, and 1982, using the dollar-value LIFO method for each year.

Problems

P–10–1   Golden Corporation has the following products:

> Beta, sales of $1,500,000, gross profit rate of 33⅓%
> Alpha, sales of $1,000,000, gross profit rate of 40%
> Rho, sales of $600,000, gross profit rate of 30%
> Tau, sales of $900,000, gross profit rate of 50%

Required:
1. Compute the composite rate of gross profit.
2. If sales of Tau increased by $100,000 with a corresponding $100,000 drop in sales of Rho, would the composite rate change? If so, what would be the new rate?

P–10–2   Roy Company has hired you, its CPA, to determine its composite rate of gross profit. Roy sells products X, Y, and Z. The following information is available:

Product	Unit Sales	Unit Cost	Sales Price
X	100,000	$5.75	$ 7.75
Y	75,000	4.00	6.00
Z	125,000	9.00	13.00

Required:
1. Compute the gross profit rate for each product.
2. Compute the composite rate of gross profit.
3. Assume there are 60,000 on hand at the end of the period. Utilizing the composite rate of gross profit with a pro rata allocation among the products, determine the ending inventory balance.

P–10–3 P-Hat Company has a composite rate of gross profit of 38.75%. Sales are $6,000,000; beginning inventory was $400,000; purchases amounted to $3,650,000; and selling expenses totaled $225,000.

Required:

Compute the value of the ending inventory.

P–10–4 Accountants frequently are asked to calculate the markup on cost and sales price.

a)   Given: Cost $27
          Markup on cost 70%
     Compute the selling price and the gross profit.

b)   Given: Cost $140
          Markup on cost 65%
     Compute the sales price and the gross profit.

c)   Given: Cost $35
          Sales price $63
     Compute the markup on cost and the gross profit.

d)   Given: Cost $100
          Gross profit on
          sales price 30%
     Compute the gross profit percentage of cost.

P-10-5 Foske's Co., a department store, uses the retail—inventory method. The ensuing data pertain to 1981 operations.

Beginning inventory at cost	$56,800
Beginning inventory at sales price	80,400
Purchases in 1981 at sales price	200,000
Purchases in 1981 at cost	130,400
Additional markups	7,600
Ending inventory at retail	89,200
Markdowns	8,800

Required:
1. Compute the 1981 sales.
2. Compute the ending inventory balance using the retail LIFO method.

P-10-6 The following information pertains to B & B Company.

	1980		1981		1982	
	Cost	Retail	Cost	Retail	Cost	Retail
Inventory, Jan. 1	$ 25,000	$ 35,000				
Purchases	120,000	200,000	$130,000	$220,000	$140,000	$240,000
Net markups		10,000		11,000		15,000
Net markdowns		2,000		1,000		2,000
Sales		160,000		170,000		250,000
Current price index		110		120		125

Assume that the January 1, 1980, current price index was equal to 100.
Required:
1. Calculate the cost of the ending inventory for the year 1980 using the dollar-value LIFO retail method. (Round to whole dollars.)
2. Same as Part 1 for 1981.
3. Same as Part 1 for 1982.

P-10-7 Zack Back Pack Shoppe is your client. It operates on a fiscal year ending June 30. On November 22, a fire destroys the entire merchandise. The owner hires you to determine the cost of the merchandise destroyed so that he can file a claim with his insurance company. You manage to obtain the following data:

Inventory on July 1	$ 93,000
Purchases, July 1 through November 22	333,000
Sales, July 1 through November 22	543,000
Markup percentage on cost	40%

Required:
1. Determine the cost of the merchandise destroyed based on the 40% markup percentage on cost.
2. Assume that instead of a 40% markup on cost, Zack had a gross profit rate of 40% of sales. Determine the cost of the merchandise destroyed.

P-10-8 Long Company is a lumber retail store. Data available from its 1981 operations consist of the following:

Beginning inventory at cost	$ 46,500
Beginning inventory at retail	77,500

Purchases and freight	231,000
Purchases at retail	384,000
Net markups	1,000
Sales	439,000
Net markdowns	2,000

Required:
1. Compute the value of the ending inventory at retail.
2. Compute the cost of the ending inventory under the FIFO inventory method.
3. Compute the cost of the ending inventory under the FIFO—LCM method.

P–10–9 Short Company's 1981 data are presented below:

Accounts receivable (Net, Jan. 1, 1981)	$ 12,740
Cash, January 1, 1981	40,300
Accounts payable (for purchases) January 1, 1981	12,000
Inventory January 1, 1981 (Cost)	39,000
Accounts receivable (Net) 12/31/81	15,680
Purchases, 1981	120,000
Cash sales, 1981	150,000
Accounts payable, 12/31/81	15,000
Selling & administrative expense, 1981	40,300
Cash on hand, 12/31/81	101,600
Markup on cost	50%
Inventory, January 1, 1981, at retail	58,500

Further inspection of the data indicates that 2% of the credit sales are uncollectible. Selling and administrative expenses are paid in cash.

Required:
1. Compute the cost of goods sold at retail average cost.
2. Compute the ending inventory at retail.

P–10–10 Durrant Company has been in operation since January 1, 1978. The controller assigns you, the junior accountant, the responsibility of preparing a schedule computing lower-of-cost-or-market inventory under the conventional retail method for December 1981. The data consist of the following:

	Cost	Retail
Inventory, January 1	$ 20,000	$ 36,000
Purchases	225,000	360,000
Freight-in	5,000	
Purchase returns	(2,500)	(4,000)
Additional markups		8,400
Markup cancellations		(400)
Markdowns (net)		2,000
Sales		294,500

Required:
Compute the cost of the ending inventory using the following:
  a) The retail average method.
  b) The retail average lower of cost or market method.
  c) The retail FIFO method.
  d) The retail FIFO—LCM method.

P–10–11   Watspice Company began operations on April 1, 1981. Its operations for the quarter ended June 30 are as follows:

			Cost	Retail
April	4	Purchase 20,000 units	$155,000	$225,000
	27	Purchase 10,000 units	80,000	112,500
May	20	Purchase 7,500 units	60,000	84,375
		Freight	3,000	
June	12	Purchase 5,000 units	44,000	56,250
	23	Purchase 8,000 units	64,000	90,000

Markups for the quarter were applied evenly throughout the quarter and amounted to $18,200. Net markdowns were $4,550. Sales amounted to 40,000 units for a total of $460,800.

Required:
1. Compute the ending inventory at retail.
2. Compute the ending inventory at cost using the following:
   a) Retail FIFO.
   b) Retail average cost.
3. Compute the ending inventory at cost using the following:
   a) Retail FIFO—LCM.
   b) Retail—average cost—LCM.

P–10–12   Jones and Smith Enterprises has been in business for years. The company uses the retail inventory method. The following data pertain to the company's 1981 operations:

Beginning inventory (at cost)	$ 36,000
Beginning inventory (at retail)	60,000
Net purchases (at cost)	118,000
Net purchases (at retail)	180,000
Freight-in	2,000
Net markups	18,000
Net markdowns	6,000
Sales	180,000

Required:
1. Compute the ending inventory at retail.
2. Compute the ending inventory at retail average cost.
3. Compute the ending inventory at retail average cost—lower-of-cost-or-market.

P–10–13   Ball'N Gunn Corporation employs a fiscal year ending June 30. The officers wish to keep full insurance coverage on the company's inventory at cost. The company has had a gross margin on net sales of about 45% over the last few years. Presented below are the data for the year ended June 30, 1982:

Sales	$500,000
Sales returns	30,000
Sales discounts	10,000
Inventory July 1, 1981	40,000
Purchase	300,000
Purchase returns	24,000
Purchase discounts	6,000
Freight-in	32,500
Selling & administrative	70,000

Required:

Assuming that the inventory is at its highest on June 30, indicate the amount of insurance needed to fully cover the inventory at cost.

P–10–14 Falls Company uses the retail average cost method. Falls's data for the year ended June 30, 1982, are presented below:

	Cost	Retail
Beginning inventory	$ 20,000	$ 30,000
Net purchases	250,000	410,000
Additional markup		20,000
Markup cancellation		5,000
Net markdown		5,000
Markdown cancellation		2,500
Sales		369,750

Required:

1. Compute the ending inventory at retail.
2. Compute the ending inventory using retail FIFO.
3. Compute the ending inventory using retail FIFO—LCM.

P–10–15 Springs Company uses the dollar value LIFO retail method. Assume that the computed price index was 120% for the current year. Springs has the following data for operations for the year ended December 31, 1982:

	Cost	Retail
Inventory, January 1, 1982	$ 40,000	$ 54,000
Purchases	125,000	194,000
Net markups		12,000
Markdowns		7,000
Markdown cancellation		1,000
Sales		185,000

Required:

Compute the value of the ending inventory at dollar value LIFO retail.

P–10–16 Assume the same data as in Problem 10–15. Springs discovers in 1983 that the price index for that year was 125%. In 1983 Springs purchases $300,000 of goods at cost with retail value of $525,000; net markups are $19,000; net markdowns are $4,000; sales amount to $480,000.

Required:

1. Compute the value of the ending inventory at dollar value retail LIFO.
2. Same as part 1. but assume sales were $500,000; goods available will not change.

P–10–17 Winmers, Inc. commenced operations on January 1, 1980. For the year 1980, everything the company bought and sold had the same cost and sales price. In 1981 fluctuations in costs and sales prices began developing. The data for Winmers, Inc. for 1981 are presented below.

	Cost	Retail
Beginning inventory	$ 35,000	$ 50,000
Purchases	150,000	250,000
Freight	6,000	
Additional markups		13,000
Markup cancellations		1,000
Markdowns		4,000

Markdown cancellations	2,000
Sales	210,000

Required:

1. Compute the ending inventory under retail FIFO method.
2. Compute the ending inventory under retail LIFO method.
3. Was there any difference in ending inventory under the two methods? If so, how much and why?

P–10–18 Zeta Co. sells four different products: A, B, C, and D. Zeta's auditor wishes to test the reasonableness of the ending inventory value. The company has been able to ascertain the following information from its records:

Product	Unit Sales	Unit Price
A	40,000	$10.00
B	10,000	25.00
C	25,000	18.00
D	5,000	30.00

The auditor has checked the past several years and found the gross profit rates to be as follows:

A—20%
B—40%
C—50%
D—30%

The auditor also has determined the beginning inventory to be $70,000; purchases during the period were $850,000.

Required:

Determine the value of the ending inventory.

P–10–19 Tanley's Men's Store was destroyed on April 10, 1980, when a fire ravaged the shopping mall containing the store. The following information is available from the company's records, which were kept at a different location:

Data for 1980 up to date of fire

Sales	$150,000
Sales returns (back on shelves)	2,500
Purchases	100,000
Purchase returns and allowances	1,500
Freight-in	4,300
Inventory, 1/1/80	30,000

The following information was available from prior years:

	Cost of Goods Sold	Gross Profit
1978	$268,200	$ 89,400
1979	283,100	104,300

Required:

Estimate the value of the inventory destroyed in the fire.

11

Plant Assets—
Acquisition,
Use, and
Disposition

Accounting in the News

Under current accounting practices, assets are reported at their unexpired cost. Many accounting theorists have argued that significant business assets are reported in the financial statements at dollar values that are out-of-date. Land is one area in which this is particularly true. Most companies own land that was purchased a long time ago and currently is reported in the financial statements at the price originally paid for the land. Generally there is a substantial difference between the original cost of the land and its current market value. This situation is illustrated in the following excerpts from a *Forbes* article:

Marvin Davis, not surprisingly, has chosen land development over filmmaking for Twentieth Century-Fox Corp.'s 63-acre studio site in Los Angeles' Century City. It makes sense for oilman Davis, a veteran of Denver real estate development, who bought the film company in June for $722 million. The value of Fox' 63 acres, west of Beverly Hills, is estimated today at some $500 million. High-rise office buildings are more likely than films to enhance that land's value, reckons Davis, who picked up other real estate worth, perhaps, an additional $200 million in the purchase of Fox. . . .

Disney, the last to build a major studio in Los Angeles, bought its 44-acre Burbank site in 1938 for $100,000—about $2,270 per acre. The site would sell today for close to $44 million—a cool $1 million per acre. Yet Disney carries it, along with the enormous landholdings of Disneyland, Disney World and a 691-acre ranch 25 miles outside of Los Angeles, on its books at a mere $16.4 million.*

*William Harris, "Someday They'll Build a Town Here, Kate" *Forbes*, October 26, 1981, p. 135.

> Current accounting practice reports the original cost rather than the market value because of the realization rule. As discussed in Chapter 3, revenue or increases in market value should not be recognized until substantially all of the earning process is complete. The earning process is not considered to be substantially complete until the property actually is sold.

This chapter, and Chapters 12 and 13, focus on long-term assets. A **long-term asset** is one that is expected to benefit the operations of the company for more than one year. These assets may be tangible items, such as property, plant, and equipment, or intangible items, such as patents and copyrights. The focus of this chapter and Chapter 12 is tangible assets, while Chapter 13 discusses accounting for intangibles.

Property, plant, and equipment have four basic characteristics: (1) they are tangible, meaning they have physical substance; (2) they are acquired for use in operations and are not intended for resale; (3) their useful life extends beyond a year, meaning their cost must be allocated over more than one accounting period (land is an exception to this allocation since it is not used up or consumed in operations); and (4) the assets provide measurable future benefits.

Valuation of Property, Plant, and Equipment

Property, plant, and equipment are usually valued on the basis of unexpired **historical cost.** Historical cost is measured at the date of acquisition and includes the cash or cash equivalent price of obtaining the asset *and* getting it ready for its intended use. Theoretically, the cost should include all costs of acquiring the asset and getting it ready for use. In practice, however, some costs may not be included because they are immaterial or the expense of tracing the cost to the asset is more than the expected benefit. For example, the costs involved in the ordering of a machine, such as the cost of the employee's time and the cost of supplies, are not significant enough to justify the record keeping expense of assigning the cost to the machine. Instead, these are expensed as normal operating costs.

After acquisition, items of property, plant, and equipment are valued at cost, reduced by the portion of the cost expensed or written off in prior periods. Some accountants believe that when the current market value of an asset is significantly above its unexpired cost, the asset should be written up to reflect its current value. However, current GAAP, expressed in APB Opinion No. 6, is that property, plant, and equipment should not be written up to reflect appraisal, market, or current values.[1] Recorded cost is the result of an actual transaction, not a hypothetical transaction as is the case with current value. Cost does not recognize increases in value until such increases are realized through a transaction. The accounting profession is currently experimenting with reporting current values as supplemental information in annual reports. These recent developments are discussed in Chapter 26.

APB #6

---

[1] "Status of Accounting Research Bulletins," *Opinions of the Accounting Principles Board No. 6* (New York: AICPA, 1965), par. 17.

Sometimes the market value of an asset may be below its book value. Some accounting theorists contend that when this situation exists the asset should be written down to market value and a loss should be recognized. Under current practice, this would not be done unless the recorded book value could not be realized through future operations. As long as the asset is expected to have future benefits equal to or greater than its current book value, no adjustment is necessary. If expected future benefits are less than book value, an adjustment would be made to record a loss on the asset.

Initial Acquisition Cost

While initial acquisition cost conceptionally should include the cost of acquiring an asset and getting it ready for its intended use, problems arise in practice in determining what amounts should be included in or excluded from the cost of an asset.

Cost of Land

The cost of land should include all expenditures made to acquire the land and get it ready for use. The cost of land consists of (1) the purchase price, including any broker's commission; (2) the cost of conveying and protecting title to the property, such as attorney's fees, recording fees, title insurance, and surveying costs; (3) assumptions of any liens or mortgages on the property—for example, a lien for past due real estate taxes; (4) the cost of getting the land ready for its intended use, such as grading, filling, and draining; and (5) the cost of land improvements that are expected to have an indefinite life, such as landscaping.

The land cost should not include the cost of investigating alternative properties that were not purchased. Neither should the cost of improvements that have limited life, such as private streets and parking lots, be included in the cost of the land. These costs should be recorded in a Land Improvements account and written off over their estimated useful life. However, a special assessment for streets, drains, lights, etc., which are to be maintained in the future by the city, should be charged to the land account because, in this case, they have an indefinite life. The key factor is whether the item has a definite or indefinite life. If indefinite, the cost is charged to the land account; otherwise, it is charged to another asset account and depreciated.

Frequently land is purchased with an existing structure. For example, an oil company that intends to build a service station may buy a corner lot with a house on it. The cost of dismantling the old house (less any salvage value that may be received) is considered a part of the land cost because it is a cost of getting the land ready for its intended use.

Land that is being used currently in the operations of the business, or that is bringing in revenue through rentals, is properly classified as part of Property, Plant, and Equipment. Land that is held for speculation or future use and is not currently benefiting the company should be classified as an investment. Theoretically, the costs of carrying such property (i.e., real estate taxes) should be charged to the cost of the property rather than expensed in the period incurred. This is logical because under the matching concept the costs (taxes) should be matched with their associated revenue (gain on sale). However, if the value of the property is declining, these costs should be written off in the year incurred because they have no expected future benefit.

Cost of Buildings

The cost of a building should include all costs of acquiring or constructing a building and getting it ready for use. This cost should include: (1) the purchase price or cost of construction; (2) costs of remodeling or altering the building for its intended use; and (3) assumptions of mortgages or payments of liens.

Costs incurred for excavation and grading relating to the building, architects' and engineers' fees, building permits, and the net cost of temporary buildings used during construction are considered part of the cost of construction. Although the cost should include unanticipated costs, such as blasting rock formations, it should not include extraordinary construction costs that may be caused by acts of God, i.e., a fire or flood. These costs have no future benefit and should be written off as a loss in the year incurred.

Exhibit 11-1 shows costs incurred by Short Cakes Company in the purchase of land and construction of a building. The proper treatment of each item is indicated in the right-hand column. The entry to record these costs is as follows:

Land	60,900	
Building	91,650	
Loss from construction accident	1,200	
Cash		153,750

Exhibit 11-1
SHORT CAKES COMPANY
Cost of Land and Building

Item	Cost	Proper Treatment
Purchase price of land	$50,000	Land
Legal fees for land purchase	1,500	Land
Payment of prior years' taxes on the land	3,000	Land
Cost of removal of old building	1,000	Land
General grading of lot	800	Land
Cost of building permits	300	Building
Cost of architects' plans	750	Building
Construction costs of building	90,000	Building
Excavation for building foundation	600	Building
Sewage line assessment (one-time cost)	3,000	Land
Cost of shrubs and trees	1,600	Land
Cost of repairing wall of building damaged by a bulldozer	1,200	Loss
Total	$153,750	

For tax purposes it is wise to separate the cost of building equipment, such as elevators, special foundations for machinery, special ventilation equipment, etc., from other costs. These may be subject to an investment tax credit and/or may have a shorter depreciable life than the building.

Cost of Equipment

Equipment consists of machinery, delivery equipment, office equipment, furniture, fixtures, and similar assets. Equipment costs include (1) the cash equivalent purchase price, including any tax; (2) charges for freight and insurance in transit; (3) installation costs; and (4) set-up or adjustment costs.

The cost should be net of any discounts allowed, whether taken or not. The objective is to record the asset at its normal cash selling price. Installation costs include not only the actual costs of installing the machine, but any special foundations or protective equipment needed. If they are material in amount, set-up or adjustment costs should include the cost of labor and materials used to get the machine properly adjusted and ready for operation.

Cost of Self-Constructed Assets

There are special difficulties in determining the acquisition cost of assets that are constructed by the company rather than acquired through purchase. Many companies construct their own assets because they have idle capacity, want to have better control over the quality of the acquired asset, or believe it will cost them less than purchasing the asset.

Raw materials and direct labor used in constructing an asset definitely should be charged to the cost of the asset. In fact, any cost that is directly traceable to the construction, meaning that it is incurred as a direct result of constructing the asset, should be included in the asset cost. This includes not only direct material and labor, but any incremental overhead costs incurred, such as special licenses or permits, engineering design, and so forth.

The major accounting problem concerning self-constructed assets is the treatment of normal overhead costs. There are essentially two schools of thought regarding the treatment of normal overhead costs: (1) charge overhead to the cost of the asset on a proportional basis with that charged to normal production, or (2) do not charge any of the normal overhead to the cost of the self-constructed asset.

Proponents of the first view believe that the overhead costs are a proper charge to the cost of the asset because current facilities are used in the asset's production. If the overhead rate is normally $3 per direct labor hour, all jobs going through the plant should be charged at this rate. To do otherwise would undervalue the self-constructed asset and would require normal production to absorb more than its fair share of overhead costs.

Those who subscribe to the second view believe these overhead costs are incurred whether or not the asset is self-constructed. Property taxes, fire insurance, etc., must be paid whether the asset is self-constructed or purchased. These costs are not incurred as a direct result of self-constructing the asset and, therefore, should not be charged to it. This approach has merit when the plant is operating at less than capacity and when constructing the asset does not interfere with normal production. However, the approach has doubtful merit when a plant is operating at capacity and part of the normal production must be curtailed to construct the asset. In this instance, the first approach is clearly preferable since the overhead could have been charged over more output units had the company produced only its normal product. This would have resulted in a lower cost per unit.

The issue has not been resolved so firms are free to use whichever method they choose. We prefer the first method because it charges plant overhead to all items produced in the plant, not just to those for resale.

On occasion, it may cost a company more to construct an asset than it would have cost to purchase it from another company. This could occur as a result of unexpected production problems or cost overruns for materials, engineering, etc. When the cost of a self-constructed asset is more than the outside purchase price of an identical asset, the self-constructed asset should be recorded at its normal cash selling price, not at the self-constructed cost. The difference between the normal selling price and the construction cost should be written off as a loss in the year incurred.

Interest Costs

Another problem area in accounting for asset acquisitions is the treatment of interest costs incurred before the asset is put into use. Interest costs incurred after acquisition are expensed in the year incurred. Frequently, however, firms must incur interest costs in purchasing an asset before it is put into service. For example, a firm that is having a plant built normally will have to make construction progress payments to the contractor during the time of construction. The firm that borrows money to make these payments incurs significant interest costs because of the large amount of money and the length of time involved in building a large building.

Within the accounting profession there has been controversy concerning whether the interest cost should be expensed as incurred, or whether it should be charged to the cost of the building and depreciated. Charging the interest cost to the cost of the asset would lower expenses and raise net income during the construction period. It would have the opposite effect after the asset is put into use; however, this would normally not be significant on a year-by-year basis since the interest cost is written off over the life of the acquired asset. While capitalization of interest has been an acceptable practice in the utility industry for years, it has not been a common practice in other industries.

In late 1979 the FASB issued Statement No. 34[2] that sets forth the treatment of interest during construction. The Statement indicates that the acquisition cost of an asset should include all costs necessarily incurred to acquire an asset and get it ready for use. If a relatively long period of time is necessary to get the asset ready for use, as in construction, the interest costs incurred during this period are considered to be a part of the acquisition cost: "In concept, interest cost is capitalizable for all assets that require a period of time to get them ready for their intended use."[3] This applies to assets for the enterprise's own use,

FASB 34

[2]"Capitalization of Interest Costs," *Statement of Financial Accounting Standards No. 34* (Stamford, Conn.: FASB, 1979).
[3]Ibid., par. 8.

whether self-constructed or constructed by others, and to assets for resale that "are constructed or otherwise produced as discrete projects (e.g., ships or real estate developments)."[4] These standards do not apply to assets that are in use or are ready for operation. The critical test is whether activity is currently being undertaken to get an asset *ready* for its intended use. Once the asset is in the condition and location necessary for its intended use, the capitalization of interest ceases. (If the effect of capitalization versus expensing is immaterial to the asset value, capitalization of interest is not required.)

Capitalization of interest will begin and will continue as long as the following three conditions exist:

1. Expenditures for the asset have been made.
2. Activities that are necessary to get the asset ready for its intended use are in progress.
3. Interest cost is being incurred.[5]

Expenditures are capitalized expenditures that required the outlay of cash, transfer of noncash assets or the incurrence of an obligation on which interest is recognized, such as notes payable.

Activities necessary to get the asset ready for its intended purpose are interpreted broadly. Such activities include more than physical construction. Administrative and technical activities that take place before construction, such as planning and obtaining building permits, are included in the definition of these activities. The definition also includes activities after construction has begun that are necessary to overcome unforeseen obstacles, such as technical problems, labor disputes, litigation, and material shortages. Interest cost may not be capitalized if substantially all activities related to acquisition of the asset have stopped. However, the standard does indicate that brief interruptions that are imposed externally and delays that are a normal part of the acquisition process should not stop the interest capitalization process.

Capitalization of interest will cease when the asset is substantially ready for its intended use. In cases in which construction is completed in parts and the completed parts can be used independently, such as a condominium, interest capitalization should stop when each unit is ready for its intended use. In those cases in which an asset must be completed in its entirety before it is ready for its intended use, interest capitalization will continue until the entire project is substantially complete. And in instances in which an asset cannot be used before a separate facility is completed, the interest capitalization would continue until the separate facility is ready for its intended use. For example, a petroleum company may build a refinery but may not be able to operate it until a pipeline leading to the refinery is completed. In this situation, interest would continue to be capitalized on the refinery as long as activities necessary to complete the pipeline were under way.

Practical problems arise in determining the amount of interest to be capitalized. When the asset expenditures are being financed by a separate borrowing, the incremental cost of that borrowing or loan should be charged to the asset. Often a new asset acquisition may not have its own identifiable loan, but may be

---

[4] Ibid., par. 9.

[5] Ibid., par. 17.

financed as part of the general borrowings of the company. In this case, it is difficult to determine the amount of interest since the company may have numerous loans at varied interest rates. When this situation exists, a weighted average interest rate should be calculated. This average rate is then applied to the average amount of accumulated expenditures for the asset during the period to determine the interest cost for the period.

For example, assume Foxboro Co. has entered into an agreement with a contractor to build a plant. Construction of the plant started in June, 1978. Foxboro halted construction from February 1, 1980, to June 1, 1980, because of some substantial uncertainties concerning future demand for its products. Construction resumed in June and was completed October 1, 1980. Although the building was ready for occupancy on October first, Foxboro did not begin using the building until November 1, 1980 because they were too busy to move. Foxboro made the following payments to the contractor:

October 1, 1979	$100,000
December 1, 1979	400,000
February 1, 1980	500,000
July 1, 1980	300,000
October 1, 1980	700,000
Total payments	$2,000,000

Foxboro borrowed all of the money from a bank at a 20% annual interest rate. The calculations of the interest to be capitalized and expensed are shown in Exhibit 11-2. Note that interest was not capitalized during the period construction was halted since activities necessary to get the asset ready for its intended use were not then in progress. This delay cannot be considered brief relative to the actual construction time, nor was the delay externally imposed such as with a labor strike. Interest was not capitalized for the month of October, 1980, either. In this instance, interest could not be capitalized because the asset was complete and ready for its intended purpose on October 1, 1980.

Exhibit 11-2
Capitalization of Interest

Payment Date	Amount	Monthly Interest Cost	Interest Capitalized Months	Interest Capitalized Amount	Interest Expensed Months	Interest Expensed Amount
October '79	$100,000	× 0.20 × ¹⁄₁₂ = $ 1,666.67	8	$ 13,333	5	$ 8,333
December '79	400,000	× 0.20 × ¹⁄₁₂ = 6,666.67	6	40,000	5	33,333
February '80	500,000	× 0.20 × ¹⁄₁₂ = 8,333.33	4	33,333	5	41,667
July '80	300,000	× 0.20 × ¹⁄₁₂ = 5,000.00	3	15,000	1	5,000
October '80	700,000	× 0.20 × ¹⁄₁₂ = 11,666.67	0	0	1	11,667
				$101,666		$100,000

Statement No. 34 also sets forth required financial statement disclosures relating to interest costs. Firms must provide footnote disclosure of the total amount of interest cost incurred during the period, and the portion thereof, if any, that has been capitalized.[6]

Method of Asset Acquisition

Assets acquired should be valued at the fair market value of the consideration given or of the asset acquired, whichever is more clearly determinable. **Fair market value** is the normal cash selling price of the asset in an arm's length transaction. The method of acquiring an asset (i.e., cash, deferred payment, exchange, etc.) can make it difficult to determine the fair market value. The effect of these alternative methods of acquisition is discussed in the following sections.

Acquisition for Cash

When assets are acquired with cash, the normal valuation for the acquired asset is the cash given up in the transaction. The only case in which this is not true is when the fair market value of the acquired asset is significantly less than the cash paid. This is an unusual situation and involves a loss on the purchase. For example, a company purchased a used truck for $5,000 believing it was in good repair. After the purchase, the company discovered that the engine was worn out and the truck was worth only $4,000. If there was no recourse against the seller, the truck would have to be written down to $4,000, and a $1,000 loss would be recorded.

Cash discounts may also create a problem. Some accountants believe that assets should be recorded net of any cash discounts, whether the discounts actually are taken or not, because this amount is the actual cash selling price. Others believe the discount should be deducted only if actually taken, since it may not always be in the company's best interest to take the discount. Although both methods currently are acceptable, the first appears to have more theoretical support and we recommended it.

The second approach results essentially in the capitalization of interest (the discount lost by delayed payment). In most cases, these interest costs will not meet the criteria set forth previously for capitalization of interest. Since the asset will be placed into service on or near the date of purchase, the interest is incurred after the asset is placed into service. Another reason for not capitalizing the discount is that it is normally an immaterial amount.

Acquisition under Deferred Payment Plans

Property, plant, and equipment are purchased frequently on a deferred payment plan. The objective in valuing the asset is still to record it at its normal cash selling price. When deferred payment plans are used, the purchase price generally is determined by using the present value of the consideration exchanged in the transaction. The present value usually will equal the sum of the cash down payment plus the present value of the deferred payments.

---

[6] Ibid., par. 21.

APB #1

APB Opinion No. 21[7] outlines the guidelines for recording notes exchanged for noncash assets. Essentially, the Opinion indicates that when a note is exchanged for goods in an arm's length transaction, there is the presumption that the rate of interest stipulated in the note is fair and that the property should be recorded at the stated face amount of the note. However, if there is no stated interest rate, or if the rate is unreasonable, the property should be valued at either the market value of the goods received or at the market value of the note given, whichever is more clearly determinable. For example, suppose on January 1 a company purchases a machine, agreeing to pay $5,000 at the end of each year for the next three years with no interest rate stipulated. Clearly, the machine cannot be valued at $15,000. This amount (three payments of $5,000) includes an implicit interest charge for delaying payment. If the normal cash selling price of the machine is $12,000, both the machine and the note should be recorded at $12,000. The following entry would be made:

Machinery	12,000	
Notes payable—machinery		12,000

The implicit interest rate of the note can be determined by calculating the present value of an annuity (see Chapter 5) using the following formula:

$$P = P_{\overline{n}|i} \times a$$
or
$$\text{Present Value} = \text{PV Factor} \times \text{Annuity}$$

In this case, the present value ($12,000) and the annuity payment ($5,000) are known, and the factor can be determined thus:

$$\$12,000 = P_{\overline{n=3}|i=?} \times \$5,000$$
$$\text{Factor} = \$12,000/\$5,000$$
$$\text{Factor} = 2.40$$

Consult Table 5-4; look across the 3-year row and you'll find the factor 2.40183 under the 12% column. Therefore, the implicit rate of the note is approximately 12%.

The year-end entry to pay the note would be as follows:

Interest expense	1,440*	
Note payable—machinery	3,560	
Cash		5,000
*($12,000 × 0.12)		

[7] "Interest on Receivables and Payables," *Opinions of the Accounting Principles Board No. 21* (New York: AICPA, 1971).

The entry for the second year payment would be:

Interest expense	1,013*	
Note payable—machinery	3,987	
Cash		5,000
*($12,000 − $3,560) 0.12		

The interest expense was calculated by taking the book value of the note times the implicit interest rate.

At times a company may enter into a similar type of transaction in which the market values of both the property received and the note given are unknown. When this occurs the property received should be valued at the discounted present value of the note. Since the note has no interest rate, or has an unreasonable one, a reasonable interest rate must be determined to apply in discounting the note. The rate used should be the rate the company would have to pay if the firm obtained the financing from a different source on the date of the purchase.

For example, assume that a company purchases the same machine discussed above, under the same financing terms, but the machine's market value is unknown. Also, assume that, as a financing alternative, the company could have borrowed the money from their bank at 15% interest. In this situation, the value of the asset received and the note given would be calculated as follows:

$$P = P_{\overline{n=3}|i=15\%} \times a$$
$$P = 2.28323 \times \$5,000$$
$$P = \$11,416$$

Acquisition with Equity Securities

Occasionally firms will acquire assets in exchange for their common or preferred stock. When an asset is received in exchange for equity securities, the account valuations will be based on the market value of either the asset received or the stock distributed, whichever is more clearly determinable.

When the stock exchanged is traded actively on the market, it is the chosen basis for valuation because it is a good indication of the current cash-equivalent price. When the stock is not traded actively, as in the case of a closely held family corporation, the stock value may not be the best valuation. Stock exchange prices that are out-of-date should not be used. Instead, the market value of the asset received should be the basis for valuation. Again, the objective is to determine the current cash-equivalent purchase price of the asset, that is, what one would have to pay if purchased today, for cash, in an arm's length transaction. This does not mean that the transaction should be valued at a "list price" or "suggested retail price." Frequently, these prices do not represent the cash purchase price. For example, how many people pay the "sticker" or "window" price for a new car? In most cases, particularly with American cars, one can buy the car for a price significantly below that on the window sticker. The same holds true for other assets. Therefore, the accountant must be careful to record the asset, and the securities given up, at the cash purchase price, not at the list or retail price.

Acquisition Through Exchanges

Assets such as property, plant, and equipment are referred to as nonmonetary assets. **Nonmonetary** means that their price or value in terms of a monetary unit (dollars) may change over time. This differs from a monetary asset such as cash, notes receivable, and notes payable whose value generally does not change.

Frequently a company will acquire a nonmonetary asset by exchanging another nonmonetary asset for the acquired asset. At times these exchanges may also involve the payment or receipt of a monetary asset (such as cash). The monetary asset is referred to as "boot."

The accounting treatment of transactions involving exchanges of nonmonetary assets is controversial. Within the accounting profession there is disagreement as to whether these transactions should be recorded at market value (which implies recognition of gains and losses) or at book value (which implies no recognition of gains and losses). While the proper theoretical treatment may still be unsettled in the minds of those in the profession, the APB issued Opinion No. 29,[8] which has brought consistent treatment in practice.

Opinion No. 29 indicates that ordinarily a transaction involving an exchange of nonmonetary assets should be valued at the fair market value of the asset surrendered or the asset received, whichever is more clearly determinable. As noted earlier, this implies recognition of any gain or loss on the transaction. This is considered proper treatment when the "earning process" is considered complete. This is always the case when dissimilar assets are exchanged, for example, when a parcel of land is exchanged for a machine.

The earning process is not considered complete when similar assets are exchanged, such as when trading in an old truck for a new one. In this case, the earning process is not considered complete because the company is still using the same type of asset in production. As discussed in earlier chapters, revenue recognition requires that the earning process be substantially complete. Therefore, there is no recognition of gains in exchanges of similar assets. Also remember that losses should be recorded in the year incurred whether or not there has been a disposal of the asset. Thus, although gains are not recognized on exchanges of similar assets, losses are recognized. In some situations there may be a partial gain when the transactions also involve the receipt of a monetary asset (boot) or a dissimilar asset; in this case the partial gain should be recognized.

Exhibit 11-3 summarizes the APB Opinion concerning the basis for valuation of asset exchanges and the recognition of gains and losses. Note that the market value basis (and recognition of gains and losses) is used in all cases except when there are similar assets exchanged and there is a gain involved. In the exchange of similar assets, the valuation is at book value if no boot is involved, or it is a combination of book and market values if boot is received. Accounting for these various circumstances is discussed in more detail in the following three sections.

Exchange of Dissimilar Assets.   When dissimilar assets are exchanged, the earning process is considered to have been completed. Exchanges involving dissimilar assets are valued at the market value of the asset surrendered or the asset received, whichever is more clearly determinable. Any resulting gain or loss is

---

[8]"Accounting for Nonmonetary Transactions," *Opinions of the Accounting Principles Board No. 29* (New York: AICPA, 1973), par. 18.

Exhibit 11-3
Asset Exchanges

Asset Exchanged For:	Valuation Basis	Recognition of Gain	Valuation Basis	Recognition of Loss
1. Dissimilar assets	Market value	Yes	Market value	Yes
2. Similar assets:				
a) Without cash boot	Book value	No	Market value	Yes
b) With cash boot	Combination market & book	Partially	Market value	Yes

recognized. In cases in which the market value of both the asset surrendered and the asset received is determinable, the value of the asset surrendered should be used. When a market value cannot be determined for either asset, the book value of the asset surrendered should be used.

For example, Kerry Cable Co. exchanged an old truck for a new machine. The truck originally cost $15,000 and had accumulated depreciation of $9,000. The truck's current market value at the time was $8,000. Since dissimilar assets are involved, the transaction should be valued at market value, and any gain or loss should be recognized. The entry at the date of exchange is as follows:

Machinery (market value of old truck)	8,000	
Accumulated depreciation—trucks	9,000	
Trucks		15,000
Gain on disposal of trucks		2,000

Note that the new machine is valued at the market value of the truck surrendered, and that the $2,000 difference between the book value of the truck ($15,000 − $9,000 = $6,000) and the market value ($8,000) is recognized as a gain.

When the exchange also involves boot, the new asset is valued at the market value of the asset surrendered plus the boot paid or minus the boot received. For example, if Kerry Cable Co. had given the old truck plus $3,000 cash, the following entry would be made:

Machinery ($8,000 + $3,000)	11,000	
Accumulated depreciation—trucks	9,000	
Trucks		15,000
Cash		3,000
Gain on disposal of trucks		2,000

Similar Assets—Loss Involved. In all cases in which a loss is involved, whether exchanging similar or dissimilar assets, the valuation is at market value and the loss is recorded. The accounting treatment of similar asset exchanges involving a loss would be the same as the treatment for dissimilar assets.

For example, assume the same original facts as above for Kerry Cable Co. (no boot situation) except that the market value of the truck surrendered is $4,000 instead of $8,000. Since the book value of the truck was $6,000 ($15,000 − $9,000), there is a $2,000 loss to record. The entry is as follows:

Machinery	4,000	
Accumulated depreciation—trucks	9,000	
Loss on disposal of trucks	2,000	
Trucks		15,000

Note that the new machine is again valued at the market value of the old machine. If the $3,000 cash boot were also paid, the entry would be:

Machinery ($4,000 + $3,000)	7,000	
Accumulated depreciation—trucks	9,000	
Loss on disposal of trucks	2,000	
Trucks		15,000
Cash		3,000

The new machine is valued at the market value of the old machine plus the boot paid, or minus the boot received, just as in the case of dissimilar assets.

Similar Assets—Gain Involved. Transactions involving exchanges of similar assets when a gain is indicated should be valued at the book value, not at the market value of the asset surrendered. Thus, no gain is recognized. This treatment is justified on the basis that the earning process is not substantially complete when similar assets are exchanged. However, if boot is also received in the transaction, part of the gain is considered to have been earned and, therefore, should be recorded.

When no boot is received in the exchange, accounting for the transaction is fairly simple. The asset acquired is valued at the book value of the asset surrendered plus any boot that may have been *given*.

For example, Chip Chocolate Co. exchanged an old mixing machine plus $4,000 cash for a new mixing machine. The old machine had an original cost of $10,000 and a book value of $3,500. The market value of the machine was $5,000.

The entry for the purchase of the new machine is as follows:

Machine—new ($3,500 + $4,000)	7,500	
Accumulated depreciation—machinery	6,500	
Machine—old		10,000
Cash		4,000

Note that the new machine is valued at the book value of the old machine plus the boot paid. The market value ($5,000) of the old machine is not used. When boot is received in the transaction, the accounting becomes more complicated. In this situation, the gain relating to the similar assets exchanged is not recognized because the earning process is not considered complete. But since the earning process is complete on the cash portion of the transaction, the gain relating to the cash received is recognized. The transaction is considered part sale (gain to be recognized) and part exchange (gain not recognized). The total gain in the transaction must be apportioned between the sale part and the exchange part. The portion of the gain to be recognized is determined using the following formula:

$$\frac{\text{Boot Received}}{\text{Boot Received} + \text{Fair Value of Assets Received}} \times \frac{\text{Total}}{\text{Gain}} = \frac{\text{Gain to be}}{\text{Recognized}}$$

The proportion of boot received to the total value received in the transaction is the portion of the gain that should be recognized. The total gain is the difference between the total value received and the book value of the object given.

To illustrate, Stacey Stove Co. traded a large stamping machine for a smaller one and received $5,000 cash. The old machine had an original cost of $25,000 and a book value of $20,000. The new, smaller machine had a normal cash selling price of $18,000. The gain ($3,000) on the sale is the excess of the total value received of $23,000 ($5,000 + $18,000) over the book value of the large machine ($20,000) exchanged. The entire $3,000 gain cannot be recognized since only the cash portion of the gain is considered to have been earned. The gain to be recognized is $652, and is calculated as follows:

$$\frac{\$5,000}{\$5,000 + \$18,000} \times \$3,000 = \$652$$

The entry to record the exchange is as follows:

Cash	5,000	
Machine—new	15,652	
Accumulated depreciation—old	5,000	
Machine—old		25,000
Gain on disposal of machine		652

The value placed on the new machine is equal to its market value ($20,000) less the portion of the gain that was not recognized, or $2,348 ($3,000 − $652). Decreasing the value of the acquired asset by the unrecognized gain has the effect of decreasing future years' depreciation and, thereby, recognizes the gain over the life of the new asset.

Summary of Asset Exchanges.   The following is a summary of the rules governing accounting for exchanges of nonmonetary assets:

1. When a loss is indicated, recognize the loss and value the acquired asset at market value.
2. When a gain is indicated, recognize the gain according to the proportion of the value of monetary assets (boot) and/or nonmonetary dissimilar assets received to the total value received. Value the acquired asset at its fair value less any portion of the gain not recognized.

Lump Sum Purchases

Businesses occasionally buy a group of dissimilar assets in a single transaction. This is referred to as a group, basket, or **lump sum purchase.** Normally, the purchase price and the market value of the assets acquired differ in a lump sum purchase. An accounting problem arises in trying to determine the cost of individual assets. The total purchase price usually is allocated among the acquired assets on the basis of their relative fair market values. The fair market values of all the assets may not always be readily available. The market value may be estimated by using appraisal values, property tax assessment values, or insurable value.

For example, assume Eagle Co. purchased a machine, a truck, and some inventory from a company that was liquidating all of its assets. The purchase price was $90,000, and the estimated market value of the acquired assets was as follows:

Assets	Market Value
Machine	$50,000
Truck	20,000
Inventory	30,000
Total	$100,000

The costs would be assigned to the individual assets as follows:

Machine $\dfrac{\$50,000}{\$100,000} \times \$90,000 = \$45,000$

Truck $\dfrac{\$20,000}{\$100,000} \times \$90,000 = \$18,000$

Inventory $\dfrac{\$30,000}{\$100,000} \times \$90,000 = \$27,000$

When the value of one of the assets is indeterminable, the assets whose values are known are assigned their market value, and any remaining cost is assigned to the asset without a market value. For example, if the value of the inventory in the above case were unknown and indeterminable, the cost assignment would be:

Machine	$50,000
Truck	20,000
Inventory	20,000 (the amount remaining after assigning other assets their market value)

The basic concept of accounting for lump sum purchases also applies to other areas, such as inventories and lump sum issuances of equity securities and/or debt.

Donated Assets

A transaction that involves the transfer of a donated asset is referred to as a **nonreciprocal transfer.** A business may be involved in such a transfer as either donee or donor. For example, a company may receive the gift of a parcel of land from a city in return for its promise to build a plant and provide jobs for the local community.

When the company is the donee, as above, a problem arises as to what value to place on the property. The cost principle would assign the property a zero cost or some minimal value reflecting costs of title transfers, etc. Such a valuation is unrealistic since the company now owns a valuable asset. APB Opinion No. 29 states that " . . . a nonmonetary asset received in a nonreciprocal transfer should be recorded at the fair value of the asset received."[9] When the fair value is recorded for the asset, an offsetting credit must be made. Three possibilities exist for the credit: (1) record the whole amount as income in the year of the transfer; (2) record the value as an unrealized revenue and recognize it over the life of the asset; or (3) record the value as an increase in owners' equity as Contributed Capital—Donated Property.

Current practice is to treat donations as additional contributed capital. Cash donations received from the government in the form of subsidies, tax credits, or rebates are one exception to this treatment. These are normally reported in the income statement in the year of receipt.

When the company is the donor, the valuation basis is the same as above. The donor should record the donation at its fair market value on the date of the gift.[10] This usually means that a gain or loss on asset disposition will have to be recorded because the book value is more or less than the fair market value. For example, Jones Steel Co. donates 10 acres of land it acquired for $20,000 to the city for a recreational park. The current market value of the land is $40,000. The transfer is recorded as follows:

Donations	40,000	
Land		20,000
Gain on disposal of land		20,000

[9]"Nonmonetary Transactions," par. 18.

[10]Ibid.

Because donations and contributions normally are not considered operating expenses, they are deducted under the "Other Expenses" category in the income statement.

Costs Incurred after Acquisition

Costs incurred after acquisition are costs that are incurred *after* an asset is in place and ready for its intended use. These additional costs may vary from normal daily maintenance to major additions to the asset. Some very difficult problems arise in accounting for these costs. The major problem is trying to determine whether the cost should be written off in the year incurred as an expense or whether it should be capitalized (recorded in an asset account) and written off over some future period. The treatment of certain costs is obvious; for example, daily maintenance costs only benefit the company for a short time (a day) and should be expensed. Other costs obviously may benefit the company for many future years and so should be recorded as an asset. An example would be the cost of doubling the size of a plant. However, many costs fall in a gray area between these. Thus, the accountant must rely heavily on his or her judgment.

Three criteria are used in practice to determine the proper treatment of these costs. Any after-acquisition cost will be capitalized and written off over the current and future years if the cost increases (1) the *useful life* of the asset, (2) the *productivity* of the asset, or (3) the *quality* of units produced with the asset. Any expenditure that makes the asset last longer, produce more units, or produce better units is considered to be a capital expenditure.

Expenditures are classified as either capital expenditures or revenue expenditures. **Capital expenditures** benefit the current and future periods and are recorded as assets in the period incurred and written off over the periods benefited. **Revenue expenditures** are expenditures that are expected to benefit only the current period and, therefore, are expensed against revenue as they are incurred.

Certain costs may meet one of the three criteria but still may be treated as a revenue expenditure because of the dollar amount of the cost involved. Most companies set a minimum cost that must be met before the cost will be capitalized. For example, a company may establish a minimum cost of $500 or $750. All costs incurred below these amounts are expensed even though they may meet one of the criteria. There is a very practical reason for this. Maintaining accounting records can be expensive. Setting up many depreciation schedules for small items may cost more than the expected benefits. Is it practical, or beneficial, for a billion dollar company to worry about depreciating a $100 chair? This would be similar to a small company depreciating a pencil or roll of tape over the period benefited. The dollar effect on assets and income is immaterial; it is also minimized by the fact that these types of small expenditures are made on a continuous basis.

Costs incurred after acquisition generally fall into one of four categories:

1. Maintenance and repairs
2. Improvements and replacements
3. Reinstallations and rearrangements
4. Additions

Maintenance and Repairs

Maintenance is the cost of recurring service on an asset; it includes such services as lubricating, cleaning, and making minor adjustments. Repairs are classified as either ordinary or major. **Ordinary repairs** are a recurring expense, such as repainting or replacing small parts that may have worn out. Maintenance and ordinary repairs generally do not last longer than a year and involve small expenditures. **Major repairs** usually are expected to last several years and are more expensive. They include overhauls and replacements of major parts.

The distinction between maintenance and the different repairs may be seen in the operation of a car. Maintenance would include oil changes, lubrication, and washing. Examples of ordinary repairs would be normal, recurring repairs such as tune-ups, replacement of burned out lights, fan belts, and so forth. A major repair would be a motor overhaul, replacement of a major portion of the front end, or a brake overhaul. The accounting treatment of most major repairs is the same as that for improvements and replacements, which is discussed in the next section. However, if the major repair were the result of an accident (such as an auto wreck) or an act of God (such as a hurricane), the cost of the repair would be charged to a loss account.

Maintenance and ordinary repair costs are revenue expenditures and so are expensed in the period incurred. While maintenance is a continuous expenditure throughout the year, ordinary repairs may be sporadic or planned for certain times of the year. Normally, companies will plan to make ordinary repairs during their slack time of the year. For example, you wouldn't expect United Parcel Service or the U.S. Post Office to schedule their fleets of delivery vehicles for tune-ups in December, their busiest month of the year. They more likely schedule service after a busy time, when deliveries are expected to slacken. Although this makes sense from a business point of view, it does create some accounting problems.

Most companies prepare quarterly or monthly financial statements. Suppose that a company's ordinary repair schedule calls for repairs to be made in the second and fourth quarters. In these quarters repair costs will be incurred which benefit more than just the quarter in which the cost is incurred. If a first quarter report were prepared, it would not include any of the repair costs, and income would be overstated. The opposite would be true in the second quarter. Thus, companies frequently estimate their annual repair costs and charge them off equally to each period, since each period benefits from the cost. The estimated cost is charged to an expense account, and an allowance for repairs account is used as the credit. The allowance account normally would be classified as a current liability in the interim balance sheets.

For example, Hodges Co. estimates that its annual ordinary repair costs will be $120,000. It expects to incur these costs in the second and fourth quarters. The entries for the year are as follows:

End of first quarter:
    Repair expense   30,000*
        Allowance for repairs   30,000
        *($120,000 × ¼)

End of second quarter ($60,000 actual costs incurred):

Allowance for repairs	60,000	
Cash, inventories, expenses payable		60,000
Repair expense	30,000	
Allowance for repairs		30,000

End of third quarter:

Repair expense	30,000	
Allowance for repairs		30,000

End of fourth quarter ($62,000 actual costs incurred):

Allowance for repairs	62,000	
Cash, inventory, expenses payable		62,000
Repair expense	32,000	
Allowance for repairs		32,000

Notice that the allowance for repairs account should have a zero balance at the end of the year and that all costs incurred should be expensed. The fourth quarter is charged with $2,000 more in expense because the fourth quarter costs were more than estimated and it was the only quarter left in which to assign the cost. If, in the second quarter, the company determined that the total costs for the year were to be $122,000 instead of $120,000, the additional $2,000 would have been expensed over the remaining quarters for which statements had not been prepared, in this case, the second, third, and fourth quarters. The cost overrun in the second quarter would cause $41,333 of expense to be charged to each of the last three quarters.

Some accountants believe that major repairs should be handled between years on the same basis that minor repairs are handled between quarters. They would contend, for example, that if a steel mill built a new blast furnace that would have to be relined in three years, at a cost of $150,000, the $150,000 cost should be charged to expense at the rate of $50,000 per year. Although this may sound appealing, it is not theoretically sound. In the first three years the company does not benefit from the future $150,000 expenditure. The company will benefit in the three years following the expenditure. If, at the end of three years, the company decides to shut down the blast furnace, the $150,000 does not have to be incurred and the first three years' output is not affected by the decision. How, then, can the future cost be associated with the revenues of the first three years? The question to ask in this type of situation is "Will the first three years' revenues be affected by a decision either to spend or not spend the money on relining?" If the answer is no, which it is, the cost should not be matched with those revenues. On the other hand, if you ask the question, "After three years will the decision to reline affect the following three years' revenues?" the answer is definitely yes. Clearly, the cost of relining should be matched with revenue earned after relining, not before relining.

Improvements and Replacements

Improvements and replacements normally extend the useful life of an asset or improve the quantity or quality of production and are, therefore, capital expenditures. Both improvements and replacements involve substitution of the parts of assets. A **replacement** substitutes a new part for a similar old part, whereas an **improvement** substitutes a new, superior part for the old part. For example, replacing an old 200-horsepower engine in a truck with a new 200-horsepower engine is a replacement, while replacing the old engine with a new 250-horsepower engine is an improvement. Replacements normally extend the asset's useful life but do not affect the productivity or quality of the product. On the other hand, improvements are expected to improve productivity or product quality.

Replacements and improvements may be capitalized using one of three methods: (1) substitution, (2) cost capitalization, or (3) accumulated depreciation adjustment.

Substitution. With the substitution approach the cost and related accumulated depreciation of the replaced part are removed from the books, and the cost of the new part is added to the asset cost. When this occurs a new depreciation schedule may have to be calculated for the asset, or a separate depreciation schedule may have to be established for the new part. Although the substitution method is considered the most theoretically correct, it is frequently difficult to apply in practice. The method requires that we know the original cost and book value of the part replaced. Often this is not known. For example, a truck that is being depreciated is usually depreciated as one item. The components of the truck normally are not depreciated as separate items. As a result, there is no book value for the components, such as the engine. When this is the case, another method of capitalization should be used.

If the cost and book value of the replaced component are known, the substitution method can be used. For example, Trax Co. replaced the heating and cooling system in their factory with a new system costing $70,000. The old system had cost $30,000 and had a book value of $2,000. Assume the company received $500 credit for the scrap value of the old system. The entry to record this transaction is as follows:

Heating and cooling system	70,000	
Accumulated depreciation—heating and cooling	28,000	
Loss on disposal of assets	1,500	
Cash		69,500
Heating and cooling system		30,000

Cost Capitalization. Under the cost capitalization approach, which is used generally for improvements, the cost of the new part is added to the asset account without removing the book value of the old asset. The entry for the replacement of the heating and cooling system, using the example above, is:

Building (or heating and cooling system)	69,500	
Cash		69,500

The new part can be added to the building account and a new depreciation schedule can be calculated for the building, or the new part can be set up in a separate account with its own depreciation.

Accumulated Depreciation Adjustment. The third alternative deducts the cost of the new part from the amount of accumulated depreciation rather than adding it to the asset account. This approach usually is used for replacements since they increase the asset's useful life but do not affect productivity or product quality. Reducing the accumulated depreciation means that more years' depreciation will have to be taken to depreciate the asset down to salvage value.

Note that both the cost capitalization and the accumulated depreciation adjustment methods result in the same net book value. For example, Jackson Co. owns a building that cost $200,000 and has accumulated depreciation of $110,000. The company replaces the roof at a cost of $30,000.

The results of recording the replacement under the cost capitalization and the accumulated depreciation adjustments are presented below. Note that both methods result in a book value of $120,000.

		After Roof Replacement	
	Before Replacement	*Cost Capitalization*	*Accumulated Depreciation Adjustment*
Cost	$200,000	$230,000	$200,000
Less Accumulated Depreciation	110,000	110,000	80,000
Book Value	$90,000	$120,000	$120,000

Reinstallments and Rearrangements

Reinstallments and **rearrangements** are costs incurred that do not result in the acquisition of a new part or tangible assets, but are expected to benefit future periods. Such costs would include expenditures for changing plant layout and moving machinery. For example, a company may have time and motion studies conducted to determine how the efficiency of its plant layout can be improved. The cost of moving and reinstalling machinery to conform to a new, more efficient plant layout would fall into the reinstallment and rearrangement category. Since the expenditure will make future operations more efficient, the cost should be written off over the future periods expected to be benefited. The cost is normally put into a deferred charge account (asset) and amortized.

Additions

Additions are expansions or enlargements of existing assets, such as putting an addition on a building. The cost of the addition should be charged to an asset account and depreciated; normally the cost is considered to include any costs of preparing the old building for the addition, such as tearing down or reinforcing walls.

If the addition is an integral part of the previous structure, it should be added to the cost of that structure and depreciated over the shorter of (1) the life of the original structure or (2) the addition. If the addition is not an integral part of the original asset, it should be set up in its own asset account and depreciated over its useful life.

Asset Dispositions

Assets may be disposed of by sale, exchange, involuntary conversion, or abandonment. Regardless of the method of disposal, depreciation should be recorded to the date of disposal. After depreciation has been updated, the disposal is recorded by eliminating the original cost of the asset from the asset account and by eliminating the accumulated depreciation on the asset. Any related gain or loss on disposition also should be recorded. According to APB Opinion No. 30,[11] gains and losses of this type are considered normal business items and are not treated as extraordinary gains and losses. The gains and losses result from a difference between book value and disposal value. This difference may be caused by using incorrect estimates in calculating depreciation or by disposing of the asset at a time other than at the end of its original estimated useful life. As is discussed in the next chapter, the purpose of depreciation is cost allocation, not asset valuation. As a result, it is normal to have gains and losses on disposition of assets.

When there is disposal of assets as part of a movement to discontinue a segment of a business's operations, the gain or loss on asset disposition should be included in the gain or loss on disposal of the segment. This segment disposal gain or loss should be shown as a separate item in the income statement, before extraordinary items.[12] This is discussed in Chapter 23.

Sale of Plant Assets

When property, plant, and equipment are sold in exchange for monetary assets, depreciation is recorded to the date of sale, and any gain or loss is recorded. For example, on June 30, 1982, Curry Co. sold for $2,250 cash a machine that was originally purchased on January 2, 1975 for $22,000. The machine had a $2,000 salvage value and an estimated useful life of eight years. The company prepares financial statements annually on December 31. The entries to record the sale are as follows:

To record six month's depreciation to June 30, 1982:
Depreciation expense   1,250*
   Accumulated depreciation—machinery   1,250

$$*\left(\frac{\$22,000 - \$2,000}{8} \times \tfrac{1}{2}\right)$$

To record the sale:
Cash   2,250
Accumulated depreciation   18,750*
Loss on disposal of machinery   1,000
   Machinery   22,000
*(7½ years at $2,500 per year)

[11] "Reporting the Results of Operations," *Opinions of the Accounting Principles Board No. 30* (New York: AICPA, 1973), par. 23.

[12] Ibid., par. 8.

Exchanges

When assets are exchanged for other assets, depreciation is still recorded to the date of disposition. Losses on the exchange are recognized and, as discussed earlier in the chapter, gains are recognized to the extent that monetary assets or dissimilar nonmonetary assets are received.

Involuntary Conversion

Occasionally, a company may have to dispose of an asset when it does not wish to do so. Such a disposal could result from some type of **involuntary conversion,** such as acts of God (fire, flood, etc.) or government condemnation. The accounting treatment of these conversions is the same as that for the sale of assets, except for possible differences in the classification and disclosure of the gains and losses. If the gains or losses resulted from acts of God, the criteria set forth in APB Opinion No. 30[13] must be applied to determine if the gains or losses are extraordinary items.

A government condemnation occurs when a governmental unit takes property for the public good. For example, the state government may take property for road construction, or the federal government may take property for federal parks or wildlife preserves. When this occurs, the governmental agency reimburses the owner in cash for the fair market value of the property taken. Thus, the transaction is similar to a cash sale. As before, any depreciation should be recorded to the date of sale, and any gain or loss on sale should be recorded.

Many in industry believe that a gain or loss should not be recorded since the condemned property must be replaced by other property. The result of replacement is that the company is not in a better financial position after the involuntary conversion. However, the FASB disagrees and requires that gains and losses be recognized.[14] These gains and losses are normally unusual and nonrecurring and are classified as extraordinary items.

Abandonment

Abandonment occurs when an asset is thrown away or sold for scrap value. Again, depreciation should be recorded to the date of disposition. If the asset is thrown away, its book value is written off as a loss. If the asset is sold for scrap, the difference between the book value and the scrap value is recognized as a gain or loss.

Discovery Value and Asset Impairment

Occasionally, an asset owned by a company will experience a drastic increase in value, called **discovery value,** or a drastic decrease in value, sometimes called **asset impairment.**

---

[13] "Results of Operations," par. 20.

[14] "Accounting for Involuntary Conversions of Nonmonetary Assets to Monetary Assets," *FASB Interpretation No. 30* (Stamford, Conn.: FASB, 1979), Summary par.

Discovery Value

An asset may increase substantially in value because of some discovery concerning the asset, such as the discovery of oil or natural gas under the land. Some accountants believe the asset then should be written up to its market value to reflect its current economic status. However, APB Opinion No. 6 states that "property, land and equipment should not be written up by an entry to reflect appraisal, market or current values which are above cost to the entity."[15] The logic behind this Opinion is that the treatment is consistent with the cost principle. To recognize the increase would also violate the revenue realization rule, since the value increase has not been realized through an exchange transaction.

Asset Impairment

Occasionally a company may own an asset whose value becomes materially impaired, such as a machine that becomes obsolete because of unexpected technological advancements. When this occurs, the company may not be able to recover the book value of the asset through use or disposal. Material impairment of an asset should be recorded as a loss in the year in which the impairment occurs. The loss classification should be viewed in light of the criteria for extraordinary items set forth in APB Opinion No. 30.

General Disclosure Requirements

Disclosure requirements relating to plant, property, and equipment come from three main sources: APB Opinion No. 12, "Omnibus Opinion—1967"; APB Opinion No. 22, "Disclosure of Accounting Policies"; and APB Opinion No. 29, "Accounting for Nonmonetary Transactions."

APB Opinion No. 12 sets forth several disclosures relating to plant, property, and equipment. One of these is that there be a disclosure of the balances of major classes of assets, by nature and function.[16] The other disclosures in the Opinion are discussed in the next chapter.

APB Opinion No. 22 requires that "a description of all significant accounting policies of the reporting entity . . . be included as an integral part of the financial statements."[17]

APB Opinion No. 29 indicates that when an enterprise has one or more nonmonetary transactions during the year, the company should disclose "the nature of the transaction, the basis of accounting for the assets transferred, and gains or losses recognized on transfers."[18]

A sample of actual disclosures can be seen in the Milton Bradley Company 1980 Annual Report. In their Consolidated Balance Sheet, under assets, they list

---

[15]"Status of Accounting Research Bulletins," par. 17.

[16]"Omnibus Opinion—1967," *Opinions of the Accounting Principles Board No. 12* (New York: AICPA, 1967), par. 5.

[17]"Disclosure of Accounting Policies," *Opinions of the Accounting Principles Board No. 22* (New York: AICPA, 1972), par. 8.

[18]"Disclosure of Accounting Policies," par. 28.

Exhibit 11-4
MILTON BRADLEY COMPANY

Milton Bradley Company
Notes to Consolidated Financial Statements

1. Summary of Significant Accounting Policies

Property, Depreciation and Amortization—Property, plant and equipment are stated at cost. Plant and plant improvements are depreciated by the straight-line method; machinery and equipment are generally depreciated by accelerated methods. Maintenance and repairs are charged to expense as incurred. Betterments and major renewals are capitalized. Cost of assets sold or retired and the related amounts of accumulated depreciation are eliminated from the accounts in the year of disposal, and the resulting gain or loss is included in earnings. Cost of assets which have become fully depreciated and the related amounts of accumulated depreciation are eliminated from the accounts.

Land improvements and buildings are depreciated over 15 to 50 years, machinery and equipment over 3 to 12 years and leasehold improvements over the shorter of the life of the lease or the improvement.

Exhibit 11-5
MILTON BRADLEY COMPANY

	1980	1979	1978
3. Property, Plant and Equipment			
Land	$ 5,955	$ 3,497	$ 3,190
Land improvements	1,721	1,148	1,034
Buildings and improvements	39,443	29,497	27,639
Machinery and equipment	54,781	40,140	31,043
Leasehold improvements	1,827	1,603	1,788
Construction in progress	1,830	5,407	1,046
	105,557	81,292	65,740
Less accumulated depreciation and amortization	35,678	28,906	24,605
Property, plant and equipment net	$ 69,879	$52,386	$41,135

Capitalized leases amounting to $3.084 million; $1.729 million and $1.837 million in 1980, 1979 and 1978 respectively, are included in land and buildings and improvements.

property, plant, and equipment as one line net of depreciation. Detail on the asset category is presented in the notes to the financial statements. Exhibit 11-4 is taken from Note 1. Summary of Significant Accounting Policies, Note 1, illustrates compliance with the requirements of APB Opinion No. 22. It describes the accounting policies related to the property, plant, and equipment classification. Exhibit 11-5 is taken from Note 3, Property, Plant, and Equipment. It illustrates compliance with APB Opinion No. 12 disclosure requirements and shows the company's assets by major category.

Concept Summary

ACQUISITION AND DISPOSITION OF TANGIBLE ASSETS

ASSET VALUATION

Assets should be valued at their unamortized cost. Cost includes all material expenditures necessary to acquire the asset and to get it ready for its intended use.

ASSET ACQUISITION

Type	Original Valuation of Asset
Cash purchase	Value at amount of cash paid.
Deferred payment	Value at normal cash selling price of asset acquired or at market value of debt, if known. When neither of above is known, value the asset and obligation at the present value of the obligation.
Purchase with equity securities	Value at market value of asset acquired or stock given up, whichever is more clearly determinable.
Lump sum purchase	Assign the total cost to the individual assets in the lump sum purchase on the basis of the relative market values of the assets purchased.
Self-constructed	Value asset at cost of construction, including a charge for overhead.

Acquisitions involving interest payments	Charge interest to the cost of the asset when the following conditions are met: 1. Expenditures for the asset have been made. 2. Activities that are necessary to get the asset ready for its intended use are in progress. 3. Interest cost is being incurred.

ASSET EXCHANGES

Type of Exchange	Gain or Loss Indicated	Accounting Treatment
Similar	Loss	Recognize loss and value new asset at its market value or at market value of old asset plus boot paid or less boot received.
	Gain	Recognize gain only in proportion to the value of boot received to total value received.
Dissimilar	Loss	Recognize loss and value new asset at its market value or at market value of old asset plus boot paid or less boot received.
	Gain	Recognize gain and value new asset at its market value or at market value of old asset plus boot paid or less boot received.

COST AFTER ACQUISITION

Type	Periods Benefited	Accounting Treatment
Capital Expenditure (Major repairs, improvements, replacements, rearrangements, reinstallations, and additions)	Current & future	Capitalize cost and depreciate over current and future years.

| Revenue Expenditure (Maintenance and ordinary repairs) | Current only | Expense cost incurred. |

Questions

Q–11–1 Define the term *long-lived asset* and give some examples.

Q–11–2 What are the four basic characteristics of plant, property, and equipment?

Q–11–3 How should plant, property, and equipment by valued at acquisition? What costs should be included in the original valuation?

Q–11–4 Indicate which of the following items should be included in the cost of plant assets:

    a) The purchase price of a new machine.

    b) Freight on the purchase of a new machine.

    c) The cost of a special concrete base for the machine.

    d) The first year's personal property tax on the machine.

    e) The cost of labor and materials used in adjusting the machine during installation.

    f) The cost of lubrication during the first month of operation.

    g) Fire and theft insurance on the machine.

Q–11–5 Which of the following costs should be included in the cost of land purchased?

    a) Attorneys' fees and recording fees.

    b) Payment of two years' back taxes on property.

    c) Payment of current year's taxes on property.

    d) Cost of landscaping.

    e) Cost of driveways and parking lot.

    f) Cost of road to property. Road will be maintained in the future by the city.

    g) Assumption of a mortgage on the land.

    h) Attorneys' fees for investigating title of alternate property not purchased.

Q–11–6 Which of the following costs should be included in the cost of a building?

    a) Architect's fees.

    b) Landscape architect's fees.

    c) Cost of a storage shed used during construction.

    d) Cost of lumber used to make forms for pouring concrete. The lumber did not become part of the building but was burned after use.

    e) Cost of digging foundation for the building.

    f) Cost of rebuilding some walls damaged by a storm occurring during the construction period.

    g) Unexpected cost of blasting rock in digging out the foundation.

Q–11–7 What is the major accounting problem in determining the cost of a self-constructed asset?

Q–11–8 Fields Co. constructed a new plant. The company was required to make progress payments during construction. The company's accountant told the president that interest incurred during the construction period should be written off as an expense in the year incurred. Do you agree?

Q–11–9 What conditions must exist in order to capitalize interest costs?

Q–11–10 How should the cost of equipment purchased under a deferred payment plan be determined when the note has no interest rate or an unreasonable one?

Q–11–11 Discuss the proper treatment of gains and losses on exchanges of assets not involving boot when (a) similar assets and (b) dissimilar assets are exchanged.

Q–11–12 What effect does the payment of boot have on the recognition of gains on exchanges of similar assets?

Q–11–13 How should the individual asset cost be determined when assets are purchased in a lump-sum purchase?

Q–11–14 Distinguish between a capital and a revenue expenditure.

Q–11–15 Under what circumstances should a cost incurred after acquisition be capitalized?

Q–11–16 Discuss the theoretical justification for quarterly accrual of normal maintenance and repair costs. Should repair costs be accrued between years?

Q–11–17 Distinguish between a repair, a replacement, and an improvement. How should each be accounted for?

Q–11–18 MSM Nursery Co. owned 25 acres of land condemned by the state. The land was to be used for a highway interchange. MSM, which originally paid $25,000 for the property, used it to raise plants and grass. The state paid MSM $100,000 for the property. MSM used the $100,000 to buy 25 acres in another location. The president of MSM told his accountant not to show the gain on the condemnation in the income statement because, in effect, the company was forced to exchange one piece of property for another. Since the properties are similar, no gain should be recognized according to APB *Opinion No. 29.* Do you agree?

Q–11–19 When should asset discovery values and impairments be recorded?

Discussion Questions and Cases

D–11–1 Some ways in which a company may acquire plant assets are for cash, on a deferred payment plan, by exchanging other assets, or by a combination of these ways.
Required: .
1. Identify six costs that should be capitalized as the cost of land. For your answer, assume that land with an existing building is acquired for cash and that the existing building is to be removed in the immediate future in order that a new building can be constructed on that site.
2. At what amount should a company record a plant asset acquired on a deferred payment plan?
3. In general, at what amount should plant assets received in exchange for other non-monetary assets be recorded? Specifically, at what amount should a company record a new machine acquired by exchanging an older, similar machine and paying cash?

(AICPA adapted)

D–11–2 Snavely Co. has designed a new machine to be used in its manufacturing operations. The design was sent to several companies to get estimates on the cost of constructing the machine. Mr. Timm, the company president, is considering constructing the machine in Snavely Co.'s own facilities. Snavely Co. has been operating at about 80% of normal capacity. Mr. Timm has come to you, the company controller, to ask what costs would have to be capitalized to the machine account if it were self-constructed by Snavely.
Required:
1. List the types of costs that would have to be capitalized under the circumstances. Give theoretical justification for your treatment of fixed factory overhead.
2. Would your treatment of fixed overhead differ if the plant currently were operating at full capacity?

D–11–3 Stamford Co. started construction on a new building in January, 1982. The company borrowed funds several times during the year to make progress payments to the builder. Construction was halted twice during the year. Construction stopped for two months because of a labor union strike and for one month because the contractor could not get needed supplies and raw materials.

Stamford Co. currently is preparing its 1982 financial statements. Mr. Stamford, owner of the company, believes that all interest incurred during the year relating to the construction project should be charged to the building and not to expense. He told his accountant, "If it weren't for constructing this building, we wouldn't have incurred any of this interest cost. I want you to charge all of the interest to the building and none of it to expense. I need to send these financial statements to our bank, and I don't want that interest decreasing our net income."

Required:
Assume that you are Stamford Co.'s accountant. What would you tell Mr. Stamford concerning the proper accounting treatment of interest incurred during construction?

D–11–4 Among the principal topics related to the accounting for the property, plant, and equipment of a company are acquisition and retirement.

Required:
1. What expenditures should be capitalized when equipment is acquired for cash?
2. Assume that the market value of equipment acquired is not determinable by reference to a similar purchase for cash. Describe how the acquiring company should determine the capitalizable cost of equipment purchased by exchanging it for each of the following:
    a) Bonds having an established market price.
    b) Common stock not having an established market price.
    c) Similar equipment having a determinable market value.
3. Describe the factors that determine whether expenditures relating to property, plant, and equipment already in use should be capitalized.
4. Describe how to account for the gain or loss on the sale of property, plant, and equipment for cash. (AICPA adapted)

Exercises

E–11–1 McGrath Co. recently began operations and incurred the following costs relative to the purchase of land and the construction of a building:

Cost of land	$ 80,000
Attorney's fees and recording fees	2,000
Cost of clearing trees and brush from land	1,000
Grading of land to eliminate low spots	500
Architect's fees for building	4,000
Building permits	150
Building materials and labor	230,000
Cost of land excavation for foundations	1,500
Cost of driveways and parking lot	25,000
Landscaping costs	10,000
Additional construction costs caused by vandalism	6,000
Tax assessment for streets and drainage*	15,000
Cost of the construction tool shed (net of salvage value)	1,500
Cost of liability insurance during construction	900
Attorney's fees for title searches of alternative properties not purchased	500

*All future costs relating to these items will be paid by the city.

Required:
Determine the cost of each of the following asset accounts: Land, Land Improvements, and Building.

E–11–2 Agudelo Coffee Co. purchased some used machinery during the current year. The following costs were incurred in acquiring the machinery (Agudelo's incremental borrowing rate is 15%):

Cash downpayment	$ 30,000
Total of five annual (year-end) installment	
payments—there is no interest rate stated on the note	100,000
Cost of constructing a special base for the machinery	3,000
Cost of replacing worn parts on machinery before	
being put into operation	10,000
Cost of labor to install machine	2,000
Maintenance costs incurred after operation began	2,500
Cost of freight on machinery purchased	500
Cost of repairing damage to machine caused when	
machine was dropped during installation	3,000

Required:
Determine the cost of the machine.

E–11–3 Sumner's Co. manufactures heavy machinery for the steel fabrication industry. During the current year Sumner's Co. needed to acquire a new machine for its operations. Sumner's engineers designed the machine, and construction of the machine was put out for bids. The lowest bid was $285,000. Sumner's decided not to accept the bid, but rather to build the machine itself. The plant was operating at normal capacity. The following costs were incurred:

Engineering design	$ 4,000	Labor	40,000
Materials	130,000	Variable overhead	20,000

The plant's normal fixed overhead rate is 150% of the direct labor costs.
Required:
1. What dollar amount should be assigned to the machine?
2. If Sumner's Co. were operating at only 60% of normal capacity, would your answer to the previous question change?

E–11–4 Kyle Co. incurred the following costs in self-constructing a machine.

Engineering design	$ 1,500	Freight on materials	2,000
Materials	20,000	Variable overhead	10,000
Direct labor	50,000		

The fixed overhead rate is 50% of the direct labor cost. Kyle Co. received the following outside bids on construction of the machine:
Alber Co., $95,000; Brook Co., $90,000; Bates Co., $92,000.
Required:
Prepare a journal entry to reflect proper treatment of the costs above.

E–11–5 Crittenden Crafts Co. had a building constructed during 1982. The contract price was $200,000 and called for payments to be made according to the following schedule:

> 25% when construction starts
> 25% when construction is 75% complete
> Balance upon completion

Crittenden Crafts Co. had to borrow all of the funds necessary to make the construction payments. The bank charged 18% interest on the funds. Construction began on June 1, 1982. The construction was 75% complete on December 1 and was completed on January 30, 1983. Occupancy of the building was delayed until April 1, 1983, because of circumstances unrelated to the building.
Required:
How should the interest costs incurred in 1982 and up to April 1, 1983, be treated for accounting purposes? Explain your reasoning.

E–11–6 G. O. Neal Co. purchased a unique machine on January 1, 1982, under the following terms:

$25,000 downpayment

$200,000 note payable—$50,000 payable at the end of each year
for four years. The payments include interest at a 4% rate.

G. O. Neal Co.'s incremental borrowing rate for this type of loan is 15%. The market value of the machine is not known.

Required:

Give all of the necessary entries for 1982 and 1983 relating to the transaction above. Assume that the machine has no salvage value and is depreciated under the straight-line method over a 10-year useful life.

E–11–7 Answer the following multiple choice questions.

a) On December 1, 1978, Dartmouth Corporation exchanged 1,000 shares of its $25 par value common stock held in treasury for a parcel of land to be held for a future plant site. The treasury shares were acquired by Dartmouth at a cost of $40, and on the exchange date the common shares of Dartmouth had a fair market value of $55 per share. Dartmouth received $5,000 for selling scrap when an existing building was removed from the site. Based upon these facts, the land should be capitalized at

    (1) $35,000.   **(3)** $50,000.

    (2) $40,000.   **(4)** $55,000.

b) In January, 1977, Action Corporation entered into a contract to acquire a new machine for its factory. The machine, which had a cash price of $150,000, was paid for as follows:

Downpayment	$ 15,000
Notes payable in 10 equal monthly installments	120,000
500 shares of Action common stock with an agreed value of $50 per share	25,000
Total	$160,000

Before using the machine, Action incurred installation costs of $4,000. The machine has an estimated useful life of 10 years and an estimated salvage value of $5,000. What should Action record as the cost of the machine?

    (1) $160,000.   **(3)** $164,000.

    (2) $154,000.   **(4)** $150,000.

c) The Ackley Company exchanged 100 shares of Burke Company common stock, which Ackley was holding as an investment, for a piece of equipment from the Flynn Company. At the date of exchange the Burke Company common stock, which Ackley had purchased for $30 per share, had a quoted market value of $34 per share. The piece of equipment had a recorded amount on Flynn's books of $3,100. What journal entry should Ackley have made to record this exchange?

		Debit	Credit
(1)	Equipment	3,000	
	Investment in Burke Co. com. stk.		3,000
(2)	Equipment	3,100	
	Investment in Burke Co. com. stk.		3,000
	Other income		100
(3)	Equipment	3,100	
	Other expense	300	
	Investment in Burke Co. com. stk.		3,400
(4)	Equipment	3,400	
	Investment in Burke Co. com. stk.		3,000
	Other income		400

d) When the fair value is determinable, a nonreciprocal transfer of a nonmonetary asset to another entity should be recorded at which of the following?

(1) The fair value of the asset received, but no gain or loss should be recognized on the disposition of the asset.

(2) The fair value of the asset transferred, and a gain or loss should be recognized on the disposition of the asset.

(3) The recorded amount of the asset transferred.

(4) The recorded amount of the asset received.

e) On January 1, 1970, Burry Corporation purchased for $76,000 equipment having a useful life of 10 years and an estimated salvage value of $4,000. Burry has recorded monthly depreciation of the equipment on the straight-line method. On December 31, 1978, the equipment was sold for $15,000. How much gain should Burry recognize as a result of this sale?

(1) $0   **(3)** $7,400

(2) $3,800   **(4)** $11,400

f) Company A and Company B exchanged nonmonetary assets with no monetary consideration involved and no impairment of value. The exchange did not culminate an earning process for either Company A or Company B. On what should the accounting for the exchange be based?

(1) The recorded amount of the asset received.

(2) The recorded amount of the asset relinquished.

(3) The fair value of the asset received.

(4) The fair value of the asset relinquished.

g) Brower Corporation owns a manufacturing plant in the country of Oust. On December 31, 1977, the plant had a book value of $5,000,000 and an estimated fair market value of $8,000,000. The government of Oust has indicated clearly that it will expropriate the plant during the coming year and will reimburse Brower for 40% of the plant's estimated fair market value. What journal entry should Brower make on December 31, 1977, to record the intended expropriation?

		Debit	Credit
(1)	Estimated loss on expropriation of		
	foreign plant	1,800,000	
	Allowance for estimated loss on		
	foreign plant		1,800,000
(2)	Estimated loss on expropriation of		
	foreign plant	3,000,000	
	Allowance for estimated loss on		
	foreign plant		3,000,000
(3)	Receivable due from foreign government	3,200,000	
	Investment in foreign plant		3,200,000
(4)	Loss on expropriation of		
	foreign plant	1,800,000	
	Receivable due from foreign government	3,200,000	
	Investment in foreign plant		5,000,000

h) Hardy, Inc. purchased certain plant assets under a deferred payment contract. The agreement was to pay $10,000 per year for five years. The plant assets should be valued at

(1) $50,000.

(2) $50,000 plus imputed interest.

(3) The present value of a $10,000 annuity for five years at an imputed interest rate.

(4) The present value of a $10,000 annuity for five years discounted at the bank prime interest rate.   (AICPA adapted)

E-11-8 On January 1, 1980, Richmond, Inc., signed a fixed-price contract to have Builder Associates construct a major plant facility at a cost of $4,000,000. It was estimated that it would take three years to complete the project. Also on January 1, 1980, to finance the construction cost, Richmond borrowed $4,000,000 payable in 10 annual installments of $400,000 each plus interest at the rate of 11%. During 1980 Richmond made deposit and progress payments totaling $1,500,000 under the contract; the average amount of accumulated expenditures was $650,000 for the year. The excess borrowed funds were invested in short-term securities from which Richmond realized investment income of $250,000.
Required:
How should the interest on the $4,000,000 obligation be reported in Richmond's 1980 financial statements?

(AICPA adapted)

E-11-9 Drance Co. acquired a new machine in exchange for 500 shares of Drance Co. common stock. The machine had a list price of $11,000. The stock had a par value of $10.
Required:
Give the entry to record the acquisition of the machine under each of the following independent cases.
    a) The normal cash selling price for the machine is $9,500.
    b) The common stock is traded actively and currently is selling for $20 per share.
    c) In a cash sale the machine normally is sold at a 10% discount. The company's stock sold for $18 a share five months ago—the last time the stock was traded.
    d) The company selling the machine originally offered to sell it to Drance Co. for $10,500 cash. After several rounds of negotiations they agreed to take the stock. The stock trades weekly and has a current price of $19 per share.

E-11-10 On January 2, 1982, Wilbur Delivery Company traded in an old delivery truck for a newer model. Data relative to the old and new trucks follow:

Old Truck

Original cost	$ 8,000
Accumulated depreciation as of January 2, 1982	6,000
Average published retail value	1,700

New Truck

List price	$10,000
Cash price without trade-in	9,000

Required:
Give the entry to record the purchase of the new truck under each of the following assumptions:
    a) The cash paid on the trade-in was $7,800.
    b) The cash paid on the trade-in was $6,500.

(AICPA adapted)

E-11-11 Good Deal Company received $20,000 in cash and a used computer with a fair value of $180,000 from Harvest Corporation in exchange for Good Deal's existing computer, which had a fair value of $200,000 and an undepreciated cost of $160,000 recorded on its books.
Required:
1. Give the entry to record the exchange.
2. Give the entry to record the exchange, assuming a machine rather than a computer was received in the exchange.

(AICPA adapted)

E–11–12   Paxson Co. owns a machine that originally cost $8,000. The current book value of the machine is $3,000. Its market value is not known. Paxson Co. traded the old machine for a new machine. The new machine has a normal cash selling price of $15,000.
Required:
Give the entry to record the acquisition of the new machine under each of the following assumptions:
  a)   The new machine is dissimilar and
      (1)   Paxson paid cash boot of $13,000.
      (2)   Paxson paid cash boot of $11,000.
  b)   The new machine is similar to the old machine and
      (1)   Paxson paid cash boot of $13,000.
      (2)   Paxson paid cash boot of $11,000.

E–11–13   The Maddox Corporation acquired land, buildings, and equipment from a bankrupt company at a lump-sum price of $90,000. At the time of acquisition, Maddox paid $6,000 to have the assets appraised. The appraisal disclosed the following values:

Land	$60,000
Building	40,000
Equipment	20,000

Required:
Give the entry to record the lump-sum purchase.

(AICPA adapted)

E–11–14   Flynn Co. owns a manufacturing plant. During the current year the elevator in the plant wore out and had to be replaced. The original elevator cost $15,000 and had an estimated useful life of 10 years and no salvage value. The old elevator was replaced at the beginning of the ninth year of service. The replacement elevator cost $22,000.
Required:
1.   Give the entry to record the replacement under each of the following methods:
  a)   The substitution approach.
  b)   The cost capitalization approach.
  c)   The accumulated depreciation adjustment approach.
2.   When should each of the three methods be used?

E–11–15   Dolcetti Co. incurred the following costs in its plant during the past month. All of the costs were charged to the Plant Maintenance Expense account.

Janitorial services	$ 600
Replacement of windows broken by vandals	110
Cost of new roof	3,600
Replaced old boiler with a new, superior, and more efficient boiler	9,500
Cost of interior painting of two rooms	250
Repair of leaking water lines	50
Replacement of old rotten door	30
Repaving parking lot	4,100
Cost of installing a concrete foundation for a new machine	1,200

Required:
Prepare the journal entry necessary to correct the Plant Maintenance Expense account.

E–11–16   Kenworthy Co. owned a small office building located on five acres. The state government condemned the property in eminent domain proceedings. The state was building an interstate highway, and an interchange was planned for the Kenworthy property.

The state paid $135,000 to Kenworthy Co. The company located another five-acre tract of land and purchased it for $80,000.

The original tract of land was purchased for $2,500. The building cost $40,000 to build and had a book value of $18,000 on the settlement date. A real estate appraisor estimated that the old land and building were worth $125,000: land—$75,000, and building—$50,000.

Required:
1. Give the entry to record the sale to the state and the purchase of the new land.
2. How should any gain or loss on the transaction be disclosed in the financial statements?

E–11–17 Two Cities Product Co. grows vegetables and markets them in two major cities. The company owns several farms and other agricultural acreage near each of the two cities. During the current year discoveries were made concerning two plots of land owned by the company. The so-called Tale Plot has been owned by the company for about 10 years and originally cost $60,000. This year it was discovered that there are substantial oil and gas reserves beneath the surface. A well has been drilled and currently is producing significant royalty income for Two Cities. It is estimated that the value of the land and the expected present value of future royalties is approximately $15,000,000.

The other plot of land, referred to as the Love Plot, is located in another state. The company bought the land last year from a chemical company for $700,000. During the current year it was discovered that the land is badly contaminated with hazardous waste materials. Hazardous waste engineers estimate that the land will not be useful, for any purpose, for at least 25 years. A real estate appraisal, made after the contamination was found, values the property at $25,000. Two Cities has no recourse against the seller.

Required:
1. Give any journal entries necessary to record the information above.
2. How should the two items be disclosed in the financial statements?

Problems

P–11–1 At December 31, 1982, certain accounts included in the property, plant, and equipment section of the Townsand Company's balance sheet had the following balances:

Land	$100,000
Buildings	800,000
Leasehold improvements	500,000
Machinery and equipment	700,000

During 1983 the following transactions occurred:

a) Land site number 621 was acquired for $1,000,000. In addition, to acquire the land Townsand paid a $60,000 commission to a real estate agent. Costs of $15,000 were incurred to clear the land. During the course of clearing the land, timber and gravel were recovered and sold for $5,000.

b) A second tract of land (site number 522), with a building, was acquired for $300,000. The closing statement indicated that the land value was $200,000 and the building value was $100,000. Shortly after acquisition, the building was demolished at a cost of $30,000. A new building was constructed for $150,000 plus the following costs:

Excavation fees	$11,000
Architectural design fees	8,000
Building permit fee	1,000
Imputed interest on funds used during construction	6,000

The building was completed and occupied on September 30, 1983.

c) A third tract of land (site number 623) was acquired for $600,000 and was put on the market for resale.

d) Extensive work was done to a building occupied by Townsand under a lease agreement that expires on December 31, 1992. The total cost of the work was $125,000, which consisted of the following:

Work Performed	Cost	Estimated Useful Life
Painting of ceilings	$ 10,000	1 year
Electrical work	35,000	10 years
Construction of extension to current working area	80,000	30 years
	$125,000	

The lessor paid one-half of the costs incurred in connection with the extension to the current working area.

e) During December, 1983, costs of $65,000 were incurred to improve leased office space. The related lease will terminate on December 31, 1985, and is not expected to be renewed.

f) A group of new machines was purchased under a royalty agreement that provides for payment of royalties based on units of production for the machines. The invoice price of the machines was $75,000, freight costs were $2,000, unloading charges were $1,500, and royalty payments for 1983 were $13,000.

Required

1. Prepare a detailed analysis of the changes in each of the following balance sheet accounts for 1983:

> Land
> Buildings
> Leasehold improvements
> Machinery and equipment

Disregard the related accumulated depreciation accounts.

2. List the items in the fact situation which were not used to determine the answer to Part 1 above, and indicate *where, or if*, these items should be included in Townsand's financial statements.

(AICPA adapted)

P–11–2 Andrew Co. was incorporated on January 2, 1982, but did not begin operations until July 1, 1983, because its new factory facilities were not completed until that date. The land and building account at December 31, 1982, was as follows:

1982

January	31	Land and building	$ 98,000
February	28	Cost of removal of old building	1,500
May	1	Partial payment on new construction	35,000
	1	Legal fees paid	2,000
June	1	Second payment on new construction	30,000
	1	Insurance premium	1,800
	1	Special tax assessment	2,500
	30	General expenses	12,000
July	1	Final payment on new construction	35,000

December 31	Interest costs relating to new construction	
	incurred during the year	10,450
31	Asset write-up	12,500
	Total	$240,750
31	Depreciation—1982—1%	2,408
	Account balance	$238,342

The following information relates to the items above.

a) To acquire the land and building the company paid $48,000 cash and 500 shares of its 5% cumulative preferred stock, par value $100 per share. The fair market value of the stock on January 31 was $100 per share.

b) The cost of removal of the old building amounted to $1,500, and the demolition company retained all materials from the building.

c) Legal fees covered the following:

Cost of organization of the company	$ 500
Examination of title covering purchase of land	1,000
Legal work in connection with the construction contract	500
Total	$2,000

d) The insurance premium covered the building for a three-year term beginning on May 1, 1982.

e) General expenses covered the following for the period from January 2, 1982, to June 30, 1982:

President's salary	$ 6,000
Plant superintendent supervision construction of the new building	5,000
Office salaries	1,000
Total	$12,000

f) The special tax assessment covered street improvements that are permanent in nature.

g) Interest costs incurred during the year that relate to the new building were as follows:

May 1 to July 1	$ 1,450
July 1 to December 31	9,000
Total	$10,450

h) Because of a general increase in construction costs after entering into the building contract, the board of directors increased the value of the buildings $12,500, believing that such an increase was justified to reflect the current market value at the time the building was completed. Retained earnings was credited for this amount.

i) The estimated life of the building is 50 years. The write-off for 1982 was 1% of the asset value since the building was in use for only half a year.

Required:

Prepare journal entries necessary to correct the land, building, and accumulated depreciation accounts at December 31, 1982.

(AICPA adapted)

P-11-3 Ellford Corporation received a $400,000 low bid from a reputable manufacturer for the construction of special production equipment needed by Ellford in an expansion program. Because the company's own plant was not operating at capacity, Ellford decided to construct the equipment there and recorded the following production costs related to the construction:

Services of consulting engineer	$ 10,000
Work subcontracted	20,000
Materials	200,000
Plant labor normally assigned to production	65,000
Plant labor normally assigned to maintenance	100,000
Total	$395,000

Management prefers to record the cost of the equipment under the incremental cost method. Approximately 40% of the corporation's production is devoted to government supply contracts, which are all based in some way on cost. The contracts require that any self-constructed equipment be allocated its full share of all costs related to the construction.

The following information is also available:

a) The production labor above was for partial fabrication of the equipment in the plant. Skilled personnel were required and were assigned from other projects. The maintenance labor would have been the idle time of nonproduction plant employees who would have been retained on the payroll whether or not their services were utilized.

b) Payroll taxes and employee fringe benefits are approximately 30% of labor cost and are included in manufacturing overhead cost. Total manufacturing overhead for the year was $5,630,000, including the $100,000 maintenance labor used to construct the equipment.

c) Manufacturing overhead is approximately 50% variable and is applied on the basis of production labor cost. Production labor cost for the year for the corporation's normal products totaled $6,810,000.

d) General and administrative expenses include $22,500 of executive salary cost and $10,500 of postage, telephone, supplies, and miscellaneous expenses identifiable with this equipment construction.

Required:

1. Prepare a schedule computing the amount that should be reported as the full cost of the constructed equipment to meet the requirements of the government contracts. Any supporting computations should be in good form.

2. Prepare a schedule computing the incremental cost of the constructed equipment.

3. What is the greatest amount that should be capitalized as the cost of the equipment? Why?

(AICPA adapted)

P-11-4 Mead Trucking Co. records show the following information in its equipment accounts for 1982:

Equipment

Beginning balance—January 1, 1982		$2,146,000
January	2—Purchased truck 204	65,000
March	15—Purchased truck 205	70,000
April	1—Purchased truck 206	78,000
May	1—Traded truck 146	(54,000)
	1—Purchased truck 207	74,000

July	16—Purchased truck	208	~~71,500~~	74000
September	1—Purchased truck	209	~~30,000~~	46 300 –
October	1—Purchased truck	210	62,000	57,000
	15—Junked truck	90	(36,000)	
Ending balance			$2,506,500	2485519

Accumulated Depreciation—Equipment

Beginning balance	$ 984,000	
May 1—Truck traded	(40,000)	
October 15—Truck junked	(36,000)	
1982 depreciation—20% of year-end asset cost	501,300	497,103
Ending balance	$1,409,300	1405,103

The following information relates to the transactions in the equipment account.

January   2—Truck 204 was purchased for $5,000 cash plus six semiannual payments of $10,000 each. Mead Co. signed a non-interest-bearing note for the amount. Mead's incremental borrowing rate is 12%.

March   15—Truck 205 was purchased for cash.

April   1—Truck 206 was purchased for $4,000 down and a $75,000 note. The note calls for three annual payments of $25,000 each, starting on December 31, 1982. The note includes interest at 4%.

May   1—Purchased truck 207 for $50,000 plus truck 146. The market value of truck 146 on this date was $24,000.

July   16—Truck 208 was purchased for 650 shares of Mead Co. 10% preferred stock. The stock has a par value of $100. The stock is not traded actively. The last sale was in early 1981 at $110 per share. Truck 208 is identical to truck 207.

September 1—Truck 209 was purchased in a lump sum purchase. It was acquired in addition to a small garage and land for $250,000. The market value of the items when purchased were as follows:

Land	$100,000
Building	120,000
Truck	50,000

The company accountant originally recorded the land and building at their market value and assigned the remaining purchase price to the truck.

October   1—Truck 210 was purchased for $42,000 cash plus a computer the company had been using until it purchased a larger computer. The old computer had a book value of $20,000 and originally cost $50,000. The market value of the old computer on the date of trade was $15,000.

October   15—Since truck 90 was old and worn out, it was junked. The company received $300 for it. It was completely depreciated.

Required:

1. Prepare journal entries necessary to correct the equipment account and related accumulated depreciation.

2. What total interest expense should be recorded in 1982 for the two trucks purchased on a deferred payment plan?

3. What amount of gain or loss should the 1982 financial statements reflect as a result of the assets exchanged for new trucks?

P–11–5 Simplicity Co. purchased a new machine from Complex Co. Simplicity exchanged an old machine and cash for a new machine. The old machine originally cost $40,000 and has a book value of $15,000. The new machine has a normal cash selling price of $60,000 and cost Complex Co. $52,000 to manufacture.

Required:

Give the entry to record the transaction on both Simplicity Co. and Complex Co. books under each of the following assumptions:

    a) The machines are similar and Simplicity paid the following:
        (1) $40,000 boot.
        (2) $55,000 boot.

    b) The machines are dissimilar and Simplicity paid the following:
        (1) $40,000 boot.
        (2) $55,000 boot.

P–11–6 On July 1, 1982, West Co. exchanged productive assets with East Co. Information concerning the two company's assets is as follows:

	West Co. Asset	East Co. Asset
Original cost	$80,000	$120,000
Accumulated depreciation to-date of exchange	50,000	60,000
Fair market value of the asset	35,000	75,000

West Co. gave East Co. $40,000 cash boot.

Required:

Prepare the entry to record the sale in both sets of books under the following two assumptions:

    a) The assets are similar.
    b) The assets are dissimilar.

P–11–7 Beams Co. exchanged equipment it owned for new equipment. The old asset cost $90,000 and had accumulated depreciation of $20,000.

Required:

Prepare journal entries to record the exchange under each of the following independent cases assuming that assets are (1) dissimilar and (2) similar.

    a) The market value of the new asset is $80,000, and Beams Co. paid $15,000 cash boot.

    b) The market value of the new asset is $60,000, and Beams Co. received $20,000 cash boot.

    c) The market value of the old asset is $80,000, and no cash boot is paid or received.

P–11–8 Yarboro Co. has never been audited. Its bank has asked the company to submit audited financial statements as part of its application for a large loan. Assume you are part of the audit staff examining Yarboro's records and that you have found the following information concerning the building and building repairs and maintenance accounts.

Building Account

Beginning balance—January 1, 1982	$430,000
Painting exterior	6,000
Addition to building	95,000
New landscaping	10,000
Cost of concrete base for new machine	3,000
Cost of materials for new roof	3,400
Cost of repairing loading dock	1,500
Ending balance	$548,900

Building Repairs and Maintenance

Annual salary of maintenance crews	$ 48,000
Fringe benefits of maintenance crews	9,600
Lubricants	2,400
Miscellaneous maintenance supplies	1,900
Cost of new boiler for building furnace	12,000
Overhaul of building elevator	6,000
Cost of interior painting	2,200
Cost of new air conditioner compressor	23,000
Interest on building mortgages	28,000
Electricity for building	14,000
	$147,100

You also have been able to find the following information:

a) The company maintenance people replaced the roof. The maintenance crew works 50 weeks a year. It took them two-and-a-half weeks to replace the roof.

b) The old loading dock was damaged heavily when one of the company trucks backed into it. The accident was not insured.

c) Fringe benefits for the maintenance crew average 20% of their base salary.

d) The old boiler does not have a book value since it is being depreciated as part of the building.

e) The new air conditioner compressor replaced one which was installed eight years ago. The old compressor originally was set up in an asset account called "air conditioning system" and was depreciated separate from the building. The old compressor cost $12,000 and had a book value of $3,000.

Required:

1. Prepare journal entries necessary to correct the two accounts above.
2. What is the correct balance for each account?

P–11–9 Presented below is a schedule of the 1982 property dispositions for Jackson Corporation

Schedule of Property Dispositions

	Cost	Accumulated Depreciation	Cash Proceeds	Fair Market Value	Nature of Disposition
Land	$22,000	—	$20,000	$20,000	Condemnation
Building	6,800	—	2,100	—	Demolition
Warehouse	60,000	$7,978	58,000	58,000	Destruction by fire
Machine	4,000	1,700	600	3,300	Trade-in
Furniture	8,200	6,560	—	1,900	Contribution
Automobile	6,000	2,250	3,000	3,000	Sale

The following additional information is available:

Land   On February 15 a condemnation award was received as consideration for unimproved land held primarily as an investment, and on March 31 another parcel of unimproved land to be held as an investment was purchased at a cost of $21,500.

Building   On April 2 land and building were purchased at a total cost of $34,000, of which 20% was allocated to the building on the corporate books. The real estate was acquired with the intention of demolishing the building, and this was accomplished during the month of November. Cash proceeds received in November represent the net proceeds from demolition of the building.

Warehouse
On June 30 the warehouse was destroyed by fire. The warehouse was purchased on January 2, 1978, and had depreciation of $7,978. On December 27 part of the insurance proceeds was used to purchase a replacement warehouse at a cost of $53,000.

Machine
On December 26 the machine was exchanged for another machine having a fair market value of $2,700, and cash of $600 was received. (Round to the nearest dollar.) The machines were similar.

Furniture
On August 15 furniture was contributed to a qualified charitable organization. No other contributions were made or pledged during the year.

Automobile
On November 3 the automobile was sold to Fred Bates, a stockholder.

Required:

1. Prepare the journal entry to record the disposition of each of the assets above.
2. Indicate any items that should be reported as extraordinary items on Jackson's income statement.

(AICPA adapted)

P–11–10 You are engaged in the examination of the financial statements of The Smoky Mountain Mfg. Co. and are auditing the machinery and equipment account and the related depreciation accounts for the year ended December 31, 1981. Your permanent file contains the following schedules:

Machinery and Equipment

Year	Balance 12/31/79	1980 Retirements	1980 Additions	Balance 12/31/80
1967–70	$ 8,000	$2,100	—	$ 5,900
1971	400	—	—	400
1972	—	—	—	—
1973	—	—	—	—
1974	3,900	—	—	3,900
1975	—	—	—	—
1976	5,300	—	—	5,300
1977	—	—	—	—
1978	4,200	—	—	4,200
1979	—	—	—	—
1980	—	—	$5,700	5,700
	$21,800	$2,100	$5,700	$25,400

Accumulated Depreciation

Year	Balance 12/31/79	1980 Retirements	1980 Provision	Balance 12/31/80
1967–70	$ 7,840	$2,100	$ 160	$ 5,900
1971	340	—	40	380
1972	—	—	—	—
1973	—	—	—	—
1974	2,145	—	390	2,535
1975	—	—	—	—
1976	1,855	—	530	2,385
1977	—	—	—	—
1978	630	—	420	1,050

1979		—		—	—	—
1980		—		—	285	285
	$12,810		$2,100		$1,825	$12,535

A transcript of the machinery and equipment account for 1981 follows:

Machinery and Equipment

Date			Item	Debit	Credit
1981 Jan.	1		Balance forward	$25,400	
Mar.	1		Burnham grinder	1,200	
May	1		Air compressor	4,500	
June	1		Power lawnmower	600	
	1		Lift truck battery	320	
Aug.	1		Rockwood saw		$ 150
Nov.	1		Electric spot welder	4,500	
	1		Baking oven	2,800	
Dec.	1		Baking oven	236	
				$39,556	$ 150
	31		Balance		39,406
				$39,556	$39,556

Your examination reveals the following information:

a) The company uses a 10 year life for all machinery and equipment for depreciation purposes. Depreciation is computed by the straight-line method. Six months' depreciation is recorded in the year of acquisition or retirement. For 1981 the company recorded depreciation of $2,800 on machinery and equipment.

b) The Burnham grinder was purchased for cash from a firm in financial distress. The chief engineer and a used machinery dealer agreed that the practically new machine was worth $2,100 in the open market.

c) For production reasons the new air compressor was installed in a small building that was erected in 1981 to house the machine and will be used also for general storage. The cost of the building, which has a 25-year life, was $2,000 and is included in the $4,500 voucher for the air compressor.

d) The power lawnmower was delivered to the home of the company president for personal use.

e) On June 1 the battery in a battery-powered lift truck was accidentally damaged beyond repair. The damaged battery was included at a price of $600 in the $4,200 cost of the lift truck purchased on July 1, 1978. The company decided to rent a replacement battery rather than buy a new battery. The $320 expenditure is the annual rental for the battery paid in advance, net of a $40 allowance for the scrap value of the damaged battery that was returned to the battery company.

f) The Rockwood saw sold on August 1 had been purchased on August 1, 1968, for $1,500. The saw was in use until it was sold.

g) On September 1 the company determined that a production casting machine was no longer needed and advertised it for sale for $1,800 after determining from a used machinery dealer that this was its market value. The casting machine had been purchased for $5,000 on September 1, 1976.

h) The company elected to exercise an option under a lease-purchase agreement to buy the electric spot welder. The welder had been installed on February 1, 1981, at a monthly rental of $100.

i) On November 1 a baking oven was purchased for $10,000. A $2,800 down payment was made, and the balance will be paid in monthly installments over a three-year period. The December 1 payment includes interest charges of $36. Legal title to the oven will not pass to the company until the payments are completed.

Required:

Prepare the auditor's adjusting journal entries required at December 31, 1981, for equipment and the related depreciation.

(AICPA adapted)

P–11–11   Adams Co. had the following events occur during 1982:

a) Littlestown gave Adams Co. a 25-acre plot of ground in the hopes that Adams would build a plant on the site. Littlestown originally paid $25,000 for the land. A recent appraisal estimated its value at $90,000.

b) Adams had some of its land condemned for use in a state highway project. The land originally cost $20,000. The state paid Adams $85,000 for the property. Adams used the proceeds plus an additional $20,000 to buy a similar-size piece of land near the condemned property.

c) Adams Co. has a machine that is two years old and originally cost $54,000. Accumulated depreciation on the machine amounted to $20,000. A new product, which makes the machine obsolete, has just come on the market. Adams estimates it could get $800 scrap value for the machine.

d) Oil and gas were discovered under some land that Adams owns. The land originally cost $75,000 and currently is estimated to be worth $1,200,000.

e) Adams Co. owns machinery which it leases out on one-year rental contracts. The machinery originally cost $340,000 and has a book value of $250,000. A new line of machinery has just been introduced which is technologically superior to the machinery owned by Adams. As a result of these developments, Adams estimates that it will have to reduce its rental charges significantly and probably will only receive future rentals with an equivalent present value of $125,000.

Required:

1. Prepare journal entries for each of the items above.
2. How will each of the items above be reported in Adams Co. 1982 financial statements?

12

Plant Assets— Depreciation and Depletion

Accounting in the News

The annual depreciation expense for many companies is substantial. This is particularly true in capital-intensive industries, such as auto manufacturing, utilities, and railroads. As this excerpt illustrates, there have been some recent changes regarding the accounting treatment of track expenditures for railroads.

> Last month the ICC proposed that from now on railroads should be able to depreciate rather than expense most of their track expenditures for reporting purposes.
>
> The goods news is that railroads' reported earnings are going to get a much needed lift. By capitalizing investment in track, firms like Burlington Northern and CSX—which have been spending heavily to upgrade their track—will start looking really good. Even such lines as Santa Fe, Southern Railway, Norfolk & Western and Union Pacific, which have been stoutly keeping up their track, will show a nice increase in earnings.
>
> How much? For the moment that's a closely guarded secret. Computing such figures from the outside is hazardous, but First Boston rail analyst Robert Long guesses it will mean a 10% to 25% increase in reported earnings for each of the top eight rails.*

Railroads currently are using the replacement method (discussed later in this chapter) of accounting for their investment in track. Under this method the cost of replacing worn out track, ties, and so forth is charged directly to expense. The asset's book value reflects the cost of the original installation of the track. The new method will allow railroads to capitalize the cost of replacing the track and to write it off over the period benefited. The new method is theoretically superior and conforms to what is done in other industries. The old method violated the matching concept.

*Gerald Odening, "They've Been Working on the Railroad," *Forbes*, July 20, 1981, p. 83.

While some assets such as antiques, gems, and land have an indefinite life and may increase in value over time, most assets have a limited life and decrease in value over time. Generally, the assets owned by a business either wear out, become technologically obsolete, or just deteriorate over time. These assets lose their value and eventually become worthless, or nearly so. The decline in the value of the asset over its life should be charged to an expense and matched with the revenues the asset generates. Writing off the cost of a long-term asset over its useful life is a process called **depreciation.** If the asset is a natural resource, the process is referred to as **depletion,** and if the asset is intangible, the process is called **amortization.**

Nature of Depreciation

Businesses acquire assets for use in their operations to generate a profit. When they acquire a long-term asset, in essence they are prepaying a cost for the life of the asset. This prepaid cost benefits the current and future years because it is a necessary cost of the operations and the revenue-generating process. The matching concept requires that costs be matched with the revenues they generate. Depreciation is the process of matching the cost of long-term assets with the revenue they generate. The cost of using the asset is the difference between the cost of acquiring it and its estimated value at the time the asset will no longer be used in the operations. This estimated value is referred to as **residual** or **salvage value.**

People who are not familiar with accounting frequently believe the purpose of depreciation is to record the annual decline in the value of the asset. They believe that the asset's book value is intended to reflect its market value. This is not the purpose of depreciation. Rather, its purpose is to *allocate the cost* of an asset to the periods that benefit from its use. Depreciation is *not* a method of annual asset valuation; it is not intended to reflect asset values on the balance sheet. It is a method of systematic and rational allocation of asset costs.

For example, suppose a machine costs $10,000 and has a five-year useful life. At the end of its life, its scrap value is expected to equal the net cost of removal. This information can be depicted as follows:

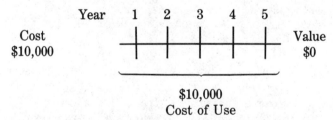

The asset cost $10,000 at the beginning of year one and will be worth zero at the end of year five. The cost of using the asset for five years is $10,000. This $10,000 cost should be assigned to the periods benefited. If the service received from the asset was equal in each of the five years, it is rational to assign $2,000 (⅕) of cost to each year. This is true even if the market value of the asset at the end of the first year were to be $8,500. The intent is to use the asset over its useful life, not to sell it at the end of the first year. Therefore, it is reasonable to assign $2,000 to each of the periods benefited. If the intent were to sell the asset at the end of the first year, a $1,500 depreciation charge would be justified because the useful life would be one year, and the residual value would be the asset's expected value at the end of the year.

Elements of Depreciation

There are four basic elements involved in the depreciation process:

1. The cost of the asset
2. The salvage value of the asset
3. The asset's useful life
4. Selection of a suitable depreciation method

Although accountants are careful that their calculations are correct, depreciation is not an exact measurement. Since there are estimates used in calculating depreciation, the depreciation figure itself is only an estimate. Each of the four elements of depreciation can affect the depreciation estimate significantly.

Cost of the Asset

Determining the cost of an asset was discussed in the previous chapter. Cost should include all of the material costs of acquiring the asset and getting it ready for its intended use. In most cases the cost is not difficult to determine. However, in some instances the determination of cost is not as easy and may involve estimates. Estimates are used often in determining the cost of self-constructed assets. The rules and procedures presented in Chapter 11 should be followed in determining an asset's cost for purposes of depreciation.

Salvage Value

Salvage value, also referred to as residual value, is the expected value of the asset at the end of its estimated useful life. Salvage value may represent the scrap, or resale, value at the time the asset is to be removed from service. In essence, it is an estimate of the net realizable value of the asset on its intended date of disposal. In other words, it is the net cash flow from disposition. For example, Land Spice Co. purchased a machine for $20,000. At the end of its useful life, it is estimated that the machine will be worth $1,000 in scrap value and will cost $300 to remove and transport. The machine, then, has a salvage value equal to the expected net cash receipts of $700.

Depreciation allocates an asset's depreciable cost over its estimated useful life. **Depreciable cost** is the asset's cost less its estimated salvage value. The depreciable cost for the Land Spice Co. machine is $19,300 ($20,000 cost − $700 salvage). This is the amount that should be written off over the asset's useful life.

Useful Life

Useful life is the period of time a company estimates an asset will be useful in an economic sense. Useful life does not refer to the actual physical life of an asset. While an asset may last a long time physically, it may not be desirable or feasible from an economic standpoint to use an asset for its physical life. Many assets currently exist that are not economically feasible to operate in the type of service for which they were originally designed; for example, steam-powered locomotives, old tube-type computers, steam ships, and so forth. These assets still exist and are operable, but they are not efficient in comparison to newer alternatives. Useful life, then, refers to an asset's economic useful life, the period of time in which the asset can be used economically for its intended purpose.

Depreciation may be caused by use or nonuse factors. Use factors are the actual wear and tear from using the machine. Over the time of use, the parts start wearing out until eventually the repairs and maintenance cost more than a new asset would cost. There are several nonuse factors. One is the deterioration and decay caused by the lapse of time or from the process of weathering. A building or car will deteriorate with the passage of time, whether it is used or not. Another nonuse factor is **obsolescence,** which is the decrease in the usefulness of the asset caused by economic factors rather than use factors. A machine may become obsolete because a new, much more efficient machine has been developed, this is referred to as **technological obsolescence.** The transistor-type computer made the tube-type computer obsolete, and the integrated circuit computer has made the transistor computer obsolete. In some areas, such as computers, technological change is rapid and has a significant effect on depreciation. Other areas, such as building construction, experience slow technological change so this type of obsolescence does not significantly affect depreciation.

Obsolescence can also occur as a result of company growth. A company may outgrow its plant and may need to replace it with a larger one. This is sometimes referred to as **inadequacy.** Inadequacy differs from technological obsolescence in that the asset may still be technologically up-to-date, but it can no longer be used by the company because it will not meet the company's needs. For example, a small company may buy a minicomputer to use for its accounting system. If the company expands substantially, it may find that the mini can no longer meet its needs for data processing even though the mini is technologically up-to-date.

One of the most recent causes of obsolescence is the increased emphasis on environmental factors. Many plants in the paper industry have been shut down because it is not economically feasible to operate them within current air and water pollution standards. The plants can still produce paper, but the cost of controlling pollution is more than the expected revenues. As a result, many plants have become obsolete and been closed.

Both use and nonuse factors should be considered in estimating useful lives. Many firms rely on their past experience with similar assets in determining useful lives. Some firms choose arbitrary lives while others use very sophisticated techniques of estimation. The major cause of depreciation for a particular asset should be considered when estimating useful lives.

Selection of Depreciation Methods

Various methods are available to calculate depreciation expense. Some provide an equal amount of depreciation per year or per unit produced while others provide more depreciation in early years and less in later years. The latter types are referred to as accelerated depreciation methods.

The selection of the method should take into account usage and obsolescence factors as well as revenue flows and anticipated repair costs. If an asset is not subject to a high degree of obsolescence and is used an equal amount each year, the use of a method which records an equal amount of depreciation each year would seem rational. This type of depreciation is referred to as **straight line depreciation.** On the other hand, if the asset is subject to rapid technological change, a method that depreciates most of the cost in the earlier years may be preferable.

Some theorists believe that the accountant should look at the total use costs (depreciation cost and repair and maintenance costs) when selecting a depreciation method. They contend that if the asset is used equally each year, an accelerated method may be preferred even if the asset is not subject to rapid technological change. They reason that accelerated depreciation coupled with increasing repair and maintenance costs will give a more uniform or stable total cost over the life of the asset. This is depicted in Exhibit 12-1, in which, for simplicity, the costs are assumed to be linear. The example also assumes that repair and maintenance costs will increase steadily over the life of the asset whereas, in fact, the changes are erratic. The graph depicts the repair costs as increasing while the depreciation expense is decreasing. Note, however, that the total of the two represents a constant cost over the life of the asset. Although this approach has merit, most companies adopt accelerated depreciation either because of obsolescence or because they are using it for tax purposes and choose to keep the books on the same method.

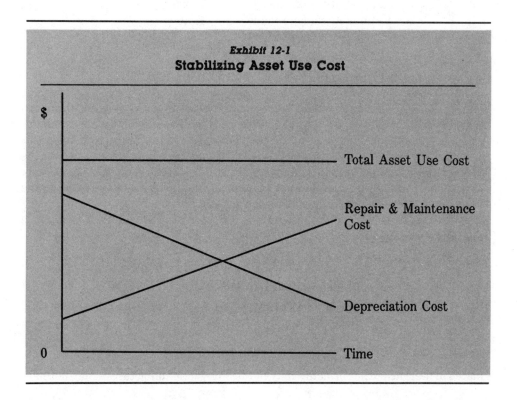

Exhibit 12-1
Stabilizing Asset Use Cost

Methods of Depreciation

Numerous depreciation methods exist. There are no established rules to determine when one method should be selected over another. However, as noted in the previous section, the method chosen should take into consideration the pattern of use and obsolescence factors. The following depreciation methods will be discussed:

1. Units of production method
2. Straight-line method
3. Accelerated methods
    a) Sum-of-the-years'-digits
    b) Fixed-percentage-on-declining-balance
    c) Double-declining-balance
    d) Accelerated cost recovery system
4. Special depreciation methods
    a) Inventory method
    b) Retirement and replacement methods
    c) Group and composite-life methods

The first three methods will be illustrated using the following data relating to a machine:

Purchase date	January 1, 1982
Cost of machine	$165,000
Estimated useful life	5 years
Estimated salvage value	$15,000
Estimated total production	600,000 units

Units of Production Method

The units of production method depreciates the asset on a per-unit-produced basis. The life of the asset is considered in terms of total productive capability expressed in units produced or hours run. This method is appropriate in instances in which the asset's use is expected to vary from year to year and in which the depreciation is caused primarily by use, not by obsolescence or passage of time. In essence, the depreciation is fixed per unit of production but is variable in the total annual depreciation. To illustrate, assume the machine above produced 150,000 units in its first year of operation. The units of production depreciation is calculated as follows:

$$\frac{\text{Cost} - \text{salvage}}{\text{Total lifetime production}} \times \frac{\text{current}}{\text{production}} = \frac{\text{depreciation}}{\text{charge}}$$

$$\frac{\$165,000 - \$15,000}{600,000 \text{ units}} \times \$150,000 = \$37,500$$

Sometimes it is difficult to use the units of production method because estimates of lifetime output or hours may not be known. Manufacturers may not have such information since operating conditions can change output drastically. For example, an automobile used as a family car in the country should give more miles in its life than the same car used as a New York taxi. When lifetime output or hour estimates cannot be determined, some other depreciation method must be selected.

Straight-Line Method

The straight-line method depreciates an asset over time on the basis of years. Depreciation is considered a function of time rather than usage. The method is appropriate when the asset's usage is relatively constant over its life and when rapid technological change is not significantly involved. The calculation of straight-line depreciation is as follows:

$$\frac{\text{Cost} - \text{salvage}}{\text{Useful life}} = \text{depreciation expense}$$

$$\frac{\$165,000 - \$15,000}{5} = \$30,000$$

Under this method $30,000 of depreciation would be recorded in each year of the asset's useful life. Straight-line depreciation is the method most used in financial reporting. The method should not be used when there are significant differences in usage from year to year or when technological obsolescence is substantial.

Accelerated Methods

The accelerated methods charge a higher amount of depreciation in the early years of an asset's useful life. Accelerated methods are used frequently for tax purposes because they provide significant tax deferrals in the early years. More depreciation can be taken under the accelerated method than is possible under straight-line depreciation. This is a tax deferral rather than a tax savings because the difference is eliminated over the life of the asset. The total depreciation and taxes (assuming no change in the tax rates) will be the same under straight-line and accelerated depreciation for the whole life of the asset. The difference is in the timing of the tax payments.

The accelerated methods should be used for financial reporting purposes when the asset is subject to rapid technological change or when significant increases in repair and maintenance costs are expected over the life of the asset. There are four accelerated methods: sum-of-the-years'-digits, fixed-percentage-on-declining-balance, double-declining-balance, and accelerated cost recovery.

Sum-of-the-Years'-Digits. This method (abbreviated SYD) uses a decreasing fraction each succeeding year to multiply by the depreciable cost. The fraction is determined by using the sum of the years as the denominator and the remaining useful life of the asset as the numerator. In the machine example the denominator is (5 + 4 + 3 + 2 + 1). The fraction applied would be 5/15 in year one, 4/15 in year two, etc. Note that the denominator remains constant while the numerator decreases by one each year. Depreciation under the SYD method is shown in Exhibit 12-2. At the end of the five years, the total accumulated depreciation is equal to the asset's depreciable cost, and the asset's book value is equal to the estimated salvage value of the asset.

When a large useful life is involved, a formula can be used to determine the sum-of-the-years'-digits. The formula is:

$$\frac{n(n + 1)}{2}$$

In our example, where n (5) equals the useful life of the asset, the formula is calculated as follows:

$$\frac{5(5 + 1)}{2} = 15$$

Fixed-Percentage-on-Declining-Balance.   The previous methods used depreciable cost (cost less salvage) as the basis for the depreciation calculation. This method and the next are declining-balance methods that use the book value of the asset instead of its depreciable cost. When calculating depreciation, you ignore the salvage value, except in the last year, when the asset is not depreciated below a book value equal to the salvage value.

The fixed-percentage-on-declining-balance method multiplies a constant percentage by the book value to get a decreasing depreciation charge. The following formula is used to determine the rate:

$$\text{Rate} = 1 - \sqrt[n]{\frac{\text{salvage value}}{\text{cost}}}$$

Exhibit 12-2
Sum-of-the-Years'-Digits Depreciation Method

Year	Depreciable Cost[a]	Remaining Life	SYD Fraction	Depreciation Expense[b]	Accumulated Depreciation	Book Value
						$165,000
1	$150,000	5	$5/15$	$ 50,000	$ 50,000	115,000
2	150,000	4	$4/15$	40,000	90,000	75,000
3	150,000	3	$3/15$	30,000	120,000	45,000
4	150,000	2	$2/15$	20,000	140,000	25,000
5	150,000	1	$1/15$	10,000	150,000	15,000
		15	$15/15$	$150,000		

[a] $165,000 − $15,000 salvage
[b] Depreciable cost times SYD fraction

The formula takes into account the cost, estimated life, and residual value of the asset. Applying the formula to the previous machine example results in an annual depreciation rate of 38.1%, computed as follows:

$$0.381 = 1 - \sqrt[5]{\frac{\$15,000}{\$165,000}}$$

Exhibit 12-3 presents an application of this method. Note that the depreciation for the last year is limited to the amount necessary to bring the asset's book value down to its salvage value.

Double-Declining-Balance. The double-declining-balance method (abbreviated DDB) is similar to the fixed-percentage method. It differs only in calculation of the percentage rate to be written off each year. The method is derived from tax laws that allowed some assets to be depreciated at double their straight-line rate. To determine the DDB percentage rate, you first must determine the straight-line rate. Salvage value is ignored in calculating the straight-line rate, which is as follows:

$$\frac{100\% \text{ of cost}}{\text{Useful life}} = \frac{100\%}{5 \text{ years}} = 20\% \text{ per year, straight-line rate}$$

Since 100% of the asset's cost is to be written off over its useful life, the useful life is divided into the 100% to determine the percentage that is written off per year. In the machine example, the rate is 20%. Since the DDB rate is twice the straight-line rate, the DDB rate is 40% (20% × 2).

An application of the DDB method to the machine example appears in Exhibit 12-4. Notice that salvage value is ignored except in the last year, when the depreciation expense is adjusted to make the ending book value equal the salvage value. Notice also that the DDB rate is applied to the book value of the asset, not to its cost or depreciable cost.

Exhibit 12-3
Fixed-Percentage-on-Declining-Balance Method

Year	Depreciation Expense	Accumulated Depreciation	Book Value
			$165,000
1	$165,000 × 0.381	$62,865	102,135
2	102,135 × 0.381	38,913	63,222
3	63,222 × 0.381	24,088	39,134
4	39,134 × 0.381	14,910	24,224
5	24,224 × 0.381	9,224*	15,000

*Rounded to limit book value to salvage

Exhibit 12-4
Double-Declining-Balance Depreciation

Year	Calculation (Book Value × DDB Rate)	Depreciation Expense	Accumulated Depreciation	Book Value
				$165,000
1	$165,000 × 0.4	$66,000	$ 66,000	99,000
2	99,000 × 0.4	39,600	105,600	59,400
3	59,400 × 0.4	23,760	129,360	35,640
4	35,640 × 0.4	14,256	143,616	21,384
5	21,384 × 0.4	6,384*	150,000	15,000

*The depreciation calculation equals $8,553. However, only the amount necessary to bring the book value to salvage value is used in the last year.

The accelerated methods of depreciation are systematic and rational. Their use is most appropriate when the productivity or earning power of an asset is greater in the early years of its life, when repair and maintenance costs are expected to increase significantly over the life of the asset, or when the asset is subject to rapid technological change.

Accelerated Cost Recovery System. The Economic Recovery Tax Act of 1981 established the Accelerated Cost Recovery System (ACRS) as a replacement for the prior laws relating to depreciation for tax purposes. ACRS is a system for recovering capital costs using accelerated methods over predetermined recovery periods. These recovery periods are generally unrelated to, and shorter than, prior law useful lives. ACRS applies to both new and used property and is mandatory for all eligible property.

Under the new system the cost of eligible personal property (movable property) must be recovered over a 15-year, 10-year, 5-year, or 3-year period, depending on the type of property. Most personal property falls into the 5-year class. Cars, light trucks, research and experimentation equipment, and certain other short-lived property are in the 3-year class. The 10-year class includes certain long-lived utility property, railroad tank cars, coal-utilization property, and certain real property. Other long-lived utility property falls into the 15-year class. Eligible real property (immovable items such as a building) is placed in a separate rate 15-year real property class.

Under the ACRS, recovery of costs is determined by using a statutory accelerated method. As an option the taxpayer may choose to recover costs using the straight-line method over the recovery period. The new system provides for recovery of the entire cost of the asset. Salvage value is not considered.

The recovery deduction for each year is determined by applying a statutory percentage to the unadjusted basis of the property. The statutory percentage depends on the property class and the number of years since the property was

Exhibit 12-5
**For Property Placed in Service, 1981–84
(Recovery Percentage)**

| | Class of Property | | | |
	3-Year	5-Year	10-Year	15-Year Public Utility Property
Recovery year:				
1	25	15	8	5
2	38	22	14	10
3	37	21	12	9
4		21	10	8
5		21	10	7
6			10	7
7			9	6
8			9	6
9			9	6
10			9	6
11				6
12				6
13				6
14				6
15				6
Total	100	100	100	100

placed in service. For personal property the law indicates that the full, relevant statutory percentage should be used in the year the asset is placed into service, regardless of the month it was placed into service. However, no recovery deduction is allowed in the year of an asset's disposition. For real property, the statutory rate varies depending on which month the asset was placed into service or taken out of service. In essence, partial year recoveries are taken for real property in the year an asset is placed into or taken out of service.

The statutory percentages for personal property for each class of asset are shown in Exhibit 12-5. For example, if a $10,000 auto were placed into service during 1981 and sold in 1984, the annual cost recovery would be as follows:

1981	$2,500	($10,000 × 25%)
1982	3,800	($10,000 × 38%)
1983	3,700	($10,000 × 37%)
1984	0	

The statutory percentages for real property are shown in Exhibit 12-6. The rows indicate the year of the asset's use. The columns represent the month of the initial

Exhibit 12-6
ACRS Cost Recovery Tables for Real Property
All 15-Year Real Property (Except Low-Income Housing)

If the Recovery Year Is:	The Applicable Percentage Is: (Use the Column for the Month in the First Year the Property is Placed in Service)											
	1	2	3	4	5	6	7	8	9	10	11	12
1	12	11	10	9	8	7	6	5	4	3	2	1
2	10	10	11	11	11	11	11	11	11	11	11	12
3	9	9	9	9	10	10	10	10	10	10	10	10
4	8	8	8	8	8	8	9	9	9	9	9	9
5	7	7	7	7	7	7	8	8	8	8	8	8
6	6	6	6	6	7	7	7	7	7	7	7	7
7	6	6	6	6	6	6	6	6	6	6	6	6
8	6	6	6	6	6	6	5	6	6	6	6	6
9	6	6	6	6	5	6	5	5	5	6	6	6
10	5	6	5	6	5	5	5	5	5	5	6	5
11	5	5	5	5	5	5	5	5	5	5	5	5
12	5	5	5	5	5	5	5	5	5	5	5	5
13	5	5	5	5	5	5	5	5	5	5	5	5
14	5	5	5	5	5	5	5	5	5	5	5	5
15	5	5	5	5	5	5	5	5	5	5	5	5
16	—	—	1	1	2	2	3	3	4	4	4	5

year the asset was placed into service. Thus, if an asset were placed into service in July, the relevant percentages for each year are those listed in the "7" column. The percent written off in year 1 is 6%, year 2 is 11%, year 3 is 10%, and so forth.

Although the ACRS has eliminated the traditional accelerated methods and useful lives for tax purposes, these methods are still used for financial reporting purposes and for tax purposes for assets acquired before 1981. There are other provisions and intricacies in the ACRS method. Further discussion is included more appropriately in income tax texts and courses.

Special Depreciation Methods

The depreciation methods just discussed are used for most assets. However, some assets have unique characteristics and may require the use of a more specialized depreciation method. Three of these methods are as follows:

1. Inventory
2. Retirement and replacement
3. Group and composite life

Inventory. The inventory method (sometimes called the appraisal method) is used when there are numerous small-unit cost items such as hand tools or utensils. The method treats these assets as though they were inventory. When assets are purchased, they are charged to an asset account with an appropriately descriptive caption, such as hand tools. At the end of the year a physical inventory of the tools is taken, and an appraisal value is placed on them. The appraisal value takes into account the quantity and condition of the tools on hand. The value is usually an estimate made by a company employee who is familiar with the cost of the items.

For example, Shanty Construction Co. began the current year with a hand tool inventory of $800. During the year, Shanty purchased more hand tools worth $500 and debited them to the hand tool account. At year-end Shanty took a hand tool physical inventory and valued the inventory at $700. Some of the hand tools, not included in the $700, were broken so Shanty sold them as scrap for $20. The entry to record the hand tool depreciation is as follows:

Cash	$ 20	
Depreciation expense—hand tools	580	
Hand tools		600

The credit is made to the asset account rather than to an accumulated depreciation account. If an accumulated depreciation account were used, the purchases of these items would accumulate in the asset account even though the items might no longer be on hand. A reduction in the quantity of assets or their value should be recorded as a direct decrease in the asset account.

Retirement and Replacement. The retirement and replacement methods have been used by public utilities and railroads in accounting for large numbers of low-cost assets such as poles, telephones, railroad ties, and so forth. These methods minimize the cost of accounting for this type of asset. The **retirement** method charges to depreciation the cost (less salvage value) of the assets retired. The **replacement** method charges to depreciation expense the cost (less salvage value of the old, replaced units) of the units purchased as replacement units. The retirement method uses a FIFO flow assumption whereas the replacement method uses a LIFO flow assumption. When the replacement method is used, the cost of the original units is maintained in the asset account until the asset is reduced or eliminated.

For example, assume that in 1982, Keystone Telephone Co. installed some telephone poles and lines at a cost of $2,000,000. Six years later, $150,000 worth of lines were replaced at a cost of $250,000. The replaced lines had a salvage value of $5,000. The entries to record these events under the retirement and replacement systems are as follows:

Retirement Method			Replacement Method		

To record original installation in 1982:

Transmission			Transmission		
Lines	2,000,000		lines	2,000,000	
Cash		2,000,000	Cash		2,000,000

To record retirement of replaced lines:

Depreciation					
Expense	145,000				
Salvage					
Inventory	5,000		No entry		
Transmission					
Lines		150,000			

To record the purchase of replacement lines:

Transmission			Depreciation		
Lines	250,000		Expense	245,000	
Cash		250,000	Salvage		
			Inventory	5,000	
			Cash		250,000

Under both methods, the salvage value of the replaced (old) units reduced the amount of depreciation expense.

These two methods have been criticized because they violate the matching concept, particularly in the early life of the asset. In our example no depreciation was recorded in the first five years of the asset's life, even though the assets were used in the company's operations. The matching concept requires a cause and effect relationship between revenues and expenditures. The first five years should have been charged with part of the cost of the transmission line. Retirement and replacement methods are useful when companies have been in existence for some time and when replacements occur more or less constantly.

Group and Composite. Depreciation is usually applied to single-asset units except when depreciating a large number of small-unit cost items. In some cases it may be desirable to lump depreciable assets together. Such combinations can decrease the bookkeeping associated with accounting for depreciation. **Group** depreciation involves combining similar assets, such as trucks, into one depreciable unit. **Composite** depreciation combines dissimilar assets, such as machinery and buildings, into one depreciable unit.

The means of determining the depreciation is essentially the same for both methods. A group or composite useful life or depreciation rate must be determined. The life or rate is an average for the unit.

To illustrate, Graham Co. depreciates trucks, assembling machinery, and dies on a composite basis. The relevant data and the depreciation calculation are presented in Exhibit 12-7. The composite depreciation rate is calculated by dividing the straight-line annual depreciation by the total cost of the assets in the composite unit. The composite useful life is determined by dividing the total depreciable cost by the total straight-line depreciation.

One difficulty with group and composite depreciation is that there is no book value for individual assets in the unit. The unit as a whole has a book value. Since the book values of individual assets are not available, gains or losses cannot be recognized on the sale of one of the assets in the unit. When an asset is sold, the original cost of the asset is credited to the unit, and accumulated depreciation is debited for any difference between the sale price and the original cost. For example, assume one of the trucks in Exhibit 12-7, which originally cost $15,000, is sold for $2,000. Here is the entry for the sale:

Cash	2,000	
Accumulated depreciation	13,000	
Equipment		15,000

Notice that no gain or loss is recorded.

The primary disadvantage of the group and composite methods is that they do not recognize gains and losses as they are realized. The methods also tend to cover up mistaken judgments concerning useful lives or salvage values.

Exhibit 12-7
Composite Depreciation Method

Asset	Cost	Salvage Value	Depreciable Cost	Useful Life	Annual Depreciation Straight-Line
Trucks	$ 80,000	$10,000	$ 70,000	5	$14,000
Machinery	150,000	10,000	140,000	8	17,500
Dies	70,000	4,000	66,000	3	22,000
	$300,000	$24,000	$276,000		$53,500

$$\frac{\$53,500}{\$300,000} = 0.1783 - \text{composite rate}$$

$$\frac{\$276,000}{\$53,500} = 5.16 \text{ years} - \text{composite life}$$

Other Aspects of Depreciation

Some special problem areas exist in depreciation accounting. These are (1) depreciation and replacement funds, (2) partial year depreciation, (3) revision in depreciation estimates, and (4) investment tax credits.

Depreciation and Replacement Funds

Many people believe, incorrectly, that depreciation generates funds or is intended to provide funds for asset replacement. The purpose of depreciation, as noted previously, is to allocate the cost of an asset to the periods benefited. Depreciation does not generate or provide funds.

This misconception probably arose from the calculation involved in determining cash or working capital funds generated from operations. These calculations are discussed in detail in Chapter 25. Basically, cash flows from operations are calculated by taking the net income and adding to it those expenses that were deducted previously, but did not require the outlay of cash. For example, assume a company has the following simplified income statement:

Revenues—cash sales		$10,000
Less:		
Expenses paid in cash	$5,000	
Depreciation	2,000	7,000
Net income		$ 3,000

Cash funds generated by operations can be calculated in one of the following ways:

A		B	
Cash revenues	$10,000	Net income	$3,000
Less: cash expenses	5,000	Add back expenses not requiring the use of cash:	
		Depreciation	2,000
Cash generated	$ 5,000		$5,000

Method B is used most in practice. It requires that depreciation be added. This addition of depreciation appears to increase the cash generated from operations. For this reason many financial statement users incorrectly perceive depreciation as source of funds (cash). As can be seen in Method A, depreciation has no effect on cash flows. It is added in Method B only because it was deducted originally to calculate net income. It should not be deducted to get cash flows from operations.

Partial Year Depreciation

Businesses buy and sell assets throughout the year, not just on January 1, as the previous examples in the chapter assumed. When assets are purchased during the year, a partial year depreciation must be calculated. Normally depreciation is

---

Exhibit 12-8
Partial Year Depreciation Accelerated Methods

Asset Life	Sum-of-Years'-Digits	Double-Declining-Balance
Year 1	$\frac{4}{10} \times \$12,000 = \$4,800$	$\$12,000 \times 0.5 = \$6,000$
2	$\frac{3}{10} \times 12,000 = 3,600$	$6,000 \times 0.5 = 3,000$
3	$\frac{2}{10} \times 12,000 = 2,400$	$3,000 \times 0.5 = 1,500$

Assume the asset is purchased on April 1, 1982. The depreciation charge for the first three calendar years is as follows:

1982 Calendar Year
$\$4,800 \times \frac{3}{4} = \$3,600$ $\$6,000 \times \frac{3}{4} = \$4,500$

1983 Calendar Year
$\$4,800 \times \frac{1}{4} = \$1,200$ $\$6,000 \times \frac{1}{4} = \$1,500$
$\$3,600 \times \frac{3}{4} = \underline{2,700}$ $\$3,000 \times \frac{3}{4} = \underline{2,250}$
$\underline{\underline{\$3,900}}$ $\underline{\underline{\$3,750}}$

1984 Calendar Year
$\$3,600 \times \frac{1}{4} = \$900$ $\$3,000 \times \frac{1}{4} = \$750$
$\$2,400 \times \frac{3}{4} = \underline{1,800}$ $\$1,500 \times \frac{3}{4} = \underline{1,125}$
$\underline{\underline{\$2,700}}$ $\underline{\underline{\$1,875}}$

---

calculated in whole months. If an asset is acquired in the first half of the month, or disposed of in the last half, depreciaiton is taken for the whole month. On the other hand, when an asset is purchased in the second half of the month, or disposed of in the first half, no depreciation is recorded.

Very large companies have frequent asset purchases and sales during the year. They may charge a full year's depreciation on assets owned at the beginning of the year and no depreciation on assets purchased during the year. Another alternative is to charge a half-year's depreciation on any assets purchased or disposed of during the year and a whole year's depreciation on assets held for the entire year.

Care must be taken in calculating partial year depreciation when the accelerated methods are used. Exhibit 12-8 shows the proper way to record partial year depreciation when using the sum-of-the-years'-digits and double-declining-balance methods. The example assumes depreciation calculations for a machine costing $12,000, with no salvage value and a four-year useful life. Each year's depreciation in terms of the asset's life, must be spread among the financial reporting periods. For example, the 1983 reporting year includes the last quarter of the first year and the first three quarters of the second year of the asset's useful life. This can be depicted as follows:

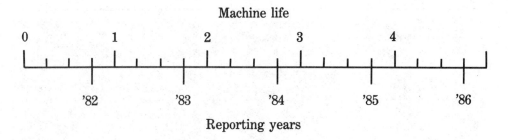

Machine life

Reporting years

Revision of Estimates

As indicated earlier, several estimates are involved in calculating depreciation. Often it is difficult to make reasonable estimates concerning assets that will last many years. Is the useful life of a building thirty or forty years? How can one estimate what it will be worth forty years from now? Some buildings are used for over a hundred years while others are torn down in twenty years.

Companies try to make reasonable estimates, but with time and more available information, it may become clear that an estimate is materially in error. A machine may have been estimated to last eight years, but after three years of use it may become apparent that it won't last more than five. When there is evidence that a previous estimate is materially in error, the estimate should be changed.

APB Opinion No. 20[1] sets forth the proper treatment of changes in accounting estimates. These are discussed in more detail in Chapter 22. Such changes should be accounted for prospectively; that is, the depreciation expense should be recalculated for the remaining life of the asset. There are no retroactive adjustments for changes in estimates. The proper treatment is to depreciate the remaining depreciable cost (cost less salvage value less accumulated depreciation as of the date of change) over the remaining life of the asset. Changes in estimates could modify the remaining depreciable cost through a change in the estimated salvage value or a change in the estimated remaining life.

For example, Jute's Juggery Co. was depreciating a machine that cost $50,000 over an eight-year life. The machine had an estimated salvage value of $7,500 and was being depreciated under the straight-line method. In the third year of the asset's useful life, it was determined that the asset would last only a total of five years and would have a salvage value of $4,000. Assume that depreciation has not been recorded for the third year. To calculate the new annual depreciation, the undepreciated depreciable cost must be determined as follows:

Asset cost	$50,000
Less: prior year's depreciation	
$\dfrac{\$50,000 - \$7,500}{8} \times 2$ years	10,625
Total	$39,375
Less: current estimated salvage	4,000
Remaining depreciable cost	$35,375

---

[1] "Accounting Changes," *Opinion of the Accounting Principles Board No. 20* (New York: AICPA, 1971).

The remaining depreciable cost is written off on a straight-line basis over the remaining life of the asset.

$$\frac{\$35,375}{5 \text{ yrs.} - 2 \text{ yrs.}} = \$11,792 \text{ per year}$$

The annual depreciation is \$11,792 for the remaining three years of the asset's useful life.

Investment Credit

The investment credit was initiated by Congress in 1962 to stimulate the economy. An investment credit allows a company to receive a credit against its income tax due if certain investments are made. The credit is simply a reduction in the taxes due. It represents a subsidy from the federal government to businesses to stimulate their purchase of certain types of assets. In theory, the credit is intended to increase the demand for durable goods and to stimulate economic growth.

To understand how the investment credit works, assume Slidell Co. anticipates it will have an income tax of \$50,000 due for the current year. In December the company buys a qualifying type asset for \$40,000 which is subject to a 10% investment credit. The purchase of the asset will give Slidell Co. a \$4,000 investment tax credit and will reduce its taxes due to \$46,000.

Some reporting problems arise in accounting for the investment credit. There are two schools of thought on how to account for the credit. The first, called the **flow-through** or tax reduction method, accounts for the investment credit as a reduction in income taxes in the year the asset is purchased. This method is consistent with the view that the credit represents a subsidy from the government in the form of reduced taxes due.

The second approach, referred to as the **deferral** or **cost reduction** method, essentially accounts for the credit as a reduction in the cost of the asset or a reduction in income tax expense over the life of the asset. The deferral viewpoint is that the benefits of the credit should be recognized over the life of the asset, not in the year of purchase as under the flow-through method. If the purchased asset is sold or disposed of before a specified, minimum number of years, the tax law requires that the company repay all or part of the tax credit. The amount of repayment depends on the number of years the asset is held. The potential repayment supports the view of proponents of the deferral method in their recognition of the credit over the life of the asset instead of in the year of purchase.

The two approaches are illustrated in the following example. Hay Brewing Co. purchases a new machine for \$150,000. The machine has a 10-year useful life, has no salvage value, and qualified for a 10% investment credit. The company will depreciate the machine using the straight-line method. For simplification, assume the company is in a 50% tax bracket and will have a taxable income of \$50,000 each year during the life of the asset. The entries to record the tax credit under both methods are as follows:

Flow-through Method			Deferral Method		
Machine purchase					
Machinery	150,000		Machinery	150,000	
Cash		150,000	Cash		150,000
Recording tax expense and payment of taxes					
Income tax			Income tax		
expense	10,000*		expense	25,000	
Cash		10,000	Deferred		
*($50,000 × 0.5) − $15,000			tax credit		15,000
			Cash		10,000
			Deferred tax		
			credit	1,500	
			Income tax		
			expense		1,500
Recording depreciation					
Depreciation			Depreciation		
expense	15,000*		expense	15,000	
Accumulated			Accumulated		
depreciation		15,000	depreciation		15,000
*$150,000 ÷ 10 years					
Annual tax entries for next nine years					
Income tax			Income tax		
expense	25,000		expense	23,500	
Cash		25,000	Deferred tax		
			credit	1,500	
			Cash		25,000

The deferral method recognizes the $15,000 tax credit as a reduction in income tax expense over the life of the asset.

There has been a strong controversy within the accounting profession and business community about the proper treatment of investment tax credits. In 1962 the Accounting Principles Board issued Opinion No. 2, indicating that the deferral method was to be used.[2] The business community strongly opposed this position, and many companies ignored the Opinion. The SEC did not support the Opinion either. In 1964 the APB issued Opinion No. 4, which stated that the deferral method was preferred but that companies were free to use either method.[3] In other words, the APB gave in under pressure from accountants, businesses, and the SEC.

The controversy died down because the tax credit was repealed from 1966 to 1967 and again from 1969 to 1971. But in 1971 the controversy heated up again before the credit was to be reinstated by Congress. The APB indicated that when the tax credit was reinstated the Board was going to issue a new Opinion requir-

[2]"Accounting for the Investment Credit," *Opinions of the Accounting Principles Board No. 2* (New York: AICPA, 1962).

[3]"Accounting for the Investment Credit," *Opinions of the Accounting Principles Board No. 4* (Ammending No. 2) (New York: AICPA, 1964).

ing use of the deferral method. When notice of this came out, business put pressure on the government to do something. The Treasury Department, with congressional support, included provisions in the tax legislation that allowed businesses to account for the investment tax credit under whichever method they wished. As a result, the new APB Opinion was never issued, and companies are free to choose whichever reporting method they prefer.

The government's involvement in the treatment of accounting for investment credits was of particular concern to the accounting profession, who shared with the Securities and Exchange Commission the responsibility for establishing rules and principles for financial reporting. This was one of the first incidents in which Congress chose to get involved in the establishment of accounting principles.

Depletion

Depletion allocates the cost of a natural resource to the revenues generated by the natural resource. Natural resources include oil and gas, timber, and minerals such as coal, iron ore, copper, and zinc. They are referred to as wasting assets because once they are used they no longer exist. Depletion is like depreciation except that it relates to natural resources rather than to other, tangible, long-lived assets. Depletion accounting uses the same type of estimates that depreciation does. The asset's cost, salvage value, and useful life (usually in terms of total production) must be estimated.

The cost of the asset is determined using the cost principle. In natural resource accounting, the cost of the asset is usually composed of three types of costs: acquisition, exploration, and development costs. Acquisition cost includes the cost of acquiring the property or acquiring the mineral rights to it. Frequently the rights are purchased before the actual existence of minerals is known. The company acquiring the mineral rights generally will run tests, such as experimental drillings and seismic tests or, in the case of oil and gas properties, will drill a well. These are the exploration costs.

The final stage is development, during which costs are incurred to extract the minerals once they are discovered. These costs could be mining costs or the costs of drilling and equipping production wells. Development costs are usually one of two types: (1) tangible equipment costs and (2) intangible costs. Tangible equipment costs are the cost of equipment needed to extract, transport, and develop the natural resources. This equipment might be conveyors, trucks, bulldozers, and so forth. Since they are not natural resources, tangible equipment costs are not depleted. Tangible equipment is depreciated over the useful life of the equipment, which may be longer or shorter than the life of the natural resource. If the life is longer but the asset cannot be moved to another site, it is depreciated over the estimated life of the natural resource. Intangible costs are the costs of drilling wells, and the costs for tunnels, shafts, and other intangible items that are necessary for production.

The depletion cost base includes the cost of the mineral rights, and the costs of exploration and intangible development. There is some controversy within the oil and gas industry about the treatment of development costs for unproductive wells. Some companies write off these costs in the year in which the well is determined unproductive, whereas other firms capitalize the cost and write it off over the life of productive wells. This is discussed in more detail in the Appendix to this chapter.

It is very difficult to estimate the reserves available in a natural resource. Imagine trying to estimate the tons of coal in a vein or the barrels of oil or cubic feet of gas in a field. This is much more difficult and less precise than estimating useful lives of tangible assets. As a result, changes in estimates are more frequent in natural resource accounting. These changes are accounted for in the same manner as that discussed earlier in the chapter.

Calculating depletion is similar to the units of production method of depreciation. The cost, less any estimated residual or salvage value, is divided by the total estimated reserves to get a dollar depletion per unit. The depletion per unit is then multiplied by the number of units produced during the period to determine the total depletion. For example, Coalition Coal Co. purchased mineral rights and developed a mine at a cost of $3,000,000. The mine is believed to contain 5,000,000 tons of coal. During the current year, Coalition mined 600,000 tons of coal. The depletion for the year is as follows:

$$\frac{\$3,000,000}{5,000,000} = \$0.60/\text{ton} \times 600,000 = \$360,000 \text{ depletion}$$

The entry to record the depletion is:

Depletion expense	360,000	
Accumulated depletion		360,000

Some companies prefer not to use an accumulated depletion account and credit the asset account directly.

Financial statement disclosures should separate investments in unproven or undeveloped property from those in producing property. For example:

Property and mineral rights:		
Undeveloped property and rights		$1,000,000
Producing property	$3,000,000	
Less: accumulated depletion	360,000	2,640,000
		$3,640,000

The depletion calculated above is called **cost depletion,** which is used for financial reporting. There also exists a **statutory depletion** under current tax law. For tax purposes, a company may take the larger of the statutory depletion or the cost depletion. Statutory depletion allows the company to deduct, as depletion, a percentage of gross income received from the sale of the natural resources. This percentage ranges from 5% to 22%, depending on the type of natural resource. Since statutory depletion is based on a percentage of revenues, it is possible for statutory depletion to be greater than the cost of the property or mineral rights. Statutory depreciation is not GAAP and may not be used in financial statements.

Many companies in natural resource industries would like to record their resources at their market value or discovery value rather than at cost. As was discussed in the previous chapter, the natural resources should not be written up to discovery values. An estimate of the total reserves of natural resources may be disclosed in the company's annual report, but it should not be included in the financial statements.

Financial Statement Disclosures

Financial statement disclosures for property, plant, and equipment are essentially governed by APB Opinions No. 12[4] and 22[5] and FASB Statement No. 33.[6] Opinion No. 12 states that the following should be disclosed:

1. Depreciation expense for the period.
2. Balances of major classes of depreciable assets, by nature or function, at the balance-sheet date.
3. Accumulated depreciation, either by major classes of depreciable assets or in total, at the balance sheet date.
4. A general description of the method or methods used in computing depreciation with respect to major classes of depreciable assets.[7]

The need for disclosure of the methods of depreciation used was reinforced in APB Opinion No. 22. It is normal practice to disclose the asset valuation basis, which is usually cost. It is generally accepted practice to disclose both the original cost of the asset and related accumulated depreciation. Both are disclosed so that a statement reader can get some indication of the age of the assets. For example, the following are the machinery-related amounts for two companies:

	Orbach Ornament Co.	Nancy's Novelty Co.
Machinery—cost	$200,000	$60,000
Accumulated depreciation	150,000	10,000
Book value	$ 50,000	$50,000

Both companies have machinery with the same book value. However, reporting only book values would lessen substantially the informational content of the disclosure. This disclosure informs the reader that Orbach Co. owns significantly more machinery than Nancy's Co. and also indicates that Orbach Co.'s machinery is substantially older and will have to be replaced soon.

Property, plant, and equipment disclosures should also include information on any pledges, liens, or other ways in which the assets may be committed. Any assets which are held for investment purposes or for future use should be disclosed as investments rather than as property, plant, and equipment.

[4]"Omnibus Opinion," *Opinion of the Accounting Principles Board No. 12* (New York: AICPA, 1967).

[5]"Disclosure of Accounting Policies," *Opinion of the Accounting Principles Board No. 22* (New York: AICPA, 1972).

[6]"Financial Reporting and Changing Prices," *Statement of Financial Accounting Standards No. 33* (Stamford, Conn.: FASB, 1979).

[7]"Omnibus Opinion," par. 5.

Exhibit 12-9 presents information from a recent Annual Report of International Harvester Co. This report meets the reporting requirements set forth in APB Opinions 12 and 22 and is representative of the type of disclosures found in annual reports. The disclosures appear in three areas: Statement of Financial Condition, Accounting Policy Footnote, and Property Footnote.

An example of a disclosure relating to the investment tax credit appears in Exhibit 12-10, which was taken from the 1981 Annual Report of the Quaker Oats Co. and appeared in the footnote relating to income taxes.

Exhibit 12-9
INTERNATIONAL HARVESTER CO.
Property, Plant, and Equipment Disclosures

STATEMENT OF FINANCIAL CONDITION

Property
  Net of accumulated depreciation and
    amortization of $1,005,125 in 1979
    and $944,425 in 1978 (Note 9)   1,039,147   889,723

SUMMARY OF ACCOUNTING POLICY FOOTNOTE

Property
  The replacement of significant items of equipment and the expenditures for tooling and pattern equipment required because of increased capacity, new products and changes in existing products or equipment are capitalized. Expenditures for major rebuilding of machine tools are also capitalized. Expenditures for maintenance and repairs and for renewals of relatively minor items are charged to costs and expenses as incurred.

  Depreciation and amortization are generally computed on the straight line basis. The useful lives of the various classes of properties are as follows:

  Building and building equipment—3 to 50 years
  Land improvements—3 to 50 years
  Automotive equipment—3 to 7 years
  Machinery—4 to 20 years
  Auxiliary equipment—1 to 13 years
  Furniture and fixtures, etc.—1 to 20 years
  Tooling and pattern equipment—1 to 8 years
  Leasehold improvements—lease term or life of asset,
      whichever is shorter.

  Gains and losses on property disposals are included in income.
  The Company capitalizes leases that transfer substantially all of the benefits and risks of ownership to the leasee. These capital leases are, in general, amortized over the terms of the respective leases. Lease amortization is included in depreciation expense.

Exhibit 12-9 (continued)
INTERNATIONAL HARVESTER CO.
Property, Plant, and Equipment Disclosures

PROPERTY FOOTNOTE

At October 31, Property includes the following:

	1979	1978
	(*Thousands of Dollars*)	
Buildings machinery and equipment, at cost		
Manufacturing	$1,521,470	$1,347,671
Distribution	220,058	213,977
Other	57,468	48,513
Total	1,798,996	1,610,161
Less accumulated depreciation	897,952	844,224
Net	901,044	765,937
Tooling and pattern equipment, at cost less amortization of $107,173,000 in 1979 and $100,201,000 in 1978	106,041	92,963
Land	32,062	30,823
Property net	$1,039,147	$ 889,723

Buildings, machinery and equipment include $54.1 million and $51.7 million at October 31, 1979 and 1978, respectively, representing gross amounts of capitalized lease obligations.

Exhibit 12-10
QUAKER OATS COMPANY
Investment Tax Credit Disclosure

INCOME TAXES. Deferred income taxes are provided on timing differences and result primarily from the use of accelerated depreciation methods for tax purposes.

In 1979, the Company changed its method of accounting for U.S. investment tax credits from the deferral to the flow-through method in order to achieve greater comparability with the general accounting practices of most other companies. The flow-through method recognizes credits in income when the assets are placed in service. The cumulative effect of this change, which was made retroactive to July 1, 1978, was to increase 1979 net income by $14.7 million, or $.74 per share.

Double-digit inflation has had a significant impact on the operations of companies. Financial information should be evaluated in light of these changes. The effects of inflation are particularly evident in accounting for long-term assets. A company may be depreciating a machine on the basis of an original cost figure that may be only a quarter or a third of the cost of replacing the asset today. Historical cost depreciation may cause a financial statement reader to overestimate the long-run profitability of a company because it matches old costs with current revenues. FASB Statement No. 33 requires disclosure of certain types of constant dollar and current cost information for the property, plant, and equipment category. The details of these disclosures are discussed in Chapter 26. The purpose of the required disclosures is to aid the financial statement readers in their evaluations of the company.

Concept Summary

DEPRECIATION OF TANGIBLE ASSETS

DEPRECIATION—PURPOSE

To *allocate* the *cost* of the asset to the periods that benefit from the asset's use—the allocation process must be systematic and rational.

DEPRECIATION—VARIABLES

Variable	Description
Asset Cost	Includes all costs necessary to acquire the asset and get it ready for its intended purpose.
Salvage Value	The estimated value of the asset at the end of its useful life.
Useful Life	The number of years it is expected that the asset can be used economically in the operations of the business.

DEPRECIATION—METHODS

Method	Calculation
Units-of-Production	$\dfrac{\text{Cost} - \text{salvage}}{\text{Lifetime production}} \times \text{current production}$

Straight-Line	$\dfrac{\text{Cost} - \text{salvage}}{\text{Useful life}}$
Sum-of-the-Years' Digits	$\text{Cost} - \text{salvage} \times \dfrac{\text{remaining useful life}}{\text{sum-of-the-years' digits}}$
Fixed-Percentage-on Declining Balance	Book value × fixed percentage
Double-Declining-Balance	Book value × (straight-line rate × 2)
Accelerated Cost Recovery System	Cost × statutory percentage
Inventory Method	Book value − year-end appraisal value
Retirement and Replacement: Retirement	Cost − salvage of assets retired
Replacement	Cost of replacement units − salvage of replaced units
Group and Composite	Cost × group (composite) rate or $\dfrac{\text{Cost}}{\text{Group (composite) life}}$

Appendix

Oil and Gas Accounting

Several unique problems develop when accounting for oil and gas properties. One problem concerns accounting for the cost of dry holes, which includes the cost of mineral rights and exploration costs. There are two ways of handling these costs: (1) the successful efforts method and (2) the full-cost method.

Successful Efforts vs. Full-Cost

The **successful efforts** method capitalizes only those costs that relate to a successful well. These costs are then amortized on a units of production basis over the life of the well. The cost of unsuccessful wells (dry holes) is written off in the period in which the well is determined to be unsuccessful. The **full-cost** approach capitalizes the cost of both successful and unsuccessful wells and writes off the cost over the production of the successful wells. With this approach the dry wells are considered necessary to get the good wells. Proponents of this view contend that if a company must drill twelve wells to get one productive well, the productive well should be charged with the cost of all the wells. There are some problems with this approach. For example, suppose that traditionally one in twelve wells was good, but that in the current year only one in twenty was good. Should the cost of the extra eight wells be considered abnormal and expensed, or should the cost be capitalized with the rest? Current practice is to capitalize all the costs when the full-cost approach is used.

Another problem with the full-cost approach is defining the "cost centers" to be used. Should the cost of an unsuccessful well in the Baltimore Canyon, off the East coast, be capitalized and written off with productive wells in the Tuscaloosa Trend, in Louisiana? Or should the cost of dry holes in the Baltimore Canyon only be written off against good wells from the same cost center or area of interest? Under the latter approach, if no productive wells are found in an area, all cost of exploration in that area would be written off. The cost center could be defined as the country, state, geological formation, or specific field. Current practice is to define a cost center by country. The cost of all wells in a single country is capitalized or written off over the life of the good wells in that country.

Cost should not be capitalized unless there is the expectation that future revenues will be sufficient to offset the costs. When this is not the case, the unrecoverable costs should be written off immediately as an impairment.

Most large oil companies use the successful efforts approach whereas many smaller oil companies use the full-cost approach. The obvious benefit to using full cost is that it can significantly increase reported income in the short run. the larger income results from writing off unsuccessful exploration costs over many years rather than in the year the well is determined to be unsuccessful.

In 1977 the FASB issued Statement No. 19, which was intended to eliminate the choice of a method. The Statement required all companies to use the successful efforts method. Companies using the full-cost method were strongly opposed to the Statement and lobbied to get relief from it. They were concerned that if the small producers were forced to use successful efforts, their financial picture would worsen and they might not be able to raise funds for additional drilling. The fear of curtailed exploration efforts during a period of energy uncertainty led the Justice Department to ask the Securities and Exchange Commission to wait in adopting one method over the other until the effects of such a move could be determined. The SEC was to determine if the adoption of one method would improve significantly the financial information presented to investors. They were also to investigate the effect of uniform accounting on the industry.

In 1978 the SEC issued three Accounting Series Releases on oil and gas accounting.[8] The SEC did not believe that either the successful efforts method or the full-cost method adequately reflects the financial condition of an oil and gas company. Instead, the SEC proposed Reserve Recognition Accounting (called RRA), which is a current value technique in which the company estimates its reserves and places a value on them. A net value of the difference between the value of reserves and the future cost of production would appear in the Income Statement in the year of discovery and would also be reported in the balance sheet. Currently the SEC is experimenting with RRA and requires RRA disclosures in a company's annual report to the SEC. RRA applies to **proven reserves,** which are those that engineering and geological data indicate, with reasonable certainty, can be recovered from known reservoirs under current economic and operating conditions. In other words, it must be fairly certain that the reserves exist and can be recovered economically with existing technology.

RRA has received substantial criticism from executives in the oil industry. Opponents of the method contend that there is so much guess work and estimation involved in arriving at the RRA figures that the method is unreliable and therefore is not useful. They indicate that their best estimate in any given year could be off in either direction by more than 50% when additional information is obtained in subsequent years. Reserves are very difficult to measure; the true amount of recoverable resources is not known until recovery is complete. Application of RRA requires that companies estimate how much they will produce from proven reservoirs *each year* in the future. The future revenue, measured at year-end prices, and the future production costs, measured at current costs of production, are discounted to the present, at a 10% rate. The net present value is reflected as the value of the reserves. This is just a brief overview of RRA. It is much more complex than this, and an in-depth presentation is beyond the scope of this text.

---

[8]"Adoption of Requirements for Financial Accounting and Reporting Practices for Oil and Gas producing Activities," *Accounting Series Release No. 253* (Washington, D.C.: SEC, 1978); "Requirements for Financial Accounting and Reporting Practices for Oil and Gas Producing Activities," *Accounting Series Release No. 257* (Washington, D.C.: SEC, 1978); and "Oil and Gas Producers—Full Cost Accounting Practices," *Accounting Series Release No. 158* (Washington, D.C.: SEC, 1978).

As a result of the SEC actions regarding oil and gas accounting, the Financial Accounting Standards Board issued Statement No. 25, which has suspended the provision in Statement No. 19 relating to successful efforts.[9] In February, 1981, the SEC announced that it was abandoning the idea of using RRA as the uniform oil and gas financial accounting method. The SEC concluded that RRA was inappropriate as the primary accounting method because of the unreliability of reserve estimates. In the announcement, the SEC asked that the FASB develop new financial statement disclosure requirements for the oil and gas industry. The SEC indicated that RRA data would continue to be required as supplemental information until the FASB issued the new disclosure requirements. Although the SEC asked the FASB to develop new disclosures, it specifically indicated that the FASB should not reconsider the successful efforts vs. full-cost issue. The SEC indicated that it would reconsider these methods after the FASB set forth disclosure requirements. The FASB is expected to issue its new disclosure requirements during 1982.

The future of oil and gas accounting is uncertain. If industry has its way, there will be no RRA, and firms will be free to choose either the successful efforts or the full-cost method. In all probability, some sort of supplemental information on reserves, either in dollars or quantities, will be required. Information on reserves and changes in reserves is extremely important in evaluating an oil and gas company. The company's profitability and future are dependent upon its ability to find oil and gas reserves.

Questions

Q–12–1   What is the purpose of depreciation?

Q–12–2   What is the difference between depreciation, depletion, and amortization?

Q–12–3   How are the concepts of depreciation and matching interrelated?

Q–12–4   What are the four elements of depreciation?

Q–12–5   What should be included in the cost of an asset?

Q–12–6   What is salvage or residual value?

Q–12–7   Should long-lived assets be written off over their physical life? Explain.

Q–12–8   What factors affect useful life?

Q–12–9   What factors should be considered in the selection of a depreciation method?

Q–12–10   Some accounting theorists contend that accelerated depreciation methods should be used for assets that will be used evenly throughout their lives because this method results in a more even *total use cost* per year throughout the assets' lives. Define total use cost and explain why this theory results in more even cost per year.

Q–12–11   Under what circumstances should each of the following depreciation methods be used?

    a)   Units of production.

    b)   Straight-line.

    c)   Accelerated depreciation.

---

[9]"Suspension of Certain Accounting Requirements for Oil and Gas Producing Companies," *Statement of Financial Accounting Standards No. 25* (Stamford, Conn.: FASB, 1979).

Q–12–12 Assume you are calculating depreciation under the sum-of-the-years'-digits method. Use the formula given in the chapter to determine the number of years' digits if the useful life is 20 years.

Q–12–13 When is the inventory method of depreciation appropriate?

Q–12–14 Explain how the retirement and replacement methods are similar to FIFO and LIFO inventory methods?

Q–12–15 Distinguish between group and composite depreciation.

Q–12–16 When are group and composite methods used?

Q–12–17 When the group or composite methods are used, do individual assets have a book value? Explain.

Q–12–18 Does depreciation provide funds for the replacement of the asset? Explain.

Q–12–19 What is an investment tax credit? What are the two methods of accounting for these credits?

Q–12–20 What is statutory depletion? Why might statutory depletion be preferred to cost depletion for tax purposes?

Q–12–21 What financial statement disclosures should be made regarding depreciation?

Q–12–22 Answer the following multiple choice questions:

a) As generally used in accounting, what is depreciation?
  (1) It is a process of asset valuation for balance sheet purposes.
  (2) It applies only to long-lived intangible assets.
  (3) It is used to indicate a decline in market value of a long-lived asset.
  (4) It is an accounting process that allocates long-lived asset cost to accounting periods.

b) Which of the following reasons provides the best theoretical support for accelerated depreciation?
  (1) Assets are more efficient in early years and initially generate more revenue.
  (2) Expenses should be allocated in a manner that smooths earnings.
  (3) Repairs and maintenance costs probably will increase in later periods, so depreciation should decline.
  (4) Accelerated depreciation provides easier replacement because of the time value of money.

c) Which of the following is a principal objection to the straight-line method of depreciation?
  (1) It provides for the declining productivity of an aging asset.
  (2) It ignores variations in the rate of asset use.
  (3) It tends to result in a constant rate of return on a diminishing investment base.
  (4) It gives smaller periodic write-offs than do decreasing charge methods.

d) A graph is set up with depreciation expense on the vertical axis and time on the horizontal axis. If you assume linear relationships, how would the graphs for straight-line and sum-of-the-years'-digits depreciation, respectively, be drawn?
  (1) Vertically and sloping down to the right.
  (2) Vertically and sloping up to the right.
  (3) Horizontally and sloping down to the right.
  (4) Horizontally and sloping up to the right.

(AICPA adapted)

****Q–12–23** What are the two methods of accounting for the cost of mineral rights and exploration costs for petroleum industry companies? Describe each.

****Q–12–24** What is an *area of interest?*

****Q–12–25** What are proven reserves?

Note: Items with an *asterisk* relate to material contained in the appendix.

Discussion Questions and Cases

D–12–1 Property, plant, and equipment (plant assets) generally represent a material portion of the total assets of most companies. Accounting for the acquisition and usage of such assets is, therefore, an important part of the financial reporting process.
Required:
1. Distinguish between revenue and capital expenditures and explain why this distinction is important.
2. Briefly define depreciation as used in accounting.
3. Identify the factors that are relevant in determining the annual depreciation and explain whether these factors are determined objectively or whether they are based on judgment.
4. Explain why depreciation usually is shown in the sources of funds section of the statement of changes in financial position.

(AICPA adapted)

D–12–2 Depreciation continues to be one of the most controversial, difficult, and important problem areas in accounting.
Required:
1. Explain the conventional accounting concept of depreciation accounting and discuss its conceptual merit with respect to (a) the value of the asset, (b) the charge(s) to expense, and (c) the discretion of management in selecting the method.
2. Explain the factors that should be considered when applying the conventional concept of depreciation to the determination of how the value of a newly acquired computer system should be assigned to expense for financial reporting purposes. (Income tax considerations should be ignored).
3. What depreciation methods might be used for the computer system?

(AICPA adapted)

D–12–3 Behrens Co. recently began operations. The company currently is preparing its first year's financial statements to submit to its bank. The company has a sizable investment in plant, property, and equipment-type assets. Mr. Behrens, the owner of the company, is not familiar with accounting methods, and he has come to you for help. He asks you how accountants determine the market value of assets at the end of each period so they know how much depreciation to record. He also indicates that he is aware of the fact that different depreciation methods exist, but he doesn't understand why there are alternatives. He would like to know what these methods are and when they should be used.
Required:
1. What is the purpose of depreciation?
2. What nonspecialized methods of depreciation exist?
3. What factors should Mr. Behrens consider when he is choosing a depreciation method?

D–12–4 Humphreys Transit Co. has been in the trucking business for a number of years. The company has been very successful and now owns a large fleet of trucks. Mr. Humphreys, the owner of the company and a neighbor of yours, mentions to you after a little league baseball game that he is thinking of changing depreciation methods for his trucks. He indicates that the bookkeeping cost of keeping depreciation on each truck is increasing, and that the benefits aren't worth the cost. He asks if he can stop by your house that evening to discuss his problem. As he is leaving, he indicates that he has heard of a depreciation method called the inventory method and that he is considering a change to this method.
Required:
What would you recommend to Mr. Humphrey's during his evening visit?

*D–12–5 Some years ago the Securities and Exchange Commission began requiring Reserve Recognition Accounting (RRA) disclosures in the financial statements of petroleum producers. The method was criticized strongly by the petroleum industry as inaccurate and misleading.

Required:

1. What is RRA?
2. What is the basis for the industry complaints that such information is inaccurate and misleading?

Note: Iems with an *asterisk* relate to material contained in the appendix.

Exercises

E–12–1 Answer the following multiple choice questions.

a) Which method excludes salvage value from the base for the depreciation calculation?

(1) Straight-line.
(2) Sum-of-the-years'-digits.
(3) Double-declining-balance.
(4) Productive-output.

b) When a fixed asset with a five-year estimated useful life is sold during the second year, how would the use of the sum-of-the-years'-digits method of depreciation instead of the straight-line method of depreciation affect the gain or loss on the sale of the fixed asset?

	Gain	Loss
(1)	Decrease	Increase
(2)	Increase	Decrease
(3)	No effect	No effect
(4)	No effect	Decrease

c) Which of the following depreciation methods is computed in the same way that depletion is computed?

(1) Straight-line.
(2) Sum-of-the-years'-digits.
(3) Double-declining-balance.
(4) Productive-output.

d) In January, 1978, Solataire Company purchased equipment for $60,000, to be used in its manufacturing operations. The equipment was estimated to have a useful life of eight years, with salvage value estimated at $6,000. Solataire considered various methods of depreciation and selected the sum-of-the-years'-digits method. On December 31, 1979, the related allowance for accumulated depreciation will have a balance that is

(1) $7,500 less than under the straight-line method.
(2) $7,500 less than under the double-declining balance method.
(3) $9,000 greater than under the straight-line method.
(4) $9,000 greater than under the double-declining-balance method.

(AICPA adapted)

E–12–2 Orbach Shelter Co. purchased a truck to haul materials for its home construction business. The initial cost was $15,000, and the truck has an estimated salvage value of $3,000. This type of truck generally is used for five years and then is replaced by a new truck. On the average the trucks are driven 100,000 miles during this time. In some cases a truck of this type may be used more extensively. The company has a policy of selling any truck that has been driven 100,000 miles before the five-year period is up.

Required:
1. Discuss the appropriateness of the units of production method of depreciation in this case.
2. Give the entry to record depreciation in years 1 and 2 assuming the following mileage: year 1—20,000 miles, year 2—28,000 miles.

E–12–3 Cash of $100,000 and notes having a present value of $75,000 are given in return for an asset with an estimated useful life of five years and salvage value of $15,000. What is the depreciation for the first year under each of the following methods:

a) Straight-line.
b) Sum-of-the-years'-digits.
c) Double-declining-balance.

E–12–4 Using the information presented below, compute the amount of depreciation expense that would be recorded in 1982 if the following depreciation methods were used.

a) Units of production.
b) Straight-line.
c) Sum-of-the-years'-digits.

Purchase date	January 1, 1982
Cost of asset	$200,000
Estimated useful life	8 years
Estimated salvage value	$10,000
Estimated total production	500,000 units
Units produced in 1982	100,000

E–12–5 Answer the following multiple choice questions.

a) On January 1, 1979, Current Company purchased a new machine for $5,000,000. The new machine has an estimated useful life of five years, and the salvage value is estimated to be $500,000. Current uses the sum-of-the-years'-digits method of depreciation. What would be the amount of depreciation expense for 1980 (the second year)?

(1) $800,000.
(2) $1,200,000.
(3) $1,333,333.
(4) $1,500,000.

b) Shaw Company purchased a machine on January 1, 1978, for $350,000. The machine has an estimated useful life of five years and a salvage value of $50,000. The machine is being depreciated using the double-declining-balance method. What should be the asset balance net of accumulated depreciation at December 31, 1979?

(1) $126,000.
(2) $158,000.
(3) $170,000.
(4) $224,000.

(AICPA adapted)

E–12–6 Why would a company switch from the double-declining-balance method to the straight-line method during the useful life of an asset if the company were trying to maximize the amount of depreciation expense recorded? Assume that prospective treatment is proper and that the asset in question has a cost of $2,500, no salvage value, and a useful life of five years.

E–12–7 Samson Water Co. has a sizable investment in water meters. The meter asset account currently shows a balance of $830,000. During the past year $170,000 was spent to buy replacements for meters that were worn out. The cost of the old meters was $80,000. The old meters have a salvage value of $2,000.

Required:
Prepare the journal entry necessary to record depreciation under each of the following methods:

a) Retirement method.

b) Replacement method.

E–12–8   Pete Anderson Co. uses composite depreciation on a group of assets, including office machines costing $50,000, office furniture costing $150,000, and company cars costing $75,000. The assets have a useful life of 5, 7, and 3 years, respectively, and all have a salvage value of 5% of cost.

Required:
1. What is the composite rate and composite life?
2. What is the amount of depreciation expense for the first two years after the assets were acquired?
3. Give the journal entry to record the sale of a company car that cost $9,000. Assume the sale was made at the beginning of the third year and the sale price was $2,000.

E–12–9   Vince's Potato Chip Co. recently acquired a machine at a cost of $125,000 and spent $25,000 to have it installed. The machine has no salvage value and a useful life of 10 years.

Required:
1. How much cash is generated in the first two years of operation as a result of depreciation on this machine assuming sum-of-the-years'-digits?
2. How much savings might you argue is generated in the first two years of operation as a result of using double-declining-balance instead of straight-line depreciation assuming a 50% tax rate?

E–12–10   Brooking Inc. has a policy of charging a full year's depreciation to assets purchased in the first half of any year and no depreciation to those purchased in the second half. Given the following purchases of depreciable assets, what amount of depreciation would be recorded under the present policy? What if the same policy were applied to each month? Assume straight-line depreciation and no salvage value.

Date	Amount	Useful Life
3/12	$21,000	5
9/21	15,000	10
5/30	12,000	10

E–12–11   On July 1, 1978, Gusto Corporation purchased equipment at a cost of $22,000. The equipment has an estimated salvage value of $3,000 and is being depreciated over an estimated life of eight years under the double-declining-balance method of depreciation. For the six months ended December 31, 1978, Gusto recorded one-half year's depreciation. What should be the charge for depreciation (rounded to the nearest dollar) of this equipment for the year ended December 31, 1979, and 1980, assuming the following methods?

a) Sum-of-the-years'-digits.

b) Double-declining-balance.

(AICPA adapted)

E–12–12   Willard, Inc. purchased some equipment on January 2, 1978, for $24,000 (no salvage). Willard used straight-line depreciation based on a 10-year estimated life. During 1981 Willard decided that this equipment would be used for only three more years and then would be replaced with a technologically superior model.

Required:
What depreciation entry, if any, should Willard make as of December 31, 1981, to reflect this change?

(AICPA adapted)

E–12–13 Eastside Corporation purchased a machine on July 1, 1980, for $75,000. The machine was estimated to have a useful life of 10 years with an estimated salvage value of $5,000. During 1983 it became apparent that the machine would become uneconomical after December 31, 1987, and that the machine would have no scrap value. Accumulated depreciation on this machine as of December 31, 1982, was $17,000.

Required:

What should be the charge for depreciation in 1983 under generally accepted accounting principles?

(AICPA adapted)

E–12–14 Turpin Co. purchased machinery three years ago for $500,000. The machinery originally was estimated to last seven years, but it now appears Turpin Co. will be unable to use the machinery for more than five years. Technological advances, however, have increased the market value of the machinery at the end of its useful life. Turpin Co. now expects to get 15% of cost instead of the originally estimated 5%.

Required:

What amount of depreciation should be recorded in year 3 assuming straight-line depreciation?

E–12–15 Irving Co. purchased a machine at the beginning of 1982 for $700,000. The machine has a seven-year useful life and a $70,000 salvage value. Irving Co. is in a 50% tax bracket and will have taxable income of $1,000,000 for the next seven years.

Required:

If you assume that Irving uses straight-line depreciation, what journal entries would be required under flow-through and deferral methods in 1982 assuming a 10% investment credit?

E–12–16 Odell Corporation quarries limestone at two locations, crushes it, and sells it for use in road building. The Internal Revenue Code provides for 5% depletion on such limestone. The company pays a royalty of $0.01 per ton of limestone quarried at Quarry No. 1, which is leased. Quarry No. 2 is owned, the company having paid $100,000 for the site. The company estimates that the property can be sold for $30,000 after production ceases. Other data follow:

	Quarry No. 1	*Quarry No. 2*
Estimated total reserves, tons	30,000,000	100,000,000
Tons quarried through December 31, 1980	2,000,000	40,000,000
Tons quarried, 1981	800,000	1,380,000
Sales, 1981	$600,000	$1,000,000

Required:

1. What is the 1981 depletion of Quarry No. 1 for financial reporting purposes?
    a) $3,000.
    b) $8,000.
    c) $30,000.
    d) $29,600.
    e) None of the above.

2. Assume the same facts as in item 1 above. What is the 1981 depletion of Quarry No. 2 for financial reporting purposes?
    a) $0.
    b) $1,380.
    c) $966.
    d) $50,000.
    e) None of the above.

3. Assume the same facts as in item 1 except that a new engineering study performed early in 1971 indicated that as of January 1, 1981, 75,000,000 tons of limestone were

available in Quarry No. 2. What, then, is the 1981 depletion of Quarry No. 2 for financial reporting purposes?

a) $772.80.
b) $840.
c) $0.
d) $50,000.
e) None of the above.

(AICPA adapted)

E–12–17 On July 1, 1974, Miller Mining, a calendar-year corporation, purchased the rights to a copper mine. Of the total purchase price, $2,800,000 was appropriately allocable to the copper. Estimated reserves were 800,000 tons of copper. Production began immediately. Miller expects to extract and sell 10,000 tons of copper per month. The selling price is $25 per ton. Miller uses percentage depletion (15%) for tax purposes.

To aid production, Miller also purchased some new equipment on July 1, 1974. The equipment cost $76,000 and had an estimated useful life of eight years. After all the copper is removed from this mine, however, the equipment will be of no use to Miller and will be sold for an estimated $4,000.

Required:

1. If sales and production conform to expectations, what is Miller's depletion expense on this mine for financial accounting purposes for the calendar year 1974?

a) $105,000.
b) $210,000.
c) $225,000.
d) $420,000.

2. If sales and production conform to expectations, what is Miller's depreciation expense on the new equipment for financial accounting purposes for the calendar year 1974?

a) $4,500.
b) $5,400.
c) $9,000.
d) $10,800.

(AICPA adapted)

*E–12–18 Wildcat Co. incurred $1,840,000 of drilling costs during the current year. These costs were incurred in the Baltimore Canyon area. The company has since abandoned the leases on this area.

The company has other productive wells in the U.S. During the current year the company produced 12% of the estimated reserves on the other proven properties.

Required:

What should be the current year's expense for the cost incurred in the Baltimore Canyon assuming each of the following:

a) The company uses the successful efforts method.
b) The company uses the full cost method and defines an area of interest as
   (1) A country.
   (2) A geological structure.

Note: Items with an *asterisk* relate to material contained in the appendix.

Problems

P–12–1 Brennan Co. just purchased a new machine. The following information relates to the machine:

Cost of machine	$80,000
Transportation cost	2,000

Installation cost	3,000
Estimated salvage value	7,000
Estimated useful life	4 years
Estimated total production capacity	1,000,000 units

During the first two years of production the machine produced the following:

1st year	350,000 units
2nd year	300,000 units

Required:
1. Calculate the first two years' depreciation under each of the following methods:
   a) Straight-line.
   b) Units of production.
   c) Sum-of-the-years'-digits.

2. Calculate the depreciation for all four years using the double-declining-balance method.

P–12–2 On January 1, 1975, Barth Company, a small machine-tool manufacturer, acquired a piece of new industrial equipment for $1,000,000. The new equipment was eligible for the 10% investment tax credit, and Barth took full advantage of the credit and accounted for the amount using the flow-through method. The new equipment had a useful life of five years, and the salvage value was estimated to be $100,000. Barth estimates that the new equipment can produce 10,000 machine tools in its first year. Production then is estimated to decline by 1,000 units per year over the remaining useful life of the equipment.

The following depreciation methods may be used:
   a) Double-declining-balance.
   b) Straight-line.
   c) Sum-of-the-years'-digits.
   d) Units-of-output.

Required:
1. Which depreciation method would result in the maximization of profits for financial statement reporting for the three-year period ending December 31, 1977? Prepare a schedule showing the amount of accumulated depreciation at December 31, 1977, under the method selected. Show supporting computations in good form. Ignore present value, income tax, and deferred income tax considerations in your answer.
2. Which depreciation method would result in the minimization of profits for income tax reporting for the three-year period ending December 31, 1977? Prepare a schedule showing the amount of accumulated depreciation at December 31, 1977, under the method selected. Show supporting computations in good form. Ignore present value considerations in your answer.

(AICPA adapted)

P–12–3 Chokum Chemical Co. recently had a chemical fire at one of its plants. Unfortunately, the fire destroyed most accounting records related to depreciation. The only information available is the total book value of all depreciable assets. After talking to some employees of Chokum, you learn that due to rapid technological change, all assets, except buildings, are depreciated using a five-year useful life. You also have learned that the Chokum Chemical Co. acquired the existing buildings and land two years ago at a cost of $1,200,000 and planned to make the present site a parking lot in 10 years from the date of acquisition. At that time Chokum replaced all other assets. Assume that Chokum always uses the DDB method of depreciation for all assets other than buildings and uses the straight-line method for buildings. The buildings are not expected to have a salvage value. The total book value of all assets is $1,700,000. The land was estimated to be worth $200,000 on the date of purchase of the land and buildings.

Required:

1. Show how the plant, property, and equipment accounts would appear on the statement of financial condition as of the end of the second year.
2. What amount of depreciation expense should be reported in the second year's income statement?

P–12–4 On January 2, 1982, the D. H. Lang Co. purchased a new machine at a cost of $200,000. The machine has a useful life of eight years and a salvage value of $10,000.

Required:

Compute the amount of depreciation to be recorded during 1982 to 1989 using the following methods of depreciation:

  a) Straight-line.
  b) Fixed-percentage-on-declining-balance (FP).
  c) Double-declining-balance.

Your answer should be in the following form:

Year	Depreciation Base			Depreciation Rate			Depreciation Expense		
	SL	FP	DDB	SL	FP	DDB	SL	FP	DDB
1									
2									
3									
4									
5									
6									
7									
8									

P–12–5 The Glow-Bright Utility Co. is under attack from Ralph's Raiders, an environmental protection group, for its plan to build a new nuclear facility. Glow-Bright claims the new plant must be a nuclear plant since it could be operated more cheaply than a conventional plant. The company cites Glow-Bright's low profit in the current year as evidence of the need to cut operating expenses related to all plants to be built in the future. You are the controller for Glow-Bright and have been asked to choose a depreciation method for the current year that will best support Glow-Bright's position. The following information is relevant and relates to the purchase of electrical wire and poles in the current year. Assume the method you choose has been used consistently in the past.

Equipment purchased	$500,000
Useful life	7 years
Book value of equipment replaced	$150,000
Salvage value of equipment replaced	10,000

Required:

Show the entries required for the method you choose.

P–12–6 On April 23, 1982, Charles James sold Joyce Dickens a machine for $36,000. James originally purchased the machine on January 1, 1979, for $50,000. He had used an estimated life of eight years for depreciation and a $2,000 salvage value. Dickens estimates the machine can be used profitably for another 10 years but will have no salvage value. Assume depreciation is recorded for any month only if an asset is purchased before the 15th of that month.

Required:

1. If James used DDB, what would be the amount of depreciation he would record for 1982?

2. If Dickens used SYD, what would be the amount of depreciation she would record for
   a) 1982?
   b) 1983?

P–12–7 The D.H. Larry Co. purchased an asset three years ago for $100,000. The company estimated the useful life of the asset to be 16 years. Estimated salvage value was $10,000. Now the company believes the asset will last only eight more years and will have a salvage value of only $5,000 at that time. Assume the company has used the double-declining balance method of depreciation for the past three years.

Required:
What is the amount of depreciation for the current year if the use of this method is continued?

P–12–8 Kuhn Co. purchased a new machine for $150,000. The machine qualifies for a 10% investment tax credit. The machine has an estimated useful life of eight years and an estimated salvage value of $2,500. The company uses the sum-of-the-years'-digits method of depreciation.

Required:
Give the entries necessary during the first two years to record depreciation and treatment of the investment tax credit under the following methods:
   a) The flow-through approach.
   b) The deferral method.

P–12–9 LeBlanc, Inc. had the following assets that it was depreciating on a composite basis.

Asset	Cost	Salvage Value	Useful Life
A	40,000	4,000	8
B	8,000	500	5
C	65,000	2,000	10
D	22,000	1,500	4
E	35,000	3,000	8
F	12,000	1,000	5

Required:
1. Calculate the composite life and the annual composite depreciation rate for the group of assets listed. Round the decimal to two places. Give the entry to record the first full year's depreciation.
2. Early in the third year it became necessary to replace asset F. It was sold for $6,000. A replacement asset was purchased for $20,000. This new asset had a useful life of six years and a salvage value of $1,000. Record the sale of asset F and the purchase of the replacement asset.
3. Give the entry to record the depreciation for the third full year.

P–12–10 Gardner Co. owns a variety of small tools that are used in its manufacturing operations. The tools have a similar useful life and cost approximately the same. The company carries these tools in a machine tools account. At the end of 1981 the company had 200 tools in the account at a cost of $4,000. During 1982 the company purchased 100 replacement tools at a cost of $2,500. The company also sold or scrapped 75 used tools and received proceeds of $400. The ending inventory of tools was estimated to be worth $2,600.

Required:
Give the entries to record the acquisitions and disposition of the above tools under the following methods:
   a) Inventory method.
   b) Retirement method.
   c) Replacement method.

P–12–11 In early 1980 Big Hole Mining Company purchased the mineral rights to property containing coal deposits for $1,500,000. The property is estimated to contain 3,000,000 tons of coal. The company also constructed buildings at a cost of $400,000. The buildings have an estimated useful life of 30 years and no salvage value. Mining equipment costing $750,000 was purchased also. It was estimated to have a useful life of 10 years and minimal salvage value. The company estimates that it can extract all of the coal deposits within 10 years. At that time the surface property must be cleared of all structures. It is estimated that the net cost of dismantling the buildings and restoring the land will be $25,000. The machinery will be scrapped after the mine is depleted. During the first year of operation the company mined 450,000 tons of coal.

Required:

Give the journal entries necessary to record depletion and depreciation. Show and label all calculations.

P–12–12 The following independent situations describe facts concerning the ownership of various assets.

a) The Apex Company purchased a tooling machine in 1971 for $30,000. The machine was being depreciated on the straight-line method over an estimated useful life of 20 years, with no salvage value. At the beginning of 1981, when the machine had been in use for 10 years, Apex paid $5,000 to overhaul the machine. As a result of this improvement, Apex estimated that the useful life of the machine would be extended an additional five years.

b) Samson Manufacturing Co., a calendar-year company, purchased a machine for $65,000 on January 1, 1979. At the date of purchase Samson incurred the following additional costs:

Loss on sale of old machine	$1,000
Freight-in	500
Installation cost	2,000
Testing costs prior to regular operation	300

The estimated salvage value of the machine was $5,000, and Samson estimated that the machine would have a useful life of 20 years, with depreciation being computed on the straight-line method. In January, 1981, accessories costing $3,600 were added to the machine in order to reduce its operating costs. These accessories neither prolonged the machine's life nor provided any additional salvage value.

c) On July 1, 1981, Gusto Corporation purchased equipment at a cost of $22,000. The equipment has an estimated salvage value of $3,000 and is being depreciated over an estimated life of eight years under the double-declining-balance method of depreciation. For the six months ended December 31, 1981, Gusto recorded one-half year's depreciation.

d) The Gunther Company acquired a tract of land containing an extractable natural resource. Gunther is required by its purchase contract to restore the land to a condition suitable for recreational use after it has extracted the natural resource. Geological surveys estimate that the recoverable reserves will be 4,000,000 tons, and that the land will have a value of $1,000,000 after restoration. Relevant cost information follows:

Land	$9,000,000
Estimated restoration costs	1,200,000
Tons mined and sold in 1981	800,000

e) In January, 1981, Action Corporation entered into a contract to acquire a new machine for its factory. The machine, which had a cash price of $150,000, was paid for as follows:

Down payment	$ 15,000	
Notes payable in 10 equal monthly installments, interest 10%	120,000	
500 shares of Action common stock with an agreed value of $50 per share	25,000	
Total	$160,000	

Before the machine's use, installation costs of $4,000 were incurred. The machine has an estimated useful life of 10 years and an estimated salvage value of $5,000. Straight-line depreciation is used.

Required:

In each case compute the amount of cost allocation for the current year, 1981.

(AICPA adapted)

P–12–13 Thompson Corporation, a manufacturer of steel products, began operations on October 1, 1972. The accounting department of Thompson has started the fixed-asset and depreciation schedule presented on the following page. You have been asked to assist in completing this schedule and have determined that the data on the schedule are correct. You have also obtained the following information about the company's records and personnel:

a) Depreciation is computed from the first of the month of acquisition to the first of the month of disposition.

b) Land A and Building A were acquired from a predecessor corporation. Thompson paid $812,500 for the land and building together. At the time of acquisition the land had an appraised value of $72,000, and the building had an appraised value of $828,000.

c) Land B was acquired on October 2, 1972, in exchange for 3,000 newly issued shares of Thompson's common stock. At the date of acquisition the stock had a par value of $5 per share and a fair value of $25 per share. During October, 1972, Thompson paid $10,400 to demolish an existing building on this land so it could construct a new building.

d) Construction of Building B on the newly acquired land began on October 1, 1973. By September 30, 1974, Thompson had paid $210,000 of the estimated total construction costs of $300,000. Estimated completion and occupancy are in July, 1975.

e) A local university donated certain equipment to the corporation. An independent appraisal of the equipment when donated placed the fair value at $16,000 and the salvage value at $2,000.

f) Machinery A's total cost of $110,000 includes installation expense of $550 and normal repairs and maintenance of $11,000. Salvage value is estimated at $5,500. Machinery A was sold on February 1, 1974.

g) On October 1, 1973, Machinery B was acquired with a down payment of $4,000. The remaining payments are to be made in 10 annual installments of $4,000 each, beginning on October 1, 1974. The prevailing interest rate is 8%.

THOMPSON CORPORATION
Fixed Asset and Depreciation Schedule
For Fiscal Years Ended September 30, 1973, and September 30, 1974

Assets	Acquisition Date	Cost	Salvage	Depreciation Method	Estimated Life in Years	Depreciation Expense Year Ended September 30, 1973	1974
Land A	October 1, 1972	$(1)	N/A	N/A	N/A	N/A	N/A
Building A	October 1, 1972	(2)	$47,500	Straight-line	(3)	$14,000	$(4)

Land B	October 2, 1972	(5)	N/A	N/A	N/A	N/A	N/A
Building B	Under construction	210,000 to-date	—	Straight-line	30	—	(6)
Donated equipment	October 2, 1972	(7)	2,000	150% Declining-balance	10	(8)	(9)
Machinery A	October 2, 1972	(10)	5,500	Sum-of-the-years'-digits	10	(11)	(12)
Machinery B	October 1, 1973	(13)	—	Straight-line	15	—	(14)

N/A—Not applicable

Required:

Number your answer sheet from 1 to 14. For each numbered item on the schedule above (numbers in parentheses) supply the correct amount next to the corresponding number on your answer sheet. Round each answer to the nearest dollar. Do not recopy the schedule. Show supporting computations in good form.

*P–12–14 International Crude Oil Co. has operations in three countries: the U.S., Canada, and Brazil. The current year and total exploration costs incurred in connection with its exploration activities and the estimated proved reserves, as of year-end, are as follows:

	Current Year	Total Cost	Oil Reserves
U.S.			
Louisiana	$ 750,000	$5,400,000	900,000 bbls.
Texas	2,000,000	7,200,000	1,400,000
Canada	1,700,000	3,000,000	400,000
Brazil	1,300,000	2,000,000	–0–

During the current year the company had production as follows:

Louisiana	200,000 bbls.
Texas	400,000 bbls.

The Brazil operations were abandoned during the year. Assume that all current and prior expenditures were successful, except for the Brazil operations. Assume the prior years' costs in Brazil were for completed wells which were unsuccessful.

Required:

How much exploration cost should be written off in the current year assuming the following:

a) Successful efforts.

b) Full cost.

Note: Items with an *asterisk* relate to material contained in the appendix.

13

Intangible
Assets

Accounting in the News

Intangible assets often are referred to as "soft" assets because of the uncertainty associated with their future benefits. This uncertainty factor poses some interesting, if not perplexing, accounting problems. One of the primary accounting issues is to decide beforehand how to allocate the cost of an intangible asset over the periods benefited. Theoretically, proper allocation of the cost of an intangible asset would require that you be able to identify the nature, amount, and timing of the benefits on a "before-the-fact" basis. However, such identification is often difficult, if not impossible. For example, consider how the future benefits will be identified and measured in the case of a recent transaction between RCA Corporation and Columbia Pictures, as described in the following excerpts from a recent article.

> In what could be among the industry's largest home video marketing agreements, RCA Corp. and Columbia Pictures Industries Inc. announced a joint venture to market videocassettes and discs in the U.S. and Canada.

> Coca Cola Co., which recently acquired Columbia, said RCA would pay Columbia more than $50 million over three years for access to Columbia's library of television programs and 1,800 to 2,000 motion pictures.

> The agreement gives RCA world-wide access to Columbia products, augmenting an agreement signed last June with Columbia to distribute video programs outside North America.*

Measurement of the cost of the intangible asset (the *right* to use Columbia's library of television programs and motion pictures) poses no particular problem in this case. However, allocating the $50 million cost among the periods to be benefited is a different matter. Consider, for example, the need to estimate videocassette sales for the various titles that will be offered.

*Lauro Landro, "RCA, Coke Unit Form Venture on Home Video," *Wall Street Journal*, June 29, 1982, p. 12. Reprinted by permission of The Wall Street Journal, © Dow Jones & Company, Inc. 1982. All Rights Reserved.

This transaction exemplifies the type of accounting problems often faced in accounting for intangible assets—the focus of this chapter. Some of these problems lend themselves to an easy solution, while others pose very complex accounting issues.

A precise accounting definition of intangible assets has proved thus far to be elusive. From a legal viewpoint, an intangible asset is any asset that lacks physical substance. Accountants, however, traditionally have restricted the intangible assets classification to *long-lived* intangibles associated with an enterprise's operations, such as patents, copyrights, trademarks, leaseholds, franchises, organization costs, and other similar items. These are classified as assets because of the future benefits derived from the ownership or control of these special rights or privileges. The specific classification as an intangible asset traditionally has required that the asset be long-lived, lack physical substance, represent future economic benefits, and be acquired for purposes of operations rather than investment. Accountants customarily have included other assets lacking physical substance in other sections of the balance sheet. For example, accounts and notes receivable and short-term investments are included in current assets, and investments in stocks and bonds are classified as long-term investments.

Accounting for Intangible Assets

The accounting issues related to intangible assets are similar to those associated with long-lived, tangible assets. The major issues involved are (1) valuation at acquisition and (2) accounting for the asset's use or other disposition. The specific accounting and disclosure requirements related to intangible assets are set forth in APB *Opinion No. 17*, "Intangible Assets."[1]

APB # 17

Valuation at Acquisition

Intangible assets may be acquired from others or they may be developed internally. Further, they may be specifically identifiable, such as a patent, or they may be unidentifiable, as in the case of goodwill. Conceptually, an asset is specifically identifiable if the asset, such as a patent, or the future benefits that it represents, can be identified separately. An intangible asset traditionally has been regarded as being specifically identifiable if it can be acquired or developed separately from other assets. For example, a patent is specifically identifiable since it can be acquired or developed separately from other assets, whereas goodwill is not specifically identifiable because it cannot be acquired or developed separately.

---

[1]"Intangible Assets," *Opinions of the Accounting Principles Board No. 17* (New York: AICPA, 1970). Certain intangible assets acquired before November 1, 1970 (the effective date of *APB Opinion No. 17*), may be accounted for in accordance with APB Opinion No. 17 or *Accounting Research Bulletin No. 43*, Chapter 5.

Purchased, Specifically Identifiable Intangible Assets. Identifiable intangible assets acquired from others should be recorded at cost on the date of acquisition. As in the case of other assets, cost is measured by the fair value of the consideration given or the fair value of the asset received, whichever is more clearly determinable.

If the identifiable intangible asset is acquired as a part of a group of assets, the total cost of the group of assets is allocated to the individual assets acquired on the basis of their relative fair values. The procedures involved are the same as those discussed in Chapter 11 for other "lump-sum" acquisitions.

Purchased, Unidentifiable Intangible Assets. The principal example of an unidentifiable intangible asset is **goodwill.** Purchased goodwill is to be recorded consistent with the historical cost principle. Purchased goodwill arises from the acquisition of all or a major part of another enterprise. Goodwill is the excess of the cost of the acquired company over the fair value of the *identifiable* tangible and intangible net assets acquired. The accounting for goodwill is discussed later in this chapter.

Internally Developed, Specifically Identifiable Intangible Assets. In general, the costs incurred by an enterprise to develop intangible assets should be capitalized if the resulting assets are specifically identifiable and have reasonably determinable economic lives. These assets are in essence "self-constructed." As discussed in Chapter 11, the amount capitalized generally should include the costs directly associated with the development of the asset as well as a reasonable allocation of any related overhead costs. However, the amount capitalized should not include any costs that FASB *Statement No. 2,* "Accounting for Research and Development Costs," would classify as research and development costs.[2] For example, the capitalizable costs for an internally developed patent would include the legal fees associated with applying for the patent but would not include the costs of researching and developing the product or process being patented. Research and development costs are expensed as incurred. These costs are discussed more fully in a later section of this chapter.

Internally Developed, Unidentifiable Intangible Assets. *Opinion No. 17* requires that the "costs of developing, maintaining, or restoring intangible assets which are not specifically identifiable, have indeterminate lives, or are inherent in a continuing business and related to an enterprise as a whole—such as goodwill—should be deducted from income when incurred."[3] Thus, the costs of internally developed, unidentifiable intangible assets, such as goodwill, should be expensed as incurred.

---

[2] "Accounting for Research and Development Costs," *Statement of Financial Accounting Standards No. 2* (Stamford, Conn.: FASB, 1974).

[3] *"Intangible Assets,"* par. 27.

Accounting Subsequent to Acquisition

The major accounting issues subsequent to acquisition are those relating to (1) normal amortization, (2) abnormal write-offs, and (3) disposals by sale or exchange.

Normal Amortization. Under normal conditions an intangible asset should be amortized systematically over its economic life. The amortization period, however, may not exceed 40 years. Thus, an intangible asset with an estimated economic life of 15 years should be amortized over 15 years, whereas one with an estimated economic life of 50 years should be amortized over 40 years (the maximum amortization period). The estimate of the asset's economic life should be based on all relevant factors, including the following considerations:

1. Legal, regulatory, or contractual provisions may limit the maximum useful life.
2. Provisions for renewal or extension may alter a specified limit on useful life.
3. Effects of obsolescence, demand, competition, and other economic factors may reduce a useful life.
4. A useful life may parallel the service life expectancies of individuals or groups of employees.
5. Expected actions of competitors and others may restrict present competitive advantages.
6. An apparently unlimited useful life may in fact be indefinite, and benefits cannot be reasonably projected.
7. An intangible asset may be a composite of many individual factors with varying effective lives.[4]

Intangible assets with an unlimited life (such as goodwill) acquired before November 1, 1970, the effective date of *Opinion No. 17,* may be either (1) retained as an asset (i.e., not amortized) as long as there is no indication of a decline in the asset's value or (2) accounted for in accordance with *Opinion No. 17* by amortizing the asset over its estimated economic life or 40 years, whichever is less.

The straight-line amortization method should be used unless the enterprise can demonstrate that another systematic method is more appropriate. The amortization entry would be a debit to amortization expense (or an account such as factory overhead if the amortization is a part of manufacturing costs) and a credit to the specific intangible asset account; the credit alternatively may be made to an accumulated amortization account. The method and period of amortization should be disclosed in the financial statements.

Opinion No. 17 requires that an enterprise continually evaluate the attendant facts to determine whether later events and circumstances warrant a revised estimate of the economic life of an intangible asset. Changes in the estimated life

---

[4] Ibid., par. 27.

of an intangible asset should be accounted for as a change in accounting estimate. The unamortized balance should be amortized over the remainder of the revised estimated life.

Abnormal Write-Offs. Sometimes a given event or a series of events may cause a substantial and possibly abrupt decline in the estimated future benefits of an intangible asset. In such cases the decline in future benefits should be recognized as a loss in the period of decline. For example, if a franchisee's exclusive right to sell a particular product in a given geographical region is revoked legally by the franchisor, the franchisee should recognize the unamortized cost of the franchise (less any refunds received from the franchisor) as a loss in the period in which the franchise is revoked. The loss usually should be classified as an ordinary loss.

Before the issuance of *Opinion No. 17*, some enterprises would properly recognize goodwill acquired in a business combination but then would write off the goodwill immediately as a loss or as a direct charge to retained earnings. Such an immediate write-off of goodwill is now prohibited. It is possible, however, that a series of reported net losses in the years after a business combination may indicate that the unamortized goodwill balance should be reduced or perhaps even written off completely.

Disposal by Sale or Exchange. Identifiable intangible assets may be sold or exchanged separately or as part of a group of assets. Such disposals should be accounted for in the same manner as the disposal of other types of assets. In the case of a sale, any difference between the proceeds received and the unamortized balance of the intangible asset should be recorded as a gain or loss in the period of the sale.

Intangible assets are nonmonetary assets. Therefore, exchanges of identifiable intangible assets should be accounted for in a manner similar to that described in Chapter 11 for exchanges of plant and equipment items.

Unidentifiable intangible assets, including goodwill, ordinarily cannot be disposed of apart from the enterprise as a whole. There may be cases, however, in which a segment of the business or group of assets sold is large enough so that all or a portion of the unamortized goodwill should be included in the cost of the assets sold.

Specifically Identifiable Intangible Assets

The preceding discussion provided an overview of the basic issues involved in accounting for intangible assets at the time of acquisition and after acquisition. This section focuses on the nature of various, specific intangible assets and accounting issues related to these assets.

Patents

A **patent** is an exclusive right granted by the U.S. Patent Office that enables the holder to use, manufacture, sell, or otherwise control the product or process patented without interference or infringement by others. The patent has a legal life of 17 years and is nonrenewable. However, in some cases the effective life of a patent may be extended beyond 17 years by obtaining a new patent on a modification of the original product or process patented.

Patents acquired from others should be recorded at cost, which is the fair value of the consideration given or the fair value of the patent received, whichever is more clearly evident. Cost also includes any legal fees and other costs incurred in obtaining the patent. Cost of an internally developed patent conceptually includes the incremental costs of developing and registering the patent, other than those costs classified as research and development costs under *Statement No. 2*. As a practical matter, the costs that should be capitalized are the legal fees and other costs related to registration of the patent.

The cost of a patent should be amortized over its estimated economic life, i.e., the period during which benefits are expected to be received. Logically, the estimated economic life would not be greater than the patent's legal life. It may be less, however, due to technological advances, changing demand, or other factors. The straight-line amortization method normally should be used.

It is often necessary to defend a patent in court against infringement by others. The cost of a successful defense should be charged to the patent account; the resulting unamortized balance should be amortized over the remaining estimated life of the patent. If the defense is unsuccessful, both the cost of the defense and the unamortized balance of the patent should be recognized as a loss.

For example, assume that a patent was purchased on January 1, 1978, at a cost of $20,000 and is being amortized on a straight-line basis over its estimated life of 10 years. During the early part of 1982, $6,000 is spent in defending the patent in a patent infringement case. If the defense is successful, the related entries in 1982 will be as follows:

Patent	6,000	
Cash		6,000
To record litigation costs incurred.		
Patent amortization expense	3,000	
Patent (or accumulated amortization—patent)		3,000
To record 1982 amortization.		

The patent amortization for 1982 is computed as follows:

Cost incurred Jan. 1, 1978	$20,000
Less amortization 1978–1981 ($2,000 per year)	8,000
Unamortized cost Jan. 1, 1982	$12,000
Cost of successful defense	6,000
Balance to be amortized over remaining six years	$18,000

$$\text{Revised annual amortization} = \frac{\$18,000}{6 \text{ years}} = \$3,000$$

If, on the other hand, the defense is unsuccessful, the entry in 1982 is as follows:

Loss from write-off of patent	18,000	
Cash		6,000
Patent		12,000

Copyrights

A **copyright** is a right granted by the federal government to creators of literary, musical, and other artistic works. It gives the creator the exclusive right to control the reproduction, sale, or other use of the copyrighted work. Like patents, copyrights may be sold or assigned to others. Before January 1, 1978, a copyright was granted for 28 years and was renewable for an additional 28 years. A new copyright law became effective on January 1, 1978, which changed the copyright period for works created after that date so that it included the life of the creator plus 50 years.

Copyrights purchased from others should be recorded at cost. The cost of an internally developed copyright should include the incremental costs incurred in developing the work and obtaining the copyright, except for those costs classified as research and development costs under *Statement No. 2*. The cost of the copyright should be amortized over its useful life, not to exceed 40 years.

Trademarks and Tradenames

A **trademark** or **tradename** is a name, symbol, or other device used to identify distinctively a given product, such as Coke, Chevette, and Formica. Registration of the trademark or tradename with the U.S. Patent Office gives the owner exclusive right to its use for a period of 20 years, with an unlimited number of renewal periods of 20 years each as long as the trademark or tradename continues to be used. The cost of the trademark or tradename should be amortized over its expected useful life or 40 years, whichever is less. As with patents and copyrights, the cost of successfully defending the trademark or tradename in court should be capitalized.

Leases

A **lease** conveys to the lessee the *right* to use property of the lessor for a specified period of time. Accordingly, you can argue that any amounts capitalized should be classified as an intangible asset. Most enterprises, however, classify capitalized leases in the plant and equipment section of the balance sheet. Accounting for leases is discussed in detail in Chapter 18.

Franchises

A **franchise** is an agreement whereby the franchisor grants to the franchisee the right to provide certain services or sell certain products. In one common type of franchise a city or other municipality grants a private enterprise the right to provide certain services, such as transportation, garbage collection, or electricity. Costs to acquire the franchise should be charged to a franchise account and amortized over its useful life, not to exceed 40 years.

Another common type of franchise is one in which one business grants another business the exclusive right to sell a given product or service in a particular geographical region. An example is the right to manufacture and sell Pepsi Cola products to retailers in a given area.

Annual payments made under a franchise agreement should be included in operating expenses as they are incurred. If a franchise is terminated, any unamortized balance in the franchise account should be recognized as a loss. For a detailed discussion of accounting for franchises, you should consult FASB *Statement No. 45*, "Accounting for Franchise Fee Revenue."[5]

Organization Costs

Certain costs incurred in the formation of a business frequently are capitalized on the basis that such costs are essential to the creation of the business and therefore represent future benefits. Examples of such costs are legal fees, accounting fees, underwriting costs, and state incorporation fees. These costs are debited to the organization costs account and amortized over a reasonable period of time, not to exceed 40 years. Current tax law allows organization costs to be written off for tax purposes over a period of five years or longer.

Deferred Charges

Long-term prepayments and other accounts with debit balances often are also classified as intangible assets. Some enterprises, however, present these items in a separate, deferred charges section of the balance sheet. Examples of these items are long-term prepaid insurance premiums, plant rearrangement costs, and deferred income tax charges.

Research and Development Costs

Each year business enterprises spend vast sums of money on research and development (R & D) activities directed at developing new or improved products and processes. In the past these enterprises followed a variety of practices in accounting for and reporting R & D costs. Some capitalized all R & D costs, others expensed all such costs, while still others capitalized certain R & D costs and expensed the rest. The magnitude of these expenditures and the lack of uniformity

---

[5]"Accounting for Franchise Fee Revenue," *Statement of Financial Accounting Standards No. 45* (Stamford, Conn.: FASB, 1981).

in accounting for R & D costs led the FASB to reexamine the accounting and reporting issues related to R & D activities. The result was the Board's issuance of FASB *Statement No. 2*.[6]

GAAP Relating to Research and Development

The basic position taken by the Board in *Statement No. 2* is specific—all research and development costs are to be expensed when incurred.

Some accountants argue that the FASB's position that all research and development costs be expensed when incurred is too extreme. Such a position, they contend, precludes the recognition of what a number of enterprises consider to be one of their most valuable assets. These accountants argue that the future benefits associated with research and development activities should be reflected on the balance sheet as an asset.

The FASB considered various alternatives for accounting for research and development costs. The FASB elected to choose one of these alternatives and thereby achieve a greater uniformity in how research and development costs are accounted for and reported. Three of the principal factors the FASB identified as being influential in its decision to require that all research and development costs be expensed when incurred were as follows:

1. The high degree of uncertainty about the future benefits of individual research and development projects.
2. The absence, in most cases, of a direct relationship between research and development costs and specific future revenue.
3. The inability to measure future benefits with any degree of certainty, even in cases in which one accepts the idea that such future benefits exist.[7]

Definition of Research and Development

One of the major difficulties relating to R & D is in deciding what constitutes an R & D cost. The FASB defined research and development as follows.

Research is planned search or critical investigation aimed at discovery of new knowledge with the hope that such knowledge will be useful in developing a new product or service . . . or a new process or technique . . . or in bringing about a significant improvement in an existing product or process.

Development is the translation of research finding or other knowledge into a plan or design for a new product or process or for a significant improvement to an existing product or process whether intended for sale or use. It includes conceptual formulation, design, and testing of product alternatives, construction of prototypes, and operation of pilot plants. It does not include routine or periodic alterations to existing products, production lines, manu-

---

[6]"Research and Development Costs."

[7]Ibid., par. 39–45.

facturing process, and other on-going operations even though those alternatives may represent improvements and it does not include market research or market testing activities.[8]

To further help identify what constitutes a research and development activity, the FASB provided the following examples of activities that would be included and those that would be excluded.

Included in R & D Activities

(a) Laboratory research aimed at new knowledge.

(b) Searching for applications of new research findings or other knowledge.

(c) Conceptual formulation and design of possible product or process alternatives.

(d) Testing in search for or evaluation of product or process alternatives.

(e) Modification of the formulation or design of a product or process.

(f) Design, construction, and testing of pre-production prototypes and models.

(g) Design of tools, jigs, molds, and dies involving new technology.

(h) Design, construction, and operation of a pilot plant that is not of a scale economically feasible to the enterprise for commercial production.

(i) Engineering activity required to advance the design of a product to the point that it meets specific functional and economic requirements and is ready for manufacture.

Excluded from R & D Activities

(a) Engineering follow-through in an early phase of commercial production.

(b) Quality control during commercial production including routine testing of products.

(c) Trouble-shooting in connection with break-downs during commercial production.

(d) Routine, on-going efforts to refine, enrich, or otherwise improve upon the qualities of an existing product.

(e) Adaptation of an existing capability to a particular requirement or customer's need as part of a continuing commercial activity.

(f) Seasonal or other periodic design changes to existing products.

(g) Routine design of tools, jigs, molds, and dies.

(h) Activity, including design and construction engineering, related to the construction, relocation, rearrangement, or start-up of facilities or equipment other than (1) pilot plants and (2) facilities or equipment whose sole use is for a particular research and development project.

(i) Legal work in connection with patent applications or litigation, and the sale or licensing of patents.[9]

[8] Ibid., par. 8.

[9] Ibid., par. 9 and 10.

The FASB also specifically excluded from the definition of R & D activities the acquisition, development, or improvement of a process by an enterprise for use in its selling or administrative activities.[10] Such costs are not R & D costs. For example, the costs incurred by an airline to develop a computerized reservation system are not R & D costs. However, these costs would be R & D costs if incurred by an enterprise developing the system to sell to airlines.

Costs associated with activities *excluded* from R & D activities are not R & D costs. Whether these non-R & D costs should be expensed or capitalized depends upon the particular set of circumstances. For example, legal work in connection with a patent application is not an R & D activity [see item (i) above in the list of excluded activities]. Therefore, the related legal fees are not R & D costs. As discussed previously, these legal fees should be capitalized as a part of the cost of the patent.

Costs Associated with R & D Activities

Costs associated with R & D activities do not qualify automatically as R & D costs. As you will recall, all R & D costs must be expensed as incurred. However, *Statement No. 2* requires that certain costs associated with R & D activities be capitalized. The key issue then is to determine the point at which costs associated with R & D activities become R & D costs. The determination of this point is discussed below for the various types of costs associated with R & D activities.

Materials. The costs of materials acquired for R & D activities should be capitalized if the materials have alternative future uses in other R & D projects or otherwise. The cost of such materials, as well as the cost of materials from the enterprise's normal inventory, is not an R & D cost until the materials are *used* in R & D activities. The cost of materials that are acquired for a particular R & D project and that have no alternative future use is an R & D cost at the time the cost is incurred.

Equipment and Facilities. The cost of equipment or facilities acquired or constructed for R & D activities should be capitalized if the equipment or facilities have alternative future uses in other R & D projects or otherwise. The cost of such equipment or facilities is not an R & D cost. However, the depreciation of such equipment or facilities is an R & D cost to the extent that the asset is used in R & D activities. The cost of equipment or facilities that are acquired or constructed for a particular R & D project and that have no alternative future use is an R & D cost and should be expensed when incurred.

Personnel. Salaries, wages, and other related costs of personnel engaged in R & D activities are R & D costs at the time the costs are incurred.

Intangibles Purchased from Others. The cost of an intangible purchased from others for use in R & D activities should be capitalized if the intangible asset has

---

[10]"Applicability of FASB Statement No. 2 to Computer Software," *FASB Interpretation No. 6* (Stamford, Conn.: FASB, 1975), par. 4.

an alternative future use in other R & D projects or otherwise. The amortization of an intangible asset is an R & D cost to the extent that the asset is used in R & D activities. The cost of an intangible asset that is purchased for use in a particular R & D project and that has no alternative future use is an R & D cost at the time the cost is incurred.

Contract Services. The cost of services performed by others in connection with an enterprise's R & D activities is an R & D cost. Similarly, the cost of R & D conducted by others in behalf of the enterprise is an R & D cost.

Indirect Costs. R & D costs should include a reasonable allocation of indirect costs, but they should not include general and administrative costs unless they are clearly related to R & D activities.

The proper accounting treatment of the various costs associated with R & D is illustrated in Exhibit 13-1. The example includes the proper treatment of the cost of supplies, depreciation, purchased patents, and contract (outside) R & D work.

Costs Outside the Scope of Statement No. 2

Statement No. 2 does not apply to costs of R & D activities conducted for others *under a contractual arrangement.* The accounting for these costs is a part of accounting for contracts in general. Generally, these costs should be capitalized and carried as an asset until the contract is completed, at which time they should be expensed as the cost of contract services performed.

The Statement also does not apply to R & D activities that are unique to enterprises in the extractive industries, such as prospecting, acquisition of mineral rights, exploration, drilling, mining, and related mineral development. It does apply, however, to the R & D activities of enterprises in the extractive industries that are similar to the R & D activities of other enterprises.

Goodwill

There are two distinctively different, but somewhat related, issues associated with goodwill. The first, and the one of paramount concern to accountants, is accounting for goodwill. From an accounting standpoint, the major concerns are (1) determining the circumstances under which goodwill should be recorded, (2) computing the amount of goodwill to be recorded, and (3) amortizing the recorded goodwill over its economic life. The second issue related to goodwill has to do with financial management. It focuses on the valuation of a business enterprise for purposes of determining the price at which the enterprise should be purchased or sold. The financial management issue stops when the purchaser and seller agree upon the negotiated purchase price of the enterprise being acquired. This negotiated purchase price then represents the starting point of accounting for goodwill, that is, it represents a "given" in calculating the amount of goodwill to be recorded in the accounts.

Exhibit 13-1
PROGRESSIVE COMPANY
Accounting for Associated R & D Costs

---

1. Supplies purchased during the year:
   Type A, which is used exclusively in
   manufacturing operations $15,000
   Type B, which normally is used both in
   manufacturing operations and in R & D
   activities 19,000
   Type C, which is used exclusively in R & D
   activities but on various projects 8,000
   Type D, which is used exclusively on a
   particular R & D project and has no
   alternative use 3,000
                                                                          $45,000

   Entry:
   Supplies inventory (Types A, B, & C) 42,000
   R & D costs (Type D) 3,000
      Cash 45,000
   To record the purchase of the supplies.

2. Supplies used during the year:
   Type A $11,000
   Type B:
      Used in manufacturing .... $ 7,000
      Used in R & D 8,000   15,000
   Type C 6,000
   Type D 2,500
                                                                          $34,500

   The following entries record the cost of
   supplies used during the year:
   Factory overhead 11,000
      Supplies inventory (Type A) 11,000
   To record the usage of Type A supplies.

   Factory overhead 7,000
   R & D costs 8,000
      Supplies inventory (Type B) 15,000
   To record the usage of Type B supplies.

   R & D costs 6,000
      Supplies inventory (Type C) 6,000
   To record the usage of Type C supplies.

3. Depreciation recognized during the year:
   On equipment used exclusively in
   manufacturing $14,200

Exhibit 13-1 (continued)
PROGRESSIVE COMPANY
Accounting for Associated R & D Costs

On equipment used 50% in manufacturing and
50% in R & D activities (on various
R & D projects) 20,000
On equipment used exclusively in R & D
activities but on various R & D projects 8,400
$42,600

Entry:
Factory overhead ($14,200 & $10,000) 24,200
R & D Costs ($10,000 & $8,400) 18,400
    Accumulated depreciation—equipment 42,600
To record depreciation on equipment for
the year.

4. Patents purchased during the year:
Patent A, which has a six-year estimated
life, is related to a machine which is
used 50% in manufacturing and 50% in
R & D activities .... $ 6,000
Patent B, which is related to a new process
that will be used exclusively in a
specific R & D project (the process and,
thus, the patent has no economic value to
other enterprises and has no alternative
use to Progressive Company). 2,200
$ 8,200

Entry:
Patent 6,000
R & D Costs 2,200
    Cash 8,200
To record the purchase of patents.

Factory overhead (patent amortization) 500
R & D Costs 500
    Patent ($6,000 ÷ 6 years) 1,000
To record the amortization of patents.

5. R & D activities performed for Progressive
Company by Second Company at a cost of
$5,400:
R & D costs 5,400
    Cash 5,400
To record R & D performed by outside
company.

Accounting for Goodwill

Conceptually, goodwill represents the excess of the value of a business over the fair value of its identifiable net assets. It represents all of those factors that cause the value of an enterprise as a whole to be greater than the sum of its identifiable parts (i.e., its identifiable net assets). There may be numerous such factors, including the following:

1. Superior management team
2. Outstanding sales organization
3. Effective advertising
4. Secret process or formula
5. Good labor relations
6. Outstanding credit rating
7. High standing in the community
8. Strategic location[11]

These are the type of factors that enable the enterprise to realize an earnings level above that of other enterprises without these factors. Thus, goodwill also can be viewed as an enterprise's excess earning power.

From a theoretical standpoint, arguments have been made for at least three different treatments of recorded goodwill:

1. Deduct the cost from stockholders' equity at the date acquired.
2. Retain the cost indefinitely as an asset unless a reduction in its value becomes evident.
3. Amortize the cost of goodwill over its estimated useful life.

Proponents of treatment (1) argue that the nature of goodwill differs significantly from that of other assets and therefore requires special treatment. They contend that the special treatment of writing off goodwill directly against stockholders' equity is justified because of the inseparability of goodwill from the business as a whole and the attendant lack of reliability of estimates of its useful life and current value. The direct write-off, they argue, avoids the subjective estimates of the value and useful life of goodwill and prevents distortions in future years' earnings that would result from these estimates.

Proponents of treatment (2) contend that goodwill is not consumed or used to produce earnings in the same manner as are other assets. Thus earnings should not be reduced by amortization of goodwill. Proponents further argue that earnings should not be reduced by *both* amortization of goodwill and current expenditures that are incurred to enhance or maintain the goodwill acquired. They maintain that any method of amortizing goodwill is arbitrary because the useful life of goodwill is indefinite and thus not measurable.

[11] George R. Catlett and Norman O. Olson, "Accounting for Goodwill," *Accounting Research Study No. 10* (New York; AICPA, 1968), pp. 17–18.

Those favoring treatment (3), which is the current official position, argue that goodwill is not unlike other assets with limited lives in that it represents future benefits that will expire within some finite period of time. Accordingly, its cost should be amortized over the periods benefited, i.e., over its useful life. Although the specific life of goodwill may be indeterminate, it is not infinite. As a practical matter, then, the asset should be amortized over some reasonable period of time.

These arguments for treatment (3) represent the underlying foundation for the current, authoritative position that in normal situations goodwill should be amortized over its useful life (if it can be determined), but the amortization period should not exeed 40 years. Of course, if there is evidence of a permanent impairment of the value of goodwill, the impairment should be recognized in the period in which it occurs by writing down goodwill to this lower value.

Only purchased goodwill may be recorded in the accounts. It is unacceptable to record internally developed goodwill. Recording internally developed goodwill would be similar to recording increases in the value of inventory before the point of sale, which in most cases is also an unacceptable practice. In addition, it would be difficult, if not impossible, to match expenditures with specific elements of goodwill such as those listed earlier. Current practice views such expenditures as being an inherent part of a continuing business and as being related to the business as a whole. These expenditures are to be expensed as incurred.

Purchased goodwill is the acquisition of an entire business (or at least a major portion of the business). It represents the excess of the purchase price of the business as a whole over the fair value of the identifiable net assets acquired. In this context, goodwill represents a "catch-all" or master valuation account.

As stated previously, the negotiated purchase price of the business as a whole represents the starting point in determining the amount of goodwill to be recorded. The negotiated purchase price establishes the fair value of the consideration given in exchange for the business. If you assume that the exchange represents an arm's-length transaction between an informed and willing buyer and an informed and willing seller, the presumption is that the fair value of the net assets received is equal to the fair value of the consideration given. Therefore, if the purchase price (i.e., the fair value of the consideration given) exceeds the fair fair value of the *identifiable* net assets acquired, one of two conclusions must be drawn: (1) the purchaser acted irrationally, or (2) the purchaser willingly paid for perceived future benefits beyond those represented by the identifiable net assets acquired.

In the absence of strong evidence to the contrary, accounting traditionally assumes an informed, willing, and rational purchaser and seller. Therefore, the first listed conclusion is not considered to be a valid one. By deduction, then, goodwill represents the portion of the purchase price paid for those future benefits (unidentifiable assets) that are not specifically identifiable or that are not susceptible to reasonable measurement for accounting purposes. These future benefits sometimes are referred to collectively as the "excess earning power" of the business acquired.

As an illustration of the calculation of goodwill, assume that Alpha Company paid $1,000,000 cash for Beta Company. The identifiable assets and liabilities of Beta at the time were as shown in Exhibit 13-2.

Exhibit 13-2
BETA COMPANY
Assets and Liabilities

	Book Value	Fair Value
Receivables	$100,000	$ 80,000
Inventory	300,000	390,000
Plant and equipment (net)	400,000	500,000
Patents	–0–	50,000
	$800,000	$1,020,000
Liabilities	150,000	150,000
Identifiable net assets	$650,000	$ 870,000

The amount of goodwill is determined as follows:

Fair value of consideration given		$1,000,000
Less fair value of identifiable net assets acquired:		
Identifiable assets	$1,020,000	
Less liabilities assumed	150,000	870,000
Goodwill (excess of cost over fair value of identifiable net assets acquired)		$ 130,000

If a balance sheet were prepared for Alpha immediately after the acquisition of Beta, goodwill of $130,000 would be shown in the intangible assets section. The other assets and liabilities acquired in the transaction would be shown at their fair values.

Negative Goodwill

It is possible, although not probable, that in the acquisition of a business the fair value of the consideration given may be less than the fair value of the identifiable net assets acquired. Such a situation raises a question about the rational behavior of the seller, who presumably could have sold the identifiable assets individually for a total price greater than the amount received for the business as a whole. Since accounting traditionally has assumed, in the absence of evidence to the contrary, an informed, willing, and rational buyer and seller, the explanation of the excess of the fair value of the identifiable net assets over the fair value of the consideration given must be (1) the imperfection of the market place, (2) an apparent advantage to the seller of a "basket sale" as opposed to selling the assets individually, or (3) the subjectivity in some cases in determining fair values.

APB *Opinion No.16* requires that any excess of the fair value of the identifiable net assets acquired over the fair value of the consideration given should be allocated to reduce proportionately the values assigned to the noncurrent assets acquired (except long-term investments in marketable securities) in determining their fair values. If the allocation reduces the noncurrent assets to zero values, the remainder of the excess fair value over cost should be classified as a deferred credit and should be amortized systematically to income over the period estimated to be benefited but not in excess of 40 years.[12]

Financial Management

The financial management issue related to goodwill focuses on determining the value of an enterprise. An integral part of the valuation of a business as a whole is the determination of the amount of goodwill, if any, associated with the enterprise.

There are numerous approaches to estimating the value of a business. They range from very sophisticated methods to simple, "seat-of-the-pants" projections. An in-depth discussion of the valuation of a business usually is included in most finance textbooks. The following discussion of the valuation of a business, and the related estimation of goodwill, is presented to emphasize the conceptual aspect of estimating goodwill. It is not intended as an exhaustive treatment of the sophisticated issues involved in valuing a business.

Perhaps the most conceptually sound approach to valuing a business is the discounted cash flow approach. The underlying idea of this approach is that at any point in time the value of a business is equal to the present value of its future cash inflows and outflows, as depicted below:

Present value of all future cash inflows	$xxx
Less present value of all future cash outflows	xxx
Value of the business	$xxx

Although this approach to valuing a business may be sound conceptually, it offers little help as a practical guide for determining the worth of a business because of the difficulty in estimating the future cash flows.

A number of approaches to estimating the value of a business are based on estimates of future earnings of the enterprise. For example, one simplistic approach is to base the estimate of the value of a business on capitalized, estimated average future earnings. Assume that estimated average future earnings are $100,000. Assume further that the purchaser requires a minimum 10% return on investment. The estimated value of the business would be:

$$\frac{\text{Estimated average future earnings}}{\text{Capitalization rate}} = \frac{\$100,000}{0.10} = \$1,000,000$$

---

[12] "Business Combinations," *Opinions of the Accounting Principles Board No. 16* (New York: AICPA, 1970), par. 91.

Goodwill, then, would be the excess of the estimated value of the business over the fair value of the identifiable net assets of the business. For example, if you assume the fair value of the identifiable net assets to be $800,000, estimated goodwill would be $200,000, determined as follows:

Estimated value of the business	$1,000,000
Fair value of identifiable net assets	800,000
Estimated goodwill	$ 200,000

Some approaches to estimating the value of a business focus on estimating the amount of goodwill directly by capitalizing estimated average future "excess" earnings as the amount of goodwill. For example, assume that in the preceding illustration "normal" earnings for an enterprise in this industry would be $85,000 per year. In this case the estimated average future earnings for this enterprise of $100,000 represents an estimated average future "excess" earnings of $15,000, as shown below.

Estimated average future earnings	$100,000
Less "normal" average earnings	85,000
Estimated average future "excess" earnings	$ 15,000

Capitalizing the "excess" earnings at a rate of 10% would yield estimated goodwill of $150,000, as computed below:

$$\frac{\text{Estimated average future ``excess'' earnings}}{\text{Capitalization rate}} = \frac{\$15,000}{0.10} = \$150,000$$

If you assume as before that the estimated fair value of the identifiable net assets is $800,000, the estimated value of the business is $950,000, determined as follows:

Fair value of identifiable net assets	$800,000
Estimated goodwill	150,000
Estimated value of the business	$950,000

In the preceding illustration the amount of estimated goodwill was calculated by dividing the estimated average future excess earnings ($15,000) by the capitalization or discount rate (10%). This calculation (i.e., dividing by the capitalization rate) implies that the excess earnings are expected to continue indefinitely (i.e., in perpetuity). Many argue that such an assumption is illogical. They contend that any excess earning power now existing will diminish within a reasonably short period of time. In that case, goodwill should be calculated based on the assumption that the excess earnings will continue for a limited number of years.

For example, assume that the average excess annual earnings of $15,000 from the preceding illustration is expected to last for five years. Assuming that

---

Exhibit 13-3
Summary of Intangible Assets Reported by Companies
Included in *Accounting Trends and Techniques*

	Intangibles Being Amortized	Intangibles Not Being Amortized
Goodwill	266	143
Patents and patent rights	56	—
Trademarks, brand names, and copyrights	22	8
Licenses, franchises, and memberships	21	—
Other	42	11

10% is considered to be an appropriate rate of return, you would calculate good-will as the present value of an annuity of $15,000 discounted at 10% for five years, as shown below:

$$\text{Goodwill} = \text{Excess Earnings} \times P_{\overline{n}|i}$$
$$= \$15,000 \times P_{\overline{5}|10\%}$$
$$= \$15,000 \times 3.791$$
$$= \$56,865$$

If you continue the assumption that the fair value of the identifiable net assets is $800,000, the estimated value of the business then is $856,865.

Disclosure of Intangibles

Enterprises have reported a variety of different types of intangible assets. The most prevalent is goodwill, as illustrated in Exhibit 13-3, which is a summary of the intangible assets reported by companies included in *Accounting Trends and Techniques*.[13]

The intangibles not being amortized were acquired before October 31, 1970, the effective date of *Opinion No. 17*. As discussed previously, the enterprise is not required to amortize these intangible assets if they have an unlimited life and are being accounted for under *Accounting Research Bulletin No. 43*. However, a permanent decline in the value of any intangible asset must be recognized by writing down the asset to its lower value.

Following are examples of intangible assets and the related notes reported in recent annual reports.

---

[13] *Accounting Trends and Technique. 1981* (New York: AICPA, 1981). p. 75.

General Mills, Inc.

Goodwill and other intangible assets $198,000,000

Notes to financial statements:

Goodwill represents the difference between the purchase prices of acquired companies and the related values of net assets acquired and accounted for by the purchase method of accounting. Any goodwill acquired after October, 1970, is amortized on a straight-line basis over not more than 40 years.

The cost of patents, copyrights, and other intangible assets is amortized evenly over their estimated useful lives by charges against earnings. Most of these costs were incurred through the purchases of businesses.

Annually, the Audit Committee of the Board of Directors reviews goodwill and other intangibles. At its meeting on May 24, 1982, the Board of Directors confirmed that the remaining amounts of these assets have continuing value.

Honeywell, Inc.

Goodwill $102,000,000

Notes to financial statements:

Goodwill arising after October, 1970, is amortized over not more than a 40-year period. Goodwill arising before November, 1970, is not amortized unless there is evidence that its value has diminished.

McDonalds Corporation

Intangible assets, net $70,692,000

Notes to financial statements:

Set forth below is the composition of the
   intangible assets.

Unlimited-term franchise rights, not being amortized	$13,599,000
Other franchise rights	55,142,000
Other intangible assets	1,951,000
Intangible assets, net	$70,692,000

Concept Summary

ACCOUNTING TREATMENT REQUIRED FOR EXPENDITURES RELATED TO INTANGIBLES

Nature of Item	Accounting Treatment at Time of Acquisition	Accounting Treatment after Acquisition
Purchased, Specifically Identifiable (and not an R & D cost)	Record as asset, at cost.	Amortize.

Internally Developed, Specifically Identifiable (and not an R & D cost)	Record as asset, at cost (e.g., cost of registering an internally developed patent).	Amortize.
Purchased, Unidentifiable (and not an R & D cost)	Record as goodwill, excess of cost over fair value of identifiable net assets acquired.	Amortize.
Internally Developed, Unidentifiable	Expense as incurred.	—
Research and Development Costs	Expense as incurred.	—

Questions

Q–13–1 What are the characteristics of items classified as intangible assets?

Q–13–2 How are the characteristics of intangible assets similar to those of property, plant, and equipment? How are they dissimilar?

Q–13–3 Since they qualify as assets and lack bodily substance, why are long-term investments in stocks and bonds not included in the intangible assets section of a balance sheet?

Q–13–4 What is the difference between an identifiable intangible asset and an unidentifiable intangible asset?

Q–13–5 Under what circumstances is it acceptable to record goodwill?

Q–13–6 Over what period of time should an intangible asset be amortized?

Q–13–7 What method should be used to amortize intangible assets?

Q–13–8 What costs are normally included in the intangible asset, organization costs?

Q–13–9 Red Company acquired a trademark from Blue Company for $50,000 cash. How should Red Company account for the $50,000 cost of the trademark?

Q–13–10 Green Company incurred costs of $50,000 in developing and registering a trademark. How should Green Company account for the $50,000 cost of developing and registering the trademark?

Q–13–11 How is the cost of purchased goodwill determined?

Q–13–12 ABC Company's balance sheet included goodwill that resulted from the acquisition of the net assets of another enterprise. However, the notes to the financial statements indicate that the goodwill reflected on ABC's balance sheet is not being amortized. If you assume that the amounts involved are material, does the fact that ABC is not amortizing goodwill mean that its financial statements are not in accordance with generally accepted accounting principles? Explain.

Q–13–13 Corporation X acquired the net assets of Corporation Y at a cost less than the fair value of Y's identifiable net assets. What is the proper accounting treatment of this excess of the fair value of identifiable net assets acquired over cost?

Q–13–14 What was the FASB's underlying reasoning for its position that research and development costs should be expensed when incurred?

Q–13–15 Can a cost that qualifies as a research and development cost under FASB *Statement No. 2* be an element of factory overhead?

Q–13–16 Select the best answer for each of the following questions.

a) On January 1, 1972, an intangible asset with a 35-year estimated useful life was acquired. On January 1, 1977, a review was made of the estimated useful life, and it was determined that the intangible asset had an estimated useful life of 45 more years. As a result of the review

    (1) The original cost at January 1, 1972, should be amortized over a 50-year life.

    (2) The original cost at January 1, 1972, should be amortized over the remaining 30-year life.

    (3) The unamortized cost at January 1, 1977, should be amortized over a 40-year life.

    (4) The unamortized cost at January 1, 1977, should be amortized over a 35-year life.

b) On January 15, 1971, a corporation was granted a patent on a product. On January 2, 1980, to protect its patent, the corporation purchased a patent on a competing product that originally was issued on January 10, 1976. Because of its unique plant, the corporation does not feel the competing patent can be used in producing a product. The cost of the competing patent should be

    (1) Amortized over a maximum period of 17 years.

    (2) Amortized over a maximum period of 13 years.

    (3) Amortized over a maximum period of 8 years.

    (4) Expensed in 1980.

c) How should goodwill be written off?

    (1) As soon as possible to retained earnings.

    (2) By systematic charges to retained earnings over the period benefited, but not in excess of 40 years.

    (3) As soon as possible as a one-time charge to expense and reported as an extraordinary item.

    (4) By systematic charges to an operating expense over the period benefited, but not in excess of 40 years.

d) In a business combination, what is the appropriate method of accounting for an excess of fair value assigned to net assets over the cost paid for them?

    (1) Record as negative goodwill.

    (2) Record as additional paid-in capital from combination on the books of the combined company.

    (3) Proportionately reduce values assigned to nonmonetary assets and record any remaining excess as a deferred credit.

    (4) Proportionately reduce values assigned to noncurrent assets and record any remaining excess as a deferred credit.

e) Which of the following is *not* a consideration in determining the useful life of an intangible asset?

    (1) Legal, regulatory, or contractual provisions.

    (2) Provisions for renewal or extension.

    (3) Expected actions of competitors.

    (4) Initial cost.

(AICPA adapted)

Q–13–17 Select the best answer for each of the following questions.

a) Goodwill represents the excess of the cost of an acquired company over the

    (1) Sum of the fair values assigned to identifiable assets acquired less liabilities assumed.

(2) Sum of the fair values assigned to tangible assets acquired less liabilities assumed.

(3) Sum of the fair values assigned to intangible assets acquired less liabilities assumed.

(4) Book value of an acquired company.

b) Goodwill from a business combination

(1) Should be expensed in the year of acquisition.

(2) Is an asset that is *not* subject to amortization.

(3) Is an intangible asset.

(4) Occurs in a pooling of interests.

c) What is the proper time or time period over which to match the cost of an intangible asset with revenues if it is likely that the benefit of the asset will last for an indeterminate but very long period of time?

(1) Forty years.

(2) Fifty years.

(3) Immediately.

(4) At such time as diminution in value can be determined quantitatively.

d) In accordance with generally accepted accounting principles, which of the following methods of amortization normally is recommended for intangible assets?

(1) Sum-of-the-years'-digits.

(2) Straight-line.

(3) Units of production.

(4) Double-declining balance.

e) Which of the following should be expensed as incurred by the franchisee for a franchise with an estimated useful life of ten years?

(1) Amount paid to the franchisor for the franchise.

(2) Periodic payments to a company, other than the franchisor, for that company's franchise.

(3) Legal fees paid to the franchisee's lawyers to obtain the franchise.

(4) Periodic payments to the franchisor based on the franchisee's revenues.

(AICPA adapted)

Q–13–18 Select the best answer for each of the following questions.

a) How should research and development costs be accounted for according to an FASB *Statement?*

(1) Must be capitalized when incurred and then amortized over their estimated useful lives.

(2) Must be expensed in the period incurred unless contractually reimbursable.

(3) May be either capitalized or expensed when incurred, depending upon the facts of the situation.

(4) Must be expensed in the period incurred unless it can be clearly demonstrated that the expenditure will have significant future benefits.

b) Which of the following principles best describes the current method of accounting for research and development costs?

(1) Associating cause and effect.

(2) Systematic and rational allocation.

(3) Income tax minimization.

(4) Immediate recognition as an expense.

c) Which of the following is an activity that would be expensed currently as research and development costs?

(1) Adaptation of an existing capability to a particular requirement or customer's need as a part of continuing commercial activity.

(2) Legal work in connection with patent applications or litigation, and the sale or licensing of patents.

(3) Engineering follow-through in an early phase of commercial production.

(4) Testing in search for or evaluation of product or process alternatives.

d) Which of the following research- and development-related costs should be capitalized and amortized over current and future periods?

(1) Research and development general laboratory building.

(2) Inventory used for a specific research project.

(3) Administrative salaries allocated to research and development.

(4) Research findings purchased from another company to aid a particular research project currently in process.

e) If a company constructs a laboratory building to be used as a research and development facility, the cost of the laboratory building is matched against earnings as

(1) Research and development expense in the period(s) of construction.

(2) Depreciation deducted as part of research and development costs.

(3) Depreciation or immediate write-off depending on company policy.

(4) An expense at such time as productive research and development have been obtained from the facility.

(AICPA adapted)

Discussion Questions and Cases

D–13–1 The Thomas Company is in the process of developing a revolutionary new product. A new division of the company was formed to develop, manufacture, and market this new product. As of year-end (December 31, 1977) the new product has not been manufactured for resale; however, a prototype unit was built and is in operation.

Throughout 1977 the new division incurred certain costs. These costs included design and engineering studies, prototype manufacturing costs, administrative expenses (including salaries of administrative personnel), and market research costs. In addition, approximately $500,000 in equipment (estimated useful life of 10 years) was purchased for use in developing and manufacturing the new product. Approximately $200,000 of this equipment was built specifically for the design of the new product; the remaining $300,000 of equipment was used to manufacture the preproduction prototype and will be used to manufacture the new product once it is in commercial production.

Required:

1. What is the definition of *research* and of *development* as defined in *Statement of Financial Accounting Standards No. 2*?

2. Briefly indicate the practical and conceptual reasons for the conclusion reached by the FASB on accounting and reporting practices for research and development costs.

3. In accordance with *Statement of Financial Accounting Standards No. 2*, how should the various costs of Thomas described above be recorded on the financial statements for the year ended December 31, 1977?

(AICPA adapted)

D–13–2 The owners of a professional football team have announced plans to move the team and its headquarters from another city to Lubbock, Texas. To enhance interest in the team, the owners conducted a "name the mascot" contest in Lubbock at a cost of $100,000. The winning entry selected the name "Lubbock Wranglers." Soon after the Wranglers started their first season in Lubbock, the owners were served notice of a lawsuit filed against them by John Plainsman for infringement on his registered tradename. A search of the official records revealed that Plainsman had indeed properly registered the name Lubbock Wranglers for his local softball team. To expedite matters and to avoid unfavorable publicity, the owners of the professional football team settled out of court with Plainsman for $80,000. Under terms of the settlement, Plainsman transferred all rights to the tradename "Lubbock Wranglers" to the owners of the professional football team.

Required:
How should the owners of the professional football team account for the following:
    a) The $100,000 cost of the "name the mascot" contest?
    b) The $80,000 paid to Plainsman?

D–13–3 Elmo Company operates several plants at which limestone is processed into quicklime and hydrated lime. The Bland Plant, where most of the equipment was installed many years ago, continually deposits a dusty white substance over the surrounding countryside. Citing the unsanitary condition of the neighboring community of Adeltown, the pollution of the Adel River, and the high incidence of lung disease among workers at Bland, the state's pollution control agency has ordered the installation of air pollution control equipment. Also, the agency has assessed a substantial penalty, which will be used to clean up Adeltown. After considering the costs involved (which could not have been reasonably estimated prior to the agency's action), Elmo decides to comply with the agency's orders, the alternative being to cease operations at Bland at the end of the current fiscal year. The officers of Elmo agree that the air pollution control equipment should be capitalized and depreciated over its useful life, but they disagree over the period(s) to which the penalty should be charged.

Required:
Discuss the conceptual merits and reporting requirements of accounting for the penalty as a
    a) Charge to the current period.
    b) Correction of prior periods.
    c) Capitalizable item to be amortized over future periods.

                                                (AICPA adapted)

D–13–4 Accounting practitioners, accounting authors, and the courts have proposed various solutions to the problems of accounting in terms of historical cost for goodwill and similar intangibles.

Required:
1. In comparing the problems of accounting for goodwill and similar intangible assets to those of other plant assets:
    a) What problems are similar? Explain.
    b) What problms are different? Explain.
2. Without regard to current authoritative pronouncements, from a conceptual standpoint what are the possible accounting treatments subsequent to the date of acquisition for the cost of goodwill and similar intangible assets? Explain.
3. Under current authoritative pronouncements, what is the required accounting treatment subsequent to the date of acquisition for the cost of goodwill and similar intangible assets?

                                                (AICPA adapted)

Exercises

E–13–1 Midland Company purchased a patent on January 1, 1971, for $160,000. On that date the patent had an estimated remaining useful life of 10 years. On January 1, 1974, Midland spent $21,000 in a successful defense of a patent infringement suit brought against the company. On December 31, 1977, Midland sold the patent to Odessa Company for $87,000.

Required:
Prepare the entries necessary on Midland's books in 1977 related to the amortization and sale of the patent.

E–13–2 Evergreen Company purchased a patent on January 1, 1980, for $178,500. The patent was being amortized over its remaining legal life of 15 years expiring on January 1, 1995. During 1983 Evergreen determined that the economic benefits of the patent would not last longer than 10 years from the date of acquisition.

Required:
Calculate the amount to be charged to patent amortization expense in each of the years 1982 and 1983.

(AICPA adapted)

E–13–3 On January 1, 1982, Robert Harrison signed an agreement to operate as a franchisee of Perfect Pizza, Inc. for an initial franchise fee of $40,000. Of this amount, $15,000 was paid when the agreement was signed, and the balance is payable in five annual payments of $5,000 each beginning on January 1, 1983. The agreement provides that the down payment is not refundable and no future services are required of the franchisor. Harrison's credit rating indicates that he can borrow money at 12% for a loan of this type. Information on present and future value factors is as follows:

Present value of $1 at 12% for 5 periods	0.567
Future amount of $1 at 12% for 5 periods	1.762
Present value of an ordinary annuity of $1 at 12% for 5 periods	3.605

Required:
Prepare the entries necessary on Harrison's books in 1982 and 1983 to account for the initial franchise fee and related payments.

(AICPA adapted)

E–13–4 Barb Company has provided information on intangible assets as follows:
a) A patent was purchased from the Lou Company for $1,500,000 on January 1, 1977. Barb estimated the remaining useful life of the patent to be 10 years. The patent was carried on Lou's accounting records at a net book value of $1,250,000 when Lou sold it to Barb.
b) During 1978 a franchise was purchased from the Rink Company for $500,000. In addition, 5% of the revenue from the franchise must be paid to Rink. Revenue from the franchise for 1978 was $2,000,000. Barb estimates the useful life of the franchise to be 10 years and takes a full year's amortization in the year of purchase.
c) Barb incurred research and development costs in 1978 as follows:

Materials and equipment	$120,000
Personnel costs	140,000
Indirect costs	60,000
	$320,000

d) On January 1, 1978, Barb, based on new events that have occurred in the field, estimates that the remaining life of the patent purchased on January 1, 1977, is only five years from January 1, 1978.

Required:
1. Prepare a schedule showing the intangibles section of Barb's balance sheet at December 31, 1978. Show supporting computations in good form.
2. Prepare a schedule showing the income statement effect for the year ended December 31, 1978, as a result of the facts above. Show supporting computations in good form.

(AICPA adapted)

E–13–5 Freeman's records show the following balances at the end of the current year.

Unamortized initial franchise fee	$15,000
Organization costs	10,000
Bond sinking fund	60,000
Excess of cost over fair value of identifiable net assets of purchased subsidiary	45,000
Discount on bonds payable	12,000
Deposits with advertising agency which will be used to promote goodwill	8,000
Trademarks	16,000
Treasury stock	10,000
Accounts payable with debit balances	2,000
Patent (related to a machine used 50% in manufacturing and 50% in research and development)	22,000

Required:

Prepare the intangible assets section of Freeman's balance sheet at the end of the current year.

E-13-6 Howard Company incurred the following costs in 1977:

Materials used in research and development projects	$ 400,000
Equipment acquired that will have alternate future uses in future research and development projects	2,000,000
Depreciation for 1977 on equipment in item above	500,000
Personnel costs of persons involved in research and development projects	1,000,000
Consulting fees paid to outsiders for research and development projects	100,000
Indirect costs reasonably allocable to research and development projects	200,000
	$4,200,000

Required:

Prepare a schedule to show the research and development costs that Howard Company should recognize in its 1977 income statement.

(AICPA adapted)

E-13-7 Tech Products, Inc. incurred the following costs during the year ended December 31, 1978:

Laboratory research aimed at discovery of new knowledge	$ 7,000
Design, construction, and testing of preproduction prototypes	9,000
Design of tools, jigs, molds, and dies involving new technology	15,000
Quality control during commercial production, including routine testing of products	18,000

Required:
1. Which of the costs above should be classified and expensed as research and development costs in 1978?
2. How should the costs not included in the first item above be accounted for in 1978?

(AICPA adapted)

E–13–8 On January 1, 1982, Frontier Company acquired three machines, identified as A, B, and C. Each machine cost $30,000 and has an estimated life of three years with no residual value. Machine A was acquired for a specific research project and has no alternative use. Machine B is used on various research projects. Machine C is used 50% of the time in research and development activities and 50% in manufacturing. Frontier uses the straight-line depreciation method.

Required:
Based only on the information above, what is the amount of research and development cost that Frontier should report on its income statement for 1982?

E–13–9 On January 1, 1982, Diamond Company acquired a patent from Gold Company in exchange for land and $10,000 cash. At the time of the exchange the land had a book value of $40,000 and a fair value of $45,000. The patent has a remaining legal life of five years.

Required:
Prepare all entries necessary on Diamond's books in 1982 related to the patent under each of the following independent assumptions:

a) The patent relates to a process that will be used in a specific research and development project. The process, and thus the patent, has no alternative future use.
b) The patent relates to a process that will be used in various research and development projects.

E–13–10 The balance sheet of Bronco Company on January 1, 1977, is as follows:

Assets

Inventories	$260,000
Building (net of accumulated depreciation of $120,000)	180,000
Land	140,000
	$580,000

Liabilities and Partners' Equity

Liabilities	$ 80,000
Partners' equity:	
Rough, capital	250,000
Rider, capital	250,000
	$580,000

On January 1, 1977, Mustang Corporation purchased all of the assets and assumed all of the liabilities of Bronco Company by paying the partners, Rough and Rider, a total of $700,000 cash. On that date the fair market value of Bronco's inventories was $300,000. The fair market values of all other assets and liabilities of Bronco were equal to their book values.

Required:
Prepare the entry necessary on Mustang Corporation's books on January 1, 1977, to record the assets acquired and liabilities assumed from Bronco Company.

E–13–11 The owners of the Zoot Suit Clothing Store are contemplating selling the business to new interests. The cumulative earnings for the past five years amounted to $450,000, including extraordinary gains of $10,000. The annual earnings based on an aver-

age rate of return on investment for this industry would have been $76,000.
Required:
Calculate the amount of implied goodwill assuming excess earnings are to be capitalized at 10%.

(AICPA adapted)

E–13–12   The owners of Central Company are considering the acquisition of Western Company. Central's financial analysts determine that Western's identifiable net assets have a fair value of $300,000. They also estimate that Western's future annual earnings will be $48,000.
Required:
Compute the implied value of goodwill under each of the following independent assumptions:

a)   The estimated future annual earnings are expected to continue in perpetuity and are to be capitalized at 12%.

b)   The normal rate of return for this industry is 8%. Any excess earnings are expected to have a life of 5 years and are to be capitalized at 10%.

E–13–13   Select the best answer for each of the following questions.

a)   The general ledger of the Flint Corporation as of December 31, 1982, includes the following accounts:

Organization costs	$ 5,000
Deposits with advertising agency (will be used to promote goodwill)	8,000
Discount on bonds payable	15,000
Excess of cost over book value of net assets of acquired subsidiary	70,000
Trademarks	12,000

In the preparation of Flint's balance sheet as of December 31, 1982, what should be reported as total intangible assets?
  (1) $87,000.
  (2) $92,000.
  (3) $95,000.
  (4) $110,000.

b)   The Plaza Company was organized late in 1978 and began operations on January 1, 1979. Plaza is engaged in conducting market research studies on behalf of manufacturers. Before the start of operations the following costs were incurred:

Attorney's fees in connection with organization of Plaza	$ 4,000
Improvements to leased offices prior to occupancy	7,000
Meetings of incorporators, state filing fees, and other organization expenses	5,000
	$16,000

Plaza has elected to record amortization of organization costs over the maximum period allowable under generally accepted accounting principles. What is the amount of organization costs amortized for 1979?
  (1) $225.
  (2) $400.
  (3) $1,800.
  (4) $3,200.

c) In January, 1975, Tracy Corporation purchased a patent for a new consumer product for $180,000. At the time of purchase the patent was valid for 15 years. Because of the competitive nature of the product, however, the patent was estimated to have a useful life of only 10 years. During 1978 the product was permanently removed from the market under governmental order because of a potential health hazard present in the product. What amount should Tracy charge to expense during 1978, assuming amortization is recorded at the end of each year?

    (1) $12,000.
    (2) $18,000.
    (3) $126,000.
    (4) $144,000.

d) On January 1, 1982, Ulmer Corporation incurred organization costs of $12,000. For financial accounting purposes, Ulmer is amortizing these costs on the same basis as the maximum allowable for federal income tax purposes. What portion of the organization costs will Ulmer defer to years subsequent to 1982?

    (1) $0.
    (2) $2,400.
    (3) $9,600.
    (4) $12,000.

e) Howe Corporation bought a cola franchise from Pennington, Inc. on January 2, 1981, for $100,000. A highly regarded independent research company estimated that the remaining useful life of the franchise was 50 years. Its unamortized cost on Pennington's books at January 1, 1981, was $15,000. Howe has decided to write off the franchise over the longest possible period. How much should be amortized for the year ended December 31, 1981?

    (1) $375.
    (2) $2,000.
    (3) $2,500.
    (4) $15,000.

(AICPA adapted)

E–13–14 Select the best answer for each of the following questions.

    a) Sherwood Corporation incurred $68,000 of research and development costs in its laboratory to develop a patent which was granted on January 2, 1982. Legal fees and other costs associated with registration of the patent totaled $13,600. Sherwood estimates that the economic life of the patent will be 8 years. What amount should Sherwood charge to patent amortization expense for the year ended December 31, 1982?

    (1) $0.
    (2) $800.
    (3) $1,700.
    (4) $10,200.

    b) In 1975 the MSA Corporation incurred research and development costs as follows:

Materials and equipment	$100,000
Personnel	100,000
Indirect costs	50,000
	$250,000

These costs relate to a product that will be marketed in 1976. It is estimated that these costs will be recouped by December 31, 1979. What is the amount of research and development costs that should be charged to income in 1975?

(1) $0.
(2) $50,000.
(3) $200,000.
(4) $250,000.

c) In 1982 Murray Corporation developed a new product that will be marketed in 1983. In connection with the development of this product, the following costs were incurred in 1982:

Research and development departmental costs	$200,000
Materials and supplies consumed	50,000
Compensation paid to research consultants	60,000
	$310,000

It is anticipated that these costs will be recovered in 1985. What is the amount of research and development costs that Murray should record in 1982 as a charge to income?

(1) $0.
(2) $60,000.
(3) $250,000.
(4) $310,000.

d) During 1977 Traco Machine Company spent $176,000 on research and development costs for an invention. This invention was patented on January 2, 1978, at a nominal cost that was expensed in 1978. The patent had a legal life of 17 years and an estimated useful life of 8 years. In January 1982, Traco paid $16,000 for legal fees in a successful defense of the patent. What should amortization for 1982 be?

(1) $0.
(2) $1,231.
(3) $4,000.
(4) $26,000.

e) During 1982 Trencher, Inc. incurred research and development costs as follows:

Experimental and development costs of a new process patented in December 1982	$250,000
Testing for evaluation of new products	300,000
Modification of the formulation of a chemical product	150,000
Research and development costs reimbursable under a contract with Quality Chemicals Corporation	500,000

What amount should Trencher report as research and development expense in its income statement for the year ended December 31, 1982?

(1) $0.
(2) $450,000.
(3) $700,000.
(4) $950,000.

(AICPA adapted)

E–13–15 Select the best answer for each of the following questions.

a) On April 1, 1979, the Jack Company paid $800,000 for all the issued and outstanding common stock of Ann Corporation in a transaction properly accounted for as a purchase. The recorded assets and liabilities of Ann Corporation on April 1, 1979, are as follows:

Cash	$ 80,000
Inventory	240,000
Property and equipment (net of accumulated depreciation of $320,000)	480,000
Liabilities	(180,000)

On April 1, 1979, it was determined that Ann's inventory had a fair value of $190,000, and that the property and equipment (net) had a fair value of $560,000. What is the amount of goodwill resulting from the business combination?

   (1) $0.
   (2) $50,000.
   (3) $150,000.
   (4) $180,000.

b) On April 1, 1982, the Ash Company paid $400,000 for all the issued and outstanding common stock of Tray Corporation in a transaction properly accounted for as a purchase. The assets and liabilities of Tray Corporation on April 1, 1982, follow:

Cash	$ 40,000
Inventory	120,000
Property and equipment (net of accumulated depreciation of $160,000)	240,000
Liabilities	(90,000)

On April 1, 1982, it was determined that the inventory of Tray had a fair value of $95,000, and that the property and equipment (net) had a fair value of $280,000.

What should be the amount recorded as goodwill by Ash as a result of the business combination?

   (1) $0.
   (2) $25,000.
   (3) $75,000.
   (4) $90,000.

c) Meredith Company and Kyle Company were combined in a purchase transaction. Meredith was able to acquire Kyle at a bargain price. The sum of the market or appraised values of identifiable assets acquired less the fair value of liabilities assumed exceeded the cost to Meredith. After Meredith revalued noncurrent assets to zero there was still some negative goodwill. Proper accounting treatment by Meredith is to report the amount as

   (1) An extraordinary item.
   (2) Part of current income in the year of combination.
   (3) A deferred credit and to amortize it.
   (4) Paid-in capital.

d) During 1982 the Henderson Company purchased the net assets of John Corporation for $800,000. On the date of the transaction, John had no long-term investments in marketable securities and had $100,000 of liabilities. The fair value of John's assets when acquired were as follows:

Current assets	$ 400,000
Noncurrent assets	600,000
	$1,000,000

How should the $100,000 difference between the fair value of the net assets acquired ($900,000) and the cost ($800,000) be accounted for by Henderson?

(1) The $100,000 difference should be credited to retained earnings.

(2) The noncurrent assets should be recorded at $500,000.

(3) The current assets should be recorded at $360,000, and the noncurrent assets should be recorded at $540,000.

(4) A deferred credit of $100,000 should be set up and then amortized to income over a period not to exceed 40 years.

(AICPA adapted)

Problems

P–13–1   Avery Company purchased a patent on January 1, 1978, for $60,000. On that date the patent had a remaining legal life of 16 years but a remaining estimated economic life of only 10 years. On July 1, 1979, Avery spent $20,400 in a successful defense against a patent infringement suit brought against the company. On January 1, 1981, Avery revised its estimate of the patent's useful life; as of this date the patent is estimated to have a remaining useful life of 5 years. On December 31, 1982, management concludes that the patent is now worthless because of a new process developed by a competitor during the latter part of December 1982.

Required:

Prepare the entries related to the patent on Avery's books for each of the years 1978–1982.

P–13–2   Listed below are some of the transactions that Imke Company entered into during the first week of January, 1982, its first week of operations.

a)   Purchased a patent from Zeek Company for $28,000. The patent had been issued to Zeek on January 1, 1979.

b)   Incurred legal fees of $10,000 related to organizing the company.

c)   Incurred legal fees of $7,000 in successfully defending the company against a patent infringement suit (related to the patent purchased in a) above).

d)   Made a donation of $20,000 to a local university for which the school's trustees agreed to display the company's name for two years on a sign located immediately below each scoreboard in the football stadium.

e)   Incurred the following costs in developing a product that will be patented:

Materials and supplies used	$10,000
Design and construction of preproduction model	14,000
Testing of preproduction model	3,000

f)   Incurred legal fees of $5,100 to register patent on product developed in e) above.

g)   Acquired a franchise giving Imke the exclusive right to sell Zigwigs in a specified geographical region. Imke agreed to pay $40,000 as the initial franchise fee plus 1% of gross sales. The franchise has an unlimited life as long as Imke does not violate the terms of the franchise. Currently, there are no indications that Imke will violate any of the terms of the franchise.

h)   Purchased a tradename for $15,000.

i)   Paid Chisholm Company $10,000 for research activities conducted for Imke.

Required:

1.   Prepare journal entries to record the transactions above.

2.   Prepare the adjusting entries necessary at December 31, 1982. All intangible assets should be amortized over the maximum period allowed.

P–13–3   Coronado Corporation just completed its first year of operations. The company's accountant, who admits to being a little "rusty" regarding current authoritative accounting pronouncements, requests that you review his work and make recommendations as to any correcting entries that you believe are necessary. In your review you determine that the accountant, among other things, recorded numerous transactions in a single account labeled intangible assets. The entries in this account during this first year, 1981, were as follows:

Debit entries:

Jan.	2	Incorporation fees	$10,000
	3	Legal fees related to organizing the company	6,000
Feb.	1	Payment to owners of local professional baseball team for displaying the company's ad on their electronic scoreboard—payment covers 19X1 and 19X2	25,000
	1	Payment to Monterey Company, a local firm that is going out of business, for the tradename "Inca Ink"	5,000
April	1	Purchase of patent (patent was originally registered on January 1, 19X1)	33,500
June	1	Internally developed goodwill (credit was to retained earnings)	40,000
	15	Payment to Aztec Company for research and development work conducted for Coronado	8,000
July	1	Purchased building in which to conduct research and development activities (building has a 10-year life with no residual value)	80,000
	2	Cost of market survey conducted to assess customers' reactions to one of Coronado's new products	4,000
	3	Materials purchased for use on various research and development projects (of these, materials costing $12,000 are still on hand at year-end)	30,000
Dec. 31		Transfer from salaries expense account for salaries of research and development personnel	42,000
		Total debits	$283,500

Credit entries:

July 15	Refund from supplier for damaged materials returned (materials were purchased on July 3, 1981)	3,500
December 31, 1981 balance		$280,000

Required:

1. Prepare the necessary correcting and adjusting entries related to the information presented in the intangible assets account. Your entries should eliminate the intangible assets account and should set up appropriately labeled individual accounts with their December 31, 1981, adjusted balances. (Assume that closing entries have not been recorded for 1981.) The patent should be amortized over its remaining legal life. All other intangible assets should be amortized over the maximum period allowed.

2. Prepare the intangible assets section of Coronado Corporation's balance sheet at December 31, 1981.

P–13–4   Newpont Corporation is a large manufacturer of electronic calculators. To enhance its competitive edge, management decided to create a separate research and development (R & D) division within the company. The accountant for Newpont identified the following costs related to the R & D division's activities during 1977, the division's first year of operations.

a) A new building was constructed in January at a cost of $2,000,000. The building has an estimated life of 20 years with no residual value. The R & D division eventually will occupy all of the building, but will occupy only half of it during the next five years; the marketing division will use the other half during this five-year period.

Dep   50,000

b) Personnel costs are as follows:

Salary of director of R & D division (all of the director's time is devoted to the R & D division)	$ 80,000	*80,000*
Salaries of full-time research scientists	250,000	*250,000*
Total salaries of clerical staff (the clerical staff spends approximately 60% of its time on work related to the R & D division and 40% on work related to the marketing division)	90,000	*54,000*
Allocated share of corporate officers' salaries (the accountant decided that 10% of the $250,000 salary of the president of Newpont should be allocated to the R & D division)	25,000	*25,000*
	$445,000	

c) Materials costing $100,000 were issued during the year by Newpont's central warehouse to the R & D division. As of the end of the year, $40,000 of these materials have not been used. Of these materials still on hand, one particular item with a cost of $5,000 was acquired for a specific research project and has no alternative use.

65,000

d) New equipment was acquired for the R & D division at a total cost of $150,000. Except for one special-ordered item, each equipment item has an estimated life of 10 years with no residual value. The special-ordered equipment item, which cost $12,000, was acquired for use on a specific research project and has no alternative use or residual value; the research project is expected to require three years to complete.

13,800

12,000

e) On January 1, 1977, Newpont purchased a patent for $30,000. On that date the patent had a remaining legal life of 15 years. The patent relates to a process which the R & D division wants to use in their research activities. Newpont's research scientists estimate that because of obsolescence the patented process will be used for only three more years after 1977.

30,000

f) Newpont allocates its utilities cost among the various departments and divisions on the basis of relative square-feet of floor space occupied. On this basis the R & D division was allocated 3% of the total utilities cost of $500,000 for 1977. (You determined that the allocation basis is reasonable.)

15,000

You determined that all of the R & D division's activities during 1977 qualify under FASB *Statement No. 2* as research and development activities. You also determined that Newpont engaged in no research and development activities other than those conducted by the R & D division.

Required:

Prepare a schedule to determine the amount Newpont should report as research and development costs in its 1977 income statement.

P–13–5 Presented below are selected transactions of Moores Company during its first three years of operations.

1/1/81:   Purchased a patent (patent #105A) for $42,000. The patent has a remaining legal life of 12 years.

1/3/81:   Paid legal fees of $15,000 related to the organization of the company.

7/1/81:   Purchased a trademark for $28,000.

3/31/82:   Incurred the following costs in developing a process that will be utilized in the company's manufacturing operations:

Materials used	$30,000
Engineering costs	20,000
	$50,000

4/1/82:   Incurred legal fees of $6,120 for registration of a patent (patent #108C) on the new process developed on 3/31/82.

12/31/82: Purchased a franchise for $80,000. The franchise has an unlimited life.

7/4/83:   Incurred costs of $2,000 for entertainment of potential new customers on a riverboat cruise.

10/1/83:   Sold patent #105A for $50,000.

Required:

1. Prepare the entries to record Moores's transactions during 1981–1983.

2. Prepare the adjusting entries necessary at the end of each of the years 1981–1983. All patents are to be amortized over their legal lives. All other intangible assets are to be amortized over 10 years.

P–13–6 The balance sheet of Alpha Company at December 31, 1981, appeared as follows:

ALPHA COMPANY
Balance Sheet
December 31, 1981

Cash		$ 400,000
Accounts receivable	$120,000	
Less: Allowance for doubtful accounts	10,000	110,000
Inventories		300,000
Prepaid expenses		15,000
Total current assets		$825,000
Land		240,000
Building	700,000	
Less: Accumulated depreciation	280,000	420,000
		$1,485,000
Current liabilities		$ 380,000
Common stock, $10 par		500,000
Retained earnings		605,000
		$1,485,000

At the start of business on January 1, 1982, Alpha Company purchased 100% of the net assets of Beta Company for $227,000. Beta Company's balance sheet at December 31, 1981, showed the following:

BETA COMPANY
Balance Sheet
December 31, 1981

Accounts receivable	$ 40,000
Inventories	70,000

Land	35,000
Patent	4,000
	$147,000
Liabilities	$ -0-
Partners' equity	147,000
	$147,000

Alpha will record the purchase of the net assets of Beta by crediting cash for the $227,000 payment to the owners of Beta and by debiting each individual asset acquired (including goodwill) for the appropriate amount.

Alpha determined that the fair values of Beta's identifiable assets at January 1, 1982, were as follows:

Accounts receivable	
(all deemed to be collectible)	$ 40,000
Inventories	80,000
Land	43,000
Patent (10-year remaining life)	24,000
	$187,000

Required:

1. Prepare a balance sheet for Alpha Company at January 1, 1982, immediately after the acquisition of the net assets of Beta Company.

2. Prepare the adjusting entries at December 31, 1982, to record the amortization of Alpha's intangible assets.

P–13–7 Kindred Corporation is considering the acquisition of Witman Company. Kindred has engaged you as a financial consultant to advise the company in negotiations regarding the purchase price to offer Witman. Your analysis of Witman reveals the following:

Fair value of Witman's identifiable net assets	$400,000
Projected future annual earnings	50,000
Normal rate of return on net assets, exclusive	
of goodwill, in this industry	10%

Required:

Compute the implied purchase price of Witman and the related implied goodwill under each of the following independent assumptions.

    a) Projected future annual earnings will continue in perpetuity and should be capitalized at the normal rate of return.

    b) Goodwill is equal to eight years' excess earnings.

    c) Goodwill is equal to projected excess annual earnings capitalized at 20%.

    d) Goodwill is equal to projected excess annual earnings capitalized at 15%.

P–13–8 Foster Company was incorporated on Janaury 3, 1981. The corporation's financial statements for its first year's operations were not examined by a CPA. You have been engaged to examine the financial statements for the year ended December 31, 1982, and your examination is substantially completed. The corporation's trial balance appears below.

FOSTER COMPANY
Trial Balance
December 31, 1982

	Debits	Credits
Cash	$ 11,000	
Accounts receivable	42,500	
Allowance for doubtful accounts		$ 500
Inventories	64,500	
Machinery	75,000	
Equipment	29,000	
Accumulated depreciation		10,000
Patents	85,000	
Prepaid expenses	10,500	
Organization costs	29,000	
Goodwill	24,000	
Licensing agreement no. 1	50,000	
Licensing agreement no. 2	49,000	
Accounts payable		147,500
Unearned revenue		12,500
Capital stock		300,000
Retained earnings, 1/1/1982	27,000	
Sales		668,500
Cost of goods sold	454,000	
Selling and general expenses	173,000	
Interest expense	3,500	
Extraordinary losses	12,000	
	$1,139,000	$1,139,000

The following information relates to accounts that may yet require adjustment.

a)   Patents for Foster's manufacturing process were acquired on January 2, 1982, at a cost of $68,000. An additional $17,000 was spent in December, 1982, to improve machinery covered by the patents and charged to the patents account. Depreciation on fixed assets has been properly recorded for 1982 in accordance with Foster's practice, which provides a full year's depreciation for property on hand June 30 and no depreciation otherwise. Foster uses the straight-line method for all depreciation and amortization and amortizes its patents over their legal life.

b)   On January 3, 1981, Foster purchased licensing agreement no. 1, which was believed to have an unlimited useful life. The balance in the licensing agreement no. 1 account includes its purchase price of $48,000 and expenses of $2,000 related to the acquisition. On January 1, 1982, Foster purchased licensing agreement no. 2, which has a life expectancy of 10 years. The balance in the licensing agreement no. 2 account includes its $48,000 purchase price and $2,000 in acquisition expenses, but it has been reduced by a credit of $1,000 for the advance collection of 1983 revenue from the agreement. In late December, 1981, an explosion caused a permanent 60% reduction in the expected revenue-producing value of licensing agreement no. 1, and in January, 1983, a flood caused additional damage that rendered the agreement worthless.

c)   The balance in the goodwill account includes (1) $8,000 paid December 30, 1981, for an advertising program it is estimated will assist in increasing Foster's sales over a period of four years following the disbursement, and (2) legal expenses of $16,000 incurred for Foster's incorporation on Janaury 3, 1981.

d)   The balance in the organization costs account properly includes costs incurred during the organizational period. The corporation has exercised its option to amortize organization costs over a 60-month period for federal income tax purposes and wishes to amortize these for accounting purposes on the same basis. (No amortization has been recorded.)

Required:

Prepare a worksheet to adjust accounts that require adjustments. The worksheet should contain debit and credit columns for (1) trial balance, (2) adjustment, (3) income statement, and (4) balance sheet. A separate account should be used for the accumulation of each type of amortization. Any correction of 1981 earnings should be debited or credited, as appropriate, directly to the 1/1/1982 retained earnings balance. Formal adjusting entries and financial statements are not required. (*Hint:* Make sure that licensing agreement no. 1 is amortized over the maximum life required in APB *Opinion No. 17* before the explosion damage is determined.)

(AICPA adapted)

P–13–9 Davis Company owns 100% of the common stock of Clancy Company. Davis has been experiencing cash flow problems. To obtain badly needed working capital, on January 1, 1983, Davis decides to sell all of the net assets of Clancy Company to Stockton Company for $270,000. The book and fair value of Clancy's assets and liabilities on January 1, 1983, are as follows:

	Book Value	Fair Value
Receivables	$ 30,000	$ 30,000
Inventories	80,000	80,000
Plant assets (net)	200,000	200,000
	$310,000	$310,000
Liabilities	$ –0–	$ –0–

Required:

Prepare the entry on Stockton Company's books to record the purchase of the net assets of Clancy Company.

P–13–10 Needles Company wants to diversify its operations. Management has decided that the best approach currently is to purchase an existing company. After an intensive search, management decides that Williams Company is the best candidate available for acquisition. Williams reported net income in each of the past five years as follows:

Year	Net Income
1978	$60,000
1979	54,000 + 10,000
1980	65,000
1981	62,000 – 4,000
1982	66,000

Your investigation of the information related to Williams reveals the following:

a) The 1979 net income includes an extraordinary loss (net of tax) of $10,000.

b) The 1981 net income includes an extraordinary gain (net of tax) of $4,000.

c) On January 1, 1983, the fair value of Williams's identifiable net assets is $500,000.

d) The normal rate of return on identifiable net assets is 10% for the industry in which Williams operates.

e) The appropriate capitalization rate for any excess earnings is 15%.

Required:
1. Compute the implied value of Williams Company on January 1, 1983, if estimated future annual earnings are based on average annual earnings of the past five years and excess earnings are expected to last five more years. (For simplicity, assume future earnings will occur at the end of the respective years.)
2. Compute the implied value of Williams Company on January 1, 1983, if estimated future annual earnings are based on average annual earnings of the past five years and excess earnings are expected to last in perpetuity.
3. Assume that after lengthy negotiations Williams accepts an offer from Needles in the amount of $560,000. What is the amount of goodwill that Needles should record on January 1, 1983, related to the purchase of the net assets of Williams?

P–13–11 Strong Company incurred the following costs during the year ended December 31, 1982:

a) Cost of routine, ongoing efforts to improve the quality of one of its existing products	$ 3,000
b) Cost of modifying the design of one of its existing products	7,000
c) Cost of constructing a pilot plant that is not of a scale economically feasible for commercial production	30,000
d) Cost of designing a new product (the product will be marketed next year)	4,500
e) Routine design of new molds and jigs	1,200
f) Attorney's fees incurred in connection with the registration of a patent on a new product developed this year	6,300
g) Cost of constructing and testing a preproduction model of a new product	1,600
h) Attorney's fees incurred in connection with a successful defense of the company in a patent infringement case (the patent relates to a new product that is being marketed this year for the first time	3,800
i) Cost of research and development activities conducted by Strong Company for Johnson Company under a contractual arrangement	12,000
j) Cost of research and development activities conducted by Jones Company for Strong Company under a contractual arrangement	8,000
k) Cost of developing a new computer software package that will be offered for sale	2,400
l) Cost of developing a new computerized payroll system for Strong's own use	1,900

Required:
Prepare a schedule to show which of the costs listed above Strong Company should report as research and development costs in its 1982 income statement.

14

Current Liabilities

Accounting in the News

Using short-term debt as a method of long-term financing can be costly and risky. As interest rates have risen and as long-term debt has dried up, many corporations have been forced to turn to short-term borrowings to meet their capital needs. The following excerpt from the *Wall Street Journal* illustrates that the result can be a decrease in a firm's credit rating and an even further increase in its interest costs.

Getting hooked on short-term debt has made U.S. corporations more vulnerable to recession than at any time since the 1930s.

That's the view of many bankers and financial analysts. Persistent high interest rates have discouraged long-term borrowing and lending and have addicted companies to short-term debt. That debt has swollen the current-liability line on their balance sheets to the point that their credit standings are endangered. Short-term borrowings, those generally due in a year or less, amounted to more than 46% of total corporate debt outstanding in the second quarter, by some estimates, up from less than 40% in 1977 and 33% in 1962.

In prosperous times with earnings on the rise, that would create no worry. But a recession could sharply reduce earnings, if it's not doing so already, and leave many companies in shaky shape. "It isn't a very healthy situation," says George Poliszczuk, a vice president of Pittsburgh's Mellon Bank. "A lot of companies out there are going to experience difficulties" in meeting their debt payments, he says.

"There's a growing potential for severe financial problems and perhaps even widespread bankruptcies," agrees David Jones, an economist for Aubrey G. Lanston & Co., a New York securities firm.*

The subject of this chapter, current liabilities, introduces you to the accounting issues related to short-term debt and to other current liabilities.

*Edward P Foldessy, "Companies Facing Severe Problems Because of Rising Short-Term Debt," *Wall Street Journal*, October 26, 1981, p. 29. Reprinted by permission of The Wall Street Journal, © Dow Jones & Company, Inc. 1982. All Rights Reserved.

In recent years, issues related to the determination and recognition of liabilities have received increased emphasis. Concerns with "off balance sheet financing," unrecorded pension liabilities, callable preferred stock, and contingent liabilities have focused considerable attention on the GAAP related to liabilities. This chapter discusses the generally accepted accounting principles and the detailed accounting for current liabilities. Long-term liabilities, income tax issues, pensions, and leases are presented in Chapters 15 through 18 respectively.

Definition of Liabilities

As part of its conceptual framework project, the FASB has attempted to develop meaningful definitions of the elements of financial statements. In *Statement of Financial Accounting Concepts No. 3*, "Elements of Financial Statements of Business Enterprises," the FASB defines liabilities as "probable future sacrifices of economic benefits arising from present obligations of a particular entity to transfer assets or provide services to other entities in the future as a result of past transactions or events."[1] In this Statement the Board also describes the three essential characteristics of a liability:

1. There is a present duty or responsibility to one or more entities that requires settlement by a probable future transfer or use of assets at a specified or determinable date, at the occurrence of a specified event, or on demand.
2. The enterprise has little or no discretion to avoid the future sacrifice.
3. The transaction or event has already happened.[2]

For a liability to be recognized, the recipient of the transferred assets does not have to be known. As long as the payment or the transfer of assets to settle the obligation is probable, the identity of the actual recipient can be unknown before the time of settlement to the enterprise incurring the liability. For example, when an enterprise guarantees or warrants a product, a liability exists even though the actual individual or enterprise that ultimately will make a claim against the guarantor is not known presently.

As long as the future transfer of cash or other assets is probable, the existence of a legally enforceable claim is not a prerequisite for an obligation to qualify as a liability. Liabilities often result from equitable or constructive obligations, and although they lack legal sanctions, these liabilities are binding because of social or moral sanctions or customs. For example, there is a question about whether future payments under lease agreements represent legally enforceable claims against the lessee. These payments are considered equitable or constructive obligations and are recognized under the criteria of SFAC No. 3.

---

[1] "Elements of Financial Statements of Business Enterprises," *Statement of Financial Accounting Concept No. 3* (Stamford, Conn.: FASB, 1980), par. 28.

[2] Ibid., par. 29. This definition is considerably different from that in *APB Statement No. 4*, "Basic Concepts and Accounting Principles Underlying Financial Statements of Business Enterprises." In this Statement the APB defines liabilities as economic obligations of an enterprise that are recognized and measured in conformity with generally accepted accounting principles. Liabilities also include certain deferred credits that are not obligations, but are recognized and measured in conformity with generally accepted accounting principles. This traditional definition is rather circular and views liabilities as arising from accounting procedures; it has little conceptual merit.

Finally, in order to be considered a liability, an event or transaction must have occurred already. This means that only present, not future, obligations represent liabilities of a particular enterprise. For example, a mere exchange of future promises of performance between two enterprises does not result in the recognition of a liability or of the corresponding asset. For example the signing of a labor contract between management and labor does not cause the enterprise to recognize a liability. The liability is recognized only when the employees perform services for the enterprise and have not been compensated.

Classification of Liabilities

For financial statement purposes liabilities are classified as either current or noncurrent. **Current liabilities** consist of those obligations "that are scheduled to mature within one year after the date of an enterprise's balance sheet or . . . within an enterprise's operating cycle that is longer than one year."[3] Generally, these liabilities require the use of existing resources that are classified as current assets or require the creation of new current liabilities. As with the definition of current assets, the operating cycle is an important concept. This cycle, which was explained in Chapter 4, is the length of time it takes to purchase or manufacture the goods that are held for resale and to turn these goods into receivables and then ultimately cash. Depending upon the particular industry, an enterprise may have several operating cycles within one year or may have one operating cycle extending several years. For example, a firm in the heavy construction industry may have an operating cycle that lasts several years, whereas a supermarket will have several operating cycles within one year. Current liabilities normally include such accounts as current maturities of long-term debt, short-term notes payable, accounts payable, taxes payable, and other accrued expenses.

Noncurrent liabilities, or **long-term debts,** are those liabilities that will not be satisfied within one year or within the operating cycle. Included in this category are mortgages payable, bonds payable, and lease obligations. The portion of these long-term liabilities due within one year, however, would be classified as current liabilities.

Valuation of Current Liabilities

Since most current liabilities are payable within a relatively short period of time, they are recorded at their face value—that is, the amount ultimately needed to discharge the liability. No recognition is given to the fact that the present value of these outlays discounted at an appropriate interest rate would be less. The difference between the face value and the present value is usually immaterial, and as a result, current liabilities are recorded at their face value. In fact, APB *Opinion No. 21*, which relates to the valuation of non-interest bearing payables and receivables, does not apply to payables resulting from transactions with customers or suppliers in the normal course of business that are due in customary trade

---

[3]"Classification of Short-term Obligations Expected to be Refinanced," *Statement of Accounting Standards No. 6* (Stamford, Conn.: FASB, 1979), par. 2.

terms not exceeding approximately one year.[4] However, non-interest bearing notes payable other than those described above should not be recorded at their face value. For these notes payable an appropriate interest rate should be imputed. The proper procedures for valuing these types of notes are discussed in Chapter 15.

Determination and Measurement of Current Liabilities

For purposes of determining their existence and measurement, liabilities are often classified as those:

1. That are definitely determinable in amount.
2. That represent collection for third parties and payrolls.
3. Liabilities conditioned on operations.
4. That are contingent upon future events.
5. That are deposits and advances from customers.
6. That are executory contracts.

Each of these categories is discussed in detail in the following sections.

Liabilities Definitely Determinable in Amount

Liabilities included in this category are definite in amount—that is, the actual amount of the liability is known at the time it is incurred. In some cases these liabilities, such as trade notes payable, bank notes and loans payable, and current maturities of long-term debt, are interest-bearing and have definite payment dates. In other cases liabilities, such as accounts payable to vendors and suppliers, are non-interest bearing and have payment dates that are at the discretion of the enterprise. In any event, the liabilities in this category have fixed payment terms and result from past transactions from which the enterprise has received benefits already; thus, they clearly meet the recognition criteria set forth in SFAC No. 3.

Accounts Payable

Accounts payable represent monies owed to the enterprise's suppliers or vendors for the purchase of goods and services. Most purchases take place on credit, and the accrual basis of accounting requires the recording of the liability when the title passes for assets purchased or when services are received. Although payment terms vary, usually full payment is due within 30 days. Cash discounts (e.g., 2/10, n/30) are a common practice in many industries.

There are few measurement problems associated with accounts payable. The amount and other payment terms are known with certainty. Cash discounts must

[4]"Interest on Receivables and Payables," *Opinions of the Accounting Principles Board No. 21* (New York: AICPA, 1971), par. 3.

be accounted for; alternative accounting treatments are discussed in Chapter 8. The significant accounting problem associated with accounts payable is determining their existence and insuring that they are recorded in the proper accounting period. Failure to record these liabilities, or failure to apply proper cutoff procedures, will result in the misstatement of the financial statements. For example, the inclusion of the cost of an item in ending inventory for which no corresponding purchase entry has been recorded will cause both cost of goods sold and total liabilities to be understated.

Trade Notes Payable

Trade notes payable are written obligations to the enterprise's suppliers and vendors. In some industries it is common to insist on trade notes payable rather than on accounts payable for inventory purchases. In other instances a particular firm's credit rating may preclude it from purchasing goods and services on open account. Trade notes payable can result also from the purchase of equipment or other personal property in which the payment terms are normally longer than is customary for an open account payable. These notes are generally interest-bearing, and the proper amount of interest expense must be accrued at the balance sheet date.

Short-Term Notes Payable

Short-term notes payable arise from cash borrowings from banks or other financial institutions. These notes may be secured partially or fully by the enterprise's assets. Notes payable have stated payment dates and are generally interest bearing. Measurement problems result when these notes are discounted at a financial institution and the cash proceeds that a firm receives are less than the face value of the note. For example, assume the Gernon Corporation borrows $50,000 by discounting a one-year note payable at the Toledo National Bank. Since the stated discount rate is 12%, the company only receives $44,000, or $50,000 less the discount of $6,000 ($50,000 × 0.12). However, 12% does not represent the true interest rate because the Gernon Corporation received proceeds of $44,000 and only has benefit of that amount for twelve months. The effective annual interest is 13.6% ($6,000 ÷ $44,000). This note could be recorded in the following manner:

Cash	44,000	
Discount on notes payable	6,000	
Notes payable		50,000

In the liability section of the balance sheet, the discount on notes payable is an offset to the note payable. The discount can be amortized monthly, or when financial statements are prepared. In this example, the monthly amortization would be $500 ($6,000 ÷ 12), and the appropriate entry would be as follows:

Interest expense	500	
Discount on notes payable		500

Alternatively, the money could have been borrowed through a type of loan that is not discounted. The discounted note frequently is referred to as a "time note" whereas a nondiscounted note is usually referred to as a "demand note." With a **time note,** the bank cannot demand payment before the due date because the interest on the note is considered to be prepaid. In the case of a **demand note,** the interest is not paid until the loan is paid or due. Since interest is not prepaid on a demand note, the note could be called for payment before the due date. With a demand note, the face value of the loan is received on the loan date. Using the previous example, if the note were a demand note, Gernon Corporation would receive $50,000 cash instead of the $44,000 it received under the time note. On the due date Gernon would repay the principal of $50,000 plus the $6,000 interest. The entries using a demand note are as follows:

The borrowing date:		
Cash	50,000	
Notes payable		50,000
Monthly interest accrual:		
Interest expense	500	
Interest payable on notes		500
The due date (including last accrual):		
Interest expense	500	
Interest payable on notes		500
Interest payable on Notes	6,000	
Note payable	50,000	
Cash		56,000

With the demand note, the effective interest cost is the same as the stated interest rate, or 12% ($6,000 ÷ $50,000). Banks prefer to loan money on a time note rather than on a demand note because the effective rate of interest earned is higher (13.6% versus 12% in the above example).

Current Maturities of Long-Term Debt

Current maturities of long-term debt represent those portions of long-term liabilities that are payable within one year of the balance sheet date and so are classified as current liabilities. As an example, the next 12 payments due on a 30-year mortgage would be classified as a current liability. The remaining portion would be considered a long-term liability. However, if the current maturity of the long-term debt is to be liquidated by noncurrent assets accumulated for this purpose, the liability should not be classified as current, since it does not require the use of assets classified as current. This would occur when the current portion of long-term debt is to be retired from a sinking fund that is classified as a noncurrent investment. Another example is when short-term obligations are to be refinanced.

Short-Term Obligations to Be Refinanced

Short-term obligations are classified as current liabilities because their liquidation will require the use of working capital during the coming year or operating cycle. In some situations, however, the enterprise may intend to refinance these obligations on a long-term basis. This decision would be based on such factors as the company's need for working capital, interest rates, and the economic environment. This refinancing could occur by replacing the short-term debt with either (1) long-term debt, (2) a series of short-term obligations with due dates extending beyond one year or the operating cycle, or (3) equity securities. Commercial paper, construction loans, and current maturities of long-term debt are examples of short-term obligations that may be refinanced on a long-term basis.

Since short-term obligations that are expected to be refinanced on a long-term basis will not require the immediate use of working capital during the coming year or operating cycle, the question arises as to how these obligations should be classified on the balance sheet. This is an important question because the classification of these obligations will affect such items as the computation of net working capital and the current ratio. For example, if these obligations were classified as current, the company's working capital and current ratio would decrease. This could affect adversely the company's credit rating and could increase its interest costs.

Before the issuance of any official pronouncements, these liabilities were shown in balance sheets either as current liabilities or as a separate class of liabilities distinct from both current and long-term liabilities. *ARB No. 43* supported the classification of "contractual obligation falling due at an early date which is expected to be refunded"[5] as noncurrent liabilities. However, the meaning of "expected to be refunded" was subject to various interpretations. In some situations an enterprise's intent and its prior ability to refinance were considered important criteria. In other situations the firm's future ability to refinance, as evidenced by an agreement for long-term financing, was considered important in determining the correct classification of these items.

The SEC became concerned about the various ways these liabilities were being classified. In 1973 the Commission issued *ASR No. 143*, which required commercial paper and other short-term obligations to be classified as current liabilities unless the following three specific conditions were met: (1) a noncancelable binding agreement to refinance the short-term debt exists; (2) the refinancing would extend the maturity date beyond one year; and (3) it is the borrower's intention to exercise this right.

Concerned that the SEC pronouncement was at variance with criteria for current liability classification as stated in *ARB No. 43*, the FASB decided to consider the issue of refinancing short-term debt. The result was *Statement No. 6*, "Classification of Short-Term Obligations Expected to be Refinanced." The State-

[5] Committee on Accounting Procedure, American Institute of Certified Public Accountants, *Accounting Research Bulletin No. 43* (New York: AICPA, 1953), Chapter 3A, par. 8.

ment notes that short-term obligations can be excluded from the current liabilities section of the balance sheet only if both of the following criteria are met:

1. The enterprise intends to refinance the obligations on a long-term basis.
2. The enterprise has the ability to consummate the refinancing and this ability is demonstrated by the following:
   a) The issuance of long-term debt or equity securities after the balance sheet date but before the balance sheet is issued, or
   b) A financing agreement that clearly permits the enterprise to refinance the short-term obligation on a long-term basis.[6]

If the refinancing occurs through the issuance of long-term obligations or of equity securities after the balance sheet date but before the balance sheet is actually issued, the amount to be excluded from the current liability section cannot exceed the proceeds from the new obligation or equity securities. For example, assume the Dorsey Corporation has $5,000,000 of current maturities of long-term debt that it intends to refinance partially through the issuance of $4,000,000 additional long-term debt. If this post-balance sheet date refinancing occurs before the issuance of the balance sheet, the Dorsey Corporation must reclassify only $4,000,000 of the current liability as noncurrent.

If refinancing is to be accomplished through a financing agreement, each of the following conditions must be met:

1. The agreement is essentially noncancelable and cannot expire within one year of the balance sheet date, or within the operating cycle if it is longer.
2. No violation of any provision of the agreement exists as of the balance sheet date. Also, there is no available information indicating that a violation has occurred after the balance sheet date but before the issuance of the balance sheet. If a violation exists, a waiver has been obtained.
3. The lender is capable of honoring the agreement.

The amount to be reclassified as a long-term liability cannot exceed the amount available under the refinancing agreement. If there are any restrictions on the funds obtainable under the agreement, the amounts reclassified as noncurrent must be reduced correspondingly. In some financing agreements the actual amounts available will fluctuate, depending upon the needs of the enterprise or the value of the collateral. In this case, the amount reclassified as long-term is limited to a reasonable estimate of the minimum amount expected to be available at any date, from the scheduled maturity of the short-term obligation to the end of the enterprise's fiscal year or operating cycle, whichever is longer. In the event that no reasonable estimate can be made of this minimum amount, the entire short-term obligation must be classified as a current liability.

For example, included in the current liability section of the December 31, 1981, balance sheet of the Stone Corporation are the following short-term obligations:

Current portion of 10% long-term debt due February, 1982 $5,000,000
9% note payable due July, 1982   3,000,000

---

[6]"Classification of Short-term Obligations," par. 11.

The Stone Corporation intends to refinance both short-term obligations on a long-term basis. Therefore, the company negotiates a revolving line of credit with City National Bank. Borrowing will be at 2% above prime and will be limited to the amount of the Company's inventory that is pledged as collateral. The loans will have stated maturities of 90 days and will be continuously renewable for 90-day periods at the company's option for up to three years. Finally, the inventory is expected to range between a high of $8,000,000 during the second quarter of 1982 and a low of $4,000,000 during the fourth quarter of 1982.

In this case only $4,000,000 can be reclassified as long-term debt. This represents the minimum amount expected to be available from February through December, 1982. The actual timing of the refinancing will determine which particular obligation will be reclassified.

In some situations a firm will have a short-term obligation that is repaid after the balance sheet date, and subsequently is replaced by long-term debt before the balance sheet is issued. The FASB pronouncement in this regard is that "if a short-term obligation is repaid after the balance sheet date and subsequently a long-term obligation or equity securities are issued whose proceeds are used to replenish current assets before the balance sheet is issued, the short-term obligation shall not be excluded from the current liabilities at the balance sheet date."[7]

FASB# 6

The disclosure requirements relating to short-term obligations expected to be refinanced are included with the discussion of financial statement presentation of current liabilities at the end of this chapter.

Dividends Payable

Corporations often issue cash dividends to common and preferred stockholders. A corporation is under no legal obligations to issue a dividend, but once it is declared, the dividend becomes a liability of the corporation. Since the liability usually is paid within a month or so, it is classified as current.

Some issues of preferred stock are cumulative—that is, preferred shareholders have a prior claim on subsequent dividends if the Board of Directors does not declare a dividend for the current year. These are called **dividends in arrears,** and although they are not legal liabilities until declared, full disclosure of the amount in arrears should be made on the balance sheet or in the footnotes to the financial statements. Accounting for dividends is discussed in detail in Chapter 20.

Collections for Third Parties and Payrolls

Enterprises often make collections for third parties such as unions and governmental agencies—that is, a tax or levy is imposed on the consumer and/or employee, and the firm is mandated by law to collect the levy on behalf of the taxing authority. Included in this category are sales taxes, payroll taxes, employee withholding taxes, and union dues. The specifics of these liabilities are discussed in the following sections.

---

[7] Ibid., par. 12.

Sales Taxes

Most states and some local political jurisdictions impose sales, excise, or use taxes. Although these taxes often are imposed on the consumer, the retailer or wholesalers must collect them on behalf of the taxing agency. There are no particular accounting problems associated with the imposition and collection of sales taxes. A separate liability account may or may not be established at the time of the sale. However, in no case does the amount of the sales tax ultimately increase sales revenues.

For example, the NAA Corporation records the sales tax liability at the time a sale takes place. The entry to record a $5,000 sale on account and a 6% sales tax would be as follows:

Accounts receivable	5,300	
Sales		5,000
Sales tax payable		300

When the sales taxes are remitted to the taxing authority, usually on a monthly or quarterly basis, the sales tax payable account is debited and cash credited.

Some enterprises initially record both the sale and the sales tax in the sales revenue account. At the end of the accounting period or when the sales taxes are due, an adjusting entry is made to record the amount of the liability. As an illustration, assume the NAA Corporation records the sales collected initially in the sales revenue account. The total in the sales account for the quarter is $500,000, including the sales tax. The sales tax rate is 6%. The adjusting entry at the end of the quarter would be as follows:

Sales	28,302	
Sales taxes payable		28,302
To record sales tax payable		
(Total Sales − Sales before tax = sales tax)		
($500,000 − ($500,000 ÷ 1.06) = $28,302)		

The $500,000 total in the sales account represents 106% of the sales before tax. To determine the sales before tax, you make the calculation $500,000 ÷ 1.06. The specific method the firm decides to use depends on its accounting system.

Payroll Taxes and Employee Withholding Taxes

As an employee earns a wage, certain federal and state taxes are incurred. Included are state and federal income taxes and social security taxes. The employer also incurs a portion of the social security tax and the federal and state unemployment taxes. The employer must account for all of these taxes and must file appropriate returns at quarterly or yearly intervals.

FICA (Federal Insurance Contributions Act) taxes commonly are called social security taxes. These taxes include Old Age, Survivor, and Disability Insur-

Exhibit 14-1
Schedule of Social Security Taxes

Year	Base Salary	Employee and Employer Rate	Maximum Tax on Employee and Employer
1978	$17,700	6.05%	$1,070.85
1979	22,900	6.13%	1,403.77
1980	25,900	6.13%	1,587.67
1981	29,700	6.65%	1,975.05
1982–1984	32,400	6.70%	2,170.80
1985	*	7.05%	*
1986–1989	*	7.15%	*

*The actual increase in the taxable wage base for these years is dependent on the cost of living benefit increase for retirees in the previous calendar year.

ance (O.A.S.D.I.) and Medicare insurance. Equal taxes are levied on both the employee and the employer on a varying salary base. Exhibit 14-1 presents the rate and salary base from 1978 through 1989.

In addition to paying a portion of the employee's social security taxes, the enterprise also must pay federal and state unemployment taxes. Federal unemployment taxes are the result of the Federal Unemployment Tax Act (F.U.T.A.) and are currently 3.4% of the employee's first $6,000 in wages. However, the employer can receive a maximum credit of 2.7% for state unemployment taxes incurred. Thus, actual federal unemployment taxes may only be 0.7%. The amount and limits of state unemployment taxes, of course, vary from state to state. In addition, the tax in most states is based on a sliding scale that depends upon the claims against specific firms. Individual state laws should be consulted for specific rates and regulations.

The federal government, as well as many states, have adopted "pay as you go" requirements for federal and state withholding taxes. This means that income taxes are withheld from each employee's paycheck. These taxes are not an expense of the employer, but are withheld by the employer on behalf of the taxing authority.

The following example illustrates the taxes just discussed. Assume the weekly payroll for the Elenor Corporation is $25,000. The entire payroll is subject to FICA taxes at the 1981 rate of 6.65%, state unemployment taxes of 2.7%, and federal unemployment taxes of 0.7%. In addition, federal income taxes of $5,400, state income taxes of $2,200, and union dues of $250 are withheld. The entries to record the payroll and related payroll tax expense are on page 538.

Each employer who is subject to social security taxes must file quarterly returns. In addition, most states require firms to file quarterly state unemployment returns. Federal unemployment returns are filed annually. Actual payments on these liabilities to the taxing authorities depend upon the size of the company's payroll. Payments can be as often as weekly if warranted by the size of the company's payroll.

Wages and salaries	25,000	
Federal withholding taxes payable		5,400.00
State withholding taxes payable		2,200.00
Union dues withheld		250.00
FICA taxes payable		1,662,50(1)
Cash or wages payable		15,487.50
To record wages incurred.		

Payroll tax expense	2,512.50	
FICA taxes payable		1,662.50
Federal unemployment taxes payable		175.00(2)
State unemployment taxes payable		675.00(3)
To record employer's payroll tax expense.		

(1) $1,662.50 = $25,000 \times 0.0665$.
(2) $175 = $25,000 \times 0.007$.
(3) $675 = $25,000 \times 0.027$.

Compensated Absences

Compensated absences do not represent collections for third parties. However, since they relate closely to payrolls, they are covered in this section. As employees work they accrue certain fringe benefits. Some of these benefits include vacation, sick, and holiday pay. These items are referred to as **compensated absences.** The FASB addressed the issue of accounting for such absences in *Statement No. 43*, "Accounting for Compensated Absences," and decided that the employer should accrue a liability for employees' compensation for future absences if the following conditions are met:

1. The employer's obligation relating to employees' rights to receive compensation for future absences is attributable to employees' services already rendered.
2. The obligation relates to rights that vest or accumulate.
3. Payment of the compensation is probable.
4. The amount can be reasonably estimated.[8]

If all the above conditions are met but it is impossible to estimate reasonably the amount of the liability, this fact must be disclosed.

Statement No. 43 does not require the accrual of a liability for sick pay that accumulates but is nonvesting. The Board thought that it would be difficult to estimate future sick pay that is contingent on the employee's absence. Further, the

---

[8]"Accounting For Compensated Absences," *Statement of Financial Accounting Standards No. 43* (Stamford, Conn.: FASB, 1981), par. 6.

Board thought that such sick pay would not normally be material. As a result, sick pay is charged to expense as incurred.

The accounting for compensated absences is illustrated by the following example. Assume that at year-end, the Giddings Co. estimates that its current employees have earned a vested right for 300 days of vacation. Wages and other fringe benefits (other than vacation pay) average $250 per day. In addition, these employees have accumulated 50 days of nonvested sick pay. During the following quarter, the Giddings Co. paid its employees for 100 days of vacation pay and 20 days of sick pay. Based on these facts the company would make the following entries:

At year-end:

Wages and salaries expense	75,000	
Estimated liability for compensated absence		75,000
To record the estimated vacation pay.		
($75,000 = $250 × 300 days)		

During the following quarter:

Estimated liability for compensated absence	25,000	
Wages payable or cash		25,000
To record vacation pay.		
($25,000 = $250 × 100 days)		

Wages and salaries expense	5,000	
Wages payable or cash		5,000
To record sick pay.		
($5,000 = $250 × 20 days)		

As the journal entries illustrate, an accrual is made only for the vacation pay. The estimated liability for compensated absence normally would be disclosed as a current liability. The sick pay is debited to an expense as incurred. However, if the contingent liability for sick pay is material, it should be disclosed in the footnote to the financial statement.

Liabilities Conditional on Operations

The amount of some liabilities is dependent on the results of operations. Liabilities such as federal income taxes are conditional upon periodic income, whereas property tax obligations are conditional upon asset valuations.

Income Taxes Payable

Federal, state, and local taxes payable are determined in accordance with the regulations of the appropriate taxing authority. Income tax expense is based upon income as determined by GAAP. Income tax expense and the relationship between tax expense and taxes payable are discussed in Chapter 16.

Property Taxes Payable

Property taxes represent a major source of revenue for local governments. They are levied on individuals and businesses based upon the value of real or personal property. In general, accounting for property taxes involves consideration of the assessment, lien and payment dates, the governmental unit's fiscal year, and the enterprise's fiscal year. There are a number of possible alternatives for accounting for property taxes. *Accounting Research Bulletin No. 43* lists eight different alternatives but does single out one particular method.

> Generally, the most acceptable basis of providing for property taxes is monthly accrual on the taxpayer's books during the fiscal period of the taxing authority for which the taxes are levied.[9]

Whatever method is adopted should be followed consistently.

As an illustration of the treatment preferred by *ARB No. 43*, assume the Raider Corporation, which is located in Los Angeles County, has a December 31 year-end. Los Angeles County's fiscal year is from July 1 to June 30. Property taxes become a lien on July 1 even though the exact amount of the assessment is not determined until November. Taxes are due in two equal installments on December 31 and April 30. On July 1, 1981, the Raider Corporation estimates that its property tax will amount to $36,000. On November 30, 1981, the Corporation receives a tax bill of $37,200 and makes its two required payments of $18,600 on December 31, 1981, and on April 30, 1982. The entries to record these events are as follows:

July 30, 1981, through October 31, 1981:

Property tax expense	3,000	
Property tax payable		3,000

To record one month of estimated property tax expense of plant ($3,000 = $36,000 ÷ 12). Entry is made each month from July to October 31.

November 30, 1981:

Property tax expense	3,150	
Property tax payable		3,150

To record property tax expense for the month

Total property taxes	37,200
Previously recorded ($3000 × 4 months)	12,000
Unrecorded property taxes	$25,200

---

[9]Committee on Accounting Procedure, Chapter 10A, par. 14.

Remaining months—(Nov. 1
through June 30th)   ÷8

Expense per month from
Nov. 1, 1981 to
June 30, 1982 $ 3,150

December 31, 1981:
    Property tax expense   3,150
    Prepaid property tax   300
    Property tax liability   15,150
        Cash   18,600
    To record property tax expense for
    December and payment of the tax bill

January 30, 1982:
    Property tax expense   3,150
        Property tax payable   2,850
        Prepaid property tax   300
    To record property tax expense

February 28 and March 30, 1982
    Property tax expense   3,150
        Property tax payable   3,150
    To record property tax expense

April 30, 1982
    Property tax expense   3,150
    Property tax payable   9,150
    Prepaid property tax   6,300
        Cash   18,600
    To record monthly property tax
    expense and tax payment

May 31 and June 31, 1982:
    Property tax expense   3,150
        Prepaid property tax   3,150
    To record monthly property tax
    expense

As this example illustrates, the Raider Corporation estimates its monthly property tax expense to be $3,000 and makes the appropriate entries for July through October. This estimate is based on available information at the time, such as last year's tax bill, and on knowledge of changes in property values and rates. On November 30, 1981, the firm receives the actual tax bill for the year and makes an entry to record the necessary adjustment. When the payments are made, the liability is reduced and the monthly expense and any prepaid taxes are recorded.

Bonus Agreements

Many enterprises offer bonuses to key executives. Often these bonuses are based on enterprise or divisional performance. Accountants are called upon frequently to interpret these agreements and to insure that proper accruals are made.

Bonus agreements can take a variety of forms; for example, they can be a percentage of pretax and prebonus income. Assume that a divisional manager of the Arnold Corporation receives a bonus of 15% of the pretax divisional income. If this income figure is $200,000, the bonus would be $30,000 or ($200,000 × 0.15). In other situations the bonus could be calculated after the bonus is deducted from the prebonus income of $200,000—the bonus is an expense which is deducted in calculating the income on which the bonus is based. In this case the bonus (X) is figured as follows:

$$X = 0.15 \times (\text{pretax income before the bonus} - \text{the bonus})$$
$$X = 0.15\ (\$200,000 - X)$$
$$X = \$30,000 - 0.15X$$
$$1.15X = \$30,000$$
$$X = \$26,087$$
$$\text{Proof: } \$26,087 = 0.15\ (\$200,000 - \$26,087)$$

There are a variety of other ways in which a bonus could be determined. For example, the bonus could be calculated after deducting the tax effects of the bonus. Other considerations could include allocation of overhead and of general and administrative expenses to the division in determining prebonus income. As noted, the accountant's job is to insure that the accrual for the bonus properly reflects the agreement between the interested parties.

The entry to record the bonus or profit-sharing accrual should be made only after all the adjustments necessitated by GAAP and/or by the provisions of the agreement have been made. Thus, this journal entry normally would be made just before the last adjusting entry to record income taxes for the period. The bonus is an expense in the period in which it is earned regardless of when and how paid. The corresponding liability is considered current because it usually will be paid shortly after year-end. Below is the journal entry to record the bonus of $26,087 calculated in the last example:

Employees' bonus expense	26,087	
Employees' bonus payable		26,087

When the bonus is paid, the following entry is made.

Employees' bonus payable	26,087	
Cash		26,087

Other Conditional Payments

Firms often enter into agreements that call for conditional payments based upon revenues or production. For example, lease or rental agreements frequently are based on a set amount plus a percentage of the gross rentals. Similar agreements are made between franchisors and franchisees. Patent or royalty agreements can be based upon either production rates or revenues earned. In all of these cases, the accountant must make sure that an accrual is made and that this accrual properly reflects the agreement between the parties.

Contingent Liabilities

The existence of some liabilities is contingent upon future events. Generally, the amounts of these liabilities must be estimated; the actual amount cannot be determined until the event confirming the liability occurs. Also, the actual payee is usually unknown until the subsequent event occurs. Liabilities of this kind are considered **contingent liabilities.** The accounting issues raised by contingent liabilities are related to the timing and manner of their recognition in the accounting records.

Accounting for Contingencies

FASB *Statement No. 5*, "Accounting for Contingencies," defines a **contingency** as an "existing condition, situation, or set of circumstances involving uncertainty as to the possible gain (a **gain contingency**) or loss (a **loss contingency**) to an enterprise that will ultimately be resolved when one or more future events occur or fail to occur."[10] Thus, a contingency is the result of an existing condition whose ultimate resolution depends on some future events.

FASB #5

Not all loss contingencies are contingent liabilities. In some cases loss contingencies relate to asset impairments, as in the collectibility of receivables or expropriation of property. These are not liabilities because they will not result in an obligation to third parties. Examples of loss contingencies include the following:

1. Collectibility of receivables.
2. Obligations related to product warranties and product defects.
3. Risk of loss or damage of enterprise property by fire, explosion, or other hazards.
4. Threat of expropriation of assets.
5. Pending or threatened litigation.
6. Actual or possible claims and assessments.
7. Risk of loss from catastrophes assumed by property and casualty insurance companies, including reinsurance companies.
8. Guarantees of indebtedness of others.
9. Obligations of commercial banks under "standby letters of credit."
10. Agreements to repurchase receivables (or to repurchase the related property) that have been sold.[11]

---

[10] "Accounting For Contingencies," *Statement of Financial Accounting Standards No. 5* (Stamford, Conn.: FASB, 1975), par. 1.

[11] Ibid., par. 4.

The uncertainties associated with the first two items (collectibility of receivables and obligations related to warranties and guarantees) are inherent in making estimates required in financial accounting for a going concern rather than solely with the occurrence of some specific future event. However, the FASB did not think it was necessary to distinguish these types of items from the other contingencies.

According to the provisions of *Statement No. 5*, there are three ways in which loss contingencies can be accounted for: (1) accrual of the liability or loss, (2) footnote disclosure only, or (3) no disclosure. The correct accounting treatment for the contingent liability depends upon (1) the probability that the future event will or will not occur and (2) whether the amount of the liability can be estimated reasonably. The FASB notes that "the likelihood that a future event or events will confirm the loss or impairment of an asset or the incurrence of a liability can range from probable to remote."[12] The Board defines these likelihoods as follows:

1. Probable—the chance of the future event or events is likely to occur.
2. Reasonably possible—the chance of the future event or events occurring is more than remote but less than likely.
3. Remote—the chance of the future event or events occurring is slight.[13]

A loss contingency should be accrued by a charge to income if the following criteria are met:

1. The information available prior to issuance of the financial statements indicates that it is probable that an asset has been impaired or a liability incurred at the date of the financial statement.
2. The amount of the loss can be reasonably estimated.[14]

Estimated liabilities under guarantees or warranties are examples of contingencies that meet the above criteria and, therefore, would be accrued. Since the liabilities are probable and their amount can be reasonably estimated from past experience, they meet the recognition criteria under SFAC No. 3. Recording these estimated liabilities insures the proper matching of income and expenses.

If one or both of the criteria are not met, and if there is at least a reasonable possibility that the loss will occur, only footnote disclosure should be made. According to *Statement No. 5*, the footnote disclosures should indicate the nature of the contingency and should give an estimate of the amount or range of the possible loss, or should state that such an estimate cannot be made. Examples of contingencies that may require this type of disclosure include pending or threatened litigation, threat of expropriation of assets, and actual or possible claims and assessments. Also, items generally referred to as contingent liabilities under current practice should continue to be disclosed in the footnotes to the financial statements regardless of the likelihood of their occurrence. These items include guar-

[12] Ibid., par. 3.

[13] Ibid.

[14] Ibid., par. 8.

antees of indebtedness of others, obligations of commercial banks under standby letters of credit, and guarantees to repurchase receivables. Finally, general or unspecified business risks do not meet the conditions for accrual and no accrual should be made. Neither should an accrual be made for self-insurance.[15]

Statement No. 5 requires a good deal of judgment on the part of management and the firm's auditors. Differing interpretations of probable, reasonably possible, and remote can lead to a variety of accrual and disclosure methods in practice. Exhibit 14-2 lists several possible loss contingencies and the probable accounting treatment for them. The correct accounting treatment required by *Statement No. 5* is summarized in Exhibit 14-3.

Some specific issues related to contingent losses, including accounting for warranties and premiums, for litigation and claims, and for self-insurance are discussed in detail in the following sections. Contingent losses involving estimated uncollectible accounts receivables were discussed in Chapter 6.

Contingent Liabilities That Are Accrued

There are numerous examples of contingent losses that usually are accrued. Included are product warranties and guarantees, premium offers to customers, and trading stamps.

Warranty and Guarantee Costs. Most enterprises that manufacture consumer products promise that their products will perform at a satisfactory level for a specified period of time. If the product fails to perform or needs repair, the firm will repair or replace the product at little or no cost to the consumer. These promises are called **warranties** or **guarantees.** Warranties in the automobile industries are a good example. Most U.S. automobile manufacturers provide a warranty on their new cars for the first 12,000 miles or for 12 months, whichever comes first.

Warranties and guarantees are contingent liabilities that usually are accrued as a charge to income at the time the product is sold. It is probable that a liability has been incurred and that the amount of the loss can be estimated reasonably. Clearly, when an automobile manufacturer produces and sells a car, certain expenses will be incurred due to the warranty provisions. Using past experience as a basis, the manufacture can estimate these expenses reasonably.

The *accrual method* can take two different forms—the expense method and the sales method. Under the *expense method*, which is the usual approach, the warranty and sales price are considered inseparable. This means that the entire sale price is considered all sales revenue rather than part sale of product and part sale of a warranty. An estimate of the warranty liability then is made at the time of sale and that amount is charged to expense. Under the *sales method*, the sales price is separated into sales revenues and unearned warranty revenues. The unearned warranty revenue is deferred at the time of sale and recognized as warranty expenses are incurred. The sales method is appropriate when the total price includes two separate items—the product and an express warranty on that prod-

---

[15] Self-insurance occurs when a company assumes the risk of loss itself rather than transferring this risk to someone else through acquisition of an insurance policy.

Exhibit 14-2
Loss Contingencies

Loss Related to	Usually Should Be Accrued	Should Not Be Accrued	Accrual Depends On Circumstances*
1. Collectibility of receivables	X		
2. Obligations related to product warranties and product defects	X		
3. Risk of loss or damage of enterprise property by fire, explosion, or other hazards		X	
4. General or unspecified business risks		X	
5. Risk of loss from catastrophes assumed by property and casualty insurance companies including reinsurance companies		X	
6. Threat of expropriation of assets			X
7. Pending or threatened litigation			X
8. Actual or possible claims and assessments**			X
9. Guarantees of indebtedness of others			X
10. Obligations of commercial banks under "standby letters of credit"			X
11. Agreements to repurchase receivables (or the related property) that have been sold			X

*Should be accrued when both criteria are met (probable and reasonably estimable).
**Estimated amounts of losses incurred prior to the balance sheet date but reported subsequent thereto should be accrued as of the balance sheet date.
Source: Ernst and Whinney, *Financial Reporting Developments*—No. 38353, August 1975, p. 4.

Exhibit 14-3
Accounting Treatment of Loss Contingencies

Ability to Estimate Loss	Probability of Event		
	Probable	Reasonably Possible	Remote
Can Be Estimated Reasonably	Accrue	Footnote Disclosure	No Disclosure Required
Cannot Be Estimated Reasonably	Footnote Disclosure	Footnote Disclosure	No Disclosure Required

uct. The best method to apply depends upon the actual, underlying transaction. Both of these methods are illustrated using the following data:

On January 2, 1983, the Dolphin Company started manufacturing combination microwave and conventional gas stoves at a per unit price of $1,200. Each stove is guaranteed for ten years. During the 1983 calendar year, the firm sold 5,000 stoves. Prior experience with similar models indicates that the Dolphin Company will incur an average of $50 in repairs expense for each stove under guarantee. In 1983 the company incurred $130,000 of warranty expenditures on these stoves.

Under the *expense method*, the following summary journal entries would be made in 1983:

Cash or accounts receivable	6,000,000	
Sales revenue		6,000,000
To record sales for the year.		
(5,000 units × $1,200 = $6,000,000)		
Guarantee expense	250,000	
Estimated liability for guarantees		250,000
To record liability for guarantee expense.		
(5,000 units × $50 = $250,000)		
Estimated liability for guarantees	130,000	
Cash supplies, accrued wages, etc.		130,000
To record actual expenditures incurred during the year.		

The expense for 1983 would be $250,000, and the balance in the estimated liability account at December 31, 1983, would be $120,000 ($250,000 − $130,000). Guarantee expenditures incurred in future years would be offset against this liability. Further, this liability would be increased in 1984 for estimated guarantee expenses resulting from 1984 sales. As is the case with all accounting estimates, the actual guarantee expense will not equal the estimated expense. As a result, the liability account will not always zero out for each product sold. If, over a period of time, there appears to be a growing balance in the liability account balance due to overestimation of prior years' expense, a change in estimate can be made. In accordance with APB *Opinion No. 20*, "Accounting Changes," these changes in estimate affect the year of change and future years—that is, they are handled prospectively with no retroactive adjustment or cumulative effect change. The issues related to accounting changes are discussed in Chapter 22.

Under the *sales method*, the total sales price is considered to be made up of two separate elements—sales revenues and revenues from guarantee services. The revenues from the guarantee services are deferred and recognized as guarantee services are performed. Given the information for the Dolphin Company and assuming 52% of the work is performed, the journal entries for this method are as follows:

Cash, accounts receivable	6,000,000	
Sales		5,750,000
Unearned guarantee revenue		250,000
($250,000 = $50 × 500)		
To record sales for year and		
unearned guarantee revenue.		
Unearned guarantee revenue	130,000	
Revenue from guarantees		130,000
To record guarantee revenue for		
period, assuming 52% of guarantee		
work is performed.		
Warranty expense	130,000	
Cash, supplies, accrued wages, etc.		130,000

The sales revenue in the period of sale is less than it would be under the expense method. In this particular example the guarantee revenue is equal to the actual expense incurred. This will vary depending upon whether there is a profit element included in the guarantee price.

The sales method should be used only when it is possible to separate sales revenues and guarantee revenues. For example, this method would be acceptable when a manufacturer sells an extended guarantee or warranty as a separate item. In most situations the expense method would be appropriate.

The *cash basis method* is an alternative to accruing the liability at the time the sale is made. Under the cash basis method warranty and guarantee costs are charged to income when they are incurred by the manufacturer. This would be similar to recognizing bad debts, not when the sale is made, but when the debt is actually declared in default. This method results in a mismatching of income and expense for a particular accounting period, and is generally used only for tax purposes.

Premiums. In order to increase the market share of an existing product or to promote the introduction of a new product, a firm may offer various premiums to customers. For example, a laundry detergent company may offer potential customers a towel in exchange for $0.10 and five detergent box tops. Although they were not mentioned specifically in *Statement No. 5*, premiums generally met the criteria to be accrued as a contingent liability. As with guarantees, the liability is probable and can be estimated reasonably; thus, the liability for these premiums and the related expense should be recorded at the time the sale is made.

For illustration purposes, assume that the Soapy Detergent Company offers customers a towel in exchange for $0.10 and five detergent box tops. The company purchased 30,000 towels at $0.60 each. The firm estimates that only 55% of the box tops will be returned. The company sold 200,000 boxes of detergent at $1.20 per box. Ninety thousand box tops were returned during 1981. The premium offer began on January 2, 1981, and ran throughout the entire year. Summary transactions for the 1981 year generally are recorded as follows:

Cash or accounts receivable	240,000	
Sales		240,000
To record sales of 200,000 boxes at $1.20 per box during the year.		
Inventory of premiums—towels	18,000	
Cash, accounts payable		18,000
To record purchase of 30,000 towels at $0.60 each.		
Cash	1,800 (1)	
Premium expense	9,000	
Inventory of premiums—towels		10,800 (2)
To record the receipt of 90,000 box tops and the issuance of 18,000 towels.		

Computations:

(1) Number of towels	18,000	
Price received	× 0.10	
Cash received	$1,800.00	
(2) Premiums issued	18,000	
Cost per premium	× 0.60	
Cost of premiums issued	$10,800	

Premium expense	2,000	
Estimated liability for premiums outstanding		2,000

To record estimated liability for premiums outstanding at December 31, 1981.

Computations:

Estimated box tops to be returned (200,000 × 55%)	110,000	
Box tops returned	90,000	
Box tops outstanding	20,000	
Number of towels to be distributed (20,000 ÷ 5)	4,000	
Net cost per towel (Cost $0.60 − $0.10 selling price)	$ 0.50	
Estimated Liability Outstanding	$2,000	

The total premium expense for 1981 is $11,000, and the current liability, estimated liability for premiums outstanding, equals $2,000. The inventory of premium towels of $7,200 ($18,000 − $10,800) would be reported in the current asset section of the balance sheet. Frequently this type of premium involves postage costs which also must be estimated and recorded.

Trading Stamps. Although trading stamps are not as popular as in the past, some firms, such as Sperry and Hutchinson Company still issue them. Accounting for trading stamps is the same as for premiums, except that the liability is the sole responsibility of the trading stamp company and all entries are made on its books. The trading stamp company buys a variety of merchandise that it records as an asset. The value of the stamps that will be redeemed then is estimated, and the related liability and expense are recorded.

Contingent Liabilities That Are Not Accrued

The previous examples illustrate contingent liabilities that usually are accrued. They are probable and the amount of the liability can be measured reasonably. There are a number of items, such as threat of expropriation, litigation, and other claims, whose proper treatment depends on interpreting whether the accrual criteria under *Statement No. 5* have been met. If the likelihood of the event is only reasonably possible or if the likelihood is probable but no reasonable estimate of the loss can be made, only footnote disclosure is required. In most cases the company's management and auditors must exercise considerable judgment in applying the criteria of *Statement No. 5*.

Litigation and Other Claims.   Litigation and asserted and unasserted claims represent special problems. **Asserted claims** are those that actually have been made against the company. If a customer sues the company for injury received from its product, it is an asserted claim. An **unasserted claim** is one in which the company believes it may have a liability but the claimant is not currently aware that s/he has a claim against the company. For example, if a drug manufacturer just determined that it has been producing a drug that may cause liver damage to certain individuals, the company is aware that there are potential claims against it. However, since the customers are not currently aware of the circumstances, their potential claims are unasserted. Accruals or disclosure of losses on litigation before the lawsuit is settled may put the company's legal position in jeopardy. In *Statement No. 5*, the FASB listed three factors to be evaluated in determining whether accrual and/or disclosure is required with regard to pending or threatened litigation and actual or possible claims and assessments:

1. The period in which the underlying cause (i.e., the cause for action) of the pending or threatened litigation or of the actual or possible claim or assessment occurred.   *FASB #5*
2. The degree of probability of an unfavorable outcome.
3. The ability to make a reasonable estimate of the amount of loss.[16]

An accrual would be inappropriate for an event that takes place after the balance sheet date. However, disclosure might be required. The second and third factors require a good deal of judgment. In evaluating the degree of probability of an unfavorable outcome, management should consider the nature of the litigation, the progress of the case after the date of financial statements but before they are issued, the opinion of the legal counsel, and the extent to which management will contest the legal action. Because of the difficulty of evaluating these factors and the problems in estimating losses, accruals for losses on lawsuits seldom are made before a final decision. In most cases disclosure of the existence of the suit is made through footnote disclosure. An example of a footnote disclosure for litigation and guarantees is included in the final section of this chapter.

Frequently in accounting for contingent liabilities such as lawsuits, information available at year-end indicates that an unfavorable outcome is probable, but the amount of the loss can be estimated only in a range between figures. If no single estimate in that range is better than any other, the minimum amount should be accrued and disclosure should be made of the additional contingency.

Unasserted claims at the balance sheet date are even more difficult to evaluate. In this situation the enterprise must determine not only the degree of probability that a suit may be filed, but also the possibility of an unfavorable outcome. The likelihood of these two possible events must be evaluated in accordance with the criteria of *Statement No. 5* to determine whether accrual and disclosure, disclosure alone, or no disclosure is required. An example of how one company disclosed the possibility of unasserted claims is illustrated in the final section of this chapter.

---

[16]"Accounting for Contingencies," par. 33.

Contingencies That Require Footnote Disclosure. Even though the probability of an event occurring is remote, *Statement No. 5* requires footnote disclosure in three situations:

1. Guarantee of the indebtedness of others.
2. Obligations of commercial banks under "stand-by letters of credit."
3. Guarantee to repurchase receivables (or any related property) that have been sold or assigned.

The FASB took this position because at the time *Statement No. 5* was adopted these loss contingencies currently were being disclosed in financial statements. The footnote disclosure should include the nature and amount of the guarantee, and if possible, an estimate of the value of any recovery that could be made.

 The Board also noted that unspecified business risks do not meet the accrual criteria for contingent liabilities. This did not prohibit the appropriation of retained earnings for these items. However, this appropriation must be shown in the stockholders' equity section of the balance sheet. Retained earnings appropriations are discussed in Chapter 20. Finally, the Board did not change the recognition criteria for gain contingencies. This means that gain contingencies should not be reflected on a company's books. Adequate disclosures of these gain contingencies are appropriate as long as misleading expectations regarding ultimate realization are avoided.

Deposits and Advances from Customers

An enterprise often receives cash as a deposit or in advance of some service. These deposits represent liabilities which would be classified as current or long-term depending upon when the deposits are likely to be returned. If all deposits are not returned or claimed, the liability account is debited and an appropriate revenue account, such as revenue from unclaimed deposits, is credited.

In some industries, certificates, tokens, and other forms of advance payment are common. These items generally represent nonmonetary liabilities in that the issuing firm promises to perform a service in exchange for the token or gift certificate. At the time the items are actually sold, cash is debited and a liability account, advances from customers, or unearned revenue is credited. Again, any unredeemed tokens or certificates would be included in income in the period in which they lapse.

Obligations Arising from Executory Agreement

Executory agreements are promises of two enterprises to perform some service. Unexecuted executory agreements result when neither party has performed any service or made any transfers. An example would be a purchase agreement in which no payments had been made nor any assets received. These transactions do not result in any asset or liability recognition. If material, unexecuted executory contracts should be disclosed in the footnotes. Permanent losses on purchase agreements should be recorded as described in Chapter 11.

Exhibit 14-4

GENERAL FOODS CORPORATION

Current Liability Disclosures

	1978	1977
	($000)	
Current Liabilities		
Notes Payable	$119,726	$105,320
Current Portion of Long-Term Debt	15,728	17,353
Accounts and Drafts Payable	310,192	294,551
Accrued Liabilities	329,013	307,071
Accrued Income Taxes	85,059	127,121
Current Liabilities	$859,718	$851,416

*NOTES TO CONSOLIDATED
FINANCIAL STATEMENTS*

Note 4: Notes Payable

	1978	1977
Commercial Paper	$ 14,023,000	$ 9,715,000
Notes Payable to Banks	105,703,000	95,605,000
Total	$119,726,000	$105,320,000
Maximum amount outstanding at any month-end during period	$314,000,000	$112,000,000
Average amount outstanding during period (based on month-end amounts)	$189,000,000	$ 72,000,000
Weighted average interest rate for period	8.2%	9.9%

At April 1, 1978, bank credit lines totaled $498,000,000. Borrowings, under these lines and through the issuance of commercial paper, are on terms and at interest rates generally extended to prime borrowers. Credit lines totaling $97,000,000 expire after fiscal 1979 while the remaining lines of $401,000,000 may be cancelled at the company's option at any time. As of April 1, 1978, notes payable amounting to $104,000,000 were outstanding under these arrangements. Pursuant to company policy, bank credit lines are maintained in full support of outstanding commercial paper. The amount of compensating balances was not material.

Please turn to the text at the bottom of page 555 for descriptions of Exhibits 14-4 through 14-7, which appear beginning above and continuing on the following pages.

Exhibit 14-5
PHILIP MORRIS INCORPORATED
Reclassification of $550,000,000 of Short-Term Debt

PHILIP MORRIS INCORPORATED

	1978	*1977*
Total current liabilities	$1,171,667,000	$ 805,153,000
Long-term debt	2,146,968,000	1,426,619,000
Deferred income taxes	149,952,000	104,429,000
Other liabilities	24,918,000	21,772,000
Total liabilities	$3,483,505,000	$2,357,973,000

NOTES TO FINANCIAL STATEMENTS

Long-Term Debt	*1978*	*1977*
Outstanding at December 31, exclusive of amounts due within one year:		
Short-term notes (see below)	$ 550,000,000	$ 500,000,000
Notes, interest principally from $8\frac{1}{4}\%$ to 8.85%, payable from 1982 to 1998	689,400,000	342,000,000
Bank term loan agreements, interest from $7\frac{7}{8}\%$ to $8\frac{1}{2}\%$ through April, 1985, and at a fluctuating rate thereafter, payable from 1980 through 1988	360,000,000	200,000,000
Sinking Fund debentures, interest from $6\frac{5}{8}\%$ to $9\frac{1}{8}\%$, payable from 1979 to 2004	369,121,000	227,100,000
Purchase money obligations, interest principally from 6% to 7%, payable through 2008	114,461,000	62,306,000
Other	63,986,000	95,213,000
	$2,146,986,000	$1,426,619,000

The Company has entered into a $300,000,000 revolving credit and term loan agreement, maturing in 1981, and a $250,000,000 Eurodollar revolving credit agreement maturing in 1982, both of which can be used to refinance short-term notes payable. Management intends to exercise its rights under these agreements in the event that it becomes advisable. Accordingly, at December 31, 1978, $550,000,000 of short-term notes payable have been classified as long-term debt in accordance with Financial Accounting Standards Board Statement No. 6.

Exhibit 14-6
LUBATOL, INC.
Footnote Disclosure of Litigation and Guarantees

LUBATOL, INC.

NOTES TO CONSOLIDATED
FINANCIAL STATEMENTS

Note 6: Commitments and Contingencies—Five lawsuits brought against the Company in the United States district courts in California, Michigan and Texas, alleging that the Company violated Federal securities laws and state laws in connection with certain repurchases or redemptions of its stock have been dismissed. Appeals in three of the actions have been dismissed or waived. The other two actions are on appeal to the United States Court of Appeals for the Ninth Circuit. One of the actions on appeal seeks an unspecified amount of money damages, the other seeks money damages aggregating more than $8,600,000, and punitive damages of $5,000,000. Another action alleging claims relating to certain repurchases of stock has been filed in the Chancery Court of Delaware and seeks compensatory and punitive damages in an indeterminate amount and alternatively, rescission. The Company believes that the allegations made in these complaints are not meritorious and that the Company has in all instances adequate legal defenses.

The Company has guaranteed the repayment of principal and interest of certain short-term notes payable of UIC Investments, Inc., a subsidiary of the Company's life and casualty insurance subsidiaries. The amount of notes payable outstanding at December 31, 1978 covered by these guarantees was $140,000,000.

Financial Statement Disclosure Current Liabilities

As discussed in this chapter, current liabilities include notes payable, current portion of long-term debt, accounts payable, and accrued payables. Although the specific order of the account within the current liability section of the balance sheet varies, most firms list secured and unsecured notes before trade and other payables. For illustration purposes the current liability section and the related footnotes from the 1978 General Foods balance sheet are reproduced in Exhibit 14-4. Relevant footnotes disclosures for short-term debt to be refinanced, litigation, and claims and unasserted claims are illustrated in Exhibits 14-5, 14-6, and 14-7 respectively.

Exhibit 14-7
ALLEGHENY LUDLUM INDUSTRIES, INC.
Disclosures of Unasserted Claims

ALLEGHENY LUDLUM INDUSTRIES, INC.

NOTES TO CONSOLIDATED FINANCIAL STATEMENTS

Note 15: Contingencies—On September 28, 1978 a Federal Grand Jury sitting in Pittsburgh, Pennsylvania handed up a one-court indictment indicting four companies and five individuals employed by those companies as defendants in a criminal case for violations of the antitrust laws; Titanium Metals Corporation of America ("TMCA"), a 50% owned affiliated company, was named as an unindicted co-conspirator in that action. As an unindicted co-conspirator, TMCA faces no criminal charges. On the same date, a civil action was filed by the United States of America, at Civil Action No. 78-1108, which named TMCA and the four companies as defendants, alleging violations of the antitrust laws. This action seeks only equitable relief. There are potential unasserted claims involving violations of the antitrust laws arising from the Grand Jury investigation, which potential unasserted claims were first brought to the attention of the management of TMCA in 1976. Management and legal counsel of TMCA are unable at this time to predict the extent of potential claims or the financial effect to TMCA, if any, should claims be asserted and determined adversely to TMCA, but the effect could be material to the financial position and results of operations of TMCA. In September, 1977 TMCA's management authorized and made provision for settlement offers with its customers in an amount up to $3,000,000. In January, 1978 the provision for settlement offers was increased to $5,000,000. The effect on Allegheny's 1977 financial statements was to reduce earnings from continuing operations by $1,253,000, or $.17 per share, with a corresponding reduction of Allegheny's investment in TMCA. Legal counsel of TMCA is unable at this time to give assurance that the ultimate liability will not exceed the amount provided.

In the opinion of legal counsel and management of Allegheny, any excess over the amount provided would not be material to the consolidated financial statements of Allegheny. Legal counsel of Allegheny has advised management of Allegheny that the activities of TMCA would not form a basis for sustaining an action against Allegheny merely because of its stock ownership of TMCA.

Concept Summary

ACCOUNTING FOR LIABILITIES

BASIC CONCEPTS RELATING TO LIABILITIES

Concept	Description
Liability Recognition Criteria	Accounting recognition is given to liabilities if the following conditions are met: 1. There is a probable future transfer of use of assets. 2. The enterprise has little discretion to avoid the future sacrifice. 3. The transaction giving rise to the obligation already has occurred. 4. The amount of the future sacrifice and the terms of the settlement can be estimated reasonably.
Current Liability Classification Criteria	Current liabilities are those liabilities that are scheduled to mature in one year or within one operating cycle if the cycle is longer than one year.
Liability Valuation Criteria	Current liabilities are recorded at their face value, the amount needed to discharge the liability. Because of materiality no recognition is given to the fact that the present value of the future cash outflows is less.
Contingent Liability Recognition Criteria	Contingent liabilities are accrued if the loss is probable and the amount can be estimated reasonably. Only footnote disclosure is required if the probability of the loss is only reasonably possible or if the loss is probable, but the amount cannot be estimated reasonably.
Classification of Short-Term Obligations Expected to be Refinanced	Classify as a current liability if (1) there is an intent to refinance on a long-term basis and (2) there is an ability to consummate refinancing, as evidenced by actual post-balance sheet date refinancing or formal approved agreement for refinancing.

TYPES OF LIABILITIES

Type	Description	Examples
Definitely Determinable	Liabilities whose amount is known at the time the liability is incurred	Accounts payable, notes payable, accrued payables
Collections for Third Parties	Liability to third parties resulting from collections of amounts on behalf of the third parties	Sales taxes and payroll taxes withheld
Conditioned on Operations	Liability whose amount is determined based on the results of operations	Income taxes and bonuses payable
Contingent	The amount of the obligations contingent upon the occurrence of some future event	Lawsuits, losses from catastrophes, guarantees of indebtedness

Questions

Q–14–1 How would you define liabilities? In doing so, explain the major elements of a liability.

Q–14–2 Distinguish current liabilities from noncurrent liabilities. Why is the classification of liabilities important to an enterprise?

Q–14–3 How are current liabilities related to the operating cycle?

Q–14–4 In practice, how are current liabilities valued on the balance sheet? From a theoretical view, is this method correct?

Q–14–5 Discuss the application of present value concepts to the valuation of current liabilities. How does this affect financial statements?

Q–14–6 What are the characteristics of liabilities that are definitely determinable in amount? Provide three examples of liabilities in this category. What are the accounting problems related to these liabilities?

Q–14–7 What is a discount on notes payable, and how does it arise?

Q–14–8 Under what circumstances are current maturities of long-term debt excluded from the current liability section of the balance sheet?

Q–14–9 Give examples of fixed amount, fixed date liabilities. What are some of their measurement problems?

Q–14–10 According to FASB *Statement No. 6*, what criteria must an enterprise use to demonstrate its ability to consummate the refinancing of a loan?

Q–14–11   Under what conditions can an enterprise reclassify short-term obligations that are being refinanced through a financing agreement? What portion of the short-term obligation can the firm reclassify?

Q–14–12   What is the potential effect on the current period's balance sheet and income statement of unrecorded liabilities? Discuss the effects of applying improper cutoff procedures to inventory purchases on open account.

Q–14–13   When do dividends become a liability of a corporation? Discuss the accounting treatment and/or disclosure requirements of undeclared, cumulative, preferred dividends. dends.

Q–14–14   List the most common payroll taxes paid by the employee and by the employer.

Q–14–15   What is a compensated absence? Under what circumstances should an employer accrue a liability for employees' compensation of future absences?

Q–14–16   How does the FASB define a *contingency?* What are some examples of loss contingencies? Of a gain contingency?

Q–14–17   Discuss ways in which loss contingencies can be accounted for.

Q–14–18   How does the likelihood of occurrence relate to a contingent liability?

Q–14–19   Under what circumstances should a loss contingency be accrued? Give some examples of contingencies likely to be accrued. Under what circumstances should a loss be disclosed? Give some examples.

Q–14–20   How should accruals for self-insurance be handled?

Q–14–21   Discuss the cash basis method and the accrual method of accounting for warrantee costs.

Q–14–22   Contrast the warrantee expense method and the warrantee sales method.

Q–14–23   Discuss the factors to be considered in the accounting treatment of pending or threatened litigation.

Q–14–24   Discuss contingencies that require disclosure regardless of probability of occurrence. Give some examples.

Q–14–25   Answer each of the following multiple choice questions.
  a)   Which of the following items should be classified as a current liability?
    (1)   An accommodation endorsement on a demand note issued by an affiliated company.
    (2)   A cash dividend declared before the balance sheet date when the date of record is subsequent to the balance sheet date.
    (3)   Unfunded past service costs of a pension plan to the extent that benefits have not vested and the costs have not been charged to operations.
    (4)   Dividends in arrears on cumulative preferred stock.
  b)   Assume that a manufacturing corporation has (1) good quality control, (2) a one-year operating cycle, (3) a relatively stable pattern of annual sales, and (4) a continuing policy of guaranteeing new products against defects for three years, which has resulted in material but rather stable warranty repair and replacement costs. How should any liability for the warranty be reported?
    (1)   As long-term.
    (2)   As current.
    (3)   As part current and part long-term.
    (4)   Need not be disclosed.
  c)   If a contingent loss is probable and can be estimated reasonably to be within a given range, but no amount within the range is a better estimate than any other amount within the range, the amount to be accrued should be which of the following?
    (1)   Zero.

(2) The upper limit of the range.

(3) The lower limit of the range.

(4) The mean of the upper and lower limits of the range.

(AICPA adapted)

Discussion Questions and Cases

D–14–1 The following three independent sets of facts relate to (a) the possible accrual or (b) the possible disclosure by other means of a loss contingency.

Situation 1: A company offers a one-year warranty for the product that it manufactures. A history of warranty claims has been compiled, and the probable amount of claims related to sales for a given period can be determined.

Situation 2: After the date of a set of financial statements but before the issuance of the financial statements, a company enters into a contract that probably will result in a significant loss to the company. The amount of the loss can be reasonably estimated.

Situation 3: A company has adopted a policy of recording self-insurance for any possible losses resulting from injury to others by the company's vehicles. The premium for an insurance policy for the same risk from an independent insurance company would have an annual cost of $2,000. During the period covered by the financial statements, there were no accidents involving the company's vehicles that resulted in injury to others.

Required:

Discuss the accrual and/or type of disclosure necessary (if any) and the reason(s) why such disclosure is appropriate for each of the three independent sets of facts above.

(AICPA adapted)

D–14–2 Anthony Herferd is in the breeding herd business. When the breeding herd matures, it is sold to farmers. It normally takes a female breeder two years to mature and produce her first calf. The company finances the breeding herds through a series of two-year bank notes. How should the breeding herds and bank notes payable be classified on Anthony Herferd's balance sheet. Why is it important that these items are classified correctly? Current liabilities - one operating cycle

D–14–3 The two basic requirements for the accrual of a loss contingency are supported by several basic concepts of accounting theory. Three of these concepts include periodicity (time periods), measurement, and objectivity.

Required:

Discuss how the two basic requirements for the accrual of a loss contingency relate to the three concepts listed above.

(AICPA adapted)

D–14–4 The following note was taken from the financial statements of the Melville Shoe Corporation:

MELVILLE SHOE CORPORATION
Notes to Financial Statements
(2) Property, Plant, and Equipment

Pursuant to an order of condemnation, a subsidiary of the company was compelled to surrender possession of certain land and building on April 20, 1971. The subsidiary has recorded as a deferred credit $6,620,000 in payments it received in 1972 toward the final award. Relocation and related expenses incurred by the company have been deferred and will be applied to the proceeds of the final award. In July, 1975, the pending litigation against the Dormitory Authority of the State of New York was decided by the Supreme Court of the State of New York, and the company was awarded an additional $6,948,539. The Dormitory Authority appealed the decision to the Appellate Division of the Supreme Court. Upon final determination of the appeal and the receipt of the additional award, the company will account for the gain from the condemnation as a prior period adjustment and accordingly will restate prior years' financial statements.

Required:
Do you agree with the accounting treatment of the proceeds from the condemnation of the company's property? Why? (Assume that FASB *Statement No. 5* was in effect. It is not necessary to comment on the possible treatment as a prior period adjustment.)

D–14–5 APB *Statement No. 4* and SFAC No. 3 have both defined liabilities. Many in the profession believe that the new definition defines liabilities differently than earlier definitions.

Required:
1. Compare and contrast the definition of liabilities in APB *Statement No. 4* with that in SFAC No. 3. Which definition do you think is preferable and why?
2. Refer to SFAC *Statement No. 3* and expand upon the three essential characteristics of liabilities described in the Statement. How do you think these characteristics relate to the current practice of classifying certain deferred income tax credits as liabilities?

Exercises

E–14–1 Presented below is a situation describing circumstances that have financial reporting consequences for the company involved.

The following items are listed under the liabilities on the balance sheet of Adams Industrial Company on December 31, 1981:

Accounts payable	$ 200,000
Notes payable	300,000
Bonds payable	1,040,000

The accounts payable represent obligations to suppliers that were due in January, 1982. The notes payable mature on various dates during 1982. The bonds payable mature on July 1, 1982.

These liabilities must be reported on the balance sheet in accordance with generally accepted accounting principles governing the classification of liabilities as current and noncurrent.

Required:
1. What is the general rule for determining whether a liability is classified as current or noncurrent?

2. Under what conditions may any of Adams Industrial Co.'s liabilities be classified as noncurrent? Explain your answer.

(CMA adapted)

E–14–2 The following events relate to inventory purchases by the R. Smith Corporation. The company uses the periodic inventory method.

a) On January 10, 1981, R. Smith purchased $5,000 of inventory, terms 2/10, net 30.

b) On January 15, 1981, R. Smith purchased $8,000 of inventory from another supplier. Smith received a quantity discount of 5%. Payment terms 2/10, net 30.

c) On January 18, 1981, R. Smith returned $1,000 of goods from January 10, 1981, that had spoiled.

d) On January 19, 1981, R. Smith paid for the remainder of the January 10, 1981, purchase.

e) On February 1, 1981, R. Smith paid for the January 15, 1981 purchase.

Required:

1. Make the required entries assuming that all purchases are recorded net.

2. Make the required entries assuming that all purchases are recorded gross.

3. What is the real cost to R. Smith for not paying the January 15, 1981, purchase within the discount period?

E–14–3 The Diamond Corporation borrowed $200,000 from the National Banks by discounting a one-year note payable at 16%.

Required:

1. What cash proceeds did the Diamond Corporation receive?

2. What is the effective interest rate?

3. Make the necessary entry to record the proceeds from this note.

E–14–4 The Artsy Art Supply Company had $500,000 of short-term debt as of June 30, 1981, the company's year-end. Artsy's financial statements are issued on August 15, 1981. The short-term debts are due on August 1, 1981. In order to liquidate the debt, Artsy Supply Company issued 10-year bonds at 10% on July 15, 1981, for which the company netted $350,000. The $350,000 in addition to $150,000 in cash was used to liquidate the $500,000 debt. The June 30 balance sheet is issued on August 15, 1981.

Required:

Show how the $500,000 short-term debt should be presented on the June 30, 1981, balance sheet. Include footnote disclosure if necessary. Explain the reason for your decisions.

E–14–5 The preliminary balance sheet of Equity, Inc., prepared on December 31, 1980, included a $3,000,000 note payable due April 20, 1981. On January 10, 1981, the company issued additional shares of its common stock for cash proceeds of $4,800,000 and used $2,300,000 of these proceeds to reduce the note payable. Audited financial statements were to be released on March 15, 1981, while management was still in the process of negotiating a line of credit that would be used to expand operations and to eliminate the remaining balance of the $3,000,000 note payable.

Required:

Show the correct December 31, 1980, balance sheet presentation for the situation above in accordance with FASB *Statement No. 6*. Explain the reasons for your decisions.

E–14–6 Where should each of the following items appear, if at all, on a classified balance sheet?

a) Cash dividends payable.

b) Stock dividends issued.

c) Accrued wages.

d) Rent received in advance.

e) Established cost of repairs to be made in the next accounting period.

f) Losses established from judgment in lawsuit case to be appealed.

g) Current installment on serial bond payable.

h) Accrual of self-insurance.
i) Estimated liability for income taxes not yet paid.
j) Estimated loss on unspecified business losses.
k) Short-term obligations to be refinanced.

E–14–7 For the first quarter of the fiscal year, Bumble Beez Honey, Inc. had $20,000 sales on account. The state has a 6% sales tax.
Required:
Show the journal entry recording the sales and any necessary adjusting entries at the end of the quarter under the following conditions:
   a) If sales taxes have not been included in the sales revenue account.
   b) If sales and sales taxes are included in the sales revenue account.
   c) Which method, if any, is preferable?

E–14–8 Delta, Inc. is a retail store operating in a state with a 5% retail sales tax. The state law provides that the retail sales tax collected during the month must be remitted to the state during the following months. If the amount collected is remitted to the state on or before the twentieth of the following month, the retailer may keep 2% of the sales tax collected. On April 10, 1980, Delta remitted $16,905 sales tax to the state tax division for March, 1980, retail sales. What was Delta's March, 1980, retail sales subject to sales tax?

(AICPA adapted)

E–14–9 The following information was obtained from the bookkeeper of Cozy Cottage Industries: the total payroll is $300,000, of which $50,000 represents salaries in excess of $29,700. Federal income taxes of $44,000 and union dues of $2,000 were withheld. The amount paid to employees in excess of $6,000 was $70,000. The state unemployment rate is 2.7%, the current FICA tax is 6.65% (on earnings up to $29,700), and federal unemployment taxes are 0.7% (on earnings up to $6,000).
Required:
As the accountant for Cozy, you must prepare journal entries for wages and salaries and for the employer payroll taxes.

E–14–10 The Brenkley Corporation provides an incentive compensation plan under which its president receives a bonus equal to 10% of the corporation's income in excess of $100,000 before income taxes, but after the bonus. Income before income tax and bonus is $320,000, and the effective tax rate is 40%.
Required:
1. Calculate the amount of the bonus and make the appropriate entry to record the bonus.
2. Calculate the bonus assuming that it is determined after income taxes and bonuses are considered.

E–14–11 Morton Mercantile's net income before taxes and bonus consideration is $250,000. The company has decided to pay a 20% bonus. The current income tax rate is 40%.
Required:
1. Calculate the bonus based on income after taxes, but before the bonus. The bonus is treated as an expense for tax purposes.
2. Calculate the bonus after taxes and after the bonus.

E–14–12 The O'Conner Company makes furniture for use in courtrooms. In addition to a regular salary, the firm's employees earn vacation pay and sick pay at a rate of $150 per day. The following events relate to these compensating absences during the period.
   a) Office employees earned rights to vested vacation of 30 days.
   b) Office employees earned rights to 10 days of accumulated but nonvested sick pay.
   c) Factory employees earned rights to 15 days of accumulated vacation days.
   d) Factory employees earned rights to 10 days of accumulated vested sick pay.

Required:

1. Make the appropriate entries to record each of the events above.
2. In your opinion, how should jury pay for an employee be handled? Why?
3. In your opinion, how should sabbatical pay be handled? Why? (*Hint:* see *Statement No. 43.*)

E–14–13   The Smith Company is being sued by Apple County for illness caused to local residents as a result of negligence on the company's part in permitting the residents to be exposed to highly toxic chemicals from its waste dump. Smith's lawyer states it is probable that Smith will lose the suit and be found liable for a judgment amounting anywhere from $1,000,000 to $2,500,000. However, the lawyer believes that the most probable judgment will be $1,750,000. How should Smith account for the situation above? Why?

E–14–14   The Smith Corporation is on a calendar year ending June 30. The corporation is located in San Francisco, which has a fiscal year that ends on June 30. Property taxes become a lien on July 1 and are payable in two equal installments on December 1 and April 1.

On July 1, 1981, the company estimates that its property taxes will be equal to last year's, which amounted to $48,000. On October 1, 1981, the firm receives its tax bill for the July 1, 1981, to June 30, 1982, period, which amounts to $49,200.

Required:

Make the appropriate journal entries to record the firm's property taxes at the following:

a) July 31, 1981.
b) October 31, 1981.
c) December 1, 1981.
d) December 31, 1981.
e) April 1, 1982.

E–14–15   The Holland Company manufactures explosives. The company is on a calendar year and distributes its financial statement by March 15 of the following year. On January 20, 1982, an explosion destroyed part of the firm's plant. In addition, there was considerable damage to surrounding commercial buildings. The company estimates that its plant suffered $1,000,000 of damage. Further, although no suits have been filed, the company's attorney believes that individuals suffering personal and property damage will file suits.

Required:

If you assume that the firm's financial statements are not issued until March, 1982, how should the Holland company report and/or disclose the events above?

E–14–16   In an effort to increase sales, Nick Razor Blade Company inaugurated a sales promotional campaign on June 30, 1981, in which Nick placed a coupon on each package of razor blades sold, the coupons being redeemable for a premium. Each premium cost Nick $0.50, and five coupons must be presented by a customer to receive a premium. Nick estimated that only 60% of the coupons issued would be redeemed. For the six months ended December 31, 1981, the following information is available:

Packages of Razor Blades Sold	Premiums Purchased	Coupons Redeemed
800,000	60,000	200,000

Required:

1. What is the estimated liability for premium claims outstanding at December 31, 1981?
2. Make the required entries for 1981.

(AICPA adapted)

E–14–17   In 1980 the Irwin Corporation began selling a new line of products that carry a two-year warranty against defects. All sales are made on account based upon past experience with other products; the estimated warranty costs related to dollar sales are as follows:

First year of warranty	1%
Second year of warranty	3%

Sales and actual warranty expenditures for 1980 and 1981 are as follows:

	1980	1981
Sales	$600,000	$750,000
Actual warranty expenditure	18,000	27,000

Required:

If you assume that the corporation uses the expense method, make the required journal entries for 1980 and 1981 to record the sales and the warranty expense.

E–14–18

a) There are two major ways of accounting for warranties: the cash method and the accrual method. Which, if either, is preferable, and why? Compare and contrast the effect of the two methods on the appropriate income statement and balance of accounts.

b) There are two different ways of employing the accrual method: the expense method and the sales method. Under each of the three independent situations below, which method should be applied and why?

(1) The Brokow Company manufactures home video recorders. These recorders are sold with a three-year unconditional warranty that requires the company to make all repairs for manufacturer's defects.

(2) The Valcun Termite Exterminator Company fumigates houses. The basic fumigation costs $700 and includes a one-year guarantee. In addition, the customer has the right to renew the guarantee at a fee of $60 per year.

(3) The Yomato Tire Company warrants its tires for 50,000 miles against all defects. If the tire cannot be fixed, the customer will be given a partial credit towards the purchase of a new tire. The credit is based on the number of miles the tire has been driven.

Problems

P–14–1 The following transactions for the Michael Corporation have occurred during the year. Michael's year-end is December 31.

a) On January 18 the corporation purchased resale goods from a vendor for $5,000, subject to cash discount terms of 2/10, net 30. Purchases and accounts payable are recorded at net amounts after cash discounts.

b) Michael purchased a van for delivery purposes on February 1 for $11,500, paying $2,000 in cash. The corporation signed a 10% note at the local bank for the balance. Principal and interest are due in one year. The van has a five-year life with no salvage value. The firm uses straight-line depreciation and takes six months depreciation in the year of purchase.

c) Inventory was purchased on January 18 and paid for on February 14.

d) On July 31 the corporation signed a $89,600 note at the local bank. It received proceeds of $80,000 from the bank. The note is due in one year.

e) On September 1, 1981, the board of directors declared a $50,000 cash dividend, payable on October 10, to stockholders of record on September 30.

f) Sales for the year all on account totaled $84,800, which includes a 6% sales tax. Sales taxes are recorded in a separate account.

g) The estimated annual federal income tax for the year was $4,500. The entire estimate was paid before year-end. At year-end the accountant determined the actual tax expense and liability to be $5,200.

Required:

1. Make journal entries to record the transactions above.
2. Prepare any year-end adjusting journal entries that are necessary to prepare the financial statements. Assume straight-line amortization of discounts.

P–14–2   The Dudley Pet Store entered into the following transactions during 1981. The firm is on a calendar year.

   a)   The store purchased a delivery van for $15,000 on January 31, 1981. The company put $3,000 down and signed a one-year, 12% note for the balance of the purchase price. The delivery van has a five-year life and no salvage value.

   b)   On February 10, 1981, Dudley purchased some office equipment from Do-It-Rite suppliers for $8,500 subject to cash discount terms of 2/10, net 60. Purchases are recorded at net amounts. The office equipment has a 10-year life with no salvage value.

   c)   Inventory purchase on open account amounted to $60,000. Terms are 2/10, net 60. The company records purchases net.

   d)   On February 19, 1981, Dudley paid Do-It-Rite for the office equipment.

   e)   Two thousand dollars worth of the inventory purchased in part c) was returned because it was spoiled on arrival. Eighty percent of the remaining inventory purchase made in part c) was paid within the discount period. The remaining 20% was paid after the discount period.

   f)   Sales for the year amounted to $120,000, of which 20% is on account and the remainder for cash. State sales tax amounts to 6%. Sales taxes are recorded in a separate account.

   g)   The firm rents a part of its store to a dog groomer. The agreement calls for a year's rent of $2,400 to be paid in advance. On October 1, 1981, the firm received the first year's rent in advance. A liability account is credited.

   h)   Payroll for the year amounted to $25,000, which was paid in cash. Applicable payroll taxes accrued as follows: federal and state withholding, $2,800; FICA taxes, 6.5%; and state unemployment taxes, 2.7%. All wages are fully taxable.

   i)   During the holiday season the Dudley Pet Store sold gift certificates. The certificates amounted to $3,000 and were paid for in cash. As of year-end only 25% of these certificates had been redeemed.

   j)   Sales and payroll taxes were paid in full before year-end.

Required:

1. Make the journal entries necessary to record the transactions properly.
2. Make any necessary adjusting entries in order to present fairly the financial statements in accordance with generally accepted accounting principles. In addition to the above data, the following information is available to you:

   a)   The company's policy is to take six months of straight-line depreciation in the year of purchase.

   b)   On November 10, 1981, Dudley decided that working capital was needed for forthcoming projects. Thus, rather than using cash to pay off a note of $50,000 that was maturing in 1982, the management decided that other means of financing the maturing note should be investigated. As a result, on November 10, 1981, Dudley entered into an agreement with the Last National Bank to borrow up to 80% of the amount of its accounts receivables. During the next fiscal year the receivables are expected to range between a low of $55,000 and a high of $80,000. This agreement runs for three years.

P–14–3   Royal Corporation's current liabilities at December 31, 1981, were as follows:

Trade accounts payable	$100,000
16% notes payable issued on November 1, 1981, maturing on July 1, 1982	30,000

14% debentures payable issued on February 1, 1981; final installment due on February 1, 1986; balance due at December 31, 1981, including annual installment of $50,000 due on February 1, 1982	300,000
	$430,000

Royal's December 31, 1981, financial statements were issued on March 31, 1982. On January 5, 1982, the entire $300,000 balance of the 14% debentures was refinanced by issuance of a long-term obligation. In addition, on March 1, 1981, Royal consummated a noncancelable agreement with the lender to refinance the 16% note payable on a long-term basis, on readily determinable terms that have not yet been implemented. Both parties are financially capable of honoring the agreement, and there have been no violations of any of the agreement's provisions.

Required:

1. What is the total amount of Royal's short-term obligations that properly may be excluded from current liabilities at December 31, 1981?

2. Draft the liability section of Royal's balance sheet. Include proper footnotes.

3. Assume the same facts for Royal Corporation's liabilities, except that the agreement with the lender to refinance the 16% note payable on a long-term basis is cancelable at any time upon 10 days notice by the lender. What is the total amount of Royal's short-term obligations that properly may be excluded from current liabilities at December 31, 1981.

(AICPA adapted)

P–14–4 Calico Corner Craft, Inc., which is on a calender year, issues its financial statement on March 15 of the following year. Below is information concerning the liability account of the company:

a) At December 31 short-term obligations include $500,000 of the current portion of 10% long-term debt maturing in February, 1982, and $300,000 of 12% notes payable issued in November, 1981, and due in July, 1986.

b) The company intends to refinance the current maturity of the 10% long-term debt and the 12% note payable.

c) Accounts payable and accruals equal $1,000,000.

d) Other long-term debt equals $2,500,000.

e) Assume that in refinancing the notes and long-term debt, the lender or prospective lender is capable of honoring the agreement. There is no evidence of any violations of the agreement, and all terms are readily determinable.

Required:

1. Assume the following facts: the company issued $800,000 of 10-year debentures to the public during January, 1982. The company's intention is to use these proceeds to liquidate $500,000 of the long-term debt maturing in February, 1982, and the $300,000 of 12% notes maturing in July, 1986. As a result, the debt maturing in February is paid before the financial statements in March. The remaining proceeds from the sale of the debentures are invested in U.S. Treasury notes maturing the same day in July as the 12% note.

    a) What amounts, if any, can be excluded from the current liability section of the 12/31/81 balance sheet? Draft the liability section of 12/31/81 balance sheet. Include appropriate footnotes.

    b) How should the 12% note payable and investment in U.S. Treasury note be classified on the March 31, 1982, interim financial statements?

2. How would your answer differ from part 1a) if instead of issuing the debentures, Calico issued $800,000 of equity securities? (All other facts remain the same.)

P–14–5 Total wages for the third quarter to employees of Go Fer Company were $500,000, of which $400,000 are wages in excess of $6,000, and $200,000 are wages in excess of $29,700 per employee. The state unemployment tax is 2.7%, and the federal unemployment rate is 3.4% before the state credit of the employee's first $6,000 in wages. A 6.65% FICA tax for both employer and employees is applied to the first $29,700 of each employee's wages. State income taxes withheld total $75,000, and federal income taxes withheld total $125,000. Union dues collected from employees total $15,000.

Required:

1. Calculate the amount of payroll taxes.

2. Prepare journal entries for the payroll and payroll taxes expense assuming that 50% goes into work in process, 30% into general and administrative, and 20% into selling expense.

P–14–6 The Lucky Laundry Company has five employees on its payroll for the fourth quarter of 1981. Because of a favorable rate the company is allowed a 1% unemployment compensation by the state (normal rate is 2.7%); the federal unemployment rate is 0.7%. The maximum unemployment wage is $6,000 for both federal and state. Lucky has determined the federal income tax rate for each employee to be 10%. Current FICA taxes are 6.7% on the first $32,100 of the current year's wage. Each employee is entitled to payment for compensated vacation pay based on his or her average weekly salary. These benefits vest. Each employee works a five-day week, and each employee receives two days a month of accumulated, nonvesting sick pay.

During your audit of Lucky Laundry you have obtained the following information:

Name	Earnings to 9/30/81	Earnings 4th Quarter 1981	Vacation Days Earned 4th Quarter	Sick Days Taken during 4th Quarter
C. Dover	$ 4,200	$2,300	4	0
L. Typer	25,400	6,000	6	1
T. Brown	16,300	5,000	5	4
D. Turnover*	3,200	1,000	—	—
B. Good	29,700	6,300	6	0
Totals	$78,800	$20,600		

*Terminated 11/7/81

All employees were employed before 1981.

Required:

1. For each employee determine the correct amount of payroll taxes for the fourth quarter and accrued expense for compensated absences.

2. Assume that the federal income tax withheld and the state income taxes withheld equaled $3,500 and $1,000, respectively for the quarter. Make the journal entries to record the payroll and related expenses for the fourth quarter.

P–14–7 Puppy Love is a large pet supply store and grooming parlor. It pays its employees on an hourly basis. For each 170 hours worked, employees receive one day of vacation pay and one day of sick pay. The firm accrues compensated absenses in accordance with FASB *Statement No. 43*. The amount of the accrual is based upon the employees' average current pay rate. Quarterly statements as of March 31, 1982, are now being prepared, and no accrual for compensated absences has been made since December 31, 1981. Accruals are only made for full days of vacation pay or sick pay earned. Remaining hours are carried over to the next accrual period. All benefits vest and accumulate.

Puppy Love's payroll register indicates the following:

Name	Salary from 1/1/82–3/31/82**	Hours Worked
Sumi	$2,362.50	525
Helene	360.00	150
Jay	1,530.00	340
Marlane	2,100.00	420
Paul*	284.00	142

*Paul was terminated on 2/1/82.
**Each employee received a 10% pay raise in 1982.

Required:
1. Make the required entries to record the compensated absence accrual at 3/31/82.
2. How would your answer differ if the sick pay did not vest but only accumulated?
3. How would your answer differ if the sick pay neither vested nor accumulated?

P–14–8 As president of Pyramid Publishers, T. Tahl receives a guaranteed annual salary of $150,000. She also receives a 10% bonus. Pyramid's average tax rate is 40%. The profit before taxes and bonus is $400,000.

Required:
1. Calculate T. Tahl's bonus based on profit before bonus and taxes.
2. Calculate the bonus if it is based on profit after taxes but before bonus.
3. Calculate the bonus based on profit after bonus but before taxes.
4. Calculate bonus based on profit after taxes and bonus.

P–14–9 Gary Stout is the store manager of the Montclair Branch of Eat-Rite Markets. In an agreement worked out with corporate management, he is to receive a salary of $30,000 plus a bonus. The bonus is to be calculated as follows:

a) Stout will receive a 20% bonus on excess earnings from the store.

b) Excess earnings are defined as net income before corporate taxes in excess of a 15% return on investment.

c) Both net assets and net income are to be calculated in conformity with generally accepted accounting principles. However, depreciable assets are to be valued at their net fair market value in determining store-wide net assets. Depreciation also is to be based on fair market values in determining net income.

The corporate office of Eat-Rite Markets has provided you with the following information:

a) The company is on a calendar year.

b) Preliminary profits before any of the adjustments required below is $400,000 for the year ended December 31, 1981. Included is depreciation expense of $100,000 based on the historical cost of the assets.

c) The net book value of the assets is $1,000,000.

d) The net fair market value of the depreciable assets exceeds their net book value by $400,000. Depreciation for 1981 based on fair market values would exceed straight-line by $50,000.

e) Ten thousand dollars of inventory shipped f.o.b. shipping point on December 28, 1981, was included in ending inventory, but was not recorded as a payable until January 1, 1982.

f) A customer of the market slipped on a banana peel and severely injured his back. The accident occurred in late December, 1981. The customer filed suit in January, 1982, and is asking for $150,000 of damages. However, Eat-Rite's attorney believes that although the company is at fault and will most likely lose the suit, she is sure damages will only be between $50,000 and $75,000.

Required:
1. Calculate the amount of the bonus due Stout.
2. Make the appropriate entry to accrue the bonus at year-end.

P–14–10 The Better Bag Co. closes its books annually on December 31. The company's property tax becomes a lien against the property on July 1. The estimated property tax for July 1, 1981, to June 30, 1981, is $18,000. The County Assessor mails the tax bills in October, with the first installment due in November, the second due in April. The tax bill received on October 15, 1981, was for $18,600, of which Better Bag pays $9,300 on November 30, 1981, and $9,300 on April 30, 1982.

Required:
Prepare monthly journal entries for Better Bag for the period July 31, 1981, to June 30, 1982.

P–14–11 The Twin Tower Nuclear Power Plant is preparing the financial statements for 1981. The following activities have occurred during the year:

a) As a result of an accidental leakage in 1981, personal injury law suits totaling $5,000,000 have been filed against Twin Towers. Corporate lawyers believe that it is highly likely that there will be unfavorable verdicts on the law suits. However, the three lawyers have not been able to come to a consensus regarding potential losses. Their estimates range from a high of $3,000,000 to a low of $1,000,000.

b) Because of past performance records, Twin Tower insurance rates have become very high. Thus, Twin Tower management has decided to self-insure and has set up a sinking fund of $2,500,000 with annual contributions to total $500,000, or the amount required to maintain at least a $2,500,000 balance, whichever is greater.

c) An irate customer went to the plant to protest his latest bill personally. While walking to the manager's office, he slipped and fell, injuring his back. The customer has filed suit against the corporation for injuries and general damages in the amount of $120,000. The corporation lawyers believe that the outcome will be unfavorable for Twin Towers, but that the customer will not be awarded more than $75,000.

d) Because of its recent bad publicity and accidents, Twin Towers management has decided that it is highly probably that 1982 also will have its share of lawsuits. Based on the prior year's activities, Twin Tower anticipates that lawsuits totaling 2.5 million will be filed against the corporation.

Required:
Indicate the financial statement for each of the situations, including footnote disclosure, if any are required. Explain your reasoning.

P–14–12 There are five independent parts to this problem.

a) Dobbin Corporation, a manufacturer of household paints, is preparing annual financial statements at December 31, 1981. Because of a recently proven health hazard in one of its paints, the government clearly has indicated its intention of having Dobbin recall all cans of this paint sold in the last six months. The management of Dobbin estimates that this recall would cost $1,000,000. What accounting recognition, if any, should be accorded this situation? Why?

b) Volner Company's fire insurance premiums were increased from $60,000 to $200,000 in 1981. To avoid paying such a substantial additional expense, Volner increased the deductible on its policy from $100,000 to $1,000,000. Volner's income tax rate is 40%. At December 31, 1981, how much of a contingent liability should Volner accrue to cover possible future fire losses? Why?

c) A truck owned and operated by Green Company was involved in an accident with an auto driven by White on November 15, 1981. Green received notice on January 10, 1982, of a lawsuit for $750,000 damages for a personal injury suffered by White. The company counsel believes it is probable that the plaintiff will be successful against the company for an estimated amount of $250,000. Counsel also believes there is a chance the plaintiff will be awarded as much as $350,000. Green's accounting year ends on December 31, and the 1981 financial statements were issued on March 15, 1982. What amount of loss, if any, must be accrued by a charge to income in 1981?

d) How should a loss contingency that is reasonably possible and for which the amount can be reasonably estimated be reported?

e) When and under what circumstances are gain contingencies recognized?

P–14–13 The Trusty Tent Corporation backs all of its products with a three-year warranty. Under the warranty, Trusty promises to repair or replace manufacturer defects for three years. In the past the company has found that warranty costs have been 1% of sales in the first year after sales, 3% of sales in the second year after sales, and 5% of sales in the third year after sales. The actual sales and warranty expenditures are as follows:

	Sales	Warranty Expenditures
1981	$750,000	$ 8,000
1982	600,000	23,000
1983	650,000	55,500

Required:
Prepare the required journal entries under the expense method and determine the liability at 12/31/83.

P–14–14 The Jigs Dog Food Company distributes to consumers coupons that may be presented on or before the declaration date to grocers for a $0.10 discount on dog food purchases. The grocers are reimbursed by Jigs when they sent the coupons to the company. Past experience indicates that 40% of such coupons are sent to Jigs for redeemption; all coupons must be presented for redeemption within one month of the expiration date. Past experience indicates that 5% of all coupons presented by grocers for redeemption are submitted past the deadline and are not honored by Jigs. During 1981 Jigs issued two separate series of coupons as follows:

Issued On	Number Issued	Expiration Date	Amount Disbursed as of 12/31/81
1/1/81	1,000,000	Varies up to 4/30/81	$34,000
7/1/81	1,200,000	Varies from 1/2/82–4/30/82	40,000

Required:
Determine the liability for unredeemed coupons as of December 31, 1981.

P–14–15 The Motley Machinery Mfg. sells a machine for $1,500. The machine has a one-year warranty to replace defective parts and provide the necessary labor at no cost to the customer. Motley sold 1,500 machines in 1981 and 2,000 in 1982, all on account. It is estimated that warranty costs will be $60 per machine, of which 60% will be for labor, 40% for parts. Sales are made evenly throughout the year with one-third of the warranty expense incurred in 1981 and two-thirds in 1982.

Required:
1. If warranty costs actually are incurred as estimated, prepare the journal entries under each of the following assumptions:
   a) The expense method, for both 1981 and 1982.
   b) The sales method for 1981.
2. What were the differences in the appropriate balance sheet and income statement accounts between these two methods in 1981?

P–14–16 The Flavorite Coffee Company introduced a new line of instant coffee. In order to spur sales, the company is offering a coffee mug as a premium for two certificates of purchase and $0.25. Each jar of coffee is sold to wholesale distributors for $0.70. The coffee mugs cost Flavorite $0.40 each. Postage and handling cost for each mug distributed is $0.20. The company estimates that proofs of purchase from 40% of all jars sold in 1981 will be returned. However, the company believes the return rate will increase to 45% on 1982 sales. Any premiums outstanding at the end of one year are assumed to be redeemed next year. The following information is also available:

	1981	1982
Coffee mugs purchased	200,000	350,000
Jars of coffee sold	1,200,000	1,500,000
Proofs of purchases redeemed	360,000	570,000

Required:
1. Prepare journal entries for the 1981 and 1982 entries relating to the premium plan.
2. Indicate how items relating to the premium plan should be shown on a classified balance sheet at 12/31/82.

P–14–17 Copy-At sells small desk top copiers that are extremely fast. Each copier is sold for $1,500. Because of its relatively inexpensive price, the copier has a very limited warranty. As a result, the company offers customers an additional four-year full warranty for $100. You have determined the following data for 1981:

		Estimated Three-Year Cost of Warranty	
Copiers Sold	Warranties Sold	Labor	Parts
600	400	$50	$30

Assume that all sales are for cash and take place on the last day of 1981. Further, during 1982 the company incurred the following warranty expenses related to 1981 sales:

Labor	Parts
$5,300	$2,400

Required:
1. What method should Copy-At use to account for warranties? Why?
2. Make the necessary journal entries for 1981 and 1982 relative to the 1981 copier sales.
3. Determine the balances and classification of balance sheet items for 1982 related copier sales.

P–14–18 The Ander Company manufactures a variety of hand tools. The company employs the calendar year for reporting purposes. Information regarding selected assets and liabilities as of December 31, 1980, before any year-end adjustments, is given below.
Cash

The Ander Company has $900,000 in various checking accounts. Of this amount, $50,000 is a compensating balance against a note with the Holly National Bank.
Securities

Ander Company has investments in the common stock of three companies and the bonds of one foreign government. The $100,000 investment in the bonds was made in January, 1980, in order to conduct business in that country. The common stock investments were made to invest temporarily excess funds. The investments in stock are with heavily traded companies listed on major exchanges. Details of these three common stock investments are presented in the following schedule:

Company	Acquisition Date	Purchase Price	Market Value December 31, 1980
Stan Co.	June 15, 1980	$180,000	$140,000
Clarmont, Inc.	September 30, 1980	90,000	80,000
Tra, Inc.	October 15, 1980	70,000	90,000

The books still contain the account "allowance for decline in market value of temporary investments" with the $40,000 credit balance established at December 31, 1979.

Accounts Receivable

The outstanding accounts receivable as of December 31, 1980, total $400,000, including $20,000 due from officers of the company. The "allowance for uncollectible accounts" account had a debit balance of $12,000 at December 31, 1980. An aging of the accounts receivable at year-end indicates that $10,000 of the accounts receivable will be uncollectible.

Notes Receivable

Ander Company holds two notes receivable. One is a $20,000 trade note receivable dated March 1, 1980. This is a one-year note that calls for payment of interest of 12% at maturity. The other note is from Rexit, a company in which Ander holds a 30% interest. This is a one-year note for $50,000 that is dated July 1, 1980. The note carries a 10% interest rate, and the interest is due at maturity.

Inventories

The company's inventory is costed on a moving average basis and totals $950,000. This amount includes $100,000 of merchandise held in foreign countries in excess of normal requirements in order to meet foreign government investment requirements. The market value for the excess foreign inventory is $180,000 and $1,200,000 for the remaining inventory.

Accounts Payable

Outstanding accounts payable as of December 31, 1980, total $500,000. Included in this balance is $60,000 due to an unconsolidated joint venture.

Notes Payable

Three notes payable are outstanding at December 31, 1980, as follows:

a) Ander has a $60,000, 12-month note with CTH Finance. The note is due on December 1, 1981. The note carries a 15% interest rate with the interest due at maturity.

b) A note covering a borrowing from PNH Insurance Co. for $100,000 is due on April 1, 1981, and carries a 10% interest rate. This note contains an agreement that permits Ander to refinance the note into a three-year note at maturity. Interest is payable annually on the anniversary date, and the current year's interest must be paid before the note can be refinanced. Ander plans to notify the insurance company early in 1981 of its intentions to refinance the note when the note becomes due.

c) Ander's third note is with Holly National Bank for $500,000. The note is dated July 1, 1980, and is due on July 1, 1985. Interest of 16% is payable annually on the anniversary date of the note.

Income Taxes Payable

The company has accrued $80,000 in income taxes related to 1980 income. In addition, there is a deferred income tax payable amounting to $40,000. This arises from the company's use of the straight-line depreciation method for the financial statements and the double-declining-balance method for the tax return.

Customer Advances

Customers are required to make advance payments for special orders. Special orders normally are filled within six weeks from the date of the order. Customer advances at December 31, 1980, total $15,000.

Required:

Ander Company is preparing its classified statement of financial position as of December 31, 1980, for presentation in its annual report to its shareholders.

  a) For each item that should be classified as a current asset, identify the account, the appropriate amount, and any additional disclosures that would be required either in the body of the statement or in the accompanying notes.

  b) For each item that should be classified as a current liability, identify the account, the amount, and any additional disclosures that would be required either in the body of the statement or in the accompanying notes.

(CMA adapted)

15

Long-Term Liabilities

Accounting in the News

Both interest rates and the cash outflows due to interest payments have escalated in recent years. As a result, businesses have been forced to devise new financing techniques. Caesars World came up with the following interesting solution.

BOSTON—Caesars World Inc. may bet that some bond buyers are gamblers and would take hotel rooms in lieu of cash interest payments.

J. Terrence Lanni, president of Caesars World, a gambling casino operator, said he has held preliminary talks with potential underwriters about a bond issue that would raise $75 million to reduce the interest costs that have made its two-year-old Caesars Tahoe hotel-casino complex unprofitable.

Under the plan, Caesars Tahoe would issue 5,000 of $15,000 face amount bonds. Each bondholder would be entitled to spend two weeks a year at the resort. Mr. Lanni noted that the plan would improve the resort's 65% occupancy rate. Moreover, he said "People who can afford $15,000 bonds" and stay at Caesars Tahoe without paying for their hotel rooms are likely to return additional money to Caesars "around the green felt" of the gambling tables.

In fiscal 1981, the hotel had a $16 million deficit, primarily because of capital costs of $27 million a year, and Mr. Lanni projected the fiscal 1982 deficit would be $10 million. If the bond plan works, the resort should reach break-even status before 1983, however, he said.*

Bonds with paid vacations in lieu of interest payments are just one way to raise capital. Other forms of more traditional long-term debt include regular term bonds, serial bonds, and mortgage notes. Accounting for such long-term liabilities is the subject of this chapter.

*William M Bulkeley, "Caesars World Inc. May Try Bond Issue Paying in Vacations," *Wall Street Journal*, January 22, 1982, p. 41. Reprinted by permission of The Wall Street Journal, © Dow Jones & Company, Inc. 1982. All Rights Reserved.

Long-term liabilities represent a major source of capital for U.S. corporations. They consist of those obligations of an enterprise that are not due within the coming year or the operating cycle if it is longer than a year. Mortgages payable, bonds payable, long-term notes payable, and pension and lease obligations are examples of long-term liabilities. This chapter will discuss the current accounting theory and practice related to long-term liabilities; the focus will be on the accounting by both the borrower and the investor. Because bonds are one of the most common forms of long-term debt, they will be used to illustrate the key concepts. Early extinguishment of debt and troubled debt restructurings will be discussed also. Accounting for serial bonds is illustrated in the Appendix to this chapter. Accounting for pensions and leases is discussed in Chapters 17 and 18, respectively.

Long-term financing decisions are important considerations of financial management. Businesses need some form of permanent or semipermanent capital to finance plant expansion, mergers, and acquisitions and to raise working capital. Profit-seeking enterprises can issue either some form of capital stock and/or some form of long-term debt to fulfill their financing needs. The decision as to whether to issue additional capital stock or long-term debt ultimately affects the firm's return on assets and the return on common stockholders' equity. If an enterprise is able to earn a greater return on its debt than the interest charge on that debt, the return to common stockholders will be increased. This is referred to as **leverage.** Effective use of leverage is one of the advantages of issuing long-term debt as a source of financing. Further, the ownership of existing shareholders is not diluted. The use of long-term debt, however, commits the enterprise to fixed interest and principal payments. In addition, the covenants or agreements the firm must make with its debt holders can reduce managerial flexibility. Thus, the financing decision is important and is the result of considering a variety of complex factors.

Valuation of Long-Term Liabilities

In general, monetary liabilities should be valued at the present value of their future cash outflows. Such valuation requires that the future cash outflows needed to discharge a liability be discounted at an appropriate interest rate. Because most current liabilities are payable in a relatively short period of time, they are recorded at their face value—that is, the amount ultimately needed to discharge the liability. No recognition is given to the fact that the present value of these outlays discounted at an appropriate interest rate would be somewhat less. Generally, the amounts involved are immaterial. However, for long-term liabilities the difference between the face value of the liability and the present value of the future cash flows can be material. As a result, long-term liabilities should be valued at the present value of their future cash outflows. The discount rate should be the appropriate market interest rate for that particular obligation at the time of its issuance. The carrying value of the liability should not be adjusted for subsequent changes in the market rate of interest.

Problems arise when an obligation has no stated interest rate or when the rate is substantially below the rate for similar liabilities. The APB noted this problem as follows: "The use of an interest rate that varies from prevailing inter-

APB #21

est rates warrants evaluation of whether the face amount and the stated interest rate of a note or obligation provide reliable evidence for properly recording the exchange and subsequent related interest."[1] In response to this problem, the Board issued APB *Opinion No. 21*, "Interest on Receivables and Payables," which outlines the appropriate accounting method for situations in which the face amount of the note does not correspond reasonably to the present value of the consideration given or received in the exchange.

This problem and the solution described in *Opinion No. 21* are illustrated by the following example. Assume that the Andrews Corporation agrees to purchase a custom piece of equipment. The agreement calls for the Andrews Corporation to make three, equal, annual payments of $4,741 each at the end of each of the next three years. No interest is stipulated in the agreement. The cash equivalent price of the equipment is $12,000, which represents the present value of the three payments of $4,741 discounted at the then current market rate of 9%. It would be *inappropriate* to record this transaction of debiting the equipment and crediting note payable for $14,223, the total amount of the cash outflows. This would over-state the cost of the equipment and subsequent depreciation expense and would understate subsequent interest expense. The equipment and note should be re-corded by discounting the payments at 9%. The journal entry is as follows:

Equipment	12,000	
Discount on note payable	2,223	
Note payable		14,223
To record the purchase of equipment.		
$4,741 \times 2.53130 =$		
$12,000 (See Table 5-4)		

The discount then is amortized over the next three years, and interest charges of $2,223 thus are incurred over the next three years. Further, future depreciation is based on a cost of $12,000.

With certain exceptions, APB *Opinion No. 21* is applicable to receivables and payables that represent contractual rights or obligations to receive or pay money on fixed or determinable dates whether or not there is any stated provision for interest. The exceptions include the following:

APB #21

1. Receivables and payables arising from transactions with customers or suppliers in the normal course of business which are due in customary trade terms not exceeding approximately one year.
2. Amounts which do not require repayment in the future, but rather will be applied to the purchase price of the property, goods or service involved (e.g., deposits or progress payments on construction contracts, advance payments for acquisition of resources and raw materials, advances to encourage exploration in the extractive industries).

[1] "Interest on Receivables and Payables," *Opinions of the Accounting Principles Board No. 21* (New York: AICPA, 1971), par. 1.

3. Amounts intended to provide security for one party to an agreement (e.g., security deposits, retainers on contracts).
4. The customary cash lending activities and demand or savings deposit activities of financial institutions whose primary business is lending money.
5. Transactions where interest rates are affected by the tax attributes or legal restrictions prescribed by a governmental agency (e.g., industrial revenue bonds, tax exempt obligations, government guaranteed obligations, income tax settlements).
6. Transactions between parent and subsidiary companies and between subsidiaries of a common parent.[2]

In addition, the *Opinion* does not apply to estimated liabilities such as warranties or to convertible debt securities.

The *Opinion* does cover three major types of obligations: (1) notes received or issued for cash, (2) notes with unstated rights or privileges, and (3) notes exchanged for noncash property, goods, or services. Each is discussed in the following sections.

Notes Issued Solely for Cash

A note issued solely for cash is presumed to have a present value at its issue date equal to the cash proceeds received. Because of a possible difference between the stated interest rate, if any, and the market rate at the date of issue, the amount received by the borrower may be more or less than the face value of the note. For cash loans such as this, the dollar amount of interest expense will be the difference between the total amount of cash received by the borrower and the total amount to be repaid. The effective interest rate is the one that equates these amounts. Because these notes are presumed to have a present value equal to their cash proceeds, no other interest is imputed. As an illustration of these concepts, assume that on January 2, 1983, the Arnold Company issues a non-interest-bearing note due in three years with a face value of $10,000. The company receives cash proceeds of $7,117.80 for the note. An interest rate of 12% equates the cash proceeds of $7,117.80 and the face value of the $10,000 to be paid at the end of three years.[3] The journal entries to record the issuance of this note and the adjusting entries for the next three years are illustrated in Exhibit 15-1.

Exhibit 15-2 illustrates how the annual interest expense is calculated using the effective interest method. This method, which is sanctioned by *Opinion No. 21*, results in a constant interest rate because the 12% interest rate is multiplied by the carrying value of the note at the beginning of each period. However, the dollar amount of interest expense increases each year as does the carrying value of the note. The effective interest method insures that the liability is always carried at the present value of the required future cash payments. An alternative

---

[2] Ibid., par. 3.

[3] This is determined by the following:

$$\text{Equation: } \frac{\text{Cash proceeds}}{\text{Face value}} = \text{factor in present value table}$$

$$\frac{\$7,117.80}{\$10,000} = 0.71178 \text{ from Table 5-2. This equals an interest rate of 12\%.}$$

Exhibit 15-1
ARNOLD COMPANY
Journal Entries—Non-Interest-Bearing Cash Note

Cash	7,117.80	
Discount on note payable	2,882.20	
Note payable		10,000
To record issuance of note.*		

Adjusting entries:

End of year	1983	1984	1985
Interest expense	854.14	956.63	1,071.43
Discount on note payable	854.14	956.63	1,071.43
To record amortization of discount.			

Note payable	10,000	
Cash		10,000
To record principal payment.		

*Alternatively, the note could be recorded net—that is, the entry would be made as follows:

Cash	7,117.80	
Note payable		7,117.80

The adjusting entry to record the interest expense is a debit to the interest expense account and a credit directly to the note payable account. If this method is used, full disclosure of the actual discount is required.

would be to use the straight-line method. The annual interest expense under the straight-line method would be $960.73 ($2,882.20 ÷ 3). This method results in a constant dollar amount of interest expense even though the carrying value of the obligation increases over its life. The straight-line amortization method is not appropriate if there is a material difference between its results and those under the effective interest method.[4]

The note payable is recorded on the balance sheet at its face value of $10,000. The appropriate balance in the discount on note payable account then is offset against the note payable account. The partial balance sheet for the Arnold Company at the end of 1983 appears in Exhibit 15-3.

Notes Issued with Unstated Rights or Privileges

There are certain situations in which notes issued for cash also include unstated rights or privileges. For example, a corporation that is dependent upon a particular supplier may lend that supplier cash to be repaid over a number of years with

[4]"Receivables and Payables," par. 15.

Exhibit 15-2
ARNOLD COMPANY
Discount Amortization—Effective Interest Method

End of Year	Interest Expense 12%	Unamortized Discount or Note Payable	Carrying Value of Note
		$2,882.20	$7,117.80
1983	$ 854.14[(1)]	2,028.06	7,971.94[(2)]
1984	956.63	1,071.43	8,928.57
1985	1,071.43	–0–	10,000.00
	$2,882.20		

[(1)]$854.14 = $7,111.80 × 0.12.
[(2)]$7,971.94 = $7,117.80 + $854.14, or alternatively, $10,000 discounted at 12% for 2 years = $7,971.94 = $10,000 × 0.797194.

no stated interest rate. In this case the non-interest-bearing loan may represent partial consideration under a purchase agreement to obtain the supplier's product below prevailing market rates; thus, accounting recognition must be given to this fact. The note should be recorded at its discounted present value using an appropriate interest rate. The resulting discount should be amortized over the life of the note. In addition, the difference between the present value of the note and the cash paid or received should be recognized as additional cost of goods sold to the lender and additional sales revenue to the borrower.

For example, the White Corporation is a major supplier of raw materials to the Smith Company. On January 2, 1982, the Smith Company agrees to lend the White Corporation a substantial amount of money so the White Corporation can maintain its present level of production. The terms of the agreement call for a $500,000 interest-free loan to be paid at the end of three years. In addition, the White Corporation agrees to supply raw materials over the next three years to

Exhibit 15-3
ARNOLD COMPANY
Partial Balance Sheet
End of Year 1983

Long-term Liabilities		
Notes payable		$10,000.00
Less: Discount on note payable		2,028.06
		$ 7,971.94

the Smith Corporation at 85% of the prevailing market price. This note should be recorded at the discounted present value of the future cash outflows. If 12% represents an appropriate interest rate, the present value of $500,000 discounted at that rate for three years equals $355,890, and the amount of the discount equals $144,110. At the time of the agreement the White Corporation (borrower) and the Smith Company (lender) would make the journal entries shown in Exhibit 15-4.

The "rights in contract with supplier" account is an asset on the lender's books whereas the "unearned revenue" account is a liability on the books of the borrower. Both the borrower and lender must amortize the discount over the life of the note. As sales are made, the White Corporation recognizes a prorated portion of the unearned revenue account as earned sales, and the Smith Company amortizes the rights in contract with supplier account as additional cost of goods sold. Given that the companies use the effective interest method and the purchases are made evenly over the next three years, the appropriate journal entries at the end of 1982 are shown also in Exhibit 15-4.

Notes Exchanged for Property, Goods, or Services

A note may be exchanged for property, goods, or services in which (1) interest is not stated, (2) the stated rate of interest is unreasonable, or (3) the stated face amount is substantially different from the current cash sales price or from the market value of the note at the date of the transaction. In these circumstances "the note, the sales price, and the cost of the property, goods or services exchanged for the note should be recorded at the fair value of the property, goods, or services or at an amount that reasonably approximates the market value of the note, whichever is more clearly determinable."[5] If neither of these amounts can be determined, the note should be recorded at its present value using an appropriate interest rate. Two examples are provided illustrating non-interest-bearing notes and notes with an unreasonably low interest rate.

Non-Interest-Bearing Notes. Assume that on January 2, 1981, the Jigs Corporation agrees to purchase a custom-ordered piece of equipment. The agreement calls for the company to make four, equal, annual payments of $16,462 each at the end of each of the next four years. No interest was stipulated in the note, and the cash equivalent price of the equipment could not be determined. Assume that the appropriate interest rate is 12%. The entries to record the equipment and the first annual payment are presented in Exhibit 15-5. The present value calculation and the amortization table for the effective interest method also are presented in the exhibit. This exhibit illustrates how each $16,462 payment is divided between interest and principal. The interest element is calculated by multiplying the carrying value of the note by 12%. The remaining portion of the payment represents a reduction in the principal.

Two important points should be noted. First, failure to record the note at its present value of $50,000 will result in an overstatement of the asset and liability values, the subsequent overstatement of depreciation, and an understatement of interest expense. Second, the determination of the appropriate rate is a difficult

[5] Ibid., par. 12.

Exhibit 15-4
Journal Entries
Notes Issued With Unstated Rights or Privileges

White Corporation (Borrower)
Issuance of Note:

Cash	500,000	
Discount on note payable	144,110	
Notes payable		500,000
Unearned revenue		144,110

To record note payable at the present value, $355,890 = $500,000 × 0.71178 (Table 5-2).

Entries at End of 1982:

Interest expense	42,707[1]	
Discount on notes payable		42,707
Unearned revenue	48,037[2]	
Sales		48,037

Smith Corporation (Lender)

Note receivable	500,000	
Rights in contract with supplier	144,110	
Discount on note receivable		144,110
Cash		500,000

To record note receivable at its present value.

Discount on note receivable	42,707[1]	
Interest income		42,707
Cost of goods sold	48,037[2]	
Rights in contract with supplier		48,037

[1] $42,707 = $355,890 × 0.12.
[2] $48,037 = $144,110 ÷ 3.

Exhibit 15-5
JIGS COMPANY
Illustration of Non-Interest-Bearing Note

Journal Entries

Jan. 2, 1981	Equipment	50,000	
	Discount on note payable	15,858	
	Note payable		65,848
	To record purchase of equipment.		
Dec. 31, 1981	Note payable	16,462	
	Interest expense	6,000	
	Discount on note payable		6,000
	Cash		16,462
	To record first annual payment.		

Note Payable—Present Value Calculation

Maturity value of note: $16,462 × 4 years = $65,848
Present value of note discounted at 12%
for four years: $16,461.72 × 3.03735 = 50,000
(See Table 5-4)
Discount $15,848

Note Payable Amortization Table—Effective Interest Method

Date	Payment	Interest Expense—12%	Principal Payment	Unamortized Discount	Present Value or Carrying Value of Note
1/ 2/81				$15,848	$50,000
12/31/81	$16,462	$6,000[1]	$10,462[2]	9,848[3]	39,538[4]
12/31/82	16,462	4,745	11,717	5,103	27,821
12/31/83	16,462	3,338	13,124	1,765	14,697
12/31/84	16,462	1,765	14,697	–0–	
	$65,848	$15,848	$50,000		

[1] $ 6,000 = $50,000 × 0.12.
[2] $10,462 = $16,462 – $6,000.
[3] $ 9,848 = $15,848 – $6,000.
[4] $39,538 = $50,000 – $10,462.

problem. The APB provides some guidance in this matter, although it does note that the variety of transactions makes it impossible to have any specific rate applicable to transactions:

> The choice of a rate may be affected by the credit standing of the issuer, restrictive covenants, the collateral, payment and other terms pertaining to the debt, and, if appropriate, the tax consequences to the buyer and seller. The prevailing rates for similar instruments of issuers with similar credit ratings will normally help determine the appropriate interest rate for determining the present value of a specific note at its date of issuance. In any event, the rate used for valuation purposes will normally be at least equal to the rate at which the debtor can obtain financing of a similar nature from other sources at the date of the transaction. The objective is to approximate the rate which would have resulted if an independent borrower and an independent lender had negotiated a similar transaction under comparable terms and conditions with the option to pay the cash price upon purchase or to give a note for the amount of the purchase which bears the prevailing rate of interest to maturity.[6]

Note Payable with Unreasonably Low Interest.   Although the procedure for recording a note with an unreasonably low interest rate is similar, the calculations are slightly more complex. For example, assume that the Jigs Corporation agreed to somewhat different terms in its equipment purchase agreement. The agreement now calls for one payment of $66,000 to be made at the end of four years and for interest at 4% per year on the unpaid balance payable at the end of each of the next four years. If 4% is an unreasonably low rate of interest, an appropriate rate must be determined. Again, if you assume that 12% represents an appropriate rate, the entries to record this transaction and the last payment are illustrated in Exhibit 15-6. This exhibit also shows the calculation of the present value of the note and the amortization of interest using the effective interest method. In this example the equipment is recorded at $49,963, the present value of the future cash outflows. Each year, journal entries are made to record the annual interest payment and the appropriate discount amortization. As Exhibit 15-6 illustrates, the annual interest expense is determined by multiplying the 12% rate by the carrying value of the note at the beginning of the year. The difference between the cash interest and the interest expense is the amortized discount. Finally, the carrying value of the note is increased by the amortized discount. Thus, by the maturity date the carrying value of the note equals its face value.

Bonds Payable

A **bond** is a written agreement between a borrower and a lender in which the borrower agrees to repay a stated sum and to make periodic interest payments at specified dates. Bonds have a number of common features, some of which are enumerated below. Although bonds can be issued in any denomination, in the past they usually have been issued in $1,000 denominations. In recent years, however,

---

[6] Ibid., par. 13.

$5,000 and $10,000 bonds have become more common. The denomination, or the principal, of the bond is often referred to as its **par value, face value,** or **maturity value.** The date that this principal payment is due is called the **maturity date** and can range from five to more than thirty years from the issue date. Bonds have a stated rate of interest that is part of the bond agreement. Although this interest rate is stated in annual terms, it is usually paid semiannually.

There are a number of different types of bonds, including term, serial, and convertible bonds. **Term bonds** are bonds in which the entire principal amount is

---

Exhibit 15-6
JIGS CORPORATION
Illustration of Note with Unreasonably Low Interest Rate

Journal Entries

Jan. 2, 1981	Equipment	49,963	
	Discount on note payable	16,037	
	Note payable		66,000
	To record purchase of equipment.		
Dec. 31, 1981	Interest expense	5,996	
	Discount on note payable		3,356
	Cash		2,640
	To record annual interest payment.		
Dec. 31, 1984	Interest expense	7,354	
	Discount on note payable		4,714
	Cash		2,640
	Note payable	66,000	
	Cash		66,000
	To record last interest payment and principal payment.		

Calculation of Discount

Face value of note		$66,000
Present value of note:		
Present value of $66,000 due at the end of 4 years discounted at 12%		
$66,000 × 0.63552 (See Table 5-2)	$41,944	
Present value of four annual interest payments of $2,640 ($66,000 × .04) at 12%		
$2,640 × 3.03735 (See Table 5-4)	8,019	49,963
Discount		$16,037

Exhibit 15-6 (continued)
JIGS CORPORATION
Illustration of Note with Unreasonably Low Interest Rate

Note Payable Amortization—Effective Interest

Date	Cash Interest Payment—4%	Effective Interest—12%	Discount Amortized	Balance of Unamortized Discount	Present Value or Carrying Value of Note
1/ 2/81				$16,037	$49,963
12/31/81	$ 2,640[1]	$ 5,996[2]	$ 3,356[3]	12,681[4]	53,319[5]
12/31/82	2,640	6,398	3,758	8,923	57,077
12/31/83	2,640	6,849	4,209	4,714	61,286
12/31/84	2,640	7,354	4,714	–0–	66,000
	$10,560	$26,597	$16,037		

[1] $ 2,640 = $66,000 × 0.04.
[2] $ 5,996 = $49,963 × 0.12.
[3] $ 3,356 = $ 5,996 − $ 2,640.
[4] $12,681 = $16,037 − $ 3,356.
[5] $53,319 = $66,000 − $12,681.

due at a single date. In contrast, **serial bonds** have principal payments that are payable at specified intervals. Bonds can either be secured or unsecured. Unsecured bonds are called **debentures,** whereas bonds that are secured by collateral or some specified assets of the borrower often are referred to as **mortgage bonds.** Other bonds, which are called **income bonds,** have variable interest payments that depend upon the issuers' operating income.

Some bonds have provisions that allow the holder to obtain eventually an equity position in the firm. These features enable a firm to issue the bond at a lower effective interest rate. A **convertible bond** is convertible into the firm's common stock. These bonds are usually callable, and thus allow the borrower or issuer to call or retire the bonds before their maturity. As a result, the bondholder is forced either to convert the bond or to have it redeemed before maturity. A similar type of bond includes detachable stock warrants. Holders of these bonds can use the warrants to purchase equity securities at a set price while still maintaining their debt position. Accounting for convertible bonds and for bonds with detachable warrants is discussed in Chapter 20.

Bearer or **coupon bonds** are not registered in the name of the holder but are negotiable by whomever holds them. In order to receive an interest payment, the current holder simply clips off a coupon and redeems it at an authorized bank. Other bonds are registered in the name of the holder and can be negotiated only by that holder.

Recently a number of corporations have started to issue **zero-coupon** or **zero-interest** bonds and notes. These are debt instruments that do not pay any annual interest. As a result, they are issued at deep discounts—that is, at amounts substantially less than their face or maturity value. For example, Pepsi-Co recently issued zero-coupon bonds with a face value of $850,000,000 for $54,000,000. The entire $850,000,000 must be repaid, and the $796,000,000 difference between the issue price and the face amount represents interest expense that is spread over the life of the bond.

These zero-coupon bonds are popular with both investors and issuers. The investor is able to lock in the bonds' total return when they are purchased. Because of this guaranteed return, investors are willing to accept lower interest rates than they would on traditional bonds. In addition to this feature, these bonds are also popular with issuers since they do not have to make annual interest payments.

Unlike common stockholders, holders of long-term debt such as bondholders generally are unable to vote for corporate management or otherwise participate in corporate affairs. As a result, they often insist upon written covenants in loan agreements. The purpose of these covenants is to help insure that the enterprise maintains a financial position that will insure timely interest and principal payments. Although these **indenture** agreements may take many forms, they usually include restrictions as to dividend payments, working capital position, and issuance of additional debt. In addition, these covenants may require that certain assets be pledged as security for the debt, or they may require the maintenance of a sinking fund. An example of the wording found in such covenants is shown in Exhibit 15-7.

The discussion in this chapter focuses on term bonds issued by profit-oriented enterprises to private or institutional investors. However, a variety of government agencies ranging from the federal government to local municipalities issue bonds for a number of purposes. Serial bonds are discussed in the Appendix to this chapter.

Exhibit 15-7
Illustration of a Covenant

The Corporation covenants that no dividend of any kind (other than dividends payable on the Preferred Stock of the Corporation) will be declared or paid on any stock of the Corporation at a time when the net working capital of the Corporation shall be less than the total amount of proceeds realized by the Corporation from the sale of 20-year 12% debentures due January 2, 1999 (of which this debenture is one), or if the payment of such dividend would reduce the net working capital of the Corporation to an amount less than such sum. "Net working capital" shall mean the excess of the current assets of the Corporation over its current liabilities as of the date when such determination is necessary.

The Corporation covenants that so long as this debenture remains unpaid, it will not, without the consent of the holders of the debentures of this issue, create or permit any indebtedness secured by mortgage or any funded obligation having priority over this issue.

Accounting for Bonds by the Borrower

The decision to issue bonds represents a major commitment by the corporation. The actual issue can be made in a number of ways. For example, large bond issues often are underwritten by investment bankers, who agree to purchase the entire bond issue at a certain price, and then assume the risks involved in selling the bonds to institutions and private investors. In some situations a price is established by the underwriters; in other situations the underwriters receive a commission for each bond sold. Bonds also can be issued directly to private investors or institutions without the aid of underwriters. Finally, a firm may issue bonds on a subscription basis in a manner similar to stock subscriptions. Regardless of the particular method used to issue the bonds, the accounting concepts and procedures are essentially the same. These include determining bond prices, accounting for the issuance of bonds at or between interest dates, amortization of any discount or premium, and accounting for early extinguishments of debt.

Determination of Bond Prices—Premium and Discount

As noted previously, bonds often are issued in $1,000 denominations; this will be assumed in future illustrations. However, the issuer may not receive the $1,000 face value for each bond. A bond issued at more than its face value is issued at a **premium.** Conversely, a bond issued at less than its face value is issued at a **discount.** Premiums or discounts are the result of the relationship between the prevailing market interest rate and the stated bond interest rate. The stated rate is specified on the bond and does not change over the life of the bond. This rate is referred to also as the **nominal interest rate.** On the other hand, the money market will establish a rate of interest for the particular bond depending upon relative risk and other factors. These two interest rates are apt to be different, and this difference will be reflected in the market price of the bond. Thus, a bond that has a stated rate of interest above the market rate of interest for an investment of similar risk will sell at a premium, whereas a bond that has a stated interest rate below the prevailing market interest rate will sell at a discount. The premium or discount equalizes the actual yield on the bond, with the appropriate yield prevailing in the market at the time of issue. There is, therefore, an inverse relationship between the prevailing market interest rate and the market price of a particular bond. In effect, any discount or premium should be thought of as additional interest expense (discount) or as a reduction in interest expense (premium) to be amortized over the life of the bond.

In the bond market, prices are quoted in percentages, with 100 meaning that the bond is selling currently at its face value. A bond selling at a discount is quoted at a percentage below 100. For example, a $1,000 bond selling at $980 is quoted at 98. Conversely, a $1,000 bond selling at $1,100 is quoted at 110.

Calculation of Bond Prices. Given the prevailing market interest rate, the stated interest rate, and the maturity date, bond prices can be calculated easily. When investors purchase bonds, they actually are purchasing two items: an annuity made up of future cash interest payments, and a single, future amount constituting the maturity value of the bond. Rational investors would not pay any more than the present value of these two types of future cash inflows, discounted at an appropriate interest rate.

For example, assume that $100,000 of five-year term bonds with a stated interest rate of 10% were issued to yield 12% on January 2 of the current year. The bonds pay interest semiannually every July 1 and January 1. The issue or purchase price of the bond is calculated in Exhibit 15-8.

An alternative method is to calculate directly the amount of the discount. In this example the bond is selling at a discount because the stated interest rate is only 10% (5% payable semiannually), whereas the investor is demanding a 12% (6% payable semiannually) rate. In effect, the investor receives a $1,000 shortfall during each semiannual interest period. This shortfall is the difference between the required interest payment of $6,000 ($100,000 × 0.06) and the actual interest payment of $5,000 ($100,000 × 0.05). Over the life of the bond there are 10 interest periods in which this shortfall occurs. The present value of this $1,000 annuity for 10 periods, discounted at 12% payable semiannually, represents the bond discount of $7,360. This can be verified by multiplying $1,000 by the factor in Table 4, which is the factor for 10 periods at 6%, or $1,000 × 7.36009 = $7,360.

Similar procedures would be followed if the desired yield rate were above the stated interest rate. For example, assume the same $100,000 of 10% bonds were issued to yield 8%. All other terms are the same as in the previous example. The issue purchase price of the bonds is calculated in Exhibit 15-9. Of course, if the bonds were issued at face, they would be sold at their face value of $100,000.

Individual investors need not make these calculations. A variety of bond tables are available that determine appropriate prices at different yield rates and maturity dates. As an example, a partial bond table is reproduced in Exhibit 15-10. The table is for bonds with a stated 10% interest rate, various yields from 6% to 14%, and maturity dates ranging from four years, nine months to six years.

Exhibit 15-8
Determination of Discount
Determination of Issue Price of $100,000 of Five-Year Bonds with Stated Interest Rate of 10% Issued to Yield 12%

Present value of $100,000 to be received at the end of 10 periods at 6% payable semiannually	
$100,000 × 0.55840 (Table 5-2)	$ 55,840
Present value at 6% of semiannual cash interest payments of $5,000 ($100,000 × 0.05) to be received at the end of each of the next 10 interest dates	
$5,000 × 7.36009 (Table 5-4)	36,800
Total issue price	$ 92,640
Face value of bonds	(100,000)
Discount	$ 7,360

Exhibit 15-9
Determination of Premium
Determination of Issue Price of $100,000 of Five-Year Bonds with Stated Rate of 10% Issued to Yield 8%

Present value of $100,000 to be received at the end of 10 periods at 4% payable semiannually	
$100,000 × 0.67556 (Table 5-2)	$ 67,556
Present value at 4% of semiannual interest payments of $5,000 ($100,000 × 0.05) to be received at the end of each of the next 10 interest dates	
$5,000 × 8.11090 (Table 5-4)	40,554
Total issue price	$108,110
Face value of bonds	(100,000)
Premium	$ 8,110

The use of this table can be illustrated by referring back to the premium example in Exhibit 15-9. The intersection of a yield rate of 8% and the maturity date of five years is the factor of 108.11. This indicates that the price of the bond is 108.11% of its face value. If this factor is multiplied by the $100,000 face value, the result represents the issue price of $108,110.

Journal Entries To Record Issuance of Bond. If bonds are issued on the interest date, the journal entries are straightforward. Exhibit 15-11 presents the journal entries at the date of issue for the three cases: bonds issued at par, at a discount, and at a premium. In each of the cases, bonds payable is recorded at $100,000, the maturity value. The difference between the maturity value and the cash proceeds is debited or credited to the discount or premium account, respectively.

Presentation of Discount or Premium on the Balance Sheet. Before the issuance of *Opinion No. 21*, discounts and premiums were classified on the balance sheet in a number of ways. Some firms classified the discount as a deferred charge, whereas others classified it as an offset to the bonds payable account. *Opinion No. 21* now requires "that the discount or premium should be reported on the balance sheet as a direct deduction from or as an addition to the face amount of the note."[7] The Board's view was that the discount or premium is not an asset or liability separable from the liability and thus should not be recorded as a deferred charge or credit. Proper balance sheet classification on January 2, 1981, the date of issue, for each case is shown in Exhibit 15-12.

[7] Ibid., par. 16.

Exhibit 15-10
Bond Table*

| Yield | | | | Years and Months | | | | 10% |
	4-9	4-10	4-11	5-0	5-3	5-6	5-9	6-0
6.00	116.30	116.55	116.81	117.06	117.77	118.51	119.19	119.91
6.20	115.41	115.65	115.88	116.12	116.79	117.48	118.13	118.80
6.40	114.53	114.75	114.97	115.20	115.82	116.47	117.07	117.71
6.60	113.65	113.86	114.07	114.28	114.86	115.47	116.03	116.62
6.80	112.79	112.98	113.17	113.37	113.91	114.48	115.00	115.55
7.00	111.93	112.11	112.29	112.47	112.97	113.50	113.98	114.50
7.20	111.08	111.24	111.41	111.58	112.04	112.53	112.97	113.45
7.40	110.23	110.39	110.54	110.70	111.12	111.58	111.98	112.42
7.60	109.40	109.54	109.68	109.83	110.21	110.63	110.99	111.39
7.80	108.57	108.70	108.83	108.97	109.31	109.69	110.02	110.38
8.00	107.75	107.87	107.99	108.11	108.41	108.76	109.05	109.39
8.10	107.35	107.45	107.57	107.69	107.97	108.30	108.57	108.89
8.20	106.94	107.04	107.15	107.26	107.53	107.84	108.10	108.40
8.30	106.54	106.63	106.74	106.84	107.09	107.39	107.62	107.91
8.40	106.14	106.23	106.32	106.42	106.66	106.93	107.15	107.42
8.50	105.74	105.82	105.91	106.01	106.22	106.48	106.69	106.94
8.60	105.34	105.42	105.50	105.59	105.79	106.03	106.22	106.46
8.70	104.94	105.02	105.10	105.18	105.36	105.59	105.76	105.98
8.80	104.55	104.62	104.69	104.77	104.93	105.14	105.30	105.50
8.90	104.16	104.22	104.29	104.36	104.51	104.70	104.84	105.03
9.00	103.77	103.83	103.89	103.96	104.08	104.26	104.39	104.56
9.10	103.38	103.43	103.49	103.55	103.66	103.83	103.93	104.09
9.20	103.00	103.04	103.09	103.15	103.24	103.39	103.48	103.63
9.30	102.61	102.65	102.70	102.75	102.83	102.96	103.04	103.16
9.40	102.23	102.26	102.30	102.35	102.41	102.53	102.59	102.70
9.50	101.85	101.88	101.91	101.95	102.00	102.10	102.15	102.25
9.60	101.47	101.49	101.52	101.56	101.59	101.68	101.71	101.79
9.70	101.09	101.11	101.14	101.17	101.18	101.26	101.27	101.34
9.80	100.72	100.73	100.75	100.78	100.78	100.84	100.83	100.89
9.90	100.34	100.35	100.37	100.39	100.37	100.42	100.40	100.44
10.00	99.97	99.97	99.98	100.00	99.97	100.00	99.97	100.00
10.10	99.60	99.60	99.60	99.61	99.57	99.59	99.54	99.56
10.20	99.23	99.22	99.22	99.23	99.17	99.17	99.11	99.12
10.30	98.86	98.85	98.85	98.85	98.78	98.76	98.69	98.68
10.40	98.50	98.48	98.47	98.47	98.38	98.36	98.27	98.25
10.50	98.13	98.11	98.10	98.09	97.99	97.95	97.85	97.82
10.60	97.77	97.75	97.73	97.72	97.60	97.55	97.43	97.39
10.70	97.41	97.38	97.36	97.34	97.21	97.15	97.02	96.96
10.80	97.05	97.02	96.99	96.97	96.82	96.75	96.61	96.53
10.90	96.70	96.66	96.62	96.60	96.44	96.35	96.20	96.11

Exhibit 15-10 (continued)
Bond Table*

Yield	Years and Months							10%
	4-9	4-10	4-11	5-0	5-3	5-6	5-9	6-0
11.00	96.34	96.30	96.26	96.23	96.06	95.95	95.79	95.69
11.10	95.99	95.94	95.90	95.86	95.68	95.56	95.38	95.27
11.20	95.64	95.58	95.54	95.50	95.30	95.17	94.98	94.86
11.30	95.29	95.23	95.18	95.14	94.92	94.78	94.58	94.44
11.40	94.94	94.87	94.82	94.77	94.55	94.39	94.18	94.03
11.50	94.59	94.52	94.46	94.41	94.17	94.01	93.78	93.63
11.60	94.24	94.17	94.11	94.06	93.80	93.63	93.38	93.22
11.70	93.90	93.83	93.76	93.70	93.43	93.24	92.99	92.81
11.80	93.56	93.48	93.41	93.34	93.07	92.87	92.60	92.41
11.90	93.22	93.13	93.06	92.99	92.70	92.49	92.21	92.01
12.00	92.88	92.79	92.71	92.64	92.34	92.11	91.82	91.62
12.20	92.20	92.11	92.02	91.94	91.61	91.37	91.06	90.83
12.40	91.54	91.43	91.34	91.25	90.90	90.63	90.30	90.05
12.60	90.88	90.76	90.66	90.57	90.19	89.90	89.55	89.28
12.80	90.22	90.10	89.99	89.89	89.49	89.18	88.80	88.52
13.00	89.57	89.44	89.32	89.22	88.80	88.47	88.07	87.76
13.20	88.93	88.79	88.67	88.55	88.11	87.76	87.34	87.02
13.40	88.29	88.15	88.01	87.89	87.43	87.06	86.62	86.28
13.60	87.66	87.51	87.37	87.24	86.76	86.37	85.91	85.55
13.80	87.03	86.87	86.73	86.59	86.09	85.68	85.21	84.83
14.00	86.41	86.25	86.09	85.95	85.43	85.00	84.51	84.11

*Source: *Expanded Bond Value Tables*, Desk Edition, (Boston, Mass.: Financial Publishing Company, 1970)

Subsequent Entries after Bond Issue Date

After the bond is issued, the enterprise must make periodic entries to record the cash interest payment as well as any amortization of the discount or premium. The entry to record the cash interest payment must be made at the interest payment date. An adjusting entry to accrue the interest payable should be made if the enterprise's year-end does not coincide with the interest payment date. Generally the entry to amortize any discount or premium is made on the interest payment or accrual date. However, an alternative is to record the amortization only at year-end or when financial statements are prepared. Illustrations in this chapter assume the entry is made on each interest payment or accrual date.

The discount or the premium represents an adjustment to the issuer's total interest expense related to the particular bond, and it must be written off over the life of the bond. This write-off can be accomplished by use of either the straight-line method or the effective interest method.

Exhibit 15-11
Bond Entries at Issue Date

Case 1—at Par

Cash	100,000	
Bonds payable		100,000

Case 2—at a Discount

Cash	92,640	
Discount on bonds payable	7,360	
Bonds payable		100,000

Case 3—at Premium

Cash	108,110	
Premium on Bonds payable		8,110
Bonds payable		100,000

Exhibit 15-12
Partial Balance Sheet
Long-term Liability Section

Case 1—at Par

Bonds payable—10% due January 1, 1986	$100,000

Case 2—at a Discount

Bonds payable—10% due January 1, 1986		$100,000
Less: Unamortized discount		7,360
		$ 92,640

Case 3—at Premium

Bonds payable—10% due January 1, 1986		$100,000
Plus: Unamortized premium		8,110
		$108,110

Exhibit 15-13
Journal Entries for Bond Issued at a Discount
Assuming Straight-Line Amortization

July 1, 1981	Interest expense	5,000	
	Cash		5,000
	To record semiannual interest payment (5% of $100,000).		
	Interest expense	736	
	Discount on bonds payable		736
	To record straight-line amortization of discount ($7,360 ÷ 10 periods = $736).		

These entries could be combined with the same result

	Interest expense	5,736	
	Discount on bond payable		736
	Cash		5,000
Dec. 31, 1981	Interest expense	5,000	
	Interest payable		5,000
	To record accrual of interest expense for six months.		
	Interest expense	736	
	Discount on bonds payable		736
	To record discount amortization for six months.		
Jan. 2, 1982	Interest payable	5,000	
	Cash		5,000
	To record the semiannual interest payment.		

The Straight-Line Amortization Method. Under this method the discount or premium is amortized proportionally at each interest payment or accrual date or alternatively at year-end. As a result, this method results in a constant dollar interest charge over the life of the bond. Assume that the bond in Case 2, Exhibit 15-11, is issued at a discount on January 2 and that the company uses the straight-line method and has a December 31 year-end. The entries in Exhibit 15-13 are made on July 1, 1981; December 31, 1981; and January 2, 1982.

Effective Interest Amortization Method. Although the straight-line method is relatively simple, it does not result in the accurate amortization of the discount or premium. The effective interest method is more accurate. As illustrated previously, this procedure results in a constant interest rate that is equal to the market rate at the time of issuance. In order to determine the interest expense for the period, you multiply the yield rate by the carrying value of the bonds at the beginning of the period. The effective interest method insures that the bonds always are carried at the present value of the required future payments. This method should be used unless there is no material difference between it and the straight-line method.[8] Exhibits 15-14 and 15-15 illustrate, for the initial data, the calculations for the amortization of the discount and premium, respectively.

In Exhibit 15-14 the effective bond interest expense is calculated by multiplying the carrying value of the bond by the semiannual yield rate. In this case the interest expense of $5,558 at July 1, 1981, is equal to $92,640 multiplied by 6%. The difference between the required cash interest payment of $5,000 ($100,000 × 5%) and the effective interest expense of $5,558 is the discount amortization of $558. Finally, the unamortized discount of $6,802 at July 1, 1981, is the original discount of $7,360 less the amortized discount of $558. The carrying value of the bond thus is increased by $558. Alternatively, the carrying value of the bond on July 1, 1981, $93,198, is equal to $100,000 less the remaining unamortized discount of $6,802.

Exhibit 15-14
Discount Amortization—Effective Interest Method

Date	Debit — Effective Bond Interest Expense 6%	Credit — Cash Interest Paid 5%	Credit — Discount Amortization	Unamortized Discount Balance	Carrying Value of Bond
1/2/81				$7,360	$ 92,640
7/1/81	$ 5,558[(1)]	$ 5,000	$ 558[(2)]	6,802[(3)]	93,198[(4)]
1/2/82	5,592	5,000	592	6,210	93,790
7/1/82	5,627	5,000	627	5,583	94,417
1/2/83	5,665	5,000	665	4,918	95,082
7/1/83	5,705	5,000	705	4,213	95,787
1/2/84	5,747	5,000	747	3,466	96,534
7/1/84	5,792	5,000	792	2,674	97,326
1/2/85	5,840	5,000	840	1,834	98,166
7/1/85	5,890	5,000	890	944	99,056
1/2/86	5,944	5,000	944	–0–	100,000
	$57,360	$50,000	$7,360		

[(1)] $5,558 = $92,640 × 0.06.
[(2)] $558 = $5,558 − $5,000.
[(3)] $6,802 = $7,360 − $558.
[(4)] $93,198 = $100,000 − $6,802, or $93,198 = $92,640 + $558.

[8] Ibid., par. 15.

Exhibit 15-15 is constructed in a similar manner. However, in the premium case the effective semiannual interest rate is 4%, and the carrying value of the bond is reduced by the amortized premium. Given that the firm has a December 31 year-end, the journal entries for both the discount and premium cases are presented for 1981, the first year, and for 1985, the last year, in Exhibit 15-16.

This notion that the effective interest method insures that the bonds always are carried at the present value of the required future payments can be proven by referring back to the discount example in Exhibit 15-14. As of July 1, 1981, the carrying value of the bonds is $93,198. Exhibit 15-17 illustrates how this figure can be calculated independently by discounting the future cash payment at 10% payable semiannually for nine interest periods.

Issuance of Bonds between Interest Dates

In the previous examples the bonds were assumed to be issued on an interest payment date. In many situations, however, bonds are issued on a date other than the interest date. In these cases the purchaser of the bond must pay the issuer for the interest that has accrued since the last interest date because the purchaser will receive the required interest payment regardless of how long the bond has been held. For example, interest usually is received by bondholders when they present their interest coupon to a bank. Banks will not honor a partial

---

Exhibit 15-15
Premium Amortization—Effective Interest Method

Date	Debit Effective Bond Interest Expense 4%	Credit Cash Interest Paid 5%	Debit Premium Amortization	Unamortized Premium Balance	Carrying Value of Bond
1/2/81				$8,110	$108,110
7/1/81	$ 4,324[1]	$ 5,000	$ 676[2]	7,434[3]	107,434[4]
1/2/82	4,297	5,000	703	6,731	106,731
7/1/82	4,269	5,000	731	6,000	106,000
1/2/83	4,240	5,000	760	5,240	105,240
7/1/83	4,210	5,000	790	4,450	104,450
1/2/84	4,178	5,000	822	3,628	103,628
7/1/84	4,145	5,000	855	2,773	102,773
1/2/85	4,111	5,000	889	1,884	101,884
7/1/85	4,075	5,000	925	959	100,959
1/2/86	4,041*	5,000	959	–0–	100,000
	$41,890	$50,000	$8,110		

[1] $4,324 = $108,110 × 0.04.
[2] $676 = $5,000 − 4,324.
[3] $7,434 = $8,110 − $676.
[4] $107,434 = $100,000 + $7,434, or $107,434 = $108,110 − $676.
* Rounding error.

Exhibit 15-16
Journal Entries

	Discount		Premium	
July 1, 1981	Interest expense	5,558	Interest expense	4,324
	Discount on bonds payable	558	Premium on bonds payable	676
	Cash	5,000	Cash	5,000
	To record interest payment.		To record interest payment.	
Dec. 31, 1981	Interest expense	5,592	Interest expense	4,297
	Discount on bonds payable	592	Premium on bonds payable	703
	Interest payable	5,000	Interest payable	5,000
	To record accrual of six months' interest.		To record accrual of six months' interest.	
Jan. 2, 1982	Interest payable	5,000	Interest payable	5,000
	Cash	5,000	Cash	5,000
	To record payment of interest.		To record payment of interest.	
July 1, 1985	Interest expense	5,890	Interest expense	4,075
	Discount on bonds payable	890	Premium on bonds payable	925
	Cash	5,000	Cash	5,000
	To record interest payment.		To record interest payment.	
Dec. 31, 1985	Interest expense	5,944	Interest expense	4,041
	Discount on bonds payable	944	Premium on bonds payable	959
	Interest payable	5,000	Interest payable	5,000
	To record accrual of six months' interest.		To record accrual of six months' interest.	
Jan. 2, 1986	Interest payable	5,000	Interest payable	5,000
	Bonds payable	100,000	Bonds payable	100,000
	Cash	105,000	Cash	105,000
	To record interest and principal payment.		To record interest and principal payment.	

Exhibit 15-17
Determination of Present Value of $100,000 of 10% Bonds
Issued to Yield 12% as of July 1, 1981

Present value of $100,000 to be received at end of
ninth period at 6%, interest payable semiannually
$100,000 × 0.59189 (Table 5-2) $59,190
Present value at 6%, interest payable semiannually,
cash payment of $5,000 to be received at the end of
each of the next nine periods
$5,000 × 6.8017 (Table 5-4)   34,008
                                                                   $93,198

---

coupon. Therefore, bondholders will receive all the interest that has accrued since the last interest date although they may be entitled to only a partial payment.

This interest element must be accounted for separately. For illustration purposes, assume that the $100,000 of five-year, 10% bonds were issued at par on March 1, 1981, rather than on January 2, 1981. Again, the interest is payable semiannually on July 1 and January 2. The correct entries to record the issuance of the bonds on March 1, 1981, and the interest payment on July 1, 1981, are shown in Exhibit 15-18.

Exhibit 15-18
Journal Entries to Record Issuance of Bonds
between Interest Dates

Mar. 1, 1981	Cash	101,667	
	Interest payable		1,667*
	Bonds payable		100,000
	To record issuance of $100,000 of 10% bonds.		
July 1, 1981	Interest payable	1,667	
	Interest expense	3,333	
	Cash		5,000
	To record semiannual interest payment of $5,000.		

*$100,000 @ 10% interest
for two months = $100,000
× 0.10 × 2/12 = $1,667.

As illustrated, the firm receives $101,667, the face value of the bond plus the interest that has accrued since the last interest date. In this example two months' interest, or $1,667, has accrued since the last interest date and is credited to the interest payable account. On July 1 cash is credited for $5,000. The interest payable is debited for $1,667 and interest expense for $3,333. The debit to interest expense represents four months of interest at 10% and is the net interest cost to the firm.

Discount or Premium on Bonds Issued between Interest Dates. Bonds are likely to be sold between interest dates at either a discount or premium. In order to determine the issue price, you can use either present value techniques or a bond table. For example, assume that the $100,000 of five-year, 10% bonds previously described were sold at a discount on March 1 to yield 10%. The issue price can be approximated closely by referring to Exhibit 15-14. The exhibit shows that if the bonds were issued on January 2, 1981, an interest payment date, the price is $92,640. Because the bonds were not issued until March, two months of the discount must be added to the $92,640 to determine the price on that date. Exhibit 15-14 indicates that the discount amortization for the six-month period—January 2, 1981, to July 1, 1981—is $558. Two-sixths of that amount, or $186, is added to $92,640 on March 1, 1981, to determine the price of $92,826. Thus, the discount is $7,174, or $100,000 minus $92,826. It should be noted that the amount is slightly different from what would be obtained if you referred to a bond table. If you use the table in Exhibit 15-10, the price is $92,790 (the intersection between 12% and the remaining life of four years, ten months). The $36 difference is due to ratably allocating the first six-month amortization in Exhibit 15-14 to each month rather than determining the monthly interest using the effective interest method.

In order to determine the cash proceeds, you must add the interest accrued since January 2, 1981, to the issue price. The calculation of the total proceeds of $94,493 is illustrated in Exhibit 15-19. The journal entry on March 1, 1981, is as follows:

Cash	94,493	
Discount on bonds payable	7,174	
Interest payable		1,667
Bonds payable		100,000
To record the bond issues on March 1.		

To calculate the price of a bond issued between interest dates at a premium, you would use a similar procedure. However, that portion of the premium that must be amortized from the initial interest date to the actual issue date ($676 × 2/6 = $225) is subtracted from the present value as of the initial interest date (price equals $107,885 or $108,110 − $225). It should be noted that the amount is slightly different from what you would obtain if referring to a bond table. If you

---

Exhibit 15-19
Calculation of Accrued Interest on Bond Sold at a Discount

Face value of Bond	$100,000
Less: Discount calculated above	7,174
Carrying value on March 1	$ 92,826
Add: Two months' accrued interest	1,667
Cash proceeds received	$ 94,493

---

use the table in Exhibit 15-10, the price is $107,870 (the intersection between 8% and the remaining life of four years, ten months). The $15 difference is due to ratably allocating the first six-month amortization in Exhibit 15-15 to each month.

Subsequent Entries. In subsequent periods the discount or premium must be amortized over the remaining life of the bond. Either the straight-line method or the preferable effective interest method may be used. For this example, if you use the straight-line method, the discount is amortized proportionately over the *remaining* 58 months at a rate of $124 per month ($7,174 ÷ 58). Based on this data, the entry on July 1, 1981, is as follows:

Interest expense	5,496	
Discount on bonds payable		496*
Cash		5,000
*$124 × 4 months = $496		

To amortize the discount using the effective interest method, you must construct an amortization table similar to that in Exhibit 15-14. If a minor adjustment is made at the first interest date, the table in this exhibit can be used to make subsequent journal entries. The first entry on July 1 is below:

Interest expense	5,372	
Discount on bonds payable		372*
Cash		5,000
*4/6 × $558 = 372		

Remember that the carrying value of the bond is $92,826 and has already been adjusted for two months of discount amortization. Thus, only four months, or $372 (4/16 × $558), of the discount must be amortized. After this entry is made, the carrying value of the bond is $93,198 ($92,826 + $372), which is the value recorded in Exhibit 15-14 for 7/1/81. Thereafter, the remaining entries can be drawn right from the table. The entry for December 31, 1981, is as follows:

Interest expense	5,592	
Discount on bonds payable		592
Interest payable		5,000

It is important to note that this entry is the same as that for December 31, 1981, illustrated in Exhibit 15-16.

Expenses Incurred When Issuing Bonds

A variety of costs are incurred when an enterprise issues bonds. These costs are referred to as **issue costs.** Examples of such costs include printing, engraving, legal, and accounting costs. Further, many bonds are marketed through investment bankers who receive a commission for underwriting the bond issue. As a result of these costs, the lenders receive less cash from the bond issue than they would have received otherwise. Current accounting practice requires that these costs be accounted for separately and not be combined with the discount or premium account. These costs are reported on the balance sheet as deferred charges and are then amortized generally using the straight-line method over the remaining life of the bond.[9]

There are theoretical problems with this treatment. As the *Statement of Financial Accounting Concepts No. 3* points out, debt issue costs are not an asset in that they provide no future economic benefit: "debt issue cost in effect reduces the proceeds of borrowing and increases the effective interest rate, and thus may be accounted for the same as debt discount."[10] This means that the lender should account only for the net cash received; thus, the issue cost becomes a liability valuation account causing a reduction of the face or maturity value of the bond. This treatment would increase the effective interest cost related to the bond issue.

Accounting procedures under current practice—treating the issue cost as a deferred charge—are illustrated by the following example. Assume that a firm issues $100,000 of five-year, 10% bonds on January 2, 1981, to yield 12%. Interest is paid semiannually on July 1 and January 2. The firm incurs issue costs of $5,000. The required entries on January 2, 1981, and July 1, 1981, using the effective interest method for amortizing the discount, are presented in Exhibit 15-20.

---

[9] Ibid., par. 16.

[10] "Elements of Financial Statements of Business Enterprises," *Statement of Financial Accounting Concepts No. 3* (Stamford, Conn.: FASB, 1980), par. 101.

Exhibit 15-20
Accounting for Bond Issue Cost—Journal Entries

Jan. 2, 1981	Cash	$87,640	
	Discount on bonds payable	7,360	
	Bond issue costs	5,000	
	Bonds payable		100,000
	To record issuance of bonds—see Exhibit 15-14.		
July 1, 1981	Bond issue expense	500[1]	
	Interest expense	5,558[2]	
	Discount on bonds payable		558
	Bond issue costs		500
	Cash		5,000
	To record semiannual interest payment and amortization of discount and bond issue cost.		

[1] $5,000 ÷ 10 interest periods = $500—straight-line method.
[2] See Exhibit 15-14—effective interest method.

Bond Sinking Fund Provisions

Many bond agreements require that the issuing corporation create and maintain a sinking fund. A **sinking fund** is a collection of cash and other assets that are set apart from the remaining assets of the firm and are used only for specified purposes. The fund is generally under the control of a trustee or agent who is independent of the issuing corporation. Provisions of the bond indenture usually require the payment of periodic sums to the fund. The trustee of the fund then invests these monies, which are used to make principal and/or interest payments. The accounting procedures relating to interest expense recognition by the issuing corporation are not affected by the existence of bond sinking funds.

Early Extinguishment of Debt

Early extinguishment of debt occurs whenever a firm's long-term debt is retired before maturity. Reacquisition and/or refunding of long-term debt are financing decisions of management and depend upon such variables as cash flows and past, existing, and anticipated interest rates. For example, it may be very advantageous for management to repurchase bonds when market interest rates have risen since the original issue date. This is illustrated by the following example. Assume that the Pacific Union Corporation issued $50,000, 6%, twenty-year bonds at face at the beginning of 1972. Because the bonds were issued at face, market interest rates were equivalent to the stated interest rates for that type of debt securities. However, by the beginning of 1980 interest rates rose to 10%, and as a result the market value of the bonds decreased to $36,201 (present value of the future cash flows—interest and principal—discounted at 5% payable semi-annually for 24 interest periods). It may be advantageous for Pacific Union to repurchase these bonds on the open market because it can liquidate a $50,000 debt for only $36,201.

This situation did occur in fact during the inflationary period of the 1970s. For example, in 1978 Caesar's World, Inc. redeemed a total of $10,915,000 of its 8% debt at 65% of par value. This transaction resulted in an extraordinary gain of $3,672,000.

Bond retirements can take place in a variety of ways and for a variety of reasons. For example, some bonds have call provisions that allow the issuer to redeem the bonds at certain dates and prices. These callable bonds permit the issuing corporation to take advantage of changing interest rates. Noncallable bonds also can be retired before their maturity through their repurchase on the open market. The accounting for early extinguishment of debt is the same regardless of the manner in which the bonds are retired.

Accounting for Early Extinguishment of Debt

When a firm extinguishes its debt before maturity, a gain or loss usually will occur. The gain or loss is the difference between the reacquisition price and the net carrying value of the debt. The **reacquisition price** of the bond or other debt is the amount actually paid, including any call premium or other reacquisition costs. The **net carrying amount** is the amount due at maturity, adjusted for the unamortized premium or discount and the issue cost. If the net carrying value exceeds the reacquisition price, a *gain* occurs. Conversely, if the reacquisition price exceeds the carrying value, a *loss* occurs. There are two issues related to the gain or loss on early extinguishment of debt: (1) the period in which the gain or loss should be recognized and (2) the nature of the gain or loss.

The Period in Which the Gain or Loss Is Recognized

Before the issuance of any official pronouncements, the gain or loss on early extinguishment could be handled in three different ways:

1. Amortization over the remaining original life of the extinguished issue.
2. Amortization over the life of the new issue.
3. Recognition currently in income as a loss or gain.

Each method has been supported in court decisions, in regulatory agency rulings, and in the professional accounting literature. In order to reduce the permissible alternatives, the APB issued *Opinion No. 26*, "Early Extinguishment of Debt," which noted that all early extinguishments of debt are fundamentally alike, and that the accounting for these transactions should be the same regardless of the

APB #26

means used to achieve the extinguishment.[11] The Opinion requires that any gain or loss be recognized currently in the period of the extinguishment. This requirement is based on the view that the market rate of interest has caused a change in the market value of the debt, which has yet to be reflected in the accounts. The entire gain or loss should be recorded in the current period when the bond is extinguished because it is related solely to past or current periods.

The Nature of the Gain or Loss

Even with the issuance of *Opinion No. 26*, considerable controversy arose over the nature of the gain or loss—that is, whether it meets the criteria to be an extraordinary item on the income statement. When *Opinion No. 26* was issued, the requirements of *Opinion No. 9* were still in effect and the gain or loss often was considered extraordinary. Shortly thereafter, the APB issued *Opinion No. 30*, which concluded that a gain or loss on early extinguishment of debt was not considered extraordinary.[12] As noted previously, the interest rates and market conditions in the 1970s caused many firms to extinguish large amounts of debt at a substantial gain. Under the criteria of *Opinion 30*, these gains were included in "income from continuing operations." After considerable pressure from the SEC and others, the FASB decided to review the classification of gains and losses arising from early extinguishment of debt and in 1975 issued *Statement No. 4*, "Reporting Gains and Losses from Early Extinguishment of Debt." This Statement requires that "gains and losses from extinguishment of debt . . . be aggregated and, if material, classified as an extraordinary item net of related income tax effect."[13] Thus, for early extinguishment of debt the Statement overrides criteria set forth in *Opinion No. 30* that extraordinary items be unusual in nature and occur infrequently. Further, this Statement requires the disclosure of the following:

APB #30

FASB #4

1. A complete description of the transaction, including how the debt was extinguished.
2. The net income tax effect.
3. The per share amount of the gain or loss net of the tax effect.

   In an example used previously in this chapter, $100,000 of five-year, 10% bonds were issued at a discount to yield 12%. Now assume that these bonds are called on July 1, 1984, at a price of 102, or for a total of $102,000. If the interest accrual or discount amortization has not been recorded yet, the journal entries in Exhibit 15-21 are made. The extraordinary loss on the redemption ($4,674) is the difference between the carrying value of the bonds on July 1, 1984, $97,326, and the reacquisition price of $102,000. It is important to note that any discount or premium must be amortized to the date of extinguishment.

---

[11] "Early Extinguishment of Debt," *Opinions of the Accounting Principles Board No. 26* (New York: AICPA, 1972).

[12] "Reporting the Results of Operations," *Opinions of the Accounting Principles Board No. 30* (New York: AICPA, 1973).

[13] "Reporting Gains and Losses from Extinguishment of Debt," *Statement of Financial Accounting Standards No. 4* (Stamford, Conn.: FASB, 1975), par. 8.

Exhibit 15-21
Journal Entries to Record Early Extinguishment of Debt

July 1, 1981	Interest expense	5,792	
	Discount on bond payable		792
	Cash		5,000
	To record interest payment and discount amortization— see Exhibit 15-14 for data.		
	Bonds payable	100,000	
	Extraordinary loss on redemption	4,674[2]	
	Discount on bonds payable		2,674[1]
	Cash		102,000
	To record the repurchase of bonds at 102.		

[1] See Exhibit 15-14.
[2] Calculation of extraordinary loss:

Redemption price	102,000
Net carrying value of bond	$ 97,326
Loss	($ 4,674)

Accounting for Bonds by the Investor

Accounting for bonds by the investor is similar to that by the issuer, except that the investor records an asset—investment in bonds—rather than a liability—bonds payable. The investment in bonds account can be classified either as a current asset or as a long-term investment depending on the marketability of the bonds and on management's intention as to when the bonds will be converted into cash.

Accounting for the Acquisition of Bonds

The acquisition price of bonds includes the purchase price, the brokerage commission, and other costs related to the purchase. The bonds may be purchased at their face value, or at a discount or premium. In practice, the debit to the bond account is made at cost, including the acquisition costs mentioned above. A separate account is not maintained for the premium or discount. This treatment of the discount and premium account varies from the recommendation made in the official pronouncements and is based on materiality considerations.[14] Examples in this chapter will not use separate premium or discount accounts. If the bonds are purchased between interest dates, the investor must pay the previous owner for

---

[14] APB *Opinion No. 21* applies to both bonds payable and investment in bonds.

Exhibit 15-22
Accounting for the Acquisition of Bonds

Case 1—at 98
(Discount)

Investment in bonds	49,000[1]
Interest receivable	1,000[2]
Cash	50,000

[1] $49,000 = $50,000 × 0.98.
[2] $ 1,000 = $50,000 × 0.12 × 2/12.

Case 2—at face

Investment in bonds	50,000
Interest receivable	1,000
Cash	51,000

Case 3—at 102
(Premium)

Investment in bonds	51,000[3]
Interest receivable	1,000[4]
Cash	52,000

[3] $51,000 = $50,000 × 1.02.
[4] $ 1,000 = $50,000 × 0.12 × 2/12.

any interest accrued since the last interest date, since the investor will collect all this interest on the next payment date. The interest element must be accounted for separately.

Accounting for bond purchases is illustrated by the following examples. Assume that on March 1, 1981, AB Investment Company purchases 12% bonds dated January 1, 1981, with a face value of $50,000. Note that the purchase date is between interest dates. Interest is payable each July 1 and January 2. Exhibit 15-22 presents the journal entries if the bonds were purchased at (1) 98, (2) face, or (3) 102. (Quoted prices include all brokerage fees.)

Discount and Premium Amortization

When a company invests in bonds as a short-term investment, no discount or premium amortization is recorded by the investor. When bonds are held as a long-term investment, the investor should amortize any premium or discount on the bond investment. The straight-line method or the effective interest method can be used to amortize the bond discount or premium. As noted previously, the effective interest method should be used unless there are no material differences between the two methods. Regardless of which method is used, the discount is amortized by debiting the investment in bond account, and the premium is amortized by crediting the investment in bond account. This insures that the investment account will reflect the maturity value of the bond after the discount or premium is fully amortized.

Straight-Line Amortization. Under the straight-line method the discount or premium is amortized ratably over the remaining life of the bond. Given that the amortization entry is made at each interest date and the bond matures in four years and ten months, the journal entries for each of the three cases as of July 1, 1981, December 31, 1981 (calendar year-end), January 2, 1982, and January 2, 1986 (maturity date) are presented in Exhibit 15-23.

As this exhibit illustrates, the amortized discount increases the carrying value of the bond. Total interest expense for the period equals the stated interest rate plus the amortized discount. From the investor's point of view, the discount represents additional interest income earned over the life of the bond. By the maturity date, January 2, 1986, the carrying value of the bond has been increased to $50,000, its maturity value. Conversely, the amortized premium decreases the carrying value of the bond and represents a decrease in interest expense over the life of the bond. Again, by the maturity date the carrying value of the bond has been decreased to its maturity value of $50,000.

Effective Interest Method. The effective interest method is the preferable amortization method. However, because an investor usually purchases only part of a bond issue, there may not be a material difference between this method and the straight-line method. The entries under the effective interest method are the same as illustrated above for the straight-line amortization. The interest revenue is determined by multiplying the effective rate times the book value of the investment. The amortization is the difference between the calculated interest revenue and the cash interest received. Thus, the calculations when using the effective interest method are similar to those made by the issuer.

Exhibit 15-23
Discount and Premium Amortization

Date	Case 1—Discount	Dr	Cr	Case 2—Face	Dr	Cr	Case 3—Premium	Dr	Cr
July 1, 1981	Investment in bond	68.97[2]					Cash	3,000.00[7]	
	Cash	3,000.00[1]		Cash	3,000.00		Interest receivable		1,000.00[8]
	Interest receivable		1,000.00	Interest receivable		1,000.00	Interest income		1,931.03[9]
	Interest income		2,068.97[3]	Interest income		2,000.00	Investment in bond		68.97[8]
Dec. 31, 1981	Investment in bond	103.44[4]					Interest receivable	2,896.56	
	Interest receivable	3,000.00		Interest receivable	3,000.00		Interest income	103.44	
	Interest income		3,108.44[5]	Interest income		3,000.00	Investment in bond		3,000.00
Jan. 2, 1982	Cash	3,000.00		Cash	3,000.00		Cash	3,000.00	
	Interest receivable		3,000.00	Interest receivable		3,000.00	Interest receivable		3,000.00
Jan. 2, 1986	Cash	53,000.00[6]		Cash	53,000.00		Cash	53,000.00[10]	
	Interest receivable		3,000.00	Interest receivable		3,000.00	Interest receivable		3,000.00
	Investment in bond		50,000.00	Investment in bond		50,000.00	Investment in bond		50,000.00

(1) $3,000 = $50,000 × 0.06.
(2) Discount of $1,000 ÷ 58 months = $17.24 per month × 4 months = $68.97.
(3) Interest income of $2,068.97 = $2,000 interest income earned from 3/1/81 to 7/1/81 plus $68.97 amortized discount.
(4) Discount amortized—$17.24 × 6 months = $103.44.
(5) Interest income = $3,000 interest earned from 7/1/81 to 12/31/81 plus amortized discount of $103.44.
(6) This entry assumes interest accruals and discount amortizations were made on 12/31/85.
(7) $3,000 = $50,000 × 0.06.
(8) Premium of $1,000 ÷ 58 months = $17.24 per month × 4 months = $68.97.
(9) Interest income of $1931.03 = $2,000 interest income earned from 3/1/81 to 7/1/81 less amortized premium.
(10) This entry assumes interest accruals and discount amortization were made on 12/31/85.

Sale of Bonds Before the Maturity Date

When bonds are sold before their maturity date, a gain or loss usually will occur. This gain or loss is the difference between the carrying value of the bond, after amortizing the discount or premium to the sale date, and the net proceeds from the sale. This gain or loss is included in income from operations and thus is not considered an extraordinary item. Any interest accrued since the last interest date must be accounted for separately.

For example, assume that a $50,000, five-year bond, dated January 1, 1981, was purchased at a price of 98 on March 1, 1981, and was sold at 101 plus accrued interest on October 1, 1983. If the AB Investment Co. uses straight-line amortization, Exhibit 15-24 shows how the gain on the sale of the bonds is determined. This exhibit also presents the journal entries that are made to record this sale. The first journal entry records the amortization of the discount since July 1, 1983, the last interest date. The second journal entry records the sale of the bonds. These journal entries could be combined.

Other Forms of Long-Term Debt

This chapter has been concerned primarily with accounting problems related to bonds. There are, however, other types of long-term debt, including convertible bonds and bonds with detachable stock warrants, mortgages payable, and short-term debt expected to be refinanced.

Exhibit 15-24
Recording Gain on Sale of Bonds

Journal Entries

Oct. 1, 1983

Investment in bond		52	
Interest income			52

To record discount amortization from 7/1/83 to 10/1/83—three months at $17.24 per month ($1,000 discount ÷ 58 mos).

Cash		52,000	
Investment in bonds			49,534
Gain on sale of bond			966*
Interest income			1,500

To record sale of bonds at 101 plus accrued interest of $1,500 ($50,000 × 0.06 × 3/6).

*Proceeds from sale of bonds without accrued interest		$50,500
Carrying value of bonds on 10/1/83:		
Original cost	$49,000	
Discount amortized from 3/1/81 to 10/1/83 = $1,000 × 31/58	534	49,534
Gain on sale		$ 966

Dilutive Debt Securities

Dilutive debt securities include convertible bonds and bonds with detachable stock warrants. These debt securities allow investors either to convert the bond holdings into equity securities or to purchase equity securities by exercising the stock warrants. They are considered dilutive because conversion to common stock will dilute the current shareholders' equity. The accounting theory and problems related to these debt securities are described in Chapter 21.

Mortgages Payable

A **mortgage** is a promissory note secured by an asset; its title is pledged to the lender. Mortgages often are used to purchase specific assets rather than to obtain cash for general purposes. Generally, they are payable in equal installments consisting of interest and principal over the life of the mortgage. Some mortgages, however, are payable in full on the maturity date. Mortgages generally range from a few years in duration to forty years.

There are no particular accounting problems associated with mortgages. As with other liabilities, a reasonable rate of interest must be stated, or the procedures under *Opinion No. 21* must be applied. If mortgages are payable in installments, the payments due within the next twelve months must be classified as a current maturity of long-term debt. The remaining portion is, of course, a long-term liability.

Short-Term Debt Expected to Be Refinanced

Chapter 14 contains a complete discussion of short-term debt expected to be refinanced. As explained in that chapter, if the provisions of FASB *Statement No. 6* are met, all or some portion of the short-term debt should be reclassified. Basically, the provisions of *Statement No. 6* allow the reclassification of short term as long term if (1) the firm intends to refinance the debt and (2) it can demonstrate its ability to do so.

Troubled Debt Restructurings

In some situations debtors are unable to meet their obligations. General economic conditions or changes in market structure may cause economic difficulties for particular firms. In these situations holders of long-term debt, banks, and other creditors face tough choices. On one hand, if financial distress forces the debtor into default, the creditor can begin bankruptcy proceedings. The outcome of such proceedings are, of course, unknown, and the creditor ultimately may receive only a few cents on each dollar of debt. On the other hand, the debtor and creditor may agree to restructure the debt by changing the payment or interest terms in order to enable the debtor to liquidate the liability eventually.

This situation is illustrated easily by two recent examples. Due to a rapidly falling U.S. automobile market, Chrysler Corporation was forced to restructure a large portion of its debt. Chrysler creditors agreed to this restructuring based on government guarantees and on the hope of keeping the firm afloat. Another case occurred in 1981 when Braniff International's financial condition deteriorated as fuel costs and interest rates soared. In an effort to keep Braniff a viable company, the company's creditors agreed to a major debt restructuring. However, Braniff is currently in bankruptcy proceedings.

This section of the chapter illustrates the proper accounting for such troubled debt restructuring.

What Is a Troubled Debt Restructuring?

FASB *Statement No. 15* defines a **troubled debt restructuring** as a debt restructuring in which the "creditor for economic or legal reasons related to the debtor's financial difficulties grants a concession to the debtor it would not otherwise consider." [15] As a result, a troubled debt restructuring may include one or a combination of the following:

1. A transfer of an asset to the creditor by the debtor to satisfy a debt fully or partially (asset swap).
2. The issuance of an equity interest to the creditor by the debtor to satisfy a debt fully or partially (equity swap).
3. Modification of terms of the debt through a change in one or more of the following:
   a The interest rate.
   b Maturity date.
   c Face value of the debt.
   d Accrued interest.

A debt restructuring will not qualify as a troubled debt restructuring just because the debtor is experiencing financial difficulties. Further, if the debtor can obtain funds from sources other than the existing creditor at current market rates similar to those for non-troubled debt, a troubled debt restructuring does not exist. Thus, according to *Statement No. 15*, a troubled debt restructuring does not occur if:

1. The fair value of the assets or equity interest transferred by the debtor to the creditor in full satisfaction of the creditor's receivable equals the creditor's recorded investment in the receivable.
2. The fair value of the assets or equity interest transferred by the debtor to the creditor in full settlement of the debtor's payable at least equals the carrying value of that payable.
3. The creditor reduces the effective interest rate to reflect current interest rates in order to maintain the relationship.
4. The debtor in exchange for old debt issues new debt with an interest rate that reflects current market rates.[16]

---

[15] "Accounting by Debtors and Creditors for Troubled Debt Restructuring," *Statement of Financial Accounting Standards No. 15* (Stamford, Conn.: FASB, 1977), par. 2.

[16] Ibid., par. 7.

Accounting for Troubled Debt Restructurings

As noted previously, there are three major types of troubled debt restructurings: (1) a transfer of assets, (2) a grant of an equity interest, or (3) a modification of terms. In general, the restructuring will result in a gain to the debtor and a loss to the creditor. However, in some situations involving a modification of terms, the Board believed that the restructuring is essentially only a continuation of the old debt, and as such no gain or loss should be recognized.

Full Satisfaction through an Asset or Equity Transfer.

These two types of troubled debt restructurings involve a transfer of assets or an equity interest in full satisfaction of the debt. The Board concluded that these debt restructurings represent completed transactions and as such should be based on fair values. As a result, the debtor will recognize a gain on the restructuring which is measured by the excess of the carrying value of the payable over the fair value of the assets or equity transferred to the creditor. These gains on troubled debt restructuring should be aggregated and, if material, should be classified as extraordinary because they represent early extinguishments of debt and fall under the criteria of *Statement No. 4*. If an asset swap is involved, the debtor also should recognize a gain or loss on the disposition of the asset. This gain or loss is measured by the difference between the fair value of the asset and its carrying value, and, according to *Opinion No. 30*, would be included in income from continuing operations.

The creditor will recognize a loss to the extent of the excess of the carrying value of the receivable over the fair value of the asset received in the exchange. This loss is considered an ordinary loss and may be offset against the allowance for doubtful accounts receivable. Finally, after the restructuring, the creditor shall account for assets received in satisfaction of a receivable the same as if the assets had been acquired for cash.

For example, the Voice Corporation, which manufactures CB radios, has been experiencing financial difficulties in recent years and is unable to meet its $100,000 debt to its local bank. Consequently, the bank agrees to accept a parcel of land owed by the Voice Corporation in full settlement of the debt. The land has a fair market value of $88,000 and a book value of $65,000. The journal entries for the Voice Corporation (the borrower) and the local bank (the creditor) are presented in Exhibit 15-25.

The ordinary gain on disposition of land ($23,000) is the difference between the fair market value of the asset ($88,000) and its book value ($65,000). The extraordinary gain from debt restructuring ($12,000) is the difference between the $100,000 note payable and the $88,000 fair value of the land. The creditor's loss on debt restructuring ($12,000) is the difference between the carrying value of the receivable ($100,000) and the fair value of the land received from the Voice Corporation ($88,000). This loss could be debited to allowance for doubtful accounts receivable rather than to the loss on restructuring account.

Issuance of equities for full satisfaction of a debt is handled in a manner similar to an asset swap. For example, assume the same facts in the above example except that the Voice Corporation issued the local bank 5,000 shares of its no-par common stock that had a fair market value of $90,000. Exhibit 15-26 presents the journal entries for the Voice Corporation and the local bank to record this transaction.

Exhibit 15-25
Journal Entries—Troubled Debt Restructuring
Asset Swap

Voice Corporation

Notes payable to local banks	100,000	
Ordinary gain on disposition of land		23,000[1]
Land		65,000
Extraordinary gain from debt restructuring		12,000[2]

Local Bank

Land	88,000	
Loss on receivables	12,000	
Notes receivable		100,000

[1]	Fair market value of land	$ 88,000
	Book value of land	65,000
	Gain on disposition	$ 23,000

[2]	Carrying value of payable	$100,000
	Fair market value of land	88,000
	Extraordinary gain	$ 12,000

Exhibit 15-26
Journal Entries—Troubled Debt Restructuring
Equity Swap

Voice Corporation

Note payable	100,000	
Common stock—no par		90,000
Extraordinary gain from debt restructuring		10,000[1]

Local Bank

Investment in common stock	90,000	
Loss on receivables	10,000	
Note receivable		100,000

[1]	Carrying value of payable	$100,000
	Fair market value of stock	90,000
	Extraordinary gain	$ 10,000

The gain to the Voice Corporation is measured by the difference between the carrying value of the note ($100,000) and the fair market value of the stock ($90,000). Conversely, the $10,000 loss to the local bank is measured by the difference between the carrying value of the receivable ($100,000) and the fair market value of the stock ($90,000).

Modification of Terms. A modification of terms is a debt restructuring that involves a reduction in the stated interest rate, an extension of the maturity date, a reduction in the face amount of the debt, or a combination of the above. In this situation the Board noted that there is no transfer of resources; in fact, there is a continuation of the existing debt. As a result, *Statement No. 15* requires that no loss to the creditor or gain to the debtor "should be recognized in a troubled debt restructuring of this type if the total future cash receipts or payments (whether designated as interest or face amount) specified by the new terms, at least equals the recorded investment or carrying amount of the debt before the restructuring."[17] The Board took its position in the belief that the creditor is interested in recovering its investment in the receivable. Thus, as long as the cash flows are large enough to recover the investment in the receivable, no gain or loss is recognized. There is, however, an adjustment in the effective interest income or expense.

In some debt restructurings involving a modification of terms, the future cash flows—including both principal and interest—are less than the debt. In this situation the debtor recognizes an extraordinary gain measured by the excess of the carrying value of the payable over the future cash outflows. The creditor recognizes an ordinary loss measured by the excess of the recorded receivable over the future cash inflows. These two different cases are illustrated below.

No Gain or Loss Recognized—Future Cash Flows Exceed Carrying Value.
Assume that the Charles Co. is unable to meet the terms of its long-term debt to the Second National Bank. The Charles Co. had borrowed $100,000 at 14% interest. The entire principal is due on December 31, 1985, and the interest is due annually. Under a restructuring plan agreed to on January 1, 1981, the bank agrees to forgive $20,000 of the principal and to reduce the interest rate from 14% to 8%. Interest is still due annually, and the principal is still due on December 31, 1985. Under the terms of this restructuring agreement, as illustrated in Exhibit 15-27, the future cash interest and principal payment exceed the prerestructuring carrying amount. Thus, no gain or loss is recognized on the restructuring. There is, however, a reduction in interest expense/income. A new effective interest rate must be calculated: the rate of return that equates the prerestructuring amount of $100,000 with the restructured cash flows of $112,000. The easiest way to calculate this interest rate given the uneven future cash flows, is to use a calculator or computer program. The cash flows include $6,400 received at the end of each of the first four years and $86,400 ($6,400 + $80,000) received at the end of year five.

A trial and error method using the present value tables can be used also to determine the new interest rate. As illustrated in Exhibit 15-28, discounting the cash flows at 2% and 3% indicate that the actual rate falls between these two

[17] Ibid., par. 30.

Exhibit 15-27
Cash Flows under Restructuring Agreement

Principal	$ 80,000
Interest	
$80,000 × 0.08 = $6,400 × 5 years	32,000
Total cash flows	$112,000
Carrying value of note and cash flows	
prerestructuring note	100,000
Excess	$ 12,000

rates. The actual rate for this example is 2.603%. The amortization table reflecting this rate is illustrated in Exhibit 15-29.

It is important to point out that interest payments of $6,400 now are divided between interest at a rate of 2.603% and principal. The relevant journal entries for December 31, 1981, and for December 31, 1985, for both the Charles Co. (the debtor) and the Second National Bank (the creditor) are presented in Exhibit 15-30.

Exhibit 15-28
Trial and Error Method to Determine Interest Rate

	3%	*2%*
Present value of maturity value of $80,000 to be received in 5 years	$80,000 × 0.86261 = $69,009	$80,000 × 0.90573 = $ 72,458
Present value of 5-year annuity of $6,408	$ 6,400 × 4.57971 = $29,310	$ 6,400 × 4.71346 = $ 30,166
	$98,319	$102,624

Exhibit 15-29
Amortization Table under Restructured Agreement

Date	Cash Flows	Prerestructured Nature of Cash Flow	New Interest Expense/Income at Effective Rate of 2.603%	Reduction in Principal Amount	Balance
January 1, 1981					$100,000
December 31, 1981	$ 6,400[(1)]	Interest	$ 2,603[(2)]	$ 3,797[(3)]	96,203[(4)]
December 31, 1982	6,400	Interest	2,504	3,896	92,307
December 31, 1983	6,400	Interest	2,403	3,997	88,310
December 31, 1984	6,400	Interest	2,299	4,101	84,209
December 31, 1985	6,400	Interest	2,191	4,209	80,000
December 31, 1985	80,000	Principal		80,000	-0-
	$112,000		$12,000	$100,000	

[(1)] $6,400 = $80,000 × 0.08.
[(2)] $2,603 = $100,000 × 2.603.
[(3)] $3,797 = $6,400 − $2,603.
[(4)] $96,203 = $100,000 − $3,797.

Recognition of Gain or Loss—Future Cash Flows Do Not Exceed Prerestructuring Amount.   Under the terms of *Statement No. 15* a gain or loss is recognized by the debtor or creditor when the restructured future cash flows do not exceed the prerestructured amount. All future cash flows reduce the note payable or receivable, and no interest expense or income is recognized. For example, assume the same facts as in the previous example except that the interest rate is reduced from 14% to 3%. As a result, as shown in Exhibit 15-31, the restructured cash flows do not exceed the prerestructured amount.

In this situation the prerestructured note is reduced by $8,000. The debtor records this $8,000 reduction as an extraordinary gain, and the creditor records it as an ordinary loss. As illustrated in Exhibit 15-32, future cash payments serve to reduce the remaining balance, and no interest expense or income is recorded.

The relevant journal entries as of January 1, 1981: December 31, 1981; and December 31, 1985, are presented in Exhibit 15-33 for both the Charles Co. and the Second National Bank.

There are a variety of ways in which the terms of a debt may be modified. The previous example included a decrease in both the interest rate and principal payment. Other modifications also could include an extension of the maturity date and the reduction or complete forgiveness of past-due interest. Regardless of the type of modification, the concepts illustrated in the previous paragraphs still apply.

Summary of Troubled Debt Transactions

Exhibit 15-34 summarizes the accounting treatment for various types of troubled debt restructurings under FASB *Statement No. 15*. This Statement has caused considerable controversy among accounting theorists and practitioners, as well as in the banking industry. The controversy has to do with the Board's decision not

Exhibit 15-30
Journal Entries—Troubled Debt Restructuring
Modification of Terms—No Gain or Loss Recognized

The Charles Co.

Dec. 31, 1981	Interest expense	2,603	
	Note payable	3,797	
	Cash		6,400
	To record $6,400 payment.		
Dec. 31, 1985	Interest expense	2,191	
	Note payable	4,209	
	Cash		6,400
	To record $6,400 payment.		
	Note payable	80,000	
	Cash		80,000
	To record principal payment of $80,000.		

The Second National Bank

Dec. 31, 1981	Cash	6,400	
	Interest income		2,603
	Note receivable		3,797
	To record receipt of $6,400.		
Dec. 31, 1985	Cash	6,400	
	Interest income		2,192
	Note receivable		4,209
	To record receipt of $6,400.		
	Cash	80,000	
	Note receivable		80,000
	To record receipt of $80,000.		

Exhibit 15-31
Cash Flows under Restructuring Agreement

Principal	$ 80,000
Interest (80,000 × 0.03 = $2,400 × 5 years)	12,000
Total cash flows	$ 92,000
Prerestructuring note carrying value	100,000
Decrease in cash flows	($ 8,000)

Exhibit 15-32
Restructured Payments

Date	Cash Flows	Prerestructured Nature of Cash Flows	Reduction in Note Principal	Balance After $8,000 Adjustment
January 1, 1981				$92,000[1]
December 31, 1981	$ 2,400[2]	Interest	$ 2,400	89,600
December 31, 1982	2,400	Interest	2,400	87,200
December 31, 1983	2,400	Interest	2,400	84,800
December 31, 1984	2,400	Interest	2,400	82,400
December 31, 1985	2,400	Interest	2,400	80,000
31, 1985	80,000	Principal	80,000	—
	$92,000		$92,000	

[1] $92,000 = $100,000 − $8,000.
[2] $2,400 = $80,000 × 0.03.

to recognize a gain or loss on certain debt restructuring involving a modification of terms on a continuing debt. As stated previously, the Board takes the position that a gain or loss should not be recognized when the restructured cash flows still exceed the prerestructured carrying value. This position is based on the Board's belief that an actual transaction involving a transfer of resources has not taken place, and as a result, there is a continuation of the debt with only an adjustment in the interest rate.

Many accountants argue that the FASB's position not only is inconsistent with the rest of *Statement No. 15*, but is unsound from a theoretical point of view. Supporters of this view argue that some recognition should be given to the revised pattern of cash flows that exists under the restructured agreement. They believe that a modification of terms is an arm's length transaction and requires an adjustment in the historical carrying value of the note. Thus, the debtor should recognize a gain and the creditor a loss on all troubled debt restructuring involving a modification of terms.

It is interesting to note that in its exposure draft the Board supported a view that would have resulted in the debtor recording a gain and the creditor a loss on all debt restructurings involving a modification of terms. After considerable pressure from bankers and others, the Board modified its view to that outlined in Exhibit 15-34.

Financial Statement Presentation of Long-Term Liabilities

Long-term liabilities are shown on the balance sheet in a separate section immediately after the current liability section. Detailed footnote disclosures describing the maturity data and interest rates of the major components of long-term debt

Exhibit 15-33
Journal Entries—Troubled Debt Restructuring
Modification of Terms—Gain and Loss Recognized

The Charles Co.

Jan. 1, 1981   Note payable   8,000
                      Extraordinary gain   8,000
                          from debt restructuring
                  To record extraordinary gain.

Dec. 31, 1981   Note payable   2,400
                      Cash   2,400
                  To record $2,400 payment.

Dec. 31, 1985   Note payable   82,400
                      Cash   82,400
                  To record $82,400 payment
                  ($2,400 + $80,000).

The Second National Bank

Jan. 1, 1981   Loss on receivables   8,000
                      Note receivable   8,000
                  To record ordinary loss.

Dec. 31, 1981   Cash   2,400
                      Note receivable   2,400
                  To record receipt of $2,400.

Dec. 31, 1985   Cash   82,400
                      Note receivable   82,400
                  To record receipt of $2,400.

are required. In addition, the maturities of long-term debt within the next five years are disclosed also. Exhibit 15-35 is an example of the proper presentation of long-term liabilities and related footnotes.

Earlier in the chapter it was mentioned that Caesars World, Inc. had a significant gain from early extinguishment of debt. The disclosures related to this gain are presented in Exhibit 15-36.

FASB *Statement No. 15* requires extensive disclosures of restructured debt of both debtors and creditors. The debtor must disclose the following:

1. A description of the principal changes in the terms and/or major features of the settlement.
2. The aggregate gain on restructuring and the related income tax effect.
3. The aggregate net gains or losses on the deposition of assets during the period related to restructurings.
4. The per share amount of the gain on restructuring.[18]

---

[18] Ibid., pars. 164–166.

Exhibit 15-34
FASB Statement No. 15 Procedures

Type of Restructuring	Debtors	Creditors
1. Full settlement of debt through asset swap.	1. Debtors recognize a) Gain or loss on asset disposition. b) Extraordinary gain on restructuring.	1. Creditors recognize ordinary loss on restructuring.[1]
2. Full settlement of debt through equity swap.	2. Debtors recognize extraordinary gain on restructuring.	2. Creditors recognize ordinary loss on restructuring.[1]
3. Modification of terms on continuing debt.	3. Debtor gain recognition.	3. Creditor loss recognition.
a) Restructured cash flows exceed prerestructured amount.	a) Debtor does not recognize gain; reduction in effective interest expense.	a) Creditor does not recognize loss; reduction in effective interest income.
b) Restructured cash flows *do not* exceed prerestructured amount.	b) Debtor recognizes extraordinary gain; no interest expense is recorded.	b) Creditor recognizes ordinary loss;[1] no interest income is recorded.

[1]FASB *Statement No. 15* allows this loss to be offset against allowance for doubtful accounts.

The creditors are required to disclose the following:

1. For the outstanding receivables that have been restructured:
   a The recorded investment.
   b The gross interest income that would have been recorded if no restructuring had taken place.
   c The actual gross interest income that was recorded during the period.
2. The amount of commitments to lend additional funds to debtors whose receivables have been restructured.[19]

Examples of the disclosures are illustrated in Exhibit 15-37.

---

[19]Ibid., pars. 167–172.

Exhibit 15-35

ALEXANDER & BALDWIN, INC. AND CONSOLIDATED SUBSIDIARIES
Balance Sheets
December 31, 1979 and 1978
(In Thousands except Share Amounts)

	1979	1978
Long-Term Liabilities:		
Long-term debt	$132,080	$ 70,085
Obligations under capital leases	46,828	48,122
Other	1,061	736
Total long-term liabilities	$179,969	$118,943

7. LONG-TERM DEBT

At December 31, 1979 and 1978, long-term debt of continuing operations consisted of the following:

	1979	1978
	(In Thousands)	
United States Goverment-insured Merchant. Marine bonds and guaranteed ship financing bonds, collateralized by containerships:		
8¾%, payable 1979/1995	$ 10,373	$11,057
7½%, payable 1979/1994	10,057	10,441
6.45%–7.95%, payable 1979/1987	15,000	17,000
8⅛%, payable 1987/2003	32,000	32,000
United States Government guaranteed ship financing notes, 13⅜%, payable 1980	49,500	—
Collateral trust ship construction notes, 12.875% and 13.05%, payable 1980	12,700	—
Bank mortgage loans, collateralized by land and buildings:		
8½%, payable 1979/1994	1,714	1,765
7%–7¾%, payable 1979/2003	40	40
Unsecured note, Federal Reserve discount rate plus 1½%, payable 1979/1985	900	1,050
Total	$132,284	$73,353
Less current portion	204	3,268
Long-term debt	$132,080	$70,085

Exhibit 15-35 (continued)
ALEXANDER & BALDWIN, INC. AND CONSOLIDATED SUBSIDIARIES
Balance Sheets
December 31, 1979 and 1978
(In Thousands except Share Amounts)

The Company includes bond maturities due in the following year in current liabilities if current funds are expected to be used for payment or in long-term debt (noncurrent) if funds are expected to be withdrawn from the capital construction fund. Accordingly, 1980 bond maturities totaling $3,368,000 were classified as noncurrent at December 31, 1979, and 1979 maturities totaling $3,068,000 were included in current liabilities at December 31, 1978.

The ship financing notes are collateralized by a security interest in the vessel under construction, and the ship construction notes are collateralized by the assets of the capital construction fund. The Company has agreements to refinance all such notes through issuance of ship financing bonds and withdrawals from the capital construction fund. Accordingly, the notes are classified as long-term debt.

At December 31, 1979 maturities of all long-term debt during the next five years totaled $65,568,000 for 1980, $3,577,000 for 1981, $3,582,000 for 1982, $3,588,000 for 1983 and $3,594,000 for 1984.

Exhibit 15-36
CAESARS WORLD, INC. (JUL)
Disclosure of Gain from Extinguishment of Debt

	1978	1977
	($000)	
Income before extraordinary item	$ 8,305	$5,076
Extraordinary gain net of income taxes (Note 15)	2,406	
Net income	$10,711	$5,076

Note 15: Extraordinary item—During fiscal 1978, the Company redeemed a total of $10,915,000 principal amount of its 8% convertible senior subordinated debentures due 1989 at 65% of par value ($7,095,000), resulting in the following extraordinary gain:

	(Thousands Omitted)
Extraordinary gain (net of unamortized loan costs of $148)	$3,672
Income taxes	1,266
Extraordinary gain net of income taxes	2,406

Exhibit 15-37
Footnote Disclosure

By Creditor

Note 10—Nonperforming Loans and Investments

The following table presents information concerning loans that are contractually past due sixty days or more as to interest or principal payments, and loans and investments that have been restructured to provide a reduction or deferral of interest or principal for reasons related to the debtors' financial difficulties.

Category	Aggregate Recorded Investment	Gross Interest Income That Would Have Been Recorded under Original terms	Gross Interest Income Recorded During the Period	Commitments for Additional funds
Loans	$75,000,000	$6,000,000	$2,250,000	$6,000,000
Investments in debt securities	10,000	625,000	200,000	–0–

By Debtor

Note 6—Debt Restructuring in Current Year

During the year the Company transferred certain real estate carried at $8,500,000 (fair value $9,000,000) to a bank in full settlement of a 12% note in the amount of $10,000,000. As a result of this transaction, the Company recognized a gain of $500,000 (included as a separate item in income before income taxes and extraordinary items)* on the disposition of real estate and a gain of $1,000,000 on the restructuring of debt. The gain on the restructuring of debt, net of related income taxes of $500,000, has been classified as an extraordinary item and increased net income by $.05 a share.*

*Source: Ernst & Whinney, "Accountant for Troubled Debt Restructuring," *Financial Reporting Developments* (1977).

Concept Summary

LONG-TERM LIABILITIES

Definition—obligations of an enterprise that fall due beyond one year or operating cycle, if longer.

Valuation—on date of incurrence the obligations are recorded at their present value.

ACCOUNTING FOR NOTES

Notes Exchanged for	Valuation
Cash	Original cash proceeds
Property goods or services 1. Stated reasonable interest rate	Face value of note
2. No interest rate stated, unreasonable interest rate or the face value of note is significantly different from the fair market value of the property goods or services	Fair market value of property goods or services or market value of note, whichever is more clearly determinable; if neither is determinable, record the obligation at its present value.

BOND DISCOUNTS AND PREMIUMS

Bonds Issued at	Description	Reason
Face	Bonds sold at face value.	Market yield equals the bonds face rate of interest.
Discount	Bond sold below its face value.	The market yield is greater than the face rate of interest on the bond.
Premium	Bond sold above its face value.	The market yield is less than the face rate of interest on the bonds.

Amortization Method	Description	Effect in Interest
Straight-Line	Write off an equal amount of discount or premium each period.	The dollar amount of interest expense remains constant, but the effective rate changes over the life of the bonds.
Effective Interest	Amortize an amount equal to the difference between the effective interest cost and the cash interest paid.	The interest rate remains the same throughout the life of the bond, but the dollar amount of interest changes.

EARLY EXTINGUISHMENT OF DEBT

Description	Accounting Treatment
Bonds, or other debt, repurchased before maturity.	Gains or losses from early extinguishment are shown as an extraordinary gain or loss, net of tax effects.

TROUBLED DEBT RESTRUCTURING

		Accounting Treatment	
Type	Description	Debtor	Creditor
Obligation settled by transfer of assets	The debtor transfers assets to the creditor in full settlement of the obligation.	Debtor must recognize the differences between book value and market price as assets transferred as an ordinary gain or loss. Any difference between the market value of the transferred property and the book value of the obligation is recognized as an extraordinary gain from early extinguishment of debt.	Recognize the difference between the market value of the assets received and the carrying amount of the receivable as an ordinary loss. The assets received are recorded at their fair market value.

Obligation settled by transfer of equity	The debtor transfers equity in the business in settlement of the obligation.	The difference between the fair market value of the equity securities and the book value of the obligation is recognized as an extraordinary gain from early extinguishment of debt.	The equity securities received are recorded at their fair market value, and the difference between this market value and the book value of the receivable is recognized as an ordinary loss.
Modification of terms	The obligation is not paid immediately. The terms such as due date, interest rate, and face amount are changed to benefit the debtor.	If future cash flows exceed the carrying amount of the obligation, determine the new implicit interest rate and recognize interest using this rate. No gain or loss is recorded. If the carrying amount exceeds the future cash flows, value the obligation at the amount of future cash flows and recognize an extraordinary gain.	If future cash flows exceed the carrying amount of the receivable, no gain or loss is recognized. Interest is recognized at the new rate implicit in the modified terms. If the carrying amount exceeds the future cash flows, value the receivable at the amount of the future cash flows and recognize an ordinary loss for the difference.

Appendix

Accounting for Serial Bonds

The main body of this chapter discussed the accounting issues related to bonds that have a single maturity date. However, many corporations issue **serial bonds,** which are bonds that mature over a period of years. These bonds are attractive to investors who wish to insure the orderly payment of principal and interest.

Accounting for the Issuance of Serial Bonds

Like term bonds, serial bonds can be issued at their face value, at a discount, or at a premium. For example, serial bonds can be issued at face value but with varying interest rates. Exhibit 15-38 illustrates the interest rates associated with $100,000 of serial bonds issued at par value on January 2, 1981, by York City. These bonds mature at the rate of $10,000 a year beginning on January 2, 1982. The interest rates increase for the bonds maturing at later dates to reflect the increased risk associated with receiving a fixed interest rate in future periods.

In the above example all the bonds were assumed to be issued at par, but

Exhibit 15-38
YORK CITY
$100,000 Serial Bonds Issued at Par

Principal Amount	Maturity Date	Interest Rate
$10,000	1/2/82	8.00%
10,000	1/2/83	8.25%
10,000	1/2/84	8.50%
10,000	1/2/85	8.75%
10,000	1/2/86	9.00%
10,000	1/2/87	9.25%
10,000	1/2/88	9.50%
10,000	1/2/89	9.75%
10,000	1/2/90	10.00%
10,000	1/2/91	10.25%
$100,000		

with varying stated interest rates. However, like single payment bonds, serial bonds can sell at a discount or at a premium. In some situations the stated interest rate remains the same for all bonds, but a different discount and/or premium can be associated with the respective maturity dates. In effect, the assumption is made that the bonds represent different issues with separate maturity dates that are combined because they are issued on the same date.

For example, assume that the Hope Corporation issues $50,000 of serial bonds on January 2, 1981. The bonds have a stated annual interest rate of 8% but are sold to yield varying rates depending upon the maturity date. Interest is paid annually on December 31, and the bonds mature at the rate of $10,000 annually beginning on December 31, 1981. These bonds are considered as five, separate, $10,000 issues having maturity dates that range from one to five years. Exhibit 15-39 demonstrates how the issue price of $44,797 and the corresponding discount of $5,203 are calculated. In effect, each of the five $10,000 series is discounted at the appropriate rate to its present value. The initial bond issue is recorded as follows:

Cash	44,797	
Discount on bonds payable	5,203	
Bonds payable		50,000

Exhibit 15-39
Calculation of Issue Face of Serial Bonds

			Present Values of			
Amount Due	Maturity Date	Yield Rate	Principal Payment	+ Interest Payment	=	Total Present Value
$10,000	12/31/81	10%	$9,090.91[1]	$ 727.27[2]		$ 9,818.18[3]
10,000	12/31/82	11%	8,116.22[4]	1,370.02[5]		9,486.24[6]
10,000	12/31/83	12%	7,117.80	1,921.47		9,039.27
10,000	12/31/84	13%	6,133.19	2,379.58		8,512.76
10,000	12/31/85	14%	5,193.69	2,746.46		7,940.15
$50,000						$44,796.60

[1] Present value of a single payment of $10,000 due in one year at 10%
$$\$9,090.91 = \$10,000 \times 0.909091.$$
[2] Present value of an annuity of $800 due in one year at 10%
$$\$727.27 = \$800 \times 0.909091.$$
[3] $9,818.18 = $9,090.91 + $727.27.
[4] Present value of a single payment of $10,000 due at the end of two years at 11%
$$\$8,116.22 = \$10,000 \times 0.81162.$$
[5] Present value of an annuity of $800 due at the end of each of the next two years at 11%
$$\$1,370.02 = \$800 \times 1.71253.$$
[6] $9,486.24 = $8,116.22 + $1,370.02.

Exhibit 15-40
Bonds Outstanding Discount Amortization

Year Ending	Bonds Outstanding During the Year	Ratio of Bonds Outstanding during the Year to Total Outstanding	Total Discount	Discount Amortized During Year
Dec. 31, 1981	$ 50,000	50/150	$5,203	$1,734
Dec. 31, 1982	40,000	40/150	5,203	1,387
Dec. 31, 1983	30,000	30/150	5,203	1,041
Dec. 31, 1984	20,000	20/150	5,203	694
Dec. 31, 1985	10,000	10/150	5,203	347
	$150,000			$5,203

In other situations it may not be possible to identify specific prices for each maturity date. For example, the entire issue could be sold as a unit to an underwriter for a single, lump sum price. In this case the entire discount or premium must be amortized as a unit. As will be demonstrated in the next section, either the bonds outstanding method or an effective interest method using an average rate for the entire issue is used in this situation.

Discount or Premium Amortization

As with single date maturity bonds, any discount or premium must be amortized over the bond life. Two methods generally are used—the bonds outstanding method and the effective interest rate method. The effective interest method should be used unless the results are not materially different from the bonds outstanding method.

Bonds Outstanding Method. This method amortizes the discount or premium by multiplying the total discount or premium by a ratio. This ratio is the bonds outstanding during the year divided by the total of all bonds outstanding over the life of the entire issue. Exhibit 15-40 presents a table calculating the discount amortization for the serial bonds issued by the Hope Corporation.

Once the yearly discount is determined, an amortization schedule for the entire bond issue can be constructed. This schedule, which combines the discount amortization and the principal payments, is illustrated in Exhibit 15-41. Based on this table, the following journal entries would be made on December 31, 1981, and December 31, 1985.

Exhibit 15-41
Serial Bonds Amortization Table— Bonds Outstanding Method

Date	Cash Principal Payment	Cash Interest Payment—8%	Discount Amortized	Interest Expense	Bonds Payable	Decrease in Bond Carrying Value	Bond Carrying Value
1/ 2/81							$44,797
12/31/81	$10,000	$ 4,000[(1)]	$1,734[(2)]	$ 5,734[(3)]	$10,000	$ 8,266[(4)]	36,531[(5)]
12/31/82	10,000	3,200	1,387	4,587	10,000	8,613	27,918
12/31/83	10,000	2,400	1,041	3,441	10,000	8,959	18,959
12/31/84	10,000	1,600	694	2,294	10,000	9,306	9,653
12/31/85	10,000	800	347	1,147	10,000	9,653	—
	$50,000	$12,000	$5,203	$17,203	$50,000	—	—

[(1)]$4,000 = $50,000 × 0.08.
[(2)]From Exhibit 15-40.
[(3)]$5,734 = $4,000 + $1,734.
[(4)]$8,266 = $10,000 − $1,734.
[(5)]$36,531 = $44,797 − $8,266.

Dec. 31, 1981	Interest expense		5,734	
	Bonds payable		10,000	
	Cash			14,000
	Discount on bonds payable			1,734
	To record interest and			
	principal payments.			
Dec. 31, 1985	Interest expense		1,147	
	Bonds payable		10,000	
	Cash			10,800
	Discount on bonds payable			347
	To record interest and			
	principal payments.			

Effective Interest Method. Unless there are no material differences, the effective interest method is preferable to the bonds outstanding method. The easiest way to use this method is to compute a single average interest rate for the entire series of bonds. For the Hope Company this interest rate is 12.52%. The present value technique for irregular cash flows or a calculator can be used to determine this rate. The amortization procedure for this method is similar to that for a single maturity date bond and is illustrated in Exhibit 15-42. The following entries would be made at December 31, 1981, and December 31, 1985, for this method.

Exhibit 15-42

Serial Bonds Amortization Table—Effective Interest Method

	Debits		Credits				
			Cash				
Date	Interest Expense— 12.52%	Bonds Payable	Principal Payments	Interest Payments—8%	Discount Amortized	Decrease in Bond Carrying Value	Bond Carrying Value
1/ 2/81							$44,797
12/31/83	$5,609[1]	$10,000	$10,000	$ 4,000[2]	$1,609[3]	$ 8,391[4]	36,406[5]
12/31/82	4,558	10,000	10,000	3,200	1,358	8,642	27,764
12/31/83	3,476	10,000	10,000	2,400	1,076	8,924	18,840
12/31/84	2,359	10,000	10,000	1,600	759	9,241	9,599
12/31/85	1,201	10,000	10,000	800	401	9,599	—
		$50,000	$50,000	$12,000	$5,203		

[1] $5,609 = $44,797 × 12.52%.
[2] $4,000 = $50,000 × 0.08.
[3] $1,609 = $5,609 − $4,000.
[4] $8,391 = $10,000 − $1,609.
[5] $36,406 = $44,797 − $8,391.

Dec. 31, 1981	Interest expense	5,609	
	Bonds payable	10,000	
	Cash		14,000
	Discount on bonds payable		1,609
	To record interest and		
	principal payment.		
Dec. 31, 1985	Interest expense	1,201	
	Bonds payable	10,000	
	Cash		10,800
	Discount on bonds payable		401
	To record interest and		
	principal payment.		

Redemption of Serial Bonds before Scheduled Redemption

Serial bonds can be redeemed before their scheduled maturity. Any difference between the carrying value and the redemption price of the bonds will result in an extraordinary gain or loss. For serial bonds, the problem is one of determining the unamortized discount or premium to be written off when the bonds are redeemed. The required procedures to be used for the bonds outstanding method and the effective interest method are illustrated below.

Bonds Outstanding Method. The proper amount of unamortized discount or premium to be written off can be determined by using the following formula:

$$\frac{\text{Number of years before maturity} \times \text{Par value of bonds} \times \text{Total discount or premium}}{\text{Total value of all bonds outstanding}}$$

For example, assume that the Hope Corporation redeems $10,000 of its bond due on December 31, 1985, on January 1, 1984, for $10,500. Thus, as of January 1, 1984, these bonds are redeemed two years early, and $694 of unamortized discount associated with these bonds should be written off.

$$\frac{2 \times \$10,000 \times \$5,203}{\$150,000} = \$694$$

In other words, 10/150 of the total discount of $5,203, or $347, is amortized each year. Since there are two years remaining on the bonds redeemed, the total that must be written off on the redemption date is $694 (2 × $347).

The journal entry to record this transaction is as follows:

Bonds payable	10,000	
Extraordinary loss	1,194	
Unamortized discount		694
Cash		10,500

The Effective Interest Method. When the effective interest method is employed, the present value or the carrying value of the bonds being redeemed must be determined. The difference between the present value of the bonds and the redemption price results in an extraordinary gain or loss. As of January 1, 1984, (the redemption date) the $10,000 bonds due on December 31, 1985, had a present value of $9,241 based on a 12.52% average discount rate for two years.

Present value of principal amount at 12% for 2 years:	
$10,000 \times 0.78984$	$7,898
Present value of interest annuity of $800 for two years at 12.52%:	1,343
Total present value	$9,241

Since the redemption price is $10,500, there is a $1,259 ($10,500 − $9,241) extraordinary loss on the transaction. The journal entry to record the redemption is as follows:

Bonds payable	10,000	
Extraordinary loss	1,259	
Discount on bonds payable		759
Cash		10,500

Questions

Q–15–1 How does the stated interest rate on a bond affect its issuance price?

Q–15–2 Several different interest rates are important in accounting for bonds. What do the following terms measure?
  a) Stated rate.
  b) Yield rate.
  c) Market rate.
  d) Nominal rate.
  e) Effective rate.
  Can any of these rates change during the life of the bond issue?

Q–15–3 What are written convenants and why are they used?

Q–15–4 Certain types of receivables and payables are exceptions to the requirements of APB *Opinion No. 21*. Identify these items.

Q–15–5   What are the major types of obligations to which APB *Opinion No. 21* applies?

Q–15–6   At what amount should property acquired in exchange for a non-interest bearing note be recorded?

Q–15–7   Define the following terms:

   a) Term bonds.
   b) Serial bonds.
   c) Debentures.
   d) Mortgage bonds.
   e) Convertible bonds.
   f) Bearer bonds.

Q–15–8   What is the proper method of presenting bonds payable and any related premium or discount on the balance sheet.

Q–15–9   Describe the straight-line interest method and the effective interest method. When is each method used?

Q–15–10   What is the proper method of recording the expenses incurred in issuing bonds?

Q–15–11   When should the gain or loss resulting from the early extinguishment of debt be recognized? What is the theory behind this method?

Q–15–12   What are the disclosure requirements of FASB *Statement No. 4?*

Q–15–13   What are the differences between a bond reacquisition, bond redemption, and refunding of a bond?

Q–15–14   What is the proper balance sheet presentation for bonds maturing within the current year?

Q–15–15   According to FASB *Statement No. 15*, what distinguishes a troubled debt restructuring from other debt restructurings?

Q–15–16   Why might a creditor consider granting concessions to the debtor by restructuring a troubled debt? Name some concessions that might be included in the restructuring of a troubled debt.

Q–15–17   What are the disclosure requirements under FASB *Statement No. 15* for the following?

   a) The debtor.
   b) The creditor.

Q–15–18   There are two methods of amortizing the bond premium or discount on serial bonds: the bonds outstanding method and the effective interest method. Describe each of these methods and indicate when each should be used.

Q–15–19   Define the following terms relative to bonds payable.

   a) Par value.
   b) Face value.
   c) Book value.
   d) Maturity value.
   e) Market value.
   f) Carrying value.

   Which, if any, of these values can change during the life of the bond?

Q–15–20   When a bond is sold at a premium, and the premium is amortized using the effective interest method, will the annual interest expense increase or decrease over the life of the bond? Why?

Q–15–21   At what value should long-term liabilities be reflected on the balance sheet? Is this different from current liabilities? Why?

Q–15–22   When is the stated rate of interest deemed not to be reasonable? What must be considered in determining an appropriate interest rate?

Q–15–23 Select the best answer for the following three questions:

a) A two-year note was issued in an arm's length transaction at face value solely for cash at the beginning of this year. There were no other rights or privileges exchanged. The interest rate is specified at 10% per year. Principal and interest are payable at maturity. The prevailing rate of interest for a loan of this type is 15% per year. What annual interest rate should be used to record interest expense for this year and next year?

	This Year	Next Year
(1)	10%	15%
(2)	10%	10%
(3)	15%	10%
(4)	15%	15%

b) When the interest payment dates of a bond are May 1 and November 1, and a bond issue is sold on June 1, the amount of cash received by the issuer will be

  (1) Decreased by accrued interest from June 1 to November 1.

  (2) Decreased by accrued interest from May 1 to June 1.

  (3) Increased by accrued interest from June 1 to November 1.

  (4) Increased by accrued interest from May 1 to June 1.

c) On May 1, 1980, a company purchased a new machine that it does not have to pay for until May 1, 1982. The total payment on May 1, 1982, will include both principal and interest. If you assumed interest at a 10% rate, the cost of the machine would be the total payment multiplied by what time value of money concept?

  (1) Future amount of annuity of 1.

  (2) Future amount of 1.

  (3) Present value of annuity of 1.

  (4) Present value of 1.

(AICPA adapted)

Discussion Questions and Cases

D–15–1 The effective interest method is the appropriate method of amortizing a premium or discount resulting from the issuance of bonds.

Required:

1. What is the effective interest method of amortization, and how is it different from similar to the straight-line method of amortization?

2. How is amortization computed using the effective interest method? Why and how do amounts obtained using the effective interest method differ from amounts computed under the straight-line method?

3. Under what conditions might the straight-line method be an appropriate method of amortizing a premium or discount?

(AICPA adapted)

D–15–2 Before the issuance of APB *Opinion No. 26*, "Early Extinguishment of Debt," three different methods of accounting for the gains and losses resulting from the refunding of debt had been supported in court decisions, rulings of regulatory agencies, and in the accounting literature:

  a) Amortized over remaining life of old debt.

  b) Amortized over the life of the new issue.

  c) Recognized in the period of extinguishment.

Required:

1. Discuss the theoretical support for each of these different methods of accounting for gains and losses from the early extinguishment of debt.

2. Which of the methods above is generally accepted and how should the appropriate amount of gain or loss be shown in a company's financial statements?

(AICPA adapted)

D–15–3 On January 1, 1981, Dixon Diecast issued its 20-year, 8% bonds for $1,106,775. The bonds have a maturity value of $1,000,000 and pay interest semiannually on January 1 and July 1. Bond issue costs were not material in amount. The following are three possible presentations of the long-term liability section of Dixon's balance sheet at the issue date:

a)	Bonds payable (maturing January 1, 2001)	$1,000,000
	Unamortized premium on bonds payable	106,775
	Total bond liability	$1,106,775

b)	Bonds payable—face value $1,000,000	
	(maturing January 1, 2001)	$ 252,572[1]
	Bonds payable—interest (semiannual payment $40,000)	854,203[2]
	Total bond liability	$1,106,775

[1] The present value of $1,000,000 due at the end of 40 (six-month) periods at the yield rate of 3½% per period.
[2] The present value of $40,000 per period for 40 (six-month) periods at the yield rate of 3½% per period.

c)	Bonds payable—principal (maturing January 1, 2001)	$1,000,000
	Bonds payable—interest ($40,000 per period	
	for 40 periods)	1,600,000
	Total bond liability	$2,600,000

Required:

1. Discuss the conceptual merit(s) of each of the date-of-issue balance sheet presentations shown above for these bonds.

2. Explain why investors would pay $1,106,775 for bonds that have a maturity value of only $1,000,000.

3. Assuming that a discount rate is needed to compute the carrying value of the obligation arising from a bond issue at any date during the life of the bonds, discuss the conceptual merit(s) of using the following for this purpose.

a) The coupon or nominal rate.

b) The effective or yield rate at the date of issue.

4. If the obligations arising from these bonds are to be carried at their present value computed by means of the current market rate of interest, how would the bond valuation at dates after the date of issue be affected by an increase or decrease in the market rate of interest?

(AICPA adapted)

D–15–4 The basic premise behind APB *Opinion No. 26*, "Early Extinguishment of Debt," is that all extinguishments of debt before scheduled maturities are fundamentally alike, and the accounting for such transactions should be uniform regardless of the methods used to accomplish the extinguishment. This conclusion is as controversial today as it was when *Opinion No. 26* was issued. Opponents claim that all early extinguishments are not alike and that the Opinion fails to recognize the economic effects of an early extinguishment of debt designed to yield a profit.

Required:

Discuss the reasoning used to support both sides of this controversy. Which do you think is theoretically sound?

D–15–5   FASB *Statement No. 15*, "Accounting by Debtors and Creditors for Troubled Debt Restructuring," basically implies that most modifications of terms in debt restructuring agreements do not result in a significant economic transaction, and therefore no gain or loss should be reported at the date of restructuring. In addition, under the provisions of FASB *Statement No. 15*, it is possible that the debtor and creditor will not record any interest income or interest expense over the life of the debt.

Required:

1. Do you agree with the FASB that no significant economic transaction has occurred? Explain your position.

2. Do you believe that FASB *Statement No. 15* is consistent with APB *Opinion No. 21*, "Interest on Receivables and Payables"? Explain your position.

D–15–6   Business transactions often involve the exchange of property, goods, or services for notes or similar instruments that may stipulate no interest rate or an interest rate that varies from prevailing rates.

Required:

1. When a note is exchanged for property, goods, or services, what value should be placed upon the note

　　a) If it bears interest at a reasonable rate and is issued in a bargained transaction entered into at arm's length? Explain.

　　b) If it bears no interest and/or is not issued in a bargained transaction entered into at arm's length? Explain.

2. If the recorded value of a note differs from the face value,

　　a) How should the difference be accounted for? Explain.

　　b) How should this difference be presented in the financial statements? Explain.

(AICPA adapted)

*D–15–7   One way for a corporation to accomplish long-term financing is through the issuance of long-term debt instruments in the form of bonds.

Required:

1. Contrast a serial bond with a term (straight) bond.

2. For a five-year term bond issued at a premium, why would the amortization in the first year of the life of the bond differ using the interest method of amortization instead of the straight-line method? Include in your discussion whether the amount of amortization in the first year of the life of the bond would be higher or lower using the interest method instead of the straight-line method.

3. When a bond issue is sold between interest dates at a discount, what journal entry is made, and how is the subsequent amortization of bond discount affected? Include in your discussion an explanation of how the amounts of each debit and credit are determined.

4. Describe how to account for and classify the gain or loss from the reacquisition of a long-term bond before its maturity.

(AICPA adapted)

Note: Items with an *asterisk* relate to material contained in the appendix.

Exercises

E–15–1   The following accounts were taken from Wayword, Inc.'s December 31, 1981, general ledger:

　　a) Loans from officers.

　　b) Dividends payable.

　　c) Customer deposits.

　　d) Notes payable due July 1, 1985.

e) Unamortized discount on bonds payable.
f) Serial bond payable, $100,000 due each April 1.
g) Cash overdraft.
h) Accrued payroll taxes.

Required:

Indicate how each one of the items above should be classified on Wayword, Inc.'s balance sheet of December 31, 1982. Explain any doubtful items.

E-15-2 Loland Company purchased a new piece of equipment from Ace, Inc. on July 1, 1981. In payment, Ace, Inc. accepted a note payable in four equal annual payments of $13,250. The first payment is due on July 1, 1982. The cash equivalent price of the equipment is $42,000.

Required:

1. Prepare the journal entry to record the purchase of the equipment.
2. How much, if any, interest expense should be reported as of December 31, 1981? (*Hint:* Determine the effective rate of interest.)
3. Prepare the journal entry to record the July 1, 1982, payment to Ace, Inc.

E-15-3 On January 1, 1981, the Carpet Company lent $100,000 to its supplier, Loom Corporation, evidenced by a note, payable in five years. Interest at 5% is payable annually, with the first payment due on December 31, 1981. The going rate of interest for this type of loan is 10%. The parties agreed that Carpet's inventory needs for the loan period would be met by Loom at favorable prices. Assume that the present value (at the going rate of interest) of the $100,000 note is $81,000 at January 1, 1981.

Required:

1. Make the journal entry to record the loan payable on the books of Loom Corporation.
2. If you assume that the merchandise is sold to the Carpet Company evenly over the next five years, make an entry to record the interest payment for December 31, 1981.

E-15-4 Dixie Lanes issued a non-interest-bearing note for $17,840 to the bank and received $15,000 in cash. The note is to be repaid in eight equal semiannual payments of $2,230 each.

Required:

Prepare the journal entry to record this transaction. Is there an implicit interest rate on this loan? If so, can it be determined from the information given?

E-15-5 Palmer Co. sold 10-year bonds on July 1, 1980, with a face value of $250,000. The stated annual interest rate is 13%, payable semiannually on June 30 and December 31. These bonds were sold to yield 15%.

Required:

Prepare the journal entry to record the issuance of these bonds.

E-15-6 The Pagano Corporation issued $100,000 of five-year, 12% bonds on January 2, 1981. Interest is payable semiannually on June 30 and December 31. These bonds were sold to yield 10%.

Required:

1. Make the entry to record the issuance of the bonds on January 2, 1981.
2. Assuming the firm uses the straight-line amortization method, make the required entries on December 31, 1981.
3. Assuming the firm uses the effective interest method, make the required entries at December 31, 1981.

E-15-7 On July 1, 1981, the Williams Corporation issued $500,000 of 10-year, 8% bonds to yield 12%. The bonds pay interest every July 1 and January 1.

Required:

1. Make the entry to record the issuance of the bonds on July 1, 1981.
2. Assuming the firm uses the straight-line method of amortization, make the required entries on July 1, 1982.

3. Assuming the firm uses the effective interest method of amortization, make the required entries on July 1, 1982.

E–15–8 On March 1, 1981, the Spring Co. issued 10-year, 9% bonds with a face value of $300,000. The bonds pay interest semiannually on January 1 and July 1 and mature on January 1, 1991. The bonds were sold at their face value.
Required:
1. Prepare the journal entry to record the issuance on March 1, 1981.
2. Prepare the journal entry to record the first interest payment on July 1, 1981.

E–15–9 On March 1, 1981, the Stover Corporation issued 5-year, 10% bonds with a face value of $500,000 to yield 12%. These bonds pay interest semiannually on January 1 and July 1.
Required:
1. Prepare the entry to record the issuance of the bonds on March 1, 1981.
2. Assuming the firm uses the straight-line method of amortization, make the required entries on July 1, 1981.
3. Assuming the firm uses the effective interest method of amortization, make the required entries on July 1, 1981.

E–15–10 Grim and Co. had outstanding bonds with a face value of $100,000. On January 31, when these bonds had an unamortized discount of $4,000, they were called at 106. To pay for these bonds, Grim had issued other bonds a month earlier bearing a lower interest rate. The newly issued bonds had a life of 10 years, face value of 100,000, and were issued at 102. Issue costs related to the new bonds were $3,000.
Required:
Calculate the amount and nature of any gain or loss Grim and Co. should report on this refunding.

E–15–11 On January 1, 1981, Provident Corporation issued 1,000 of its 9%, $1,000 callable bonds for $1,040,000. The bonds are dated January 1, 1981, and mature on January 1, 1991. Interest is payable semiannually on July 1 and January 1. The bonds can be called by the issuer at 101 at any time after December 31, 1985.

On July 1, 1986, Provident called in all of the bonds and retired them. Assume that Provident uses the straight-line method of amortizing bond premium.
Required:
1. Make the entry to record the issuance of the bonds on January 1, 1981.
2. Make the required entry to record the interest payment January 1, 1985.
3. Make the required entries to record the retirement of the bonds on July 1, 1986.
(AICPA adapted)

E–15–12 The December 31, 1981, the general ledger of the North Company contained an account "6% bonds payable." This account had a balance of $95,000 as of that date. Further examination revealed that the bonds had a face value of $100,000, a yield of 8%, and were issued at a discount. The amortization of the bond discount was recorded under the effective interest method. Interest was paid on January 1 and July 1 of each year. On July 1, 1982, several years before their maturity, North retired the bonds at 102, excluding accrued interest of issuing new bonds. The new bonds have a face value of $100,000 and were issued at $110,000.
Required:
1. Compute the gain or loss, if any, on the retirement of the bonds.
2. Make the entry to record the retirement of the old bonds and the issuance of the new bonds.

(AICPA adapted)

E–15–13 Using the facts in Exercise 15–7, answer the required parts for the purchase of the bonds issued by the Williams Corporation.

E–15–14   On December 31, 1980, Josha, Inc. issued $2,000,000 of 10%, 10-year bonds to yield 12%. Interest is paid semiannually on December 31 and June 30. The firm incurred costs of $10,000. The firm uses the straight-line method of amortization.

Required:

1.   Make the entry to show the issuance of the bonds.

2.   Make the required entry at June 30, 1981.

E–15–15   Shaid Corporation purchased $100,000 of 10-year, 6% bonds on June 1, 1981, at 98 plus accrued interest. The bonds were dated April 1, 1981, with interest payable April 1 and October 1. Bond discount is amortized semiannually on a straight-line basis.

Required:

1.   Make the required entry on June 1, 1981, to record the issuance of the bonds.

2.   Make the entry needed at December 31, 1981.

3.   Make the entry to record the interest payment and discount amortization on April 1, 1982.

E–15–16   The Silva Company has been experiencing serious financial difficulties and is about to default on its $120,000, 10% note payable to Logan Screens, Inc. After much negotiating Logan agrees to accept a parcel of land with a fair market value of $105,000 from Silva in exchange for the note plus the six months' accrued interest now due. The land had been purchased by Silva several years ago for $65,000.

Required:

Prepare the journal entries to record the exchange by both the Silva Company and Logan Screens, Inc. in accordance with FASB *Statement No. 15*.

E–15–17   Melody Lanes Estates is considering entering voluntary bankruptcy because of its inability to meet the terms of a debt agreement with its major creditor, Estesse Fund Development. The five-year, $200,000, 8% note is payable today, December 31, 1981, along with six months' accrued interest. After hearing of Melody Lanes' condition, Estesse decided to extend the note for five years and to reduce the interest rate to 5%. The interest payment is due each December 31, and the note now matures on December 31, 1986. Should either Melody Lane Estates or Estesse Land Development report a gain or loss on this transaction? Support your position.

*E–15–18   The Dryer Drum Company issued $300,000 in serial bonds on April 1, 1978. The bonds mature at a rate of $100,000 each May 31 beginning on May 31, 1979. Interest at 10% is paid each May 31. The bonds were sold to yield 8%.

Required:

1.   Calculate the proceeds collected by the Dryer Drum Company on the issuance of these bonds.

2.   Prepare the journal entry to record this transaction.

3.   Compute the premium to be amortized each year using the bonds outstanding method.

*E–15–19   On January 1, 1978, MyKoo Corporation issued $1,000,000 in five-year, 5% serial bonds to be repaid in the amount of $200,000 on January 1, 1979, 1980, 1981, 1982, and 1983. Interest is payable at the end of each year. The bonds were sold to yield a rate of 6%.

Required:

1.   Prepare a schedule showing the computation of the total amount received from the issuance of the serial bonds.

2.   Assume the bonds were sold originally with a discount of $26,247. Prepare an amortization schedule for the first two years after issuance using the effective interest method.

(AICPA adapted)

E–15–20   The Instant Gold Company makes and sells a powder that turns into one ounce of gold when mixed with an ounce of water. For many years its business was booming, but when the price of gold fell, the company's business almost stopped completely. As a result, the company is having difficulty meeting its obligation to its main creditor, Silver National

Bank. The Instant Gold Company owes the bank $500,000 at 14% interest. The entire principal is now due and payable; accrued interest, however, has been paid fully. Because of the difficulties the company is experiencing, the bank agrees to make certain concessions regarding the note.

Required:

1. If the bank agrees to any modification of terms, does this qualify as a troubled debt restructuring under FASB *Statement No. 15?* Why? What differentiates a troubled debt restructuring from other debt restructurings?

2. Assume that the bank agreed to accept land with a fair market value of $450,000 in full satisfaction of the note. The land had a book value of $300,000 on Instant Gold's books. Make the required journal entries for both the company and the bank.

3. Now assume that the bank agreed to accept 5,000 shares of Instant Gold's $5 par value preferred stock in full satisfaction of the note. The stock currently has a fair market value of $90 per share. Make the required entries for the company and the bank.

Note: Items with an *asterisk* relate to material contained in the appendix.

Problems

P-15-1   Under which of the following sets of facts would APB *Opinion No. 21* require recognition of an interest rate other than the one stated in the debt agreement? Explain your reasons.

  a)   Toyland bought Christmas toys costing $500,000 from the manufacturer in July. The terms of the agreement require Toyland to pay the $500,000 note in full on January 10 of the following year.

  b)   Gravel, Inc. purchased a new truck on credit. The company agreed to make three annual payments of $18,000 each, beginning one year from the date of sale. The cash price of the truck was $42,825.

  c)   Western Gear bought $200,000 in corporate bonds paying 6% interest. The prevailing market rate of interest is 10% for similar bonds.

  d)   Big Lakes made an interest-free loan to Little Lakes, one of its wholly owned subsidiaries. The current rate of interest on a loan of that nature is 12%.

  e)   Churchall purchased $1,000,000 of California residence bonds paying 6% interest. The prevailing market rate at the time is 11%.

P-15-2   On July 1, 1981, Wilson Brothers, Inc. purchased a piece of equipment. A non-interest-bearing note was issued as payment for the equipment, calling for four semiannual payments of $10,000 each, beginning on January 1, 1982. The cash equivalent price of the equipment could not be determined. The current interest rate on this type of note is 10%.

Required:

1. Prepare the journal entry to record the purchase of the equipment.

2. Prepare an amortization table for this note using the effective interest method.

3. Prepare the journal entry to record the first payment.

4. How would this note be reported on the December 31, 1982, balance sheet?

P-15-3   On January 2, 1980, the Flynn Corporation purchased a plot of land from the Mets Company. The agreement calls for the Flynn Corporation to make one $200,000 payment at the end of five years. Interest of 6% per year is required to be paid on the unpaid balance at the end of each of the next five years. Current interest rates for equivalent loans are 18% per year. The corporation's year-end is December 31. The company uses the effective interest method.

Required:

1. Prepare an amortization table similar to the one illustrated in the chapter.
2. Make all necessary entries for 1980 and 1981.

P–15–4 The Pulpy Paper Company plans to expand its production in order to meet the growing demand for its fine products. The My-T-Fine Machinery Corp has offered to supply Pulpy with the new machinery it will need. My-T-Fine offers three options to Pulpy for the purchase of the machine:

Option A—Cash purchase, $100,000
Option B—15 equal annual payments of $14,682
Option C—A note for $150,000 requiring annual interest payments
        at 8% for 10 years and payment of the face amount at the
        end of 10 years.

Required:
Prepare journal entries under each available option to record the purchase of the equipment. The current interest rate for the industry is 12%.

P–15–5 On July 1, 1981, the Willis Company purchased a patent that will revolutionize its industry. The sales contract calls for the Willis Company to pay You Got It, Inc., the seller, a single payment of $120,000 on June 30, 1986. Interest at the rate of 5% per year on the unpaid balance is to be paid on June 30 of each of the next five years. The cash equivalent and price of the patent could not be determined. The current market interest rate on this type of note is 14%.

Required:

1. Prepare the journal entry to record the purchase of the patent and issuance of the note.
2. Prepare an amortization schedule for this note using the effective interest method.
3. Prepare the journal entries to record the last interest payment and principle payment on June 30, 1986.

P–15–6 The following information relates to the issuance of 10-year bonds. Interest is paid semiannually. From the information given calculate the missing figures in the following independent situations:

	#1	#2	#3	#4
Face value	$100,000	$100,000	$250,000	$300,000
Nominal interest	6%		12%	
Effective yield	8%	12%	10%	12%
Issue price		$ 77,060		$300,000
Premium				
Discount				

P–15–7 On April 1, 1980, Essex, Inc. issued $150,000 face value, five-year bonds payable on April 1, 1985. Interest accrues at 10% per year and is payable each April 1 and October 1. The bonds were issued to yield 12% annual interest.

Required:

1. Compute the issue price and any premium or discount at issuance.
2. Prepare the journal entry necessary to record the issuance of these bonds.
3. Prepare an amortization table for the term of the bond showing the following amounts

at the issuance date and at each one of the interest payment dates using the straight-line
interest method:

Issue price 138,960
Disc. 11,040
Int. Exp. 8604

   a) Interest expense.
   b) Interest paid.
   c) Amortization of discount or premium.
   d) Unamortized discount or premium.
   e) Carrying value of the bond.
4. Rework Part 3 using the effective interest method.

P–15–8 On January 1, 1981, the Arnold Corporation issued $200,000 five-year, 12%
bonds payable. The bonds were issued to yield 10%, and interest is payable each July 1 and
January 1.
Required:
1. Compute the issue price and any premium or discount at issuance.
2. Prepare the journal entry necessary to record the issuance of these bonds.
3. Prepare an amortization table for the term of the bond showing the following amounts
at the issuance date and at each one of the interest payment dates using the straight-line
interest method:
   a) Interest expense.
   b) Interest paid.
   c) Amortization of discount or premium.
   d) Unamortized discount or premium.
   e) Carrying value of the bond.
4. Rework Part 3 using the effective interest method.

P–15–9 On March 1, 1981, the Craft Company issued $100,000 of five-year, 10% bonds.
The bonds were issued to yield 14%. Interest is payable on July 1 and January 1.
Required:
1. Record the issuance of the bonds on March 1, 1981.
2. Assuming the firm uses the straight-line amortization method, prepare the necessary
journal entries on January 1, 1982.
3. Assuming the firm uses the effective interest method, prepare an amortization table
similar to the one in the text. Prepare the required journal entries on January 1, 1982.

P–15–10 Jiffy Delight, Inc. issued five-year, 10% bonds on April 1, 1978. The bonds
have a face value of $200,000 and are callable at 102. They were issued to yield 11%.
Interest is payable semiannually on April 1 and October 1. On October 1, 1981, Jiffy
Delight called the bonds.
Required:
1. Record the issuance of the bonds on April 1, 1978.
2. Prepare an amortization schedule for the Jiffy Delight bonds using the effective interest method.
3. Prepare the journal entry to record the redemption of the bonds on October 1, 1981.

P–15–11 On January 1, 1981, the Hopewell Company sold its 8% bonds that had a face
value of $1,000,000. Interest is payable at December 31, each year. The bonds mature on
January 1, 1991. The bonds were sold to yield a rate of 10%.
Required:
1. Prepare a schedule to compute the total amount received from the sale of the bonds.
Show supporting computations in good form.
2. Make the journal entry needed at issuance.

P–15–12 On December 1, 1981, the Cone Company issued its 7%, $2,000,000, face value
bonds for $2,200,000, plus accrued interest. Interest is payable on November 1 and May 1.
On December 31, 1983, the book value of the bonds, inclusive of the unamortized premium,
was $2,100,000. On July 1, 1984, Cone reacquired the bonds at 98 plus accrued interest.
Cone appropriately uses the straight-line method for the amortization of bond premium
because the results do not differ materially from using the interest method.

Required:

Prepare a schedule to compute the gain or loss on this early extinguishment of debt.

(AICPA adapted)

P–15–13 On July 1, 1977, Pliney Co. issued $500,000 of 10-year, 8% bonds at 103. The bonds are callable at Pliney's option at 104. The amortization of the bond premium has been recorded on the straight-line method (which was not materially different from the effective interest method).

On June 30, 1980, Pliney repurchased $250,000 of the bonds in the open market at 96.

Required:

1. Record the issuance of the bonds on July 1, 1977.
2. Record the semiannually interest and amortization on June 30, 1980.
3. Record the reacquisition of the bonds on June 30, 1980.
4. How should this reacquisition be reflected on Pliney's financial statements?

(AICPA adapted)

P–15–14 The National Fender Bender Co. is a major supplier of fenders to the Ace Automobile Co. Because National is experiencing cash flow problems, Ace agrees to lend it $1,000,000 interest-free to be repaid at the end of four years. As a result of this agreement, National agrees to supply Ace with bumpers at 90% of the current market price. In recent years Ace has borrowed funds at an average of 10% and has lent funds to various suppliers at 12%. National Fender recently received a three-year term loan from the bank at 14%.

Required:

1. Make the necessary entries on the books of both National and Ace for the entire first year of this transaction. (Assume Ace makes purchases evenly over the term of the agreement.)
2. Prepare partial balance sheets at the end of year 1 to reflect this transaction.
3. What would be the effect of not giving accounting recognition to the unstated rights and privileges?

P–15–15 April 1, 1981, Consolidated Corp. issued a 10-year, 10%, $300,000 face value nonconvertible bond at 103 plus accrued interest. Interest is payable semiannually on June 30 and December 31.

Required:

1. Prepare the journal entry to record the bond issuance on April 1, 1981.
2. Prepare the journal entries to record the interest payments on June 30 and December 31, 1981 (use the straight-line method).
3. Repeat Parts 1 and 2, only record the investment in bonds from the purchaser's point of view.

P–15–16 On March 31, 1981, George Co. purchased $100,000, five-year, 10% bonds dated January 1 and due on December 31, 1985. The bonds were bought to yield 12%, and interest is payable each January 1.

Required:

1. Compute the issue price and any premium or discount.
2. Prepare the journal entry necessary to record purchase of these bonds.
3. Prepare an amortization table for the term of the bond using the effective interest method.
4. Prepare the journal entries for December 31, 1981, and December 31, 1985.
5. Assume now that the bonds were redeemed on December 31, 1984, at a price of 104 plus accrued interest. Prepare any necessary journal entries.

P–15–17 Apel, Inc. has agreed to restructure the debt owed to it by Plante Co., a financially troubled motor home dealer. The existing, $500,000 note pays 15% annual interest on June 30 and matures on July 1, 1984, three years from today. Apel has reduced the principle by $150,000, lowered the interest rate to 7%, and extended the maturity date to July 1, 1986.

Required:

1. Prepare any journal entries necessary to reflect this transaction on both Apel's and Plante's books on July 1, 1981.

2. Prepare the journal entries for both Apel and Plante for the payments made on June 30, 1982, and 1986.

3. Prepare the journal entries to record the repayment of the note on July 1, 1986.

P–15–18 The Larsen Corporation entered into the following agreement with California National Bank: on December 31, 1982, the corporation's $1,000,000 note is restructured by (1) forgiving $100,000 of principal and $120,000 of accrued interest, (2) extending the maturity date from December 31, 1982, to December 31, 1987, and (3) reducing interest from 12% to 2%.

Required:

1. Is a gain or loss recognized on this restructuring? Why or why not?

2. Make the required entries for 1982, 1983, and 1987 on the books of the Larsen Corporation and the bank.

3. If the interest rate had only been reduced to 6%, how would this effect your answer to Part 1? Why? Assuming the new effective interest rate is 0.968%, make the entries on the books of both the Larsen Corporation and the bank for 1982, 1983, and 1987.

P–15–19 Murphy's Manufacturing Co. has been experiencing financial difficulties in recent years and is unable to meet its debt to Valley National Bank. Murphy's Manufacturing Co. currently owes the bank $500,000 at 12% interest. The principal and the year's accrued interest are now due and payable.

Required:

Make the required entries on Murphy's books to record each of the following independent restructurings:

    a) Assume Valley National Bank agrees to accept a parcel of land from Murphy's in full settlement of the debt. The land has a book value of $240,000 and a fair market value of $530,000.

    b) Now assume Valley National Bank agrees to accept 50,000 shares of Murphy's common stock in full settlement of the debt. The common stock has a par value of $5 per share and a market value of $9.75 per share.

    c) Now assume that Valley agrees to the following restructuring plan:

The bank will accept 10,000 shares of common stock with a current fair market value of $9.75.

The accrued interest and $100,000 of the principal will be forgiven. In addition, the maturity date of the loan will be extended three full years, and interest will be reduced to 4%. Interest is payable annually, beginning in one year. Is a gain or loss recognized on this restatement? Why?

    d) Now assume that instead of receiving 10,000 shares, Valley National receives 20,000 shares of stock. All other facts remain the same. In this siutation is a gain or loss recognized? Why?

*P–15–20 On July 1, 1979, the Araujo Corporation issued $1,000,000 in five-year, 8% serial bonds to be repaid at $200,000 on July 1 of 1980, 1981, 1982, 1983, and 1984. Interest is payable annually on June 30. The bonds were sold to yield a rate of 10%.

Required:

1. Prepare a schedule showing the computation of the amount of cash received from the issuance of the serial bonds.

2. Prepare the journal entry to record the issuance of the serial bond on July 1, 1979.

3. Prepare a schedule of amortization of the bond discount for the first three years using the bonds outstanding method.

(AICPA adapted)

Note: Items with an *asterisk* relate to material contained in the appendix.

16

Accounting
for Income Taxes

Accounting in the News

Income taxes represent a major expense to most U.S. corporations. Yet, do corporations actually pay to the government all those taxes shown as expenses on their income statements? Perhaps not. As the following article indicates, a good portion of what a corporation records as tax expense never gets paid to the government.

The liability side of Anheuser-Busch's 1980 balance sheet shows "deferred income taxes, $267.7 million." That's no small sum—equal to 19% of total liabilities and 26% of stockholders' equity. Anheuser is not an isolated case. But are deferred taxes really a *liability*?

That's a question many accountants are asking themselves these days. Says Harvey D. Moskowitz, national director of accounting and auditing for Seidman & Seidman, "The deferred taxes on the balance sheet bear no relationship to what is actually going to be owed. So the current method of income tax accounting makes it impossible for the investor to evaluate a company's liquidity, solvency or cash flow."

Here's the explanation for this curious state of affairs: Anheuser-Busch had pretax income of $271.5 million, so, using standard corporate tax rates (less credits), it owed $99.7 million to Uncle Sam. That's what it set aside as "provision for income taxes" on its income statement. But it's not what the company actually paid. Like most businesses Anheuser keeps two sets of books, one for tax purposes, one for stock owners. It uses accelerated depreciation for taxes but straight line for reporting to investors. It expenses interest for tax purposes but often capitalizes it on the books. So, out-of-pocket, it really had to pay only $31.9 million in taxes in 1980—the line marked "current" on the income statement. The other $67.8 million, called "deferred," represents cash that's squirreled away in liabilities on the balance sheet, under the assumption that the company will pay those taxes *eventually*—when accelerated depreciation runs out, for example.

That assumption is probably wrong, though. As long as the company keeps growing—in real terms or because of inflation—it will keep adding new assets and new interest costs to replace the ones that are running out. That means those deferred taxes, instead of getting paid, will simply roll over. And over and over and over. It could almost make you dizzy.*

*Jane Carmichael, "Rollover," *Forbes*, January 18, 1982, p. 75.

This chapter, whose subject is interperiod income tax allocation, explains how and why a corporation's income tax expense is not always the same as its income tax payable.

Business enterprises are subject to a variety of federal, state, local, and in some cases, foreign income taxes. Accounting for these taxes, which involves determining the proper balances in both the income tax expense (based on accounting income) and the income taxes payable (based on taxable income) accounts, is an important aspect of financial reporting and of managerial decision making. The amount of income tax expense for the period depends on the selection of the set of generally accepted principles used to determine the pretax accounting income. However, the amount of taxable income and the actual taxes payable are related to the provisions of the Internal Revenue Code (IRC). Because of the significant difference between the objectives of determining pretax accounting income, as defined by GAAP, and the objectives of determining taxable income, as defined by the IRC, the tax expense and the tax liability of a particular enterprise are apt to be different. The subject of this chapter is accounting for the interplay between these two accounts, which is called **interperiod income tax allocation** (apportioning income taxes between accounting periods).

Income tax is allocated also between items within the income statement. For example, income tax related to current operating income is separate from income tax related to extraordinary gains or losses. This type of tax allocation is referred to as **intraperiod tax allocation.** Intraperiod allocations are discussed in Chapter 23.

Differences between Pretax Accounting Income and Taxable Income

There are significant differences between generally accepted accounting principles and the provisions of the IRC; these differences stem from their varying objectives. GAAP are aimed at providing investors and other users with reliable and relevant financial information for decision making. The provisions of the Code are the result of various objectives, such as equity, ability to pay, ease of administration, and political considerations. Even when there is an overlap between the two, management is free to select one accounting method for reporting purposes and another for tax purposes, and it is usually in its best interest to do so.[1] Generally, for tax purposes management will select that set of accounting methods permissible under the IRC that will minimize the cash outflow for the payment of tax. For financial reporting purposes management generally will select that set of accounting principles under GAAP that will provide reliable and rele-

---

[1] The LIFO inventory method is an exception to this choice. IRC provisions require the use of LIFO for financial statement purposes before it can be selected for tax purposes. However, the LIFO conformity requirements have been eased substantially, and management can disclose the difference between LIFO inventories on the balance sheet and their current replacement cost.

vant information to financial statement users about the firm's periodic performance and financial position.

There are three major classes of items that cause differences between pretax accounting income and taxable income. These are permanent differences, timing differences, and loss carryback and carryforward provisions. Permanent differences and timing differences will be discussed in the sections following.

Loss carrybacks and carryforwards result from the fact that the IRC allows losses in the current year to offset prior or future years' income. As a result, a firm can claim a refund against prior years' taxes and/or can offset future years' taxes. These are discussed later in the chapter.

Permanent Differences

Permanent differences result from items that enter into the determination of accounting income but *never* into the determination of taxable income, or items that are included in taxable income but *never* in accounting income. These differences arise from transactions that will not reverse or turn around in future periods. They represent permanent statutory differences between the IRC and GAAP and can be classified into two major types. One major group of permanent differences is the result of the fact that certain revenues or expenses are included in pretax accounting income but not in taxable income. Examples of this type of permanent differences are listed below.

1. Revenues included in pretax financial accounting income but not in taxable income:
    a) Proceeds received on life insurance policies on corporate officers.
    b) Interest received on state and local bonds.
    c) Interest on certain tax-free "All Savers" certificates.
2. Expenses included in pretax financial accounting income but not in taxable income:
    a) Amortization of goodwill.
    b) Premiums paid on life insurance policies on corporate officers.
    c) Illegal payments, fines, and expenses resulting from violations of the law.

In another group of permanent differences, certain items are included in the determination of both pretax accounting income and taxable income, but there are permanent differences in the amount included under each. These are as follows:

1. Statutory percentage depletion in excess of cost depletion.
2. Depreciation or amortization on certain assets that have a tax basis different from their accounting basis, resulting from the nonrecognition of gain provisions in the IRC for these assets.
3. A special deduction for certain dividends received by a corporation.

The APB concluded that since permanent differences do not reverse or otherwise affect other periods, interperiod income tax allocation is not appropriate for these items. Therefore, in computing the annual tax expense, the accountant must adjust the pretax accounting income for the effects of these items. The

---

Exhibit 16-1
JOBS CORPORATION
Effect of Permanent Differences

Income before taxes	$250,000
Income tax expense	88,000
Net Income	$162,000

The tax expense of $88,000 is determined by the following calculations:

Pretax accounting income	$250,000
Add: Amortized goodwill	10,000
Less: Interest on state bonds	(40,000)
Pretax accounting income adjusted for permanent differences. Also equal to taxable income.	$220,000
Statutory tax rate	0.40
Tax expense and tax liability	$ 88,000

---

current tax rate then is applied to this figure. If you assume that there are no other differences, the income tax expense and income tax liability would be the same. However, because of the difference in income the actual effective tax rate on accounting income will differ from the statutory tax rate. *Opinion No. 11* and the SEC rules require the disclosure of the major differences between these rates.

The effect of permanent differences is illustrated by the following example. Included in the $250,000 pretax accounting income of the Jobs Corporation is $40,000 of interest income received on California State Bonds and $10,000 of amortized goodwill. The company's statutory tax rate is 40%. A partial income statement for the corporation and the determination of the tax expense of $88,000 appear in Exhibit 16-1.

Since the amortization of goodwill never is allowed to be deductible for tax purposes, it must be added to pretax income in calculating the taxes payable. On the other hand, the interest on state bonds is never included in taxable income and therefore must be subtracted from pretax income. Because there are no other differences, both the tax expense and tax liability equal $88,000. In this example the effective tax rate on accounting income is only 35.2% ($88,000 ÷ $250,000) compared to the statutory rate of 40%.

Timing Differences

Timing differences result from the fact that some transactions affect taxable income in a different period from when they affect pretax accounting income. *Opinion No. 11* maintains that "timing differences originate in one period and reverse or 'turn around' in one or more subsequent periods. Some timing differ-

APB#11

ences reduce income tax that would otherwise be payable currently; others increase income taxes that would otherwise be payable currently."[2] An example of a timing difference that would reduce current income taxes payable is the use of straight-line depreciation based on the asset's economic life for financial reporting purposes and the use of Accelerated Cost Recovery System (ACRS) depreciation for tax purposes on a recently purchased asset. In the first few years the ACRS depreciation exceeds the straight-line depreciation, and book income exceeds taxable income. In the later years of the asset's life, the timing difference reverses; straight-line depreciation then exceeds ACRS depreciation, and taxable income exceeds book income. It is important to realize that timing differences affect two or more periods: the period in which the timing difference originates and later period(s) when the initial difference reverses. The four major groups of timing differences are listed in Exhibit 16-2.

The Need for Interperiod Income Tax Allocation

Financial reporting problems for income taxes result from the fact that timing differences cause some transactions to affect the determination of net income for financial accounting purposes in one period and the computation of taxable income in a different period. The purpose of interperiod income tax allocation is to deal with this problem by allocating all applicable taxes against the income for the period, irrespective of when these taxes actually are paid. The need for this allocation is based on two arguments: (1) income taxes are an expense of a business, and (2) the taxes determined to be payable in any one period do not reflect necessarily the appropriate amount of expense incurred in the period.

The first assumption behind the need for interperiod income tax allocation is that income taxes are as much an expense of a business as are wages or depreciation. This is the view proposed by official accounting pronouncements.[3] Many accounting theorists argue, however, that income taxes are not an expense. They maintain that unlike other expenses, income taxes do not generate revenue but are, in fact, the result of pretax revenues in excess of pretax expenses. These theorists believe that because taxes are incurred only if income is earned, they more closely resemble dividends than other expenses. This argument has not been resolved theoretically and may await the development of new accounting concepts.[4]

Official pronouncements, then, consider income taxes to be an expense of doing business. The question arises as to whether the amount of the tax expense should be based on taxable income or on pretax financial accounting income—that is, should the tax expense of the period be the cash that is due the government. Proponents of interperiod income tax allocation think that the amount of income taxes determined to be payable in any one period does not reflect necessarily the appropriate amount of tax expense incurred in that period. They believe that

---

[2]"Accounting for Income Taxes," *Opinions of the Accounting Principles Board No. 11* (New York: AICPA, 1967), par. 13.

[3]Ibid., par. 146.

[4]See Weeler James and Willard Galliart, *An Appraisal of Interperiod Income Tax Allocation* (New York: Financial Executive Research Institute, 1974).

Exhibit 16-2
Major Groups of Timing Differences

1. Revenues or gains that are included in taxable income later than they are included in pretax accounting income. Examples include:
   a) Gross profits on installment sales recognized for accounting purposes in the period of sale, but reported for tax purposes in the period in which the installments are collected.
   b) Gross profits on long-term construction contracts recognized for accounting purposes on the percentage-of-completion method, but recognized for tax purposes on the completed-contract basis.
   c) Use of the equity method of accounting for investments for accounting purposes and use of the cost method for tax purposes.
2. Expenses or losses that are deducted in determining pretax accounting income. The major example of this item is the estimated costs of warranties, guarantees, and other estimated expenses that are recognized for accounting purposes in the period in which the expense is probable and can be estimated; these costs are not reported for tax purposes until the actual liability has been determined.
3. Revenues or gains that are included in taxable income earlier than they are included in pretax accounting income. Prepaid income is the major group of items included in this category. For example, rents collected in advance are reported for tax purposes in the period in which they are received, but are reported for accounting purposes in the periods in which the rent is earned.
4. Expenses or losses that are deducted in determining taxable income earlier than they are deducted in determining pretax accounting income. Included in this category are the following:
   a) The use of accelerated depreciation for tax purposes and the use of straight-line for accounting purposes.
   b) Certain interest and taxes during construction that are deducted in tax returns when incurred and are capitalized for accounting purposes as part of the cost of the assets.

using actual taxes payable would result in a mismatching of revenue and expense. The argument is made that interperiod tax allocation improves matching, and matching improves the prediction of future income.

Thus, the purpose of interperiod income tax allocation is to allocate the income tax expense to the periods in which revenues are earned and in which expenses are incurred. In effect, interperiod tax allocation ensures that the total income tax paid over the life of the enterprise is allocated to the proper accounting period. Without this procedure there would be improper matching of revenue and expense, resulting in misleading profitability figures.

The need for interperiod income tax allocation is illustrated in the following example, which compares a series of income statements without income tax allocation with those in which there is income tax allocation. Assume that the Brokow Company commenced business on January 2, 1981. At that time the company purchased equipment costing $100,000. For tax purposes the company uses ACRS, and the asset falls into the three-year class. For financial reporting purposes the asset has a five-year life and no salvage value; straight-line depreciation is used. The current tax rate is 40% and remains constant over the next five years. For the sake of simplicity, assume that the Brokow Company has constant revenues of $200,000 and expenses, other than depreciation, of $75,000 over the five-year period. The computation of the Company's taxable income is portrayed in Exhibit 16-3.

The condensed income statements for the Brokow Company without interperiod income tax allocation are illustrated in Exhibit 16-4. These statements are constructed using straight-line depreciation, but the income taxes are based upon ACRS depreciation and are drawn from Exhibit 16-3. This means that the tax expense is equal to the taxes payable as computed in that exhibit.

For comparison purposes Exhibit 16-5 presents the same series of income statements, but this time employing interperiod income tax allocation. This means that the tax expense is based on accounting income before taxes, rather than on taxable income. An examination of the two sets of income statements in

Exhibit 16-3
BROKOW COMPANY
Computation of Taxable Income and Income Tax Liability

	1981	1982	1983	1984	1985	Total
Net revenues	$200,000	$200,000	$200,000	$200,000	$200,000	$1,000,000
Expense—other than depreciation	75,000	75,000	75,000	75,000	73,000	375,000
Depreciation—ACRS*	25,000	38,000	37,000	–0–	–0–	100,000
Total expenses	$100,000	$113,000	$112,000	$ 75,000	$ 75,000	$ 475,000
Taxable income	100,000	87,000	88,000	125,000	125,000	525,000
Income taxes— liability, 40%	$ 40,000	$ 34,800	$ 35,200	$ 50,000	$ 50,000	$ 210,000
Tax expense as a % of income before taxes	40%	40%	40%	40%	40%	40%

*Under ACRS the depreciation percentage write-off per year for property placed in service in 1981–1984 is as follows:

Recovery Year	Applicable Percentage
1	25%
2	38%
3	37%
	100%

Exhibit 16-4

BROKOW COMPANY

Condensed Income Statements without Interperiod Income Tax Allocation for the Years Ended 1981–1985

	1981	1982	1983	1984	1985	Total
Net revenues	$200,000	$200,000	$200,000	$200,000	$200,000	$1,000,000
Expense—other than depreciation	75,000	75,000	75,000	75,000	75,000	375,000
Depreciation—straight-line	20,000	20,000	20,000	20,000	20,000	100,000
Total expenses	$ 95,000	$ 95,000	$ 95,000	$ 95,000	$ 95,000	$ 475,000
Income before taxes	105,000	105,000	105,000	105,000	105,000	525,000
Tax expense— ACRS basis (See Exhibit 16-3)	40,000	34,800	35,200	50,000	50,000	210,000
Net income	$ 65,000	$ 70,200	$ 69,800	$ 55,000	$ 55,000	$ 315,000
Tax expense as a % of income before taxes	38%	33%	34%	48%	48%	40%

Exhibits 16-4 and 16-5 points out the need for interperiod income tax allocation. In both series of statements the total amount of income before taxes ($525,000), tax expense ($210,000), and net income ($315,000) are equal when all five years are combined. However, each of these items is apportioned differently for each series of statements within the five years. The statements in Exhibit 16-4 that are constructed without interperiod income tax allocation show higher net incomes in the first three years and lower net incomes in the last two years than those in Exhibit 16-5 that are prepared using interperiod income tax allocation. The higher reported income in the first three years is misleading because it is due solely to the immediate tax benefits from the use of ACRS depreciation. Thus, it might appear to investors, potential investors, or other users that the Brokow Company is more profitable in the first three years than it really is if its income were reported under GAAP. Interperiod tax allocation solves this problem and ensures that the tax expense on the income statement is based on the actual expenses incurred during the period. This means that both the depreciation and the tax expense are based on the use of straight-line depreciation.

The counter argument is that matching puts too much emphasis on income determination at the expense of the balance sheet. Also, other allocations of doubtful validity, such as depreciation, make statements tentative, and they are not improved by allocating income taxes.[5] Further, the current emphasis on predicting cash flows makes it more reasonable for income taxes to be based on the

[5] Eldon Hendrickson, *Accounting Theory*, 4th ed. (Homewood, Illinois: Irwin, 1982), pp. 433–436.

Exhibit 16-5
BROKOW COMPANY
Condensed Income Statement with Interperiod Income Tax Allocation for the Years Ended 1981–1985

	1981	1982	1983	1984	1985	Total
Net revenues	$200,000	$200,000	$200,000	$200,000	$200,000	$1,000,000
Expense—other than depreciation	75,000	75,000	75,000	75,000	75,000	375,000
Depreciation— straight-line	20,000	20,000	20,000	20,000	20,000	100,000
Total expense	$ 95,000	$ 95,000	$ 95,000	$ 95,000	$ 95,000	$ 475,000
Income before taxes	105,000	105,000	105,000	105,000	105,000	525,000
Tax expense—40%	42,000	42,000	42,000	42,000	42,000	210,000
Net income	$ 63,000	$ 63,000	$ 63,000	$ 63,000	$ 63,000	$ 315,000
Tax expense as a % of income before taxes	40%	40%	40%	40%	40%	40%

cash outflows that will take place within or just after the end of the period. However, the APB believed that the arguments and concepts behind interperiod income tax allocation were persuasive and adopted it in *Opinion No. 11*.

Procedures for Applying Income Tax Allocation

In order to illustrate the interperiod income tax allocation procedures with both permanent and timing differences, we have provided the following example. The condensed income statements for the Quick Corporation for the years ended December 31, 1981, through 1985 are portrayed in Exhibit 16-6. Revenues include interest received on nontaxable bonds of $15,000, $12,000, $16,000, $18,000, and $20,000 for each respective year. The company purchased a new piece of equipment for $120,000 on January 2, 1981. For tax purposes, the asset falls into the three-year class under the ACRS. For financial reporting purposes, the equipment has a five-year life with no salvage value, and straight-line depreciation is used. Exhibit 16-6 also shows the correct amount of depreciation under each method.

Exhibit 16-7 shows how the income tax expense and income taxes payable are calculated. The journal entries for 1981 through 1985 and the "T" account for the deferred tax account are illustrated in Exhibit 16-8. A number of points should be noted about these illustrations. The interest on the nontaxable bonds represents a permanent difference; thus, no income tax allocation is required. As a result the interest income is subtracted from the accounting pretax income in determining the current year's income tax expense. However, the difference in the straight-line depreciation and ACRS depreciation is a timing difference.

The difference between the tax expense recorded on the income statements and the liability recorded on the balance sheet is either a debit or a credit to a

Exhibit 16-6
QUICK CORPORATION
Condensed Income Statements
For the Years Ended December 31, 1981–1985

	1981	1982	1983	1984	1985
Revenues	$500,000	$530,000	$510,000	$550,000	$560,000
Expenses	400,000	440,000	430,000	460,000	465,000
Pretax accounting income	$100,000	$ 90,000	$ 80,000	$ 90,000	$ 95,000

Depreciation Expense
For the Years Ended December 31, 1981–1985

	1981	1982	1983	1984	1985
Straight-line	$24,000	$24,000	$24,000	$24,000	$24,000
ACRS	30,000	45,600	44,400	–0–	–0–
Difference	($ 6,000)	($21,600)	($20,400)	$24,000	$24,000

deferred tax account. In this example, as illustrated in Exhibit 16-8, a credit is made to the deferred tax account in the first three years, and a debit is made in the last two years. At the end of the five-year period the total depreciation is the same for both methods, and the result is a zero balance in this deferred tax account. When the deferred tax account has a credit balance, it is shown on the liability section of the balance sheet. Conversely, when the account has a debit balance, it is shown on the asset side of the balance sheet. In reality the deferred tax account does not zero out. Remember that this example illustrates deferred taxes using only one timing difference. The use of straight-line depreciation vis-a-vis ACRS ensures that the deferred tax account will have a zero balance at the end of the asset's useful life. There is, however, considerable evidence that as firms replace existing assets with higher-priced assets, the balance in the deferred credit account will continue to increase. This has led to considerable debate about the exact nature of the deferred tax credit account, and about the appropriateness of comprehensive income tax allocation, the method required by the APB in *Opinion No. 11*. These issues will be explored in depth in the sections following.

Partial Versus Comprehensive Allocation

The extent to which income tax allocation should be applied is embodied in the argument concerning partial versus comprehensive allocation.

Exhibit 16-7

QUICK CORPORATION
Computation of Income Tax Expense and Taxes Payable
For the Years Ended December 31, 1981–1985

	1981	1982	1983	1984	1985
Income per books	$100,000	$90,000	$80,000	$90,000	$95,000
Adjustment for permanent differences, tax-free interest income	15,000	12,000	16,000	18,000	20,000
Adjusted pretax accounting income	$ 85,000	$78,000	$64,000	$72,000	$75,000
Income tax rate, 40%	0.40	0.40	0.40	0.40	0.40
Tax expense	$ 34,000	$31,200	$25,600	$28,800	$30,000
Adjusted pretax accounting income from above	$ 85,000	$78,000	$64,000	$72,000	$75,000
Difference in depreciation expense	(6,000)	(21,600)	(20,400)	24,000	24,000
Taxable income	$ 79,000	$56,400	$43,600	$96,000	$99,000
Income tax rate, 40%	0.40	0.40	0.40	0.40	0.40
Taxes payable	$ 31,600	$22,560	$17,440	$38,400	$39,600
Deferred tax (credit) charge	($ 2,400)	($ 8,640)	($ 8,160)	$ 9,600	$ 9,600

Partial Income Tax Allocation. Proponents of partial income tax allocation argue that there is a presumption that income tax expense for the period usually should be the same for financial accounting purposes as the taxes payable for the period. Individuals who hold this view classify timing differences as either recurring or nonrecurring. Recurring differences between taxable income and pretax accounting income result in an indefinite reduction or postponement of tax payments. Thus, under partial income tax allocation, no allocation is required for recurring differences. In effect they are treated as permanent differences. A common example of a recurring difference is the difference that arises when a company with a relatively stable or growing investment in depreciable assets uses straight-line depreciation in determining pretax accounting income but uses ACRS in determining taxable income. The continued investment in higher-priced assets indefinitely postpones the reversal of the timing difference. The view that recurring differences do not require income tax allocation is based on the assumption that the taxes resulting from these differences are not expected to be payable or recoverable from the government, and thus, they should not affect income.

Conversely, nonrecurring differences do turn around eventually, and so do not cause an indefinite postponement of taxes. An example of a nonrecurring difference might be an isolated installment sale of a productive facility in which

Exhibit 16-8
QUICK CORPORATION
Tax Journal Entries

	1981	1982	1983
Income tax expense	34,000	31,200	25,600
Deferred tax credit	2,400	8,640	8,160
Income taxes payable	31,600	22,560	17,440

	1984	1985
Income tax expense	28,800	30,000
Deferred tax credit	9,600	9,600
Income taxes payable	38,400	39,600

Deferred Taxes

1984	9,600	2,400	1981
1985	9,600	8,640	1982
		8,160	1983
	19,200	19,200	

the gross profit is reported for financial statement purposes on the date of sale and for tax purposes when the installments are collected. Proponents of partial tax allocation argue that nonrecurring differences should be allocated between periods in order to avoid materially misstating income tax expense and net income. Thus, under partial income tax allocation, income tax expense for the period equals the taxes payable for the period plus or minus the tax effects of specific, nonrecurring timing differences that are expected to turn around in three to five years. Partial tax allocation recently has been adopted by the Accounting Standards Committee of the Institute of Chartered Accountants in England and Wales and by the International Accounting Standard Committee.

Comprehensive Income Tax Allocation. The APB rejected these views and required the use of comprehensive income tax allocation. Under the comprehensive income tax allocation method, income tax expense for a period includes the tax effects of all transactions affecting the determination of pretax accounting income for that period even though some of these transactions may affect the determination of taxes payable in a different period. As a result, all timing differences, recurring or nonrecurring, are included in determining deferred taxes. The proponents of this view argue that the actual amount of income taxes payable does not measure necessarily the appropriate amount of income tax expense for the period. This view is based primarily on the matching principle and on the belief that the partial allocation method, which stresses cash flows, is a departure from the accrual basis of accounting.

The APB's Position.   The APB's position on comprehensive income tax allocation is summed up as follows:

> The Board has considered the various concepts of accounting for income taxes and has concluded that comprehensive interperiod tax allocation is an integral part of the determination of income tax expense . . . Since permanent differences do not affect other periods, interperiod tax allocation is not appropriate to account for such differences.[6]

This *Opinion* has not quieted debate on the issue of comprehensive versus partial tax allocation; a number of Board members dissented from it. Three of these members noted that to the extent that this method deviates from the income tax reasonably expected to be paid or recovered, it would result in accounts carried either as assets that have no demonstrable value and that are never expected to be recovered or as liabilities that are mere contingencies. A number of empirical studies support this view. The findings from one study indicate that "deferred tax balances have increased steadily over the years and represent a large item in the liability section of the balance sheet."[7] Because of these arguments many accountants continue to press for the adoption of partial tax allocation.

Differing Methods of Income Tax Allocation

Regardless of whether partial or comprehensive tax allocation is used, there are three different methods that can be adopted to measure the amount of deferred taxes: (1) the deferred method, (2) the liability method, and (3) the net of tax method. If tax rates change or are expected to change in the future, these three methods will result in a different measurement of the deferred tax amount. Each method is described briefly next.

The Deferred Method.   Interperiod tax allocation under the **deferred method** emphasizes the tax effects of timing differences on income in the period they originate. Under this method, the only method sanctioned by the APB, the measurement of the deferred credit or charge is determined on the basis of the tax rates currently in effect. When the timing differences reverse, there is no adjust-

---

[6]"Accounting for Income Taxes," par. 146.

[7]Schwartz, Bill, "Income Tax Allocation: It is Time for a Change," *Journal of Accounting Auditing and Finance* (Spring, 1981), p. 243.

ment for subsequent changes in rates; the deferred taxes simply are allocated to the periods in which the reversals occur, based on the original rates. For example, in Exhibit 16-8 the deferred tax credit account was debited by $9,600 when the timing difference began to reverse in 1984. Under the deferral method, this journal entry would remain even if the tax rate had increased to 45% or decreased to 30% in 1983. This method is consistent with the matching principle and was supported by the Board, because in its view "it provides the most useful and practical approach to interperiod tax allocation and the presentation of income taxes on the balance sheet."[8]

Liability Method. The **liability method** attempts to measure the taxes at the amount that ultimately will be paid in future periods. Thus, the income taxes that are expected to be paid in the future on pretax accounting income are accrued in the current period. Under this method, differences between income tax expense and taxes payable in the period of origination are considered as either liabilities for taxes payable in the future or assets for prepaid taxes. They are not considered deferred credits or charges to be amortized to future periods as they are under the deferred method. Therefore, the tax liability or prepaid taxes are computed at the tax rate expected to be in effect in the period in which they reverse. When the timing differences actually reverse, adjustments are made for any subsequent changes in the actual tax rates.

The procedures for the liability method can be illustrated by returning to the example in Exhibit 16-7. Assume now that the tax rate in 1981 through 1983 remains at 40%, but at that time (1981) the rate for the years 1984 through 1985 is expected to decrease to 30%. However, when the timing difference first begins to reverse in 1984, the actual tax rate in effect is 35%. The tax rate is also 35% in 1985. Under the liability method the journal entries as shown in Exhibit 16-9 would be made.

In 1981, 1982, and 1983, the credit to the deferred tax account is based on a tax of 30%, the rate expected to be in effect at the time of the reversal. This should be compared to the deferred method that computes the deferral based on 40%, the actual tax rate in existence at the time of the difference.

In 1984, and 1985, the debit to the deferred tax credit account is based on a tax rate of 35%, the actual rate in effect at the time of the reversal. Under the deferred method, the rate would again be 40%, the rate in existence when the timing difference originated in 1981, 1982, and 1983. In this particular case the balance in the deferred tax account does not zero out because the expected rate of 30% does not equal the actual rate of 35%.

The APB rejected the liability method, maintaining that "deferred charges and deferred credits relating to timing differences represent the cumulative recognition given to their tax effects, and as such do not represent receivables or payables in the usual sense."[9]

The Net of Tax Method. The **net of tax method** is the third method of measuring the deferred tax account. Under this alternative the tax effects of timing differences are recognized in the valuation of the respective asset or liability

[8] "Accounting for Income Taxes," par. 35.

[9] Ibid., par. 57.

Exhibit 16-9
Journal Entries for the Liability Method

	1981		1982	
Income tax expense	33,400		29,040	
Deferred tax credit		1,800[a]		6,480[c]
Taxes payable		31,600[b]		22,560[d]

	1983	
Income tax expense	23,560	
Deferred tax credit		6,120[e]
Taxes payable		17,440[f]

	1984		1985	
Income tax expense	25,200		26,250	
Deferred tax credit	8,400[g]		8,400[i]	
Taxes payable		33,600[h]		34,650[j]

[a] $6,000 timing difference × 0.30 = $1,800.
[b] Given in Exhibit 16-7.
[c] $21,600 timing difference × 0.30 = $6,480.
[d] Given in Exhibit 16-7.
[e] $20,400 timing difference × 0.30 = $6,120.
[f] Given in Exhibit 16-7.
[g] $24,000 difference in depreciation × 0.35 = $ 8,400.
[h] $96,000 taxable income × 0.35 = $33,600.
[i] $24,000 difference in depreciation × 0.35 = $ 8,400.
[j] $99,000 taxable income × 0.35 = $34,650.

---

accounts. For example, the tax effects of excess depreciation are used to reduce the related asset account. This is based on the reasoning that the depreciation currently deducted for tax purposes reduces the future value of the asset because future depreciation benefits are lessened. The use of accelerated depreciation quickens this process; thus, the asset cost must be reduced by the tax effect of this accelerated depreciation.

These concepts are illustrated by the following example. Assume that in January 1979, the Hasty Corporation purchased a piece of equipment for $30,000. The machine has a five-year life and no salvage value. The company uses straight-line depreciation for financial accounting purposes and ACRS for tax purposes. The tax rate is 40%. In the first year straight-line depreciation is $6,000, and ACRS depreciation is $7,500 (25% × $30,000). At a 40% tax rate, the tax effect of the excess depreciation is $600 [0.40 × ($7,500 − $6,000)]. The appropriate journal entry and balance sheet presentation to reflect the method are as follows:

Entry:
Depreciation expense	6,600	
Accumulated depreciation		6,000
Deferred taxes		600
To record income taxes		
for 1979.		

Balance Sheet Presentation:
Equipment		$30,000
Less: Accumulated depreciation	$6,000	
Deferred taxes	600	6,600
		$23,400

It is important to note that in *Statement of Financial Accounting Concepts No. 3,* "Elements of Financial Statement of Business Enterprises," the Board concludes that both the liability method and the net of tax method are compatible with the definitions of assets and liabilities contained in the Statement, and that the deferred method does not fit these definitions.[10] If these definitions are implemented, there would be a substantial change in the current accounting practice related to interperiod tax allocation. Applying a liability view would imply the discounting of deferred taxes to some present value amount. However, the deferred method is still the only method sanctioned in the official pronouncements.

Applications of the Deferred Method of Comprehensive Income Tax Allocation in Practice

Previous illustrations in this chapter focused on relatively straightforward examples with one timing difference and a constant tax rate. In practice, applying deferred income tax allocation is more complicated. A firm is likely to be experiencing simultaneously originating and reversing differences from a variety of items. **Originating differences,** which represent the initial difference between taxable income and pretax accounting income due to a particular timing difference, could result in either a deferred credit or a deferred charge. For example, in an earlier example (Exhibit 16-7) a firm purchased a piece of equipment for $120,000. The company assumed the asset had a five-year life with no salvage value, and took straight-line depreciation for book purposes and ACRS depreciation for tax purposes. In 1981 there was an originating difference of $2,400

---

[10] "Elements of Financial Statements of Business Enterprises," *Statement of Financial Concepts No. 3* (Stamford, Conn.: FASB, 1980), pars. 163 and 164.

[0.40 × ($30,000 − $24,000)], due to the excess of ACRS over straightline depreciation. Although in this example the originating differences resulted in a deferred credit because book income exceeded taxable income, it is also possible for a deferred charge to occur in cases in which taxable income exceeds book income.

A **reversing difference** occurs when the original timing difference begins to turn around. In the situation just discussed, this happens in 1984 when straight-line depreciation exceeds the ACRS depreciation, and as a consequence taxable income exceeds book income. The result is a debit to the deferred credit account of $9,600. Again, a reversing difference may either be a debit or credit, depending upon the nature of the originating difference.

If a firm has a number of originating and reversing differences, the computation of the correct deferred tax entry can be complex. There are two major methods that have been developed to deal with these problems: (1) the individual item basis (2) and the group-of-similar-items basis. Both of these methods are sanctioned by the APB.

Individual Item Basis

The **individual item basis** treats each originating difference and its subsequent reversing difference as an item distinct from other timing differences. Thus, for each timing difference it is necessary to calculate the tax effect of the originating and subsequent reversing differences. The deferred tax account is increased and decreased accordingly. Obviously, given a number of different originating and reversing differences, the record keeping required to apply this method can be burdensome. Thus, in practice this method can be difficult to apply unless there are large, distinct, nonrecurring timing differences, or unless computers are used.

Group-of-Similar-Items Basis

In practice the **group-of-similar-items basis** is far more common. Under this method, all similar items are grouped and deferred taxes are determined for the group. That is, all items using accelerated depreciation would be grouped together, all installment sales would be grouped together, and so forth. This clearly simplifies the computation process. The two variants of this method that are common in practice are the gross change method and the net change method. If a change in tax rates occurs, these methods will result in a different balance in the deferred tax account.

Gross Change Method.   Under the **gross change method** the net change to the deferred tax account is computed by separately calculating the tax effect of the originating differences, at the current rate, and the tax effect of the reversing differences, at the rate in effect at the time of origination. These originating and reversing differences then are offset to determine the actual net change on the deferred tax account.

If tax rates have changed since the originating difference, it is necessary to make some flow assumption as to tax rates in order to calculate the tax effect of the reversing difference. Usually a FIFO or average rate assumption is made. On a FIFO basis, reversals to the deferred tax account are computed based on the earliest tax rate since the originating differences. If the reversal is large enough, the next earliest tax rate would be used and so forth. Hence, it is necessary to keep records of all layers of originating differences. A slightly easier method to calculate the effects of the reversal is to use a rate based on the average taxes that have been incurred since the differences originated.

Net Change Method.   The **net change method** is easier to apply. The originating and reversing differences are netted together, and the current tax rate is applied to calculate the change in the deferred tax account. This means that originating and reversing differences are grouped together, and a single, current tax rate is applied. The applications of the net change method and both variants of the gross change method are illustrated below.

Illustration Of The Two Methods.   The St. Joseph's Construction and Development Company, a land developer that constructs planned residential communities, began business on January 2, 1978. The company uses straight-line depreciation and the percentage-of-completion method for accounting purposes and uses sum-of-the-year's-digits and the completed-contract method for tax purposes. The company's deferred tax account is presented in Exhibit 16-10.

At the end of 1980 the deferred tax account had a credit balance of $15,680. During 1981 the firm had pretax accounting income of $250,000 from construction based on the percentage-of-completion method, land sales, and other nonconstruction sources. In addition, at the beginning of 1981 the firm purchased a fleet of 20 new cars for its salesmen. Because of this purchase, an originating difference of $25,000 resulted from the excess of ACRS depreciation over straight-line depreciation. In 1981 the first reversing difference (relating to differences in accounting for construction revenues) occurred when the company completed its first project. As a result, the gross profit on the contract for tax purposes (completed-contract method) exceeded the gross profit for book purposes (percentage-of-completion method) by $10,000. Finally, assume that the current tax rate

---

Exhibit 16-10
ST. JOSEPH'S CONSTRUCTION AND DEVELOPMENT CO.
Deferred Tax Account

Year	Timing Differences	Tax Rate at Time of Differences	Credit to Deferred Tax Account
1978	$10,000	40%	$ 4,000
1979	14,000	44%	6,160
1980	12,000	46%	5,520
	$36,000		$15,680
	Average Rate	43.6%	($15,680 ÷ $36,000)

Exhibit 16-11
ST. JOSEPH'S CONSTRUCTION
AND DEVELOPMENT COMPANY
Computation of Taxes Payable

Pretax accounting income	$250,000
Originating difference—excess depreciation	(25,000)
Reversing difference—excess gross profit on	
completed contract	10,000
Taxable income	$235,000
Tax rate	0.46
Taxes payable	$108,100

(1980) remains at 46% and that there were no permanent differences. Exhibit 16-11 reconciles book income with taxable income and determines the taxes payable for the year.

Exhibits 16-12 and 16-13 illustrate the computation of the current year deferred tax amount using the gross change average rate and FIFO rate method, respectively. As is evident from the illustration, the only difference between these two variants of the gross change method is the calculation of the reversing amount. The average rate method uses the average tax rate over the period, whereas the FIFO method uses the first tax rate of 40%. There is no need to go to the 1979 layer since the reversing amount uses only the 1978 layer of $10,000

Exhibit 16-12
ST. JOSEPH'S CONSTRUCTION
AND DEVELOPMENT COMPANY
Gross Change Method—Average Rate

Taxes payable	$108,100
Originating difference	
$25,000 × 0.46	11,500
Reversing difference	
$10,000 × 0.436[1]	(4,360)
Tax expense—1981	$115,240
Increase in deferred credit	
$115,240 − $108,100	$ 7,140

[1]$15,680 ÷ $36,000 = 0.436.

Exhibit 16-13
ST. JOSEPH'S CONSTRUCTION
AND DEVELOPMENT COMPANY
Gross Change Method—FIFO

Taxes payable	$108,100
Originating difference	
$25,000 × 0.46	11,500
Reversing difference	
$10,000 × 0.40	(4,000)
Tax expense—1981	$115,600
Increase in deferred credit	
$115,600 − $108,100	$ 7,500

(See Exhibit 16-10). Had the reversal been for $15,000, $10,000 would have come from the 1978 layer and $5,000 would have come from the 1979 layer. The journal entries for the two methods would be as follows:

	Average Rate		FIFO	
Taxes expense	115,240		115,600	
Deferred tax credit		7,140		7,500
Taxes payable		108,100		108,100
To record taxes for the year.				

Exhibit 16-14 illustrates the computation of the amount of tax expense and the increase in the deferred credit accounting using the net change method. In this example the originating and reversing difference are offset. The difference of $15,000 is multiplied by the current tax rate of 46% to cause an increase of $6,900 in the deferred tax account. The appropriate journal entry is as follows:

Tax expense	115,000	
Deferred tax credit		6,900
Taxes payable		108,100
To record taxes for the year.		

Exhibit 16-14
ST. JOSEPH'S CONSTRUCTION
AND DEVELOPMENT COMPANY
Net Change Method

Taxes payable		$108,100
Originating difference	$25,000	
Reversing difference	(10,000)	
	$15,000	
Current tax rate	0.46	6,900
Tax expense—1981		$115,000

If you apply the net change method, it is possible that the deferred tax account would not zero out even with a complete reversal of a single timing difference. Tax rates changes cause reversing differences to decrease the deferred tax account at the current tax rate, whereas the originating difference is computed at the rate in effect at that time. Thus, there may be no direct relationship between the originating and reversing rates.

In summary, all three methods result in a credit to taxes payable of $108,100. The difference lies in the debit to the tax expense account and the credit to the deferred tax account. Exhibit 16-15 illustrates these differences. Both the gross change and net change methods are used in practice. However, expectations of changing tax rates would make the gross change method preferable to the net change method.

The With and Without Method

The previous examples assumed a tax rate that remains constant across all levels of taxable income. This is not the situation in reality. Corporate tax rates, as illustrated in Exhibit 16-16, are graduated. Further, not all items affecting taxa-

---

Exhibit 16-15
ST. JOSEPH'S CONSTRUCTION
AND DEVELOPMENT COMPANY
Summary of Deferred Tax Method

	Gross Change		Net Change Method
	Average Rate	*FIFO Rate*	
Tax expense	$115,240	$115,600	$115,000
Deferred tax credit	(7,140)	(7,500)	(6,900)
Taxes payable	(108,100)	(108,100)	(108,100)

| | | | 1983 |
Step	1981 Rates	1982 Rates	and Beyond Rates
First $25,000 of taxable income	17%	16%	15%
Second $25,000 of taxable income	20%	19%	18%
Third $25,000 of taxable income	30%	30%	30%
Fourth $25,000 of taxable income	40%	40%	40%
Taxable income in excess of $100,000	46%	46%	46%

Exhibit 16-16
Corporate Tax Rates

ble income are taxed at the same rate. For example, capital gains are subject to an alternative rate of 20%. As a result, timing differences can cause the actual tax rate to change, depending upon what level or type of income is involved. An allocation procedure called the **with and without method** has been developed to deal with this situation.

To apply this **method,** you determine pretax accounting income with and without the appropriate timing differences. The difference between the tax computed on these amounts represents the current deferred tax provision. For example, assume the Mesh Corporation has pretax accounting income of $60,000. Included is nontaxable interest income of $5,000. Further, the corporation has an originating difference of $10,000 due to the excess of ACRS depreciation over straight-line depreciation. The tax rates in Exhibit 16-16 apply for 1982. Exhibit 16-17 illustrates the computation of the taxes payable and the deferred tax provision. The journal entry to record the tax is an follows:

Tax expense	10,250	
Deferred tax credit		2,450
Taxes payable		7,800
To record taxes for the year.		

As this exhibit indicates the credit to the deferred tax account is $2,450. If this method had not been used, the credit would have been $3,000 ($10,000 × 0.30), because the highest step rate of 30% would have been applied to the difference. However, this would be incorrect since the $10,000 difference straddles two tax rates, 19% and 30%.

Exhibit 16-17
MESH CORPORATION
Determination of Taxes Payable and Deferred Tax

Pretax accounting income	$60,000
Less: Permanent difference—interest income	(5,000)
Adjusted pretax income	$55,000
Less: Timing difference—excess depreciation	(10,000)
Taxable income	$45,000

Taxes Payable

Amount	Rate	Total
$25,000	16%	$4,000
20,000	19%	3,800
$45,000		$7,800

Tax without Timing Difference			*Tax with Timing Difference*		
Amount	Rate	Total	Amount	Rate	Total
$25,000	16%	$ 4,000	$25,000	16%	$4,000
25,000	19%	4,750	20,000	19%	3,800
5,000	30%	1,500			
$55,000		$10,250	$45,000		$7,800

Deferred tax = $10,250 − $7,800 = $2,450

Accounting for Net Operating Losses

The provisions of the IRC permit a corporation to carry back and/or carry forward a net operating loss incurred in the current period. This allows a corporation that has fluctuating earnings to spread out these earnings and thus reduce its overall tax burden. Under these provisions the loss can be carried back three years (to the earliest year first), and if some loss still remains can be carried forward fifteen additional years. The carryback offsets previous years' income, which results in a reduction in taxes from those years and a definitely determinable tax fund. Tax carryforwards offset future years' income; the realization of carryforward benefits depends on the corporation's ability to generate income in the future.

A corporation may elect to forego the carryback and to use the carryforward immediately. This decision would be based on tax planning considerations. For example, when carried back, the current year's loss may wipe out tax credits used in previous years. If these tax credits have expired and can no longer be carried forward, the corporation would lose its benefit from them. In this situation the firm may decide to forego the carryback and may elect an immediate carryforward.

In *Opinion No. 11* the APB differentiates between the accounting treatment for loss carrybacks and loss carryforwards. In the Board's view a loss carryback results in a refund of taxes that is both measurable and currently realizable, whereas the realization of benefits from carryforwards is questionable. Thus, it prescribes different accounting treatments for carrybacks and forwards.

APB # 11

Accounting for Loss Carrybacks

Net operating losses incurred in the current period can be carried back three years. This carryback offsets prior year's income, and the corporation can claim a refund for taxes paid in those years. The net operating loss is carried back first to the earliest year, and so forth. *Opinion No. 11* clearly defines the accounting for loss carrybacks:

> The tax effects of any realizable loss carrybacks should be recognized in the determination of net income (loss) of the loss periods. The tax loss gives rise to a refund (or claim for refund) of past taxes, which is both measurable and currently realizable; therefore, the tax effect of the loss is properly recognizable in the determination of net income (loss) for the loss period.[11]

APB # 11

The APB took this view to achieve proper matching inasmuch as current realization of the refund is assured. Therefore, a receivable is recorded for the tax refund, and a corresponding decrease in the current year's loss is reported.

For example, assume that the Michele Corporation suffered a $150,000 net operating loss in 1981. Since past years have been profitable, the loss can be carried back and the corporation elects to do so. The prior three year's taxable income and tax rates are presented below:

Year	Taxable Income	Rate
1978	$ 80,000	44%
1979	60,000	44%
1980	120,000	46%

The corporation can claim a $63,000 refund due to the carryback. As illustrated in Exhibit 16-18, the $150,000 is offset first against the 1978 income of $80,000. The remaining $70,000 loss ($150,000 − $80,000) then is offset against the 1979 income of $60,000 and against $10,000 of the 1980 income. Because of changing tax rates, each year's refund must be calculated separately. The corporation still has $110,000 ($120,000 − $10,000) of 1980 taxable income available to be offset

---

[11] "Accounting for Income Taxes," par. 44.

Exhibit 16-18
MICHELE CORPORATION
Computation of Tax Refund

Year	Taxable Income	Taxable Income Offset		Rate	Refund
1978	$ 80,000	$ 80,000	×	40%	$32,000
1979	60,000	60,000	×	44%	26,400
1980	120,000	10,000	×	46%	4,600
		$150,000			$63,000

against any future net operating losses in 1982 or 1983. The journal entry for 1981 is below:

Income to refund	63,000	
Income tax refund due to loss carryback		63,000
To record operating loss carryback		

The proper income statement presentation is presented in Exhibit 16-19.

Finally, if the net operating loss is large enough to wipe out earnings in all three carryback years, the remainder can be carried forward. In that case, the rules for carryforwards are applied.

Accounting For Loss Carryforwards

Net operating losses that are not carried back or fully used up by the previous three year's profits are eligible to offset future years' profits. This means that the loss can be carried forward fifteen years; it is applied first to the initial year of

Exhibit 16-19
MICHELE CORPORATION
Partial Income Statement
For the Year Ended December 31, 1981

Loss before taxes	($150,000)
Less: Income tax refund on prior years' taxes due to carryback	63,000
Net loss	($ 87,000)

Exhibit 16-20
GERNON CORPORATION
Partial Income Statement
For the Year Ended December 31, 1982
Tax Benefit Not Assured

Income before taxes	$140,000
Less: Income taxes—46%	(64,400)
Income before extraordinary item	$ 75,600
Extraordinary item—tax carryforward	36,800
Net income	$112,400

future profits. Since the ultimate benefit of a carryforward is dependent on future earnings, the APB concluded that, the tax benefits of a carryforward generally should not be recognized in the year of loss, but only when it actually is realized in future. The Board stated that the only exception to this rule should be when the benefit is "assured beyond a reasonable doubt."[12]

The following example illustrates both of these cases. The Gernon Corporation has been in operation for several years and generally has been profitable. In 1981, however, the corporation reported a pretax accounting and taxable loss of $80,000 because of recession. The year 1982 was profitable, with pretax accounting and taxable income of $140,000. The tax rate in all years is 46%. Assume the company had decided to forgo the carryback.

Tax Benefit Not Assured. The most common situation is that the tax benefit is not assured. In this case no recognition is given to the tax loss, and 1981's reported loss would remain at $80,000. However, footnote disclosure of the $36,000 ($80,000 × 0.46) tax benefit from the loss carryforward would be appropriate.

In 1982 the Gernon Corporation has a pretax income of $140,000 and would obtain a benefit from the loss carryforward. The tax benefit from this carryforward is recognized as an extraordinary gain. The 1982 partial income statement for the Gernon Corporation appears in Exhibit 16-20. The journal entry to record the tax is as follows:

Tax expense	64,400	
Extraordinary item—tax carryforward		36,800
Taxes payable		27,600
To record income taxes for 1982.		

---

[12] Ibid., par. 45.

Since the entire loss was used in 1982 to offset that year's income, 1983 is not affected.

In requiring that the benefits from loss carryforwards be recognized in the year of realization rather than in the year of loss, the APB believed that the realization concept should take precedence over the matching concept. In this case the emphasis on realization is based on the difficulty of assessing objectively the probability of future income in the year of the loss. Further, the Board required the tax benefit when recognized be considered an extraordinary item. This is due to the fact that in the year in which the benefit is realized, the income tax expense includes both the current year's taxes and prior years' tax benefits—the carryforward. Hence, the reduction in taxes due to the carryforward is separated from other taxes and is considered an extraordinary item. This enables financial statement users to better predict income from continuing operations.

Tax Benefit Assured Beyond a Reasonable Doubt.   The APB recognized that in some situations the benefits from a loss carryforward could be assured beyond a reasonable doubt in the year of loss. *Opinion No. 11* defines these situations as follows:

> Realization of the tax benefit of a loss carryforward would appear to be assured beyond any reasonable doubt when both of the following conditions exist: (a) the loss results from an identifiable, isolated and nonrecurring cause and the company either has been continuously profitable over a long period or has suffered occasional losses which were more than offset by taxable income in subsequent years, and (b) future taxable income is virtually certain to be large enough to offset the loss carryforward and will occur soon enough to provide realization during the carryforward period.[13]

It is important to emphasize that the Board believed these criteria would be met only in unusual situations. They intended to rule out recognition of loss carryforwards from general unsuccessful business operations, depressed economic conditions, or changes in consumer preferences or technology. Following is an example of a loss carryforward that may qualify for recognition in the loss year:

> Losses resulting from the expropriation of a foreign subsidiary, or from the abandonment of one of several operations where the continuing operations are and have been profitable and are virtually certain to be profitable enough to offset the loss carryforwards.[14]

For purposes of illustration assume the same facts as in the previous example except that now the tax benefit is considered to be assured beyond a reasonable doubt. In this situation the company can record an asset (the estimated future tax benefits from loss carryforward). The amount of this asset is based upon the

---

[13] Ibid., par. 47.

[14] "Accounting for Income Taxes," *Accounting Interpretation of APB Opinion No. 11* (New York: AICPA, 1972), Section 13.

estimated tax rate at the time of expected realization. Given a tax rate of 46%, the Gernon Corporation would make the following entry in 1981:

Estimated future tax benefits from loss carryforward	36,800	
Reduction of loss from loss carryforward		36,800
To record operating loss carryforward.		

Because the realization is expected in 1982, the estimated future tax benefit account would be classified as a current asset. The reduction of the loss account is an income statement account. The partial income statement for 1981 appears in Exhibit 16-21.

In the following year, 1982, the company had pretax income of $140,000 and tax expense of $64,400 (0.46 × $140,000). The $36,800 tax benefit is realized, reducing the taxes payable to $27,600 ($64,400 − $36,800), while the expense for 1982 remains at $64,400 (0.46 × $140,000). These points are reflected in the following journal entry:

Income tax expense	64,400	
Estimated future tax benefit from loss carryforward		36,800
Income taxes payable		27,600
To record income taxes for the year.		

The Effect of Timing Differences

Up to this point the assumption has been made that the pretax accounting income equals the taxable income; timing differences were not considered in the discussion. When timing differences exist, the carryback and carryforward procedures

---

Exhibit 16-21
GERNON CORPORATION
Partial Income Statement
For the Year Ended December 31, 1981
Tax Benefit Assured

Loss before tax effects	$80,000
Less: Tax benefits due to loss carryforward	36,800
Net loss	$43,200

are similar, although somewhat more complicated. In these situations the carry-back results in a tax refund based upon taxable income. The corresponding reduction in the current period's tax expense account is based upon pretax accounting income. The difference between the debit to the asset account, the tax refund receivable, and the credit to the reduction in tax expense account is allocated to the deferred tax account. It will be a debit or credit depending upon the nature of the timing difference. Tax loss carryforwards are treated in a similar manner.

For example, in 1980 the Expo Corporation suffered a $70,000 pretax accounting loss and a $90,000 taxable loss. At the beginning of 1980 the balance in the deferred tax account was $32,000. The tax rate in all years is 40%. Exhibit 16-22 shows how the loss carryback is offset against the existing deferred tax credit. The $90,000 taxable loss when carried back to 1977, 1978, and 1979 wipes out all previous taxable income of $30,000 in those years. As a result, a $12,000 ($30,000 × 0.40) refund results. The loss cannot be carried back to 1976 because of the three-year limitation. The $70,000 accounting loss, when carried back to the previous three years, causes the total tax expense to be reduced by $28,000 ($70,000 × 0.40). The difference of $16,000 ($28,000 − $12,000) is a debit to the deferred tax account. These computations result in the following journal entry:

Refund for prior years' taxes	12,000	
Deferred tax credit ~back~	16,000	
Reduction of loss from loss carryforward		28,000
To record income taxes for 1980.		

Exhibit 16-22
THE EXPO CORPORATION
Application of Loss Carryback

Year	Income (Loss) Before Income Taxes		Income Tax Expense (CR)—40% Rate			Cumulative Net Deferred Tax
	Accounting	Taxable	Current	Deferred	Total	Credit
1976	$30,000	$10,000	$ 4,000[1]	$ 8,000[2]	$12,000[3]	$ 8,000
1977	30,000	10,000	4,000	8,000	12,000	16,000[4]
1978	30,000	10,000	4,000	8,000	12,000	24,000
1979	30,000	10,000	4,000	8,000	12,000	32,000
1980	(70,000)	(90,000)	(12,000)	(16,000)	(28,000)	16,000
Balance at end of 1980			$ 4,000	$16,000	$20,000	
1981	10,000	30,000	$ −0−	$ 4,000	$ 4,000	20,000

[1] $4,000 = $10,000 × 0.40.
[2] $8,000 = ($30,000 − $10,000) × 0.40.
[3] $12,000 = $4,000 + $8,000.
[4] $16,000 = $8,000 + $8,000.

forward

After the application of the carryback, a $60,000 taxable loss carryback exists. This is the difference between the original $90,000 taxable loss and the $30,000 used in the 1980 carryback. There is no remaining accounting carryback because the entire $70,000 was used in the 1980 carryback.

During 1981 assume the company had taxable income of $30,000 and accounting income of $10,000. There are no current taxes payable due because at the end of 1980 the loss carryforward of $60,000 existed, which wiped out the 1981 taxable income. The accounting income of $10,000 in 1981 is taxed at 40% since there is no accounting loss carryforward. Thus, a $4,000 deferred tax credit results ($10,000 × 0.40). In 1981 the following journal entry would be made:

Tax expense	4,000	
Deferred tax credit		4,000
To record income taxes for 1981.		

Financial Statement Disclosures Related to Interperiod Income Tax Allocation

Disclosures related to income taxes are the result of the requirements of APB *Opinion No. 11*, and for public companies.[15]

APB Opinion No. 11 Disclosures

According to APB *Opinion No. 11* deferred changes and credits due to timing differences represent the cumulative recognition given to their tax effects and as such do not represent receivables or payables in the usual sense. However, though many accountants feel that it is inappropriate to do so, deferred tax credits customarily are included in the liability section of the balance sheet. Criticism of this treatment is especially relevant when the deferred credit account continues to increase, and there is no reasonable expectation of a subsequent decrease in that account.

Regardless of whether a deferred tax credit should or should not be included in the liability section, the question arises as to the current–noncurrent classification. *Opinion No. 11* concluded that deferred charges and credits should be classified in two categories—one for the net current amount and the other for the net noncurrent amount. FASB *Statement No. 37* addressed the criteria to be applied in determining whether deferred accounts are current or noncurrent.[16] According to this Statement, a deferred charge or credit that is related to an asset or liability should be classified as current or noncurrent based on the classification of the related asset or liability. The deferred charge or credit is related to an asset or liability if reduction of the asset or liability causes the timing differences to reverse. In some situations a deferred charge or credit is not related to an asset or liability because (1) there is no associated asset or liability, or (2) reduction of an

FASB # 37

---

[15] *Accounting Series Release No. 149* (SEC, 1973).

[16] "Balance Sheet Classification of Deferred Income Taxes," *Statement of Financial Accounting Standards No. 37* (Stamford, Conn.: FASB, 1980).

associated asset or liability will not cause the timing difference to reverse. In these cases the current noncurrent classification should be based on the expected reversal date of the specific timing difference.

Following is an example of a situation in which the deferred tax credit or charge is related to an asset or liability. Assume that a firm uses the installment method for tax purposes, but recognizes income at the time of sale for financial reporting purposes. The company uses a one-year time basis to classify current assets and liabilities. At December 31, 1981, the appropriate account balances are as follows:

Asset section:
   Installment receivables:

Due within one year	$100,000
Due after one year	300,000
	$400,000

Liability section:
   Accumulated Deferred Income
      Tax credit-related installment receivables $80,000

According to *Statement No. 37*, the firm should classify the deferred income tax credit in the same manner as the related receivables. Since 25% of the related receivables ($100,000 ÷ $400,000) are current, 25% of the deferred credit, or $20,000 (0.25 × $80,000), would be classified as current.

In some situations no relationship exists between the deferred tax account and the asset or liability account. For example, a firm may report profits on construction contracts based on the completed contract method for tax purposes and on the percentage of completion for financial reporting purposes. The deferred income tax credit does not relate to an asset or liability that appears on the firm's balance sheet. The timing difference reverses only when the contracts are complete. They are not affected by progress billings or payment of receivables. Thus, the firm would classify the deferred tax credit based on its estimated reversal dates.

In addition, APB *Opinion No. 11* requires the following income statement disclosures:

1. Taxes estimated to be payable.
2. Tax effects of timing differences.
3. Tax effects of operating losses.

These amounts should be allocated to income before extraordinary items in the income statement or allocated as combined amounts, with disclosure of the components parenthetically or in a note to the financial statements.[17]

Finally, the following disclosures also should be made:

1. Amounts of any operating loss carryforwards not recognized in the loss period, together with expiration dates (indicating separately amounts which, upon recognition, would be credited to deferred tax accounts);

[17]"Accounting For Income Taxes," par. 60.

Exhibit 16-23
Disclosure of Income Taxes
Union Pacific 1980 Annual Report

5. Federal Income Taxes

Components of Federal income tax expense are as follows:

Thousands of Dollars	1980	1979	1978
Current	$ 6,084	$ 69,046	$ 46,234
Deferred	148,669	111,216	87,235
	$154,753	$180,262	$133,469

The tax effect of differences in the timing of revenues and expenses for tax and financial statement purposes is as follows:

Thousands of Dollars	1980	1979	1978
Excess of tax over book depreciation	$ 79,305	$ 49,633	$47,049
Intangible drilling costs	52,557	41,139	20,363
Interest capitalized	16,390	—	—
Surrender of offshore Florida leases	—	—	29,514
Incentive per diem	448	(872)	(13,005)
Other	(31)	21,316	3,314
	$148,669	$111,216	$87,235

A reconciliation between statutory and effective tax rates follows:

	1980	1979	1978
Statutory tax rate	46.0%	46.0%	48.0%
Investment tax credit	(13.9)	(11.9)	(11.6)
Depletion of natural resources	(.9)	(.8)	(1.3)
Other	(3.5)	(1.3)	(1.5)
Effective tax rate	27.7%	32.0%	33.6%

2. Significant amounts of any other unused deductions or credits, together with expiration dates; and

3. Reasons for significant variations in the customary relationships between income tax expense and pretax accounting income, if they are not otherwise apparent from the financial statements or from the nature of the entity's business.[18]

---

[18] Ibid., par. 63.

SEC Required Disclosure—ASR No. 149

In 1973 the SEC issued *ASR No. 149*, which increased the disclosure requirements pertaining to income taxes for public companies. This release required registrants to reconcile the enterprise's effective tax rate with the statutory federal income tax rate and to disclose the components of the deferred income tax expense account. These requirements were in response to pressure from analysts and investors who were having difficulty determining the effective tax rates of corporations. The objectives of *ASR No. 149* were to overcome these problems by enabling users of financial statements to understand better the basis for the registrant's tax accounting and the degree and reasons why the registrant's actual level of tax rate is different from the statutory tax rate. By developing such an understanding, the SEC believed that investors could distinguish more easily between a one-time tax advantage and continuing tax advantages enjoyed by a company and would be able to appraise the significance of changing effective tax rates.

These disclosures are illustrated in the footnote to the 1980 Union Pacific Annual Report, which is presented in Exhibit 16-23.

Concept Summary

INTERPERIOD INCOME TAX ALLOCATION

Purpose of Allocation—to allocate income tax expense to the period in which the tax is incurred irrespective of when the tax is paid. Allocation is necessary to achieve a proper matching of revenues and expenses.

Method of Allocation—current GAAP require the use of comprehensive tax allocation. Under this method, income tax expense for a period includes the tax effects of all transactions affecting the determination of pretax accounting income for that period even though some of these may affect the determination of taxes payable in a different period. All timing differences are included in the determination of deferred taxes.

DIFFERENCES BETWEEN ACCOUNTING AND TAX

Type	Description	Example	Treatment
Permanent	A difference between accounting and tax income that always will remain a difference	Interest on municipal bonds	No tax allocation is made for permanent difference. Tax expense is calculated in the same manner as taxes payable for these items.

Timing	Difference that occurs because of a difference in the timing of the recognition of an item between accounting and tax income calculations	Use of different depreciation in inventory methods for accounting and tax income measurements	Allocate income taxes. Record tax expense based on reported accounting income. Record tax liability based on taxable income. Record difference between tax expense and tax liability as a deferred charge or credit.

OPERATING LOSS CARRYBACK AND CARRYFORWARD

Type	Accounting Treatment
Carryback	Recognize effect of carryback in income in year of loss and record a tax receivable.
Carryforward	Do not recognize the effect of a carryforward in the year of loss unless the company had been experiencing profitability, the loss was an isolated and nonrecurring event, and future profits sufficient to offset the carryforward are assured.

Questions

Q–16–1   What are the determinants of income tax expense and income taxes payable?

Q–16–2   What is the objective of determining pretax accounting income, and how does it differ from the objective of determining taxable income?

Q–16–3   What are the three major classes of difference between taxable income and pretax accounting income?

Q–16–4   Explain permanent differences between taxable income and pretax accounting income. List three examples and describe what adjustments to accounting income must be made for each of them.

Q–16–5   Discuss timing differences and their relation to interperiod income tax allocation. List four examples of timing differences.

Q–16–6   Explain the need for interperiod income tax allocation.

Q–16–7   Discuss the conceptual reasons given for requiring interperiod income tax allocation.

Q–16–8   How are deferred tax charges and credits handled on the financial statements?

Q–16–9   The APB requires the use of comprehensive income tax allocation under the deferred method. Discuss comprehensive versus partial allocation.

Q–16–10   What are the arguments for and against the use of both partial and comprehensive allocation?

Q–16–11   Discuss the three methods of measuring the amount of deferred taxes. Discuss the conceptual rationale for each of these methods and the reason why the APB chose the deferral method.

Q–16–12   Explain the following two methods of interperiod tax allocation:
   a)   Individual item basis.
   b)   Group-of-smaller-items method.

Q–16–13   How is the gross change method applied?

Q–16–14   Explain the implementation of the net change method.

Q–16–15   When is it most appropriate to use the gross change method? The net change method?

Q–16–16   Explain loss carrybacks and carryforwards and the reasons they are included in the Internal Revenue Code.

Q–16–17   How does the APB differentiate between the accounting treatment for loss carrybacks and loss carryforwards? What accounting concepts are involved?

Q–16–18   Discuss the method of accounting for loss carrybacks.

Q–16–19   How are loss carryforwards handled?

Q–16–20   What is the effect of timing differences on loss carrybacks and loss carryforwards?

Q–16–21   Discuss the disclosure requirements under APB *Opinion No. 11*, and FASB *Statement No. 37* and also include a discussion of the SEC-required disclosure under *ASR No. 149.*

Q–16–22   Answer the following multiple choice questions.
   a)   When you account for income taxes, interest received on municipal obligations is an example of
      (1)   Intraperiod tax allocation.
      (2)   Interperiod tax allocation.
      (3)   A permanent difference.
      (4)   A timing difference.
   b)   The books of the Hazel Company for the year ended December 31, 1979, showed income of $180,000 before provision for income tax. In computing the taxable income for federal income tax purposes, Hazel took the following timing differences into account:

Depreciation deducted for tax purposes in excess of depreciation recorded on the books	$8,000
Income from installment sale reportable for tax purposes in excess of income recognized on the books	6,000

What should Hazel record as its current federal income tax liability at December 31, 1979, assuming a corporate income tax rate of 50%?
      (1) $86,000.
      (2) $89,000.
      (3) $90,000.
      (4) $91,000.
   c)   Which of the following interperiod tax allocation methods uses the tax rates in

effect at the origination of the timing differences and does not adjust for subsequent changes in tax rates?

   (1) Deferred method.

   (2) Liability method.

   (3) Net of tax method.

   (4) Net present value method.

d) Interperiod income tax allocation is justified by the basic theory that income taxes should be treated as which of the following?

   (1) An expense.

   (2) A distribution of earnings.

   (3) A distribution of earnings for the current portion and an expense for the deferred portion.

   (4) An expense for the current portion and a distribution of earnings for the deferred portion.

e) Interperiod income tax allocation in corporate financial statements can best be justified by which of the following accounting concepts or principles?

   (1) Conservatism.

   (2) Matching.

   (3) Realization.

   (4) Objectivity.

(AICPA adapted)

Discussion Questions and Cases

D-16-1 Deferred income taxes are required under generally accepted accounting principles. APB *Opinion No. 11* requires the use of the deferred method of comprehensive interperiod tax allocation. Two ways to account for timing differences under the deferred method are: (1) gross change method, and (2) net change method.

Required:
Describe the gross change method, and the net change method.

(AICPA adapted)

D-16-2 Under each of the following situations decide whether interperiod allocation is required. If interperiod allocation is required, discuss the appropriate method of handling the allocation.

   a) The portion of dividends reduced by the dividends-received deduction by corporations under existing federal income tax law.

   b) The excess of accelerated depreciation used for tax purposes over straight-line depreciation used for financial reporting purposes.

   c) Extraordinary gains or losses as defined by the Accounting Principles Board.

   d) All differences between taxable income and financial statement earnings.

(AICPA adapted)

D-16-3 Income tax allocation is an integral part of generally accepted accounting principles. The applications of intraperiod tax allocation (within a period) and interperiod tax allocation (among periods) are both required.

Required:

1. Explain the need for interperiod tax allocation.

2. Accountants who favor interperiod tax allocation argue that income taxes are an expense rather than a distribution of earnings. Explain the significance of this argument. Do not merely define *expense* or *distribution of earnings*. (Continued on next page.)

3. Indicate and explain whether each of the following independent situations should be treated as a timing difference or a permanent difference.

a) Estimated warranty costs (covering a three-year warranty) are expenses for accounting purposes at the time of sale but deducted for income tax purposes when incurred.

b) Depreciation for accounting and income tax purposes differs because of different bases of carrying the related property. The different bases are a result of a business combination treated as a purchase for accounting purposes and as a tax-free exchange for income tax purposes.

c) A company properly uses the equity method to account for its 30% investment in another company. The investee pays dividends that are about 10% of its annual earnings.

4. Discuss the nature of the deferred income tax accounts and possible classifications in a company's statement of financial position.

(AICPA adapted)

D–16–4 The Stockman Corporation is an emerging business. In prior years the company has invested about $25,000 a year in new plant and equipment as an equal amount of old equipment is retired. This year the company expects to increase its investment in plant and equipment to exceed the amount of planned retirement. It expects to continue this process in the future. The Stockman Corporation has been reporting income for both tax and financial statement purposes by using straight-line depreciation, but has now decided to change to accelerated depreciation.

Required:

1. The opponents of comprehensive income tax allocation argue that in situations such as those described above, comprehensive allocation leads to amounts carried as liabilities which are mere contingencies. Explain what they mean by that comment and how this liability arises.

2. What alternatives do these opponents propose and why?

3. What counter arguments do the proponents of comprehensive income tax allocation make?

D–16–5 In preparing financial statements a corporation is expected to follow the practice of comprehensive income tax allocation. At various times three methods of allocation have been used: the deferred method, the liability method, and the net of tax method.

Required:

1. Discuss the theoretical justification for interperiod income tax allocation.

2. Describe briefly each of the above-mentioned three methods of tax allocation and give reasons why each method is now acceptable or unacceptable.

(AICPA adapted)

D–16–6 The following differences enter into the reconciliation of financial net income and taxable income of A. P. Baxter Corp. for the current year.

a) Tax depreciation exceeds book depreciation by $30,000.

b) Estimated warranty costs of $6,000 applicable to the current year's sales have not been paid.

c) Percentage depletion deducted on the tax return exceeds cost depletion by $45,000.

d) Unearned rent revenue of $25,000 was deferred on the books but appropriately included in taxable income.

e) A book expense of $2,000 for life insurance premiums on officers' lives is not allowed as a deduction on the tax return.

f) Gross profit of $80,000 was excluded from taxable income because Baxter had appropriately elected the installment sale method for tax reporting while recognizing all gross profit from installment sales at the time of the sale for financial reporting.

Required:
Consider each reconciling item independently of all others and explain whether each item would enter into the calculation of income taxes to be allocated. For any which are included in the income tax allocation calculation, explain the effect of the item on the current year's income expense and how the amount would be reported on the balance sheet. (Tax allocation calculations are not required.)

(AICPA adapted)

D–16–7   The Securities and Exchange Commission (SEC) has stated, "financial statements may be filed in such form and order, and may use such generally accepted terminology as will best indicate their significance." However, the SEC has regulatory power to specify certain disclosure requirements of material information that should appear in published annual reports that are issued to security holders of companies subject to proxy solicitation.

The SEC has specific disclosure requirements for income tax expense that appears on the income statement.

Required:
1.   Identify the SEC's major disclosure requirements for income tax expense.
2.   Disclosure requirements are intended to benefit users of financial information. What specific benefits do users gain from the disclosure of income tax expense?

(CMA adapted)

D–16–8   The Internal Revenue Code (IRC) has significant impact on accounting reporting practices. The accounting methods selected for the purpose of reducing taxable income are often used in the measurement of financial reporting income. If different methods are used for book and tax purposes, the provision for the income tax liability and the income tax charge must be adjusted accordingly. Therefore, the income tax laws influence reported income whether the same or different methods are used for both book and tax purposes.

Required:
Present a discussion supporting the conclusions of the preceding statement. Include in your support an example of:

a)   An accounting method that became popular for financial reporting purposes (although not required to be used by the IRC) following its inclusion in the IRC.

b)   An accounting method that must be used for financial reporting purposes if it is selected for income tax purposes.

(CMA adapted)

D–16–9   Professor R. W. Shattke stated (*Accounting Review*, April, 1972), when commenting on APB *Statement No. 4:*

Liabilities apparently should be related to economic obligations and, in addition, should be measured at discounted amounts. The message is clear: the APB should amend Opinion No. 11 and get rid of the strange animal it created in the pronouncement.

Although this statement was made 10 years prior to the issuance of *Statement of Financial Accounting Concepts No. 3* it is still relevant today.

Required:
1.   Define liabilities under current GAAP. In doing so describe the major elements of liabilities, and how deferred taxes relate to this definition.
2.   Comment on the remark above by Professor Shattke and indicate your views on the matter. What alternatives are available?

Exercises

E–16–1 In 1981 Harper Company paid the annual premiums of $80,000 on officers' life insurance (on which the company is the beneficiary) and received interest income of $120,000 on municipal obligations. Harper also collected $200,000 in royalties in 1981. For income tax reporting, the royalties are taxed when collected. For financial statement reporting, the royalties are recognized as income in the period earned. The unearned portion of the royalties collected in 1981 amounted to $150,000 at December 31, 1981. The tax rate is 40%.

Required:
Prepare the required journal entry for 1981 to record the income tax expense according to APB *Opinion No. 11*.

(AICPA adapted)

E–16–2 The JIGS Corporation reported the following taxable and pretax accounting income:

	1981	1982	1983
Taxable income	$180,000	$200,000	$290,000
Pretax accounting income	220,000	210,000	240,000

The tax rate is 40% for each year. All differences between taxable income and pretax accounting income are due to timing differences.

Required:
Prepare the required journal entries for 1981 through 1983 to properly record the company's tax expense and taxes payable.

E–16–3 LAX Helicopter flies passengers from Los Angeles International Airport to various locations in Southern California. Below is the condensed income statement for the last four years:

	1981	1982	1983	1984
Revenues	$300,000	$320,000	$360,000	$450,000
Expenses	210,000	240,000	290,000	370,000
Pretax accounting income	$ 90,000	$ 80,000	$ 70,000	$ 80,000

Expenses include amortized goodwill of $5,000 in each of the four years. At the beginning of 1981 LAX purchased a new piece of equipment with a cost of $120,000. The company uses straight-line depreciation for financial statement purposes but has elected to use sum-of-the-years'-digits for tax purposes. The asset has a four-year life and no salvage value. The tax rate is 40%.

Required:
Determine the amount of taxable income each year and make the appropriate journal entries to record the tax expense and tax liability each year.

E–16–4 The Arthur Company reported the following taxable income and pretax accounting income for 1981 through 1983:

	1981	1982	1983
Taxable income	$110,000	$140,000	$125,000
Pretax accounting income	95,000	105,000	135,000

The tax rate for all three years is 30%, and all the differences in income are timing differences.

Required:

1. Make the required journal entries to record the tax expense and taxes payable for all three years.

2. Determine the ending balance in the deferred tax account and prove that the balance is correct.

E–16–5 Jacob's Fancy Fruit Shop reports the following taxable income and pretax accounting income for 1981 through 1984:

	1981	1982	1983	1984
Taxable income	$ 90,000	$125,000	$285,000	$240,000
Pretax accounting income	160,000	185,000	235,000	220,000
Tax rate	40%	45%	45%	45%

Included in pretax accounting income is $10,000 per year of interest on New York state bonds. All other differences in income are the result of differences in depreciation expense due to the use of ACRS depreciation for tax purposes. The reversing differences in 1983 and 1984 originated in 1981 and 1982. Assume a FIFO flow.

Required:

1. For each of the four years determine the income figure upon which the tax expense should be calculated.

2. Make the required journal entries for all four years to record the proper amount of tax expense and taxes payable.

E–16–6 Complete the table below by determining whether the following items are timing differences or not and by determining their effect on the deferred tax account.

	Timing Difference		Deferred Taxes		
	Yes	No	Credit	Debit	No Effect
1. Estimated warranty expense deducted for financial reporting purposes but not for tax purposes.					
2. Premiums on officers' life insurance expensed on the financial statements but not on the tax return.					
3. Rental revenue received in advance included in income for tax purposes but not included for financial statement purposes.					
4. ACRS depreciation used on a new asset for tax purposes, and straight-line for financial purposes.					
5. Fine for polluting included in determination of pretax accounting					

(Continued on next page.)

income but not deducted
for tax purposes.
6. 85% deduction for dividends
received.
7. Gross margin on
installment sales
reported for tax
purposes exceeds
sales on accrual basis
for financial reporting
purposes.
8. Current year's estimated
expenses for repairs
accrued for financial
statement purposes. For
income tax reporting, they
will be deducted in the
following year when
paid.
9. Excess of expense on tax
return over expense on
books for estimated
uncollectible accounts.
10. Percentage depletion on
gas in excess of cost
depletion.

E-16-7   The Sumi Corporation's tax return for 1980 through 1982 disclosed the following information:

Year	Taxable Income
1980	$100,000
1981	150,000
1982	140,000

In addition, the following information is available:

a)   In the beginning of 1980, the Sumi Corporation purchased new equipment costing $40,000. The equipment has a four-year life and no salvage value. The corporation uses straight-line depreciation for financial reporting purposes and sum-of-the-years'-digits depreciation for tax purposes.

b)   The Sumi Corporation owns a building that it leases for $24,000 for three years. In accordance with the lease terms, the lessee paid for the entire three-year lease at the beginning of the first year, 1980.

c)   Purchased goodwill on the corporation's books is amortized at a rate of $5,000 per year.

d)   The tax rate is 35% in all three years.

Required:

1.   Determine the amount of pretax accounting income.

2.   Determine the proper balance in the deferred tax account at the end of 1980, 1981, and 1982.

E-16-8   The Bob and Ken Company purchased a new piece of equipment for $120,000 on January 2, 1981. The asset has a five-year life and no salvage value. The firm uses straight-line depreciation for financial accounting purposes and sum-of-the-years'-digits for tax purposes. The tax rate during 1981, 1982, and 1983 is 45%. At the time of purchase, however, the company is aware of legislation that will reduce the tax rate to 40% in 1984 and after. There are no other differences between accounting and taxable income. The following data relate to the company's income and depreciation:

	Year				
	1981	*1982*	*1983*	*1984*	*1985*
Pretax accounting and taxable income before depreciation	$200,000	$200,000	$240,000	$270,000	$300,000
Depreciation:					
Straight-line	24,000	24,000	24,000	24,000	24,000
Sum-of-the-years'-digits	40,000	32,000	24,000	16,000	8,000

Required:
1. Prepare the appropriate journal entries to record tax expense and taxes payable for the five-year period applying the deferred method.
2. Prepare the same entries applying the liability method.

E–16–9 The Mangard Company, an installment seller of furniture, records sales on the accrual basis for financial statement purposes but on the installment basis for tax purposes. As a result, $50,000 of the deferred taxes have been accrued at December 31, 1981. In accordance with practices within the industry, installment accounts receivable from customers are shown as current assets on the balance sheet, even though the average collection period is three years.

Also, at December 31, 1981, the Mangard Company has recorded a $20,000 deferred income tax debit arising from a book accrual of noncurrent deferred compensation expense that will not be tax-deductible until 1983. Finally, at December 31, 1981, Mangard has $15,000 of deferred income taxes resulting from the use of accelerated depreciation for tax purposes and the use of straight-line for financial accounting purposes.

Required:
What is the balance in the deferred taxes account and how should it be classified on the balance sheet?

(AICPA adapted)

E–16–10 The Waco Company, an installment seller, earns a $3,000 pretax gross profit on each installment sale. For financial accounting purposes, the entire $3,000 is recognized at the time of sale. For income tax purposes, however, the installment method of accounting is used.

Assume that the Waco Company only makes one sale in 1981, one in 1982, and one in 1983. In each case one-third of the gross sales price is collected in the year of sale, one-third in the next year, and the final installment in the next year.

Required:
1. If the income tax rate is 50%, determine the amount to be shown on the company's December 31, 1983, balance sheet as deferred income taxes.
2. Now assume that on January 1, 1983, the tax rate increases from 50% to 60%.
   a) If the company uses the gross charge method, determine the appropriate amount of deferred income tax as of December 31, 1983.
   b) If the company uses the net charge method, determine the appropriate amount of deferred taxes as of December 31, 1983.

(AICPA adapted)

E–16–11 The Hawkins Company is involved in a number of transactions that result in timing differences. The following data are available:

Pretax accounting income	$500,000
Originating difference	(75,000)
Reversing difference	45,000
Taxable income	$470,000

Tax rates:	
Current year	40%
All prior years	45%

There are no permanent differences.

Required:
1. Determine the change in the deferred tax account using the
   a) Gross change method.
   b) Net change method.
2. Prepare the necessary journal entries for both methods.

E–16–12 The Cherry Company is in the light machinery manufacturing business. At the beginning of the current year, 1982, the company purchased a new stamping press for $300,000. Under current tax laws (ACRS depreciation) the asset has only a three-year life. However, for financial reporting purposes, the asset has a five-year life. In both cases there is no salvage value, and straight-line depreciation is used.

There are no other timing differences, and the firm has elected to use the gross charge method of determining the change in the deferred taxes account.

Required:
1. Assume that the tax rate for all five years is 40%. Determine the yearly balance in the deferred tax account and state whether the change is a debit or credit using the
   a) FIFO method of applying tax rates.
   b) Average method of applying tax rates.
2. Now assume the following tax rates:

1982	45%	1984	40%	1986	35%
1983	45%	1985	40%		

Calculate the change in the deferred tax account under both the FIFO and average method of applying tax rates.

E–16–13 The following data pertaining to the financial and tax records are available for the Bond Company:

	1980	*1981*	*1982*	*1983*
Income per financial statements:				
Pretax accounting income	$80,000	$100,000	$70,000	$110,000
Depreciation—straight-line	(15,000)	(15,000)	(15,000)	(15,000)
Rental income	5,000	5,000	5,000	5,000
Income before taxes	$70,000	$ 90,000	$60,000	$100,000
Income per tax returns:				
Pretax income	$80,000	$100,000	$70,000	$110,000
Depreciation—sum-of-the-years'-digits	(24,000)	(18,000)	(12,000)	(6,000)
Rental income	20,000	–0–	–0–	–0–
Taxable income	$76,000	$ 82,000	$58,000	$104,000

There are no other timing or permanent differences. In addition, the following tax rates apply:

1980	50%
1981	45%
1982	45%
1983	40%

Required:
Compute the change in the deferred tax account using the following:
  a) Net change method.
  b) Gross change method.
   (1) FIFO rate method.
   (2) Average rate method.

E–16–14 The management of the Stout Company chooses accounting policies that reduce its taxable income. It reports 1980 taxable income of $40,000. In addition, the following information is available:

  a) The company purchased a new truck at the beginning of 1979. The truck cost $60,000 and has no salvage value. The firm uses straight-line depreciation for both book and tax purposes. However, for tax purposes the asset has a three-year life, whereas for financial accounting purposes it has a six-year life.

  b) The company invests in Indiana state bonds. Income from these bonds amounted to $15,000.

The current tax rates are 20% on the first $45,000 of income and 30% on all income above $45,000.

Required:
Make the necessary entry to record the tax expense and tax payable for 1980 using the with and without method.

E–16–15 The Maryann Company reported the following results for its first three years of operations:

1979	$ 10,000
1980	(200,000)
1981	350,000

There were no permanent or timing differences for these three years. The tax rate for all three years is 45%. In 1980 there is no reasonable assurance that there will be future profits.

Required:
1. What should the Maryann Company record as its current income tax liability and tax expense for all years?
2. Prepare the journal entry for 1981 and the bottom portion of the income statement for 1981 starting with income before taxes.

E–16–16 The Sally Corporation sells office equipment. The following information concerning the corporation's taxable and pretax accounting income is available:

Year	Income	Rate
1976	$10,000	50%
1977	15,000	50%
1978	20,000	45%
1979	10,000	45%

1980	(60,000)	40%
1981	30,000	40%
1982	35,000	45%
1983	20,000	40%
1984	(25,000)	30%

Required:
1. Make the required journal entries for 1980 through 1984 to record the tax expense and taxes payable assuming the following:
  a) There is no reasonable assurance of income in future years.
  b) There is reasonable assurance of future years' income. (The company will utilize any carryback before utilizing a carryforward.)
2. Prepare the portion of the income statements for 1980 and 1981 beginning with income before taxes for both cases.

E–16–17 The Pat Corporation is a successful secretarial service company. During the economic recession in 1979–1980, however, business dropped off and the company suffered a loss. The following income figures are available:

Year	Income	Tax Rates
1976	$50,000	50%
1977	60,000	50%
1978	70,000	45%
1979	(40,000)	40%
1980	(90,000)	40%
1981	20,000	35%

In 1980 because of heavy losses the company does not believe it can assure itself of future earnings.
Required:
1. Determine the tax refund due the Pat Corporation for 1979 and 1980.
2. Make the required journal entries for 1979 through 1981 to record the tax expense and tax payable for each year.

Problems

P–16–1 As the auditor for the Anthony Company, you have prepared the partial income statement illustrated below:

ANTHONY COMPANY
Partial Income Statement
For the Year Ended December 31, 1981

Sales	$1,000,000
Cost of goods sold	600,000
Gross margin	$ 400,000
Operating expenses	250,000
Income before taxes	$ 150,000

In addition, you have determined the following facts:
  a) The company uses straight-line depreciation for financial reporting purposes and

double-declining-balance for tax purposes. During 1981 double-declining-balance depreciation exceeded straight-line depreciation by $25,000.

b) On January 2, 1981, the company agreed to rent a building it owns to the Welch Corporation for three years. The yearly rental fee is $12,000. However, the Welch Corporation was required to prepay all three years upon the signing of the lease on January 2, 1981.

c) Included in operating expenses is $5,000 of amortized goodwill.

d) The company accrued a contingent liability for guarantee expenses. The amount of this accrual was $5,000. During the year the company actually paid $3,500 in guarantee expenses.

e) The current tax rate is 40%.

Required:

1. Prepare a schedule determining taxable income.
2. Prepare the journal entry to record the tax expense and taxes payable for 1981.

P–16–2 MNC is a multinational corporation. For 1981 the firm reported pretax earnings of $250,000. You have determined the following additional information:

a) The company owns a 30% interest in the Wang Corporation. Based on the equity method of accounting the firm included earnings of $40,000 from the Wang Corp. Actual cash dividends received from Wang by MNC amounted to $25,000.

b) Until the end of 1980 the company used the same depreciation method for tax and financial reporting purposes. However as of January, 1981, the Company began using sum-of-the-years-digits for tax purposes but continued to use straight line for financial reporting purposes. On that date MNC purchased $110,000 of assets that have a 10-year life and no salvage value.

c) The firm amortizes goodwill of $10,000 from the purchase of another subsidiary.

d) MNC received other dividend income of $10,000 that is subject to the 85% dividend exclusion provision of the code.

e) The company sold a large parcel of land in 1981. The land cost $50,000 and was sold for $150,000. The firm received a 25% downpayment in 1981, and the remainder will be payable over 10 years beginning in 1982 at 10% interest. The firm elects to use the installment basis for tax purposes.

Required:

1. Prepare a schedule determining taxable income, assuming the tax rate is 45%.
2. Prepare the journal entry to record the tax expense and the taxes payable for 1981.

P–16–3 The Tax Free Corporation was organized at the beginning of 1981. The corporation is involved in a variety of real estate transactions, including rental revenues and real estate sales.

Selected figures from the company's 1981 and 1982 tax returns are presented below:

	1981	1982
Rental revenue	$640,000	$700,000
Gain on sale of land	–0–	50,000
Total revenues	$640,000	$750,000
Expenses, other than depreciation	200,000	260,000
Depreciation—sum-of-the-years'-digits	100,000	90,000
Total expenses	$300,000	$350,000
Taxable income	$340,000	$400,000

The following information is also available:

a) The company owns one building, which it purchased at the beginning of 1981. The building has a 10-year life with no salvage value. The firm uses sum-of-the-years'-digits depreciation for tax purposes and straight-line for accounting purposes.

b) The company has a policy of demanding rental payments in advance. These payments are taxable when received but recorded as income for financial statement purposes when earned. An analysis of the unearned rental revenue account follows:

Unearned Rental Income Account

Balance, January 1, 1981	$ –0–
Rents received during 1981	640,000
	$640,000
Rental income earned	(620,000)
Balance, December 31, 1981	$ 20,000
Rents received during 1982	700,000
	$720,000
Rental income earned	660,000
Balance, December 31, 1982	$ 60,000

c) The firm has invested excess cash in California state bonds. Interest earned in 1981 and 1982 is $10,000 and $12,000, respectively.

d) The Tax Free Corporation accrues estimated repairs expense at the end of the year. At the end of 1981 the firm accrued $10,000 of estimated repairs to be paid in 1982. The 1982 accrual for expense to be paid in 1983 was $15,000.

e) At the end of 1982 the firm sold a parcel of land. The gain was $50,000. This is considered a capital gain and is taxed at 25%.

f) The normal tax rate is 40% for 1981 and 1982.

Required:

1. Prepare a schedule determining pretax accounting income for 1981 and 1982.
2. Make the necessary journal entries to record tax expense and taxes payable.

P–16–4 Solar Hot Tubs sells hot tubs that run on solar energy. The firm sells the tubs on an installment basis over a four-year period. Forty percent of the sale price is collected in the year of sale. The remaining 60% is collected ratably over the remaining three years. The gross margin on each hot tub is $500. Since the firm started business in 1979, it has sold the following tubs:

Year	Units Sold
1979	500
1980	650
1981	725
1982	1,000

The firm reports income on the installment basis for tax purposes. For financial accounting purposes the company recognizes the entire gross profit in the year of sale. Installment receivables are classified as current assets under industry practice.

Solar Hot Tubs owns a fleet of automobiles purchased at the beginning of 1979. These cars are used by its salespersons. The total cost was $100,000. The firm uses straight-line depreciation for both tax and financial accounting purposes. However, the cars have a four-year life for tax purposes and an eight-year life for financial statement purposes.

The firm purchases life insurance on its officers. Yearly premiums amount to $5,000.

Operating expenses other than depreciation amounted to the following:

1979	$ 70,000
1980	100,000
1981	150,000
1982	175,000

Required:

1. Prepare a schedule determining taxable income and pretax accounting income for each of the four years.

2. Record the appropriate journal entry to record the tax expense and taxes payable for 1982. The tax rate for all years is 30%.

3. How should the change in the deferred tax account that results from the 1982 transactions be classified on the balance sheet?

P–16–5 Answer each of the following four questions.

a) In 1982 the Chrol Company formed a foreign subsidiary. Income before United States and foreign income taxes for this wholly owned subsidiary was $500,000 in 1982. The income tax rate in the country of the foreign subsidiary was 40%. None of the earnings of the foreign subsidiary has been remitted to Chrol; however, there is nothing to indicate that these earnings will not be remitted to Chrol in the future.

The country of the foreign subsidiary does not impose a tax on remittances to the United States. A tax credit is allowed in the United States for taxes payable in the country of the foreign subsidiary.

If you assume the income tax rate in the United States is 48%, what is the total amount of income taxes relating to the foreign subsidiary that should be shown in the income statement of Chrol in 1982? (*Hint:* see APB *Opinion No. 23.*)

b) Baker, Inc. owns 35% of the outstanding stock of Cable, Inc. During the calendar year 1981, Baker's "investment in cable" account appeared as follows:

Balance, January 1, 1981	$650,000
Equity in 1981 earnings of Cable	100,000
Dividends received from Cable—1981	(20,000)
Balance, December 31, 1981	$730,000

Baker believes that its equity in Cable's undistributed earnings will be realized in the form of future dividends. If you assume a 40% income tax rate, by how much should deferred income taxes be affected because of these facts?

(1) $4,800.

(2) $6,000.

(3) $7,200.

(4) $9,000.

c) The Hutch Company sells household furniture. Customers who purchase furniture on the installment basis make payments in equal monthly installments over a two-year period, with no down payment required. Hutch's gross profit on installment sales equals 60% of the selling price of the furniture.

For financial accounting purposes, sales revenue is recognized at the time the sale is made. For income tax purposes, however, the installment method is used. There are no other book and income tax accounting differences, and Hutch's income tax rate is 50%.

If Hutch's December 31, 1981, balance sheet includes a deferred tax credit of $30,000 arising from the difference between book and tax treatment of the installment sales, it should also include installment accounts receivable of how much?

d) The Skipper Company, a calendar-year company, began operations in 1981 and, for that year, reported an operating loss of $140,000. For 1982 the company reported operating income (before income taxes) of $300,000. Assuming an income tax rate of 50%, what should Skipper record in 1982 as a tax benefit arising from the operating loss carryforward?

(AICPA adapted)

P–16–6 The Peachy Delight Ice Cream Parlor sells ice cream cones and other products. The firm opened at the beginning of 1978 when it purchased the business from the former owners. In completing your audit for 1981, you have been able to determine the following information:

a) $120,000 of freezers and other equipment was purchased at the beginning of 1978 when the firm opened for business. Because of an expansion, an additional $150,000 of new freezers was purchased at the beginning of 1981. For both these purchases the firm uses straight-line depreciation for financial accounting purposes and sum-of-the-years'-digits for tax purposes. The assets have a four-year life with no salvage value.

b) At the beginning of 1980 the firm leased a new store. The lease required the firm to prepay three years' rent. The yearly rental is $12,000. The rent is recorded as an expense when incurred for financial statement purposes; it is deducted for tax purposes when paid.

c) When the firm was purchased, goodwill amounting to $100,000 was recorded. It is amortized over 40 years.

d) Tax rates are as follows:

Year	Rate
1978	50%
1979	50%
1980	40%
1981	35%

e) Pretax accounting income for each is presented below:

Year	Pretax Accounting Income
1978	$200,000
1979	250,000
1980	310,000
1981	270,000

f) There are no other differences between taxable income and pretax accounting other than those listed above.

Required:

1. Compute the balance in the deferred tax account at the end of each year using the
    a) Net change method.
    b) Gross change method.
       (1) FIFO rate method.
       (2) Average rate method.
2. Make the appropriate journal entries to record the deferred taxes each year for the net change method.

P–16–7 The Jackson Company began business at the beginning of 1979. The company follows certain accounting policies for tax purposes and different policies for financial accounting purposes. The principle differences are summarized below:

	Accounting Policy	Tax Reporting	Financial Reporting
Income from subsidiaries	Cost method	Equity method
Depreciation	Double-declining-balance	Straight-line

You have been able to determine the following additional information:
a) All the firm's equipment was purchased in 1980 at a cost of $200,000. The useful life is five years, and there is no salvage value.
b) Income recorded from subsidiaries is as follows:

Year	Equity Method	Cost Method
1979	–0–	–0–
1980	$50,000	$40,000
1981	60,000	70,000

c) Pretax accounting income totaled $400,000 in 1980. In 1981 the pretax accounting income totaled $500,000.
d) The following year tax data pertain to the Jackson Company:

Year	Expected Rate	Actual Rate
1980	45%	45%
1981 & beyond	40%	40%

Required:
1. Determine the balance deferred tax account at the end of 1980 and 1981 using the liability method. Make the appropriate journal entries to record the deferred taxes.
2. Determine the balance in the deferred tax account at 1981, assuming the required method is used, under the following:
a) The net change method.
b) The gross change method—FIFO.
3. How should the balance in the deferred tax account be classified on the balance sheet of the Jackson Company?

P–16–8 The Ray Corporation owns a foreign subsidiary. The firm makes a provision for U.S. income taxes on the unremitted earnings of the subsidiary that are not considered to be reinvested permanently in that subsidiary. These foreign earnings are included in U.S. taxable income in the year the dividends are actually paid. The accounting policy of the firm is to use one year as the time basis for classifying current assets and liabilities. The firm prepares consolidated financial statements with its subsidiary.

At December 31, 1981, an analysis of the accumulated amount of unremitted earnings on which taxes have been accrued indicate the following:

Accumulated unremitted earnings on which taxes have been accrued:	
Expected to be remitted within one year	$2,000,000
Not expected to be remitted within one year	1,000,000
	$3,000,000
Accumulated deferred income Tax credits related to unremitted earnings	$ 125,000

Required:
1. How should the deferred income tax credits be classified on the consolidated balance sheet? Why?

2. How would your answer differ if the Ray Company used the equity method rather than prepared consolidated financial statements? Why?

P–16–9 The Wyatt Corporation began business in 1980. It suffered a pretax accounting loss of $500,000 during the year. In 1981 and 1982 the company earned pretax income of $300,000 and $400,000. However, during 1980 these profits could not be assured beyond a reasonable doubt. The tax rate is 40% for all three years.

Required:
1. Prepare the required tax journal entries for 1980 through 1982.
2. Prepare the partial income statements for 1980 through 1982. Start with income before taxes.
3. Prepare appropriate footnotes to the income statement.

P–16–10 The Castro Company had the following pretax accounting income for the years 1979 through 1984. Assume there are no permanent or timing differences.

Year	Pretax Accounting Income	Tax Rate
1979	$100,000	45%
1980	20,000	45%
1981	5,000	40%
1982	(180,000)	40%
1983	40,000	40%
1984	200,000	35%

Required:
1. Assume the corporation elects to carry back the loss in 1982. Make the appropriate tax entries for 1982 through 1984. Also assume that the corporation in 1982 is not assured beyond a reasonable doubt of future earnings.
2. Now assume the corporation elects not to carry back the loss but to take immediate advantage of the carryforward. Make the necessary tax entries for 1982 through 1984 if the corporation is assured beyond a reasonable doubt of future earnings.

P–16–11 PSK Electronics, Inc. has a November 30 fiscal year. The corporate controller is responsible for preparing the financial statements, which will be audited by PSK's independent public accountant. PSK's pretax consolidated income for the year ended November 20, 1981, includes $80,000 from its own operations and $20,000 from its wholly owned domestic manufacturing company, for a total of $100,000. The consolidated corporate income tax return for the 1980–1981 fiscal year, which has not been filed yet, reveals the following facts:

a) PSK has used the LIFO inventory method for tax purposes since the 1979–1980 fiscal year.

b) The corporation uses accelerated depreciation methods for tax purposes and uses straight-line for financial reporting purposes. Consequently, depreciation on the tax return is $10,000 greater than the depreciation on the corporation's income statement.

c) PSK has a $5,000 investment credit for the current tax year; the corporation uses the flow-through method for investment credit.

d) PSK has the premiums on life insurance policies on key corporate officers, and the corporation is the beneficiary of these policies. Premiums paid on these policies amounted to $3,000 in the current fiscal year, of which $2,000 was expensed and $1,000 represented an increase in the cash surrender value of the policies.

The LIFO election for tax purposes has resulted in a substantial tax savings, but it also has had a depressing effect on earnings per share (EPS). The president of PSK would like to use the FIFO inventory method for the 1980–1981 financial statements or, at least, disclose in the notes to the financial statements what the EPS would have been had the FIFO method been used. The use of FIFO would have increased PSK's book inventory by $20,000 as of November 30, 1981.

For ease in calculation, assume that PSK Electronics, Inc. is subject to a federal income tax rate of 40% and that the provision and current liability for state income taxes is $4,000.

Required:

1. For each of the four lettered items presented above explain whether the treatment for income tax purposes would be different from the treatment used in preparing the financial statements which are to be audited.

2. Calculate the income tax provision that will be reflected on PSK Electronics, Inc.'s income statement prepared for the year ended November 30, 1981.

3. From the data in the problem, calculate the change in the deferred tax account(s) of PSK Electronics, Inc. from December 1, 1980, to November 30, 1981.

(CMA adapted)

P–16–12   The Mikis Company has supplied you with the following information regarding its 1981 income tax expense for financial statement reporting:

a)   The provision for current income taxes (exclusive of investment tax credits) was $600,000 for the year ended December 31, 1981. Mikis made estimated tax payments of $550,000 during 1981.

b)   Investment tax credits of $100,000, arising from fixed assets put into service in 1981, were taken for income tax reporting in 1981. Mikis defers investment tax credits and amortizes them to income over the productive life of the related assets for financial statement reporting. Unamortized deferred investment tax credits amounted to $400,000 at December 31, 1981, and $375,000 at December 31, 1980.

c)   Mikis generally depreciates fixed assets using the straight-line method for financial statement reporting and various accelerated methods for income tax reporting. During 1981, depreciation on fixed assets amounted to $900,000 for financial statement reporting and $950,000 for income tax reporting. Commitments for the purchase of fixed assets amounted to $450,000 at December 31, 1981. Such fixed assets will be subject to an investment tax credit of 10%.

d)   For financial statement reporting, Mikis has accrued estimated losses from product warranty contracts prior to their occurrence. For income tax reporting, no deduction is taken until payments are made. At December 31, 1980, accrued estimated losses of $200,000 were included in the liability section of Mikis's balance sheet. Based on the latest available information, Mikis estimates that this figure should be 30% higher at December 31, 1981. Payments of $250,000 were made in 1981.

e)   In 1976 Mikis acquired another company for cash. Goodwill resulting from this transaction was $800,000 and is being amortized over a 40-year period for financial statement reporting. The amortization is not deductible for income tax reporting.

f)   Mikis has a wholly owned foreign subsidiary. In 1981 this subsidiary had income before U.S. and foreign income taxes of $175,000 and a provision for taxes in its own country of $70,000. No earnings were remitted to Mikis in 1981. For U.S. income tax reporting, Mikis will receive a tax credit for $70,000 when these earnings are remitted. Mikis provides taxes on the unremitted earnings of this subsidiary for financial statement reporting.

g)   Premiums paid on officers' life insurance amounted to $80,000 in 1981. These premiums are not deductible for income tax reporting.

h)   Assume that the U.S. income tax rate is 48%.

Required:

1. What amounts should be shown for (a) provision for current income taxes, (b) provision for deferred income taxes, and (c) investment tax credits recognized in Mikis's income statement for the year ended December 31, 1981? Show supporting computations in good form.

2. Identify any information in the Mikis Company situation which was not used to determine the answer to Part 1 above and explain why this information was not used.

(AICPA adapted)

P–16–13 Your CPA firm has been appointed to examine the financial statements of Clark Engineering, Inc. (CEI) for the two years ended December 31, 1980, and December 31, 1981, in conjunction with an application for a bank loan. CEI was formed on January 2, 1973, by the nontaxable incorporation of the Clark family partnership.

Early in the engagement you learned that CEI's controller was unfamiliar with income tax accounting and that no income tax allocations have been recorded. During the examination considerable information was gathered from the accounting records and from client employees regarding interperiod income tax allocation. This information has been audited and is as follows (with dollar amounts rounded to the nearest $100):

a) CEI uses the direct write-off method for income tax purposes and a full accrual method for financial accounting purposes. The balance of the allowance for doubtful receivables account at December 31, 1979, was $62,000. Following is a summary of the accounts written off and the corresponding year(s) in which the related sales were made.

	Year in Which Accounts Written Off	
Year(s) in Which Sales Were Made	1981	1980
Year 79 and prior	$19,800	$20,000
Year 80	7,200	
Year 81		
Totals	$27,000	$29,000

The following is an analysis of changes in the allowance for doubtful receivables account for the two years ended December 31, 1981.

	Year Ended December 31	
	1981	1980
Balance at beginning of year	$66,000	$62,000
Accounts written off during the year	(27,000)	(29,000)
Doubtful receivables expense for the year	38,000	33,000
Balance at end of year	$77,000	$66,000

b) Following is a reconciliation between pretax accounting income and taxable income:

	Year Ended December 31	
	1981	1980
(1) Net income per accounting records	$333,100	$262,800
(2) Federal income tax payable during year	182,300	236,800
(3) Taxable income not recorded on the accounting records this year		
Deferred sales commission	10,000	
(4) Expenses recorded on the accounting records this year not deducted on the tax return:		

(a) Allowance for doubtful receivables	11,000	4,000
(b) Amortization of goodwill	8,000	8,000

(5) Total of lines (1) through (4) — $544,400 | $511,600

(6) Income recorded on the accounting records this year not included on the tax return:

Tax exempt interest— Watertown 5% Municipal Bonds — 5,000

(7) Deductions on the tax return not charged against pretax accounting income this year: depreciation — 83,700 | 38,000

(8) Total of lines (6) and (7) — $ 88,700 | $ 38,000

(9) Taxable income [line (5) less line (8)] — $455,700 | $473,600

c) Assume that the effective tax rates are as follows:

1979 and prior years	60%
1980	50%
1981	40%

d) In December, 1981, CEI entered into a contract to serve as distributor for Brown Manufacturer, Inc.'s engineering products. The contract became effective on December 31, 1981, and $10,000 of advance commissions on the contract was received and deposited on December 31, 1981. Because the commissions had not been earned, they were accounted for as a deferred credit on the balance sheet at December 31, 1981.

e) Goodwill represents the excess of cost over fair value of the net tangible assets of another company that were acquired for cash on January 2, 1976. The original balance was $80,000.

f) Depreciation on plant assets transferred at incorporation and acquisitions through December 31, 1979, have been accounted for on a straight-line basis for both financial and tax reporting. Beginning in 1980 all additions of machinery and equipment have been depreciated under the declining-balance method for tax reporting and under the straight-line method for financial reporting. Company policy is to take a full year's depreciation in the year of acquisition and none in the year of retirement. There have been no sales, trade-ins, or retirements since incorporation. Following is an analysis disclosing significant information about depreciable property and related depreciation:

Asset	Cost	Estimated Economic Life	Annual Straight-Line Amount	Declining-Balance Depreciation		Depreciation Taken Through Dec. 31, 1979
				1981	1980	1979
Building	$1,190,000	20 & 50 yrs.	$31,000			$380,000
Machinery and equipment: Transferred at incorporation or acquired through Dec. 31, 1979	834,000	Various	45,900			495,800

Acquisitions since
Dec. 31, 1979

1980	267,000	6 years	38,700	$ 63,700	$76,000
1981	395,000	6 years	58,000	116,000	
Total asset cost	$2,686,000				

Total Depreciation Expense

	1981	1980	*through Dec. 31, 1979*
For financial accounting purposes	$172,900	$114,900	$875,800
For income tax purposes	$256,600	$152,900	$875,800

Required:

1. Prepare a schedule calculating (a) the balance of deferred income taxes at December 31, 1980, and 1981, and (b) the amount of the timing differences between actual income tax payable and financial accounting income tax expense for 1980 and 1981. Round all calculations to the nearest $100 and use the gross change method.

2. Independent of your solution to part 1., and assuming data shown below, prepare the section of the income statement beginning with pretax accounting income to disclose properly the income tax expense for the years ended December 31, 1981, and 1980.

	1981	1980
Pretax accounting income	$480,400	$465,600
Taxes payable currently	182,300	236,800
Year's net timing difference—Dr. (Cr.)	28,100	(24,500)
Balance of deferred tax at end of year—Dr. (Cr.)	(44,200)	(16,100)

(AICPA adapted)

17

Accounting
for Pension Costs

Accounting in the News

Determining pension costs is not an easy task. Assumptions must be made concerning employee turnover, interest rates, life expectancy, salary increases, and so forth. Collectively these are referred to as actuarial assumptions. If significant changes occur in these assumptions, they can cause dramatic changes in a company's financial statements, as the following article excerpt indicates:

> In the face of disastrous losses for Pan Am and Braniff, Eastern Air Lines looked good in April with a first-quarter profit of $4.1 million. However, had the accountants and actuaries not changed one or two assumptions in Eastern's pension plan it would have been a different story. The airline's pension plan funding in 1981 will be reduced from 1980's $100 million to around $75 million. That's a "saving" of $25 million.
>
> Bet you thought this kind of cookie jar stuff was illegal. Welcome to the rarefied world of actuarial assumptions, where crystal-ball gazing is accepted practice. Simply put, Eastern's squad of actuaries merely penciled in a change in their assumptions of what Eastern's pension fund might earn on its capital in the future. Obviously, if you assume that interest rates will stay high and that you're going to earn more on the money in your fund, then you need to put in less now to meet future obligations. That means you can decrease your annual contribution, as Eastern did.
>
> Is this legitimate? Perfectly. Companies are free to pick any number that feels right to them. "There was a rash of increases in actuarial assumptions in the mid-Seventies, the last bout of high inflation," recalls Ed Davis of Buck Consultants, a New York-based actuarial firm. "People were looking for places to improve earnings. I have to expect that there is going to be another rash."[*]

This chapter discusses the problems encountered in accounting for pension plan costs.

[*]Thomas Baker, "Reading the Tea Leaves," *Forbes*, June 22, 1981, p. 76.

In recent decades there has been a significant increase in the number of companies adopting pension plans for their employees. Today most large companies and many medium and small companies have adopted pension plans, and pension costs have become a significant expense. As a result, there is a need for adequate financial reporting of these costs. Before 1965 there were varied approaches to accounting for pension plans. Little, if any, comparability existed among companies regarding pension costs reporting and financial statement disclosures.

Two publications issued in 1965–1966 addressed accounting for pension plans: *Accounting Research Study No. 8* (AICPA)[1] and *APB Opinion No. 8*.[2] The *Opinion* attempted to eliminate the wide diversity of accounting practice and to standardize financial statement disclosures. Additional statements issued by the FASB are discussed in this chapter.

Nature of Pension Plans

In general, a **pension plan** is

> an arrangement whereby a company undertakes to provide its retired employees with benefits that can be determined or estimated in advance from the provisions of a document or documents or from the company's practices.[3]

The economic importance of pension funds can be seen by looking at data compiled by the SEC for private, noninsured pension plans. At the end of 1979 the surveyed plans' total assets amounted to $225 billion. This was more than double the 1968 total and eight times the 1958 total.[4] Specific pension plan arrangements have individual characteristics that can be identified by the following factors:

1. Method used to determine benefits.
2. Entity that controls the receipts and disbursements for the plan.
3. Groups making payments to the plan.
4. The time when employees have a right to pension benefits without continued employment.
5. Tax treatment.

Each of these factors is discussed in the following paragraphs.

There are two general methods of determining benefits—that using specific criteria identified in the pension plan and that using the amounts available to be paid at the time of retirement. The first method is called a **defined benefit plan**

---

[1] Ernest L. Hicks, "Accounting for the Cost of Pension Plans," *Accounting Research Study No. 8* (New York: AICPA, 1965).

[2] "Accounting for the Cost of Pension Plans," *Opinions of the Accounting Principles Board No. 8* (New York: AICPA, 1966).

[3] Ibid., par. 3.

[4] Securities and Exchange Commission, *Statistical Bulletin*, July 1979 and May 1980 as reported in "An Analysis of Issues Related to Employers' Accounting for Pensions and Other Postemployment Benefits," *Financial Accounting Standards Board Discussion Memorandum* (Stamford, Conn.: FASB, 1981), p. 3.

since the amount of payments (benefits) can be determined by reference to specific documents. The criteria used to determine benefits and their relative importance (or credit given) may differ among plans. In general, the criteria include length of service and salary. Salary usually consists of the highest earnings for a specified time period, normally three to five years.

The other method of determining benefits is called a **defined contribution plan.** For these plans, the amount of the payment (contribution) made to the pension plan each year is set by the pension agreement. Usually this is a specified percentage of an employee's salary. The amount of retirement income provided to an employee will be based upon the accumulated value of the contributions (including interest[5]) made for that employee.

Defined benefit plans are more common than defined contribution plans; hence, most of this chapter will be spent discussing defined benefit plans. Large defined contribution plans do exist, however, including TIAA-CREF (Teachers Insurance and Annuity Association and College Retirement Equities Fund), a retirement plan in which a large number of university faculty participate.

In most cases an organization separate from the employer receives payments from the employer, invests pension assets, and disburses payments to retired employees. This organization is called a **funding agency.** A plan that has a funding agency is called a **funded plan.** Funding occurs when an employer makes payments to the funding agency. The term **fund** is used to refer to the assets maintained by the funding agency. A plan is **unfunded** if the employer does not make payments directly to a funding agency.

Certain pension agreements require employees to make payments (contributions) toward their own retirements in addition to the employers' payment (contribution). These plans are called **contributory plans.** Other agreements require only employer payments and are called **noncontributory plans.**

In general, pension agreements provide a time (or times) when pension benefits become irrevocable. An employee's benefits are then said to be **vested.** This can occur at one point in time or gradually over several time periods. Until an employee's benefits are vested, no pension benefits will be received upon retirement if an employee resigns or is terminated. If the plan is a contributory plan, all employee contributions usually are returned in the case of resignation or termination. When an employee's benefits are vested and the employee subsequently resigns or is terminated, at normal retirement age s/he will receive appropriate benefits based upon salary and years of service with the employer.

Some agreements provide for complete vesting at one specific point in time, usually after a specified number of years of employment. Other agreements provide an increasing scale of vesting to a specific time when complete vesting occurs. To determine the amount vested, you should refer to a **vesting schedule** provided in the pension agreement.

If the plan meets certain qualification requirements, specific tax advantages are allowed the employer, the employees, and the pension fund. A **qualified plan** allows the employer to take the contributions as deductions in determining taxable income. The income of the pension fund is exempt from federal income taxes. Also, employees are taxed only when benefits are received or made available. In

---

[5]Throughout this chapter **interest** is used to refer to earnings, including gains on securities of a pension fund.

certain situations these benefits may be taxed at capital gains rates. Finally, death benefits made from employer contributions may not be subject to federal estate taxes.[6]

In order to qualify, pension plans must:

1. Be for the exclusive benefit of employees.
2. Not discriminate in favor of a specific group of employees.
3. Cover a reasonable proportion of employees.
4. Vest employee contributions immediately.
5. Meet one of three, alternative, minimum vesting requirements for employer's contributions.[7]

Historical Development of Pension GAAP

During the last three decades, pensions have received substantial attention from accounting policy-making bodies. In 1956 the Committee on Accounting Procedure issued *Accounting Research Bulletin No. 47*, "Accounting for Costs of Pension Plans." This bulletin recommended that pension expense be recognized when benefits are earned instead of the **"pay-as-you-go"** or **terminal funding method** in which pension expense is recognized when retirement payments are made. In the 1960s the APB again addressed the pension issue "because of the increasing importance of pensions and variations in accounting."[8] Unreasonable increases and decreases in the amount of pension expense recorded by companies were found between years. Here is an example cited:

> A company with a stable or growing employee group to have pension expense of $50,000 one year, $100,000 the next and $10,000 the next. Although not usually so extreme, fluctuations of this sort did occur in many cases found in practice.[9]

The APB commissioned a research study that was published as Accounting Research Study No. 8, "Accounting for the Cost of Pension Plans."[10] Over a year after the publication of this study, *APB Opinion No. 8* was issued. This opinion is still the primary authoritative source for accounting by a company (an employer) for pension costs. To reduce the fluctuations in pension accounting, *Opinion No. 8* addressed three major issues:

1. Accounting for actuarial gains and losses.
2. The relationship of funding to pension expense.
3. The economic substance and legal form of a pension plan.

These issues are discussed later in this chapter.

---

[6]Prentice-Hall, Inc., *Prentice-Hall Federal Taxes* (Englewood Cliffs: Prentice-Hall, Inc., 1981), par. 19.006(a).

[7]W. H. Hoffman and L. C. Phillips, eds., *West's Federal Taxation: Individual Income Taxes 1982 Annual Edition* (St. Paul: West Publishing Co., 1981), pp. 663–666.

[8]"Cost of Pension Plans," par. 5.

[9]*AICPA Professional Standards—Accounting* (New York: AICPA, 1981), par. U4063.020.

[10]Hicks, "Cost of Pension Plans."

Pensions again became an important topic in the 1970s, and the FASB undertook further study of the issue. Among the significant events of the 1970s affecting pensions were the **Employee Retirement Income Security Act** of 1974 **(ERISA)** and the expansion of eligibility for tax-deferred retirement plans.[11] ERISA was passed to address some of the abuses that were found with some pension plans and some employers. It set participation, vesting, and funding requirements. *FASB Interpretation No. 3* considered the impact of ERISA on *Opinion No. 8* and concluded that while compliance with ERISA might modify certain requirements that in turn might change the amount of pension expenses, *Opinion No. 8* was not affected by ERISA.[12]

Criticism of *Opinion No. 8* generally addressed the following issues:

1. Acceptance of a variety of actuarial methods and amortization practices.
2. Failure to recognize certain obligations as liabilities.
3. Artificial leveling of pension expense.
4. Latitude in the selection of actuarial assumptions.[13]

In 1980 *FASB Statement No. 36* was issued as an "interim measure" until the issuance of a discussion memorandum that would examine the pension issue further.[14] Also in 1980 the first statement on reporting by a pension plan, *FASB Statement No. 35*, was issued.[15] In 1981 the FASB issued a discussion memorandum, "Employers' Accounting for Pensions and Other Postemployment Benefits" as a step in considering accounting for significant postemployment benefits.

Pension Accounting

Pensions have evolved as a form of deferred compensation provided by employers to employees. Given this view of pensions, pension costs must be allocated or matched with the services provided. Two fundamental issues must be addressed: (1) the amount that should be allocated to expense in a particular period, and (2) the amount that should be recognized as a liability at a particular point in time.

The recent FASB discussion memorandum states that the fundamental accounting problem is one of measuring, valuing, or otherwise determining the amount of the exchange occurring in a period or before a certain date.[16] It indicates different views of the way in which the exchange between employer and employees takes place and of the nature of the obligation and expense that result.[17]

---

[11] To solve some of the problems of multi-employer pension plans created by ERISA, Congress passed the Multi-Employer Pension Plan Amendments Act of 1980.

[12] "Accounting for the Cost of Pension Plans Subject to the Employee Retirement Income Security Act of 1974," *FASB Interpretation No. 3* (Stamford, Conn.: FASB, 1974), par. 5.

[13] "Pensions and Other Postemployment Benefits," p. 2.

[14] "Disclosure of Pension Information," *Statement of Financial Accounting Standards No. 36* (Stamford, Conn.: FASB, 1980).

[15] "Accounting and Reporting any Defined Benefit Pension Plans," *Statement of Financial Accounting Standards No. 35* (Stamford, Conn.: FASB, 1980).

[16] "Pensions and Other Postemployment Benefits," p. 13.

[17] Ibid.

Accounting for Defined Contribution Plans

Accounting for defined contribution plans is relatively uncomplicated compared to accounting for defined benefit plans. Consider the defined contribution plan for employees of Axe Company in which Axe provides a contribution based upon 8% of an employee's salary. Axe's pension plan, which is a funded, noncontributory plan, covers all its full-time employees. Payments are made yearly to an insurance company that administers the pension plan. When an employee retires from Axe Company, the contributions made by Axe based upon the employee's salary plus accrued interest are available to pay the retirement benefits. To determine the monthly benefits at retirement, one must estimate the employee's expected age at death, a specific contribution level, and a specific interest rate for the contributions to date and future contributions. Estimates of these uncertainties are made by **professional actuaries,** individuals who have advanced training in probability and statistics and who are able to make these needed estimates. Estimates of age at death are made by using **mortality tables.** In this situation, Axe Company has no liability for the pensions as long as the required contributions are made. Hence, the pension expense for any period should be 8% of employee salaries.

Here is an example of how employee retirement benefits are estimated. Mr. Smith is covered by a defined contribution plan in which he contributes 5.5% of his gross income and his employer contributes an equal amount. For 1981 his statement from the retirement plan indicates a total of $3,025.00 contributed to the plan. This represents equal contributions of 5.5% of his salary of $27,500 ($27,500 $\times$ 5.5% = $1,512.50 $\times$ 2). The pension plan statement also indicates that if a like amount were contributed until 2013, Mr. Smith would receive a retirement income of $3,500 per month. This was based upon actuarial estimates of Mr. Smith's life expectancy and an estimate of earnings of the contributions.

Accounting for Defined Benefit Plans

Several uncertainties affect the amount that a specific employee or group of employees will receive as retirement income under a defined benefit plan. These uncertainties include employee turnover, future employee salaries, employee mortality rates, the rate of return on pension fund assets, and the amount of expenses, if any, that will be incurred by the pension fund. These uncertainties typically are resolved by professional actuaries who make needed estimates called **actuarial assumptions,** with the expectation that actual turnover, salaries, and mortality rates will closely approximate the estimates. If the actual amounts differ from the estimate, an **actuarial gain or loss** occurs.

When pension plans are established by existing companies, employees usually are given credit for service from their initial employment date. For example, if an employee has worked for the company for ten years, he usually will get credit in his retirement pay for these years and for those worked after the retirement plan was initiated. The company must pay a sufficient amount into the pension fund to cover the retirement benefits earned by the employee during his employment before the date the plan was initiated. The cost of providing this credit is called **past service cost.** At the time of initial adoption of a pension plan, actuaries estimate the past service costs based upon the benefits provided in the pension plan documents and their actuarial assumptions.

Questions have been raised about the appropriate treatment of past service costs. Alternatives that could be used are to write off past service costs as a prior period adjustment, to expense them in the year of adoption, or to amortize them as an expense to periods after the adoption of the plan.

The first approach assumes that the cost relates to prior years and should be charged against prior years' revenues. This approach is illogical since prior employees' services have been received and paid for already. If the company closed down or decided not to initiate a pension plan, no additional costs would be incurred. The second approach, to expense the costs immediately, assumes the cost either benefits the current year only or has no benefit at all. Companies initiate pension plans to benefit the future through such factors as lower employee turnover, lower training costs, and higher productivity. It is difficult to understand why a company would initiate a pension plan if it expected no future benefits. Therefore, the immediate write-off also seems illogical. The logical approach is to write off the cost over the period of expected benefit, the future. *APB Opinion No. 8* recognized that past service costs should be allocated to periods after the adoption of the plan. This is consistent with the view adopted in *Accounting Research Bulletin No. 43*:

> . . . even though the calculation is based on past service, costs of annuities based on such service are incurred in contemplation of present and future services, not necessarily of the individual affected but of the organization as a whole, and therefore should be charged to the present and future periods benefited.[18]

The cost of providing future pension benefits for any year after the adoption of a pension plan is called **normal cost.** Normal costs also are estimated by actuaries based upon the benefits provided in the pension plan documents and on actuarial assumptions.

After initial adoption, pension plans usually are amended to provide for increased retirement benefits. These amendments usually are retroactive for all employees. The new normal cost normally is higher than the current normal cost. The costs of providing retroactive increases are called **prior service costs.** *APB Opinion No. 8* accounts for prior service costs in a manner similar to past service costs.

Determining Pension Expense. *Opinion No. 8* presents two general views of pensions without indicating any preference. In the first, pensions are viewed "as a form of supplemental benefit to employees at a particular time."[19] This view leads to a matching of pension costs, including past service costs, of particular employees. In the other view, pensions are viewed as (1) a means of promoting efficiency by providing for systematic retirement of older employees or (2) the fulfillment of a social obligation expected of business enterprises, the cost of which, as a practical matter, constitutes a business expense that must be incurred.[20] This view leads to a matching of costs amounting to normal cost plus inter-

---

[18]"Restatement and Revision of Accounting Research Bulletin," *Accounting Research Bulletin No. 43* (New York: AICPA, 1953), Chapter 13, par. 3.

[19]"Cost of Pension Plans," par. 11.

[20]"Cost of Pension Plans," par. 11.

est on unfunded prior service costs since this amount normally will meet the benefits required under the plan. While indicating a preference for the first view, the APB concluded the following:

1. All pension costs should be allocated to periods after the adoption of the plan.
2. Annual pension expense should
   a) Use one of the five acceptable actuarial cost methods.
   b) Be greater than the total of:
      (1) Normal cost
      (2) Interest on unfunded prior and past service costs.[21]
      (3) A provision for vested benefits if they are greater than the total of the pension fund plus any balance sheet pension accruals minus balance sheet prepayments or deferred charges.[22]
   c) Be less than the total of:
      (1) Normal cost.
      (2) 10% of past service costs (until amortized).
      (3) 10% of prior service costs (until amortized).
      (4) Interest equivalents for the difference between the expenses recorded and the amounts funded.

Notice that the maximum provision, (c), represents the first viewpoint, whereas the minimum provision, (b), represents the second viewpoint. The APB accepted this approach to determining pension expense because of a belief that "accounting for pension cost is in a transitional stage, (and) that the range of practices would be significantly narrowed if pension costs were accounted for at the present time within limits. . . ."[23] The 10% amortization rates represent rates that appear to be determined by an APB compromise to prevent rapid amortization.

For example, Monroe Company adopted a pension plan on January 1, 1981. At that time the actuaries estimated the following:

Unfunded past service cost	$550,000
Normal cost—1981	92,000
Interest rate	8%

The minimum expense for 1981 is as follows:

Normal cost	$ 92,000
Unfunded past service cost × 8%	44,000
	$136,000

[21] This type of interest is called an interest equivalent. It attempts to measure the interest cost related to the obligation for the unfunded prior or past service costs. It is essentially equivalent to interest on debt.

[22] The provision for vested benefits is used rarely because vested benefits are usually less than the pension fund plus balance sheet pension items.

[23] "Cost of Pension Plans," par. 17.

The maximum expense for 1981 is as follows:

Normal cost	$ 92,000
Unfunded past service cost × 10%	55,000
	$147,000

The actual expense recorded by Monroe in 1981 must be between $136,000 and $147,000 and must be determined based upon an acceptable actuarial cost method.

Actuarial Cost Methods. In *Opinion No. 8* five actuarial cost methods are considered acceptable. These five methods belong to one of two different types:

1. The **accrued benefit cost method**—the amount assigned to the current year usually represents the present value of the increase in present employees' retirement benefits resulting from that year's service.
2. The **projected benefit cost methods**—the amount assigned to the current year usually represents the level amount (or an amount based on a computed level percentage of compensation) that will provide for the estimated projected retirement benefits over the service lives of either the individual employees or the employee group, depending on the method selected.[24]

The **unit credit method** is the only acceptable accrued benefit cost method. This method results in increasing yearly costs for an individual employee. However, for all employees covered by the plan, the yearly cost tends to increase only if the number of employees, their average age, or their salary tends to increase.

The projected benefit cost methods include four acceptable methods: **entry age normal, individual level premium, aggregate,** and **attained age normal** methods. The costs computed under these four methods tend either to be stable or to decline over time.[25]

Recording Pension Expense. Once the amount of pension expense has been determined, the funding policy also must be analyzed to determine the proper accounting entry. The amount funded and the amount expensed do not have to be equal. In general, normal service costs are funded on a yearly basis. Funding policies on past service costs vary. ERISA established requirements that any plan existing at January 1, 1974, fund all past service costs within forty years. All plans started after January 1, 1974, must fund all past service costs within thirty years. ERISA also establishes yearly funding requirements.

Given that funding and accounting policies can differ, one of three relationships can occur. These alternatives are illustrated in Exhibit 17-1.

Harmar Corporation is in the process of instituting a pension plan for all employees in 1982. The plan will provide employees credit for all years employed by Harmar, including those before 1982. Harmar has worked out all arrange-

[24] Ibid., par. 20.

[25] Ibid.

Exhibit 17-1
Effects of Relationship Between Funding and Amortization

Relationship	*Result*
1. Funding period and amortization period are equal.	1. The expense and cash disbursed by the employer are equal.
2. Funding period is shorter than the amortization period.	2. In the early years, the cash disbursed to the plan is greater than the expense recognized. The difference represents a prepaid asset which is amortized in later years.
3. Funding period is longer than the amortization period.	3. In the early years, the expense recognized exceeds the amount of cash disbursed to the plan. The difference represents a deferred liability which is extinguished by payments in later years.

---

ments for the plan except for the amortization period. Three alternative amortization periods are being considered. The following information has already been determined by the consulting actuaries:

Normal cost—1982	$ 35,000
Normal cost—1983	36,500
Past service cost, January 1, 1982	150,000
Funding period	25 years
Interest rate (expected earnings on fund)	6%
Vested benefits—1982	$ 4,000
Vested benefits—1983	10,000

By using a present value of an annuity table, you can determine the amount of the yearly payment for past service costs:

$$p = P_{\overline{n = 25}|\, i = 6\%} \times r$$
$$\$150,000 = 12.78336 \times r$$
$$r = \$150,000/12.78336$$
$$r = \$11,734$$

The payment of $11,734 is designed to provide interest and a reduction in the total past service cost due the pension plan. Interest payments are made to recognize

Exhibit 17-2
Past Service Cost Amortization Table

Year	Beginning of Year Balance[1]	Payment[2]	Interest[3]	Principal[4]	End of Year Balance[5]
1982	$150,000.00	$11,734.00	$9,000.00	$2,734.00	$147,265.94
1983	147,265.94	11,734.00	8,835.95	2,898.05	144,367.87
1984	144,367.87	11,734.00	8,662.07	3,071.93	141,295.94
1985	141,295.94	11,734.00	8,477.75	3,256.25	138,039.69
1986	138,039.69	11,734.00	8,282.38	3,451.62	134,588.06
1987	134,588.06	11,734.00	8,075.28	3,658.72	130,929.31
1988	130,929.31	11,734.00	7,855.76	3,878.24	127,051.06
1989	127,051.06	11,734.00	7,623.06	4,110.94	122,940.12
1990	122,940.12	11,734.00	7,376.41	4,357.59	118,582.50
1991	118,582.50	11,734.00	7,114.95	4,619.05	113,963.44
1992	113,963.44	11,734.00	6,837.80	4,896.20	109,067.19
1993	109,067.19	11,734.00	6,544.03	5,189.97	103,877.19
1994	103,877.19	11,734.00	6,232.63	5,501.37	98,375.81
1995	98,375.81	11,734.00	5,902.55	5,831.45	92,544.31
1996	92,544.31	11,734.00	5,552.66	6,181.34	86,362.94
1997	86,362.94	11,734.00	5,181.77	6,552.23	79,810.69
1998	79,810.69	11,734.00	4,788.64	6,945.36	72,865.31
1999	72,865.31	11,734.00	4,371.92	7,362.08	65,503.23
2000	65,503.23	11,734.00	3,930.19	7,803.80	57,699.43
2001	57,699.43	11,734.00	3,461.97	8,272.03	49,427.39
2002	49,427.39	11,734.00	2,965.64	8,768.36	40,659.04
2003	40,659.04	11,734.00	2,439.54	9,294.46	31,364.58
2004	31,364.58	11,734.00	1,881.87	9,852.12	21,512.46
2005	21,512.46	11,734.00	1,290.75	10,443.25	11,069.21
2006	11,069.21	11,734.00	664.79	11,069.21	0.0

[1] For the beginning of first year the balance is given. For the beginning of each subsequent year, the beginning balance is equal to the balance at the end of the previous year.
[2] Given.
[3] Beginning of year balance times 6%.
[4] Difference between payment and interest.
[5] Beginning of year balance minus principal payment.

the lost interest income that would have been earned by the plan if the past service costs were funded immediately. Exhibit 17-2 provides an amortization table for Harmar's past service costs.

The following three examples illustrate the three different funding/amortization alternatives.

Alternative #1—Amortization over 25 years (Equal amortization and funding periods)

For the year ended December 31, 1982, Harmar will record as pension expense the past service costs of $11,734 plus the normal costs of $35,000 in the following journal entry:

Pension expense   46,734
    Cash   46,734
    To record pension
    expense for 1982.

Assuming that the $46,734 was determined by an acceptable actuarial cost method, the expense must be checked against the maximum and minimum. As can be seen in Exhibit 17-3, the computed expense is between the maximum and minimum pension expense established in *Opinion No. 8*.

Alternative #2—Amortization over 30 years (Funding period is shorter than amortization period)

Harmar will record the past service costs at an amount that will amortize the $150,000 over 30 years. If you use the present value of an annuity table, where $P_{\overline{n = 30}|i = 6\%}$, the factor is 13.76483, and the amount for the first year is

$$r = \$150,000/13.76483 = \$10,897.39$$

Notice that for the funding period (the first 25 years) the cash paid to the plan will be greater than the expense recorded. Hence a deferred pension expense is debited for the difference. For the last five years no payments for past service costs are made so the credit from recording the expense will be made to deferred pension expense.

Exhibit 17-3
Computation of Maximum/Minimum for 1982

	Minimum	Maximum
Normal cost	$35,000	$35,000
Past service cost:		
Interest on unfunded portion		
($150,000 × 6%)	9,000	
10% of costs		
($150,000 × 10%)		15,000
Vested benefits		
Interest equivalents		
	$44,000	$50,000

For the first year, pension expense of $45,897.39 ($10,897.39 + $35,000) and payment of $46,734.00 ($11,734.00 + $35,000) is recognized:

Pension expense	45,897.39	
Deferred pension expense	836.61	
Cash		46,734.00
To record pension		
expense for 1982.		

Notice once again that the expense recorded is within the limits established by *APB Opinion No. 8.* The debit to deferred pension expense is the difference between the cash paid and the expense recognized. After the first year the amount of pension expense recognized for past service cost is the amortization amount reduced by the interest on the deferred expense account. For the second year, pension expense is $10,397.39 (amortization) − $50.20 (interest $836.61 × 6%) + $36,500 (normal cost). The journal entry for the second year is as follows:

Pension expense	47,347.19	
Deferred pension expense	886.81	
Cash		48,234.00
To record pension		
expense for 1983.		

The debit to the deferred pension expense of $886.81 is the difference between the cash paid and the expense recorded.

Exhibit 17-4 presents an expense/asset amortization schedule for each of the 30 years. The amounts for 1982 and 1983 are the same as those computed above.

If the normal cost remains at $36,500, in 2007 Harmar will record pension expense of $44,643.38 ($8,143.38 + $36,500) in the following journal entry:

Pension expense	44,643.38	
Deferred pension expense		8,143.38
Cash		36,500.00
To record pension expense		
for the year 2007.		

The credit to deferred pension expense is the difference between the cash paid and the expense recorded. The balances in the deferred account arise from the cumulative timing differences between funding and amortization. Deferred pension expense appears on the balance sheet in the deferred charges section.

Exhibit 17-4
Expense/Asset Amortization Schedule

Year	Cash Credit[1]	Amort. Amount[2]	Deferred Pension Account Balance Jan. 1[3]	Interest on Balance[4]	Deferred Pension Expense Debit – Credit[5]	Deferred Pension Account Balance Dec. 31[6]	Pension Expense[7]
1982	11,734.00	10,897.39	0.0	0.0	836.61	836.61	10,897.39
1983	11,734.00	10,897.39	836.61	50.20	886.81	1,723.43	10,847.19
1984	11,734.00	10,897.39	1,723.43	103.41	940.02	2,663.45	10,793.98
1985	11,734.00	10,897.39	2,663.45	159.81	996.42	3,659.87	10,737.58
1986	11,734.00	10,897.39	3,659.87	219.59	1,056.21	4,716.07	10,677.79
1987	11,734.00	10,897.39	4,716.07	282.96	1,119.58	5,835.65	10,614.42
1988	11,734.00	10,897.39	5,835.65	350.14	1,186.75	7,022.41	10,547.25
1989	11,734.00	10,897.39	7,022.41	421.34	1,257.96	8,280.37	10,476.04
1990	11,734.00	10,897.39	8,280.37	496.82	1,333.44	9,613.80	10,400.56
1991	11,734.00	10,897.39	9,613.80	576.83	1,413.44	11,027.25	10,320.56
1992	11,734.00	10,897.39	11,027.25	661.63	1,498.25	12,525.50	10,235.75
1993	11,734.00	10,897.39	12,525.50	751.53	1,588.14	14,113.64	10,145.86
1994	11,734.00	10,897.39	14,113.64	846.82	1,683.43	15,797.07	10,050.57
1995	11,734.00	10,897.39	15,797.07	947.82	1,784.44	17,581.51	9,949.56
1996	11,734.00	10,897.39	17,581.51	1,054.89	1,891.50	19,473.02	9,842.50
1997	11,734.00	10,897.39	19,473.02	1,168.38	2,005.00	21,478.01	9,729.00
1998	11,734.00	10,897.39	21,478.01	1,288.68	2,125.30	23,603.31	9,608.70
1999	11,734.00	10,897.39	23,603.31	1,416.20	2,252.81	25,856.12	9,481.19
2000	11,734.00	10,897.39	25,856.12	1,551.37	2,387.98	28,244.10	9,346.02
2001	11,734.00	10,897.39	28,244.10	1,694.65	2,531.26	30,775.36	9,202.74
2002	11,734.00	10,897.39	30,775.36	1,846.52	2,683.14	33,458.50	9,050.86
2003	11,734.00	10,897.39	33,458.50	2,007.51	2,844.12	36,302.62	8,889.87
2004	11,734.00	10,897.39	36,302.62	2,178.16	3,014.77	39,317.40	8,719.23
2005	11,734.00	10,897.39	39,317.40	2,359.04	3,195.66	42,513.06	8,538.34
2006	11,734.00	10,897.39	42,513.06	2,550.78	3,387.40	45,900.46	8,346.60
2007	0.0	10,897.39	45,900.46	2,754.03	−8,143.36	37,757.10	8,143.36
2008	0.0	10,897.39	37,757.10	2,265.43	−8,631.96	29,125.14	8,631.96
2009	0.0	10,897.39	29,125.14	1,747.51	−9,149.87	19,975.26	9,149.87
2010	0.0	10,897.39	19,975.26	1,198.52	−9,698.87	10,276.39	9,698.87
2011	0.0	10,897.39	10,276.39	621.00	−10,276.39	0.0	10,276.39

[1] Given (see text).
[2] Given (see text).
[3] Equal to December 31 balance of prior year.
[4] Balance on Jan. 1 times 6%.
[5] Cash credit less amortization amount plus interest on balance.
[6] Beginning balance plus (minus) deferred pension expense.
[7] Amortization amount less interest on balance.

Alternative #3—Amortization over 20 years (Funding period is longer than amortization period.)

Harmar will record as past service costs an amount that will amortize the $150,000 over 20 years. Using the present value of an annuity table, for $P_{\overline{n=20}|i=6\%} = 11.46992$, you'll find that the amount for the first year is

$$r = \$150,000/11.46992$$
$$r = \$13,077.69$$

Notice that the amount of expense recorded for the first year is greater than the amount paid. Hence, a deferred pension liability account is credited. The journal entry to record pension expense is as follows:

Pension expense ($13,077.69 + $35,000)	48,077.69	
Deferred pension liability		1,343.69
Cash		46,734.00
To record pension expense for 1982.		

After the first year the amount of the pension expense recognized for past service cost is the amortization amount increased by the interest on the deferred pension liability. For the second year the pension expense is the $13,077.69 (amortization amount) + $80.62 (interest—$1,343.69 × 0.06) + $36,500 (normal cost) = $49,658.31. The journal entry for the second year is as follows:

Pension expense	49,658.31	
Deferred pension liability		1,424.31
Cash		48,234.00
To record pension expense for 1983.		

The credit to deferred pension liability is the difference between the cash paid and the expense recorded.

Exhibit 17-5 presents an expense/liability amortization schedule for each of the 25 years. The amounts for 1982 and 1983 are the same as those computed above. From the 21st through 25th years, the only pension expense recorded is for the amount of interest on the deferred liability account.

In 2002, assuming normal costs of $36,500, Harmar will record pension expense of $36,500 plus $2,965.71, which represents the interest on the beginning balance in the deferred liability account. The difference between the cash pay-

Exhibit 17-5
Expense/Liability Amortization Schedule

Year	Cash Credit[1]	Amort. Amount[2]	Deferred Pension Liability Balance Jan. 1[3]	Interest on Balance[4]	Deferred Pension Liability Debit – Credit[5]	Deferred Pension Liability Balance Dec. 31[6]	Pension Expense[7]
1982	11,734.00	13,077.69	0.0	0.0	−1,343.69	−1,343.69	13,077.69
1983	11,734.00	13,077.69	−1,343.69	80.62	−1,424.31	−2,768.00	13,158.31
1984	11,734.00	13,077.69	−2,768.00	166.08	−1,509.77	−4,277.76	13,243.77
1985	11,734.00	13,077.69	−4,277.76	256.67	−1,600.35	−5,878.11	13,334.35
1986	11,734.00	13,077.69	−5,878.11	352.69	−1,696.37	−7,574.48	13,430.37
1987	11,734.00	13,077.69	−7,574.48	454.47	−1,798.16	−9,372.64	13,532.16
1988	11,734.00	13,077.69	−9,372.64	562.36	−1,906.04	−11,278.68	13,640.04
1989	11,734.00	13,077.69	−11,278.68	676.72	−2,020.41	−13,299.09	13,754.41
1990	11,734.00	13,077.69	−13,299.09	797.95	−2,141.63	−15,440.72	13,875.63
1991	11,734.00	13,077.69	−15,440.72	926.44	−2,270.13	−17,710.85	14,004.13
1992	11,734.00	13,077.69	−17,710.85	1,062.65	−2,406.34	−20,117.19	14,140.34
1993	11,734.00	13,077.69	−20,117.19	1,207.03	−2,550.71	−22,667.90	14,284.71
1994	11,734.00	13,077.69	−22,667.90	1,360.07	−2,703.76	−25,371.66	14,437.76
1995	11,734.00	13,077.69	−25,371.66	1,522.30	−2,865.98	−28,237.64	14,599.98
1996	11,734.00	13,077.69	−28,237.64	1,694.26	−3,037.95	−31,275.59	14,771.95
1997	11,734.00	13,077.69	−31,275.59	1,876.54	−3,220.22	−34,495.81	14,954.22
1998	11,734.00	13,077.69	−34,495.81	2,069.75	−3,413.43	−37,909.25	15,147.43
1999	11,734.00	13,077.69	−37,909.25	2,274.55	−3,618.24	−41,527.49	15,352.24
2000	11,734.00	13,077.69	−41,527.49	2,491.65	−3,835.34	−45,362.82	15,569.34
2001	11,734.00	13,077.69	−45,362.82	2,721.77	−4,065.45	−49,428.28	15,799.45
2002	11,734.00	0.0	−49,428.28	2,965.70	8,768.30	−40,659.98	2,965.70
2003	11,734.00	0.0	−40,659.98	2,439.60	9,294.40	−31,365.58	2,439.60
2004	11,734.00	0.0	−31,365.58	1,881.93	9,852.06	−21,513.52	1,881.93
2005	11,734.00	0.0	−21,513.52	1,290.81	10,443.19	−11,070.33	1,290.81
2006	11,734.00	0.0	−11,070.33	663.67	11,070.33	0.0	663.67

[1] Given (see text).
[2] Given (see text).
[3] Equal to December 31 balance of prior year.
[4] Balance on Jan. 1 times 6%.
[5] Amortization amount less cash credit plus interest on balance.
[6] Beginning balance plus (minus) deferred pension liability credit (debit).
[7] Amortization amount plus interest on balance.

ment of $11,734.00 and the interest represents a reduction in the deferred liability account. In 2002 the following journal entry will be made:

Pension expense ($36,500 + $2,965.71)	39,465.71	
Deferred pension liability	8,768.29	
Cash ($11,734 + 36,500)		48,234.00
To record pension expense for year 2002.		

The balances in the deferred liability account arise initially from the timing differences between funding and amortization. Only in the last five years is the recorded balance sheet liability equal to the present value of the employer's liability for past service costs.

For the first year all three alternatives are within the maximum and minimum expenses set by *APB Opinion No. 8*. All other years would have to be checked also. If Harmar had decided to consider a fourth alternative, amortization over ten years, the yearly amount would be as follows:

$$r = \$150,000/P_{\overline{n = 10}|\, i\, =\, 6\%}$$
$$r = \$150,000/7.36009 = \$20,380.19$$

In this case the computed amount is greater than the maximum allowable by *Opinion No. 8*.[26]

The only difference in the three methods is the amortization period for past service costs. If the funding period is the same as the amortization period, no balance sheet recognition of the pension plan is given. If the funding period is not the same as the amortization period, balance sheet recognition of the pension plan occurs as either an asset or liability. If the funding period is longer than the amortization period, a pension liability is reported on the balance sheet. If the amortization period is longer than the funding period, a pension asset account is reported on the balance sheet. Interest is also computed on the beginning balance in the asset or liability account. When a deferred pension account is recorded, interest reduces the pension expense. When a deferred pension liability account is recorded, interest increases pension expense.

There is no balance sheet recognition of the unfunded past service costs except to the extent of differences between the amortization and funding of these costs. If the amortization and funding are over the same period of time, there is no liability for the unfunded portion reported in the balance sheet. Some in the profession have argued that since unfunded past service costs are to be paid in the future, they are liabilities. They contend that the present value of this obligation should be recorded on the books and should be reported in the liability section of the balance sheet. This same value would be reported as an asset (deferred pension cost) and would be amortized over the period of expected benefit. The accounting treatment would be essentially the same as discussed in Chapter 18 for capitalized leases. Although current GAAP do not recognize the asset and liability, the area of pension reporting currently is being reexamined by the FASB.

Actuarial Gains and Losses

Since actuaries estimate factors and since deviations between actual experience and the estimates may occur, the value of pension funds and the amount of pension expense may have to be adjusted. In addition, estimates made by actuaries

---

[26] In this case the maximum would be used. If past service cost is unfunded and if the interest rate is greater than 10%, the minimum will exceed the maximum. However, the mandatory funding requirements of ERISA tend to make this situation rare.

may change before actual events occur. These adjustments are called actuarial gains and losses.

These gains and losses result from changes in actuarial assumptions or estimates. For example, assume an actuary estimated a 10% turnover rate among employees when estimating the pension cost for the company. If subsequent experience shows a 5% rate, the cost would have been underestimated and a loss would result. Since actuarial assumptions are made about a wide range of factors, such as employee salary, employee turnover, life expectancies, and interest revenue, adjustments to any of these factors can result in actuarial gains and losses.

In discussing the accounting for actuarial gains and losses, *APB Opinion No. 8* indicated that "the primary question concerns the timing of their [gain and loss] recognition in providing pension cost."[27] The APB concluded that actuarial gains and losses should be included in pension expense "in a consistent manner that reflects the long-range nature of pension cost."[28] Two approaches, **spreading** and **averaging,** are acceptable for most actuarial gains and losses. Under spreading, gains or losses in a specific year are "spread" over or allocated to a specific number of future years. For example, an actuarial gain of $2,000 was incurred in 1981 and a $4,000 gain was incurred in 1982; if a ten-year, straight-line spreading were used, a $200 gain would be recognized in 1981 and a $600 gain would be recognized in 1982 ($2,000/10 + $4,000/10). Under averaging, an average based upon past changes and/or expected future conditions is used. For example, Pane Company had actuarial gains of $8,000 for the past four years and $7,000 for 1981. Using a five-year moving average $\dfrac{(\$32,000 + \$7,000)}{5}$ Pane would recognize a $7,800 gain in 1981. If a $2,000 actuarial loss were incurred in 1982 and a $1,000 actuarial gain were incurred in 1983, a $4,400 gain $\left[\dfrac{(\$8,000 + \$8,000 + \$7,000 - \$2,000 + \$1,000)}{5}\right]$ would be recognized in 1983.

The APB also concluded that certain actuarial gains and losses should be recognized immediately if the gain or loss results from "a single occurrence not directly related to the operation of the pension plan and not in the ordinary course of the employer's business."[29] Examples provided in the *Opinion* are plant closings and business combinations. The APB resolved that the gains or losses incurred are part of other costs (expenses) and should be recognized immediately because they are not related to future operations. For example, the closing of a plant normally results in a gain. The gain should be recognized immediately because it is a result of a current event (plant closing) that is unrelated to the incurrence of future pension costs.

Accounting and Reporting by Defined Benefit Plans

In March of 1980 *FASB Statement No. 35,* "Accounting and Reporting by Defined Benefit Pension Plan" was issued. This Statement is the result of several exposure drafts issued by the FASB and comments received in reply to the drafts. The

[27] "Cost of Pension Plans," par. 26.

[28] Ibid., par. 30.

[29] Ibid., par. 31.

FASB issued its first exposure draft on this subject in 1977 and received over 700 comments. In 1979 the FASB issued a revised draft that received almost 300 comments.

The Statement indicates that the primary objective of the financial statements of a defined benefit plan is to provide useful information in evaluating the plan's current and future ability to pay required benefits. Therefore, the financial statements should provide information on the following:

1. Plan resources and how the stewardship responsibility for those resources has been changed.
2. The accumulated plan benefits of participants.
3. The results of transactions and events that affect the information regarding those resources and benefits.
4. Other factors necessary for users to understand the information provided.[30]

This Statement applies to all defined benefit plans, regardless of size, that present financial statements. These financial statements must include the following:

1. A statement that includes information regarding the net assets available for benefits as of the end of the plan year.
2. A statement that includes information regarding the changes during the year in the net assets available for benefits.
3. Information regarding the actuarial present value of accumulated plan benefits as of either the beginning or end of the plan year.
4. Information regarding the effects, if significant, of certain factors affecting year-to-year change in the actuarial present value of accumulated plan benefits.[31]

Disclosure

The pension disclosure requirements of *APB Opinion No. 8* were amended by *FASB Statement No. 36*. This Statement set certain disclosure requirements for all employers having a pension plan and set differential disclosure requirements for smaller and larger employers. All employers must disclose the following information:

1. Employee group(s) covered.
2. Accounting policies.
3. Funding policies.
4. Pension expense.
5. Significant matters affecting the comparability among all periods for which financial statements are presented.[32]

---

[30] "Defined Benefit Pension Plan," par. 5.

[31] Ibid., par. 6.

[32] "Pension Information," par. 7.

Exhibit 17-6
General Motors Annual Report
Pension Disclosures

Note: Pension Expense
Total pension expense of the Corporation and its consolidated subsidiaries amounted to $1,922.1 million in 1980. $1,571.5 million in 1979 and $1,326.7 million in 1978. The increase in pension expense for 1980 and 1979 primarily reflects the impact of amendments to the U.S. and Canadian plans, as approved by the stockholders in 1980. For purposes of determining pension expense, the Corporation uses a variety of assumed rates of return on pension funds in accordance with local practice and regulations, which rates approximate 6%. The following table compares accumulated plan benefits and plan net assets for the Corporation's defined benefit plans in the United States and Canada as of October 1 generally, the plans' anniversary dates of both 1980 and 1979:

(Dollars in Millions)	*1980*	*1979*
Actuarial present value of accumulated plan benefits:		
Vested	$17,438.5	$18,156.5
Nonvested	2,234.1	2,521.0
Total	$19,672.6	$20,677.5
Market value of assets available for benefits:		
Held by trustees	$10,584.6	$ 9,066.0
Held by insurance companies	2,769.2	2,501.7
Total	$13,353.8	$11,567.7

The assumed rates of return used in determining the actuarial present value of accumulated plan benefits (shown in the table above) were based upon those published by the Pension Benefit Guaranty Corporation, a public corporation established under the Employee Retirement Income Security Act (ERISA). Such rates averaged approximately 8¼% for 1980 and 7% for 1979.

The Corporation's foreign pension plans are not required to report to certain governmental agencies pursuant to ERISA, and do not otherwise determine the actuarial value of accumulated benefits or net assets available for benefits as calculated and shown above. For those plans, the total of the plans' pension funds and balance sheet accruals, less pension prepayments and deferred charges, exceeded the actuarially computed value of vested benefits by approximately $215 million at both December 31, 1980 and December 31, 1979.

Disclosure of additional information must be made by employers whose pension plans are required by ERISA to file reports with the federal government. The additional information that must be disclosed in financial statements by larger employers generally is already available in the reports required by ERISA. Employers whose pension funds have 100 or more participants should have the information available. The additional information required includes the following:

1. Actuarial present value of vested and nonvested accumulated benefits.[33]
2. The interest rates used in determining the amount in #1.
3. The plan's net assets available for benefits.
4. The date that items #1 through #3 were determined.[34]

Other disclosures are required for those employers whose pension plans do not meet the ERISA requirements. The employer must disclose "the excess, if any, of the actuarially computed value of vested benefits over the total of the pension fund and any balance sheets pension accruals, less any pension prepayments or deferred charges."[35] It is also required that the employer state the reason for the disclosure of this information instead of the previous information.

The pension disclosures contained in a recent General Motors Annual Report are presented in Exhibit 17-6.

Concept Summary

ACCOUNTING FOR PENSION COSTS

PENSIONS—INCOME AND BALANCE SHEET EFFECTS

Plan	Expense Recognized	Balance Sheet Effect
Defined Contribution Plan	Contribution rate times eligible compensation	None, if yearly payments are made
Defined Benefit Plan	Based upon one of the five actuarial cost methods *and* be greater than normal cost + interest on unfunded prior and past service	None, unless the amortization period and the funding period for past service costs are different. If the

---

[33] Accumulated plan benefits are benefits that are "attributable under the provisions of a pension plan to employees' service rendered to the benefit information date." "Defined Benefit Pension Plans," par. 280.

[34] "Pension Information," par. 8.

[35] Ibid., par. 8.

costs[1] *and* be less than
normal cost + 10% of past
service costs (until
amortized) + 10% of prior
service costs (until
amortized) + interest
equivalents.

amortization period is
shorter, a pension liability
will be reported. If the
funding period is shorter,
a pension asset account
will be reported.

PENSION PLAN DISCLOSURE REQUIREMENTS

Firms That Are not Required to File Pension Reports Under ERISA	Firms That Are Required to File Pension Reports Under ERISA
Employee group(s) covered	Employee group(s) covered
Accounting policies	Accounting policies
Funding policies	Funding policies
Pension expense	Pension expense
Matters affecting comparability	Matters affecting comparability
Excess of the actuarially computed value of vested benefits over the total of the pension fund and any balance sheet pension accruals, less any pension prepayments or deferred charges.	Actuarial present value of vested and nonvested accumulated benefits.
	The interest rates used in determining the actuarial present value.
	The plan's net assets available for benefits
	The date of the actuarial determination.

[1] Plus a provision for vested benefits if vested benefits are greater than the total of the pension fund plus (minus) any balance sheet pension accruals (prepayments or deferred charges).

Questions

Q-17-1 When a company adopts a pension plan, what accounting treatment should be applied to past service costs?

Q-17-2 How do vested benefits differ from nonvested benefits?

Q-17-3   What is the difference between past service costs and prior service cost? How does the accounting for each differ?

Q-17-4   Why is the terminal funding method of accounting for pension plans not a generally accepted accounting principle?

Q-17-5   How are defined benefit plans different from defined contribution plans? How are they similar?

Q-17-6   What pension expense is recorded for a defined contribution plan?

Q-17-7   What is the relationship over time between the amounts paid for past service costs and pension expense given each of the following?
   a)   The amortization and funding periods are the same.
   b)   The amortization period is longer than the funding period.
   c)   The amortization period is shorter than the funding period.

Q-17-8   What are the maximim and minimum amounts that can be recorded as pension expenses?

Q-17-9   What treatments can be used to account for actuarial gains and losses?

Q-17-10   What are actuarial cost methods? What are the acceptable methods?

Q-17-11   Under what circumstances should an actuarial loss be recognized immediately for accounting purposes?

Q-17-12   How do the pension disclosure requirements for larger corporations differ from those of smaller corporations?

Q-17-13   What estimates of uncertainties must be made in order to establish pension expense for a defined benefit plan?

Q-17-14   How could two defined benefit pension plans differ? What impact will these differences have on accounting for the plans?

Q-17-15   What parties are involved in a pension plan? How does their accounting differ?

Q-17-16   What events are treated as actuarial gains and losses?

Q-17-17   What are interest equivalents? How are they used in pension accounting?

Q-17-18   What is normal cost?

Q-17-19   How does the computation of the maximum and minimum provisions differ?

Q-17-20   What pension disclosures are required of employers?

Discussion Questions and Cases

D-17-1   One of your friends asks you to evaluate the following alternative pension plans called Plan 1 and Plan 2 that are available through his employer.
Required:
What factors will you tell your friend are important to consider?

Comparison of Provisions of Plan 1 and Plan 2

Plan 1	*Plan 2*
Contributions	
The member contributes 5% of gross salary covered by Social Security and 5½% of salary in excess of	The member pays 5% of gross salary. The employer pays 7.06%.

that covered by Social Security. The employer matches the member's contributions.

Portability
Each member has a personal contract and may continue contributing at other educational institutions. Individuals may also contribute extra payments whether employed by a participating institution or not.

Plan 2 has no portability.

Vesting
Both employer and employee contributions are 100% vested from the date of contribution.

There is no vesting until the member has accrued 10 or more years creditable service.

Formula Benefits
No formula benefits are available.

A formula using average salary and creditable service is used to compute all retirement allowances.

Refund
If a member terminates and is not moving to another participating institution, he/she may repurchase a contract of less than 5 years. If the contract is more than 5 years old, a refund is available only if the total accumulation is less than $2,200. Upon refund, the member receives only the employee share.

Any terminated member or employed member who has changed to part-time may request a refund of his/her contributions plus interest at any time until retirement. The member forfeits the employer share.

Variable Retirement Income
Plan 1 includes a variable annuity which may decrease or increase retirement income in accordance with investment earnings. Its primary investments are in common stock. Although part of Plan 1 includes a fixed annuity, income payments may vary due to interest and dividends. Amount of income payable at retirement is based on the value of the accumulation and the person's age and sex.

Plan 2 is a defined benefit plan. Since income is computed with a formula and not based on the value of an accumulation, the income is fixed except for changes in the formula and cost-of-living increases.

Cost-of-Living Increases
There are no cost-of-living increases as such. Instead there may be variances in annuity income as stated in the preceding item.

Adjustments in income to reflect increases or decreases in the CPI may be made. Such adjustments may not exceed 3%.

D–17–2 Sarr Corporation is considering the establishment of a pension plan for senior management. (None of the other company employees are or will be covered by a pension plan.) The plan will provide for credit for all service to the company. Past service costs will be funded over 3 years and normal costs will be funded yearly. Sarr has proposed to amortize past service costs over 40 years and average normal costs over 10 years.

Required:

What questions are raised by Sarr's proposal?

D–17–3 Jay Company is looking at several alternatives in deciding the exact character of their new pension plan. The following is a summary of the alternatives:

- **a)** Funding—over 15 or 20 years
- **b)** Amortization—over 20 or 25 years
- **c)** Contributory (employees paying 20% of the cost) v. noncontributory

Required:

Discuss the impact of each of these alternatives on the recording of pension transactions and the financial statements components involving the pension transactions.

D–17–4 Sheldon Enterprises is considering the establishment of either a defined benefit or defined contribution plan. The defined benefit plan will not give credit for past service.

Required:

How will accounting for the plans differ?

Exercises

E–17–1 The Thoughtful Corporation adopted an employee pension plan on January 1, 1981, for all of its eligible employees. Thoughtful has agreed to make annual payments to a designated trustee at the end of each year. Data relating to the plan follow:

Normal cost	$100,000
Past service cost on January 1, 1981	500,000
Funds held by trustee are expected to earn a 5% return	

In accordance with APB *Opinion No. 8*, what is the maximum provision for pension cost that Thoughtful can record for 1981?

(AICPA adapted)

E–17–2 The following terms are relevant to accounting for the cost of pension plans. Define or explain briefly each of the following:

- **a)** Normal cost.
- **b)** Past service cost.
- **c)** Prior service cost.
- **d)** Funded plan.
- **e)** Vested benefits.
- **f)** Actuarial gains and losses.
- **g)** Interest.

(AICPA adapted)

E–17–3 Liberty, Inc., a calendar-year corporation, adopted a company pension plan at the beginning of 1980. This plan is to be funded and is noncontributory. Liberty used an appropriate actuarial cost method to determine its normal annual pension cost for 1980 and 1981 as $15,000 and $16,000, respectively, which was paid in the same year.

Liberty's actuarially determined past service costs were funded on December 31, 1980, at an amount properly computed as $106,000. These past service costs are to be amortized at the maximum amount permitted by generally accepted accounting principles. The interest factor assumed by the actuary is 6%.

Required:
Prepare journal entries with supporting computations to record the funding of past service costs on December 31, 1980, and the pension expenses for the years 1980 and 1981.

(AICPA adapted)

E-17-4 The Never Last Corporation has proposed the following pension plan note for its financial statements for the year ended December 31, 1981.

Note 5: For many years the company has maintained a pension plan for certain of its employees. Before the current year, pension expense was recognized as payments were made to retire employees. There was no change in the plan in the current year. However, based upon an actuarial estimate, the company provided $64,000 for pensions to be paid in the future to current employees.

Required:
Evaluate the adequacy of the note.

(AICPA adapted)

E-17-5 Answer the following multiple choice questions.

a) When a pension plan is adopted, what should the past service benefit cost of employees be charged to?
   (1) Retained earnings.
   (2) Expense only as paid.
   (3) Expense in current and future periods.
   (4) Expense in the current period only.

b) If a company has a legal obligation for pension cost in excess of amounts paid and amounts accrued, the excess should be shown on the statement of financial position as
   (1) Both a liability and a deferred charge.
   (2) A liability only.
   (3) A deferred charge only.
   (4) Neither a liability nor a deferred charge, but the excess should be disclosed in a note to the financial statements.

c) If you follow the guidelines set by the APB, what is the minimum charge to expense permitted in accounting for pension plan expense?
   (1) Normal cost.
   (2) Normal cost plus a prescribed percentage of prior (or past) service cost.
   (3) Normal cost, plus interest on unfunded prior (or past) service cost, plus a prescribed percentage of any increase in prior service costs arising from amendments to the plan.
   (4) Normal cost, plus interest on unfunded prior (or past) service cost, plus a possible provision for vested benefits.

d) A pension fund actuarial gain or loss that is caused by a plant closing should
   (1) Be recognized immediately as a gain or loss.
   (2) Be spread over the current year and future years.
   (3) Be charged or credited to the current pension expense.
   (4) Be recognized as a prior period adjustment.

e) Which of the following actuarial cost methods is *not* an acceptable method for determining pension cost?
   (1) Unit credit.
   (2) Individual level premium.
   (3) Terminal funding.
   (4) Entry age normal.

f) Which of the following disclosures of pension plan information would *not* normally be required by the APB or FASB to be included in the financial statements?
   (1) The estimated pension expense for the period.
   (2) The amount paid from the pension fund to retirees during the period.

(3) A statement of the company's accounting and funding policies for the pension plan.

(4) The nature and effect of significant pension plan matters affecting comparability for all periods presented.

(AICPA adapted)

E–17–6 In examining the costs of pension plans, a CPA encounters certain terms. The elements of pension costs that the terms represent must be dealt with appropriately if generally accepted accounting principles are to be reflected in the financial statements of entities with pension plans.

Required:

1. Discuss the theoretical justification for accrual recognition of pension costs.
2. Discuss the relative objectivity of the measurement process of accrual versus the terminal funding (pay-as-you-go) method of accounting for annual pension costs.

(AICPA adapted)

E–17–7 Explain the following terms as they apply to accounting for pension plans:

a) Actuarial valuations.

b) Actuarial cost methods.

c) Vested benefits.

d) Funding.

(AICPA adapted)

E–17–8 Terri Corporation established a pension plan on January 1, 1981. Past service costs at January 1, 1981, were $165,000. Eight percent interest is the appropriate rate to use for the plan. The past service costs are being funded over 20 years. Normal costs for 1981 are $20,000.

Required:

Compute the minimum and maximum provisions for 1981.

E–17–9 Being a progressive firm, Joan Company established a pension plan on the day the company started operations. The pension plan provides that normal costs will be funded yearly.

Required:

What in general will be the yearly pension expense? In the case of Joan Company, how does the yearly pension expense relate to the minimum and maximum provisions?

E–17–10 Peter Corporation has an unfunded past service pension liability at January 1 of $85,000. During the current year the company made a payment of $55,000 to the pension fund ($20,000 of which is for current year normal cost). At the time of inception, past service costs were $890,000, and an 8% interest rate was set.

Required:

If Peter Corporation follows the practice of equal funding and amortization policies, prepare journal entries to record the pension transactions.

E–17–11 Difficult Corporation amended its pension plan at the beginning of its twentieth year of existence. The amendment provided prior service costs of $88,000 that are to be amortized and funded over 12 years. At the time of amendment a 5% interest rate is appropriate. Normal cost for the twentieth year was $68,000. Difficult had funded and amortized past service costs over 12 years.

Required:

1. Compute the minimum and maximum provisions for the year of amendment.
2. Prepare the journal entries for the twentieth year pension transactions.

E–17–12 Liss Company established a pension plan on January 1, 1981. At that time past service costs were $50,000, which Liss funded immediately. Liss has decided to amortize past service costs over three years.

Required:

Using a 5% interest rate and disregarding the maximum and minimum provisions of APB *Opinion No. 8*, prepare an amortization schedule for the past service costs.

E–17–13   Mike Company is considering the adoption of a pension plan for its employees. If Mike adopts the plan, past service costs will be $150,000. If an 8% interest rate is appropriate, what will be the yearly funding payment and amortization amount in the following cases:

   a)   Amortization and funding over 20 years.
   b)   Amortization over 20 years and funding over 30 years.
   c)   Funding over 25 years and amortization over 15 years.

E–17–14   In 1981 Judy Corporation had its first pension actuarial gain or loss. The gain amounted to $2,000 and reduced the cash payment to $50,000 for normal and past service in 1981. If actuarial gains and losses are to be spread over 10 years, and Judy currently has no pension accounts on the balance sheet, prepare the journal entry to record the gain for 1981.

E–17–15   Adam Corporation has had the following actuarial gains and (losses) for the years indicated:

1970	$2,000
1971	(500)
1972	3,000
1973	–0–
1974	800
1975	200
1976	–0–
1977	100
1978	(100)
1979	(100)
1980	(300)
1981	100

Required:
If Adam spreads gains and losses over 10 years and has no balance sheet recognition of pensions except for the gains and losses, prepare the journal entries for the yearly amortization for 1979, 1980, and 1981.

Problems

P–17–1   Norm Food Products established a pension plan on October 1, 1981, the first day of its fiscal year. The plan is noncontributory and provides for employee credit since the employee's date of employment. Past service costs are $150,000 at October 1, 1981. Norm is going to fund and amortize these costs over 20 years. The actuaries have established a 12% interest rate for the fund. Normal costs for the first year are $28,000.
Required:
1.   Prepare the journal entries for the first year.
2.   What are the appropriate pension balances that will be shown on the financial statements for the year ended September 30, 1982?

P–17–2   AHL has decided to establish a pension plan for all employees on July 1, 1981. AHL's fiscal year ends on June 30. The plan is noncontributory and gives employees credit for all past service with the company. The actuarially determined past service cost is $100,000 at July 1, 1981. AHL is going to fund the past service costs over 20 years and amortize these costs over 16 years. The actuaries determined that a 5% rate is appropriate.

Required:

1. If normal costs are $22,000 for the first year, prepare the necessary journal entries for the first year.

2. If normal costs are $30,000 for each year after the 15th year, and if no changes are made in the plan, prepare the necessary journal entries for the 16th and 21st years. (Assume that the pension liability balance at the beginning of the 16th year is $35,000.)

P–17–3 Smithfield Corporation established a pension plan for all nonhourly employees on January 1, 1981. (Hourly employees already were covered by a union pension plan.) The plan is noncontributory and gives employees credit either from their date of employment or from January 1, 1960. The actuarially determined past service cost is $80,000 at January 1, 1981. Smithfield is going to fund the past service costs over 16 years and amortize these costs over 20 years. The actuaries have determined that a 6% rate is appropriate. Normal costs are anticipated to be $20,000 for the first three years and $25,000 thereafter.

Required: (Assume that the actual normal costs are equal to the anticipated normal costs, and that no plan changes occur):

1. Prepare the journal entries for each of the first two years.

2. Prepare the journal entries for the 21st year.

P–17–4 AB Delta Company established a pension plan for all employees on January 1, 1981. The plan is noncontributory and gives employees credit since their date of initial employment. The actuarially determined past service cost is $65,000 at January 1, 1981. Delta has decided to fund and amortize the past service costs over 15 years and has determined a 5% interest rate to be appropriate. Normal costs that are fully funded are $10,000 for 1981 and $15,000 for 1982.

Required:

1. Prepare journal entries for each of the first two years.

2. If normal costs are $22,000 in the 16th year and if no plan changes occur, prepare journal entries for the 16th year.

P–17–5 On January 1, 1981, the Johnson & Jackson Company established a funded, noncontributory pension plan that gives employees credit for all past service to the company. At January 1, 1981, the past service cost is $1,255,000. This amount will be funded over 15 years. The consulting actuaries believe a 10% interest rate is appropriate. For 1981, normal cost is $85,000.

Required:

1. Compute the maximum and minimum pension expense for 1981.

2. Prepare journal entries to record the pension transactions for 1981 if the company uses
   a) The maximum amount.
   b) The minimum amount.

P–17–6 Casey & Lewis Printers, Inc. was organized in 1955 and established a formal pension plan on January 1, 1977, to provide retirement benefits for all employees. The plan is noncontributory and is funded through a trustee, the First National Bank, which invests all funds and pays all benefits as they become due. Vesting occurs when the employee retires at age 65. Original past service cost of $110,000 is being amortized over 15 years and funded over 10 years on a present value basis at 5%. The company also funds an amount equal to the current normal cost net of actuarial gains and losses. There have been no amendments to the plan since inception. The independent actuary's report appears below.

Required:

1. On the basis of requirements for accounting for the cost of pension plans, evaluate the treatment of actuarial gains and losses and the computation of pension cost for financial statement purposes. Ignore income tax considerations.

2. Independent of your answer to part 1., assume that the total amount to be funded is $32,663, the total pension cost for financial statement purposes is $29,015, and all amounts presented in Parts II, III, and IV of the actuary's report are correct. Write a footnote for

the financial statements of Casey & Lewis Printers, Inc. for the year ended June 30, 1981, if Casey & Lewis are not required to file reports under ERISA. How would your answer have differed if Casey & Lewis were required to file reports under ERISA?

(AICPA adapted)

CASEY & LEWIS PRINTERS, INC.
Basic Noncontributory Pension Plan
Actuarial Report as of June 30, 1981

I. *Current Year's Funding and Pension Cost*
Normal cost (before adjustment for actuarial gains) computed under the entry-age-normal method

Normal cost (before adjustment for actuarial gains) computed under the entry-age-normal method		$34,150
Actuarial gains:		
Investment gains (losses):		
Excess of expected dividend income over actual dividend income		(350)
Gain on sale of investments		4,050
Gains in actuarial assumptions for:		
Mortality		3,400
Employee turnover		5,050
Reduction in pension cost from closing of plant		8,000
Net actuarial gains		$20,150
Normal cost (funded currently)	$14,000	14,000
Past service costs:		
Funding	14,245	
Amortization		10,597
Total funded	$28,245	
Total pension cost for financial-statement purposes		$24,597

II. *Fund Assets*

Cash	$ 4,200
Dividends receivable	1,525
Investment in common stock, at cost (market value, $177,800)	$162,750
	$168,475

III. *Actuarial Liabilities*

Number of employees	46
Number of employees retired	0
Yearly earnings of employees	$598,000
Actuarial liability	$145,000

IV. *Actuarial Assumptions*

Interest	5%
Mortality	1951 group Annuity tables
Retirement	Age 65

P–17–7   Mar Corporation established a noncontributory pension plan the first day of the current fiscal year. During the year, Mar's payment to the plan was composed of the following: normal cost, $56,000; past service cost, $265,000; and actuarial loss on a plant closing, $16,000.

Required:

If the past service costs are funded and amortized over the same period (and if the $265,000 is within the maximum and minimum), prepare the journal entry to record the pension transactions.

P–17–8 Jackson Company adopted a noncontributory pension plan from the day the company started operations. In the plan's first year the normal cost was $65,000. Actuarial gains for the first year were $1,000. Jackson made a net contribution of $64,000 for the first year. Actuarial gains are being spread over 10 years.

Required:

Prepare the journal entry for pensions during the first year.

P–17–9 Dane Enterprises, which started operations in 1970, instituted a pension plan on January 1, 1975. The insurance company that is administering the pension plan has computed the present value of past service costs at $100,000 for the five years of operations through December 31, 1974. The pension plan provides for fully vested benefits when employees have completed 10 years of service. Therefore, there will be no vested benefits until December 31, 1979.

The insurance company proposed that Dane Enterprises fund the past service cost in equal installments over 15 years calculated by the present value method. If Dane used an interest rate of 5%, the annual payment for past service cost would be $9,634. The company's treasurer agreed to this payment schedule. In addition, the controller concluded that a 15-year period was a reasonable period for amortizing the past service costs for book purposes. Consequently, the past service costs also will be amortized at the annual rate of $9,634 for 15 years.

The normal cost for the pension fund is estimated to be $30,000 each year for the next four years. The annual payment to the insurance company, covering the current year's normal cost and the annual installment on the past service cost, is payable on December 31 of each year, which is the end of Dane Enterprises's fiscal year. The insurance company was paid $39,634 ($30,000 + 9,634) on December 31, 1975, to meet the company's pension obligations for 1975.

Required:

1. Calculate and label the components that comprise the maximum and minimum 1975 financial statement pension expense limits in accordance with generally accepted accounting principles for Dane Enterprises.

2. Assume Dane Enterprises will be unable to remit the full pension payment ($39,634) in 1976 and will only submit $30,000 (the normal cost) to the insurance company. If Dane Enterprises can recognize $39,634 as pension expense in 1976, show the entry required. If the company cannot recognize the $39,634 as pension expense in 1976, explain why not.

(CMA adapted)

P–17–10 Marx Corporation established a pension plan for its employees on January 1, 1981. Marx decided to amortize and fund the past service costs of $75,000 over two years using an 8% interest factor. Normal costs for 1981 and 1982 are $30,000 per year.

Required (disregard the maximum and minimum provisions of APB *Opinion No. 8*):

1. Prepare an amortization schedule for 1981 and 1982.

2. Prepare the appropriate pension journal entries for 1981 and 1982.

3. Determine the balance sheet and income statement pension account balances for each of the two years.

P–17–11 Morse Corporation established a pension plan for its employees on January 1, 1980. Morse decided to fund the past service costs of $110,000 over two years and to amortize them over three years using an 8% interest factor. Normal costs for 1980, 1981, and 1982 are $40,000 per year.

Required (disregard the maximum and minimum provisions of APB *Opinion No. 8*):

1. Prepare an amortization and funding schedule for 1980, 1981, and 1982.

2. Prepare the appropriate pension journal entries for 1980, 1981, and 1982.

3. Determine the balance sheet and income statement pension account balances for each of the three years.

P–17–12 Randall Corporation established a pension plan for its employees on January 1, 1980. Randall decided to fund the past service costs of $110,000 over three years and to amortize them over two years using an 8% interest factor. Normal costs for 1980, 1981, and 1982 are $40,000 per year.

Required (disregard the maximum and minimum provisions of APB *Opinion No. 8*):

1. Prepare an amortization and funding schedule for 1980, 1981, and 1982.

2. Prepare the appropriate pension journal entries for 1980, 1981, and 1982.

3. Determine the balance sheet and income statement pension account balances for each of the three years.

18

Accounting for Leases

Accounting in the News

Many companies enter into leasing arrangements for a variety of reasons. One of the major reasons, as shown below, is to take advantage of some benefits under the tax law.

> You would think that any tax deal that interests such big companies as IBM and General Electric would be thoroughly thought out. And ordinarily you would be right. But in their haste to get in under the Nov. 13 deadline for retroactive treatment on the new leasing deals permitted by the Reagan tax act, a lot of companies are rushing in before they have even had a chance to consider the impact on their books. It could be significant. . . .
>
> The leasing deals are based on the old proposition that them that has, gets. Companies with little or no income obviously have no use for tax credits or accelerated depreciation; they simply have no income to shelter. But such firms may have all sorts of tax credits and accelerated depreciation coming to them as they make capital investments in plant and equipment. So the Reagan tax act permits the unprofitable company to sell these credits to a profitable firm that can use them.
>
> Here's how that works: The well-off company buys the equipment from the less profitable company, takes the tax credits itself and then leases the equipment back. It's all done on paper—no equipment actually changes hands. The seller of the credits picks up a profit and the buyer picks up the tax benefits.
>
> Unfortunately, the accounting for these deals plays tricks with earnings.*

This chapter presents the proper accounting treatment for various types of lease contacts.

*Richard Greene, "Every Silver Lining Has a Cloud," *Forbes*, December 7, 1981, p. 152.

A **lease** represents a contractual agreement between a lessor and a lessee that provides the lessee the right to use the property subject to lease for a specified time period in return for designated cash payments to be made to the lessor over the term of the lease. Several financial and operating advantages to leasing exist, such as the following:

1. Securing the use of property without significant down payments.
2. Maintaining technologically current equipment, thereby avoiding, or at least reducing, the risk of obsolescence.
3. Obtaining a more flexible debt arrangement.
4. Incurring a lease obligation that often is not formalized in the financial statements; that is, the lease obligation under certain leases need be disclosed only in the financial statement footnotes.

Although this listing is by no means all-inclusive, these advantages are indicative of why leasing has become increasingly popular throughout the past two decades.

Because the nature of lease agreements is so complex, authoritative rule-making bodies in accounting have devoted a significant amount of literature to explaining how to account for and disclose leases in the financial statements. A glossary of terms appears at the end of this chapter that should be studied before attempting to understand the technical intricacies of lease accounting. The Appendix discusses a particular form of capital leases from the lessor's perspective: leveraged leases.

The Development of Authoritative Lease Accounting Literature

Before 1964 leases were not considered capitalizable in most cases, and basically the accounting treatment afforded lease agreements was to charge the payments to expense as accruable for the lessee and to recognize revenue as receivable for the lessor. Then, the Accounting Principles Board initiated the issuance of four lease accounting pronouncements that governed lease accounting until November, 1976. These four documents were as follows:

1. APB *Opinion No. 5*, "Reporting Leases in Financial Statements of Lessee"
2. APB *Opinion No. 7*, "Accounting for Leases in Financial Statements of Lessors"
3. APB *Opinion No. 27*, "Accounting for Lease Transactions by Manufacturer or Dealer Lessors"
4. APB *Opinion No. 31*, "Disclosure of Lease Commitments by Lessees"

Although these four documents were theoretically sound in general, there were at least two major problems with them. First, there existed a significant amount of what was termed "off balance sheet financing" available. **Off balance sheet financing** refers to the acquisition of assets without currently paying for them or recording a liability on the books. A lease is an example of off balance sheet financing. Lease commitments, for whatever duration and regardless of cancelability, in many cases were being disclosed only in the footnotes to financial statements (refer back to leasing advantage No. 4), but these lease commitments were just as real as some obligations being termed liabilities on the balance sheet. Second, inconsistencies in the four Opinions existed, primarily as related to classification. This latter problem has been labeled the "nonsymmetrical lease classification problem"—the criteria outlined in APB *Opinion No. 5* for what constitutes a capital lease for lessees were not the same as the capital lease criteria for lessors in APB *Opinion No. 7*. The problem that resulted from these nonsymmetrical classification criteria was that lessees could analyze a lease agreement and determine that an asset and related obligation should not be established, whereas lessors could analyze the same agreement and conclude that substantially all the risks and rights of ownership applicable to the property subject to lease transferred to the lessee. Thus, in this case the lessee would not establish the property as an asset, but the lessor would write off the property as if sold, and it would not be reflected in the financial statements of either party. Conversely, the lease agreement classification could result in both lessee and lessor reflecting the same asset on two separate balance sheets.

Because of these and other problems in classifying and accounting for leases, the Financial Accounting Standards Board issued *Statement No. 13*, "Accounting for Leases," in an attempt to codify lease accounting into one document.[1] The fundamental objective of *Statement No. 13* was to account for lease agreements as the acquisition of an asset and incurrence of a liability by the lessee and as a sale or financing by the lessor (a capital lease) if substantially all the benefits and risks incident to ownership of the property subject to lease transfer from the lessor to the lessee. All other leases should be accounted for as operating leases. However, implementing this fundamental notion has been difficult in practice both from a classification and an accounting perspective. As a result, *Statement No. 13* has been amended and interpreted thirteen times, so there now exists a total of 14 promulgated pronouncements that govern lease accounting. The remainder of this chapter is devoted to explaining the technical classification, accounting, and disclosure provisions currently in effect applicable to leases.

Lease Classification Criteria

Lessees should classify leases as either operating or capital in nature. Lessors should make the same distinction except that they should subclassify capital leases as sales-type, direct financing, or leveraged.

Statement No. 13 itemizes four criteria for lease classification, only one of which must be met before a *lessee* will capitalize an asset and obligation to reflect the substance of a lease agreement. All other leases would be operating leases. The last two criteria are not applicable if the beginning of the lease term falls within the last 25% of the *total estimated economic life* of the leased property. *Statement No. 13* itemizes two more criteria from the *lessor's* perspective that are to be utilized *in addition to* the criteria used by lessees in determining whether the lessor has a capital or operating lease. If at least one of the first four criteria is met, and if *both* of the second criteria are met, the lessor has a **capital lease** (either sales-type, direct-financing, or leveraged).

The four criteria applicable to both lessees and lessors are summarized as follows (refer to the Glossary for important definitions):

---

[1] "Accounting for Leases," *Statement of Financial Accounting Standards No. 13* (Stamford, Conn.: FASB, 1976).

1. The lease transfers ownership of the property to the lessee by the end of the lease term.
2. The lease contains a bargain purchase option.[2]
3. The lease term is equal to 75% or more of the estimated economic life of the leased property.
4. The present value of the minimum lease payments at the beginning of the lease term, excluding that portion of the payments representing executory costs such as insurance, maintenance, and taxes to be paid by the lessor, equals or exceeds 90% of the excess of the fair value of the leased property at the inception of the lease over any related investment tax credit retained and expected to be realized by the lessor. A lessor should compute the present value of the minimum lease payments using the interest rate implicit in the lease. A lessee should compute the present value of the minimum lease payments using the lessee's incremental borrowing rate unless (a) it is practicable for the lessee to learn the implicit rate computed by the lessor, *and* (b) the implicit rate computed by the lessor is less than the lessee's incremental borrowing rate. If both of these conditions are met, the lessee should use the rate of interest implicit in the lease.[3]

The additional lessor criteria are as follows:

1. Collectibility of the minimum lease payments is reasonably predictable.
2. No important uncertainties surround the amount of unreimbursable costs yet to be incurred by the lessor under the lease. Examples of such uncertainties might include commitments by the lessor to guarantee performance of the leased property in a manner more extensive than the typical product warranty or to protect the lessee effectively from obsolescence of the leased property. However, the necessity of estimating executory costs such as insurance, maintenance, and taxes to be paid by the lessor should not within itself constitute an important uncertainty.[4]

FASB *Statement No. 27* provides that a renewal or extension of an existing sales-type lease, or direct financing lease that otherwise qualifies as a sales-type lease, should be classified as a direct financing lease unless the renewal or extension occurs at or near the end of the original term specified in the existing lease. In that case the lease should be classified as a sales-type lease.[5] A renewal or extension that occurs *in the last few months* of an existing lease is considered to have occurred at or near the end of the existing lease term. Changes in estimates or circumstances should not give rise to lease reclassification for accounting purposes.

Both lessors and lessees should classify leases as capital or operating; however, from the lessor's perspective, capital leases may take one of three forms:

---

[2] A provision in the lease giving the lessee the option to buy the property for a price significantly below the expected fair market value of the property at the date the option is exercisable.

[3] Ibid., par. 7.

[4] Ibid., par. 8.

[5] "Classification of Renewals or Extensions of Existing Sales-Type or Direct Financing Leases," *Statement of Financial Accounting Standards No. 27* (Stamford, Conn.: FASB, 1979).

1. **A sales-type lease** gives rise to manufacturer or dealer profit (or loss). Operationally, this means that the fair value of the leased property at the inception of the lease is greater (or less) than the cost or carrying value of the property.
2. **A direct financing lease** is a capital lease agreement (other than a leveraged lease) that does not give rise to manufacturer or dealer profit (or loss). In such a case the fair value of the leased property at the inception of the lease equals the cost or carrying value of the property.
3. **A leveraged lease** is a three-party lease agreement involving a lessee, a lessor, and a long-term creditor. The financing provided by the long-term creditor is sufficient to give the lessor substantial "leverage" in the transaction and is a nonrecourse transaction as far as the general credit of the lessor is concerned. The lessor's net investment declines during the early years of the lease (maybe even to a negative amount) once the investment has been completed, and rises in subsequent years of the lease term. A leveraged lease meets all of the characteristics listed below, provided the lessor chooses to defer any applicable investment tax credit and to allocate it to income over the lease term. If the lease agreement meets the characteristics itemized below but the investment tax credit is not deferred and allocated to income over the lease term, the lease agreement should be classified and accounted for as a direct financing lease with the nonrecourse debt shown as a liability in the balance sheet. The following are the characteristics of a leveraged lease:
    (a) The lease agreement meets the criteria for classification as a direct financing lease (sales-type leases cannot be leveraged leases).
    (b) The lease involves a third-party, long-term creditor in addition to the lessee and lessor.
    (c) The financing provided by the long-term creditor is nonrecourse to the general credit of the lessor (although the creditor may have recourse to the property or related rentals) and is sufficient to provide the lessor with "substantial leverage" in the transaction.
    (d) The lessor's net investment in the leveraged lease declines during the early years once the investment has been completed and rises in later years of the lease, a pattern that may occur more than once.

See the Appendix of this chapter for a discussion of the accounting associated with leveraged leases.

Remember, a lease must meet only one of the first four criteria to constitute a capital lease—lessors then must apply the additional two criteria.

Lessee Accounting and Reporting

This section summarizes the general accounting and disclosure requirements for lessees related to both capital and operating leases. Special categorizations of leases (e.g., real estate leases, subleases, and sale-leasebacks) will be discussed later in this chapter.

Capital Leases

For leases classified as capital leases, an asset and an obligation should be recorded at the inception of the lease in the amount of the present value of the minimum lease payments to be made during the lease term. Executory costs, such as insurance, maintenance, and taxes, should be excluded from this computation and charged to expense as these costs become payable. The interest rate to be used by lessees in recording the asset and obligation should be the same interest rate used in applying the 90% lease classification criterion—that is, the lessee's incremental borrowing rate or the lessor's implicit rate.

In no case should the capitalized amount of a lease exceed the fair value of the property at the inception of the lease. If the present value of the minimum lease payments, as computed by the lessee, exceeds the lessee's estimate of the fair value of the property subject to lease, the leased asset should be recorded at fair value. For example assume that on January 1, 1978, Eagle Company (as lessor) entered into a noncancelable lease with Tide Company (as lessee) for a machine with a book value to Eagle of $6,000,000. Minimum lease payments in the lease agreement aggregated to $10,652,430, of which $7,200,000 represents the present value of the minimum lease payments and the fair value of the machine. The lease agreement expires on December 31, 1987. Payments of $1,065,243 are due each January 1 with the first payment due January 1, 1978. The lessee's incremental borrowing rate and the lessor's implicit rate both are 10%. Tide expects the machine to have a 10-year useful life and no salvage value, and the asset is to be depreciated on a straight-line basis.

Exhibit 18-1 represents a lease amortization schedule applicable to this lease, and Exhibit 18-2 provides the journal entries applicable to the lessee for this lease. Note that this lease is a capital lease since the present value of the minimum lease payments ($7,200,000) is at least equal to the fair value of the property (also $7,200,000) and the 75% criterion is met $\left(\dfrac{\text{10-year lease}}{\text{10-year useful life}} = 100\%, \text{which} \right.$ is more than 75% of the remaining life of the asset).

Capitalized assets and obligations should be segregated or identified separately in the balance sheet of the lessee or related footnotes. Lease obligations are subject to the same current/noncurrent classification status applicable to other liabilities. Also, the lease obligation should be amortized by determining the appropriate periodic interest to be recognized under the effective interest method as discussed in Chapter 15.

The amortization period of capitalized assets is dependent on criteria used to indicate capitalization of the lease. If the property subject to lease transfers title during the lease term, or if the lease agreement contains a bargain purchase option, there is a presumption that the lessee will have use of the property throughout its economic life. Therefore, such properties should be amortized over their remaining useful lives without being limited by the lease term. Conversely, if a leased asset were capitalized because of the 75% or 90% criterion, the asset should be amortized over the lease term. This conclusion results since the property subject to lease will revert back to the lessor at the end of the lease term. In the above example the asset did not transfer title, and no bargain purchase option existed, so the leased asset should be amortized over the lease term.

Operating Leases

In accounting for operating leases, lessees should not recognize either an asset or an obligation related to the leasing arrangement. Rather, lease (rent) expense should be recognized, normally on a straight-line basis, over the life of the lease.

Exhibit 18-1
Lessee's Amortization Schedule for Capital Lease

Payment	Annual Payment	Annual Interest Expense	Obligation Reduction	Present Value at Beginning of Year
Initial value				$7,200,000[a]
1	$1,065,243	–0–	$1,065,243	6,134,757[b]
2	1,065,243	$613,476[c]	451,767[d]	5,682,990[e]
3	1,065,243	568,299	496,944	5,186,046
4	1,065,243	518,605	546,638	4,639,408
5	1,065,243	463,941	601,302	4,038,106
6	1,065,243	403,811	661,432	3,376,674
7	1,065,243	337,667	727,576	2,649,098
8	1,065,243	264,910	800,333	1,848,765
9	1,065,243	184,877	880,336	968,399
10	1,065,243	96,844*	968,399	–0–

[a] $1,065,243 × 6.75902 = $7,200,000.
[b] $7,200,000 – $1,065,243 = $6,134,757.
[c] $6,134,757 × 10% = $613,476.
[d] $1,065,243 – $613,476 = $451,767.
[e] $6,134,757 – $451,767 = $5,682,990.
*Rounded

Although the FASB states a preference for recognizing lease rentals on a straight-line basis, another systematic and "rational" approach may be used if it results in recognizing expenses that are more indicative of the benefits received under the lease.

As an example of how to account for operating leases, assume that Salvage Leasing Company leased some heavy equipment to Maxwell Drilling Company under a five-year, noncancelable lease beginning on January 1, 1978. The lease agreement stipulates that a $15,000 payment is to be made each December 31, starting December 31, 1978. Salvage Leasing is responsible for any executory costs associated with the lease. The equipment subject to the lease has a remaining estimated useful life of 12 years, an estimated fair value of $120,000, and an acquisition cost to Salvage Leasing of $120,000. At the end of the lease term the equipment is estimated to have a fair value of $60,000. No bargain purchase or renewal clauses are included in the lease agreement. Both Salvage Leasing and Maxwell Drilling operate on a calendar year basis. Collectibility of the minimum rentals is reasonably assured to Salvage Leasing and, no significant uncertainties exist concerning unreimbursable costs yet to be incurred under this arrangement. The implicit rate of interest in this lease is 10%, which is also Maxwell Drilling Company's incremental borrowing rate.

Since there is no mention of a title transfer or a bargain purchase option in

---

Exhibit 18-2
Journal Entries for Capital Lease (Lessee)

YEAR 1

Jan. 1, 1978

Leased property under capital lease	7,200,000	
Obligation under capital lease		7,200,000

To record asset and obligation at inception of capital lease.

Obligation under capital lease	1,065,243	
Cash		1,065,243

To record first payment (in advance) under capital lease.

Dec. 31, 1978

Lease interest expense	613,476	
Interest payable		613,476

To record annual interest expense on leased asset. ($6,134,760 × 10% = $613,476)

Amortization of leased property	720,000	
Accumulated amortization— leased property		720,000

To record amortization expense on leased asset (straight-line). ($7,200,000 ÷ 10 years = $720,000 annual amortization)
NOTE: Amortize over the term of the lease since neither title transfered nor bargain purchase option existed.

YEAR 2

Jan. 1, 1979

Obligation under capital lease	451,767	
Interest payable	613,476	
Cash		1,065,243

To record second payment under capital lease.
($1,065,243 − $613,476 = $415,767)

Exhibit 18-2 (continued)
Journal Entries for Capital Lease (Lessee)

Dec. 31, 1979	Lease interest expense	568,299	
	Interest payable		568,299
	To record annual interest expense on leased asset. ($5,682,990 × 10% = $568,299)		
	Amortization of leased property	720,000	
	Accumulated amortization— leased property		720,000
	To record annual amortization of leased asset.		

this lease, Maxwell Drilling needs to apply the 75% and 90% criteria to determine whether a capital lease exists. In applying the 75% criterion, Maxwell divides the lease term (5 years) by the remaining useful life of the property from the inception of the lease (12 years) to result in 41.67%. Since this resulting number is less than 75%, the Maxwell Drilling Company needs to apply the 90% criterion. The present value of the minimum lease payments of $56,862 ($15,000 × 3.7908) is substantially less than 90% of the fair value of the property ($108,000), so the 90% criterion is not met. Since, from the lessee's perspective, none of these four tests is met, the lease agreement constitutes an operating lease. The journal entries to be made on Maxwell Drilling Company's books are summarized in Exhibit 18-3.

Lessor Accounting and Reporting

The lease accounting and disclosure requirements applicable to lessors depend on the type of lease that has been signed. Lessors should apply the classification criteria discussed previously to determine whether the lease is capital or operating in nature. With capital leases, the specific categorization—that is, sales-type, direct financing, or leveraged—also must be determined. The accounting and disclosure requirements for these leases are discussed below with the exception of leveraged leases, which are illustrated in the Appendix.

Capital Leases—Sales-Type

For sales-type leases the lessor should record as a receivable the minimum rentals during the lease term plus the unguaranteed residual value accruing to the lessor's benefit. The present value of the minimum rentals should be recorded as the sales price, while the cost or carrying value of the property (less the present value of any residual value plus any direct costs of negotiating and closing the lease) should be charged against income in the same period (see the discussion of

---

Exhibit 18-3
Journal Entries for Operating Lease (Lessee)

Jan. 1, 1978	No entry		
Dec. 31, 1978	Lease rental expense	15,000	
	Cash		15,000
	To record first lease payment.		
Dec. 31, 1979	Lease rental expense	15,000	
	Cash		15,000
	To record second lease payment.		
Dec. 31, 1980	Lease rental expense	15,000	
	Cash		15,000
	To record third lease payment.		
Dec. 31, 1981	Lease rental expense	15,000	
	Cash		15,000
	To record fourth lease payment.		
Dec. 31, 1982	Lease rental expense	15,000	
	Cash		15,000
	To record final lease payment.		

---

initial direct costs later in this chapter). The difference between the receivable and its present value should be recorded as unearned income. This unearned income should appear as a deduction from the receivable and should be amortized to income over the life of the lease to produce a constant rate of return.

For example, assume that J.T. Corporation manufactures heavy-duty drilling equipment that has an estimated economic life of 12 years. On January 1, 1978, J.T. Corporation entered into a 10-year lease with Dry Hole Company for water drills. The normal selling price for these drills is $364,547. The J.T. Corporation incurs $250,000 of cost to manufacture the drills. The company's history of collecting lease payments has been very good, and no important uncertainties exist concerning the amount of unreimbursable costs yet to be incurred by J.T. Corporation. Dry Hole Company will pay annual rentals of $50,000 at the beginning of each year and will pay all executory costs. The unguaranteed residual value at the end of the lease term is estimated to be $35,000. J.T. Corporation's implicit interest rate is 9%.

This lease is a sales-type lease for J.T. Corporation. It is a capital lease because both the 75% and the 90% criteria are met (remember, only one of the tests must be met):

1. $\dfrac{\text{Lease term} = 10 \text{ years}}{\text{Useful life} = 12 \text{ years}} = 83\frac{1}{3}\%$, which is greater than the required 75%.

2. Present value of minimum lease payments = ($50,000 × 6.99525) = $349,763. 90% of fair value $364,547 = $328,092. Since $349,763 is greater than $328,092, the 90% criterion is met.

The required criteria applicable to rent collectibility and unreimbursable costs are met also. So the lease is a sales-type lease to J.T. Corporation. Exhibit 18-4 presents a lease amortization schedule applicable to this lease, and Exhibit 18-5 illustrates the journal entries on J.T. Corporation's books to record this transaction.

Capital Leases—Direct Financing Type

For direct financing leases the lessor should record as a receivable the minimum rentals during the lease term plus any unguaranteed residual value accruing to the lessor. Any difference between this receivable and the cost or carrying amount of the property under lease should be recorded as unearned income and amortized to income over the life of the lease to produce a constant rate of return.

Exhibit 18-4
Amortization Schedule for Sales-Type Lease (Lessor)

Payment	Annual Lease Payment	Interest Revenue (9%)	Reduction (Increase) of Net Asset	Present Value of Asset at End of Year
Initial value				$364,547[a]
1	$50,000	–0–	$50,000	314,547[b]
2	50,000	$28,309[c]	21,691[d]	292,856[e]
3	50,000	26,357	23,643	269,213
4	50,000	24,229	25,771	243,442
5	50,000	21,910	28,090	215,352
6	50,000	19,382	30,618	184,734
7	50,000	16,626	33,374	151,360
8	50,000	13,622	36,378	114,982
9	50,000	10,348	39,652	75,330
10	40,000	6,780	43,220	32,110
End of lease term	–0–	2,890	(2,890)	35,000

[a] ($50,000 × 6.99525) + ($35,000 × 0.42241) = $364,547.
[b] $364,547 − $50,000 = $314,547.
[c] $314,547 × 9% = $28,309.
[d] $50,000 − $28,309 = $21,691.
[e] $314,547 − $21,691 = $292,856.

Exhibit 18-5
Journal Entries for Sales-Type Lease (Lessor)

YEAR 1

Jan. 1, 1978	Minimum lease payments receivable	535,000	
	Cost of goods sold	235,216	
	Sales		349,763
	Inventory		250,000
	Unearned interest		170,453

To record sales-type lease at
date of inception.
Sales is the present value of the
MLP ($50,000 × 6.99525).
Cost of goods sold is the
inventory cost less the present
value of the unguaranteed residual
[$250,000 − ($35,000 × 0.42241)].

	Cash	50,000	
	Minimum lease payments		
	receivable		50,000

To record first lease payment
received (in advance).

Dec. 31, 1978	Unearned interest	28,309	
	Interest revenue from		
	capital lease		28,309

To record accrued interest
revenue from lease at year-end.

YEAR 2

Jan. 1, 1979	Cash	50,000	
	Minimum lease payments		
	receivable		50,000

To record receipt of lease
payment.

Dec. 31, 1979	Unearned interest	26,357	
	Interest revenue from		
	capital lease		26,357

To record accrued interest
revenue from July 15 to
year-end.

For example, assume that J.T. Corporation enters into a lease similar to that in the previous example for sales-type leases. However, in this case the cost to manufacture the drills is $364,547, which equals the fair value of the leased asset. All other facts are the same as in the previous example.

Since the 75% criterion is met and the rent collectibility and unreimbursable costs tests are satisfied, this lease is a capital lease. Also, since the present value of the minimum lease payments equals the cost or carrying amount of the equipment, this lease would constitute a direct financing lease to J.T. Corporation. Illustrative journal entries to be made by J.T. Corporation are presented in Exhibit 18-6.

Exhibit 18-6
Journal Entries for Direct Financing Lease (Lessor)

YEAR 1

Jan. 1, 1978

Minimum lease payment receivable		535,000	
	Equipment		364,547
	Unearned interest		170,453
To record direct financing lease at date of inception.			

Cash		50,000	
	Minimum lease payments receivable		50,000
To record first payment received on direct financing lease.			

Dec. 31, 1978

Unearned interest		28,309	
	Interest revenue from capital lease		28,309
To record accrued interest revenue at year-end. ($364,547 − $50,000) × 9% = $28,309			

YEAR 2

Jan. 1, 1979

Cash		50,000	
	Minimum lease payments receivable		50,000
To record receipt of second lease payment.			

Dec. 31, 1979

Unearned interest		26,357	
	Interest revenue from capital lease		26,357
To record accrued interest revenue for the year.			

Exhibit 18-7
Journal Entries for Operating Lease (Lessor)

YEAR 1			
Jan. 1, 1978	No entry at date of lease agreement		
Dec. 31, 1978	Depreciation expense	10,000	
	Accumulated depreciation		10,000
	To record annual depreciation expense on leased asset. $120,000 ÷ 12 years = $10,000 annual straight-line depreciation.		
	Cash	15,000	
	Rental revenue		15,000
	To record receipt of first lease payment.		
YEAR 2			
Dec. 31, 1979	Depreciation expense	10,000	
	Accumulated depreciation		10,000
	To record annual depreciation expense on leased asset.		
	Cash	15,000	
	Rental revenue		15,000
	To record receipt of second lease payment.		

Operating Leases

For operating leases the cost or carrying amount of the property under lease should be included in the property, plant, and equipment section of the lessor's balance sheet and should be depreciated or amortized in the normal manner. Rental receipts should be reported as income over the lease term on a straight-line basis unless another "systematic and rational" basis is more indicative of the leased property's diminishing value.

Data from the operating lease example for lessees presented earlier in the chapter will be used for the lessors' journal entries illustrated in Exhibit 18-7.

Accounting for Initial Direct Costs

Initial direct costs (the Glossary) are applicable only to lessors and represent those costs that are associated directly with negotiating and consummating *completed* leasing transactions; for example, commissions and costs of preparing documents. The central question concerning these costs relates to how they should be matched with corresponding lease revenues.

For sales-type leases this problem is minimal since manufacturer or dealer profit will offset initial direct costs and thus will avoid any undue penalization of earnings. The FASB concluded that to the extent that initial direct costs exist relative to a sales-type lease, they should be expensed as incurred.

A complicating problem exists for direct financing leases in that no lease revenue generally is recognized by the lessor in the period in which initial direct costs are incurred. Therefore, while the FASB requires immediate expensing of initial direct costs, lessors should recognize a portion of the unearned revenue (interest) immediately in an amount equal to initial direct costs incurred. For example, if you assume that a lessor incurs $4,500 of properly identified initial direct costs applicable to a direct financing lease, the journal entries to record those costs with a corresponding revenue offset would be as follows:

1.	Initial direct costs	4,500	
	Cash (payable)		4,500
	To recognize the initial direct costs.		
2.	Unearned lease revenue	4,500	
	Lease revenue		4,500
	To offset the initial direct costs with lease revenue.		

Since this second entry reduces the amount of interest income to be recognized over the life of the lease by a lessor, a new effective interest rate must be determined. This new rate then would be used to recognize interest throughout the lease term under the effective interest method.

For operating leases, lessors should defer recognition of initial direct costs and should allocate the costs over the lease term to be matched against rental revenue. The reason for this is that no manufacturer or dealer profit is recognized on operating leases, and there is no unearned revenue to be brought back to offset initial direct costs. Therefore, to properly match revenues and expenses applicable to operating leases, you should defer initial direct costs and allocate them over the lease term.

Accounting for Subleases

FASB *Statement No. 13* includes a discussion of accounting and reporting for subleases and similar transactions.[6] The following types of leasing transactions represent subleases:

[6]"Accounting for Leases," par. 35–40.

1. The property subject to lease is re-leased by the original lessee, and the lease agreement between the original lessor and the original lessee remains in effect.
2. A new lease is substituted under the original lease agreement. The ultimate lessee becomes the primary obligor under the agreement, and the original lessee may or may not be secondarily liable.
3. A new lessee is substituted through a new agreement, and the original lease agreement is canceled.

Accounting by the Original Lessor

In many sublease arrangements the original lessor is unaffected by the agreement between the sublessor and the ultimate lessee. When the sublessor enters into a sublease, or if the original lease agreement is sold or transferred by the original lessee to a third party, the original lessor should not alter his or her accounting for the original lease.

However, if the original lessee is replaced by a new agreement with a new lessee, the original lessor should account for the termination of the original lease and should classify and account for the new lease as a separate agreement. The lease termination should be accounted for by removing the net investment in the lease from the accounts; recording the leased asset at the lower of its original cost, present fair value, or present carrying amount; and charging the net adjustment to income of the period.

Accounting by the Original Lessee (Sublessor)

The major accounting and reporting problems of subleases are experienced by the original lessee, who must address both lessee and lessor accounting issues. The decision making processes to be followed by the original lessee are discussed next.

When a new lease agreement is constructed such that the original lessee is no longer the primary obligor under the original lease, accounting for the termination of the original lease depends on its classification. If the original lease were a capital lease, the asset and obligation related to that lease should be negated, and any gain or loss should be recognized immediately in income. If the original lessee is secondarily liable under the new agreement, the loss contingency should be treated in accordance with FASB *Statement No. 5*, "Accounting for Contingencies."[7] Any consideration paid or received upon termination of the original lease should be included in the determination of gain or loss to be recognized. If the original lease were an operating lease and if the original lessee is secondarily liable under the new lease, the loss contingency should again be treated in accordance with *Statement No. 5*.

When a new lease is agreed upon such that the original lessee still has the primary obligation under the original lease, original lessee accounting and report-

---

[7]"Accounting for Contingencies," *Statement of Financial Accounting Standards No. 5* (Stamford, Conn.: FASB, 1975).

ing once again is dependent on how the original lease was classified.[8] If the original lease contained a transfer of title or a bargain purchase option clause, the original lessee should classify the sublease agreement based upon all the criteria applicable to lessors in *Statement No. 13*. The original lessee as sublessor now must also meet the lessor predictability criteria in *Statement No. 13* in addition to the lessee criteria initially applied to determine classification of the original lease. If the new lease meets the capitalization criteria for lessors, the sublessor should classify the new lease as a sales-type or direct financing lease contingent on whether any manufacturer or dealer profit is evident. The unamortized balance of the leased asset under the original lease should be treated as the cost of property subject to the sublease. If the sublease does not qualify as a capital lease to the sublessor, the new lease should be considered an operating lease. In either case, the sublessor should continue to account for the obligation under the original lease as if the sublease had not transpired.

If the original lease met either the 75% or the 90% criterion but did not contain a transfer of title or a bargain purchase option, the sublessor, with one exception, should classify the new lease in accordance with the 75% criterion and lessor predictability criteria only. If these criteria are met, the sublease should be classified as a direct financing lease. This requirement precludes the use of the 90% criterion in classifying a sublease of this nature and also seemingly precludes the recognition of any manufacturer or dealer profit. In any event, the unamortized cost of the leased property to the sublessor should be treated as the cost of property subject to the sublease. If the sublease does not meet the capitalization requirements imposed for subleases, the new lease should be accounted for as an operating lease. In the case of either a capital lease or an operating lease, the sublessor should continue to account for the obligation under the original lease as before.

The exception to this general rule arises when the timing and other circumstances related to the sublease indicate that the new lease was intended as an integral part of an overall lease arrangement in which the sublessor serves only as an intermediary. For these leasing transactions, the sublease should be classified according to the criteria relating to the 75%, 90%, and lessor predictability criteria. When you apply the 90% criterion, the fair value of the leased property should be the fair value of the property to the original lessor at the inception of the original lease.

If the original lease were considered an operating lease, the sublessor should account for it and the sublease as an operating lease. In essense, the FASB precludes the sublessor from transferring more property rights than were indicated in the original lease.

Real Estate Leases

Real estate leases may involve properties such as land, buildings, parts of buildings, and equipment included in a real estate lease package.

---

[8] FASB *Interpretation No. 27* (November, 1978) concludes that paragraph 39 of *Statement No. 13* does not prohibit recognition of a loss by an original lessee who disposes of leased property or who mitigates the cost of an existing lease commitment by subleasing the property.

Leases Involving Land Only

If a lease agreement is applicable to land only, the real estate lessee should consider the lease a capital lease only if the lease transfers title to the lessee during the lease term or if the lease agreement contains a bargain purchase option (the 75% and 90% criteria are not applicable to land leases from either the lessee's or lessor's perspective). If the lease contains either of these provisions, the real estate lessee should capitalize an asset and related obligation in the amount of the present value of the minimum lease payments to be made during the lease term. If the lease agreement contains neither a title transfer nor a bargain purchase option, the lessee accounts for the transaction as an operating lease, and therefore charges rental payments against income as they are incurred.

Lessors should apply the same classification criteria to land lease agreements that lessees do, but before a lessor concludes that a lease agreement is a capital lease, the two additional lessor predictability criteria also must be met. Under capital leases related to land, the lessor should write off the land and substitute a receivable in the amount of the present value of the minimum lease payments. Land operating leases do not necessitate the write-off of property and the substitution of a receivable. Instead, rental payments should be recognized as revenue when earned.

Leases Involving Land and Building

Land and building agreements that contain title transfer or bargain purchase option provisions must be accounted for by the lessee as capital leases. The land and building elements of the lease should be accounted for separately based on their relative fair values at the inception of the lease. Because the lessee presumes ownership of both the land and the building by the end of the lease term, the properties must be segregated so that the building may be depreciated and the land may be maintained at undepreciated cost. The building should be depreciated over its estimated economic life without regard to the length of the lease term.

If the lease agreement contains neither a title transfer nor a bargain purchase option provision, the parties involved must assess the relative significance of the land element to the total value of the lease package. The FASB has defined the materiality threshold in these situations to be 25%. When the fair value of the land is less than 25% of the aggregate fair value of the leased properties, the land element is presumed immaterial. Conversely, if the land element comprises 25% or more of the aggregate fair value of the leased properties, the land is presumed material. The FASB utilizes this materiality standard in operationalizing the requirements of *Statement No. 13*.

When the land portion of the lease is deemed immaterial and the lease term is 75% or more of the estimated economic life of the building, or the present value of the minimum lease payments equals or exceeds 90% of the excess fair value of the leased property over any investment tax credit retained and expected to be realized by the lessor, the lease agreement is a capital lease and should be accounted for as a single lease unit. In these cases the lessee will depreciate the cost of the land as well as the cost of the building. Although this approach lacks theoretical merit, it may be defended on the grounds that the land element in the lease package is deemed immaterial. The cost of these properties should be amortized over the lease term since the overall estimated life of the property is not relevant to a lessee who does not gain ultimate title to the leased properties.

In land and building agreements in which the land portion is considered material, the lessee should consider the land and building separately when applying the 75% and 90% criteria, and the land element always should be considered an operating lease. If the building element meets either of these capitalization criteria, the present value of the minimum lease payments associated with the building should be recorded as the initial value of the building to be depreciated over the lease term by the lessee. Otherwise, both the land and building constitute operating leases to the lessee. The following example illustrates how lessees and lessors classify and account for real estate leases involving buildings.

On January 1, 1980, Lessor Corp. entered into a noncancelable lease with Lessee Corp. for land and a building for a term of 10 years. Lease payments of $40,000 are to be paid at the end of each year. There is no transfer of title or bargain purchase option at the end of the lease term. Both Lessor's implicit interest rate and Lessee's incremental borrowing rate are 12%. The land has a cost and fair value of $26,000. Lessor's undepreciated cost of the building is $100,000, and its fair value is $200,000 at the date of the lease agreement. Lessor is certain that all future lease payments will be received from Lessee. The building has an estimated remaining economic life of 13 years.

Since the fair value of the land is less than 25% of the aggregate fair value of the leased property, Lessee should treat both land and building as a single unit ($26,000 ÷ $226,000 = 11.5%). The lease term is 75% or more of the life of the building (10 years ÷ 13 years = 76.9%); thus, Lessee will classify the lease as a capital lease. The 90% criterion also is met since the present value of the minimum lease payments is $226,000, which is 100% of the fair value of the leased assets. This allows the lessee to depreciate the cost of the land as well as the building over the lease term because the land element is considered immaterial per *SFAS No. 13*.

Lessee's journal entries would be as follows:

Jan. 1, 1980	Leased property under capital lease	226,000	
	Obligation under capital lease		226,000
	To record asset and obligation at inception of capital lease. The asset should be recorded at the present value of the minimum lease payments.		
Dec. 31, 1980	Obligation under capital lease	12,880	
	Lease interest expense ($226,000 × 12%)	27,120	
	Cash		40,000
	To record first lease payment and interest expense for the year.		

Amortization of leased property	22,600	
Accumulated amortization— leased property		22,600

To record amortization of
cost of leased property.
$226,000 ÷ 10 years = $22,600
annual amortization using
straight-line

In addition to meeting the 75% and 90% criteria, Lessor also has met the two predictability tests. Thus, Lessor also accounts for the lease as a capital lease. The land and the building will be treated as a single unit since the same 25% materiality threshold also applies to the lessor. Further breakdown of the capital lease must be made to either a sales-type or direct financing lease. Since the fair value of the leased property ($226,000) is greater than the carrying value ($126,000), there is a dealer profit. Thus, Lessor will classify the lease as a sales-type lease and will credit the $100,000 dealer profit into income in the current period. The remaining $174,000 unearned income will be amortized over the lease term.

Lessor's journal entries are as follows:

Jan. 1, 1980	Minimum lease payments receivable	400,000	
	Unearned income		174,000
	Land		26,000
	Building		100,000
	Gain on sale of assets		100,000
	To record capital lease at date of inception and remove assets from Lessor's books.		
Dec. 31, 1980	Cash	40,000	
	Unearned income ($226,000 × 12%)		27,120
	Minimum lease payments receivable		12,880
	To record first lease payment received.		

Leases Involving Equipment and Real Estate

When a lease agreement involves both real estate and equipment or machinery, the lessee and the lessor should consider the equipment element in the lease package separately. If any one of the lessee capitalization criteria is met, the lessee should consider the equipment portion of the lease package to be a capital lease regardless of whether the remaining properties meet the criteria. Similarly, the lessor should consider the equipment element a capital lease if any one of the four capitalization criteria is met and if the lessor predictability criteria are met. All other equipment leases are operating leases. The FASB has concluded that the inclusion of equipment in a real estate lease package should not alter the accounting process specified for real estate transactions. Therefore, non-real estate properties are considered as if a separate lease document specified the agreements between the lessee and the lessor related to the equipment.

Leases Involving Only Part of a Building

It is common to find lease agreements covering only part of a large facility, such as shopping mall locations. From the lessee's perspective, if the fair value of the leased space is objectively determinable, the classification and accounting provisions applicable to land and building leases should be followed. FASB *Interpretation No. 24*, "Leases Involving Only Part of a Building," specifies that for purposes of determining the fair market value of part of a building, reasonable estimates based upon objective independent appraisals or estimated replacement cost information may be utilized.[9] *Interpretation No. 24* will allow more lease agreements to be considered capital leases since the 90% criterion should be met more often. However, if the fair value of the leased property is not objectively determinable, but the lease agreement meets the 75% criterion, the lessee should capitalize the lease agreement using the estimated economic life of the building in which the leased property is located. If neither the 90% nor the 75% criterion is met, the lease agreement should be considered an operating lease.

From the perspective of the lessor, both the cost and the fair value of the leased property must be objectively determinable before the land and building lease provisions are applicable since both of these amounts must be used in lessor classification. *Interpretation No. 24* is equally applicable to lessors in determining fair value. If the cost or fair value of the leased property is not objectively determinable, the lease agreement should be considered an operating lease.

Profit Recognition of Sales-Type Leases of Real Estate

Statement No. 13 provides "predictability" criteria that require lessors to assess both the collectibility of lease receivables and the predictability of future costs before classifying a lease as a sales-type lease. However, *Statement No. 13* provides little operational guidance in determining whether a lease receivable is, in fact, collectible. FASB *Statement No. 26*, "Profit Recognition on Sales-Type Leases of Real Estate," provides that unless a sales-type lease involving real estate meets the requirements of the AICPA accounting guide entitled *Accounting for Profit Recognition on Sales of Real Estate* for full and immediate recognition of profit, the lease should be accounted for as an operating lease.[10] The

---

[9] "Leases Involving Only Part of a Building," *FASB Interpretation No. 24* (Stamford, Conn.: FASB, 1978).

[10] "Profit Recognition on Sales-Type Leases of Real Estate," *Statement of Financial Accounting Standards No. 26* (Stamford, Conn.: FASB, 1979).

provisions of this guide may be summarized as follows:

1. Is the real estate lease closed? If no, *Statement No. 26* does not apply; if yes, go to Step 2.
2. Is the seller's continuing involvement with the property indicative of retained ownership risks? If yes, lease is an operating lease; if no, go to Step 3.
3. Is the buyer's down payment adequate? If no, lease is an operating lease; if yes, go to Step 4.
4. Is the composition of the down payment cash or properly supported notes? If no, lease is an operating lease; if yes, go to Step 5.
5. Is receivable collectibility highly uncertain? If yes, lease is an operating lease; if no, go to Step 6.
6. Are the buyer's continuing investments adequate? If no, lease is an operating lease; if yes, rent collectibility criterion is met.

Statement No. 26 does not modify the accounting for losses on sales-type leases of real estate. You should consult the accounting guide for an in-depth analysis of these profit recognition issues.

Accounting for Sales with Leasebacks

A **sale with leaseback** involves the sale of the property by the owner and lease of the property by the purchaser back to the seller. *Statement No. 13* generally requires the treatment of a sale-leaseback as a single financing transaction in which any profit or loss on the sale is deferred and amortized by the seller-lessee. However, operationalizing this provision when the leaseback covers only a relatively small part of the property sold or when the leaseback is only for a short period of time has proven difficult. In some cases the profit on the sale might exceed the total rentals under the leaseback, resulting in a negative rental if the provisions of *Statement No. 13* are followed.

The technical provisions of FASB *Statement No. 28* may be summarized in the following sequence:

1. Is the sale-leaseback transaction finalized? If no, *Statement No. 28* does not apply; if yes, go to Step 2.
2. Is the fair value of the property subject to leaseback less than the carrying value? If yes, recognize loss to the extent of the excess carrying value over the fair value and go to Step 3; if no, go to Step 3.
3. Does the seller/lessee retain only a "minor portion" of the use of the property subject to lease ("minor portion" should be ascertained using the 90% criterion in *Statement No. 13*)? If yes, go to Step 4; if no, go to Step 7.
4. Are lease payments reasonable? If yes, go to Step 6; if no, go to Step 5.
5. Adjust rentals to a reasonable amount by deferring or accruing (and amortizing) rental payments and adjusting profit or loss. Go to Step 6.
6. Recognize profit or loss on sale.
7. Does the seller/lessee retain "substantially all" of the use of the property subject to lease ("substantially all" should be ascertained by the 90% criterion in *Statement No. 13*)? If yes, go to Step 8; if no, go to Step 10.

8. Defer and amortize profit or loss. Go to Step 9.
9. Is the leaseback classified as a capital lease? If yes, amortize any profit or loss in proportion to amortization of the leased asset; if no (i.e., operating lease), amortize any profit or loss in proportion to the rental expense.
10. Seller/lessee retains more than a minor but less than substantially all of the use of the property subject to lease. Go to Step 11.
11. Is there "excess" profit realized ("excess" profit is profit on sale of the property in excess of (a) the present value of the minimum lease payments if the lease is an operating lease or (b) the recorded amount of the leased asset if the lease is a capital lease)? If yes, go to Step 12; if no, go to Step 13.
12. Recognize excess profit immediately. Go to Step 13.
13. Defer nonexcess profit and amortize it in relation to amortization of the leased asset if lease is a capital lease or in proportion to rental expense if lease is an operating lease.[11]

The following example illustrates a sale-leaseback in which the "more than minor but less than substantially all" criterion is applicable. On January 1, 1980, XX Corp. sold equipment to ZZ Corp. for $550,000 and immediately leased back the equipment for a ten-year term. The equipment had a cost to XX Corp. of $250,000 with a remaining estimated life of 12 years. There is no bargain purchase option or title transfer in the lease agreement. XX Corp. uses straight-line depreciation. The equipment has a fair value of $550,000, and the present value of the minimum lease payments is $280,000.

Step 1. Once the sale-leaseback agreement is finalized, compare the present value of the minimum lease payments to the fair value of the leased equipment.

$$\frac{\text{Present value of minimum lease payments}}{\text{Fair value of property}} = \frac{\$280,000}{\$550,000} = 51\%$$

Since the seller/lessee leased back 51% of the equipment, the purchaser/lessor is deemed to have surrendered "more than a minor portion but less than substantially all" of the use of the equipment.

Step 2. The lease now should be classified as either a capital lease or an operating lease. Since the lease term is 75% or more of the estimated life of the leased equipment (10 years ÷ 12 years = 83.3%), the seller/lessee has a capital lease.

Step 3. Determine the amount of profit to be realized and recognized.

Sales price	$550,000
Book value of equipment	250,000
Profit realized on sale	$300,000

Since only "excess" profit is recognized on a "more than minor but less than substantially all" sales-leaseback, the remaining profit is deferred and amortized over the lease term.

[11]"Accounting for Sales with Leasebacks," *Statement of Financial Accounting Standards No. 28* (Stamford, Conn.: FASB, 1979).

Profit realized on sale	$300,000
Recorded amount of the leased asset	280,000
Excess profit recognized	$ 20,000

Thus, only the excess profit of $20,000 will be recognized, while the remaining $280,000 realized profit will be deferred and amortized.

The journal entries for XX Corp. are presented in Exhibit 18-8.

Exhibit 18-8
Journal Entries for Seller/Lessee (XX Corp.)

Jan. 1, 1980	Cash	550,000	
	Equipment		250,000
	Profit on sale		20,000
	Deferred profit		280,000
	To record sale of equipment.		
	Equipment under capital lease	280,000	
	Obligation under capital lease		280,000
	To record leaseback of equipment.		
Dec. 31, 1980	Amortization expense	28,000	
	Accumulated amortization— leased equipment		28,000
	To record amortization of the cost of leased equipment. ($280,000 ÷ 10 years = $28,000) NOTE: Amortize cost over the lease term (not the estimated life of equipment) using straight-line amortization.		
	Deferred profit	28,000	
	Profit on sale		28,000
	To record amortization of deferred profit. ($280,000 ÷ 10 years = $28,000) NOTE: Deferred profit is recognized in the same manner as amortization of the leased equipment.		

Financial Statement Disclosures

Financial statement disclosure requirements concerning leases can be broken down into the following areas:

Lessee:
1. Capital leases
2. Operating leases
Lessor:
1. Capital leases
   (a) Sales-type
   (b) Direct financing
2. Operating leases

The disclosure requirements for each of the above are presented below.
   LESSEE
   Capital leases
   For leases capitalized per *Statement No. 13* as amended, lessees should make, at a minimum, the following disclosures:

1. The gross amount of the assets recorded as of the date of each balance sheet presented, in the aggregate and by major classes (by nature or function).
2. Minimum future payments required as of the date of the latest balance sheet presented, in the aggregate and for each of the five succeeding fiscal years (reduced by executory costs, which are expensed as incurred).
3. The total of minimum sublease rentals to be received in the future under noncancelable subleases as of the date of the latest balance sheet presented.
4. Total contingent rentals actually incurred during each period for which an income statement is presented. Contingent rentals are not included in minimum lease payments, but rather are expensed as incurred (see Glossary definition from FASB *Statement No. 29*).
5. A general description of the leasing arrangements, including the basis on which contingent rentals are determined, the existence and terms of renewal or purchase options and escalation clauses, and the restrictions imposed by the lease agreements.

Operating leases
   For operating leases, lessees should make the following financial statement disclosures:

1. For leases with terms in excess of one year—the minimum future payments required as of the date of the latest balance sheet, in the aggregate and for each of the five succeeding fiscal years.
2. For leases with terms in excess of one year—the total minimum rentals to be received in the future under noncancelable subleases as of the latest balance sheet date.
3. For all leases—rental expense in each period for which an income statement is presented, with separate disclosure of minimum rentals, contingent rentals, and sublease rentals.

4. For all leases—a general description of the leasing arrangements, including the basis on which contingent rentals are determined, the existence and terms of renewal or purchase options and escalation clauses, and the restrictions imposed by the lease agreements.

An example of a financial statement disclosure for lessee capital and operating leases appears in Exhibit 18-9. The disclosures were taken from a recent annual report of Mobil Oil Corporation.

LESSOR

Capital leases—sales-type

The following disclosures are required for sales-type leases:

1. Minimum rents receivable as of the date of each balance sheet presented, with separate deductions from the total for amounts representing executory costs that are included in the minimum rentals and the accumulated allowance of uncollectible rentals.
2. Unguaranteed residual values.
3. Unearned income.
4. Future minimum lease payments to be received for each of the five succeeding fiscal years.
5. Contingent rentals included in income.
6. A general description of the leasing arrangements.

Capital leases—direct financing type

In addition to the requirements for sales-type leases, the lessor also must disclose any amounts of unearned income included in income to offset the initial direct costs charged against income for each period in which an income statement is presented.

Operating leases

For operating leases, the lessor should make the following financial statement disclosures:

1. As of the latest balance sheet date, the cost of the property held for leasing, by major category of property, less any related accumulated depreciation.
2. Minimum future rentals on noncancelable leases as of the latest balance sheet presented, in the aggregate and for each of the five succeeding fiscal years.
3. Total contingent rentals included in income for each period in which an income statement is presented.
4. A general description of the leasing arrangements.

A sample disclosure of the lessor's operating lease appears in Exhibit 18-10. This disclosure appeared in the 1980 annual report of Safeco Corporation.

Exhibit 18-9
MOBIL OIL CORPORATION
Lessee Lease Disclosures

Leases

Mobil leases real estate, service stations, tankers, and other equipment through noncancelable capital and operating leases.

Net rent expense charged to earnings was $501 million in 1980, $408 million in 1979, and $369 million in 1978, after deducting rentals from subleases of $60 million in 1980, $50 million in 1979, and $45 million in 1978. Contingent lease rentals for operating and capital leases were included in net rent expense as incurred and were $46 million in both 1980 and 1979, and $35 million in 1978. These contingent lease rentals are determined generally by volumetric measurement or sales revenue. Some rental agreements contain escalation provisions that may require higher future rent payments. Mobil does not expect that such rent increases, if any, will have a material effect on future earnings.

Capital leases included in net properties, plants, and equipment were $440 million at December 31, 1980 and $483 million at December 31, 1979.

Future minimum lease payments under
noncancelable leases
at December 31, 1980:

(In millions)	Operating Leases	Capital Lease Obligations
1981	$ 247	$ 62
1982	204	59
1983	172	51
1984	131	46
1985	113	41
Later years	712	611
Future minimum lease payments	$1,579	$870
Less		
—executory costs		(66)
—interest		(464)
Capital lease obligations		$340

Exhibit 18-10
SAFECO CORPORATION
Lessor Lease Disclosures

Property Held for Lease—Real Estate Companies

The real estate companies receive rental income principally from the lease of shopping centers, hospital and health care facilities, and office space under leases which expire at various dates through 2047. These leases are accounted for as operating leases. Minimum future rentals from leases in effect at December 31, 1980 are as follows:

Years Receivable	*Amount*
	(Thousands Omitted)
1981	$ 23,495
1982	22,513
1983	21,700
1984	20,148
1985	18,887
1986 and thereafter	188,097
Total	$294,840

The above does not include contingent rentals, based on a percentage of sales in excess of stipulated minimums or increases in the Consumer Price Index. Contingent rentals totaled $5,254,000 in 1980, $5,158,000 in 1979, and $4,130,000 in 1978.

The real estate companies' investment in rental property and the related accumulated depreciation at December 31, 1980, is as follows:

	(Thousands Omitted)
Shopping Centers	$127,596
Hospital and Health Care Facilities	27,644
Office Space	30,250
Other	15,735
	201,225
Less: Accumulated Depreciation	27,919
Total	$173,306

Concept Summary

IMPACT OF EVENTS ON LEASE ACCOUNTING

Event	Impact on Lessor	Impact on Lessee
Transfer of Title or Bargain Purchase Option	Capital lease to lessor if "predictability tests" met; since property belongs to lessee at end of lease, unguaranteed residual values not important.	Capital lease to lessee; amortize asset over useful life of property since asset owned by lessee beyond lease term.
75% and/or 90% Test Met	Capital lease to lessor if "predictability tests" met; must estimate residual value of property since asset reverts back to lessor at end of lease term.	Capital lease to lessee; amortize property over lease term since asset reverts back to lessor at end of lease term.
Collectibility of Payments and No Important Unreimbursable Costs ("Predictability Tests")	Both tests must be met before lessor may classify lease as capital lease.	Tests are not relevant to lessee classification of the lease.
Initial Direct Costs (Insurance, Maintenance, Taxes)	Expensed as incurred in sales-type leases; offset by unearned interest in direct financing leases; capitalized and amortized in operating leases.	Concept is not relevant to lessees; if these type costs are incurred by lessee, expense as incurred.
Capital Lease	Write off asset as if sold to lessee; any profit inherent in lease should be recognized immediately.	Establish asset and obligation as if acquired from lessor; classify asset as fixed asset and segregate obligation into current/noncurrent as with other liabilities.
Operating Lease	Maintain asset on financial statements and recognize rent revenue as earned.	Do not establish asset or obligation and recognize rent expense as accruable.

Glossary of Lease Terminology

Before attempting to understand the technical accounting provisions of FASB *Statement No. 13* and amending documents, you should become familiar with the specific terminology used in the pronouncements. The definitions discussed below are an integral part of *Statement No. 13* and related authoritative literature.

Related Parties in Leasing Transactions Related parties include a parent company and its subsidiaries, an owner company and its joint ventures and partnerships, and investor/investees provided that the investor has the ability to exercise significant influence over the operating and financing policies of the related party (see Chapter 7).

Inception of the Lease A lease agreement is presumed to have its inception at the date of the lease agreement or commitment, whichever is earlier. A lease commitment must be in writing, must be signed by the parties to the transaction, and must establish specifically the principal terms of the transaction.

Fair Value of the Leased Property Fair value is the price for which the leased property could be sold in an arm's-length transaction between unrelated parties. When the lessor is a manufacturer or dealer, the fair value of the property at the inception of the lease ordinarily will be its normal selling price, reflecting any volume or trade discounts that may be applicable. However, the determination of fair value should be made in light of the market conditions prevailing at the time, which may indicate that the fair value of the property is less than the normal selling price and, in some cases, less than the cost of the property. When the lessor is not a manufacturer or dealer, the fair value of the property at the inception of the lease ordinarily will be its cost, reflecting any volume or trade discounts that may be applicable. However, when there has been a significant lapse of time between the acquisition of the property by the lessor and the inception of the lease, the determination of fair value should be made in light of the market conditions prevailing at the inception of the lease.

Bargain Purchase Option A bargain purchase option allows the lessee the right to purchase the leased property for an amount significantly less than the estimated fair value of the property at the date the option becomes exercisable. The "bargain" part of the purchase option should be sufficient to indicate at the inception of the lease that exercise of the option is reasonably assured.

Bargain Renewal Option A bargain renewal option allows the lessee the right to renew the lease for a rental significantly less than the fair rental of the property at the date the option becomes exercisable. The "bargain" part of the renewal option should be sufficient to indicate at the inception of the lease that exercise of the option is reasonably assured.

Lease-Term The lease term is defined as all of the following:

1. The fixed noncancelable term.
2. All periods covered by bargain renewal options.
3. All periods for which failure to renew the lease would impose a penalty sufficient to make the renewal reasonably assured.

4. All periods covered by ordinary renewal options during which the lessee guarantees the lessor's debts with respect to leased property (other than indirectly through agreement to make regularly scheduled lease payments).
5. All periods covered by ordinary renewal options up to the date that any bargain purchase option becomes exercisable.
6. All renewals or extensions of the lease which are at the option of the lessor.

The lease term never should extend beyond the date a bargain purchase option becomes exercisable. A cancelable lease should be considered noncancelable for purposes of defining the lease term if cancellation is conditional on any of the following provisions:

1. Only upon the occurrence of some remote contingency.
2. Only with the lessor's permission.
3. Only if the lessee enters into a new lease with the same lessor.
4. Only upon payment by the lessee of a penalty such that the continuation of the lease is reasonably assured.

Estimated Economic Life of Leased Property   The economic life of leased property is the estimated remaining period during which the property is expected to be economically usable by one or more users, with normal repairs and maintenance, for the purpose for which it was intended at the inception of the lease, without limitation by the lease term.

Estimated Residual Value of Leased Property   The estimated residual value of leased property is the estimated fair value of the property at the end of the lease term.

Unguaranteed Residual Value   The unguaranteed residual value is the estimated residual value of the leased property exclusive of any portion guaranteed by the lessee or a third party unrelated to the lessor. A guarantee by a third party related to the lessee should be considered a lease guarantee; if the guarantor is related to the lessor, the residual value should be considered unguaranteed.

Minimum Lease Payments (Lessee)   The lessee's minimum lease payments represent payments the lessee is obligated to make or can be required to make plus the payment stipulated in any bargain purchase option. If the lease agreement does not contain a bargain purchase option, the minimum lease payments would include all of the following:

1. The minimum rental payments over the lease term.
2. The amount of any residual value guarantee at the end of the lease term, whether or not such guarantee constitutes a purchase of the leased property.
3. Any payment the lessee must make or can be required to make upon failure to renew or extend the lease at its expiration, whether or not such payment constitutes a purchase of the leased property.

Minimum Lease Payments (Lessor)   The lessor's minimum lease payments are the same as those of the lessee except that any guarantee of the residual value or of rental payments beyond the lease term by a third party unrelated to either the lessee or lessor must be added, provided the third party is financially capable of discharging the obligation that may arise as a result of the guarantee.

Interest Rate Implicit in the Lease   The rate of interest implicit in a lease agreement is the discount rate that, when applied to (1) the minimum lease payments, excluding that portion of the payments representing executory costs to be paid by the lessor, and any profit thereon, and (2) the unguaranteed residual value accruing to the benefit of the lessor, causes the aggregate present value at the beginning of the lease term to be equal to the fair value of the leased property to the lessor at the inception of the lease, less any investment tax credit retained and expected to be realized by the lessor.

Lessee's Incremental Borrowing Rate   The incremental borrowing rate is the rate that the lessee would have incurred at the inception of the lease to borrow, over a similar term, the funds necessary to purchase the leased property.

Initial Direct Costs   FASB *Statement No. 17*, "Accounting for Leases—Initial Direct Costs," supersedes the definition of initial direct costs in *Statement No. 13* and defines these costs as follows:

> Those costs incurred by the lessor that are directly associated with negotiating and consummating completed leasing transactions. Those costs include, but are not necessarily limited to, commissions, legal fees, costs of credit investigations, and costs of preparing and processing documents for new leases acquired. In addition, that portion of salespersons' compensation, other than commissions, and the compensation of other employees that is applicable to time spent in the activities described above with respect to completed leasing transactions shall also be included in initial direct costs. The portion of salespersons' compensation and the compensation of other employees that is applicable to the time spent in negotiating leases that are not consummated shall not be included in initial direct costs. No portion of supervisory and administrative expenses or other indirect expenses, such as rent and facilities costs, shall be included in initial direct costs.[12]

Contingent Rentals   FASB *Statement No. 29*, "Determining Contingent Rentals," amends *Statement No. 13* by adding the following subparagraph:

> (Contingent rentals represent) the increases or decreases in lease payments that result from changes occurring subsequent to the inception of the lease in the factors (other than the passage of time) on which lease payments are based, except as provided in the following sentence. Any escalation of minimum lease payments relating to increases in construction or acquisition cost of the leased property or for increases in some measure of cost or value during the construction or pre-construction period. . . . shall be excluded from contingent rentals. Lease payments that depend on a factor directly related to the future use of the leased property, such as machine hours of use or sales volume during the lease term, are contingent lease payments in their entirety. However, lease payments that depend on an existing index or rate, such as the consumer price index or the prime interest rate, shall be included in the minimum lease payments based on the index or rate existing at the inception of the lease; any increases or decreases in the lease payments that result from subsequent changes in the index or rate are contingent rentals and thus affect the determination of income as accruable.[13]

---

[12]"Accounting for Leases—Initial Direct Costs," *Statement of Financial Accounting Standards No. 17* (Stamford, Conn.: FASB, 1977), par. 8.

[13]"Determining Contingent Rentals," *Statement of Financial Accounting Standards No. 29* (Stamford, Conn.: FASB, 1979), par. 11.

Appendix

Accounting for Leveraged Leases

A unique form of financing productive assets, known as "leveraged leasing," is being utilized increasingly in the business community. The growing use of this method of financing reflects the significant advantages of leveraged leasing for lessors: (1) a majority of the funds used to purchase the property subject to lease is supplied by a third-party creditor; (2) the loan from the creditor is nonrecourse to the general credit of the lessor; (3) during the early years of the lease term, depreciation and interest deductions should exceed annual lease income, thereby providing excess deductions to be applied against other income; (4) the lessor receives the benefit of the investment tax credit; (5) the leased asset reverts back to the lessor at the end of the lease term; and (6) no liability to the creditor is recorded in the liability section of the balance sheet of the lessor, thus enabling a better debt-to-equity ratio. While this list of advantages may not be all-inclusive, it does indicate why leveraged leasing is growing in popularity among lessors.

The particular nature of leveraged leases influenced the FASB to devote extensive coverage to them in *Statement No. 13*. The purpose of this Appendix is to examine the accounting requirements of *Statement No. 13* related to leveraged leasing in an attempt to provide some guidance in applying these technical accounting provisions.

What Is a Leveraged Lease?

A lease agreement is classified as a **leveraged lease** when the lessor elects to defer recognition of any investment tax credit and to allocate the credit to income over the lease term *and* when the following conditions are evident in the lease agreement:

1. The lease agreement contains criteria that indicate that a direct financing lease has been negotiated. Sales-type leases cannot constitute leveraged leases in that no manufacturer of dealer profit may be recognized.
2. The lease agreement involves at least three parties: a lessee, a lessor, and a long-term creditor. The relationship among these three parties is diagrammed in Exhibit 18-11.
3. The financing provided by the long-term creditor must be nonrecourse to the general credit of the lessor (although the creditor may have recourse to the leased property and related rental payments). The financing should be sufficient to provide the lessor with "substantial leverage" in the transaction. *Statement No. 13* does not specify what constitutes substantial leverage, although as a general rule, if the creditor provides financing for 50% or more of

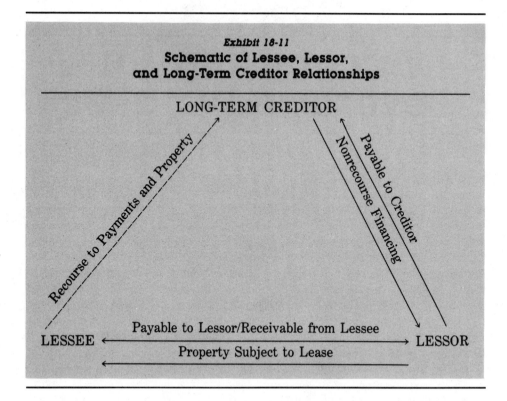

Exhibit 18-11
**Schematic of Lessee, Lessor,
and Long-Term Creditor Relationships**

LONG-TERM CREDITOR

Recourse to Payments and Property

Payable to Creditor
Nonrecourse Financing

LESSEE

Payable to Lessor/Receivable from Lessee

Property Subject to Lease

LESSOR

the lessor's investment in the leased property, the lessor's leverage may be considered substantial.

4. The lessor's net investment in the lease declines during the early years of the lease once the investment has been completed and rises during the lease's later years. This investment pattern may occur more than once.

   In attempting to determine whether a lease agreement produces the required net investment pattern, the lessor first should determine the future net cash flows and their application to recovery of the net investment and to income. Therefore, it often is desirable to utilize a sequential decision making process in trying to determine whether the lease is considered leveraged. Stated differently, since *all* of the aforementioned characteristics must be present before a lease agreement is considered leveraged, the existence of the investment pattern characteristics should be determined after the lessor is satisfied that other specified conditions are present.

   The "investment with separate phases" method should be used in determining positive and negative net investment periods (separate phases). Income then will be recognized at a constant rate of return on the net investment only in the periods in which the net investment is positive, thereby associating lease income with the unrecovered balance of the earning asset.

   Lessor recovery of the net investment in the early years of the lease term is due to the inclusion in lease income of cash flows from the tax benefits of the investment tax credit, accelerated depreciation, and interest deductions. As a result of this cash flow stream, the net investment balance usually is negative during the middle years of the lease term, and the lessor has temporary use of funds for reinvestment. It should be emphasized that earnings on these reinvested funds (secondary earnings) are considered separate from leveraged lease income and are reported in income only when realized.

In later years of the lease term, the cash flows are influenced by net tax liabilities; the investment tax credit will have been utilized, and the tax benefits from depreciation and interest deductions diminish. In these years the lessor has a net cash outflow since the tax obligations exceed any excess of rental receipts over debt interest and principal payments to the third-party creditor.

Accounting for Leveraged Leases

Lessors should record their investment in a leveraged lease net of the nonrecourse debt. The net of the following account balances represents the lessor's initial and continuing investment in a leveraged lease:

1. Rents receivable, less principal and interest applicable to the nonrecourse debt.
2. A receivable for the amount of the investment tax credit to be realized.
3. The estimated residual value of the leased property.
4. Unearned and deferred income (consisting of the estimated pretax lease income or loss), after deducting initial direct costs, that remains to be allocated to income over the lease term *plus* any investment tax credit that remains to be allocated to income over the lease term.

The initial lessor journal entry to record the leveraged lease (including the lessor's equity investment—cash) would appear as follows:

Lease payments receivable	XXX	
Estimated residual value	XXX	
Investment tax credit receivable	XXX	
Cash		XXX
Unearned and deferred income		XXX

The lessor's investment in a leveraged lease, less any deferred taxes resulting from differences between pretax accounting income and taxable income, represents the lessor's net investment in leveraged leases to be utilized in computing periodic lease income. Since the amounts to be recorded as lease income and the changes in the net investment each period are dependent on amounts associated with other lease periods, the amounts applicable to all periods must be determined simultaneously. Amounts applicable to the net investment must reduce or increase that investment each period by the difference between the period net cash flow and the income recognized for the period. Income under leveraged leases should be recognized to produce a constant rate of return only in periods of positive net investment.

The net income to be recognized under a leveraged lease is composed of three elements: (1) pretax lease income (or loss) allocated in proportionate amounts from unearned and deferred income, (2) investment tax credit allocated in proportionate amounts from unearned and deferred income, and (3) the related tax effect of any pretax lease income (or loss) recognized which should be reflected in current period tax expense. In lease arrangements in which projected net cash receipts are less than the lessor's initial investment, a loss for the difference should be recognized immediately at the inception of the lease.

As an example of leveraged leasing, assume that MR Corporation entered into a lease agreement in which it leased equipment to Atmo Supply. MR Corporation borrowed a significant portion of the funds to buy the equipment from Credit Co. Other information is as follows:

Cost of equipment to MR Corporation	$200,000
Fair value of equipment at inception of lease	$200,000
Lease term	15 years
Useful life of equipment	17 years
Inception of lease	January 1, 1980
Annual lease payments by lessee	$ 38,000
Estimated residual value accruing to MR Corporation	$ 40,000
Long-term nonrecourse debt	$150,000 bearing interest at 10%, payable in annual installments of $19,721 beginning on December 31, 1980
Equity investment by MR Corporation	$ 50,000
Tax rate for MR Corporation	40%
Investment tax credit	10% of equipment cost, which is realized on December 31, 1980, by MR Corporation
Rate of return to MR Corporation	9%

Cashflows accruing to MR Corporation are assumed to be as follows for the first two years:

For 1980

	Cash Inflows		Cash Outflows
Received from lessee	$38,000	Paid to third party	$19,721
Investment tax credit realized	20,000		
Tax savings	6,721		
	$64,721		$19,721

For 1981

	Cash Inflows		Cash Outflows
Received from lessee	$38,000	Paid to third party	$19,721
Tax savings	5,279		
	$43,279		$19,721

The journal entries for MR Corporation are as follows:

Jan. 1, 1980	Lease payments receivable	274,185[a]	
	Estimated residual value	40,000	
	Investment tax credit receivable	20,000	
	Cash		50,000
	Unearned and deferred income		284,185[b]
	To record the lease.		

[a]38,000 × 15 = $570,000 Total Lease Receipts
  19,721 × 15 = 295,815 Loan Payments
             $274,185 Net Receivable

[b]$264,185 Total interest
 −20,000 Investment tax credit
 $284,185

Dec. 31, 1980	Cash	38,000	
	Lease payments receivable		38,000
	To record payment from lessee.		
	Lease payments receivable	19,721	
	Cash		19,721
	To record payment on long term note.		
	Tax payable	20,000	
	Investment tax credit receivable		20,000
	To record reduction in taxes from investment tax credit.		
	Unearned and deferred income	504[c]	
	Investment tax credit		504
	To recognize investment tax credit earned.		

[c]$50,000 investment $\times$ 9% = \$4,500

$$\$ 4{,}500 \times \left(\frac{\$20{,}000 \text{ Investment Credit}}{\$178{,}511^*} \right) = \$504$$

*264,185 total interest
+20,000 investment tax credit
−105,674 Tax effect of interest ($264,185 $\times$ .4)
$178,511 Unearned and deferred income net of tax

Unearned and deferred income	6,660[d]	
Interest (lease) income		6,660
To record interest income.		

[d]50,000 investment $\times$ 9% = \$4,500

$$\$4{,}500 \times \left(\frac{\$264{,}185 \text{ Interest}}{\$178{,}511 \text{ See footnote c above}} \right) = \$6{,}660$$

Tax expense	2,664[e]	
Tax payable	6,721[f]	
Deferred taxes		9,385
To record tax effect of lease.		

[e]$6,660 (see previous entry) $\times$ .4(tax) = \$2,664
[f]Given under cash inflows as the tax savings

The net investment in leveraged lease at January 1, 1981, is as follows:

Lease payments receivable	$255,906[g]
Investment tax credit receivable	0
Estimated residual value	40,000
	$295,906
Less: Unearned and deferred income	(277,021)[h]
Deferred taxes	(9,385)
Net investment	$ 9,500

[g]($274,185 − $38,000 + $19,721)
[h]($284,185 − ($504 + $6,660))

The journal entries for MR Corporation for December 31, 1981, are as follows:

Dec. 31, 1981	Cash	38,000	
	Lease payments receivable		38,000
	To record payment from leasee.		
	Lease payments receivable	19,721	
	Cash		19,721
	To record payment of long term note.		

Unearned and deferred income	96[i]	
Investment tax credit recognized		96
To record recognition of investment tax credit		

[i]$95,000 (net investment) $\times$ 9% = $855

$$\$855 \times \left(\frac{\$20,000}{\$178,511} \right) = \$96$$

Unearned and deferred income	1,265[j]	
Interest (lease) income		1,265
To record lease interest income.		

[j]$9,500 (net investment) $\times$ 9% = 855

$$\$855 \times \left(\frac{\$264,185}{\$178,511} \right) = \$1,265$$

Tax expense	506[k]	
Tax payable	5,279[l]	
Deferred taxes		5,785
To record tax effect of lease.		

[k]$1,265 (interest) $\times$ .4(tax) = $506
[l]Given under cash flows as tax savings for second year.

The net investment in leveraged lease at January 1, 1982, is presented below:

Lease payments receivable	$237,627[m]
Investment tax credit receivable	0
Estimated residual value	40,000
	$277,627
Less: Unearned and deferred income	(275,660)[n]
Deferred taxes	(15,170)
Net investment	$(13,203)

[m]($255,906 − $38,000 + $19,721)
[n]($277,021 − ($96 + $1,265))

The accounting requirements applicable to leveraged leasing include the following disclosure standards peculiar to these agreements:

1. In the balance sheet, deferred income taxes should not be netted against the investment in leveraged leases.
2. In the income statement or related footnotes, net income and its components from leveraged leases are to be classified or disclosed separately as pretax income, investment tax credit recognized, and tax effects of pretax lease income.

3. When leveraged leasing is material to the lessor in terms of revenue, net income, or assets, the components of the net investment balance should be disclosed in the footnotes.

Questions

Q–18–1 List some of the advantages and disadvantages of leasing an asset rather than purchasing an asset.

Q–18–2 Identify the classification of leases from the standpoint of the lessee, and the criteria that must be met to meet the requirements of each classification.

Q–18–3 Identify the classification of leases from the standpoint of the lessor, and the criteria that must be met to meet the requirements of each classification.

Q–18–4 Describe the accounting procedures involved in applying the operating method by the lessee, by the lessor.

Q–18–5 Describe the accounting procedures involved in applying the capital lease method by the lessee, by the lessor.

Q–18–6 Define and explain the incremental borrowing rate and determine when and by whom it is used.

Q–18–7 Explain and define the interest rate implicit in the lease.

Q–18–8 Explain and define the minimum lease payment.

Q–18–9 Explain and define the term *unguaranteed residual value.*

Q–18–10 Explain how a change in the estimated residual value of leased property is handled by the lessor and the lessee.

Q–18–11 Explain and define *bargain purchase option* and *bargain renewal option.*

Q–18–12 Define a *leverage lease*, and explain how it differs from other types of leases.

Q–18–13 Your client constructed an office building at a cost of $500,000. He sold this building to Jones at a material gain and then leased it back from Jones for a stipulated annual rental. How should this gain be treated?
  a) Recognized in full as an ordinary item in the year of the transaction.
  b) Recognized in full as an extraordinary item in the year of the transaction.
  c) Amortized, net of tax, as an adjustment of the rental cost, an ordinary item, over the life of the lease.
  d) Amortized as an ordinary item over the life of the lease, but with the tax effect.
    (AICPA adapted)

Q–18–14 What is the cost basis of an asset acquired by a lease that is in substance an installment purchase?
  a) The net realizable value of the asset determined at the date of the lease agreement plus the sum of the future minimum lease payments under the lease.
  b) The sum of the future minimum lease payments under the lease.
  c) The present value of the amount of future minimum lease payments under the lease (exclusive of executory costs and any profit thereon), discounted at an appropriate rate.
  d) The present value of the market price of the asset, discounted at an appropriate rate as an amount to be received at the end of the lease.
    (AICPA adapted)

Q–18–15 Generally accepted accounting principles require that certain lease agreements be accounted for as purchases. The theoretic basis for this treatment is that a lease of this type

a) Effectively conveys all of the benefits and risks incident to the ownership of property.

b) Is an example of form over substance.

c) Provides the use of the leased asset to the lessee for a limited period of time.

d) Must be recorded in accordance with the concept of cause and effect.

(AICPA adapted)

Q–18–16 Based solely upon the sets of circumstances indicated below, which set gives rise to a sales type or direct financing lease of a lessor?

	Transfers Ownership by End of Lease?	*Contains Bargain Purchase Provisions?*	*Collectibility of Lease Payments Assured?*	*Any Important Uncertainties?*
a)	No	Yes	Yes	No
b)	Yes	No	No	No
c)	Yes	No	No	Yes
d)	No	Yes	Yes	Yes

(AICPA adapted)

Discussion Questions and Cases

D–18–1 Milton Corporation entered into a lease arrangement with James Leasing Corporation for a certain machine. James's primary business is leasing, and it is not a manufacturer or dealer. Milton will lease the machine for a period of three years, which is 50% of the machine's economic life. James will take possession of the machine at the end of the initial three-year lease and will lease it to another smaller company that does not need the most current version of the machine. Milton does not guarantee any residual value for the machine and will not purchase the machine at the end of the lease term.

Milton's incremental borrowing rate is 10%, and the implicit rate in the lease is 8½%. Milton has no way of knowing the implicit rate used by James. With either rate, the present value of the minimum lease payments is between 90% and 100% of the fair value of the machine at the date of the lease agreement.

Milton has agreed to pay all executory costs directly, and no allowance for these costs is included in the lease payments. James is reasonably certain that Milton will pay all lease payments, and, because Milton has agreed to pay all executory costs, there are no important uncertainties regarding costs to be incurred by James.

Required:

1. With respect to Milton (the lessee), answer the following:

   a) What type of lease has been entered into? Explain the reason for your answer.

   b) How should Milton compute the appropriate amount to be recorded for the lease or asset acquired?

   c) What accounts will be created or affected by this transaction, and how will the lease or asset and other costs related to the transaction be matched with earnings?

   d) What disclosures must Milton make regarding this lease or asset?

2. With respect to James (the lessor), answer the following:

   a) What type of leasing arrangement has been entered into? Explain the reason for your answer.

   b) How should this lease be recorded by James, and how are the appropriate amounts determined?

   c) How should James determine the appropriate amount of earnings to be recognized from each lease payment? (Continued on next page.)

d) What disclosures must James make regarding this lease?

(AICPA adapted)

D–18–2 In completing your work applicable to CJR Corp., several questions have arisen related to the appropriate accounting and disclosure requirements for some of CJR's leases. Respond as to how these problem areas should be resolved.

a) On January 1, 1980, CJR Corp. sold drilling equipment with a book value of $250,000 to Dry Hole Drilling for $550,000 and immediately leased back the equipment for 10 years. The equipment has a fair value of $400,000. The present value of the minimum lease payments is $280,000, and the equipment has a remaining life of 12 years. The lease agreement does not stipulate a transfer of title or a bargain purchase option. CJR Corp. amortizes the cost of similar properties that are owned on a straight-line basis. What should CJR do applicable to this lease on January 1, 1980, and at the end of the first year?

b) Management of CJR is concerned about the accounting treatment applicable to initial direct costs. Explain the composition of initial direct costs, promulgated accounting treatment for these costs, and the rationale (objective) underlying the promulgated conclusions.

c) Management of CJR is aware of the FASB's objective of creating increased symmetry applicable to lease classification. Discuss how the FASB attempted to increase classification symmetry and identify and discuss several ways leases may not be classified symmetrically.

D–18–3 The Jackson Company manufactured a piece of equipment at a cost of $7,000,000 that it held for resale from January 1, 1976, to June 30, 1976, at a price of $8,000,000. On July 1, 1976, Jackson leased the equipment to the Crystal Company. The lease is appropriately recorded as an operating lease for accounting purposes. The lease is for a three-year period expiring June 30, 1979. Equal monthly payments under the lease are $115,000 each and are due on the first of the month. The first payment was made on July 1, 1976. The equipment is being depreciated on a straight-line basis over an eight-year period with no residual value expected.

Required:

1. What expense should Crystal appropriately record as a result of the facts above for the year ended December 31, 1976? Show supporting computations in good form.

2. What income or loss before income taxes should Jackson appropriately record as a result of the facts above for the year ended December 31, 1976? Show supporting computations in good form.

(AICPA adapted)

D–18–4 The Truman Company leased equipment from the Roosevelt Company on October 1, 1976. The lease is appropriately recorded as a purchase for accounting purposes for Truman and as a sale for accounting purposes for Roosevelt. The lease is for an eight-year period expiring on September 30, 1984. Equal annual payments under the lease are $600,000 each and are due on October 1, 1976. The cost of the equipment on Roosevelt's accounting records was $3,000,000. The equipment has an estimated useful life of eight years with no residual value expected. Truman uses straight-line depreciation and takes a full year's depreciation in the year of purchase. The rate of interest contemplated by Truman and Roosevelt is 10%. The present value of an annuity of $1 in advance for eight periods at 10% is 5.868.

Required:

1. What expense should Truman appropriately record as a result of the facts above for the year ended December 31, 1976? Show supporting computations in good form.

2. What income or loss before income taxes should Roosevelt appropriately record as a result of the facts above for the year ended December 31, 1976? Show supporting computations in good form.

(AICPA adapted)

Exercises

E-18-1 Benedict Company leased equipment to Mark, Inc. on January 1, 1978. The lease is for an eight-year period expiring on December 31, 1985. The first of eight equal annual payments of $600,000 each was made on January 1, 1978. Benedict had purchased the equipment on December 29, 1977, for $3,200,000. The lease is appropriately accounted for as a sales-type lease by Benedict. Assume that the present value at January 1, 1978, of all rent payments over the lease term discounted at a 10% interest rate was $3,520,000.
Required:
Compute the amount of interest income Benedict should record in 1979 (the second year of the lease period) as a result of the lease.

(AICPA adapted)

E-18-2 Arrow Company purchased a machine on January 1, 1979, for $1,440,000 for the purpose of leasing it. The machine is expected to have an eight-year life from the date of purchase, no residual value, and is expected to be depreciated on the straight-line basis. On February 1, 1979, the machine was leased to Baxter Company for a three-year period ending on January 31, 1982, at a monthly rental of $30,000. In addition, Baxter paid $72,000 to Arrow on February 1, 1979, as a lease bonus.
Required:
Compute the amount of income before income taxes that Arrow should report on this leased asset for the year ended December 31, 1979.

E-18-3 Fox Company, a dealer in machinery and equipment, leased equipment to Tiger, Inc. on July 1, 1979. The lease is appropriately accounted for as a sale by Fox and as a purchase by Tiger. The lease is for a 10-year period (the useful life of the asset) expiring on June 30, 1989. The first of 10 equal annual payments of $500,000 each was made on July 1, 1979. Fox had purchased the equipment for $2,675,000 on January 1, 1979, and had established a list selling price of $3,375,000 on the equipment. Assume that the present value at July 1, 1979, of the rent payments over the lease term discounted at 12% (the appropriate interest rate) was $3,165,000.
Required:
1. Compute the amount of profit on the sale and the amount of interest income that Fox should record for the year ended December 31, 1979.
2. If you assume that Tiger uses straight-line depreciation, what is the amount of depreciation and interest expense that Tiger should record for the year ended December 31, 1979?

(AICPA adapted)

E-18-4 The Morn Company leased equipment to the Lizard Company on May 1, 1978. At that time the collectibility of the minimum lease payments was not reasonably predictable. The lease expires on May 1, 1980. Lizard could have bought the equipment from Morn from $900,000 instead of leasing it. Morn's accounting records showed a book value for the equipment on May 1, 1978, of $800,000. Morn's depreciation on the equipment in 1978 was $200,000. During 1978 Lizard paid $240,000 in rentals to Morn and incurred maintenance and other related costs under the terms of the lease of $18,000 in 1978. After the lease with Lizard expires, Morn will lease the equipment to the Cold Company for another two years.
Required:
1. Compute the income before income taxes derived by Morn from this lease for the year ended December 31, 1978.
2. Compute the amount of expense incurred by Lizard from this lease for the year ended December 31, 1978.

(AICPA adapted)

E–18–5 On January 1, 1976, the Anson Company leased a machine to Scovil Company. The lease was for a 10-year period, which approximated the useful life of the machine. Anson purchased the machine for $80,000 and expects to earn a 10% return on its investment, based upon an annual rental of $11,836, payable in advance each January 1.

Required:

If you assume that the lease was a financing lease, what should be the interest entry on Anson's books on December 31, 1976?

E–18–6 An office equipment representative has a machine for sale or lease. If you buy the machine, the cost is $7,596. If you lease the machine, you will have to sign a noncancellable lease and make five payments of $2,000 each. The first payment will be paid on the first day of the lease. At the time of the last payment you will receive title to the machine. The present value of an ordinary annuity of $1 is as follows:

Number of Periods	Present Value		
	10%	12%	16%
1	0.909	0.893	0.862
2	1.736	1.690	1.605
3	2.487	2.402	2.246
4	3.170	3.037	2.798
5	3.791	3.605	3.274

Required:
Compute the interest rate implicit in the lease.

E–18–7 The Standard Company leased a piece of equipment to the Piping Company on July 1, 1977, for a one-year period expiring on June 30, 1978, for $90,000 a month. On July 1, 1978, Standard leased this piece of equipment to the Tacking Company for a three-year period expiring on June 30, 1981, for $100,000 a month. The original cost of the piece of equipment was $6,000,000. The piece of equipment, which has been continually on lease since July 1, 1973, is being depreciated on a straight-line basis over an eight-year period with no salvage value.

Required:
Assuming that both the lease to Piping and the lease to Tacking are recorded appropriately as operating leases for accounting purposes, compute the amount of income (expense) before income taxes that each would record as a result of the facts above for the year ended December 31, 1978.

E–18–8 On January 1, 1970, the Cougar Company signed a 20-year noncancelable lease agreement to lease a building from the Mustang Corporation. The lease agreement contains the following terms:

a) Rental payments of $50,000 are to be made on December 31 of each year.
b) The fair market value of the building on January 1, 1970, is $800,000.
c) The building estimated economic life is 20 years. There is no estimated residual value.
d) The building will be depreciated using the straight-line method.
e) Cougar's incremental borrowing rate is 8% per year. The Mustang Corporation's annual rent insures the company a 10% rate of return.

Required:
1. Prepare the entries on the lessee's and lessor's books to record the initial lease transaction.
2. Prepare the entries necessary to record the lease transactions for 1971, 1972.

E–18–9 On January 1, 1973, Ramos Co. signed a 10-year noncancelable lease for certain machinery. The terms of the lease call for payments of $10,000 per year to be made by

Ramos for 10 years. The machinery has a 20-year life and no salvage value. Ramos uses the straight-line depreciation method on all depreciable assets.

Assume that, in substance, this lease is an installment purchase of the machinery by Ramos, and accordingly should be capitalized. If you assume a 10% discount rate, the lease payments have a present value of $61,440.

Required:

Relative to the capitalized lease described above, Ramos' 1973 income statement should include interest expense and depreciation in what amount?

(AICPA adapted)

E–18–10 On January 2, 1974, Lessor Corporation leased some equipment to Lessee Corporation. Both corporations are on a calendar year. This equipment had cost Lessor $45,000. There were no other significant costs associated with the lease. Lessor appropriately accounted for this transaction as a lease equivalent to a sale, and Lessee appropriately treated it as a capitalized lease under an installment purchase. The lease is for a noncancelable term of eight years, with $10,000 rent payable at the beginning of each year. Lessee made the first payment on January 2, 1974. The implicit interest rate is 10%, and the present value of an annuity of $1 in advance for eight years at 10% is 5.868. The "interest" method of amortization is used. The equipment is expected to have a 10-year life, no salvage value, and to be depreciated on a straight-line basis.

Required:

1. What journal entry should Lessor have made on January 2, 1974, to reflect the transaction as a lease equivalent to a sale?

2. What journal entry should Lessor have made on January 2, 1974, if this lease were to have been accounted for as an operating lease?

3. Assume that Lessee treated this transaction as an operating (true) lease rather than as a purchase of the equipment. By how much would 1974 income before income taxes differ between these two methods?

(AICPA adapted)

E–18–11 On January 2, 1973, Kirk Manufacturing Company leased some equipment from Quarter Corporation. This lease was noncancelable and was in substance an installment purchase. The initial term of the lease was 12 years, with title passing to Kirk at the end of the twelfth year upon payment of $1. Kirk must pay an annual rental of $10,000 at the beginning of each year. The first rental payment was made on January 2, 1973, and no deposit was required. The equipment has an estimated useful life of 20 years with no anticipated salvage value. The prevailing interest rate for Kirk on similar financing arrangements is 8%.

Present Value of an Annuity in Advance of $1 at 8%

11 years	$ 7.710
12 years	8.139
19 years	10.372
20 years	10.604

Required:

1. At what amount should Kirk have capitalized this equipment?

2. Prepare the required journal entries for Kirk and Quarter to record the lease initially.

3. If the equipment had been capitalized at $90,000 and all other facts remain as originally stated, how much interest expense should Kirk have recorded in 1973?

(AICPA adapted)

E–18–12 Beth Co. leased equipment to Wolf, Inc. on April 1, 1977. The lease is recorded appropriately as a sale for accounting purposes for Beth. The lease is for an eight-year period expiring on March 31, 1985. The first equal annual payment of $500,000 was made on April 1, 1977. Beth had purchased the equipment on January 1, 1977, for $2,800,000. The equipment has an estimated useful life of eight years with no residual value expected. Beth uses straight-line depreciation and takes a full year's depreciation in the year of purchase. The cash selling price of the equipment is $2,934,000.

Required:

1. If you assume an interest rate of 10%, what amount of interest income should Beth record in 1977 as a result of the lease?

2. Prepare the journal entries required at Beth and Wolf to record the 1977 interest applicable to this lease.

(AICPA adapted)

E–18–13 On January 1, 1981, MR Corporation sold drilling equipment with a book value of $175,000 to Dry Hole Drilling Co. for $200,000 and immediately leased back the equipment for two years. The equipment had a fair value of $200,000 on the date of this transaction. The present value of the minimum lease payments is $17,500, and the remaining useful life of the equipment is estimated to be 12 years. The lease agreement does not stipulate a title transfer or bargain purchase option.

Required:

Prepare any required entry(ies) to record this sale-leaseback on the books of MR Corporation.

Problems

P–18–1 Buyco and Sellco entered into a lease agreement that called for Sellco to build a jet airplane for Buyco. The lease term is 15 years. The lease is noncancelable, becomes effective January 1, 1978, and requires annual payments each December 31 of $102,965. The total cost of building the asset to Sellco is $700,000.

Buyco has an incremental borrowing rate of 8%, while the rate implicit in the lease is 6%. (Buyco does not have knowledge of this rate). The economic life of the jet is 20 years. Its estimated residual value is $5,000 after 15 years and zero after 20 years. Buyco and Sellco depreciate similar assets on a double-declining-balance basis. At the end of the lease Buyco assumes title to the jet. Collectibility is reasonably assured, and there are no uncertainties relative to Sellco's costs.

Relevant present value factors are:

Present Value of Ordinary Annuity Factors

	6%	8%
15 periods	9.712	8.559
20 periods	11.470	9.818

Required:

1. What type of lease agreement does this constitute from Buyco's perspective?

2. What type of lease agreement does this constitute from Sellco's perspective (be specific)?

3. Without prejudice to your answers in Parts 1 and 2 assume this lease agreement is a capital lease from Buyco's perspective. Over what period of time should Buyco depreciate the asset?

4. If the lease agreement had not contained a transfer of title at the end of the lease term, what type of lease would this constitute from Buyco's perspective? Why?

5. What is the fair value of the asset on January 1, 1978?

6. How much profit would Sellco recognize under this agreement on January 1, 1978?
7. Make all of the journal entries required by Buyco on January 1, 1978.
8. Make all of the journal entries required by Sellco on January 1, 1978.
9. Make all of the journal entries required by Buyco on December 31, 1978.
10. Make all of the journal entries required by Sellco on December 31, 1978.

P–18–2   On Jan. 1, 1979, Lessor Co. leased equipment to Lessee Co. The equipment had a cost to Lessor Co. of $100,000. The lease term is 10 years, at which time the equipment will have a zero residual value. The economic life of the equipment is also 10 years. Its fair market value is $100,000. Lessee Co. uses straight-line depreciation on similar assets. Both the implicit interest rate and the lessee's incremental borrowing rate are 10%. The annual payments are $16,274 beginning on Dec. 31, 1979.

On Jan. 1, 1980, Lessee Co. subleases the equipment to Subco. The original lease term remains in effect, with Lessee Co. remaining the primary obligor. The sublease agreement has a 7-year lease term. The equipment has a fair value of $95,000 on this date. The interest rate implicit in the sublease and Subco's incremental borrowing rate are 12%. The lease payments of $20,816 are due each December 31 beginning on Dec. 31, 1980.

Required:
1. Make all of the entries necessary on the books of Lessee Co. in 1980.
2. Make all of the entries necessary on the books of Lessor Co. on Jan. 1, 1980.
3. Make all of the entries necessary on the books of Subco on Jan. 1, 1980.

P–18–3   In 1977 the Archibald Freight Company negotiated and closed a long-term lease contract for newly constructed truck terminals and freight storage facilities. The buildings were erected to the company's specifications on land owned by the company. On January 1, 1978, Archibald Freight Company took possession of the leased properties. On January 1, 1978, and 1979, the company made cash payments of $1,200,000, which were recorded as rental expenses.

Although the terminals have a composite useful life of 40 years, the noncancellable lease runs for 20 years from January 1, 1978, with a favorable purchase option available upon expiration of the lease. You have determined that the leased properties and related obligations should be accounted for as a capital lease. Internal Revenue Service agents have indicated that purchase accounting will be required for tax purposes and that an assessment will be made for deficiencies in 1978 income taxes.

The 20-year lease is effective for the period from January 1, 1978, through December 31, 1997. Advance rental payments of $1,000,000 are payable to the lessor on January 1 of each of the first 10 years of the lease term. Advance rental payments of $300,000 are due on January 1 for each of the last 10 years of the lease. The company has an option to purchase all of these leased facilities for $1 on December 31, 1997. It also must make annual payments to the lessor of $75,000 for property taxes and $125,000 for insurance. The lease was negotiated to assure the lessor a 6% rate of return. Archibald, who is aware of the lessor's rate of return, has an incremental borrowing rate of 8%.

Required:
Assume that the discounted present value of terminal facilities and related obligation at January 1, 1978, was $10,000,000. Prepare journal entries for Archibald Freight Company to record the following:
  a) Cash payment to the lessor on January 1, 1980.
  b) Depreciation expense for the year ended December 31, 1980.
  c) Interest expense for the year ended December 31, 1980.

(AICPA adapted)

P–18–4   On January 1, 1975, the Green Company entered into a noncancelable lease agreement with the Blatt Company for a machine that was carried on the accounting records of Green at $2,000,000. Total payments under the lease agreement, which expires on December 31, 1984, aggregate $3,550,800, of which $2,400,000 represents the cost of the machine to Blatt. Payments of $355,080 are due each January 1. The first payment was made on January 1, 1975, when the lease agreement was finalized. The interest rate of 10%, which was stipulated in the lease agreement, is considered fair and adequate compensation to Green for the use of its funds. The "interest" method of amortization is being used. Blatt expects the machine to have a 10-year life, no salvage value, and to be depreciated on a straight-line basis. The lease agreement should be accounted for as a lease equivalent to a sale by Green and as a lease that is in substance a purchase by Blatt.

Required:

1. What should be the income before income taxes derived by Green from this lease for the year ended December 31, 1975?

2. Ignoring income taxes, what should be the expenses incurred by Blatt from this lease for the year ended December 31, 1975?

(AICPA adapted)

P-18-5 The Tall Company leased equipment from the Small Company on July 1, 1978, for an eight-year period expiring on June 30, 1986. Equal annual payments under the lease are $500,000 and are due on July 1 of each year. The first payment was made on July 1, 1978. The rate of interest contemplated by Tall and Small is 10%. The cash selling price of the equipment is $2,934,000, and the cost of the equipment on Small's accounting records was $2,500,000.

Required:

Assuming that the lease is appropriately recorded as a sale for accounting purposes by Small, what is the amount of profit on the sale and the interest income that Small would record for the year ended December 31, 1978?

(AICPA adapted)

P-18-6 On January 1, 1977, Flip Corporation signed a 10-year noncancelable lease for certain machinery. The terms of the lease called for Flip to make annual payments of $30,000 for 10 years with title to pass to Flip at the end of this period. The machinery has an estimated useful life of 15 years and no salvage value. Flip uses the straight-line method of depreciation for all of its fixed assets. Flip accordingly accounted for this lease transaction as an installment purchase of the machinery. The lease payments were determined to have a present value of $201,302 with an effective interest rate of 10%.

Required:

With respect to this capitalized lease, what expenses should Flip record for 1977?

(AICPA adapted)

P-18-7 On January 1, 1981, LGR Corporation entered into a sale-leaseback transaction with Thomas Company. The transaction involved land that cost LGR $200,000 and a building that was constructed at a cost to LGR of $768,500. The construction on the building was completed on November 22, 1980, and the cost of the construction is indicative of the fair value of the building on January 1, 1981. The fair value of the land on January 1, 1981, is $220,000. Terms of the sale-leaseback transaction are as follows:

a) The sales price for the land and building is $988,500.

b) The lease is a 10-year, noncancelable lease. The estimated useful life of the building at January 1, 1981, is 30 years with no salvage value estimated. The building will be depreciated under the straight-line method.

c) Lease payments in the amount of $146,249 are due each January 1, with the first payment due on January 1, 1981.

d) Thomas Company's implicit rate in this lease is 10%, and this rate is known to LGR Corporation.

e) LGR has the option to reacquire the property at the end of the lease term for a negligible amount.

f) Thomas Company will have no unreimburseable costs, and the company is virtually certain of collecting the lease payments.

Required:

1. Prepare a lease amortization schedule through 1984 for this lease. The same schedule will be used by the lessee and the lessor.

2. Prepare journal entries required of LGR and Thomas to record this transaction on January 1, 1981.

3. Prepare all of the journal entries required of LGR and Thomas on December 31, 1981, applicable to this lease.

4. Determine the balance sheet classifications and the amounts to be disclosed in these classifications for LGR and Thomas at December 31, 1981.

P–18–8 The following data relate to equipment leased by Lessor Corporation to Lessee Corporation:

Cost of equipment to Lessor	$400,000
Fair value of equipment at inception of lease	400,000
Lease term	15 years
Inception of lease	January 1, 1980
Annual rental payment from Lessee	$80,000 (paid each December 31)
Residual value	$10,000
Financing	
Equity investment by Lessor	$50,000
Long-term nonrecourse debt	$350,000 (interest at 10% payable in installments of $60,000, beginning on December 31, 1980)
Lessor effective tax rate	40%
Investment tax credit	10% of equipment cost, which is realized by lessor on December 31, 1980

Additional data are as follows:

a) The lease meets the criteria for a leveraged lease to Lessor Corporation.

b) The following cash flows accrue to Lessor Corp. on December 31:

     1980: $68,825
     1981: 31,825
     1982: 33,825

c) The rate of return at which Lessor Corp. recognizes income is 10%.

Required:

Prepare all of the journal entries for Lessor Corp. applicable to this lease on the following dates:

  a) January 1, 1980.
  b) December 31, 1980.
  c) December 31, 1981.

19

Stockholders' Equity—Issuance and Reacquisition

Companies often raise funds for growth and expansion through the sale of equity securities. Frequently, a fast-growing closely held corporation will have to "go public" (sell stock to the general public and investors) to raise capital. Such was the case with Apple Computer.

CUPERTINO, Calif.—Not since Eve has an apple posed such temptation. But this time it's Apple Computer, Inc. which filed its long-awaited registration with the Securities and Exchange Commission for an initial public offering of 4.5 million common shares. The tentative offering price will be between $14 and $17 a share.

The hot manufacturer of personal computer systems for the home, business and educational markets, said the offering is planned for early December. Apple announced its intent to go public last August, and investor appetite for the new issue has been keen ever since.

The company will sell four million shares, and certain holders will sell 500,000 shares. Morgan Stanley & Co. and Hambrecht & Quist will lead a group of underwriters. As previously reported, Apple said it plans to use proceeds mainly for working capital.*

The subject of this chapter is how to account for issues of stock and other equity-related items.

*Marilyn Chase, "Apple Computer Registers Its First Offer Of 4.5 Million Shares at $14 to $17 Apiece," *The Wall Street Journal*, November 7, 1980, p. 7. Reprinted by permission of The Wall Street Journal, © Dow Jones & Company, Inc. 1980. All Rights Reserved.

In the prior chapter, long-term debt was described as an important source of capital for a business. A second source of capital, and one that is more important for most businesses, are the funds obtained from the owners. This capital is included in the balance sheet under the "owners' equity" section. The exact heading given to this section will depend on the form of the business organization. For instance, the section entitled "owners' equity" in a partnership or proprietorship balance sheet is replaced by "stockholders' equity" on a corporation's balance sheet.

Forms of Business Organization

A business may be organized as a proprietorship, partnership, or corporation. The corporate form of business organization is dominant in the United States as well as in many other countries. This form of business differs significantly from either the proprietorship or the partnership. Foremost is the corporation's status as a separate legal entity. Over a century ago Chief Justice John Marshall defined a **corporation** as "an artificial being, invisible, intangible and existing only in contemplation of the law."[1]

Advantages of the Corporate Form

With rare exceptions, the fact that a corporation is regarded as a separate entity means that the owners of the corporation have no personal liability for its debts or other obligations. Any personal financial loss is limited to the amount of the owner's investment in the corporation. In the proprietorship and partnership forms of business organization, the organization is not regarded as a legal entity, separate from its owners. Therefore, the owner's liability is not limited to the amount invested.

Another important feature of a corporation is its status as a separate entity for tax purposes. A variety of regulations exist at the federal level, and at some state levels, that have an impact on the income tax that is levied on the corporation. However, for many owners of business the tax rates on corporate income are lower than the tax rates that would have to be paid if the business income were taxed as the personal income of the owner. Corporations distribute their income to the owners in the form of dividends. A disadvantage of the corporate form is that the dividend income is subject to tax at personal income tax rates to the person receiving the dividend. Nevertheless, for many owners of business the status of the corporation as a separate entity for tax purposes is desirable.

Corporations have other characteristics that are regarded as advantageous. Ownership of a corporation is evidenced by stock. Usually, the transferability of the stock from one buyer, or investor, to another is unrestricted. This enables the corporation to have an indefinite life span, because the business entity does not have to be reformed each time the ownership interest changes. This feature also makes it practical for a corporation to have a large number of owners, or stockholders. Of course, for practical purposes the existence of a large number of owners results in the separation between the owners of a corporation and its

---

[1] *Trustees of Dartmouth College v. Woodward*, 17 U.S. (4 Wheat) 518, 636, 4 L.Ed. 629 (1819).

management. However, these characteristics of the corporation enable a business to raise larger amounts of capital than could be obtained from only one or a few owners.

The **proprietorship** form of organization does not have the status of a separate legal entity. The income of the proprietorship is considered the personal income of the owner for tax purposes. The owners decide if there is a separation between ownership and management, and they are personally responsible for the debts of the business. Ownership interest is not transferable except by sale of all or a part of the proprietor's interest. In the event of such a sale, the business is reorganized under the new owners. The **partnership** form of organization is comparable to the proprietorship form, but there are two or more owners.

A comparison of the characteristics of the proprietorship, partnership, and corporate forms of organization is illustrated in Exhibit 19-1.

Forming a Corporation

Corporations are formed in accordance with the laws of individual states. Those wishing to form a corporation must file an application for a corporate charter with an appropriate state official. The application usually must contain a description of (1) the nature of the business to be conducted, (2) the capital stock to be issued and the rights of the stockholders, and (3) the incorporators. The corporation

Exhibit 19-1
Characteristics of Forms of Business Organization

Characteristic	Proprietorship	Partnership	Corporation
Separate legal entity	No	No	Yes
Separate entity for income tax purposes	No	No	Yes
Separate entity for accounting purposes	Yes	Yes	Yes
Double taxation of income— tax on income of the entity and again when distributions are made to owner(s)	No	No	Yes
Owner personally liable for debts of entity	Yes	Yes	No
Ownership interest easily transferred	No	No	Yes
Reformation of entity necessary when ownership changes	Yes	Yes	No
Ownership separate from management	Not usually	Not usually	Usually

becomes legal when the application is approved and the state has issued a charter, also known as articles of incorporation. Then the incorporators and others who previously have agreed to buy stock in the new corporation elect a board of directors, approve bylaws (general guidelines for operating the corporation), and select officers. The officers execute the corporate policies established by the directors and are responsible for the day-to-day operations.

Corporations may exist in several forms. They may be owned by individuals or by the government. Private corporations may be for-profit or not-for-profit. For-profit corporations issue stock whereas not-for-profit corporations usually don't. For-profit corporations may have many or few stockholders. A privately held, or closed, corporation has relatively few shareholders.

Those corporations having many stockholders are regarded as publicly *held*. A common definition of a publicly held company is one whose securities are traded publicly. Corporations whose stock is traded publicly are subject to the financial reporting requirements of the Securities and Exchange Commission (SEC).

The transactions in which a corporation may engage are described in its articles of incorporation. They may be described in broad terms, or the description may be specific. Often this will depend on the laws of the state in which the entity is incorporated. These state laws or regulations may have an impact on a variety of corporation transactions. For instance, they often have an impact on the conduct of transactions affecting the owners' equity accounts of the corporation. Even the methods of accounting for such transactions may be specified or implied by state statute. This implies that the accountant for any individual corporation must be knowledgeable about the applicable laws that may affect the accounting in the state in which the entity is incorporated.

Nature of the Capital Stock

At the time of its incorporation, an entity is authorized to issue one or more classes of capital stock. A corporation must have at least one class of stock. If a corporation has only one class of stock, the stock is regarded as **common stock.** It is unusual for a corporation to have more than one class of common stock.

To attract investors, corporations may issue two or more classes of capital stock. The classes differ in order to accommodate the differing goals of investors. The distinction between classes is made on the basis of the "rights" of the stockholder in such matters as voting for directors and sharing in the distribution of profits. The specific rights may be determined by state statute, the corporate charter, or the bylaws. Each share of stock in a class has the same rights as every other share in that class. Generally, special classes of stock are designated as **preferred stock;** they are characterized by the granting of certain privileges not accorded to common stockholders.

Unless specifically restricted, the ownership interest represented by the shares of stock may be sold by one investor to another at any time. The corporation, of course, must maintain records of individual ownership interests. To facilitate this, a new stock certificate indicating the number of shares purchased is issued to the new owner whenever shares are traded. Maintenance of up-to-date stockholder records, in the form of a stockholder ledger, is important for making proper dividend payments and for other legal purposes.

Par and No-Par Stocks

Authorization for a class of stock to be issued by a corporation is found in its articles of incorporation. Under the laws of most states, each class of stock must have a designated value per share. If a value per share is designated in the articles of incorporation, the stock is known as **par value** stock. The issuance of no-par value stock is permitted by the Model Corporation Act that is in effect in most states. However, there is a requirement that the stock be assigned a stated value. This value usually is established by the board of directors. Both common stock and preferred stock may be par value or no-par value stock.

The significance of the par or stated value of a stock has its origin in the concept of **legal capital,** which exists in some form in all states. The legal capital is the portion of the owners' equity in the corporation that state law requires to be maintained for the protection of creditors. The exact composition of legal capital is determined by the laws of the state of incorporation. It is a basic rule of law in most states that the corporation cannot make distributions of assets to shareholders that will result in reducing owners' equity below the amount of legal capital except in very rare situations. Examples of exceptions include a corporate liquidation or reorganization, although these steps also are subject to state laws.

Historically, it was the par value times the number of shares outstanding that constituted the legal capital of the corporation. Since the purpose of legal capital is to provide a measure of protection to creditors, the issuance of stock at less than this value is illegal in virtually all states. In the event of corporate insolvency, the initial purchasers of the stock may be liable to the corporation for the amount of the discount (i.e., the difference between par value and issue price) if the stock originally was issued for an amount less than par value.

The par value of a stock has little, if any, economic significance. Practically, it represents the minimum amount for which a share of stock initially may be issued by a corporation to an investor. In practice, at the time a class of stock initially is sold, it usually will have a par value well below the price for which it is expected to sell. This avoids the potential problem of selling the stock at a discount. Once the stock has been issued, the subsequent price at which it sells in the market will depend on investors' appraisal of its worth. This may have no relationship either to par value or to the initial selling price.

Common Stock

Common stockholders possess the basic rights of ownership in the corporation. These rights are determined by the laws of the state in which the company is incorporated, and by its charter and bylaws. Generally, these rights include the following:

1. The right to vote for directors and through this to be represented in the management of the company.
2. The right to share in the profits of the corporation through dividends declared by the board of directors.
3. The right to share in the distribution of the residual assets of the corporation

(i.e., those remaining after claims of creditors or preferred shareholders are satisfied) upon liquidation.

4. The pre-emptive right, or the right to maintain one's proportional share of ownership in the company by purchasing that proportional share in any newly authorized issues of stock.

If the common stock does have the pre-emptive feature, then "rights" to purchase shares in a newly authorized stock issue must be issued to common stockholders when additional shares are to be sold. The number of rights a stockholder receives is based on the number of common shares owned. The rights give the holder the privilege of buying, for a limited time, shares in the new issue of stock at a price below market. This process is obviously time-consuming, and many corporations have discontinued the pre-emptive right.

Other variations on the rights of common shareholders may be encountered in individual cases. The right that is the least likely to vary is the right to vote for directors. Common stockholders frequently are the only stockholders entitled to vote.

Common stockholders also bear the major risk of loss of their investment in the corporation. In the event of bankruptcy or liquidation, common shareholders receive the residual assets, if any, after the claims of all other suppliers of capital have been satisfied. On the other hand, the common stockholders also benefit the most if the corporation is successful. This benefit may be realized by appreciation in the market value of the common stock and by the receipt of dividends paid on the stock.

Preferred Stock

Preferred stock is a special class of stock in which preferences, or rights, are granted in exchange for certain restrictions that do not exist on the common stock. The rights and restrictions of the preferred stock, which vary among companies, are described in the preferred stock contract.

Rights of Preferred Stock

The rights of preferred shareholders usually include one or more of the following:

1. Preference as to dividends
2. Conversion rights
3. Preference as to assets in the event of liquidation

Dividend Preference. The most frequent right that preferred stock carries is a preference as to dividends of a specified amount. This does not provide assurance that the dividend will be paid, for any dividend must first be approved by the board of directors. Before declaring a dividend, the board must determine if the company (1) has adequate cash to pay a dividend and (2) will not impair its legal capital if one is paid. However, the preference does assure that preferred stockholders will be paid the dividends to which they are entitled before dividends are paid to common stockholders.

The amount of the preferred dividend usually is specified in the title of the stock. If the preferred stock has a par value, the dividend may be stated as a percentage of this value. For example, a 6%, $100 par preferred stock is entitled to a $6 dividend per year. Alternatively, the dividend may be stated as a fixed amount. An example is a $5.50 preferred stock. This stock is entitled to a $5.50 dividend per year.

The dividend on the preferred stock also may have other features. First, it may be cumulative or noncumulative. Second, the amount may or may not vary with the dividend paid on the common; that is, the preferred stock may be participating or nonparticipating. These preferences are described next.

Cumulative and Noncumulative Dividend. Typically, dividends on preferred stock are **cumulative** unless specifically made noncumulative. This means that any dividend not paid in a given year accumulates and must be paid in the future before any dividend is paid on the common stock. If the stock is **noncumulative,** the directors can avoid paying a dividend on the preferred stock simply by not declaring it. It is unlikely that such a stock would be attractive to investors. If a stock is cumulative, unpaid dividends are known as **dividends in arrears.** The amount of dividends in arrears is not a liability if the dividend has not been declared by the board of directors. However, because knowledge of the amount of dividends in arrears may be important to users of financial statements, it is disclosed either in the owners' equity section of the balance sheet or in the footnotes to the financial statements.

Suppose that a corporation has outstanding 1,000 shares of 7%, $50 par value preferred stock in the total amount of $50,000. There are 2,000 shares of $100 par value common stock outstanding for a total of $200,000. Assume that dividends on the preferred stock are two years in arrears. If $25,000 is to be distributed as dividends in the given year, the allocation between the two classes of stock is shown below.

	Preferred	*Common*
(1) The preferred stock is noncumulative		
To Preferred: current year's dividend only (7% × $50,000)	$ 3,500	
To Common: remainder		$21,500
Total	$ 3,500	$21,500
(2) The preferred stock is cumulative		
To Preferred: dividends in arrears— $3,500 per year for two years	$ 7,000	
To Preferred: current dividend	3,500	
To Common: remainder		$14,500
Total	$10,500	$14,500

Participating or Nonparticipating Dividend. Another feature of preferred stock to make it attractive to investors is the right to receive additional dividends beyond the stated rate. This type of preferred stock is known as **participating** preferred stock. Preferred stock is assumed to be nonparticipating unless the participation feature is specified.

The preferred stock with such a right may be fully participating or partially participating. If, in addition to the stated rate, a preferred stock is entitled to receive total dividends equivalent to the dividend rate paid on common stock, the preferred stock is said to be fully participating. For example, if X Company pays the stated $7 dividend on its 7%, $100 par value fully participating preferred stock and also pays a $7 dividend on its $100 par value common stock, then additional dividends would be shared equally by the two classes of securities. When the two classes do not have the same par value, the dividends commonly are shared on a pro rata basis, which is based on the par value per share.

For an illustration of the participating dividend feature, refer again to the data provided for the preceding illustration of a cumulative dividend. Assume also that the preferred stock is fully participating and that a total of $25,000 is to be distributed as dividends.

	Preferred	*Common*
(1) The preferred stock is noncumulative		
To Preferred: current year's dividend		
(7% × $50,000)	$ 3,500	
To Common: equivalent dividend		
(7% × $200,000)		$14,000
Remainder of dividend:		
($25,000 − $3,500 − $14,000 = $7,500)		
To Preferred: $\dfrac{\$50,000}{\$50,000 + \$200,000}$ × $7,500	1,500	
To Common: $\dfrac{\$200,000}{\$50,000 + \$200,000}$ × $7,500	——	6,000
Total	$ 5,000	$20,000
(2) The preferred stock is cumulative		
To Preferred: dividends in arrears		
($3,500 per year for 2 years)	$ 7,000	
To Preferred: current year's dividend		
(7% × $50,000)	3,500	
To Common: 7% × $200,000		$14,000
Remainder: $500 divided as follows:		
To Preferred stock: ⅕ × $500	100	
To Common stock: ⅘ × $500	——	400
Total	$10,600	$14,400

A preferred stock also may be partially participating. In this case the preferred stock participates in dividends paid to common stock above the preferential rate, but only up to a specified limit. For example, a company may issue a 7%, $100 par value preferred stock with a participating right up to a total of 9%. In this case the right of the preferred stock to participate in additional dividends paid on common stock is limited to an additional 2% dividend. If the dividend paid on the preferred stock is limited to the stated preference rate, the stock is nonparticipating.

Illustrations of dividend distributions with partially participating and nonparticipating preferred stock are provided below using the data from the preceding example.

	Preferred	*Common*
(3) The preferred stock is noncumulative with a participation rate of 9%		
To Preferred: current year's dividend	$ 3,500	
To Common: 7% × $200,000		$14,000
Remainder: ($25,000 − $3,500 − $14,000 = $7,500)		
To Preferred: 2% × $50,000	1,000	
To Common: Remainder		6,500
Total	$ 4,500	$20,500
(4) The preferred is noncumulative and is nonparticipating		
To Preferred: current year's dividend	$ 3,500	
To Common: Remainder		$21,500

The number of preferred stock issues with a participating feature is relatively small. Those with the fully participating feature sometimes are found in family-owned companies. The use of such a stock enables all stockholders to participate equally in the growth in dividends that the company may realize. Voting privileges, however, are limited to a smaller number of stockholders who own the common stock.

Convertible Preferred Stock. A **conversion** feature frequently is incorporated into preferred stock to make it more attractive to investors. This grants the shareholder the right to exchange the preferred stock for some other security (usually common stock) at a specified ratio. The preferred stockholder then can share in the distribution of corporate earnings beyond the stipulated preference rate at such time as the growth in earnings makes ownership of the common stock more attractive. The right to exercise the conversion feature may be limited to a specified time period or otherwise may be restricted.

Convertible preferred stocks have been used most commonly in connection with the acquisition of one corporation by another, also known as a corporate takeover. The dividend preference rate on the stock to be issued is set at a level sufficient to make it attractive to holders of the securities in the target company. The conversion feature provides these security holders with the opportunity to share in the potentially higher earnings that may be realized in the future by the combined companies. By receiving a preferred stock equivalent in value to the stock that the acquiring company seeks, the shareholders of the target company are provided with reasonable assurance of receiving a dividend equal to (and frequently greater than) the dividend being paid on their present investment. This provides an inducement to the shareholder to sell the stock to the acquiring company. An illustration of a convertible preferred stock is provided later in Chapter 21.

Asset Preference.   A preferred stock often has a preference as to assets in the event the corporation is dissolved. This feature gives the shareholders of the preferred stock a right over common stockholders to receive distributions of any assets remaining after creditors are paid. The right of the preferred shareholders to receive distributions of assets is limited to the par value of the preferred stock or to another specified amount.

Limitations of Preferred Stock

In return for its preferences, the preferred stock has other features that limit its rights compared to those of the common stock. The typical restrictions that may exist on preferred stock include the following:

1.   Absence of voting rights
2.   No right to share in the distributions of earnings beyond the stated rate
3.   Callable at the option of the issuing corporation
4.   Mandatory redemption

Absence of Voting Rights.   The absence of voting rights is the most common restriction of preferred stock. However, if preferred dividends are in arrears, preferred stockholders may be granted a voting privilege that will enable them to elect one or more directors to the board.

Limitation on Dividends.   A second restriction is the limitation on the amount of dividends that may be paid on the preferred stock. Most preferred stock issues are **nonparticipating.** A nonparticipating stock may not share in the distribution of income in amounts in excess of the stated dividend rate. The limitations on preferred stock with respect to dividends have an impact on the market price of the preferred stock. The amount that investors will be willing to pay for the preferred stock will depend on the amount of dividend to which the preferred stock has a claim. To this extent, the market price of a preferred stock may behave in a manner similar to bonds. This means that as investors require higher rates of return on their investments, the market price of the preferred stock will tend to decline if its dividend feature is limited.

Callable Preferred Stock.   Another feature common to preferred stock is that it may be **callable.** This means that the issuing corporation has the right to call (or retire) the stock at a specified price. This has the effect of limiting any increase in market value of the preferred stock to approximately the call price, which usually is set only slightly higher than the price at which the security was issued. If dividends are in arrears on a preferred stock, they usually must be paid if the call option is exercised.

   The call feature is advantageous to the issuing company because it provides it with the option of redeeming the preferred stock. This option is likely to be exercised at the time when the capital provided by preferred shareholders no longer is needed or when other sources of capital become more advantageous. If the callable preferred stock also has a conversion feature, a company might exercise its option to call the stock in order to force conversion. Of course, the preferred shareholders would have the right to receive cash for their securities instead.

Mandatory Redemption.   Another feature incorporated into preferred stocks in recent years is **mandatory redemption.** Customarily, this feature provides that the preferred stock must be redeemed, or retired, at a specified date. If the issue is to be retired serially, both the amounts and dates will be specified. This is in contrast to the "call" feature, which allows the issuing corporation the option of redeeming the shares.

Mandatory redemption may make the preferred stock, in substance, indistinguishable from a bond. There is a difference, however, in the accounting treatment of the "cost" of these two types of securities. Interest on debt is treated as an expense by the corporation for purposes of determining net income and income tax expense. Dividends on stock are not regarded as an expense and are not considered in computing net income. Instead, dividends are regarded as distributions of the net earnings of the corporation.

The hybrid nature of preferred stocks with a mandatory redemption feature has resulted in controversy over the manner of their presentation in the financial statements. Ordinarily, preferred stock is regarded as a form of owners' equity and so is included under the stockholders' equity section of the balance sheet. However, in 1979 the SEC issued a requirement (ASR 268) that preferred stock with a mandatory redemption feature be disclosed separately from other preferred and common stock. ASR 268 requires that the amount of capital contributed by the holders of preferred stock with a mandatory redemption feature be excluded in determining stockholders' equity. The preferred stock may be included as long-term debt or it may be presented as a separate item of capital between long-term debt and stockholders' equity. There also must be disclosure of the terms of the redemption, including the amount and timing of redemptions scheduled over the succeeding five years.

The special features of preferred stock that have been described here are those that are more common. Variations on these, and additional features, exist. State laws also may affect the rights of preferred shareholders. A complete description of the specific privileges or rights of a preferred stock appears on the stock certificate issued by the corporation.

Accounting for Contributed Capital

Accounting for the owners' equity, in the case of a corporation, presents unique problems not encountered in a sole proprietorship or partnership. A single equity account represents the interest of the sole proprietor. Individual equity accounts represent the equity interest of each partner in a partnership. In a corporation, several accounts are needed to show adequately the owners' equity.

In the stockholders' equity section of a corporation's balance sheet, the intent is to present the status of the ownership interests at the balance sheet date. If more than one class of stock exists, the status of each class is shown. The presentation includes details about each source of capital.

Corporations have two major classifications of capital: (1) contributed capital and (2) retained earnings. Usually, these two classifications are shown separately, as follows:

I. Contributed capital
   A. Capital stock, representing the par or stated value of the share times the number of shares issued
   B. Additional paid-in capital, representing
      1. Capital contributed in excess of the par value of the shares
      2. Capital contributed from other sources
II. Retained earnings

To aid in complying with the statutes governing legal capital, separate stockholders' equity accounts are established for each source of contributed capital. The importance of maintaining accounts that show the amount and source of the various components of contributed capital will become evident later in the chapter.

Capital stock is the ordinary security issued by corporations to raise equity capital. Corporations also may raise capital by issuing other types of securities known as dilutive debt securities. Two common types of such securities are convertible bonds and bonds with detachable warrants. These securities are discussed in Chapter 21.

Accounting for Capital Stock

The classes of stock, together with their respective rights or privileges, that a corporation is authorized to issue are described in its corporate charter or articles of incorporation. Before the issuance of any stock, it is common to note the authorization of the class by a memorandum entry in the appropriate journal. In the absence of a specific title for the stock, such as common stock or preferred stock, the term capital stock will be used.

Memorandum entry: Capital stock—par value $50 per share; 10,000 shares authorized. (Specific features of the stock also may be described.)

At the time the stock is issued, the capital stock account is credited for an amount equal to the par value of the stock times the number of shares issued. The excess of the proceeds received over the par or stated value of the stock is recorded in another contributed capital account, appropriately described. The commonly used account titles are "paid-in capital in excess of par" or "capital contributed in excess of par (or stated) value." Sometimes the account title "premium on capital stock" is used, as well as other terms. This terminology is used for both common and preferred stock.

The total amount to be recorded for capital contributed from issuance of stock usually is measured by (1) the amount of cash received or (2) the fair value of noncash assets received. The fair value of noncash assets received may be measured by the fair market value of the shares of stock issued if that market value is more readily determinable. If the corporation receives capital in the form of claims to money, or if it has liabilities canceled, the measure of contributed capital is the discounted present value of the money claim or liability canceled.[2]

Stock Issued for Cash.   The most common situation is the sale of stock for cash. Assume that one share of common stock with a $50 par value is sold for $60. The following journal entry would be made:

Cash	60	
Common stock—par value $50		50
Paid-in capital in excess of par—common stock		10

If a preferred stock is issued instead of a common stock, the account titles used here would be revised appropriately as follows:

Cash	60	
Preferred stock—par value $50		50
Paid-in capital in excess of par—preferred stock		10

The term "stated value" would be substituted for "par value" if the stock is a no-par issue. If the issuance is for a no-par stock with no requirement for a stated value, the entire proceeds are credited to the capital stock account.

Cash	60	
Capital stock		60

Separate accounts, appropriately described, are used to record the transactions for each class of stock.

If stock is issued for less than its par value, the difference is referred to as a **discount.** A negative (debit balance) contributed capital account, such as "discount on common stock," is used to record the discount amount. Because the laws of most states prohibit the issuance of stock at a discount, it is unlikely that this situation will be encountered.

Stock Issued for Noncash Consideration.   In addition to issuing stock for cash, a corporation also may issue stock for assets or services. A problem may arise in assigning a value to this noncash consideration. The amount recorded as proceeds should be either the current value of the stock issued or the value of the assets or services received, whichever is more clearly evident. If the shares of a corpora-

[2]"Basic Concepts and Accounting Principles Underlying Financial Statements of Business Enterprises," *APB Statement No. 4* (New York, AICPA, 1970), Chapter 7, par. 182, M–2.

tion are traded publicly, the market value of the shares usually will be used. In a closely held company, the value of whatever is received may be more readily determinable.

Suppose that 1,000 shares of a $10 par value common stock are to be issued for a parcel of land. The fair market value of the land is not firmly determinable, but the fair market value of the stock is known to be $16,000. The following journal entry would be made:

Land	16,000	
Common stock		10,000
Paid-in capital in excess of par—common stock		6,000
To record the issuance of stock for land.		

If, on the other hand, the fair market value of the stock was not readily determinable, but the fair market value of the land was known to be $15,500, the following entry would be made:

Land	15,500	
Common stock		10,000
Paid-in capital in excess of par—common stock		5,500
To record the issuance of stock for land.		

A special problem exists in the absence of information about market value. In some cases it may be possible to obtain an appraisal value of the assets or services. In other cases the board of directors may establish a value using whatever information is available. In the absence of fraud, the law will uphold the value established by the board of directors.

The potential for abuse exists when stock is issued for consideration other than cash. Overvaluation of the assets received results in an overstatement of the capital of the corporation. This condition is referred to as **watered** stock. That abuse was more likely to occur in days before the establishment of the Securities and Exchange Commission.

The opposite condition, undervaluation of consideration received for stock, also may occur. This is referred to as a situation in which there is a **secret reserve**. Secret reserves also are created by other accounting practices that result in artificially higher rates of write-offs for assets or other artificial understatements of assets or overstatements of liabilities. The misstatement that results from either watered stock or secret reserves may be corrected by applying the appropriate accounting correcting entry.

Issuance of Securities in a "Package".   Corporations sometimes issue two or more classes of securities as a "package" in exchange for cash or other consideration. The "package" may be composed of one or more classes of stock and bonds or notes. A valuation problem arises from the need to allocate the value of the consideration received among the classes of securities. A corporation may sell such a package for cash, or may exchange the package when acquiring a special property or another corporation.

When securities are issued as a package, there are two recognized methods for making an allocation of values if this is needed: (1) the proportional method and (2) the incremental method.

The **proportional method** is used when there are known market values for all the securities in the package. The value of the proceeds received is allocated among the individual securities on a basis that is in proportion to the market value of the individual securities.

For example, suppose a corporation decides to issue a package of authorized, but previously unissued, securities to a new investor in exchange for cash. The package consists of 500 shares of common stock, par value $10, with a current market value of $80 per share; and 1,000 shares of preferred stock, par value $12, with a current market value of $20 per share. If the proceeds from the issuance of the shares are $57,000, the transaction will be recorded as follows:

Allocation of Purchase Price

Fair market value of common stock ($80 × 500)	$40,000
Fair market value of preferred stock ($20 × 1,000)	20,000
Total market value	$60,000
Allocation to common stock: $\dfrac{\$40,000}{\$60,000} \times \$57,000$	$38,000
Allocation to preferred stock: $\dfrac{\$20,000}{\$60,000} \times \$57,000$	$19,000
	$57,000

The journal entry would be:

Cash	57,000	
Common stock		5,000
Paid-in capital in excess of par—common stock		33,000
Preferred stock		12,000
Paid-in capital in excess of par—preferred stock		7,000
To record the issuance of stock.		

In this example a question may be asked as to why the consideration received is not equal to the market value of the individual securities in the package. The explanation is that the market value of a security usually is established by transactions in which relatively small quantities of the security are traded. When larger amounts of securities are involved, they customarily trade at a somewhat lower price.

If the fair market value of all the securities in a package is not known, the **incremental method** is used. For those securities in the package for which market value is known, that value is assigned to the respective securities. The remainder is assigned to the security for which the market value is not known.

For example, refer to the data provided for the preceding example. Assume, however, that the market value for the preferred stock is not known.

> *Allocation of Purchase Price*
>
> | | |
> |---|---|
> | Fair market value of common stock ($80 × 500) | $40,000 |
> | To preferred stock—remainder | 17,000 |
> | Total | $57,000 |

The journal entry would be:

Cash	57,000	
Common stock		5,000
Paid-in capital in excess of par—common stock		35,000
Preferred stock		12,000
Paid-in capital in excess of par—preferred stock		5,000
To record the issuance of stock.		

A different kind of problem arises when there is no known market value for any of the securities in the package. If it is expected that a market value will become established for one or more of the securities in the future, then a temporary allocation may be made. This temporary allocation may be based on the face value of the securities. When a market value becomes established, the temporary basis is adjusted to conform with one of the two methods described above.

In the event that no market value is expected to be established, the board of directors may assign a value to the securities, perhaps with the advice of an investment banker or other specialist.

Stock Subscriptions

To this point, it has been assumed that stock has been issued as part of a completed exchange transaction. The receipt of cash or other consideration has occurred simultaneously with the issuance of the shares. However, stock also may be sold by a **subscription contract,** which is regarded as a legal document. Stock subscriptions commonly occur at the time a corporation is organized. In some states, the preincorporation subscribers to the capital stock must be identified in the incorporation application.

Two accounts are created at the time a stock subscription contract is negotiated. The contract indicates the number of shares to which the purchaser is subscribing and usually indicates whether payment is to be made in cash or other consideration. Assume that an organizer of a corporation subscribes to 100 shares of its $50 par value common stock for $50 per share. The following entry would be made:

Subscriptions receivable—common stock	5,000	
Common stock subscribed		5,000
To record issuance of subscribed stock.		

The financial statement presentation of stock subscriptions to be collected within one year appears below.

Current Assets		*Stockholders' Equity*	
Subscriptions receivable—		Common stock	
Common stock	$5,000	subscribed	$5,000

In the balance sheet, the capital stock subscribed account is classified as a component of owner's equity. The stock subscription receivable account usually is classified as a current or noncurrent asset, depending on when the corporation expects to receive the consideration.

This accounting treatment recognizes the corporation's obligation to issue the shares when the subscription has been collected. Also, in most states the subscriber has the legal rights and privileges of a stockholder, even though the stock has not yet been paid for and the stock certificate has not yet been issued. If there is no intention that the holder of the subscription will pay for the stock, then the stock subscription receivable is not an asset, and it should be reported as an offset against the capital stock subscribed account in the stockholders' equity section of the balance sheet.

Generally, accounting for stock subscriptions follows procedures similar to those described for stock issuance for cash. For example, assume that subscriptions are received for 100 shares of common stock, par value $10, at $50 per share.

Stock subscriptions receivable—common stock	5,000	
Common stock subscribed		1,000
Paid-in capital in excess of par—common stock		4,000
To record stock subscriptions.		

The excess of the subscription price over the par value is entered directly into the "paid-in capital in excess of par" account, even though the cash has not been collected at this point. This presentation reflects the status of the subscription receivable as a legal contract.

When payment for the stock is collected from the subscriber, an appropriate entry is made. For example, assume that one-half the balance in the subscription receivable account illustrated above is paid.

Cash	2,500	
Common stock subscriptions receivable		2,500
To record collection of subscriptions.		

Usually, the stock certificate is not issued until the full amount of the subscription is collected. At that time, an entry to record the issuance of the stock is made. Assume that the subscriber in the illustration above pays the balance of the contract, and that the corporation issues the 100 shares of $10 par value common stock.

Cash	2,500	
Common stock subscriptions receivable		2,500
To record collection of subscription.		
Common stock subscribed	1,000	
Common stock		1,000
To record issuance of subscribed stock.		

It is important to maintain accounts for stockholders' equity in adequate detail to permit the identification of each source of capital. For instance, the account "capital stock subscribed" may or may not be a component of legal capital, depending on the state of incorporation.

Unpaid Stock Subscriptions. If the subscriber defaults and does not pay the full amount of the capital stock subscription, the actions taken will depend on the laws of the state of incorporation and on the nature of the subscription contract. The corporation may be able to (1) issue shares equivalent to the number paid for or (2) refund any amounts that have been paid. If these options are available and if either is chosen, the balances relating to uncollected stock subscriptions are eliminated by making an entry to reverse the canceled portion of the subscription. Continuing the example above, assume that the subscriber defaults after making the first payment of $2,500 for the subscription. Assume also that the state law requires the issuance of capital stock equivalent to the portion of the subscription for which payment has been made and that the remainder of the subscription is canceled. The following entries will be made:

Common stock subscribed	500	
Common stock		500
To record the issuance of stock to the		
subscriber.		
Common stock subscribed	500	
Paid-in capital in excess of par—common stock	2,000	
Subscriptions receivable—common stock		2,500
To record the cancellation of a stock		
subscription.		

State law may provide other alternatives. In some cases the subscription right is forfeited and any amount paid by the subscriber is transferred to a paid-in capital account appropriately described. Alternatively, the corporation may sell the shares to a new buyer, refunding any excess to the original subscriber.

Costs of Issuing Stock

Implicit in the illustrations provided so far is the assumption that the costs connected with stock issuance are immaterial. No entries to record the costs of issuing stock have been illustrated. In the case of a large stock sale, however, the costs of issuance are significant and cannot be overlooked. Fees must be paid for printing documents and for other matters related to the sale. Professional fees also may be paid for underwriting, accounting, and legal services. The accepted accounting practice for these fees is to deduct them from the proceeds received from the issuance of the sale of the stock.

An exception to this accounting practice occurs in newly formed companies. In such cases the costs associated with the initial issuance of capital stock are regarded as part of the costs of organizing the company. All such costs are recorded as organization costs. Usually, the organization costs are relatively small in amount. The conventional accounting practice is to conform to tax regulations in this matter; these regulations permit amortization of the costs over a period of five years.

For example, assume that an existing company issues 10,000 shares of $10 par value common stock for $61 per share. Expenses in connection with the issue total $40,000. These expenses will be accounted for as if they have been paid out of the proceeds received from the sale of the stock. Only the net amount of the proceeds will be recorded.

Cash	570,000	
Common stock		100,000
Paid-in capital in excess of par—common stock		470,000
To record the issuance of stock.		

Reacquisition of Stock—Treasury Stock

A corporation may reacquire its own stock by purchasing it from existing shareholders. This stock, which may be either common or preferred, is known as **treasury stock.** The characteristics of treasury stock are as follows: (1) it has been outstanding before its repurchase by the company and (2) it is on hand, i.e., it has not been resold or formally canceled. The repurchase of its own stock by a corporation does not result in a reduction in the number of shares of stock issued, but it is a reduction in the number of shares outstanding. Treasury stock is not regarded as an asset of the company; it is a reduction in stockholders' equity.

A corporation may repurchase its own stock with the intent of later reissuing the shares. The stock will be reissued if it were purchased for the purpose of satisfying the requirements of an employee stock option plan, a bonus arrangement, or a stock purchase plan. Shares also may be reissued in connection with the acquisition of another corporation or in exchange for other assets.

Treasury shares also may be acquired with the intent to retire them formally. The stock will be retired formally if it were purchased for a planned contraction in the ownership of the corporation. The purchase may be made to buy out the ownership interest of a particular stockholder, or to buy a proportional interest of all stockholders. The intent of the latter may be to enhance the market value of the remaining stock by reducing the number of outstanding shares.

Cost Method

There are two accepted methods of accounting for the acquisition of treasury stock: (1) the cost method and (2) the par value method. The two methods affect individual accounts in the stockholders' equity section differently. However, the total amount of stockholders' equity is the same under both. Because it is more widely used, the cost method is described first. The cost method is required or implied in the states that have adopted the Model Corporation Act.

Cost Method—Acquisition of Shares.   The **cost method** of accounting for treasury stock is based on the assumption that the treasury stock transaction occurs in two parts: (1) the acquisition of its own shares by the corporation and (2) a later disposition of those shares either by reissuance or retirement. The basis for recording both the acquisition and disposal of the treasury shares is their actual purchase price, or cost, to the corporation.

Consider a company in which the stockholders' equity section appears as shown in Exhibit 19-2. Assume that the company chooses to reacquire 100 shares of its stock. If the 100 shares, par value $10, are reacquired for $60 per share, the following entry is made to record the acquisition:

Treasury stock (100 shares @ $60)	6,000	
Cash		6,000
To record the purchase of		
treasury stock.		

Exhibit 19-2
Stockholders' Equity

Contributed capital	
Common stock, $10 par value; 10,000 shares	
authorized and outstanding	$100,000
Paid-in capital in excess of par	470,000
Total contributed capital	$570,000
Retained earnings	100,000
Total stockholders' equity	$670,000

Exhibit 19-3
Stockholders' Equity

Contributed capital	
Common stock, $10 par value; 10,000 shares	
authorized and issued, of which 100 are	
held in treasury	$100,000
Paid-in capital in excess of par	470,000
	$570,000
Retained earnings	100,000
	$670,000
Deduct: cost of treasury shares	(6,000)
Total stockholders' equity	$664,000

If a corporation has more than one class of stock outstanding, separate accounts are established for each class of stock acquired as treasury stock.

In the financial statements of the corporation, treasury stock accounted for by the cost method is shown as a reduction of the total stockholders' equity. This reflects the reduction in total capitalization due to the purchase of treasury stock.

The preceding example may be used to illustrate the presentation of treasury stock on the balance sheet using the cost method (see Exhibit 19-3). The example assumes that 100 shares of this stock issue were reacquired as treasury stock for $60 per share.

Cost Method—Reissuance of Shares. If the treasury stock is reissued later, the process described above is reversed. It is unlikely that the reissue price will be exactly the same as the acquisition cost of the stock. However, no "gain" or "loss," in the accounting sense, may be realized by a corporation as a result of transactions in its own shares. Instead, any difference between acquisition cost and reissue price is regarded as an adjustment of the stockholders' equity in the corporation.

If the treasury stock is reissued at an amount greater than the original acquisition cost, the excess is recorded as an additional component of paid-in capital. Referring to the illustration above, assume that 50 of the shares of common stock that were purchased for $60 per share are reissued later for $78 per share.

Cash	3,900	
Treasury stock		3,000
Paid-in capital—treasury stock transactions		900
To record the sale of treasury stock.		

A separate account is used to identify the source of this new component of contributed capital. If treasury shares have been acquired at various prices, a method for identifying the cost of the shares sold must be established. Either the specific identification, fifo, or average cost methods may be used. Normally, the fifo method is followed unless another method is specified.

Treasury stock also may be issued for an amount less than its cost to the corporation. In this case the difference between the cost and the selling price is recorded as a reduction of the appropriate stockholders' equity accounts. If there is a paid-in capital account resulting from previous treasury stock transactions in that class of stock, the difference may be charged to this account to the extent that it has a sufficient balance. Suppose that the 50 shares referred to above, acquired for $60 per share, later were reissued for $50 per share instead of $78. Assume that the corporation does have an account, "paid-in capital—treasury stock transactions," with a balance of $900.

Cash	2,500	
Paid-in capital—treasury stock transactions	500	
Treasury stock		3,000
To record the reissuance of treasury stock.		

If there is no paid-in capital account resulting from such treasury stock transactions, or if the account balance is exhausted, any additional difference may be charged to retained earnings.[3] For example, assume that the remaining 50 shares of treasury stock were later reissued for $40 per share. The $2000 from reissuance is $1000 less than the $60 per share cost of the stock. Again, assuming that the company has an account, "paid-in capital—treasury stock transactions," with a balance of $900, the following entry is made:

Cash	2,000	
Paid-in capital—treasury stock transactions	900	
Retained earnings	100	
Treasury stock (50 shares @ $60)		3,000
To record the reissuance of treasury stock.		

The remaining difference of $100 is charged to retained earnings.

The cost method of accounting for treasury stock commonly is used when a corporation has acquired its own stock with the intent of reissuing it or when the exact use of the treasury shares has not been decided yet.[4]

[3]"Status of Accounting Research Bulletins," *Opinions of the Accounting Principles Board No. 6* (New York: AICPA, 1965), par. 12b.

[4]Ibid.

Par Value Method

The **par value** method views the treasury stock purchase as if it is a completed transaction in which the corporation has acquired and constructively retired the stock. The stock actually is not retired; instead, it is carried at par value, rather than cost, until a decision about final disposition is made. The difference between the acquisition cost of the stock and its par value is recorded as an adjustment to the appropriate stockholders' equity accounts at the time the shares are acquired. In the balance sheet, the treasury stock, at par value, is shown as a reduction of the related capital stock account.

Par Value Method—Acquisition of Shares. In the usual transaction, the cost of treasury shares will exceed their par value. In this case there are two methods of accounting for the excess of the purchase price of the treasury shares over their par value. Both methods are acceptable.

Under *Method 1* the intent is to eliminate from the stockholders' equity accounts the portion of contributed capital that is applicable to the reacquired shares.

When the purchase price of the treasury shares exceeds the par value of the shares, the excess is allocated between (1) paid-in capital in excess of par for this class of stock and (2) retained earnings.[5] The amount of the purchase price allocated to the paid-in capital is an average, or pro rata, amount per share based on the number of shares outstanding.

An illustration may clarify this; refer to Exhibit 19-2. That company has 10,000 shares of stock outstanding and a total contributed capital of $570,000, or $57 per share. The par value is $10 per share, and the average paid-in capital is $47 per share.

Assume that the company reacquires 100 shares of this stock for $60 per share. The excess of the cost ($60) over par value ($10) is $50 per share. Of this excess, $47 will be charged to the paid-in capital account, and the remainder will be charged to retained earnings.

Treasury stock	1,000	
Paid-in capital in excess of par—common stock	4,700	
Retained earnings	300	
Cash		6,000
To record the reissuance of treasury stock.		

After reacquisition of the shares, the stockholders' equity section would appear as shown in Exhibit 19-4.

The total stockholders' equity has been reduced from $670,000 to $664,000. The amount of the reduction is equal to the cost of the treasury stock.

A company may also have an account for paid-in capital arising from previous treasury stock transactions. In this case the excess of the cost of the treasury

[5] Ibid., par. 12a.

Exhibit 19-4
Stockholders' Equity

Contributed capital	
Common stock: $10 par value; 10,000 shares authorized and issued	$100,000
Less: treasury stock, 100 shares at par	1,000
Common stock outstanding (9900 shares)	99,000
Paid-in capital in excess of par	465,300
Total contributed capital	$564,300
Retained earnings	99,700
Total stockholders' equity	$664,000

---

stock over its par value may be allocated between (1) the paid-in capital created when the shares originally were issued and (2) the paid-in capital account arising from previous treasury stock transactions. The charge to the former of these accounts is determined in the manner already described. The excess of cost over par value is offset against the paid-in capital arising from previous treasury stock transactions to the extent of the balance in that account. Any remainder is charged to retained earnings.

For example, refer to the data in Exhibit 19-3. Assume, however, that the company does have a paid-in capital in excess of par account arising from treasury stock transactions, and that the balance in this account is $900. The journal entry to record the purchase of 100 shares at $60 per share under these conditions is as follows:

Treasury stock (100 shares @ $10 share)	1,000	
Paid-in capital in excess of par—common stock (100 shares @ $47)	4,700	
Paid-in capital—treasury stock transactions	300	
Cash		6,000
To record the reissuance of treasury stock.		

In this example, it was not necessary to charge any of the cost on the purchase of the treasury stock to retained earnings.

As mentioned previously, there is a second way in which the par value method of accounting for treasury stock is applied. Under *Method 2* the excess of the cost of the treasury stock over its par value is charged directly to retained earnings. Use of this method avoids the need to allocate a portion of the excess to additional paid-in capital accounts. The rationale for the alternative method is that the corporation always can reallocate retained earnings to paid-in capital by declaring a stock dividend.[6] This type of transaction is explained in the next chapter. The following entry illustrates *Method 2* using the example above, in which 100 shares of common stock, par value $10, are acquired for $60 per share:

Treasury stock (1,000 shares @ $10)	1,000	
Retained earnings	5,000	
Cash (1,000 shares @ $60)		6,000

It is possible that treasury stock may be purchased at a cost less than its par value. In this case an entry also is made in the treasury stock account for the par value of the shares purchased. The difference between this amount and the purchase price is credited to a paid-in capital account.

For example, assume that a company purchases 100 shares of $10 par value stock for $9 per share. The entry to record the acquisition would be as follows:

Treasury stock	1,000	
Paid-in capital—treasury stock transactions		100
Cash		900
To record the reissuance of treasury stock.		

Under the par value method of accounting, an entry is made to paid-in capital-treasury stock at the time the treasury shares are acquired. The reason is that the company has reacquired $1,000 par value of its stock for only $900. The difference between the par value of the original issue and its reacquisition cost is reclassified within the stockholders' equity section as paid-in capital arising from treasury stock transactions.

Par Value Method—Reissuance of Shares. Under the par value method, the reissuance of shares of treasury stock is accounted for in the same manner as the issuance of new capital stock. The difference between the par or stated value of the shares and their selling price is entered in a paid-in capital account just as if the shares were newly issued. Any excess of issue price over par value is recorded as an increase in the account "paid-in capital" arising from the sale of stock. Should the stock be issued for an amount less than par value, the difference would be charged to the same account to the extent of its balance. Any excess loss would be charged to retained earnings. It would not be appropriate to record a discount on the issuance of treasury stock. The discount may be recorded only at the time the shares are originally issued.

To illustrate the entries for the reissuance of treasury stock accounted for by the par value method, refer again to the preceding illustration. The balance in the treasury stock account is $1,000, representing the 100 shares of common stock, $10 par value, being held in the treasury. Assume that the 50 shares held in the

[6] Ibid., par. 12a.

treasury are reissued for $70 per share. The following journal entry would be made:

Cash	3,500	
Treasury stock		500
Paid-in capital in excess of par		3,000
To record the reissuance of		
treasury stock.		

The purchase of treasury stock by a corporation must be carried out in accordance with state law or other established regulations. Since the purchase of treasury shares results in a distribution of assets to the selling shareholder, most state laws prohibit the purchase of treasury shares, except under rare circumstances, if the effect would be to impair legal capital. Regardless of the method of accounting used for treasury stock, the shares are nonvoting and do not receive cash dividends as long as they continue to be held by the corporation.

Donated Treasury Stock

Occasionally, shareholders may donate all or a portion of their stock to the corporation. Donated stock also is considered treasury stock. The donation may be for the purpose of enabling the corporation to raise additional capital through resale of these shares, or it may be for some other purpose.

There are three methods of accounting for donated shares. Two methods are variations on the "cost" and "par value" methods of accounting for treasury stock previously described. The third method is to make only a memorandum entry for the receipt of the shares.

Under the variation of the cost method, the receipt of the donated shares is recognized by recording them at market value, and by crediting a separate paid-in capital account for a corresponding amount. Under the variation of the par value method, the donated stock is recorded at its par value with a corresponding credit to the same paid-in capital account. These two methods of accounting are illustrated below.

Assume that 100 shares of common stock, par value $10, are donated to the company by a shareholder. The market value of the shares is $15 per share at the time of the donation. With the variation of the cost method, the following entry would be made:

Treasury stock	1,500	
Paid-in capital—donated stock		1,500
To record donated stock.		

If the variation of the par value method is used, the entry would be as follows:

Treasury stock	1,000	
Paid-in capital—donated stock		1,000
To record donated stock		

Entries are made in the accounts to reflect the final disposition of the donated stock. If the shares are reissued subsequently, the transaction is accounted for using either the cost or par value methods, depending on the method used to record the original donation. Both these methods of accounting for reissuance of treasury stock have been described in the previous section.

If only a memorandum entry were made to record receipt of the donated shares, the entire proceeds from issuance are credited to an account for paid-in capital from donated stock. Suppose that no entry previously has been made to record the receipt of the 100 donated shares described in the previous example. If these 100 shares are reissued now for $20 per share, the following entry would be made:

Cash	2,000	
Paid-in capital—donated shares		2,000
To record the sale of donated		
stock.		

Retirement of Treasury Stock

When treasury stock is retired formally, the effect is to return the shares to the status of unissued shares. Normally, shares of stock that are to be retired can be viewed initially as treasury shares. The accounting method used to record the retirement depends on whether the cost or par value method were used to record the acquisition of the shares.

If the par value method of accounting were used, only one entry is needed to record the retirement. Since the treasury stock is carried at par or stated value, a credit can be made to the treasury stock account and a debit can be made to the original paid-in capital account. For example, assume that 100 shares of capital stock, $100 par value, are being held as treasury stock. Under the par value method of accounting, the treasury stock account balance is $10,000. The retirement would be recorded as follows:

Capital stock	10,000	
Treasury stock		10,000
To record the		
retirement of		
treasury stock.		

If the shares were accounted for using the cost method, the difference between cost and par or stated value is allocated among the paid-in capital accounts and, if necessary, retained earnings in the manner described for the acquisition of treasury shares using the par value method.

Restriction of Retained Earnings for Treasury Stock

Normally treasury stock purchases are limited to the amount of the corporation's retained earnings and paid-in capital. The purpose of this limitation is to prevent the corporation from impairing its legal capital by distributing assets to owners through the purchase of treasury shares. This has the effect of requiring that a restriction be placed upon retained earnings in an amount equal to the cost of the treasury shares. The restriction is to preclude the corporation from making other disbursements of assets in excess of the amount of "free" retained earnings. The restriction may be noted by formally restricting a portion of the retained earnings equal to the cost of the treasury stock or by disclosure in the footnotes to the financial statements. Exhibit 19-5 illustrates such a disclosure.

In states that have adopted the Model Corporation Act it also may be possible to purchase treasury stock in an amount equal to the paid-in capital in excess of par. When this occurs the paid-in capital account must also be restricted as long as the treasury stock is held.

In most states the circumstances under which a corporation can acquire its own stock are prescribed by statute. The method of accounting for the stock acquisition also is governed by statute. If the methods of accounting prescribed

---

Exhibit 19-5
Restriction of Retained Earnings
for Cost of Treasury Stock
Cost Method
Stockholders' Equity

Contributed capital	
Common stock, $10 par value; 10,000 shares authorized and issued, of which 100 shares are held as treasury stock	$100,000
Paid-in capital in excess of par	470,000
Total contributed capital	$570,000
Retained earnings—restricted for cost of treasury shares	6,000
—unrestricted	94,000
Total retained earnings	$670,000
Less: cost of treasury shares	6,000
Total stockholders' equity	$664,000

by the state differ from the methods described here, the accounting followed should conform to applicable state law.[7]

Other Retirements of Stock

There are two major ways in which a corporation may retire its own stock. One method is to purchase, or otherwise acquire, the shares for the purpose of retirement. In this case the transaction can be viewed as one in which the stock being retired initially acquires the characteristics of treasury stock. This is true even if the stock issue has been "called" by the corporation for retirement. Under the second method, such as a preferred stock with a convertible feature, the stock is retired by exchange for shares of another class of stock. Convertible preferred stock is discussed in Chapter 21.

If the stock is purchased for retirement, the accounting method used to record the retirement is analogous to that described for the purchase of treasury stock using the par value method. The procedure is to remove all capital account balances related to the shares being retired. Any excess cost is debited to retained earnings, and any "gain" is recorded in a separate paid-in capital account.

For example, assume that a preferred stock issue of 1,000 shares with a par value of $20, and an original issue price of $21, is called at $22 for retirement. The journal entry is as follows:

Preferred stock	20,000	
Paid-in capital in excess of par—preferred	1,000	
Retained earnings	1,000	
Cash		22,000
To record the retirement of preferred stock.		

If, instead, the call price is $20,000, the journal entry would be:

Preferred stock	20,000	
Paid-in capital in excess of par—preferred	1,000	
Additional paid-in capital—retirement of preferred		1,000
Cash		20,000
To record the retirement of preferred stock.		

In both cases, the original paid-in capital accounts applicable to the shares being retired are eliminated. The additional paid-in capital account arising from the retirement of an entire stock issue at a "gain" becomes applicable to the common stock.

[7] Ibid., par. 13.

Financial Statement
Disclosures of Contributed Capital

In the balance sheet of a corporation, the presentation of contributed capital is designed to show the total amount and source of each component of capital. The specific manner of presentation must be one that satisfies any statutory or corporate charter requirements.

Within the stockholders' equity section, separate contributed capital accounts are provided for (1) the par or stated value of the shares issued, (2) capital contributed in excess of par or stated value for the shares issued, and (3) contributed capital from other sources. Examples of other sources are contributed capital arising from treasury stock transactions or from donated treasury stock. If an

---

Exhibit 19-6
Stockholders' Equity

Contributed capital		
Capital stock		
Preferred stock—5% cumulative; par value $100; authorized 10,000 shares; issued and outstanding 5,000 shares.		$ 500,000
Class A preferred stock—$2 cumulative; no par value; redeemable value $30; authorized, issued, and outstanding 7,000 shares.		210,000
Common stock—no par value; stated value, $10; authorized 50,000 shares; issued 25,000 shares, of which 500 are in the treasury.		250,000
Total		$960,000
Paid-in capital:		
In excess of par or redemption value of preferred stock	$ 15,000	
In excess of stated value of common stock	100,000	
Arising from treasury stock transactions	12,000	127,000
Total contributed capital		$1,087,000
Retained earnings		$2,100,000
Total		$3,187,000
Deduct cost of 500 shares of treasury stock		11,300
Total stockholders' equity		$3,175,700

Note: Retained earnings are restricted for dividends in the amount of $11,300, the cost of the treasury stock.

entire issue of stock is retired at a "gain," a contributed capital account also will exist for this; this component of capital is considered part of paid-in capital of the common stock.

Disclosures also are presented for each class of stock. These include the number of shares authorized, issued, and outstanding. The number of shares held as treasury stock also is reported. Any special rights or privileges of a class of stock are described in detail. Typically, these rights relate to preferred stock and include information about the dividend rate and whether it is cumulative or participating, the existence of any voting rights, and asset preference in the event of liquidation. If the preferred stock is callable or convertible, descriptions of these features also are provided.

Exhibit 19-6 shows a common presentation of contributed capital.

It is common practice, as shown in this illustration, to limit the amount of detail breakdown provided for the additional paid-in capital accounts. For instance, only one amount is shown for the paid-in capital from the sale of preferred stock. Of course, the company would be required to keep separate accounts for the paid-in capital arising from the issuance of each of the two classes of preferred stock. But this additional detail probably will not be relevant to the users of the financial statements.

If changes occur in any of the contributed capital accounts during the period covered by the financial statements, the details of the changes must be shown. Usually this is done in a separate statement of changes in stockholders' equity.

In the stockholders' equity section of the balance sheet, a distinction is made between the two major sources of owners' capital: (1) contributed, or paid-in, capital and (2) retained earnings. The distinction is made primarily to show the sources of capital, rather than because it has any practical economic significance. Also, disclosure of capital by source is required under the laws of most states. As is illustrated in this chapter and in Chapter 20, the distinction between contributed capital and retained earnings is not always a permanent one. Corporations can engage in transactions that result in reclassifying an amount of capital from one of these two sources to the other.

Exhibit 19-7 shows the stockholder's equity disclosures from a recent annual report of Alexander & Baldwin, Inc. The company is located in Hawaii and is involved in ocean transportation, property development and management, investments and merchandising, trucking, and storage. Part I of Exhibit 19-7 shows the stockholder's equity section from the company's balance sheet. Part II consists of a Statement of Stockholder's Equity. This Statement illustrates the detail of the changes in equity as discussed above. Notice that the Statement shows the changes for the two years financial data presented in the financial statements.

Exhibit 19-7
Equity Disclosures

Part I	1979	1978
Stockholders' Equity:		
Capital stock—authorized, 30,000,000 shares of common stock without par value; stated value, $2-2/9 per share; outstanding, 9,083,228 and 9,097,060 shares	$ 21,837	$ 21,762
Additional capital	20,306	19,788
Retained earnings	243,710	219,530
Cost of treasury stock	(13,583)	(12,810)
Total stockholders' equity	$272,270	$248,270

Part II

ALEXANDER & BALDWIN, INC. AND CONSOLIDATED SUBSIDIARIES
STATEMENTS OF STOCKHOLDERS' EQUITY
For the years ended December 31, 1979 and 1978
(In thousands except share amounts)

| | Capital Stock | | | | | |
| | Issued | | In Treasury | | | |
	Shares	Stated Value	Shares	Cost	Additional Capital	Retained Earnings
Balance, December 31, 1977	9,731,901	$21,626	496,279	$(9,185)	$18,937	$197,813
Changes in 1978:						
Stock options exercised	6,850	15			72	
Purchased minority interest in subsidiary	54,588	121			779	
Treasury stock purchased			200,000	(3,625)		
Net income						32,811
Cash dividends— $1.20 per share						(11,094)
Balance, December 31, 1978	9,793,339	21,762	696,279	(12,810)	19,788	219,530
Changes in 1979:						
Stock options exercised	33,610	75			391	
Treasury stock purchased			70,000	(1,207)		
Treasury stock issued			(22,558)	434	127	
Net income						35,296
Cash dividends— $1.22½ per share						(11,116)
Balance, December 31, 1979	9,826,949	$21,837	743,721	$(13,583)	$20,306	$243,710

Concept Summary

STOCKHOLDERS' EQUITY—
ISSUANCE AND REACQUISITION

TYPES OF CAPITAL

Type	Description	Source
Contributed	Capital derived from means other than the earnings of the entity, primarily from stockholder investments	Common stock; preferred stock; additional paid-in capital from treasury stock transactions, stock retirements, and donated assets
Earned	Capital generated from the operations and retained for use in the entity	Retained prior earnings

PREFERRED STOCK FEATURES

Features	Description
Voting	Preferred may be voting or nonvoting. In some cases nonvoting preferred may become voting upon the occurrence of some event, such as nonpayment of dividends for a specified period of time.
Callable	Preferred is callable when the company has a right to repurchase the shares at a stipulated price.
Convertible	A convertible preferred stock is one that can be exchanged for common stock shares.
Cumulative	When preferred is cumulative, dividends in arrears must be paid before common shareholders can participate in dividend distributions.
Participating	Participating preferred may share in a distribution of earnings in an amount in excess of the stipulated dividend rate.

TREASURY STOCK

Definition—the company's own stock that has been issued and repurchased by the company.

Accounting Method	Description
Cost	Repurchased stock is recorded at cost.
Par	Repurchased treasury stock is treated as if it were to be retired. It is recorded at its par value.

Questions

Q–19–1 What are the differences between the three major forms of business organization?

Q–19–2 Discuss the advantages and disadvantages of the corporate form of business organization.

Q–19–3 What are the basic requirements for an entity to incorporate? Discuss the pervasive role that a state plays in the activities of the corporation.

Q–19–4 What are the differences between privately held and publicly held corporations?

Q–19–5 Explain the differences between common stock and preferred stock. Discuss how these are separate ownership classes, yet within these classes each share is equal.

Q–19–6 Define *legal capital*. How and why is it restricted?

Q–19–7 What are the four basic rights of common stock shareholders? Which one of these rights is most likely to have been discontinued? What is the value of this right to the common stock shareholder?

Q–19–8 What theory of ownership equity is enumerated by the following equation: assets minus liabilities minus preferred stock equity equals common stock equity?
  a) Fund.
  b) Enterprise.
  c) Entity.
  d) Residual equity.

(AICPA adapted)

Q–19–9 Describe the differences between the following features of preferred stock:
  a) Cumulative vs. noncumulative.
  b) Participating vs. nonparticipating.
  c) Convertible vs. nonconvertible.
  d) Callable vs. noncallable.
  e) Redeemable vs. nonredeemable.

Q–19–10 Explain how fully participating preferred stock takes on a preference that generally is reserved for the holders of common stock.

Q-19-11 Discuss the advantages of convertible preferred stock to the shareholder. Discuss the advantages of callable preferred stock to the issuing corporation.

Q-19-12 Discuss preferred stocks' priority claim to corporate assets in the event of liquidation. Who does their claim defeat and up to what amounts?

Q-19-13 List and briefly explain the typical restrictions on the holders of preferred stock.

Q-19-14 Explain how the features of limited dividend participation and mandatory redemption cause the equity security of preferred stock to take on the characteristics of a debt security.

Q-19-15 Describe the special accounting treatment for and disclosure requirements of preferred stock with a mandatory redemption feature.

Q-19-16 At the issuance of capital stock, total contributed capital should be credited for what amount?

Q-19-17 Discuss the potential accounting abuses that could arise when issuing stock for a consideration without a clearly determinable market value.

Q-19-18 Differentiate between the two methods used to account for the issuance of securities in a package.

Q-19-19 What are the two alternative methods of recording the initial costs of issuing stock? When is each more appropriate?

Q-19-20 Explain the characteristics of treasury stock. For what purposes do companies reacquire their own stock?

Q-19-21 How are the cost method and par value method of accounting for treasury stock different?

Q-19-22 List and explain three methods of accounting for the receipt of donated stock.

Q-19-23 Discuss the accounting treatment for the repurchase and retirement of a complete class of outstanding stock. How is this different from a repurchase to acquire treasury shares?

Q-19-24 Which of the following statements *best* describes the net effect on retained earnings of the purchase and subsequent sale of treasury stock?
  a) Retained earnings may never be increased, but sometimes is decreased.
  b) Retained earnings may never be increased or decreased.
  c) Retained earnings sometimes is increased, but may never be decreased.
  d) Retained earnings always is affected unless the selling price is exactly equal to cost.

(AICPA adapted)

Q-19-25 How should a gain from the sale of treasury stock be reflected when using the cost method of recording treasury stock transactions?
  a) As ordinary earnings shown on the earnings statement.
  b) As paid-in capital from treasury stock transactions.
  c) As an increase in the amount shown for common stock.
  d) As an extraordinary item shown on the earnings statement.

(AICPA adapted)

Q-19-26 How does the par-value method of accounting for treasury stock differ from the cost method?
  a) *No* gains or losses are recognized on the sale of treasury stock using the par value method.
  b) Any gain is recognized upon repurchase of stock, but a loss is treated as an adjustment to retained earnings.
  c) It reverses the original entry to issue the common stock, with any difference

between carrying value and proceeds adjusted through paid-in capital, and treats a subsequent resale like a new issuance of common stock.

d) It reverses the original entry to issue the common stock, with any difference being shown as an ordinary gain or loss, and does *not* recognize any gain or loss on a subsequent resale of the stock.

(AICPA adapted)

Discussion Questions and Cases

D-19-1 Capital stock is an important area of a corporation's equity section. Generally the term *capital stock* embraces common and preferred stock issued by a corporation.
Required:
1. What are the basic rights inherent in ownership of common stock, and how are they exercised?
2. What is preferred stock? Discuss the various preferences afforded preferred stock.

D-19-2 Define the following terms.
   a) Treasury stock.
   b) Legal capital.

D-19-3 It has also been said that "watered stock" is the opposite of a "secret reserve."
Required:
1. What is a "secret reserve"?
2. What is "watered stock"?
3. Describe the general circumstances in which "watered stock" can arise.
4. What steps can be taken to eliminate "water" from a capital structure?

(AICPA adapted)

D-19-4 Ms. Thinbody owns 5,000 shares of common stock in Joe's Fitness Emporium, a small, closely held corporation. Mr. Healthy Clubs, a national chain of fitness studios, has offered to purchase Joe's for an amount agreeable to all the stockholders but Ms. Thinbody. Joe's articles of incorporation require that at least 90% of the outstanding shares of common stock must vote in favor of a corporate reorganization before it can take place. In a secret meeting, the consenting stockholders approved and issued enough stock to reduce Ms. Thinbody's holding to only 10%. Joe's Fitness Emporium's balance sheet before dilution of Ms. Thinbody's holdings is as follows:

	Assets	Liabilities & Stockholders' Equity	
Cash	$ 7,000	Liabilities	$ 3,000
Other Assets	18,000	Common Stock	
		($1 Par Value)	25,000
		Retained Earnings	(3,000)
	$25,000		$25,000

Required:
1. How many shares of common stock are needed to be issued to reduce Ms. Thinbody's ownership to the required 10%?
2. What general rights of common stock did the other stockholders violate when they issued these additional shares?
3. Explain how these rights would protect Ms. Thinbody's interests.
4. Discuss why you think one of the historic rights of common stock is being eliminated by larger corporations.

D–19–5 In an effort to better the company's cash position, the board of directors of Express Printing Company is contemplating the issuance of one of two different securities. The first alternative is to issue preferred stock with limited dividend participation and a mandatory redemption feature. Second, it has looked into selling long-term bonds. As the company accountant, you have been asked to prepare a presentation for the next board meeting that explains:

a) The advantages and disadvantages of both alternatives.

b) The special accounting treatment required by the first alternative.

D–19–6 For numerous reasons a corporation may reacquire shares of its own capital stock. When a company purchases treasury stock, it has two options as to how to account for the shares: (1) cost method, and (2) par value method.

Required:

Compare and contrast the cost method with the par value method for each of the following:

a) Purchase of shares at a price less than par value.

b) Purchase of shares at a price greater than par value.

c) Subsequent resale of treasury shares at a price less than purchase price, but more than par value.

d) Subsequent resale of treasury shares at a price greater than both purchase price and par value.

e) Effect on net income.

(AICPA adapted)

D–19–7 The president of the Big A Corporation has suggested repurchasing a pro rata portion of each stockholder's shares at a price well above the current market price. This, he believes, will both satisfy the stockholders' demands for a dividend and maintain the company's strong financial appearance by showing a large surplus of retained earnings.

Required:

1. As the accountant for Big A, you must explain to the president how, if generally accepted accounting principles are followed, his scheme will fail.

2. In addition to restricting retained earnings, when might it also be necessary to disclose a restriction on paid-in capital in excess of par?

Exercises

E–19–1 The Culture Corporation had the following classes of stock outstanding as of December 31, 1979:

> Common stock, $20 par value, 20,000 shares outstanding.
> Preferred stock, at 6% interest, $100 par value, cumulative
> and fully participating, 1,000 shares outstanding.

Dividends on preferred stock have been in arrears for 1977 and 1978. On December 31, 1979, a total cash dividend of $90,000 was declared. What are the amounts of dividends payable on both the common and preferred stock, respectively?

(AICPA adapted)

E–19–2 No dividends had been paid by the Boomer Corporation for the past three years. Its capital stock issued and outstanding during these three years and at December 31, 1983, was as follows:

> Common stock, $50 par value, 15,000 shares outstanding.
> Preferred stock, at 4% interest, $100 par value, 5,000 shares outstanding.

Retained earnings at the end of 1983 is $80,000.

Required:

1. Assume the preferred stock is cumulative and compute the maximum dividend payments to both classes of stock.

2. Assume the preferred stock is noncumulative and compute the maximum dividend payments to both classes of stock.

E–19–3 The outstanding capital stock of M. F. Edwards Company at May 11, 1985, consisted of the following:

> 15,000 shares of common stock, no par value, stated value $20 per share.
> 5,000 shares of 5% preferred stock, $20 par value.

Required:

Under each of the following assumptions, calculate the amount of dividends to be distributed to each class of stock.

a) The preferred stock is cumulative and nonparticipating. No dividends were paid in the previous year, and $50,000 is to be distributed this year.

b) The preferred stock is cumulative and fully participating. Dividends are one year in arrears, and $65,000 is available for distribution this year.

c) The preferred stock is noncumulative and partially participating, up to 10%. Dividends were not paid in the previous year, and $75,000 is to be distributed this year.

E–19–4 On July 14, 1983, JX Corporation exchanged 1,000 shares of its $8 par value common stock for a plot of land. JX's common stock is listed on the New York Stock Exchange and traded at an average price of $21 per share on July 14. The land was appraised by independent real estate appraisers on July 14 at $23,000. Record the journal entry to reflect this transaction.

E–19–5 Use the proportional method to allocate the values and record the journal entry for these securities issued in a package:

> 600 shares common stock, stated value $5, current market value $11.
> 110 shares preferred stock, at 5% interest, $10 par value, current market value $20.

This package was issued for $8,000.

E–19–6 Use the incremental method to allocate the values and record the journal entry for these securities issued in a package:

> 800 shares common stock, $10 par value, current market value $15.
> 75 shares preferred stock, at 4% interest, $5 par value, no current market value.

This package was issued for $12,800.

E–19–7 Maw Company received subscriptions for 7,500 shares of its preferred stock ($40 par value) at a price of $55 per share. Subscriptions for 70,000 shares of its $2 par value common stock also were received at a price of $10 per share.

Required:

Record the journal entries for each of the transactions as listed below:

a) Receipt of all the subscriptions as above.

b) Full payment of the subscriptions.

c) Issuance of the stock.

E–19–8 Chas Corporation issued 5,000 shares of $10 par value common stock for $47 per share. Issue costs, including printing fees, attorney fees, and accounting fees, amounted to $4,000.

Required:
Record the journal entry necessary to reflect the transaction above assuming the following:

a) Chas Corporation is an existing corporation that made a further issuance of common stock.

b) Chas Corporation is a new corporation initially offering the securities above.

E–19–9 Baker Corporation has 80,000 share of $50 par value common stock authorized, issued, and outstanding. All 80,000 shares were issued at $55 per share. Retained earnings of the company amounts to $160,000.

Required:
If $1,000 shares of Baker common stock are reacquired at $62, show the journal entry necessary to reflect the treasury stock acquisition using the methods below:

a) Par value method. (Make entries for both methods.)

b) Cost method.

E–19–10 An analysis of the stockholders' equity of Barton Corporation as of January 1, 1982, is as follows:

Common stock, par value $20; authorized, 200,000 shares; issued and outstanding, 120,000 shares	$2,400,000
Paid-in capital in excess of par	280,000
Retained earnings	1,540,000
Total	$4,220,000

Barton uses the *cost method* of accounting for treasury stock and during 1982 recorded the following transactions:

a) Acquired 2,000 shares of its stock for $70,000.

b) Sold 1,200 treasury shares at $40 per share.

c) Retired the remaining treasury shares.

Required:
Record the transactions above in general journal form.

E–19–11 Jenny Corporation was organized on January 1, 1988, with an authorization of 500,000 shares of common stock with a par value of $5 per share. During 1988 the corporation had the following capital transactions:

January	5	Issued 100,000 shares @ $5 per share.
April	6	Issued 50,000 shares @ $7 per share.
June	8	Issued 15,000 shares @ $10 per share.
July	28	Repurchased 25,000 shares @ $4 per share.
December	31	Sold 20,000 shares held in treasury @ $8 per share and retired the remaining 5,000 shares.

Jenny used the par value method to record the purchase and reissuance of the treasury shares.

Required:
Record the transactions above in general journal form.

(AICPA adapted)

E–19–12 Goodel Corporation was organized on January 1, 1981, with authorized capital of 500,000 shares of $10 par value common stock. During 1981, Goodel had the following transactions affecting stockholders' equity:

January	10	Issued 10,000 shares @ $12 per share.
May	8	Repurchased 1,000 shares of treasury stock @ $13 per share.
September	10	Sold 1,000 shares of treasury stock @ $14 per share.

Required:
Goodel uses the cost method for recording treasury stock transactions. Show the necessary entries.

(AICPA adapted)

E–19–13 Elaine Corporation was organized on January 1, 1979, with an authorization of 1,000,000 shares of common stock with a par value of $5 per share. During 1979, the corporation had the following capital transactions:

January	4	Issued 200,000 shares @ $5 per share.
April	8	Issued 100,000 shares @ $7 per share.
June	9	Issued 30,000 shares @ $10 per share.
July	29	Repurchased 50,000 shares @ $4 per share.
December 31		Sold 50,000 shares held in treasury @ $8 per share.

Required:
Elaine used the par value method to record the purchases and reissuance of the treasury shares. Show the necessary entries.

(AICPA adapted)

E–19–14 On September 22, 1983, Robert Warren, the major stockholder of C. S. Consultants, Inc., donated 1,500 shares of $10 par value common stock back to the corporation. This stock previously had sold at a *premium* of $18. The current market price is $31.
Required:
1. Record the journal entries for this donated treasury stock under the three following alternatives:
    a) Cost method.
    b) Par value method.
    c) Memorandum entry.
2. Now assume this donated stock is sold later at a price of $29 per share. Again record the necessary entry under the three methods above.

E–19–15 In 1982 Mark Albert and Associates, Inc. purchased 5,000 shares of their $10 par value outstanding common stock for $45 per share to meet the needs of future employee stock options. Later that year the option plan was eliminated, and the treasury shares were retired. The common stock originally had been issued for $42.

Required:
Make the necessary entries to reflect the acquisition and retirement under both cost and par value methods of handling treasury stock.

E–19–16 Forrest Insurance Company purchased for retirement its complete issue of 2,000 shares of $5 par value preferred stock. The preferred stock had been sold originally at $17 less $1 per share original issuance costs.
Required:
Record the appropriate journal entries for the repurchase of the stock at a call price of
    a) $18 per share.
    b) $12 per share.

E–19–17 Midl Company records all its treasury stock transactions under the par value method. Midl had repurchased 5,000 shares of $10 par value common stock for $77,000. On Midl company's year-end balance sheet, retained earnings was restricted for treasury stock in the amount of $50,000.
Required:
1. Briefly explain why this restriction is inadequate.
2. What should be the amount of restricted retained earnings?

E–19–18 Newton Corporation was organized on January 1, 1983. On that date it issued 200,000 shares of its $10 par value common stock at $15 per share (400,000 shares were authorized). During the period of January 1, 1983, through December 31, 1985, Newton reported net income of $750,000 and paid cash dividends of $380,000. On January 5, 1985, Newton purchased 12,000 shares of its common stock at $12 per share. On December 31, 1985, 8,000 treasury shares were sold at $8 per share. Newton used the cost method of accounting for treasury shares.

Required:

Prepare the stockholders' equity section of Newton Corporation's December 31, 1985, balance sheet in good form.

(AICPA adapted)

Problems

P–19–1   The Amlin Corporation was incorporated on January 1, 1984, with the following authorized capitalization:

20,000 shares of common stock, no par value, stated value $40 per share.
5,000 shares of 5% cumulative preferred stock, no par value, $10 per share.

During 1984 Amlin issued 12,000 shares of common stock for a total of $600,000 and 3,000 shares of preferred stock at $16 per share. In addition, on June 30, 1984, subscriptions for 1,000 shares of preferred stock were taken at a purchase price of $17. By December 1, half of the subscriptions were fully paid and the stock issued, while the remaining were defaulted and written off the books with no stock issued. Amlin Corporation paid no dividends in 1984 and had income after taxes of $43,500.

Required:

1. Record the journal entries to reflect the events above.
2. Prepare in good form the stockholders' equity section of Amlin's December 31, 1984, balance sheet.
3. If the subscriptions not paid for had not been written off, how would Amlin's year-end balance sheet be different?

(AICPA adapted)

P–19–2   The stockholders' equity section of Goetz Company's December 31, 1982, balance sheet was as follows:

Common stock, $20 par value; authorized 150,000 shares; issued and outstanding 100,000 shares	$2,000,000
Additional paid-in capital	400,000
Retained earnings	100,000
	$2,500,000

The following independent situations also refer to Goetz Company:

a)   During 1983 Goetz suffered a net loss of ($75,000). The current market price of the common stock is $42.50. Goetz purchased 1,000 shares of its common stock at the current market price.   *10,000 shares*

b)   During 1983 Goetz had net income of $60,000 for the year, and paid dividends of $75,000. Goetz purchased 1,000 shares of its common stock at the current market price.   *11,411 shares*

Required:

For each of the situations above, calculate the following:

a)   The maximum shares of stock that could be repurchased without impairing legal capital, assuming the state has passed the Model Corporation Act.   *10,000*

b) The amounts of any restrictions that would be disclosed in the company's balance sheet for the stock purchased in each situation.

P–19–3 Tomasco, Inc. began operations in January, 1978, and had the following reported net income or loss for each of its five years of operations:

1978	$ 150,000	loss
1979	130,000	loss
1980	120,000	loss
1981	250,000	income
1982	1,000,000	income

At December 31, 1982, the Tomasco capital accounts were as follows:

Common stock, par value $10 per share; authorized 100,000 shares; issued and outstanding 50,000 shares	$ 500,000
4% nonparticipating, noncumulative preferred stock, par value $100 per share; authorized, issued, and outstanding 1,000 shares	100,000
8% fully participating, cumulative preferred stock, par value $100 per share; authorized, issued, and outstanding 10,000 shares	1,000,000

Tomasco has never paid a cash or stock dividend. There has been no change in the capital accounts since Tomasco began operations. The appropriate state law permits dividends only from retained earnings.

Required:

Prepare a work sheet showing the *maximum* amount available for cash dividends on December 31, 1982, and how it would be distributable to the holders of the common shares and each of the preferred shares. Show supporting computations in good form.

(AICPA adapted)

P–19–4 You have been assigned to the audit of Wright, Inc., a manufacturing company. You have been asked to summarize the transactions for the year ended December 31, 1983, affecting stockholders' equity and other related accounts. The stockholders' equity section of Wright's December 31, 1982, balance sheet is as follows:

Stockholders' Equity

Common stock, par value $10; shares authorized 500,000; shares issued 90,000	$ 900,000
Capital in excess of par value	11,250
Retained earnings	424,689
Less cost of 1,210 shares of common stock in treasury	(36,300)
Total	$1,299,639

You have extracted the following information from the accounting records and audit working papers.

a) On January 15, 1983, 650 shares of treasury stock were sold for $20 per share. The 1,210 shares of treasury stock on hand at December 31, 1982, were purchased in one block in 1978. Wright used the cost method for recording the treasury shares purchased.

b) On March 6, 1983, subscriptions for 1,400 shares of common stock were issued at $22 per share, payable 50% down and the balance by March 20. On March 20 the balance due on 1,200 shares was received, and those shares were issued. The subscriber who defaulted on the 200 remaining shares forfeited his downpayment in accordance with the subscription agreement.

c) On August 31, 1983, Wright exchanged 12,400 previously authorized but unissued shares of its common stock for a 100-acre tract of land. There was no readily determinable market value for the land, but it had been kept on the owner's books at $248,000.

d) On November 11, 1983, 500 shares of the treasury stock were retired.

e) On December 3, 1983, 1,000 shares of the outstanding common stock were donated back to the company. These shares were recorded using the par value method.

Other data:

The market price at which Wright's common stock traded on a Midwest exchange at various dates follows:

January 2	$19	August 31	$33
January 15	20	October 1	33
January 26	21	November 1	36
March 30	22	December 3	38
August 1	32	December 31	42

Required:

1. Record the journal entries to reflect all of the transactions above for 1983.

2. Prepare a presentation of stockholders' equity in good form including all required amounts and disclosures as of December 31, 1983.

(AICPA adapted)

P–19–5 The following are transactions of the Illinois Corporation:

a) The board of directors authorized 10,000 shares of $10 par value common stock.

b) One-half of the shares in Part a) were issued for $72,000.

c) The other half of the common stock was issued on a subscription basis at $25 per share with a 20% down payment.

d) Issued 15,000 shares of 7%, no par value preferred stock, stated value of $40 per share. Sold at a "premium" of $15 per share.

e) 90% of common stock shares subscribed were paid in full.

f) The remaining 10% of the shares subscribed to by Mr. Brooke were defaulted, and he did not pay the remaining 80% due. Illinois Corporation issued shares equivalent to the partial payments and canceled the balances relating to the remaining uncollected subscriptions.

Required:

Prepare entries in journal form to record the transactions above.

P–19–6 The Commerce Company has two issuances of *nonparticipating*, par value preferred stock outstanding. One is cumulative, 5% preferred stock, $10 par, 20,000 shares outstanding. The other is noncumulative 7% preferred stock, $20 par, 30,000 shares outstanding. The 50,000 shares of common stock outstanding have a par value of $1 per share. Retained earnings of the company are 125,000.

Required:

1. Compute the amount of *dividends per share* that would be received this year if all retained earnings were paid out and if

a) Dividends are in arrears for three years.

b) All dividends had been paid previously.

2. If the preferred stock had the right of participation in any dividend that exceeded 10% on common stock, up to an additional 2% for preferred stockholders, how much could each class of stock receive if no dividends were in arrears and all retained earnings were paid out?

P-19-7 Presented below is the stockholders' equity section of Caper Corporation at December 31, 1983:

Common stock, par value $20; authorized	
50,000 shares; issued and outstanding 30,000 shares	$600,000
Capital in excess of par	150,000
Retained earnings	230,000
Total stockholders' equity	$980,000

During 1984 the following transactions occurred relating to stockholders' equity:
a) 1,000 shares were reacquired at $28 per share.
b) 900 shares were reacquired at $30 per share.
c) 1,500 shares of treasury stock were sold at $32 per share.
For the year ended December 31, 1984, Caper reported net income of $110,000. The state in which Caper is incorporated places a restriction on the distribution of retained earnings equal to the cost of treasury stock. Assuming Caper accounts for treasury stock under the par value method, record the necessary journal entries to reflect the transactions above and prepare the stockholders' equity section of the December 31, 1984, balance sheet.

P-19-8 Buyback Corporation was organized on January 1, 1984. On that date it issued 100,000 shares of $10 par value common stock at $12 per share (200,000 shares were authorized). During the period from January 1, 1984, through December 31, 1986, Buyback earned net income of $400,000 and declared and paid cash dividends of $150,000. On January 10, 1986, Buyback purchased 5,000 shares of its common stock at $10 per share. On December 31, 1986, 3,000 treasury shares were sold at $7 per share. Buyback used the cost method in accounting for treasury stock.
Required:
Prepare the stockholders' equity section of the December 31, 1986, balance sheet. (Journal entries are not required.)

P-19-9 As the new accountant for Kate's Fashions, Inc. you discover during the year that no entries have been recorded in the treasury stock accounts despite the treasury stock activity. The related capital stock accounts had the following ongoing balances:

Common stock ($50 par value)	$90,000
Contributed capital in excess of par	28,000
Retained earnings	15,000

Required:
You are to record the following treasury stock transactions under the two generally accepted accounting methods as a proposal for the controller. (Use the FIFO flow assumption as needed.)
a) Repurchased 350 shares at $59 per share.
b) Repurchased 200 shares at $65 per share.
c) Sold 275 treasury shares at $63 per share.
d) Repurchased 100 shares at $66.50 per share.
e) Sold 150 treasury shares at $66 per share.

P-19-10 On June 15, 1982, Triple-A Advertising was organized and authorized to issue the following equity securities:

Common stock, 10,000 shares, $5 par value.
Preferred stock, 7,500 shares, 6%, $8 par value.

During the company's first half-year of operation, the following capital stock transactions occurred:

June   30   Issued one-half of the common stock at $15 per share.

July   26   Issued the remaining half of the authorized common stock in exchange for assets with the following fair market values:

Furniture and fixtures	$ 9,000
Machinery and equipment	18,000
Land	23,000

August   17   Subscriptions for the preferred stock were received at a price of $15 per share. All subscribers made a 50% downpayment on this date.

September 29   The second installment on the subscribed shares was received, and the preferred stock was issued.

December 31   The income summary account, with a debt balance of $13,000, was closed to retained earnings.

Required:

Record the journal entries reflecting the events above and prepare a year-end balance sheet.

P–19–11   The following information was taken from the equity accounts of R. Lindbeck Co.:

Common stock, $5 par value, $10,000 shares issued and outstanding	$50,000
Preferred stock, $3 par value, 2,000 shares issued and outstanding	6,000
Paid-in capital common stock	75,000
Paid-in capital preferred stock	14,000
Paid-in capital defaulted subscriptions	10,000

The issuance of the preferred stock was handled completely on subscription basis. When the stock was subscribed (4,000 shares at $10), 50% was paid as a downpayment. When the second installment was due, half the subscribers defaulted. The applicable state law allows the corporation to retain any incomplete payments on stock subscriptions, while the subscriber forfeits any rights to partial issuance or refund. The common stock was issued outright to the purchasers.

Required:

The account balances above represent all the transactions affecting the capital stock of the corporation during its first three months of operation. From these balances and from the information above, recreate in chronological order the journal entries underlying those balances.

P–19–12   The following accounts represent the total stockholders' equity of Trooper Company as of July 1, 1982:

Preferred stock, 8%, cumulative, $10 par value	$100,000
Paid-in capital—preferred stock	25,000
Common stock, $50 par value	500,000
Paid-in capital—common stock	125,000
Retained earnings	85,000

During the fiscal year the following transactions affecting stockholders' equity occurred:

   a) Issued 2,000 shares of preferred stock at $17 per share.

   b) Issued 7,500 shares of common stock at $74 per share.

c) Purchased 2,000 shares of common stock for the treasury at $82 per share—recorded at cost.

d) Retired 1,000 treasury shares in item c).

e) Reissued 500 shares of treasury stock at $85 per share.

f) Net income for the year was $130,000.

Required:

Based on the data above, prepare the stockholders' equity section of the balance sheet as of June 30, 1983.

P–19–13 On February 13, 1983, Lakeside's application for a corporate charter was approved by the appropriate state agencies with the following proposed capitalization:

> 75,000 shares of 6% preferred stock, convertible, $50 par value
> 200,000 shares of common stock, $10 par value

The following transactions in capital stock occurred throughout the first year:

a) Two-thirds of the preferred stock were subscribed for at $58 per share, payable 50% down with the balance due in one more payment.

b) 100,000 shares of the common stock were subscribed for at $25 per share; two-fifths of this amount was paid for immediately, with the balance due within three months.

c) 10,000 shares of common stock were issued in exchange for 10 railroad cars. The rail cars had no determinable market value, but were on the books of the selling company at $75,000 net of accumulated depreciation. Market value of the common stock on this day was $17 above par value.

d) The balance on the preferred stock subscriptions was received, and the stock was issued.

e) The balance on the common stock subscriptions was fully paid, except for 500 shares. The partial payment on these shares was returned to the subscriber, and the related accounts were eliminated.

f) 1,000 shares of common stock were reacquired for $26 per share and accounted for using the par value method.

g) Net income for the first year was $85,000.

Required:

1. Record the journal entries necessary to reflect the transactions above.
2. Prepare a statement of stockholders' equity at year-end.

P–19–14 From the following information prepare the stockholders' equity section of the balance sheet:

Common stock	$10,000
Paid-in capital in excess of par—common stock	2,000
Preferred stock—6%	30,000
Preferred stock—8%	40,000
Paid-in capital in excess of par—6% preferred stock	12,000
Paid-in capital in excess of par—8% preferred stock	8,000
Treasury stock—donated common stock (at cost, 100 shares)	1,500
Treasury stock—common stock (at cost, 100 shares)	1,750
Treasury stock—6% preferred (at cost, 500 shares)	5,500
Paid-in capital in excess of par—donated common stock	1,500
Retained earnings	25,000

P–19–15   On April 14, J. R. Oil Company was organized and received authority from the state to issue the following capital stock:

   $8 preferred stock, cumulative, nonparticipating, $75 par value, 100,000 shares

   Common stock, $10 par value, 100,000 shares

The following transactions involving stockholders' equity occurred throughout the year:

April	25	50,000 shares of the preferred stock were subscribed for at $100 per share. $20 per share was received as a downpayment with the balance due on June 1.
May	1	Sold 75,000 shares of the common stock at $32 per share.
June	1	Received the full balance due on the preferred stock subscriptions and issued those shares.
August	12	Issued 2,000 shares of common stock and 500 shares of preferred stock in exchange for land valued at $121,000. The market value of the common stock was $35 per share. No fair value of the preferred stock could be determined.
September	1	$600,000 in dividends was declared by the board of directors.

Required:

Prepare journal entries to reflect the transactions above.

20

Stockholders' Equity—Retained Earnings and Dividends

Accounting in the News

Dividend payments are important sources of income to many investors. Some people in the financial community believe a decrease in dividends could adversely affect a company's stock price. For this reason many companies try at least to maintain stable dividend levels during bad times.

Any company that paid more than $300 million of common stock dividends last year must be the picture of health—or at the very least, not terribly troubled, right?

Wrong. Not if that company is the Ford Motor Co.

Last year Ford lost almost $3 billion pretax on its North American operations. That's half again as much as crippled Chrysler lost in North America pretax, and three times what General Motors lost here. It took $800 million of tax credits and $600 million of overseas profits to keep Ford's net loss down to a mere $1.5 billion. . . .

Despite the cash squeeze and the prospect of more difficult times to come, Ford is still clinging to its common stock dividend. At the current level of 30 cents a quarter (cut from $1 last July), the dividend on its 120 million shares runs Ford more than $140 million a year. That's money Ford has to borrow at today's outrageous interest rates.*

This chapter discusses items that should be considered in declaring dividends and accounting for various types of dividends.

*Allan Sloan, "A Fault?" *Forbes*, April 13, 1981, p. 31.

This chapter covers the major types of events and transactions affecting retained earnings. These include dividend transactions, including cash and other forms of dividends; appropriations of retained earnings; and quasi reorganizations. Certain of these may involve adjustments to both the contributed capital and retained earnings accounts.

Functions of Retained Earnings

Retained earnings has its source in the earnings of the corporation. The account reflects the accumulated undistributed earnings of the corporation. The measurement of earnings is important because generally it is only from earnings that dividends may be distributed to shareholders. If a corporation has had no other transactions affecting its capital accounts except earnings and dividends, then the amount of retained earnings represents the difference between total income and dividends since the beginning of the corporation. If a corporation has had losses in excess of income, then the retained earnings account has a debit balance and is referred to as the **accumulated deficit.** This is subtracted from other stockholders' equity accounts in the balance sheet.

Earning an adequate income is of primary importance to most business organizations. This income has two uses: first, it may be distributed to the owners of the business and thus represents a return on the capital invested by the owners; second, the income may be retained in the business as the basis for expansion. The purpose of retaining income within the business is to finance the growth of the business.

The original purchasers of the corporation's stock have contributed capital to the business. These original investors, or any subsequent purchasers of their stock, may realize a return on their investment in two ways. The first is through receiving dividends on their stock. Dividends are a return on the stockholder's investment—they represent a distribution of assets that have resulted from the earnings of the corporation. Stockholders also realize a return on their investment if the market value of their stock increases. If earnings are retained within the corporation, it is expected that the corporation's value will increase and thus the market price of its stock will increase also.

It is evident that the use of earnings for paying dividends and for expanding the business is important. Many successful corporations have a continuing need for additional funds to enable the business to expand. In order to increase its assets, the corporation must have a source for funding the growth. Retaining the earnings within the business, rather than distributing them as dividends, is the only internal source of funds for expansion. All other sources must be provided by outsiders, either creditors or owners. On the other hand, a dividend is important to investors because it represents a current return on their investment. Although an increase in the market value of the stock may be attractive, the investor must sell the stock to realize this form of return. In many businesses these two uses of earnings are in competition.

It is the responsibility of the corporation's directors to decide the extent to which earnings will be paid out currently as dividends or reinvested in the corporation. When a corporation pays a dividend, generally no distinction is made about whether the dividend is from current or past earnings.

Factors Affecting Dividend Decisions

The decision to declare a dividend must take into consideration a number of factors. These include (1) the legality of the dividend, (2) the availability of cash, (3) contractual restrictions on the payment of dividends, and (4) dividend policy.

Legality of the Dividend

The first factor affecting the dividend decision is whether or not it is legal under the laws of the state of incorporation. In most states a corporation is required to maintain a minimum amount of capital, known as **legal capital,** for the protection of creditors. A corporation cannot make distributions of assets to stockholders if the effect is to reduce the legal capital below this minimum amount.

As mentioned in the previous chapter, the definition of legal capital varies among the states. In some states it is defined as the par or stated value of the shares issued. In this specific case, it may be possible for a corporation to declare dividends on the basis of an additional paid-in capital account, rather than on the basis of retained earnings. The dividend would represent a return of a portion of the capital originally invested by stockholders and would not be classified as income for the investor receiving it. Unless advised to the contrary, stockholders assume that the dividend represents a payout of earnings and not a return of capital.

To satisfy the laws of the state of incorporation, the corporation maintains separate accounts for each source of capital included in stockholders' equity. This provides a basis for determining whether a dividend legally can be declared. If a dividend is distributed illegally by the board of directors, both the individual directors and the stockholders may have a liability for the amount of the dividend. For instance, if a dividend is paid by an insolvent corporation, or if the dividend would cause the corporation to become insolvent, state law may provide that the stockholder has a contingent liability to the extent of the dividend received. Accordingly, determining the legality and the source of the dividend is important.

The statutory restrictions on the declaration of dividends have no practical impact on the profitable companies. These companies have substantial retained earnings legally available for dividends. Whether or not dividends can be paid will be determined by the availability of cash and by the existence of other restrictions arising from loan or other agreements.

Availability of Cash

The existence of retained earnings does not mean that a corporation has cash or other assets available for paying dividends. The reason is that the increase in net assets that results from retaining earnings in the business ordinarily is not in the form of cash. Instead, the growth in net assets may be reflected by increases in accounts receivable, inventories, or other assets. Also, the liabilities of the corporation may have been reduced.

A complete picture of all the factors affecting the change in the net assets of a corporation for a specified period is provided by the Statement of Changes in Financial Position, described in Chapter 25. This statement shows how a business has utilized the earnings and other sources of funds.

The payment of a dividend represents a major use of cash. Before deciding to pay a dividend, the corporation's board of directors must determine if sufficient cash is available. A corporation must maintain adequate cash and other liquid assets to enable it to meet its payroll, pay the accounts payable, and satisfy other continuing obligations. A dividend also competes with other possible uses of cash, such as replacing existing equipment or financing an expansion of working capital or plant assets. Advance financial planning is important to assure that adequate cash will be available when a dividend is to be paid.

Contractual Restrictions

When a corporation borrows money, particularly on a long-term basis, it is not uncommon for lenders to place restrictions on the payment of dividends. The intention of the restriction is to provide assurance that the corporation's current level of credit-worthiness will be maintained in the future. The effect is that increases in the corporation's net assets, to the extent specified in the lending agreement, must be retained in the business. Such a restriction does not guarantee that the company will be able to repay the loan upon maturity. Even if the net assets of the corporation are greater, the increase may not be in cash or other liquid form. However, the restriction does provide assurance that such assets— to the extent that they do exist—will not be distributed to shareholders in the form of dividends.

Restrictions specified in a lending agreement may extend also to other matters. For instance, a corporation may be required to maintain a certain amount of working capital or a specified current ratio. In addition, limitations may be placed on additional borrowings. The terms of the lending agreement specify the exact nature and extent of all restrictions.

Dividend Policy

Corporations often establish policies with regard to the timing and amount of dividend distributions. The policy will reflect the extent to which the earnings of the business are to be distributed to stockholders or retained for expansion. The intent of setting a specified amount of earnings to be distributed usually is to provide shareholders with a consistent, predictable dividend. Most corporations are reluctant to lower their rate of dividend. Therefore, the directors will establish dividends at a level that they believe can be maintained during periods of good business or moderate decline. Over time, the amount of the dividend may be expected to grow. Before deciding on such increases, however, the directors of the corporation usually seek to determine if the new dividend rate can be maintained.

The decision of individual investors to buy stock in a company often is influenced by its dividend policy. Investors who are interested primarily in current income will choose to invest in a company that pays out a relatively high proportion of its earnings as dividends. Other investors seek only appreciation in the value of their stock investment through the retention of earnings within the company. These investors will select a company in a growing industry that needs capital for expansion and, as a result, retains all or most of its earnings within the business. The decisions of investors are influenced in part by the income tax consequences of their choice of investment. Dividends received in cash generally are taxed at ordinary income tax rates to the person receiving the dividend. A gain realized from the sale of stock held on a long-term basis is taxed at the capital gains rate, which usually is much lower than the ordinary income tax rate. For these reasons, knowledge of the company's dividend policy is important.

Accounting for Dividends

The action of the board of directors in authorizing a dividend is referred to as the **declaration** of the dividend. This action creates a legal obligation to pay the dividend, and an accounting entry must be made to reflect it. A separate dividends account is used to record the dividends declared on a class of stock during the period. As stated previously, dividends are not considered an expense of the company. Instead, they are considered a distribution of earnings. Therefore, the dividends account is closed directly to retained earnings at the end of the accounting period. The accounting for a typical dividend transaction is illustrated below. It is assumed that the dividend represents a distribution of the earnings of the company and will be paid in cash.

Entry on date the dividend is declared:
    Dividends
        Dividends payable

Entry on date the dividend is paid:
    Dividends payable
        Cash

Entry on date the dividend account is closed:
    Retained earnings
        Dividends

If a balance sheet is prepared after the date of declaration and before the date of payment, the dividend payable balance is included in current liabilities since payment requires the use of current assets.

At the time a dividend is declared, two additional dates are important: (1) the date of record and (2) the ex-dividend date. The **date of record** is important because it is the stockholders on this date who will receive the dividend. The date of record usually is several weeks before the date of payment of the dividend. This time period is needed to permit the corporation to prepare an up-to-date listing of its stockholders at the date of record and to process the dividend checks. The **ex-dividend date** is significant because purchasers of the stock on or after this date do not receive the dividend. In the case of smaller companies, the ex-dividend date usually is the day following the date of record. However, in companies whose stock is traded on the New York Stock Exchange, the stock is traded ex-dividend on the third business day before the date of record.

This additional time is needed for the stock trades to be settled. For example, if the date of record falls on a Friday, an investor who buys the stock on the preceding Monday will receive the dividend, and the investor who buys on Tuesday will not. This is because Tuesday is the third business day before the date of record. Accordingly, it is likely that the price of the stock will drop by the amount of the dividend on the day the stock trades ex-dividend. No journal entries are made by the company on either the date of record or the ex-dividend date.

Kinds of Dividends

Dividend distributions may take several forms. The most common is cash. Distributions also may be made in the form of (1) property, (2) scrip (i.e., a promise to pay cash), and (3) shares of the company's own stock. If the dividend is in a form other than cash, the term "dividend" is accompanied by a descriptive word or phrase, such as **stock dividend** or **property dividend,** indicating the exact nature of the dividend. Also, unless otherwise indicated, the origin of the dividend is assumed to be retained earnings. Following are illustrations of the accounting practices followed in recording these different types of dividends.

Cash Dividends. The term "dividend" used without modification implies the **cash dividend.** This is the most common kind of dividend and the accounting is straightforward. In the example following, the significant dates and entries in a dividend transaction are illustrated.

Assume that on December 15, the directors of Adams Company declare a dividend of $1 per share, payable to stockholders of record on December 28, and that the dividend will be disbursed on January 15. Adams Company has 5,000 shares of capital stock outstanding. The following entries will be made:

At date of declaration:

| December 15 | Dividends | 5,000 | |
| | Dividends payable | | 5,000 |

At date of record:

December 28   No entry

At date of payment:

| January 15 | Dividends payable | 5,000 | |
| | Cash | | 5,000 |

Since the dividend is payable in cash, the dividend payable account is classified as a current liability.

Property Dividends. Occasionally, a dividend is distributed in a form other than cash. A **property dividend,** or dividend-in-kind, may be the product produced by the company, securities of another company that have been held as an investment, or some other asset. Practical limitations on the divisibility of most kinds of noncash assets make property dividends uncommon. When they do occur, it is most often in smaller companies with only a few stockholders. If a property dividend is declared in a large company, the asset that is distributed to stockholders usually is the stock of another company that has been held as an investment. For instance, at one time the DuPont Corporation held a significant investment in the common stock of General Motors Corporation. These shares of GM were distributed as a dividend to the holders of DuPont's common stock. Such a distribution is known as a **spin-off.** The desire to spin off an investment is the reason for most of the property dividends that occur in large corporations.

When a property dividend is declared, a decision must be made about the value of the property being disbursed as a dividend. According to *APB Opinion No. 29*, the dividend is to be recorded at the fair market value of the assets to be distributed.[1] This is the value that the entity would realize in an outright sale at or near the time of the distribution. In the absence of a known market value, an estimated value, based on an independent appraisal, may be used. For example, if items from the inventory of a company are distributed as a dividend, the basis for recording the dividend is the selling price of the inventory.

The difference between the market value of the asset being distributed and the amount at which the asset is carried on the books of the company is recognized as a gain or loss. Thus, the fair market value of the property to be distributed is determined at the date of the declaration of the dividend. The amount of the gain or loss is included in the determination of income for the period in which the declaration is made.

Assume that the directors of the Adams Company have declared as a dividend the stock of Barker Company that has been held as an investment. The stock has a current market value of $10 per share and a cost to the company of $6 per share. If Adams Company owns and is distributing 5,000 shares of Barker Company stock, the declaration of the dividend is recorded as follows. In the first entry you increase the asset account balance by $4 per share to adjust the investment account balance from its book value of $30,000 (5,000 shares × $6) to $50,000 (5,000 shares × $10).

Investment in stock of Barker Company	20,000	
Gain on investment in stock of Barker Company		20,000
To record the increase in the value of investments.		
Property dividend	50,000	
Dividends payable		50,000
To record declaration of a property dividend.		

If the securities to be distributed are classified as a current asset, the dividend payable account is a current liability.

[1]"Accounting for Nonmonetary Transactions," *Opinions of the Accounting Principles Board No. 29* (Stamford, Conn.: FASB, 1973), par. 18.

Scrip Dividends.   A type of dividend rarely encountered is a **scrip dividend.** Scrip dividends have occurred in a few cases when a company wished to declare a dividend but lacked the cash to pay it currently. The **scrip** is the equivalent of a note payable, and it represents an obligation. If the scrip is interest-bearing, the interest is recorded as an expense of the period in which it accrues. It is not a part of the dividend.

Stock Dividends.   A **stock dividend** is the distribution of additional shares of stock to the stockholders of the corporation. Unlike other kinds of dividends, it does not involve the distribution of any assets by the corporation. A stock dividend does increase the number of shares of stock outstanding, but the corporation receives nothing in return for the issuance of the shares. As a result, there is no change in the *total* amount of stockholder's equity. The stock dividend has no economic impact on the corporation.

Ordinarily, the shares distributed as a stock dividend are from the same class as the stock on which the dividend is being issued. The shares distributed usually are from authorized but previously unissued shares, and they are issued on a pro rata basis. For example, if a 10% stock dividend is declared, each stockholder receives one share as a dividend for each ten shares owned. From the investor's viewpoint, the stock dividend simply increases the number of shares of stock representing the investment.

A stock dividend also has no effect on the percentage of ownership of the corporation by individual stockholders. This is illustrated below for a stockholder who owns 100 shares of stock in a company that pays a 10% stock dividend. Assume that before the dividend declaration the company had 10,000 shares of stock issued and outstanding.

	Number of Shares Owned	Total Number of Shares	Percent of Ownership
Before the 10% stock dividend	100	10,000	1%
After the 10% stock dividend	110	11,000	1%

It is apparent that a stock dividend has no impact on either the corporation's assets or an individual investor's percentage of ownership. Nor is a stock dividend regarded as taxable income of the investor who receives it. However, accounting entries do need to be made to reflect the fact that additional shares of stock are being issued. The effect of the accounting entry is to capitalize, or reclassify, a portion of the retained earnings to the contributed capital accounts.

Accountants have disagreed about the amount of retained earnings that should be capitalized to reflect a stock dividend. Some accountants believe that the amount of retained earnings that should be capitalized is the fair market value of the additional shares of stock to be issued. In their view a stock dividend results in this amount of retained earnings not being available for future dividends. Other accountants believe that only the par, or stated value, of the shares to be distributed should be capitalized. Their reasoning is that a stock dividend has no economic impact on the corporation and that only the entry required by state law should be made. Typically, the only legal requirement is to increase contributed capital by the par value of the new shares being issued. The amount of retained earnings to be capitalized is different under the "fair market value" and "legal basis" methods of accounting.

Under the fair market value basis, the amount of retained earnings that should be capitalized is the fair market value of the additional shares issued. This is supported by the fact that many recipients of stock dividends believe they are receiving a distribution of corporate earnings equal to the fair market value of the stock received. Because of this belief, retained earnings should have the fair market value removed so that this amount will not be available for future dividend distributions.

The legal basis requires that only the par or stated value of the stock be capitalized from retained earnings. This theory is supported by the argument that a stock dividend has no economic impact on the corporation and, therefore, the only entry that should be made is that required by law. This theory is also based on the fact that a stock dividend merely distributes the stockholder's interest in the corporation over a larger number of shares. Selling the shares received would reduce the stockholder's proportionate share of the ownership in the corporation.

Advocates of both views of accounting sometimes refer to the behavior of the stock's market price to support their arguments. The question of how to account for stock dividends is not readily answered by referring to the market price of the stock. It is difficult to prove that a change in the market price of a company's stock is due only to the announcement of a stock dividend. Similarly, the absence of a change in the market price of the stock after such an announcement cannot be taken as evidence that the stock dividend represents income to the stockholder. A change or lack of change in the market price of a company's stock may be due to a variety of other factors.

The disagreement over the method of accounting for stock dividends was settled by the AICPA's Committee on Accounting Procedure.[2] Under their pronouncement, stock dividends are classified first as either "small" or "large." A stock dividend is regarded as small if it involves a distribution of less than 20 to 25% of the existing number of shares outstanding. Otherwise it is regarded as large.

This range of percentages was chosen as the dividing line between a small and large stock dividend because it was believed that a noticeable change in the market price of the stock would occur for distributions larger than 20 or 25%. As a result, stockholders would be less likely to regard a large stock dividend as income even if they did regard a small stock dividend as income. The Committee on Accounting Procedure specified that different accounting methods be used for small and large stock dividends.

If a stock dividend is classified as small, retained earnings in the amount of the fair market value of the dividend is transferred to contributed capital. The previous example may be continued to illustrate this. The company has 10,000 shares of stock outstanding, par value $10 per share. Before declaring the dividend, the company has additional paid-in capital of $140,000 and retained earnings of $90,000. Assume the market value is $18 per share before the declaration

---

[2]"Chapter 7: Capital Account," *Accounting Research Bulletin Number 43* (New York: AICPA, 1934), Section B, par. 11.

of a 10% stock dividend and that the market value of the shares is unchanged by this announcement. The stock dividend will be 1,000 shares (10% of 10,000 shares outstanding). The total amount of retained earnings transferred to contributed capital will be $18,000 (1,000 shares times the $18 market value). Of the amount transferred to contributed capital, $10,000 will be recorded in the par value account (1,000 shares times $10 par value), and the remaining $8,000 will be recorded in an additional paid-in capital account. The entry on the date of declaration appears below.

Stock dividend (retained earnings)	18,000	
Stock dividend distributable		10,000
Paid in capital in excess of par		8,000
To record the declaration of		
a stock dividend.		

The following entry is made at the date of distribution of the stock dividend.

Stock dividend distributable	10,000	
Common stock, $10 par value		10,000
To record the distribution of		
a stock dividend.		

The effect of this stock dividend on the stockholders' equity section of the balance sheet appears in Exhibit 20-1. The effect on an individual stockholder who is assumed to own a 1% interest, or 100 shares, before issuance of the dividend also is illustrated. Since this company has only common stock outstanding, the book value per share is computed easily by dividing total stockholders' equity by the number of shares issued and outstanding.

It should be noted that the Committee on Accounting Procedure suggested that this accounting practice be followed only by publicly held companies. It was presumed that stockholders of closely held companies would not confuse a stock dividend with a dividend in which actual assets of the company are distributed.

For all large stock dividends, the "legal" method of accounting is to be followed. Under this method, retained earnings in the amount of the par or stated value of the stock distributed as a dividend is transferred to contributed capital. This method of accounting also is to be followed for small stock dividends declared by closely held companies.

This also may be illustrated by referring to the preceding example. Assume that the company, with 10,000 shares of $10 par value stock outstanding, declares a 50% stock dividend. Because this is a large dividend, the amount of retained earnings transferred to contributed capital is only the par value of the shares to be distributed. Knowledge of the market value of the stock following the announcement of the dividend is not needed. In this case $50,000 (5,000 shares to be distributed times $10 par value per share) will be transferred from retained earnings. On the date of declaration the following entry will be made:

Stock dividend (retained earnings)	50,000	
Stock dividend distributable		50,000
To record the declaration of a large stock dividend.		

Exhibit 20-1
Illustration of Stock Dividend

Stockholders' equity—before 10% stock dividend

Contributed capital	
Common stock, $10 par value; 20,000 shares authorized; 10,000 shares issued and outstanding	$100,000
Paid-in capital in excess of par	140,000
Total contributed capital	240,000
Retained earnings	90,000
Total stockholders' equity	$330,000

Stockholders' equity—after distribution of 10% stock dividend

Contributed capital	
Common stock, $10 par value; 20,000 shares authorized; 11,000 shares issued and outstanding	$110,000
Paid-in capital in excess of par	148,000
Total contributed capital	258,000
Retained earnings	72,000
Total stockholders' equity	$330,000

Book Value of 1% Ownership

	Number of Shares	Book Value per Share	Book Value of 1% of Share
Before stock dividend	100	$33	$3300
After stock dividend	110	30	3300

When the stock is distributed, the entry will be as follows:

Stock dividend distributable	50,000	
Capital stock, $10 par value		50,000
To record the distribution		
of a stock dividend.		

If a balance sheet is prepared after the date of declaration of a stock dividend and before the stock actually is distributed, a stock dividend distributable account is included in the stockholders' equity section. It is not a liability because its settlement does not require the use of assets or the creation of a liability.

In the case of large stock dividends, the Committee on Accounting Procedure also recommended that the word "dividend" not be used in the related announcements.[3] If this recommendation cannot be followed because of legal requirements, the Committee suggested that the transaction be described as a stock "split-up" effected in the form of a dividend. Stock split-ups are discussed in a later section.

Dividends on Treasury Stock

Treasury stock, as described in the previous chapter, has the status of issued but not outstanding. It does not receive ordinary dividends that represent a distribution of the assets of the company. Whether or not treasury stock will participate in stock dividends or in a stock split depends on the laws of the state of incorporation. If the stock is split, generally the treasury shares also are changed. It is less likely that a stock dividend will be permitted on treasury shares.

Liquidating Dividends

A **liquidating dividend** is not a dividend in the usual sense in which that term is used. Rather, it represents a return to the shareholder of all or a portion of the capital originally invested in the corporation at the time of the issuance of the stock.

The board of directors may declare a liquidating dividend for the purpose of reducing the amount of the company's capital; they may also do so when the company is going out of business. Another reason for declaring a liquidating dividend occurs in the case of companies in the extractive industries such as ore mining. Generally, these companies are permitted by law to include in dividends an amount equal to the cost of the ore mined, or the depletion allowance. The reasoning is that the original investment, and the original legal capital, will not be needed once the resource has been depleted. In a strict sense, then, a liquidating dividend is not a dividend.

[3] Ibid., par. 11.

Liquidating dividends are accounted for as a reduction of contributed capital rather than as a distribution of retained earnings. A separate account, such as capital repaid, may be established as a contra account to the contributed capital section of the balance sheet. Or an additional paid-in capital account may be reduced first. The extent to which a dividend represents a return of capital should be disclosed in the financial statements of the company and in the dividend notice sent to shareholders.

A liquidating dividend may be partially a distribution of income and partially a distribution of capital. Suppose that Zano Company distributes an $8,000 dividend to its shareholders. The announcement of the declaration includes a statement that $5,000 is a distribution of income and $3,000 is a distribution of capital paid in on common stock. Assume that the liquidating dividend is charged against additional paid-in capital. The following entry would be made:

Dividends	5,000	
Paid-in capital in excess of par	3,000	
Dividends payable		8,000
To record dividends declared.		

The dividend account reflects only the amount of the income distribution and is closed to retained earnings. The debit to paid-in capital in excess of par reduces its balance.

Stock Split

Another decision that the directors of a corporation may make is to split up the company's stock. A **stock split-up,** or **split,** is similar to a stock dividend in that both involve the issuance of additional shares of stock to existing stockholders. The corporation receives nothing in exchange for the shares issued. However, in the case of a stock split, the corporation ordinarily reduces the par or stated value of its shares. Usually the reduction in par value is in proportion to the number of additional shares to be issued. For example, if a stock with a par value of $10 is to be split two for one (i.e., two shares are issued in exchange for each share held), the corporation may be expected to change the par value of the new shares to $5 per share.

Ordinary Stock Split

In the case of the **ordinary stock split,** there is no change in the total amount of contributed capital or the total par value of the stock. There is, however, a change in the description of the stock and in the number of shares outstanding.

For example, suppose a company has 10,000 shares of $10 par value common stock outstanding. The company decides to split the stock two for one. Usually the company will change the par value of the stock to $5 per share and will issue

20,000 shares of new stock in exchange for the 10,000 shares of the old stock issue. In such a case the following journal entry might be made:

Common stock, $10 par value	100,000	
Common stock, $5 par value		100,000
To record a two for one stock split.		

Because there has been no change in the total amount of the contributed capital account, a company may decide not to make a formal journal entry to record the split. Instead, the company simply may change the description of the capital stock account to reflect the new par value and the new number of shares outstanding.

To effect the ordinary stock split, several actions are possible. The company may call in the old shares and exchange them for the new shares. Or, the company may issue stickers that show the new par value to be attached to the old shares; the necessary number of additional shares then will be issued. Under either of these alternatives, however, it is unlikely that the company will succeed in getting all shareholders to make the change in their certificates in a timely manner.

Alternative Form of Stock Split

In the case of the ordinary stock split described above, the shareholder usually exchanges shares from the existing stock issue for shares of the new stock issue. This process may be inconvenient both for the shareholder and for the company. Also, the state laws governing additional distributions of stock may prevent a company from declaring the ordinary stock split.

The alternative method is to use a stock dividend to effect a stock split. As said previously, a stock dividend is similar in some respects to a stock split. However, in a stock split, it clearly is the company's intention to reduce the market price per share by issuing the additional shares of stock. A large stock dividend also is expected to have the effect of lowering the market price of the stock noticeably. For this reason the Committee on Accounting Procedure recommended that large stock dividends be described as a "stock split effected in the form of a dividend."[4] Either method of issuing additional shares can be expected to have the same effect on the market price per share.

For example, consider again a company that has 10,000 shares of $10 par value common stock outstanding. The company could achieve the effect of a two for one stock split by issuing a 100% stock dividend. Under this approach, the company would issue 10,000 additional shares of $10 par value common stock. Because twice as many shares of stock will be outstanding, the economic impact on the market price per share will be the same as in an ordinary two for one stock split.

An illustration of a stock split effected in the form of a stock dividend may be provided by referring to the previous example. The company has 10,000 shares of

[4] Ibid., par. 11.

common stock, par value $10, outstanding. The company decides to split its stock two for one by issuing a 100% stock dividend. Assume that state law requires that a transfer be made from retained earnings to the par value capital account. The following journal entry will be made to record the issuance of a 10,000 share, $10 par value common stock dividend:

Retained earnings	100,000	
Common stock, $10 par value		100,000
To record a 100% stock dividend.		

In those cases where the reduction in the par value of the shares is not in proportion to the number of additional shares issued, the usual entry would be to reclassify a portion of retained or additional paid-in-capital to the par or stated value account. The actual accounts affected would be determined by the laws of the state of incorporation.

Reverse Stock Split

A **reverse stock split** is the opposite of the ordinary stock split. The par or stated value of the shares is increased rather than decreased, and there is a reduction in the number of shares outstanding. The usual purpose of a reverse split is to increase the per share market value of the shares outstanding. This might be necessary in the case of a company whose stock is traded on a stock exchange. As a condition for continued trading, the exchange may require that the stock have at least a minimum per share market value. Should the stock fall below this value, the company might consider a reverse split in an effort to achieve the required minimum.

Accounting recognition for a reverse split is analogous to that for a split-up. In the usual case, the decrease in the number of shares is proportional to the increase in par or stated value. Consider, for example, the entry that may be made to reflect the creation of a new class of capital stock in place of the former class. Suppose a company has 2,000 shares of $5 par value common stock outstanding. The directors of the company declare a reverse stock split of 50% and a change in par value to $10 per share. In this case, the company will have 1,000 shares of $10 par value common stock outstanding. The company either may change the title of its capital stock account to reflect the new par value or it may make the following journal entry:

Common stock—$5 par value	10,000	
Common stock—$10 par value		10,000
To record a reverse stock split.		

In either case, there is no change in the total amount of the capital stock account.

If the change in the number of shares outstanding is *not* in proportion to the increase in the par or stated value, a journal entry must be made. The journal entry is needed because this transaction involves a transfer between the capital stock account and either retained earnings or a paid-in capital account.

Appropriations of Retained Earnings

The appropriation of retained earnings is another action a company's board of directors may take. The purpose of the action is to indicate that the portion of retained earnings appropriated is restricted for a specific purpose. As a result of the appropriation, the retained earnings are divided into two parts: (1) appropriated for the reason(s) cited and (2) unappropriated. The effect of an appropriation of retained earnings is to reduce the amount of retained earnings available for any other purpose, such as declaring dividends. Because it involves only a reclassification of a portion of retained earnings, the action itself has no effect on the assets or liabilities of the company. The total of retained earnings is unchanged.

There are two ways to indicate appropriations of retained earnings on the balance sheet of a company. One is to make a journal entry recording the appropriation. This method results in the creation of a separate account that is presented within the retained earnings section of the balance sheet. Unless an entry formally is required in a particular circumstance, restrictions on retained earnings also may be disclosed in a note to the financial statements. This alternative method is more common today. For purposes of illustration, the journal entry method of indicating restrictions of retained earnings is used in this section.

There are three major business reasons for appropriating retained earnings. The appropriation may be (1) necessary to comply with a legal restriction found in state statute, (2) required by a contractual restriction arising from a lending or other agreement entered into by the company, or (3) voluntarily made by the directors of the company to signify that a portion of the assets is unavailable for dividends.

Legal Restriction

A legal restriction may be found in the laws of the state of incorporation. If a company purchases treasury stock, for example, there may be a statutory requirement that retained earnings formally be restricted in the amount of the cost of the treasury stock. This is intended to prevent the company from making additional distributions to shareholders to the extent of the cost of treasury stock. This form of an appropriation of retained earnings was illustrated in the previous chapter.

Contractual Restriction

If a restriction of retained earnings is required as part of a lending agreement, all or a specified portion of the retained earnings account balance may be appropriated, according to the term of the agreement under which the loan was negotiated. Here is an example of a restriction that may be made to help preserve the credit-worthiness of a company.

When a bank makes a substantial loan to a company, the lending agreement may contain restrictions on future dividends until the loan is repaid. As one illustration, consider a lending agreement that prohibits payment of dividends from retained earnings existing at the date of the loan. In this case, dividends may be paid only out of company earnings after this date. The company may indicate this restriction by appropriating the balance of retained earnings at the date of the agreement. Suppose the loan was for $100,000 and that the balance of the retained earnings account is $560,000. In addition to recording the loan transaction, you would make the following journal entry to record the restriction of retained earnings:

Retained earnings	560,000	
Retained earnings—appropriated under terms		
of lending agreement		560,000
To record appropriation of retained earnings.		

Assume that the stockholders' equity section of the company's balance sheet appears as follows:

Stockholders' Equity

Contributed capital:		
Common stock, $10 par value;		
20,000 shares authorized;		
10,000 shares issued	$100,000	
Paid-in capital in excess of par	140,000	$240,000
Retained earnings:		
Appropriated under terms of lending		
agreement	$560,000	
Unappropriated	—	560,000
Total stockholders' equity		$800,000

Earnings subsequent to the date of the lending agreement will be closed to the unappropriated retained earnings account.

In some cases a company may be accumulating a fund of assets for a particular purpose. To signify that these assets are not available for dividends, the company may consider it desirable to indicate that a corresponding portion of the retained earnings is restricted and unavailable for dividends. The company also may be required to make such an appropriation.

For example, a company has a long-term bond issue outstanding. Under the terms of the bond indenture, the company must accumulate a sinking fund to retire the bonds at maturity. Assume that a $100,000 contribution must be made to the sinking fund in the current year. The following entry illustrates this.

Bond sinking fund cash	100,000	
Cash		100,000
To record payment to the bond sinking fund.		

In this case the company actually is accumulating a fund for a special purpose.

Assume further that the bond indenture requires that an appropriation of retained earnings be made in the amount of each contribution to the bond sinking fund. In this case the following entry is made to record the restriction on retained earnings in the amount of the contribution for the current year.

Retained earnings	100,000	
Retained earnings—appropriated for bond retirement		100,000
To record appropriation for bond issue.		

This appropriation of retained earnings serves only to notify financial statement readers that a portion of the retained earnings is restricted and unavailable for dividends. By itself, an appropriation of retained earnings provides no assurance that any assets are available for the purpose indicated. If assets are to be accumulated for a special purpose, this must be done by separate actions of company management.

Voluntary Restriction

Appropriations of retained earnings also may be established at the discretion of the board of directors. In this case there is no intent to accumulate assets for a particular use. Historically, the purpose of such discretionary appropriations was to inform shareholders that dividends could not be paid even though the company had accumulated earnings. This practice may have been undesirable if it caused shareholders to think that retained earnings not appropriated were available for dividends. Suppose, for example, that a company plans to construct a new plant. The cost of the construction is estimated at $400,000. The board of directors may elect to appropriate retained earnings in the amount of $400,000 as a means of notifying financial-statement readers of the planned expansion. The following entry would be made:

Retained earnings	400,000	
Retained earnings—appropriated for		
plant expansion		400,000
To appropriate retained earnings.		

The entry does not provide any assurance that the company has sufficient assets to proceed with the planned expansion. Today the practice of appropriating retained earnings for such purposes largely has been discontinued. It is assumed that users of financial statements are not likely to believe that the existence of retained earnings implies that a company has assets available for payment of a corresponding amount of dividends.

Under GAAP, appropriations of retained earnings cannot be used to absorb any charges or losses incurred by the company. Instead, the amount of any loss incurred must be included in the determination of income for the period. When the reason for the appropriation no longer exists, the appropriated amount is reclassified back to unappropriated retained earnings by reversing the original entry.

Quasi Reorganizations

It is not unusual for businesses to experience problems in maintaining a cash balance sufficient to pay all their obligations on a timely basis. This is particularly common in times of economic stagnation or decline. Sometimes the business can be maintained only if it is reorganized in such a way that the financial difficulties are overcome. The reorganization is carried out under the supervision of the board of directors. Stockholder, and usually creditor, approval also must be obtained. A quasi reorganization is an alternative to a bankruptcy proceeding or to a formal, court-supervised reorganization. In a quasi reorganization, the corporate entity remains unchanged. Under the other alternatives, the existing corporation is dissolved, and the assets may be sold to repay creditors. In a bankruptcy proceeding, any remaining assets are distributed to shareholders. In a formal reorganization, the remaining assets are the basis for the formation of a new corporation. Both these alternatives are more expensive and time-consuming than is a quasi reorganization.

Typically, the company that undergoes a quasi reorganization has favorable prospects for the future, in spite of its past difficulties. As a result of past operating losses, the company may have defaulted on its debt or other obligations. If the company has preferred stock, the dividends may be in arrears. Additional capital is needed to enable the company to continue in operations. Investors, however, may be unwilling to provide new capital if there is little hope for an appropriate return on the capital, particularly in the near future. The outlook for a return on

---

Exhibit 20-2
ABC CORPORATION
Balance Sheet Prior to Reorganization
September 30, 1982

Assets

Cash	$ 30,000
Other current assets	137,000
Land	30,000
Plant and equipment, net	303,000
	$500,000

Liabilities and Net Worth

Accounts payable	$ 70,000
Notes payable	250,000
Common stock, $10 par value	250,000
Paid-in capital in excess of par	125,000
Retained earnings	(195,000)
	$500,000

---

new investment may be unfavorable even if the company is restored to profitability as a result of the investment. One reason is that future profits earned by a company first may have to be applied to satisfy past obligations. Or, if a company has an accumulated deficit, future earnings first may offset that deficit and may not be available for distribution as dividends. For these or other reasons, the corporation may be unable to attract new financing necessary to continue its operations.

The major benefit to the corporation occurs when the quasi reorganization process results in eliminating an accumulated deficit. Usually the quasi reorganization also involves a net write-down of assets, thus increasing any existing deficit. To effect a quasi reorganization, a corporation must have total contributed capital in an amount that is sufficient to absorb the accumulated deficit. After all revaluations have been made to the assets and, if appropriate, to the liabilities, the debit balance in retained earnings is eliminated. The deficit is charged to an additional paid-in capital account. It may not be charged to the account for the par or stated value of the outstanding stock. If the amount of additional paid-in capital is insufficient to absorb the deficit, the par value of the stock is restated downward in order to permit the creation of additional paid-in capital.

After a quasi reorganization is completed, the corporation should have no retained earnings or deficit. A new retained earnings account is established, and it is dated as of the date of the reorganization. The dating of retained earnings eventually is discontinued, usually after ten years.

An example of the accounting procedures in a quasi reorganization follows. The balance sheet at September 30, before the quasi reorganization, is presented in Exhibit 20-2. Under the plan of reorganization, the following changes will be made in the assets, liabilities, and capital accounts of the company:

1. The land account will be written up to $80,000, which is its current market value.
2. Plant and equipment will be written down to $240,000, which is its fair value, based on an independent appraisal.
3. The $250,000 in debt will be exchanged for $150,000 in new long-term notes payable and $100,000 in preferred stock.
4. The 25,000 shares of $10 par value common stock outstanding will be exchanged for 25,000 shares of $5 par value capital stock.

The following journal entries reflect the above agreements:

1. To write up the land account from $30,000 to $80,000:

Land	50,000	
Retained earnings		50,000

2. To write down the plant and equipment from $303,000 to $240,000:

Retained earnings	63,000	
Plant and equipment		63,000

3. To record the issuance of $150,000 in new long-term notes and $100,000 in preferred stock in exchange for cancellation of the existing $250,000 debt:

Notes payable	250,000	
Notes payable—long-term		150,000
Preferred stock		100,000

4. To record restatement of the capital stock account from $10 par value to $5 par value for 25,000 shares of stock outstanding:

Capital stock	125,000	
Paid-in capital in excess of par		125,000

Exhibit 20-3
ABC CORPORATION
Balance Sheet After Reorganization
September 30, 1982

Assets

Cash	$ 30,000
Other current assets	137,000
Land	80,000
Plant and equipment	240,000
	$487,000

Liabilities and Net Worth

Accounts payable	$ 70,000
Notes payable—long-term	150,000
Preferred stock	100,000
Common stock	125,000
Paid-in capital in excess of par	42,000
Retained earnings—September 30, 1982	–0–
	$487,000

---

5. The final entry is to eliminate the deficit in the retained earnings account. The new balance in the deficit of $208,000 ($195,000 − $50,000 + $63,000) is eliminated against the paid-in capital.

Paid-in capital in excess of par	208,000	
Retained earnings		208,000

A new retained earnings account is created. It is dated as of the time of the reorganization—"Retained Earnings—September 30, 1982."

As a result of the above readjustments, the balance sheet of the company appears as illustrated in Exhibit 20-3.

Disclosure

Changes in retained earnings have been disclosed (1) in the equity section, (2) as part of a combined statement of earnings and retained earnings, (3) as a separate retained earnings schedule, or (4) as part of a schedule of changes in stockholders' equity. APB *Opinion No. 12* indicated that the financial statements should provide disclosure of changes in the separate accounts comprising stockholders' eq-

APB #12

uity.[5] Thus, firms are required to disclose changes in retained earnings as well as in other equity accounts. The *Opinion* did not specify the form of the disclosures.

Historically, changes in retained earnings generally were disclosed under one of the first three methods listed above. For example, Exhibit 20-4, which was

[5]"Omnibus Opinion 1967," *Opinions of the Accounting Principles Board No. 12* (New York: AICPA, 1967), par. 9, 10.

Exhibit 20-4
Northern Natural Gas Company and Subsidiaries
Consolidated Statements of Income

	Year Ended December 31,	
	1979	1978
	(Thousands of Dollars)	
Income:		
Operating revenues	$2,499,202	$1,918,988
Other income, net (Notes 1 and 11)	17,856	10,873
	$2,517,058	$1,929,861
Costs and Expenses:		
Costs and operating expenses	$1,919,448	$1,470,868
Depreciation and amortization (Note 7)	144,482	117,023
Taxes, other than income	43,731	34,937
Interest and related charges	56,956	59,195
Allowance for borrowed funds used during construction (Note 1)	(2,328)	(3,285)
	$2,162,289	$1,678,738
Income before income taxes	$ 354,769	$ 251,123
Taxes on income (Note 6)	169,231	109,375
Net Income	$ 185,538	$ 141,748
Average number of common shares outstanding	22,365,818	22,541,902
Earnings per share of common stock	$ 8.17	$ 6.15
Consolidated Statements of Retained Earnings		
Balance at beginning of year	$ 608,019	$ 525,730
Net income	185,538	141,748
Cash dividends:		
Common stock	(62,543)	(56,351)
Preferred stock	(2,739)	(3,108)
Balance at end of year	$ 728,275	$ 608,019

The accompanying notes are an integral part of these statements.

Exhibit 20-5
Revlon, Inc. and Subsidiaries
Consolidated Statements of Stockholders' Equity

Year ended December 31, 1980 (thousands of dollars)	Common Stock Issued		Additional Paid In Capital	Retained Earnings	Treasury Stock, At Cost
	Shares	Amount			
1980					
Balance—January 1	$35,734,053	$35,734	$138,538	$651,068	$5,686
Net Earnings				192,407	
Dividends declared:					
Common Stock				(56,734)	
Convertible Preferred Stock				(14,741)	
Capital transactions of pooled company prior to acquisition			1,480		
Common stock issued:					
Non-Qualified Stock Option Plan	103,923	104	(317)		(411)
Executive Stock Option Plan	133,407	133	4,056		
Employees' Stock Purchase Plan	177,807	178	5,323		
Conversion of debentures	177,807	178	6,636		
Conversion of debentures	37,635	38	6,636		
In connection with merger			1,370		
Amortization of the excess of the stated redemption value over the fair value of the Convertible Preferred Stock				(2,873)	
Purchase of treasury stock					1,241
Balance—December 31	$36,186,825	$36,187	$157,086	$769,127	$6,516

taken from a recent annual report of Northern Natural Gas, discloses changes in retained earnings as an addition to the statement of income. Since the issuance of *Opinion No. 12* there appears to be a growing trend toward a separate columnar disclosure of the changes in each of the accounts comprising the equity section. This approach is illustrated in Exhibit 20-5, which is a part of the equity change disclosure presented in a recent annual report of Revlon, Inc.

Concept Summary

ACCOUNTING FOR DIVIDENDS AND RETAINED EARNINGS

DIVIDENDS

Definition—distribution of assets to stockholders, representing either a distribution of income (regular dividend) or a distribution of the owner's investment in the company (a liquidating dividend).

Form	Description	Valuation
Cash	Distributing cash of the corporation	Value at the amount of cash distributed
Property	Distribution of some noncash asset, such as investments or inventory	Valued at the market value of the asset distributed
Stock	Distribution of additional shares of the company's stock as a dividend	Small—valued at market value of shares on the date of declaration if a publicly held company Large—valued at par value or stated value

RETAINED EARNINGS APPROPRIATIONS

Definition—setting aside part of retained earnings as not available for distribution to shareholders. Restrictions may be voluntary or imposed by law or contractual obligations.

QUASI REORGANIZATION

Description—a method of revising capital structure, usually to eliminate a deficit in retained earnings.

Procedure

1. Revalue assets through charges to retained earnings.
2. Lower par value of stock to provide sufficient paid-in capital to offset retained earnings deficit.
3. Eliminate deficit by an offset to paid-in capital.

Questions

Q–20–1 Describe the relationship between the two uses of a corporation's income and the two returns the stockholder receives on his or her investment.

Q–20–2 Describe the various accounting entries discussed in this chapter that reduce retained earnings.

Q–20–3 What are the four factors affecting dividend distributions?

Q–20–4 What is the difference between a return of capital and a return on capital?

Q–20–5 What legal constraints generally affect the declaration of a dividend?

Q–20–6 Distinguish between the four important dates relevant to the accounting for dividends. On which dates are journal entries required?

Q–20–7 Explain how a highly profitable corporation with a large accumulation of retained earnings may not be able to declare a cash dividend.

Q–20–8 Distinguish between dividends declared by the board and dividends in arrears on cumulative preferred stock.

Q–20–9 What is the ex-dividend date? How does it differ depending on the type of corporation?

Q–20–10 Explain the differences between cash dividends, property dividends, scrip dividends, and stock dividends.

Q–20–11 What adjustments must be made to record a property dividend of appreciated assets?

Q–20–12 How can it be said that a stock dividend has no economic effect on the issuing corporation?

Q–20–13 Explain the theory supporting the fair market value basis and the legal basis of recording stock dividends.

Q–20–14 How does the effect of a stock split differ from the effect of a stock dividend on stockholders' equity?

Q–20–15 What distinguishes a small stock dividend from a large stock dividend? How does the accounting for each differ?

Q–20–16 How is a stock split effected in the form of a dividend?

Q–20–17 Why is a liquidating dividend not actually a dividend in the usual sense in which the term is used?

Q–20–18 Explain the accounting for and purpose of a reverse stock split.

Q–20–19   For what three reasons are retained earnings appropriated?

Q–20–20   What are the basic steps in accounting for a quasi reorganization?

Q–20–21   What is the purpose of a quasi reorganization?

Q–20–22   Conditions warranted that a company have a quasi reorganization. What is the status of the retained earnings account immediately after the quasi reorganization?

  a) Has a zero balance.
  b) Remains the same as it was before the quasi reorganization.
  c) Is frozen and dated, and subsequent transactions will be shown separately.
  d) Has a debit balance equal to the write-down of the assets that were overstated.

(AICPA adapted)

Q–20–23   The issuer should charge retained earnings directly for the market value of the shares issued in a (an)

  a) Pooling of interests.
  b) Two for one stock split.
  c) Employee stock bonus.
  d) 10% stock dividend.

(AICPA adapted)

Q–20–24   Milner Company issued what is called a "100% stock dividend" on its common stock. Milner did *not* change the par value of the common stock. At what amount per share, if any, should either paid-in capital or retained earnings be reduced for this transaction?

  a) Zero because no entry is made.
  b) Par value.
  c) Market value at the declaration date.
  d) Market value at the date of issuance.

(AICPA adapted)

Q–20–25   For a time after undergoing a quasi reorganization, the retained earnings of a corporation must be

  a) Appropriated.
  b) Dated when presented on a balance sheet.
  c) Maintained at zero.
  d) Considered as belonging to the company's creditors.

(AICPA adapted)

Discussion Questions and Cases

D–20–1   A CPA often encounters problems in accounting for transactions involving the stockholders' equity section of the balance sheet.

Required:

1. Explain the significance of the dates that are important in accounting for cash dividends to stockholders. State the journal entry, if any, needed at each date.

2. Assume retained earnings can be used for stock dividends distributable in shares. What is the effect of an ordinary 10% common stock dividend on retained earnings and total stockholders' equity?

3. What is the effect of a 35% common stock dividend on retained earnings and the stockholders' equity?

(AICPA adapted)

D–20–2   P. K. Corporation notified its stockholders of the dividends that had been distributed to them for the year. In 1982, the company's statements revealed that $8.40 had been distributed for each share. Of that amount, though, $2.60 was listed as a liquidating dividend.

Required:

1.   Explain the difference between the liquidating dividend and the regular cash dividend.
2.   If P. K. Corporation has 20,000 shares of common stock issued and outstanding, what entry was made to record the declaration of the dividend?
3.   What entry was made to record the payment of the dividend?

D–20–3   Stock splits and stock dividends may be used by a corporation to change the number of shares of its stock outstanding.

Required:

1.   What is meant by a stock split effected in the form of a dividend?
2.   From an accounting viewpoint, explain how the stock split effected in the form of a dividend differs from an ordinary stock dividend.
3.   How should a stock dividend which has been declared but not yet issued be classified in a statement of financial position? Why?

(AICPA adapted)

D–20–4   P. K. Corporation has accumulated a large deficit over the last three years. Excess depreciation on overvalued assets has contributed to the recurring losses. Recent cash shortages have forced late payments on accounts and creditors have tightened their financing policies. Even though sales are at an all-time high, the board of directors has been forced to consider filing for statutory bankruptcy.

Required:

As the accountant for P. K., you must explain to the board how a quasi reorganization might be a solution to their problems, including:

a)   Its advantages over bankruptcy proceedings.
b)   The authorization required.
c)   The basic accounting steps involved.
d)   Disclosure requirements.

D–20–5   Fortune Company continually shows large year-end profits and has accumulated a large balance in retained earnings. Fortune's stockholders are becoming disgruntled because once again the board passed on declaring a quarterly dividend.

Required:

Explain how the existence of retained earnings in no way exhibits an ability to pay a dividend.

D–20–6   L. Sharks, Inc. loans money out with the stipulation that no dividends can be paid out of retained earnings existing at the date of the loan. The company believes that this appropriation will protect them completely against losses on defaults.

Required:

1.   Discuss how this appropriation does not insure payment of the obligation when due.
2.   Briefly explain what other types of appropriations occur frequently in practice.

Exercises

E–20–1   On January 1, 1987, Wilson, Inc. declared a 5% stock dividend on its common stock when the market value of the common stock was $15 per share. Stockholders' equity *before* the stock dividend was declared consisted of the following:

Common stock, $10 par value; authorized, 200,000 shares; issued and outstanding, 100,000 shares	$1,000,000
Paid-in capital in excess of par on common stock	150,000
Retained earnings	700,000
Total stockholders' equity	$1,850,000

Required:
Prepare the journal entries to record the declaration and subsequent payment of the stock dividend.

(AICPA adapted)

E–20–2 George Corporation declared a cash dividend of $10,000 on January 17, 1981. This dividend was payable to stockholders of record on February 10, 1981, and payment was made on March 2, 1981.
Required:
What journal entry would be recorded on the following dates:
  a) January 17.
  b) February 10.
  c) March 2.

(AICPA adapted)

E–20–3 The directors of Corel Corporation, whose $40 par value common stock currently is selling at $50 per share, have decided to issue a stock dividend. The corporation has an authorization for 200,000 shares of common stock, has issued 110,000 shares—10,000 of which are now held as treasury stock, and desires to capitalize $400,000 of the retained earnings balance.
Required:
To accomplish this, what percentage of stock dividend should the directors declare?

(AICPA adapted)

E–20–4 Below are selected accounts of Bucky Company, which was incorporated on January 1, 1981.

Cost of treasury stock	$16,000
Net income since January 1, 1981	94,000
Appropriation for bond sinking fund	25,000
Subscriptions receivable	12,000
Total cash dividends paid	13,000
Total stock dividends paid at fair market value	17,000
Total stock split-up effected in the form of a dividend	12,000

Required:
From the accounts above determine the current balance of the following:
  a) Appropriated retained earnings.
  b) Unappropriated retained earnings.
  c) Total retained earnings.

E–20–5 On June 30, 1982, Rickert Corporation declared and issued a 10% common stock dividend. Before this dividend, Rickert had 10,000 shares of $5 par value common stock issued and outstanding. The market price of Rickert's common stock on June 30 was $12 per share.
Required:
Show the journal entry required to record this declaration and issuance.

(AICPA adapted)

E–20–6   Blue Ribbon Co. distributed the following dividends to its common stockholders:

a)   Investment in Bud Co. carried at $250,000; fair market value of the 10,000 shares is $190,000.

b)   Investment in Miller Co. carried at $175,000; fair market value of the 5,000 shares is $245,000.

Required:

Record the journal entries necessary to record the property dividends above at both declaration and distribution.

E–20–7   Doe Corporation owned 1,000 shares of Spun Corporation. These shares were purchased in 1977 for $9,000. On September 15, 1981, Doe declared a property dividend of one share of Spun for every 10 shares of Doe held by a stockholder. On that date, when the market price of Spun was $14 per share, there were 9,000 shares of Doe outstanding.

Required:

What gain and net reduction in retained earnings would result from this property dividend?

(AICPA adapted)

E–20–8   On December 31, 1979, the stockholders' equity section of Mercedes Corporation was as follows:

Common stock, par value $5; authorized, 30,000 shares; issued and outstanding, 9,000 shares	$ 45,000
Paid-in capital in excess of par	58,000
Retained earnings	73,000
Total stockholders' equity	$176,000

On April 1, 1980, when the fair market value of the stock was $8 per share, the board of directors declared a 10% stock dividend, and accordingly 900 additional shares were issued. For the three months ended March 31, 1980, Mercedes sustained a net loss of $16,000.

Required:

1.   Record the entry necessary to reflect the stock dividend declared.
2.   What amount should Mercedes report as retained earnings as of April 1, 1980?

(AICPA adapted)

E–20–9   Sprint Company has 1,000,000 shares of common stock authorized with a par value of $3 per share, of which 600,000 shares are outstanding. When the market value was $8 per share, Sprint issued a stock dividend in which for each six shares held one share was issued as a stock dividend. The par value of the stock was not changed.

Required:

What entry should Sprint make to record this transaction?

(AICPA adapted)

E–20–10   On June 30, 1981, when the Perry Company's stock was selling at $40 per share, its capital accounts were as follows:

Capital stock (par value $25, 50,000 shares issued)	$1,250,000
Premium on capital stock	600,000
Retained earnings	3,550,000

A 100% stock dividend was declared, and the par value per share remained at $25. (Treat as an alternative form of a stock split.)

Required:

What entry should Perry make to record this transaction?

(AICPA adapted)

E–20–11 On June 30, 1983, the stockholders' equity section of Comet Corporation was as follows:

Common stock, par value $25; authorized, 500,000 shares; issued and outstanding, 300,000 shares	$ 7,500,000
Paid-in capital in excess of par	1,400,000
Retained earnings	1,890,000
	$10,790,000

On July 1, 1983, the board of directors of Comet declared a 5% stock dividend on common stock to be distributed on August 10, 1983, to shareholders of record on July 31, 1983. The market price of Comet's common stock on each of these dates was as follows:

July 1	$30
July 31	31
August 10	32

Required:
Prepare the appropriate journal entry to record the transactions on the following dates:
a) July 1.
b) July 31.
c) August 10.

(AICPA adapted)

E–20–12 Drums, Inc. is contemplating three different distributions to increase outstanding capital stock. They are as follows:
a) Declare a stock dividend of 15%.
b) Declare a stock dividend of 100%; treat as a large stock dividend.
c) Declare a two for one stock split.
The capital accounts of Drums, Inc. are as follows:

Common stock, $5 par value; 50,000 shares authorized; 25,000 issued and outstanding	$125,000
Contributed capital in excess of par	75,000
Retained earnings	230,000

The current market price of the common stock is $9.
Required:
What entries would be made in each situation above?

E–20–13 On December 31, 1983, the stockholders' equity section of the balance sheet of Mason Co. was as follows:

Common stock (par value $1; 1,000 shares authorized; 300 shares issued and outstanding)	$ 300
Paid-in capital in excess of par	1,800
Retained earnings	$2,000
	$4,100

On January 2, 1984, the board of directors declared a stock dividend of one share for each three shares owned. Accordingly, 100 additional shares of stock were issued. On January 2 the fair market value of Mason's stock was $10 per share.

Required:

Record the necessary journal entry and prepare a presentation of stockholders' equity following the issuance of the additional shares.

(AICPA adapted)

E-20-14 Effective April 27, 1981, the stockholders of Bennett Corporation approved a two for one split of the company's common stock, and an increase in authorized common shares from 100,000 shares (par value $20 per share) to $200,000 shares (par value $10 per share). Bennett's stockholders' equity accounts immediately before issuance of the stock split shares were as follows:

Common stock, par value $20; 100,000 shares authorized; 50,000 shares outstanding	$1,000,000
Additional paid-in capital in excess of par	150,000
Retained earnings	1,350,000

Required:

What should be the balances in Bennett's additional paid-in capital and retained earnings accounts immediately after the stock split is effected?

(AICPA adapted)

E-20-15 Smith Company has 1,000,000 shares of common stock authorized with a par value of $3 per share, of which 300,000 shares are outstanding. Smith authorized a stock dividend when the market value was $8 per share, entitling its stockholders to one additional share for each share held. The par value of the stock was *not* changed.

Required:

What entry, if any, should Smith make to record this transaction?

(AICPA adapted)

E-20-16 On July 1, 1982, Boulevard Corporation split its common stock four for one when the market value was $80 per share. Before the split, Boulevard had 50,000 shares of $12 par value common stock issued and outstanding.

Required:

After the split:

1. How many total shares are outstanding?
2. What is the par value of these shares?

(AICPA adapted)

E-20-17 On December 31, 1984, when the Conn Company's stock was selling at $36 per share, its capital accounts were as follows:

Capital stock (par value $20; 100,000 shares issued)	$2,000,000
Premium on capital stock	800,000
Retained earnings	4,550,000

A 100% stock dividend was declared, and the par value per share remained at $20.

Required:

What journal entry, if any, should be made to reflect the stock dividend above?

(AICPA adapted)

E-20-18 Wohco, Inc. has an accumulated deficit of $75,000. The board of directors is seeking to enter into a quasi reorganization. They believe the company's future will be favorable enough to warrant this fresh start. Wohco's balance sheet before the reorganization is as follows:

Assets

Cash and other current assets	$ 82,000
Warehouse (net of depreciation)	320,000
Factory equipment (net of depreciation)	180,000
	582,000

Liabilities & Stockholders' Equity

Liabilities	$327,000
Common stock ($30 par)	300,000
Paid-in capital in excess of par	30,000
Retained earnings (accumulated deficit)	(75,000)
	$582,000

The fair market value of the factory equipment is $110,000. Common stock par value is to be reduced to $15 par value.

Required:

Prepare the journal entries to record the quasi reorganization.

E–20–19 Livingston Corporation has incurred losses from operations for several years. At the recommendation of the newly hired president, the board of directors voted to implement a quasi reorganization, subject to stockholder approval. Immediately before the restatement, on June 30, 1982, Livingston's balance sheet was as follows:

Current assets	$ 350,000
Property, plant, and equipment (net)	1,350,000
Other assets	400,000
	$2,100,000
Total liabilities	$ 800,000
Common stock—$8 par value	1,600,000
Paid-in capital in excess of par	300,000
Retained earnings (deficit)	(600,000)
	$2,100,000

The stockholders approved the quasi reorganization effective on July 1, 1982, to be accomplished by a reduction in other assets of $150,000; a reduction in property, plant, and equipment (net) of $350,000; and reduction by halving the par value of the outstanding common stock.

Required:

Record the journal entries necessary to implement the quasi reorganization.

(AICPA adapted)

E–20–20 The following data were taken from the books of Ritter Co.:

Common stock—$10 par value; 25,000 shares issued and outstanding	$250,000
Paid-in capital in excess of par	25,000
Retained earnings (deficit)	(105,000)

Plant assets are overvalued by $35,000, and land is overvalued by $10,000. As of January 1, 1984, the corporation's stockholders and creditors agreed to permit a quasi reorganization. The new management reissued all of the outstanding common stock at a $4 par value.

Required:

Prepare the journal entries required to implement the reorganization.

Problems

P–20–1   The board of directors of Rez Company declared the following dividends:

> 7% stock dividend:
>> Date of declaration, March 1; market price, $54
>> Date of record, March 15; market price, $56
>> Date of distribution, March 26; market price, $57
> $0.75 cash dividend per share:
>> Date of declaration, March 30
>> Date of record, April 14
>> Date of distribution, April 21

The stockholders' equity section of Rez's March 1, 1982, balance sheet is as follows:

Common stock, $20 par value; authorized 100,000 shares; issued and outstanding 65,000 shares	$1,300,000
Paid-in capital in excess of par	3,000,000
Retained earnings	1,700,000

Net income for the month of March was $74,000.

Required:
1. Give the journal entries to record the foregoing transactions for March and April.
2. Prepare the stockholders' equity section of the balance sheet as it would appear at the end of March.

P–20–2   The following accounts appeared in the December 31, 1985, balance sheet of Jeglum Company:

Common stock, $20 par value *2000 shares*	$40,000
Paid-in capital in excess of par—common stock	12,000
Preferred stock, 8%, $50 par value *1000 sh*	50,000
Paid-in capital in excess of par—preferred stock	25,000
Common stock dividend distributable	10,000
Dividend payable—preferred stock	4,000
Investment in Betco Company (2,500 shares)	35,000

The following transactions occurred during 1985:

January	15	Issued the previous year's stock dividend.
February	13	Paid the dividend on preferred stock.
April	1	Declared a property dividend on common stock payable in one share Betco Company stock for every common share held, when Betco's market value was $85 per share.
May	1	Paid the property dividend.
June	15	Declared a 6% stock dividend on common stock payable August 1; current market price is $28.
August	1	Issued common stock dividend; market price is $32.
December	20	Declared annual cash dividend on preferred stock; payment on Feb. 13, 1986.

Required:
Prepare the journal entries necessary to record the transactions above.

P–20–3 Old Town Corporation is considering recommendations for declaring two differ- *25000 sh.* ent stock dividends. Old Town's stockholders' equity is made up of $125,000 in $5 par common stock, $100,000 in contributed capital in excess of par, and $50,000 in retained earnings.

The first recommendation is to declare and issue a 10% stock dividend; the second is to issue a 35% stock dividend. Both of these are being considered at a time when the market value share is $12.

Required:

Prepare the journal entries required for each alternative at both the date of declaration and the date of issuance. Also prepare a display of stockholders' equity under each alternative after the issuance of new shares.   *SE = 275000*

P–20–4 Orange and Blue Company recorded two dividend transactions in 1983. The first was a declaration of a 100% stock dividend on both common and preferred shares. The second dividend occurred after issuance of the stock dividend above. The second dividend consisted of the declaration and payment of a $2 per share dividend on common stock and payment of the annual dividend on preferred stock at the stated rate. This cash dividend was declared after the 100% stock dividend on both common and preferred shares had been distributed.

Orange and Blue's stock was listed as follows:

>   Common stock, $50 par value; 500 shares issued; 100 shares treasury stock
>   Preferred stock, 6%, $10 par value, 500 shares issued and outstanding
>   Treasury stock, common, $5,000 at par

The applicable state law permits issuance of a 100% stock dividend on treasury shares, but not the payment of a cash dividend on those shares.

Required:

Assuming that a sufficient amount of retained earnings exists, prepare the journal entries to record the transactions above.

P–20–5 The following transactions involving the Medicine Shop, Inc. occurred sequentially during 1985:

a) A 65% stock dividend was declared on the 20,000 shares of outstanding, $50 par value common stock.

b) $500,000 was transferred to the MacArthur State Bank, establishing a sinking fund to retire serial bonds due over the next 10 years. An appropriation of retained earnings also was authorized.

c) The stock dividend in item a) was issued.

d) The current year's serial bonds were retired in the amount of $50,000, thus eliminating that portion of the appropriation.

e) A $1.50 cash dividend per share of common stock outstanding was declared. One-third of this dividend liquidated a portion of contributed capital.

Required:

Prepare the appropriate journal entries for each of the transactions above.

P–20–6 The following is a presentation of the stockholders' equity accounts of Simon Corporation at July 1, 1984:

Common stock, no par value, stated value $20; 2,000 shares authorized, 1,000 shares issued, of which 100 are held as treasury stock	$ 20,000
Paid-in capital in excess of par—common stock	35,000
Cumulative preferred stock, $5 par value; 8% cumulative, authorized 10,000 shares; 5,000 shares issued and outstanding	25,000

Paid-in capital in excess of par—preferred stock		10,000
Total contributed capital		$ 90,000
Retained earnings:		
Restricted for cost of treasury stock	$ 6,000	
Unrestricted	104,000	110,000
Total capital and retained earnings		$200,000
Less cost of treasury stock at cost		6,000
Total stockholders' equity		$194,000

The following transactions occurred during Simon's fiscal year:

July	25	50 shares of treasury stock were sold at $58 per share.
August	15	Entered into loan agreement which stipulated that $50,000 in retained earnings is restricted from dividend payments.
September	22	Issued 500 shares of common stock at $65 per share.
December	28	Declared 15% stock dividend on outstanding common stock—(does not include treasury shares). Market value is $65 per share.
January	30	Declared annual dividend on preferred stock, including that which had not been paid in the previous year.
February	1	Issued the stock dividend.
March	1	Declared and immediately recorded a two-for-one stock split of the preferred stock. The market price was $8 per share, and the par value was charged to $2.50.
March	6	Paid the cash dividend on preferred stock to stockholders of record on February 28.
April	26	Acquired 200 shares of common stock for $55 per share. Simon Co. uses the cost method.
June	30	Net income for the year was $180,000.

Required:
1. Record the journal entries for the transactions above.
2. Prepare a new stockholders' equity statement as of June 30, 1985.   394,400

P-20-7 The Gaston Company has sustained heavy losses over a period of time, and conditions warrant that Gaston undergo a quasi-reorganization at December 31, 1983.

Selected balance sheet items prior to the quasi reorganization are as follows:

a) Inventory was recorded in the accounting records at December 31, 1983, at its market value of $6,000,000. Cost was $6,500,000.

b) Property, plant, and equipment was recorded in the accounting records at December 31, 1983, at $12,000,000, net of accumulated depreciation. The appraised value was $8,000,000.

c) Stockholders' equity on December 31, 1983, was as follows:

Common stock, par value $10 per share; authorized, issued, and outstanding 700,000 shares	$7,000,000
Paid-in capital in excess of par	1,600,000
Retained earnings (deficit)	(900,000)
	$7,700,000

d) Under the terms of the quasi reorganization, the par value of the common stock is to be reduced from $10 per share to $5 per share.

Required:
Record the journal entries necessary to reflect the quasi reorganization.

(AICPA adapted)

P-20-8 Campbell Company has the following outstanding capital stock: 10,000 shares, $10 par value common stock. The current market price is $23 per share. Assume unrestricted retained earnings exist as needed. The following are independent situations to be considered in your solution:

Situation 1:

Campbell Company, a small, closely held corporation, declares a 15% stock dividend.

Situation 2:

Campbell Company, a large publicly held corporation, declares a 15% stock dividend.

Situation 3:

Campbell Company, a large publicly held corporation, declares a 75% stock dividend.

Situation 4:

Campbell Company, a large publicly held corporation, declares a 100% stock dividend.

Situation 5:

Campbell Company, a small closely held corporation, declares a two-for-one stock split with a reduction of the par value to $5 per share.

Required:

For each of the situations above, record the necessary journal entry.

P-20-9 The Dalton Corporation had the following balances in its stockholders' equity accounts at December 31, 1985:

Common stock, $50 par value	$ 50,000
Paid-in capital in excess of par—common stock	75,000
Preferred stock, 8%, $40 par value	40,000
Paid-in capital in excess of par—preferred stock	24,000
Retained earnings	120,000

Dalton's board of directors is considering the following different dividend declarations:

a) A cash dividend on both common and preferred stock. One-half of the preferred stock dividend and one-fourth of the $0.80 dividend per common share would be out of contributed capital.

b) A five-for-two stock split on common stock, reducing the par value appropriately, when the market price was $130 per share.

c) A 45% stock dividend on preferred stock when the market price was $70 per share.

d) A 12% stock dividend on common stock when the market price was $128 per share.

Required:

Record the journal entries for each alternative at both the date of declaration and the date of issuance.

P-20-10 High Risk, Inc. is seeking financial relief through a quasi reorganization. An in-depth examination of the company's assets revealed the following information:

a) An investment in Fred Company is overvalued by $15,000.

b) 25% of the $80,000 inventory is obsolete.

c) Certain land holdings have appreciated $10,000 since acquisition.

d) Selected patents carried at $17,000 have expired and have no value.

High Risk's stockholders' equity accounts are as follows:

Common stock, $6 par value; 30,000 shares issued	$180,000
Paid-in capital in excess of par—common stock	30,000
Accumulated deficit	(48,000)
	$162,000

The common stockholders have consented to a reduction in the par value of their stock to $4.

Required: $\int \! \mathcal{B}$

From the information above prepare the journal entries necessary to effect the quasi reorganization.

P–20–11 Tayler Company has accumulated a deficit of $130,000 over the last three years. After an analysis of Tayler's accounts, the following facts were revealed:

   a) $12,000 in accounts receivable should be written off as worthless.
   b) Inventories need to be reduced $15,000 to be at lower of cost or market.
   c) Certain investments are undervalued by $17,000.

The company's board of directors, stockholders, and creditors have agreed to a quasi reorganization that implements the following steps:

   a) Adjust the asset accounts as needed to their fair market values.
   b) Allocate the $42,000 contributed capital in excess of par to offset the deficit.
   c) Change the par value of the 20,000 shares of common stock from $15 to $10 and apply to the deficit.
   d) Allocate any excess capital to an account entitled, "excess reorganization capital."

Required:

Prepare the journal entries to record this quasi reorganization.

P–20–12 The following transactions need to be recorded on the books of Perry Company:

   a) One-half of the net income for the year is to be appropriated for the construction of a new plant.
   b) A $50,000 appropriation for a bond sinking fund that is also established by opening a special bank account.
   c) The appropriation for self-insurance is to be eliminated since the company has purchased adequate coverage from various agencies.
   d) A 15% stock dividend on the $100,000 of common stock (par value $50) is declared and issued at a time when the market price is $80 per share.
   e) Net income for the year was $230,000.

Before making the entries above, look at the following related accounts, which appeared in Perry's ledger:

Total retained earnings	$600,000
Retained earnings appropriated for self-insurance	125,000

Required:

1. Prepare the necessary journal entries to record the transaction above.
2. What amount of retained earnings appears to be available for dividends?

P–20–13 The stockholders' equity accounts of Frick, Inc. had the following balances:

Preferred stock, 5%, $20 par value, 10,000 shares issued	
and outstanding	$200,000
Paid-in capital in excess of par—preferred stock	25,000
Common stock, $25 par value; 15,000 shares issued and	
outstanding	375,000
Paid-in capital in excess of par—common stock	75,000
Retained earnings	250,000

During the subsequent year, the following transactions affecting stockholder's equity occurred:

   a) Declared and issued a stock dividend on common stock whereby each holder of 10 shares received an additional share of common stock. The current market price was $30 per share.

b) Declared and issued a stock dividend on preferred stock whereby each holder of three shares received an additional share of preferred stock. The current market price was $25 per share.

c) Net income for the year was $100,000.

Required:

1. Prepare entries in general journal form to record both the declaration and issuance of the stock dividends above.

2. Prepare a new stockholder's equity section of the balance sheet.

P–20–14 Rose Company had the following balances in its stockholders' equity accounts at December 31, 1985:

Common stock, $20 par value; 100,000 shares issued and outstanding	$2,000,000
Paid-in capital in excess of par	1,200,000
Retained earnings	5,000,000

The current market price of Rose Company stock is $28.

Required:

Under each of the following assumptions, prepare the necessary journal entries to record the dividend at both declaration and issuance.

a) A 15% stock dividend.

b) A five-for-one stock split.

c) A 100% stock dividend.

d) A two-for-one stock split.

21

Dilutive Securities and Earnings Per Share

Accounting in the News

Few, if any, indicants of earning power ever have received the attention that earnings per share (EPS) numbers have. From quotations in prestigious journals to comparisons of industry in professional business meetings, EPS information has become a benchmark for comparing and determining profitability.

Most discussions of how enterprise policy changes should work involve an analysis of EPS effects. EPS data always are included in these discussions, which cover such topics as the disposition of a corporate division, acquisition of a new subsidiary, and emphasizing or deemphasizing a product line. The following excerpts from a recent article illustrate the focus on EPS information:

> Jack Eckerd Corp.'s sales probably will increase 20% in fiscal 1982, but per-share earnings may fall about 10% from last year's results. Stewart Turley, chairman and president, said.
>
> Mr. Turley said the drugstore and retailing chain's sales in the year ending July 31 probably would total about $2.1 billion. Eckerd had net income of $78.5 million, or $2.19 a share, on revenue of $1.75 billion in fiscal 1981.
>
> Mr. Turley blamed the projected earnings decline on operating losses related to Eckerd's acquisition of American Home Video. Eckerd completed its previously announced acquisition of the closely held Denver concern that operated 61 video specialty stores in a stock swap in September.
>
> High interest costs and lower than normal increases in Eckerd Drug Co.'s profit also will contribute to the earnings decline, Mr. Turley said.
>
> But the company is optimistic about an earnings improvement in fiscal 1983. . . .*

*"Jack Eckerd Expects Per-Share Net to Fall About 10% in Fiscal '82," *Wall Street Journal*, May 11, 1982, p. 26. Reprinted by permission of The Wall Street Journal, © Dow Jones & Company, Inc. 1982. All Rights Reserved.

> The accounting computations involved in developing these often-quoted per share amounts are complex and involve the use of several estimations and approximations. While the numbers are quoted simplistically, they often are extremely difficult to generate as a matter of practice.

Earnings per share data, in conjunction with other financial information, constitute a measure of profitability that investors typically rely on in their investment decision process. Investors use earnings per share information in evaluating corporate income and trends in income in relation to the shares held. Consideration of the widespread use of earnings per share data and the significance attached to it by the users of financial statements led the Accounting Principles Board to conclude in APB *Opinion No. 15* that earnings per share data or net loss per share data should be presented on the face of the income statement.[1]

Before the issuance of *Opinion No. 15*, the APB strongly recommended in *Opinion No. 9*, that earnings per share data be disclosed in the income statement.[2] *Opinion No. 15* changed the recommendation to a requirement applicable to corporations that present the results of operations in conformity with generally accepted accounting principles.[3]

Earnings per share is a financial ratio that expresses the amount of earnings available to each share of common stock outstanding. Often a corporation has outstanding securities in the form of convertible debt, convertible preferred stock, stock options, and warrants that enable the holder to obtain common stock when the securities are converted or exercised. The conversion or exercise of these securities has a potentially dilutive effect on the earnings per share that must be disclosed. Dilutive securities will be discussed in detail in the first part of this chapter. The second part of the chapter will focus on the computation of earnings per share.

Dilutive Securities

Dilutive securities are those securities that will cause earnings per share to decrease or loss per share to increase. Dilutive securities include convertible debt, convertible preferred stock, and stock options and warrants.

Convertible Debt

In order to raise capital at a lower interest rate than would be available by issuing nonconvertible debt securities, corporations often will issue debt securities that may be converted into capital stock at a specified future date (usually an interest

---

[1] "Earnings per Share," *Opinions of the Accounting Principles Board No. 15* (New York: AICPA, 1969).

[2] "Reporting the Results of Operations," *Opinions of the Accounting Principles Board No. 9* (New York: AICPA, 1966).

[3] The requirement to disclose earnings per share information was suspended for nonpublic enterprises by "Suspension of the Reporting of Earnings Per Share and Segment Information by Nonpublic Enterprises," *Statement of Financial Accounting Standards No. 21* (Stamford, Conn.: FASB, 1978).

date). These securities are called **convertible debt,** and upon their issuance represent a liability of the issuing corporation. The terms of such securities generally include the following:

1. An interest rate that is lower than the issuing corporation could obtain for nonconvertible debt.
2. An initial conversion price that is greater than the market value of the common stock at the issue date of the convertible security.
3. A conversion price that does not decrease except to protect against dilution.
4. A callable feature, usually at the option of the issuer. (For example, the issuing corporation may reserve the right to redeem the security before its maturity date.)

It is important to note that convertible bonds are subordinate to nonconvertible debt because of the equity potential involved. The privilege of converting the debt security into an equity security is included to make the bonds more attractive to the investor. If the activities of the issuing corporation are profitable, the holders of convertible debt are in a position to share in the profits by converting their debt into stock. The anticipation of sharing in the profits of the issuing corporation not only induces the investor to accept a subordinate position (i.e., increased risk of loss upon dissolution), the investor also is willing to accept a lower effective interest rate than would be accepted on a nonconvertible debt security.

In summary, convertible debt can be sold at an interest rate lower than that for nonconvertible debt because investors who desire the security of a bond holding but wish the added option of sharing in future profits place a value on the conversion privilege. Further, since a convertible debt security combines the benefits of a bond with the option of converting it into an equity interest, it is subordinate to debt that does not provide such privilege.

The dual nature of convertible debt securities gives rise to theoretical problems relating to the proper accounting treatment upon their issuance. Since convertible bonds possess the characteristics of both debt and equity, the question presented is whether convertible debt securities should be accounted for by the issuer solely as debt, or should the equity element (the conversion privilege) receive separate accounting recognition at the time of issuance.

An argument for separate accounting recognition of the conversion privilege can be based on the premise that there is an economic value inherent in the conversion privilege.[4] The economic value is reflected by the consideration given by the investors, and, therefore, it would be appropriate to allocate a portion of the proceeds from the sale of convertible bonds to the contingent equity feature. The amount so allocated then would receive separate accounting recognition in the equity section of the balance sheet.

The alternative argument is that the debt and equity elements are inseparable and cannot coexist. Stated differently, at any given time the security is either all debt or all equity. The APB adopted this view in *Opinion No. 14,* which states

---

[4]"Accounting for Convertible Debt and Debt Issued with Stock Purchase Warrants," *Opinions of the Accounting Principles Board No. 14* (New York: AICPA, 1969), par. 9.

that no portion of the proceeds from the issuance of convertible debt should be accounted for as attributable to the conversion feature.[5] This means that convertible debt should be accorded the same accounting treatment upon issuance as nonconvertible debt issues. The difference between the cash proceeds from the sale of the convertible debt and the face amount should be recorded as a discount or premium as appropriate. The discount or premium then should be amortized over the life of the debt using the effective interest method.[6]

When the convertible debt subsequently is exchanged for equity securities, the problem becomes the determination of the amount at which to record the securities exchanged for the debt. There are two methods of valuing the new securities issued in the exchange:

1. **The book value method**—the new securities (stock) may be valued at the carrying value of the old securities (bonds).
2. **The market value method**—the new securities may be valued at cost, i.e., the fair value of the securities given up (stock) or the fair value of the securities received (bonds), whichever is more easily determinable.

As an illustration of the accounting for convertible debt, assume Red, Inc. issued 1,000, five-year, 10% convertible bonds with a $1,000 face value, callable when the market price per share of outstanding common stock ($100 par) reaches $120. The exchange ratio specified on the bonds is 10 shares of stock for each $1,000 bond. If you assume that Red, Inc. sold the convertible bonds for $1,100 each, the entry to record the initial issuance would be as follows:

Cash	1,100,000	
Bonds payable		1,000,000
Premium on bonds payable		100,000
To record the issuance of bonds.		

The premium then would be amortized over the five-year life of the bonds. However, if it is assumed that the investors will exercise their conversion rights at a time when the carrying value of the bonds is $1,080,000 (after adjusting for accrued interest and premium amortization) and the market value of the stock is $115 per share, the entry would be as follows:

Book Value Method

Bonds payable	1,000,000	
Premium on bonds payable	80,000	
Common stock		1,000,000
Paid-in capital		80,000
To record the bond conversion.		

[5] Ibid., par. 12.

[6] "Omnibus Opinion—1967," *Opinions of the Accounting Principles Board No. 12* (New York: AICPA, 1967), par. 17.

Market Value Method

Bonds payable	1,000,000	
Premium on bonds payable	80,000	
Loss on redemption	70,000	
Common stock		1,000,000
Paid-in capital		150,000
To record the bond conversion.		

It is important to observe that under the market value method the issuing corporation must recognize a loss or gain upon the issuance of its common stock in exchange for the bonds. Many accountants contend this treatment is inappropriate, and therefore the market value method has not received widespread acceptance.

Conversely, the book value method has gained general acceptance among practitioners for the following reasons:

1. It does not require the recognition of a loss (or gain) on the issuance of the equity securities.
2. It views the issuance of the equity securities as the final step of the transaction whereby the debt securities were issued.
3. It recognizes that the conversion does not represent the culmination of a completed earnings cycle; rather, it is merely the transformation of contingent shareholders into shareholders.

The primary conceptual weakness of the book value method is that it fails to give accounting recognition to the total value that investors have attributed to the equity security. However, the accounting profession deems the three advantages of the book value method mentioned above to be strong enough to outweigh the weakness noted.

To continue the illustration, assume that the investors held the bonds until the market price of the common stock reached $120 (rather than exercising their conversion option), and Red, Inc. reacquired the bonds by exercising the call provision at a time when the carrying value of the bonds was $1,060,000. Since the convertible bonds were reacquired at the option of Red, Inc. (the issuer) rather than by conversion (at the option of the investors), the transaction must be accounted for under the provisions of APB *Opinion No. 26*[7] and *SFAS No. 4*.[8] The extinguishment of convertible debt before maturity does not transform the debt security into an equity security. Therefore, the difference between the cash acquisition price ($120 in the example) of the debt and its carrying value should be recognized currently in income as an extraordinary loss (or gain). The entry would be as follows:

[7]"Early Extinguishment of Debt," *Opinions of the Accounting Principles Board No. 26* (New York: AICPA, 1972).

[8]"Reporting Gains and Losses from Extinguishment of Debt," *Statement of Financial Accounting Standards No. 4* (Stamford, Conn.: FASB, 1975).

Bonds payable	1,000,000	
Premium on bonds payable	60,000	
Loss on early extinguishment	140,000	
Cash		1,200,000
To record the		
reacquisition of bonds.		

Debt Issued with Stock Warrants

An alternative to issuing convertible debt is to issue debt securities with stock purchase warrants. **Warrants** are certificates that grant the holder the right to purchase a stated number of shares of stock at a specified price within a specified time period. Like the conversion feature of convertible debt, stock purchase warrants are included to enhance the marketability of the bonds; they enable the issuer to obtain financing at a lower rate than would be possible through the issuance of nonconvertible debt without the warrants.

Debt securities may be issued with nondetachable stock purchase warrants or with detachable stock purchase warrants. **Nondetachable warrants** require that the security (bond or preferred stock) with which the warrants were issued be surrendered when the warrants are exercised, whereas **detachable warrants** may be separated from the security with which they were issued and exercised separately. Since the warrants represent a contingent equity interest, it is necessary to determine when it is appropriate to give accounting recognition to the equity feature represented by such warrants. Remember that when the debt and equity elements are inseparable and cannot coexist, no portion of the proceeds from a debt issue with contingent equity features should be attributed to the equity feature. Thus, accounting for debt with nondetachable warrants depends on whether the debt must be surrendered in order to obtain the stock. If the debt must be surrendered, no portion of the proceeds should be attributed to the stock purchase warrants. The accounting requirements would be identical to the requirements for accounting for convertible debt securities. However, if the debt security does not have to be surrendered in order to obtain the stock, the security will be accounted for in the same manner as debt securities issued with detachable warrants.

Debt issued with detachable warrants may be distinguished from convertible debt in that the warrants may be separated from the debt security and subsequently traded independently in the open market. Also, debt issued with detachable warrants usually is issued with the expectation that the debt will not be repaid until the maturity date. The fact that the debt and contingent equity features are represented by two independent securities leads to the conclusion that the proceeds from the sale of bonds with detachable warrants should be allocated to the two elements for accounting purposes. The allocation should be based on their relative fair values at the time of issuance. The portion allocated to the warrants should be recorded as paid-in capital. The remainder represents the proceeds from the issuance of debt.

For example, assume Rollo, Inc. issued 100, five-year, 10% face value bonds. Each $1,000 bond contains one detachable warrant that entitles the holder to purchase one share of common stock ($50 par) for $75. At the time of sale it is

Exhibit 21-1
ROLLO, INC.
Allocation of Proceeds

		Allocation %	×	Total Proceeds	=	Relative Value
$\dfrac{\text{FMV of bonds}}{\text{FMV of bonds + FMV of warrants}}$	$= \dfrac{\$975}{\$975 + \$51} =$	0.95	×	$100,000	=	$95,000 (bonds)
$\dfrac{\text{FMV of warrants}}{\text{FMV of bonds + FMV of warrants}}$	$= \dfrac{\$51}{\$975 + \$51} =$	0.05	×	$100,000	=	$5,000 (warrants)

estimated that the bonds would sell for $975 independent of the warrants, and that the warrants would sell for $51 independent of the bonds. The bonds were issued at their face amount of $1,000.

The first step is to allocate the proceeds to the two separate elements as shown in Exhibit 21-1.

The journal entry to record the issuance of the bonds with detachable warrants would be as follows:

Cash	100,000	
Discount on bonds payable	5,000	
Bonds payable		100,000
Stock warrants outstanding		5,000
To record the issuance of bonds with detachable warrants.		

To continue the illustration, assume that 80 warrants were tendered for the purchase of 80 shares of common stock; the entry would be:

Cash	6,000	
Stock warrants outstanding	4,000	
Common stock (80 shares × $50 par)		4,000
Paid-in-capital in excess of par		6,000*
To record the exercise of stock warrants.		

*($6,000 proceeds + $4,000 value of warrants − $4,000 allocated to stock = $6,000)

Finally, assume that the remaining 20 warrants outstanding are never tendered. The entry to be made following the expiration date would be as follows:

Stock warrants outstanding	1,000	
Paid-in-capital—expired stock warrants		1,000
To record the experation of stock warrants.		

Pervasive Concepts

It should be observed that in both the issuance of convertible debt and the issuance of debt with detachable warrants, the investor has acquired the right to purchase an equity interest at a future date. The only significant difference between them is the form of payment to be made in exchange for the stock. The convertible debt holder pays the issuing corporation by releasing it from an interest-bearing liability, whereas the warrant holder is required to pay cash. This distinction is a case of emphasizing form over substance and, conceptually, should not be considered justification for ignoring the equity feature of convertible debt.

It should be noted also that the APB's conclusion in *Opinion No. 14* that the equity feature should not receive accounting recognition seemingly is inconsistent with its recommendations in *Opinion No. 15*. In the latter Opinion the APB recommends that the equity feature of convertible debt should be treated as common stock in computing fully diluted earnings per share, and in many instances the convertible debt may even attain the status of common stock equivalent to be included in computing primary earnings per share.[9] This inconsistency is mitigated partially in *Opinion No. 14*, which reads: "When convertible debt is issued at a substantial premium, there is a presumption that such premium represents paid-in capital."[10]

While the FASB has acknowledged the conceptual problems inherent in the position that currently is promulgated concerning debt issued with contingent equity interest, the Board has deferred restating its position until a comprehensive review of all the related issues can be accomplished.[11]

Thus, for the time being, contingent equity interest included with debt securities will be recognized separately only (1) in computing earnings per share and/or (2) when evidenced by a stock purchase warrant that does not require the surrender of the debt security in order to obtain the equity security.

Convertible Preferred Stock

When preferred stock is issued with terms and conditions that allow the holder to exchange the preferred stock for common stock in a specified ratio, it is known as **convertible preferred stock.** Holders of convertible preferred stock have the

[9] These concepts and terms will be discussed in detail in the second part of the chapter.

[10] "Accounting for Convertible Debt," par. 18.

[11] "Reporting Gains and Losses," par. 4.

security of regular dividends and the option of conversion if the value of the common stock increases.

The existence of a convertible feature does not affect the recording of the issuance of the preferred stock. When the conversion privilege is exercised, no gain or loss is recognized because the transaction involves only a change within the stockholders' position in liquidation preference; it has no economic effect on the corporation as a whole. For example, assume that Curatola, Inc. issued 2,000 shares of $20 par preferred stock for $25 per share and made the following entry:

Cash	50,000	
Preferred stock		40,000
Paid-in capital in excess of par—preferred		10,000
To record the issuance of preferred stock.		

At a later date 1,000 shares of preferred stock (half of the original issue) are exchanged for 5,000 shares of $5 par common stock. Curatola, Inc. then would make the following entry:

Preferred stock	20,000	
Paid-in capital in excess of par—preferred	5,000	
Common stock		25,000
To record the conversion of preferred stock.		

Note that the paid-in capital that relates to the preferred stock must be removed from the accounts when conversion occurs.

Stock Options

Many corporations follow the practice of granting corporate employees options to purchase, or rights to subscribe for, shares of a corporate capital stock. While the names and terms of these plans may vary, they generally are referred to as **stock option plans** and typically grant the employees the option to purchase a fixed number of shares of capital stock at a stated price during a specified period. The purpose of such a plan may be to raise capital, allow employees to become owners, or provide additional compensation.[12]

Stock option plans that require the employees to pay cash as the consideration for the stock they receive are referred to as **noncompensatory plans,**

---

[12] For a detailed discussion of accounting for stock appreciation rights, see "Accounting for Stock Appreciation Rights and Other Variable Stock Option or Award Plans," *FASB Interpretation No. 28* (Stamford, Conn.: FASB, 1978).

whereas plans in which employees receive stock for current or future services without paying a significant amount of cash are designated as **compensatory plans.** The accounting treatment for these two types of stock option plans differs in that under noncompensatory plans, the corporation does not recognize any compensation cost, and, therefore, the stock issued is treated as any other stock issue (except that the cash proceeds may be withheld from the employees' pay rather than paid directly).

APB *Opinion No. 25* requires the following characteristics to be present for a plan to be considered noncompensatory:

1. Substantially all the employees must be eligible to participate.
2. The stock must be offered to eligible employees equally or based on a uniform percentage of salary or wages.
3. The time permitted for exercising an option must be limited to a reasonable period.
4. The exercise price must be approximately equal to the market price.[13]

If the plan does not contain all four of these characteristics, it must be classified as compensatory.

The principal problem in accounting for compensatory plans is the measurement of compensation. In other words, the following determinations must be made:

1. At which point in time should the compensation cost be measured?
2. What is the total amount of compensation cost?
3. To what accounting period should the compensation cost be allocated as an expense?

In *Opinion No. 25* the APB offers guidelines to be used in making these determinations. The APB suggests that the date for determining compensation cost is the first date on which both of the following are known:

1. The number of shares that the employee is entitled to receive.
2. The option or purchase price, if any.

In most cases the date, commonly referred to as the **measurement date,** is the date on which the option or purchase right is granted to the employee. However, it should be noted that the measurement date may be later than the **date of grant** (the date options are given to employees) if the terms of the plan depend on subsequent events.

The amount of compensation cost is determined by deducting the amount (if any) the employee is required to pay from the quoted market price of the stock at the measurement date. While the APB acknowledged that this approach to valuing stock options does not measure precisely the fair value of the services giving rise to the compensation, it does offer a practical solution to a difficult problem. Furthermore, if a quoted market price is unavailable, the best estimate of the market value of the stock may be used to measure compensation.

---

[13] "Accounting For Stock Issued to Employees," *Opinions of the Accounting Principles Board No. 25* (New York: AICPA, 1972), par. 7.

The determination of the proper accounting period to which the compensation cost should be allocated is based on the matching principle. Stated differently, once the compensation cost is determined, the expense should be allocated to the periods benefited by the employees' services. If an employee performs services before receiving any stock, the employer corporation should accrue compensation expense in each period in which the services are performed. Conversely, if stock is issued under the plan before some or all of the services have been performed, part of the cost of compensation depends on events after the date of grant. An illustration for each situation is presented next.

Compensation Costs Measured at Date of Grant (measurement date is the same as the date of grant). Assume that on January 1, 1980, White, Inc. granted a stock option to each member of its accounting staff, which consisted of 20 professionals, for 1,000 shares of common stock ($4 par) at an option price of $5. The purpose of the plan is to provide additional compensation for services for the years 1980 through 1982. The services are expected to remain equal throughout the three-year life of the plan. The market price per share at the date of grant (January 1, 1980) is $7.

Since the plan is compensatory, and since both the number of shares that each employee is entitled to receive (1,000 each) and the option price ($7) are known at the date of grant, the compensation cost can be measured as follows:

Quoted market price (at measurement date)	$	7
Less: Option price		5
Compensation cost per share	$	2
Times: Number of shares (1,000 × 20)		×20,000
Total compensation costs		$40,000

The entry at the date of grant would be as follows:

Deferred compensation cost[14]	40,000	
Stock options outstanding		40,000
To record the granting of		
stock options.		

If it is assumed that none of the options had been exercised at December 31, 1980, the entry to record the annual allocation of compensation cost to accountants' compensation expense would be as follows:

Accountants' compensation expense	13,333	
Deferred compensation costs		13,333
To record compensation expense.		
($40,000/3 years = $13,333)		

---

[14] Presented as a contra-equity account in the balance sheet.

If it is assumed that on December 31, 1981, when the market value of the stock is $15, all of the accountants exercise their options, White would make the following entry:

Cash	100,000	
Stock options outstanding	40,000	
Common stock ($4 par × 20,000)		80,000
Paid-in capital in excess of par		60,000
To record the exercise of stock options.		

Note that the $15 market value of the stock at the exercise date is irrelevant.

Date of Grant and Measurement Date Differ.   Assume that on January 1, 1982, White, Inc. granted its sales manager the option to purchase 5,000 shares of common stock ($30 par), exercisable after two years (from the date of grant) at an option price to be established at the end of that period by reducing the market price per share at the date of grant by the percentage that sales increased during the specified compensation period of two years. The market price per share on January 1, 1982, is $40. Since the option price cannot be determined at the date of grant, no journal entry is required at that date.

If it is assumed that at the end of 1982 it is estimated, based on current trends, that sales will increase by 20% by the end of 1983 and that the market price per share is expected to reach $52, the entry to record the accrued compensation expense would be as follows:

Compensation expense	50,000	
Sales manager stock option outstanding		50,000
To record compensation expense.		

The calculation of the expense is shown in Exhibit 21-2.

If at the end of 1983 it is determined conclusively that sales actually increased by only 15% and that the market price per share is actually $45, the entry would be as follows:

Compensation expense	5,000	
Stock option outstanding		5,000
To record compensation expense.		

Exhibit 21-2
Calculation of Accrued Compensation Expense

Estimated market price at measurement date	$ 52
Less: Estimated option price ($40 × (1 − 0.2))	32
Estimated compensation per share	$ 20
Times: Number of shares subject to option	×5,000
Total estimated compensation cost	$100,000
Divided by: Number of periods	÷2
Equals: Accrued compensation expense	$ 50,000

The calculation of the expense appears in Exhibit 21-3.

If we assume that the sales manager exercises his options on January 1, 1984, the entry required by White, Inc. would be the following:

Cash	170,000	
Stock options outstanding	55,000	
Common stock ($30 par)		150,000
Paid-in-capital in excess of par		75,000
To record the exercise of		
stock options.		

Disclosure Requirements

Full disclosure is required as to the status of the option at the end of the accounting period, including the number of shares under option, the option price, and the number of shares exercisable. With regard to options exercised during the period, the number of shares involved and the option price must be disclosed.[15]

ARB # 43

Earnings Per Share

The method of reporting earnings per share before 1953 had no particular accounting authority. With the issuance of *ARB No. 43*, "Restatement and Revision of Accounting Research Bulletins," the term "income per share" was introduced. Because the term "share" never was given any interpretive meaning, there were many different creative applications in practice. However, the Committee on Accounting Procedures (CAP) strongly urged that a per share amount be presented for extraordinary items. In 1958 the CAP issued *ARB No. 49*, "Earnings

---

[15] "Compensation Involved in Stock Option and Stock Purchase Plans," *Accounting Research Bulletin No. 43* (New York: AICPA, 1953), Chapter 13, Section B.

Exhibit 21-3
Calculation of Compensation Expense

Estimated market price at measurement date	$ 45
Less: Option price ($40 × (1 − 0.15))	34
Compensation cost per share	$ 11
Times: Number of shares subject to option	×5,000
Total compensation costs	$55,000
Less: Compensation cost expensed in prior period	50,000
Compensation expense for current year	$ 5,000

Per Share," which introduced the term "earnings per share" and the concept of weighted average common stock. *ARB No. 49* strongly recommended that an earnings per share figure be shown on the income statement.

In 1966 the APB issued *Opinion No. 9*, which also strongly recommended the disclosure of an earnings per share figure.[16] However, the APB addressed the issue of convertible securities, options, and warrants and recommended that an earnings per share figure be presented considering any of these possible dilutions. Finally, in 1969 the APB issued *Opinion No. 15*, changing its recommendation for disclosure to a requirement.[17]

With this new posture came dual presentation: (1) earnings per common and common equivalent shares and (2) fully diluted earnings per share. The APB also defined some key terms and offered an extensive set of rules for application. This chapter does not include all of these rules, only the most commonly applied ones.

Simple vs. Complex Capital Structures

A corporation's capital structure can be either simple or complex, depending upon the nature of the securities that compose it. A **simple capital structure** consists of common stock only or includes no potentially dilutive convertible securities, options, warrants, or other rights that in the aggregate could dilute earnings per common share upon conversion or exercise. For this type of structure a single earnings per share presentation is appropriate. It is expressed in terms such as "earnings per common share" on the face of the income statement.

For a capital structure to be regarded as **complex,** it must include securities that have a dilutive effect on earnings per common share. A dilutive effect is one that will cause the earnings per share to decrease. Complex capital structures require dual presentation of earnings per share shown with equal prominence on the face of the income statement. These presentations are expressed in terms such as "earnings per common share—assuming no dilution" and "earnings per

---

[16]"Reporting the Results of Operations."

[17]"Earnings per Share."

common share—assuming full dilution." These two presentations commonly are referred to as "primary earnings per share" and "fully diluted earnings per share."

Regardless of the type of capital structure, earnings per share amounts must be shown for all periods presented. Further, *Opinion No. 15* specifically prohibits the retroactive restatement of the earnings per share amounts unless they (1) give effect to prior period adjustments,[18] (2) give effect to stock dividends and stock splits, including those occurring after the close of the period being reported upon,[19] (3) give effect to a pooling of interest,[20] (4) give effect to changes in the number of shares contingently issuable or issued when such changes are caused by changes in the market price of the stock,[21] and (5) give effect to a reduction in the number of shares contingently issuable when the term of an agreement to issue additional shares expires and the conditions have not been met.[22]

Weighted Average Common Shares

The computation of the earnings per share data should be based on the weighted average number of common shares outstanding during the periods presented. It is necessary to use the weighted average so that the effect of increases or decreases in outstanding common and common equivalent shares on earnings per share data is related to the portion of the period during which the related income (loss) is affected. In computing the weighted average, you weight any shares issued during the period by the fraction of the period they were outstanding, and weight any shares that are reacquired during the period by the fraction of the period they were not outstanding (1 − period outstanding).

For example, assume that Hoffman, Inc. had 500 common shares outstanding on January 1. The company issued 100 shares on March 31 and 60 shares on August 1. Also, they reacquired 200 shares on October 1. The computation of the weighted average common shares outstanding on December 31 is presented in Exhibit 21-4.

The 550 weighted average represents the amount of equivalent common shares outstanding during the period. It should be noted that more precise methods of computation could be used to compute weighted average, such as weighting on a daily basis the shares issued or reacquired. However, if the difference between these methods is immaterial, either computation is acceptable.

When the number of common shares outstanding increases due to a stock dividend or stock split, or decreases due to a reverse split, a retroactive recognition of an appropriate equivalent change in the capital structure should be computed for all periods presented. As an illustration, assume that Price, Inc. had 100,000 shares of common stock outstanding on January 1, 1982. During the year Price, Inc. reacquired 6,000 shares on March 1 and issued 1,000 shares on July 1. On July 15 a 10% stock dividend was declared and distributed. On August 18 a

[18] Ibid., par. 18.

[19] Ibid., par. 48.

[20] Ibid., par. 49.

[21] Ibid., par. 63.

[22] Ibid., par. 62.

Exhibit 21-4
HOFFMAN, INC.
Computation of Weighted Average Shares

Dates Applicable	No. of Shares	Fraction Outstanding	Product
Jan. 1 to Dec. 31	500	12/12	500
Mar. 31 to Dec. 31	100	9/12	75
Aug. 1 to Dec. 31	60	5/12	25
Oct. 1 to Dec. 31	(200)*	3/12	(50)
		Weighted average shares	550

*Note that the reacquired shares are weighted for the portion of the period that they were not outstanding.

two for one stock split occurred. The computation of the weighted average common shares outstanding is as presented in Exhibit 21-5.

The 10% stock dividend declared on July 15 was based on the 95,500 weighted shares outstanding at the date of declaration (100,000 − 5000 + 500). Thus, an additional 9550 (95,500 × 0.10) shares of common stock were issued on that date. Since the stock dividend should be restated retroactively for all periods presented, these additional shares should be weighted for the whole period. The equivalent change in the capital structure should be computed as 9550 × 12/12 = 9550. When the two for one stock split occurred, Price, Inc. had

Exhibit 21-5
PRICE, INC.
Computation of Weighted Average Shares

Dates	Transactions	No. of Shares	Fraction Outstanding	Product
Jan. 1	Outstanding	100,000	12/12	100,000
Mar. 1	Purchased	(6,000)*	10/12	(5,000)
Jul. 1	Issued	1,000	6/12	500
Jul. 15	10% stock dividend	9550**	12/12	9550
Aug. 18	Two for one stock split	105,050**	12/12	105,050
			Weighted average	210,100

*Note that the reacquired shares are weighted for the portion of the period that they were not outstanding.
**Based on the weighted average number of shares as of the date of issue.

weighted average shares of 105,050 (100,000 − 5000 + 500 + 9,550). Therefore, an additional 105,050 shares of common stock were equivalently issued on that date. As previously mentioned, a retroactive recognition for the entire period is required when a stock split occurs. The equivalent change in the capital structure would be computed as 105,050 × 12/12 = 105,050. Therefore, the weighted average number of shares outstanding for the period would be 210,100.

If a stock dividend or stock split occurs after the end of the year but before the issuance of financial statements, the weighted average number of shares outstanding for all periods presented must be restated. Refer to the previous example and assume that a 10% stock dividend occurred on January 12, 1983, before the issuance of financial statements for year 1982. The stock dividend would be based on the weighted average shares, *not* on the number of shares outstanding. It should be noted that when you compute the weighted shares at the end of 1983, the stock dividend will be based on the number of weighted average shares on January 12. The purpose of this requirement is to restate weighted average shares for transactions that occur after year-end but before the financial statements actually are issued.

Simple Capital Structure

As discussed previously, a corporation has a simple capital structure if during the period it had no securities outstanding (or agreement to issue securities) that in the aggregate dilute earnings per outstanding common share. Because there are many intricate calculations involved in the dual presentation amounts (i.e., primary and fully diluted), the APB established a 3% materiality level as to when significant dilution is deemed to exist. Therefore, aggregate dilution from all aforementioned securities, which is less than 3% of earnings per common share outstanding, need not be reported for either primary or fully diluted earnings per share.

In the case of a simple capital structure, a single presentation of earnings per outstanding common share is required. A simple capital structure also may include preferred stock that is not convertible to common stock. In computing earnings per outstanding common share in this situation, you must make two calculations: (1) reduce income by the preferred stock dividend claims (declarations, cumulations, or payments), and (2) divide income by the weighted average number of shares outstanding during the year. For example, assume the following facts:

Common stock, par $10, authorized 300,000 shares:	
Outstanding at beginning of year—100,000 shares	$1,000,000
Shares issued during the year—5,000 on July 1	50,000
Preferred stock, par $50, 8% nonconvertible, authorized 10,000 shares, outstanding during entire year—5,000 shares; dividends are paid yearly	$ 250,000
Net income	$ 300,000

Given these facts, the EPS is calculated as follows:
1. Calculation of the numerator:

Net income	$300,000
Less: Portion of the net income available to preferred stock ($250,000 × 0.08)	20,000
Earnings available to common stockholders	$280,000

2. Calculation of the denominator:

	Months	No. of Shares	Product
January 1 to December 31	12/12	100,000	100,000
July 1 to December 31	6/12	5,000	2,500
Weighted average shares outstanding			102,500

3. Earnings per common share:
   Earnings per share available to common stockholders $2.73
   ($280,000/102,500)

Notice that net income is reduced by dividends that either are declared or will be paid to preferred stockholders in order to reflect the actual earnings that will be available to common stockholders. These earnings then are divided by the number of common shares outstanding (weighted according to the time they were outstanding).

Complex Capital Structure—Introduction

A corporation has a complex capital structure for purposes of computing earnings per share if, in addition to common stock, it has issued securities that have a dilutive effect on earnings per outstanding common share by at least 3%. Among the securities that may have a dilutive effect are convertible preferred stock, convertible debt, options, warrants, participating securities, different classes of common stock, and agreements to issue such securities or shares of common stock in the future.[23]

As discussed previously, corporations that have a complex capital structure must compute and present a dual presentation of earnings on outstanding common shares, consisting of primary and fully diluted earnings per share. In computing only **primary earnings per share** you include common stock and dilutive common stock equivalents. **Fully diluted earnings per share** computations include not only common stock and dilutive common stock equivalents, but also any other potentially dilutive securities. They include as well any exercises or conversions for which common stock was issued during the period, whether their effect is dilutive or antidilutive.

The fully diluted earnings per share computation reflects the maximum dilution of all potentially dilutive issuances of common stock and their effect on current earnings per share on a prospective basis. Therefore, the difference between primary and fully diluted earnings per share shows (1) the maximum extent of

---

[23] "Computing Earnings per Share," *Interpretation of Opinion No. 15 of the APB* (New York: AICPA, 1970), par. 18.

potential dilution of current earnings that would occur from the conversions of securities that are not common stock equivalents or the contingent issuance of common stock not included in the computation of primary earnings per share and (2) the effect of all issuances of common stock on exercises or conversions during the year as if the issuance had occurred at the beginning of the year.[24] The following discussion will clarify the meaning and implementation of the terms and concepts introduced above.

Primary Earnings Per Share and Common Stock Equivalents

Primary earnings per share is the amount attributable to each share of common stock outstanding and common stock equivalents assumed to be outstanding during the period. In this text we have used primary earnings per share as a convenient means to express the presentation of this data when dual presentation is required. Thus, "primary" is merely a communication tool used to identify this earnings per share data and is not intended to place a greater significance on this data than is attributed to the fully diluted earnings per share data. Primary earnings per share, in essence, is based on common stock and dilutive common stock equivalents.

A **common stock equivalent** is a security that is, in substance, equivalent to common stock, based on its terms or the circumstances under which it was issued. Thus, a common stock equivalent is not common stock in form, yet it derives its status from its common stock characteristics or conversion privileges. These securities are unique in that they enable their holders to become common stockholders. Some examples of common stock equivalents are options, warrants, preferred stock or debt that is convertible into common stock, and agreements to issue common stock with the passage of time as the only condition for issuance. Options and warrants are always common stock equivalents. Convertible stock and debt issues are common stock equivalents providing the stock or debt yields less than 66⅔% of the average Aa corporate bond yield at the time of issuance.[25] The determination of whether a security is a common stock equivalent is made only at the time of issuance and should not be changed as long as the security remains outstanding. However, convertible securities outstanding or issued subsequently with the same terms as those of a common stock equivalent also should be classified as common stock equivalents.[26]

Fully Diluted Earnings Per Share

Fully diluted earnings per share is a pro forma presentation that reflects the possible dilution of earnings per share that would have occurred if all contingent issuances of common stock that would have reduced earnings per share had taken place at the beginning of the period (or time of issuance, if later). According to the APB, the purpose of fully diluted earnings per share is to show the maximum potential dilution of current earnings per share on a prospective basis. Therefore,

---

[24] Ibid., par. 21.

[25] "Determining Whether a Convertible Security Is a Common Stock Equivalent," *Statement of Financial Accounting Standards No. 55* (Stamford, Conn.: FASB, 1982), par 7.

[26] "Earnings per Share," par. 28.

any security that would upon conversion, exercise, or other contingent issuance increase earnings per share (or decrease loss per share) would be considered antidilutive and should not enter into the computation of primary or fully diluted earnings per share.[27] Fully diluted earnings per share computations include both common stock equivalents and non-common stock equivalents as long as their effect on earnings per share is *not* antidilutive. Any potential dilution of less than 3% in the aggregate need not be considered in the computation and presentation of dual earnings per share. In applying this 3% dilution test, you must consider all dilutive securities in total, not individually. Furthermore, any security that is antidilutive should be excluded in computing aggregate dilution.

For example, Best, Inc. has earnings per share (base) of $3.00 without regard to any dilutive securities (earnings available to common stockholders ÷ weighted average number of shares). In order for a dual presentation to be required, computed fully diluted earnings per share would have to be less than or equal to (≤) $2.91 [$3.00 − ($3.00 × 0.03)] or ($3.00 × 0.97). If the dilution of earnings per share would not be considered material, a single presentation of $3.00 would be appropriate.

Convertible Securities

As noted previously, convertible securities enter into the computation of primary earnings per share if they are considered to be common stock equivalents and are potentially dilutive. Convertible securities should be considered common stock equivalents if the cash yield at the time of issuance is significantly below what would be a comparable rate for a similar security without the conversion option. To aid in the classification the FASB concluded that if at the time of issuance a security has a cash yield (based on market price) of less than 66⅔% of the average Aa corporate bond yield, it will be considered a common stock equivalent. The term **"cash yield"** refers to the ratio of the annual dollar interest to the market price paid for the security. For example, assume that a convertible $1,000 bond is issued with a coupon rate of 8% and a market price of $1,400. Cash yield at the time of issuance would be 5.7% ($1,000 × 0.08 ÷ $1,400). If the current Aa bond yield were 10%, this security would be classified as a common stock equivalent because the cash yield (5.7%) is less than 66⅔% of the Aa bond yield rate (6.7%). It is assumed that by accepting an effective interest rate at any amount significantly less than the stated coupon rate, the investor purchased the security primarily for its conversion privilege.

For convertible securities to be considered dilutive, each issue must individually reduce base earnings per share if converted into common stock during the period. That is, the incremental effect on earnings divided by the incremental effect on weighted average shares must be less than the base earnings per share. Examples of incremental changes in earnings available to common stockholders

---

[27] There are exceptions in which antidilutive securities can be included in earnings per share computations. These exceptions are (1) when common stock is issued during the period on an antidilutive conversion or exercise, (2) when a security is antidilutive in earnings per share for income before extraordinary items but is dilutive in earnings per share for net income or vice versa, and (3) when aggregate computation is required which has a net dilutive effect but which may include antidilutive securities or antidilutive computations (i.e., the 20% test for options and warrants).

are interest on bonds (after tax) and preferred dividends. The number of common shares issuable in a convertible issue represents the incremental change in weighted average shares.

For example, assume that Robe, Inc. had base earnings per share of $2.50. Robe, Inc. also had 100, 4% convertible bonds, $1,000 par, each bond convertible into 10 shares of common stock. The effective tax rate is 50%. This bond issue is dilutive because the after-tax interest ($0.04 \times \$100,000 \times 0.5$) divided by the number (1,000) of issuable common shares $\left(\dfrac{\$2,000}{1,000} = \$2.00\right)$ is less than base earnings per share of $2.50.

The "if converted" method, which assumes conversion of the securities at the beginning of the period (or date of issuance, if later), is used in the computation of both primary and fully diluted earnings per share for convertible securities. This assumption requires the elimination of related bond interest and preferred dividends from the earnings available to common stockholders.

In addition, securities must be convertible within five years of the date of the financial statement to be included in primary earnings per share and convertible within ten years to be included in fully diluted earnings per share. Accordingly, the conversion rate or exercise price in effect during each period should be used in computing primary earnings per share. If securities are not immediately exercisable or convertible, the earliest effective price or rate during the succeeding five years should be used. Fully diluted earnings per share computations should be based on the most advantageous or highest price or rate within ten years of the date of the financial statement. Any conversion or exercise of securities beyond these periods is considered to be insignificant and should not be included in either primary earnings per share or fully diluted earnings per share.

Convertible securities that require cash payments upon conversion are considered to be the equivalent of warrants. Therefore, in computing primary and fully diluted earnings per share, you should use the treasury stock method. Dual earnings per share computations and the "if converted" method are illustrated in the following example.

Assume that Jax, Inc. reported net income of $900,000 in 1982 and weighted average number of shares outstanding of 100,000. In computing the earnings per share for the period, Jax, Inc. also offered the following information:

1. The Board of Directors decided that current earnings should be retained for further expansion. Therefore, no preferred dividends were declared or paid.
2. Jax, Inc. currently has cumulative, 8% preferred stock, par value $10, 25,000 shares issued and outstanding. The stock originally was issued at par when the Aa bond yield was 10%. Each preferred share is convertible into 2 shares of common stock.
3. Also outstanding are 5,000, 9% bonds, par value $1,000. Each bond is convertible into 3 shares of common stock. These bonds were issued at a time when the Aa bond yield was extremely high and were classified as common stock equivalents.
4. On January 1, 1982, Jax, Inc. issued 10,000 shares of 6% preferred stock, $15 par, at a market price of $20 per share. Each preferred share is convertible into 2 shares of common stock.

5. On July 1, 1982, 1,000, 7% bonds were issued at a market price of $1,200 per bond. Each bond has a par value of $1,000 and is convertible into 5 shares of common stock.
6. The Aa corporate bond yield has remained constant during the year at 9%.
7. Jax, Inc. has a corporate tax rate of 50%.

In this situation EPS is calculated as follows:

	Primary EPS Incremental Changes in Income	Incremental Changes in Shares
Before adjustments	$880,000*	100,000
6% Preferred	–0–	20,000
7% Bonds	17,500	2,500
Adjusted earnings and weighted average shares	$897,500	122,500

Primary earnings per share ($897,500/122,500) = $7.33

*Income available to common shareholders (net income less dividends to non-common stock equivalent preferred shareholders, i.e., 8% preferred).

Net income is adjusted for the dividends on the 8% preferred stock because they are cumulative. This issue is not included in the calculation of primary earnings per share because they are not common stock equivalents. The cash yield (8% because issued at par) is not less than $\frac{2}{3}$ of the Aa bond yield ($\frac{2}{3} \times 10\% = 6.6\%$). The 6% preferred issues are common stock equivalents since the cash yield $\left(\frac{0.06 \times 15}{20} = 4.5\%\right)$ is less than $\frac{2}{3}$ of the Aa bond yield ($\frac{2}{3} \times 9\% = 6\%$). This issue is also dilutive $\left(\frac{0.06 \times \$150,000}{20,000} = \$.45 \text{ per share compared to } \$8.80 \text{ per}\right.$

share base$\Big)$; thus, it is included in primary earnings per share.

Although the 9% bond issue is classified as a common stock equivalent, the effects on earnings are antidilutive $\left(\frac{0.09 \times \$5,000,000 \times 0.5}{15,000} = \$15 \text{ per share}\right.$

compared to the $8.80 base per share$\Big)$ and therefore are not included. Notice that the amount of annual interest (0.09 × $5,000,000 par) is reduced by the tax rate (50%) to reflect the actual effect on income. The 7% bond issue qualifies as a common stock equivalent. $\left(\text{Cash yield: } \frac{0.07 \times \$1,000}{\$1,200} \le \frac{2}{3} \times 9\%.\right)$ The 7% bonds are also dilutive $\left(\frac{\frac{1}{2} \text{ year} \times 0.07 \times \$1,000,000 \times 0.5}{5,000 \times \frac{1}{2}} = \$7 \text{ per share com-}\right.$

pared to the $8.80 per share base$\Big)$ and are included in the computation. Note that the effects on income and weighted average shares are adjusted by the time outstanding ($\frac{1}{2}$ year). The fully diluted EPS is computed as follows:

Fully Diluted EPS

	Incremental Changes in Income	Incremental Changes in Shares
Before adjustments	$880,000	100,000
8% Preferred	20,000	50,000
6% Preferred	–0–	20,000
7% Bonds	17,500	2,500
Adjusted earnings and weighted average shares	$917,500	172,500

Fully diluted earnings per share ($917,500/172,500) = $5.32

Notice that the 8% preferred stock issue is included in the computation of fully diluted earnings per share. Even though this issue was not a common stock equivalent and was not included in primary earnings per share, it is, however, dilutive $\left(\dfrac{0.08 \times \$250,000}{50,000} = \$.40 \right)$. Also, the cumulative preferred dividends associated with this issue have to be added back to income attributable to common stock because the issue is assumed to be converted at the beginning of the period. As noted previously, the 6% preferred stock and the 7% bonds were common stock equivalents and dilutive; therefore, they were included in both primary and fully diluted earnings per share. The 9% bonds are also antidilutive for fully diluted earnings per share $\left(\dfrac{0.09 \times \$5,000,000 \times 0.5}{15,000} = \$15 \right)$, and therefore are not included in the computation.

In concluding the computation of earnings per share, it must determine if the aggregate effect on income of the convertible securities is significant enough to require a dual presentation. This task is accomplished by the 3% test as follows:

$8.80 (Base EPS) × 97% = $8.54
$5.32 (FD EPS) < $8.54

Fully diluted earnings per share is less than 97% (1 − 0.03) of the base earnings per share; therefore, Jax, Inc. has a complex capital structure. Dual presentation of earnings per share is required.

Stock Options and Warrants

Options and warrants usually have no cash yield but give the holder the right to purchase common stock at a specified price. For the most part these securities derive their value from the fact that they represent a right to buy common stock. Therefore, these securities always are classified as common stock equivalents and, if dilutive, are included in both primary and fully diluted earnings per share. Further, other securities that require the payment of cash upon exercise or conversion (regardless of the yield at the time of issuance) are considered the equivalents of options or warrants and are classified also as common stock equivalents at all times. Examples of some of these securities are stock purchase contracts, stock subscriptions not fully paid, deferred compensation plans providing for the issuance of common stock and some convertible debt and convertible preferred stock.

Options and warrants are considered dilutive in the computations of primary earnings per share if the exercise price is below the average market price during the period. The APB recommended as a materiality threshold that these securities are not assumed to be exercised until the market price has been in excess of the exercise price for substantially all of three consecutive months, ending with the last month of the period of the earnings per share computation.[28] For fully diluted earnings per share computations, the exercise price must be below the average market price or the market price at the end of the period, whichever is greater. The use of the greater of the average market price or ending market price in the fully diluted earnings per share computation reflects the maximum potential dilution that can occur if all options and warrants are exercised.

Whenever options and warrants are antidilutive, they are not included in the computations of either primary or fully diluted earnings per share. Antidilution generally occurs when the exercise price exceeds the average market price for primary EPS and, for fully diluted EPS, exceeds the year-end price, if it is greater than the average market price. The exclusion of these antidilutive securities is reasonable in that the stock could be purchased in the open market for less than it could be purchased by exercising the option or warrant.

As with convertible securities, options and warrants must be exercisable within five years of the date of the financial statements to be included in primary earnings per share and exercisable within ten years to be included in fully diluted earnings per share. Accordingly, the exercise price in effect during each period should be used in computing primary earnings per share. If the securities are not immediately exercisable, the earliest effective price during the succeeding five years should be used. Fully diluted earnings per share computations should be based on the most advantageous or highest price within ten years of the date of the financial statement. Any exercise of options and warrants beyond these periods is considered to be insignificant and should not be included in either primary earnings per share or fully diluted earnings per share.

The computation of earnings per share involving options and warrants requires the use of one of two methods, depending upon the results of the "20% test." If the number of shares obtainable upon exercise of the options and warrants in the aggregate is less than or equal to 20% of the common shares outstanding, the treasury stock method must be used.[29] However, if the number of obtainable shares (in theory) is greater than 20% of the outstanding common stock, the modified treasury stock method is required. This latter requirement reflects the fact that when a substantial number (20%) of common shares can be obtained through the exercise of the options and warrants, the treasury stock method may not reflect potential dilution adequately. The treasury stock and modified treasury stock methods will be discussed in the following sections.

---

[28] "Substantially all" means essentially 11 of 13 weeks.

[29] If the capital structure includes options and warrants containing provisions that (1) require or permit the tendering of debt or (2) require retirement of specified debt or other securities and convertible securities that require or permit payment of cash, the "if converted" method should be applied first, and then any excess proceeds should be applied to the purchase of common stock under the treasury stock method.

Treasury Stock Method. The **treasury stock method** assumes that all options and warrants are exercised at the beginning of the period (or at the time of issuance, if later) and that the proceeds obtained through each individual exercise are used to purchase common stock. When primary EPS is being computed, these proceeds are assumed to be used to repurchase shares at the average market price for the year. However, the proceeds are assumed to be used to repurchase shares at the greater of the average market price or the year-end market price (reflecting maximum potential dilution) when fully diluted EPS is being computed.

For example, consider the following information as relates to Forb, Inc.

Net income	$250,000
Weighted average shares	95,000
Number of shares outstanding—December 31, 19X1	100,000
Options and warrants outstanding	1,000
Each option and warrant exercisable into 5 shares of common stock	5,000
Exercise price	$ 20
Average market price	$ 25
Market price—December 31, 19X1	$ 23
Proceeds from exercise: ($20 × 5,000 shares)	$100,000
Number of shares proceeds can repurchase at $25 per share ($100,000 ÷ $25)	4,000

Note that the average market price would be used to repurchase common shares for both primary earnings per share and fully diluted earnings per share, since it is greater than the ending market price. Therefore, the maximum number of shares that can be repurchased with the available proceeds ($100,000) is 4,000. Also notice that the number of shares assumed exercised (5,000) is less than 20% of the outstanding stock at the end of the period (20% × 100,000 = 20,000). Hence, the treasury stock method is appropriate.

Weighted average shares are adjusted by the incremental shares (i.e., common shares issued through exercise less any shares assumed to be repurchased). No adjustments in earnings are required. If you refer to the previous example, primary and fully diluted earnings per share are calculated as follows:

	Incremental Changes in Earnings	*Incremental Changes in Shares*
Before adjustments	$250,000	95,000
Required adjustments	—	1,000
Adjusted	$250,000	96,000

Primary and fully diluted earnings per share $\left(\dfrac{\$250,000}{96,000}\right) = \underline{\underline{\$2.60}}$

Notice that the change in weighted average shares (1,000) is the difference between the number of shares to be issued (5,000) and the number of shares assumed repurchased (4,000).

For further illustration of the treasury stock method, see Exhibit 21-6, which shows the calculations for primary EPS.

In the exhibit the 20% test is not met since the number of shares to be issued from the exercise (20,000) is less than 20% of the shares outstanding (125,000 × 0.2); therefore, the treasury stock method is required and each issue must be considered individually. Notice that the Series A options are antidilutive since the exercise price ($20) is greater than the average price ($15), and so are not included in primary earnings per share. The proceeds from the exercise of the

---

Exhibit 21-6
Treasury Stock Method—Primary EPS

Common shares outstanding—December 31, 19X5	125,000
Weighted average shares—December 31, 19X5	95,000
Net income	$ 140,000
Debt outstanding (10%)	$1,000,000
Income tax rate	40%
Common stock prices: average	$ 15
ending	$ 21

Stock Options

Series A—January 1, 19X5, 10,000 options authorized and issued.
    One option plus $20 is needed to acquire one common share.

Series B—January 1, 19X2, 10,000 options authorized and issued.
    One option plus $10 is needed to acquire one common share.

None of the options has been exercised.

Earnings per Share Calculations

Primary EPS

	Incremental Changes in Earnings	Incremental Changes in Shares
Before adjustments	$140,000	95,000
Series B*	—	3,333
Adjusted	$140,000	98,333

$$\text{Primary earnings per share} \left(\frac{\$140,000}{98,333} \right) = \underline{\$1.42}$$

*20% test not met, consider individually.

Proceeds:	Issued from exercise	10,000
10,000 × $10 = $100,000	Acquired treasury shares	6,667 ($100,000/$15)
		3,333

Series B options are used to acquire common shares at the average market price, thereby having no effect on earnings and an incremental effect (3,333) on weighted average shares.

Exhibit 21-7 presents the calculation of fully diluted EPS using the treasury stock method. Notice that the Series A options are now dilutive for fully diluted earnings per share (exercise, $20 < market, $21). Again, there are no adjustments to net income, and there is an incremental adjustment to weighted average shares (issued from exercise less acquired treasury stock). Primary and fully diluted earnings per share are below base earnings per share ($1.47) and therefore are included in the dual presentation. Also, the 3% test is met (fully diluted, $1.39 < $1.43) and a dual presentation is required.

Modified Treasury Stock Method. As discussed previously, if the number of obtainable shares through the exercise of options and warrants is, in the aggregate, greater than 20% of the outstanding common shares, the modified treasury stock method is required. The **modified treasury stock method** requires *all* op-

---

Exhibit 21-7
Treasury Stock Method—Fully Diluted EPS

	Fully Diluted EPS	
	Incremental Changes in Income	*Incremental Changes in Shares*
Before adjustments	$140,000	95,000
Series A	—	476
Series B	—	5,238
Adjusted	$140,000	100,714

$$\text{Fully diluted earnings per share} \left(\frac{\$140,000}{100,714} \right) = \$1.39$$

Series A
Proceeds:
$10,000 \times \$20 = \$200,000$

Issued from exercise	10,000
Acquired treasury shares ($200,000 \div \$21$)	9,524
	476

Series B
Proceeds:
$10,000 \times \$10 = \$100,000$

Issued from exercise	10,000
Acquired treasury shares ($100,000 \div \$21$)	4,762
	5,238

$$\text{3\% test: Base EPS} \left(\frac{\$140,000}{95,000} \right) = \$1.47 \times 0.97 = \$1.43$$

tions and warrants to be considered in the aggregate when you compute earnings per share. Like the treasury stock method, the modified treasury method assumes that the proceeds from the exercise are employed to repurchase common stock using the average market price for primary earnings per share and the greater of the average or ending market price for fully diluted earnings per share. In assuming the repurchase of shares, you use the aggregate proceeds to purchase common shares, but these are not to exceed 20% of the outstanding number of shares at year-end. Any remaining proceeds then are used to (1) retire any short-term or long-term debt and then (2) invested in government securities or commercial paper. If any debt is retired, earnings must be adjusted for the net-of-tax effect on income.

For example, if Canyon, Inc. retires a 6% debt issue (par $100,000), net income must be adjusted to reflect the after tax interest saved since the debt is assumed to be repurchased as of the beginning of the period. The calculations would be as follows (assuming a 50% tax rate): $6\% \times \$100,000 \times 0.5 = \$3,000$. This $3,000 would be added to earnings since it represents a reduction in interest that otherwise would have been paid. The modified treasury stock method also requires the weighted average shares to be adjusted for the incremental shares (common shares obtained through exercise, less any shares assumed to be repurchased). Primary and fully diluted earnings per share then are computed. If these aggregate computations are less than the base earnings per share, they are included in the dual presentation. Conversely, if they are greater than the base earnings per share, they are excluded. For example, assume that Canyon, Inc.'s base earnings per share was computed to be $2.85. The aggregate computation of primary earnings per share was $2.50, and the aggregate fully diluted earnings per share was $2.45. Both would be included in the computation of a dual presentation. Further illustration of the modified treasury stock method is presented in Exhibit 21-8.

Notice that the number of exercised shares (20,000) exceeds 20% of the shares outstanding (85,000); therefore, the options must be considered in the aggregate regardless of their individual effects. If you assume exercise, the proceeds were used first to acquire treasury stock (17,000 is the maximum since $20\% \times 85,000 = 17,000$) at the average market price (for primary earnings per share), and then to retire outstanding debt. Net income is adjusted by the effects of the reduction in interest expense. Weighted average shares are adjusted for the difference between the shares issued in the assumed exercise (20,000) less the acquired treasury stock (17,000).

Application of the modified treasury stock method for fully diluted EPS is presented in Exhibit 21-9. When computing fully diluted earnings per share, you must assume repurchase of the treasury stock at the ending market price because it is higher. Notice that the fully diluted earnings per share is lower than the primary earnings per share, thus showing the maximum possible dilution.

Primary and fully diluted calculations are less than the base earnings per share ($1.67), and so are included in the dual presentation. Also note that the 3% test is met ($1.61 < $1.62); therefore, a dual presentation is required.

Under the modified treasury stock method, it is possible for an antidilutive option or warrant issue to be included in the aggregate computations of primary and fully diluted earnings per share. For example, consider the following facts presented in Exhibit 21-10.

Exhibit 21-8
Modified Treasury Stock Method—Primary EPS

Common shares outstanding—December 31, 19X5	85,000
Weighted average shares—December 31, 19X5	60,000
Net income—December 31, 19X5	$ 100,000
Debt outstanding (10%)	$1,000,000
Income tax rate	40%
Common stock prices: average	$ 14
ending	$ 16

Stock Options

Series A—January 1, 19X5, 10,000 options authorized and issued.
One option plus $20 is needed to acquire one common share.

Series B—January 1, 19X2, 10,000 options authorized and issued.
One option plus $10 is needed to acquire one common share.

None of the options has been exercised.

Earnings per Share Calculations

	Primary EPS	
	Incremental Changes in Income	*Incremental Changes in Shares*
Before adjustments	$100,000	60,000
Series A and B*	3,720	3,000
Adjusted	$103,720	63,000

$$\text{Primary earnings per share} \left(\frac{\$103,720}{63,000} \right) = \underline{\underline{\$1.65}}$$

*20% test met, consider in the aggregate.

Proceeds:			Proceeds	$300,000
10,000 × $20 =	$200,000		Acquired treasury stock**	
10,000 × $10 =	100,000		(17,000 × $14)	238,000
20,000	$300,000		Remaining proceeds	$ 62,000
			Retire debt	62,000
			Interest avoided	×10%
				$ 6,200
			Tax ($6,200 × 40%)	2,480
			Change in income	$ 3,720

**Reacquisition limited to 20% of outstanding shares.

Exhibit 21-9
Modified Treasury Stock Method—Fully Diluted EPS

	Fully Diluted EPS	
	Incremental Changes in Income	*Incremental Changes in Shares*
Before adjustments	$100,000	60,000
Series A and B	1,680	3,000
Adjusted	$101,680	63,000

$$\text{Fully diluted earnings per share} \left(\frac{\$101,680}{63,000} \right) = \underline{\underline{\$1.61}}$$

Proceeds	$300,000
Acquired treasury stock (17,000 × $16)	272,000
Remaining proceeds	$ 28,000
Retire debt	28,000
Interest avoided	× 10%
	$ 2,800
Tax ($2,800 × 40%)	1,120
Change in income	$ 1,680

$$3\% \text{ test: Base EPS} \left(\frac{\$100,000}{6,000} \right) = \$1.67 \times 97\% = \underline{\underline{\$1.62}}$$

Primary and fully diluted earnings per share ($1.69) is less than base earnings per share ($1.75), and therefore is dilutive in the aggregate. However, note that Option B is antidilutive ($20 > $16) when considered individually, but it is still included in the dual computation. Also note that if base earnings per share had been $1.60, primary and fully diluted earnings per share would have been antidilutive, and Options A and C would have been excluded in the computation even though they were individually dilutive ($10 and $15 < $16).

It should be noted also that the materiality factor of 20% used in APB *Opinion No. 15* refers to both a "test" and a "limit."[30] The 20% "test" refers to the situation in which the total number of common shares obtained through the exercise of options and warrants (in the aggregate) exceeds the outstanding common stock at the end of the period. The 20% "limit" is the limit placed on the number of common shares that can be assumed repurchased with the proceeds from the exercised options and warrants.

We wish to reemphasize also that if, in the aggregate, fully diluted earnings per share dilute base earnings per share less than 3%, a dual presentation would *not* be required. This test must be applied as well when options and warrants are included.

---

[30] "Earnings per Share," par. 30.

Exhibit 21-10
Antidilutive Issues in the Modified Treasury Stock Method

	Exercise Price	*# Shares Obtainable*	*Proceeds*
Option A	$10	10,000	$100,000
Option B	20	3,000	60,000
Option C	15	5,000	75,000
		18,000	$235,000

Average and ending market price: $16
Weighted average and shares outstanding: 100,000
Net income: $175,000

	Incremental Changes in Income	*Incremental Changes in Shares*
Before adjustment	$175,000	100,000
Adjustment		
$18,000 - \left(\dfrac{\$235,000}{\$16}\right)$	—	3,312
	$175,000	103,312

Primary and fully diluted earnings per share $\left(\dfrac{\$175,000}{103,312}\right) = \$1.69$

Contingent Issuances

There may be times when corporations agree to issue additional common stock based upon some future event. Such conditional agreements are referred to as **contingent agreements.** Because such agreements involve the issuance of common stock, earnings per share computations are affected. Examples of some common conditions that might need to be met for the issuance of contingent shares are as follows:

1. Passage of time.
2. Maintenance or attainment of some level of earnings.
3. Changes in market price.

When contingent shares are based upon the mere passage of time, they should be considered outstanding for both primary and fully diluted earnings per share. The weighted average shares are increased by the number of shares contingently issuable. No adjustment would be required to the earnings available to common stockholders.

If the contingent agreement is based upon maintenance or attainment of some future level of earnings, and if that level is being attained currently, the additional shares should be considered as outstanding for the purpose of computing both primary and fully diluted earnings per share. If the required level of earnings is not being met currently, the contingent shares will *not* enter into primary earnings per share but may enter into fully diluted earnings per share if dilutive. The critical factor is the meeting of the required conditions.

If the required earnings conditions are being met, weighted average shares are adjusted for the number of contingently issuable common shares in computing both primary and fully diluted earnings per share. If the conditions are not being met, earnings available to common shareholders must be adjusted for the difference between the required earnings level and the earnings level currently being attained when computing fully diluted EPS. For example, assume that Kart, Inc. entered into an agreement in which its average earnings must reach a certain amount in 1982 for an additional 50,000 common shares to be issued. There are 100,000 weighted average shares, and current average earnings are $100,000. Based on these conditions, consider each of the following cases.

CASE 1

Average income required: $90,000

	Incremental Changes in Income	Incremental Changes in Shares
Actual	$100,000	100,000
Contingency adjustment	—	50,000
Adjusted	$100,000	150,000

Primary and fully diluted earnings per share $\left(\dfrac{\$100,000}{150,000}\right) = \underline{\underline{\$0.67}}$

The required earnings are being met currently; therefore, the number of shares issuable is considered in calculating both primary and fully diluted earnings per share.

CASE 2

Average income required: $170,000

	Incremental Changes in Income	Incremental Changes in Shares
Actual	$100,000	100,000
Contingency adjustment	70,000	50,000
Adjusted	$170,000	150,000

Fully diluted earnings per share $\left(\dfrac{\$100,000}{100,000}\right) = \underline{\underline{\$1.00}}$

Net income is adjusted for the difference in net income ($100,000) and the desired level of income ($170,000), and the weighted average shares are adjusted for the issuable shares. These adjustments would only enter into the calculation of fully diluted earnings per share if the desired level of earnings is not met currently. However, the effects of these adjustments are antidilutive ($170,000 ÷ 150,000 = $1.13 > $1.00), and therefore they cannot be included.

CASE 3

Average income required: $130,000

	Incremental Changes in Income	*Incremental Changes in Shares*
Actual	$100,000	100,000
Contingency adjustment	30,000	50,000
Adjusted	$130,000	150,000

Fully diluted earnings per share $\left(\dfrac{\$130,000}{150,000} \right) = \underline{\underline{\$0.87}}$

The required conditions are not being met currently (primary is therefore not reported), and the effects are not antidilutive ($0.87 < $1.00); therefore, fully diluted earnings per share must reflect the contingency.

The last major type of contingent agreements involves guaranteed market prices. A corporation may agree to issue additional common stock if the market price of its stock falls below a certain price or does not reach a certain price. You should compare the required market price to the market price at the close of the reportable period in determining the effects on earnings per share computations. If the guaranteed market price is not attained, the number of contingent shares will be included in the weighted average shares in the computation of both primary and fully diluted earnings per share. Adjustments to earnings available to common stockholders are not required.

For example, assume that North, Inc. issued stock in exchange for equipment. The agreement to consummate the exchange specified that 500 additional shares would be issued if North, Inc.'s market price per share did not reach $80 in one year. If the market price were $75 at the financial statement date, the issuable shares (500) would be used in computing both primary and fully diluted earnings per share. No adjustment to earnings would be required. Conversely, if the market price were $85 at the financial statement date, the issuable shares would *not* enter into the computation of earnings per share.

Financial Statement Disclosure of EPS

The earnings per share data are required to be presented prominently in the financial statements due to the significance that investors and others place upon the data. Therefore, the APB concludes in *Opinion No. 15* that earnings per share or net loss per share data should be shown on the face of the income statement. When dual presentation of earnings per share is required, the primary and fully diluted earnings per share amounts should be presented with equal prominence. Earnings per share amounts are required to be presented only for earnings before extraordinary items and net income. However, it is desirable to show per share data on extraordinary items, on cumulative effects of changes in accounting principles, and on discontinued operations.

Corporations with complex capital structures are required to disclose information in addition to the earnings per share data in the footnotes to the financial statements. Some of the more common disclosures are as follows:

1. Bases upon which primary and fully diluted earnings per share were calculated.
2. Issues that are common stock equivalents.
3. Issues that are other potentially dilutive securities.
4. Shares issued upon conversion, exercise, and conditions met for contingent issuances.
5. Assumptions and adjustments made for earnings per share data.
6. Restatement for a prior period adjustment.[31]

For example, the following data have been taken from the annual financial report to the stockholders of the H. J. Heinz Company and Consolidated Subsidiaries:

	April 30, 1980	*May 2, 1979*
Per common share amounts:		
Primary	$6.24	$4.80
Fully diluted	$6.00	$4.64

CAPITAL STOCK

The number of shares authorized, outstanding, issued, retired, or converted, and the par values of the company's capital stock appear in the table following this note.

The 3.65% cumulative preferred stock is callable or redeemable through the sinking fund at $102.75 per share. Payments (or open market purchases of such stock) aggregating $200,000 are required to be made to the sinking fund on or before October 1 of each year.

The company currently has outstanding 2,394 shares of $3.50 first and second series cumulative preferred stock, par value $18.50 per share. The total par value of these shares, $44,000 ($46,000 at May 2, 1979), has been included in sundry liabilities in the Consolidated Balance Sheets. The company is retiring these shares on the basis of annual sinking fund requirements. The involuntary liquidation value of these shares is $239,000. Each share has voting rights on an equal basis with the common stock.

The $1.70 first series, third cumulative preferred stock is convertible into common stock at any time at a conversion rate of $0.75 share of common stock or may be redeemed by the company at $30.50 per share beginning on December 1, 1982, and at decreasing prices thereafter until December 1, 1986, when it may be redeemed at $28.50 per share. Each share entitles the holder to one-half vote.

---

[31] For further required disclosures, see "Computing Earnings per Share," *Unofficial Accounting Interpretations of APB Opinion No. 15* (New York: AICPA, 1970), pars. 100 and 101.

At April 30, 1980, 2,270,552 shares (2,365,462 at May 2, 1979) of common stock were reserved for conversion of convertible preferred stock outstanding and for outstanding options or for the granting of options under the employees' stock option plans.

Concept Summary

EARNINGS PER SHARE

TYPES OF EARNINGS PER SHARE

Type	Basis of Calculation
Primary	Earnings attributable to common shares as well as securities that derive a substantial portion of their value from their ability, through exercise or conversion, to become shares of common stock.
Fully Diluted	Earnings attributable to shares in primary EPS and other securities that may be convertible into common stock.

COMMON STOCK EQUIVALENCY TEST

Item	Test
Convertible Stock	Yield is less than $2/3$ the average Aa bond yield at the issuance date.
Options and Warrants	The market value of the stock is above the exercise price for substantially all of a three-month period, with the last month being the last month of the reporting period.

IMPACT OF SECURITIES ON EPS CALCULATIONS

	Impact on	
Securities	Primary EPS	Fully Diluted EPS
Outstanding Common Stock	Included in computation at weighted average shares outstanding	Included in computation at weighted average shares outstanding

Common Stock Equivalents	If dilutive, included in computation from beginning of period or time of issuance, if later; assume conversion or exercise at average market price	If dilutive, included in computation from beginning of period or time of issuance, if later; assume conversion or exercise at average market price or end of period price, whichever is higher
Convertible Securities (Preferred Stock and/or Bonds)	Included in computation only if deemed common stock equivalent and dilutive	Included in computation if dilutive
Contingent Shares	Considered outstanding shares if issuable upon passage of time; otherwise, considered outstanding when contingency resolved	Considered outstanding shares if issuable upon passage of time; otherwise, considered outstanding when contingency resolved
Antidilutive Securities	Not included in computation	Not included in computation

Appendix

Comprehensive Earnings Per Share Illustration

The following schedule sets forth the short-term debt, long-term debt, and stockholders' equity of Red, Inc. as of December 31, 1981. The president of Red, Inc. has requested that you assist the controller in preparing figures for earnings per share computations.

Short-term debt:	
Notes payable—banks	$ 4,000,000
Current portion of long-term debt	10,000,000
Total short-term debt	$ 14,000,000
Long-term debt:	
4% convertible debentures due April 15, 1993	$ 30,000,000
Other long-term debt less current portions	20,000,000
Total long-term debt	$ 50,000,000
Stockholders' equity:	
$4.00 cumulative, convertible preferred stock; par value $20 per share; authorized 2,000,000 shares; issued and outstanding 1,200,000 shares	$ 24,000,000
Common stock; par value $1 par share; authorized 20,000,000 shares; issued 7,500,000 shares including 600,000 shares held in treasury	7,500,000
Additional paid-in capital	4,200,000
Retained earnings	76,500,000
Total	$112,200,000
Less: Cost of 600,000 shares of common stock held in treasury (acquired before 1981)	900,000
Total stockholders' equity	$111,300,000

Additional Information:

1. The "Other long-term debt" and the related amounts due within one year are amounts due on unsecured promissory notes which require payments each

year to maturity. The interest rate on these borrowings is 6½%. At the time that these monies were borrowed, the Aa corporate bond yield was 7%.

2. The 4% convertible debentures were issued at their face value of $30,000,000 in 1963 when the Aa bond yield was 5%. The debentures are due in 1993 and until then are convertible into the common stock of Red, Inc. at the rate of 40 shares for each $1,000 debenture.

3. The $4.00 cumulative, convertible preferred stock was issued in 1980. The stock had a market value of $60 at the time of issuance when the Aa bond yield was 9%. On July 1, 1981, and on October 1, 1981, holders of the preferred stock converted 80,000 and 20,000 preferred shares, respectively, into common stock. Each share of preferred stock is convertible into 1.2 shares of common stock.

4. On April 1, 1981, Red, Inc. issued 800,000 shares of common stock.

5. Series A options were issued in 1975 to purchase 200,000 shares of Red, Inc.'s common stock at a price of $25 per share. None of these options has been exercised.

6. On October 1, 1980, the company granted Series B options to its officers and selected employees to purchase 100,000 shares of Red Inc.'s common stock at a price of $32 per share. The options are *not* exercisable until 1988.

7. The average and ending market prices during 1981 of Red, Inc. common stock were as follows:

    Average for the year $33
    December 31, 1981   34

8. Dividends on the preferred stock have been paid through December 31, 1981, on a quarterly basis (i.e., $1 each quarter). Dividends paid on the common stock were $0.50 per share for each quarter.

9. The net income of Red, Inc. for the year ended December 31, 1981, was $8,600,000. There were *no* extraordinary items, changes in accounting principles, or discontinued operations. The provision for income taxes was computed at a rate of 48%.

Required: Compute earnings per share.

(AICPA adapted)

SOLUTION

Weighted average shares:

1-1-81	Outstanding	$5,980,000^{(1)} \times 12/12 =$	5,980,000
4-4-81	Issue	$800,000 \times 9/12 =$	600,000
7-1-81	Conversion	$96,000^{(2)} \times 6/12 =$	48,000
10-1-81	Conversion	$24,000^{(3)} \times 3/12 =$	6,000
			6,634,000

(1)7,500,000 12-31-81
   (600,000) Treasury stock
   (920,000) Issued during year and included in the ending outstanding shares.
   5,980,000 12-1-81

(2)80,000 × 1.2.
(3)20,000 × 1.2.

Base EPS:

Net income	$8,600,000
Preferred dividend	5,020,000*
Unadjusted earnings	$3,580,000

$3,580,000 ÷ 6,634,000 = $0.54

*1st quarter	1,300,000 × $1 =	$1,300,000
2nd quarter	1,300,000 × $1 =	1,300,000
7–1 conversion	(80,000)	
3rd quarter	1,220,000 × $1 =	1,220,000
10–1 conversion	(20,000)	
4th quarter	1,200,000 × $1 =	1,200,000
		$5,020,000

Calculation of Adjustments for Non-Common Stock Securities:

1. "Other long-term debt":
   Issue is not convertible—exclude

2. 4% convertible debentures:
   30,000 bonds × 40 shares = 1,200,000
   $30,000,000 par × 4% interest = $1,200,000 × 48% tax rate = $576,000

   $$\frac{\$576,000}{1,200,000} = \$0.48 \quad \text{Dilutive ($0.48 < $0.54)}$$

   67% × 5% Aa bond yield = 0.03
   4% > 3%—therefore not a CSE[1]
   These securities are included in FDEPS[2], but *not* in PEPS[3].

[1] Common stock equivalent.
[2] Fully diluted earnings per share.
[3] Primary earnings per share.

3. $4.00 cumulative, convertible preferred stock:
   1,200,000 shares × 1.2 conversion rate = 1,440,000
   Dividend (see base EPS calculation) = $5,020,000

   $$\frac{\$5,020,000}{1,440,000} = \$3.49 \quad \text{Antidilutive ($3.49 > $0.54)}$$

   Not included in PEPS or FDEPS.

5. Issuable from Series A: 200,000
   Issuable from Series B: 100,000
   Total 300,000

   20% of common shares outstanding: 1,380,000*
   *(7,500,000 − 600,000 treasury × 20%)
   20% test not met, consider warrants individually.

Series A:

Dilutive—exercise price ($25) is below average and ending market prices. Include in both PEPS and FDEPS.

Proceeds:	200,000 × $25 = $5,000,000	
PEPS:	$5,000,000 ÷ $33(avg.) = 151,515 assumed repurchased	
	200,000 − 151,515 = 48,485 incremental shares	
FDEPS:	$5,000,000 ÷ $34(end.) = 147,059 assumed repurchased	
	200,000 − 147,059 = 52,941 incremental shares	

No adjustments to income are required.

6. *Series B*

Dilutive—exercise price ($32) is below average and ending market prices. Include in FDEPS but not PEPS because these options are not exercisable for eight years.

Proceeds:	100,000 × $32 = $3,200,000	
FDEPS:	$3,200,000 ÷ $34 = 94,118 assumed repurchased	
	100,000 − 94,118 = 5,882 incremental shares	

No adjustments to income are required.

Calculation of EPS:
Adjustments

Primary EPS

	Incremental Changes in Income	Incremental Changes in Shares
Before adjustments	$3,580,000	6,634,000
Series A options	–0–	48,485
Adjusted	$3,580,000	6,682,485

Primary EPS—$0.53

Fully Diluted EPS

	Incremental Changes in Income	Incremental Changes in Shares
Before adjustments	$3,580,000	6,634,000
4% Convertible debentures	576,000	1,200,000
Series A options	–0–	52,941
Series B options	–0–	5,882
Adjusted	$4,156,000	7,892,823

Fully diluted EPS—$0.52
3% test: Base EPS $0.54 × 97% = $0.52

Not a complex capital structure. FDEPS is not less than $0.52; therefore, a single presentation is required.

Earnings per common share—$0.54

Questions

Q–21–1 Explain the term *dilutive security*.

Q–21–2 Why would an investor be willing to purchase convertible debt securities with a 9% interest rate when he could purchase straight debt securities with a 11% interest rate? What benefits will the issuing company derive from selling convertible debt securities versus straight debt securities?

Q–21–3 What are two methods of valuing the securities issued when convertible debt is exchanged for equity securities? Which method is used more widely in practice? Why?

Q–21–4 What are warrants? Distinguish between debt securities issued with detachable warrants and convertible debt securities.

Q–21–5 When is it appropriate to give accounting recognition to the equity feature represented by warrants?

Q–21–6 Discuss the appropriate accounting for the issuance of convertible preferred stock and for the conversion of convertible preferred stock.

Q–21–7 What is the purpose of a stock option plan? Distinguish between a compensatory and a noncompensatory stock option plan.

Q–21–8 What conditions must be met for a stock option plan to be considered a noncompensatory plan under APB *Opinion No. 25?*

Q–21–9 Define *measurement date*. Is the measurement date always the date on which the option is granted to the employee? Why?

Q–21–10 Discuss the disclosure requirements for stock option plans.

Q–21–11 Define *primary earnings per share* and *fully diluted earnings per share*.

Q–21–12 Discuss and distinguish between a simple capital structure and a complex capital structure.

Q–21–13 Explain how to determine if convertible preferred stock and convertible debt could be considered common stock equivalents?

Q–21–14 Explain the treasury stock method as it applies to options and warrants in computing earnings per share.

Q–21–15 Define the term *senior security* and explain how senior securities that are not convertible enter into the determination of earnings per share data.

Q–21–16 How do stock dividends and splits affect the weighted average number of shares?

Q–21–17 What is the modified treasury stock method? How and when is it applied?

Q–21–18 To what extent is treasury stock assumed to be acquired by a corporation applying the treasury stock method in earnings per share calculations?

   a) To the maximum extent possible.

   b) Up to 20% of earnings for the period being reported on.

   c) None, until all long-term debt in effect has been retired; then, to the maximum extent possible.

   d) Up to 20% of outstanding common stock.

(AICPA adapted)

Q–21–19 Which of the following statements best describes the effect of cash yield at issuance of convertible securities on calculating earnings per share (EPS)?

   a) If less than two-thirds of the then current Aa bond interest rate, these securities are used to calculate primary EPS but not fully diluted EPS.

   b) If less than two-thirds of the then current Aa bond interest rate, these securities are used to calculate fully diluted EPS but not primary EPS.

   c) If greater than two-thirds of the then current Aa bond interest rate, these securities are used to calculate primary EPS and fully diluted EPS. (Continued)

d) If greater than two-thirds of the then current Aa bond interest rate, these securities are used to calculate fully diluted EPS but not primary EPS.

(AICPA adapted)

Q-21-20 In computing earnings per share, the equivalent number of shares of convertible preferred stock are added as an adjustment to the denominator (number of shares outstanding). If the preferred stock is preferred as to dividends, which amount then should be added as an adjustment to the numerator (net earnings)?

a) Annual preferred dividend.

b) Annual preferred dividend times one minus the income tax rate.

c) Annual preferred dividend times the income tax rate.

d) Annual preferred dividend divided by the income tax rate.

(AICPA adapted)

Q-21-21 The computation of earnings per share in accordance with generally accepted accounting principles may involve the consideration of securities deemed common stock equivalents. Common stock equivalents are an example of which of the following?

a) Form over substance.

b) Substance over form.

c) Form over accounting principle.

d) Substance over accounting principle.

(AICPA adapted)

Discussion Questions and Cases

D-21-1 Public enterprises are required to present earnings per share data on the face of the income statement.

Required:

Compare and contrast primary earnings per share with fully diluted earnings per share for each of the following:

a) The effect of common stock equivalents on the number of shares used in the computation of earnings per share data.

b) The effect of convertible securities that are not common stock equivalents on the number of shares used in the computation of earnings per share data.

c) The effect of antidilutive securities.

D-21-2 *Earnings per share* (EPS) is the most featured single financial statistic about modern corporations. Daily published quotations of stock prices recently have been expanded to include a *times earnings* figure, which is based on EPS, for many securities. Often, the focus of analysts' discussions will be on the EPS of the corporations receiving their attention.

Required:

1. Explain how dividends or dividend requirements on any class of preferred stock that may be outstanding affect the computation of EPS.

2. One of the technical procedures applicable in EPS computations is the *treasury-stock method*.

a) Briefly describe the circumstances under which it might be appropriate to apply the treasury-stock method.

b) There is a limit to the extent to which the treasury-stock method is applicable. Indicate what this limit is and give a succinct indication of the procedures that should be followed beyond the treasury-stock limits.

3. Under some circumstances convertible debentures would be considered *common stock equivalents*, whereas under other circumstances they would not.

a) When is it proper to treat convertible debentures as common stock equivalents? What is the effect on computation of EPS in such cases?

b) In case convertible debentures are not considered as common stock equivalents, explain how they are handled for purposes of EPS computations.

(AICPA adapted)

D–21–3 Incurring long-term debt with an arrangement whereby lenders receive an option to buy common stock during all or a portion of the time the debt is outstanding is a frequently used corporate financing practice. In some situations the result is achieved through the issuance of convertible bonds; in others, the debt instruments and the warrants to buy stock are separate.

Required:

1. Describe the differences that exist in current accounting for original proceeds of the issuance of convertible bonds and of debt instruments with separate warrants to purchase common stock.

2. Discuss the underlying rationale for the differences described in part 1 above.

3. Summarize the arguments that have been presented for the alternative accounting treatment.

(AICPA adapted)

D–21–4 Jones has adopted a traditional stock option plan for its officers and other employees. This plan is properly considered a compensatory plan.

Required:

Discuss how accounting for this plan will affect net earnings and earnings per share. Ignore income tax considerations and accounting for income tax benefits.

(AICPA adapted)

Exercises

E–21–1 On March 1, 1979, Danna Corporation issued $500,000 of 8% nonconvertible bonds at 103 which are due on February 28, 1999. In addition, each $1,000 bond was issued with 30 detachable stock warrants, each of which entitled the bondholder to purchase, for $50, one share of Danna common stock, par value $25. On March 1, 1979, the fair market value of Danna's common stock was $40 per share, and the fair market value of each warrant was $4.

Required:

1. What amount of the proceeds from the bond issue should Danna record as an increase in stockholders' equity?

2. Prepare all required journal entries for Danna Corporation on March 1, 1979.

E–21–2 Weaver Company had 100,000 shares of common stock issued and outstanding at December 31, 1978. On July 1, 1979, Weaver issued a 10% stock dividend. Unexercised stock options to purchase 20,000 shares of common stock (adjusted for the 1979 stock dividend) at $20 per share were outstanding at the beginning and end of 1979. The average market price of Weaver's common stock (which was not affected by the stock dividend) was $25 per share during 1979. Net income for the year ended December 31, 1979, was $550,000. What should be Weaver's 1979 primary earnings per common share, rounded to the nearest penny?

(AICPA adapted)

E–21–3 Information relating to the capital structure of Vauxhall Corporation is as follows:

	December 31,	
	1978	1979
Outstanding shares of:		
Common stock	200,000	200,000
Preferred 6% stock, $100 par; convertible into three shares of common stock for each share of preferred	10,000	10,000

The preferred stock was issued at par on July 1, 1978, when the Aa bond interest rate was 9.5%. During 1979 Vauxhall paid dividends of $6 per share on its preferred stock. The net income for the year ended December 31, 1979, is $860,000. What is the primary earnings per common share, rounded to the nearest penny, for the year ended December 31, 1979?

(AICPA adapted)

E-21-4   At December 31, 1974, the Back Company had 350,000 shares of common stock outstanding. On September 1, 1975, an additional 150,000 shares of common stock were issued. In addition, Back had $10,000,000 of 8% convertible bonds outstanding at December 31, 1974, which are convertible into 200,000 shares of common stock. The bonds were not considered common stock equivalents at the time of their issuance, and no bonds were converted into common stock in 1975. The net income for the year ended December 31, 1975, was $3,000,000. If you assume the income tax rate was 50%, what should be the fully diluted earnings per share for the year ended December 31, 1975?

(AICPA adapted)

E-21-5   Information concerning the capital structure of the Petrock Corporation is as follows:

	December 31,	
	1975	1976
Common stock	90,000 shares	90,000 shares
Convertible preferred stock	10,000 shares	10,000 shares
8% convertible bonds	$1,000,000	$1,000,000

During 1976 Petrock paid dividends of $1.00 per share on its common stock and $2.40 per share on its preferred stock. The preferred stock is convertible into 20,000 shares of common stock, but is not considered a common stock equivalent. The 8% convertible bonds are convertible into 30,000 shares of common stock and are considered common stock equivalents. The net income for the year ended December 31, 1976, was $285,000. Assume that the income tax rate was 50%.

Required:
1.   What should be the primary earnings per share for the year ended December 31, 1976, rounded to the nearest penny?
2.   What should be the fully diluted earnings per share for the year ended December 31, 1976, rounded to the nearest penny?

(AICPA adapted)

E-21-6   On July 1, 1976, Austin Company granted Harry Ross, an employee, an option to buy 500 shares of Austin common stock at $30 per share. The option was exercisable for five years from the date of the grant. Ross exercised his option on October 1, 1976, and sold his shares on December 2, 1976. The quoted market prices of Austin common stock during 1976 were as follows:

July 1	$30 per share
October 1	35 per share
December 2	37 per share

As a result of the option granted to Ross, Austin should recognize additional compensation expense for 1976 on its books in what amount?

(AICPA adapted)

E–21–7 At December 31, 1975, the Hilery Company had 2,000,000 shares of common stock outstanding. On January 1, 1976, Hilery issued 1,000,000 shares of convertible preferred stock, which were considered common stock equivalents at the time of their issuance. During 1976 Hilery declared and paid $2,000,000 cash dividends on the common stock and $1,000,000 cash dividends on the preferred stock. Net income for the year ended December 31, 1976, was $9,000,000. If you assume an income tax rate of 50%, what should be earnings per share for the year ended December 31, 1976?

(AICPA adapted)

E–21–8 On June 30, 1973, Leaf Corporation granted compensatory stock options for 10,000 shares of its $24 par value common stock to certain of its key employees. The market price of the common stock on that date was $31 per share, and the option price was $28. The options are exercisable beginning on January 1, 1976, providing those key employees are still in the employ of the company at the time the options are exercised. The options expire on June 30, 1977.

On January 4, 1976, when the market price of the stock was $36 per share, all 10,000 options were exercised. What should be the amount of compensation expense recorded by Leaf Corporation for the calendar year 1975?

(AICPA adapted)

E–21–9 Fountain, Incorporated, has 5,000,000 shares of common stock outstanding on December 31, 1976. An additional 1,000,000 shares of common stock were issued on April 1, 1977, and 500,000 more on July 1, 1977. On October 1, 1977, Fountain issued 10,000 convertible bonds, at 7% interest and $1,000 face value. Each bond is convertible into 40 shares of common stock. The bonds were not considered common stock equivalents at the time of their issuance, and no bonds were converted into common stock in 1977. What is the number of shares to be used in computing primary earnings per share and fully diluted earnings per share, respectively?

(AICPA adapted)

E–21–10 At December 31, 1978, the Suppa Company has 500,000 shares of common stock issued and outstanding, 400,000 of which had been issued and outstanding throughout the year and 100,000 of which were issued on October 1, 1978. Net income for the year ended December 31, 1978, was $2,144,000. What should be Suppa's 1978 earnings per common share, rounded to the nearest penny?

(AICPA adapted)

E–21–11 The Madden Company had 600,000 shares of common stock issued and outstanding at December 31, 1977. During 1978 no additional common stock was issued. On January 1, 1978, Madden issued 400,000 shares of nonconvertible preferred stock. During 1978 Madden declared and paid $200,000 cash dividends on the common stock and $110,000 on the nonconvertible preferred stock. Net income for the year ended December 31, 1978, was $750,000. What should be Madden's 1978 earnings per common share, rounded to the nearest penny?

(AICPA adapted)

E–21–12 Faucet Company has 2,500,000 shares of common stock outstanding on December 31, 1977. An additional 500,000 shares of common stock were issued on April 1, 1978, and 250,000 more on July 1, 1978. On October 1, 1978, Faucet issued 5,000 convertible bonds, at 7% interest and $1,000 face value. Each bond is convertible into 40 shares of common stock. The bonds were not considered common stock equivalents at the time of their issuance, and no bonds were converted into common stock in 1978. What is the number of shares to be used in computing primary earnings per share and fully diluted earnings per share, respectively, for the year ended December 31, 1978?

(AICPA adapted)

E–21–13 During all of 1971, Pachta Corporation had outstanding 100,000 shares of common stock and 5,000 shares of noncumulative, $7 preferred stock. The preferred stock, which is a common stock equivalent, is convertible into three shares of common shares. In 1971 Pachta Corporation had $230,000 income from continuing operations, and $575,000 extraordinary losses. There were no dividends declared or paid.
Required:
Compute the primary earnings per share for income (loss) for 1971.

E–21–14 The Sledge Company's net income for 1972 was $10,000. During 1972 Sledge Company declared and paid $1,000 dividends on preferred stock and $1,750 dividends on common stock. On January 1, 1972, Sledge Company had 10,000 shares of common stock outstanding. Two thousand additional shares were issued on July 1, 1972. There were no other stock transactions during the year.
Required:
Compute the earnings per share for 1972.

E–21–15 Space Corporation had two issues of securities outstanding: common stock and a 5% convertible bond issue in the face amount of $10,000,000. Interest payment dates on the bond issue are June 30 and December 31. The conversion clause in the bond indenture entitles the bondholder to receive 40 shares of $20 par value common stock in exchange for each $1,000 bond. On June 30, 1978, the holders of $900,000 face value bonds exercised the conversion privilege. The market price of the bonds on that date was $1,100 per bond, and the market price of the common stock was $35. The total unamortized bond discount at the date of conversion was $500,000.
Required:
In applying the book value method, prepare the journal entry(ies) Space should make to reflect this conversion.

E–21–16 On April 7, 1975, the Script Corporation sold a $1,000,000, 20-year bond issue, at 8% interest, for $1,030,000. Each $1,000 bond has a detachable warrant that permits the purchase of one share of the corporation's common stock for $30. The stock has a par value of $25 per share. Immediately after the sale of the bonds, the corporation's securities had the following market values:

8% bond without warrants	$1,020
Warrants	10
Common stock	28

Required:
Prepare the journal entry Script should make to record the sale of the bonds.

(AICPA adapted)

E–21–17 In 1976 Orlando, Inc. issued for $105 per share, 8,000 shares of $100 par value convertible preferred stock. One share of preferred stock can be converted into three shares of Orlando's $25 par value common stock at the option of the preferred shareholders. In August, 1977, all of the preferred stock were converted into common stock. The market value of the common stock at the date of the conversion was $30 per share. What entry should Orlando make as a result of this conversion?

(AICPA adapted)

Problems

P–21–1 Red, Inc. issued $1,000,000 of its 9%, 10-year convertible bonds on January 1, 1981, at 104. Each $1,000 bond may be converted into 10 shares of $100 par value common stock after December 31, 1982. Interest is payable annually at December 31.

On January 1, 1983, $500,000 of the bonds were converted. The market price of the stock on that date was $110. On July 1, 1983, when the stock was selling at $106, an additional $100,000 of the bonds were converted.

Assume that the bond premium is amortized on a straight-line basis and that accrued interest was paid in cash at the time of conversion.

Required:
Prepare journal entries for the following dates:
  a) January 1, 1981.
  b) December 31, 1982.
  c) January 1, 1983 (use the book value method and the market value method).
  d) July 1, 1983 (use the book value method and the market value method).

P–21–2 Brown Corporation issued 500, $1,000 bonds at par. In order to enhance the marketability of the bonds, two detachable warrants were issued with each bond. Each warrant entitled the holder to purchase one share of $100 par common stock for $120. Brown's investment counselor estimated that on the date of issuance the approximate value of the bonds independent of the warrants was $485,000 and the value of the warrants independent of the bonds was $42,000.

Required:
1. Prepare the entry necessary at the date of issuance of the bonds.
2. Assuming the warrants are not detachable, prepare the entry necessary at the date of issuance of the bonds.

P–21–3 On January 1, 1981, Clay Corporation granted a stock option to each of its 10 managers for 500 shares of $5 par value common stock at an option price of $6. The market price per share on January 1, 1981, was $8. The option plan is designed to supplement the managers' compensation for the next two years.

On December 31, 1981, when the market value of Clay's stock was $9.50, none of the options was exercised. On December 31, 1982, when the market value of Clay's stock was $11, all of the options were exercised.

Required:
Prepare the journal entries for the following:
  a) The date of grant.
  b) December 31, 1981.
  c) December 31, 1982.

P–21–4 Rodeo Corp's year ends on Dec. 31, 1981. At the beginning of 1981 Rodeo had 70,000 shares of common stock outstanding. On Oct. 1, 1981, Rodeo issued an additional 30,000 shares. In addition, Rodeo had 10,000 stock options outstanding, which are convertible into 10,000 common shares. The exercise price is $10 per share, and the average and ending market price for the year was $12.50 per share. Rodeo also had $100,000 of 9% convertible bonds outstanding on December 31 that were not CSE. Each bond was convertible into 100 shares of common stock. Reported net income for the year was $50,000.

Required: *PEP S = 63¢   FDEPS = 61¢*
Compute primary and fully diluted EPS. Rodeo's tax rate is 50%.

P–21–5 The Gumball Company had 20,000 shares of common stock outstanding on January 1, 1981. On March 1, 4,000 additional shares were issued, and on September 1, 6,000 shares were redeemed from the shareholder. The Gumball Company had $108,000 net income during the year and paid dividends of $18,000 during 1981.

Required:

Compute the weighted average of shares outstanding for 1974, and compute earnings per share.

P–21–6 On January 1, 1980, as an incentive to greater performance in their duties, J.J. Walker Company adopted a qualified stock option plan to grant corporate executives non-transferable stock options to 500,000 shares of its unissued, $1.00 par value common stock. The options were granted on May 1, 1980, at $25 per share, the market price on that date. All of the options were exercisable one year later and for four years thereafter providing that the executive was employed by the Company at the date of exercise.

The market price of this stock was $40 per share on May 1, 1981. All options were exercised before December 31, 1981, at times when the market price varied between $40 and $50 per share.

Required:

1. What information on this option plan should be presented in the financial statements of J.J. Walker Company at (a) December 31, 1980, and (b) December 31, 1981? Explain why this is acceptable.

2. It has been said that the exercise of such stock option would dilute the equity of existing stockholders in the corporation.

   a) Discuss how this could happen.

   b) Discuss what could prevent a dilution of existing securities from taking place in this transaction.

P–21–7 On January 1, 1980, the McKee Company issued $6,000,000 of 7% notes along with warrants to buy 400,000 shares of its $10 par value common stock at $18 per share. The notes mature over the next 10 years starting one year from the date of issuance, with annual maturities of $600,000. At the time McKee Company had 3,200,000 shares of common stock outstanding, and the market price was $23 per share. The company received $6,680,000 for the notes and the warrants. For McKee Company, 7% was a relatively low borrowing rate. If offered alone at this time, the notes would have been issued at a 20 to 24% discount.

Required:

Prepare the journal entries for the issuance of the notes and the warrants for the cash consideration received.

P–21–8 The Harris Manufacturing Company reports long-term debt and stockholders' equity balances at December 31, 1978, as follows:

Convertible 4% bonds (sold at par)	$ 500,000
Common stock, $25 par, 100,000 shares issued and outstanding	2,500,000

Additional information is determined as follows:

Conversion terms of bonds—40 shares for each $1,000 bond	
Income before extraordinary gain—1978	$80,000
Extraordinary gain (net of tax)	10,000
Net income—1978	$90,000

Required:

What are the primary earnings per share for the company for 1978 assuming that the tax rate is 40% and that the Aa bond interest rate at the date of the bonds were sold was 7–1/2%? No changes occurred during 1978 in the debt and equity balances above.

P–21–9 Throughout 1972, J. Co. had 10,000 shares of common stock outstanding. There was no potential dilution of earnings per share except as follows:

In 1971, J. Co. agreed to issue 2,000 additional shares of its stock to the former stockholders of S. Company if the acquired company's earnings for any of the five years, 1972 through 1976, exceeded $5,000.

Results of operations for 1972 were as follows:

Net income of J. Co.	$10,000
Net income of S. Co.	4,000
Consolidated net income	$14,000

Required:

Compute the primary and fully diluted earnings per share for 1972.

P EPS = 1.40   FDEPS = 1.25

P–21–10 The following schedule sets forth the short-term debt, long-term debt, and stockholders' equity of Darren Company as of December 31, 1974. The president of Darren has requested that you assist the controller in preparing figures for earnings per share computations.

Short-term debt	
Notes payable—banks	$ 4,000,000
Current portion of long-term debt	10,000,000
Total short-term debt	$ 14,000,000
Long-term debt	
4% convertible debentures due on	
April 15, 1986	$ 30,000,000
Other long-term debt less current portions	20,000,000
Total long-term debt	$ 50,000,000
Stockholders' equity	
$4.00 cumulative, convertible preferred stock; par value $20 per share; authorized 2,000,000 shares; issued and outstanding 1,200,000 shares; liquidation preference $30 per share aggregating $36,000,000	24,000,000
Common stock, par value $1 per share; authorized 20,000,000 shares; issued 7,500,000 shares, including 600,000 shares held in treasury	7,500,000
Additional paid-in capital	4,200,000
Retained earnings	76,500,000
Total	$112,200,000
Less cost of 600,000 shares of common stock held in treasury (acquired prior to 1974)	900,000

Total stockholders' equity	$111,300,000
Total long-term debt and stockholders' equity	$161,300,000

The "other long-term debt" and the related amounts within one year are amounts due on unsecured promissory notes that require payments each year to maturity. The interest rates on these borrowings range from 6% to 7%. At the time these monies were borrowed, the Aa bond interest rate was 7%.

The 4% convertible debentures were issued at their face value of $30,000,000 in 1956 when the Aa bond interest rate was 5%. The debentures are due in 1986 and until then are convertible into the common stock of Darren at the rate of 25 shares for each $1,000 debenture.

The $4.00 cumulative, convertible preferred stock was issued in 1973. The stock had a market value of $75 at the time of issuance when the Aa bond interest rate was 9%. On July 1, 1974, and on October 1, 1974, holders of the preferred stock converted 80,000 and 20,000 preferred shares, respectively, into common stock. Each share of preferred stock is convertible into 1.2 shares of common stock.

On April 1, 1974, Darren acquired the assets and business of Brett Industries by issuing 800,000 shares of Darren common stock in a transaction appropriately accounted for as a purchase. On October 1, 1973, the company granted options to its officers and selected employees to purchase 100,000 shares of Darren's common stock at a price of $33 per share. The options are not exercisable until 1976.

The average and ending market prices during 1974 of Darren common stock were as follows:

	Average Market Price	Ending Market Price
First quarter	$31	$29
Second quarter	33	32
Third quarter	35	33
Fourth quarter	37	34
Average for the year	34	—
December 31, 1974	—	34

Dividends on the preferred stock have been paid through December 31, 1974. Dividends paid on the common stock were $0.50 per share for each quarter. The net income of Darren Company for the year ended December 31, 1974, was $8,600,000. There were no extraordinary items. The provision for income taxes was computed at a rate of 48%.

Required:

1. Prepare a schedule that shows the adjusted number of shares for 1974 to compute the following:

   a) Primary earnings per share.

   b) Fully diluted earnings per share.

2. Prepare a schedule that shows the adjusted net income for 1974 to compute the following:

   a) Primary earnings per share.

   b) Fully diluted earnings per share.

Do not compute earnings per share.

(AICPA adapted)

P–21–11 On January 2, 1973, Lang Co. issued at par $10,000 of 4% bonds, convertible in total into 1,000 shares of Lang's common stock. These bonds are common stock equivalents for purposes of computing earnings per share. No bonds were converted during 1973.

Throughout 1973 Lang had 1,000 shares of common stock outstanding. Lang's 1973 net income was $1,000. Lang's income tax rate is 50%. No potentially dilutive securities other than the convertible bonds were outstanding during 1973.

Required:

Compute Lang's primary earnings per share for 1973.

(AICPA adapted)

P–21–12 The Hint Corporation granted stock options for 10,000 shares of its $20 par value common stock to certain of its key employees on January 1, 1975, when the fair market value of the common stock was $35 per share. The options, which can be exercised at $38 per share, became exercisable on January 1, 1976, and expire on December 31, 1978. Those employees receiving the options must be employed by the corporation at the time the options are exercised.

Required:

Compute the amount of additional compensation Hint should record in 1975.

(AICPA adapted)

P–21–13 The Bryant Corporation adopted a stock option plan on October 20, 1978, as follows:

a) 60,000 shares of $10 par value stock are available to grant options to corporate executive officers at a price of $14 per share.

b) The market value of the shares at October 20, 1978, was $19.

c) On February 15, 1979, options to purchase 15,000 shares were granted to the corporate president—one-half for services to be performed in 1979 and the remainder for services in 1980.

d) On March 1, 1979, options to purchase 10,000 shares were granted to the corporate financial vice-president—8,000 for services to be performed during 1979 and the remainder for services to be performed during 1980.

e) The market value of the stock on February 15, 1979, was $16 and on March 1, 1979, was $17.

f) The options are exercisable for a period of one year following the year the services were rendered.

g) During 1980 neither executive exercised any options when the options for 1979 services lapsed. The market value of the options on December 31, 1980, was $13 per share.

h) On December 15, 1981, both executives exercised their remaining options when the market price of the stock option was $16 per share.

Required:

1. Prepare all journal entries Bryant should make applicable to this plan during 1978, 1979, 1980, and 1981.

2. Assuming the options are a material financial statement component, what disclosures should Bryant make applicable to the plan in the 1978 and 1979 financial statements?

22

Accounting Changes and Correction of Errors

Accounting in the News

The Financial Accounting Standards Board strives continually to provide statement users with more informative and reliable financial statements. Frequently, accounting principles are changed to meet this objective. However, as the following article excerpt shows, these accounting changes sometimes have a detrimental effect on a company's apparent financial condition.

> The ability to raise interest rate assumptions may have allowed companies to breathe easier about their unfunded pension liabilities, but there's a new proposal in the works that should strike the fear of God in their hearts.
>
> The Financial Accounting Standards Board is thinking seriously about forcing companies to put their past service liabilities directly on the balance sheet. This isn't exactly the same as the more inclusive unfunded pension liabilities. . . .
>
> If the FASB finally passes this accounting change—and there will be a great deal of argument before that happens—all sorts of traditional ratios will be thrown awry.
>
> Take debt-to-equity, used to tell if a company has any more borrowing capacity or too much debt outstanding. Firms that include sizable chunks of past service liabilities on their balance sheets will see debt-to-equity ratio go through the ceiling, since pension liability will be treated as a form of long-term debt. Stockholders' equity won't change at all.*

This chapter presents the accounting and disclosures necessary to implement the various types of accounting changes.

*Richard Greene, "Balance Sheet Blockbuster," *Forbes*, August 2, 1982, p. 67.

Management sometimes finds it desirable or necessary to go back and make adjustments to previously reported financial statements. For example, management may discover a mistake in the initial recording of a transaction that requires correction, or may decide that the approach used in reporting a given event is not as desirable as another approach that is equally acceptable under generally accepted accounting principles.

The major theoretical problem created by such an accounting change concerns the method to be used in reporting on financial statements the effects of the change. Since it is likely that a particular change will affect financial reporting in a number of past and future periods, it is important that the effects of the change be disclosed adequately in the financial statements. In searching for a solution to this problem, the accounting profession has supported three approaches.

1. **Retroactive restatement.** This requires that financial statements previously issued be recast to reflect the impact of the change. For example, if, in Year 5 of operations, management found a recording error made in Year 1, retroactive restatement would mandate that a prior period adjustment be made to correct the previously prepared financial statements.

   The major advantage of retroactive restatement is the fact that it produces a consistent set of financial statements. Users can be sure that accounting changes improve the comparability of published financial data. On the other hand, critics of this approach argue that retroactive restatement undermines public confidence in financial statements. If financial statement users are confronted constantly with changes in prior financial reports, how can they be expected to rely upon the data contained in current statements?

2. **Cumulative restatement.** This requires that the entire effect of an accounting change be reported in the current period as a separate item of gain or loss. If, for instance, management decides in Year 5 of operations that it is desirable to use the FIFO rather than the weighted average method of inventory valuation, the cumulative effect of the change—for all prior years—would be expressed as a single line item on the Year 5 financial statements.

   The advantage of cumulative restatement is that the effect of the change is reported and explained in one place on the financial statements. Since prior years' financial statements remain unchanged, the user does not run the risk of being confused or alienated by multiple changes on prior and current statements.

   Although cumulative restatement may avoid some of the problems of retroactive restatement, it fails to maintain the degree of comparability present under the retroactive approach. Since cumulative restatement makes no adjustments to prior financial statements, a user who analyzes comparative data will be confronted with information that has been prepared on the basis of two different assumptions.

3. **Prospective restatement.** This requires that the effects of an accounting change be integrated into the current and future financial statements. For example, if management decides in Year 5 of operations that certain operating assets should have been depreciated over fifteen years rather than ten

years, prospective restatement merely requires that the remaining depreciable cost of the asset be expensed over the remaining life of the asset. Under a prospective approach, no attempt is made to report what the past effect of the change would have been; instead, the change is implemented and the effects are left to work themselves out in later periods.

The greatest advantage of prospective restatement is its simplicity. Since no "correcting entry" is required immediately, there is no need to engage in the tedious task of prior financial statement reconstruction. On the other hand, prospective restatement lacks the element of comparability attained through retroactive restatement and the degree of simplified disclosure present in cumulative restatement.

Although all of the above methods of implementing accounting changes and corrections of errors have disadvantages, many of these disadvantages are reduced through supplemental disclosures (i.e., footnotes). Whenever the face of the financial statements provides an inadequate description of a particular transaction, a footnote disclosure should be added to provide a more complete description. These footnotes will "fill the gaps" that often result from the mechanical process of financial statement preparation.

Given the unique advantages and disadvantages of each of the methods of implementing accounting changes and correcting errors, it should be obvious that each method is suited most particularly to certain types of fact situations. The remainder of this chapter explains how the retroactive, cumulative, and prospective approaches are applied to varying types of accounting changes.

APB *Opinion No. 20*, "Accounting Changes," describes three types of accounting changes: (1) change in accounting principle, (2) change in accounting estimate, and (3) change in reporting entity.[1] Also, included in *Opinion No. 20* is the proper treatment for correcting accounting errors.

Change in an Accounting Principle

A **change in an accounting principle** occurs anytime a reporting entity changes from one generally accepted accounting principle to another generally accepted accounting principle. It should be noted that a change from an *unacceptable* method of accounting to an acceptable method is considered a correction of an error and is not to be treated as a change in an accounting principle. In addition, changes in principle that are mandated by the promulgation of new financial accounting standards may be dealt with directly in the new standard itself. If so, the procedures for implementing the change that are described in the standard, and not those generally applicable to changes in accounting principles, are to be used in the preparation of subsequent financial statements.

Before a change in an accounting principle can be made, the financial reports produced through the use of the new principle must be deemed "preferable" to those produced by the old principle. In determining what is preferable, the APB noted a desire to enhance the usefulness of financial statements. More specifi-

[1] "Accounting Changes," *Opinions of the Accounting Principles Board No. 20* (New York: AICPA, 1971).

cally, the APB contended that new APB Opinions and AICPA Industry Audit Guides constitute evidence supporting the preferability of a change in an accounting principle.[2] Recently, the FASB has said that AICPA Statements of Position (SOPs) and Guides on accounting and auditing matters (Guides) present preferable principles for purposes of applying the accounting change rules of APB *Opinion No. 20*.[3]

General Rules for Accounting Principle Changes

Once it is established that a change from one generally accepted accounting principle to another generally accepted principle is preferable, the general rules dictate that the entire effect of the change be accounted for on a cumulative basis. In other words, the entire effect of the change should be shown as income (or loss) in the income statement of the period in which the new accounting principle is adopted.

The cumulative effect of the change is determined by comparing the amount in the retained earnings account at the beginning of the year to what that amount would have been if the new accounting principle had been used in all prior years. The following example will help to explain accounting on a cumulative basis in the year of the change.

On June 1, 1983, Lee Corporation decides that it is preferable to switch from the declining-balance method to the straight-line method of computing depreciation. The Lee balance sheet as of the beginning of 1983 is presented in Exhibit 22-1. If Lee had used the straight-line method of depreciation since it commenced operations, the balance sheet would appear as in Exhibit 22-2. Despite the fact that the company did not decide to make the change until June 1, the effect of the change is measured as of the beginning of the current period, January 1, 1983. Therefore, the effect of the change is that accumulated depreciation should be reduced by $6,750 to reflect the appropriate straight-line balance of $7,500, and net income should be increased by $6,750 (straight-line retained earnings of $37,500 less declining-balance retained earnings of $30,750). To reflect the change properly, Lee would make the following entry in its general journal:

June 1, 1983	Accumulated depreciation	6,750	
	Cumulative effect of change in accounting principle		6,750
	To record the cumulative effect of changing from the declining-balance method to the straight-line method of computing depreciation.		

[2] Ibid., pars. 15 and 16.

[3] "Specialized Accounting and Reporting Principles and Practices in AICPA Statements of Position and Guides on Accounting and Auditing Matters," *Statement of Financial Accounting Standards No. 32* (Stamford, Conn.: FASB, 1979).

Exhibit 22-1
LEE CORPORATION
Balance Sheet—Declining Balance Method
January 1, 1983

Cash		$10,000	Accounts payable	$15,000
Buildings	$75,000		Total liabilities	$15,000
Accumulated depreciation	(14,250)	60,750		
			Common stock ($25 par)	25,000
			Retained earnings	30,750
			Stockholders' equity	$55,750
Total assets		$70,750	Total equities	$70,750

Lee Corporation's income statement for 1983 will report both the depreciation expense computed using the straight-line method *for the entire year* and the special income item generated by the accounting change. This special income item is reported on the face of the income statement between extraordinary items and net income.

The existence of a change in an accounting principle presents three additional problems: changes in income tax, presentation of comparative financial statements, and interim financial reporting.

Changes in Income Tax. If a change in an accounting principle is implemented for financial statement purposes, but a similar change is not made for purposes of computing tax liability, a previously unaccounted for timing difference may result. The impact of this timing difference on the balance sheet must be considered in determining the cumulative effect of the change in an accounting principle. A simple modification of the previous example will demonstrate this process.

Lee Corporation, a taxpayer subject to a 40% marginal tax rate, has used and

Exhibit 22-2
LEE CORPORATION
Balance Sheet—Straight Line Method
January 1, 1983

Cash		$10,000	Accounts payable	$15,000
Buildings	$75,000		Total liabilities	$15,000
Accumulated depreciation	(7,500)	67,500		
			Common stock ($25 par)	25,000
			Retained earnings	37,500
			Stockholders' equity	$62,500
Total assets		$77,500	Total equities	$77,500

Exhibit 22-3

LEE CORPORATION
Balance Sheet
January 1, 1983

Cash		$10,000	Accounts payable	$15,000
Buildings	$75,000		Deferred taxes payable	2,700
Accumulated depreciation	(7,500)	67,500	Total liabilities	$17,700
			Common stock ($25 par)	25,000
			Retained earnings	34,800
Total assets		$77,500	Stockholders' equity	$59,800
			Total equities	$77,500

will continue to use the declining-balance method of computing depreciation for tax purposes. On June 1, 1983, Lee decides that it is preferable to switch from declining-balance to straight-line depreciation for financial statement purposes. If you assume the use of declining-balance depreciation, the January 1, 1983, balance sheet is the same as that shown in Exhibit 22-1. The balance sheet on January 1, 1983, assuming the change to straight-line depreciation (net of tax effect), would be as presented in Exhibit 22-3.

The deferred tax account that now appears on Lee Corporation's postchange balance sheet is the result of a $6,700 timing difference produced by the use of straight-line depreciation for financial statement purposes and declining-balance depreciation for tax purposes. Since Lee Corporation is subject to a 40% marginal tax rate, a $2,700 tax deferral (40% × $6,750) resulted from the accounting change.

Given the fact that accounting changes and the taxing system will interact, the accountant must be careful to identify all of the effects of a change in an accounting principle. In the case of Lee Corporation, these effects now include both a decrease in the accumulated depreciation account of $6,750 and an increase in the deferred taxes payable account of $2,700. Further, the difference in the prechange and postchange retained earnings account of $4,050 ($34,800 − $30,750) must be recognized as an addition to the income of the current period.

All of these effects can be recorded properly through the following general journal entry:

June 1, 1983	Accumulated depreciation	6,750	
	Deferred taxes payable		2,700
	Cumulative effect of change		
	in accounting principle		4,050
	To record the net cumulative		

effect of changing from the
declining-balance method
to the straight-line method of
computing depreciation.

As in the prior example, the 1983 income statement will show all computations (depreciation expense and income tax expense) as if the straight-line method had been in use for the entire year. In addition, the cumulative effect of change in accounting principle account will be reflected on the face of the 1983 income statement.

Presentation of Comparative Statements.   A second problem produced by the existence of a change in an accounting principle concerns the presentation of comparative financial statements. Since a change in an accounting principle is accounted for on a cumulative basis, prior period financial statements are not adjusted to reflect the new accounting principle. Yet, if prior period statements are issued for comparative purposes in conjunction with current statements, readers may be confused by the use of two, different accounting principles. At a minimum, the comparability of the different sets of financial statements will be severely restricted.

To overcome this problem, generally accepted accounting principles dictate that certain **pro forma** information be added to the prior period financial statements. This *pro forma* information tells readers what would have appeared on the financial statements if the new accounting principle had been in use in the prior periods. Thus, financial statement users are provided a basis upon which to build comparisons of the current and past years. GAAP specifically require that income before extraordinary items, net income, and earnings per share should be restated on such a *pro forma* basis. The following example will best explain the presentation of *pro forma* information.

At the end of 1983 Lee Corporation decides to publish comparative income statements for 1981 through 1983. Before the inclusion of any *pro forma* information, the statements would be as presented in Exhibit 22-4.

Since the 1983 income statement uses straight-line depreciation whereas the other income statements use declining-balance, Lee Corporation must add supplemental *pro forma* data to the 1981 and 1982 statements. The *pro forma* numbers must reflect the fact that if straight-line depreciation had been used in 1981 and 1982, income before extraordinary items, net income, and earnings per share would have been materially different.

The *pro forma* data required for the Lee comparative income statements would be shown at the bottom of the 1981 and 1982 statements as follows:

Pro Forma Data Based upon Assumed Application of
New Accounting Principle in Prior Years

	1/1/82–12/31/82	*1/1/81–12/31/81*
Net income before extraordinary items	$10,350.00	$7,350.00
Net income	27,450.00	7,350.00

Exhibit 22-4

LEE CORPORATION
Comparative Income Statements
For the Years

	1/1/83–12/31/83		1/1/82–12/31/82		1/1/81–12/31/81	
Sales		$ 150,000		$ 125,000		$100,000
Cost of goods sold		(125,000)		(100,000)		(80,000)
Gross margin		$ 25,000		$ 25,000		$ 20,000
Salaries expense	$6,000		$4,000		$4,000	
Depreciation expense	3,750	(9,750)	6,750	(10,750)	7,500	(11,500)
Net income before taxes		$ 15,250		$ 14,250		$ 8,500
Income tax expense (40%)		(6,100)		(5,700)		(3,400)
Income before extraordinary items		$ 9,150		$ 8,550		$ 5,100
Extraordinary gains (losses)		(1,000)		17,100		—
Cumulative effect of gain in accounting principle		4,050		—		
Net income		$ 12,200		$ 25,650		$ 5,100
Earnings per share						
Income before extraordinary items		$ 9.15		$ 8.55		$5.10
Extraordinary items				17.10		0
Cumulative effect of change		4.05		0		0
Net income		$13.20		$25.65		$5.10

Earnings per share		
before extraordinary items	10.35	7.35
Net income	27.45	7.35

The 1982 differences of $1,800 in income ($1.80 per share) can be explained by noting that if straight-line depreciation had been used in 1982, only $3,750 of depreciation expense would have been recognized. When this $3,000 reduction in depreciation expense (increase in income) is subjected to a 40% tax rate, income tax expense increases by $1,200. The net result is an $1,800 increase in income. Likewise, the $2,250 change in 1981 income ($2.25 increase per share) can be explained by the $3,750 reduction in depreciation expense ($7,500 − $3,750) and by the $1,500 increase in income tax expense ($3,750 × 40%) that would have resulted if the straight-line method had been in use. At this point it should be noted that when the *pro forma* increases and/or decreases in income are aggregated, they will equal the cumulative effect of the change that is reported on the current income statement ($1,800 + $2,250 = $4,050).

In addition to reporting the cumulative effect of the change and the required *pro forma* restatements, a company's financial statements should include a footnote that explains the justification for and effects of the accounting principle change. If for some reason either the cumulative effect of the change or the required *pro forma* data cannot be calculated, the entity should implement the change in accounting principle for the current year and should explain the reason for not reporting the required information in a footnote to the financial statements.

Below is the footnote disclosure that should be included in the 1983 Lee Corporation financial statements:

> During 1983 the management of Lee Corporation decided to change from the declining-balance method to the straight-line method of recording depreciation. It is management's belief that the straight-line method of depreciation produces a better allocation of the cost of fixed assets over the period of their usefulness.
>
> The financial information reported for 1983 reflects the adoption of the straight-line method of depreciation for the entire year. In addition, the cumulative effect of the change, measured as of January 1, 1983, is reported on the income statement as a cumulative effect of a change in accounting principle. The impact of this change on both net income and earnings per share is specified on the face of the 1983 income statement.
>
> The financial information reported for 1982 and 1981, presented for comparative purposes, has not been adjusted to reflect the change in accounting principle. Therefore, this financial information is based upon the use of the declining-balance method of depreciation, and thus, is not directly comparable. Supplemental information, included at the bottom of the 1982 and 1981 income statements, reflects the *pro forma* impact of a retroactive implementation of the change in accounting principle.

Notice that the footnote presents the reason for the change, the effect of the change on the current year, and a reference to comparability problems and the *pro forma* information.

Interim Financial Reporting.   A final problem presented by the general rules of accounting for changes in principles concerns interim financial reporting. APB *Opinion No. 28* requires a firm to prepare and disseminate quarterly financial statements.[4] However, APB *Opinion No. 20* dictates that the cumulative effect of a change in an accounting principle be measured as of the beginning of the period, regardless of the actual date on which the change was adopted. The problem created by these two opinions is demonstrated clearly by the Lee Corporation example: if a firm adopts a change in an accounting principle in the middle of an annual reporting period, in what interim period should the change be implemented *and* in what interim period should the cumulative effect of that change be reported?

In *Statement No. 3* the FASB provided a two-part answer to these questions. First, the Board mandated that the cumulative effect of an accounting principle change made in the first interim period be reported as part of the net income of that interim period.[5] Thus, in the Lee Corporation example, if the change had been implemented during the first quarter of the year, the cumulative effect of the change *and* the new accounting principle would have been reflected on the first quarter's interim financial statements.

Second, the FASB decided that when a change in an accounting principle is implemented during any interim period after the first, no cumulative effect should be recognized in the financial statements of that interim period. Instead, the interim financial statements of prior periods are to be restated to show the use of the new accounting principle; the cumulative effect of the change is to be shown in income of the first interim period. In other words, regardless of the date on which the change is implemented, a "cumulative effect" accounting change is to be treated as if it had been implemented during the first interim reporting period.[6]

With respect to the Lee Corporation accounting principle change, the June 1 decision date becomes insignificant. Even though interim financial statements for the first quarter of 1983 have been published already, upon republication at the end of the second quarter those statements will be recast to reflect the accounting principle change as if it had been introduced during the first interim period.

Exceptions to the General Rules

Although most changes in an accounting principle are dealt with on the cumulative basis described above, there are four exceptions to this general rule. They are as follows:

1. A change from the last-in-first-out (LIFO) inventory pricing method to any other generally accepted inventory pricing method.
2. A change in the method of accounting for long-term, construction-type con-

---

[4] "Interim Financial Reporting," *Opinions of the Accounting Principles Board No. 28*, (New York: AICPA, 1973).

[5] "Reporting Accounting Changes in Interim Financial Statements," *Statement of Financial Accounting Standards No. 3* (Stamford, Conn.: FASB, 1974), par. 9.

[6] Ibid., par. 10.

tracts (e.g., a change from the percentage-of-completion method of accounting for long-term construction to the completed-contract method).

3. A change to or from the "full cost" method of accounting used in the extractive industries.

4. A change in any accounting method that accompanies the first public issuance of financial statements in order to obtain additional capital, effect a business combination, or register securities.

In each of these four special circumstances, *retroactive restatement* is used to reflect the effects of the change. Under retroactive restatement, a prior period adjustment is made to account for the total effect of the change on retained earnings as of the beginning of the current period. In addition, retroactive restatement mandates that the financial statements of prior periods be recast so as to report information as it would have been reported if the new accounting principle had been in use in the prior periods. Finally, retroactive restatement requires that footnotes be used to explain the justification for any major effects of the account-principle change. The following example will demonstrate the implementation of a special accounting principle change through retroactive restatement.

On August 1, 1983, Sherman Corporation decides to change from the LIFO method of inventory valuation to the FIFO method. At the beginning of 1983 (January 1), the corporation's balance sheet revealed the information presented in Exhibit 22-5. If the FIFO method of inventory valuation had been in use previously, assume that the January 1, 1983, balance sheet would have included inventory and retained earnings that were $5,000 higher than under the LIFO method.

To implement the accounting change, Sherman must recognize a prior period adjustment equal to the difference between the beginning retained earnings balance and the balance that would have existed if the new accounting principle had been used previously. In addition, the beginning inventory account must be adjusted to reflect the proper FIFO balance. Therefore, the following entry must be recorded in the general journal:

Exhibit 22-5
SHERMAN CORPORATION
Balance Sheet
January 1, 1983

Cash	$12,000	Current liabilities	$ 9,000
Inventory (LIFO)	8,000	Total liabilities	$ 9,000
Other assets	10,000		
		Common stock ($10 par)	5,000
		Retained earnings	16,000
		Stockholders' equity	$21,000
Total assets	$30,000	Total equities	$30,000

Aug. 1, 1983	Inventory	5,000	
	Prior period adjustment		5,000
	To record a change to		
	the FIFO from the LIFO		
	method of valuing		
	inventory.		

Like a general change in an accounting principle, the net of tax effect of a special change is accounted for at the beginning of the period. The prior period adjustment account is reflected on the statement of retained earnings as an adjustment to the beginning retained earnings balance. And the 1983 financial statements are presented using the new accounting principle.

Unlike a general change in an accounting principle, a special change requires retroactive restatement of all prior period financial statements. This retroactive restatement means that all prior financial statements must be *changed* to reflect the new accounting principle. Thus, all of Sherman Corporation's prior financial statements must be recast to reflect the use of the FIFO method of valuing inventory. In addition, a footnote must be included to explain both the justification for the change and the effect of the change on income before extraordinary items, net income, and earnings per share. It should be noted that since the cumulative effect of the change, measured as of January 1, 1983, was treated as a prior period adjustment, the 1983 income statement does not reflect this amount. Instead, the cumulative effect of the change represents a direct adjustment to the January 1, 1983, retained earnings balance. The only effect of the change to be reflected in the 1983 income statement is the effect of the implementation of the accounting change in that period.

Change in an Accounting Estimate

Although published financial statements often give users the impression that they are precise measurements, those statements generally are built upon a series of estimates. The useful lives and salvage values of depreciable assets, the allowance for doubtful accounts, and the liability for future performance under product warranties are all examples of **estimates** used in the preparation of financial statements.

Since estimates must be based upon the best information available at a given time, they are subject to change as the available information changes. The occurrence of new events, the availability of additional information, and the acquisition of more experience are all bases upon which a change in an accounting estimate can be justified.

When a change in an accounting estimate is necessary, that change should be handled on a *prospective basis*. In other words, no attempt should be made to correct prior period financial statements or to reflect the cumulative effect of the estimate change in current period statements. Instead, the new accounting estimate should be integrated into the preparation of the current and all future years' financial statements.

Single-Period Estimate Changes

If an accounting estimate is one that normally is made in each period, a change in that estimate need only be implemented in preparing the financial statements of that period. Therefore, changes in the estimates of uncollectible accounts, inventory obsolescence, product warranty liability, and so forth should affect only the accounting for the current period financial statements. Neither the financial statements of future periods nor the supplemental disclosures (footnotes) accompanying the current statements should be affected by such a change. An example will demonstrate more fully the accounting to be used for a single-period estimate change.

On December 31, 1983, Jackson Corporation undertakes an aging analysis of the $600,000 of accounts receivable currently shown on the books. Even though such an analysis conducted in 1981 and 1982 revealed that 4% of the outstanding accounts were uncollectible, this year's analysis reveals that 5% are uncollectible. Since this is clearly a change in an accounting estimate, Jackson will use prospective restatement. Therefore, no attempt will be made to change the statements of 1981 and 1982 or to show any cumulative effect of the change in 1983. Instead, Jackson merely will use the new estimate of 5% in preparing the 1983 financial statements.

If it is assumed that the unadjusted balance in the allowance for doubtful accounts were $6,500, the 1983 adjusting entry would be recorded as follows:

Dec. 31, 1983	Bad debts expense	23,500	
	Allowance for doubtful accounts		23,500
	To adjust allowance for doubtful accounts to reflect the uncollectibility of 5% of accounts receivable.		

Given the fact that Jackson probably will undertake a new aging analysis in 1984, it must be assumed that the 1983 estimate is not to be viewed as affecting future years. Therefore, this change in estimate does not affect future financial statements *and* does not require any supplemental footnote disclosure.

Multi-Period Estimate Changes

If a single accounting estimate affects a number of future periods, a change in that estimate will affect both the current and the future periods. In such an instance both the current and future period financial statements must reflect the new estimate. The current period financial statements also must include a footnote that discloses the effect of the estimate change on income before extraordinary items, net income, and earnings per share. The following example will demonstrate the accounting technique to be used in implementing a multi-period estimate change.

Meade Corporation acquired depreciable assets on January 1, 1981, at a cost of $60,000. At that time Meade executives estimated that the assets would have a useful life of ten years and a salvage value of $10,000. Meade employed the straight-line method of depreciation in 1981 and 1982, which produced the following result:

$$\frac{(\$60,000 - \$10,000)}{10 \text{ years}} = \$5,000 \text{ depreciation expense per year}$$

On December 31, 1983, Meade realized that its original estimates were incorrect. At this point Meade estimated that the asset would have a useful life of 16 years and a $2,400 estimated salvage value. This change in an accounting estimate means that Meade must recompute its 1983 depreciation expense to reflect the new estimates. In addition, since it is unlikely that Meade will reevaluate annually the facts surrounding the depreciation of fixed assets, the new estimates will be used in computing depreciation expense in future years. No attempt will be made to correct the prior statements or to adjust for the cumulative effect of the inaccurate estimate used in previous years. The estimates used in those years were the best available, were based upon existent information, and thus, are not subject to change when more precise information becomes available.

To implement the new estimate, Meade will use the following formula:

$$\frac{\text{Remaining depreciable cost}}{\text{Remaining useful life}} = \begin{array}{l} \text{Per year depreciation expense to be} \\ \text{recognized in future periods} \end{array}$$

This formula reflects the fact that an accounting estimate change is implemented "on top of" all prior financial reporting. In other words, when there is a change in an estimate, the new estimate simply is applied to the already existent financial data. The application of this formula to the Meade facts yields the following results:

$$\frac{(\$60,000 - \$10,000 - \$2,400)}{(16 \text{ years} - 2 \text{ years})} = \$3,400 \text{ depreciation expense per year}$$

Notice that the numerator above calculates the remaining depreciable cost as of the beginning of the period of change. It is calculated by subtracting prior years' depreciation and the new estimate of salvage value from the original cost. In 1983, and in all future years (assuming that there are no further estimate changes) Meade will report a depreciation expense of $3,400. The following adjusting entry will be made:

Dec. 31, 1983	Depreciation expense	3,400	
	Accumulated depreciation		3,400
	To record depreciation expense for 1983.		

Since the Meade Corporation change in estimate will affect both the current and future periods, footnote disclosure of the effect on income before extraordinary items, net income, and earnings per share is required. Although it would appear that these effects would be represented simply by the $1,600 ($5,000 − $3,400) change in depreciation expense, you must remember that this change will have a tax effect. Meade must take this tax effect into account when preparing the required footnote disclosure.

The following is an example of the type of footnote disclosure Meade would have to make:

> During 1983 management obtained certain additional information regarding assumptions previously used in calculating depreciation expense. Based upon the additional information, management concluded that prior estimates concerning depreciable assets acquired in 1981 should be changed. Specifically, management decided that the remaining useful life of these assets should be increased from eight years to fourteen years, and that estimated salvage value should be decreased from $10,000 to $2,400. Similar changes in estimates were not made for purposes of federal taxation.
>
> The implementation of the new estimates resulted in a $1,600 decrease in depreciation expense in 1983. After management allowed for a 40% marginal tax rate, the changes resulted in a $960 increase in both net income and income before extraordinary items. In addition, the changes resulted in a 55¢ per share increase in earnings per share.

Combined Estimate-Principle Change

In some instances a change in an accounting principle and a change in an accounting estimate are combined in a single accounting change. When the effects of each of the underlying changes are identifiable, the accounting changes should be dealt with separately. In this case cumulative restatement will be used to recognize the effect of the change in an accounting principle, and prospective restatement will be used to record the change in an accounting estimate. The following example will demonstrate the application of this dual reporting system.

On June 1, 1983, Smith Corporation decides to switch from the declining-balance method to the straight-line method of computing depreciation on fixed assets that were acquired on January 1, 1981, for $100,000 and that have no salvage value. At the same time Smith decides to change the useful life of these assets from five to ten years.

In making this decision Smith has implemented two accounting changes. The first is a change in an accounting principle—the change from the declining-balance method to the straight-line method of depreciation. The separable effects of this accounting principle change must be reported on a cumulative basis. This cumulative effect can be isolated by determining what the January 1, 1983, retained earnings balance would have been if the new accounting principle had been in use during the prior years.

If the new accounting principle had been in use during the prior years, it would have been applied in conjunction with the old estimates. Therefore, if you assume that Smith is in a 45% tax bracket and that it does not change its method of computing its income tax liability, the cumulative effect of the accounting principle change on January 1, 1983, retained earnings can be determined to be $13,200. This figure is derived from the fact that two years of straight-line application will yield $24,000 less depreciation expense, calculated as follows:

$$\text{Double-declining-balance depreciation:}$$
$$\$100,000 \times 0.40 = \$40,000$$
$$(\$100,000 - \$40,000) \times 0.40 = \underline{24,000}$$
$$\text{Total} \qquad \$64,000$$
$$\text{Straight-line depreciation:}$$
$$\frac{\$100,000}{5 \text{ years}} = \$20,000/\text{year} \times 2 \text{ years} = 40,000$$

$$\underline{\underline{\$24,000}}$$

Income tax expense would be $10,800 (45% × $24,000) more than it would be under the declining-balance method. To record the cumulative effect of this change, Smith would make the following entry:

June 1, 1983	Accumulated depreciation	24,000	
	Cumulative effect of change in accounting principle		13,200
	Deferred taxes payable		10,800
	To record the effect of a change from the declining-balance method to the straight-line method of computing depreciation.		

As of January 1, 1983, Smith will use the straight-line method of computing depreciation, but, as of that date Smith also will recognize that there has been a change in an accounting estimate—a change in the useful life of the depreciable asset—which will be reported on a prospective basis. Hence, depreciation expense for 1983, and for all later years, will reflect the fact that the remaining straight-line depreciable cost of $60,000 ($100,000 − $40,000) must be allocated evenly over the remaining useful life of eight years (new life of ten years less two years of depreciation previously recognized). On December 31, 1983, the following adjusting entry will be needed to recognize the annual depreciation expense of $7,500 ($60,000 ÷ 8 years):

Dec. 31, 1983	Depreciation expense	7,500	
	Accumulated depreciation		7,500

To adjust for annual
depreciation expense.

Since the above accounting change was treated as two distinct changes, two distinct sets of supplemental disclosures will be required. With respect to the change in accounting principle, all of the previously described *pro forma* and footnote information must be presented. The previously described footnote disclosures also will be required for the change in accounting estimate.

The effects of a change in an accounting principle and a change in an accounting estimate sometimes are combined inextricably. In such situations the entire accounting change is treated as a change in an accounting estimate. The following example will demonstrate this system of accounting.

On June 1, 1983, McClellan Corporation decides to change its policy regarding the expensing of certain assets. In the past McClellan has capitalized the assets upon acquisition and has depreciated them over a period of five years. McClellan now believes that the assets should be expensed upon acquisition.

McClellan could argue that this is a change in an accounting principle justifying cumulative restatement—a change in a principle regarding the capitalization of assets. On the other hand, McClellan could argue that this is simply a change in the estimated useful life of the assets, which requires prospective restatement. The APB concluded that such situations are more like a change in estimate. Therefore, McClellan would expense the cost of the affected assets in the current and all future periods. No effort should be made to report the cumulative effect of this change or to recast prior financial statements.

Change in a Reporting Entity

When one entity owns a substantial equity interest in another, the two entities often report their *combined* financial position and results of operations through the use of consolidated financial statements. While the preparation of consolidated statements will be dealt with in a separate, more advanced course, the possibility of a change in the underlying consolidated reporting entity raises issues that can be dealt with best in the context of accounting changes.

A **change in a reporting entity** is effected by any one of the three following occurrences:

1. The first presentation of consolidated or combined statements in place of statements of individual companies.
2. A change in the specific subsidiaries that comprise the group for which consolidated statements are prepared.
3. A change in the group of companies included in the consolidated financial statements.

The major problem associated with a change in a reporting entity concerns comparability. If the financial statements of corporations A, B, and C are combined to produce consolidated statements, users of those statements will be unable to compare the consolidated information with that available in prior periods—periods in which the financial statements of A, B, and C were presented on an individual basis.

Retroactive restatement will eliminate this problem of comparability. The financial statements of the individual members of the consolidated group are not in need of adjustment. Each individual set of financial statements accurately reflects the financial position and results of operations of a particular firm. Therefore, a unique form of retroactive restatement must be used to reflect the effects of the change on the group, without affecting the separate financial statements of individual members.

This unique form of retroactive restatement requires no formal journal entries. Instead, a change in a reporting entity is reflected retroactively by reconstructing the consolidated financial statements (not adjusting individual statements) for each prior period that is reported currently. In other words, if the members of the new reporting entity decide to present financial statement users with three years of prior comparative data, those data are consolidated to show the results of operations and the financial position that would have existed if the new reporting entity had existed in those prior periods. Thus, all of the consolidated data given to financial statement users are prepared as if the new entity had always existed. As a result, the desired degree of comparability is achieved.

In addition to the retroactive restatement described above, certain supplemental footnote disclosures are necessitated by a change in a reporting entity. First, the nature of the change and the reasons for it must be explained in a footnote to the current financial statements. Second, the effect of the change on income before extraordinary items, net income, and earnings per share must be disclosed in a footnote to the statements of all presented fiscal periods. These supplemental disclosures, when combined with the required retroactive restatement, help to assure that financial statement users will not be confused by changes in reporting entities.

Correcting Accounting Errors

An accounting error results from an incorrect implementation of some stage of the accounting process; it represents an inaccuracy in the financial data that must be corrected. The general rule that must be applied to all accounting errors is that once discovered, the error must be corrected and its effects removed from the financial statements.

Accounting errors may result from any aspect of the financial statement preparation process. Mathematical mistakes, mistakes in the application of accounting principles, and oversight or misuse of facts that previously existed may result in errors. Given the virtually infinite number of varied sources from which errors can be derived, it would be impossible to analyze the error correction process by discussing each of the separate sources. Instead, the correction of errors can be understood most easily if emphasis is placed upon the reporting period in which the error is discovered. Errors can be discovered in the same period in which the error was made or in subsequent periods.

Errors Made and Discovered in the Same Period

If an accounting error is made and discovered in the same reporting period, the books of the company will not have been closed. Therefore, the income effect of the error still will be isolated in the revenue and expense accounts (i.e., the effect will not have been transferred to retained earnings by way of the closing process).

To correct such errors you can use a simple, three-step process. First, the journal entry that was used originally to record the erroneous information should be reversed. Second, any other journal entries that were based upon the erroneous information should be reversed also. Finally, the correct information should be recorded in the form of replacement journal entries.

For example, on January 1, 1982, Grant Corporation purchased $100,000 of machinery. The Grant bookkeeper erroneously recorded the transaction by debiting the machinery account for $90,000. Although cash was credited for $100,000, the bookkeeper decided that $10,000 paid for transportation and installation should be debited to freight expense. On December 31, 1982, the $90,000 balance in the machinery account was used to calculate straight-line depreciation over a five-year useful life.

Before closing the books on December 31, the bookkeeper discovered his mistake. Since the mistake was made and discovered in the same period, the bookkeeper can use the simple, three-step correction process. First, the initial entry should be reversed as follows:

Dec. 31, 1982	Cash	100,000	
	Freight expense		10,000
	Machinery		90,000
	To remove the effects of an error made in recording the acquisition of machinery.		

Second, any "secondary effects" of the error should be removed from the books as follows:

Dec. 31, 1982	Accumulated depreciation	18,000	
	Depreciation expense		18,000
	To remove the effects of an accounting error.		

If the error affected the computation of income tax expense, that effect also would have had to be removed from the books.

Finally, the proper entries should be recorded in the following manner:

Dec. 31, 1982	Machinery	100,000	
	Cash		100,000
	To record the acquisition of machinery for cash.		
Dec. 31, 1982	Depreciation expense	20,000	
	Accumulated depreciation		20,000
	To record annual straight-line depreciation on machinery.		

It should be noted that all of the above adjustments, including the effects of the reversal entries, could have been recorded through the following simple entry:

Dec. 31, 1982	Machinery	10,000	
	Depreciation expense	2,000	
	Freight expense		10,000
	Accumulated depreciation		2,000
	To adjust books for error made in the recording and depreciating of machinery.		

Although the simple entry would have shortened the process of journalization substantially, the underlying analysis used to determine the contents of the entry is fundamentally the same as that used to implement the three-step correction process.

Since errors made and discovered in the same period are corrected before the preparation of published financial statements, there is no need to be concerned about the comparability of previously published data. Therefore, there is no need to provide financial statement users with any form of supplemental data concerning this type of error.

Errors Made and Discovered in Different Periods

If an error is made in one reporting period but is not discovered until a later period, that error has affected one or more previously published sets of financial statements. To correct the erroneous information and to insure the comparability of the published financial statements, you must use retroactive restatement.

As with other situations in which retroactive restatement is required, a journal entry must be made to reflect the necessary **prior period adjustment.** This journal entry must correct the beginning retained earnings balance and adjust other balance sheet accounts to their proper beginning-of-the-year levels. In addition, the correction of an error through retroactive restatement requires supplemental disclosure in the form of a footnote explaining the nature of the error and the effect of its correction on income before extraordinary items, net income, and earnings per share.

Errors Requiring Balance Sheet Adjustment. In almost all cases, errors that are made and discovered in different periods will require a balance sheet adjustment to implement the necessary corrections. A brief example of the implementation of this process of balance sheet adjustment follows.

On January 1, 1981, Grant Corporation purchased machinery with a five-year useful life for $100,000 cash. As in the previous example, the bookkeeper erroneously recorded this transaction by debiting machinery for $90,000 and freight expense for $10,000 while crediting cash for $100,000. The error was not discovered until June 1, 1983. If you assume that Grant Corporation is subject to a 40% tax rate, the financial statements presented in Exhibit 22-6 would have been published in 1981 and 1982.

If the transaction had been recorded properly in 1981, the financial statements would have appeared as shown in Exhibit 22-7.

Note that the error caused the 1981 reported income statement to show $4,800 less income, determined as follows:

Overstated freight expense	$10,000
Understated depreciation ($10,000 ÷ 5 years)	2,000
Net overstated expenses	$ 8,000
Less tax savings ($8,000 × 0.4)	3,200
Understatement of income	$ 4,800

In 1982 the depreciation expense is again understated by $2,000, which overstates taxes by $800 ($2,000 × 0.4) and net income by $1,200.

In the balance sheet as of Jan. 1, 1983, the following are understated: machinery by $10,000, accumulated depreciation by $4,000, and retained earnings by $3,600 (1981 income understatement of $4,800 less the 1982 overstatement of $1,200). The tax liability is understated by $3,200 in 1981 and overstated by $800 in 1982.

The correction of Grant Corporation's multi-period error can be accomplished in four simple steps. First, a prior period adjustment must be made to correct the Grant Corporation balance sheet as of January 1, 1983. This entry would be recorded as follows:

June 1, 1983	Machinery	10,000	
	Taxes payable	800	
	Accumulated depreciation		4,000
	Liability for prior unpaid taxes		3,200
	Prior period adjustment		3,600

Exhibit 22-6
GRANT CORPORATION
Financial Statements

Income Statement	1/1/81–12/27/81	1/1/82–12/31/82
Sales	$ 65,000	$ 85,000
Cost of goods sold	(25,000)	(38,000)
Gross margin	$ 40,000	$ 47,000
Freight expense	(10,000)	0
Depreciation expense	(18,000)	(18,000)
Net income before taxes	$ 12,000	$ 29,000
Income tax expense	(4,800)	(11,600)
Net income	$ 7,200	$ 17,400

Balance Sheet	12/31/81	12/31/82
Cash	$ 10,000	$ 52,200
Machinery	90,000	90,000
Accumulated depreciation	(18,000)	(36,000)
Total assets	$ 82,000	$106,200
Current taxes payable	$ 4,800	$ 11,600
Total liabilities	$ 4,800	$ 11,600
Common stock	$ 70,000	$ 70,000
Retained earnings	$ 7,200	$ 24,600
Total stockholders' equity	$ 77,200	$ 94,600
Total equities	$ 82,000	$106,200

While the adjustments made in the machinery, accumulated depreciation, taxes payable, and prior period adjustment accounts can be understood simply by considering the direct effects of the error, the adjustment to the liability for prior unpaid taxes account may need some further explanation. In 1981 Grant Corporation reported a tax liability of $4,800. This tax liability was computed on the basis of an error made in the processing of the accounting records—an error that was not discovered until 1983. If the error had been discovered in 1981, Grant's tax liability would have been $8,000. Since the error was not discovered, Grant paid what it thought the 1981 tax liability to be. A similar series of events affected the computation of Grant's tax liability for 1982.

Exhibit 22-7
GRANT CORPORATION
Financial Statements

Income Statement	1/1/81–12/31/81	1/1/82–12/31/82
Sales	$ 65,000	$ 85,000
Cost of goods sold	(25,000)	(38,000)
Gross margin	$ 40,000	$ 47,000
Freight expense	0	0
Depreciation expense	(20,000)	(20,000)
Net income before taxes	$ 20,000	$ 27,000
Income tax expense	(8,000)	(10,800)
Net income	$ 12,000	$ 16,200

Balance Sheet	12/31/81	12/31/82
Cash	$ 10,000	$ 52,200
Machinery	100,000	100,000
Accumulated depreciation	(20,000)	(40,000)
Total assets	$ 90,000	$112,200
Current taxes payable	$ 8,000	$ 10,800
Liability for prior unpaid taxes	0	3,200
Total liabilities	$ 8,000	$ 14,000
Common stock	$ 70,000	$ 70,000
Retained earnings	12,000	28,200
Total stockholders' equity	$ 82,000	$ 98,200
Total equities	$ 90,000	$112,200

Under federal tax law, when an error is discovered, taxpayers must amend their prior returns and must pay any additional taxes due. Therefore, in the restated 1982 financial statements, Grant must report not only the actual tax liability for 1982, but also the excess of 1981 taxes actually incurred ($8,000) over those actually paid ($4,800). This amount is reported on the December 31, 1983, balance sheet as "liability for prior unpaid taxes."

As a second step in the correction process, all published prior period financial statements should be recast to reflect the correction of the error. Therefore, the data that are based upon a correct date of acquisition entry should be substituted for the incorrect data in any comparative statements or historical summaries that are published.

Third, a footnote that provides the necessary supplementary disclosure should be prepared. That footnote should explain clearly the error and the impact of its correction on Grant's current income before extraordinary items, net income, and earnings per share. The footnote required for the Grant Corporation error would read as follows:

> In 1981 Grant Corporation's bookkeeper incorrectly recorded the acquisition of machinery. The error was not discovered until the current period. The correction of the error resulted in an increase in retained earnings, through a prior period adjustment, of $3,600.

> Prior year financial statements have been recast to reflect the correction of the error. The correction in the current period has resulted in an increase of $2,000 in depreciation expense. This increased expense has resulted in a decrease in after-tax income before extraordinary items and net income of $1,200. In addition, the correction has resulted in a decrease in 1983 earnings per share of 13¢.

Finally, the corrected financial data should be used as the basis for all future computations. In computing 1983 depreciation expense and income tax expense, Grant should make sure that an asset with an historical cost of $100,000 is being depreciated over a useful life of five years.

Errors Not Requiring Balance Sheet Correction.

In some isolated instances the effects of an accounting error will "reverse out" over a number of periods. In those rare situations the entity's current balance sheet will be no different from the balance sheet that would have appeared had the error not been made. Thus, no entry will be needed to correct the current balance sheet. However, because prior financial statements will reflect the misleading impact of the error, retroactive restatement still is required when the prior years' statements are presented for comparative purposes. Retroactive restatement will be used to recast the prior financial statements. In addition, a footnote to the current financial statement will be used to explain the nature of the error and the fact that its correction had no effect upon the current statements. The following example will demonstrate the application of this form of retroactive restatement.

On December 31, 1981, Thompson Corporation conducted its periodic count of inventory, which revealed the presence of $50,000 of merchandise. On December 31, 1982, Thompson made another periodic count and found $75,000 of merchandise on hand. On June 1, 1983, Thompson discovered that $10,000 of merchandise that was properly included in the 1982 count also had been on hand in 1981 but had not been included in the 1981 count. Selective information from the published financial statements for the three years appears in Exhibit 22-8. If the error had not been made in counting the 1981 inventory, the selective data would have been as presented in Exhibit 22-9.

It should be noted that the December 31, 1983, financial information is the same, despite the 1981 error. The December 31, 1982 (January 1, 1983), balance sheets are the same also. The reason for these identical sets of data lies in the functioning of the periodic inventory system. Since the 1981 ending inventory became the 1982 beginning inventory, the effects of the counting error canceled themselves out over the course of the two-year period. Therefore, once the 1982 ending inventory was counted accurately and entered onto the balance sheet, the effects of the 1981 error had been "washed out."

Exhibit 22-8

THOMPSON CORPORATION
Financial Statements

Income Statement	1/1/81–12/31/81	1/1/82–12/31/82	1/1/83–12/31/83
Sales	$50,000	$60,000	$90,000
Beginning inventory	$10,000	$ 50,000	$ 75,000
Purchases	85,000	50,000	30,000
Cost of goods available	$95,000	$100,000	$105,000
Ending inventory	(50,000)	(75,000)	(65,000)
Cost of goods sold	(45,000)	(25,000)	(40,000)
Gross margin	$ 5,000	$35,000	$50,000
Other expenses	(1,000)	(5,000)	(10,000)
Income before taxes	$ 4,000	$30,000	$40,000
Income tax expense	(1,600)	(12,000)	(16,000)
Net income	$ 2,400	$18,000	$24,000

Balance Sheet	12/31/81	12/31/82	12/31/83
Cash	$10,000	$13,400	$ 51,400
Merchandise inventory	50,000	75,000	65,000
Total assets	$60,000	$88,400	$116,400
Taxes currently payable	$ 1,600	$12,000	$ 16,000
Total liabilities	$ 1,600	$12,000	$ 16,000
Common stock	$56,000	$56,000	$ 56,000
Retained earnings	2,400	20,400	44,400
Total stockholders' equity	$58,400	$76,400	$100,400
Total equities	$60,000	$88,400	$116,400

Page 948   West's Intermediate Accounting

Exhibit 22-9

THOMPSON CORPORATION
Financial Statements

Income Statement	1/1/81–12/31/81		1/1/82–12/31/82		1/1/83–12/31/83	
Sales		$50,000		$60,000		$90,000
Beginning inventory	$10,000		$ 60,000		$ 75,000	
Purchases	85,000		50,000		30,000	
Cost of goods available	$95,000		$110,000		$105,000	
Ending inventory	(60,000)		(75,000)		(65,000)	
Cost of goods sold		(35,000)		(35,000)		(40,000)
Gross margin		$15,000		$25,000		$50,000
Other expenses		(1,000)		(5,000)		(10,000)
Income before taxes		$14,000		$20,000		$40,000
Income tax expense		(5,600)		(8,000)		(16,000)
Net income		$ 8,400		$12,000		$24,000

Balance Sheet	12/31/81		12/31/82		12/31/83	
Cash		$10,000		$13,400		$ 51,400
Merchandise inventory		60,000		75,000		65,000
Total assets		$70,000		$85,000		$116,400
Taxes currently payable		$ 5,600		$ 8,000		$ 16,000
Liability for prior unpaid taxes		0		4,000		0
Total liabilities		$ 5,600		$12,000		$ 16,000
Common stock		$56,000		$56,000		$ 56,000
Retained earnings		8,400		20,400		44,400
Total stockholders' equity		$64,400		$76,400		$100,400
Total equities		$70,000		$88,400		$116,400

Since the January 1, 1983 (December 31, 1982), balance sheet accurately reflects Thompson Corporation's financial position, there is no need for an entry to record a prior period adjustment. However, Thompson Corporation still must implement retroactive restatement. This retroactive restatement will consist of making corrections on any published prior financial statements (1981 and 1982) and reporting the nature of the error and effects of its correction in a footnote to the 1983 financial statements.

Computational Analysis for Cumulative and Retroactive Restatement

One of the most difficult tasks associated with both cumulative and retroactive restatement is to determine the amounts and accounts that should be used in preparing the appropriate adjusting entry. The following brief example will be used to demonstrate two different systems of analysis.

On January 1, 1981, Sherman Corporation, a 40% bracket taxpayer, purchased $100,000 of machinery with a five-year useful life. On January 1, 1982, and January 1, 1981, Sherman purchased similar machines at costs of $150,000 and $200,000, respectively. In recording these acquisitions, the bookkeeper inadvertently expensed the cost of each purchase. This error was not discovered until January 1, 1984.

Journal Entry Approach

One method of determining the amounts and accounts to be used in preparing a cumulative or retroactive restatement journal entry is to compare those journal entries that actually were made in the prior years to those that should have been made. An analysis of the retroactive restatement needed by Sherman Corporation is presented in the journal entry reconstruction shown in Exhibit 22-10. Once the journal entries are reconstructed, a comparison of those entries that should have been made to those that actually were made will reveal the necessary adjustments. In the case of Sherman Corporation, such a comparative analysis can be carried out as follows:

1. Cash account

Correct entries	$450,000 credits
Actual entries	450,000 credits
Needed adjustment	$ 0

2. Machinery account

Correct entries	$450,000 debits
Actual entries	0
Needed adjustment	$450,000 debits

3. Accumulated depreciation

Correct entries	$160,000 credits
Actual entries	0
Needed adjustment	$160,000 credits

Exhibit 22-10

SHERMAN CORPORATION

Journal Entry Analysis

	Actual Entries				*Correct Entries*	
Jan. 1, 1981	Expense	100,000		Machinery	100,000	
	Cash		100,000	Cash		100,000
	To record initial acquisition expenditure.					
Dec. 31, 1981	—			Depreciation expense	20,000	
				Accumulated depreciation		20,000
	To record annual depreciation expense.					
31, 1981	Taxes payable	40,000		Taxes payable	8,000	
	Income tax expense		40,000	Income tax expense		8,000
	To record tax effect of machinery.					
Jan. 1, 1982	Expense	150,000		Machinery	150,000	
	Cash		150,000	Cash		150,000
	To record 1982 acquisition expenditure.					

Dec. 31, 1982	Depreciation expense*	50,000	
	Accumulated depreciation		50,000
	To record annual depreciation expense.		
31, 1982	Taxes payable	20,000	
	Income tax expense		20,000
	To record tax effect of machinery.		
Jan. 1, 1983	Machinery	200,000	
	Cash		200,000
	To record 1983 acquisition expenditure.		
Dec. 31, 1983	Depreciation expense*	90,000	
	Accumulated depreciation		90,000
	To record annual depreciation expense.		
31, 1983	Taxes payable	36,000	
	Income tax expense		36,000
	To record tax effect of machinery.		

*Includes depreciation on prior year's purchase(s) as well as the current year purchase.

4. Taxes Payable

Correct entries	$ 64,000 debits
Actual entries	180,000 debits
Needed adjustment	$116,000 credits

This simple analysis of balance sheet accounts will yield the following entry for the implementation of retroactive restatement as of January 1, 1984:

Jan. 1, 1984	Machinery	450,000	
	Accumulated depreciation		160,000
	Taxes payable		116,000
	Prior period adjustment		174,000
	To retroactively restate		
	financial statements for		
	errors made in the		
	recording of the		
	acquisition of machinery.		

The $174,000 prior period adjustment can be proved in any one of three ways. First, it could be said that the $174,000 credit is a "plug figure" needed to make the adjusting entry balance. Second, it could be said that since the net changes in the balance sheet accounts resulted in an increase in net assets of $174,000, that amount also must represent a needed adjustment to retained earnings. Such a needed adjustment to retained earnings is recognized through a prior period adjustment. Finally, the $174,000 can be shown to be the difference between the total expenses actually recognized on prior financial statements and the expenses that should have been recognized ($270,000 − $96,000 = $174,000). Since the prior years' expense accounts have been closed to retained earnings, the only way to recognize the needed correction is through a prior period adjustment.

Worksheet Approach

The major problem inherent in the use of the journal entry system of analysis is that entry reconstruction, especially in complex situations, is cumbersome and time-consuming. The worksheet method attempts to reduce the analysis of cumulative and retroactive changes to a single, simple worksheet. The worksheet used for this analysis should include columns for (1) a description of the desired adjustment, (2) the income effect of the adjustment for each of the prior affected years, and (3) the balance sheet affect of the adjustment. A worksheet analysis prepared for the Sherman Corporation situation is presented in Exhibit 22-11.

Once the worksheet is set up, the needed adjustments are entered into the proper columns on a piecemeal basis. The errors for Sherman Corporation would be entered into the worksheet columns as follows:

1. Adjustment for acquisition of machinery. Since the bookkeeper originally placed machinery acquisition costs in expense accounts, these costs must be transferred to an asset account. This could be done by increasing the balance

Exhibit 22-11

SHERMAN CORPORATION
Error Analysis Worksheet
January 1, 1984

	Net Income Effect			Balance Sheet Effect Account	
Needed Adjustment	*1981 DR(CR)*	*1982 DR(CR)*	*1983 DR(CR)*	*DR(CR)*	
1. Adjust for acquisition of machinery					
a) 1981	$(100,000)				
b) 1982		$(150,000)			
c) 1983			$(200,000)	$450,000	Machinery
2. Adjust for proper depreciation					
a) 1981	20,000				
b) 1982		50,000			Accumulated
c) 1983			90,000	(160,000)	depreciation
Effect on income before taxes	$ (80,000)	$(100,000)	$(110,000)	$290,000	
3. Tax effect at 40% rate					
a) 1981	32,000				
b) 1982		40,000			
c) 1983			44,000	(116,000)	Taxes payable
Effect on net income	$ (48,000)	$ (60,000)	$ (66,000)	$174,000	

sheet machinery account by $450,000 and by reducing the expenses (increasing the net income) recognized in 1981, 1982, and 1983 by $100,000, $150,000 and $200,000, respectively.

2. Adjustment for depreciation. Since there were no assets on the balance sheet, no depreciation expense had been recognized. To correct this error, Sherman must recognize accumulated depreciation of $160,000 and must increase the expenses for the three years (net income must be reduced) by $20,000, $50,000, and $90,000, respectively.

At this point the primary effects of the error have been accounted for by the adjustment process. The effect of the error on net income before taxes can be determined simply by adding the amounts in the annual net income columns. The error has secondary effects on income tax that have not been accounted for in the analysis; these effects are discussed next.

3. Adjustment for tax effect. Since the error did affect net income, it also will have affected income tax expense and taxes payable. You can determine the amount of the needed adjustment simply by applying the tax rate of 40% to the net income before tax effect of the adjustments. In other words, if the prior entries had been made, Sherman Corporation would have been liable for additional taxes of $116,000 because income tax expense for 1981, 1982, and 1983 would have been increased (net income would have been decreased) by $32,000, $40,000, and $44,000, respectively.

After completing the worksheet, you can determine the necessary adjusting entry by looking at the changes that are required on the balance sheet and at the aggregate net income effect produced by those changes. Although the balance sheet accounts can be adjusted directly, the specific income statement accounts of prior years have been closed. Therefore, the net income effect will have to be reported as a prior period adjustment. As with the journal entry analysis, the correction of Sherman Corporation's books would require the following entry:

Jan. 1, 1984	Machinery	450,000	
	Accumulated depreciation		160,000
	Taxes payable		116,000
	Prior period adjustment		174,000
	To retroactively restate financial statements for errors made in recording the acquisition of machinery.		

The journal entry and worksheet systems are equally applicable to the analysis of error corrections or to changes in accounting principles. If the analyst is confronted with a change in an accounting principle that requires cumulative restatement, the only needed adjustment to the process described above is that a cumulative effect item (an item of current income) rather than a prior period adjustment item should be recognized. Therefore, when confronted with a situation requiring cumulative or retroactive restatement, the analyst should use that system with which s/he is most comfortable.

Financial Statement Disclosures

The specifics for financial statement disclosures of accounting changes were discussed earlier in the chapter because they were so closely related to the illustrations and to the financial statement presentations. Exhibit 22-12 and 22-13 show recent actual financial statement disclosures for McCormick & Company, Inc. and Macmillan, Inc.

Exhibit 22-12
McCORMICK & COMPANY, INC.
Accounting Change Disclosure

---

13. Change in Accounting Method for Vanilla Inventory: In the fourth quarter of 1980, the Company changed from the first-in, first-out (FIFO) method to the last-in, first-out (LIFO) method of valuing vanilla inventory effective from December 1, 1979. The Company believes the LIFO method is preferable because it more closely matches the current cost of vanilla beans, which has fluctuated widely in the world market during the past two years, with current selling prices of vanilla products. The change reduced 1980 net income by $3,666,000 or $.32 per common share.

There was no cumulative effect of the change on prior years since the November 30, 1979, vanilla inventory valuation under the FIFO method is the same as the beginning inventory under LIFO.

Exhibit 22-13
MACMILLAN, INC.
Accounting Change Disclosure

2. Changes in Accounting Principles

Effective January 1, 1979, the Company adopted new accounting principles which it believes will provide a better matching of costs and revenues in these highly inflationary times. The accounting principles that were changed involve adopting accelerated depreciation for financial statement purposes, establishing an accrual for future vacation pay, expensing as incurred advertising and promotion costs and valuing substantially all inventory on the last-in, first-out (LIFO) method.

The $8.0 million ($.64 per share) cumulative effect of the change to accelerated depreciation on prior years (after reduction for deferred income taxes of $7.3 million) is a one-time charge to income for 1979. Such charge represents the excess accelerated depreciation recorded for tax return purposes in prior years over straight-line depreciation recorded for financial statement purposes on substantially all the Company's property, plant, and equipment. The effect of the depreciation change was to reduce income from continuing operations by $.8 million ($.06 per share) and to reduce net income by $8.8 million ($.70 per share).

The Financial Accounting Standards Board is currently studying the matter of requiring all companies to accrue for vacation pay. In anticipation of such a requirement, the Company has decided to change from its acceptable alternative accounting practice of recognizing such costs when paid to accruing for these costs when earned by employees. The $1.2 million ($.10 per share) cumulative effect of the change on prior years (after the related deferred income tax benefit of $1.1 million) is a one-time charge to income for 1979. This charge provides for accrued vacation pay applicable to prior years on substantially all of the Company's eligible employees. The effect of the vacation pay change was to reduce income from continuing operations by $.1 million ($.01 per share) and to reduce net income by $1.3 million ($.11 per share).

The $4.5 million ($.36 per share) cumulative effect on prior years of the change to expensing advertising and promotion costs (after reduction for deferred income taxes of $4.1 million) is a one-time charge to income. Such charge represents advertising and promotion costs previously recorded in prepaid expenses and other assets in prior years. The effect of this change was to reduce income from continuing operations by $1.2 million ($.10 per share) and to reduce net income by $5.7 million ($.46 per share).

Effective January 1, 1979, the Company adopted the last-in, first-out (LIFO) method of inventory accounting for most of its domestic subsidiaries. Prior to 1979, such inventories had been accounted for at the lower of cost (generally actual or average) or market. This change was made because management believes that the LIFO method (which charges current earnings with current costs) minimizes inflation-induced inventory profits

Exhibit 22-13 (continued)
MACMILLAN, INC.
Accounting Change Disclosure

and more appropriately reflects operating results. The change had no effect on prior periods since the December 31, 1978 inventories were the opening inventories under the LIFO method. The effect of this change was to reduce income from continuing operations and net income by $2.0 million ($.16 per share).

Pro forma earnings (loss) per share, assuming that the changes in accounting principles are applied retroactively (other than the change to LIFO which is not retroactively applied), are as follows:

	1979		*1978*	
	Actual	*Pro Forma*	*Actual*	*Pro Forma*
Earnings (loss) per common and common equivalent share:				
Continuing operations	$ 1.31	$ 1.31	$2.01	$1.88
Discontinued operations	(4.73)	(4.73)	(.30)	(.30)
Cumulative effect of accounting changes	(1.10)			
Net income (loss)	**$(4.52)**	**$(3.42)**	**$1.71**	**$1.58**
Earnings (loss) per common share, assuming full dilution:				
Continuing operations	$ 1.31	$ 1.31	$1.93	$1.81
Discontinued operations	(4.73)	(4.73)	(.28)	(.28)
Cumulative effect of accounting changes	(1.10)			
Net income (loss)	**$(4.52)**	**$(3.42)**	**$1.65**	**$1.53**

Concept Summary

ACCOUNTING CHANGES
CHANGE IN ACCOUNTING PRINCIPLE

Description	Required Entries	Statement Effect	Supplemental Disclosure
A change from one generally accepted accounting principle to another generally accepted accounting principle.			

| a. Most changes | Current cumulative restatement—total prior income effect is shown as an "effect of change in accounting principle." Balance sheet accounts are adjusted to reflect proper balance as of the beginning of the current year. Current and all future years are accounted for under new principle. | "Effect of change in accounting principle" is an income statement account reported between operating income and extraordinary items. Effects in current and future years are reflected through normal accounting procedures. | Income before extraordinary items, extraordinary items, net income, and earnings per share are disclosed *pro forma* for any prior financial statements presented. Current financial statements should include an explanation of the change and its effects. |
| b. Exceptions 1. Change from LIFO 2. Change in long-term contract accounting 3. Change from full-costing in extractive industry 4. Initial public disclosure | Retroactive restatement—total prior income effect is reported as a "prior period adjustment." Balance sheet accounts are adjusted to reflect proper balances as of the beginning of the current period. Current and all future periods are accounted for on the basis of the new principle. | Prior period adjustment is reflected on the current statement of retained earnings. Prior year(s)'s financial statements are presented with amounts restated to reflect the change. Effect in current and future years is reflected through normal accounting procedures. | Explanation of the change and a summary of its effects should be provided in notes to current financial statements. |

CHANGE IN AN ACCOUNTING ESTIMATE

Description	Required Entries	Statement Effect	Supplemental Disclosure
A change in accounting based upon the receipt of new and more accurate information concerning a particular transaction that was subject to estimation in prior years	Prospective restatement—no attempt is made to change the accounting presented in prior periods. Instead, the new information is used to develop more accurate estimates in the current and future periods.	Current and future financial statements are adjusted to reflect the use of the new estimate.	Effect of new estimate on income before extraordinary items, extraordinary items, net income, and earnings per share is disclosed in a note to the current financial statements.

CHANGE IN ACCOUNTING ENTITY

Description	Required Entries	Statement Effect	Supplemental Disclosure
The first presentation of consolidated or combined statements in place of the statements of individual companies

A change in the specific subsidiaries that comprise the group for which consolidated statements are prepared

A change in the group of companies included in the consolidated financial statements | No entries are needed to adjust the records of any of the reporting entities. | Retroactive restatement is used to show the prior period statements as if the current reporting entity had existed in all prior periods. | An explanation of the change and its effects should accompany the current statements. |

CORRECTION OF ERRORS

Description	Required Entries	Statement Effect	Supplemental Disclosure
The improper application of a generally accepted accounting principle to a particular transaction.			
a. Errors made and corrected in the same period.	Current adjustment—the original entry should be reversed and the proper entry substituted.	Financial statements are not affected.	No supplemental disclosure is required.
b. Errors made and corrected in different periods.	Retroactive restatement—total prior income effect is shown as a prior period adjustment. Balance sheet accounts are	Prior period adjustment is reflected on the current statement of retained earnings. If prior years' statements	Explanation of the error and a summary of its effect on income before extraordinary items, extraordinary items,

| adjusted to reflect the proper amount as of the beginning of the current period. Current and future years are accounted for on the basis of the corrected application of accounting principles. | are presented, those statements are corrected to reflect what would have been if the error had not been made. | net income, and earnings per share should be included in a note to the current statements. |

Questions

Q–22–1 Explain the advantages and disadvantages of each of the following methods of dealing with an accounting change:

   a) Retroactive restatement.

   b) Cumulative restatement.

   c) Prospective restatement.

Q–22–2 What is a *change in an accounting principle?*

Q–22–3 Why is a change from an unacceptable method of accounting to an acceptable method of accounting not treated as a change in an accounting principle?

Q–22–4 On what date is the cumulative effect of a change in an accounting principle measured?

Q–22–5 Where is the cumulative effect of a change in an accounting principle reported on the financial statements?

Q–22–6 What types of changes in accounting principles require the use of retroactive restatement?

Q–22–7 What type of supplemental disclosures are required with respect to a change in an accounting principle?

Q–22–8 When are *pro forma* disclosures required with respect to changes in an accounting principle?

Q–22–9 How are changes in accounting principles reported in interim financial statements?

Q–22–10 What is an *accounting estimate?*

Q–22–11 What types of supplemental disclosure are required when there is a change in an accounting estimate?

Q–22–12 How often may a firm implement changes in accounting estimates?

Q–22–13 Which financial statements are affected by changes in accounting estimates?

Q–22–14 How should an accountant treat a situation in which an accounting estimate and an accounting principle are changed at the same time?

Q–22–15 What standards must an accountant use in determining whether changes in accounting estimates and changes in accounting principles are acceptable for financial statement purposes?

Q–22–16 Why do accountants use prospective restatement when dealing with changes in accounting estimates?

Q–22–17   What is a *change in an accounting entity?*

Q–22–18   What problems do changes in entities create for the users of financial statements?

Q–22–19   What types of journal entries are needed to implement a change in an accounting entity?

Q–22–20   Why is retroactive restatement used to report the effects of a change in an accounting entity?

Q–22–21   What is an *accounting error?*

Q–22–22   Why is it important that the correction of errors be implemented through the use of retroactive restatement?

Q–22–23   What is the difference between an error in accounting for a given fact situation and a change in an accounting estimate?

Q–22–24   What type of supplemental disclosure is required with respect to errors that have affected prior period financial statements?

Q–22–25   Where is the correction of an error reported on the financial statements?

Q–22–26   Is there any disclosure needed when an accounting error affects a number of periods but has no effect on the current period financial statements?

Q–22–27   Why are cumulative restatement and retroactive restatement implemented through an analysis of only balance sheet accounts?

Discussion Questions and Cases

D–22–1   The Smith Corporation was formed in 1967 to manufacture a product invented by the founder, Mr. Smith. By the end of 1981, the company was firmly established as the leader in its industry. More important, the company, now publicly held, was earning substantial profits.

The manufacturing process used by Smith is capital intensive. Therefore, the major expenses incurred by Smith are related to the depreciation of manufacturing equipment and the cost of the materials used to produce finished goods. Since the passage of the new tax law, Smith has very little flexibility with respect to the depreciation method to be used for tax purposes. In fact, Smith's tax advisers have concluded that no additional tax savings can be achieved through "depreciation planning."

In the middle of 1981, Smith's advisers began to study the costs associated with inventory. The advisers concluded that while the first-in first-out system used by Smith was quite adequate for purposes of management decision making and third party reporting, it did not produce the most beneficial results for purposes of taxation. Therefore, the advisers concluded that Smith should give serious consideration to changing to the last-in first-out method of measuring inventory costs.

Initially, Smith rejected the idea. It was his belief that LIFO was nothing more than a gimmick. Yet, when as president he was forced to sign the checks needed to pay the 1981 income tax bill, he began to reconsider the suggestion of his advisers.

In July, 1981, the president decided that the change to LIFO should be implemented for tax purposes. His advisers then informed him that if LIFO were adopted for tax purposes, it would also have to be used for financial reporting purposes. This required change in accounting principle troubled the president. Specifically, the president is concerned about the acceptability of this change for financial accounting purposes.

Required:

Prepare a brief memo explaining the factors that would have to be considered in determining the acceptability of this change in accounting principle.

D–22–2 The Jackson Corporation was formed in 1972 to provide services to major manufacturing entities. By 1975, the company had grown substantially. In fact, the rate of corporate growth had been so great that in 1974, executives decided to form two new subsidiaries. By 1976, one of the subsidiaries had formed a subsidiary of its own.

Jackson Corporation—now a holding company with three subsidiaries on two separate tiers—is a publicly held entity. Therefore, the corporation regularly prepares financial statements for distribution to the general public. These financial statements have traditionally been prepared on a consolidated basis.

During the early part of 1982, the company again undertook a major reorganization. This reorganization was accomplished in two distinct steps:

1. One of the Jackson subsidiaries had developed a patented production process that had a substantial market value. Jackson did not desire to use the process; therefore, it sold the process to another manufacturer. The process had been developed in 1979, and to some extent had been used by Jackson in the past.

    The sale of the process was implemented by forming a new subsidiary. The new subsidiary received a contribution of capital from Jackson in the form of the patented process. The stock of the subsidiary (100%) was then sold to the purchaser of the process. The transaction was structured this way on the advice of competent tax counsel.

2. Jackson decided that administrative costs could be eliminated if two of the three existing subsidiaries were merged. Therefore, Jackson took action to liquidate one of its existing subsidiaries and transfer all of its property and activity to another existing subsidiary.

The management of Jackson Corporation has expressed concern about the proper way of reporting these transactions in the financial statements.

Required:

Prepare a brief memo addressing the question of whether either of these transactions is an accounting change within the scope of APB *Opinion No. 20*.

D–22–3 In 1953, the Meade Manufacturing Company constructed a factory in West Virginia. The factory consisted of seven buildings, numerous parking lots, and several roads. The factory operated efficiently until 1976.

In 1976, engineers discovered that the factory had been built above several abandoned coal mines. These mines had not been considered in preparing the original factory design. More important, the mines had begun to deteriorate, and as they did, the foundation of several of the factory buildings began to crack.

In late 1976, management hired a team of engineers to perform a detailed study of the problem. The engineers concluded that three of the buildings were subject to damage due to the mines. In addition, the engineers estimated that at least one of the three buildings was not safe for use.

In response to the engineer's report, Meade abandoned the unsafe factory building and implemented a major repair program for the other two buildings. The book value of the abandoned building was expensed in 1977.

Early this year, management discovered that the engineers had been negligent in the preparation of their 1976 report. Specifically, a new study discovered that none of the three affected buildings was safe for use. The new report indicated that this conclusion should have been reached after the 1976 study was performed. All of the information was available in 1976; the prior engineers had just ignored or overlooked that information in reaching their conclusion.

Upon receiving the most recent report, Meade abandoned the two buildings. Meade executives are convinced that the book value of these two buildings must be written off in the current period, but management cannot decide upon the proper method of implementing the write-off.

At least one executive has argued that the discovery of the damage to the two additional buildings should be considered a change in a prior estimate, and therefore reported in the financial statements on a prospective basis. Another executive has argued that the accounting problem is the result of an error, and therefore should be dealt with retroactively.

Required:
Prepare a brief memo describing the issues involved and making suggestions as to the proper treatment of the building write-off.

D–22–4   Since its formation in 1974, Grant Corporation has established its allowance for doubtful accounts and bad debt expense by using a fixed percentage of credit sales. As of the end of 1981, Meade financial statements show a credit balance of $6,000 in the allowance for doubtful accounts account.

During early 1982, management decided that the system used in the past was not producing useful information. Therefore, management decided to change its method of estimating bad debts expense and the allowance for doubtful accounts. Under the new system, the annual estimate will be based upon an aging of year-end accounts receivable. If this method had been in use in 1981, the ending balance in the allowance for doubtful accounts account would have been $8,000.

The company accountant has become confused as to whether this is merely a change in an accounting estimate or a change in an accounting principle. He realizes that the process of determining annual bad debts expense is nothing more than a process of estimation, but he also realizes that the change from a "credit sales" to an "accounts receivable" basis of estimation may constitute a change in an accounting principle.

Required:
Prepare a brief memo that outlines the basic arguments for each of these alternative positions and summarizes the proper approach to this issue.

D–22–5   In 1981, Pickett Corporation changed from the first-in first-out method of valuing inventory to the weighted-average method of valuing inventory. A similar change was made for purposes of taxation.

The 1981 change resulted in a decline in the book value of inventory of $35,000. For financial statement purposes, this decline was considered the result of a change in an accounting principle and was reported by way of cumulative restatement. For federal income tax purposes, the $35,000 decline in net income will not be deductible in 1981. Instead, the $35,000 will be deducted over a period of ten years, at a rate of $3,500 per year.

In preparing the entry to record the change, the Pickett bookkeeper recorded the $35,000 net of its effect on Pickett's income tax liability. The entry was recorded as follows:

7/1/81	Taxes currently payable	14,000	
	Cumulative effect of a change in an accounting principle	21,000	
	Merchandise inventory		35,000
	To record the effects of a change in an accounting principle.		

Upon examining this entry, the corporate treasurer questioned the treatment of the tax effect of the entry. It was the treasurer's belief that since the benefit of the decline in inventory value would be realized—for federal income tax purposes—over a period of ten years, the book effect of that tax benefit should also be amortized over a period of ten years.

Required:
Prepare a brief memo explaining the proper approach to this issue. If you feel that the bookkeeper's entry was incorrect, prepare the appropriate adjusting entry.

Exercises

E–22–1 Answer the following multiple choice questions.

a) On January 1, 1975, an intangible asset with a 35-year estimated useful life was acquired. On January 1, 1980, a review was made of the estimated useful life, and it was determined that the intangible asset had an estimated useful life of 45 more years. As a result of the review

 (1) The original cost at January 1, 1975, should be amortized over a 50-year life.

 (2) The original cost at January 1, 1975, should be amortized over the remaining 30-year life.

 (3) The unamortized cost at January 1, 1980, should be amortized over a 40-year life.

 (4) The unamortized cost at January 1, 1980, should be amortized over a 35-year life.

b) Pro forma effects of retroactive application usually would be reported on the face of the income statement for a change.

 (1) In the service lives of depreciable assets.

 (2) In the salvage value of a depreciable asset.

 (3) From the straight-line method of depreciation to the double-declining-balance method.

 (4) From presenting statements for individual companies to presenting consolidated statements.

c) A company changes from the double-declining-balance method of depreciation for previously recorded assets to the straight-line method. The cumulative effect of the change on the amount of retained earnings at the beginning of the period in which the change is made should be reported separately as a (an)

 (1) Extraordinary item.

 (2) Component of income after extraordinary items.

 (3) Component of income from continuing operations.

 (4) Prior period adjustment.

d) An example of a special change in accounting principle that should be reported by restating the financial statements of prior periods is the change from the

 (1) Straight-line method of depreciating plant equipment to the sum-of-the-years'-digits method.

 (2) Sum-of-the-years'-digits method of depreciating plant equipment to the straight-line method.

 (3) LIFO method of inventory pricing to the FIFO method.

 (4) FIFO method of inventory pricing to the LIFO method.

(AICPA adapted)

E–22–2 On June 1, 1981, Sheridan Corporation discovered an error that had been made in recording inventory. In 1980 merchandise had been purchased and paid for by the company, but instead of debiting the merchandise inventory account, Sheridan's bookkeeper debited the office supplies account. As a result of this error, on August 1, 1980, the merchandise inventory account was understated, and the office supplies account was overstated by $15,000. At the end of 1980 a physical count of both merchandise inventory and office supplies was taken. Although the error was not discovered at this time, a *proper* count was taken, and the adjustments indicated were made before preparing year-end financial statements.

Required:
1. Calculate the effect of this error on the 1980 Sheridan financial statements.
2. Calculate the effect of this error on the 1981 Sheridan financial statements.
3. Prepare any journal entries that would be made on June 1, 1981, to correct this error.

E-22-3 State whether each of the following transactions will result in an increase, decrease, or no change in the information shown on the face of the current income statement.

a) Lee Company changes from the FIFO to the LIFO method of computing ending inventory. Since Lee Company was formed in 1967, the company has experienced constantly rising prices with respect to materials and labor used in the manufacturing process.

b) Lee Company accountants discovered that the bookkeeper negligently had forgotten to recognize depreciation expense during the prior period. Although the current year depreciation expense computations are correct, as of the beginning of the year, accumulated depreciation was understated by the amount of the prior year's depreciation expense.

c) Lee Company accountants estimated that bad debts expense should be estimated at 2% of credit sales for the current year. In the past Lee Company used an estimate of 3% of credit sales.

E-22-4 Answer the following multiple choice questions.

a) Presenting consolidated financial statements this year when statements of individual companies were presented last year is which of the following?
    (1) A correction of an error.
    (2) An accounting change that should be reported prospectively.
    (3) An accounting change that should be reported by restating the financial statements of all prior periods presented.
    (4) Not an accounting change.

b) Accounting changes often are made, and the monetary impact is reflected in the financial statements of a company even though, in theory, this may be a violation of which accounting concept.
    (1) Materiality.
    (2) Consistency.
    (3) Conservatism.
    (4) Objectivity.

c) When a company makes a change in accounting principle, prior year financial statements generally are not restated to reflect the change. The Accounting Principles Board decided that this procedure would prevent a dilution of public confidence in financial statements but recognized that this procedure conflicts with which accounting concept?
    (1) Materiality.
    (2) Conservatism.
    (3) Objectivity.
    (4) Comparability.

d) Which of the following is (are) the proper time period(s) to record a change in accounting estimate?
    (1) Current period and prospectively.
    (2) Current period and retroactively.
    (3) Retroactively only.
    (4) Current period only.

e) Which of the following describes a change in reporting entity?
    (1) A company acquires a subsidiary that is to be accounted for as a purchase.
    (2) A manufacturing company expands its market from regional to nationwide.

(3)   A company acquires additional shares of an investee and changes from the equity method of accounting to consolidation of the subsidiary.

(4)   A business combination is made using the pooling of interests method.

(AICPA adapted)

E–22–5   Bond Company purchased a machine on January 1, 1975, for $3,000,000. At the date of acquisition the machine had an estimated useful life of six years with no salvage. The machine is being depreciated on a straight-line basis. On January 1, 1978, Bond determined, as a result of additional information, that the machine had an estimated useful life of eight years from the date of acquisition, with no salvage. An accounting change was made in 1978 to reflect this additional information.

Assume that the direct effects of this change are limited to the effect on depreciation and the related tax provision, and that the income tax rate was 50% in 1975, 1976, 1977 and 1978.

Required:

Give the journal entry to record the change and the depreciation expense for the current year.

(AICPA adapted)

E–22–6   Evergreen Company purchased a patent on January 1, 1977, for $178,500. The patent was being amortized over its remaining legal life of 15 years expiring on January 1, 1992. During 1980 Evergreen determined that the economic benefits of the patent would not last longer than 10 years from the date of acquisition.

Required:

Give the journal entry to record the amortization expense for 1980.

(AICPA adapted)

E–22–7   In 1979 and all prior years, Grant Company accountants estimated bad debts expense on the basis of an aging of receivables. The activity in the bad debts expense and the allowance for doubtful accounts accounts is summarized below:

	1976	1977	1978	1979
Bad debts expense	$27,000	$36,000	$42,000	$18,000
Allowance—Jan. 1	3,000	4,500	6,000	(1,800)
Write-offs	25,500	34,500	49,800	15,000
Allowance—Dec. 31	4,500	6,000	(1,800)	1,200

In preparing the 1980 adjusting entry, Grant Company decided to estimate the bad debts expense as a fixed percentage of gross sales. If this method had been in use in the prior years, the following would have been reported:

	1976	1977	1978	1979
Bad debts expense	$28,000	$34,000	$40,000	$26,000
Allowance—Jan. 1	3,000	5,500	5,000	(4,800)
Write-offs	25,500	34,500	49,800	15,000
Allowance—Dec. 31	5,500	5,000	(4,800)	6,200

Required:

1.   Determine the effect that this accounting change will have on the 1980 Grant Company financial statement.

2.   If comparative statements are presented, will this change affect the information reported on prior years' financial statements?

E–22–8   Sherman Corporation has used the completed-contract method of accounting for construction projects. Since the company began operations, the following information has been reported:

	1979	1980	1981
Costs incurred	$65,000	$285,000	$452,000
Profit on			
contracts completed	—	240,000	25,000
Costs associated with			
completed contracts	—	210,000	275,000

In 1981 Sherman elected to change to the percentage-of-completion method *for financial statement purposes only*. An analysis of the two contracts in-progress at the end of 1981 and the one project completed in 1981 reveals the following:

	1/1/81			12/31/81		
Contract #	1	2	3	1	2	3
Costs						
incurred	$ 0	$ 40,000	$ 0	$140,000	$235,000	$117,000
Additional costs						
to complete	300,000	235,000	250,000	160,000	0	143,000
Contract						
price	500,000	300,000	350,000	500,000	300,000	350,000

Required:
Prepare a journal entry to complete this accounting change assuming that Sherman Company is in a 40% tax bracket.

E–22–9 Determine whether each of the following accounting changes requires retroactive, prospective, or current restatement of financial statements.

a) Smith Company decides to change methods of depreciation. In the past the straight line method was used. Now, Smith Company wants to use the sum-of-the-years'-digits method.

b) In conjunction with the change in depreciation methods, Smith Company wants to reduce the life of all assets by 10%.

c) Smith Company changes from the completed-contract to the percentage-of-completion method of accounting for long-term construction contracts.

d) Smith Company accountants erroneously valued ending inventory on the basis of a first-in-first-out assumption. Smith traditionally has used the weighted average method.

e) In the middle of the year, Smith Company accountants realized that generally accepted accounting principles required that they use cost depletion. In the past they had used percentage depletion.

E–22–10 For the past 12 years Randolph Company has used the weighted average—perpetual method of recording inventory. On February 1 of the current year, Randolph decided to change to the FIFO periodic system. The following information was taken from the Randolph Company records:

	12/31/1	2/1/2
Inventory—average	$227,000	$301,000
Cost of goods sold	936,000	203,000
Inventory—FIFO	201,000	292,000

Required:
1. Assuming that Randolph is subject to taxes at a 55% rate, prepare the general journal entries that would be needed to record this accounting change.
2. What disclosures are necessary in the financial statements?

E–22–11   Using the following format, prepare a table that summarizes the effect of the following changes.

Effect on Current Income Statement		Effect on Current Balance Sheet	
Account	Amount	Account	Amount

a)   During the current year Meade Corporation changed from the straight-line to the declining-balance method of depreciating assets for tax purposes. Before this year, accumulated depreciation showed a credit balance of $29,000. If the new system had been in use, the balance would have been $47,000. So far this year, $4,000 of depreciation expense has been recognized. If the new method had been in use, depreciation expense would have been $6,000.

b)   Company accountants have decided that the allowance method (as opposed to the direct write-off method) of handling bad debts expense should be in use. If such a method had been used in the past, an allowance for doubtful accounts of $6,200 would have existed at the beginning of the year. During this period $2,100 of bad accounts have been written off. Assume that Meade accrues taxes annually at a rate of 45%.

E–22–12   In 1978 Thompson Pipe Foundry relined some of its melting pots at a cost of $2,600,000. Since relining was a process that was required regularly, Thompson elected to expense these costs immediately. In 1981 Thompson decided to change this accounting technique. Thompson now believes that the costs should have been capitalized and depreciated over a 12-year life using the sum-of-the-years-digits' method.

Required:

Assuming that Thompson is subject to a 40% tax rate and that no change will be made for tax purposes

    a)   Show the general journal entries that should have been made in years 1978 through 1981.

    b)   Show the general journal entries actually made.

    c)   Prepare an entry to implement the desired change.

E–22–13   Freeman, Inc. has used the first-in first-out periodic inventory system for the past five years. At the end of 1981 the Freeman auditors discovered that the company had failed consistently to include in ending inventory the cost of goods purchased on credit and in transit at the end of each year. In addition, no entry had been made to record the accounts payable associated with those goods. A summary of the dollar cost of inventory in transit at the end of each of the last five years follows:

1977	1978	1979	1980	1981
$4,000	$18,000	$26,000	$19,000	$21,000

Required:

1.   Determine the income effect caused in each year by the failure to include these goods in inventory.

2.   Prepare the journal entry that would be needed to correct this error

    a)   In 1981 before the books are closed.

    b)   In 1982.

E–22–14   Pickett Savings and Loan Association opened its doors to the general public in May, 1979. At the time of opening, the Association spent $45,000 on computer equipment. The bookkeeper expensed this equipment immediately, even though the computer was estimated to have a five-year life.

On June 1, 1981, management discussed this mistake while reviewing fixed asset policies. In addition, management decided that the life of computer equipment should be reduced from five to three years.

Required:
Assuming that Pickett reports to shareholders on the basis of a March 31 fiscal year, prepare the entries that will be needed in 1981. You may ignore taxes and use straight-line depreciation when required.

E–22–15 State whether each of the following is a change in accounting principle, a change in accounting estimate, or a change in accounting entity:
- **a)** A change from the FIFO to the LIFO method of valuing inventory.
- **b)** A change from the unit LIFO method to the dollar value LIFO method.
- **c)** A change in the percentage of accounts receivable charged to bad debts expense.
- **d)** The acquisition of a new subsidiary.
- **e)** A change in the method used to depreciate fixed assets.
- **f)** A change in the useful life of fixed assets.
- **g)** A change from the percentage-of-completion to the completed-contract method of accounting for construction contracts.
- **h)** The sale of an old subsidiary.

E–22–16 An analysis of accounts receivable for Sheridan Corporation revealed the following information:

	12/31/78	12/31/79	12/31/80	12/31/81
Accounts receivable	$28,000	$62,000	$102,000	$97,000
Allowance for doubtful accounts	(2,800)	(6,200)	(10,200)	(9,700)
Bad debts expense	2,800	5,600	10,300	9,200
Credit sales	146,000	251,000	306,000	301,000

Throughout this period Sheridan has recognized 10% of year-end accounts receivable as uncollectable. In 1978 the Sheridan bookkeeper was instructed to write off the $12,000 account of Richard Roe. The bookkeeper failed to do so.

Required:
1. Reconstruct the schedule above to reflect the changes that would have resulted if the Roe account had been written off properly.
2. Calculate the effect that the proper write-off in 1978 would have had on pretax net income in 1978, 1979, 1980, and 1981.
3. Prepare the general journal entry that is needed to implement the error correction assuming that the error was discovered after making the 1981 adjusting entries. You may ignore the potential tax effect of the error.

E–22–17 In 1975 Montgomery Corporation purchased a building for $285,000. The building was to be depreciated using the straight-line method over a period of 15 years. The corporation estimated the building to have a salvage value of $47,000.

Between 1975 and 1978 the bookkeeper failed to allow for salvage value in the computation of depreciation expense. At the end of 1978, this error was discovered by a new employee. The new employee decided that the best way to handle the problem was to allocate the remaining depreciable cost of the asset over its remaining useful life. This system of calculating depreciation expense was used in 1979 and 1980.

Required:
Assuming that the problem was discovered in early 1981, prepare a schedule showing the effects of the prior errors on net income for 1975, 1976, 1977, 1978, 1979, 1980, and 1981. You may assume that the declining-balance method of depreciation was used for tax purposes and that the company is subject to taxation at a marginal rate of 45%. You may assume also that the declining-balance method was applied properly.

Problems

P–22–1   On June 1, 1981, the executives of Scott Corporation decided to change from the weighted average—perpetual to the First-In First-Out—periodic method of computing merchandise inventory. In addition, the executives decided to alter the method by which their lower of cost or market assumptions were applied. In the past, the lower of cost or market method was applied by assuming that merchandise inventory on hand at the end of a period had a fair market value of 1% below cost. Management has decided that the 1% allowance is insufficient. Therefore, management has decided that a 3% allowance for decline in market value should be adopted. A summary of relevant information on merchandise inventory follows:

	12/31/79	12/31/80	6/01/81
Merchandise inventory (Weighted average—perpetual)	$ 48,000	$ 62,000	$74,000
Allowance for decline in market value	(480)	(620)	(740)
Cost of goods sold—perpetual	162,000	195,000	86,000
Loss from decline in market value	480	140	120
Merchandise inventory (FIFO—periodic)	52,000	68,000	76,000
Allowance for decline in market value—1%	(520)	(680)	(760)

Required:
Prepare the general journal entry that is needed to implement the accounting changes made by company executives. You may assume that the company is not subject to any form of taxes.

P–22–2   The cost of goods sold section of the Sherman Corporation income statement for the past five years is shown below:

	12/31/76	12/31/77	12/31/78	12/31/79	12/31/80
Beginning inventory					
Raw materials	$ 10,000	$ 12,000	$ 14,000	$ 13,000	$ 18,000
Goods in process	15,000	22,000	18,000	19,000	17,000
Finished goods	35,000	42,000	16,000	68,000	82,000
Raw materials purchased	92,000	88,000	76,000	98,000	97,000
Direct labor applied	56,000	62,000	62,000	73,000	74,000
Overhead applied	41,000	34,000	42,000	36,000	61,000
Cost of goods manufactured	$249,000	$260,000	$228,000	$307,000	$349,000

Less: ending inventory					
Raw materials	12,000	14,000	13,000	18,000	21,000
Goods in process	22,000	18,000	19,000	17,000	32,000
Finished goods	42,000	16,000	68,000	82,000	91,000
Cost of goods sold	$173,000	$212,000	$128,000	$190,000	$205,000

In June, 1981, management consultants discovered that company personnel had been using inaccurate techniques in counting ending inventory. The company personnel had failed to take into account the raw materials inventory that had been purchased by the company and was in transit to company facilities under f.o.b. shipping point contracts. In addition, company personnel had failed to consider the allocation of certain overhead items in valuing the merchandise classified as finished goods. A recalculation of the raw materials and finished goods accounts for each of the years above revealed the following information:

	12/31/76	12/31/77	12/31/78	12/31/79	12/31/80
Ending inventory					
Raw materials	$ 14,000	17,000	17,000	21,000	27,500
Finished goods	43,500	18,000	71,000	82,500	93,000

The amount not included originally in the raw materials inventory balance was properly recorded in the raw materials purchased account. The overhead not properly included in the finished goods inventory account was properly shown in the overhead applied account. The same errors were made on both the tax return and the financial statements.

Required:

1. Recast the cost of goods sold section of the Sherman Corporation income statements for the years 1976 to 1980.

2. Prepare the footnote that would be included in the 1981 financial statements explaining the inventory errors that were made in prior years and discovered in the current year.

3. Prepare the general journal entry that would be needed in 1981 to correct the Sherman Corporation books. You may assume that Sherman Corporation is subject to a 35% marginal tax rate.

P–22–3 On June 1, 1981, the management of Lee Corporation made the following decisions regarding the accounting system used by the company:

   a) The company decided that the LIFO—periodic system of recording finished goods inventory was no longer appropriate. Instead, the corporate managment felt that the FIFO—periodic system should be used. A historical summary of inventory information is shown below.

	12/31/79	12/31/80	6/1/81
LIFO inventory	$52,000	$61,000	$48,000
FIFO inventory	75,000	82,000	61,000

   b) In 1980 office supplies purchased by the company for $27,000 cash were recorded incorrectly in the miscellaneous expense account. At the end of 1980 a proper count of office supplies was made, and the following entry was recorded on the books:

Dec. 31, 1980	Office supplies expense	18,000	
	Office supplies		18,000
	To adjust office supplies account to reflect amount on hand at time of physical count.		

c) In 1979, equipment was purchased for $35,000 cash. At the time of acquisition the equipment was estimated to have a useful life of 10 years and a salvage value of $2,000. The equipment should have been depreciated on the double-declining method for both accounting and tax purposes. Unfortunately, the bookkeeper recorded the acquisition of the equipment by debiting miscellaneous expense.

d) Company management decided that it was inappropriate to account for raw materials inventory on a perpetual basis. Instead, management felt that a periodic system would best serve the needs of the corporation. A summary of information relevant to the raw materials inventory account follows:

	12/31/79	12/31/80	6/1/81
Perpetual inventory	$ 86,000	$ 92,000	$ 66,000
Cost of goods sold	127,000	165,000	122,000
Periodic inventory	86,000	92,000	92,000
Cost of goods sold	127,000	165,000	–0–

Required:
1. Prepare the general journal entries that are needed to implement the accounting changes above. You may assume that the company is subject to a 45% marginal tax rate.
2. Prepare any explanations that would be necessary for these accounting changes.

P–22–4 McClellan Corporation has engaged in many major construction projects during the last five years. The company consistently has reported earnings for both accounting and tax purposes on the completed-contract basis. In June of 1981, company management decided that the completed-contract method of accounting was still desirable for tax purposes, but that the percentage-of-completion method better reflected the true financial position of the firm for financial statement purposes. Therefore, the company decided to adopt the percentage-of-completion method as of the preparation of the December 31, 1981, financial statements. To facilitate the change, McClellan assembled the following information:

Project A: Started on June 1, 1976; completed on August 2, 1979. Total contract price, $1,500,000. Total cost incurred to complete, $1,300,000.

	12/31/76	12/31/77	12/31/78	12/31/79
Costs actually incurred	$ 50,000	$400,000	$700,000	$150,000
Estimated costs to complete	1,100,000	800,000	100,000	0
Collections from client	250,000	350,000	700,000	200,000

Project B: Started on July 1, 1978; completed on February 1, 1981. Total contract price, $3,000,000. Total cost incurred to complete, $2,500,000.

	12/31/78	12/31/79	12/31/80	12/31/81
Costs actually incurred	$ 200,000	$ 800,000	$1,000,000	$ 500,000
Estimated costs to complete	2,300,000	1,600,000	550,000	0
Collections from client	50,000	600,000	900,000	1,450,000

Project C: Started on July 1, 1980; completion expected in 1983. Total contract price, $2,500,000. Estimated total cost, $1,900,000 (as of December 31, 1981).

	12/31/80	12/31/81
Costs actually incurred	$ 450,000	$ 300,000
Estimated costs to complete	1,400,000	1,150,000
Collections from client	350,000	350,000

Required:
1. Analyze the transactions above and determine the effect of the accounting change. You may assume that McClellan Corporation is subject to taxes at a 40% rate. *Hint:* a comparative journal entry approach may be best suited to the analysis of this problem. Consult Chapter 8 Appendix to review the journal entries involved in long-term construction accounting.
2. Prepare a general journal entry to implement the accounting change decided upon by McClellan management.
3. Prepare an adjusting entry to recognize the "construction activity" of McClellan Corporation in 1981. You may assume that taxes will be dealt with in a separate adjusting entry.

P–22–5 The following information was taken from the financial statements of Kirby Corporation:

	12/31/78	12/31/79	12/31/80	12/31/81
Merchandise inventory	$ 18,000	$ 32,000	$ 47,000	$ 36,500
Cost of goods sold	175,000	186,000	192,000	155,000
Accounts receivable	16,000	28,000	42,000	38,000
Allowance for uncollect.	(1,600)	(2,800)	(4,200)	(3,800)
Bad debts expense	1,400	2,200	4,400	3,600
Equipment	82,000	82,000	168,000	143,000
Accumulated depreciation	(32,000)	(38,000)	(47,000)	(54,000)
Depreciation expense	6,000	6,000	9,000	9,000
Taxes currently payable	(4,000)	(6,000)	(8,000)	(5,000)
Deferred taxes payable	(6,000)	(12,000)	(13,000)	(15,000)
Income tax expense	5,000	12,000	9,000	7,000

On December 31, 1981, after the books had been adjusted but before closing, corporate management reached the following decisions on accounting policies:

a) An error had been made in the way in which the merchandise inventory account was valued. The error had resulted in an understatement of the 1978 and 1979 ending inventories of $10,000 and $18,000, respectively, and an overstatement of the 1980 and 1981 ending inventories of $12,000 and $22,000, respectively.

b) Uncollectible accounts that traditionally were estimated to be 10% of year-end receivables had dropped substantially. During the past four years, uncollectibles had averaged only 5% of year-end receivables. The company decided to use the new estimate for purposes of determining bad debts expense.

c) Equipment traditionally depreciated over a fixed useful life should have been depreciated by using a production method based on the number of hours that the equipment is in use. Based on the service hours method, accumulated depreciation and depreciation expense would have appeared as follows:

	12/31/78	12/31/79	12/31/80	12/31/81
Depreciation expense	$ 8,000	$12,000	$18,000	$17,000
Accumulated depreciation	(30,000)	(42,000)	(60,000)	(75,000)

Required: (Assume a 40% tax rate.)

1. Prepare a schedule that shows the effect that each of the described accounting changes would have had in each of the four years on the following accounts:

a) Merchandise inventory.
b) Cost of goods sold.
c) Accounts receivable.
d) Allowance for uncollectibles.
e) Bad debts expense.
f) Equipment.
g) Accumulated depreciation.
h) Depreciation expense.
i) Taxes currently payable.
j) Deferred taxes payable.
k) Income tax expense.

2. Explain the disclosure that would be required to implement the three accounting changes above. Note: disclosure would be required on both the face of the financial statements and the footnotes to the financial statements.

P–22–6 On June 30, 1981, the interim financial statements of Grant Corporation revealed the following information concerning the first two quarters of 1981 operations:

GRANT CORPORATION
Interim Balance Sheet

Assets	3/31/81	6/30/81	Liabilities & Stockholders' Equity	3/31/81	6/30/81
Cash	$ 10,000	$ 10,000	Short-term payables	$ 12,000	$ 14,000
Net receivables	8,000	12,000	Long-term		
Land	42,000	42,000	Liabilities	31,000	23,000
Net plant,			Capital stock—		
property, & eq.	62,000	60,000	$5 par	25,000	25,000
Intangibles	3,500	3,000	Paid in cap. in		
Total assets	$125,500	$127,000	excess of par	5,000	5,000
			Retained earnings	52,500	60,000
			Tot. Liabilities &		
			stk. eq.	$125,500	$127,000

GRANT CORPORATION
Interim Income Statement

	1/1/81—3/31/81	3/31/81—6/30/81
Net revenue from sales	$120,000	$140,000
Cost of goods sold	(84,000)	(92,000)
Gross margin	$ 36,000	$ 48,000
Operating expenses		
Salaries	12,000	12,000
Depreciation	2,000	2,000
Amortization of intangibles	500	500
Sales commissions	16,000	18,500
Operating income before taxes	$ 5,500	$ 15,000
Income tax expense (50%)	2,750	7,500
Net income	$ 2,750	$ 7,500

Before the distribution of these statements on June 30, 1981, management discovered the following information:

a) On January 1, 1981, the company paid a short-term payable of $6,000. The bookkeeper accidentally debited salaries expense instead of short-term payables.

b) On June 30, 1980, the company purchased $4,000 of equipment from a supplier. At the time of acquisition the equipment was estimated to have a 20-year useful life and a $500 salvage value. All equipment was depreciated using the straight-line method for both tax and accounting purposes. Management has now decided that this particular equipment should have been depreciated on the basis of a declining-balance method. Company management decided to make this change for purposes of financial statements only as of June 1, 1981.

Required:
1. Prepare the general journal entries that are needed to properly reflect the transactions above on the books of Grant Corporation.
2. Recast the interim financial statements to properly reflect the financial status of Grant Corporation on March 31, 1981, and June 30, 1981.

P–22–7 During the 1981 year, the executives of Davis Corporation made the following decisions regarding the company's financial accounting system:

a) On August 1, 1981, Davis discovered that merchandise purchased on January 21, 1981, for $18,000 had been improperly recorded. The merchandise had been debited to the office equipment account instead of to merchandise inventory. When half of the merchandise was sold on June 1, 1981, the bookkeeper recorded the receipt of $12,000 cash and recognized a gain on the sale of office equipment of $3,000.

b) Davis management decided that company policy with respect to the capitalization of office furniture should be changed. In the past the company expensed office furniture when acquired. The company now feels that such furniture should be capitalized and depreciated over five years without any salvage value. The company purchased $8,000 of office furniture in 1978, $12,000 in 1979, $2,000 in 1980, and $5,000 in 1981.

c) In the past, company management has estimated that 1% of accounts receivable (recorded using the gross method) existent at the end of the year will be paid off in time to take advantage of the company's 3% cash discount. In the past few years, customers have tended to take the cash discount more often than expected. Therefore, in 1981 company management has decided to increase the estimate of those who will take the discount to 2% of year-end accounts receivable. A summary of the past history of cash discounts is shown on page 976.

	1979	1980	1981
Year-end accounts receivable	$22,000	$38,000	$47,000
Estimated discounts @ 1%	220	380	470
Estimated discounts @ 2%	440	760	940
Discounts actually taken	380	700	?

The December 31, 1981, balance in the allowance for cash discounts account is zero ($0).

d) On September 1, 1981, management discovered a series of prior errors that had been made in recording office supplies. In some instances, supplies purchased and paid for were not recorded. In other instances, office supplies acquisitions were recorded improperly. A summary of the errors is shown below.

	12/31/79	12/31/80	9/1/81
Actual supplies on hand	$3,000	$8,000	$2,000
Office supplies—per books	4,500	6,200	1,300
Supplies expense—per books	6,200	8,700	0
Unrecorded payables	0	800	200

e) On December 31, 1981, company management decides that the lower of cost or market method of accounting for long-term investments would be preferrable to the cost method that is currently in use. A summary of the company's long-term investment account is shown below.

	12/31/78	12/31/79	12/31/80	12/31/81
Investments at cost	$18,000	$19,000	$17,000	$27,500
Investments at market	18,000	16,500	14,000	27,000

Required:

1. Prepare general journal entries to implement each of the accounting changes above. You may ignore the effect of income taxes on Davis Corporation.

2. Explain the types of supplemental disclosure and financial restatement that would be required to properly reflect each of the accounting changes above.

P–22–8 On December 31, 1981, members of the accounting and auditing committee of Meade Corporation reached the following decisions with regard to accounting policies:

a) The method of measuring inventory should be changed from the weighted average to the First-In First-Out method. The company will continue to use the periodic system. A summary of the inventory values used in the past showed the following information:

	1979	1980	1981
January 1, weighted average inventory	$50,000	$85,000	$32,000
January 1, FIFO inventory	45,000	72,000	38,000
December 31, weighted average inventory	85,000	32,000	61,000
December 31, FIFO inventory	72,000	38,000	56,000

b) Company buildings (previously depreciated using the straight-line method) should be depreciated using the double-declining-balance method. A summary of the buildings and accumulated depreciation—buildings accounts showed the following information:

	1979	1980	1981
January 1, buildings account	$75,000	$92,000	$ 99,000
Additions made during the year	17,000	12,000	15,000
Retirements made during the year	0	5,000	2,000
December 31, buildings account	$92,000	$99,000	$112,000
January 1, accumulated depreciation	0	4,900	9,550
December 31, accumulated depreciation	4,900	9,550	15,150

The company depreciates all buildings over a 20-year life and assumes that there will be no salvage value. Company policy always has stated that additions should be treated as if on hand during the entire year, and retirements should be treated as if on hand for no part of the year. The entire building account is treated as a single group account for depreciation purposes.

c) The company decided that equipment with an acquisition cost of between $5,000 and $10,000 should be capitalized and depreciated over a five-year life with no salvage value. In the past such equipment has been expensed at the date of acquisition. The company acquired $150,000 of such equipment in 1975 (at least 10 different items), $250,000 of such equipment in 1976 (at least 25 different items), $50,000 in 1977 and 1978 (at least 5 different items in each year), and $175,000 of such equipment in 1981 (at least 18 different items).

d) The company decided to change the method of handling long-term construction projects. In the past the company used the percentage-of-completion method of recording long-term construction projects. In the future the company has decided to use the completed-contract method. The following information relates to the two long-term construction projects in which the firm is involved:

	1978	1979	1980	1981
Project A—contract price is $560,000				
Costs expended this period	0	$ 175,000	$ 200,000	$100,000
Estimated cost to complete	$ 450,000	280,000	95,000	0
Amount actually received on contract	50,000	150,000	200,000	160,000
Project B—contract price is $2,000,000				
Costs expended this period	0	0	275,000	500,000

Estimated cost to complete	1,500,000	1,500,000	1,300,000	900,000
Amount actually received on contract	0	300,000	400,000	500,000

Required: (Assume the books have not been closed.)

1. Prepare the general journal entries that will be needed to implement each of the changes in accounting principles above. You may assume that the company is subject to a 45% tax rate and that the financial statements and tax records rely upon the same methods of accounting.

2. Prepare the financial statement footnotes that will be needed for the 1981 financial statements because of the accounting changes above. You may assume that the following information applies to the prior years of company operations:

	1975	1976	1977	1978	1979	1980	1981
Earnings per share	$3.0	$3.5	$4.2	$4.0	$5.0	$5.5	$5.7
Shares outstanding	1,000	1,500	1,250	1,750	1,750	1,900	1,900

P–22–9 The following represent the *partially adjusted* financial statements of Jackson Corporation:

JACKSON CORPORATION
Balance Sheet
December 31, 1981

Assets			*Liabilities*	
Cash	$ 5,000		Accounts payable	$ 50,000
Accounts rec.	10,000		Short-term notes	
Allowance for doubt.			payable	300,000
accts.	?		Contingent liability	
Land	100,000		for pending legal	
Buildings	75,000		action	?
Accumulated			Total liabilities	$?
depreciation	?		*Stockholders' Equity*	
Equipment	125,000		Common stock—$5 par	100,000
Accumulated			Cont. cap. in excess	
depreciation	?		of par	50,000
Mineral deposits	350,000		Retained earnings	?
Allowance for			Total stockholders'	
depletion	?		equity	?
Total assets	$?		Total liabilities and equity	?

JACKSON CORPORATION
Income Statement
January 1, 1981—December 31, 1981

Sales revenue	$1,350,000
Sales returns	(200,000)
Net sales	$1,150,000

Operating expenses		
Employee salaries		150,000
Depreciation—buildings		?
Depreciation—equipment		?
Depletion		?
Bad debt expense		?
Operating income before taxes	$	?
Income tax expense		?
Net income from operations	$	?
Loss due to pending legal action—net of taxes		?
Net income	$	?

After preparing these statements, the accountants found that the following information was relevant to the remaining adjusting entries:

a) Bad debts expense (with a current balance of $0) has not been adjusted since December 31 of the prior year. At present the allowance for doubtful accounts shows a balance of $500 (Dr.). In the past the company has estimated that 2% of year-end accounts receivable will be uncollectable. Based on past experience, the company has decided to change its estimate. Starting with the current year, the company feels that it will be necessary to recognize 8% of year-end accounts receivable as uncollectable.

b) Accumulated depreciation—buildings (with a current balance of $15,000) has not been adjusted since December 31 of the prior year. In the past, depreciation on the buildings has been calculated by using the double-declining-balance method and a life of 10 years. The company now feels that this original estimate was incorrect and that the property should originally have been estimated to have a 20-year useful life.

c) Accumulated depreciation—equipment (with a current balance of $40,000) has not been adjusted since December 31 of the prior year. In the past, depreciation on the equipment has been calculated by using the sum-of-the-years'-digits method, a five-year useful life, and a $5,000 salvage value. The company now believes that the sal-vage value estimate was incorrect and that the equipment will be worth $35,000 at the end of its useful life.

d) Allowance for depletion (with a current balance of $100,000) has not been ad-justed since December 31 of the prior year. The mineral deposits were acquired two years ago. At that time, engineers estimated that 180,000 tons of minerals would be extracted from the property and that once all minerals were removed, the property would be worth $50,000. During the first two years of operations, 60,000 tons of minerals were extracted. During the current year, 15,000 tons of minerals were ex-tracted, but at the beginning of this year a new engineering study revealed that only 45,000 tons remained. The new engineering study indicated that the original $50,000 residual value was accurate.

e) Last year a client was injured while visiting one of the company's plants. The client sued the company for $50,000, and the corporate attorneys estimated that the company would lose between $10,000 and $20,000 due to the litigation. Therefore, a contingent liability for pending legal action of $10,000 was recognized in the prior year. Attorneys have now reexamined the case and believe that the company will lose between $15,000 and $35,000.

Required:

1. Prepare the adjusting entries that remain to be made on the books of Jackson Corpora-tion. You may assume that the company is subject to a 40% tax rate and that all items are handled in the same manner for purposes of the financial statements and the tax return.

2. Complete the 1981 financial statements of Jackson Corporation.

(Continued on next page.)

3. Prepare the financial statement footnotes that would be needed to disclose the accounting estimate changes made with respect to

a) Depreciation on equipment.

b) Depletion.

c) Bad debts.

d) Contingent liabilities.

P–22–10   Before closing the books for 1981, Moore Company's accountants discovered the following information:

a) The 1981 beginning inventory was understated by $35,000. The reason for the understatement was that in counting the 1980 ending inventory, employees had failed to count merchandise on the receiving dock which had been paid for by Moore Company. The company uses the periodic method of accounting for inventory. There were no similar problems encountered in the count of the 1981 ending inventory.

b) A copying machine was purchased on January 2, 1980, for a total cost of $12,000. The machine was recorded on the books of Moore Company by debiting office expense. The machine should have been properly recorded in the office equipment account and depreciated using the straight-line method over a useful life of 10 years. At the time of acquisition, company management thought that the machine had a $2,000 salvage value.

c) In 1979 the account of R.J. Johnson was written off as uncollectable. Although the account was uncollectable, the $14,000 amount was recorded by debiting bad debts expense and crediting accounts receivable. The following is a summary of the activity in the allowance for doubtful accounts account from 1979 to the present:

	1979	1980	1981
Beginning balance	$18,000	$21,000	$34,000
Reductions from write-offs	(6,000)	(14,000)	(21,000)
Additions from adjustments	9,000	27,000	19,000
Ending balance	$21,000	$34,000	$32,000

During the three-year period, the company consistently estimated bad debts expense as a fixed percentage of the end of the period accounts receivable.

e) On February 1, 1981, $18,000 was paid to part-time laborers. The payment was debited accidentally to executive compensation expense instead of to wages.

f) Since 1978 the company bookkeeper has been placing all expenditures made on research and development in an asset account called research & development. In addition, the bookkeeper has been expensing 10% of the ending balance in research & development each year. The table below summarizes the actual expenditures made on research and development and the approach taken by the bookkeeper:

Year	Actual Expenditure	Amount Added to "Research & Development"	Amount Expensed
1978	$15,000	$15,000	$1,500
1979	22,000	22,000	3,550
1980	8,050	8,050	4,000
1981	42,000	42,000	7,800

Required:

1. Prepare a worksheet (as illustrated in the chapter) to determine the effect that the correction of each of these errors will have on the restated 1978, 1979, 1980, and 1981 income statements and on the 1981 balance sheet. You may assume that Moore Company is subject to taxes levied at a 40% rate.

2. Prepare the general journal entries that would be needed to correct the Moore Company financial statements.

P–22–11 You have been engaged to examine the financial statements of Zurich Corporation for the year ended December 31, 1976. In the course of your examination you have ascertained the following information:

a) A check for $1,500 representing the repayment of an employee advance was received on December 29, 1976, but was not recorded until January 2, 1977.

b) Zurich uses the allowance method of accounting for uncollectible trade accounts receivable. The allowance is based upon 3% of past due accounts (over 120 days) and 1% of current accounts as of the close of each month. Due to a changing economic climate, the amount of past due accounts has increased significantly, and management has decided to increase the percentage based on past due accounts to 5%. The following balances are available:

	As of Nov. 30, 1976 Dr. (Cr.)	As of Dec. 31, 1976 Dr. (Cr.)
Accounts receivable	$390,000	$430,000
Past due accounts (included in accounts receivable)	12,000	300,000
Allowance for uncollectible accounts	(28,000)	9,000

c) The merchandise inventory on December 31, 1975, did not include merchandise having a cost of $7,000, which was stored in a public warehouse. Merchandise having a cost of $3,000 was erroneously counted twice and included twice in the merchandise inventory on December 31, 1976. Zurich uses a periodic inventory system.

d) On January 2, 1976, Zurich had a new machine delivered and installed in its main factory. The cost of this machine was $97,000, and the machine is being depreciated on the straight-line method over an estimated useful life of 10 years. When the new machine was installed, Zurich paid for the following items, which were not included in the cost of the machine but were charged to **repairs and maintenance:**

Delivery expense	$ 2,500
Installation costs	8,000
Rearrangement of related equipment	4,000
	$14,500

e) On January 1, 1975, Zurich leased a building for 10 years at a monthly rental of $12,000. On that date Zurich paid the landlord the following amounts:

Rent deposit	$ 6,000
First month's rent	12,000
Last month's rent	12,000
Installation of new walls and offices	80,000
	$110,000

The entire amount was charged to rent expense in 1975.

f) In January, 1975, Zurich issued $200,000 of 8%, 10-year bonds at 97. The discount was charged to interest expense in 1975. Interest on the bonds is payable on December 31 of each year. Zurich has recorded interest expense of $22,000 for 1975 and $16,000 for 1976.

g) On May 3, 1976, Zurich exchanged 500 shares of treasury stock (its $50 par value common stock) for a parcel of land to be used as a site for a new factory. The treasury stock had cost $70 per share when it was acquired and on May 3, 1976, it had a fair market value of $80 per share. Zurich received $2,000 when an existing building on the land was sold for scrap. The land was capitalized at $40,000, and Zurich recorded a gain of $5,000 on the sale of its treasury stock.

h) The account "advertising and promotion" included an amount of $75,000, which represented the cost of printing sales catalogues for a special promotional campaign in January, 1977.

i) Zurich adopted a pension plan on January 2, 1976, for eligible employees to be administered by a trustee. Based upon actuarial computations, the annual normal pension cost was $70,000, and the present value of past service cost on that date was $900,000. The company has decided to use the maximum provision for pension expense and to fund past service cost. On December 31, 1976, Zurich remitted $970,000 to the trustee and charged this amount to the account "pension expense."

j) Zurich was named as a defendant in a law suit by a former customer. Zurich's counsel has advised management that Zurich has a good defense and that counsel does not anticipate that there will be any impairment of Zurich's assets or that any significant liabilities will be incurred as a result of this litigation. Management, however, wishes to be conservative, and therefore has established a loss contingency of $100,000.

Required:

Prepare a schedule showing the effect of errors upon the financial statements for 1976. The items in the schedule should be presented in the same order as the facts are given, with corresponding numbers 1 through 10. Use the following columnar headings for your schedule:

No.	Explanation	*Income Statement* Dr. (Cr.)	*Balance Sheet December 31, 1976* Dr. (Cr.)	Account

(AICPA adapted)

P–22–12 The Noble Corporation is in the process of negotiating a loan for expansion purposes. The book and records have never been audited, and the bank has requested that an audit be performed. Noble has prepared the following comparative financial statements for the years ended December 31, 1977, and 1976:

Balance Sheet
As of December 31, 1977, and 1976

	1977	1976
Assets		
Current assets		
Cash	$163,000	$ 82,000
Accounts receivable	392,000	296,000
Allowance for uncollectible accounts	(37,000)	(18,000)
Marketable securities, at cost	78,000	78,000
Merchandise inventory	207,000	202,000
Total current assets	$803,000	$604,000

Fixed assets		
Property, plant, and equipment	167,000	169,500
Accumulated depreciation	(121,600)	(106,400)
Total fixed assets	45,400	63,100
Total assets	$848,400	$703,100

Liabilities and Stockholders' Equity

Liabilities		
Accounts payable	$121,400	$196,100

Stockholders' equity		
Common stock, par value $10; authorized 50,000 shares;		
issued and outstanding 20,000 shares	200,000	200,000
Paid-in capital in excess of par	60,000	60,000
Retained earnings	467,000	247,000
Total stockholders' equity	$727,000	$507,000
Total liabilities and stockholders' equity	$848,400	$703,100

Statement of Income
For the Years Ended December 31, 1977, and 1976

	1977	*1976*
Sales	$1,000,000	$900,000
Cost of sales	430,000	395,000
Gross profit	$ 570,000	$505,000
Operating expenses	210,000	205,000
Administrative expenses	140,000	105,000
	$ 350,000	$310,000
Net income	$ 220,000	$195,000

During the course of the audit, the following additional facts were determined:

a) An analysis of collections and losses on accounts receivable during the past two years indicates a drop in anticipated losses due to bad debts. After consultation with management it was agreed that the loss experience rate on sales should be reduced from the recorded 2% to 1%, beginning with the year ended December 31, 1977.

b) An analysis of marketable securities revealed that this investment portfolio consisted entirely of short-term investments in marketable equity securities that were acquired in 1976. The total market valuation for these investments as of the end of each year was as follows:

December 31, 1976	$81,000
December 31, 1977	62,000

c) The merchandise inventory at December 31, 1976, was overstated by $4,000, and the merchandise inventory at December 31, 1977, was overstated by $6,100.

d) On January 2, 1976, equipment costing $12,000 (estimated useful life of ten years and residual value of $1,000) was charged incorrectly to operating expenses. Noble records depreciation on the straight-line method. In 1977 fully depreciated equipment (with no residual value) that originally cost $17,500 was sold as scrap for $2,500. Noble credited the proceeds of $2,500 to property and equipment.

e) An analysis of 1976 operating expenses revealed that Noble charged to expense a three-year insurance premium of $2,700 on January 15, 1976.

Required:

1. Prepare the journal entries to correct the books at December 31, 1977. The books for 1977 have not been closed. Ignore income taxes.

2. Prepare a schedule showing the computation of corrected net income for the years ended December 31, 1977, and 1976, assuming that any adjustments are to be reported on comparative statements for the two years. The first items on your schedule should be the net income for each year. Ignore income taxes. (Do not prepare financial statements.)

(AICPA adapted)

23

Reporting Income and Retained Earnings

Accounting in the News

Any discussion of the financial viability of an enterprise invariably focuses on income statement components. Gains and losses applicable to continuing operations, discontinued operations, extraordinary items, and even the effects of certain accounting changes are reflected on the statement. As the following excerpts from a recent article indicate, the income statement is affected significantly when a company decides to discontinue the operations of certain business segments.

Charter Co. said earnings from continuing operations plummeted 90% in the first period and it announced an agreement in principle to sell two communications operations, including Redbook magazine, to Hearst Corp.

Charter, which also has interests in oil and insurance, said profit fell to $1.9 million on a 27% drop in revenue to $819.6 million. Earnings from continuing operations in the 1981 period was $18.5 million, or 60 cents a share, on a $1.13 billion in revenue. A loss from discontinued operations of $3.7 million in the year earlier period made net income $14.8 million, or 47 cents a share. . . .

Once a glamor stock, Charter has seen its profit eroded by weak markets for refined products, a glut of crude oil and losses in some of its communications activities. Recently the company said it would reduce its interests in communications, choosing instead to concentrate on oil refining and insurance marketing.

In the past year Charter has announced the pending sale of six of its seven radio stations, sold Sport magazine, phased out its Dayton Press operations and closed the Philadelphia Bulletin. Remaining in its communications group are Ladies Home Journal magazine, Discount Merchandiser magazine, a mail-order business and one radio station that the company says it plans to sell. . . .*

*"Charter has 90% Drop In Earnings, Plans Sale Of Redbook to Hearst," *Wall Street Journal,* May 3, 1982, p. 7. Reprinted by permission of The Wall Street Journal, © Dow Jones & Company, Inc. 1982. All Rights Reserved.

> There continues to be a primary focus on earnings numbers in financial statement analysis. The many rules associated with income statement preparation make preparing the statement as difficult as understanding the results.

A general objective of financial accounting and financial statements is to provide reliable financial information about the economic resources and obligations of a business enterprise. Financial activities are reported as two basic types of information:

1. Financial position, which relates to a point in time.
2. Changes in financial position, which relate to a period of time.

The following statements are required to be presented with each annual report and are regarded as minimum disclosures:

1. Balance sheet (discussed in Chapter 24).
2. Statement of changes in financial position (discussed in Chapter 25).
3. Income statement.

The **balance sheet** presents the assets, liabilities, and owners' equity of an enterprise at a particular point in time. The **statement of changes in financial position** presents the changes in financial position in terms of sources (inflows) and uses (outflows) of funds during the period. The **income statement** presents the revenues, expenses, gains (losses), and net income (net loss) recognized, and thus, the results of operations of an enterprise during the period. The information presented in an income statement usually is considered very important because a significant number of decisions made in the business community involve predicting, comparing, and evaluating earnings. The best single basis for predicting future earnings are the current and past earnings of a firm. The income statement measures the firm's current earnings. The **statement of retained earnings** presents the accumulated earnings of a firm. It generally is included in the financial statements to provide the statement reader with additional information about both current and past earnings.

Concept of Income

There are four basic elements of the income statement of an enterprise: (1) revenues, (2) expenses, (3) gains (losses), and (4) net income (net loss). **Revenue** is a gross concept; in the case of ordinary sales, revenue generally is stated after deducting returns, allowances, and other similar items. Revenue from the ordinary course of business is sometimes described as **operating revenue.** APB *Statement No. 4* has defined revenue as the following:

> . . . gross increases in assets or gross decreases in liabilities recognized and measured in conformity with generally accepted accounting principles that result from those types of profit-directed activities of an enterprise that can change owners' equity.[1]
>
> Revenue under present generally accepted accounting principles is derived from three general activities: (a) selling products; (b) rendering services and permitting others to use enterprise resources, which result in interest, rent, royalties, fees and the like; and (c) disposing of resources other than products—for example, plant and equipment or investments in other entities. Revenue does not include receipt of assets purchased, proceeds of borrowing, investments by owners, or adjustments of revenue of prior periods.[2]

As discussed in Chapter 3, revenue generally is realized when both of the following conditions are met:

1. The earnings process is virtually complete.
2. An exchange has taken place.

The realization principle requires that revenue be earned before it can be recorded. Revenue recognized under the realization principle is recorded at the amount received or expected to be received.

The APB's definition of **expenses** is as follows:

> . . . gross decreases in assets or gross increases in liabilities recognized and measured in conformity with generally accepted accounting principles that result from those types of profit-directed activities of an entrprise that can change owners' equity.[3]
>
> Important classes of expenses are (1) costs of assets used to produce revenues (for example, cost of goods sold, selling and administrative expenses, and interest expense; (2) expenses from nonreciprocal transfers and casualties (for example, taxes, fires, and theft); (3) costs of assets other than products (for example, plant and equipment or investments in other companies) disposed of; (4) costs incurred in unsuccessful efforts; and (5) declines in market prices of inventories held for sale. Expenses do not include repayments of borrowing, expenditures to acquire assets, distributions to owners (including acquisition of treasury stock), or adjustments of expenses of prior periods.[4]

---

[1] "Basic Concepts and Accounting Principles Underlying Financial Statements of Business Enterprises," *Accounting Principles Board Statement No. 4* (New York: AICPA, 1970), par. 134.

[2] Ibid., par. 148.

[3] Ibid., par. 134.

[4] Ibid., par. 154.

Expenses of a period are listed below:

1. Costs directly associated with the revenues of the period.
2. Costs associated with the period on some basis other than a direct relationship with revenue.
3. Costs that cannot, as a practical matter, be associated with any other period.[5]

Costs directly associated with the revenues of the period include sales commissions and costs of products sold or services provided, when a direct association with revenues can be drawn. Costs associated with the revenues of a period on some basis other than a direct relationship include those cost associated with a period based on a systematic and rational basis of allocation. These costs benefit more than the period in which the cost was incurred and should be allocated to all periods benefited. An example of such a cost would be depreciation of a fixed asset. Costs that cannot be associated with the current period or future periods based on a direct relationship or a systematic and rational allocation should be charged to income in the current period. Examples of such expenses include officers' salaries, administrative expenses, amounts paid to settle lawsuits, and the costs of resources used in unsuccessful efforts.

Gains (losses) are another component of the income statement and can be differentiated from revenue and expense in two ways:

1. They do not occur in the ordinary course of business.
2. They are a result of a netting transaction.

A "netting" transaction simply means that the carrying value of the item is netted against the related sales price to arrive at a gain or loss. Only the resulting gain or loss will be shown in the income statement, not both the sales price and related carrying value of the item. For example, if an asset with a book value of $50,000 is sold for $75,000, the gain realized would be $25,000. As a matter of practice, gains are not differentiated from revenues in the income statement in many cases. Similarly, losses sometimes are reported "net" and are reflected as expenses in the income statement.

Income is the difference between revenues (including gains) and expenses (including losses). The terms "earnings" and "profits" also are used interchangeably to indicate income. *Statement No. 4* defines net income (net loss) as follows:

> The excess (deficit) of revenue over expenses for an accounting period, which is the net increase (net decrease) in owners' equity (assets minus liabilities) of an enterprise for an accounting period from profit-directed activities that is recognized and measured in conformity with generally accepted accounting principles.[6]

[5] Ibid., par. 155.
[6] Ibid., par. 134.

Income Statement Format

As mentioned previously, income is the difference between revenues and expenses. When presenting income, you can use various formats to group revenues, expenses, and other items of income. The detail of presentation varies under each of these formats, yet the final income figure always will be the same. Generally, there are two formats for presenting income: the single-step format and the multiple-step format. These in turn may be reported using single-year or comparative statements.

Single-Step Format

Many accountants prefer the **single-step format** because classification problems are minimized and presentation is simplified. This format has only two basic sections—revenues (including gains) and expenses (including losses). It is called a single-step statement because there is only one step in determining income—revenues minus expenses. Exhibit 23-1 illustrates a single-step format in which all revenues, including gain on the sale of an asset, are grouped under one classification. All expenses, including loss on the sale of an asset, also are grouped under

---

Exhibit 23-1
ARLEDGE, INC.
Income Statement
For the Year Ended December 31, 1983
Single-Step Format

Revenues		
Sales (net of returns and allowances of $125,000)		$2,850,000
Rent		67,000
Interest and dividends		95,000
Gain from sale of securities		125,000
Total revenue		$3,137,000
Expenses		
Cost of goods sold	$ (800,000)	
Administrative expenses	(145,000)	
Selling expenses	(87,000)	
Interest	(105,000)	
Income taxes (assume a 50% tax rate)	(1,000,000)	(2,137,000)
Net income		$1,000,000
Earnings per share (Assume 100,000 common shares outstanding for the entire year)		$10.00

one broad section. Gains and losses, as previously noted, are reported "net" in contrast to revenues, which are reported "gross," with the related expenses deducted separately.

Potential variations in the single-step format may include the following:

1. Reporting income taxes separately from expenses.
2. Reporting more than one caption for certain revenues and expenses (such as financial items—interest revenue and interest expenses; other revenues and expenses—dividends, gains, and losses, interest; and other credits and charges).

Multiple-Step Format

The **multiple-step format** provides greater classification detail and creates a more informative relationship between revenues and expenses. This format (as illustrated in Exhibit 23-2), has various subsections, such as net sales, cost of goods sold, gross margin on sales, operating expenses, other revenues, other expenses, income before income taxes, and net income. These sections provide the statement user with additional information. For example, the gross margin figure is used frequently to see if the enterprise is maintaining the same margin in sales from period to period. A change in this figure could have implications for future years' profits.

The multiple-step format also separates the results of regular operations from secondary or nonoperating activities. This separation is useful in helping the statement reader assess and predict the results of normal continuing operations. In addition the multiple-step format separates expenses by function. The cost of merchandise or of manufacturing goods that have been sold is included in the cost of goods sold. The selling and administration costs are shown separately as well. The functional breakdown allows quick comparisons from year to year to help determine when costs may be getting out of line.

Although the multiple-step format can be more informative to the users of the financial statement, it has been criticized as being relatively inflexible. The AICPA reported that of the 600 major companies surveyed in 1978, 62% used the single-step format, and 38% used the multiple-step format.[7] A substantial number of income statements, both single-step and multiple-step, presented income taxes and equity in earnings or losses of investees as separate captions immediately preceding net income.

Like the single-step format, the multiple-step format has many variations. For a manufacturing firm, for example, "inventory purchases" are replaced by "cost of goods manufactured," and a separate schedule of these manufacturing costs (including direct materials, direct labor, and factory overhead) usually is presented with the income statement. Frequently, one or more supplementary schedules also are presented in the footnotes to the financial statements to provide detailed information of the amounts shown on the income statement.

---

[7] *Accounting Trends and Techniques* (New York: AICPA, 1978), p. 219.

Exhibit 23-2
ARLEDGE, INC.
Income Statement
For the Year Ended December 31, 1983
Multiple-Step Format

Sales			
Sales revenue			$2,975,000
Less: Sales returns and allowances			(125,000)
Net sales			$2,850,000
Cost of Goods Sold			
Beginning inventory		$1,635,000	
Purchases	$440,000		
Less: Purchases, returns, and discounts	(2,500)		
Net purchases		437,500	
Freight in		28,350	
Goods available for sale		$2,100,850	
Less: Ending Inventory		(1,300,850)	
Cost of goods sold			800,000
Gross margin on sales			$2,050,000
Operating Expenses			
Advertising and selling expense		$ (87,000)	
General and administrative expenses		(145,000)	
Total operating expenses			(232,000)
Income from operations			$1,818,000
Other Revenues			
Rent		$ 67,000	
Interest and dividends		95,000	
Gain from sale of marketable securities		125,000	287,000
Other Expenses			
Interest			(105,000)
Income before taxes			$2,000,000
Income taxes (50% rate assumed)			1,000,000
Net income			$1,000,000
Earnings per share (Assume 100,000 common shares outstanding for entire year)			$10.00

Comparative Income Statements

Comparative statements involve the presentation of financial statements for the current and one or more prior periods; they facilitate comparisons by the statement user. The Securities Exchange Act of 1934 specified that annual reports furnished to stockholders in connection with the stockholders' annual meeting include "certified" comparative financial statements of two or more periods. *Accounting Research Bulletin (ARB) No. 43* discusses the benefits of comparative financial statements as follows:

> The presentation of comparative financial statements in annual and other reports enhances the usefulness of such reports and brings out more clearly the nature and trends of current changes affecting the enterprise. Such presentation emphasizes the fact that statements for a series of periods are far more significant than those for a single period and that the accounts for one period are but an installment of what is essentially a continuous history.
>
> In any one year it is ordinarily desirable that the balance sheet, the income statement, and the surplus statement be given for one or more preceding years, as well as for the current year. Footnotes, explanations, and accountants' qualifications which appeared on the statements for the preceding years should be repeated, or at least referred to, in the comparative statements to the extent that they continue to be of significance.[8]

Exhibit 23-3 presents the comparative income statements for O'Neal, Inc. Notice that the current-year results in the first column are presented directly beside the previous-year results to facilitate comparison.

Five or ten-year summaries also may be presented for the interested financial reader. These long-term summaries provide the user with valuable information of how the company has performed in the past and may provide clues as to how it will perform in the future.

Sections of the Income Statement

The income statement should be reported in a manner that is consistent from period to period and that affords comparability. You can achieve these objectives by reporting the elements of income in the same section of the income statement from period to period.

Below is an outline of the sections of the income statement:

I. Operating section. This section includes the revenues and expenses of the company's continuing operations.
   A. Sales or revenue subsection. This section provides all items of revenue from normal recurring operations net of allowances for discounts, returns, or other items deducted to arrive at net sales.

---

[8]"Restatement and Revision of Accounting Research Bulletins," *Accounting Research Bulletin No. 43* (New York: AICPA, 1953), Chapter 2, pars. 1 and 2.

Exhibit 23-3
O'NEAL, INC.
Income Statement
Comparative Financial Statements

	1983		1982	
Revenues				
Sales (net of returns and allowances)		$2,850,000		$2,005,000
Rent		67,000		63,000
Interest and dividends		95,000		60,000
Gain from sale of securities		125,000		40,000
Total revenues		$3,137,000		$2,168,000
Expenses				
Cost of goods sold	$ 800,000		$693,000	
Administrative expenses	145,000		157,000	
Selling expenses	87,000		90,000	
Interest	105,000		128,000	
Income taxes	1,000,000	2,137,000	550,000	1,618,000
Net income		$1,000,000		$ 550,000

B. Cost of goods sold subsection. This section discloses the cost of the assets sold to produce the sales. The components of this cost figure should be disclosed in detail.

C. Selling expenses. This subsection discloses the expenses associated with the sales of the period.

D. Administrative and general expenses. This subsection discloses the general and administrative expenses of the period.

II. Nonoperating section. This section discloses the gains and losses from operations of an auxiliary or secondary nature. This section would include elements of revenue or expenses that are unusual or infrequent in nature but do not warrant segregation from continuing operations.

A. Other income. This subsection includes any item of revenue or gain (net of related expenses) that results from nonoperating transactions.

B. Other expenses. This subsection includes any item of expense or loss (net of related revenues) that results from nonoperating transactions.

III. Income taxes. This section discloses the amount of taxes levied on income.

IV. Nonroutine gains and losses. This section discloses those items, specifically defined below, that warrant segregation from income from continuing operations due to their nature. Nonroutine gains and losses are not included in income from continuing operations because they do not reflect the results of normal ongoing operations.
   A. Discontinued operations. This subsection discloses the gain or loss attributable to the disposal of a segment of a business.
   B. Extraordinary items. This subsection discloses the gain or loss that is both unusual and infrequent.
   C. Cumulative effect of a change in accounting principle. This subsection discloses the effect on income resulting from using a different generally accepted accounting principle in the current period from the generally accepted principle employed in prior periods.
V. Earnings per share.

The nonroutine gains and losses are reported separately in the income statement, net of tax. The nature of these items warrants separate disclosure from continuing operations. Including such items in continuing operations would distort the income that results from normal ongoing operations. Separate disclosure of these items provides the statement user with greater information for evaluating the results of operations, provides consistency, and affords comparability for income from period to period.

As discussed in Chapter 3, a question existed for years as to whether certain nonrecurring gains and loses and corrections of prior years' income and expenses (1) should be closed directly to retained earnings and therefore not be reflected in the income statement (current operating concept), or (2) should be closed to the revenue and expense summary and then carried to retained earnings and therefore reflected in the income statement (all-inclusive concept).

In 1967 the APB issued *Opinion No. 9*, "Reporting the Results of Operations," which favored the all-inclusive concept.[9] Subsequent pronouncements were issued that directly or indirectly involved the classification and reporting of nonrecurring gains and losses and other items. The items, which are listed below, will be discussed in the following sections.

1. Discontinued operations.
2. Extraordinary items.
3. Accounting changes.
4. Income taxes.
5. Earnings per share.
6. Prior period adjustments.

Each of these items must be considered in reporting income. Discontinued operations will be discussed in detail, whereas only an overview of the other items will be presented since they were discussed in detail in earlier chapters.

---

[9]"Reporting the Results of Operations," *Opinions of the Accounting Principles Board No. 9* (New York: AICPA, 1967).

Discontinued Operations

Discontinued operations are defined as the operations of a segment of a business that has been sold, abandoned, spun off, or otherwise disposed of or, although still operating, is the subject of a *formal plan* of disposal. APB *Opinion No. 30*, "Reporting the Results of Operations," concludes that a formal plan of disposal should include the following:

1. Identification of the major assets to be disposed of.
2. Expected method of disposal.
3. Period expected to be required for completion of the disposal (usually completed within one year from the measurement date).
4. An active program to find a buyer if disposal is to be by sale.
5. Estimated results of operations of the segment from the measurement date to the disposal date.
6. Estimated proceeds or salvage to be realized upon disposal.[10]

Disposal of a Segment of a Business.   APB *Opinion No. 30* specifies the accounting and reporting requirements for the disposal of a segment of a business. The APB contends that the usefulness of the income statement is enhanced by reporting the results of continuing operations of an entity separately from the operations of a segment of the business that has been or will be discontinued. The potential investor thus is provided with a differentiation between normal operating income or loss and nonroutine gains or losses (i.e., disposal of a segment of a business). The gain or loss from the disposal of a segment of a business should be reported with the operations of the segment and not as an extraordinary item.

A **segment** of a business is defined as a component of an entity whose activities represent a separate major line of business or separate major class of customer. The segment may be a subsidiary, division, department, or other specifically identifiable component of the business. However, the assets, results of operations, and activities of the discontinued segment must be distinguished clearly (physically, operationally, and for financial reporting purposes) from the entity's other assets, results of operations, and activities. If the component cannot be distinguished clearly, it is not a business segment. Exhibit 23-4 provides several examples of disposals that *are* and *are not* classified as segment dispositions.

If a particular event or transaction is not a disposal of a segment of a business, the criteria for extraordinary item classification (see a later section of this chapter) should be considered.

Determination of Gain or Loss on Disposal of a Segment of a Business.   On the face of the income statement there are actually two amounts reported as a result of the discontinued operations: (1) income or loss from discontinued operations and (2) gain or loss on the disposal of discontinued operations.

Income or loss from discontinued operations is simply the separate, discontinued segment's income or loss, net of tax, from the first day of the entity's fiscal

---

[10]"Reporting the Results of Operations," *Opinions of the Accounting Principles Board No. 30* (New York: AICPA, 1973), par. 14.

Exhibit 23-4
Examples of Business Segment Disposals

Disposals Classified as Segment Dispositions	Disposals Not Classified as Segment Dispositions
1. A sale by a diversified company of a major line of business that represents the company's only investment in that industry. The assets and results of operations of the division are clearly segregated for internal financial reporting purposes from the other assets and results of operations of the company.	1. The sale of a major foreign subsidiary engaged in silver mining by a mining company that represents all of the company's activities in that particular country. Even though the subsidiary being sold may account for a significant percentage of gross revenue of the consolidated group and all of its revenues in the particular country, the fact that the country continues to engage in silver mining activities in other countries would indicate that there was a sale of a part of a line of business.
2. A sale by a meat packing company of a 25% interest in a professional football team, which has been accounted for under the equity method. All other activities of the company are in the meat packing business.	2. The sale by a petrochemical company of a 25% interest in a petrochemical plant, which is accounted for as an investment in a corporate joint venture under the equity method. Since the remaining activities of the company are in the same line of business as the 25% interest that has been sold, there has not been a sale of a major line of business, but rather, a sale of part of a line of business.
3. A sale by a communications company of all its radio stations, which represent 30% of the company's gross revenues. The company's remaining activities are three television stations and a publishing company. The assets and results of operations of the radio stations are clearly distinguishable physically, operationally, and for financial reporting purposes.	3. A diversified company sells a subsidiary that manufactures furniture. The company has retained its other furniture manufacturing subsidiary. Therefore, the disposal of the subsidiary is not a disposal of a segment of the business, but rather, a disposal of part of a line of business.

Exhibit 23-4 (continued)
Examples of Business Segment Disposals

Disposals Classified as Segment Dispositions	Disposals Not Classified as Segment Dispositions
4. A food distributor disposes of one of its two divisions. One division sells food wholesale primarily to supermarket chains, and the other division sells food through its chain of fast food restaurants, some of which are franchised and some of which are company-owned. Both divisions are in the business of distribution of food. However, the nature of selling food through fast-food outlets is vastly different from that of wholesaling food to supermarket chains. By having two major classes of customers, the company has two segments of its business.	4. A manufacturer of children's wear discontinues all of its operations in Italy, which were composed of designing and selling children's wear for the Italian market. In the context of determining a segment of a business by class of customer, the nationality of customers or slight variations in product lines in order to appeal to particular groups are not determining factors.

year to the measurement date. The **measurement date** is the date on which management, having authority to approve the action, commits itself to a formal plan to dispose of a segment of the business, whether by sale or abandonment. For example, if a calendar year corporation approves a formal plan of disposal on November 24, 1983, the gain or loss from discontinued operations would encompass the period from January 1, 1983, to the measurement date, November 24, 1983.

The gain or loss on the disposal of discontinued operations (shown net of income taxes) has two components:

1. Income or loss from operations from the measurement date to the disposal date (commonly referred to as the phase-out period).

2. Gain or loss from the actual disposal.

The **disposal date** is the date of closing the sale of the disposed segment if the disposal is by sale, *or* the date operations of the disposed segment cease if the disposal is by abandonment. The disposal date is the last date of operations of the disposed segment under present ownership. For example, if a calendar year corporation adopts a formal plan of disposal on November 24, 1983, and plans to cease operations of the segment by February 25, 1984, the profit or loss from operations of the disposed segment from November 24, 1983 (measurement date), to February 25, 1984 (disposal date), will be included as part of the gain or loss on disposal of discontinued operations ("1" above).

The gain or loss from the actual disposal ("2" above) is equal to the sales price of the disposed segment less both the costs directly associated with the disposal and the book value of the net assets of the disposed segment. Costs directly associated with the disposal must be the direct result of the decision to dispose of the segment, for example, severance pay, additional pension costs, employee relocation expenses, etc. These costs should *not* result from the adjustment of carrying amounts, costs, or expenses that should have been recognized on a going-concern basis before the measurement date, such as adjustments of accruals on long-term contracts and write-down or write-off of receivables, inventories, property, plant, and equipment, or other intangible assets.

The determination of whether a gain or loss exists on the disposal of the discontinued operations is based on estimates as of the measurement date. These include an estimate of income or loss during the phase-out period and an estimate of the net realizable value of the segment after giving consideration to any estimated costs and expenses directly associated with the disposal. If these estimates are deemed incorrect in a future period (all periods through the period of disposal), their correction should be treated as a change in accounting estimate.

If the disposal of the discontinued segment results in a loss (sum of "1" and "2" noted previously), the loss should be recognized as of the measurement date. If the disposal results in a net gain, the gain *should not* be recognized at the measurement date. If the net gain results from a gain on the sale of the segment, the net gain should not be recognized until the disposal date. If the net gain results from income during phase out in excess of a disposal loss, the gain should be recognized as realized—that is, during the phase-out period as income is earned. If the net gain on disposal is from both income during the phase-out period and a gain on the sale, the income should be recognized as earned, and the gain on sale should be recognized on the disposal date. This method of income recognition is consistent with the concepts of realization and conservatism because it requires the accountant to estimate and provide for losses as of the measurement date in the current period and to postpone gain recognition until actually realized. The determination of the net gain or loss in disposal of a segment of the business is summarized in Exhibit 23-5.

For example, a calendar year pesticide company, ZAPP, Inc. has decided to abandon its grain division. This abandonment qualifies as a disposal of a business segment. ZAPP, Inc. adopted a formal plan of disposal by abandonment on November 24, 1982. As of this date the grain division had lost $50,000 for the year. On December 10, 1982, the management of ZAPP, Inc. decided that the grain division's allowance for doubtful accounts had been understated by $20,000 at November 24, 1982. Therefore, the total loss of the grain division through the measurement date was actually $70,000.

The company plans to cease all operations of its grain business by February 25, 1983. ZAPP, Inc. expects to lose an additional $30,000 from the grain operation for the period from November 24, 1982, to February 25, 1983. The book value of the assets of the grain division will be $100,000 on the disposal date.

Excluding its grain division, ZAPP, Inc. has income from continuing opera-

---

Exhibit 23-5
Determining Net Gain or Loss
on Disposal of a Segment

	Operating *Loss*	*Operating* *Income*
Disposal *Loss*	Total loss recognized on measurement date.	Result: 1. Net loss—recognize on measurement date. 2. Net income—recognize throughout the period.
Disposal *Gain*	Result: 1. Net loss—recognize on measurement date. 2. Net gain—recognize as realized (on disposal date).	Gain and income recognized as realized (gain on disposal date and income throughout as earned).

---

tions of $1,000,000. ZAPP, Inc.'s effective tax rate is 50%. The computation of loss is shown below:

Loss from Discontinued Operations

Loss from January 1, 1982, to November 24, 1982	$70,000
Less: Related income tax benefit ($70,000 × 50%)	(35,000)
Loss from discontinued operations	$35,000

Loss on Disposal of Discontinued Operations

Loss from November 24, 1982, to February 25, 1983	$ 30,000
Book value of abandoned assets on February 25, 1983	100,000
Loss on disposal before income tax benefit	$130,000
Less: Related income tax benefit ($13,000 × 50%)	(65,000)
Loss on disposal of discontinued operations	$65,000

The loss from discontinued operations *includes* the $20,000 allowance for doubtful accounts adjustment because it is associated with normal business activities and is not a direct result of the decision to dispose of the segment. If the adjustment had been a direct result of the decision to dispose of the segment, the expense would become part of the gain or loss on disposal of discontinued operations and would be omitted from the income or loss from discontinued operations calculation. A partial income statement for Zapp, Inc. appears in Exhibit 23-6.

An additional example is the case of Cliffe, Inc., a highly diversified calendar year manufacturing company, which has decided to sell its liquor processing division. The sale of the division qualifies as a disposal of a business segment.

Exhibit 23-6
ZAPP, INC.
Partial Income Statement
For the Year Ended December 31, 1982

Income from continuing operations		$1,000,000
Discontinued operations		
Loss from operations of discontinued division (less applicable income tax benefit of $35,000)	$(35,000)	
Loss on disposal of discontinued division, including a provision of $30,000 for operating losses before abandonment (less tax benefit relating to the net loss on disposal of $65,000)	(65,000)	(100,000)
Net income		$ 900,000

Cliffe, Inc. adopted a formal plan of disposal on April 22, 1982. As of this date the liquor processing division had income of $450,000. The company plans to sell its liquor processing division on March 1, 1983, for $3,000,000. The expected book value of the assets of the division as of this date is $5,500,000. Because of the disposal, pension costs of the division will increase by $120,000. Cliffe, Inc. expects the division to earn an additional $300,000 during the phase-out period.

Exhibit 23-7
CLIFFE, INC.
Partial Income Statement
For the Year Ended December 31, 1982

Income from continuing operations		$12,000,000
Discontinued operations		
Income from operations of discontinued segment (less applicable income taxes of $225,000)	$ 225,000	
Loss on disposal of discontinued division, including a provision of $300,000 for operating income during the phase-out period (less tax benefit relating to the net loss on disposal of $1,160,000)	(1,160,000)	(935,000)
Net income		$11,065,000

All other income from Cliffe, Inc. is generated from continuing operations and amounts to $12,000,000. The company's effective tax rate is 50%. The computation of loss is shown below:

Income from Discontinued Operations

Income from January 1, 1982, to April 22, 1982		$450,000
Less: Related income taxes ($450,000 × 50%)		(225,000)
Income from discontinued operations		$225,000

Loss on Disposal of Discontinued Operations

Income from April 22, 1982, to March 1, 1983		$300,000
Sales price of division	$3,000,000	
Less: Increased pension costs	(120,000)	
Amount realized	$2,880,000	
Less: Book value of assets	(5,500,000)	(2,620,000)
Loss on disposal before income taxes		$(2,320,000)
Less: Related income tax benefit ($2,320,000 × 50%)		1,160,000
Loss on disposal of discontinued operations		$(1,160,000)

As mentioned earlier, only a loss on disposal can be recognized as of the measurement date. If a disposal results in a gain, it cannot be recognized until realized. Therefore, in this example, if the disposed segment had income in excess of $2,620,000 for the period from April 22, 1982, to March 1, 1983 (phase-out period), this would cause a gain on the disposal of discontinued operations to be recognized as earned during the phase-out period. A partial income statement for Cliffe, Inc. appears in Exhibit 23-7.

Disclosures. The income or loss from discontinued operations should be shown on the income statement after income from continuing operations and before both extraordinary items and the cumulative effect of accounting changes. The amount of income tax or income tax benefit applicable to both income or loss from discontinued operations and gain or loss on disposal of discontinued operations should be shown either on the face of the income statement or in a footnote. Revenues applicable to the discontinued operations should be shown either on the face of the income statement or in a footnote. The footnotes also should disclose the following:

1. The identity of the segment of business that has been or will be discontinued.
2. The expected disposal date (if known).
3. The expected manner of disposal.

4. A description of the remaining assets and liabilities of the segment at the balance sheet date.[11]
5. The income or loss from operations and any proceeds from disposal of the segment during the period from the measurement date to the balance sheet date.[12]

For periods subsequent to the period that includes the measurement date through the period of disposal, the information in items 1 through 4 above should be disclosed in addition to the actual disposal results from item 5 above compared with prior estimates.

Earnings per share is optional for a disposal of a business segment. However, earnings per share must be shown for income from continuing operations and net income. If earnings per share is shown for a business segment disposal, it should be included on either the face of the income statement or in a footnote.

If the financial statements of periods before the period that includes the measurement date also are included (comparative statements), the income statement should show a separate line item for the results of operations of the disposed segment, less applicable taxes or tax benefits, directly beneath income from continuing operations.

For example, assume the same facts that were used for Cliffe, Inc. above for the year ended December 31, 1982. For the year ended December 31, 1981, Cliffe, Inc. had income from continuing operations of $11,000,000 exclusive of the $800,000 earned by the liquor processing division. A comparative partial income statement is shown in Exhibit 23-8.

Extraordinary Items—Overview

Accounting for extraordinary items was covered in detail in Chapter 3. A brief review is presented here. *Opinion No. 30* defined **extraordinary items** as follows:

> Extraordinary items are events and transactions that are distinguished by their unusual nature *and* by the infrequency of their occurrence. Thus, *both* of the following criteria should be met to classify an event or transaction as an extraordinary item:
>
> (1) Unusual nature—the underlying event or transaction should possess a high degree of abnormality and be of a type clearly unrelated to, or only incidentally related to, the ordinary and typical activities of the entity, taking into account the environment in which the entity operates.
>
> (2) Infrequency of occurrence—the underlying event or transaction should be of a type that would not reasonably be expected to recur in the foreseeable future, taking into account the environment in which the entity operates.[13]

---

[11] APB *Opinion No. 30* indicated the following regarding item 4: Consideration should be given to disclosing this information by segregation in the balance sheet of the net assets and liabilities (current and noncurrent) of the discontinued segment. Only liabilities which will be assumed by others should be designated as liabilities of the discontinued segment. If the loss on disposal cannot be estimated within reasonable limits, this fact should be disclosed.

[12] "Reporting the Results of Operations," par. 18.

[13] Ibid., par. 20.

Exhibit 23-8
CLIFFE, INC.
Partial Income Statement
For the Years Ended December 31, 1982,
and December 31, 1981

	1982	1981
Income from continuing operations	$12,000,000	$11,000,000
Discontinued operations		
Income from operations of discontinued segment (less applicable income taxes of $225,000 in 1982 and $400,000 in 1981)	225,000	400,000
Loss on disposal of discontinued division, including a provision of $300,000 for operating income during the phase-out period (less tax benefit relating to the net loss on disposal of $1,160,000)	(1,160,000)	—
	(935,000)	400,000
Net income	$11,065,000	$11,400,000

It is apparent that the environment in which an entity operates is a key factor to consider in determining whether the event or transaction should be classified as an extraordinary item. An entity's environment includes the characteristics of the industry in which it operates, the geographic location of its operations, and the nature and extent of government regulations.

Extraordinary items should be disclosed in a separate section of the income statement, directly below the section for discontinued operations. The extraordinary gain or loss should be shown net of income taxes. For example, assume that DAP, Inc. suffered a loss due to the total destruction of a building as a result of an earthquake. The building was on DAP's balance sheet as follows:

Building	$250,000
Less: Accumulated depreciation	50,000
	$200,000

The journal entry to record the loss is below:

Extraordinary loss	200,000	
Accumulated depreciation—building	50,000	
Building		250,000

Exhibit 23-9
DAP, INC.
Partial Income Statement
For the Year Ended December 31, 1983

Income before income taxes and extraordinary item	$2,000,000
Income taxes ($2,000,000 × 50%)	1,000,000
Income before extraordinary item	$1,000,000
Extraordinary loss (less applicable income taxes of $100,000)	(100,000)
Net income	$ 900,000

This entry will remove the building and related accumulated depreciation from the balance sheet, and the extraordinary loss will flow through to the income statement. If you assume a 50% tax rate, a partial income statement would be presented as illustrated in Exhibit 23-9.

Accounting Changes—Overview

Reporting the results of operations of an entity requires recognition of accounting changes, which were discussed in detail in Chapter 22. APB *Opinion No. 20*, "Accounting Changes," defines what constitutes an accounting change and now it should be reported. For purposes of this chapter, accounting changes will be discussed in the context of the income statement (i.e., reporting accounting changes).

Income statement presentation of an accounting change depends on the type of change. The three type of changes are as follows:

1. A change in accounting principle.
2. A change in accounting estimate.
3. A change in reporting entity.

A Change in Accounting Principle. **A change in accounting principle** is a change from one generally accepted accounting principle to another generally accepted accounting principle. In general, you account for a change in accounting principle by reporting the cumulative effect of the change in accounting principles, based on retroactive calculation, in the net income of the period of the change. The cumulative effect is reported "net of tax" and should appear after extraordinary items, but before net income, as a separate line item on the income statement. The company also must disclose in the footnotes the nature of the change, the justification of the change, certain pro forma information, and the effect of the change on current operations.

The pro forma information essentially is a restatement of prior statements presented and is viewed as supplemental information to the cumulative effect presentation. Restatement of prior financial statements, under some circumstances, is considered appropriate; however, presentation of the cumulative effect of a change in accounting principle is generally appropriate. Restatement of financial statements should occur when the significance of a change in accounting principle outweighs the benefits of reporting the cumulative effect of the change.

The benefits of the cumulative effect presentation stem from the APB's belief that restatement of prior financial statements results in the dilution of public confidence in the statements. The cumulative effect establishes consistent application of accounting principles in comparative statments.

Restatement of financial statements should occur when the change in principle has a significant impact on income in the year of change. *Opinion No. 20* identifies four special changes that require restatement of prior financial statements.

1. A change from LIFO to some other inventory method.
2. A change to or from the percentage-of-completion method of accounting for long-term construction contracts.
3. A change to or from the full-cost method of accounting used in the extractive industry.[14]
4. Special cases in which companies are involved in initial public offerings of securities.[15]

Restatement requires that the prior financial statements are to be reconstructed under the assumption that the new accounting principle was in effect. When statements are restated retroactively, pro forma information is not necessary. The notes to the financial statements for both the cumulative effect and the retroactive restatement should disclose the nature of the change, justification of the change, the effect on income before extraordinary items, net income, and the earnings per share for all periods presented.

A Change in Accounting Estimate. The second type of accounting change identified by *Opinion No. 20* is a **change in accounting estimate,** which is a necessary consequence of periodic presentation of financial statements. Preparing financial statements requires estimating the effects of future events. For example, estimating the useful life or the salvage value of a depreciable asset, and estimating the collectibility of accounts receivable are all integral procedures in reporting the results of operations.

In order to reflect the results of operations properly, you must revise estimates to reflect the new events, or the additional experience or information that is obtained. Because of the nature of a change in estimate, the APB specified "prospective" treatment of a change in estimate—that is, a change in estimate, due to its normal, recurring nature should be accounted for (1) in the period of the change if the change affects that period only or (2) in the period of the change and future periods if the change affects both.

---

[14]"Accounting Changes," *Opinions of the Accounting Principles Board No. 20* (New York: AICPA, 1971), par. 27.

[15]Ibid., par. 29.

A Change in Reporting Entity.   **A change in reporting entity** occurs when the financial statements of a company reflect a different group of enterprises than were presented in previous financial statements. Accounting for a change in reporting entity requires a restatement of the financial statements for all prior periods presented, using the new reporting entity. The company must disclose the nature of the change, the reasons for the change, and the effect of the change on operations and related earnings per share for all reporting periods presented. Retroactive restatement is required so that the reader of the financial statements can have comparable information for all the periods presented.

Examples of changes in reporting entities are as follows:

1. Presenting consolidated financial statements in lieu of statements of individual companies.
2. Changing specific subsidiaries comprising the group of companies for which consolidated financial statements are presented.
3. Changing the companies included in the combined financial statements.
4. Accounting for a pooling of interests.
5. Changing the cost, equity, or consolidation method of accounting for subsidiaries and investments. A change in the reporting entity doesn't result from creation, cessation, purchase, or disposition of a subsidiary or other business unit.

Correction of an Error.   The correction of an error is not an accounting change but is included in *Opinion No. 20* because of the relation between changes in principles and errors, and changes in estimates and errors.

A change in accounting principle does not include a change from a non-generally accepted accounting principle to a generally accepted accounting principle; this is considered a correction of an error. Likewise, a change in estimate that results from the correction of an oversight or the misuse of facts is not a change in estimate, but rather, a correction of an error.

Examples of accounting errors are listed below:

1. A change in accounting principle that is not generally accepted to an accounting principle that is generally accepted.
2. Mathematical mistakes.
3. Changes in estimate that result from estimates that were not prepared in good faith.
4. An oversight, such as failure to defer certain assets and liabilities at the end of the period.
5. A misuse of facts.
6. The incorrect classification of a cost as an expense instead of an asset and vice versa.

Such errors are reported as prior period adjustments, which will be discussed later in this chapter.

Income Taxes—Overview

Income taxes are a significant expense for many business enterprises. Because accounting for income taxes requires measurement and identification with time periods, it involves deferral, accrual, and estimation concepts. Accounting for income taxes was discussed in detail in Chapter 16.

The principal problems in accounting for income taxes arise from the special treatment given to some transactions. These transactions may affect the determination of net income for financial purposes in one reporting period while affecting the determination of taxable income and income taxes payable in a different period. Therefore, the amount of income taxes expense applicable to transactions for financial accounting purposes does not necessarily represent the amount of income taxes payable during that same period. Tax allocation usually can be classified into two major categories:

1. Interperiod tax allocation.
2. Intraperiod tax allocation.

Interperiod tax allocation is the process of apportioning income taxes among periods; the reason for this is that certain revenues and expenses are included in the income statement either before or after they affect the income tax return. Hence, the amount of income taxes payable for a period does not necessarily represent the income taxes expense for that period.

Intraperiod tax allocation is the process of apportioning income tax expense to specific items on the income statement. This is done to provide informative disclosures to the users of the financial statements. Related income tax expense should be apportioned to the following items that affect tax provisions:

1. Income from continuing operations.
2. Discontinued operations.
3. Income before extraordinary items and the cumulative effect of accounting changes.
4. Extraordinary items.
5. Changes in accounting principles.
6. Net income.
7. Prior period adjustments.

Income tax expense relating to "income from continuing operations" is computed by determining the income tax expense related to the revenue and expense transactions involved in determining income. The income tax expense for the other items is determined by the tax results of the transactions involving those items.

Earnings Per Share—Overview

Many financial statement users consider earnings per share, which was discussed in detail in Chapter 21, to be of great importance. Earnings per share is presented on the face of the income statement for all public enterprises. For an enterprise with a simple capital structure (i.e., only common stock outstanding), earnings per share can be defined as net income divided by the weighted average number of shares outstanding. The items on the income statement for which earnings per share amounts must be presented are as follows:

1. Income from continuing operations.
2. Accounting changes.
3. Net income.

Although earnings per share is not required for discontinued operations and extraordinary items, many enterprises report these figures on their income statements.

The dilution (reduction) of the earnings per share amounts is complicated. Some problems may arise if an enterprise has issued preferred stock, options, warrants, or other items that may affect either the numerator or the denominator of the basic earnings per share equation. These were discussed in detail in Chapter 21.

Prior Period Adjustments—Overview

FASB *Statement No. 16*, "Prior Period Adjustments," outlined the criteria concerning the types of items to be considered prior period adjustments. The two items identified are as follows:

1. The correction of accounting errors.
2. Adjustments that result from the realization of income tax benefits of preacquisition operating loss carryforwards of purchased subsidiaries (for example, if Company A has a net operating loss carryforward when Company B buys Company A, then B is the new entity that recognizes the operating loss carryforward as a prior period adjustment).[16]

When a material error occurs, it should be corrected in the year found. The correction should be reflected as an adjustment of the opening balance of retained earnings. If comparative financial statements are presented, appropriate adjustments should be made to the net income and retained earnings for all the years presented in order to reflect the retroactive application of the prior period adjustments.

Statement of Retained Earnings

The statement of retained earnings is an essential financial statement for any enterprise. A detailed discussion of retained earnings was presented in Chapter 19. Because important items may be overlooked in the income statement, it is beneficial to examine the statement of retained earnings and the income statement together—for example, the income statement does not reveal the prior period adjustments made to retained earnings.

[16] "Prior Period Adjustments," *Statement of Financial Accounting Standards No. 16* (Stamford, Conn.: FASB, 1977), par. 11.

Exhibit 23-10
BEST, INC.
Model Income Statement Format
For the Year Ended December 31, 1983

Income from operations		$1,875,000
Sale of marketable equity securities		125,000
[a] Income from continuing operations before income taxes		$2,000,000
Provision for income taxes		(1,000,000)
Income from continuing operations		$1,000,000
[b] Discontinued operations		
Loss from operations of discontinued division (less applicable income tax benefit of $35,000)	$(35,000)	
Loss on disposal of discontinued division, including a provision of $30,000 for operating losses before abandonment (less tax benefit relating to the net loss on disposal of $65,000)	(65,000)	(100,000)
Income before extraordinary items and cumulative effect of accounting change		$ 900,000
[c] Loss from destruction of physical facility due to earthquake (less applicable income taxes of $100,000)		(100,000)
[d] Cumulative effect of a change in accounting method of depreciation (less applicable income taxes of $43,080)		43,080
Net income		$ 843,080
[e] Earnings per common share (assuming 100,000 shares standing for the entire year)		
*Income from continuing operations		$10.00
Discontinued operations		(1.00)
*Income before extraordinary items		$ 9.00
Extraordinary items		(1.00)
*Cumulative effect of change in accounting principle		0.43
*Net income		$ 8.43

*Minimum required captions

Authoritative Source
[a] Unusual or infrequently occurring items: APB *Opinion No. 30*
[b] Discontinued operations: APB *Opinion No. 30*
[c] Extraordinary items: APB *Opinion No. 30*, APB *Opinion No. 11*, FASB *Statement No. 4*
[d] Accounting changes: APB *Opinion No. 20*
[e] Earnings per share: APB *Opinion 15*, APB *Opinion No. 20*, APB *Opinion No. 30*

The dividend distribution for the current year, as well as other transfers to and from retained earnings, can be important factors for investment decisions. Users of the financial statements often are interested in the relationship between current income and dividends distributed. Shareholders and investors can discern whether management is distributing the profits or reinvesting the profits for expansion purposes.

Details of the amount of retained earnings appropriated should be available to interested parties. Only the unappropriated portion of retained earnings is available for dividend distributions. Appropriations (restrictions) of retained earnings may be imposed by management decisions, contracts with outsiders, or legal requirements. Often these appropriations are made for debt agreements, capital expenditures, treasury stock purchases, or future expansions. Appropriations are reported either as separate items on the statement of retained earnings or via footnote disclosure.

Comprehensive Illustration

This chapter has presented the reporting requirements of several authoritative pronouncements. The model income statement presented in Exhibit 23-10 displays the format to be used in reporting the complete range of nonroutine gains and losses.

Notice the order in which the items are presented. Unusual or infrequently occurring items and any provision for income taxes are two disclosures that affect income from continuing operations. Discontinued operations, extraordinary items, and accounting changes are presented below income from continuing operations. Discontinued operations is composed of two figures: the first relates to the operations of the discontinued segment, and the second relates to the gain (loss) on the disposal of the discontinued segment. Extraordinary items are presented after discontinued operations but before accounting changes, while accounting changes are presented immediately preceding net income. All items presented below income from continuing operations (discontinued operations, extraordinary items, and accounting changes) are to be presented net of any related tax effects.

Appropriate earnings per share information must be disclosed also. (The chapter lists the required earnings per share disclosures.) Any prior period adjustments are reflected in the statement of retained earnings.

Concept Summary

REPORTING INCOME AND RETAINED EARNINGS
INCOME STATEMENT CLASSIFICATIONS

Classification	Examples	Required Income Statement Disclosure
Discontinued Operations	Disposal of separate major line of business or separate major	Separate two-tier disclosure between income from

	class of customer	continuing operations and extraordinary items, net of tax, and with EPS effects
Extraordinary items	Items, events, and transactions that are both unusual in nature and infrequently occurring, considering the business environment	Separate disclosure between discontinued operations and cumulative effect of accounting change (if any)
Unusual or Infrequently Occurring Items	Items, events, and transactions that meet one but not both extraordinary item criteria	Separate disclosure within income from continuing operations; cannot be disclosed net of tax or with EPS effects
Cumulative Effect of Accounting Change	General-type changes in accounting principle, e.g., changing depreciation methods and certain inventory changes	Separate disclosure as last component in income statement before net income, net of tax, with EPS effects, and with *pro forma* disclosures

Questions

Q–23–1 Define the term *revenue* and discuss when revenue is considered realized.

Q–23–2 Define the term *expenses* and discuss when expenses are considered realized.

Q–23–3 Define *net income* and discuss its importance in financial accounting reporting.

Q–23–4 Over time, two distinguishable concepts of income determination have developed: the *current operating performance* concept and the *all-inclusive* concept. Briefly describe the primary difference between the two concepts.

Q–23–5 List the advantages and disadvantages of a *single-step* and *multiple-step* income statement, and briefly discuss the format of each.

Q–23–6 Define a *segment* of a business.

Q–23–7 Define *discontinued operations* and discuss the components of a formal plan of disposal.

Q–23–8 Discuss the accounting procedures in recording gains (losses) of a disposal of a segment of a business.

Q–23–9 Define an *extraordinary item* and discuss the requirements for classification as such. Also, discuss the appropriate accounting disclosures for extraordinary items.

Q-23-10 List the different types of accounting changes and discuss the income statement presentation for each type of accounting change.

Q-23-11 Explain the term *prior period adjustment* and give an example of such. Also, discuss the accounting presentation for prior period adjustments.

Q-23-12 Explain the difference between *interperiod income tax allocation* and *intraperiod income tax allocation* and discuss when each method becomes necessary to be applied.

Q-23-13 Discuss the importance of the presentation of the statement of retained earnings.

Q-23-14 Which of the following is an example of an extraordinary item in reporting the results of operations?
  a) A loss incurred because of a strike by employees.
  b) The write-off of deferred research and development costs believed to have no future benefit.
  c) A gain resulting from the devaluation of the U.S. dollar.
  d) A gain resulting from the state exercising its right of eminent domain on a piece of land used as a parking lot.

(AICPA adapted)

Q-23-15 How should the gain or loss from an event or transaction that meets the criteria for infrequent occurrence but not unusual nature be disclosed?
  a) Separately in the earnings statement immediately after earnings from continuing operations.
  b) On a net-of-tax basis in the earnings statement immediately after earnings from continuing operations.
  c) As an extraordinary item and treated accordingly in the earnings statement.
  d) Separately in the earnings statement as a component of earnings from continuing operations.

(AICPA adapted)

Q-23-16 When reporting the disposal of a segment of the business, which of the following is a required disclosure in the earnings statement?
  a) The gain or loss on disposal should be reported as an extraordinary item.
  b) Results of operations of a discontinued segment should be disclosed immediately below extraordinary items.
  c) Earnings per share from both continuing operations and net earnings should be disclosed on the face of the earnings statement.
  d) Revenue and expenses applicable to the discontinued operations should be disclosed in the earnings statement.

(AICPA adapted)

Q-23-17 Under which of the following conditions would flood damage be considered an extraordinary item for financial reporting purposes?
  a) Only if floods in the geographical area are unusual in nature and occur infrequently.
  b) Only if floods are normal in the geographical area but do not occur frequently.
  c) Only if floods occur frequently in the geographical area but have been insured against.
  d) Under any circumstances flood damage should be classified as an extraordinary item.

(AICPA adapted)

Discussion Questions and Cases

D-23-1 The Century Company, a diversified manufacturing company, had four separate operating divisions engaged in the manufacture of products in each of the following areas: food products, health aids, textiles, and office equipment.

Financial data for the two years ended December 31, 1975, and December 31, 1974, are presented below:

Net Sales

	1975	1974
Food products	$3,500,000	$3,000,000
Health aids	2,000,000	1,270,000
Textiles	1,580,000	1,400,000
Office Equipment	920,000	1,330,000
	$8,000,000	$7,000,000

Cost of Sales

	1975	1974
Food products	$2,400,000	$1,800,000
Health aids	1,100,000	700,000
Textiles	500,000	900,000
Office Equipment	800,000	1,000,000
	$4,800,000	$4,400,000

Operating Expenses

	1975	1974
Food products	$ 550,000	$ 275,000
Health aids	300,000	125,000
Textiles	200,000	150,000
Office Equipment	650,000	750,000
	$1,700,000	$1,300,000

On January 1, 1975, Century adopted a plan to sell the assets and product line of the office equipment division and expected to realize a gain on this disposal. On September 1, 1975, the division's assets and product line were sold for $2,100,000 cash resulting in a gain of $640,000 (exclusive of operations during the phase-out period).

The company's textiles division had six manufacturing plants which produced a variety of textile products. In April 1975, the company sold one of these plants and realized a gain of $130,000. After the sale, the operations at the plant that was sold were transferred to the remaining five textile plants which the company continued to operate.

Required:

Discuss your proposed accounting treatment applicable to the above situations. Be sure to discuss the theoretically preferable treatment of these items as well as any pragmatic implications you may suggest.

(AICPA adapted)

D-23-2 In the final stages of your audit of FMM Company, you have decided to discuss several accounting and disclosure problems discovered during the course of your engagement with top management of FMM. The company is a large public company and the financial statements you are about to release will have a wide circulation. Among the problems you wish to discuss are the ones outlined below.

Assume a calendar year for reporting purposes and that you have not been restricted in any way in fulfilling your audit requirements. Assume a 40% effective tax rate throughout for FMM.

Area 1: FMM operates several cement plants throughout the Southwest. The Luckenbach plant was built in 1974 and included all the modern technological developments. However, due to lack of demand for the products produced at the plant, operations have only been at 50% of capacity. FMM received an offer to purchase the plant from Hard Rock Corporation on November 30, 1980. FMM had been seeking a buyer for the plant and pursued the offer from Hard Rock Corporation. The sale was completed February 17, 1981, prior to the issuance of FMM's 1980 financial statements. Additional facts about the sale and the Luckenbach operations follow:

1. The plant incurred an operating loss of $260,000 for 1980.
2. The net assets of the plant on December 31, 1980 were $4,300,000.
3. The plant generated $780,000 of revenues and incurred $840,000 of expenses from January 1 to February 17, 1981.
4. The sales agreement included the following factors:
   a. There is to be a physical inventory to determine missing inventory and other assets. The inventory had not been taken prior to the issuance of the 1980 financial statements, but it is estimated that the inventory will disclose approximately $20,000 of missing assets.
   b. All equipment is to be serviced so it will be operating efficiently. This service has not been performed, but the maintenance foreman estimates the costs to service all the equipment will be $15,000.
5. The Hard Rock Corporation has agreed to pay $3,760,000 for the assets of the Luckenbach plant.

Area 2: In July 1980 the assets, net of related liabilities of Miller Manufacturing Incorporated, a wholly owned subsidiary, were sold. Miller manufactured and marketed various sprayers and components for tractors. The effective date of the sale was June 30, 1980. Additional information on operations and the sale of the subsidiary follows:

	Six Months Ended June 30, 1980	Fiscal Year Ended December 31, 1979
	(Thousands of dollars)	
Sales	$15,430	$13,948
Cost of goods sold	10,467	10,661
Selling & administrative expenses	5,277	4,464
Interest expense	110	91

1. There was a $182,000 loss before taxes on operations that was incurred after April 30, 1980, the date FMM made the decision to dispose of the company.
2. Assets sold (net of liabilities) had a book value of $2,630,000.
3. Sales price of the subsidiary was $1,000,000.
4. Finders fee and other selling expenses were $145,000.
5. FMM is still the primary obligor for trade accounts payable, purchase commitments for imported materials, and lease contracts in the amount of $2,989,000; $2,109,000; and $3,241,000 respectively.

Area 3: During 1980, FMM disposed of some productive assets from one of its manufacturing plants. These assets were disposed of in order to acquire more modern equipment. FMM incurred significant losses on these disposals and FMM management is asserting that the magnitude of these losses would distort income from continuing operations if included therein. Therefore, management is suggesting classification of these losses, in the aggregate, as an extraordinary item.

Area 4: Management decided that a significant advertising expenditure from 1979 has no future benefits beyond 1980. It was initially believed that the advertising campaign would be beneficial through 1981. The expenditure was capitalized in 1979 and one-third of the cost was amortized during 1979 with the remainder to be amortized during 1980 and 1981.

Required:

For each of the four areas listed, describe your proposed treatment of each case with FMM management; justify your comments using promulgated generally accepted accounting principles.

D–23–3 The following four cases involve financial statement items considered to be extraordinary by the Salem Company.

Situation 1: The extraordinary item relates to shutdown expenses the company incurred during a major strike by its operating employees during 1974.

Situation 2: The extraordinary item relates to a loss incurred in the abandonment of outmoded equipment formerly used in the business.

Situation 3: The extraordinary item relates to a loss sustained as a result of damage caused by a tornado to the company's merchandise at its main warehouse in Locust City. This natural disaster was considered to be an unusual and infrequent occurrence for that geographic section of the country.

Situation 4: The extraordinary item relates to a settlement agreement between Salem and the Internal Revenue Service in which Salem was assessed and agreed to pay additional income taxes of $60,000 for 1973 and $340,000 for the years 1969–72.

Required:

Analyze each situation separately; discuss whether the case warrants extraordinary item classification. Discuss how each item will be classified in the financial statements if deemed not to be extraordinary.

(AICPA adapted)

D–23–4 The Chance Company, a holding company, has two operating subsidiaries; one manufactures wheelbarrows and the other manufactures toothbrushes. The wheelbarrow subsidiary has been unprofitable, and in late December 1975, Chance contracted to sell that subsidiary to another company for $60,000. The sale will be effective on April 1, 1976. Chance will continue to operate the wheelbarrow subsidiary during the first three months of 1976, even though those operations are expected to result in a $10,000 loss (before income taxes) during that period.

At December 31, 1975, the carrying amount of Chance's investment in the wheelbarrow subsidiary is $100,000. Both the $40,000 loss on the sale of the investment and the $10,000 operating loss will be deductible on Chance's 1976 income tax return, resulting in an anticipated tax savings of $25,000 at an assumed 50% tax rate.

Required:

Discuss how the gain or loss on disposal of the wheelbarrow subsidiary should be determined and disclosed.

(AICPA adapted)

Exercises

E-23-1 Changes in account balances of the Mustard Company are presented below, except for the change in retained earnings.

Accounts	Increase (Decrease)	Accounts	Increase (Decrease)
Cash	$50,000	Accounts payable	$(15,000)
Accounts receivable	10,000	Bonds payable	45,000
Inventory	57,000	Income tax payable	5,000
Investments	(15,000)	Common stock	75,000
Property, plant, and equipment	(5,000)	Additional paid-in capital	4,000

Required:
Compute the net income for the current year using the changes in the account balances. Assume dividends were paid from retained earnings in an amount of $15,000.

E-23-2 Presented below is information pertaining to the Valentine Company. There were 5,000 shares outstanding of common stock during 1975. Assume that the loss from the tornado is an extraordinary item.

Sales	$100,000
Interest income	5,000
Dividend income	5,000
Purchases	35,000
Transportation	4,000
Loss due to tornado (net of tax)	10,000
Selling expense	20,000
Income tax expense	15,000
General administrative expenses	5,000
Cash dividend declared and paid	2,000
Inventory, January 1, 1975	4,000
Inventory, December 31, 1975	6,000
Accrued rent payable	1,000

Required:
1. Prepare a single-step income statement.
2. Prepare a multiple-step income statement.

E-23-3 The following condensed statement of income of Worth Corporation, a diversified company, is presented for the two years ended December 31, 1977, and 1976:

	1977	1976
Net sales	$5,000,000	$4,800,000
Cost of sales	3,100,000	3,000,000
Gross profit	$1,900,000	$1,800,000
Operating expenses	1,100,000	1,200,000
Operating income	$ 800,000	$ 600,000
Gain on sale of division	450,000	—
Income before income taxes	$1,250,000	$ 600,000
Provision for income taxes	625,000	300,000
Net income	$ 625,000	$ 300,000

On January 1, 1977, Worth entered into an agreement to sell for $1,600,000 the assets and product line of one of its separate operating divisions. The sale was consummated on December 31, 1977, and resulted in a pretax gain on disposition of $450,000. This division's contribution to Worth's reported operating income before income taxes for each year was as follows:

1977 $(320,000) loss

1976 $(250,000) loss

Assume an income tax rate of 50%.

Required:

1. In the preparation of a revised comparative statement of income, Worth should report income from continuing operations (after income taxes) for 1977 and 1976, respectively, in what amount?

2. In the preparation of a revised comparative statement of income, Worth should report under the caption "discontinued operations" for 1977 and 1976, respectively, what amount?

(AICPA adapted)

E–23–4 Tob Corporation purchased certain machinery on January 1, 1973. At the date of acquisition, the machinery had an estimated useful life of 10 years with no salvage. The machinery was being depreciated using the double-declining-balance method for both financial statement reporting and income tax reporting. On January 1, 1978, Tob changed to the straight-line method of depreciation of the machinery for financial statement reporting but not for income tax reporting. Assume that Tob can justify the change.

The accumulated depreciation from January 1, 1973, through December 31, 1977, under the double-declining-balance method was $200,000. If the straight-line method had been used, the accumulated depreciation from January 1, 1973, through December 31, 1977 would have been $140,000.

Required:

Assuming that the income tax rate for the years 1973 through 1978 is 50%, compute the amount shown in the 1978 income statement for the cumulative effect of changing from the double-declining-balance method to the straight-line method.

(AICPA adapted)

E–23–5 A review of the December 31, 1978, financial statements of Rhur Corporation revealed that under the caption "extraordinary losses," Rhur reported a total of $260,000. Further analysis revealed that the $260,000 in losses was comprised of the following items:

    a) Rhur recorded a loss of $50,000 incurred in the abandonment of equipment formerly used in the business.

    b) In an unusual and infrequent occurrence, a loss of $75,000 was sustained as a result of hurricane damage to a warehouse.

    c) In 1978 several factories were shut down during a major strike by employees. Shutdown expenses totaled $120,000.

    d) Uncollectible accounts receivable of $15,000 were written off as uncollectible.

Required:

If you ignore income taxes, what amount of loss should Rhur report as extraordinary on its 1978 statement of income?

(AICPA adapted)

E–23–6 The Park Company is disposing of a segment of its business. At the measurement date the net loss from the disposal is estimated to be $950,000. Included in the $950,000 are severance pay of $100,000 and employee relocation costs of $50,000, both of which are directly associated with the decision to dispose of the segment; also included are estimated net losses from operations from the measurement date to the expected disposal

date of $200,000. Net losses from operations of $150,000 from the beginning of the year to the measurement date are not included in the estimated net loss from the disposal.
Required:
Compute the loss on discontinued operations.

(AICPA adapted)

E-23-7 Glow Company's December 31 year-end financial statements contained the following errors:

	December 31, 1973	December 31, 1974
Ending inventory	$2,000 understated	$1,800 overstated
Depreciation expense	$400 understated	

An insurance premium of $1,500 was prepaid in 1973 covering the years 1973, 1974, and 1975. The entire amount was charged to expense in 1973. In addition, on December 31, 1974, fully depreciated machinery was sold for $3,200 cash, but the sale was not recorded until 1975. There were no other errors during 1973 or 1974 and no corrections have been made for any of the errors. Ignore income tax considerations.
Required:
1. What is the total effect on the errors on 1974 net income?
2. What is the total effect on the errors on December 31, 1974, retained earnings?

E-23-8 During 1980 the Brown Company had earnings before tax of $500,000 and a loss of $50,000 from the early extinguishment of debt (extraordinary item). The depreciation expense was understated in 1975 by $50,000. Retained earnings at January 1, 1980, was $750,000. Dividends on common stock of $100,000 were paid in 1980. There were 100,000 shares of common stock outstanding during 1980. The income tax was 50% in all relevant years presented.
Required:
Prepare a combined statement of income and retained earnings.

E-23-9 Presented below is information from the Turkey Company:

Retained earnings, January 1, 1977	$ 550,000
Cost of goods sold	600,000
Sales	1,550,000
Extraordinary gain	75,000
Loss on discontinued operations	100,000
Selling expenses	125,000
Administrative expenses	60,000
Extraordinary loss	32,000
Cash dividends declared	25,000
Correction of error (depreciation expense)	15,000

The income tax rate applicable to income from continuing operations, loss and gain on extraordinary items, and loss on a disposal of a segment is 50%. The income tax rate applicable to the correction of an error is 40%.
Required:
Prepare a single-step income statement.

Problems

P–23–1 The following information pertains to the Wolf Company's disposition of a segment of their business:

10/1/77	4/1/78
Measurement date	Disposal date

Estimated proceeds from "sale" of segment	$1,000,000
Book value of net assets of segment at 10/1/77	1,400,000
Estimated expenses directly associated with disposal	100,000
Estimated loss from operations of segment, 10/1/77–4/1/78	80,000
Loss from operations of segment, 1/1/77–10/1/77	130,000
Income from continuing operations, before income taxes	800,000
Income tax rate	40%

Required:

Prepare a multistep income statement.

P–23–2 Chip Co. reported a 1983 income from continuing operations of $260,000. On April 1, 1983, the company decided to dispose of its auto parts manufacturing operations. The auto parts operations incurred a $100,000 loss up to April 1. The company decided to continue the auto parts operation on a scaled-down basis until a sale of the operations could be made. In November of 1983 the company signed a purchase agreement with Kerrie Co. Kerrie agreed to purchase the auto parts operations for $700,000. The book value of the related assets was $900,000. Chip Co. incurred an additional operating loss of 90,000 from April 1 to December 31, 1983. The sale is to take place February 1, 1984, and Chip estimates that the operating loss can be held to $8,000 for January, 1984. Chip Company had 100,000 shares of stock outstanding during 1983.

Required:

Prepare a partial 1983 income statement for Chip Co. reflecting proper treatment of the items above. (Ignore income taxes.)

P–23–3 Genie Garments Co. has been manufacturing apparel for approximately 30 years. Several years ago Genie began to manufacture tennis and running shoes. The operations were never as profitable as had been hoped for. In the last year or so, this segment of the business operated at a loss because of the strong competition in this line of business. In 1982 Genie Garment Co. decided to sell its tennis and running shoes operations. The formal decision to dispose of the operations occurred on October 1, 1982, when the company signed a contract to sell. The operations had resulted in a $30,000 loss for the year up to October 1. The actual sale was for cash and took place on March 1, 1983.

The following independent cases refer to Genie Garments Co.

a) The operations were sold for a $200,000 gain, and the results of operations during the phase out period were as follows:

October 1 to December 31—$10,000 loss
January 1 to March 1—$12,000 loss

Assume these amounts could be estimated as of October 1, 1982.

b) The operations were sold for a $100,000 loss, and the results of operations were as presented in Part a) above.

c) The operations were sold for a $150,000 gain, and the results of operations during the phase-out period were as follows: *not recognize until 83*

October 1 to December 31—$10,000 income *on Dec 31 inc. st*
January 1 to March 1—$5,000 income *recognize in 83*

Again, assume these could be estimated on October 1.

d) The operations were sold at a $10,000 loss. The results of operations were the same as in Part c) above. *loss on Dec 31, also 10,000 inc. $5000 in 83*

Required:

For each of the cases above, indicate the amount of gain (loss) or income (loss) that should be recognized in 1982 and 1983. Also indicate how the amounts would be disclosed.

P–23–4 Welton Co. is a small manufacturer of oil well equipment. The business has been growing rapidly as a result of the tremendous increase in drilling activity. The company has expanded into several new areas, most of which have been very successful. One area that was not successful is the Welton Drilling Mud operations—Welton never developed the full technical expertise needed in this area. As a result of the need for funds and technical personnel in other operating areas, the company decided on October 15, 1982, to phase out the drilling mud operations. Instead of selling the operations as a unit, the company decided to sell the machinery to a competitor, and to sell the inventories at reduced prices to former customers.

Operations were phased down until January 15, 1983, when the equipment was sold for $800,000. The book value of the equipment was $1,100,000. In January the company also disposed of its remaining inventory for $150,000; its book value was $175,000. The drilling mud operations earned an income of $34,000 up to October 15; the operations from October 15 to December 31 resulted in a $10,000 loss. No operations, other than disposal of equipment and inventory, took place in January.

During 1982 the company's other operating units generated a profit of $1,400,000. Also during the year, the company wrote off $300,000 of parts inventory because they became obsolete. The company incurred as well an uninsured loss of $180,000 as a result of an explosion in one of its manufacturing buildings. The explosion was caused by a leaking natural gas line. Natural gas is used to heat the buildings. Welton Co. currently has 1,000,000 shares of common stock outstanding.

Required:

Prepare a 1982 partial income statement for Welton Co. starting with income before operating gains and losses. Assume a 30% tax rate applicable to all items.

P–23–5 The following information was extracted from the records of Mead Company. Unless otherwise indicated, the information relates to 1978 events and activities.

a) Retained earnings, Jan. 1, 1978	$450,000
b) Loss from tornado damage (considered to be unusual and infrequent—loss is fully deductible for tax purposes)	80,000
c) Proceeds from settlement of litigation begun in 1976 (proceeds are fully taxable)	100,000
d) Cash dividends declared in 1978	58,400
e) Gain on sale of land (considered to be nonrecurring but not unusual—gain is fully taxable)	15,000

f) On November 1, 1978, Mead entered into a contract to sell one of its divisions (representing all of Mead's operations in that type of activity) for $100,000 cash. The division was transferred to its new owner on December 31, 1978, at which time it had a book value of $180,000.

g) Operating revenues and expenses (excluding income taxes) for 1978 were as follows:

	Applicable to Discontinued Segment		Applicable to Continuing Operations
	1/1/78—10/31/78	11/1/78—12/31/78	
Revenues	$40,000	$10,000	$500,000
Expenses	15,000	16,000	250,000

h) The accountant for Mead failed to record the amortization of goodwill of $13,000 in 1976 and 1977. Thus, the operating expenses of 1976 and 1977 are understated by $13,000 in each year. Since the amortization of goodwill is not deductible for tax purposes, there is no tax effect related to the 1976 and 1977 errors. Since the goodwill should have been fully amortized by the end of 1977, no goodwill amortization is included in the 1978 expenses.

i) Unless otherwise indicated, all revenues and gains are fully taxable, and all expenses and losses are fully deductible for tax purposes. The income tax rate is 40%.

Required:
Prepare a formal income statement (single-step) and a statement of retained earnings.

P-23-6 The PM Corp. (a Lubbock, Texas-based firm) is in the process of preparing income statements on a comparative basis for the calendar years 1979 and 1978. You, as the competent expert, have been asked to help prepare the statement in accordance with promulgated GAAP.

You are given the following additional information:

a) Assume all amounts are material unless otherwise stated.

b) The following amounts relate to the entire enterprise:

	1979	1978
Sales	$5,000,000	$3,000,000
Operating expenses	1,900,000	2,100,000
Loss from hurricane damage	400,000	—
Retained earnings, January 1, as previously reported	7,540,000	7,000,000

c) All amounts are before tax. The effective tax rate for both 1978 and 1979 is 40%.

d) No dividends were paid in either 1978 or 1979.

e) On April 1, 1979, PM Corp. entered into an agreement to dispose of a major line of its business by abandonment. Operations are to cease on February 29, 1980. The following estimates regarding the segment were made on April 1, 1979.

	1/1/78—12/31/78	1/1/79—3/31/79	4/1/79—12/31/79	1/1/80—2/29/80
Sales	$ 10,000	$ 4,000	$15,000	$ 2,000
Operating expenses	100,000	60,000	75,000	27,000

Severance pay to employees	$ 30,000
Book value of net assets on April 1, 1979	170,000

f) PM Corp. also had two changes in accounting principle effective for 1979. In each case the new principle was used in computing 1979 income. PM Corp. changed from accelerated depreciation to straight-line depreciation. The data follow:

	Excess of Accelerated over
Year	Straight-Line Depreciation
1975	$ 20,000
1976	80,000
1977	70,000
1978	50,000
Total at beginning of 1979	$220,000

PM Corp. also changed from LIFO inventory to weighted-average inventory. Data are as follows:

		Cost of Goods Sold Using:	
Year	LIFO	Weighted Average	Difference
1975	$180,000	$130,000	$50,000
1976	90,000	80,000	10,000
1977	70,000	100,000	(30,000)
1978	80,000	60,000	20,000
Total at the beginning of 1979	$420,000	$370,000	$50,000

Required:

Using the above information, prepare a combined statement of income and retained earnings on a comparative basis for 1979 and 1978. Since this is a nonpublic enterprise, you may omit earnings per share data.

P–23–7 Shown below are the financial statements issued by Allen Corporation for its fiscal year ended October 31, 1978:

ALLEN CORPORATION
Statement of Financial Position
October 31, 1978

Assets

Cash	$ 15,000
Accounts receivable, net	150,000
Inventory	120,000
Total current assets	$285,000
Trademark (Note 3)	250,000
Land	125,000
Total assets	$660,000

Liabilities

Accounts payable	$ 80,000
Accrued expenses	20,000
Total current liabilities	$100,000
Deferred income tax payable (Note 4)	80,000
Total liabilities	$180,000

Stockholders' Equity

Common stock, par $1 (Note 5)	$100,000	
Additional paid-in capital	180,000	
Retained earnings	200,000	480,000
Total liabilities and stockholders' equity		$660,000

ALLEN CORPORATION
Earnings Statement
For the Fiscal Year Ended October 31, 1978

Sales		$1,000,000
Cost of goods sold		750,000
Gross margin		$ 250,000
Expenses		
Bad debt expense	$ 7,000	
Insurance	13,000	
Lease expenses (Note 1)	40,000	
Repairs and maintenance	30,000	
Pensions (Note 2)	12,000	
Salaries	60,000	162,000
Earnings before provision for income tax		$ 88,000
Provision for income tax		28,740
Net earnings		$ 59,260
Earnings per common share outstanding		$ 0.5926

ALLEN CORPORATION
Statement of Retained Earnings
For the Fiscal Year Ended October 31, 1978

Retained earnings, November 1, 1977	$150,000
Extraordinary gain, net of income tax	25,000
Net earnings for the fiscal year ended October 31, 1978	59,260
	$234,260
Dividends ($0.3426 per share)	34,260
Retained earnings, October 31, 1978	$200,000

FOOTNOTES

Note 1—Long-term lease

Under the terms of a 5-year noncancelable lease for buildings and equipment, the company is obligated to make annual rental payments of $40,000 in each of the next four fiscal years. At the conclusion of the lease period, the company has the option of purchasing the leased assets for $20,000 (a bargain purchase option) or entering into another five-year lease of the same property at an annual rental of $5,000.

Note 2—Pension plan

Substantially all employees are covered by the company's pension plan. Pension expense is equal to the total of pension benefits paid to retired employees during the year.

Note 3—Trademark

The company's trademark was purchased from Apex Corporation on January 1, 1976, for $250,000.

Note 4—Deferred income tax payable

The entire balance in the deferred income tax payable account arose from tax-exempt municipal bonds that were held during the previous fiscal year giving rise to a difference between taxable income and reported net earnings for the fiscal year ended October 31, 1977. The deferred liability amount was calculated on the basis of expected tax rates in future years.

Note 5—Warrants

On January 1, 1977, one common stock warrant was issued to stockholders of record for each common share owned. An additional share of common stock is to be issued upon exercise of 10 stock warrants and receipt of an amount equal to par value. For the six months ended October 31, 1978, the average market value for the company's common stock was $5 per share, and no warrants had yet been exercised.

Note 6—Contingent liability

On October 31, 1978, the company was contingently liable for product warranties in an amount estimated to aggregate $75,000.

Required:

Review the preceding financial statements and related footnotes. Identify any inclusions or exclusion from them that would be in violation of generally accepted accounting principles, and indicate corrective action to be taken. Do not comment as to format or style. Respond in the following order:

a) Earnings statement.
b) Statement of retained earnings.
c) General.

(AICPA adapted)

P–23–8 The following information was taken from the records of Bear Company. The information relates to 1980 events and activities.

a) Sales, cost of goods sold, and operating expenses (excluding income taxes) for 1980 are as follows:

	Applicable to Division X		Applicable to Other Divisions	Total for Bear Company
	1/1/80— 8/31/80	9/1/80— 12/31/80	1/1/80—12/31/80	
Sales	$50,000	$20,000	$500,000	$570,000
Cost of goods sold	60,000	24,000	260,000	344,000
Operating expenses	20,000	9,000	50,000	79,000

b) On September 1, 1980, Bear Company entered into a contract to sell one of its divisions, Division X (representing all of Bear Company's operations in that type of activity), for $120,000 cash. The division is to be transferred to its new owner on March 1, 1981, until which time it will be operated by Bear Company. Bear estimates that Division X will have a book value of $200,000 on March 1, 1981, and that Division X will result in a $9,000 loss from operations (before income taxes) during the period of Jan. 1, 1981, to March 1, 1981. Bear further estimates that it will incur $18,000 of employee relocation costs directly associated with its sale of Division X.

c) Pretax loss from hurricane damage; considered to be unusual and infrequent. The loss is fully deductible for income tax purposes. $ 35,000

d) Pretax gain on settlement of litigation begun in 1976. The gain is fully taxable.   50,000

e) Pretax loss on sale of land; considered to be an infrequent event for Bear Company but not unusual for the industry in which Bear operates. The loss is fully deductible for income tax purposes.   36,000

f) The accountant for Bear Company discovered in 1980 that he had inadvertently failed to record depreciation of $15,000 in 1979. The error is being corrected this year, including the filing of an amended income tax return for 1979.

g) Cash dividends declared in 1980   38,000

h) Retained earnings, January 1, 1980   500,000

i) During 1980 Bear Company had 10,000 shares of common stock outstanding.

j) Unless otherwise indicated, all revenues and gains are fully taxable, and all expenses and losses are fully deductible for income tax purposes. The income tax rate is 40%.

Required:

Using good form, prepare (a) a single-step income statement and (b) a retained earnings statement for Bear Company for 1980. You may omit any required footnotes; however, any required disclosures of applicable income taxes *must be* disclosed in the body (i.e., on the face) of the income statement.

P–23–9 MR Corp., a nonpublic entity, is in the process of preparing financial statements for the year ended December 31, 1980. Assume that the following data refer to the entire enterprise (assume all items are material):

	For the years ended December 31,	
	1980	*1979*
Sales	$500,000	$600,000
Cost of goods sold	150,000	150,000
Other operating expenses	40,000	20,000
Gain from fire damage	15,000	—
Loss from extinguishment of debt	—	5,000
Loss on sale of assets	6,000	—
Effective tax rate	30%	40%
Retained earnings, January 1 as previously reported	341,000	100,000
Dividends declared	20,000	20,000

On February 29, 1980, MR Corp. committed itself to a formal plan to dispose of a major line of its business by sale. The sale will be consummated on January 31, 1981. Management made the following estimates relative to the segment on February 29, 1980:

	1/1/79— *12/31/79*	*1/1/80—* *2/29/80*	*3/1/80—* *12/31/80*	*1/1/81—* *1/31/81*
Sales	$ 7,000	$1,000	$12,000	$2,000
Operating expenses*	11,000	800	18,000	6,000

*This segment has no cost of goods sold.

Book value of net assets on February 29, 1980	$600,000
Selling price	640,000
Severance pay to employees	10,000

MR Corp. also had the following accounting changes:

a) MR Corp. changed from accelerated to straight-line depreciation on January 1, 1979.

For the year ending December 31	Excess of Accelerated over Straight-Line Depreciation
Prior to 1979	$10,000
1979	7,000
1980	5,000

b) On January 1, 1980, MR Corp. changed from LIFO inventory to FIFO inventory for costing its retail inventory.

For the year ending December 31	Cost of Goods Sold Using	
	LIFO	FIFO
Prior to 1979	$300,000	$200,000
1979	75,000	50,000
1980	100,000	80,000

MR Corp. also discovered that it had made the following errors:

1978 Misrecorded warranty expense. Recorded $10,000 as an asset rather than an expense.

1979 Misrecorded warranty expense. Recorded $5,000 as an asset rather than an expense.

Required:
Based on the information provided above, you are to prepare, *in good form*, a combined statement of income and retained earnings for the years ended December 31, 1979, and 1980 on a comparative basis in accordance with current promulgated GAAP. Do *not* prepare footnotes, just the statement.

P–23–10 The following information was taken from the records of Sherman Company. Unless otherwise indicated, the information relates to 1979 events and activities.

a) Operating revenues and expenses (*excluding* income taxes) for 1979 were as follows:

	Total	Applicable to Discontinued Segment		Applicable to Continuing Operations
		1/1/79— 9/31/79	10/1/79— 12/31/79	
Revenues	$ 40,000	$30,000	$10,000	$360,000
Expenses	220,000	40,000	15,000	165,000

b) On October 1, 1979, Sherman entered into a contract to sell one of its divisions (representing all of Sherman's operations in that type of activity) for $80,000 cash. The division was transferred to its new owner on December 31, 1979, at which time it had a book value of $115,000.

c) Pretax loss on settlement of litigation begun in 1977 (the loss is fully deductible for tax purposes). $ 60,000

d) Pretax loss from hurricane damage (considered to be unusual and infrequent; loss is fully deductible for tax purposes).   45,000

e) Pretax gain on sale of land (considered to be infrequent event for Sherman, but not unusual for the industry in which Sherman operates. The gain is fully taxable at the normal income tax rate).   100,000

f) The accountant for Sherman discovered this year that he had inadvertently failed to record depreciation of $20,000 in 1978. The error is being corrected this year, including the filing of an amended tax return for 1978.

g) Cash dividends declared in 1979.   32,000

h) Retained earnings, January 1, 1979.   600,000

i) During 1979 Sherman had 10,000 shares of common stock outstanding.

j) Unless otherwise indicated, all revenues and gains are fully taxable, and all expenses and losses are fully deductible for income tax purposes. The income tax rate is 50%.

Required:

Using good form, prepare (a) a single-step income statement and (b) a retained earnings statement for Sherman Company for 1979. You may omit any required footnotes; however, any required disclosures of applicable income taxes *must be* disclosed in the body (on the face) of the appropriate financial statement.

24

Balance Sheet Presentations

Accounting in the News

Analysis of financial statements always should include a thorough examination of the footnotes, which provide the special disclosures required by the various accounting rules. Even though there are numerous disclosure requirements, items sometimes are omitted that should be included.

Here's a footnote U.S. Steel Corp. neglected to include in its recently mailed 1981 annual report: As a result of its $6 billion-plus acquisition of Marathon Oil, U.S. Steel also got as part of the bargain a contingent liability of more than $369 million. That's more than one third of the profits U.S. Steel reported last year.

Here's a footnote Du Pont should be including in its latest annual: As a result of its $7.8 billion purchase last year of Conoco, Du Pont inherited a contingent liability of about $315 million. That's more than one fifth of the combined corporations' reported earnings in 1981.

The $315 million contingent liability appeared in Conoco's last quarterly report issued for the second quarter of last year, just before its accounts were consolidated with Du Pont's. Marathon reported its $369 million potential liability in its last annual report. . . .

Du Pont's latest annual, however, shows audited, consolidated financial results of Conoco and Du Pont since the Conoco purchase occurred last summer. But there's not even a mere mention of the potential liability or of any provisions made for it. Why not? "The company decided that no disclosure was necessary, and we fully agreed with that decision," says Harold Shreckengast, a partner with Price Waterhouse. Negotiations with the Department of Energy are continuing, and an agreement, says a spokesman for Du Pont, is close at hand. Du Pont believes that the eventual settlement will "be so minimal as not to be a contingent liability."

Maybe so. But that, after all, is counting your chickens before they hatch. Even if Du Pont settles for substantially less, $315 million contingent liability should not disappear overnight without a word of explanation. That is material.*

*John A. Byrne, "Missing Footnotes," *Forbes*, April 26, 1982, p. 70.

Analyzing financial statements is a very difficult process, and a detailed examination of the footnotes is a necessity.

Throughout this text a great deal of emphasis has been placed on disclosure requirements because the accounting profession has adopted the principle of **full disclosure,** which means that all significant events and financial data that could have a significant effect on decisions should be reported. Therefore, we have emphasized and provided examples of disclosure in each chapter.

As the disclosure requirements have increased both in volume and in complexity, questions have been raised regarding the need for and desirability of these requirements, and attention is being directed at the cost involved in meeting them. For example, when the SEC released *ASR No. 190,* which required that placement cost data for inventories, fixed assets, and so forth be reported by certain large companies, the costs of compliance were estimated at over $100,000,000. The sheer volume of information presented is questioned also. In almost every annual report issued by a publicly owned company, the notes to the financial statements are several pages long and extremely complex. This is necessary because businesses today are complex, and the footnotes to the financial statements are the basic means of communicating the complex events of the business. The footnotes are also the means of presenting information for comparative purposes, such as inventory valuation methods, depreciation methods, and other significant accounting policies employed.

In this chapter we will look first at the information conveyed in the balance sheet and at the general format of its presentation. Second, we will examine the type of information that typically is disclosed in the financial statements and in the footnotes of an annual report under the principle of full disclosure. Third, we will address the requirements of interim reporting. Finally, segment reporting requirements will be illustrated. Both interim and segment reporting are topics that belong in the province of disclosure requirements. They are discussed separately here because of their scope and importance.

The Balance Sheet

An article that appeared in the July 1, 1982, edition of the *Wall Street Journal* indicated that many companies are trying to "clean-up" their balance sheets by exchanging common stock for long-term debt.[1] An investment broker will buy up old, outstanding long-term debt that is selling at a fraction of the face value because the debt was issued some years earlier when interest rates were much lower. The investment broker and the company then will issue common stock to

[1] George Anders, "Corporations Find Help for Balance Sheets: Swap Costly Debt for Low-Yielding Stock," *Wall Street Journal,* June 30, 1982, p. 25.

generate sufficient funds to retire the bonds. The net effect of the transactions is to reduce the company's outstanding debt and to increase the outstanding owners' equity. In addition, the companies are able to recognize a gain on the bond retirement that increases income. However, the stock issue also increases the outstanding shares that will ultimately dilute earnings per share. To understand the motivation of a company involved in a transaction of this type, we must understand the purpose and uses of the balance sheet and the kind of information it conveys.

Purpose and Usefulness of the Balance Sheet

The purpose of the balance sheet is to present the financial position of a company at a particular date. For this reason the balance sheet often is referred to as the **statement of financial position.** The balance sheet sets forth the assets, liabilities, stockholders' equity, and other pertinent information as of a specific date.

The information conveyed in the balance sheet is useful to short- and long-term creditors, and to current and potential owners. The balance sheet information allows evaluation of corporate liquidity, the amount of financial leverage employed, and the composition of the assets. Together with income statment data it also can provide profitability measures.

Analysis of the firm's current assets and current liabilities provides an indication of its short-term liquidity. Analysis of the long-term liabilities in relation to the owners' equity offers a measure of the financial leverage employed by the company and also gives some indication of whether the company may be overextended in debt. Financial leverage refers to the use of debt and preferred stock financing to increase the returns to common shareholders. Analysis of the property, plant, and equipment may give some indication of the need to replace these assets and of the long-run impact this will have on solvency. Potential owners and long-term creditors are concerned with the amount of existing debt and the maturities of that debt. This is one of the reasons a company might want to "clean-up" its balance sheet.

Limitations of the Balance Sheet

The balance sheet is basically a historical cost statement—that is, the assets are recorded at historical cost. Generally accepted accounting principles prescribe the use of historical cost. For many years there has been a great deal of discussion about restating all the assets at current values. There is, however, some disagreement as to which valuation basis should be employed. Proponents of some form of current value argue that restatement to current value will be an improvement over historical cost because it will give a better indication of the company's current worth. Chapter 26 contains a more detailed discussion of current value reporting.

Classifications in the Balance Sheet

The balance sheet accounts are arranged in logical groupings and in order of liquidity to assist the readers in analysis. The major groups are assets, liabilities, and owners' equity.

Assets represent economic resources that have been acquired through a past transaction or event associated with the enterprise and that will provide some future benefit. **Liabilities** are obligations, resulting from past transactions of the enterprise, to transfer economic resources to another entity. **Owners' equity** represents the residual interest in the assets of the owners after all of the liabilities and obligations have been satisfied.

These major groupings usually are subdivided into smaller groups for more informative presentation. Such a presentation is referred to as a **classified balance sheet.** A typical subdivision would be as follows:

Assets:
A. Current assets
B. Long-term investments
C. Property, plant, and equipment
D. Intangible assets
E. Other assets
Liabilities:
A. Current liabilities
B. Long-term liabilities
C. Other liabilities
Owners' Equity:
A. Contributed capital
　　1. Capital stock
　　2. Paid-in capital
B. Earned capital (retained earnings)

The Appendix to this chapter contains the complete financial statements, including the consolidated balance sheet for Ogden Corporation. We will refer to this balance sheet in the discussion that follows.

Current Assets.　**Current assets** include cash and those other assets that reasonably can be expected to be converted to cash or used in operations within one year or one operating cycle. An operating cycle is the normal time it takes for a company to expend cash for raw materials (or inventory), convert the raw material to a finished product, sell the product and collect the receivables, thus starting and ending the cycle with cash. Most companies have normal operating cycles that are less than one year. Current assets usually consist of cash, marketable securities, receivables, inventories, and prepaid items. The current assets of Ogden Corporation (see Appendix) include the items mentioned and show a total of $603,456,000.

Cash includes cash on hand, in checking accounts, and in unrestricted savings accounts. Marketable securities are listed at the lower of cost or market value and include stocks, bonds, or other certificates that are held as temporary investments and that will be converted to cash within one operating cycle. The distinction between long-term investments and marketable securities is basically a matter of management intent. If management intends to hold the securities for a period longer than a year or one operating cycle, the securities should be classified as long-term investments. If the intent is to convert them to cash within the year or operating cycle, they may be classified as current assets. Receivables are stated at their net realizable value, that is, net of the allowance for bad debts.

Any pledged or discounted receivables should be shown in a footnote or paren-thetically. Inventories are those assets held for future sale in the ordinary course of business, or held for use in the production of goods or services for future sale. Inventories may include raw materials, work-in-process, finished goods, and sup-plies. They are listed at the lower of cost or market. Prepaid expenses are listed at cost and include items such as prepaid insurance, taxes, and rent. They gener-ally are not material in amount and are classified as current assets even though they may not strictly meet the definition of a current asset. For example, insur-ance may be prepaid two or three years in advance, and the total amount techni-cally should not be classified as a current asset. Ogden's prepaid expenses are only $10,952,000 out of total current assets of $603,456,000.

As a group, current assets are considered to be the resources that will be used to pay the current liabilities of the company. They are analyzed very care-fully by short-term (and long-term) creditors to be certain that adequate re-sources exist to meet current obligations.

Long-Term Investments. **Long-term investments** are investments that man-agement intends to hold for more than one year and usually include the following:

1. Investments in equity securities (stocks, bonds, or notes) of unaffiliated com-panies.
2. Investments in equity securities (stocks, bonds, or notes) of affiliated uncon-solidated companies.
3. Investments in fixed assets not currently used in operations.
4. Special fund investments, such as sinking funds, pension funds, cash surren-der value of life insurance, and so forth.

The Ogden Corporation's financial statements in the Appendix do not list any long-term investments on the balance sheet. A typical investments section would appear as follows:

Investments	
Investment in A company bonds (cost)	$ 9,800
Investment in B company subsidiary, 1,000 shares	
common stock (equity method)	18,500
Land for future expansion (cost)	2,300
Sinking fund to retire Series 100 bonds payable,	
due 1990 to 1995	20,000
Total long-term investments	$50,600

Property, Plant, and Equipment. The **property, plant, and equipment** section of the balance sheet sometimes is referred to as the **fixed assets** section. The name implies that these assets will continue in existence indefinitely; that is, they continually will be replaced with other long-lived assets. This section includes the tangible assets used in the operation of the business. These tangible assets consist of land, buildings and improvements, machinery and equipment, furniture, tools, natural resources, and capitalized leases. The assets are reported at historical cost and, where appropriate, less the accumulated depreciation. For Ogden Corporation, the total property, plant, and equipment reported is $923,650,000 less accumulated depreciation of $329,897,000 for a net amount of $593,753,000.

Intangible Assets.   **Intangible assets** are long-lived resources that lack physical substance. They include items such as patents, trademarks, copyrights, franchises, and goodwill. Intangible assets are required to be amortized over their useful life, not to exceed 40 years. The initial cost is the cost of acquisition in an arms-length transaction.

Other Assets.   **Other assets** is a section of the balance sheet in which all of the miscellaneous assets are reported; these are assets that do not fit any of the other categories. Some examples would be noncurrent receivables, restricted funds of any sort, and advances to subsidiaries.

Ogden Corporation combined the intangibles and other assets sections. This section was used to report noncurrent receivables, restricted funds, intangibles, and miscellaneous items in the total amount of $142,993,000.

Current Liabilities.   **Current liabilities** are obligations that are expected to be satisfied either through the use of existing current assets or by creation of other current liabilities. Ogden Corporation lists five, different current liability accounts in the total amount of $378,033,000. In general, three types of liabilities should be included as current liabilities:

1. Short-term payables that have arisen from the acquisition of goods and services, that is, accounts payable, wages and salaries payable, taxes payable, and so forth.
2. Collections received in advance for the future delivery of goods or services, that is, prepaid rental income or prepaid subscriptions revenue.
3. Other liabilities that will be liquidated within one year or the current operating cycle; for example, the current portion of long-term debt.

There are some exceptions to the third category above. Some obligations would not be classified as current even though they would be due and payable within one year. These would be obligations that will be refinanced by issuing other long-term obligations or that will be retired from noncurrent assets. These liabilities are not classified as current liabilities because they will not be retired through the use of existing current assets or by creating new current liabilities.

Long-Term Liabilities.   **Long-term liabilities** are those obligations that are not current liabilities. They are usually payable in longer than one year or the current operating cycle. Long-term liabilities include items such as bonds payable, notes payable, deferred income taxes, and the long-term portion of lease payments. Because long-term liabilities are often subject to restrictions by the lenders, a great deal of supplementary disclosure often is required. For example, Ogden Corporation lists long-term debt of $456,352,000 in a single line in the balance sheet. Footnote 5, however (see Exhibit 24-4), provides details about the long-term debt and the restrictions associated with it.

Other Liabilities. The **other liabilities** section is used to report liabilities that cannot be classified as current or long-term liabilities. This section might include deferred liabilities, such as taxes or investment credits. Ogden Corporation reports other liabilities separately from deferred taxes. Other liabilities amounted to $22,709,000, and deferred taxes amounted to $50,810,000. The company's footnotes did not indicate which accounts were included in the other liabilities section.

Contributed Capital. The **owners' equity** section generally is divided into two primary categories: contributed capital and earned capital. **Contributed capital** includes funds invested in the enterprise by owners and funds that may have been contributed to the enterprise. Contributed capital usually is subdivided into capital stock and paid-in capital.

   Capital stock includes amounts invested by common and preferred shareholders. These amounts generally represent the par, or stated, value of the stocks issued. When a stock issue has no par or stated value, the amount represents the total amount received for the shares from the stockholders. The capital stock section should list each type of stock outstanding. The listing should include a description of the features of the issue, such as dividend rate; par or stated value; and the number of shares authorized, issued, and outstanding. Any reacquired shares (treasury stock) must be shown as a reduction in stockholders' equity.

   Paid-in capital consists of amounts there were invested in excess of the par or stated value of the stock issued. The section also includes donated capital arising from transactions, such as when a city gives land to a company to entice it to build a factory in the city. Included as well is additional capital from items such as treasury stock transactions and preferred stock retirements.

Earned Capital. The **earned capital** section, usually referred to as retained earnings, includes capital resulting from reinvestment of the company's prior earnings. A less desirable term, earned surplus, is used also by many companies. Ogden Corporation reported an earned surplus of $398,043,000. Occasionally, retained earnings is broken down into unrestricted and restricted. This means that only the unrestricted portion is available for dividend declaration. Restrictions on retained earnings are often the result of a legal or contractual requirement. The terms of a bond issue, for example, may require the establishment of a sinking fund for retirement of the bonds, and the concurrent restriction of retained earnings.

   Ogden Corporation reports total stockholders' equity of $404,859,000 in its balance sheet. However, footnotes 8 and 9 (see Exhibits 24-7 and 24-8 in the next section) provide additional detailed data about these items.

Other Information Reported. The balance sheet and the other financial statements are not complete by themselves. The notes to the financial statements are an integral part of the information presented to the readers, and they should be used in conjunction with the financial statements. In the next section of this chapter, we will analyze the information disclosed in the financial statements and the accompanying footnotes to those statements for Ogden Corporation.

Disclosure of Financial Information

The financial statements for Ogden Corporation presented in the Appendix are from a recent annual report of the company. The Appendix includes statements of consolidated income and earned surplus, the statements of changes in financial position, and the consolidated balance sheets, all for a three-year period. Ogden is a large company with operations in transportation and shipbuilding, industrial products, services, and food products.

Looking at the income statement, you can see that the income for 1980 was $58,249,000, and that earnings per common share were $4.56 and $3.99, fully diluted. As you will recall from the discussion in previous chapters, there are many alternative methods of accounting that could have been used to arrive at the income numbers. The same is true for the balance sheet—many, different, alternative accounting methods could have been used to arrive at the total asset figure of $1,340,202,000. For example, the inventory valuation method, the depreciation method, and the method of revenue recognition for the shipbuilding operation must be selected to provide meaningful financial statements. Further, if we want to compare Ogden with another company, an intelligent and meaningful comparison can be made only if the accounting policies and methods of the two companies are known and understood. It is vital, therefore, that we have information pertinent to accounting methods and any significant factors that affect the company's performance. This information is found in the notes to the financial statements. Generally, the first footnote sets forth the general accounting policies and methods used by the company. The other footnotes provide detail relative to specific accounts or other pertinent information. We will examine some of the notes accompanying the financial statements of Ogden Corporation.

Note 1. Summary of Significant Accounting Policies

Exhibit 24-1 is an illustration of Note 1 in Ogden's report, the summary of significant accounting policies. This section sets forth the specific accounting methods followed by the company.

Consolidation. The first part of the note indicates that Ogden made two acquisitions, one in 1979 and one in 1978, and accounted for them both as purchases instead of using the pooling of interest method. The note also indicates the amount of Goodwill acquired in each purchase, and the effect on income and earnings per share if the companies had been acquired at the beginning of the year. Finally, it indicates that Ogden sold several companies in 1978 and 1979.

Goodwill. Goodwill acquired after 1970 is being amortized over 40 years, while goodwill acquired before 1970 is not being amortized. Some companies may choose to amortize goodwill over a shorter period than 40 years; for analysis purposes, it is helpful to know the number of years.

Contracts. This portion of Note 1 refers to the revenue recognition method selected for Ogden's long-term construction contracts at its Avondale Shipyard and for its foreign shipping operations. Ogden uses the percentage-of-completion method for recognizing income on the shipbuilding, and the completed voyage method for its shipping line.

Exhibit 24-1
OGDEN CORPORATION AND SUBSIDIARIES
Notes to Financial Statements*

1. Summary of Significant Accounting Policies

Principles of
Consolidation:

The consolidated financial statements include the accounts of Ogden Corporation and its subsidiaries.

In separate transactions accounted for as purchases, Ogden acquired, as of March 31, 1979, the Progresso Foods Division of Imasco Foods Corporation for $34,800,000, and during 1978 acquired Yuba Heat Transfer Corporation and Ramirez & Feraud Chili Co., Inc. for $24,700,000. Goodwill of $2,539,000 and $18,312,000, respectively, arose in connection with the 1979 and 1978 acquisitions.

If Ogden had acquired these companies at January 1, 1978, consolidated sales, net income and earnings per share would have increased by $22,647,000, $673,000, and $.05, respectively, for 1979, and $115,195,000, $4,120,000, and $.32, respectively, for 1978.

During 1979 Ogden sold Better Built Machinery Corporation, Aviation Power Supply, Inc., and International Products Corporation and, in October, 1978, Ogden sold Shaker Savings Association.

Goodwill:

Goodwill acquired subsequent to 1970 is being amortized over 40 years. Goodwill acquired prior to 1970 is not being amortized. Where there has been a loss of value, goodwill is written off. In 1980, $4,358,000 of such goodwill was charged to operations.

Contracts:

Subsidiaries engaged in shipbuilding and the operation of foreign ships record income on the percentage of completion method of accounting and recognize income as the work progresses. Domestic shipping companies record income on the terminated voyage method of accounting and recognize income at the completion of each voyage. Under both methods of accounting, estimated losses are provided in full.

Inventories:

Inventories are recorded principally at the lower of cost (average; actual; retail; first-in, first-out; last-in, first-out) or market.

Exhibit 24-1 (continued)
OGDEN CORPORATION AND SUBSIDIARIES
Notes to Financial Statements*

Property, Plant, and Equipment:	Property, plant, and equipment is stated at cost. Depreciation is provided principally on the straight-line method on the estimated useful lives of the assets for financial reporting. Accelerated depreciation is generally used for Federal income tax purposes.
	Leasehold improvements are generally amortized on the straight-line method over the terms of the leases or the estimated useful lives of the improvements as appropriate.
Retirement Plans:	Ogden and certain subsidiaries have several pension plans covering substantially all salaried employees and certain hourly employees. Ogden's general policy is to fund pension costs accrued. Past service costs are amortized over periods up to 30 years.
Federal and Foreign Income Taxes:	Ogden files a consolidated Federal income tax return which includes all eligible United States subsidiary companies. Foreign subsidiaries are taxed according to regulations existing in the countries in which they do business. In most instances, these foreign subsidiaries pay lower taxes (if any) than they would if they operated in the United States.
	Provision has not been made for U.S. income taxes on distributions which may be received from foreign subsidiaries that would be substantially offset by foreign tax credits, or on undistributed earnings of foreign shipping companies and Domestic International Sales Corporations (DISC), which earnings are considered to be permanently invested in the related operations.
	Investment credits are accounted for on the "flow through" method, and provisions for income taxes have been reduced by the amount of investment credits earned.

*Ogden Corporation Annual Report.

Inventories. Inventories are valued by Ogden at lower of cost or market. Note 3 gives a more detailed description of the inventory valuation and indicates what effect the use of LIFO has on the valuation of certain inventories compared to the average cost method.

Property, Plant, and Equipment. These assets are stated at cost, and depreciation is recorded on the straight-line basis. Accelerated depreciation is used for tax purposes. Straight-line is used also for leasehold improvements.

Retirement Plans. The general company policies for pension and retirement plans are stated here. It indicates that Ogden funds accrued costs and amortizes past service costs over 30 years. Note 7 provides a further explanation of Ogden's retirement plans.

Federal and Foreign Income Taxes. This portion of the note indicates the composition of the income taxes account. It also indicates that Ogden uses the "flow through" method for investment tax credits. Note 6 provides a detailed analysis of Ogden's taxes.

Note 2. Accounts Receivable

Exhibit 24-2 depicts the accounts receivable on long-term shipbuilding contracts for Ogden.

Notice that Ogden discloses the receivables from the U.S. government separate from the other receivables so that the statement reader will know that a significant amount of the receivables is from one customer. Also notice that Ogden shows amounts recoverable on contracts as a receivable even though they have not been billed. This classification is not the normal practice for long-term construction contracts accounted for using the percentage-of-completion method. The usual practice (as discussed in the Appendix to Chapter 8) is to show these amounts as inventory. The footnote disclosure is sufficient to allow the statement reader to reclassify the proper amount to inventory if s/he feels it is necessary for analysis purposes.

Note 3. Inventories

The inventories, illustrated in Exhibit 24-3, are broken down into finished goods; raw materials, supplies, and products in progress; and scrap metals. This note also indicates the impact on the inventory valuation (and consequently on the cost of goods sold) of using LIFO to value certain inventories instead of current cost.

Notes 4 and 5. Short- and Long-Term Debt

The short- and long-term borrowings are described in Notes 4 and 5 and are reproduced in Exhibit 24-4. Note 4 indicates that Ogden has $96,500,000 in available short-term credit. Note 5 details the long-term debt and also provides other information about the debt, restrictions on net worth, refinancing of some notes, pledging of some properties as collateral, and the amounts of debt maturing over the next five years.

Exhibit 24-2
OGDEN CORPORATION
Notes to Financial Statements

2. Accounts Receivable

The following tabulation (expressed in thousands of dollars) shows the elements of accounts receivable from long-term shipbuilding contracts:

	1980	1979
U.S. Government:		
Amounts billed	$ 8,755	$ 7,642
Recoverable costs and accrued profit on progress completed—not billed	18,061	21,936
Total Government Receivables	26,816	29,578
Commercial Customers:		
Amounts billed	20,868	18,053
Recoverable costs and accrued profit on progress completed—not billed	116,487	68,769
Total Commercial Receivables	137,355	86,822
Total Accounts Receivable	$164,171	$116,400

Recoverable costs and accrued profit on progress completed, not billed, represent work performed on contracts which were not billable to customers at the balance sheet dates under the terms of the respective contracts.

Exhibit 24-3
OGDEN CORPORATION
Notes to Financial Statements

3. Inventories

Inventories (expressed in thousands of dollars) consist of the following:

	1980	1979
Finished goods	$ 99,200	$102,172
Raw materials, supplies and products in progress	84,772	75,286
Scrap metals, etc.	10,144	11,486
Total	$194,116	$188,944

Certain inventories were valued at LIFO. If such inventories were shown at current cost (determined by the average cost method) inventories would have been $5,588,000 and $6,443,000 higher than reported at December 31, 1980 and 1979, respectively.

Exhibit 24-4
OGDEN CORPORATION
Notes to Financial Statements

4. Short-Term Borrowings

Ogden and its subsidiaries maintain accounts with a number of banks which provide lines of short-term credit at the prime borrowing rate. Ogden is not required to maintain compensating balances against these lines of credit; however, Ogden pays a fee of 5% of the average prime rate for the line of credit and an additional 5% of the average prime rate on borrowings on these lines.

At December 31, 1980, Ogden had unused available borrowings under these lines of $96,500,000.

5. Long-Term Debt

Long-term debt (expressed in thousands of dollars) consists of the following:

	1980	*1979*
8.25% notes payable in annual installments of $5,000 to 1986 and $6,000 in 1987 to 1996	$ 85,000	$ 90,000
8.5% notes payable in semi-annual installments in 1982 to 1985	31,625	36,000
Mortgage notes on vessels:		
5.4% to 9.0% payable in installments to 1989	43,330	53,296
At variable rates above floating prime, payable in varying installments to 1986	36,321	37,694
15.6% interim notes	60,000	
Eurodollar notes at 1% to 1½% over London or Nassau interbank offering rate, payable in varying installments to 1986	55,000	53,000
Notes up to 1% above floating prime, payable in varying installments to 1987	102,928	45,183
8.8% and 9.3% mortgage notes on drydock, payable in semi-annual installments to 2000	14,744	15,520
Industrial Revenue Bonds:		
6.3% due 1994	9,000	9,000
60% to 62% of prime, due 1983 and 1995	10,900	
Capitalized leases	4,628	4,794
Miscellaneous	2,876	4,229
Total	$456,352	$348,716

Exhibit 24-4 (continued)
OGDEN CORPORATION
Notes to Financial Statements

The 8.5% notes of Ogden Corporation were issued under an agreement which contains various restrictions, the most significant being the requirement to maintain "Tangible Net Worth" of $260,000,000. At December 31, 1980, Ogden had approximately $139,000,000 in excess of the required amount.

The interim ship mortgage notes issued under the Title XI program are to be refinanced in 1981 with U.S. Government Agency guaranteed long-term bonds.

Property, plant, and equipment having a net book value of $214,095,000 has been pledged as collateral for several long-term debt issues.

The maturities on the long-term debt (expressed in thousands of dollars) for the five years following December 31, 1980, are as follows:

1981	$34,427
1982	46,808
1983	67,154
1984	62,375
1985	75,706

Note 6. Federal and Foreign Income Taxes

Exhibit 24-5 illustrates Ogden's Note 6, which is related to U.S. and foreign income taxes. By looking at the income statement in the Appendix, you see that the provision for income tax was $9,464,000 in 1980, $32,465,000 in 1979, and $42,141,000 in 1978. Note 6 gives the detail of how these amounts were determined. In 1980, for example, the $9,464,000 was a result of some fairly complex computations, and was not the amount of tax paid, but the amount of tax charged as an expense against income of the current period. The disclosure shows the amount of tax or credits relative to various items. Note that the tax rates (tax as a percent of income) are shown also. The bottom part of the disclosure indicates the source of the $15,844,000 deferred tax.

Note 7. Retirement Plans

Ogden's Note 7 about retirement plans appears in Exhibit 24-6. The data in Note 7 indicates that Ogden computes pension expense on an actuarial basis as opposed to a pay-as-you-go basis. The assets available for benefits exceed the actuarial computed total; thus, the plan is in good condition at this time.

Notes 8, 9, 10. Equity Financing

Notes 8, 9, and 10 of Ogden's report all provide details about the equity in the company. Note 8 (Exhibit 24-7) illustrates the changes in common stock and capital surplus for the years presented. Note 9 provides detail on the two preferred stock issues. The note indicates that the $1.875 preferred stock is convertible, redeemable (callable), and cumulative. The number of shares redeemed and converted during each year is presented as well. The $2 preferred stock also is convertible and redeemable and has cumulative dividends. Note 10 sets forth the provisions relating to the 5% convertible debentures. Both of these notes are presented in Exhibit 24-8. The reader of the financial statements is interested in knowing the potential dilution of the common stockholder's equity if all of the convertible securities are traded-in.

Notes 11 and 12. Interest Capitalized and Foreign Exchange

Notes 11 and 12 are illustrated in Exhibit 24-9. Note 11 indicates the amount of interest incurred during construction that was capitalized as a cost of the asset. The net foreign exchange gains and losses for the year, which were included in income, are presented in Note 12.

Other Footnotes

In addition to these 12 notes, Ogden also presented information about the number of shares used to compute earnings per share, information about business segments (which will be discussed in detail in a later section of this chapter), a note on contingent liabilities (which Ogden believed would not have a material effect on its financial position), and supplementary information on changing prices. The purpose of all of these notes is to allow the user to make intelligent and rational decisions. By studying the information contained in the annual report, including all the footnotes to the financial statements, the reader is given the opportunity to compare Ogden's performance with other similar companies. Even if the other companies use different accounting methods and procedures, disclosure of those accounting policies will allow the informed reader to estimate the impact of the policies on the financial statements.

As businesses grow, they become more complex and more involved in different industries through diversification. Because businesses have become so diverse, the accounting profession believes that it would be useful for companies to disclose information about their various lines of business. This has come to be known as segment reporting and will be discussed in the next section.

Segment Reporting

Many businesses are engaged in operations in more than a single industry. They have diversified for several reasons: attractive investment opportunities, reduction of the effects of seasonality in a business, counterbalancing the cyclical nature of a business, or other similar reasons. Investors trying to make intelligent investment decisions are faced with the task of trying to compare companies that had major positions in different industries. Until recently, no significant information was being provided for the different lines of business or segments of the business operation. Investors were given only aggregate data for the whole company in the form of consolidated financial statements.

Exhibit 24-5
OGDEN CORPORATION
Notes to Financial Statements

6. Federal and Foreign Income Taxes

The provision (credit) for Federal and foreign income taxes (expressed in thousands of dollars) was as follows:

	1980	1979	1978
Current	$ (6,380)	$63,805	$ 6,866
Deferred	15,844	(31,340)	35,275
Total	$ 9,464	$32,465	$42,141

The provision for income taxes (expressed in thousands of dollars) varied from the Federal statutory income tax rate due to the following:

	1980		1979		1978	
	Amount of Tax	Percent of Income Before Taxes	Amount of Tax	Percent of Income Before Taxes	Amount of Tax	Percent of Income Before Taxes
Taxes at statutory rate	$31,147	46.0%	$41,384	46.0%	$46,302	48.0%
Investment tax credit	(10,784)	(15.9)	(3,220)	(3.6)	(2,677)	(2.8)
Earnings of foreign shipping companies	(3,225)	(4.8)	(5,377)	(5.9)	(819)	(.8)

	1980					
Application of capital construction funds	(7,883)	(11.6)			(665)	(.7)
Write-off of goodwill	2,005	3.0				
Other—net	(1,796)	(2.7)	(322)	(.4)		
Federal and foreign income taxes	$ 9,464	14.0%	$32,465	36.1%	$42,141	43.7%

Earnings of foreign shipping companies and Domestic International Sales Corporations (DISC) considered permanently invested amounted to $8,158,000, $12,735,000 and $2,398,000 for 1980, 1979, and 1978, respectively. At December 31, 1980, earned surplus included untaxed undistributed earnings of these subsidiaries amounting to $72,807,000.

Deferred income taxes charge (credit), expressed in thousands of dollars, arising from differences between tax and financial reporting were as follows:

	1980	1979	1978
Long-term contracts	$ 6,303	$(35,237)	$29,339
Depreciation	5,160	4,292	3,623
Accrued expenses, etc.—net	1,036	(3,456)	(80)
Transactions in capital construction			
Funds—net	1,864	1,950	2,340
Other—net	1,481	1,111	53
Total	$15,844	$(31,340)	$(35,275)

Exhibit 24-6
OGDEN CORPORATION
Notes to Financial Statements

---

7. Retirement Plans

Total pension expense for the years 1980, 1979, and 1978 was $10,999,000, $10,232,000 and $10,346,000, respectively.

Accumulated benefits and net assets of the various defined benefit plans of Ogden and its subsidiaries compiled from independent actuarial valuation reports (expressed in thousands of dollars) as of January 1, 1980, are as follows:

Actuarial present value of
accumulated plan benefits:

Vested	$68,785
Non-vested	7,736
Total	$76,521
Net assets available for benefits	$83,082

The assumed rates of return used in determining the actuarial present value of accumulated plan benefits of the various plans ranged from 5% to 8%.

As an example, consider Katy Industries, Inc. Katy is a medium-sized corporation that had total assets in 1979 of $258,674,000 and total sales of $247,388,000.[2] Katy operated in four principal industries: electrical equipment and products, industrial machinery and equipment, oil field and other services, and consumer products. The industrial machinery group was the largest in terms of sales, with consumer products the smallest. In terms of assets, however, the consumer products group was largest. Suppose that you were looking at Katy as a prospective investor. To make an intelligent decision, you would want to know that Katy was engaged in these different industries and would want to know the extent of its involvement. If you were given only the aggregate data, you would be unable to make a reasonable investment decision.

Because of investors' need for segment data, the profession has required that segment data be included in the annual report. A business **segment** is defined as "a component of an enterprise engaged in providing a product or service or a group of related products and services primarily to unaffiliated customers for a profit."[3] The rules for segment reporting are contained in FASB *Statements No. 14, 18, 21, 24,* and *30.*[4] The basic rules for reporting are contained in *State-*

[2] Katy Industries, Inc. Annual Report, p. 31.

[3] "Financial Reporting for Segments of a Business Enterprise," *Statement of Financial Accounting Standards No. 14* (Stamford, Conn.: FASB, 1976), par. 10.

[4] Ibid., and "Financial Reporting for Segments of a Business Enterprise—Interim Financial Statements," *Statement of Financial Accounting Standards No. 18* (Stamford, Conn.: FASB, 1977); "Suspension of the Reporting of Earnings Per Share and Segment Information by Nonpublic Enterprises," *Statement of Financial Accounting Standards No. 21* (Stamford, Conn.: FASB, 1978); "Reporting

---

Exhibit 24-7
OGDEN CORPORATION
Notes to Financial Statements

---

8. Common Stock and Capital Surplus

In December, 1980, Ogden issued to shareholders 4,109,366 shares of common stock in connection with a three for two stock split effected in the form of a 50% stock dividend. All references in the financial statements and notes as to number of shares of common stock, related prices, dividends, and per share amounts have been restated for this stock distribution.

Changes in common stock and capital surplus (expressed in thousands of dollars) are as follows:

	1980	1979	1978
Common stock:			
Balance at beginning of year as originally reported			$ 4,395
Adjustment—3 for 2 stock split			2,197
Balance at beginning of year, as adjusted	$6,253	$6,366	6,592
Exercise of stock options		11	30
Conversion of preferred shares	147	142	75
Conversion of Debentures	74		
Purchase of treasury shares	(343)	(266)	(331)
Balance at end of year	$6,131	$6,253	$6,366
Capital Surplus:			
Balance at beginning of year	$ Nil	$ Nil	$10,988
Exercise of stock options		203	550
Conversion of preferred shares	(23)	(22)	(11)
Conversion of Debentures	4,914		
Purchase of treasury shares	(4,891)	(181)	(11,527)
Balance at end of year	$ Nil	$ Nil	$ Nil

---

ment No. 14, and *Statement No. 18, 21, 24*, and *30* are clarifications or modifications of *Statement No. 14*.

   Statement No. 18 modified *Statement No. 14* by indicating that segment data were not required for interim reports. *Statement No. 21* further modified 14 by indicating that nonpublic companies were not required to disclose segment data. Segment disclosure requirements for companies that were affiliates of other com-

Segment Information in Financial Statements that are Presented in Another Enterprise's Financial Report," *Statements of Financial Accounting Standards No. 24* (Stamford, Conn.: FASB, 1978); "Disclosure of Information About Major Customers," *Statement of Financial Accounting Standards No. 30* (Stamford, Conn.: FASB, 1979).

Exhibit 24-8
OGDEN CORPORATION
Notes to Financial Statements

9. Preferred Stock

The outstanding $1.875 cumulative convertible preferred stock is convertible at any time at the rate of 2.31255 common shares for each preferred share. Ogden may redeem the outstanding shares of preferred stock at $50.75 per share during the year commencing March 29, 1980, which price shall decline by $.25 on March 29 of each year thereafter to $50 per share, plus all accrued dividends. These preferred shares are entitled to receive cumulative annual dividends at the rate of $1.875 per share, plus an amount equal to 75% of the excess, if any, by which the dividend paid or any cash distribution made on the common stock in the preceding calendar quarter exceeded $.1333 per share. In 1980, 1979, and 1978, dividends of $2.50, $2.40, and $2.20, respectively, were paid on these preferred shares. During 1980, 1979, and 1978, Ogden purchased 600, 200, and 26,800 shares, respectively. 127,512, 122,978, and 64,613 shares were converted into 294,758, 284,244, and 149,353 shares of common stock in 1980, 1979, and 1978, respectively.

The outstanding $2 cumulative convertible preferred stock is convertible at any time at the rate of 1.5 common shares for each preferred share. Ogden may redeem the outstanding shares of preferred stock at any time at $51 per share during the year commencing February 28, 1980, which price shall decline by $.25 on February 28 of each year thereafter to $50 per share, plus all accrued dividends. These preferred shares are entitled to receive cumulative annual dividends at the rate of $2 per share.

10. 5% Convertible Subordinated Debentures

The 5% Convertible Subordinated Debentures are convertible into Ogden common stock at the rate of one share for each $33.3333 principal amount of Debentures. The Debentures are redeemable at Ogden's option at 102.6% of principal amount during the year commencing June 1, 1980 and at decreasing prices thereafter. The Indenture provides that on or before May 31 of each year through 1992, Ogden will make a sinking fund payment in an amount sufficient to retire 5% of the aggregate principal amount of the Debentures outstanding at December 31, 1978. During 1980, $4,989,000 face value of Debentures were converted into 149,669 shares of common stock. At December 31, 1980, Ogden had $17,548,000 of these Debentures on hand, which may be used to meet future sinking fund requirements.

Exhibit 24-9
OGDEN CORPORATION
Notes to Financial Statements

---

11. Interest Capitalized

Ogden and its subsidiaries charge to the cost of capital assets, interest incurred during the period of construction. These assets are amortized over their estimated useful lives. For the years ended December 31, 1980, 1979, and 1978, $7,547,000, $1,464,000 and $53,000, respectively, of interest costs were charged to assets during construction.

12. Foreign Exchange

Long-term ship mortgage debts payable in foreign currencies are covered by long-term ship charters collectible in the related foreign currency, or hedged with future exchange contracts, thus eliminating exposure to exchange fluctuations with respect to such debt.

Net exchange gains (losses) of $122,000, $3,285,000, and $(3,983,000) for 1980, 1979, and 1978, respectively, have been included in income.

---

panies that presented consolidated financial statements were eliminated by *Statement No. 24*. *Statement No. 30* required that information about major customers be disclosed—that is, sales to a single customer amounting to 10% or more of total revenues.

Identification of a Reportable Segment

Exhibit 24-10 illustrates the segment data disclosure for Katy Industries. The first information presented identifies four reportable segments for Katy: (1) electrical equipment and products, (2) industrial machinery, equipment, and products, (3) oil field and other services, and (4) consumer products.

Statement No. 14 concludes that a company may identify its industry segments by use of the federal Standard Industrial Classification scheme, by the nature of the product, or by the market served. If the industry segment is of significant size and importance, it will be considered a reportable segment, and information about it will be disclosed in accordance with *Statement No. 14*. An industry segment is a **reportable segment** if it meets *any one* of the following criteria:

1. Its revenues are 10% or more of the combined revenue of all segments of the business entity.
2. The absolute amount of its operating profit or loss is 10% or more of either of the following:
   (a) The combined operating profit of all segments of the entity that had a profit.
   (b) The combined operating loss of all industry segments of the entity that had a loss.

Exhibit 24-10
KATY Industries, Inc.
Industry Segments and Geographic Information

13. Industry Segments and Geographic Information:

The Company operates principally in four industries: Electrical Equipment and Products; Industrial Machinery, Equipment and Products; Oil Field and Other Services; and Consumer Products.

Electrical Equipment And Products—Katy Industries, Inc. manufactures and sells testing and measuring instruments for the electrical and electronic markets and various types of transformers.

Industrial Machinery, Equipment And Products—Katy Industries, Inc. manufactures and sells production machinery for the sugar, shoemaking, chemical, food and packaging industries and components and supplies such as bearings, pumps, springs, abrasive components, and metal cutting and forming tools and equipment.

Oil Field And Other Services—Katy Industries, Inc. provides oil production field services, manufactures and repairs gas engine parts to serve petroleum industry requirements, and pressure treats wood derivatives to preserve them against decay and insect damage.

Consumer Products—Katy Industries, Inc. is engaged in the harvesting and sale of shrimp; the processing and sale of cheese; assembling of watches and jewelry; and the manufacture and sale of sewage lift stations and treatment plants, recreational vehicle trailers, leathers and leather products.

Total revenue by industry includes only sales to unaffiliated customers as reported in the Company's consolidated statement of income. Sales between individual subsidiaries occur on an intrasegment basis only.

Operating income by business segment is before taxes on income, minority interest, and equity in net income of unconsolidated affiliates. The following income and expense items are not specifically identified with any of the reporting business segments: interest expense, general corporate expenses, net and other income/deductions, net.

Export sales of products, primarily to Central and South America, Western Europe and Canada, were $17,300,000 and $12,479,000 in 1979 and 1978.

Operating results by industry segment for 1979 and 1978 follow:

3. The identifiable assets are 10% or more of the identifiable assets of all the segments of the entity.[5]

The four reportable segments for Katy Industries in Exhibit 24-10 meet at least one of the three criteria listed above. The first criterion (10% or more of total sales) was met by each of the segments. The total sales for 1979 were

[5] "Segments of a Business Enterprise," par. 15.

Exhibit 24-10 (continued)
KATY Industries, Inc.
Industry Segments and Geographic Information

	1979		1978	
	Net sales	*Operating income*	*Net sales*	*Operating income*
	(Thousands of dollars)			
Industry segments:				
Electrical Equipment and Products	$ 56,296	$ 2,645	$ 60,269	$ 4,170
Industrial Machinery, Equipment and Products	100,457	13,999	70,606	7,819
Oil Field and Other Services	24,895	1,320	22,244	2,928
Consumer Products	65,740	10,169	36,754	4,698
	$247,388	28,133	$189,873	19,615
Other income (expense), net		(3,167)		(389)
Interest expense		(7,549)		(5,035)
Corporate expenses, net		(4,166)		(2,832)
		$13,251		$11,359

Other information by industry segment follows:

	Assets	*Depreciation*	*Capital expenditures*
	(Thousands of dollars)		
At December 31, 1979			
Industry segments:			
Electrical Equipment and Products	$ 35,476	$ 829	$ 851
Industrial Machinery, Equipment and Products	76,231	3,049	3,750

Exhibit 24-10 (continued)
KATY Industries, Inc.
Industry Segments and Geographic Information

Oil Field and Other Services	16,306	884	2,051
Consumer Products	87,633	2,048	6,947
Total	215,646	6,810	13,599
Corporate	43,028(1)	47	61
Consolidated	$258,674	$6,857	$13,660

At December 31, 1978
Industry segments:

Electrical Equipment and Products	$ 33,593	$ 811	$ 875
Industrial Machinery, Equipment and Products	58,536	2,673	2,853
Oil Field and Other Services	16,780	660	1,585
Consumer Products	43,509	1,745	3,134
Total	152,418	5,889	8,447
Corporate	31,400(1)	214	90
Consolidated	$183,818	$6,103	$ 8,537

(1) Corporate assets are principally investments in non-consolidated subsidiaries, cash and marketable securities.

The Company operates businesses both in the United States and in foreign countries. The operations for 1979 and 1978 of businesses within major geographic areas are summarized as follows:

	United States	Central and South America	Other	Consolidated
		(Thousands of dollars) 1979		
Sales to unaffiliated customers	$182,207	$32,619	$32,562	$247,388
Operating profit	$ 11,726	$13,655	$ 2,752	$ 28,133

Exhibit 24-10 (continued)
KATY Industries, Inc.
Industry Segments and Geographic Information

Other income (expense), net				(3,167)
Interest expense				(7,549)
Corporate expenses, net				(4,166)
				$ 13,251
Identifiable assets	$153,097	$35,649	$26,900	$215,646
Corporate assets				43,028
				$258,674

	United States	Central and South America	Other	Consolidated
		(Thousands of dollars) 1978		
Sales to unaffiliated customers	$151,549	$20,136	$18,188	$189,873
Operating profit	$ 13,719	$ 5,376	$ 520	$ 19,615
Other income (expense), net				(389)
Interest expense				(5,035)
Corporate expenses, net				(2,832)
				$ 11,359
Identifiable assets	$ 97,043	$28,744	$26,631	$152,418
Corporate assets				31,400
				$183,818

Net sales for each geographic area include sales of products produced in that area to unaffiliated customers, as reported in the Company's consolidated statement of earnings. Interarea sales are not significant. Operating profit is defined consistent with that of industry segments.

*Source: Katy Industries, Inc. Annual Report.

$247,388,000, and the segment proportions were as follows (dollar amounts are in thousands of dollars):

$$\text{Electrical equipment:} \quad \frac{\$56,296}{\$247,388} = 22.8\%$$

$$\text{Industrial machinery:} \quad \frac{\$100,457}{\$247,388} = 40.6\%$$

$$\text{Oil field:} \quad \frac{\$24,895}{\$247,388} = 10.1\%$$

$$\text{Consumer products:} \quad \frac{\$65,740}{\$247,388} = 26.5\%$$

The second criterion, that the operating profit or loss of the segment be 10% or more of the total operating profit, was met by only two of Katy's segments—the industrial machinery, equipment, and products segment, and the consumer products segment. The total operating profit reported for 1979 was $28,113,000, and the segment proportions were as follows (dollar amounts are in thousands):

$$\text{Electrical equipment:} \quad \frac{\$2,645}{\$28,133} = 9.4\%$$

$$\text{Industrial machinery:} \quad \frac{\$13,999}{\$28,133} = 49.8\%$$

$$\text{Oil field:} \quad \frac{\$1,320}{\$28,133} = 4.7\%$$

$$\text{Consumer products:} \quad \frac{\$10,169}{\$28,133} = 36.1\%$$

The third criterion in the determination of a reportable segment was that the identifiable assets of the segment be 10% or more of the total assets of all the segments. The total assets of the four segments for Katy are $215,646,000. All the segments of Katy except the oil field segment meet this criterion (dollar amounts are in thousands):

$$\text{Electrical equipment:} \quad \frac{\$35,476}{\$215,646} = 16.5\%$$

$$\text{Industrial machinery:} \quad \frac{\$76,231}{\$215,646} = 35.4\%$$

$$\text{Oil field:} \quad \frac{\$16,306}{\$215,646} = 7.6\%$$

$$\text{Consumer products:} \quad \frac{\$87,633}{\$215,646} = 40.6\%$$

Of the four segments reported by Katy Industries, the smallest group is the oil field and other services. This group meets only one of the criteria (sales) to be reported as a segment, while each of the others meets at least two of the criteria.

Disclosure

The disclosure provisions of *Statement No. 14* require the following information for each reportable segment of the company and in the aggregate for the remaining industry segments:

1. Revenues. Sales to outsiders or other segments. Intersegment sales are to be based on internal transfer prices but exclude common or joint costs.
2. Industry segment's operating profit or loss. Operating profit or loss is defined as revenue minus operating expenses. Operating expenses are the direct costs traceable to the revenues plus allocated costs that are assigned on a reasonable basis. Excluded are costs such as general corporate expenses, interest expense unless the segment's principal operation is financial, income taxes, gains or losses on discontinued operations, extraordinary items, minority interests, and cumulative effects of accounting principle changes.
3. Identifiable assets. The identifiable assets are the tangible and intangible assets used by the segment, or the allocated portion of the assets used jointly.[6]

FASB #14

The data for Katy Industries in Exhibit 24-10 provide illustrations of these three disclosure items. Katy discloses the sales of each of the four segments, their operating profits, and their identifiable assets. This same information is provided for major geographic areas. Katy reports three major geographic regions: the United States, Central and South America, and other.

In addition to the primary disclosures above, the FASB also indicated that the following other related disclosures should be set forth for each segment:

1. Aggregate amount of depreciation, depletion, and amortization.
2. Capital expenditures.
3. Net income from an investment in the net assets of unconsolidated subsidiaries and other equity method investees whose operations are integrated vertically with the operations of that segment.
4. Effect on operating profit of a change in accounting principle in the segment.[7]

Evaluation

The purpose of segment reporting is to provide users of financial statements with more detailed information about a company's operations. Although segment reporting has achieved the objective of dissemination of more detailed information, there are still some unresolved issues. For example, intersegment sales are based on internal transfer prices (see disclosure requirement no. 1. above). Transfer prices, however, can be many different numbers, including cost, cost plus a fixed percentage markup, market price, or some other figure used by the segment. Other problems involve allocation of costs and identification of assets. Cost allocation can be very difficult when there is no direct relationship between the cost and the segment or manufacturing process. Furthermore, common costs for many

[6] Ibid., pars. 23–26.
[7] Ibid., par. 27.

companies can be very significant as a percentage of sales. If you refer again to Katy Industries, for 1979 the common costs were 6.02% of total sales:

$$\frac{\$3,167 + \$7,549 + \$4,166}{\$247,388} = 6.02\%$$

Net income, however, was only 5.36% of sales:

$$\frac{\$13,251}{\$247,388} = 5.36\%$$

Another problem occurs with assets when a particular asset may be shared by several segments. This takes place when two or more operating processes are housed in the same buildings and share not only the facility, but machinery and equipment as well.

Overall, the segment information now provided in financial statements seems to be beneficial to users. A good deal of flexibility in defining segments is allowed to the reporting corporations, and the information appears to be well-received.

Interim Reporting

Throughout this text the emphasis of the discussion has been on annual reporting requirements. Annual data are provided to investors in the annual report and in the 10-K report filed with the SEC. Annual data are not, however, always useful to investors because the data are not as current and timely as they could be. To make the financial information as current as possible and to provide investors with that information on a timely basis, interim reports are issued. **Interim reports,** which are usually quarterly, provide information during the period between the issuance of annual reports.

Presentation of interim reports creates some additional problems. *The major issue is whether each interim period should be viewed as a separate, discrete time period that stands by itself, or whether it should be treated as an integral part of an annual period.* If the interim period were viewed as a separate or discrete time period, the results presented could be much different than if it were treated as an integral part of an annual period. Suppose, for example, that a company is engaged in a highly seasonal business such as a toy manufacturer. In the first quarter after the Christmas season, the revenues may be extremely low so that operating income is also very low. This is in contrast to the third and fourth quarters when the company is shipping and selling to retailers anticipating the Christmas buying season. Should the toy manufacturer use the lower tax rate in the first quarter to calculate income tax expense or a higher rate that would reflect the rate necessary for the annual period income? If the interim period were viewed as a discrete, independent period, the company would use the lower rate. If it were viewed as an integral part of an annual period, the company would use a higher annual rate.

Three official pronouncements related to interim reporting requirements have been issued: APB *Opinion No. 28*, FASB *Statement No. 3*, and FASB

Interpretation No. 18. Opinion No. 28 sets forth the general rules and requirements for interim reporting; FASB *Statement No. 3* provides interpretations and special rules for cumulative effect changes; and FASB *Interpretation No. 18* is concerned with the special rules for income tax provisions in interim reporting. All three pronouncements took the position that interim reports should be viewed as integral parts of annual periods and not as discrete time periods. The generally accepted accounting principles relating to annual accounting periods are to be followed in interim reporting periods with only limited exceptions.

Requirements of APB Opinion No. 28

Opinion No. 28 outlines the general rules and guidelines for interim reporting.[8] The general thrust of the pronouncement was to narrow the alternatives and to make interim reporting more uniform. With only a few exceptions, the same accounting principles used for annual reporting should be used for interim reporting. Some of the specific provisions of *Opinion No. 28* will be explained in the following paragraphs.

Revenue Recognition. The Opinion provides that recognition of revenue should be on the same basis in the interim report as is used for the annual report.[9] For example, if the company uses the installment method for certain sales transactions on an annual basis, it also should use the installment method on an interim basis. The purpose of this provision is to provide consistency between the interim periods and the annual period.

Seasonality and Period Costs. *Opinion No. 28* requires businesses that have significant seasonal fluctuations to disclose the seasonal nature of their business, and that the interim period should be treated as an integral part of the annual period.[10] Seasonality creates an accounting problem of matching costs and revenues if costs are incurred evenly throughout the year. During an interim period of heavy sales, large profit would be shown, while in a period of slow sales, large losses would be shown. The major factor contributing to the problem is the fixed cost.

Fixed manufacturing costs usually are applied to production at a predetermined rate based on either the expected activity for the year or the expected activity for several years. Therefore, the fixed manufacturing costs normally do not contribute to the seasonality problem. However, fixed operating costs (e.g., selling, general, administrative, and others) generally are treated as period costs and are expensed as incurred; these are the costs that contribute to the seasonality problem.

By treating these costs as period costs and expensing them as incurred, a seasonal business often will show large, fixed operation expenses in periods with relatively low sales activity. Conversely, the business also may have low fixed

---

[8]"Interim Financial Reporting," *Opinions of the Accounting Principles Board No. 28* (New York: AICPA, 1973).

[9]Ibid., par. 11.

[10]Ibid., par. 18.

operating expenses in periods with relatively high sales volume. Even if the fixed costs are incurred evenly throughout the year, individual quarters can show large variations in income. For example, examine the following illustration:

	1st Qtr.	2nd Qtr.	3rd Qtr.	4th Qtr.	Year
Sales	$100,000	$120,000	$150,000	$230,000	$600,000
Cost of sales (40%)	(40,000)	(48,000)	(60,000)	(92,000)	(240,000)
Gross profit	$ 60,000	$ 72,000	$ 90,000	$138,000	$360,000
Variable operating expense (30%)	(30,000)	(36,000)	(45,000)	(69,000)	(180,000)
Fixed operating expense (actual)	(40,000)	(40,000)	(40,000)	(40,000)	(160,000)
Income (loss)	($10,000)	($ 4,000)	$ 5,000	$ 29,000	$20,000

This example illustrates the seasonality problem when the fixed operating costs are incurred uniformly, but sales are not. The first three quarters indicate losses or a small income, while the fourth quarter shows a large income. If this company used the same information but allocated the fixed operating expense proportionately to sales instead of evenly, the following results would occur:

	1st Qtr.	2nd Qtr.	3rd Qtr.	4th Qtr.	Year
Sales	$100,000	$120,000	$150,000	$230,000	$600,000
Cost of sales (40%)	(40,000)	(48,000)	(60,000)	(92,000)	(240,000)
Gross profit	$ 60,000	$ 72,000	$ 90,000	$138,000	$360,000
Variable operating expense (30%)	(30,000)	(36,000)	(45,000)	(69,000)	(100,000)
Fixed operating exp. $160,000 ×: $\frac{100}{600}, \frac{120}{600}, \frac{150}{600}, \frac{230}{600}$	(26,667)	(32,000)	(40,000)	(61,333)	(160,000)
	$ 3,333	$ 4,000	$ 5,000	$ 7,667	$ 20,000

As illustrated above, allocation of the $160,000 fixed operating expenses based on sales gives a better indication of the annual results at an interim period. The example clearly shows the difference between viewing the interim statement as part of a discrete time period and viewing it as an integral part of the whole year. *Opinion No. 28* also recommends disclosing the seasonal nature of the business, and supplementing the quarterly data with twelve-month data through the end of the current period.[11]

Product Costs and Expenses. *Opinion No. 28* provides that **product costs,** those costs that can be associated directly with production or services provided, should be matched with or allocated to revenues generated in the interim period. Further, during the interim periods companies should use the same inventory pricing methods as used for the annual period. The Opinion allows *departure from these general rules in the following circumstances:*

1. Companies that use the gross profit method or other methods to estimate inventories in lieu of a physical inventory at an interim date should disclose the method used. The company also must disclose any significant adjustments made to reconcile with the annual physical inventory.
2. For companies that use the LIFO method, if a base period LIFO inventory layer is liquidated temporarily at an interim date and is expected to be replaced by the end of the accounting period, the replacement cost of the layer should be used to determine the cost of goods sold.
3. Permanent losses of inventory values that result in lower of cost or market write-downs should be included in the interim period in which they occur. Gains in subsequent periods should be recognized only to the extent of the loss recognized in previous interim periods. Temporary declines should be ignored.
4. Companies using standard cost systems as their product costing system should report and dispose of the variances in the same manner as in annual procedures. An exception to this is made for variances that are expected to be absorbed by the end of the annual period—for example, volume variances in seasonal businesses.[12]

Other Costs and Expenses. All costs and expenses other than product costs should be charged or allocated to revenues to allow a fair presentation for income and financial statements in interim periods. The following is a summary of the procedures set forth in *Opinion No. 28:*

1. The general rule is that costs and expenses that benefit more than one period should be allocated to the affected periods using the same methods as in annual reporting.
2. Unusual and infrequent (but not "extraordinary") transactions should be reported in the interim period in which they occur.
3. Extraordinary items and disposals of business segments should be disclosed separately and recognized in the period in which they occur.
4. All pertinent information relative to accounting changes, contingencies, seasonal results, purchase or pooling transactions, and so forth, should be disclosed to provide a proper understanding of interim statements.

[11] Ibid., par. 18.

[12] Ibid., par. 14.

5. Costs and expenses should not be assigned arbitrarily. Estimates should be reasonable and should be based on all available information applied consistently from period to period.

Again, the general thrust of the above five rules is that the interim period be viewed as an integral part of the annual period. Thus, the same method of cost allocation used on an annual basis is required for interim reporting, while unusual transactions should be reported in the period in which they occur.

Disclosure Requirements of Opinion No. 28. *Opinion No. 28* requires disclosure of the following items on an interim basis:

1. Sales, provisions for income taxes, extraordinary items, cumulative effect of accounting principle changes, and net income.
2. Primary and fully diluted EPS for each period presented.
3. Seasonal revenues, costs, and expenses.
4. Significant changes in estimates or provisions for income taxes.
5. Disposal of a segment of a business and extraordinary, unusual, or infrequently occurring items.
6. Contingent items.
7. Changes in accounting principles of estimates.
8. Significant changes in financial position.[13]

Requirements of FASB Statement No. 3

FASB *Statement No. 3* addresses the reporting of accounting principle changes during interim periods. The Statement requires that cumulative effect changes be reflected in the income of the first interim period regardless of when the change is made.

1. For cumulative effect changes made during the first interim period, the cumulative effect of the change in beginning retained earnings should be included in the income of the first interim period. Subsequent interim periods should use the new principle.
2. For cumulative effect changes made in interim periods other than the first interim period, the cumulative effect at the beginning of the year should be computed and the first interim period restated. Subsequent periods would follow the new principle but would not reflect a cumulative effect adjustment.
3. Disclosure of cumulative effect changes in interim reports should include the nature and the justification of the change in the interim period of change. Disclosure also should include the effect of the change on income from operations, on net income in the period of the change, and on the related per share amounts.[14]

---

[13] Ibid., par. 30.

[14] "Reporting Accounting Changes in Interim Financial Statements," *Statement of the Financial Accounting Standards Board No. 3* (Stamford, Conn.: FASB, 1974), pars. 9–11.

Requirements of FASB Interpretation No. 18

FASB *Interpretation No. 18* is concerned with income tax provisions during interim periods. It was issued because not all companies were following the recommendations of *Opinion No. 28*, which suggested that companies use the estimated annual rate for the interim period. *Interpretation No. 18* requires that this rate be used during interim periods.[15] The estimated rate is to be applied to the year-to-date ordinary income at the end of each interim period to determine the year-to-date tax. The amount of tax for the latest interim period would be the tax computed as of the end of the period less the tax accumulated through the beginning of the period. The estimated rate is determined by dividing the total estimated tax liability for the year by the estimated income for the year. The percentage obtained by this calculation then would be applied to the quarterly income. For example, if the estimated annual rate is 40%, and income is as follows:

1st quarter	$100,000
2nd quarter	120,000
3rd quarter	80,000

the tax would be computed as shown below:

	Year-to-Date Income	*Year-to-Date Tax*	*Tax in Current Quarter*
1st Qtr.	$100,000	$ 40,000	$40,000
2nd Qtr.	220,000	88,000	48,000
3rd Qtr.	300,000	120,000	32,000

The income on which the tax is calculated as the "ordinary income," which refers to income or loss before income taxes, excluding extraordinary items, discontinued operations, or cumulative effect changes of accounting principles.

Evaluation

The profession has been and continues to be vitally concerned with the quality of interim reporting. *Opinion No. 28*, FASB *Statement No. 3*, and FASB *Interpretation No. 18* have improved significantly the quality and the consistency of interim reporting. However, not all agree with the currently existing rules, particularly in the area of cost allocation. The premise of the existing rules is that an interim period should be viewed as a portion of the annual period, and some would disagree with this premise. The FASB is continuing its study of the requirements for interim reporting.

---

[15]"Accounting for Income Taxes in Interim Periods," *FASB Interpretation No. 18* (Stamford, Conn., FASB, 1977), par. 9.

Concept Summary

THE BALANCE SHEET AND RELATED DISCLOSURES

BALANCE SHEET CLASSIFICATIONS

Item	Description
Assets	
Current Assets	Cash and noncash assets that will be converted to cash or consumed in operations within an operating cycle
Long-Term Investments	Investments in securities or other assets that are to be held for more than one year
Property, Plants, and Equipment	Tangible long-lived assets that are used in business operations
Intangibles	Intangible long-lived assets that are used in business operations
Other	Assets that do not fit into the classifications above
Liabilities	
Current Liabilities	Those that will be paid within one year or operating cycle, if longer
Long-Term Liabilities	Those that will be paid in longer than one year or operating cycle, if longer than a year
Other Liabilities	Those that do not fit into the other liability classifications
Equity	
Capital Stock	The par or stated value of shares issued and outstanding
Contributed Capital	Sources of capital in excess of par or stated value or from other sources except earnings
Retained Earnings	Prior earnings that have been retained in the business

SEGMENT REPORTING

Characteristics of Reportable Segment	Required Disclosures
Revenues are 10% or more of the total of all segment revenues.	Segment sales
Absolute amount of segment profit or loss is 10% or more of either 1. Combined profit of all segments having a profit. 2. Combined loss of all segments having a loss.	Segment operating profit or loss
Identifiable assets are 10% or more of the total of all segments.	Segment identifiable assets

INTERIM REPORTS

Description	Accounting Treatment
Financial statements issued between the time annual reports are issued.	Interim reports are viewed as an integral part of the annual period. Basically the same principles used in preparation of annual reports are used also for interim reports.

Appendix

OGDEN CORPORATION AND SUBSIDIARIES Financial Statements*

Statements of Consolidated Income
and Earned Surplus

For the years ended December 31,

	1980	1979	1978
Income:			
Net sales	$1,760,274,000	$1,869,249,000	$1,506,999,000
Service revenues	427,062,000	372,159,000	327,616,000
Total net sales and service revenues	2,187,336,000	2,241,408,000	1,834,615,000
Interest income	23,895,000	12,667,000	8,857,000
Other income	7,144,000	19,802,000	11,857,000
Total income	2,218,375,000	2,273,877,000	1,855,329,000
Costs and Expenses:			
Costs of goods sold	1,617,154,000	1,698,853,000	1,360,816,000
Operating expenses	346,890,000	307,238,000	252,090,000
Selling, administrative, and general expenses	134,404,000	124,616,000	100,010,000
Interest expense	43,832,000	37,747,000	34,280,000
Other deductions	8,382,000	15,458,000	11,670,000
Federal and foreign taxes on income	9,464,000	32,465,000	42,141,000
Total costs and expenses	2,160,126,000	2,216,377,000	1,801,007,000
Net income	58,249,000	57,500,000	54,322,000
Earned Surplus, Beginning of Year, as originally reported			309,093,000
Adjustment—3 for 2 stock distribution			(2,198,000)
Earned Surplus, Beginning of Year, as adjusted	372,143,000	343,709,000	306,895,000
Total	430,392,000	401,209,000	361,217,000

Less:

	1980	1979	1978
Cash Dividends:			
$1.875 preferred stock	977,000	1,279,000	1,445,000
$2.00 preferred stock	643,000	643,000	643,000
Common stock—1980, $1.40 per share; 1979, $1.27 per share; 1978, $1.03 per share	17,425,000	16,049,000	13,204,000
Cost of treasury stock in excess of par value	13,304,000	11,095,000	2,216,000
Total	32,349,000	29,066,000	17,508,000
Earned Surplus, End of Year	$ 398,043,000	$ 372,143,000	$ 343,709,000
Earnings Per Common Share	$4.56	$4.39	$4.04
Earnings Per Common Share—Assuming Full Dilution	$3.99	$3.79	$3.47

See Notes to Financial Statements.

Statements of Changes in
Consolidated Financial Position

For the years ended December 31,

	1980	1979	1978
Source of Working Capital:			
Operations:			
Net income	$ 58,249,000	$ 57,500,000	$ 54,322,000
Depreciation and amortization	46,201,000	46,008,000	42,697,000
Write off of goodwill	4,358,000		
Increase (decrease) in non-current deferred taxes	(8,073,000)	2,560,000	6,220,000
Other—net	8,531,000	7,896,000	(2,180,000)
Working capital provided from operations	109,266,000	113,964,000	101,059,000
New long-term borrowings	142,797,000	93,329,000	71,280,000
Proceeds from sale of unconsolidated subsidiary		55,962,000	37,137,000
Sales and retirements of property, plant, and equipment	3,666,000		7,191,000
Issuance of common stock on conversion of Debentures	4,989,000		
Other—net	2,280,000	20,963,000	17,482,000
Total	262,998,000	284,218,000	234,149,000

Application of Working Capital:			
Additions to property, plant, and equipment	124,080,000	102,731,000	68,940,000
Reduction in long-term debt	35,161,000	75,674,000	75,398,000
Dividends	19,045,000	17,971,000	15,292,000
Purchase of treasury stock	18,472,000	11,542,000	14,100,000
Deposits to restricted and capital construction funds—net	12,776,000	4,844,000	7,323,000
Increase in goodwill from purchase of subsidiaries		2,539,000	18,312,000
Conversion of Debentures	4,989,000		
Other—net	16,117,000	24,050,000	32,331,000
Total	230,640,000	239,351,000	231,696,000
Increase in Working Capital	$ 32,358,000	$ 44,867,000	$ 2,453,000
Changes in Working Capital:			
Increase (decrease) in current assets:			
Cash	$ (14,526,000)	$ (699,000)	$ (7,642,000)
Marketable securities	(6,855,000)	(19,257,000)	46,639,000
Receivables	67,657,000	42,696,000	86,763,000
Inventories	5,172,000	5,630,000	(14,337,000)
Prepaid expenses, etc.	753,000	1,226,000	241,000
Net change in current assets	52,201,000	29,596,000	111,664,000
Increase (decrease) in current liabilities:			
Notes payable—banks	36,000,000	(15,505,000)	16,653,000
Current portion of long-term debt	(388,000)	(8,734,000)	31,105,000
Accounts payable	31,770,000	475,000	43,699,000
Federal and foreign taxes on income	(50,906,000)	8,493,000	17,754,000
Accrued expenses, etc.	3,367,000		
Net change in current liabilities	19,843,000	(15,271,000)	109,211,000
Increase in Working Capital	$ 32,358,000	$ 44,867,000	$ 2,453,000

See Notes to Financial Statements.

Consolidated Balance Sheets

Assets—December 31,

	1980	1979
Current Assets:		
Cash	$ 21,992,000	$ 36,518,000
Marketable securities—at cost, which approximates market	43,154,000	50,009,000
Receivables (less allowances: 1980, $4,827,000 and 1979, $5,139,000)	333,242,000	265,585,000
Inventories	194,116,000	188,944,000
Prepaid expenses, etc.	10,952,000	10,199,000
Total current assets	603,456,000	551,255,000
Property, Plant, and Equipment:		
Land	18,898,000	19,307,000
Buildings and improvements	133,327,000	121,357,000
Machinery and equipment	307,202,000	282,389,000
Vessels	353,039,000	354,322,000
Construction in progress	98,766,000	20,025,000
Capitalized leases	12,418,000	11,928,000
Total	923,650,000	809,328,000
Less accumulated depreciation and amortization	329,897,000	292,262,000
Property, plant and equipment—net	593,753,000	517,066,000
Other Assets:		
Non-current receivables (less allowances: 1980, $1,331,000 and 1979, $1,622,000)	10,502,000	11,730,000
Goodwill and other intangible assets	36,964,000	41,934,000
Restricted and capital construction funds	57,469,000	44,693,000
Miscellaneous	38,058,000	33,240,000
Total other assets	142,993,000	131,597,000
Total	$1,340,202,000	$1,199,918,000

See Notes to Financial Statements.

Liabilities and Shareholders' Equity—December 31,

	1980	1979
Current Liabilities:		
Notes payable—banks	$ 36,000,000	$ 34,815,000
Current portion of long-term debt	34,427,000	170,896,000
Accounts payable	202,666,000	62,519,000
Federal and foreign taxes on income	11,613,000	89,960,000
Accrued expenses, etc.	93,327,000	
Total current liabilities	378,033,000	358,190,000
Long-Term Debt (exclusive of amounts due within one year)	456,352,000	348,716,000
Other Liabilities, etc.	22,709,000	22,492,000
Deferred Taxes	50,810,000	58,883,000
5% Convertible Subordinated Debentures—Due 1993	27,439,000	32,428,000
Shareholders' Equity:		
Serial preferred stock par value $1 per share; authorized, 4,000,000 shares:		
$1.875 cumulative convertible shares; outstanding, 1980, 364,000 shares; 1979, 492,000 shares; aggregate involuntary liquidation value, 1980, $7,330,000	364,000	492,000
$2.00 cumulative convertible shares; outstanding, 1980 and 1979, 321,000 shares; aggregate involuntary liquidation value, $6,427,000	321,000	321,000
Common stock, par value $.50 per share; authorized 20,000,000 shares; outstanding, 1980, 12,262,000 shares; 1979, 12,506,000 shares	6,131,000	6,253,000
Earned surplus	398,043,000	372,143,000
Total shareholders' equity	404,859,000	379,209,000
Total	$1,340,202,000	$1,199,918,000

*Ogden Corporation Annual Report.

Questions

Q–24–1   What does the principle of full disclosure mean?

Q–24–2   What is the purpose of the balance sheet?

Q–24–3   Of what use is the information conveyed in the balance sheet?

Q–24–4   What is the major limitation or problem associated with the balance sheet?

Q–24–5   What are the major groups of accounts on the balance sheet?

Q–24–6   Define assets, liabilities, and owners' equity.

Q–24–7   What are current assets?

Q–24–8   Define an operating cycle.

Q–24–9   Which specific assets usually are included with current assets?

Q–24–10   What is implied by the title "fixed assets" (or "property, plant, and equipment") in the balance sheet?

Q–24–11   What is the distinction between short-term and long-term liabilities?

Q–24–12   What are the disclosure requirements for capital stock?

Q–24–13   Note 6 in Ogden Corporation's annual report (Exhibit 24-5) is related to Ogden's federal and foreign income taxes. What was the journal entry for income tax made by Ogden in 1980? Explain what it means.

Q–24–14   Interim reporting has been the subject of considerable debate. What is the major issue being addressed with repect to interim reporting?

Q–24–15   What are the official pronouncements dealing with interim reporting? What was each concerned with generally?

Q–24–16   What was the overall approach followed in the official pronouncements related to interim reporting?

Q–24–17   APB *Opinion No. 28* addressed the issue of revenue recognition for interim reporting. What was the Board's conclusion?

Q–24–18   Answer the following multiple choice questions related to interim reporting.

a)   The computation of a company's third quarter provision for income taxes should be based upon earnings

(1)   For the quarter at an expected annual effective income tax rate.

(2)   For the quarter at the statutory rate.

(3)   To-date at an expected annual effective income tax rate less prior quarters' provisions.

(4)   To-date at the statutory rate less prior quarters' provisions.

b)   How did the Accounting Principles Board conclude that interim financial reporting should be viewed?

(1)   As a "special" type of reporting that need not follow generally accepted accounting principles.

(2)   As useful only if activity is spread evenly throughout the year so that estimates are unnecessary.

(3)   As reporting for a basic accounting period.

(4)   As reporting for an integral part of an annual period.

c)   Which of the following methods of inventory valuation is allowable at interim dates but not at year-end?

(1)   Weighted average.

(2)   Estimated gross profit rates.

(3)   Retail method.

(4)   Specific identification.

d) Which of the following is an inherent difficulty in determining the results of operations on an interim basis?

(1) Cost of sales reflects only the amount of product expense allocable to revenue recognized as of the interim date.

(2) Depreciation on an interim basis is a partial estimate of the actual annual amount.

(3) Costs expensed in one interim period may benefit other periods.

(4) Revenues from long-term construction contracts accounted for by the percentage-of-completion method are based on annual completion, and interim estimates may be incorrect.

(AICPA adapted)

Q–24–19 Answer the following series of multiple choice questions related to segment reporting.

a) Selected data for a segment of a business enterprise are to be reported separately in accordance with FASB *Statement No. 14* when the revenues of the segment exceed 10% of the

(1) Combined net income of all segments reporting profits.

(2) Total revenues obtained in transactions with outsiders.

(3) Total revenues of all of the enterprise's industry segments.

(4) Total combined revenues of all segments reporting profits.

b) In financial reporting for segments of a business enterprise, the operating profit or loss of a segment should include which of the following?

(1) Federal income taxes.

(2) Interest expense even though the segment's operations are not principally of a financial nature.

(3) Revenue earned at the corporate level.

(4) Common costs allocated on a reasonable basis.

c) The profitability information that should be reported for each reportable segment of a business enterprise consists of which of the following?

(1) An operating profit or loss figure consisting of segment revenues less traceable costs and allocated common costs.

(2) An operating profit or loss figure consisting of segment revenues less traceable costs but not allocated common costs.

(3) An operating profit or loss figure consisting of segment revenues less allocated common costs but not traceable costs.

(4) Segment revenues only.

d) In financial reporting for segments of a business enterprise, the operating profit or loss of a segment should include, among other items, which of the following?

(1) Traceable costs.

(2) Foreign income taxes.

(3) Extraordinary items.

(4) Loss on discontinued operations.

(AICPA adapted)

Discussion Questions and Cases

D–24–1 Assume that you are the owner of a small accounting practice and are in the process of finding and developing new clients. You have been in business for a six-month period, and have been spending a great deal of time making contact with potential clients.

One of the persons whom you have met has spoken with you about plans to open a specialty women's fashion store. You invited her to call you if she desired any assistance.

She called you this morning and said that she had met with a banker and was in the process of arranging a loan with the bank. The banker has asked her to fill out some forms, one of which is a balance sheet. She asked you some specific questions in regard to the balance sheet and asked that you prepare a written response. Her questions were:

a) What are current liabilities?

b) What types of liabilities should be classified as current?

c) What exceptions are there to the classification scheme for current liabilities?

d) What is the essential difference between a marketable security and a long-term investment?

e) What is usually included as an investment on the balance sheet?

D–24–2 Segment reporting has become a very important topic in financial accounting. Proponents of segment reporting have argued that disclosure of segment data is essential to present and potential investors. They argue that segment information is necessary to make rational investment decisions.

Accordingly, the FASB has promulgated rules pertaining to segment reporting. While the FASB statements have provided some guidance for segment reporting, there are still several unresolved issues.

Required:

1. Which of the FASB statements deal with segment reporting and what do they say?

2. What are the disclosure requirements for reportable segments?

3. What are some of the unresolved issues relating to segment reporting?

D–24–3 Interim financial reporting has become an important topic in accounting. There has been considerable discussion as to the proper method of reflecting results of operations at interim dates. Accordingly, the Accounting Principles Board issued an opinion clarifying some aspects of interim financial reporting.

Required:

1. Discuss generally how revenue should be recognized at interim dates. Specifically address how revenue should be recognized for (a) industries subject to large seasonal fluctuations in revenue, and (b) for long-term contracts using the percentage-of-completion method at annual reporting dates.

2. What are the disclosure requirements of Accounting Principles Board *Opinion No. 28* regarding interim reporting?

(AICPA adapted)

D–24–4 The APB and the FASB have issued opinions and statements regarding interim reporting. One of the issues which was particularly troublesome was how product and period costs should be recognized at interim dates. This issue is still subject to a great deal of discussion and controversy. A corollary issue is the treatment of inventory and cost of goods sold at interim dates.

Required:

Discuss generally how product and period costs should be recognized at interim dates. Also discuss how inventory may be afforded special accounting treatment at interim dates.

(AICPA adapted)

D–24–5 Income taxes and the provision for income taxes have been a particularly troublesome issue for interim reporting purposes. One of the major questions was whether the interim period should be viewed as an integral part of the year or as a separate, discrete period. The APB declared that it would be viewed as an integral part of a whole year.

Required:

Discuss how the provision for income taxes is computed and reflected in interim financial statements.

(AICPA adapted)

Exercises

E–24–1 From the following data, prepare the current asset section of the balance sheet.

Cash	$ 1,500
Prepaid insurance	600
Income tax payable	(1,200)
Deferred income tax	(4,500)
Accounts receivable	7,200
Marketable securities	12,500
Buildings	101,000
Accounts payable	(7,100)
Allowance for bad debts	(600)
Inventories	14,500
Prepaid rent	1,200

E–24–2 Find the missing amounts. You are given the following data:

Cash	$2,000
Accounts receivable 5000	50% of inventories
Marketable securities	$2,500
Inventories 10000	50% of total current assets
Prepaid expenses 500	10% of accounts receivable
Total current assets	?
Cash	10% of total current assets

$2000 + 2500 + \frac{1}{3}A + \frac{1}{4}A +$

$\frac{1}{40}A = P$

$4500 \ell \frac{9}{40} A$

$\frac{500}{4500 \times 40} = 20000$
$\frac{}{9\lambda}$

E–24–3 Indicate the proper balance sheet classification for each of the following accounts:
  a) Common stock
  b) Raw materials
  c) Land held for future building
  d) Goodwill
  e) Unearned rental income (six months)
  f) Notes payable (three years)
  g) Accounts receivable
  h) Bond sinking fund
  i) Premium on bonds payable
  j) Retained earnings—restricted
  k) Organization costs
  l) Treasury stock
  m) Stock owned in affiliated company
  n) Note receivable (nine months)
  o) Preferred stock

E–24–4 Alpha Company had the following account balances at the beginning of 1982:

6% preferred stock ($10 par)	$ 50,000
Additional paid-in capital—preferred	150,000
Common stock ($10 par)	200,000
Additional paid-in capital—common	150,000
Deficit	(20,000)

During 1982 Alpha had the following transactions:
  a) Earned net income of $180,000.
  b) Issued 1,000 shares of preferred stock at $15 per share.

c) Purchased 1,000 shares of Alpha Company common stock on the open market at $16 per share.

d) Declared and paid the regular dividend on the preferred stock.

e) Declared a year-end dividend on the common of $2 per share.

Required:

Prepare the stockholders' equity section of Alpha at the end of 1982.

E–24–5 ABC Company has the following:

Checking account at First City Bank	$ 5,400
Savings account at First City Bank	10,000
Certificate of Deposit (90-day), First City Bank	100,000
Petty cash account	1,200
Bond sinking fund account at Fidelity Bank	50,000
Checking account at Fidelity Bank	21,000
Line of credit at Fidelity Bank, of which $35,000 is used and $65,000 is available	100,000

Required:

Determine the correct cash account balance.

E–24–6 The current asset section of Beta Company at December 31, 1982, contains the following:

Cash		$ 18,400
Marketable securities		45,000
Accounts receivable	$80,000	
Less: Allowance for bad debts	(3,200)	76,800
Inventories		180,000
Prepaid expenses		4,500
Total current assets		$314,700

The following errors have been discovered:

a) Marketable securities include $20,000 of common stock of an affiliated company.

b) Cash includes $10,000 of negotiable bonds.

c) The petty cash of $500 was not included.

d) Merchandise of $4,000 out on consignment was neglected.

e) Purchases of $10,000 were not recorded; the merchandise was received and inventoried.

f) The allowance for bad debts should be equal to 6% of receivables.

Required:

1. Prepare the corrected current asset section for Beta Company.

2. Calculate the net effect of the corrections on income; assume that Beta uses a periodic inventory system.

E–24–7 On January 1, 1979, Builder Associates entered into a $1,000,000, long-term, fixed-price contract to construct a factory building for Manufacturing Company. Builder accounts for this contract under the percentage-of-completion method, and estimated costs of completion at the end of each quarter for 1979 were as follows:

Quarter	Estimated Percentage of Completion	Estimated Costs at Completion
1	10%	$750,000
2*	10%	750,000
3	25%	960,000
4*	25%	960,000

*No work performed in the 2nd and 4th quarters.

Required:

What amounts should be reported by Builder as "income on construction contract" in its quarterly income statements based on the information above?

(AICPA adapted)

E–24–8 Bailey Company, a calendar-year corporation, has the following income before income tax provision and estimated effective annual income tax rates for the first three quarters of 1979:

Quarter	Income Before Income Tax Provision	Estimated Effective Annual Tax Rate at End of Quarter
First	$60,000	40%
Second	70,000	40%
Third	40,000	45%

Required:

What amount should be Bailey's income tax provision in its interim income statement for the third quarter?

(AICPA adapted)

E–24–9 In August, 1978, Ella Company spent $150,000 on an advertising campaign for subscriptions to the magazine it sells on getting ready for the skiing season. There are only two issues—one in October and one in November. The magazine is sold only on a subscription basis, and the subscriptions started in October, 1978. If you assume that Ella's fiscal year ends on March 31, 1979, what amount of expense should be included in Ella's quarterly income statement for the three months ended December 31, 1978, as a result of this expenditure?

(AICPA adapted)

E–24–10 Plains, Inc. engages in three lines of business, each of which is considered to be a significant industry segment. Company sales aggregated $1,800,000 in 1980, of which Segment No. 3 contributed 60%. Traceable costs were $600,000 for Segment No. 3 out of a total of $1,200,000 for the company as a whole. In addition, $350,000 of common costs are allocated based on the ratio of a segment's income before common costs to the total income before common costs. What should Plains report as operating profit for Segment No. 3 in 1980?

(AICPA adapted)

E–24–11 On January 1, 1976, Perry, Inc. paid property taxes on its plant for the calendar year 1976 amounting to $40,000. In March, 1976, Perry made its annual major repairs to its machinery amounting to $120,000. These repairs will benefit the entire calendar year's operations. How should these expenses be reflected in Perry's quarterly income statements?

Three Months Ended

	March 31, 1976	June 30, 1976	September 30, 1976	December 31, 1976
a)	$ 22,000	$46,000	$46,000	$46,000
b)	$ 40,000	$40,000	$40,000	$40,000
c)	$ 70,000	$30,000	$30,000	$30,000
d)	$160,000	$0	$0	$0

(AICPA adapted)

E–24–12 The Jonas Company is a diversified company that discloses supplemental financial information relating to industry segments of its business. The following information is available for 1979:

	Sales	Traceable Costs	Allocable Costs
Product A	$400,000	$225,000	
Product B	300,000	240,000	
Product C	200,000	135,000	
	$900,000	$600,000	$150,000

Cost allocations are based on the ratio of a segment's income before allocable costs to total income before allocable costs. What is the operating profit for product B for 1979?

(AICPA adapted)

E–24–13 RX Company has the following results available for the first three quarters of its fiscal year:

Quarter	Income Before Income Tax Provision	Estimated Effective Annual Tax Rate at End of Quarter
First	$ 40,000	30%
Second	100,000	45%
Third	60,000	40%

Required:
What should be the amount provided for income tax by RX in each of the first three quarters?

E–24–14 VCB Company has income before provision for income tax of $100,000 in the first quarter and $30,000 in the second quarter. VCB estimates the effective annual tax rate to be 45% at the end of the first quarter and 30% at the end of the second quarter.
Required:
1. What is the amount that should be provided for income tax in the second quarter?
2. What journal entry would be required?

E–24–15 Gerard Corporation is a decentralized marketing company with a home office in Chicago. Gerard is organized into four regions or quadrants that cover the continental U.S. The regional offices have the following results for 1982:

	Sales	Direct Costs
Northeast	$3,800,000	$2,500,000
Northwest	3,200,000	2,700,000
Southeast	7,500,000	6,000,000
Southwest	5,500,000	4,800,000

In addition to the direct costs, Gerard has incurred a total of $2,500,000 of allocable common costs. In the past, common costs have been allocated based on sales. Management is thinking of trying some other basis for allocating these costs.
Required:
1. Allocate the common costs to the regions based on sales.
2. Allocate the common costs to the regions based on income before allocation.
3. What would be your recommendations to management?

Problems

P–24–1 The December 31, 1982, balance sheet of Zen Company contains the following major sections:
   a) Current assets
   b) Long-term investments

c) Property, plant, and equipment
d) Intangible assets
e) Other assets
f) Current liabilities
g) Long-term liabilities
h) Other liabilities
i) Stockholders' equity

Following is a list of accounts. Indicate in which section each account should be classified. Use the letter k for any contra account.

1. _a_ Cash
2. _b_ Investments in affiliated companies
3. _f_ Accrued taxes payable
4. _g_ Deferred federal income taxes
5. _i_ Additional paid-in capital—preferred stock
6. _i_ Treasury stock
7. _e_ Bond sinking fund
8. _f_ Unearned rent (for six months)
9. _a_ Allowance for bad debts
10. _c_ Land
11. _b_ Land held for plant expansion
12. _i_ Donated capital from plant site
13. _i_ Treasury stock (at cost)
14. _e_ Advances to employees
15. _e_ Note receivable (due in two years)
16. _c_ Furniture and office equipment
17. _a_ Work in process
18. _d_ Organization costs
19. _d_ Patents
20. _g_ Bonds payable

P–24–2 From the following accounts and information prepare a balance sheet for Peterson Co. for the year ended December 31, 1982.

CA – 1
LTI – 2
PPE 3
IA   4
OA   5

Cash	$ 1,500	CA
Patents	15,000	IA
Land	60,000	PPE
Finished goods	44,000	CA
Common stock	200,000	SE
Accounts payable	15,000	CL
Notes payable	5,000	LTL
Marketable securities	4,000	CA
Raw materials	35,000	CA
Investment in Randall Co. stock	40,000	LTI
Prepaid insurance	3,000	CA
Supplies	12,000	CA
Additional paid-in capital—common stock	80,000	SE
Deferred income tax payable	12,000	LTL
Mortgage payable	70,000	LTL .& CL
Allowance for bad debts	2,500	CA
Work in process	21,000	CA
Buildings _–120,000_	250,000	PPE
Retained earnings	?	

Bonds payable	110,000	LTL
Machinery and equipment	~~175,000~~	PPE
Notes receivable (short-term)	~~10,000~~	CA
Accounts receivable	~~45,000~~	CA
Goodwill	~~18,000~~	IA
Copyrights	~~4,000~~	IA

(handwritten: Machinery and equipment −85,000; Accounts receivable (−2500))

There is accumulated depreciation of $120,000 on the buildings and $85,000 on the machinery and equipment. The mortgage payable is due in equal installments from 1983 to 1989. The bonds payable are 12% bonds due in 1991. The common stock is $10 par; there are 40,000 shares authorized; and 20,000 shares issued and outstanding.

P–24–3 The James Company listed the following account balances at January 1, 1982:

Contributed capital	
6% preferred stock, $50 par;	
20,000 shares authorized, 10,000 outstanding	$ 500,000
Common stock, $10 par	
500,000 shares authorized;	
200,000 issued	2,000,000
Paid-in capital—preferred	1,000,000
Paid-in capital—common	4,500,000
Total contributed capital	$ 8,000,000
Retained earnings	2,000,000
Total stockholders' equity	$10,000,000

During 1982 the following transactions took place:
  a) Issued an additional 5,000 shares of preferred stock in March at an issue price of $50 per share.
  b) In July, James issued 50,000 shares of common stock at $50 per share.
  c) Declared a two-for-one stock split of the common stock in November.
  d) Earnings for 1982 were $3,500,000.
  e) Declared and paid the year-end dividends on preferred stock.
  f) Declared and paid a $2 per share dividend on common stock at year-end.
  g) Accepted a $1,000,000 land donation to be used for a future plant site at the end-of-year board of directors meeting.
  h) Appropriated $1,000,000 of retained earnings in conjunction with the land donation.

Required:
Prepare the stockholders' equity section of the balance sheet at December 31, 1982.

P–24–4 Listed below are the balance sheet accounts related to certain parts of the balance sheet for Zee Company:

Inventories	$126,500
Marketable securities	68,700
Property, plant, and equipment (net)	675,000
Cash	180,000
Accounts receivable (net)	190,000
Prepaid expenses	20,000

Additional information is as follows:
  a) Inventories are listed at lower of cost or market using average cost. The inventories include raw materials, $26,750; work-in-process, $64,750; and finished goods, $35,000.

b) The marketable securities have a cost of $74,200.

c) The property, plant, and equipment account includes land of $100,000; buildings, which are 30% depreciated, at a cost of $450,000; and equipment, which is 50% depreciated, at a cost of $520,000. Zee uses straight-line depreciation.

d) The net accounts receivable represent 95% of the total.

Required:

1. Prepare the current asset section and the property, plant, and equipment section of the balance sheet, including any necessary parenthetical notations.

2. Prepare any footnotes necessary to accompany the information above. (Assume this is year-end.)

P–24–5 The Butler Company has prepared the following balance sheet as of December 31, 1982:

Current assets	$100,000	Current liabilities	$100,000
Long-term investment	100,000	Long term liabilities	100,000
Fixed assets	500,000	Stockholders' equity	600,000
Intangible assets (net)	100,000		
	$800,000		$800,000

You discover the following pertinent information:

a) Current assets include cash of $15,000; marketable securities with a cost of $10,000 and market value of $12,000; accounts receivable of $22,000 less the allowance account of $2,000; and inventories at lower of cost or market using LIFO cost of $55,000, including $15,000 in raw materials, $25,000 in work-in-process, and $15,000 in finished goods.

b) The long-term investment represents 2,500 shares of common stock in Johnson Corporation, an affiliate.

c) The fixed assets include land at a cost of $150,000; buildings at a cost of $400,000 less accumulated depreciation of $100,000; and equipment at a cost of $75,000 less accumulated depreciation of $25,000.

d) The current liabilities are all trade accounts payable.

e) The long-term liabilities represent a mortgage payable in 10 annual installments with interest at the rate of 18%, and the first payment due on January 1, 1985.

f) The stockholders' equity represents 10,000 shares of $10 par common stock issued and outstanding; 15,000 shares authorized; $300,000 of additional paid-in capital on the common stock; and $200,000 of retained earnings.

g) The retained earnings include a $50,000 restriction according to the terms of the mortgage bond.

Required:

Prepare a properly classified balance sheet.

P–24–6 In order to properly understand current generally accepted accounting principles with respect to accounting for and reporting upon segments of a business enterprise, as stated by FASB *Statement No. 14*, it is necessary to be familiar with certain unique teminology.

Required:

With respect to segments of a business enterprise, explain the following terms:

a) Industry segment.

b) Revenue.

c) Operating profit and loss.

d) Identifiable assets.

(AICPA adapted)

P–24–7 A central issue in reporting on industry segments of a business enterprise is the determination of which segments are reportable.

Required:

1. What are the tests to determine whether or not an industry segment is reportable?
2. What is the test to determine if enough industry segments have been separately reported upon, and what is the guideline on the maximum number of industry segments to be shown?

(AICPA adapted)

P–24–8 James Nolan, M.D., and Louis Ferrara, M.D., are applying for a $115,000 loan to purchase additional equipment for their medical practice. The bank has requested a personal statement of assets and liabilities as of June 30, 1973, from Dr. and Mrs. Nolan. Pertinent facts about the Nolans follow. Unless stated otherwise, all facts are presented as of June 30, 1973.

a) The Nolans have $8,000 in a checking account and $30,000, including interest through June 30, 1973, in a savings account.

b) The Nolans paid $7,500 in 1971 for a 15% interest in Crown Corporation, which has 100,000 shares outstanding. The stock is traded on a midwestern exchange. In recent months the stock has traded in blocks of 100 shares or less at $1.50 per share. Dr. Nolan was offered $1.10 per share for all his shares on June 22, 1973. The offer is still outstanding.

c) Dr. Nolan and Dr. Ferrara each own 50% interest in the Suburban Medical Group, a partnership. The balance sheet of Suburban Medical Group, prepared on a modified cash basis, follows:

Assets

Cash (in non-interest-bearing account)	$ 10,400
30-day treasury bills (maturing on July 30, 1973)	11,000
Drugs and supplies inventory	6,100
Equipment and office furniture (net of $14,000 accumulated depreciation)	66,000
Automobiles (net of $1,150 accumulated depreciation)	10,800
Buildings (purchased June 28, 1973)	55,000
Total	$159,300

Liabilities

6% notes payable (principal and interest) payable monthly until 1980	$ 39,000
Capital	120,300
Total	$159,300

Other data are presented below:

a) As of June 30, 1973, there were unrecorded accounts receivable of $12,451 and unrecorded accounts payable of $1,327. Payments on the notes are current. The partnership prepares its tax returns on the accrual basis.

b) Dr. Ferrara and Dr. Nolan were offered $260,000 for their practice by the Rural Medical Center. The offer is still outstanding. Counsel has advised that if the offer is accepted, any difference between the proceeds and the partners' tax bases in the partnership will be taxed as ordinary income.

c) The Nolans purchased their residence in 1970 for $85,000. The balance of the 30-year, 6-3/4% mortgage is $64,498. The current rate charged on similar mortgages is 6-3/4%. Payments on the mortgage are current. Similar homes in the area have increased in value approximately 30% since 1970. The assessed real-estate value was determined in March, 1973, to be $108,500 based on fair value.

d) Mrs. Nolan owns a 1972 automobile that cost $5,950. Current newpaper advertisements indicate that her car could be sold for $4,800.

e) In 1955 the Nolans received a painting as a wedding present from Mrs. Nolan's aunt, an internationally known artist. At the date of gift, the painting was appraised at $6,000. The painting was appraised in June, 1973, at $16,000.

f) The Nolans have maintained cost records on their major household effects. The costs aggreggate $27,500. A local business that specialized in auctioning this type of merchandise estimated in July, 1973, that the household effects have a net realizable value of $12,000. Other household effects are of nominal value.

g) Dr. Nolan has a vested interest of $14,175 in a group-participating pension plan. The present value of the vested benefits is $6,818. Dr. Nolan's contributions to the plan (tax basis) have been $5,432.

h) On July 1, 1970, Dr. Nolan paid $9,000 for 25% of the capital stock of Medical Instruments, Inc. A summary of the financial data of the corporation follows:

Balance Sheet (June 30, 1972)		Earnings for Years Ended		Dividends Paid
Assets	$112,800	June 30, 1971	$12,050	
Liabilities	46,650	June 30, 1972	18,100	
Equity	66,150	June 30, 1973	28,050	$6,200
	$112,800			

i) Similar businesses in the area have been sold recently for 10 times the average of the last three years' earnings.

j) The Nolans owed $810 on charge accounts and $220 on a national credit card account at June 30, 1973.

k) In early July, 1973, the Nolans estimated their federal income tax for their 1973 return to be $26,000. Estimated tax payments of $8,000 had been made as of June 30, 1973. A tax rate of 40% is assumed for all tax considerations.

Required:

Prepare a personal statement of assets and liabilities in good form as of June 30, 1973, for Dr. and Mrs. Nolan. Supporting calculations should be in good form; footnotes are not required.

(AICPA adapted)

P–24–9 Alpha Corporation operates in five different industries and provides the following information relative to those industries:

Industry	Revenues		Traceable Costs	Identifiable Assets
	Outsiders	Intersegment		
A	$400,000	$100,000	$300,000 + 58,1	$350,000
B	750,000	50,000	650,000 + 92,7	580,000
C	120,000	–0–	70,000 14	210,000
D	900,000	–0–	700,000 104.3	460,000
E	650,000	50,000	400,000 81,2	480,000
	2820	200	2120	2080

In addition to the costs listed above as traceable costs, Alpha incurred the following costs: 2470 Total Cost

Operating expenses not traceable to segments	$350,000
Corporate interest expense	50,000
Corporate income tax expense	170,000

Required:
Determine which of the segments above are reportable segments. Alpha allocates corporate operating expenses on the basis of income before allocation.

P–24–10 Beta Corporation is a diversified manufacturing concern with operations in seven different industries. For 1982 Beta reports (in thousands of dollars) the following information:

Division	Revenues	Operating Profit (loss)	Identifiable Assets
Lumber	$ 5,000	$ 600	$ 2,000
Paper	6,000	450	4,000
Printing	1,000	(50)	1,000
Toys	2,500	(400)	1,200
Foods	3,000	150	500
Textiles	1,500	20	800
Entertainment	1,200	80	1,700
Combined	$21,200	$ 950	$11,200

Required:
Determine which of the segments above are reportable segments.

P–24–11 The Anderson Manufacturing Company, a California corporation listed on the Pacific Coast Stock Exchange, budgeted activities for 1975 as follows:

	Amount	Units
Net sales	$6,000,000	1,000,000
Cost of goods sold	3,600,000	1,000,000
Gross margin	$2,400,000	
Selling, general, and administrative expenses	1,400,000	
Operating earnings	$1,000,000	
Nonoperating revenues and expenses	–0–	
Earnings before income taxes	$1,000,000	
Estimated income taxes (current and deferred)	550,000	
Net earnings	$ 450,000	
Earnings per share of common stock	$4.50	

Anderson has operated profitably for many years and has experienced a seasonal pattern of sales volume and production similar to the following, forecasted for 1975. Sales volume is expected to follow a quarterly pattern of 10%, 20%, 35%, 35%, respectively, because of the seasonality of the industry. Also, because of production and storage capacity limitations, it is expected that production will follow a pattern of 20%, 25%, 30%, 25%, per quarter, respectively.

At the conclusion of the first quarter of 1975, the controller of Anderson has prepared and issued the following interim report:

	Amount	Units
Net sales	$ 600,000	100,000
Cost of goods sold	360,000	100,000
Gross margin	$ 240,000	240,000
Selling, general, and administrative expenses	275,000 –	140,000
Operating loss	$(35,000)	100,000
Loss from warehouse fire	(175,000)	155,000
Loss before income taxes	(210,000)	45,000
Estimated income taxes	–0–	178,750
Net loss	$(210,000)	(33,750)
Loss per share of common stock	$(2.10)	(.34)

(Handwritten annotations: "income", "Loss from wh fire (net of 96,250 taxes)", "(33,750) Loss", "(.34) Loss per share")

The following additional information is available for the first quarter just completed, but was not included in the public information released:

a) The company uses a standard cost system in which standards are set at currently attainable levels on an annual basis. At the end of the first quarter there was underapplied fixed factory overhead (volume variance) of $50,000 that was treated as *—cost of inventory* an asset at the end of the quarter. Production during the quarter was 200,000 units, of which 100,000 were sold.

b) The selling, general, and administrative expenses were budgeted on a basis of $900,000 fixed expenses for the year plus $0.50 variable expenses per unit of sales.

c) Assume that the warehouse fire loss met the conditions of an extraordinary loss. The warehouse had an undepreciated cost of $320,000; $145,000 was recovered from insurance on the warehouse. No other gains or losses are anticipated this year from similar losses in preceding years; thus, the full loss will be deductible as an ordinary loss for income tax purposes.

d) The effective income tax rate, for federal and state taxes combined, is expected to average 55% of earnings before income taxes during 1975. There are no permanent differences between pretax accounting earnings and taxable income.

e) Earnings per share were computed on the basis of 100,000 shares of capital stock outstanding. Anderson has only one class of stock issued, no long-term debt outstanding, and no stock option plan.

Required:

1. Without reference to the specific situation described above, what are the standards of disclosure for interim financial data (published interim financial reports) for publicly traded companies? Explain.

2. Identify the weaknesses in form and content of Anderson's interim report without reference to the additional information.

3. For each of the five items of additional information, indicate the preferable treatment of each item for interim-reporting purposes and explain why that treatment is preferable.

(AICPA adapted)

P–24–12 Many accountants and financial analysts contend that companies should report financial data for segments of the enterprise.

Required:

1. What does financial reporting for segments of a business enterprise involve?

2. Identify the reasons for requiring financial data to be reported by segments.

3. Identify the possible disadvantages of requiring financial data to be reported by segments.

4. Identify the accounting difficulties inherent in segment reporting.

(AICPA adapted)

P–24–13 The following two cases provide information about income and tax rates for interim periods.

Case A Annual operating income is expected to be $300,000. Of this amount, $260,000 represents ordinary income to be taxed at 45%, and $40,000 is a capital gain to be taxed at 25%. In addition, there is an investment credit of $12,000 available.

Case B Annual operating income is expected to be a loss of $150,000. This loss can be used to offset $120,000 of income which previously had been taxed at the rate of 35%.

Required:
Compute the effective tax rate for each case.

P–24–14 Jacobson, Incorporated is a medium-sized manufacturing company in the Midwest. Jacobson has had the following results for fiscal 1981:

Interim Period	Ordinary Income (Loss)	Estimated Tax Rate
1st quarter	$120,000	45%
2nd quarter	(70,000)	25%
3rd quarter	(20,000)	
4th quarter	100,000	30%

Required:
Calculate the amount of income tax expense for each quarter for Jacobson.

P–24–15 Alexander Corporation has already issued its first quarter interim report, which reflected ordinary income in the amount of $50,000 and income tax expense of $20,000, at an estimated rate of 40%.

In the second quarter, Alexander adopted a formal plan for disposal of its textile segment. The income of the first quarter included a $10,000 loss from the textile division. Alexander had operating income of $40,000 in the second quarter, which includes $5,000 income from the discontinued textile segment before its sale in the second quarter.

The operating income in the third and fourth quarters was $60,000 and $70,000, respectively. The textile segment was sold at a net loss of $50,000 in the second period.

It may be assumed that any loss traceable to the discontinued segment will have tax benefits. It may be assumed also that the effective tax rate of 40% used in the first quarter should be revised to 45% in the remaining quarters. This increase is attributable to the removal of an unprofitable segment.

Required:
Determine the amount of tax that should be allocated to the continuing operations and the amount of tax that should be allocated to the discontinued operations for each quarter.

P–24–16 Following is the complete set of financial statements prepared by Oberlin Corporation:

OBERLIN CORPORATION
Statement of Earnings and
Retained Earnings
For the Fiscal Year Ended August 31, 1976

Sales	$3,500,000
Less: Returns and allowances	35,000
Net Sales	$3,465,000
Less: Cost of goods sold	1,039,000
Gross margin	$2,426,000

Less
  Selling expenses $1,000,000

Less		
Selling expenses	$1,000,000	
General and administrative expenses (Note 1)	1,079,000	2,079,000
Operating earnings		$ 347,000
Add other revenue		
Purchase discounts	10,000	
Gain on increased value of investments in real estate	100,000	
Gain on sale of treasury stock	200,000	
Correction of error in last year's statement	90,000	400,000
Ordinary earnings		$ 747,000
Add extraordinary item—gain on sale of fixed asset		53,000
Earnings before income tax		$ 800,000
Less income tax expense		380,000
Net earnings		$ 420,000
Add beginning retained earnings		2,750,000
		$3,170,000
Less		
Dividends (12% stock dividend declared but not		
yet issued)		120,000
Contingent liability (Note 4)		300,000
Ending unappropriated retained earnings		$2,750,000

OBERLIN CORPORATION
Statement of Financial Position
August 31, 1976

Assets

Current assets		
Cash	$ 80,000	
Accounts receivable, net	110,000	
Inventory	130,000	
Total current assets		$ 320,000
Other assets		
Land and building, net	4,000,000	
Investments in real estate (current value)	1,508,000	
Investment in Gray, Inc. at cost (Note 2)	160,000	
Goodwill (Note 3)	250,000	
Discounts on bonds payable	42,000	
Total other assets		5,960,000
Total assets		$6,280,000

Liabilities and Stockholders' Equity

Current liabilities		
Accounts payable	$ 140,000	
Income taxes payable	320,000	
Stock dividend payable	120,000	
Total current liabilities		$ 580,000

Other liabilities

Due to Grant, Inc. (Note 4)	300,000	
Liability under employee pension plan	450,000	
Bonds payable (including portions due within one year)	1,000,000	
Deferred taxes	58,000	
Total other liabilities		1,808,000
Total liabilities		$2,388,000
Stockholders' equity		
Common stock	1,000,000	
Paid-in capital in excess of par	142,000	
Unappropriated retained earnings	2,750,000	
Total stockholders' equity		3,892,000
Total liabilities and stockholders' equity		$6,280,000

Footnotes

1. Depreciation expense is included in general and administrative expenses. During the fiscal year the company changed from the straight-line method of depreciation to the sum-of-the-years'-digits method.
2. The company owns 40% of the outstanding stock of Gray, Inc. Because the ownership is less than 50%, consolidated financial statements with Gray cannot be presented.
3. As per federal income tax laws, goodwill is not amortized. The goodwill was "acquired" in 1973.
4. The amount due to Grant, Inc. is contingent upon the outcome of a lawsuit that is pending currently. The amount of loss, if any, is not expected to exceed $300,000.

Required:

Identify and explain the deficiencies in the presentation of Oberlin's financial statements. There are no arithmetical errors in the statements. Organize your answer as follows:

    a) Deficiencies in the statement of earnings and retained earnings.

    b) Deficiencies in the statement of financial position.

    c) General comments.

If an item appears on both statements, identify the deficiencies for each statement separately.

(AICPA adapted)

P–24–17 Refer to the financial statements presented in Problem P–23–7 (Chapter 23).

Required:

Review the financial statements and related footnotes. Identify any inclusions or exclusions from them that would be in violation of generally accepted accounting principles, and indicate corrective action to be taken. Do *not* comment as to format or style. Respond in the following order:

    a) Statement of financial position.

    b) Footnotes.

(AICPA adapted)

25

Statement of Changes in Financial Position

Accounting in the News

While the balance sheet, income statement, and retained earnings statement present valuable information about a business enterprise, a statement of changes in financial position is also essential to investors and creditors in their assessment of an enterprise's current and future economic health. As exemplified in the following excerpts from a recent article, an unfavorable cash flow can contribute to the downfall of an enterprise.

> Braniff International Corp. sees a chance for "rehabilitation" under the protection of federal bankruptcy laws. . . .
>
> Only a few hours after the airline suspended service and became the first major carrier ever to file for reorganization under Chapter 11 of the federal Bankruptcy Act, Braniff sounded the rallying cry. "I did not come over here—to Braniff—to preside over its liquidation," declared Howard Putnam, chairman and president. . . .
>
> Mr. Putnam also told a news conference that Braniff didn't have enough money even to meet its payroll. . . .
>
> A lack of operating cash apparently was what forced Braniff's hand, although the company also blames the recession and rapidly dropping passenger boardings as other culprits.*

The statement of changes in financial position reports an enterprise's sources and uses of financial resources. Accordingly, it may be helpful in identifying current or future problem areas, as well as current or future economic strengths.

*Brent R. Schlender et al., "Braniff Files to Reorganize Under Federal Protection, Declares Intention to Resume Operations or to Merge," *Wall Street Journal*, May 14, 1982, p. 3, 14. Reprinted by permission of The Wall Street Journal, © Dow Jones & Company, Inc. 1982. All Rights Reserved.

The balance sheet, income statement, and statement of changes in financial position are required financial statements. To fulfill the requirement that all material changes in owners' equity be disclosed, most enterprises also present a retained earnings statement or statement of changes in stockholders' equity. All four of these financial statements place significant emphasis on reporting information about an enterprise's financial position or about changes in its financial position.

The financial position of an enterprise refers to the status of its assets and claims to those assets (i.e., its liabilities and owners' equity) at a specific point in time. Changes in an enterprise's financial position refer to flows or changes in its assets or claims to those assets over a period of time.[1]

The balance sheet presents the financial position of an enterprise at a specific point in time. The other three financial statements report information about changes in financial position during a particular period of time. The income statement presents revenues, expenses, gains, losses, and net income or net loss recognized during the period. In so doing, it reports detailed information about one aspect of changes in financial position, namely the change in retained earnings resulting from operations. The retained earnings statement summarizes all changes in retained earnings.

The statement of changes in financial position, as its name suggests, also presents information about changes in an enterprise's financial position. It is designed to complement rather than duplicate the information reported in the other financial statements. Emphasis in the statement of changes in financial position is placed on the *flow* of financial resources, that is, on the sources and uses of an enterprise's financial resources.[2] The specific objectives of a statement of changes in financial position are "(1) to summarize the financing and investing activities of the entity, including the extent to which the enterprise has generated funds from operations during the period, and (2) to complete the disclosure of changes in financial position during the period."[3]

Evolution of the Statement of Changes in Financial Position

For decades business enterprises have prepared various types of funds statements. Although initially most were prepared for management's internal use, some enterprises included these statements in their annual reports in addition to the other financial statements. As might be expected, there was significant variation in the format and content of the funds statements presented. There was also a lack of consensus about the definition of funds used. Some used the term "funds"

---

[1] "Elements of Financial Statements of Business Enterprises," *Statements of Financial Accounting Concepts No. 3* (Stamford, Conn.: FASB, 1980), footnote 6.

[2] Used broadly, financial resources represent the elements (items) over which an enterprise has control that allow it to command goods and services in the marketplace. In this sense, they represent the assets that may be used and the liabilities and owners' equity that may be increased to acquire services or other assets or to reduce other liabilities or owners' equity. Financial resources, therefore, include, but are not limited to, funds, whether funds are considered to be cash, working capital, or some other accepted definition.

[3] "Reporting Changes in Financial Position," *Opinions of the Accounting Principles Board No. 19* (New York: AICPA, 1971).

to mean cash, others used it to mean working capital, while still others used it to mean some other concept of funds.

Interest in the funds statement increased when in 1961 the AICPA published *Accounting Research Study No. 2*, "'Cash Flow' Analysis and the Funds Statement," by Perry Mason.[4] The study recommended that the funds statement be included in annual reports as a major financial statement. In 1963 the APB issued *APB Opinion No. 3*, "The Statement of Source and Application of Funds," in which it recommended that a statement of source and application of funds be presented as supplementary information in financial reports.[5] Even though the Board did not make the inclusion of the statement mandatory, it did recommend that when a funds statement was presented, funds should be defined as "all financial resources" so that the statement would include the financial aspects of all significant transactions.

In 1970 the SEC issued *Accounting Series Release No. 117* requiring companies under its jurisdiction to include a funds statement in certain financial reports it required them to file.[6] Finally, in 1971 the APB issued *APB Opinion No. 19*, "Reporting Changes in Financial Position," which made the inclusion of a statement of changes in financial position mandatory for all profit-oriented business entities. Specifically, the Board stated:

> When financial statements purporting to present both financial position (balance sheet) and results of operations (statement of income and retained earnings) are issued, a statement summarizing changes in financial position should also be presented as a basic financial statement for each period for which an income statement is presented.[7]

The APB recommended use of the title, "Statement of Changes in Financial Position." The Board also concluded that the statement should be based on a broad concept embracing all changes in financial position associated with an enterprise's financing and investing activities, regardless of whether cash or other elements of working capital are affected directly.

Measuring Changes in Financial Position

Opinion No. 19 requires that the statement of changes in financial position disclose all important changes in financial position, including the effects of all significant financing and investing activities. The specific categories of information to be disclosed are as follows:

1. The sources and uses of funds, with funds being defined as cash, cash and temporary investments combined, all quick assets (i.e., cash, marketable se-

---

[4] Perry Mason, "'Cash Flow' Analysis and the Funds Statement," *Accounting Research Study No. 2* (New York: AICPA, 1961), p. 89.

[5] "The Statement of Source and Application of Funds," *Opinions of the Accounting Principles Board No. 3* (New York: AICPA, 1963).

[6] U.S. Securities and Exchange Commission, *Accounting Series Release No. 117* (Washington, D.C.: U.S. Government Printing Office, 1970).

[7] "Changes in Financial Position," par. 7.

curities, short-term notes receivable, and accounts receivable), or working capital. Funds provided by, or used in, operations should be identified separately, as should all other major sources and uses of funds.

2. The effects of other transactions that represent significant financing and investing activities even though they had no direct effect on funds as defined in (1) above. These transactions affect the financial resources of an enterprise and represent changes in its financial position even though they have no direct or immediate effect on its funds.

3. The amount of change in each individual component of funds as defined in (1) above.

Thus, if funds are defined as working capital (current assets minus current liabilities), the categories of information to be disclosed are as follows:

1. The sources and uses of working capital. Working capital provided by, or used in, operations should be identified separately, as should each other major source and use of working capital.

2. The effects of other transactions that represent significant financing and investing activities even though they had no direct effect on working capital.

3. The changes in each component of working capital—that is, the change in each current asset and current liability.

Information regarding category (1) disclosures is derived from analyzing those transactions that changed the amount of working capital. Transactions that increased working capital represent sources of working capital; those that decreased working capital represent uses of working capital.

Information for category (2) disclosures is obtained by identifying those transactions that had no effect on working capital but that nevertheless represent a significant financing and investing activity. An example of this type of transaction is the acquisition of land (a noncurrent asset) by issuing a long-term note payable (a noncurrent liability). If you assume the land has a fair market value of $50,000, the entry to record this transaction is:

Land	50,000	
Notes payable		50,000

Even though this transaction has no effect on working capital, it represents both a significant financing activity (the issuance of long-term debt) and a significant investing activity (the acquisition of land). It is therefore an important change in financial position and should be disclosed.

Other examples of these "nonfund" transactions that must be reported on the statement of changes in financial position are (1) the acquisition of noncurrent assets by transferring other noncurrent assets or by issuing stock; (2) the extinguishment of long-term debt by issuing new long-term debt, by issuing stock, or by transferring noncurrent assets; and (3) the conversion of preferred stock into common stock. Each of these transactions involves a direct exchange of one non-current item (i.e., asset, liability, or owners' equity) for another noncurrent item. In practice, the effects of these transactions often are disclosed as if they involve both an inflow (source) of funds and an outflow (use) of funds. For example, the above-mentioned acquisition of land by issuing a long-term note would be reported both as a source of working capital (as if the note was issued for $50,000 cash) and as a use of working capital (as if the land was acquired for $50,000 cash).

Information for category (3) disclosures, the amount of change in each current asset and current liability account, is obtained by comparing each account's end-of-year balance with its beginning-of-year balance.

Preparing the Statement of Changes in Financial Position

From a conceptual standpoint, the preparation of a statement of changes in financial position involves six major steps, which are described below:

Step 1: Decide how funds will be defined for purposes of disclosing the sources and uses of funds.

Step 2: Identify all transactions of the enterprise.

Step 3: Identify and analyze those transactions that caused a change in the amount of funds as defined in Step 1; those that increased funds represent sources, and those that decreased funds represent uses.

Step 4: Identify and analyze all other transactions that represent significant financing and investing activities even though they had no direct effect on funds as defined in Step 1.

Step 5: Determine the amount of change in each component of funds as defined in Step 1.

Step 6: Assemble the information obtained in the previous steps in a statement of changes in financial position format acceptable under APB *Opinion No. 19.*

Collectively, these steps represent a general model for the preparation of a statement of changes in financial position. The general model focuses attention on the objective of each type of activity rather than on the detailed procedures of how any given step is accomplished. Discussing the general model first allows attention to be directed to the underlying nature of the data presented in a statement of changes in financial position without getting bogged down in the procedural details of how the data are accumulated.

To demonstrate the general model, assume that Brooks Corporation's balance sheet at December 31, 1981, appeared as shown in Exhibit 25-1. Assume also that Brooks Corporation had the following transactions during 1982:

1. Billed customers for $80,000 of professional services performed.
2. Collected $70,000 of accounts receivable.
3. Paid accounts payable of $15,000.

Exhibit 25-1
BROOKS CORPORATION
Balance Sheet
December 31, 1981

Assets		Liabilities and Stockholders' Equity	
Cash	$ 80,000	Accounts payable	$ 15,000
Land	20,000	Common stock, $10 par	60,000
		Retained earnings	25,000
	$100,000		$100,000

---

4. Salaries earned by employees amounted to $38,000, of which $3,000 was unpaid as of December 31, 1982.
5. Sold half of its land (cost $10,000) for $12,000.
6. Acquired a building by issuing 2,000 new shares of common stock having a market value of $14 per share.
7. Acquired office equipment for $12,000 cash.
8. Recorded the following depreciation expense: building, $2,500; office equipment, $1,500.
9. Declared and paid a cash dividend of $6,400 ($.80 per share on all 8,000 shares).
10. Recorded income taxes for the year of $16,000, which will be paid in early 1983. Assume an income tax rate of 40%.

Step 1: Brooks Corporation will measure changes in financial resources in terms of working capital; that is, it will define funds to be working capital.

Steps 2, 3, and 4: For discussion purposes these steps are presented below on a transaction-by-transaction basis. First, the entry to record the transaction is presented (Step 2). Each entry (transaction) is then analyzed to identify those that increased or decreased working capital (Step 3) and those that represented a significant financing and investing activity even though working capital was not affected (Step 4).

---

1. Professional services performed:
   Accounts receivable   80,000
       Professional services revenue   80,000

Current assets (accounts receivable) increased, with no change in current liabilities. This transaction increased working capital and therefore represents a source of working capital.

---

2. Collection of accounts receivable:

Cash	70,000	
Accounts receivable		70,000

An increase in one current asset (cash) was offset by a decrease in another current asset (accounts receivable). The amount of working capital did not change. The collection of accounts receivable changed the composition of working capital but not the amount. In fact, any transaction that involves only working capital accounts (i.e., only current assets and/or current liabilities) has no effect on the amount of working capital.

---

3. Payment of accounts payable:

Accounts payable	15,000	
Cash		15,000

This transaction also involves only current accounts. Working capital did not change because the decrease in current liabilities (accounts payable) was offset by a decrease in current assets (cash).

---

4. Salaries incurred:

Salaries expense	38,000	
Cash		35,000
Salaries payable		3,000

The decrease in current assets (cash) and the increase in current liabilities (salaries payable) both decreased working capital. Therefore, salaries represent a use of working capital of $38,000.

---

5. Sale of land:

Cash	12,000	
Land		10,000
Gain on sale of land		2,000

The only working capital account affected was cash, which increased $12,000. Since working capital increased, the sale of land represents a source of working capital of $12,000.

6. Acquisition of building:

Building	28,000	
Common stock (2,000 × $10 par)		20,000
Capital in excess of par		8,000

Since this entry includes only noncurrent accounts (i.e., accounts other than current assets and current liabilities), the amount of working capital is not affected. However, this transaction represents both a significant financing activity (issuance of stock) and a significant investing activity (acquisition of building). The effects of this transaction must be included in the statement of changes in financial position.

7. Acquisition of office equipment:

Office equipment	12,000	
Cash		12,000

The decrease in a current asset (cash) with no change in current liabilities resulted in a decrease in working capital. Thus, the acquisition of office equipment represents a use of working capital.

8. Depreciation expense:

Depreciation expense	4,000	
Accumulated depreciation—building		2,500
Accumulated depreciation—office equipment		1,500

This entry is similar to entry 6 above (acquisition of building) in that it involves only noncurrent accounts and has no effect on working capital. [All income statement accounts (e.g., depreciation expense) are temporary owners' equity accounts and are therefore noncurrent accounts.] It is unlike entry 6, however, in that it does not represent a financing or investing activity. As you can observe, it would be illogical to view this entry as representing in substance both an inflow and an outflow of working capital.

9. Declaration and payment of cash dividend:

Retained earnings	6,400	
Cash		6,400

Working capital decreased since a current asset (cash) decreased with no change in current liabilities. The cash dividends represent a use of working capital.

10. Recognition of income taxes:		
Income taxes expense	16,000	
Income taxes payable		16,000

A current liability (income taxes payable) increased with no change in current assets, resulting in a decrease in working capital. This transaction represents a use of working capital.

The results of Steps 2, 3, and 4 are presented below in summary form (with the transaction numbers noted in parentheses in order to facilitate subsequent discussion.

Transactions involving sources of working capital:

(1) Professional services	$80,000
(5) Sale of land	12,000
	$92,000

Transactions involving uses of working capital:

(4) Salaries	$38,000
(7) Acquisition of office equipment	12,000
(9) Cash dividends	6,400
(10) Income taxes	16,000
	$72,400

Transactions having no effect on working capital but that represent significant financing and inventory activities:

(6) Acquisition of building by issuing stock	$28,000

Other transactions having no effect on working capital:
Those involving only current accounts:
(2) Collection of accounts receivable
(3) Payment of accounts payable
Those involving only noncurrent accounts:
(8) Depreciation

Step 5: This step consists of determining the change in each working capital account. In practice these changes would be determined from the ledger accounts or from comparative years' balance sheets, which at this point in the process already would have been prepared. The use of comparative years' balance sheets is discussed in detail later in the chapter. For purposes of the current discussion, the changes in Brooks Corporation's working capital accounts during 1982 are summarized in the T accounts below, with the 1982 transaction number noted in parentheses:

Cash

1/1/82 balance	$80,000	(3)	$15,000
(2)	70,000	(4)	35,000
(5)	12,000	(7)	12,000
		(9)	6,400
12/31/82 balance	93,600		

Accounts Receivable

1/1/82 balance	$ -0-	(2)	$70,000
(1)	80,000		
12/31/82 balance	10,000		

Accounts Payable

(3)	$15,000	1/1/82 balance	$15,000
		12/31/82 balance	-0-

Income Taxes Payable

		1/1/82 balance	$ -0-
		(10)	16,000
		12/31/82 balance	16,000

Salaries Payable

		1/1/82 balance	$ -0-
		(4)	3,000
		12/31/82 balance	3,000

Step 6: The final step in the general model for preparing a statement of changes in financial position consists of assembling the data developed in the previous steps in an acceptable format. In order to highlight specific requirements of *Opinion No. 19* and to emphasize the areas in which the preparer has flexibility regarding form, we have presented Brooks Corporation's statement of changes in financial position under two, different, acceptable formats. These statements are designated (immediately below the heading) as "Format A" (Exhibit 25-2) and "Format B" (Exhibit 25-3), respectively. These designations obviously would not appear on a formal statement.

Several points are noted below about these statements and about the reporting requirements of *Opinion No. 19*.

1.   The statement of changes in financial position should prominently disclose working capital (or whatever definition of funds is used) provided by operations, exclusive of "special" items such as discontinued operations, extraordinary items, and the cumulative effect of a change in accounting principle. There are two alternative ways of doing this. The first is to disclose in the operations section of the statement only those revenues that represented a source of working capital and those expenses that required the use of working capital. This is the approach taken in Format A. The other approach, shown in Format B, is to start the operations section with income from continuing operations (or net income if there are no "special" items) and add to that (or deduct) those items that appropriately are included in the determination of income from continuing operations but that do not represent a source or use of working capital. Whichever approach is used, the operations section nor-

Exhibit 25-2
BROOKS CORPORATION
Statement of Changes in Financial Position
For the Year Ended December 31, 1982
(Format A)

Sources of working capital
Operations
    Sources of working capital from operations:
        Professional services $80,000
    Uses of working capital in operations:
        Salaries   (38,000)
        Income Taxes   (16,000)
    Working capital provided by operations $26,000
Sale of land   12,000
    Total sources of working capital $38,000

Uses of working capital
    Acquisition of office equipment $12,000
    Declaration of cash dividends   6,400
    Increase in working capital   19,600
    Total uses of working capital $38,000

Other significant financing and investing activities:
    Acquisition of building by issuing common stock $28,000

Changes in working capital accounts:

Accounts	Balances, December 31, 1981	Balances, December 31, 1982	Change in Working Capital Increase (Decrease)
Cash	$80,000	$ 93,600	$13,600
Accounts receivable	–0–	10,000	10,000
Current assets	$80,000	$103,600	$23,600
Accounts payable	$15,000	$ –0–	$15,000
Income taxes payable	–0–	16,000	(16,000)
Salaries payable	–0–	3,000	(3,000)
Current liabilities	$15,000	$ 19,000	$ (4,000)
Working capital	$65,000	$ 84,600	$19,600

mally should appear as the first item on the statement. The final caption of the operations section should be "Working capital provided by, or used in, operations." If the income statement includes any "special" items, the final caption of the operations section in the statement of changes in financial position should be labeled appropriately; for example, "Working capital provided

Exhibit 25-3
BROOKS CORPORATION
Statement of Changes in Financial Position
For the Year Ended December 31, 1982
(Format B)

Financial resources provided by	
Operations	
Net income	$24,000
Add (deduct) items not affecting working capital:	
Depreciation expense	4,000
Gain on sale of land	(2,000)
Working capital provided by operations	$26,000
Issuance of common stock (for building)	28,000
Sale of land	12,000
Total financial resources provided	$66,000
Financial resources applied to	
Acquisition of building (by issuing common stock)	$28,000
Acquisition of office equipment	12,000
Declaration of cash dividends	6,400
Total financial resources used	$46,400
Increase in working capital	$19,600
Changes in working capital accounts	
Current assets—increase (decrease):	
Cash	$13,600
Accounts receivable	10,000
	$23,600
Current liabilities—(increase) decrease:	
Accounts payable	$15,000
Income taxes payable	(16,000)
Salaries payable	(3,000)
	$ (4,000)
Increase in working capital	$19,600

by, or used in, operations, exclusive of discontinued operations, extraordinary items, and the cumulative effect of changes in accounting principle.[8] The effects of all "special" items (i.e., discontinued operations, extraordinary items, and the cumulative effect of changes in accounting principle) on the income statement should be disclosed separately on the statement of changes in financial position.

[8] The caption should be consistent with the type of "special" items, if any, included on the enterprise's income statement. For example, if there are no "special" items, the caption should be "working capital provided by operations." If there are extraordinary items but no other "special" items, the caption should be "working capital provided by operations, exclusive of extraordinary items."

2. If funds are defined as working capital, the change in each working capital account must be disclosed, either in the body of the statement or in a separate schedule accompanying the statement. Format A (Exhibit 25-2) shows the beginning and ending balances in each working capital account, with the change (expressed in terms of the change in working capital) shown in the last column. Format B (Exhibit 25-3) shows only the change in each account, with the total change in working capital shown on the last line. Although both forms, as well as others, are acceptable, a single-column presentation, such as the one in Format B, is essential if comparative years' statements are to be presented.

3. Format A is in balanced form; that is, the total sources of working capital are shown as being equal to the total uses of working capital. This is accomplished by showing the net increase in working capital ($19,600) as the balancing amount in the uses of working capital section. Under this approach a net decrease in working capital would be shown as the balancing amount in the sources of working capital section. On the other hand, Format B emphasizes the change in working capital by showing the amount of the change as the concluding total of the top portion of the statement. For Brooks Corporation, the increase of working capital ($19,600) is shown as the difference between the total financial resources provided ($66,000) and the total financial resources used ($46,400). Under either format, note that the net increase in working capital ($19,600) which is shown in the sources and uses section in Format A and in the top part of the statement in Format B must be equal to the net increase in working capital ($19,600) which is shown on the last line of the changes in working capital accounts section in Format A and in the bottom part of the statement in Format B.

4. Format A reports in a separate section the effects of those transactions that represent significant financing and investing activities even though they had no direct effect on working capital. The acquisition of the building by issuing common stock is disclosed in the "other significant financing and investing activities" section presented below the sources and uses of working capital sections. On the other hand, Format B reports this transaction as both a source of financial resources (working capital) and a use of financial resources.

5. Both formats disclose all important changes in financial position. They report (1) the sources and uses of working capital, (2) the financial effects of other significant financing and investing activities, and (3) the change in each component of working capital. The terminology used in Format B ("financial resources") perhaps better emphasizes that all important changes in financial position are disclosed.

The previously described, six-step approach to preparing a statement of changes in financial position is a general approach that includes the essential processes involved in preparing a statement regardless of (1) the way in which funds are defined for purposes of expressing the changes in financial position and (2) the specific procedures followed in carrying out a given step. The approach focuses attention on the conceptual aspects of what is included in a statement of changes in financial position. It also emphasizes that the key aspect of developing the data for the statement is the identification and analysis of the enterprise's transactions.

From a practical standpoint, analyzing each individual transaction in the manner demonstrated earlier would prove in most cases to be laborious, if not impossible. A more formal approach normally is used for identifying and analyzing an enterprise's transactions; it incorporates the essential elements of the six-step approach but does so in a more efficient manner. Two such approaches are (1) the worksheet approach and (2) the T-account approach. The worksheet approach, the most widely used in practice, is discussed in the following section. The T-account approach is presented in the Appendix to this chapter.

Worksheet Approach—Working Capital Basis

A statement of changes in financial position in which changes in financial position are expressed in terms of working capital discloses three basic types of information:

1. Sources and uses of working capital.
2. Other significant financing and investing activities.
3. Changes in the components of working capital.

Worksheet Approach—Underlying Foundation

The worksheet approach is based on the idea that the first two types of information listed above can be determined by analyzing the changes in the *noncurrent* accounts. Central to this idea is the fact that all accounts may be classified as being either current (i.e., current assets and current liabilities) or noncurrent. Income statement accounts and accounts shown directly on the retained earnings statement, such as dividends and prior period adjustments, are temporary retained earnings accounts and are therefore noncurrent.

Given this classification of current and noncurrent, transactions may be grouped into the following three categories:

1. Transactions involving only current accounts.
2. Transactions involving both current accounts and noncurrent accounts, i.e., at least one current account and at least one noncurrent account.
3. Transactions involving only noncurrent accounts.

Transactions involving only current accounts (category 1) change the composition of working capital but not the amount. These transactions do not represent sources or uses of working capital, nor do they provide information about other significant financing and investing activities. Brooks Corporation had two transactions of this type:

Collection of accounts receivable (transaction #2)
Payment of accounts payable (transaction #3)

Transactions that involve both current and noncurrent accounts (category 2) represent a source or use of working capital. Brooks Corporation had six transactions of this type:

Professional services performed (transaction #1)
Salaries incurred (transaction #4)
Sale of land (transaction #5)
Purchase of office equipment (transaction #7)
Declaration of cash dividends (transaction #9)
Income taxes recognized (transaction #10)

Transactions that involve only noncurrent accounts (category 3) do not change working capital. However, some of these transactions may represent significant financing and investing activities. For example, Brooks Corporation's acquisition of a building by issuing common stock (transaction #6) is included in this category.

Thus, all transactions involving sources or uses of working capital or representing other significant financing and investing activities must of necessity involve a change in at least one noncurrent account. Therefore, an analysis of all changes in noncurrent accounts should ensure that (1) all sources and uses of working capital and (2) all other significant financing and investing activities are identified. This conclusion is the fundamental idea underlying the worksheet approach.

Worksheet Approach—Format and Procedures

The starting point for preparing the worksheet is the data contained in comparative years' balance sheets. Data from the income statement and the retained earnings statement (or statement of changes in stockholders' equity) are also utilized. Additional information about the nature of the changes in specific accounts also may be necessary.

The preparation of a worksheet for a statement of changes in financial position will be demonstrated now for Brooks Corporation. The comparative years' balance sheets at December 31, 1982, and December 31, 1981, are presented in Exhibit 25-4. The income statement for 1982 is shown in Exhibit 25-5, and the statement of changes in stockholders' equity for 1982 is presented in Exhibit 25-6. You may wish to verify the amounts included in these statements, which are based on the data for Brooks Corporation that were presented earlier in the chapter.

The worksheet to prepare the statement of changes in financial position for Brooks Corporation is presented in Exhibit 25-7. There are two major sections in the worksheet: (1) the balance sheet section, which comprises the top half of the worksheet and (2) the changes in working capital section, which comprises the bottom half. The balance sheet section includes the amount of working capital and each noncurrent balance sheet account. For convenience, the balance sheet items are divided into two groups—those with debit balances and those with credit balances. The changes in working capital section of the worksheet lists the sources and uses of working capital.

The worksheet has four columns. The beginning-of-year balances for the balance sheet items are presented in the first column, and the end-of-year balances are shown in the last column. The two middle columns, labeled "debit" and "credit," provide the means for analyzing the changes in the noncurrent accounts and for identifying the sources and uses of working capital.

Exhibit 25-4
BRROKS CORPORATION
Balance Sheet
December 31, 1982 and 1981

	1982	1981	*Change* Debit (Credit)
Current assets			
Cash	$ 93,600	$ 80,000	$ 13,600
Accounts receivable	10,000	–0–	10,000
	$103,600	$ 80,000	$ 23,600
Noncurrent assets			
Building	$ 28,000	$ –0–	$ 28,000
Accumulated depreciation— building	(2,500)	–0–	(2,500)
Office equipment	12,000	–0–	12,000
Accumulated depreciation— office equipment	(1,500)	–0–	(1,500)
Land	10,000	20,000	(10,000)
	$ 46,000	$ 20,000	$ 26,000
Total assets	$149,600	$100,000	$ 49,600
Current liabilities			
Accounts payable	$ –0–	$ 15,000	$ 15,000
Income taxes payable	16,000	–0–	(16,000)
Salaries payable	3,000	–0–	(3,000)
	$ 19,000	$ 15,000	$ (4,000)
Stockholders' equity			
Common stock	$ 80,000	$ 60,000	$(20,000)
Capital in excess of par	8,000	–0–	(8,000)
Retained earnings	42,600	25,000	(17,600)
	$130,600	$ 85,000	$(45,600)
Total liabilities and stockholders' equity	$149,600	$100,000	$(49,600)

The essential steps involved in completing the worksheet are discussed below.

1. List the item "working capital" as the first line in the debits portion of the balance sheet section if the amount of working capital is positive (i.e., if current assets are greater than current liabilities); if it is negative, list it as the first line in the credits section. Enter the amount of working capital at the beginning of the year in the first column and enter the end-of-year amount in the last column. These amounts are determined from the comparative years'

Exhibit 25-5
BROOKS CORPORATION
Income Statement
For the Year Ended December 31, 1982

Revenues and gains		
Professional services		$80,000
Gain on sale of land		2,000
		$82,000
Expenses		
Salaries	$38,000	
Depreciation	4,000	42,000
Income before income taxes		$40,000
Income taxes		16,000
Net income		$24,000
Earnings per common share		$3.00

balance sheets. For example, Brooks Corporation's comparative years' balance sheets (Exhibit 25-4) show that working capital was $65,000 at December 31, 1981 (current assets, $80,000, less current liabilities, $15,000), and $84,600 at December 31, 1982.

2. List each noncurrent balance sheet account with a debit balance in the debits portion of the balance sheet section and with a credit balance in the credits portion. Enter the respective beginning-of-year balances in the first column and the end-of-year balances in the last column. These balances are taken from the comparative years' balance sheets.

Exhibit 25-6
BROOKS CORPORATION
Statement of Changes in Stockholders' Equity
For the Year Ended December 31, 1982

	Common Stock	Capital in Excess of Par	Retained Earnings
Balance, January 1	$60,000	$ –0–	$25,000
Add			
Net income			24,000
Issuance of stock	20,000	8,000	
Deduct			
Cash dividends			(6,400)
Balance, December 31	$80,000	$8,000	$42,600

Exhibit 25-7
BROOKS CORPORATION
Worksheet for Preparation of Statement of Changes
in Financial Position
For the Year Ended December 31, 1982

	Balance January 1, 1982	Changes Debit	Changes Credit	Balance December 31, 1982
Debits				
Working capital	$65,000	(7) $19,600		$ 84,600
Building	–0–	(5-b) 28,000		28,000
Office equipment	–0–	(6) 12,000		12,000
Land	20,000		(4) $10,000	10,000
Total debits	$85,000			$134,600
Credits				
Accumulated depreciation— building	$ –0–		(3) 2,500	$ 2,500
Accumulated depreciation— office equipment	–0–		(3) 1,500	1,500
Common stock	65,000		(5-a) 20,000	80,000
Capital in excess of par	–0–		(5-a) 8,000	8,000
Retained earnings	25,000	(2) 6,400	(1) 24,000	42,600
Total credits	$85,000	$66,000	$66,000	$134,600
Sources of working capital				
Operations				
Net income		(1) $24,000		
Adjustments to net income:				
Depreciation		(3) 4,000		
Gain on sale of land			(4) $ 2,000	
Sale of land		(4) 12,000		
Issuance of common stock		(5-a) 28,000		
Uses of working capital				
Declaration of cash dividends			(2) 6,400	
Acquisition of building			(5-b) 28,000	
Acquisition of office equipment			(6) 12,000	
Increase in working capital			(7) 19,600	
		$68,000	$68,000	

3. Make sure that the total debits in the first column are equal to the total credits in the first column. Do likewise for the last column.

4. Determine the nature of the change in each noncurrent account. This information often can be determined by examining the other financial statements. For example, the portion of the change in accumulated depreciation that relates to the current year's depreciation usually can be determined by referring to the depreciation expense shown in the income statement. In other cases it may be necessary to examine the specific account in the general ledger to determine the nature of the change.

5. Enter in the debit and credit columns of the worksheet the summary entries that account for the changes in the noncurrent accounts. These entries are in substance a recreation of the original transaction entries, with the exception that debits to working capital accounts in the original entries are entered on the worksheet as debits to "sources of working capital," credits to working capital accounts are entered as credits to "uses of working capital," and debits or credits to items on the income statement that did not affect working capital (e.g., depreciation) are entered as adjustments to net income.
6. After all the changes have been accounted for, make sure that (1) the total of the debits column in the balance sheet section equals the total of the credits column in that section, and that (2) the total debits in the changes in working capital section equal the total credits in that section.

The entries on Brooks Corporation's worksheet are explained in the following discussion. For each entry, the counterpart original transaction entry is presented first, followed by the worksheet entry.

---

(1)

Transaction entry:

Income summary	24,000	
Retained earnings		24,000

Worksheet entry:

Sources of working capital—operations	24,000	
Retained earnings		24,000

The most convenient starting point for the worksheet entries is the change in retained earnings due to net income (loss). This entry substitutes for the many individual entries in which revenues and expenses were recognized. The net income entry is entered as if all items on the income statement affected working capital. Adjustments for items on the income statement that had no effect on working capital are included in subsequent worksheet entries.

---

(2)

Transaction entry:

Retained earnings	6,400	
Cash		6,400

Worksheet entry:

Retained earnings	6,400	
Uses of working capital		6,400

In the case of Brooks Corporation, this dividend declaration entry accounts for the remaining change in retained earnings. At this point all of the changes in the retained earnings of Brooks Corporation have been accounted for on the worksheet.

---

(3)

Transaction entry:
 Depreciation expense   4,000
  Accumulated depreciation—building   2,500
  Accumulated depreciation—office equipment   1,500
Worksheet entry:
 Adjustment—sources of working capital—operations   4,000
  Accumulated depreciation—building   2,500
  Accumulated depreciation—office equipment   1,500

The particular sequence of worksheet entries is a matter of personal preference. However, after accounting for the changes in retained earnings, you may find it convenient to account next for those changes involving income statement items that do not represent sources or uses of working capital. A review of the income statement should help to identify these items. The most common of these nonworking capital income statement items is depreciation. Since depreciation does not represent a use of working capital but is included in the determination of net income, and since the worksheet entry for net income (entry 1) is made as if all items on the income statement did affect working capital, an entry must be made on the worksheet to adjust the sources of working capital—operations for the amount of depreciation. The title of the debit portion of the worksheet entry emphasizes that this debit represents an adjustment to operations and does not represent a source of working capital.

---

(4)

Transaction entry:
 Cash   12,000
  Land   10,000
  Gain on sale of land   2,000
Worksheet entry:
 Sources of working capital   12,000
  Land   10,000
  Adjustments—sources of working capital—
   operations   2,000

The sale of the land resulted in an inflow of working capital of $12,000, which is the amount shown in the worksheet entry as a source of working capital. The $2,000 gain on the sale of land is included in the determination of net income on the income statement, but it does not represent a source or use of working capital. Therefore, the worksheet entry includes an adjustment to sources of working capital—operations for the amount of the gain. A less desirable, but sometimes used, practice is to leave the $2,000 gain in sources of working capital—operations as if it represented a source of working capital and to show the sale of land as a source of working capital of $10,000, which is the book value of the land sold.

(5-a) and (5-b)

Transactions entry:

Building	28,000	
Common stock		20,000
Capital in excess of par		8,000

Worksheet entries:

Sources of working capital	28,000	
Common stock		20,000
Capital in excess of par		8,000
Building	28,000	
Uses of working capital		28,000

This transaction represents both a significant financing activity (issuance of stock) and a significant investing activity (acquisition of building). On the worksheet it is entered as both a source of working capital (entry 5-a) and a use of working capital (entry 5-b). Identifying the worksheet entries with the same number (5), followed by different letters ("a" for entry 5-a and "b" for entry 5-b), represents a convenient way of noting that these entries represent "other significant financing and investing activities." Thus, they can be easily identified later if the preparer wishes to disclose them in a separate section on the statement of changes in financial position, as Brooks Corporation did in Format A (Exhibit 25-2), or if the preparer wishes to cross-reference the two related activities, as shown in Format B (Exhibit 25-3).

---

(6)

Transaction entry:

Office equipment	2,000	
Cash		12,000

Worksheet entry:

Office equipment	12,000	
Use of working capital		12,000

The acquisition of office equipment represents the only change in the office equipment account in this case. In many cases, however, there will be several different types of transactions that account for the change in a given account. In practice you would determine the nature of the changes in a given account by reviewing the entries to the account in the general ledger. Such a review of a plant asset account might reveal, for example, that the change in the account consists of both a purchase and a sale of that type of plant asset. If so, these represent two different transactions. The purchase should be shown as a use of working capital and the sale as a source of working capital.

---

(7)

Transaction entry:
  (none)
Worksheet entry:
  Working capital   19,600
    Uses of working capital   19,600

This entry is the final entry on the worksheet. It reconciles the beginning-of-year working capital balance with the end-of-year balance and serves as the balancing amount in both the balance sheet section and the changes in working capital section of the worksheet. If working capital had decreased during the year, this entry would have been shown as a credit to "working capital" and as a debit to "decrease in working capital" in the sources of working capital section.

After you complete the worksheet, the statement of changes in financial position can be prepared. Information for the statement is obtained from two sources. First, information about the sources and uses of working capital and the other significant financing and investing activities is taken from the changes in working capital section (i.e., the sources and uses sections) of the worksheet. Second, the change in the components of working capital is obtained from the comparative years' balance sheets. As you should expect, Brooks Corporation's statement of changes in financial position is the same as that prepared earlier using the six-step approach. The statement, under two different formats, is in Exhibits 25-2 and 25-3.

Special Problem Areas

The preceding discussion about the preparation of Brooks Corporation's statement of changes in financial position provides a framework for the discussion of certain additional problem areas that may be encountered. These problem areas are discussed in the following order:

1. Special gains and losses in general
2. Extraordinary items
3. Discontinued operations
4. Cumulative effect of a change in accounting principle
5. Gains (losses) on sale of current assets
6. Investments in equity method investees
7. Deferred income taxes
8. Amortization of discount/premium on bonds payable
9. Amortization of discount/premium on bond investments

Unless noted otherwise, funds are defined as working capital in this discussion.

"Special" Gains and Losses in General. *APB Opinion No. 19* requires that the effects of extraordinary items be reported on the statement of changes in financial position separately from the effects of recurring or "normal" operations. It is important to note that at the time the Opinion was issued extraordinary items were the only type of gain or loss requiring separate or "special" disclosure on the income statement.

After the issuance of *Opinion No. 19*, the APB issued *APB Opinion No. 20*, "Accounting Changes," which requires that the cumulative effect of certain changes in accounting principle be disclosed separately on the income statement, between extraordinary items and net income.[9] Later the APB also issued *APB Opinion No. 30*, "Reporting the Results of Operation," which requires that discontinued operations be reported on the income statement separately from income from continuing operations.[10] Thus, there are now three "special" items that must be reported separately on the income statement: (1) extraordinary items, (2) discontinued operations, and (3) the cumulative effect of certain changes in accounting principle.

Given the APB's position in *Opinion No. 19* that funds provided by, or used in, operations should be reported exclusive of extraordinary items, it is logical to assume that funds provided by, or used in, operations also should be reported exclusive of all other "special" items included on the income statement. Therefore, funds provided by, or used in, operations should be reported exclusive of extraordinary items, discontinued operations, and the cumulative effect of changes in accounting principle. The sources or uses of funds related to these special items also should be reported separately on the statement of changes in financial position.

Extraordinary Items. The effects of extraordinary items must be reported separately from the effects of recurring operations. For example, assume that Brooks Corporation's $2,000 gain on sale of land qualifies as an extraordinary gain. In that case, Brooks Corporation's income statement for 1982 would appear as shown in Exhibit 25-8.

The operations and extraordinary items sections of Brooks' statement of changes in financial position would appear as shown below:

Sources of working capital:	
Operations	
Income before extraordinary items	$22,800
Add (deduct) items not affecting working capital:	
Depreciation	4,000
Working capital provided by operations, exclusive	
of extraordinary items	26,800
Extraordinary items	
Sale of land, net of applicable income taxes	
of $800	11,200
Other sources	xxx,xxx

[9] "Accounting Changes," *Opinions of the Accounting Principles Board No. 20* (New York: AICPA, 1971).

[10] "Reporting the Results of Operations," *Opinions of the Accounting Principles Board No. 30* (New York: AICPA, 1973).

Exhibit 25-8
BROOKS CORPORATION
Income Statement
For the Year Ended December 31, 1982

Revenues		
Professional services		$80,000
Expenses		
Salaries	$38,000	
Depreciation	4,000	42,000
Income before income taxes and extraordinary items		38,000
Income taxes		15,200
Income before extraordinary items		22,800
Extraordinary items		
Gain on sale of land (net of applicable income taxes of $800)		1,200
Net income		$24,000

The related worksheet entries for the statement of changes in financial position would be:

(1) Sources of working capital—operations	22,800	
Retained earnings		22,800
(2) Adjustment—sources of working capital— operations	4,000	
Accumulated depreciation		4,000
(3) Sources of working capital—extraordinary item	11,200	
Land		10,000
Retained earnings ($2,000 gain less $800 tax effect)		1,200

The statement of changes in financial position should begin with income before extraordinary items, or with the type of income before the "special" items caption that is most appropriate for the circumstances. It is convenient to prepare the worksheet entries consistent with this requirement. Thus, the first worksheet entry should be for income before extraordinary items. Entry (1) above recognizes the entire amount of income before extraordinary items as a source of working capital from operations. The entry is prepared as if all items included in the determination of income before extraordinary items affected working capital. Any items included therein that did not affect working capital will be adjusted separately. For example, entry (2) shows the adjustment for depreciation. The

$4,000 depreciation is included in the determination of income before extraordinary items, but it had no effect on working capital.

As indicated in worksheet entry (3), the effects of extraordinary items are recognized separately. To better understand how entry (3) is derived, you will find it helpful to review the related transaction entries, as shown below.

Cash	12,000	
Land		10,000
Extraordinary gain		2,000
(To record the sale of the land)		
Extraordinary gain	800	
Income taxes payable (or cash)		800
(To record the income taxes applicable to the gain)		

These transactions increased working capital by $11,200, which is the net increase resulting from the $12,000 increase from the sale of land and the $800 decrease from the income taxes applicable to the extraordinary gain. The $11,200 inflow of working capital is reflected in worksheet entry (3) above as a source of working capital from extraordinary items. The $1,200 extraordinary gain was closed to retained earnings (through the Income Summary account); therefore, entry (3) also shows a $1,200 credit to retained earnings.

In practice some companies would report the extraordinary item on the statement of changes in financial position as follows:

Sources of working capital	
Operations	
Income before extraordinary items	$22,800
Add (deduct) items not affecting working capital:	
Depreciation	4,000
Working capital provided by operations, exclusive of extraordinary items	26,800
Extraordinary items	
Extraordinary gain on sale of land, net of applicable income taxes of $800	1,200
Other sources	
Book value of land sold	10,000

The essence of this approach is that the gain is left in the extraordinary items section as if it represented a source of working capital, with the book value of the land sold being shown separately as an "other" source of working capital. This approach may make it easier to prepare the statement; however, it is a less desirable approach from the standpoint of reporting sources and uses of working capital in the most meaningful manner.

Discontinued Operations. The effects of discontinued operations should be reported on the statement of changes in financial position separately from the effects of recurring operations. To illustrate, assume that ABC Company's partial income statement for the current year is as follows:

Income from continuing operations		$100,000
Discontinued operations		
Loss from operations (net of $4,000 income taxes)	$ 6,000	
Loss on disposal of Division X (net of $20,000 income taxes)	30,000	36,000
Income before extraordinary items		$ 64,000

Assume further that the loss on disposal was computed as follows (assuming no operations after measurement date):

Proceeds from sale of Division X		$ 40,000
Less book value of assets sold		
Inventory	$25,000	
Land	65,000	90,000
Loss before income taxes		(50,000)
Less reduction in income taxes currently due		20,000
Loss on disposal of Division X		$(30,000)

The transaction entry to record the disposal is:

Cash	40,000	
Income tax payable	20,000	
Loss on disposal of Division X (after tax)	30,000	
Inventory		25,000
Land		65,000

This entry increases working capital by $35,000, illustrated below:

Increase in cash	$40,000
Decrease in income taxes payable	20,000
Decrease in inventory	(25,000)
Increase in working capital	$35,000

The loss from operations of the discontinued segment before the measurement date represents a use of working capital of $6,000 (net of tax). This amount would have to be adjusted for any nonworking capital items, such as depreciation, included in its computation.

The net effect of discontinued operations on working capital was a $29,000 increase: $35,000 increase from the disposal and $6,000 decrease from operations. The entries on the statement of changes in financial position worksheet would be:

Sources of working capital—continuing operations	100,000	
Retained earnings		100,000
Retained earnings	36,000	
Sources of working capital—discontinued operations	35,000	
Uses of working capital—discontinued operations		6,000
Land		65,000

The partial statement of changes in financial position for ABC Company is presented below:

Sources of working capital
    Continuing operations
        Income from continuing operations $100,000
        Add (deduct) items not affecting
            working capital

            .
            .   XXX
            .   —————

        Working capital provided by
            continuing operations   XXXX
    Discontinued operations
        From disposal of Division X   35,000
        Less working capital used in
            operations of Division X   6,000
        Working capital provided by
            discontinued operations $29,000

Alternatively, you may choose to disclose for discontinued operations only the net amount of $29,000.

Cumulative Effect of a Change in Accounting Principle. A change in accounting principle is accounted for by including the cumulative effect of the change in the determination of net income. On the statement of changes in financial position, the effects of such accounting changes should be reported separately from the effects of recurring operations. For example, assume that XYZ Company changes from the straight-line depreciation method to an accelerated method and that the cumulative effect of the change is $50,000 before taxes and $30,000 after taxes. If you assume the change was made for both financial and tax purposes, the transaction entry would be as follows:

Cumulative effect	30,000	
Income taxes payable (or refund receivable)	20,000	
Accumulated depreciation		50,000

The related worksheet entry for a statement of changes in financial position would be:

Retained earnings	30,000	
Source of working capital—change in accounting principle	20,000	
Accumulated depreciation		50,000

The $20,000 source of working capital stems from the reduction in income taxes payable (or increase in income taxes receivable) resulting from making the change for tax purposes.

If XYZ had made the change for financial purposes but not for tax purposes, the transaction entry would have been as follows:

Cumulative effect	30,000	
Deferred income taxes	20,000	
Accumulated depreciation		50,000

In this case, the transaction had no effect on working capital and therefore represented neither a source nor a use of working capital. The related worksheet entry for a statement of changes in financial position would have been:

Retained earnings	30,000	
Deferred income taxes	20,000	
Accumulated depreciation		50,000

Gains (Losses) on Sale of Current Assets. In order to calculate the working capital provided by operations, you should adjust net income (or, if applicable, the appropriate income before the "special" items caption) for any ordinary gains or losses on the sale of *noncurrent* assets; gains are deducted, and losses are added. The entire proceeds are shown separately as a source of working capital.

Gains and losses arising from the sale of *current* assets are treated differently. For example, assume that current, marketable equity securities with a cost of $10,000 are sold for $12,000. The transaction entry is as follows:

Cash	12,000	
Marketable equity securities—current		10,000
Gain on sale of securities		2,000

The net effect of this transaction is a $2,000 increase in working capital; one current asset (cash) increased by $12,000, while another (marketable equity securities—current) decreased by $10,000. The gain recognized is equal to the increase in working capital and is therefore left in net income as a source of working capital. Stated generally, net income is not adjusted on the statement of changes in financial position for gains or losses on the sale of current assets when the proceeds are received in the form of other working capital items (current assets or decreases in current liabilities).

Investments in Equity Method Investees. Accounting for an investment in the common stock of an investee under the equity method usually involves two types of transaction entries: (1) recognition of the investor's share of the investee's earnings and (2) recognition of the investor's share of dividends declared by the investee. Assume, for example, that Alpha Company owns 30% of the outstanding common stock of Beta Company. Assume also that during the current year Beta Company reported net income of $100,000 and declared and paid cash dividends of $60,000. Alpha Company would record the following transaction entries:

Investment in Beta Company	30,000	
Equity in earnings of Beta Company		30,000
Cash	18,000	
Investment in Beta Company		18,000

The first transaction entry has no effect on working capital; however, the revenue item, "equity in earnings of Beta Company," is included in Alpha's net income. Conversely, the second transaction entry increased working capital, but the increase is not reflected in Alpha's net income. As a result, the following two entries would be necessary on the worksheet to prepare a statement of changes in financial position:

Investment in Beta Company	30,000	
Adjustment—sources of working capital— operations		30,000
Adjustment—sources of working capital—operations	18,000	
Investment in Beta Company		18,000

The first worksheet entry adjusts net income for a revenue item that had no effect on working capital. Conversely, the second worksheet entry includes in sources of working capital from operations an item that increased working capital but is not included in net income on the income statement. These two worksheet entries often are combined into one entry, shown below:

Investment in Beta Company ($30,000 − $18,000)	12,000	
Adjustment—sources of working capital—		
operations		12,000

This single worksheet entry accomplishes the same end result as the two separate entries. It fully accounts for the change in the investment account and adjusts net income for the net amount of the investor's share of the undistributed earnings of the investee (i.e., the excess of the investor's share of earnings, $30,000, over the dividends received by the investor, $18,000).

Deferred Income Taxes. Depending upon the circumstances involved, deferred income taxes may assume any of the following classifications on the balance sheet:

1. Noncurrent liability—net noncurrent deferred tax credits
2. Noncurrent asset—net noncurrent deferred tax charges
3. Current liability—net current deferred tax credits
4. Current asset—net current deferred tax charges

Changes in *noncurrent* deferred income taxes (classifications 1 and 2) affect net income but have no effect on working capital. Consequently, working capital provided by operations must be adjusted for the change in noncurrent deferred income taxes. For example, a $3,000 increase in deferred income tax credits (noncurrent liability) is recorded in the following transaction entry:

Income tax expense	3,000	
Deferred income taxes—noncurrent liability		3,000

This transaction entry decreased net income by increasing income tax expense but had no effect on working capital. Therefore, working capital provided by operations must be adjusted as reflected in the following worksheet entry for the preparation of a statement of changes in financial position:

Adjustment—sources of working capital—operations	3,000	
Deferred income taxes—noncurrent liability		3,000

The effect of the worksheet entry is to adjust working capital provided by operations by adding an amount equal to the increase in deferred income taxes—noncurrent liability. Conversely, a decrease in this account increases net income (by decreasing income tax expense) but has no effect on working capital. Accordingly, decreases in deferred income taxes—noncurrent liability are deducted from net income in the working capital provided by operations section of the statement of changes in financial position.

The adjustments to working capital provided by operations for changes in deferred income taxes classified as noncurrent assets are just the opposite of those for changes in deferred income taxes classified as noncurrent liabilities. Increases are deducted from working capital provided by operations, whereas decreases in noncurrent deferred income taxes are added.

Changes in deferred income taxes classified as current assets or current liabilities represent sources or uses of working capital and therefore require no adjustments on the worksheet for a statement of changes in financial position.

Amortization of Discount/Premium on Bonds Payable. The amortization of discount/premium on bonds payable classified as noncurrent liabilities is included in the determination of net income as an increase/decrease in interest expense but has no effect on working capital. Since it has no effect on working capital, the amortization of the discount/premium must be added to/deducted from working capital provided by operations. For example, assume that during the current year $10,000 of interest was paid and $1,000 of premium on noncurrent bonds payable was amortized. The transaction entries are:

Interest expense	10,000	
Cash		10,000
Premium on bonds payable	1,000	
Interest expense		1,000

The payment of interest represents a $10,000 use of working capital. However, after amortization of the premium, the interest expense account correctly shows a balance of only $9,000, which is the amount included in the determination of net income. This means that the working capital provided by operations is actually $1,000 less than the amount of net income reported. Therefore, the amount of the premium amortization must be deducted from working capital provided by operations, as reflected in the following statement of changes in financial position worksheet entry:

Premium on bonds payable	1,000	
Adjustment—sources of working capital—operations		1,000

Conversely, the worksheet entry to adjust for a similar amount of amortization of *discount* on noncurrent bonds payable would be:

Adjustment—sources of working capital—operations	1,000	
Discount on bonds payable		1,000

The discount amortized would be added to working capital provided by operations.

The amortization of discount/premium on bonds classified as *current* liabilities represents an increase/decrease in a current liability (i.e., in the bonds payable net of the discount or premium) and therefore represents a use/source of working capital. Accordingly, no adjustment to working capital provided by operations is necessary if the discount/premium relates to bonds payable classified as a current liability.

Amortization of Discount/Premium on Bond Investments. The amortization of discount/premium on bond investments classified as noncurrent assets affects net income but has no effect on working capital. For example, the transaction entry for the amortization of premium on a long-term bond investment of $1,500 is as follows:

Interest revenue	1,500	
Bond investment (or premium on bond investment)		1,500

Since this entry decreased interest revenue, and thereby decreased net income, but had no effect on working capital, the $1,500 premium amortized must be added to working capital provided by operations on the statement of changes in financial position. The related worksheet entry is:

Adjustment—sources of working capital—operations	1,500	
Bond investment (or premium on bond investment)		1,500

The amortization of discount on long-term bond investments increases interest revenue, and thus net income, but has no effect on working capital. Accordingly, the amount of any such discount amortized would be deducted from working capital provided by operations.

Normally the discount/premium on bond investments classified as current assets is not amortized. However, if it is, the amortization of the discount/premium increases/decreases the bond investment (a current asset) and therefore represents a source/use of working capital. Thus, no adjustment to working capital provided by operations is necessary if the discount/premium relates to a bond investment classified as a current asset.

Comprehensive Illustration:
Worksheet Approach—Working Capital Basis

In this section a comprehensive illustration of the preparation of a statement of changes in financial position is presented for Caprock Corporation. The worksheet approach is used, and changes in financial position are expressed in terms of working capital. Presented first for Caprock are (1) comparative years' balance sheets at December 31, 1982, and 1981 (Exhibit 25-9); (2) 1982 income statement (Exhibit 25-10); (3) 1982 retained earnings statement (Exhibit 25-11); and (4) additional information about changes in specific accounts. Next is the worksheet for preparing Caprock's statement of changes in financial position (Exhibit 25-12). This comprehensive illustration incorporates most of the various types of transactions that have been discussed thus far in this chapter. You should review the

Exhibit 25-9
CAPROCK COMPANY
Balance Sheet
December 31, 1982 and 1981

	1982	1981
Current assets		
Cash	$ 23,000	$ 20,000
Accounts receivable (net)	36,000	32,000
Inventory	50,000	60,000
Supplies	6,500	10,000
Prepaid expenses	2,900	5,000
Total current assets	$118,400	$127,000
Plant and equipment		
Building	$ 80,000	$ 80,000
Accumulated depreciation—building	(24,000)	(20,000)
Equipment	31,000	25,000
Accumulated depreciation—equipment	(12,000)	(15,000)
Land	74,000	32,000
Total plant and equipment	$149,000	$102,000
Other assets		
Patent	$ 8,000	$ 12,000
Investment in Alpha Co. stock	56,000	50,000
Investment in Beta Co. bonds	97,000	96,000
Long-term marketable equity securities	23,000	23,000
Allowance for unrealized loss on long-term marketable equity securities	(2,800)	(2,000)
Total other assets	$181,200	$179,000
Total assets	$448,600	$408,000

Exhibit 25-9 (continued)
CAPROCK COMPANY
Balance Sheet
December 31, 1982 and 1981

Current liabilities		
Accounts payable	$ 34,000	$ 30,000
Notes payable—trade	24,000	18,000
Salaries payable	2,800	–0–
Income taxes payable	13,200	12,000
Accrued operating expenses	4,000	6,800
Total current liabilities	$ 78,000	$ 66,800
Long-term liabilities		
8% bonds payable	$ –0–	$ 70,000
12% bonds payable	50,000	–0–
Discount on 12% bonds payable	(4,500)	–0–
Deferred income taxes	4,900	3,200
Total long-term liabilities	$ 50,400	$ 73,200
Stockholders' equity		
Convertible preferred stock, $100 par	$ –0–	$ 50,000
Common stock, $10 par	180,000	100,000
Capital in excess of par—common	48,000	20,000
Retained earnings	113,000	100,000
Treasury stock, at cost	(18,000)	–0–
Unrealized loss on long-term marketable equity securities	(2,800)	(2,000)
Total stockholders' equity	$320,200	$268,000
Total liabilities and stockholders' equity	$448,600	$408,000

illustration carefully, paying particular attention to the worksheet entries and the resulting statement of changes in financial position (Exhibit 25-13).

One item on Caprock's statement of changes in financial position deserves special note—the treatment of the extraordinary item. *FASB Statement No. 4,* "Reporting Gains and Losses from Extinguishment of Debt," specifies that gains and losses on extinguishment of debt shall be aggregated and, if material, disclosed as an extraordinary item.[11] Accordingly, the $3,000 loss (net of tax) on the retirement of the 8% bonds payable is disclosed appropriately on the income statement as an extraordinary loss. The loss did not represent a source or use of working capital; rather the $73,000 payment (net of tax) represented the use of working capital. Technically, *APB Opinion No. 19* requires that on the statement

---

[11] "Reporting Gains and Losses from Extinguishment of Debt," *Statement of Financial Accounting Standards No. 4* (Stamford, Conn.: FASB, 1975), par. 10.

Exhibit 25-10
CAPROCK COMPANY
Income Statement
For the Year Ended December 31, 1982

Revenues and gains		
Sales		$280,000
Equity in earnings of Alpha Company		10,000
Interest income		8,000
Gain on sale of equipment		2,500
		$300,500
Expenses		
Cost of goods sold		$150,000
Salaries		42,000
Supplies used		12,000
Depreciation		11,000
Interest expense		8,000
Patent amortization		4,000
Miscellaneous operating expenses		3,500
		$230,500
Income before income taxes and extraordinary items		$ 70,000
Income taxes		
Current	$26,300	
Deferred	1,700	28,000
Income before extraordinary items		$ 42,000
Extraordinary items:		
Loss on retirement of bonds (net of applicable income taxes of $2,000)		3,000
Net income		$ 39,000
Earnings per common share:		
Income before extraordinary items		$3.23
Net income		$3.00

of changes in financial position the working capital provided by operations, exclusive of extraordinary items, "should be immediately followed by working capital or cash provided or used by income or loss from extraordinary items, if any; extraordinary income or loss should be similarly adjusted for items recognized that did not provide or use working capital or cash during the period."[12] Thus, the extraordinary items would be presented in the following manner:

[12]"Changes in Financial Position," par. 10.

Exhibit 25-11
CAPROCK COMPANY
Retained Earnings Statement
For the Year Ended December 31, 1982

Retained earnings, January 1	$100,000
Net income	39,000
Cash dividends	(10,000)
Stock dividends	(16,000)
Retained earnings, December 31	$113,000

Working capital provided by operations, exclusive of extraordinary items		$49,700
Extraordinary items		
Extraordinary loss (net of income taxes of $2,000)	($3,000)	
Adjustment for items not affecting working capital:		
Loss on retirement of bonds (before tax)	5,000	
Working capital provided by extraordinary items		2,000

The net $2,000 provided by extraordinary items results from the tax savings from the $5,000 (before tax) loss on the retirement of the bonds. Under this approach the $75,000 (before tax) paid to retire the bonds would be shown separately as a use of working capital.

We believe that a more meaningful presentation of these items is to record the $73,000 (net of related tax) paid to retire the bonds as a use of working capital and to label the item clearly as to its nature (extraordinary) and composition. This presentation, as illustrated in Caprock's statement of changes in financial position, emphasizes the flow of financial resources and includes the related aspects in the same proximate area of the statement.

The other worksheet entries and items on the statement of changes in financial position are similar to those discussed previously in the chapter; therefore, they will not be discussed further.

Additional information about changes in specific accounts is listed below:

1. Depreciation expense for 1982 was $11,000, of which $7,000 related to buildings and $4,000 to equipment.
2. The 8% bonds payable were retired on January 2, 1982, at a price of $75,000. The 12% bonds were issued on July 1, 1982, for $45,000; the $5,000 discount is being amortized over the 5-year life of the bonds on a straight-line basis.

Exhibit 25-12
CAPROCK COMPANY
Worksheet for Preparation of Statement of Changes in Financial Position
For the Year Ended December 31, 1982

	Balance December 31, 1981	Changes				Balance December 31, 1982
			Debit		Credit	
Debits						
Working capital	$ 60,200			(19)	$ 19,800	$ 40,400
Building	80,000					80,000
Equipment	25,000	(10)	$ 20,000	(4)	14,000	31,000
Land	32,000	(11-a)	42,000			74,000
Patent	12,000			(8)	4,000	8,000
Investment in Alpha Co. stock	50,000	(2)	6,000			56,000
Investment in Beta Co. bonds	96,000	(3)	1,000			97,000
Long-term marketable equity securities	23,000					23,000
Discount on 12% bonds payable	–0–	(12)	5,000	(7)	500	4,500
Treasury stock	–0–	(13)	18,000			18,000
Unrealized loss on long-term marketable equity securities	2,000	(14)	800			2,800
	$380,200					$434,700
Credits						
Accumulated depreciation— building	$ 20,000			(5)	4,000	$ 24,000
Accumulated depreciation— equipment	15,000	(4)	10,000	(6)	7,000	12,000
Allowance for unrealized loss on long-term marketable equity securities	2,000			(14)	800	2,800
8% bonds payable	70,000	(15)	70,000			–0–
12% bonds payable	–0–			(12)	50,000	50,000
Deferred income taxes	3,200			(9)	1,700	4,900
Convertible preferred stock	50,000	(16-a)	50,000			–0–
Common stock	100,000			(11-b)	30,000	180,000
				(16-b)	40,000	
				(17)	10,000	
Capital in excess of par— common	20,000			(11-b)	12,000	48,000
				(16-b)	10,000	
				(17)	6,000	
Retained earnings	100,000	(15)	3,000	(1)	42,000	113,000
		(17)	16,000			
		(18)	10,000			
	$380,200		$251,800		$251,800	$434,700

Exhibit 25-12 (continued)
CAPROCK COMPANY
Worksheet for Preparation of Statement of Changes in Financial Position
For the Year Ended December 31, 1982

	Balance December 31, 1981	Changes		Balance December 31, 1982
		Debit	*Credit*	
Sources of working capital				
Income before extraordinary items		(1) $ 42,000		
Adjustments to income before extraordinary items				
Increase in equity method investment account			(2) $ 6,000	
Amortization of discount on bond investment			(3) 1,000	
Gain on sale of equipment			(4) 2,500	
Depreciation—building		(5) 4,000		
Depreciation—equipment		(6) 7,000		
Amortization of discount on bonds payable		(7) 500		
Patent amortization		(8) 4,000		
Increase in deferred income taxes		(9) 1,700		
Sale of equipment		(4) 6,500		
Issuance of common stock for land		(11-b) 42,000		
Issuance of 12% bonds		(12) 45,000		
Issuance of common stock for preferred		(16-b) 50,000		
Decrease in working capital		(19) 19,800		
Uses of working capital				
Retirement of bonds (extraordinary)			(15) 73,000	
Purchase of equipment			(10) 20,000	
Acquisition of land			(11-a) 42,000	
Purchase of stock for the treasury			(13) 18,000	
Conversion of preferred stock			(16-a) 50,000	
Cash dividends			(18) 10,000	
		$222,500	$222,500	

3. The 500 shares of preferred stock were converted on July 1, 1982, into 4,000 shares of common stock; capital in excess of par—common was credited for the $10,000 excess of the par value of the preferred stock converted ($50,000) over the par value of the common stock issued ($40,000).

4. A 10% stock dividend of 1,000 shares was declared and issued on January 1, 1982, when the market price of the common stock was $16 per share.

5. Land having a fair market value of $42,000 was acquired on December 30, 1982, in exchange for 3,000 shares of common stock.

6. Equipment with a book value of $4,000 (cost, $14,000; accumulated depreciation, $10,000) was sold for $6,500. New equipment was acquired during the year at a cost of $20,000.
7. Caprock Company uses the equity method to account for its investment in Alpha Company. Caprock received cash dividends of $4,000 from Alpha during 1982.

Exhibit 25-13
CAPROCK COMPANY
Statement of Changes in Financial Position
For the Year Ended December 31, 1982

Financial resources provided by	
Operations	
Income before extraordinary items	$ 42,000
Add (deduct) items not affecting working capital	
Increase in equity in undistributed earnings	
of investee	(6,000)
Amortization of discount on bond investment	(1,000)
Gain on sale of equipment	(2,500)
Depreciation	11,000
Amortization of discount on bonds payable	500
Patent amortization	4,000
Increase in deferred income taxes	1,700
Working capital provided by operations, exclusive	
of extraordinary items	$ 49,700
Sale of equipment	6,500
Issuance of common stock	
For land acquired	42,000
For conversion of preferred stock	50,000
Issuance of bonds payable	45,000
Total financial resources provided	$193,200
Uses of financial resources	
Extraordinary item	
Retirement of bonds, net of $2,000 income tax	
savings related to the $5,000 loss on retirement	$ 73,000
Purchase of equipment	20,000
Acquisition of land	42,000
Reacquisition of the Company's own stock	18,000
Conversion of preferred stock	50,000
Cash dividends	10,000
Total financial resources used	$213,000
Decrease in working capital	$ 19,800

Exhibit 25-13 (continued)
CAPROCK COMPANY
Statement of Changes in Financial Position
For the Year Ended December 31, 1982

Changes in working capital accounts	
Current assets—increase (decrease)	
Cash	$ 3,000
Accounts receivable	4,000
Inventory	(10,000)
Supplies	(3,500)
Prepaid expenses	(2,100)
	$ (8,600)
Current liabilities—(increase) decrease	
Accounts payable	$ (4,000)
Notes payable—trade	(6,000)
Salaries payable	(2,800)
Income taxes payable	(1,200)
Accrued operating expenses	2,800
	$(11,200)
Decrease in working capital	$(19,800)

8. The Beta Company bonds have a face amount of $100,000 and mature on December 31, 1985. The discount is being amortized on a straight-line basis of $1,000 per year.
9. Caprock did not sell or acquire any long-term marketable equity securities during the year.
10. During the year 1,000 shares of Caprock's common stock was reacquired at a price of $18,000; the shares are being held as treasury stock.

Statement of Changes in Financial Position—Cash Basis

The statement of changes in financial position in which changes in financial position are expressed in terms of working capital is the most widely used form for external reporting purposes. However, a number of enterprises use the form of statement in which changes in financial position are expressed in terms of cash. This form is particularly popular for internal reports for management.

Comparison of Procedures for Cash and Working Capital

Conceptually, the approach to preparing a cash basis statement of changes in financial position is the same as that discussed previously for a working capital basis statement. First, funds are defined as cash rather than working capital.

Second, the enterprise's transactions are analyzed to identify (1) those that represent sources and uses of cash and (2) those that represent significant financing and investing activities even though they had no direct effect on cash. The worksheet approach can be used in the analysis of the transactions for a cash basis statement in essentially the same manner in which it is used for a working capital basis statement. The key difference in the worksheet for a cash basis statement is that it would include each working capital account in addition to the noncurrent balance sheet accounts. Finally, the statement format for a cash basis statement is similar to that for a working capital basis statement, except that changes in the noncash working capital accounts are incorporated into the body of the statement rather than shown in a separate schedule.

From a practical standpoint, the transition from the working capital basis to the cash basis is accomplished easily by analyzing the changes in the noncash working capital accounts. Changes in these accounts represent either (1) additional sources and uses of cash or (2) adjustments to cash provided by operations. For example, an increase in accounts receivable means that the cash collected from customers is less than the reported sales amount. Therefore, the increase in accounts receivable must be deducted from sales to determine the cash received from customers. The increase in accounts receivable would be shown on the statement of changes in financial position in the operations section as a deduction from income before extraordinary items.

Just as the change in accounts receivable is related to sales, changes in most of the noncash working capital accounts are related to operating items on the income statement. Accordingly, changes in these accounts will be presented on the statement of changes in financial position as adjustments in the operations section in arriving at cash provided by operations.

Computing Cash Flows

As an example of cash flow computations, the data presented in the preceding section for Caprock Company were used to prepare Caprock's statement of changes in financial position on a cash basis, as shown in Exhibit 25-14. The adjustment related to the change in each noncash working capital account is explained in the discussion that follows.

Accounts Receivable (Net). Net sales (i.e., net of sales discounts, sales returns, and uncollectible accounts expense) are reported on the income statement on an accrual basis. The increase in accounts receivable (net) means that net sales on a cash basis are less than the amount reported on the income statement. Therefore, the increase in accounts receivable (net) must be deducted from income before extraordinary items in arriving at the cash provided by operations.

Inventory. A decrease in inventory means that less goods were purchased than were sold. If we assume for the moment that all purchases were for cash, the amount of cash paid during the year for purchases was less than the cost of goods sold as reported on the income statement. This means that with respect to the decrease in inventory, the net cash provided by operations is greater than the accrual basis amount reported on the income statement. Therefore, the decrease in inventory is added to income before extraordinary items in the operations

Exhibit 25-14
CAPROCK COMPANY
Statement of Changes in Financial Position
For the Year Ended December 31, 1982

Financial resources provided by	
Operations	
Income before extraordinary items	$ 42,000
Add (deduct) items not affecting cash	
Increase in equity in undistributed earnings	
of investee	(6,000)
Amortization of discount on bond investment	(1,000)
Gain on sale of equipment	(2,500)
Depreciation	11,000
Amortization of discount on bonds payable	500
Patent amortization	4,000
Increase in deferred income taxes	1,700
Increase in accounts receivable (net)	**(4,000)**
Decrease in inventory	**10,000**
Decrease in supplies	**3,500**
Decrease in prepaid expenses	**2,100**
Increase in accounts payable	**4,000**
Increase in notes payable—trade	**6,000**
Increase in salaries payable	**2,800**
Increase in income taxes payable	**1,200**
Decrease in accrued operating expenses	**(2,800)**
Cash provided by operations, exclusive of	
extraordinary items	72,500
Sale of equipment	6,500
Issuance of common stock	
For land acquired	42,000
For conversion of preferred stock	50,000
Issuance of bonds payable	45,000
Total cash provided	$216,000
Financial resources used	
Extraordinary item	
Retirement of bonds, net of $2,000 income tax savings	
related to the $5,000 loss on retirement	$ 73,000
Purchase of equipment	20,000
Acquisition of land	42,000
Reacquisition of the Company's own stock	18,000
Conversion of preferred stock	50,000
Cash dividends	10,000
Total cash used	213,000
Increase in cash	$ 3,000

section of the statement of changes in financial position. The adjustment for the change in inventory is made as if all purchases were for cash. Any adjustment necessary because of purchases on account is made in conjunction with the analysis of the change in accounts payable.

Supplies. The decrease in supplies on hand means that less supplies were purchased than were used. Again, if we assume for the moment that all purchases of supplies were for cash, the amount of cash paid during the year for supplies was less than the amount of supplies used as reported on the income statement. Since the cash outflow was less than the expense amount included in net income, the net cash provided by operations was greater than the earnings figure reported on the income statement. Therefore, the decrease in supplies is added to income before extraordinary items.

Prepaid Expenses. Since the prepaid expenses decreased, expenses on a cash basis are less than expenses on an accrual basis. This also means that the net cash provided by operations is larger than the amount of earnings reported. Accordingly, the decrease in prepaid expenses is added to income before extraordinary items on the statement of changes in financial position.

Accounts Payable. The increase in accounts payable indicates that more goods were purchased than were paid for during the year. Since the cash outlay was less than the amount of purchases included in the determination of net income, the net cash inflow from operations was greater than reported earnings. Therefore, the increase in accounts payable is added to income before extraordinary items.

Notes Payable—Trade. Since the notes payable relate to purchases of inventory items, changes in this account are handled in the same manner on the statement of changes in financial position as are changes in accounts payable.

Salaries Payable. The increase in salaries payable indicates that salaries expense was greater than the amount of salaries paid during the year. Since the cash outlay was less than the amount of expense, the increase in salaries payable is added to income in the operations section of the statement of changes in financial position.

Income Taxes Payable. The cash outlay for taxes during the year was less than the expense recognized on the income statement (i.e., the current portion recognized, $26,300), which means that the net cash provided by operations was greater than the earnings figure reported. Therefore, the increase in income taxes payable is added to income before extraordinary items.

Accrued Operating Expenses. The decrease in accrued operating expenses indicates that expenses on a cash basis were greater than expenses on an accrual basis. This means that the cash outflow was larger than the amount reported as expense on the income statement. Income before extraordinary items is adjusted by deducting the decrease in accrued operating expenses.

As noted previously, changes in most noncash working capital accounts are related to items included in income from continuing operations. Therefore,

Exhibit 25-15
Adjustments to "Operations" for Changes in Noncash Working Capital Accounts

Type of Change in Noncash Working Capital Account	Required Adjustment to Income from Continuing Operations
Increase in current assets	Add
Decrease in current liabilities	Add
Decrease in current assets	Deduct
Increase in current liabilities	Deduct

changes in these accounts are shown in the cash provided by operations section of the cash basis statement of changes in financial position, as adjustments to income from continuing operations. The adjustments required for changes in noncash working capital accounts *related to operations* are summarized in Exhibit 25-15.

Changes in other noncash working capital accounts must be analyzed to determine their proper treatment, if any, in the statement of changes in financial position. In general, changes associated with receipts of cash would be shown as "other" sources of cash, and changes associated with disbursements of cash would be shown as "other" uses of cash. For example, a decrease in cash dividends payable would be shown as an "other" use of cash if the reduction in the cash dividends payable resulted from the payment of the dividend in the form of cash.

On the other hand, changes in these noncash working capital accounts (i.e., those unrelated to operations) that are *not* associated with receipts or disbursements of cash have no direct effect on cash. Such changes must be analyzed, however, to determine if they represent significant financing and investing activities even though they had no direct effect on cash. For example, the issuance of, or increase in, short-term notes payable in exchange for equipment has no direct effect on cash. However, the transaction represents both a significant financing activity (issuance of the short-term note payable) and a significant investing activity (acquisition of equipment). Therefore, it would be reported in the "other significant financing and investing activities" section of the statement of changes in financial position or, alternatively, reported as both a source and use of cash. In the latter case, the increase in short-term notes payable would be shown as a source of cash and the acquisition of equipment as a use of cash.

A separate schedule of changes in working capital accounts is not required for a statement of changes in financial position prepared in a cash basis format. As illustrated for Caprock Company (Exhibit 25-14), changes in these accounts are disclosed in the body of the statement as sources or uses of cash, or as adjustments to cash provided by operations.

Financial Statement Disclosures

APB Opinion No. 19 indicates that whether or not working capital flow is presented, the net changes in each component of working capital should be disclosed for at least the current year. Also, the effects of other financing and investing

Exhibit 25-16
MCDONALD'S CORPORATION
Statement of Changes in Financial Position

Years ended December 31,	1980	1979	1978	1977	1976
			(In thousands of dollars)		
Source of working capital					
Operations—					
Net income	$220,893	$188,608	$162,669	$136,696	$109,180
Items not involving working capital					
Depreciation and amortization	119,848	96,967	79,831	65,387	53,717
Deferred income taxes	31,090	24,178	13,945	10,089	11,828
Other—net	5,341	1,450	(457)	(7)	(2,525)
Total from operations	377,172	311,203	255,988	212,165	172,200
Issuance of common stock on exercise of options	751	584	4,719	690	2,604
Long-term debt additions	408,709	506,937	312,066	156,632	130,599
Property and equipment disposals (gains and losses included in operations)	19,383	18,682	16,976	14,825	14,602
Security deposits by franchisees	6,486	8,059	7,236	6,735	5,470
Other	20,881	24,135	22,085	20,663	11,152
Total source of working capital	833,382	869,600	619,070	411,710	336,627
Use of working capital					
Property and equipment additions	410,457	437,754	354,095	301,636	233,127
Non-current assets of businesses purchased	12,760	52,399	7,833	21,869	6,132
Notes receivable due after one year	29,806	30,741	19,425	11,134	14,704
Long-term debt reductions	401,929	321,611	215,052	64,298	80,680
Cash dividends	29,731	20,516	12,949	6,073	4,021
Treasury stock purchases	3,320	13,633	1,416	5,096	885
Other	16,484	11,974	10,110	9,015	8,627
Total use of working capital	904,487	888,628	620,880	419,121	348,176
Decrease in working capital	$(71,105)	$(19,028)	$ (1,810)	$ (7,411)	$(11,549)

Exhibit 25-16 (continued)
MCDONALD'S CORPORATION
Statement of Changes in Financial Position

Years ended December 31,	1980	1979	1978	1977	1976
			(In thousands of dollars)		
Changes in elements of working capital Increase (decrease) in current assets:					
Cash and certificates of deposit	$(47,000)	$ 29,680	$ 33,466	$ 3,715	$ 6,992
Short-term investments	19,161	(45,582)	(9,205)	12,481	6,562
Accounts and notes receivable	10,145	7,478	5,995	10,863	4,411
Inventories	3,050	3,466	1,920	1,295	1,433
Prepaid expenses and other current assets	1,854	8,230	3,212	3,548	388
	(12,790)	3,272	35,388	31,902	19,786
Increase (decrease) in current liabilities:					
Accounts and notes payable	24,955	21,392	17,085	29,765	22,770
Income taxes	29,832	(5,779)	(2,918)	(4,129)	7,710
Other accrued liabilities	9,015	6,100	6,191	6,213	1,922
Current maturities of long-term debt	(5,487)	587	16,840	7,464	(1,067)
	58,315	22,300	37,198	39,313	31,335
Decrease in working capital	$(71,105)	$(19,028)	$ (1,810)	$ (7,411)	$(11,549)

activities should be disclosed separately. For example, both new borrowings and repayments of long-term debt should be disclosed; they should not be reported as a net figure.

The *Opinion* also indicates that in addition to showing the working capital or cash provided by operations, the following should be disclosed:

1. Outlays for purchase of long-term assets. . . .
2. Proceeds from sale . . . of long-term assets . . . not in the normal course of business, less related expenses involving the current use of working capital or cash.

3. Conversion of long-term debt or preferred stock to common stock.

4. Issuance, assumption, redemption, and replayment of long-term debt.

5. Issuance, redemption, or purchase of capital stock for cash or for assets other than cash.

6. Dividends in cash or in kind, or other distributions to shareholders . . . .[13]

An example of statement disclosure of changes in financial position appears in Exhibit 25-16. The statement was taken from a recent annual report of McDonald's Corporation. Notice that McDonald's chose to disclose more than just the most recent two years; they report five years of data. The statement includes the sources of working capital, the uses of working capital, and the net change in working capital for the period. The bottom part of the statement shows the changes in the elements of working capital, the results agree with the increase or decrease in working capital computed in the top part of the statement.

[13] Ibid., par. 14.

Concept Summary

PRINCIPAL ISSUES RELATED TO STATEMENT OF CHANGES IN FINANCIAL POSITION

Issue	Current Position
When statement is required	If the financial report includes both a balance sheet and an income statement, the statement of changes in financial position must be presented for each period for which an income statement is presented.
Definition of *funds*	As long as the statement discloses all significant financing and investing activities, the changes in financial resources may be expressed in terms of (i.e., *funds* may be defined as) (1) cash, (2) cash and temporary investments combined, (3) all quick assets, or (4) working capital.
Presentation of *funds* provided by operations	*Funds* provided by operations must be presented separately and should exclude the effects of *special* gains and losses.
Presentation of *special* gains and losses	The effects of *special* gains and losses (i.e., extraordinary items, discontinued operations, and the cumulative effect of a change in accounting principle) should be presented separately. The presentation

	should identify the effect the related transaction or event had on financial resources.
Presentation of significant financing and investing activities that had no effect on funds	These activities may be presented either (1) within the sources and uses of *funds* sections by including the financing aspect as a source of *funds* and the investing aspect as a use of *funds* or (2) in a separate section of the statement.
Techniques to aid in the preparation of a statement of changes in financial position	The two most popular approaches are (1) the worksheet approach and (2) the T-account approach. The worksheet approach is the most widely used in practice. However, the T-account approach may prove to be less time-consuming and thus the best approach for purposes of the CPA examination.

Appendix

The T-Account Approach

The T-account approach for preparing a statement of changes in financial position differs from the worksheet approach in form but not in substance. The primary advantage of the T-account approach is that in some cases it may be less time-consuming.

Like the worksheet approach, the T-account approach facilitates the analysis of changes in the accounts in an orderly and systematic manner. Further, it also is applicable regardless of how funds are defined. The approach is demonstrated below under the assumption that changes in financial position are expressed in terms of working capital. The data for Brooks Corporation presented earlier will be used to illustrate the T-account approach.

Since Brooks Corporation measures changes in financial position in terms of working capital, a T-account is constructed for (1) working capital and (2) each noncurrent account. The working capital T-account is used to summarize the sources and uses of working capital, much like the bottom part of the worksheet was used. The change in working capital during the year is computed and entered on the appropriate side of the T-account. Brooks Corporation's working capital increase of $19,600 is entered on the debit side; a decrease would be entered on the credit side. A line is then drawn below the amount of the change as shown. Sources of working capital and debit adjustments (additions to) to working capital provided by operations will be entered on the debit side of the working capital account. Uses of working capital and credit adjustments to (deductions from) working capital provided by operations will be entered on the credit side of the working capital account.

For each noncurrent account, the change in the account is entered on the appropriate side of its T-account. Increases in assets and decreases in liabilities and owners' equity accounts represent debit changes and are entered on the debit side. Decreases in assets and increases in liabilities and owners' equity accounts represent credit changes and are entered on the credit side. A line is drawn beneath the amount of change as shown.

Like the worksheet approach, the essence of the T-account approach is to account for the changes in the noncurrent accounts. The transaction entries are reconstructed and entered in the appropriate accounts; the sources and uses of working capital are shown in the working capital T-account. The change entered at the top of each noncurrent account represents the change that must be accounted for or explained. For each account, when all of the changes in that account have been accounted for, the net debits or net credits resulting from the entries "below the line" will equal the net change in the account shown at the top ("above the line").

Exhibit 25-17
T-Account Approach

Working Capital

	$19,600			
(Sources)			**(Uses)**	
(1) Net income	$24,000	(2)	Cash dividends	$ 6,400
(3) Adjustment—		(4)	Adjustment—gain	
depreciation	4,000		on sale of land	2,000
(4) Sale of land	12,000	(5-b)	Acquisition of	
(5-a) Common stock			building	28,000
issued	28,000	(6)	Acquisition of	
			office equipment	12,000
	$68,000			$48,400

Building

	$28,000	
(5-b) Acquisition of		
building	$28,000	

Accumulated Depreciation—Building

		$2,500
	(3) 1982 depreciation	$2,500

Office Equipment

	$12,000	
(6) Acquisition of		
office equipment	$12,000	

Accumulated Depreciation—Office Equipment

		$1,500
	(3) 1982 depreciation	$1,500

Land

		$10,000
	(4)	$10,000

Exhibit 25-17 (continued)
T-Account Approach

Common Stock

			$20,000
	(5-a)		$20,000

Capital in Excess of Par

			$8,000
	(5-a)		$8,000

Retained Earnings

				$17,600
(2) Cash dividends	$6,400	(1) Net income		$24,000

The T-account entries for Brooks Corporation are the same as the entries recorded on Brooks' worksheet for the preparation of a statement of changes in financial position (Exhibit 25-7), except that entry (7) on the worksheet as a balancing entry is not needed under the T-account approach. The use of the T-account approach is illustrated in Exhibit 25-17. Entry (1), for example, shows a debit to the working capital T-account as a source of working capital (net income) with the credit to retained earnings. Entries that involve adjustments to net income are entered in the appropriate column (debit or credit) of the working capital account. For example, entry (3) reflects the adjustment for depreciation and is entered as a debit in the working capital account and a credit in the accumulated depreciation accounts. Notice that the debit to the working capital account is labeled "Adjustment—depreciation" to indicate that it represents a nonworking capital item adjustment to net income rather than a source of working capital.

Transactions that represent "other significant financing and investing activities" are entered both as a source and a use of working capital. For example, Brooks Corporation's acquisition of land by issuing common stock is shown as a source of working capital from issuance of stock (entry 5-a) and as a use of working capital for the acquisition of land (entry 5-b).

The changes in the noncurrent accounts are analyzed, and the appropriate entries are entered until all changes have been accounted for or explained. At this point, the difference between the total debits and total credits entered in the working capital account should be equal to the net change in working capital, as shown at the top of the account.

The entries in the working capital account provide the basis for preparing the statement of changes in financial position; the schedule of changes in the individual working capital accounts would be obtained for the comparative years' balance sheet. Brooks Corporation's statement of changes in financial position was presented under two different formats in Exhibits 25-2 and 25-3.

Questions

Q-25-1 What are the objectives of a statement of changes in financial position?

Q-25-2 What is meant by the term *financial position?*

Q-25-3 Is the statement of changes in financial position the only required financial statement that presents information about changes in an enterprise's financial position? Briefly explain.

Q-25-4 In a statement of changes in financial position, the changes in financial position may be expressed in terms of any one of a number of concepts of funds. Working capital is one of these acceptable concepts of funds. What are the others?

Q-25-5 The statement of changes in financial position must disclose all significant financing and investing activities regardless of whether cash or other elements of working capital were affected directly. Give three examples of transactions that must be disclosed on the statement of changes in financial position even though they had no direct effect on cash or other elements of working capital.

Q-25-6 All significant financing and investing activities must be disclosed in the statement of changes in financial position even if they had no direct effect on cash or other elements of working capital. Give one example of this type of transaction for each of the following categories:

    a) Increase in a noncurrent asset and decrease in another noncurrent asset.
    b) Increase in a noncurrent asset and increase in a noncurrent liability.
    c) Increase in a noncurrent asset and increase in stockholders' equity.
    d) Increase in a noncurrent liability and decrease in stockholders' equity.
    e) Increase in stockholder's equity and decrease in a noncurrent liability.
    f) Decrease in a noncurrent asset and decrease in a noncurrent liability.

Q-25-7 Give seven examples of items added back to income from continuing operations to arrive at working capital provided by operations.

Q-25-8 Give four examples of items deducted from income from continuing operations to arrive at working capital provided by operations.

Q-25-9 Certain changes in accounting principles are accounted for by including the cumulative effect of the change, net of tax, in the determination of net income in the year of the change. How are such changes in accounting principles reported in a statement of changes in financial position (working capital basis)?

Q-25-10 Assume a company prepares a statement of changes in financial position (working capital basis) in which working capital provided by operations is presented by showing net income and the adjustments to net income for nonworking capital items. Explain how the current year's change in deferred income taxes should be reported, if at all, under each of the following independent assumptions:

    a) Increase in deferred tax credits (noncurrent liability).
    b) Increase in deferred tax credits (current liability).
    c) Increase in deferred tax charges (noncurrent asset).
    d) Increase in deferred tax charges (current asset).
    e) Decrease in deferred tax credits (noncurrent liability).

Q-25-11 During the current year a company reported a net loss of $40,000, but the statement of changes in financial position (working capital basis) correctly showed working capital provided by operations of $15,000. Explain how this difference could occur.

Q-25-12 During the current year a company reported net income of $20,000, but the statement of changes in financial position correctly showed working capital used in operations of $10,000. Explain how this difference could occur.

Q-25-13 How should the effects of extraordinary items be presented in a statement of changes in financial position (working capital basis)?

Q–25–14 "All changes in current asset and current liability accounts must be added to or deducted from (depending on the direction of the change) net income in computing the cash provided by or used in operations." Do you agree with this statement? If you disagree, explain why.

Q–25–15 A company prepares its statement of changes in financial position on a working capital basis. The company may use either of two approaches in the presentation of working capital provided by or used in operations. What are these two approaches? Which do you prefer and why?

Q–25–16 Select the best answer for each of the following questions.

a) A statement of changes in financial position should be issued by a profit-oriented business

(1) As an alternative to the statement of income and retained earnings.
(2) Only if the business classifies its assets and liabilities as current and noncurrent.
(3) Only when two-year comparative balance sheets are not issued.
(4) Whenever a balance sheet and a statement of income and retained earnings are issued.

b) The statement of changes in financial position discloses changes in financial position during the year and also

(1) Summarizes the financing and investing activities of an entity.
(2) Reports the changes in net working capital as opposed to cash.
(3) Relates changes in net monetary assets to net working capital.
(4) Reflects transactions that affect current financial position.

c) If a company issues both a balance sheet and an income statement with comparative figures from last year, a statement of changes in financial position

(1) Is no longer necessary, but may be issued at the company's option.
(2) Should not be issued.
(3) Should be issued for each period for which an income statement is presented.
(4) Should be issued for the current year only.

d) The working capital format is an acceptable format for presenting a statement of changes in financial position. Which of the following formats is (are) also acceptable?

	Cash	*Quick assets*
(1)	Acceptable	Not acceptable
(2)	Not acceptable	Not acceptable
(3)	Not acceptable	Acceptable
(4)	Acceptable	Acceptable

e) Which of the following items is included on a statement of changes in financial position only because of the all financial resources concept?

(1) Depreciation.
(2) Issuance (sale) of common stock.
(3) Purchase of treasury stock.
(4) Retirement of long-term debt by issuance of preferred stock.

f) Which of the following must be disclosed in a statement of changes in financial position or in a related tabulation for at least the current period?

(1) Net changes in each balance sheet account.
(2) Net change in each element of working capital.
(3) Gross changes in depreciable assets.
(4) Earnings per share.

(AICPA adapted)

Q–25–17 Select the best answer for each of the following questions.

a) On a statement of changes in financial position, depreciation is treated as an adjustment to reported net earnings because depreciation

    (1) Is a direct source of funds.

    (2) Reduces reported net earnings but does not involve an outflow of funds.

    (3) Reduces reported net earnings and involves an inflow of funds.

    (4) Is an inflow of funds to a reserve account for replacement of assets.

b) How should the amortization of bond discount for a bond issuer be shown on the statement of changes in financial position (defining funds as working capital)?

    (1) Need not be shown.

    (2) Use of funds.

    (3) Expense not requiring the use of funds.

    (4) Contra-expense item not providing funds.

c) The amortization of bond discount on long-term debt should be presented in a statement of changes in financial position as a (an)

    (1) Use of funds.

    (2) Source and a use of funds.

    (3) Addition to income.

    (4) Deduction from income.

d) A loss on the sale of machinery in the ordinary course of business should be presented in a statement of changes in financial position as a (an)

    (1) Deduction from income.

    (2) Addition to income.

    (3) Source and a use of funds.

    (4) Use of funds.

e) The amortization of patents should be presented in a statement of changes in financial position as a (an)

    (1) Source and use of funds.

    (2) Use of funds.

    (3) Addition to net income.

    (4) Deduction from net income.

f) Which of the following would be subtracted in converting net earnings to working capital provided by operations in the current period in a consolidated statement of changes in financial position?

    (1) Amortization of premium on bonds payable.

    (2) Amortization of goodwill.

    (3) Increase in deferred income tax liability.

    (4) Minority interest's share of net earnings.

(AICPA adapted)

Q–25–18 Select the best answer for each of the following questions.

    a) Which of the following items represents a potential use of working capital?

    (1) Goodwill amortization.

    (2) Sale of fixed assets at a loss.

    (3) Net loss from operations.

    (4) Declaration of a stock dividend.

    b) Which one of the following transactions would affect a statement of changes in financial position in which funds are defined as cash, but not one in which funds are defined as working capital?

    (1) Recording a net loss from operations.

    (2) Amortizing a premium on bonds.

    (3) Acquiring treasury stock.

    (4) Paying last year's federal income tax liability.

    c) In a statement of changes in financial position (defining funds as working capital) bad debt expense should be added back to net income when it relates to

	Current Receivables	Long-term Receivables
(1)	Yes	Yes
(2)	Yes	No
(3)	No	No
(4)	No	Yes

d) When preparing a statement of changes in financial position using the cash basis for defining funds, an increase in ending inventory over beginning inventory will result in an adjustment to reported net earnings because

(1) Funds were increased since inventory is a current asset.

(2) The net increase in inventory reduced cost of goods sold but represents an assumed use of cash.

(3) Inventory is an expense deducted in computing net earnings, but is not a use of funds.

(4) All changes in noncash accounts must be disclosed under the all financial resources concept.

e) Which of the following need not be disclosed in a statement of changes in financial position as a source and use of funds?

(1) Acquisition of fixed assets in exchange for capital stock.

(2) Dividend paid in capital stock of the company (stock dividend).

(3) Retirement of a bond issue through the issuance of another bond issue.

(4) Conversion of convertible debt to capital stock.

(AICPA adapted)

Discussion Questions and Cases

D–25–1 The statement of changes in financial position is normally a required basic financial statement for each period for which an earnings statement is presented. The reporting entity has flexibility in the form, content, and terminology of this statement to meet the objectives of differing circumstances. For example, the concept of *funds* may be interpreted to mean, among other things, cash or working capital. However, the statement should be prepared based on the *all financial resources* concept.

Required:

1. What is the *all financial resources* concept?

2. What are two types of financial transactions that would be disclosed under the all financial resources concept that would not be disclosed without this concept?

3. What effect, if any, would each of the following seven items have on the preparation of a statement of changes in financial position prepared in accordance with generally accepted accounting principles using the cash concept of funds?

a) Accounts receivable—trade.

b) Inventory.

c) Depreciation.

d) Deferred income tax credit from interperiod allocation.

e) Issuance of long-term debt in payment for a building.

f) Payoff of current portion of debt.

g) Sale of a fixed asset resulting in a loss.

(AICPA adapted)

D–25–2 There have been considerable discussion and research in recent years concerning the reporting of changes in financial position (sources and applications of funds). APB *Opinion No. 19* concluded:

> . . . That the statement summarizing changes in financial position should be based on a broad concept embracing all changes in financial position and that the title of the statement should reflect this broad concept. The Board therefore recommends that the title be Statement of Changes in Financial Position.

Required:
1. What are the two common meanings of *funds* as used when preparing the statement of changes in financial position? Explain.
2. What is meant by ". . . a broad concept embracing all changes in financial position . . ." as used by the APB in its *Opinion No. 19?* Explain.

(AICPA adapted)

D–25–3 Chen Engineering Company is a young and growing producer of electronic measuring instruments and technical equipment. You have been retained by Chen to advise the company in the preparation of a statement of changes in financial position. For the fiscal year ended October, 31, 1975, you have obtained the following information concerning certain events and transactions of Chen:

a) The amount of reported earnings for the fiscal year was $800,000, which included a deduction for an extraordinary loss of $93,000 (see part e below).

b) Depreciation expense of $240,000 was included in the earnings statement.

c) Uncollectible accounts receivable of $30,000 were written off against the allowance for uncollectible accounts. Also, $37,000 of bad debts expense was included in determining earnings for the fiscal year, and the same amount was added to the allowance for uncollectible accounts.

d) A gain of $4,700 was realized on the sale of a machine; it originally cost $75,000, of which $25,000 was undepreciated on the date of sale.

e) On April 1, 1975, a freak lightning storm caused an uninsured inventory loss of $93,000 ($180,000 loss, less reduction in income taxes of $87,000). This extraordinary loss was included in determining earnings as indicated in part a above.

f) On July 3, 1975, building and land were purchased for $600,000; in payment Chen gave $100,000 cash, $200,000 market value of its unissued common stock, and a $300,000 purchase-money mortgage.

g) On August 3, 1975, $700,000 face value of Chen's 6% convertible debentures were converted into $140,000 par value of its common stock. The bonds originally were issued at face value.

h) The board of directors declared a $320,000 cash dividend on October 20, 1975, payable on November 15, 1975, to stockholders of record on November 5, 1975.

Required:
For each of the eight (8) lettered items above, explain whether each item is a source or use of working capital and explain how it should be disclosed in Chen's statement of changes in financial position for the fiscal year ended October 31, 1975. If any item is neither a source nor a use of working capital, explain why it is not and indicate the disclosure, if any, that should be made of the item in Chen's statement of changes in financial position for the fiscal year ended October 31, 1975.

(AICPA adapted)

D–25–4 The following statement was prepared by the accountant for the E. R. Roycie Corporation:

E. R. ROYCIE CORPORATION
Statement of Changes in Financial Position
For the Year Ended September 30, 1982

Sources of funds	
Net income	$ 52,000
Depreciation and depletion	59,000
Increase in long-term debt	178,000
Common stock issued under employee option plans	5,000
Changes in current receivables and inventories less current liabilities (excluding current maturities of long-term debt)	3,000
	$297,000

Application of funds	
Cash dividends	$ 33,000
Expenditures for property, plant, and equipment	202,000
Investments and other uses	9,000
Change in cash	53,000
	$297,000

The following additional information is available on the E. R. Roycie Corporation for the year ended September 30, 1982:

a) The balance sheet of Roycie Corporation distinguishes between current and non-current assets and liabilities.

b)	Depreciation expense	$ 58,000
	Depletion expense	1,000
		$ 59,000

c)	Increase in long-term debt	$600,000
	Retirement of debt	422,000
	Net increase	$178,000

d) The corporation received $5,000 in cash from its employees on its employee stock option plans, and wage and salary expense attributable to the option plans was an additional $22,000.

e)	Expenditures for property, plant, and equipment	$212,000
	Proceeds from retirements of property, plant, and equipment	10,000
	Net expenditures	$202,000

f) A stock dividend of 10,000 shares of Roycie Corporation common stock was distributed to common stockholders on April 1, 1982, when the per-share market price was $6 and par value was $1.

g) On July 1, 1982, when its market price was $5 per share, 16,000 shares of Roycie Corporation common stock was issued in exchange for 4,000 shares of preferred stock.

Required:
1. In general, what are the objectives of a statement of the type shown above for the Roycie Corporation? Explain.

2. Identify the weaknesses in the form and format of the Roycie Corporation's statement of changes in financial position without reference to the additional information.

3. For each of the seven (a–g) items of additional information for the statement of changes in financial position, indicate the preferable treatment and explain why the suggested treatment is preferable.

(AICPA adapted)

D–25–5 This question concerns the various interrelationships among financial statements, accounts (or groups of accounts) among those statements, and accounts (or groups of accounts) within each statement. The following information is presented for Woods Company for the year ended December 31, 1974:

a) The statement of changes in financial position.

b) Selected information from the income statement.

c) Selected information regarding the January 1 and December 31 balance sheets.

d) Information regarding the correction of an error.

e) Partially completed balance sheets at January 1 (prior to restatement) and December 31. The omitted account and groups-of-account balances are numbered from (1) through (16) and can be calculated from the other information given.

Statement of Changes in Financial Position

Working capital, January 1, 1974		$16,500
Add resources provided		
Operations		
Net loss for 1974	$(2,885)	
Adjustments not involving working capital:		
Bond premium amortization	(500)	
Deferred income taxes	(200)	
Depreciation expense	3,000	
Goodwill amortization for 1974	2,000	
Total from operations	$1,415	
Portion of proceeds of equipment sold representing		
undepreciated cost	10,000	
Proceeds from reissue of treasury stock	11,400	
Par value of common stock issued to reacquire preferred stock	7,500	
Total resources provided	$30,315	
Subtract resources applied		
Purchase of land	14,715	
Current maturity of long-term bond debt	7,200	
Par value of preferred stock reacquired by issuing common stock	7,500	
Total resources applied	$29,415	
Increase in working capital		900
Working capital, December 31, 1974		$17,400

Information from the Income Statement

Bad debt expense	$ 750
Bond interest expense (net of amortization of bond premium)	$3,500
Loss before tax adjustment	$(3,900)

Less

Income tax adjustment (refund due)	$815	
Deferred income taxes	200	1,015
Net loss after tax adjustment		$(2,885)

Information Regarding January 1 and December 31 Balance Sheets

The book value of the equipment sold was two-thirds of the cost of that equipment.

Selected Ratios

	January 1, 1974 (prior to restatement)	December 31, 1974
Current ratio	?	3 to 1
Total stockholders' equity divided by total liabilities	4 to 3	?

Information Regarding the Correction of an Error

Woods Company had neglected to amortize $2,000 of goodwill in 1973. The correction of this material error has been apropriately made in 1974.

Balance Sheet

	January 1, 1974 (prior to restatement)	December 31, 1974
Current assets	$22,000	$ (5)
Building and equipment	92,000	(6)
Accumulated depreciation	(25,000)	(7)
Land	(1)	(8)
Goodwill	12,000	(9)
Total assets	$ (?)	$ (?)
Current liabilities	$ (2)	(10)
Bonds payable (8%)	(3)	(11)
Bond premium	(?)	(12)
Deferred income taxes	(4)	1,700
Common stock	66,000	(13)
Paid-in capital	13,000	(14)
Preferred stock	16,000	(15)
Retained earnings (deficit)	(6,000)	(16)
Treasury stock (at cost)	(9,000)	0
Total liabilities and stockholders' equity	$ (?)	$ (?)

Required:
Number your answer sheet from (1) through (16). Place the correct balance for each balance-sheet account or group of accounts next to the corresponding number on your answer sheet. Show supporting computations in good form. (One account balance and the totals are shown as a question mark (?). Calculation of these amounts may be necessary to calculate the numbered balances, but is not required to be shown separately in your numbered answers.) Do not recopy the balance sheets. Calculation of answers need not follow the numerical order of these blanks 1 through 16. Do not restate the January 1 balance sheet for the error.

(AICPA adapted)

Exercises

E–25–1 Indicate in the space provided whether each of the following independent transactions or events represents a source of *funds* (S), a use of *funds* (U), or has no effect on *funds* (NE).

	Assuming *funds* are defined as working capital	Assuming *funds* are defined as cash
a) Declaration of a cash dividend.	_____	_____
b) Payment of the dividend declared in a) above.	_____	_____
c) Acquisition of equipment by issuance of short-term note payable.	_____	_____
d) Sale of current marketable equity securities below cost.	_____	_____
e) Collection of an account receivable from a customer.	_____	_____
f) Recording adjusting entry to recognize uncollectible accounts expense using the allowance method.	_____	_____
g) Write-off of uncollectible account against the allowance for uncollectible accounts account.	_____	_____
h) Declaration of a stock dividend.	_____	_____
i) Purchase of merchandise on account.	_____	_____
j) Sale of land for less than book value.	_____	_____

E–25–2 Blue Company owns 40% of the outstanding common stock of Red Company. During the current year Blue recorded the following entries related to its investment in Red:

Investment in Red Company	40,000	
Equity in earnings of Red Company		40,000
To record Blue's share of earnings of Red.		
Cash	24,000	
Investment in Red Company		24,000
To record Blue's share of dividends paid by Red.		

Assume that a) Blue Company reported net income for the current year of $150,000 and b) all other revenues and expenses (i.e., other than those related to Blue's investment in Red) affected working capital.

Required:

Prepare a schedule to compute the working capital provided by operations for Blue Company for the current year.

E–25–3 Comparative balance sheets, an income statement, and additional information are presented below for Martha Company:

MARTHA COMPANY
Balance Sheets

| | December 31, | |
	1983	1982
Cash	$ 15,000	$ 10,000
Accounts receivable	33,000	20,000
Inventory	50,000	40,000
Building	65,000	60,000
Accumulated depreciation	(16,000)	(12,000)
	$147,000	$118,000
Accounts payable	$ 25,000	$ 20,000
Common stock	100,000	80,000
Retained earnings	22,000	18,000
	$147,000	$118,000

MARTHA COMPANY
Income Statement
For the Year Ended December 31, 1983

Sales		$100,000
Cost of goods sold		65,000
Gross margin on sales		$ 35,000
Operating expenses		
Depreciation	$ 4,000	
Other operating expenses	11,000	15,000
Income before income taxes		$ 20,000
Income taxes		6,000
Net income		$ 14,000

Additional information is as follows:
a) Net income and a cash dividend accounted for the change in retained earnings.
b) Common stock was issued at par for cash during 1983.
c) All accounts receivable relate to the sale of merchandise on account. All accounts payable relate to the purchase of merchandise on account.

Required:
1. Prepare a schedule to compute the working capital provided by operations in 1983. The schedule should begin with net income.
2. Prepare a schedule to compute working capital provided by operations in 1983. The schedule should show the individual revenue items that represented a source of working capital and the individual expense items that represented a use of working capital.
3. Prepare a schedule of changes in working capital accounts for 1983.

E–25–4 Use the data presented in E–25–3.
Required:
1. Prepare a statement of changes in financial position (working capital basis) for Martha Company for 1983. (Do not prepare a schedule of changes in working capital accounts.)
2. Prepare a statement of changes in financial position (cash basis) for Martha Company for 1983.

E–25–5   You are provided the following information concerning the operations of Neeley Company for 1983.

NEELEY COMPANY
Income Statement
For the Year Ended December 31, 1983

Sales	$500,000
Gain on sale of land	30,000
Interest income	20,000
	$550,000
Cost of merchandise sold	$220,000
Depreciation	40,000
Patent amortization	25,000
Loss on sale of short-term marketable securities	10,000
Interest expense	8,000
Loss on sale of equipment	5,000
	$308,000
Income before income taxes	$248,000
Income taxes	114,000
Net income	$134,000

Additional information is as follows:

a)   Land with a book value of $45,000 was sold for $75,000.

b)   Equipment with an original cost of $30,000 and a book value of $18,000 was sold for $13,000.

c)   Premium on long-term bond investments amortized during 1983 was $1,200.

d)   Premium on long-term bonds payable amortized during 1983 was $600.

e)   On December 1, 1983, Neeley sold all of its short-term marketable securities. These securities were acquired on January 15, 1983, at a cost of $33,000.

f)   The provision for income taxes of $114,000 consists of (1) $100,000 currently due and (2) $14,000 deferred. The deferred income tax relates to the use of an accelerated depreciation method for tax purposes and the straight-line method for financial reporting purposes.

Required:

Prepare a schedule to compute the working capital provided by operations for Neeley Company for 1983.

E–25–6   Comparative balance sheets of Raider Company at December 31, 1983, and 1982, are presented below:

RAIDER COMPANY
Comparative Balance Sheets
December 31, 1983, and 1982

	1983	1982	Increase (Decrease)
Cash	$ 21,900	$ 28,100	$ (6,200)
Accounts receivable (net)	32,000	29,700	2,300
Merchandise inventory	82,400	94,500	(12,100)
Prepaid expenses	2,600	2,950	(350)
Plant and equipment	198,000	150,000	48,000

Accumulated depreciation	(46,000)	(64,000)	(18,000)
	$290,900	$241,250	$49,650
Accounts payable	$ 46,800	$ 26,900	$19,900
Mortgage note payable (due 1986)	—	50,000	(50,000)
Common stock, $10 par	150,000	100,000	50,000
Capital in excess of par value	10,000	—	10,000
Retained earnings	84,100	64,350	19,750
	$290,900	$241,250	$49,650

Additional information follows:

a) Net income (no extraordinary items), $49,750.

b) Depreciation, $12,000.

c) An addition to the building was completed at a cost of $78,000. Fully depreciated equipment costing $30,000 was discarded with no salvage being realized.

d) The mortgage note payable was not due until 1986; however, management decided in late 1983 to pay off the note early.

e) During 1983, 5,000 shares of common stock were issued for cash. No other stock transactions occurred in 1983.

f) Cash dividends of $30,000 were declared in 1983.

Required:

Prepare a statement of changes in financial position for 1983 (working capital basis) for Raider Company. You may omit the schedule of changes in working capital accounts.

E–25–7 Explain how each of the following independent items should be disclosed, if at all, in a statement of changes in financial position (working capital basis). Assume the "working capital provided by (used in) operations" section is of the form that begins with income or loss from continuing operations and shows the adjustments for revenues and expenses that had no effect on working capital.

a) Cash dividends of $20,000 were declared. The dividends will be paid during the early part of next year.

b) During the current year a $12,000 cash dividend was paid. The dividend was declared during the preceding year.

c) A 10% (10,000 shares) stock dividend was declared and issued. The stock, which has a par value of $10 per share, had a market value of $18 per share on the date the stock dividend was declared.

d) Land that cost $50,000 was sold for $80,000. The sale of land is not unusual.

e) Bonds with a face amount of $100,000 and a carrying value of $110,000 were reacquired for $104,000 and retired. Assume an applicable income tax rate of 40% and that any resulting gain or loss is material.

f) The company incurred a $30,000 net loss. The only adjustments for items not affecting working capital were as follows: depreciation, $12,000; and amortization of discount on long-term bonds payable, $2,000.

g) A building was acquired by issuing 1,000 shares of $10 par value common stock. The stock had a market value of $25 per share.

h) During the year the company exchanged equipment and cash for land. The exchange was recorded correctly by the following entry:

Land	100,000	
Accumulated depreciation	20,000	
Loss on exchange	14,000	
Equipment		60,000
Cash		74,000

i) At the end of the current year the company wrote down its inventory from cost, $60,000, to market, $45,000. The loss was included in net income.

E–25–8 The following items relate to APB *Opinion No. 19*. Your answers pertain to data to be reported in the statement of changes in financial position of Retail Establishment for the year ended December 31, 1976. Balance sheets and income statements for 1976 and 1975 follow:

RETAIL ESTABLISHMENT, INC.
Balance Sheets

	December 31, 1976	December 31, 1975
Assets		
Current assets		
Cash	$ 150,000	$100,000
Marketable securities	40,000	
Accounts receivable—net	420,000	290,000
Merchandise inventory	330,000	210,000
Prepaid expenses	50,000	25,000
	$ 990,000	$625,000
Land, buildings and fixtures	$ 565,000	$300,000
Less: Accumulated depreciation	55,000	25,000
	$ 510,000	$275,000
	$1,500,000	$900,000
Equities		
Current liabilities		
Accounts payable	$ 265,000	$220,000
Accrued expenses	70,000	65,000
Dividends payable	35,000	
	$ 370,000	$285,000
Note payable—due 1979	$ 250,000	
Stockholders' equity		
Common stock	$ 600,000	$ 450,000
Retained earnings	280,000	165,000
	$ 880,000	$615,000
	$1,500,000	$900,000

RETAIL ESTABLISHMENT, INC.
Income Statements

	Year Ended December 31, 1976	Year Ended December 31, 1975
Net sales—including service charges	$3,200,000	$2,000,000
Cost of good sold	2,500,000	1,600,000
Gross profit	$ 700,000	$ 400,000
Expenses (including income taxes)	500,000	260,000
Net income	$ 200,000	$ 140,000

Additional information available included the following:

a) Although Retail Establishment will report all changes in financial position, management has adopted a format emphasizing the flow of cash.

b) All accounts receivable and accounts payable relate to trade merchandise. Cash discounts are not allowed to customers, but a service charge is added to an account for late payment. Accounts payable are recorded net and always are paid to take all of the discount allowed. The allowance for doubtful accounts at the end of 1976 was the same as at the end of 1975; no receivables were charged against the allowance during 1976.

c) The proceeds from the note payable were used to finance a new store building. Capital stock was sold to provide additional working capital.

Required:

Calculate the following items for Retail Establishment.

    a) Cash collected during 1976 from accounts receivable.

    b) Cash payments during 1976 on accounts payable to suppliers.

    c) Cash provided by operations during 1976.

    d) Cash dividend payments during 1976.

    e) Cash receipts during 1976 that were not provided by operations.

    f) Cash payments for assets during 1976 that were not reflected in operations.

                                       (AICPA adapted)

E–25–9 Use the data given in E–25–8.

Required:

1. Use the worksheet approach to develop the information necessary to prepare a statement of changes in financial position (working capital basis) for Retail Establishment for 1976.

2. Prepare a statement of changes in financial position (working capital basis) for Retail Establishment for 1976.

E–25–10 Use the data given in E–25–8.

Required:

*1. Use the T-account approach to develop the information necessary to prepare a statement of changes in financial position (working capital basis) for Retail Establishment for 1976.

2. Prepare a statement of changes in financial position (working capital basis) for Retail Establishment for 1976.

E–25–11 You are provided the following selected information about Wimberley Company for 1983:

    a) Net income, $57,400.

    b) Amortization of premium on long-term bonds payable, $1,200.

    c) Purchase of equipment, $16,000.

    d) Depreciation expense, $4,000.

    e) Decrease in accounts receivable, $1,400.

    f) Decrease in accounts payable (for merchandise), $2,900.

    g) Issuance of long-term notes payable, $30,000.

    h) Increase in inventories, $6,000.

    i) Gain on sale of land (ordinary), $8,000.

    j) Increase in prepaid insurance, $700.

    k) Cash dividends declared, $2,200.

    l) Increase in wages payable, $900.

    m) Amortization of patent, $1,500.

    n) Increase in deferred tax charges, $3,300. (Deferred tax charges classified as non-current asset.)

    o) Increase in deferred tax credits $1,100. (Deferred tax credits classified as current liability.)

Required:

Prepare a schedule to compute cash provided by or used in operations for Wimberley Company for 1983.

E–25–12 Presented below for North Company for 1983 are (a) the cash provided by operations and (b) the beginning and ending balances of selected accounts.

Cash collected from customers		$14,000
Cash paid to merchandise suppliers		8,000
		$ 6,000
Less:		
Salaries paid	$ 1,500	
Income taxes paid	1,200	2,700
Cash provided by operations		$ 3,300

	Balance January 1 Dr. (Cr.)	Balance December 31 Dr. (Cr.)
Accounts receivable	$2,000	$2,500
Inventory	3,200	2,700
Accumulated depreciation	(4,000)	(4,400)
Accounts payable	(1,000)	(1,600)
Salaries payable	(600)	(400)
Income taxes payable	(400)	(550)

You also determine the following data to be relevant:

a) All purchases and sales of merchandise are made on account. Only purchases of merchandise on account are recorded in the accounts payable account, and only sales of merchandise on account are recorded in the accounts receivable account. All accounts receivable are deemed to be collectible.

b) There were no acquisitions or disposals of plant assets during 1983.

Required:

Prepare an accrual basis income statement for North Company for 1983. The income statement should show separately each revenue and expense and should include a detailed presentation of the cost of goods sold.

E-25-13 During the current year, ABC Company sold one of its leather goods division for $400,000 cash. The sale qualified as a disposal of a segment under APB *Opinion No. 30*. The division did not operate between the measurement date and the disposal date. The assets of the division at the disposal date (there were no liabilities) were as follows:

	Book Value at Disposal Date
Inventory	$ 50,000
Land	100,000
Building (net)	80,000
Equipment (net)	25,000
	$255,000

Required:

Show how the sale of the leather goods division would be reported on ABC Company's statement of changes in financial position (working capital basis) for the current year. Assume the gain or loss on disposal is fully taxable or deductible at an income tax rate of 40%.

E-25-14 Select the best answer for each of the following questions.

a) The following information on selected cash transactions for 1983 has been provided by the Smith Company:

Proceeds from short-term borrowings	$1,200,000
Proceeds from long-term borrowings	4,000,000
Purchases of fixed assets	3,200,000

Purchases of inventories	8,000,000
Proceeds from sale of Smith's common stock	2,000,000

What is the increase in working capital for the year ended December 31, 1983, as a result of the information above?

    (1) $800,000.
    (2) $2,000,000.
    (3) $2,800,000.
    (4) $4,000,000.

b) The working capital of Rogers Company at December 31, 1982, was $10,000,000. Selected information for the year 1983 for Rogers is as follows:

Working capital provided from operations	$1,700,000
Capital expenditures	3,000,000
Proceeds from short-term borrowings	1,000,000
Proceeds from long-term borrowings	2,000,000
Payments on short-term borrowings	500,000
Payments on long-term borrowings	600,000
Proceeds from issuance of common stock	1,400,000
Dividends paid on common stock	800,000

What is Rogers' working capital at December 31, 1983?

    (1) $10,700,000.
    (2) $11,200,000.
    (3) $11,500,000.
    (4) $12,000,000.

c) Kirt, Incorporated had net income for 1983 of $3,000,000. Additional information is as follows:

Amortization of goodwill	$ 80,000
Depreciation on fixed assets	3,200,000
Long-term debt	
Bond discount amortization	130,000
Interest expense	2,600,000
Provision for doubtful accounts	
Current receivables	700,000
Long-term receivables	210,000

Assuming funds are defined as working capital, what should be the working capital provided from operations in the statement of changes in financial position for the year ended December 31, 1983?

    (1) $6,200,000.
    (2) $6,410,000.
    (3) $6,620,000.
    (4) $9,220,000.   (AICPA adapted)

E–25–15 The balance sheets for Magnolia, Inc. are as follows:

MAGNOLIA, INC.
Balance Sheets

	December 31,	
	1976	*1975*
Current assets	$ 474,000	$ 320,000
Equipment	1,230,000	1,200,000
Accumulated depreciation	(436,000)	(420,000)
Goodwill	480,000	500,000
Total assets	$1,748,000	$1,600,000

Current liabilities	$ 360,000	$ 160,000
Bonds payable	400,000	600,000
Discount on bonds	(12,000)	(20,000)
Common stock	1,112,000	1,112,000
Retained earnings (deficit)	(112,000)	(252,000)
Total liabilities and stockholders' equity	$1,748,000	$1,600,000

You have discovered the following facts:

a) During 1976 Magnolia sold, at no gain or loss, equipment with a book value of $76,000 and purchased new equipment costing $150,000.

b) During 1976 bonds with a face and book value of $200,000 were extinguished, with no gain or loss. They were not current liabilities before their extinguishment.

c) Retained earnings was affected only by the 1976 net income or loss.

Required:

1. How much working capital was provided by operations during 1976?

   a) $208,000.

   b) $212,000.

   c) $220,000.

   d) $228,000.

2. Assume that $200,000 face value of bonds became current at December 31, 1976, to be repaid in early 1977. What should be the change in working capital under this assumption after considering all changes in financial position?

   a) $46,000 increase.

   b) $46,000 decrease.

   c) $246,000 increase.

   d) $246,000 decrease.

(AICPA adapted)

E–25–16 Select the best answer for each of the following questions.

   a) An analysis of the machinery accounts of the Pending Company for 1983 is as follows:

	Machinery	Accumulated Depreciation	Machinery, Net of Accumulated Depreciation
Balance at January 1, 1983	$1,000,000	$400,000	$600,000
Purchases of new machinery in 1983 for cash	500,000	—	500,000
Depreciation in 1983	—	250,000	(250,000)
Balance at December 31, 1983	$1,500,000	$650,000	$850,000

Assuming that funds are defined as working capital, the information concerning Pending's machinery accounts should be shown in Pending's statement of changes in financial position for the year ended December 31, 1983, as

   (1) A subtraction from net income of $250,000 and a source of funds of $500,000.

   (2) An addition to net income of $250,000 and a use of funds of $500,000.

(3) A source of funds of $250,000.

(4) A use of funds of $500,000.

b) Token Company sold some of its fixed assets during 1983. The original cost of the fixed assets was $750,000, and the allowance for accumulated depreciation at the date of sale was $600,000. The proceeds from the sale of the fixed assets were $210,000. Assuming funds are defined as working capital, the information concerning the sale of the fixed assets should be shown on Token's statement of changes in financial position for the year ended December 31, 1983, as

(1) A subtraction from net income of $60,000 and a source of $150,000.

(2) An addition to net income of $60,000 and a source of $150,000.

(3) A subtraction from net income of $60,000 and a source of $210,000.

(4) A source of $150,000.

c) The working capital provided from operations in Seat's statement of changes in financial position for 1983 was $8,000,000. For 1983, depreciation on fixed assets was $3,800,000, amortization of goodwill was $100,000, and dividends on common stock were $2,000,000. Based on the information given above, Seat's net income for 1983 was

(1) $2,100,000.

(2) $4,100,000.

(3) $8,000,000.

(4) $11,900,000.

d) The stockholders' equity of the Spain Company at December 31, 1982, was as follows:

Convertible preferred stock, $20 par value; each share convertible into 2 shares of common stock; authorized 6,000 shares; issued and outstanding 5,000 shares	$100,000
Premium on convertible preferred stock	15,000
Common stock, $10 par value; authorized 30,000 shares; issued and outstanding 20,000 shares	200,000
Additional paid-in capital on common stock	25,000
Retained earnings	650,000
Total stockholders' equity	$990,000

During 1983 a total of 2,000 shares of the convertible preferred stock were converted into common stock. Also during 1983, a total of 5,000 shares of common stock were issued at $15 per share. If you assume funds are defined as working capital, how should the information above be shown on Spain's statement of changes in financial position for the year ended December 31, 1983?

	Source	Use
(1)	$46,000	$96,000
(2)	$46,000	$121,000
(3)	$121,000	$0
(4)	$121,000	$46,000

e) The following information was taken from the accounting records of Oregon Corporation for 1983:

Proceeds from issuance of preferred stock	$4,000,000
Dividends paid on preferred stock	400,000

Bonds payable converted to common stock	2,000,000
Purchases of treasury stock—common	500,000
Sale of plant building	1,200,000
2% stock dividend on common stock	300,000

Oregon's statement of changes in financial position for the year ended December 31, 1983, should show the following sources and uses of funds, based on the information above.

	Sources	Uses
(1)	$5,200,000	$1,200,000
(2)	$5,500,000	$1,200,000
(3)	$7,200,000	$2,900,000
(4)	$7,500,000	$3,200,000

(AICPA adapted)

E–25–17   Select the best answer for each of the following questions.

a)   Selected information from Brook Corporation's accounting records and financial statements for 1977 is as follows:

Working capital provided by operations	$1,500,000
Mortgage payable issued to acquire land and building	1,800,000
Common stock issued to retire preferred stock	500,000
Proceeds from sale of equipment	400,000
Cost of office equipment purchased	200,000

On the statement of changes in financial position for the year ended December 31, 1977, Brook should disclose the total sources of funds in the amount of

(1) $1,700,000.
(2) $2,400,000.
(3) $3,700,000.
(4) $4,200,000.

b)   The net income for the year ended December 31, 1983, for the Kenny Company was $2,100,000. Additional information is as follows:

Capital expenditures	$6,200,000
Depreciation on fixed assets	2,400,000
Dividends paid on common stock	700,000
Net increase in noncurrent deferred income tax liability	200,000
Amortization of goodwill	75,000

Based on the information given above, what should be the working capital provided from operations in the statement of changes in financial position for the year ended December 31, 1983?

(1) $4,075,000.
(2) $4,375,000.
(3) $4,700,000.
(4) $4,775,000.

c)   Selected information from the 1983 accounting records of the Soccer Company is as follows:

Working capital provided from operations	$ 2,000,000
Collection of short-term receivables	40,000,000
Payments of accounts payable	30,000,000
Capital expenditures	2,800,000

Proceeds from long-term borrowings	1,500,000
Payments on long-term borrowings	500,000
Dividends on common stock	900,000
Purchases of treasury stock	200,000
Sales of stock to officers and employees	100,000
Working capital at December 31, 1982	18,000,000

If you assume that funds are defined as working capital, what should be the working capital at December 31, 1983, shown on Soccer's statement of changes in financial position for the year ended December 31, 1983?

(1) $17,200,000.
(2) $17,300,000.
(3) $18,200,000.
(4) $27,200,000.

d) Information concerning the debt of the Gallery Company is as follows:

Short-term borrowings
Balance at December 31, 1974	$ 1,200,000
Proceeds from borrowings in 1975	1,500,000
Payments made in 1975	(1,400,000)
Balance at December 31, 1975	$ 1,300,000

Current portion of long-term debt
Balance at December 31, 1974	$ 5,500,000
Transfers from "long-term debt"	6,000,000
Payments made in 1975	(5,500,000)
Balance at December 31, 1975	$ 6,000,000

Long-term debt
Balance at December 31, 1974	$42,500,000
Proceeds from borrowings in 1975	18,000,000
Transfers to "current portion of long-term debt"	(6,000,000)
Payments made in 1975	(10,000,000)
Balance at December 31, 1975	$44,500,000

If you assume that funds are defined as working capital, how should the information above be shown on Gallery's statement of changes in financial position for the year ended December 31, 1975?

	Source	Use
(1)	$16,000,000	$18,000,000
(2)	$17,400,000	$19,500,000
(3)	$18,000,000	$16,000,000
(4)	$25,500,000	$22,900,000

e) The following information for 1983 has been provided by the Edward Company:

Proceeds from short-term borrowings	$ 600,000
Proceeds from long-term borrowings	2,000,000
Purchases of fixed assets	1,600,000
Purchases of inventories	4,000,000
Proceeds from the sale of Edward's common stock	1,000,000

If you assume that funds are defined as working capital, what is the increase in working capital for the year ended December 31, 1983, as a result of the information above?

(1) $400,000
(2) $1,000,000
(3) $1,400,000
(4) $2,000,000

(AICPA adapted)

Note: Items with an *asterisk* relate to material contained in the appendix.

Problems

P–25–1 The management of Ingalls Company has provided you with the following comparative analysis of changes in account balances during 1982:

	December 31 1982	December 31 1981	Increase (Decrease)
Debits			
Cash	$ 39,000	$ 25,150	$13,850
Accounts receivable	37,300	38,200	(900)
Inventory	52,000	42,000	10,000
Prepaid insurance	240	150	90
Land	30,000	—	30,000
Buildings	50,000	35,000	15,000
Equipment	89,500	87,400	2,100
Discount on bonds payable	1,000	—	1,000
	$299,040	$227,900	$71,140
Credits			
Allowance for uncollectible accounts	$ 410	$ 460	$ (50)
Accumulated depreciation—building	10,500	8,000	2,500
Accumulated depreciation—equipment	24,100	26,200	(2,100)
Accounts payable	6,230	9,240	(3,010)
Notes payable (short-term)	1,500	2,000	(500)
Dividends payable	8,000	7,000	1,000
Bonds payable (due 1992)	20,000	—	20,000
Common stock, $100 par	137,500	100,000	37,500
Capital in excess of par value	31,250	25,000	6,250
Retained earnings	59,550	50,000	9,550
	$299,040	$227,900	$71,140

The following information was also available:

a) Net income in 1982 was $17,550; there were no extraordinary items.

b) During January, 1982, common stock with a par value of $25,000 was exchanged for land, which was recorded at its fair market value of $30,000.

c) On July 1, 1982, 125 shares of common stock were sold for $110 per share.

d) Bonds payable with a face value of $20,000 were issued on December 31, 1982. The bonds mature on December 31, 1992.

e) Uncollectible accounts expense for 1982 was $210.

f) The only disposal of depreciable assets during 1982 was the sale of equipment for $2,000. The equipment had an original cost of $7,000 and accumulated depreciation of $5,500.

g) Cash dividends of $8,000 were declared in 1982.

h) The short-term notes payable relate to the purchase of merchandise.

Required:

1. Use the worksheet approach to develop the information necessary to prepare a statement of changes in financial position (working capital basis) for Ingalls Company for 1982.

2. Prepare a statement of changes in financial position (working capital basis) for Ingalls Company for 1982.

P–25–2 Use the data given in P–25–1.

Required:

*__1.__ Use the T-account approach to develop the information necessary to prepare a statement of changes in financial position (working capital basis) for Ingalls Company for 1982.

2. Prepare a statement of changes in financial position (working capital basis) for Ingalls Company for 1982.

P–25–3 Use the data given in P–25–1.

Required:

1. Use the worksheet approach to develop the information necessary to prepare a statement of changes in financial position (cash basis) for Ingalls Company for 1982.

2. Prepare a statement of changes in financial position (cash basis) for Ingalls Company for 1982.

P–25–4 Use the data given in P–25–1.

Required:

*__1.__ Use the T-account approach to develop the information necessary to prepare a statement of changes in financial position (cash basis) for Ingalls Company for 1982.

2. Prepare a statement of changes in financial position (cash basis) for Ingalls Company for 1982.

P–25–5 The management of Hatfield Corporation, concerned over a decrease in working capital, has provided you with the following comparative analysis of changes in account balances between December 31, 1982, and December 31, 1983:

| | December 31 | | Increase |
	1983	1982	(Decrease)
Debit Balances			
Cash	$ 145,000	$ 186,000	$(41,000)
Accounts receivable	253,000	273,000	(20,000)
Inventories	483,000	538,000	(55,000)
Securities held for plant expansion			
purposes	150,000	—	150,000
Machinery and equipment	927,000	647,000	280,000
Leasehold improvements	87,000	87,000	—
Patents	27,800	30,000	(2,200)
	$2,072,800	$1,761,000	$311,800
Credit Balances			
Allowance for uncollectible accounts			
receivable	$ 14,000	$ 17,000	$ (3,000)
Accumulated depreciation of machinery			
and equipment	416,000	372,000	44,000
Allowance for amortization of lease-hold			
improvements	58,000	49,000	9,000
Accounts payable	232,800	105,000	127,800
Cash dividends payable	40,000	—	40,000

Current portion of 6% serial bonds payable	50,000	50,000	—
6% serial bonds payable	250,000	300,000	(50,000)
Preferred stock	90,000	100,000	(10,000)
Common stock	500,000	500,000	—
Retained earnings	422,000	268,000	154,000
Totals	$2,072,800	$1,761,000	$311,800

You have received the following additional information:

During 1983 the following transactions occurred:

a) New machinery was purchased for $386,000. In addition, certain obsolete machinery, having a book value of $61,000, was sold for $48,000. No other entries were recorded in machinery and equipment or in related accounts other than provisions for depreciation.

b) Hatfield paid $2,000 in legal costs in a successful defense of a new patent. Amortization of patents amounting to $4,200 was recorded.

c) Preferred stock, par value $100, was purchased at 110 and subsequently cancelled. The premium paid was charged to retained earnings.

d) On December 10, 1983, the board of directors declared a cash dividend of $0.20 per share payable to holders of common stock on January 10, 1984.

e) A comparative analysis of retained earnings as of December 31, 1983, and 1982, is presented below:

	December 31	
	1983	*1982*
Balance, January 1	$268,000	$131,000
Net income	195,000	172,000
	$463,000	$303,000
Dividends declared	(40,000)	(35,000)
Premium on preferred stock repurchased	(1,000)	—
	$422,000	$268,000

Required:

1. Use the worksheet approach to develop the information necessary to prepare a statement of changes in financial position (working capital basis) for Hatfield Corporation for 1983.

2. Prepare a statement of changes in financial position (working capital basis) for Hatfield Corporation for 1983.

(AICPA adapted)

P–25–6 Use the data given in P–23–5.

Required:

*1. Use the T-account approach to develop the information necessary to prepare a statement of changes in financial position (working capital basis) for Hatfield Corporation for 1983.

2. Prepare a statement of changes in financial position (working capital basis) for Hatfield Corporation for 1983.

P–25–7 Use the data given in P–23–5.

Required:

1. Use the worksheet approach to develop the information necessary to prepare a statement of changes in financial position (cash basis) for Hatfield Corporation for 1983.

2. Prepare a statement of changes in financial position (cash basis) for Hatfield Corporation for 1983.

P–25–8 Use the data given in P–23–5.

Required:

*1. Use the T-account approach to develop the information necessary to prepare a statement of changes in financial position (cash basis) for Hatfield Corporation for 1983.

2. Prepare a statement of changes in financial position (cash basis) for Hatfield Corporation for 1983.

P–25–9 Presented below are comparative statements of financial position of Kenwood Corporation as of December 31, 1983, and December 31, 1982, respectively:

KENWOOD CORPORATION
Statement of Financial Position

	December 31, 1983	December 31, 1982	Increase (Decrease)
Assets			
Current assets			
Cash	$ 100,000	$ 90,000	$ 10,000
Accounts receivable (net of allowance for uncollectible accounts of $10,000 and $8,000, respectively)	210,000	140,000	70,000
Inventories	260,000	220,000	40,000
Total current assets	$ 570,000	$ 450,000	$120,000
Land	325,000	200,000	125,000
Plant and equipment	580,000	633,000	(53,000)
Less: Accumulated depreciation	(90,000)	(100,000)	10,000
Patents	30,000	33,000	(3,000)
Total assets	$1,415,000	$1,216,000	$199,000
Liabilities and Shareholders' Equity			
Liabilities			
Current liabilities			
Accounts payable	$ 260,000	$ 200,000	$ 60,000
Accrued expenses	200,000	210,000	(10,000)
Total current liabilities	$ 460,000	$ 410,000	$ 50,000
Deferred income taxes	140,000	100,000	40,000
Long-term bonds (due December 15, 1994)	130,000	180,000	(50,000)
Total liabilities	$ 730,000	$ 690,000	$ 40,000
Shareholders' equity			
Common stock, par value $5; authorized 100,000 shares; issued and outstanding 50,000 and 42,000 shares, respectively	250,000	210,000	40,000
Additional paid-in capital	233,000	170,000	63,000
Retained earnings	202,000	146,000	56,000
Total shareholders' equity	$ 685,000	$ 526,000	$159,000
Total liabilities and shareholders' equity	$1,415,000	$1,216,000	$199,000

Following is the income statement of Kenwood Corporation for the year ended December 31, 1983:

KENWOOD CORPORATION
Income Statement
For the Year Ended December 31, 1983

Sales	$1,000,000
Expenses	
Cost of sales	$ 560,000
Salary and wages	190,000
Depreciation	20,000
Amortization	3,000
Loss on sale of equipment	4,000
Interest	16,000
Miscellaneous	8,000
Total expenses	$ 801,000
Income before income taxes and extraordinary item	199,000
Income taxes	
Current	50,000
Deferred	40,000
Provision for income taxes	$ 90,000
Income before extraordinary item	109,000
Extraordinary item—gain on repurchase of long-term bonds (net of $10,000 income tax)	12,000
Net income	$ 121,000
Earnings per share	
Income before extraordinary item	$2.21
Extraordinary item	0.24
Net income	$2.45

Additional information is as follows:

a) On February 2, 1983, Kenwood issued a 10% stock dividend to shareholders of record on January 15, 1983. The market price per share of the common stock on February 2, 1983, was $15.

b) On March 1, 1983, Kenwood issued 3,800 shares of common stock for land. The common stock and land had current market values of approximately $40,000 on March 1, 1983.

c) On April 15, 1983, Kenwood repurchased long-term bonds with a face value of $50,000. The gain of $22,000 was reported as an extraordinary item on the income statement.

d) On June 30, 1983, Kenwood sold equipment costing $53,000, with a book value of $23,000, for $19,000 cash.

e) On September 30, 1983, Kenwood declared and paid a $0.04 per share cash dividend to shareholders of record on August 1, 1983.

f) On October 10, 1983, Kenwood purchased land for $85,000 cash.

g) Deferred income taxes represent timing differences relating to the use of accelerated depreciation methods for income tax reporting and straight-line depreciation methods for financial statement reporting.

Required:

1. Use the worksheet approach to develop the information necessary to prepare a statement of changes in financial position (working capital basis) for Kenwood Corporation for 1983.

2. Prepare a statement of changes in financial position (working capital basis) for Kenwood Corporation for 1983.

(AICPA adapted)

P–25–10   Use the data given in P–25–9.

Required:

*1. Use the T-account approach to develop the information necessary to prepare a statement of changes in financial position (working capital basis) for Kenwood Corporation for 1983.

2. Prepare a statement of changes in financial position (working capital basis) for Kenwood Corporation for 1983.

P–25–11   Use the data given in P–25–9.

Required:

Prepare a statement of changes in financial position (cash basis) for Kenwood Corporation for 1983.

P–25–12   The following schedule showing net changes in balance sheet accounts at December 31, 1983, compared to December 31, 1982, was prepared from the records of the Sodium Company. The statement of changes in financial position for the year ended December 31, 1983, has not yet been prepared.

Assets	Net Change Increase (Decrease)
Cash	$ 50,000
Accounts receivable, net	76,000
Inventories	37,000
Prepaid expenses	1,000
Property, plant, and equipment, net	64,000
Total assets	$228,000
Liabilities	
Accounts payable	$(55,500)
Notes payable—current	(15,000)
Accrued expenses	33,000
Bonds payable	(28,000)
Less: Unamortized bond discount	(1,200)
Total liabilities	$(64,300)
Stockholders' equity	
Common stock, $10 par value	$500,000
Capital contributed in excess of par value	200,000
Retained earnings	(437,700)
Appropriation of retained earnings for possible future inventory price decline	30,000
Total stockholders' equity	292,300
Total liabilities and stockholders' equity	$228,000

Additional information is as follows:

a)   The new income for the year ended December 31, 1983, was $172,300. There were no extraordinary items.

b) During the year ended December 31, 1983, uncollectible accounts receivable of $26,400 were written off by a charge to allowance for doubtful accounts.

c) A comparison of property, plant, and equipment as of the end of each year follows:

	December 31,		Net Increase (Decrease)
	1983	1982	
Property, plant, and equipment	$570,500	$510,000	$60,500
Less: Accumulated depreciation	224,500	228,000	(3,500)
Property, plant, and equipment, net	$346,000	$282,000	$64,000

During 1983 machinery was purchased at a cost of $45,000. In addition, machinery that was acquired in 1979 at a cost of $48,000 was sold for $3,600. At the date of sale, the machinery had an undepreciated cost of $4,200. The remaining increase in property, plant, and equipment resulted from the acquisition of a tract of land for a new plant site.

d) The bonds payable mature at the rate of $28,000 every year.

e) In January, 1983, the company issued an additional 10,000 shares of its common stock at $14 per share upon the exercise of outstanding stock options held by key employees. In May, 1983, the company declared and issued a 5% stock dividend on its outstanding stock. During the year a cash dividend was paid on the common stock. On December 31, 1983, there were 840,000 shares of common stock outstanding.

f) The appropriation of retained earnings for possible future inventory price decline was provided by a charge against retained earnings, in anticipation of an expected future drop in the market related to goods in inventory.

Required:

*1. Use the T-account approach to develop the information necessary to prepare a statement of changes in financial position (working capital basis) for Sodium Company for 1983.

2. Prepare a statement of changes in financial position (working capital basis) for Sodium Company for 1983.

(AICPA adapted)

P–25–13 Use the data given in P–25–12.

Required:

Prepare a statement of changes in financial position (cash basis) for Sodium Company for 1983.

P–25–14 Presented below are comparative statements of financial position of Area Corporation as of December 31, 1983, and December 31, 1982, respectively:

	December 31,		Increase (Decrease)
	1983	1982	
Assets			
Current assets			
Cash	$ 450,000	$ 287,000	$163,000
Notes receivable	45,000	50,000	(5,000)
Accounts receivable (net of allowance for uncollectible accounts of $17,100 and $24,700, respectively)	479,200	380,000	99,200
Inventories	460,000	298,000	162,000
Total current assets	$1,434,200	$1,015,000	$419,200

Investment in common stock of Reading Company	—	39,000	(39,000)
Investment in common stock of Zip Corporation	246,300	—	246,300
Total	$ 246,300	$ 39,000	$207,300
Machinery and equipment	455,000	381,000	74,000
Less: Accumulated depreciation	(193,000)	(144,000)	49,000
Total	$ 262,000	$ 237,000	$ 25,000
Patents (less accumulated amortization)	26,000	19,000	7,000
Total assets	$1,968,500	$1,310,000	$658,500
Liabilities and shareholders' equity			
Liabilities			
Dividends payable	$ 181,000	$ —	$181,000
Accounts payable	156,000	40,800	115,200
Accrued expenses	92,000	84,000	8,000
Total liabilities	$ 429,000	$ 124,800	$304,200
Shareholders' equity			
Preferred stock, par value $2; authorized 50,000 shares; issued and outstanding, 30,000 shares and 26,500 shares, respectively	60,000	53,000	7,000
Capital contributed in excess of par— preferred stock	6,000	2,500	3,500
Common stock, par value $10; authorized 100,000 shares; issued and outstanding, 75,200 shares and 70,000 shares, respectively	752,000	700,000	52,000
Capital contributed in excess of par— common stock	20,000	9,600	10,400
Earnings appropriated for contingencies	85,000	—	85,000
Retained earnings	616,500	420,100	196,400
Total shareholders' equity	$1,539,500	$1,185,200	$354,300
Total liabilities and shareholders' equity	$1,968,500	$1,310,000	$658,500

Additional information is as follows:

a) For the year ended December 31, 1983, Area Corporation reported net income of $496,000.

b) Uncollectible accounts receivable of $4,000 were written off against the allowance for uncollectible accounts receivable.

c) Area's investment in the common stock of Reading Company was made in 1979 and represented a 3% interest in the outstanding common stock of Reading. During 1983 Area sold this investment for $26,000.

d) Amortization of patents charged to operations during 1983 was $3,000.

e) On January 1, 1983, Area acquired 90% of the outstanding common stock of Zip Corporation (45,000 shares, par value $10 per share) in a transaction appropriately accounted for as a purchase. To consummate this transaction, Area paid $72,000 cash and issued 3,500 shares of its preferred stock and 2,400 shares of its common stock. The consideration paid was equal to the underlying book value of the assets acquired.

The fair market value of Area's stock on the date of the transaction was as follows:

Preferred $ 3
Common   12

Zip Corporation is considered to be an unrelated business and not compatible with the operations of Area Corporation; therefore, consolidation of the two companies is not required. For the year ended December 31, 1983, Zip Corporation reported net income of $150,000.

f) During 1983 machinery and equipment that were acquired in 1978 at a cost of $22,000 were sold as scrap for $3,200. At the date of sale this machinery had an undepreciated cost of $4,400.

In addition, Area acquired new machinery and equipment at cost of $81,000. The remaining increase in machinery and equipment resulted from major repairs made to machinery that were accounted for as capital expenditures.

g) On January 1, 1983, Area declared and issued a 4% stock dividend on its common stock. The market value of the shares on that date was $12 a share. The market value of the shares was not affected by the dividend distribution. On December 31, 1983, cash dividends were declared on both the common and preferred stock as follows:

Common $145,000
Preferred   36,000

h) In December 1983, a reserve for a contingent loss of $85,000 arising from a law suit was established by a charge against retained earnings.

Required:

1. Use the worksheet approach to develop the information necessary to prepare a statement of changes in financial position (working capital basis) for Area Corporation for 1983.

2. Prepare a statement of changes in financial position (working capital basis) for Area Corporation for 1983. Do not prepare a schedule of working capital.

(AICPA adapted)

P–25–15   Use the data given in P–25–14.

Required:

*1. Use the T-account approach to develop the information necessary to prepare a statement of changes in financial position (working capital basis) for Area Corporation for 1983.

2. Prepare a statement of changes in financial position (working capital basis) for Area Corporation for 1983. Do not prepare a schedule of working capital.

P–25–16   Use the data given in P–25–14.

Required:

1. Use the worksheet approach to develop the information necessary to prepare a statement of changes in financial position (cash basis) for Area Corporation for 1983.

2. Prepare a statement of changes in financial position (cash basis) for Area Corporation for 1983.

P–25–17   Use the data given in P–25–14.

Required:

*1. Use the T-account approach to develop the information necessary to prepare a statement of changes in financial position (cash basis) for Area Corporation for 1983.

2. Prepare a statement of changes in financial position (cash basis) for Area Corporation for 1983.

P–25–18   Bencivenga Company has prepared its financial statements for the year ended December 31, 1982, and for the three months ended March 31, 1983. You have been asked to prepare a statement of changes in financial position on a working capital basis for the three months ended March 31, 1983. The company's balance sheet data at December 31, 1982, and March 31, 1983, and its income statement data for the three months ended

March 31, 1983, follow. Previously you have satisfied yourself as to the correctness of the amounts presented.

Balance Sheet

	December 31, 1982	March 31, 1983
Cash	$ 25,300	$ 87,400
Marketable investments	16,500	7,300
Accounts receivable, net	24,320	49,320
Inventory	31,090	48,590
Total current assets	$ 97,210	$192,610
Land	40,000	18,700
Building	250,000	250,000
Equipment	—	81,500
Accumulated depreciation	(15,000)	(16,250)
Investment in 30%-owned company	61,220	67,100
Other assets	15,100	15,100
Total	$448,530	$608,760
Accounts payable	$ 21,220	$ 17,330
Dividend payable	—	8,000
Income taxes payable	—	34,616
Total current liabilities	$ 21,220	$ 59,946
Other liabilities	186,000	186,000
Bonds payable	50,000	115,000
Discount on bonds payable	(2,300)	(2,150)
Deferred income taxes	510	846
Preferred stock	30,000	—
Common stock	80,000	110,000
Dividends declared	—	(8,000)
Retained earnings	83,100	147,118
Total	$448,530	$608,760

*Income Statement Data
for the Three Months
Ended March 31, 1983*

Sales	$242,807
Gain on sale of marketable investments	2,400
Equity in earnings of 30%-owned company	5,880
	$251,087
Cost of goods sold	138,407
General and administrative expenses	22,010
Depreciation	1,250
Interest expense	1,150
Income taxes	32,812
	$195,629
Income before extraordinary items	55,458
Extraordinary item:	
Gain on condemnation of land	
(less income taxes of $2,140)	8,560
Net income	$ 64,018

Your discussion with the company's controller and a review of the financial records have revealed the following information:

a) On January 8, 1983, the company sold marketable securities for cash.

b) The company's preferred stock is convertible into common stock at a rate of one share of preferred for two shares of common. The preferred stock and common stock have par values of $2 and $1, respectively.

c) On January 17, 1983, three acres of land were condemned. An award of $32,000 in cash was received on March 22, 1983. Purchase of additional land as a replacement is not contemplated by the company. Assume that the gain qualifies as an extraordinary item and is taxed at capital gains rates.

d) On March 25, 1983, the company purchased equipment for cash.

e) On March 29, 1983, bonds payable were issued by the company at par for cash.

f) The investment in 30%-owned company included an amount attributable to goodwill of $3,220 at December 31, 1982. Goodwill is being amortized at an annual rate of $480.

g) The company's tax rate is 40% for regular income and 20% for capital gains.

Required:

1. Use the worksheet approach to develop the information necessary to prepare a statement of changes in financial position (working capital basis) for Bencivenga Company for the three months ended March 31, 1983.

2. Prepare a statement of changes in financial position (working capital basis) for Bencivenga Company for the three months ended March 31, 1983.

(AICPA adapted)

P–25–19 Use the data given in P–25–18.

Required:

*1. Use the T-account approach to develop the information necessary to prepare a statement of changes in financial position (working capital basis) for Bencivenga Company for the three months ended March 31, 1983.

2. Prepare a statement of changes in financial position (working capital basis) for Bencivenga Company for the three months ended March 31, 1983.

P–25–20 Use the data given in P–25–18.

Required:

Prepare a statement of changes in financial position (cash basis) for Bencivenga Company for the three months ended March 31, 1983.

P–25–21 The comparative balance sheets for Plainview Corporation are presented below:

PLAINVIEW CORPORATION
Comparative Balance Sheets
December 31, 1977, and 1976

	1977	1976	Increase (Decrease)
Assets			
Cash	$ 142,100	$ 165,300	$ (23,200)
Marketable securities (at cost)	122,800	129,200	(6,400)
Accounts receivable (net)	312,000	371,200	(59,200)
Inventories	255,200	124,100	131,100
Prepaid expenses	23,400	22,000	1,400
Bond sinking fund		63,000	(63,000)
Investment in subsidiary (at equity)	134,080	152,000	(17,920)
Plant and equipment (net)	1,443,700	1,534,600	(90,900)
	$2,433,280	$2,561,400	$(128,120)

Equities

Accounts payable	$ 227,100	$ 213,300	$ 13,800
Notes payable—current		145,000	(145,000)
Accrued payables	16,500	18,000	(1,500)
•Income taxes payable	97,500	31,000	66,500
Deferred income taxes (noncurrent)	53,900	43,400	10,500
6% mortgage bonds (due 1989)		300,000	(300,000)
Premium on 6% mortgage bonds		10,000	(10,000)
8% debentures (due 1991)	125,000		125,000
Common stock, $10 par	1,033,500	950,000	83,500
Capital in excess of par value	67,700	51,000	16,700
Retained earnings	846,580	843,200	3,380
Treasury stock (at cost of $3 per share)	(34,500)	(43,500)	9,000
	$2,433,280	$2,561,400	$(128,120)

Your workpapers disclose the following additional information:

a) The retained earnings account was analyzed as follows:

Retained earnings, December 31, 1976		$ 843,200
Net income, 1977		236,580
		$1,079,780
Less:		
Cash dividends	$130,000	
10% stock dividend	100,200	
"Loss" on reissue of treasury stock	3,000	233,200
Retained earnings, December 31, 1977		$ 846,580

b) A partial income statement for 1977 shows the following:

Income before income taxes and extraordinary items		$434,300
Provision for income taxes		
Current	$157,220	
Deferred	16,500	173,720
Income before extraordinary items		$260,580
Extraordinary items		
Fire loss—warehouse, less income tax effect of $14,000 (current $8,000, deferred $6,000)		(21,000)
Loss on extinguishment of 6% mortgage bonds, less income tax effect of $2,000		(3,000)
Net income		$236,580

c) On January 2, 1977, marketable securities costing $110,000 were sold for $127,000. The proceeds from this sale, the $63,000 in the bond sinking fund, and the $125,000 received from the issuance of the 8% debentures were used to retire the 6% mortgage bonds on that same date.

d) The treasury stock was reissued on February 28, 1977.

e) The stock dividend was declared on October 31, 1977, when the market price of Plainview Corporation's stock was $12 per share.

f) On January 1, 1977, a fire destroyed a warehouse that cost $100,000. The book value of the warehouse was $35,000 for financial reporting purposes but $20,000 for income tax purposes; an accelerated depreciation method was used for tax purposes, and the straight-line method was used for financial reporting purposes. The related deferred income tax as of the date of the fire was $6,000. The fire loss is deductible for tax purposes. Assume that the loss qualifies as an extraordinary item.

g) Plant and equipment transactions consisted of the sale of a building at its book value of $4,000 and the purchase of machinery for $28,000.

h) Depreciation expense for 1977 was $79,900.

i) Accounts receivable written off as uncollectible was $16,300 in 1976 and $18,500 in 1977. Expired insurance recorded in 1976 was $4,100 and $3,900 in 1977.

j) The subsidiary, which is 80% owned, reported a loss of $22,400 for 1977.

Required:

1. Use the worksheet approach to develop the information necessary to prepare a statement of changes in financial position (working capital basis) for Plainview Corporation for 1977.

2. Prepare a statement of changes in financial position (working capital basis) for Plainview Corporation for 1977.

(AICPA adapted)

P–25–22 Use the data given in P–25–21.

Required:

*1. Use the T-account approach to develop the information necessary to prepare a statement of changes in financial position (working capital basis) for Plainview Corporation for 1977.

2. Prepare a statement of changes in financial position (working capital basis) for Plainview Corporation for 1977.

P–25–23 Use the data given in P–25–21.

Required:

Prepare a statement of changes in financial position (cash basis) for Plainview Corporation for 1977.

Note: Items with an *asterisk* relate to material contained in the appendix.

26

Financial Reporting and Changing Prices

Accounting in the News

One of the biggest problems facing businesses as well as individuals has been the high rate of inflation. Until recently, accounting statements did not include measurements relating to the impact of inflation on a company. As a result, it was difficult for investors to evaluate a company's performance in a given economic climate. As the following article excerpt indicates, financial statement disclosures have changed.

> Inflation is not new. In its present virulent form it has been around for more than a decade, having had its most damaging impact on corporate earnings and balance sheets in the early 1970s. SEC disclosure requirements of 1976 and FASB Statement No. 33, Financial Reporting and Changing Prices, have generated more widespread understanding of the problem and significantly increased the accuracy of data for estimating the replacement costs of plant and inventory profits. The reported earnings per share figure will never be replaced, but inevitably professional investors will increasingly look for inflation adjusted accounting in formulating their buy and sell decisions.
>
> Among the more corrosive effects of inflation is its impact on capital values. One need look no further than the stock market for confirmation. The total real return on stocks has been close to zero over the past 15 years. Investors have lost confidence in equities and businessmen have curtailed their spending because of the uncertainties caused by inflation. A system of accounting cannot by itself change this state of affairs, but the first step in developing a solution is understanding the problem.*

This chapter presents the profession's current approach to providing information concerning the effect of price movements on the operations of a business.

*Gerald R. Smith, "Inflation Accounting and The Financial Executive," *Financial Executive*, December 1980, p. 17.

Primary financial statements are based on the historical cost concept. An important assumption behind this concept is that the monetary unit is stable—that is, the value of the dollar will remain constant. If the stable monetary assumption is realistic, then it is reasonable to aggregate on a balance sheet those items purchased with 1950 dollars and those items purchased with 1980 dollars. This facilitates interpretations of financial statement data and allows investors or creditors to make meaningful interperiod or interfirm comparisons. If, however, the monetary unit is not stable, the aggregation of the cost of land purchased in 1950 and inventory purchased in 1980 would have little meaning for financial statement users.

Until the 1970s it was reasonable to assume that in the United States the dollar was a relatively stable monetary unit. In the last decade, however, increasing price levels, leading to double-digit inflation, have become a chronic problem for the United States economy. Many accountants argue that supplying only historical cost information in a period of changing prices does not provide relevant information. As a result, alternative methods of accounting have been developed to deal with the problem of changing prices. The purposes of this chapter are to discuss the nature of changing prices and their effect on historical cost financial statements, and to illustrate alternative solutions, including a complete discussion of *Statement of Financial Accounting Standards No. 33*, "Financial Reporting and Changing Prices."[1]

Types of Price Changes

There are two types of price changes that are relevant to financial reporting: (1) general price-level changes and (2) specific price-level changes. Since both of these changes affect traditional historical cost statements in a different manner, it is important to understand the distinction between them.

General Price-Level versus Specific Price-Level Changes

General price-level changes are intended to provide a measure of the changes in the value of the dollar in terms of its ability to purchase a variety of goods and services—that is, as the general price level increases, the purchasing power of the dollar declines. Thus, when people speak of inflation they generally are referring to a rise in the general price level. Conversely, if the general purchasing power of the dollar increases, deflation occurs. **Specific price changes** reflect the change in value of a specific good or service vis-a-vis other goods or services. Thus, these changes reflect an adjustment in the price of a particular asset such as a building or an item of inventory. In addition to being caused by inflation, these changes are caused by market dynamics such as increased demand or decreased supply.

The way in which general and specific price-level changes are calculated helps to clarify the distinction between them. General price-level changes are measured through price indexes such as the Gross National Product Implicit Price Deflator and the Consumer Price Index for All Urban Consumers. These

---

[1]"Financial Reporting and Changing Prices," *Statement of Financial Accounting Standards No. 33* (Stamford, Conn.: FASB, 1979).

Exhibit 26-1
Calculation of General Price Level

	January 1, 1981	December 31, 1981	Percentage Increase in Industrial Items
Hamburger—pound	$1.10	$1.30	+18%
Heating oil—gallon	0.75	0.80	+7%
Milk—quart	0.95	0.90	−5%
Gasoline—gallon	1.30	1.52	+17%
Cotton fabrics—yard	1.70	1.60	−6%
	$5.80	$6.12	
Price index (assuming January 1, 1981, prices equal 100)	$6.12 ÷ $5.80 = 106		

indexes take a representative basket of goods and services and compare its current price to a base-year price. This ratio of the current-year's price to a base-year's price forms an index that measures the weighted average general price-level changes in the economy.

Exhibit 26-1 illustrates how general price indexes are calculated. This example assumes that the price index begins on January 1, 1981, at which time the index was 100. The end-of-the-year index of 106 is calculated by dividing December 31 prices by January 1 prices. It is important to recognize that the 6% increase represents an average increase over all five items. The Consumer Price Index for All Urban Consumers for the last twenty years is reproduced in Exhibit 26-2.

Specific price changes are measured by looking at the change in the current cost or value of individual items. Exhibit 26-1 also lists the specific price changes of the five items used in the example. These individual price changes range from an increase of 18% to a decrease of 6%. Current cost data can be determined by using specific price indexes, net realizable values, replacement costs, or the present value of future cash flows. Exhibit 26-3 lists the specific price indexes for three selected items.

The Relationship Between General Price Changes and Specific Price Changes

In a dynamic economy such as exists in the United States, price changes for all goods and services do not move together. For example, the price of hand calculators has declined drastically while the general price level has risen just as drastically. The relationship between general and specific price changes is illustrated further by the following example. Assume that a plot of land is purchased at the beginning of the current year for $50,000. At the end of the current year the value of the land is determined to be $60,000. During that time the general price level

Exhibit 26-2
Consumer Price Index*
All Urban Consumers—(CPI-U)
U.S. City Average
All Items
(1967 = 100)

Year	Jan	Feb	Mar	Apr	May	Jun	Jul	Aug	Sep	Oct	Nov	Dec	Avg
1961	89.3	89.3	89.3	89.3	89.3	89.4	89.8	89.7	89.9	89.9	89.9	89.9	89.9
1962	89.9	90.1	90.3	90.5	90.5	90.5	90.7	90.7	91.2	91.1	91.1	91.0	90.6
1963	91.1	91.2	91.3	91.3	91.3	91.7	92.1	92.1	92.1	92.2	92.3	92.5	91.7
1964	92.6	92.5	92.6	92.7	92.7	92.9	93.1	93.0	93.2	93.3	93.5	93.6	92.9
1965	93.6	93.6	93.7	94.0	94.2	94.7	94.8	94.6	94.8	94.9	95.1	95.4	94.5
1966	95.4	96.0	96.3	96.7	96.8	97.1	97.4	97.9	98.1	98.5	98.5	98.6	97.2
1967	98.6	98.7	98.9	99.1	99.4	99.7	100.2	100.5	100.7	101.0	101.3	101.6	100.0
1968	102.0	102.3	102.8	103.1	103.4	104.0	104.5	104.8	105.1	105.7	106.1	106.4	104.2
1969	106.7	107.1	108.0	108.7	109.0	109.7	110.2	110.7	111.2	111.6	112.2	112.9	109.8
1970	113.3	113.9	114.5	115.2	115.7	116.3	116.7	116.9	117.5	118.1	118.5	119.1	116.3
1971	119.2	119.4	119.8	120.2	120.8	121.5	121.8	122.1	122.2	122.4	122.6	123.1	121.3
1972	123.2	123.8	124.0	124.3	124.7	125.0	125.5	125.7	126.2	126.6	126.9	127.3	125.3
1973	127.7	128.6	129.8	130.7	131.5	132.4	132.7	135.1	135.5	136.6	137.6	138.5	133.1
1974	139.7	141.5	143.1	143.9	145.5	146.9	148.0	149.9	151.7	153.0	154.3	155.4	147.7
1975	156.1	157.2	157.8	158.6	159.3	160.6	162.3	162.8	163.6	164.6	165.6	166.3	161.2
1976	166.7	167.1	167.5	168.2	169.2	170.1	171.1	171.9	172.6	173.3	173.8	174.3	170.5
1977	175.3	177.1	178.2	179.6	180.6	181.8	182.6	183.3	184.0	184.5	184.5	186.1	181.5
1978	187.2	188.4	189.8	191.5	193.3	195.3	196.7	197.8	199.3	200.9	202.0	202.9	195.4
1979	204.7	207.1	209.1	211.5	214.1	216.6	218.9	221.1	223.4	225.4	227.7	229.9	217.5
1980	233.2	236.4	239.8	242.5	244.9	247.6	247.8	249.4					

*Source: U.S. Department of Labor, Bureau of Labor Statistics, Washington, D.C. 20212.

Exhibit 26-3
Specific Price Indexes*

	New Cars	Food and Beverages	Energy
1974	117.5	158.7	159.7
1975	127.6	172.1	176.6
1976	135.7	177.4	189.3
1977	142.9	188.0	207.3
1978	153.8	206.3	220.4
1979	166.0	228.5	275.9
1980	179.3	248.0	361.1
1981	190.2	267.3	410.0
1981: Apr	186.1	265.0	409.8
May	189.9	265.4	411.3
June	192.0	266.0	414.0
July	192.8	267.7	415.7
Aug	192.8	269.1	416.1
Sept	193.7	270.9	417.1
Oct	194.0	271.5	414.9
Nov	194.6	271.9	414.1
Dec	196.1	272.1	414.6
1982: Jan	196.0	274.1	416.4
Feb	194.5	275.8	413.0
Mar	194.6	274.9	406.1
Apr	196.0	275.7	395.7

*Source: Joint Economic Committee, *Economic Indicators*, May, 1982, Washington, D.C.

rose 15%. Thus, of the $10,000 increase, $7,500 ($50,000 × 0.15) is attributable to a general price rise whereas the remaining $2,500 is attributable to a specific price increase above the general price-level rise. In this particular example the changes moved in the same direction, but as is clear from Exhibit 26-1, general and specific prices can move in opposite directions.

Problems with Financial Statements Not Adjusted for Price Changes

Historical cost-based financial statements are not adjusted for changes in either general or specific prices. As a result, the usefulness of these statements is limited when significant price changes do occur in the economy. There are, however, differences in the way in which general and specific price changes affect financial statements. These limitations and differences are discussed next.

Limitations of Financial Statements
Not Adjusted for General Price Changes

The FASB refers to traditional historical cost statements that are not adjusted for purchasing power changes as **historical cost/nominal dollar** statements. (Hereafter referred to as historical cost statements.) There are a number of limitations associated with these statements.[2] Because it is not meaningful to aggregate dollars that represent different purchasing powers, the dollar value of total assets on the balance sheet loses its significance. As a result, it is difficult to compare a firm's performance over a period of time in which the general price level has changed. Because firms with varying asset compositions are affected differently by inflation, interfirm comparisons become difficult. Further, in a period of inflation, a firm that holds net monetary assets (i.e., cash and rights to receive cash) in excess of monetary liabilities suffers a purchasing power loss. In an inflationary economy $5,000 clearly will purchase more goods and services today than it will in one year. On the other hand, a firm in a net liability position will gain in a period of inflation as it pays back a fixed amount of dollars with declining purchasing power. This gain or loss is not measured on historical cost financial statements. Thus, income can be over or understated, leading among other things to unrealistic demands by shareholders for dividends and by unions for wage adjustments.

Financial statements adjusted for price-level changes can overcome some of the limitations. The FASB refers to these adjusted statements as **historical cost/constant dollar** statements. (Hereafter referred to as constant dollar statements.) They are prepared by adjusting historical cost dollars by a general price index. This results in statements prepared in dollars with the same purchasing power, and in the determination of a purchasing power gain or loss.

Limitations of Financial Statements
Not Adjusted for Specific Price Changes

There are a number of limitations associated with financial statements that do not reflect specific price changes.[3] A firm's management makes a number of decisions, such as pricing and the timing of asset purchases and sales, that are based upon current values. If financial statements are not adjusted for specific prices, it is impossible to evaluate management's effectiveness in these areas.

Limitations result from the fact that traditional financial statements are based upon the realization principle. This means that assets and liabilities are recorded at historical cost and generally are not adjusted to current value until an exchange has taken place. For example, assume that an item of inventory is purchased for $80 and is held until the end of the year, at which time its value has increased to $100. It is finally sold at the beginning of the next year for $110. Traditional financial statements would not recognize any income in the first year and would recognize $30 ($110 − $80) income in the second year.

---

[2] For a further discussion of these issues see Paul Rosenfield, "GPP Accounting—Relevance and Interpretability," *Journal of Accountancy* (August, 1975), pp. 55–59.

[3] For a further discussion of these issues see Edgar O. Edwards and Phillip W. Bell, *The Theory and Measurement of Business Income* (Berkeley: University of California Press, 1961).

Some accounting theorists argue that the historical cost income of $30 is misleading because it does not isolate properly two separate components of income—a holding gain and an operating profit. The holding gain of $20 took place in the first year when the asset's value increased from $80 to $100. The operating profit of $10 did not take place until the second year and is the result of offsetting the current cost of the asset against its sales price. In order to evaluate management's decisions in the year the economic activity took place, the company must isolate and report each of these income components in the year it occurred. Financial statements that reflect changes in specific prices separate these income components and report the current value of net assets on the balance sheet. The FASB refers to financial statements adjusted for specific price changes as **current cost/nominal dollar** statements. (Hereafter referred to as current cost statements.)

Limitations of Financial Statements
Not Adjusted for Both General and Specific Prices

Many accountants argue that to reflect economic reality properly financial statements should be adjusted for both specfic and general price-level changes.[4] Thus, holding gains calculated from specific price adjustments would be adjusted for general price-level changes and would represent real, not inflationary, gains. For example, in the previous land illustration the holding gain before removing the inflationary gain equaled $10,000 ($60,000 current cost less $50,000 historical cost). However, the real holding gain after taking out the increase due to the declining purchasing power of the dollar is only $2,500. The FASB refers to financial statements adjusted for both price changes as **current cost/constant dollar** statements.

The following summarizes the accounting alternatives developed to deal with the effect of changing prices on traditional financial statements.

Type of Price Change	*Accounting Alternatives Available*
None or slight	Historical cost/nominal dollar accounting
General	Historical cost/constant dollar accounting
Specific	Current cost/nominal dollar accounting
General and specific	Current cost/constant dollar accounting

Official Pronouncements
Concerning Accounting for Price Changes

The concept of accounting for changing prices is not a new one. In his book, *Stabilized Accounting* (1936), Henry Sweeney was one of the first accountants to develop a conceptual framework for adjusting financial statements for general price-level changes.[5] The thrust of his work grew out of the high rate of inflation

---

[4] For a further discussion of these issues see Robert Sterling, "Relevant Financial Reporting in a Period of Changing Prices," *Journal of Accountancy* (February, 1975), pp. 42–51.

[5] Henry Sweeney, *Stabilized Accounting* (New York: Harper and Bros., 1936).

many countries experienced between World Wars I and II. However, his work had little practical effect in the United States, and the stock market crash and the advent of the Securities and Exchange Commission (SEC) in the 1930s insured the continual prominence of the historical cost model. As a result, there was little activity in the U.S. concerning accounting for price changes until the 1960s.

Developments Since the 1960s

In 1963 the AICPA published *Accounting Research Study No. 6*, "Reporting the Effects of Price-Level Changes," which recommended the supplemental disclosure of the effects of general price-level changes.[6] It was not until 1969 that the APB acted upon some of the recommendations proposed in *Research Study No. 6* In *APB Statement No. 3*, "Financial Statements Restated for General Price-Level Changes," the Board recommended the supplemental disclosure of financial statements adjusted for general price-level changes:

> . . . General price-level financial statements or pertinent information extracted from them present useful information not available from basic historical dollar financial statements. General price-level information may be presented in addition to the basic historical dollar financial statements, but general price-level financial statements should not be presented as the basic financial statements. The Board believes that general price-level information is not required at this time for fair presentation of financial position and results of operations in conformity with generally accepted accounting principles in the United States.[7]

These supplemental disclosures were not mandatory and few companies experimented with them, although companies such as Indiana Telephone did prepare complete financial statements adjusted for price-level changes that were included in their annual report to shareholders. Professional accounting organizations continued to study the issue of general price-level adjusted statements, and accounting bodies in England and Canada began to issue proposals for constant dollar accounting. In this country the FASB issued an exposure draft in 1974 entitled, "Financial Reporting in Units of General Purchasing Power."[8] This exposure draft, which eventually was withdrawn, would have required supplemental disclosure of specified financial information stated in units of general purchasing power.

Development of Current Value Accounting

While these events were taking place, some accounting organizations began to advocate different variations of current value as the best way to adjust financial statements for price changes. In the United States the SEC issued *ASR No. 190*

---

[6]"Reporting the Financial Effects of Price-Level Changes," *Accounting Research Study No. 6* (New York: AICPA, 1963).

[7]"Financial Statements Restated for General Price-Level Changes," *Accounting Principles Board Statement No. 3* (New York: AICPA, 1969).

[8]"Financial Reporting in Units of General Purchasing Power," *Exposure Draft* (Stamford, Conn.: FASB, 1974).

in 1975, which required the supplemental disclosure of certain replacement cost data.[9] In particular, this release required all firms whose total inventories and gross property, plant, and equipment were more than $100 million and more than 10% of their total assets to disclose the replacement cost of their inventories, their productive capacity, and the related cost of goods sold and depreciation expense. According to the SEC, "These proposals were designed to enable investors to obtain more relevant information about the current economics of a business enterprise in an inflationary economy than provided solely by financial statements prepared on the basis of historical costs."[10]

ASR No. 190 signaled the SEC's clear intention to press for replacement cost disclosures rather than general price-level disclosures. The FASB, faced with the prospect of being in conflict with the SEC, withdrew its exposure draft on general price-level changes and began to reconsider its position on accounting for changing prices. The eventual outcome of this process was the issuance of Statement No. 33, "Financial Reporting and Changing Prices," which requires large public companies to disclose supplemental financial information on both a constant dollar and current cost basis.[11] The Board noted that this Statement is experimental in nature and will be evaluated at specified intervals. As the result of the issuance of this Statement, the SEC withdrew the requirements of ASR No. 190 for those firms that fully comply with Statement No. 33.

The Constant Dollar Accounting Model

The objective of **constant dollar accounting** is to prepare financial statements that are adjusted for general price-level changes. This means that financial statement balances are stated in terms of dollars of the same purchasing power. The historical cost model is maintained, but the measuring unit is a constant dollar rather than a nominal dollar. The traditional realization principle is not violated; historical costs are adjusted to dollars of equal purchasing power but not adjusted for changing asset values.

The theoretical justification for the constant dollar model rests on a specific, capital maintenance approach to income measurement. Under the capital maintenance approach, income generally can be defined as the change in the entity's wealth position over time without regard for additional capital investments or withdrawals. Thus, income represents the amount of wealth that can be disposed of during a given period while leaving the entity as well off at the end of the period as at the beginning of the period. That is, before income can be earned, the entity must maintain the same value of net assets at the end of the period as at the beginning of the period. The proponents of the constant dollar accounting model argue that income cannot be earned until an enterprise maintains its capital in terms of purchasing power rather than historical costs.

These concepts are illustrated by the following example. Assume that an entity begins the year with net assets of $10,000 and ends the year with net assets

[9]"Disclosure of Certain Replacement Cost Data," Accounting Series Release No. 190 (Washington: SEC, 1976).

[10]Ibid., p. 1.

[11]"Financial Reporting and Changing Prices."

of $15,000, both measured in historical costs. There were no capital investments or withdrawals by the owners. The historical cost net income for the period equals $5,000. However, if the general price level increased during the period, the net income of $5,000 overstates the income available to the firm. Part of that income is needed just to maintain the firm's ability to purchase goods and services. If during the year the price level rose 20%, the firm needs $12,000 ($10,000 × 1.20) at the end of the period just to maintain its capital in terms of purchasing power. Therefore, income is only $3,000 ($15,000 − $12,000). The proponents of constant dollar accounting believe that the $3,000 net income figure is more representative of economic reality in a period of rising prices than is the historical net income of $5,000.

The procedures required to restate nominal dollar statements to constant dollar statements differ for monetary, nonmonetary, and income statement items.

Monetary and Nonmonetary Items

Monetary assets are defined as cash or the right to receive a fixed amount of cash at a future date. Thus, monetary assets include cash, receivables, and investments, such as preferred stock or bonds that pay a specified dividend or interest rate. Most liabilities are **monetary liabilities** and are defined as those obligations payable in fixed amounts of dollars.

Nonmonetary assets and **liabilities** are those items that are not considered monetary. They do not represent fixed claims to or for cash. For example, buildings, inventories, and prepayments are nonmonetary assets. Advances from customers, which are payable in services rather than cash, represent an example of a nonmonetary liability. A list of monetary and nonmonetary items is presented in Exhibit 26-4.

Purchasing Power Gains and Losses on Net Monetary Items

As noted above, monetary items already are stated in dollars of current puchasing power and thus do not have to be restated. For example, a balance of $10,000 in accounts receivable represents $10,000 of current purchasing power and would be stated at $10,000 in both historical cost/nominal dollar and historical cost/constant dollar statements. However, these items are subject to purchasing power gains and losses when held over a period of time. For example, a person who holds $500 for an entire year when the price level rises from 100 to 110 suffers a $50 purchasing power loss. It will take $550 ($500 × 110/100) to purchase the same amount of goods and services that $500 did at the beginning of the year. Thus, a person who holds net monetary assets in a period of rising prices suffers a purchasing power loss. Conversely, a person who holds net monetary liabilities in a period of rising prices will enjoy a purchasing power gain. This individual will be repaying a fixed amount in dollars of declining purchasing power. The procedures for calculating a purchasing power gain or loss are illustrated later in a comprehensive example.

Exhibit 26-4
Monetary and Nonmonetary Items*

Balance Sheet Accounts	Monetary	Nonmonetary
Assets		
Cash	X	
Marketable securities		
Common stock		X
Preferred stock	X	
Bonds	X	
Accounts and notes receivable	X	
Allowance for doubtful accounts	X	
Inventories		X
Prepaids—claims to future services		X
Prepaids—deposits and advance payments	X	
Long-term receivables	X	
Property, plant, and equipment		X
Accumulated depreciation		X
Cash surrender value of life insurance	X	
Deferred income tax charges	X	
Intangible assets		X
Other deferred charges		X
Liabilities		
All payables—accounts, notes, dividends, and so forth	X	
Bonds payable and other long-term obligations	X	
Warranties		X
Deferred income tax credits	X	
Deferred investment tax credits		X
Stockholders' Equity		
Common stock		X
Retained earnings		X
Minority interest		X

*Source: "Financial Reporting and Changing Prices," *Statement of Financial Accounting Standards No. 33* (Stamford, Conn.: FASB, 1979).

Restating Nonmonetary Assets and Liabilities

Nonmonetary assets and liabilities do not represent fixed claims to or for dollars. Unlike monetary items, nonmonetary items retain their purchasing power as the general price level increases, and therefore must be adjusted upward. For example, if land were purchased for $100,000 in 1970 when the price-level index was 100, and if the price level rose to 180 in 1980, land would be shown on the balance sheet as $180,000, or $100,000 × 180/100. This indicates that the purchasing power of $180,000 in 1980 is equivalent to $100,000 in 1970. This increase does not represent a gain but is merely a restatement in dollars to those of equal purchasing power.

Restating Nonmonetary Items

The procedure for restating nonmonetary items is relatively straightforward. The historical cost of each item is multiplied by the following ratio:

$$\frac{\text{Consumer Price Index for Urban Consumers at the end of the year}}{\text{Consumer Price Index for Urban Consumers at the date of purchase}}$$

There are a number of different indexes that could be used. In *Statement No. 33*, the FASB chose to use the Consumer Price Index for Urban Consumers (CPI–U). Nonmonetary items are adjusted to year-end constant dollars. The following illustration shows the restatement procedures for several parcels of land purchased by the Price Corporation.

Date Acquired	Historical Cost	Price Index	Ratio	Restated Amount
June 30, 1975	$100,000	125	200/125	$160,000
April 1, 1978	250,000	140	200/140	357,143
September 31, 1979	200,000	180	200/180	222,222
December 31, 1980	—	200		—
	$550,000			$739,365

Thus, on a constant dollar balance sheet the $550,000 cost of the land would be restated to $739,365.

Restating Income Statement Items

The assumption is made that all income and expense items, other than the cost of goods sold and depreciation, occur evenly throughout the year. Based on this assumption the restatement ratio is as follows:

$$\frac{\text{CPI at year-end}}{\text{Average CPI for current year}}$$

The adjustment for the cost of goods sold and depreciation is related to the dates of inventory and fixed-asset purchases and must be analyzed separately. The relevant index would be:

$$\frac{\text{CPI at year-end}}{\text{CPI at time of purchase}}$$

Exhibit 26-5 summarizes the restatement procedures for constant dollar statements.

Constant Dollar Restatement Procedures—Comprehensive Illustration

The historical cost financial statements for the Stout Corporation, and the assumed CPI–U are illustrated in Exhibits 26-6, 26-7, and 26-8, respectively. This data will be used to illustrate constant dollar restatement procedures.

Monetary Assets and Liabilities

In preparing 1980 and 1981 single-year, constant dollar balance sheets, you don't need to restate either the monetary assets (cash, receivables, and investment in bonds) or the monetary liabilities (accounts payable, taxes payable, and bonds payable). However, when preparing comparative 1980 and 1981 balance sheets for inclusion in the 1981 annual report, you must restate the 1980 monetary items and nonmonetary items to 1981 dollars. This is necessary in order to show all balances in dollars of comparative purchasing power. Using the data from Exhibits 26-6 and 26-8, Exhibit 26-9 shows the restatement process for 1980 monetary items to be included in 1980 and 1981 comparative statements.

Exhibit 26-5
Restatement Procedures for Constant Dollar Statements

---

1. Monetary items
   a) No restatement necessary for current year's statements.
   b) Must restate prior year's balance for inclusion in comparative financial statements.
   c) Must calculate a purchasing power gain or loss that results from holding monetary items during the year.
2. Nonmonetary items
   a) Must restate balances to year-end constant dollars.
   b) Consumer Price Index for Urban Consumers is the index recommended by *Statement No. 33*.
3. Income statement items
   a) Must be restated to year-end constant dollars.
   b) Assume that most expenses take place evenly throughout the year.
   c) Depreciation and cost of goods sold are exceptions.

Exhibit 26-6
STOUT CORPORATION
Historical Cost Balance Sheet
For the Year Ended December 31

	1981	1980
Assets		
Current asset		
Cash	$ 150,000	$ 100,000
Receivables, net	250,000	175,000
Inventories—FIFO cost	180,000	190,000
Total current assets	$ 580,000	$ 465,000
Investments		
Common stock—at cost which is below market	100,000	75,000
Bonds—at cost	125,000	125,000
Total investments	$ 225,000	$ 200,000
Property, plant, and equipment		
Land	150,000	150,000
Building (net of accumulated depreciation)	170,000	175,000
Equipment (net of accumulated depreciation)	59,000	50,000
Total property, plant, and equipment	$ 379,000	$ 375,000
Total assets	$1,184,000	$1,040,000
Liabilities & Stockholders' Equity		
Current liabilities		
Accounts payable	$ 160,000	$ 140,000
Taxes payable	120,000	120,000
Total current liabilities	$ 280,000	$ 260,000
Long-term liabilities		
Bonds payable—10%	300,000	300,000
Total liabilities	$ 580,000	$ 560,000
Stockholders' equity		
Common stock ($5 par value) 20,000 shares issued and outstanding	100,000	100,000
Additional paid-in capital	200,000	200,000
Retained earnings	304,000	180,000
Total stockholders' equity	$ 604,000	$ 480,000
Total liability and stockholders' equity	$1,184,000	$1,040,000

Exhibit 26-7
STOUT CORPORATION
Historical Cost Financial Statements
For the Year Ended December 31, 1981

Historial Cost Income Statement

Sales		$2,000,000
Cost of goods sold		
Beginning inventory	$ 190,000	
Purchases	1,190,000	
Goods available for sale	$1,380,000	
Less ending inventory	180,000	1,200,000
Gross margin on sales		$ 800,000
Operating expenses		
Selling expense	200,000	
General and administrative	254,000	
Depreciation	16,000	
Interest	30,000	
Total operating expenses		500,000
Income before taxes		$ 300,000
Taxes, 40%		120,000
Net income		$ 180,000

Retained Earnings Statement

Retained earnings, balance January 1, 1981	$180,000
Net income	180,000
	$360,000
Less dividends	56,000
Retained earnings balance, December 31, 1981	$304,000

Nonmonetary Items

As stated previously, all nonmonetary items must be restated to dollars of current purchasing power. Restatement procedures for the individual items are discussed next.

Inventories. Inventories require special analysis. The proper restatement procedure depends upon the inventory cost method employed (i.e. FIFO, LIFO, or average cost) and on the inventory turnover.

As Exhibit 26-6 indicates, the Stout Company uses the FIFO cost method in costing and valuing its inventories. In order to determine when the ending inventories were acquired, you calculate an inventory turnover ratio by applying the following formula:

$$\frac{\text{Cost of goods sold}}{\text{Average inventory}}$$

The Stout Company's inventory ratio is approximately 6.5 [$1,200,000 ÷ ($190,000 + $180,000)/2]. This indicates that the firm holds its inventory for about 56 days or about two months. If inventories are acquired evenly throughout the year, then both beginning and ending inventories were purchased during the last two months of the prior and current year, respectively. As Exhibit 26-8 indicates, the beginning inventory was acquired when the average price level was 180, and the ending inventory was acquired when the average price level was 215. The relevant calculations are as follows:

	Historical Cost		1980 Ratio		Restated 12/31/80 Amount		1981 Ratio		Restated 12/31/81 Amount
12/31/80 Ending inventories	$190,000	×	185/180	=	$195,278	×	220/185	=	$232,222
12/31/81 Ending inventories	$180,000					×	220/215	=	$184,186

If a firm uses either LIFO or average cost, a different denominator, representing a different acquisition date, would be used. LIFO, which is preferred by an increasing number of companies, requires a different restatement ratio for each layer. Thus, the initial restatement procedure for LIFO can be quite complex depending on the length of time the company has been using LIFO.

Exhibit 26-8
Relevant Price Indexes—Data Assumed

January 2, 1976	
Date of incorporation and purchase of all assets before 1981	120
1980	
January 2, 1980	160
Average for 1980	175
Average for November and December when ending inventory purchased	180
1981	
January 2, 1981	185
March 1, 1981—purchase of investment in common stock—$25,000	188
July 1, 1981—purchase of equipment—$20,000	200
Average for 1981	205
Average for November and December when 1981 ending inventory purchased	215
December 31, 1981—$56,000 dividends issued	220

Exhibit 26-9
Restatement of Monetary Items
to be Included in Comparative Statements

Accounts	Single-Year Statement Balances December 31 1981[1]	December 31 1980[1]	Ratio			Comparative Statement Balances 1980[2]	1981[2]
Cash	$150,000	$100,000	×	220/185	=	$118,919	$150,000
Receivables	250,000	175,000	×	220/185	=	208,108	250,000
Bonds	125,000	125,000	×	220/185	=	148,649	125,000
Accounts payable	160,000	140,000	×	220/185	=	166,486	160,000
Taxes payable	120,000	120,000	×	220/185	=	142,703	120,000
Bonds payable	300,000	300,000	×	220/185	=	356,757	300,000

[1]As these balances would appear on single-year 1981 and 1980 constant dollar statements (Exhibit 26-12 and 26-13).
[2]As these balances would appear on comparative 1981 and 1980 statements (Exhibit 26-12).

Finally, if inventories are valued at the lower of cost or market and are written down to market, they would be considered monetary and no restatement would be required. This is because inventories valued at market already are stated in dollars of current purchasing power.

Investment in Common Stock. The investment in common stock shown in Exhibit 26-6 represents a long-term investment of less than 20% in the Newton Company, and therefore is recorded at the lower of cost or market. The investment must be restated to constant dollars because it is valued at cost, which is lower than market. The original investment was made on January 2, 1976, the date of incorporation. An additional purchase was made on March 1, 1981. The restatement procedures for 1980 and 1981 are as follows:

	Historical Cost	1980 Ratio	Restated 12/31/80 Amount	1981 Ratio	Restated 12/31/81 Amount
12/31/80 Investment	$ 75,000	× 185/120 =	$115,625	× 220/185 =	$137,500
3/1/81 Purchase	25,000			× 220/188 =	29,225
	$100,000				$166,755

As this example illustrates, the investment in the common stock account must be restated in two steps: the initial $75,000 first must be restated to 1980 dollars for 1980 statement purposes and then to 1981 dollars for 1981 statement purposes. Because the second purchase did not take place until March 1, 1981, it is adjusted for price-level changes from that date to the end of the year.

Bonds. As noted previously, the investment in bonds is considered a monetary asset, and thus, no restatement is required.

Land. The restatement procedure for the land account is straightforward and is illustrated below:

	Historical Cost		1980 Ratio		Restated 12/31/80 Amount		1981 Ratio		Restated 12/31/81 Amount
12/31/80 Land	$150,000	×	185/120	=	$231,250	×	220/185	=	$275,000

Buildings. Stout Corporation purchased the building for $200,000 on January 2, 1976, the date the corporation was formed. The company's policy is to take straight-line depreciation, based on a 40-year life with no salvage value. As of 12/31/80, the net book value of $175,000 is calculated as follows:

Historical cost $200,000
Less accumulated depreciation
     from 1/2/76—12/31/80 (5 years):
$$\frac{\$200,000}{40 \text{ years}} = \$5,000 \text{ per year} \times 5 \text{ years}$$

                                          25,000
                                       $175,000

The net book value as of December 31, 1981, would be reduced another $5,000 to $170,000. The building account is restated for both the 1980 statement and 1981 comparative statements as follows:

	Balance		1980 Ratio		Restated 12/31/80		1981 Ratio		Restated 12/31/81
Net book value—12/31/80	$175,000	×	185/120	=	$269,792	×	220/185	=	$320,833
Net book value—12/31/81	170,000					×	220/120	=	311,667

Equipment. The restatement of the equipment account is more complicated because of the additional $20,000 purchase of equipment on June 30, 1981. The original equipment was acquired for $100,000 when the corporation was formed. The Stout Company uses straight-line depreciation, estimates that the equipment has a ten-year life with no salvage value, and takes six months' depreciation in the year of purchase.

The historical cost book values on December 31, 1980, and 1981 are calculated in Exhibit 26-10.

The 1980 equipment account restated for 1980 financial statement purposes and for 1981 comparative financial statement purposes is as follows:

	Historical Cost		1980 Ratio		Restated 12/31/80 Amount		1981 Ratio		Restated 12/31/81 Amount
Net book value 12/31/80	$50,000	×	185/120	=	$77,083	×	220/185	=	$91,667

Exhibit 26-10
STOUT CORPORATION
Calculation of Book Value of Equipment

	Historical Cost 1/1/80	Less	Accumulated Depreciation to 12/31/80	=	Net Book Value 12/31/80	Plus	Purchase on 7/1/80	Less	Depreciation Expense for 1981	=	Net Book Value 12/31/81
1. Original purchase	$100,000										
2. Accumulated depreciation to 12/3/80 $\dfrac{\$100,000}{10} = \$10,000/\text{yr}$ $\times 5 \text{ yr}$			$(50,000)$		$50,000						$50,000
3. Purchase on 7/1/81							$20,000				20,000
4. 1981 depreciation on original purchase									$10,000		(10,000)
5. 1981 depreciation on purchase 1/2 year $\dfrac{\$20,000}{10} = \$2,000/\text{year}$									1,000		(1,000)
Total	$100,000	—	$50,000	=	$50,000	+	$20,000	—	$11,000	=	$59,000

The restatement procedure for the 1981 net book value of $59,000 is illustrated below:

	Historical Cost	1981 Ratio	Restated 12/31/81 Amount
Net book value 12/31/81			
Original balance	$40,000	220/120	$73,333
Purchase	19,000	220/200	20,900
	$59,000		$94,233

Liabilities. All liabilities are monetary, and thus are not restated on single-year statements. For comparative statement purposes they are restated in Exhibit 26-6.

Common Stock and Additional Paid-In-Capital. These balances result only from transactions on the date the corporation was formed, since there have been no additional issues of capital stock. Restatement procedures are as follows:

	Historical Cost		1980 Ratio		Restated 12/31/80 Amount		1981 Ratio		Restated 12/31/81 Amount
Common stock 12/31/80	$100,000	×	185/120	=	$154,167	×	220/185	=	$183,333
Additional paid-in-capital	200,000	×	185/120	=	308,333	×	220/185	=	366,667

Retained Earnings. Restated retained earnings on 12/31/80 can simply be calculated as that amount necessary to make the total of liabilities and stockholders' equity equal the total of assets. Thus, restated retained earnings for 1980 must equal $266,528. The same procedure could be followed in 1981. As an alternative,

---

Exhibit 26-11
STOUT CORPORATION
Retained Earnings Statement

Account	Historical Cost	Ratio	Restated Dollars 12/31/81
Beginning balance	$304,000	Exhibit 26-12	$316,952
Net income	180,000	Exhibit 26-18	165,889
Dividends	56,000	220/220	(56,000)
Ending retained earnings, December 31, 1981			$426,841

total stockholders' equity could be treated as one residual figure. In this case, restated stockholders' equity is the difference between restated assets and restated liabilities. The retained earnings statement for the year ended December 31, 1981, is presented in Exhibit 26-11.

Restated Balance Sheet

The constant dollar comparative balance sheets for 1981 and 1980 for the Stout Company are illustrated in Exhibit 26-12. These are the comparative statements that would appear in the 1981 annual report. The constant dollar balance sheet for 1980, as it would appear in the 1980 annual report, is presented in Exhibit 26-13.

Restatements of the Income and Retained Earnings Statements

Other than the cost of goods sold and depreciation expense, restatement of income statement items is straightforward. If the assumption is made that all income and expense items other than the cost of goods sold and depreciation take place evenly throughout the year, the adjustment rate is $\frac{\text{CPI at year-end}}{\text{Average CPI for year}}$. Restatement procedures for all income statement items are illustrated next.

Income Statement Items Other Than Cost of Goods Sold and Depreciation. The schedule in Exhibit 26-14 illustrates the restatement procedures for these income statement items. The adjustment ratio for all items is 220/205.

Cost of Goods Sold. Each item in the cost of goods sold must be adjusted separately because beginning and ending inventories and current-year purchases all are acquired at difference dates. The acquisition dates for the beginning and ending inventory are given in Exhibit 26-8. Purchases are assumed to take place evenly throughout the year.

The schedule in Exhibit 26-15 outlines the correct restatement procedures for the cost of goods sold.

Depreciation Expense. The ratio used to adjust depreciation expense is based on the index at the time the related assets were purchased. Because Stout purchased the building in 1976, the related depreciation expense must be restated from that date to 1981. Exhibit 26-16 illustrates the restatement procedures for the building depreciation and for the equipment depreciation. The procedures to calculate constant dollar depreciation for the equipment must be made in two steps because of the 1981 purchase. Total constant dollar depreciations for both items equal $28,600.

Calculation of Purchasing Power Gain or Losses

A firm incurs a purchase power gain or loss from holding net monetary items, and this amount is included on a restated income statement. The gain or loss is indicative of management's ability to adopt adequate financing policies to offset the effect of general price-level changes.

Exhibit 26-12
STOUT CORPORATION
Constant Dollar Comparative Balance Sheet
as of December 31

	1981	1980
Assets		
Current assets		
Cash	$ 150,000	$ 118,919
Receivables, net	250,000	208,108
Inventories—FIFO cost	184,186	232,222
Total current assets	$ 584,186	$ 559,249
Investments		
Common stock at cost—which is below market	166,755	137,500
Bond—at cost	125,000	148,649
Total investment	$ 291,755	$ 286,149
Property, plant, and equipment		
Land	275,000	275,000
Building (net of accumulated depreciation)	311,667	320,833
Equipment (net of accumulated depreciation)	94,233	91,667
Total property, plant, and equipment	$ 680,900	$ 687,500
Total assets	$1,556,841	$1,532,898
Liabilities and Stockholders' Equity		
Current liabilities		
Accounts payable	$ 160,000	$ 166,486
Taxes payable	120,000	142,703
Total current liabilities	$ 280,000	$ 309,189
Long-term liabilities		
Bond payable—10%	300,000	356,757
Total liabilities	$ 580,000	$ 665,946
Stockholders' equity		
Common stock ($5 par value) 20,000 shares issued and outstanding	183,333	183,333
Additional paid-in capital	366,667	366,667
Retained earnings	426,841	316,952
Total stockholders' equity	$ 976,841	$ 866,952
Total liabilities and stockholders' equity	$1,556,841	$1,532,898

Exhibit 26-13
STOUT CORPORATION
Constant Dollar Balance Sheet
December 31, 1980

Assets

Current assets

Cash	$ 100,000
Receivable, net	175,000
Inventory—FIFO cost	195,278
Total current assets	$ 470,278

Investments

Common stock at cost—which is below market	115,625
Bonds, at cost	125,000
Total investments	$ 240,625

Property, plant, and equipment

Land	231,250
Building (net of accumulated depreciation)	269,792
Equipment (net of accumulated depreciation)	77,083
Total property, plant, and equipment	$ 578,125
Total assets	$1,289,028

Liabilities and Stockholders' Equity

Current liabilities

Accounts payable	$ 140,000
Taxes payable	120,000
Total current liabilities	$ 260,000

Long-term liabilities

Bonds payable, 10%	300,000
Total liabilities	$ 560,000

Stockholders' equity

Common stock ($5 par value) 20,000 shares issued and outstanding	154,167
Additional paid-in capital	308,333
Retained earnings	266,528
Total stockholders' equity	$ 729,028
Total liabilities and stockholders' equity	$1,289,028

Exhibit 26-14
STOUT CORPORATION
Restatement of Income Statement Items

Account	Balance	×	Ratio	=	Restated Balance
Sales	$2,000,000		220/205		$2,146,341
Selling expense	200,000		220/205		214,634
General and administrative	254,000		220/205		272,585
Interest	30,000		220/205		32,195
Income taxes	120,000		220/205		128,780

To calculate a purchasing power gain or loss, you employ a procedure similar to that used to prepare a statement of changes in financial position. However, you analyze changes in net monetary items rather than changes in working capital. In effect, you compare the actual balance of net monetary items to the restated balance, and the difference represents a purchasing power gain or loss. These relationships are exemplified in the following table:

Net Monetary Position at Year End

	Net Monetary Asset Position	Net Monetary Liability Position
Restated amount exceeds actual amount	Loss	Gain
Restated amount less than actual method	Gain	Loss

As the table illustrates, if a firm is in a net liability position and if the restated balance exceeds the actual balance, the firm has a purchasing power gain.

Exhibit 26-15
STOUT CORPORATION
Restatement of Cost of Goods Sold

Account	Historical Cost	×	1981 Ratio	=	Restated Balance
Beginning inventory	$ 190,000		220/180		$ 232,222
+ Purchases	1,190,000		220/205		1,277,073
= Goods available for sale	$1,380,000				$1,509,295
− Ending inventory	180,000		220/215		184,186
= Cost of goods sold	$1,200,000				$1,325,109

Exhibit 26-16
STOUT CORPORATION
Restatement of Depreciation Expense

Building
    $5,000 × 220/120 = $9,167

Equipment

Purchase	Historical Cost	Depreciation Expense	Ratio	Restated Amount
Original—1976	$100,000	$10,000	220/120	$18,333
7/1/81	20,000	1,000	220/200	1,100
				$19,433

Total restated depreciation expense:
    Building $ 9,167
    Equipment   19,433
                $28,600

This is because the actual amount of the firm's debt is less than what the firm would have to repay in dollars of current purchasing power. Conversely, if the value of the firm's net monetary asset is less than the restated amount, the firm suffers a purchasing power loss. This is because the actual net monetary assets are less than they should be to retain their purchasing power.

Exhibit 26-17 illustrates the calculation of the purchasing power gain for the Stout Corporation. When reviewing this exhibit, you should keep in mind several points. The net monetary liability position of $160,000 at December 31, 1980, must be restated for the entire year because the firm held the balance throughout the year. Income and expenses that increase or decrease the firm's net monetary position are assumed to be earned or incurred evenly throughout the year. As a result, restatement must be made for only half a year. Depreciation is not included because it does not affect monetary items. Finally, other items, such as noncurrent asset purchases, dividend payments, or issuance of long-term equities, that affect a firm's monetary position are restated from the date of payment or receipt.

The Income Statement and Retained Earnings Statement

The restated income statement for the Stout Company is illustrated in Exhibit 26-18. All of the figures are derived from the adjustment procedures previously described.

The retained earnings statement is the final statement to be prepared in the restatement procedure. The adjustment procedure is illustrated in Exhibit 26-11.

Exhibit 26-17
STOUT CORPORATION
Computation of Purchasing Power Gain
For the Year Ended December 31, 1981

	Unadjusted Balance	1981 Ratio[1]	Restated Balance
Net monetary liability position 12/31/80	$ (160,000) ×	220/185 =	$ (190,270)
Additions to net monetary item			
sales	2,000,000 ×	220/205 =	2,146,341
	$1,840,000		$1,956,071
Deductions from net monetary item			
Purchases	(1,190,000) ×	220/205 =	(1,277,073)
Selling expense	(200,000) ×	220/205 =	(214,634)
General & Administrative	(254,000) ×	220/205 =	(272,585)
Interest	(30,000) ×	220/205 =	(32,195)
Income taxes	(120,000) ×	220/205 =	(128,780)
Dividends	(56,000) ×	220/220 =	(56,000)
Purchase of investment	(25,000) ×	220/188 =	(29,255)
Purchase of equipment	(20,000) ×	220/200 =	(22,000)
	$1,895,000		($2,032,522)
Net monetary liability position restated 12/31/81			(76,451)
Actual net monetary position 12/31/81			55,000
Purchasing power gain			$ 21,451

Net Monetary Position

	12/31/80	12/31/81
Monetary assets		
Cash	$ 100,000	$ 150,000
Receivables, net	175,000	250,000
Bonds	125,000	125,000
	$ 400,000	$ 525,000
Monetary liabilities		
Accounts payable	$ 140,000	$ 160,000
Taxes payable	120,000	120,000
Bonds payable	300,000	300,000
	$(560,000)	$(580,000)
Net monetary liabilities	$(160,000)	$ (55,000)

[1] See Exhibit 26-8 for relevant indexes.

Exhibit 26-18 STOUT CORPORATION Constant Dollar Income Statement For the Year Ended December 31, 1981		
Sales		$2,146,341
Cost of goods sold		1,325,109
Gross margin		$ 821,232
Operating expense		
Selling expense	$214,634	
General and administrative	272,585	
Depreciation	28,600	
Interest	32,195	
Total operating expense		$ 548,014
Income before taxes		273,218
Income taxes		128,780
Income before purchasing power loss		$ 144,438
Purchasing power gain		21,451
Net income		$ 165,889

The Constant Dollar Accounting Model: A Retrospective

The proponents of the constant dollar model argue that the benefits provided by restating nominal dollar statements to constant dollar far outweigh the costs involved. They believe that although the initial restatement procedures are complicated, subsequent restatement is relatively simple. Additional analysis is required only for current-year transactions. Other advantages of the constant dollar model are listed below:

1. Interfirm and intraperiod comparison are improved as all dollars are stated in the same purchasing power. Thus, financial statement analysis is improved.
2. A purchasing power gain or loss is determined.
3. The historical cost model and accepted principles for revenue realization remain intact. Only the measuring unit is changed.
4. Price indexes such as the CPI for all Urban Consumers represent objective evidence as to general price changes.
5. Users, such as potential and present investors and creditors, find their information useful and can interpret it properly.

There are several problems associated with this model. Opponents note that the effect of specific price changes is ignored. Further, there are problems with interpreting purchasing power gains and losses, which are dependent on the firm's business and may not be related to management actions. For example, Sears is likely to suffer large purchasing power losses due to its installment receivables, whereas utility companies are likely to have purchasing power gains due to their leveraged position. Other disadvantages are as follows:

1. Adjustments are made for general inflation effects rather than for changes in specific prices. Management makes decisions based on specific price changes affecting the mix of its net assets.
2. Holding and operating gains are not separated.
3. Assets are not valued at current value.
4. Purchasing power gains and losses are unrealized and difficult to interpret, and they should not be included in income.

Regardless of these arguments, the FASB now requires certain constant dollar disclosures. Whether these disclosures provide useful information for present and potential investors is a subject of future research.

The Current Value Model

Current value accounting focuses on the specific price changes that affect the firm. The objective of this model is to isolate operating income from holding gains and losses, and to value net assets at some measure of current value. That is, the attribute to be measured is current value rather than historical cost, whether adjusted or unadjusted for general price changes.

There are four different methods of determining current value: (1) present value of future cash flows, (2) net realizable value, (3) replacement cost, and (4) current costs.

Present Value of Future Cash Flows

Under the **present value method,** assets and liabilities are valued at the present value of future cash inflows or outflows. These cash flows are discounted to their present value by using an appropriate interest rate. Many theorists argue that this valuation method is the most appropriate way to value assets. If investors are interested in the timing, amount, and probability of future cash flows, assets ideally should be measured at their present value.

There are a number of problems in applying this method to the valuation of net assets. Clearly, there are significant interactions between assets, and it is difficult to measure the cash flow stream generated by individual assets. Even if you could identify the specific cash flow stream associated with individual assets, it would be difficult to project, with any certainty, this stream into the future. Finally, the appropriate discount or interest rate is open to debate.

There are circumstances, however, in which this method is currently in use. For example, in *Statement No. 33* the FASB requires that assets should be valued at the lower of their current cost or recoverable amount. For assets that are expected to be used rather than sold, the FASB defines the recoverable amount as value in use:

Value in use is the net present value of future cash flows (including the ultimate proceeds of disposal) expected to be derived from the use of an asset by an enterprise . . . Value in use shall be estimated by discounting expected future cash flows at an appropriate discount rate that allows for the risk of the activities concerned.[12]

In addition, long-term liabilities generally are measured at their present values at the time they are issued.

Net Realizable Value

Net realizable value is an alternate method of determining current value; it is defined as the selling price of an asset less the cost of disposal, and often is referred to as current cash equivalent or exit value. Under this method, assets are valued at their net realizable value, and any changes in these values are reflected in the current period's income. Advocates of this method, contend that it provides information about the enterprise's ability to adjust to changing market conditions.[13] If primary or secondary markets for the assets do not exist, however, it is difficult, if not impossible, to determine the net realizable value of certain assets.

The FASB has suggested that net realizable value be used when determining the recoverable amount of assets expected to be sold. It explains this position as follows:

Net realizable is the amount of cash, or its equivalent, expected to be derived from sale of an asset net of costs required to be incurred as a result of the sale. It shall be considered as a measurement of an asset only when the asset concerned is about to be sold.[14]

Replacement Cost

The FASB defines **replacement cost** as the amount of cash (or its equivalent) that would have to be paid to acquire currently the best asset available to undertake the function of the asset owned (less depreciation or amortization, if appropriate). In determining replacement costs, a firm would look at the assets currently available that serve the same function, even though the assets may be technologically superior to the assets currently in use. Adjustments are made for depreciation, but not for the improved technological capacities or operating savings.

For example, if U.S. Steel were calculating the replacement cost of a blast furnace, it would look at the cost of the new types of furnaces currently available even though they may be technologically superior. Adjustment would be made for the amount of depreciation on the existing asset, but no allowance would be made for increased capacities or cost savings.

---

[12] Ibid., par. 63b.

[13] See for example, Raymond Chambers, *Accounting, Evaluation and Economic Behavior* (Houston: Scholars Book Company, 1974).

[14] Financial Reporting and Changing Prices," par. 63a.

The SEC required the disclosure of certain replacement costs under the requirement of *ASR No. 190*. As noted previously, this release has been withdrawn for those firms that fully comply with FASB *Statement No. 33*.

Current Cost

The fourth method of determining current value is **current cost,** which is the method selected by the FASB in *Statement No. 33*. The Board defines current cost as the cost equal to the current replacement cost of the assets owned, adjusted for the value of any operating advantages or disadvantages of the asset owned: "Current cost differs from current replacement cost in that current cost measurement focuses on the cost of the service potential embodied in the asset owned by the enterprise, whereas current replacement cost may be the measurement of a different asset, available for use in place of the asset owned."[15]

The FASB suggests two broad methods of determining current cost:

1. Indexation
   a) Externally generated price indexes for the class of goods or services being measured.
   b) Internally generated price indexes for the class of goods or services being measured.
2. Direct pricing
   a) Current invoice prices.
   b) Vendor's price listing or other quotations or estimates.
   c) Standard manufacturing costs that reflect current costs.[16]

The Current Cost Model

Because the FASB requires certain current cost disclosures, this model is discussed in detail. The attribute to be measured in this model is current cost rather than historical cost. Under the current cost model a gain or loss is recognized as the value of the asset increases or decreases. Thus, income or loss can be recognized before the time of sale. Both a holding gain or loss (due to value changes) and an operating gain or loss (due to a sale) are recorded.

Like the constant dollar model, the current cost model rests on the theory of capital maintenance. However, the particular concept of capital maintenance is different. Remember, the pupose of constant dollar accounting is to maintain capital in terms of the firm's ability to purchase goods and services. The purpose of current cost accounting is to maintain capital in terms of the firm's productive capacity; that is, income is not earned until the firm's operating capacity at the end of the period is at least as great as it was at the beginning of the period.

As an illustration of the basic concepts behind the current cost model, assume that the Newton Corporation purchased an item of inventory in early 1980 for $10,000. The inventory was held until 1982 when it was sold for $17,500. The following current cost data are also available.

---

[15] Ibid., par. 99f.
[16] Ibid., par. 60.

	Current Cost		
	December 31 1980	December 31 1981	June 15 1980 (date of sale)
Current value	$12,000	$15,000	$16,000

Simplified current cost income statements for 1980 through 1982 are illustrated in Exhibit 26-19. For comparison, traditional historical cost statements are presented as well.

It is important to note that over the three-year period illustrated, the total income of $7,500 is the same under both methods. However, the timing and com-

---

Exhibit 26-19
THE NEWTON COMPANY
Current Cost and Historical Cost Income Statements
For the Years Ended December 31, 1980, 1981, and 1982

	Current Cost			
	December 31 1980	December 31 1981	December 31 1982	Total
Sales revenue	0	0	$17,500	
Cost of goods sold	0	0	16,000	
Gross margin	0	—	$ 1,500	$1,500
Holding gain	$2,000[1]	$3,000[2]	1,000[3]	6,000
Net income	$2,000	$3,000	$ 2,500	$7,500

[1] Current cost—12/31/80 $12,000
    Less: Historical cost   10,000
                              $ 2,000

[2] Current cost—12/31/81 $15,000
    Less: Current cost 12/31/80 12,000
                              $ 3,000

[3] Current cost—12/31/81 $16,000
    Less: Current cost 12/31/81 15,000
                              $ 1,000

	Historical Cost			
	12/31/80	12/31/81	12/31/82	Total
Sales revenues	0	0	$17,500	
Cost of goods sold	0	0	10,000	
Gross margin	0	0	$ 7,500	
Holding gain	0	0	0	
Net income			$ 7,500	$7,500

ponents of the income are different. Under the current cost model, holding gains of $6,000 are reported while the gross margin on sale is only $1,500. Under the traditional historical cost models, no holding gains are recorded but the gross margin on sales totals $7,500.

In practice, current cost income statements are more complicated than the illustration above indicates. There are three major components to a current cost income statement: (1) current cost operating margin, (2) traditional net income, and (3) current cost net income. These items are defined as follows:

Current cost operating margin: sales less operating expenses calculated on current cost basis.

Traditional net income: current cost operating margin plus or minus realized holding gains or losses. Realized holding gains or losses are the difference between the current cost of an item and its historical cost at the time it is sold or consumed.

Current cost net income: traditional net income plus or minus unrealized holding gains or losses. Unrealized holding gains and losses result from increases and decreases in the current cost of assets and liabilities. The unrealized holding gains or losses for the period are the difference between the cumulative unrealized gain or loss at the end of the period and the cumulative unrealized gain or loss at the beginning of the period. Unrealized holding gains and losses become realized when the related asset or liability is sold or liquidated.

These income statement concepts are illustrated by the following example. Assume that the Peterson Company is a retailer. The historical cost balance sheet for 1980, as well as additional data for 1981, are presented in Exhibit 26-20.

The current cost income statement is presented in Exhibit 26-21. The current cost operating margin of $580 is equal to sales less expenses at their current cost. Realized holding gains are calculated by taking the difference between operating expenses at their current cost and their historical cost. Realized holding gains added to current operating margin equals conventional net income. (This can be verified by calculating the historical net income of $770, which is equal to sales of $2,400 less historical cost of goods sold of $1,530 and depreciation of $100.)

The Current Cost Model—A Complete Illustration

In order to illustrate the current cost model, we will continue with the example of the Stout Company. (The historical cost financial statements are presented in Exhibits 26-6 and 26-7.) The data concerning the current cost of the various assets and liabilities are found in Exhibit 26-22. This exhibit also calculates unrealized gains and losses for these items for use in constructing the current cost income statement.

Balance Sheet Items

In preparing a current cost balance sheet, the enterprise records its assets and liabilities at their current cost. As noted previously, the FASB suggests a number of ways to determine current costs. These include specific price indexes,

Exhibit 26-20
THE PETERSON COMPANY
Historical Cost Balance Sheet
December 31, 1980

Cash	$ 200	Stockholders' equity	$2,000
Inventory	800		
Fixed assets	1,000		
Total assets	$2,000	Total stockholders equity	$2,000

Additional data:
1. The fixed asset has a life of 10 years. The firm uses straight-line depreciation with no salvage value. The asset was purchased on December 31, 1980, at a cost of $1,000. The current cost of the building as of December 31, 1981, is $1,200.
2. Current data for 1981:

	Historical Cost	Current Cost
Sales for 1981	$2,400	$2,400
December 31, 1980, inventory	800	850
December 31, 1981, inventory	920	1,050
Cost of goods sold	1,530	1,700
Depreciation expense	120	100

direct pricing, and appraisal techniques. The balance in retained earnings is the amount needed to balance the statement. It is not necessary to restate other items in stockholders' equity; they are left at historical cost, with the total adjustment made to retained earnings. As an alternative, all stockholders' equity accounts could be collapsed into one account, which would be reported at the amount needed to balance the financial statement.

The comparative current cost balance sheets for the Stout Company as of December 31, 1981, and December 31, 1980, are presented in Exhibit 26-23. Items that need additional clarification include buildings, equipment, and bonds payable. Since these accounts are related to their income statement counterparts of depreciation and interest expense, they are discussed in the next section.

Income Statement Items

As noted previously, the current cost income statement is divided into three major categories: (1) current cost operating margin, (2) traditional net income, and (3) current cost net income. The determination of the individual accounts included in each of these three categories is discussed in the following sections.

Exhibit 26-21
PETERSON COMPANY
Current Cost Income Statement
For the Year Ended December 31, 1981

Sales		$2,400
Cost of goods sold		1,700
Gross margin		$ 700
Depreciation		120
Current cost operating margin		$ 580
Realized holding gain		
Cost of goods sold	$170[1]	
Depreciation	20[2]	190
Conventional net income		$ 770
Unrealized holding gain		
Inventory	80[3]	
Building, net	180[4]	260
Current cost net income		$1,030

[1] Cost of goods sold current cost $1,700
   Cost of goods sold historical cost   1,530
                          $ 170

[2] Depreciation current cost
   $1,200 ÷ 10 = $ 120
   Depreciation historical cost
   $1,000 ÷ 10 =   100
                         $ 20

[3] Unrealized holding gain—inventory
   Cumulative unrealized gain, December 31, 1981
      Ending inventory at current cost $1,050
      Ending inventory at historical cost   920 $130
   Cumulative unrealized gain, December 31, 1980
      Ending inventory at current cost   850
      Ending inventory at historical cost   800   50
                         $ 80

[4] Unrealized holding gain—building
   Net building at current cost $1,080 ($1,200 − $120)
   Net building at historical cost   900 ($1,000 − $100)
                  $ 180

Current Cost Operating Margin. The current cost operating margin is determined by subtracting current cost operating expenses from sales. Sales already are reported at their current price and need no adjustment on a current cost statement. Expenses other than the cost of goods sold, depreciation, and interest also are reported at their current cost when incurred and require no adjustment.

Exhibit 26-22
THE STOUT COMPANY
Selected Historical and Current Cost Data
Balance Sheet Items

December 31, 1981

	Historical Cost	Current Cost	1981 Cumulative Unrealized Holding Gain (Loss)
Inventories	$180,000	$245,000	$ 65,000
Common stock	100,000	200,000	100,000
Bonds	125,000	125,000	—
Land	150,000	325,000	175,000
Building, net	170,000	357,000	187,000
Equipment, net	59,000	134,800	75,800
Bonds, payable	300,000	227,177	(72,823)

December 31, 1980

	Historical Cost	Current Cost	1980 Cumulative Unrealized Holding Gain (Loss)	Increase in Cumulative Unrealized Holding Gain (Loss) for 1981[1]
Inventories	$190,000	$240,000	$ 50,000	$15,000
Common stock	75,000	180,000	105,000	(5,000)
Bonds	125,000	125,000	—	—
Land	150,000	300,000	150,000	25,000
Building, net	175,000	350,000	175,000	12,000
Equipment, net	50,000	125,000	75,000	800
Bonds, payable	300,000	225,546	74,454	(1,631)

[1] 1981 cumulative unrealized holding gain (loss) minus 1980 cumulative unrealized holding gain (loss).

Thus, sales, selling expenses, and general and administrative expenses are reported as they were on the historical cost statement. Exhibi 26-24 lists the historical and current costs of the cost of goods sold, depreciation expense, and interest expense. In addition, this exhibit presents the realized holding gain for these items.

The current cost adjustments for the cost of goods sold is relatively straight-

Exhibit 26-23
STOUT CORPORATION
Comparative Current Cost Balance Sheet
As of December 31

	1981	1980
Assets		
Current assets		
Cash	$ 150,000	$ 100,000
Receivables, net	250,000	175,000
Inventories—FIFO	245,000	240,000
Total current assets	$ 645,000	$ 515,000
Investments		
Common stock—at cost which is below market	200,000	180,000
Bonds—at cost	125,000	125,000
Total investment	$ 325,000	$ 305,000
Property, plant, and equipment		
Land	325,000	300,000
Buildings (net of accumulated depreciation)	357,000	350,000
Equipment (net of accumulated depreciation)	134,800	125,000
Total property, plant, and equipment	$ 816,800	$ 775,000
Total assets	$1,786,800	$1,595,000
Liabilities & Stockholders' Equity		
Current liabilities		
Accounts payable	$ 160,000	$ 140,000
Taxes payable	120,000	120,000
Total current liabilities	$ 280,000	$ 260,000
Long-term liabilities		
Bonds payable	227,177	225,546
Total liabilities	$ 507,177	$ 485,546
Stockholders' equity		
Common stock ($5 par value) 20,000 shares issued and outstanding	100,000	100,000
Additional paid-in-capital	200,000	200,000
Retained earnings	979,623	809,454
Total stockholders' equity	$1,279,623	$1,109,454
Total liabilities and stockholders' equity	$1,786,800	$1,595,000

Exhibit 26-24
STOUT CORPORATION
Income Statement Items
For the Year Ended December 31, 1981

	Current Cost	Historical Cost	Realized Holding Gain
Cost of goods sold	$1,300,000	$1,200,000	$100,000
Depreciation	37,750	16,000	21,750
Interest	31,631	30,000	1,631
			$123,381

forward. The current cost of the goods sold at the time of sale must be determined, and that figure is used in determining the current cost operating margin. In this example, the current cost of goods sold is determined to be $1,300,000.

Depreciation expense is based upon the current cost of the building and equipment. However, in *Statement No. 33* the FASB argues that the expense should be based upon the asset's average current costs during the year. The current cost depreciation data are presented in Exhibit 26-24. However, the actual calculation of current cost depreciation and the appropriate current cost balance in the related asset and accumulated depreciation account are quite complex and are illustrated in the Appendix to this chapter.

The bonds payable were issued at face on January 2, 1976, when the corporation was formed. The stated interest rate is 10%, and they mature 20 years from 1976 or in 1996. The bonds had a current market value of $225,546 and $227,177 on January 1, 1980, and December 31, 1981, respectively. The market value of the bonds (i.e., their current cost) is a function of the current market interest rate, which averaged 14% throughout both 1980 and 1981. For example, as of January 1, 1981, the bonds had 15 years, or 30 interest payments, to maturity. The present value of the cash outflows (i.e., interest payments and maturity value) discounted at 7% interest payable semiannually on January 1, 1981, equals $225,546. The determination of this amount and the related current cost interest expense are presented in Exhibit 26-25.

Finally, like general and administrative expenses and selling expenses, income taxes are not adjusted. They are assumed to be at a current cost.

Traditional Net Income. The next major section in a current cost income statement is traditional net income. For the Stout Corporation this amount is $180,000; it is calculated by adding the realized holding gain of $123,381, determined in Exhibit 26-24, to the current cost operating margin of $56,619 (Exhibit 26-26).

Current Cost Net Income. The final component of the current cost income statement is current cost net income, which is determined by adding the unrealized holding gains and losses to traditional net income. Unrealized holding gains and

---

Exhibit 26-25
STOUT CORPORATION
Determination of Bond Value and Interest

Determination of Current Value of Bonds—1980

Present value of $15,000 annuity for 30 periods at 7%	
$15,000 × 12.40904 (Table 5-4)	$186,135
Present value of $300,000 maturity value to be received in 30 periods at 7%	
$300,000 × 0.13137 (Table 5-2)	39,411
	$225,546

Determination of Interest Expense and Subsequent Carrying Value

Date	Carrying Value	×	Current Interest Rate	=	Interest Expense	−	Cash Interest 5%	=	Addition to Carrying Value
1/2/81	$225,546		0.07		$15,788		$15,000		$ 788
7/31/81	226,334		0.07		15,843		15,000		843
					$31,631		$30,000		$1,631
1/2/82	227,177								

---

losses for the year represent the change in cumulative gains and losses during the year and are calculated in Exhibit 26-22. The current cost income statement and retained earnings statement for the Stout Corporation are presented in Exhibits 26-26 and 26-27, respectively.

In recent years the current cost model has attained more importance. In issuing *ASR No. 190* the SEC clearly believed that replacement cost data benefit present and potential investors. In addition, the FASB in *Statement No. 33* requires the supplemental disclosure of selected current cost data. In future years you are likely to see more and more disclosures of current cost data. The following is a summary of the important advantages and disadvantages of the current cost model.

Advantages
1. Income is divided into two major components—current cost operating margins and holding gains and losses. Thus, users can determine management's effectiveness in dealing with specific price changes.
2. Assets and liabilities are reported at current cost, which provides a better indication of economic value.
3. Current cost income provides a better indication of future cash flows to the enterprise and ultimately to the investor or creditor.

Exhibit 26-26
STOUT CORPORATION
Current Cost Income Statement
For the Year Ended December 31, 1981

Sales		$2,000,000
Cost of goods sold		1,300,000
		$ 700,000
Operating expenses		
Selling expense	$200,000	
General and administrative	254,000	
Depreciation expense	37,750	
Interest expense	31,631	
Income taxes	120,000	
Total operating expenses		643,381
Current cost operating margin		$ 56,619
Realized holding gain[1]		
Cost of goods sold	100,000	
Depreciation	21,750	
Interest	1,631	123,381
Traditional net income		$ 180,000
Unrealized holding gains and losses[2]		
Inventories	15,000	
Common stock	(5,000)	
Land	25,000	
Buildings	12,000	
Equipment	800	
Bonds	(1,631)	46,169
Current cost net income		$ 226,169

[1] See Exhibit 26-33.
[2] See Exhibit 26-22.

---

4. Current cost income from continuing operations may be regarded as a guide to the assessment of whether an enterprise has maintained its operating capability.

Disadvantages
1. Current costs must be estimated and often are difficult to determine. Thus, comparability and reliability are sacrificed.
2. The current cost model fails to recognize the effect of general price-level changes that may be different from specific price changes.
3. The current cost model fails to recognize purchasing power gains and losses.
4. Unrealized holding gains and losses can be misinterpreted. They cannot be distributed in the form of dividends without impairing the firm's capital.

Exhibit 26-27
STOUT CORPORATION
Retained Earnings Statement
For the Year Ended December 31, 1981

Retained earnings		
January 1, 1981, historical cost		$180,000
Add:		
Cumulative holding gains and losses of previous year[1]		
Inventories	$ 50,000	
Common stock	105,000	
Land	150,000	
Building net	175,000	
Equipment, net	75,000	
Bond payable	74,454	
		629,454
Retained earnings		
January 1, 1981, current cost		$809,454
Net income, current cost		226,169
Less: Dividends		(56,000)
Retained earnings, current cost		$979,623

[1]See Exhibit 26-22.

The Current Cost/Constant Dollar Model

The introduction to this chapter noted that many accountants argue that in order to reflect economic reality properly, financial statements should be adjusted for both specific and general price-level changes. Thus, holding gains calculated from specific price changes are adjusted for general price-level changes and represent real, not inflationary, gains. The current cost/constant dollar method accomplishes this purpose because income is not assumed to be earned until the productive capacity of the firm, measured in constant dollars, is maintained.

In current cost/constant dollar financial statements all items are restated to current cost in constant year-end dollars. Using the data for the Stout Corporation, we will discuss the current cost/constant dollar restatement procedures next.

Balance Sheet

For assets and liabilities, current cost and current cost/constant dollar amounts are the same. This is because these amounts are already in current year-end costs, and thus no further adjustment is necessary. Therefore, the asset and liability balances in the single-year 1981 current cost/constant dollar balance sheet are the same as in the current cost balance sheet.

However, two balance sheet adjustments are necessary. Common stock and additional paid-in-capital must be restated to year-end dollars, since they have not been adjusted in the current cost model. They are restated by multiplying their historical cost by the change in general price levels since incorporation. The relevant calculations are as follows:

Common stock	$100,000 \times 220/120 = \$183,333$
Additional paid-in-capital	$200,000 \times 220/120 = \ \ 366,667$

In addition, current cost retained earnings must be adjusted. The retained earnings are calculated as the amount necessary to balance the financial statement.

When comparative statements are presented, prior years' current cost asset and liability balances must be adjusted to the now current year-end constant dollars. In this example, 1980 current cost balances must be multiplied by the ratio, 220/185. This ratio is the end of the 1981 index divided by the beginning-of-the-year index. The required calculations for the Stout Corporation are presented in Exhibit 26-28.

Income Statement Items

All current cost income statement items must be adjusted to year-end dollars. Remember, the assumption is made that these items were issued evenly throughout the year, and thus must be adjusted to year-end dollars. The numerator of the

---

Exhibit 26-28
STOUT CORPORATION
Restatement to 1981 Constant Dollars
For Comparative Statement Purposes

Account	1980 Current Cost Amount	Restatement Ratio	Restated Amount
Cash	$100,000	220/185[1]	$118,919
Receivables, net	175,000	220/185	208,108
Inventories	240,000	220/185	285,405
Common stock	180,000	220/185	214,054
Bonds	125,000	220/185	148,649
Land	300,000	220/185	356,757
Building, net	350,000	220/185	416,216
Equipment, net	125,000	220/185	148,649
Accounts payable	140,000	220/185	166,486
Taxes payable	120,000	220/185	142,703
Bonds payable	225,546	220/185	268,217
Common stock	100,000	220/120[2]	183,333
Additional paid-in-capital	200,000	220/120	366,667

[1] In 1980 dollars—must be restated to 1981.
[2] In 1976 dollars—must be restated to 1981.

	Exhibit 26-29		
STOUT CORPORATION			
Restatement of Income Statement Items			

Account	Current Cost Amount	Restatement Ratio	Restated Amount
Sales	$2,000,000	220/205	$2,146,341
Cost of goods sold	1,300,000	220/205	1,395,122
Selling expense	200,000	220/205	214,634
General administration	254,000	220/205	272,585
Depreciation	37,750	220/205	40,512
Interest	31,631	220/205	33,945
Income taxes	120,000	220/205	128,780

ratio is the index at the end of the year, and the denominator is the index at midyear. Thus, the ratio is 220/205. Exhibit 26-29 illustrates this restatement procedure.

Realized Holding Gains and Losses

In a current cost/constant dollar statement, realized holding gains or losses on inventories, depreciable assets, and bonds payable are the difference between these amounts on a current cost/constant dollar basis and on a constant dollar basis. Thus, they represent realized gains and losses, net of inflation. For the Stout Corporation these realized gains and losses are determined as follows:

Account	Current Cost/ Constant Dollar (1)	Constant Dollar (2)	Realized Holding Gain Loss
Cost of goods sold	$1,395,122	$1,325,109	$70,013
Depreciation	40,512	28,600	11,912
Interest expense	33,945	32,195	1,750

(1) See Exhibit 26-29.
(2) See Exhibit 26-18.

Unrealized Gains and Losses

Unrealized gains and losses on a current cost/constant dollar basis are the incremental unrealized gains and losses that occurred during the year and are measured by determining the difference between current cost/constant dollar amounts and the constant dollar amounts. Thus, these unrealized holding gains and losses are also net of inflation. The necessary calculations for the Stout Corporation are illustrated in Exhibit 26-30.

To complete the income statement you must include the purchasing power gain of $21,451 (Exhibit 26-17) in income. Finally, financial statements for the

Exhibit 26-30

STOUT CORPORATION
Determination of Unrealized Gain (Loss) for 1981

	Inventories	Common Stock	Bonds	Land	Building	Equipment	Bonds Payable	Total
1981 Current cost/ constant dollar[1]	$245,000	$200,000	$125,000	$325,000	$357,000	$134,800	$(227,177)	$1,159,623
Constant dollar[2]	184,186	166,755	125,000	275,000	311,667	94,233	(300,000)	856,841
Cumulative unrealized holding gain (loss)	(a)$ 60,814	$ 33,245	$ 0	$ 50,000	$ 45,333	$ 40,567	$ 72,823	$ 302,782
1980 Current cost/ constant dollar[3]	$285,405	$214,054	$148,649	$356,757	$416,216	$148,649	$(268,217)	$1,301,513
Constant dollar[2]	232,222	137,500	148,649	275,000	320,833	91,667	(356,757)	849,114
Cumulative unrealized holding gain (loss)	(b)$ 53,183	$ 76,554	$ 0	$ 81,757	$ 95,383	$ 56,982	$ 88,540	$ 452,399
Increase in cumulative unrealized gain (loss) for 1981	(a – b)$ 7,631	$(43,309)	$ 0	$(31,757)	$(50,050)	$(16,415)	$(15,717)	$ (149,617)

[1] See Exhibit 26-22.
[2] See Exhibit 26-12.
[3] See Exhibit 26-28.

Exhibit 26-31
STOUT CORPORATION
Comparative Current Cost/Constant Dollar Balance Sheet
As of December 31

	1981	1980
Assets		
Current assets		
Cash	$ 150,000	$ 118,919
Receivables, net	250,000	208,108
Inventories—FIFO cost	245,000	285,405
Total current assets	$ 645,000	$ 612,432
Investments		
Common stock—at cost which is below market	200,000	214,054
Bonds	125,000	148,649
Total investments	$ 325,000	$ 362,703
Property, plant, and equipment		
Land	325,000	356,757
Building (net of accumulated depreciation)	357,000	416,216
Equipment (net of accumulated depreciation)	134,800	148,649
Total property, plant, and equipment	$ 816,800	$ 921,622
Total assets	$1,786,800	$1,896,757
Liabilities & Stockholders' Equity		
Current liabilities		
Accounts payable	$ 160,000	$ 166,486
Taxes payable	120,000	142,703
Total current liabilities	$ 280,000	$ 309,189
Long-term liabilities		
Bonds payable, 10%	227,177	268,217
Total liabilities	$ 507,177	$ 577,406
Stockholders' equity		
Common stock ($5 par value) 20,000 shares issued and outstanding)	183,333	183,333
Additional paid-in capital	366,667	366,667
Retained earnings	729,623	769,351
Total stockholders' equity	$1,279,623	$1,319,351
Total liabilities and stockholders' equity	$1,786,800	$1,896,757

Exhibit 26-32
STOUT CORPORATION
Current Cost/Constant Dollar Income Statement
For Year Ended December 31, 1981

Sales		$2,146,341
Cost of goods sold		1,395,122
		$ 751,219
Operating expense		
Selling	$214,634	
General and administrative	272,585	
Depreciation	40,512	
Interest	33,945	
Income taxes	128,780	
		690,456
Current cost/constant dollar		
operating income		$ 60,763
Realized holding gain, net of inflation[1]		
Inventory sold	70,013	
Depreciation	11,912	
Interest	1,750	
		83,675
Constant dollar income before purchasing		
power gain		$ 144,348
Unrealized holding loss, net of inflation[2]		(149,617)
		$ (5,179)
Purchasing power gain[3]		21,451
Current cost/constant dollar income		$ 16,272

[1] See page 1212 in text.
[2] See Exhibit 26-30.
[3] See Exhibit 26-17.

Stout Corporation on a current cost/constant dollar basis are presented in Exhibits 26-31, 26-32, and 26-33.

Theorists argue that the current cost/constant dollar model produces the best of both worlds. The FASB has recognized this and requires that certain current cost/constant dollar information be disclosed on a supplemental basis. The advantages and disadvantages of this model are listed below:

Advantages
1. In addition to current costs being reported, the measuring unit is standardized. Thus, the effects of both specific and general price changes are reported.

> ### Exhibit 26-33
> ### STOUT CORPORATION
> ### Current Cost/Constant Dollar Retained Earnings Statement
> ### For the Year Ended December 31, 1981
>
> | | |
> |---|---:|
> | Retained earnings, January 1, 1981 | $769,351 |
> | Add: Net income for 1981—Exhibit 24-32 | 16,272 |
> | Less: Dividends for 1981 | (56,000) |
> | Retained earnings, December 31, 1981 | $729,623 |

2. Both holding gains and losses and purchasing power gains and losses are supported.

Disadvantages

1. Difficulties in understanding and interpreting this data.

2. The cost of preparation, especially in the first year.

3. Use of subjective data in determining current cost and constant dollar data.

FASB Statement No. 33— Financial Reporting and Changing Prices

After years of discussion, experimentation, and argumentation, the accounting profession finally took an official position regarding accounting for changing prices when in September, 1979, the FASB issued *Statement No. 33*. This Statement requires certain public companies to disclose on a supplemental basis both constant dollar and current cost data. As noted in the Statement:

> Preparers and users of financial reports have not yet reached a consensus on the general practical usefulness of constant dollar information and current cost information. It seems unlikely that a consensus can be reached until further experience has been joined with the use of both types of information in systematic applications. This statement, therefore, requires certain enterprises to present information both on a constant dollar basis and on a current cost basis.[17]

Application of FASB Statement No. 33

Statement No. 33 does not require enterprises to present complete financial statements on a constant dollar and/or a current cost basis. Rather, the Statement requires partial application, with the information to be disclosed on a supplemental basis. Thus, restatement procedures are to be applied only to invento-

---

[17] Ibid., par. 13.

ries and properties and to the related cost of goods sold and depreciation. According to the Statement, the following items are to be disclosed:

1. Information on income from continuing operations for the current fiscal year on a historical cost/constant dollar basis.
2. The purchasing power gain or loss on net monetary items for the current fiscal year (not to be included in income from continuing operations).
3. Information on income from continuing operations for the current fiscal year on a current cost basis.
4. The current cost amounts of inventory and property, plant, and equipment at the end of the current fiscal year.
5. Increases or decreases for the current fiscal year in the current cost amounts of inventory and of property, plant, and equipment, net of inflation.
6. A summary of selected data for the five most recent fiscal years.

The FASB believed that the benefits of such disclosures would outweigh the preparation cost for certain companies. As a result, *Statement No. 33* only applies to public enterprises that have one of the following at the beginning of each fiscal year:

1. Inventories and property, plant, and equipment (before accumulated depreciation) amounting to more than $125 million.
2. Total assets amounting to more than $1 billion (after deducting accumulated depreciation).

Differences in FASB Procedures

There are significant differences in the restatement procedures required in *Statement No. 33* and those outlined in this chapter. As noted, the FASB does not require complete restatement, only restatement of inventories, property, plant, and equipment, cost of goods sold, and depreciation is required. Second, in restating nominal balances to a constant dollar basis, you should use the average-of-the-current-year index in the numerator. The ratio is as follows:

$$\frac{\text{CPI average for the year}}{\text{CPI at date of acquisition}}$$

If you use the average-of-the-current-year index, the Board contends that it is not necessary to adjust revenue and expenses other than the cost of goods sold and depreciation. If these revenues and expenses are assumed to occur evenly throughout the year and if an average-for-the-year index is used, the nominal dollar amount and the constant dollar would be the same. Thus, it is not necessary to restate these income statement items. Finally, the Board requires that increases in the current cost of inventories and properties be shown net of inflation; however, no provision is made for distinguishing realized and unrealized gains and losses.

Restatement Procedures
Required by FASB Statement No. 33

Consistent with previous examples, the restatement procedures required by FASB *Statement No. 33* are illustrated by using the data from the Stout Corporation. The original historical cost financial statements are presented in Exhibits 26-6 and 26-7.

Income Statement Items. *Statement No. 33* only requires restatement to constant dollar and to current cost for the cost of goods sold and depreciation expense. Adjustment is made to average-for-the-year dollars. The average index for 1981 is 205. All other income statement items are assumed to be incurred evenly throughout the year (whether realistic or not), and no adjustment is required to restate these items to average-for-the-year dollars.

Exhibit 26-34 restates the *cost of goods sold* to average-for-the-year dollars. The relevant price indexes are taken from Exhibit 26-8. The cost of goods sold on a current cost basis is the same as was determined previously. Below are the relevant *Statement No. 33* data:

	Constant Dollar	Current Cost
Cost of goods sold	$1,234,761	$1,300,000

On a constant dollar basis, *depreciation expense* also is adjusted to average-for-the-year dollars. Exhibit 26-35 illustrates the restatement procedures for the depreciation expense related to the building and equipment. Total *Statement No. 33* constant dollar depreciation equals $26,650.

Exhibit 26-34
STOUT CORPORATION
Restatement of the Cost of Goods Sold
to Average-for-the-Year Prices

Account	Historical Cost	×	1981 Ratio	=	Restated Balance Average-for-the-Year
Beginning inventory	$ 190,000		205/180	=	$ 216,389
+ Purchases	1,190,000		205/205	=	1,190,000
= Goods available for sale	$1,380,000				$1,406,389
− Ending inventory	180,000		205/215	=	171,628
= Cost of goods sold	$1,200,000				$1,234,761

The FASB argues that current cost depreciation expense should be based on the asset's average current cost during the year. The current cost depreciation of $37,750 was calculated using the average current cost, so no further adjustment is required. (See the Appendix for the derivation of this figure.) In summary, the relevant *Statement No. 33* data are as follows:

	Constant Dollar	Current Cost
Depreciation	$26,650	$37,750

In order to comply with *Statement No. 33* requirements, the Stout Corporation must recalculate its *purchasing power gain*, using average-for-the-year dollars. Exhibit 26-36 illustrates how the purchasing power gain of $19,900 is calcu-

---

Exhibit 26-35
STOUT CORPORATION
Restatement of Depreciation Expense
to Average-for-the-Year Dollars

Building:
  $5,000 × 205/120 = $8,542

Equipment:

Purchase	Historical Cost	Depreciation Expense	1981 Ratio	Restated Balance Average-for-the-Year
Original—1976	$100,000	$10,000	205/120	$17,083
7/1/81	20,000	1,000	205/200	1,025
Total				$18,108

Total restated depreciation expense:
  Building $ 8,542
  Equipment   18,108
          $26,650

Realized holding gains (losses):

	Current Cost	Constant Dollar	Realized Holding Gains (Losses)
Cost of goods sold	$1,300,000	$1,234,761	$65,239
Depreciation	37,750	26,650	11,100
			$76,339

Exhibit 26-36
STOUT CORPORATION
Determination of Purchasing Power Gain
Average-for-the-Year Dollars

	Unadjusted Balance	1981 Ratio		Restated Balance
Net monetary liability position 12/31/80	$ (160,000) ×	205/185	=	$ (177,297)
Additions to net monetary item				
Sales	$2,000,000 ×	205/205	=	2,000,000
	$1,840,000			$1,822,703
Deductions from net monetary item				
Purchases	(1,190,000) ×	205/205	=	(1,190,000)
Selling expense	(200,000) ×	205/205	=	(200,000)
General & administrative	(254,000) ×	205/205	=	(254,000)
Interest	(30,000) ×	205/205	=	(30,000)
Income taxes	(120,000) ×	205/205	=	(120,000)
Dividends	(56,000) ×	205/220	=	(52,182)
Purchase of investment	(25,000) ×	205/188	=	(27,261)
Purchase of equipment	(20,000) ×	205/200	=	(20,500)
Total	$1,895,000			$1,893,943
Net monetary position restated 12/31/81				$ (71,240)
Net monetary position 12/31/81—restated to average-for-the-year dollars	(55,000) ×	205/220	=	(51,250)
Purchasing power gain				$ 19,990

Net Monetary Liability Position

	12/31/80	12/31/81
Monetary assets		
Cash	$ 100,000	$ 150,000
Receivables, net	175,000	250,000
Bonds	125,000	125,000
	$ 400,000	$ 525,000
Monetary liabilities		
Accounts payable	144,000	160,000
Taxes payable	120,000	120,000
Bonds payable	300,000	300,000
	$(560,000)	$(580,000)
Net monetary liabilities	$(160,000)	$ (55,000)

lated. For illustrative purposes a ratio of 205/205 was used to restate most of the items. However, because the result of using this ratio is that these items are left at their historical cost, the original historical cost could have been used.

Balance Sheet Items. Under the provisions of *Statement No. 33* a complete current cost balance sheet is not required. However, enterprises must report the current cost of inventory and property, plant, and equipment. The enterprises must also report any increases or decreases in the current cost amounts of inventory and of property, plant, and equipment, net of inflation, that occurred during the current fiscal year. This requires adjustment to these particular balance sheet items.

Beginning and ending *inventories* must be restated to average-for-the-year constant dollars. The relevant calculations are as follows:

	Historical Cost	1980 Ratio	Restated 12/31/80 Amount	1981 Ratio	Restated 12/31/81 Constant Dollar Amount
12/31/80— Ending inventories	$190,000	× 175/180	= $184,722	× 205/175	= $216,389
12/31/81— Ending inventories	180,000			× 205/215	= 171,628

It should be noted that because 12/31/81 ending inventories were purchased during the last two months of 1981, they must be deflated to average-for-the-year dollars. Thus, $180,000 is multiplied by the ratio of average-for-the-year dollars over average-for-the-last-two-months dollars, or 205/215.

When assets are stated at current cost, they are already at end-of-the-year dollars. However, the FASB requires disclosures of current cost in average-for-the-year dollars. As a result, the relevant assets must be deflated from year-end dollars to average-for-the-year dollars. The relevant current cost data for inventories, deflated to average-for-the-year dollars, are illustrated below:

	Current Cost	1980 Ratio	Restated 12/31/80 Current Cost Amount	1981 Ratio	Restated 12/31/81 Current Cost Amount
12/31/80— Ending inventories	$240,000	× 175/185	= $227,027	× 205/175	= $265,946
12/31/81— Ending inventories	245,000			× 205/220	= 228,295

The computations required to restate land, buildings, and equipment to FASB constant dollar and current cost amounts are similar to those used to restate the inventories. The procedures to restate these accounts to FASB constant

Exhibit 26-37
STOUT CORPORATION
Restatement to FASB Constant Dollars

	Historical Cost	1980 Ratio		Restated 12/31/80 Amount	1981 Ratio		Restated 12/31/81 Constant Dollar Amount
Land	$150,000	× 175/120	=	$218,750	× 205/175	=	$256,250
Buildings— net book value							
12/31/80	$175,000	× 175/120	=	$255,208	× 205/175	=	$298,958
12/31/81	$170,000				× 205/120	=	$290,417
Equipment— net book value							
12/31/80	$ 50,000	× 175/120	=	$ 72,917	× 205/175	=	$ 85,417
12/31/81 Original purchase	$ 40,000				× 205/175	=	$ 46,857
Purchase 7/1/81	19,000				× 205/200	=	19,475
	$ 59,000						$ 66,332

dollars are illustrated in Exhibit 26-37, while Exhibit 26-38 shows the restatement to FASB current cost.

The required data now can be accumulated to compute the current year's increase or decrease in the current cost amounts of inventory and property, plant, and equipment, net of inflation. This increase or decrease is based on the total holding gains or losses incurred during the year, on assets held, and on assets sold. As a result, both realized and unrealized holding gains must be combined. The determination of the unrealized holding gains is presented in Exhibit 26-39. The combined computation is presented in Exhibit 26-40, and indicates that the effect of inflation totaled $156,161. Finally, Exhibit 26-41 determines the firm's net assets on a constant dollar and current cost basis. These data are required for the five-year summary.

FASB Disclosures for the Stout Corporation

Statement No. 33 requires companies to prepare (1) a supplemental statement of income from continuing operations adjusted for changing prices and (2) a five-year comparison of selected supplementary financial data adjusted for the effect

Exhibit 26-38
STOUT CORPORATION
Restatement to FASB Current Cost

	Current Cost	1980 Ratio	Restated 12/31/80 Current Cost Amount	1981 Ratio	Restated 12/31/81 Current Cost Amount
Land					
12/31/80	$300,000	× 175/185	= $283,784	× 205/175	= $332,422
12/31/81	$325,000			× 205/220	= $302,841
Buildings— net book value					
12/31/80	$350,000	× 175/185	= $331,081	× 205/175	= $387,838
12/31/81	$357,000			× 205/220	= $332,659
Equipment— net book value					
12/31/80	$125,000	× 175/185	= $118,243	× 205/175	= $138,514
12/31/81	$134,800			× 205/220	= $125,609

of changing prices. These two statements for the Stout Corporation are presented in Exhibits 26-42 and 26-43, respectively. Actual disclosures made by the General Electric Company are reproduced in Exhibit 26-44.

The Future

Although the methods used in *Statement No. 33* are experimental and controversial, the Statement itself reflects substantial agreement that financial reporting of changing prices is necessary. The FASB's Director of Research, Michael Alexander, further outlines the objectives of *Statement 33:*

> The objectives of Statement 33 recognize that information about the effects of changing prices should be available to investors, creditors, and others involved in resource allocation decisions, including those in government policymaking. The information is intended to help in assessing future cash flows, evaluating enterprise performance and operating capability, and judging erosion of general purchasing power.[18]

[18] Michael Alexander, "Statement 33 and the Future: Research and Decision," *FASB Viewpoints* (Stamford, Conn.: FASB, October, 1981).

Exhibit 26-39
STOUT CORPORATION
Determination of Unrealized Holding Gains and Losses

	Inventory	Land	Buildings	Equipment	Total
1981					
Current cost	$228,295	$302,841	$332,659	$125,609	$ 989,404
Constant dollar	171,628	256,250	290,417	66,332	784,627
1981 Total	$ 56,667	$ 46,591	$ 42,242	$ 59,277	$ 204,777
1980					
Current cost	$265,946	$332,443	$387,838	$138,514	$1,124,741
Constant dollar	216,389	256,250	298,958	85,417	857,014
1980 Total	$ 49,557	$ 76,193	$ 88,880	$ 53,097	$ 267,727
Increase (decrease)	$ 7,110	$(29,602)	$(46,638)	$ 6,180	$ (62,950)

Much research needs to be conducted in order to assess the usefulness of this data to investors and others. As Alexander notes, the "decision (on the usefulness of current cost information) will depend on the relevance in predicting future cash flows and its reliability, that is, representational faithfulness and verifiability. As for constant dollar information—even if relevance and reliability can be demonstrated—it must also pass the test of understandability."[19] The *Statement 33* experiment will be assessed within five years, and at that time the FASB will have to confront these questions.

[19] Ibid.

Exhibit 26-40
STOUT CORPORATION
Computation of Total Holding Gains (Losses)
For FASB Statement No. 33 Disclosures

	Current Cost[1]	Increase in Specific Prices Over General Prices	Effect of Inflation
Realized gains (losses)	$123,381	$76,339[2]	$ 47,042
Unrealized gains (losses)	46,169	(62,950)[3]	109,119
	$169,550	$13,389	$156,161

[1] See Exhibit 26-26.
[2] See Exhibit 26-35.
[3] See Exhibit 26-39.

Exhibit 26-41

STOUT CORPORATION
Computation of Net Assets for FASB Disclosure
As of December 31, 1981

	Historical Cost (See Exhibit 26-6)	Constant Dollar (See Exhibit 26-12)	Current Cost (See Exhibit 26-23)
Inventory	$180,000	$184,186	$ 245,000
Land	150,000	275,000	325,000
Building	170,000	311,667	357,000
Equipment	59,000	94,233	134,800
	$559,000	$865,086	$1,061,800
Stockholders' equity (net assets) at historical cost on 12/31/81	$604,000		
Increase to constant dollar ($865,086 − $559,000)	306,086		
Constant dollar stockholders' equity— 12/31/81		$910,086	
Increase to current cost ($1,061,800 − $865,086)		196,714	
Current cost—stockholders' equity—12/31/81			$1,106,800
Adjustment to average dollar—constant dollar $910,086 × 205/220		$848,035	
Current cost $1,106,800 × 205/220			$1,031,336

Exhibit 26-42

STOUT CORPORATION
Statement of Income from Continuing Operations
Adjusted for Changing Prices
For the Year Ended December 31, 1981

	As Reported in Primary Financial Statements	Adjusted for General Inflation (Constant Dollar)	Adjusted for Changes in Specific Prices (Current Cost)
Sales	$2,000,000	$2,000,000	$2,000,000
Cost of goods sold	1,200,000	1,234,761	1,300,000
Depreciation expense	16,000	26,650	33,750
Selling expense	200,000	200,000	200,000
General and administrative	254,000	254,000	254,000
Interest	30,000	30,000	30,000
Provision for income taxes	120,000	120,000	120,000
	$1,820,000	$1,865,411	$1,937,750
Income from continuing operations	$ 180,000	$ 134,589	$ 62,250
Gain from decline in purchasing power of net amounts owed		$ 19,990	$ 19,990
Increase in specific prices (current cost) of inventories, and property, plant, and equipment held during the year[1]			$ 169,550
Effect of increase in general price level			156,161
Excess of increase in specific prices over increase in general price level			$ 13,389

[1] At December 31, 1981, the current cost of inventory was $245,000, and the current cost of property, plant, and equipment, net of accumulated depreciation, was $1,786,000.

Exhibit 26-43
STOUT CORPORATION
Five-Year Comparison of Selected
Supplementary Financial Data Adjusted for
Effects of Changing Prices
(In Average 1981 Dollars)

	Years Ended December 31,				
	1977	1978	1979	1980	1981
Net sales and other operating revenues					$2,000,000.00
Historical cost information adjusted for general inflation					
Income (loss) from continuing operations					134,589.00
Income (loss) from continuing operations per common share					6.73[1]
Net assets at year-end					848,035.00
Current cost information					
Income (loss) from continuing operations					62,250.00
Income (loss) from continuing operations per common share					3.11[1]
Excess of increase in specific prices over increase in the general price level					13,389.00
Net assets at year-end					1,013,336.00
Gain from decline in purchasing power of net amounts owed					19,990.00
Cash dividends declared per common share					$2.80
Market price per common share at year-end					50.00
Average consumer price index					205

[1] Based on 20,000 common shares outstanding.

Exhibit 26-44

GENERAL ELECTRIC COMPANY
Disclosures

Table 1: supplementary information—effect of changing prices (a)

(In millions, except per-share amounts)

The notes on page 30 are an integral part of this statement.

For the Year Ended December 31, 1979	As Reported in the Traditional Statements	Adjusted for General Inflation	Adjusted for Changes in Specific Prices (Current Costs) (b)
Sales of products and services to customers	$22,461	$22,461	$22,461
Cost of goods sold	15,991	16,093	16,074
Selling, general and administrative expense	3,716	3,716	3,716
Depreciation, depletion and amortization	624	880	980
Interest and other financial charges	258	258	258
Other income	(519)	(519)	(519)
Earnings before income taxes and minority interest	2,391	2,033	1,952
Provision for income taxes	953	953	953
Minority interest in earnings of consolidated affiliates	29	16	13
Net earnings applicable to common stock	$ 1,409	$ 1,064	$ 986
Earnings per common share	$ 6.20	$ 4.68	$ 4.34
Share owners' equity at year end (net assets) (c)	$ 7,362	$10,436	$11,153

Table 2: supplementary information—effect of changing prices (a)

(In millions, except per-share amounts)

Current Cost Information in Dollars of 1979 Purchasing Power (b)
(All Amounts Expressed in Average 1979 Dollars)

	1979	1978	1977	1976	1975
Sales of products and services to customers	$22,461	$21,867	$20,984	$20,015	$19,022
Cost of goods sold	16,074	15,548	14,793	14,145	13,914
Selling, general and administrative expense	3,716	3,566	3,606	3,360	3,018
Depreciation, depletion and amortization	980	1,000	986	979	1,006
Interest and other financial charges	258	249	238	222	251
Other income	(519)	(466)	(467)	(350)	(235)
Earnings before income taxes and minority interest	1,952	1,970	1,828	1,659	1,068
Provision for income taxes	953	995	926	853	620
Minority interest in earnings of consolidated affiliates	13	13	20	26	26
Net earnings applicable to common stock	$ 986	$ 962	$ 882	$ 780	$ 422
Earnings per common share	$ 4.34	$ 4.22	$ 3.88	$ 3.45	$ 1.88
Share owners' equity at year end (net assets) (c)	$11,153	$11,020	$10,656	$10,526	$10,056
Other inflation information					
Average Consumer Price Index (1967 = 100)	217.4	195.4	181.5	170.5	161.2
(Loss)/gain in general purchasing power of net monetary items	$(209)	$(128)	$ (61)	$ (20)	$ 19
Dividends declared per common share	2.75	2.78	2.52	2.17	2.16
Market price per common share at year end	47⅞	50½	58¼	69⅜	60¼

Exhibit 26-44 (continued)

GENERAL ELECTRIC COMPANY
Disclosures

Notes to supplementary information—Tables 1 and 2

(a) This information has been prepared in accordance with requirements of the Financial Accounting Standards Board (FASB). Proper use of this information requires an understanding of certain basic concepts and definitions.

The heading "As reported in the traditional statements" refers to information drawn directly from the financial statements presented on pages 32 to 44. This information is prepared using the set of generally accepted accounting principles which renders an accounting based on the number of actual dollars involved in transactions, with no recognition given to the fact that the value of the dollar changes over time.

The heading "Adjusted for general inflation" refers to information prepared using a different approach to transactions involving inventory and property, plant and equipment assets. Under this procedure, the number of dollars involved in transactions at different dates are all restated to equivalent amounts in terms of the general purchasing power of the dollar as it is measured by the Consumer Price Index for all Urban Consumers (CPI-U). For example, $1,000 invested in a building asset in 1967 would be restated to its 1979 dollar purchasing power equivalent of $2,174 to value the asset and calculate depreciation charges. Similarly, 1978 purchases of non-LIFO inventory sold in 1979 would be accounted for at their equivalent in terms of 1979 dollars, rather than in terms of the actual number of dollars spent.

The heading "Adjusted for changes in specific prices (current costs)" refers to information prepared using yet another approach to transactions involving inventory and property, plant and equipment assets. In this case, rather than restating to dollars of the same general purchasing power, estimates of current costs of the assets are used.

In presenting results of either of the supplementary accounting methods for more than one year, "real" trends are more evident when results for all years are expressed in terms of the general purchasing power of the dollar for a designated period. Results of such restatements are generally called "constant dollar" presentations. In the five-year presentations shown above, dollar results for earlier periods have been restated to their equivalent number of constant dollars of 1979 general purchasing power (CPI-U basis).

Since none of these restatements is allowable for tax purposes under existing regulations, income tax amounts are the same as in the traditional statements (but expressed in constant dollars in the five-year summary).

There are a number of other terms and concepts which may be of interest in assessing the significance of the supplementary information shown in Tables 1 and 2. However, it is management's opinion that the basic concepts discussed above are the most significant for the reader to have in mind while reviewing this information.

(b) Principal types of information used to adjust for changes in specific prices (current costs) are (1) for inventory costs, GE-generated indices of price changes for specific goods and services, and (2) for property, plant and equipment, externally generated indices of price changes for major classes of assets.

(c) At December 31, 1979, the current cost of inventory was $5,251 million, and of property, plant and equipment was $7,004 million. Estimated current costs applicable to the sum of such amounts held during all or part of 1979 increased by approximately $1,111 million, which was $329 million less than the $1,440-million increase which could be expected because of general inflation.

Concept Summary

ACCOUNTING FOR CHANGING PRICES

Type of Price Change	Accounting Alternatives Available	Characteristics
None or Slight	Historical cost/ nominal dollar	No adjustment for general or specific price changes; all aspects of historical cost model maintained.
General	Historical cost/ constant dollar	Financial statements adjusted to constant dollars by use of CPI for all Urban Consumers. Purchasing power gain or loss recognized on monetary items. Other elements of historical cost model maintained.
Specific	Current cost/ nominal dollar	Financial statements adjusted for specific price changes by use of specific price indexes or current cost data. Realized and unrealized holding gains and losses are recognized, and assets and liabilities are revalued to current cost.
General and Specific	Current cost/ constant dollar	Financial statements adjusted for both general and specific prices. Purchasing power gain or loss recognized. Unrealized and realized holding gains net of inflation are recognized, and assets and liabilities are revalued to current cost.
	FASB *Statement No. 33*	Partial restatement; disclosures made on supplemental basis only.

Appendix

Calculation of Current Cost Depreciation

The procedures to determine the current cost depreciation are complex. Depreciation expense is based upon the current cost of the assets, and as noted in the chapter, the FASB argues that the expense should be based upon the asset's average cost during the year. Further, it is necessary to maintain parity between the gross cost of the asset and the related accumulated depreciation. This requires the computation of backlog or catch-up depreciation.

Buildings

Exhibit 26-45 lists the historical and current cost information that pertains to the building, and the calculation of the current cost depreciation of $10,250. As noted previously, the determination of the proper balance in the accumulated depreciation is complicated by the need to retain parity between the gross asset cost and the related accumulated depreciation account. In order to maintain this relationship, you must calculate backlog or catch-up depreciation. This calculation is illustrated also in Exhibit 26-45.

   The net current cost at the end of the year can be determined by adding the gross current cost increase during the year to the net current cost at the beginning of the year. The current cost depreciation and backlog depreciation then are subtracted from this amount to determine the net current cost at the end of the year. The calculation is presented in Exhibit 26-45. It is important to note that the backlog depreciation of $2,750 is not added to the current year's depreciation expense on the income statement. Rather, it is netted against the gross increase of $20,000 to produce the net increase of $17,250 in the current cost. Another way to view this computation is to recognize that the net current cost on 1/1/81 is $350,000 ($400,000 − $50,000). At 12/31/81, the net current cost is $357,000 ($420,000 − $63,000). This net current cost at the end of the year is equal to the beginning net current cost of $350,000, plus the holding gain of $17,250, less the depreciation expense of $10,250. The holding gain of $17,250 is equal to the increase in the asset's current cost, $20,000, less backlog depreciation of $2,750.

Equipment

Current cost depreciation expense is calculated on the equipment in a similar manner. This calculation is illustrated in two separate components: the original equipment purchase on 1/2/76 and the purchase on 7/1/81.

Exhibit 26-45
STOUT CORPORATION
Current Cost Depreciation—Building

Data

Historical cost acquired—1/2/76	$200,000
Current cost—1/1/81	$400,000
Current cost—12/31/81	$420,000
Asset life	40 years
Depreciation method (0.025% per year)	Straight-line
Years depreciated to 1/1/81	5 years
Accumulated depreciation—1/1/81	$25,000
Historical cost	$25,000
Current cost	$50,000

The current cost depreciation for the year, $10,250, is calculated on the average current cost for 1981.

$$\frac{\$400,000 + \$420,000}{2} = \$410,000 \times 0.025 = \$10,250$$

Backlog Depreciation

Current cost at 12/31/81		$420,000
6/40 (0.150%) of life expired		0.150
Required accumulated depreciation		$ 63,000
Less: Balance—1/1/81	$50,000	
Current cost depreciation for 1981	10,250	(60,250)
Backlog depreciation		$ 2,750

Determination of Net Current Cost—12/31/81

Net current cost—1/1/81		$350,000
Plus: Gross increase in current cost		20,000
		$370,000
Less: Current cost depreciation	$10,250	
Backlog depreciation	2,750	(13,000)
Net current cost—12/31/81		$357,000

The relevant calculations for the original $100,000 equipment balance are illustrated in Exhibit 26-46. Exhibit 26-47 presents the current cost depreciation for the $20,000, 1981 purchase, while Exhibit 26-48 reconciles the equipment account. It should be noted that for the 1981 purchase the current cost depreciation for 1981 is $1,000 (10% of $20,000 for 6 months) based on 6 months of depreciation. Because the asset was purchased at midyear, its cost is assumed to be the average current cost for the year of $20,000. The net current cost of the equipment account is determined in the same manner as it is in the building account.

Exhibit 26-46
STOUT CORPORATION
Current Cost Depreciation—Equipment—Original Balance

Data

Historical cost—acquired 1/1/76	$100,000
Current cost—1/1/81	$250,000
Current cost—12/31/81	$280,000
Asset life	10 years
Depreciation method (10% per year)	Straight-line
Years depreciated to 1/1/81	5 years
Accumulated depreciation—1/1/81	
Historical cost	$50,000
Current cost	$125,000

The current cost depreciation for 1981 is $26,000, calculated on the average current cost of 1981.

$$\frac{\$250,000 + \$280,000}{2} = \$265,000 \times 10\% = \$26,500$$

Backlog Depreciation

Current cost at 12/31/81		$280,000
6/10 or 60% of life spent		0.60
Required accumulated depreciation		$168,000
Less: Balance—1/1/81	$125,000	
Current cost depreciation for 1981	26,500	(151,500)
Backlog depreciation		$ 16,500

Determination of Net Current Cost—12/31/81

Net current cost—1/1/81		$125,000
Plus: Gross increase in current cost		30,000
		$155,000
Less: Current cost depreciation	$26,500	
Backlog depreciation	16,500	(43,000)
Net current cost—12/31/81		$112,000

Exhibit 26-47
STOUT CORPORATION
Current Cost Depreciation—Equipment—1981 Purchase

Data

Historical cost—acquired 7/1/81	$20,000
Current cost—12/31/81	$24,000
Asset life	10 years
Depreciation method (10% per year)	Straight-line
Accumulated depreciation to 1/1/81	$0

Backlog Depreciation

Current cost at 12/31/81		$24,000
½ year life expired		0.05
Required accumulated depreciation		$ 1,200
Less: Balance—1/1/81	$ 0	
Current cost depreciation for year	1,000	(1,000)
Backlog depreciation		$ 200

Determination of Current Cost—12/31/81

Net current cost at purchase date		$20,000
Plus: Gross increase in current cost		4,000
		$24,000
Less: Current cost depreciation	$1,000	
Backlog depreciation	200	(1,200)
Net current cost, 12/31/81		$22,800

Exhibit 26-48
STOUT CORPORATION
Reconciliation of Equipment Account

	Net Current Cost 1/1/81	+	1981 Current Cost Increase	−	1981 Current Cost Depreciation	−	1981 Backlog Depreciation	=	Net Current Cost 12/31/81
Original Purchase	$125,000		$30,000		($26,500)		($16,500)		$112,000
1981 Purchase	—		20,000		(1,000)				19,000
Increase			4,000				(200)		3,800
	$125,000	+	$54,000	−	($27,500)	−	($16,700)	=	$134,800

Questions

Q–26–1 Describe the two major types of price changes that affect a firm. What is the relationship between these types of price changes?

Q–26–2 Describe the major problems with historical cost financial statements that are not adjusted for general and/or specific price changes.

Q–26–3 What alternative accounting models are available to deal with the effect of changing prices on traditional financial statements? Compare and contrast these models.

Q–26–4 What are price indexes, and how are they constructed? Give examples of several price indexes that are currently in use.

Q–26–5 What is constant dollar accounting, and how does it differ from historical cost accounting? What theory of capital maintenance is implied?

Q–26–6 Define monetary and nonmonetary assets and liabilities. Give several examples of each item.

Q–26–7 What is a purchasing power gain or loss, and how is it calculated?

Q–26–8 Under what circumstances is it necessary to restate monetary items? Describe these restatement procedures.

Q–26–9 Describe the restatement procedures necessary to adjust inventories and cost of goods sold to constant dollars. How does the inventory cost method that the firm uses affect the restatement procedure?

Q–26–10 List and describe the main advantages and disadvantages of the constant dollar model.

Q–26–11 What is the rationale behind the use of the current cost model? What theory of capital maintenance is implied?

Q–26–12 What is the difference between current cost and replacement cost? Provide an example.

Q–26–13 Describe the various methods of determining current value. Provide an example in which each of these methods would be used.

Q–26–14 What are the major components of a current cost income statement? Describe each of these components.

Q–26–15 Define and contrast realized and unrealized gains and losses.

Q–26–16 List and describe the major advantages and disadvantages of the current cost model. Is this model currently in use on a comprehensive basis?

Q–26–17 How does the current cost/constant dollar model differ from both the current cost and the constant dollar model?

Q–26–18 How are realized and unrealized holding gains and losses determined under the current cost/constant dollar model?

Q–26–19 List and describe the advantages and disadvantages of the current cost/constant dollar model.

Q–26–20 What firms must comply with requirements of FASB *Statement No. 33?* Describe these requirements.

Q–26–21 What was the FASB rationale for adapting *Statement No. 33?* Do you agree with the rationale?

Q–26–22 Describe the major accounting pronouncements leading to FASB *Statement No. 33.* Why do you think it took so long for concepts embodied in *Statement No. 33* to become part of GAAP?

Q–26–23 There are several differences between the restatement procedures outlined in this chapter and those required by FASB *Statement No. 33.* Describe and explain the reasons for these differences.

Q–26–24 Describe the disclosure requirements of FASB *Statement No. 33.*

Q–26–25 Answer the following multiple choice questions.

a) Constant dollar financial statements have been a controversial issue in accounting. Which of the following arguments in favor of such financial statements is not valid?

(1) Constant dollar financial statements use historical cost.

(2) Constant dollar financial statements compare uniform purchasing power among various periods.

(3) Constant dollar financial statements measure current value.

(4) Constant dollar financial statement measure earnings in terms of a common dollar.

b) In preparing constant dollar financial statements, monetary items consist of which of the following?

(1) Cash items plus all receivables with a fixed maturity date.

(2) Cash, other assets expected to be converted into cash, and current liabilities.

(3) Assets and liabilities whose amounts are fixed by contract or otherwise in terms of dollars regardless of price-level changes.

(4) Assets and liabilities that are classified on the balance sheet as current.

c) During a period of deflation an entity would have the greatest gain in general purchasing power by holding

(1) Cash.

(2) Plant and equipment.

(3) Accounts payable.

(4) Mortgages payable.

d) Which of the following is true regarding current cost financial statements?

(1) Purchasing power gains or losses are recognized on net monetary items.

(2) Amounts are always stated in common purchasing power units of measurements.

(3) All balance sheet items are different in amount from what they would be in a historical cost balance sheet.

(4) Holding gains are recognized.

(AICPA adapted)

Discussion Questions and Cases

D–26–1 In *Financial Accounting Concept Statement No. 1,* the FASB states:

Financial reporting should provide information that is useful to present and potential investors and creditors and other users in making rational investment, credit and similar decisions.

Many accounting theorists argue that because of the impact of changing prices, historical-based financial statements do not meet this objective. Others disagree.

Required:

1. What impact do specific and general price level changes have on historical-cost-based balance sheets and income statements?

2. How can the following overcome the impact of changing prices:

a) Constant dollar/historical cost statements;

b) Current cost statements and;

c) Current cost/constant dollar statements?

3. List and discuss the arguments against adjusting financial statements for price level changes.

D–26–2 Published financial statements of United States companies are currently prepared on a stable-dollar assumption even though the general purchasing power of the dollar has declined considerably because of inflation in recent years. To account for this changing value of the dollar, many accountants suggest that financial statements should be adjusted for general price-level changes. Three independent unrelated statements regarding constant dollar financial statements follow. Each statement contains some fallacious reasoning.

Statement 1: The accounting profession has not seriously considered constant dollar financial statements before because the rate of inflation usually has been so small from year to year that the adjustments would have been immaterial in amount. Constant dollar financial statements represent a departure from the historical-cost basis of accounting. Financial statements should be prepared from facts, not estimates.

Statement 2: If financial statements were adjusted for general price-level changes, depreciation charges in the earnings statement would permit the recovery of dollars of current purchasing power and thereby equal the cost of new assets to replace the old ones. Constant dollar adjusted data would yield statement-of-financial-position amounts closely approximating current values. Furthermore, management can make better decisions if constant dollar financial statements are published.

Statement 3: When adjusting financial data for general price-level changes, a distinction must be made between monetary and nonmonetary assets and liabilities, which under the historical-cost basis of accounting have been identified as "current" and "noncurrent." When using the historical-cost basis of accounting, no purchasing power gain or loss is recognized in the accounting process, but when financial statements are adjusted for general price-level changes, a purchasing-power gain or loss will be recognized on monetary and nonmonetary items.

Required:
Evaluate each of the independent statements; identify the areas of fallacious reasoning in each and explain why it is incorrect.

(AICPA adapted)

D–26–3 The financial statements of a business entity could be prepared by using historical cost or current value as a basis. In addition, the basis could be stated in terms of unadjusted dollars or dollars restated for changes in purchasing power. The various permutations of these two separate and distinct areas are shown in the following matrix:

	Unadjusted Dollars	Dollars Restated for Changes in Purchasing Power
Historical cost	1	2
Current value	3	4

Block number 1 of the matrix represents the traditional method of accounting for transactions in accounting today, wherein the absolute (unadjusted) amount of dollars given up or received is recorded for the asset or liability obtained (relationship between resources). Amounts recorded in the method described in block number 1 reflect the original cost of the asset or liability and do not reflect any change in value of the unit of measure (standard of comparison). This method assumes the validity of the accounting concepts of going concern and stable monetary unit. Any gain or loss (including holding and purchasing power gains or losses) resulting from the sale of satisfaction of amounts recorded under this method is deferred in its entirety until sale or satisfaction.

Required:

For each of the remaining matrix blocks (2, 3, and 4) respond to the following questions. Limit your discussion to nonmonetary assets only.

    a) How will this method of recording assets affect the relationship between resources and the standard of comparison (unit of measure)?

    b) What is the theoretic justification for using each method?

    c) How will each method of asset valuation affect the recognition of gain or loss during the life of the asset and ultimately from the sale or abandonment of the asset? Your response should include a discussion of the timing and magnitude of the gain or loss and conceptual reasons for any difference from the gain or loss computed using the traditional method.

                                           (AICPA adapted)

D–26–4 Valuation of assets is an important topic in accounting theory. Suggested valuation methods include the following:

    Historical cost
    Constant dollar/historical cost
    Discounted cash flow
    Market price
    Replacement cost or current cost

Required:

1. Why is the valuation of assets a significant issue?
2. Explain the basic theory underlying each of the valuation methods cited above.

                                           (AICPA adapted)

D–26–5 Differing theories of capital maintenance underlie various asset valuation methods. Explain the theory of capital maintenance as it pertains to:

    a) Historical cost accounting.

    b) Constant dollar/historical cost accounting.

    c) Current cost accounting.

D–26–6 Asset measurement is a concept that involves the valuation or pricing of the future service of an asset. Receivables are particular assets that represent future claims to fixed amounts of monies.

Required:

1. Discuss how the asset measurement concept is applied to receivables (short-term and long-term).

2. Describe how a company that has a significant amount of receivables during an inflationary period sustains a general price-level loss. Include in your answer an example of how such a loss would be computed when a $100,000 receivable exists at the beginning and end of a year that had an inflation rate of 10%.

                                           (AICPA adapted)

D–26–7 You are currently an employee of the Essen Corporation. Because of its current size, the corporation must now comply with the requirements of FASB *Statement No. 33*. The president calls you into her office. She is rather concerned about the possible effects FASB *Statement No. 33* disclosure might have on the corporation's financial statements.

Required:

The president asks you to write a memo addressing the following issues:

1. Explain the disclosure requirements of *FASB Statement No. 33*.

2. Explain what financial characteristics of the company (i.e., age, type of assets, monetary versus nonmonetary items, and so forth) could affect the magnitude and type of price-level disclosures.

3. How can the current cost information required by FASB *Statement No. 33* be gathered?

D-26-8 Barden Corporation, a manufacturer with large investments in plant and equipment, began operations in 1938. The company's history has been one of expansion in sales, production, and physical facilities. Recently, some concern has been expressed that the conventional financial statements do not provide sufficient information for decisions by investors. After considering proposals for various types of supplementary financial statements to be included in the 1982 annual report, management has decided to present a balance sheet as of December 31, 1982, and a statement of income and retained earnings for 1982, both restated for changes in the general price level.

Required:
1. On what basis can management contend that Barden's conventional statements should be restated for changes in the general price level (constant dollar)?
2. Distinguish between financial statements restated for general price level changes and current cost financial statements.
3. Distinguish between monetary and nonmonetary assets and liabilities, as the terms are used in general price level accounting. Give examples of each.
4. Outline the procedures Barden should follow in preparing the proposed supplementary statements.
5. Indicate the major similarities and differences between the proposed supplementary statements and the corresponding conventional statements.
6. Assuming that in the future Barden will want to present comparative supplementary statements, can the 1982 supplementary statements be presented in 1983 without adjustment? Explain.
7. If Barden must comply with the provisions of FASB *Statement No. 33*, what changes would be required in their constant dollar statement?

(AICPA adapted)

Exercises

E-26-1 As an accountant in the cost department of the Cerf Company, you are asked by the controller to determine the effect of inflation on the raw materials used in the production of your main product. He provides you with the following data:

Raw Material	January 1	December 31
Rubber (pound)	$ 4.20	$ 4.40
Copper (pound)	5.20	4.90
Steel (pound)	16.00	16.80
Silver (ounce)	14.00	14.40
Oil (barrel)	32.00	31.50

Required:
1. Determine the December 31 price index for this product. Assume the January 1 index equals 100.
2. What does this new price index mean when some prices are rising, some are falling, and some remain stable?
3. In addition to constructing its own index, how else can a firm determine changes in price levels?

E-26-2 Sutter Manufacturing Corporation purchased land at the beginning of the current year for $60,000. At the end of the year the value of the land is determined to be $75,000. During the year the general price index rose 10%.

Required:
1. Determine the general and specific price changes.
2. Explain the meaning of the price changes you determined above.

E–26–3 The Montana Company purchased a plot of land for $50,000 on January 1, 1982. At that time the Consumer Price Index was 195. At December 31, 1982, the current cost of the land is $75,000, and the Consumer Price Index is 235.

Required:
Determine the value of the land to be reported on the balance sheet at year-end, and the amount of the holding gain to be included on the income statement under each of the following assumptions:
  a) Historical cost.
  b) Constant dollar/historical cost.
  c) Current cost.
  d) Current cost/constant dollar.

E–26–4 The following selected accounts are taken from the trial balance of the Mitchell Company as of December 31, 1982, when the price index was 125.

Cash	$ 25,000
Notes receivable	50,000
Land	90,000
Building	400,000
Accounts payable	35,000
Bonds payable (due 1990)	200,000
Depreciation expense—building	15,000
Inventory (LIFO basis)	65,000
Sales (made evenly throughout the year)	350,000

During 1982 the average price index was 120. The land was purchased in 1974 when the price index was 80, and the building was constructed in 1978 when the index was 100. The bonds were issued in 1977 when the index was 96. The LIFO inventory was accumulated during 1979 when the average index was 102.

Required:
Determine at what amounts these accounts would be presented in single year (December 31, 1982), constant dollar financial statements.

E–26–5 Answer each of the following independent questions.
  a) Dart Company was formed on January 1, 1981. Selected balances from the historical cost balance sheet at December 31, 1982, were as follows:

Land (purchased January 1, 1981)	$90,000
Marketable securities, nonconvertible bonds (purchased July 1, 1981, and expected to be held to maturity)	50,000
Long-term debt	70,000

The average Consumer Price Index was 100 for 1981, and 110 for 1982. In a supplementary constant dollar balance sheet (adjusted for changing prices) at December 31, 1982, these selected account balances should be shown at what amounts?
  b) Index Co. was formed on January 1, 1980. Selected balances from the historical dollar balance sheet at December 31, 1980, were as follows:

Cash	$60,000
Marketable securities, stock (purchased January 1, 1980)	70,000

| Marketable securities, bonds (purchased January 1, 1980, and held for price speculation) | 80,000 |
| Long-term receivables | 90,000 |

If the Consumer Price Index for all Urban Consumers were 100 at December 31, 1979, and if it averaged 110 during 1980, at what amounts should these selected accounts be shown in a constant dollar balance sheet at December 31, 1980?

(AICPA adapted)

E–26–6 Below is an analysis of the Gallant Corporation's machinery and equipment account as of December 31, 1980:

Machinery and Equipment

Acquired in December, 1977	$400,000
Acquired in December, 1979	100,000
Balance	$500,000

Accumulated Depreciation

On equipment acquired in December, 1977	$160,000
On equipment acquired in December, 1979	20,000
Balance	$180,000

Consumer Price Indexes

12/31/77	110
12/31/79	120
Average 1980	140

Required:

1. Determine the amount of depreciation expense for 1980. (Assume straight-line depreciation.)
2. What amount should be included under the heading of machinery and equipment net of accumulated depreciation on a constant dollar balance sheet prepared as of December 31, 1980?

(AICPA adapted)

E–26–7 The Morland Company was formed several years ago. Recently the president of the company has become very concerned about the effects of inflation on the company's purchasing power. She asks you to (a) determine the firm's purchasing power gain or loss for the year ended December 31, 1982, and (b) to prepare a constant dollar income statement for the year ended December 31, 1982.

You have been provided with the following information:

Income Statement
THE MORLAND COMPANY
For the Year Ended December 31, 1982

Sales		$160,000
Cost of goods sold		
Beginning inventory	$ 10,000	
Purchases	140,000	
Goods available for sale	$150,000	
Ending inventory	30,000	120,000
Gross margin		$40,000
Operating expenses		
Selling	10,000	

General/administrative	15,000		
Depreciation	5,000	30,000	
Income before taxes		$ 10,000	
Income taxes		2,500	
Net income		$ 7,500	
Beginning retained earnings		40,000	
		$ 47,500	
Dividends		(4,000)	
Ending retained earnings		$ 43,500	

Additional data are as follows:

a) Relevant price indexes:
   (1) January 2, 1982   115
   (2) Date when beginning inventory acquired   110
   (3) Date when ending inventory acquired   122
   (4) July 1, 1982   120
   (5) December 31, 1982   125

b) Depreciation is relative to fixed assets, which were all purchased on January 2, 1980, when the price level was 100.

c) Common stock of $50,000 was issued on October 1, 1982, when the price level was 122.

d) The dividend was declared and paid on December 31, 1982.

e) All other items were earned or incurred evenly throughout the year.

f) Net monetary asset position:

January 1, 1982	$25,000
December 31, 1982	63,500

E-26-8 Wheat Company is a new business enterprise that started operations on January 1, 1983. Although the operating returns are below industry average, company management is pleased with the first two years' results.

The economy experienced a high rate of inflation in each of the past two years. The management believes that reports of the operating results and financial position distort the true picture because the effect of inflation is not recognized fully in the statements. They would like to communicate the magnitude of this distortion to the stockholders. Consequently, the company is considering issuing supplementary financial statements restated for price-level changes.

The company accountant has assembled the following information:

a) Wheat Company's sales, purchases, and expenses occur evenly throughout the year.

b) The inventory is valued at cost using the first-in, first-out (FIFO) method. The inventory on December 31, 1983, was acquired at June 30, 1983, prices; the inventory on December 31, 1984, was acquired at September 30, 1984, prices.

c) All of the fixed assets were acquired on January 1, 1983.

d) The indexes that measure the change in the price level for selected dates are as follows:

	Index Number
January 1, 1983	100
January 1, 1984	110
December 31, 1984	130

The price level has risen evenly thoughout each year.

The income statement for fiscal year 1984 and comparative balance sheets for 1983 and 1984 appear below.

WHEAT COMPANY
Income Statement 1984

Revenue from sales		$84,000
Costs of goods sold		
Inventory 1/1/84	$21,000	
Purchases	48,000	
Costs of goods available	69,000	
Inventory 12/31/84	25,000	44,000
Gross margin		$40,000
Operating expenses		
Wages and salaries	24,000	
Depreciation	7,000	31,000
Net income before taxes		$ 9,000
Income taxes		1,800
Net income		$ 7,200

WHEAT COMPANY
Balance Sheet, December 31

	1983	*1984*
Assets		
Cash	$10,000	$13,800
Accounts receivable	20,000	17,000
Inventory	21,000	25,000
Fixed assets (net)	45,000	38,000
Total assets	$96,000	$93,800
Equities		
Accounts payable	$19,000	$ 9,600
Long-term debt	33,000	33,000
Contributed capital	40,000	40,000
Retained earnings	4,000	11,200
Total equities	$96,000	$93,800

(CMA adapted)

Required:

1. Prepare an historical cost/constant dollar balance sheet for December 31, 1984.

2. Prepare historical cost/constant dollar comparative balance sheets for December 31, 1983, and 1984.

3. Prepare an historical cost/constant income statement for the year ended December 31, 1984. Include a statement of purchasing power gain or loss.

E–26–9 Answer each of the following two questions.

a) Lacy Corporation was formed on January 1, 1980, when common stock of $300,000 was issued for cash of $50,000, and land valued at $250,000. Lacy did not begin operations until 1981, and no transactions occurred in 1980 except the recording of the issuance of the common stock.

Required:

If the Consumer Price Index were 105 at December 31, 1979, and averaged 110 during 1980, what would be the purchasing power gain or loss in Lacy's 1980 constant dollar income statement?

   b)   At the beginning of 1980, when the Consumer Price Index was 100, Bland, Inc. had total assets of $100,000, consisting of $25,000 in cash and $75,000 in silver, purchased on January 1, 1980. At the end of 1980, when the Consumer Price Index was 140, the silver sold for $100,000.

Required:

Compute the purchasing power gain or loss for 1980 and the "real" gain or loss on the sale of the silver.

E–26–10   CAB, Inc. purchased land in early 1980 for $15,000. The land was sold later in 1982 for $29,000. The following current cost data are also available:

	December 1980	December 1981	March 15 1982 (date of sale)
	$18,000	$24,000	$28,000

Required:

1.   Determine the holding gains or losses for each of the three years.
2.   Determine the current cost gain or loss on the sale in 1982.

E–26–11   The Fenton Company began operations on January 2, 1982. Immediately thereafter the firm purchased 1,000 units of inventory at a cost of $12 per unit. In addition, the Fenton Company purchased one piece of equipment with a cost of $10,000. The company gave the asset a 10-year life with no salvage value. The company uses the straight-line method of depreciation. During the year the firm sold 800 units at $20 per unit.

   In addition, the following data are available:
   a)   Current cost of goods sold is $15 per unit.
   b)   Current cost of inventory at December 31, 1982, is $18 per unit.
   c)   Current cost of equipment is $12,000.
   d)   Other expenses totaled $1,500.

Required:

Prepare a current cost income statement for the year ended December 31, 1982. (Calculate the current cost depreciation on the December 21, 1982, current cost of the equipment.)

E–26–12   You have been provided with the following data pertaining to the DZW Company:

	1982	
Account	Current Cost	Historical Cost
Depreciation expense	$ 16,400	$ 15,000
Cost of goods sold	118,000	112,000

	1982		1981	
Account	Current Cost	Historical Cost	Current Cost	Historical Cost
Inventory	$220,000	$200,000	$185,500	$150,000
Property, plant, & equipment, net	234,000	180,000	240,000	200,000

Required:

Determine the amount of the realized and unrealized holding gains or losses to be included in a current cost income statement for the year ended December 31, 1982.

E–26–13   As the controller for the Montana Corporation, which has been in operation for one year, you currently are preparing current cost/constant dollar statements. You have obtained the following data:

Current Cost Balance Sheet
MONTANA CORPORATION
December 31, 1982

Assets		Equities	
Cash	$ 10,000	Accounts payable	$ 18,000
Accounts receivable	15,000	Wages payable	10,000
Inventory	25,000	Common stock*	50,000
Property, plant, & equipment, net	60,000	Retained earnings	32,000
	$110,000		$110,000

*At historical cost.

Current Cost Income Statement
MONTANA CORPORATION
For the Year Ended December 31, 1982

Sales		$60,000
Cost of goods sold		40,000
Gross margin		$20,000
Operating expenses, excluding depreciation	$ 5,000	
Depreciation	12,000	17,000
Current operating income		$ 3,000
Realized gains		5,000
Historical cost income		$8,000
Unrealized gains		4,000
Current cost net income		$12,000

Additional data are below:

a) Constant dollar data

Account	Amount
Inventory	$24,000
Property, plant, & equipment	55,000
Cost of goods sold	42,500
Depreciation	5,400

b) The price level at 12/31/81   100
The price level at 12/31/82   110

c) Purchasing power loss   ($1,000)

d) All income and expense items including depreciation were accrued evenly throughout the year.

Required:

1. Prepare a current cost/constant balance sheet.
2. Prepare a current cost/constant dollar income statement.

E–26–14 The cost of goods sold for 1981 totaled $1,000,000 for the Rice Corporation. Beginning inventory at January 1, 1981, was $200,000, and purchases amounted to $1,200,000.

The following Consumer Price Indexes are known:

1980:	Average for period in which beginning inventory was purchased	112
	Average 1980	110
	December, 1980	115
1981:	January, 1981	116
	Average for period in which ending inventory was purchased	122
	Average 1981	120
	December, 1981	124

The current cost of cost of goods sold is determined to be $1,300,000.

Required:

Restate the cost of goods sold according to the constant dollar model and according to FASB *Statement No. 33*.

E–26–15 Details of Monmouth Corporation's fixed assets at December 31, 1980, are as follows:

Asset	Year Acquired	Percent Depreciated	Historical Cost	Estimated Current Cost
(1)	1978	30	$50,000	$70,000
(2)	1979	20	15,000	19,000
(3)	1980	10	20,000	22,000

Monmouth calculates depreciation at 10% per annum, using the straight-line method. A full year's depreciation is charged in the year of acquisition. There were no disposals of fixed assets. Monmouth prepares supplementary information for inclusion in its 1980 annual report as required by the FASB. In Monmouth's supplementary information restated into current cost, how should the net current cost (after accumulated depreciation) of the fixed assets be stated?

(AICPA adapted)

E–26–16 Using the data from Exercise 26–15 as well as the following additional information, calculate the depreciation expense and the backlog depreciation for each individual asset using the procedures required by FASB *Statement No. 33*.

Asset	Current Cost 1/1/80	Accumulated Depreciation 1/1/80
(1)	$60,000	$12,000
(2)	18,000	1,800
(3)	20,000	–0–

E–26–17 On January 1, 1975, Risky Corporation purchased a building for $150,000. The building is expected to last 40 years and is depreciated by the straight-line method.

Current cost as of January 1, 1980	$300,000
Current cost as of December 31, 1980	340,000
Accumulated depreciation as of January 1, 1980	
Historical cost	18,750
Current cost	37,500

Required:

Determine the current cost depreciation for 1980 and the net current cost of the building at December 31, 1980, using the provisions of FASB *Statement No. 33*.

E–26–18 At the beginning of 1981 the Cook Company had net monetary assets of $100,000. During this period the following events occurred:

  a) Sales of $100,000 were made evenly throughout the period.

  b) Purchases of $75,000 were made evenly throughout the period. The company maintains no inventory.

  c) Selling expenses (excluding depreciation) of $25,000 were incurred in the first quarter.

  d) Equipment was purchased in the first quarter for $10,000.

  e) Dividends of $5,000 were paid on December 31, 1981.

The Consumer Price Index was as follows:

January 1, 1981	100
First quarter, 1981	110
Average, 1981	125
December 31, 1981	140

Required:

1. Compute the purchasing power gain or loss for 1981 according to the constant dollar model.

2. Compute the purchasing power gain or loss for 1981 according to FASB *Statement No. 33*.

Problems

P–26–1 The accountants for Fats, Inc. produced the following income statement (in historical dollars):

FATS, INC.
Income Statement
For the Year Ended December 31, 1981

Sales (net)		$1,000,000
Cost of goods sold		
Inventory, Jan. 1 (LIFO method)	$ 80,000	
Purchases	470,000	
Goods available for Sale	$550,000	
Less: Inventory, Dec. 31	90,000	460,000
Gross profit on sales		$ 540,000
Operating expenses		
Selling	30,000	

General	25,000	
Depreciation	35,000	90,000
Income before taxes		$ 450,000
Income tax expense (40%)		180,000
Net income		$ 270,000

All purchases and expenses were incurred evenly. The beginning inventory and depreciable assets were acquired when the general price-level index was 125. The LIFO layer of $10,000 added to the inventory during the current year consists of goods acquired evenly throughout the year.

Relevant consumer price indexes are as follows:

January, 1981	150
Average, 1981	169
December, 1981	175

Required:
Prepare a constant dollar income statement. Assume that the purchasing power loss for the year is $9,250.

P–26–2 Farmington Hardware had a net monetary asset position of $350,000 on January 1, 1980. Transactions during 1980 are listed below:

a) Purchases made evenly throughout the year, all on account, totaled $600,000.
b) Sales made evenly throughout the year, all on account, totaled $1,000,000.
c) Collections from customers occurred in the third quarter, $700,000.
d) Payments to suppliers occurred in the third quarter, $400,000.
e) Declaration of a $200,000 dividend in December, payable during January 1981.

Relevant consumer price indexes are as follows:

January, 1980	115
Third quarter, 1980	120
Average, 1980	121
December, 1980	125

Required:
1. Calculate the purchasing power gain or loss for 1980.
2. Repeat Part 1, but assume a net monetary liability position of $350,000 on January 1, 1980.

P–26–3 Frontier Corp. acquired a plot of land in July, 1980, for $90,000. The land sold for $170,000 on July 31, 1981. The consumer price indexes and the current cost of the land on various dates are as follows:

	CPI	Current Cost
July 1, 1980	100	$ 90,000
December 30, 1980	110	100,000
July 1, 1981	112	170,000
December 31, 1981	114	

Calculate the total gain or loss for 1981 relating to this land (ignore unrealized gains and losses) based on each of the following alternatives:
a) Historical cost.

b) Constant dollar/historical cost.
c) Current cost.
d) Current cost/constant dollar.

P–26–4   Skadden, Inc., a retailer, was organized during 1977. Skadden's management has decided to supplement its December 31, 1980, historical dollar financial statements with constant dollar (end-of-year) statements. The following general ledger trial balance (historical dollar) and additional information have been furnished:

SKADDEN, INC.
Trial Balance
December 31, 1980

	Debit	Credit
Cash and receivables (net)	$ 540,000	
Marketable securities (common stock)	400,000	
Inventory	440,000	
Equipment	650,000	
Equipment—accumulated depreciation		$ 164,000
Accounts payable		300,000
6% first mortgage bonds, due in 1988		500,000
Common stock, $10 par		1,000,000
Retained earnings, December 1, 1979	46,000	
Sales		1,900,000
Cost of sales	1,508,000	
Depreciation	65,000	
Other operating expenses and interest	215,000	
	$3,864,000	$3,864,000

a) Monetary assets (cash and receivables) exceeded monetary liabilities (accounts payable and bonds payable) by $445,000 at December 31, 1979. The amounts of monetary items are fixed in terms of numbers of dollars regardless of changes in specific prices or in the general price level.
b) Purchase ($1,840,000 in 1980) and sales are made uniformly throughout the year.
c) Depreciation is computed on a straight-line basis, with a full year's depreciation being taken in the year of acquisition and none in the year of retirement. The depreciation rate is 10%, and no salvage value is anticipated. Acquisitions and retirements have been made fairly evenly over each year, and the retirements in 1980 consisted of assets purchased during 1978 that were scrapped. An analysis of the equipment account reveals the following:

Year	Beginning Balance	Additions	Retirements	Ending Balance
1978	—	$550,000	—	$550,000
1979	$550,000	10,000	—	560,000
1980	560,000	150,000	$60,000	650,000

d) The bonds were issued in 1978, and the marketable securities were purchased fairly evenly over 1980. Other operating expenses and interest are assumed to be incurred evenly throughout the year.

e) Assume that the consumer price indexes (1969 = 100) were as follows:

Annual Average	Index	Conversion Factors (1980 4th Qtr. = 1.000)
1977	113.9	1.128
1978	116.8	1.100
1979	121.8	1.055
1980	126.7	1.014

Quarterly Averages		Index	Conversion Factors
1979	4th	123.5	1.040
1980	1st	124.9	1.029
	2nd	126.1	1.019
	3rd	127.3	1.009
	4th	128.5	1.000

Required:

1. Prepare a schedule to convert the equipment account balance at December 31, 1980, from historical cost to constant dollar.

2. Prepare a schedule to analyze in historical dollars the Equipment—accumulated depreciation account for the year 1980.

3. Prepare a schedule to analyze in constant dollars the equipment—accumulated depreciation account for the year 1980.

4. Prepare a schedule to compute Skadden, Inc.'s purchasing power gain or loss on its net holdings of monetary assets for 1980 (ignore income tax implications). The schedule should give consideration to appropriate items on or related to the balance sheet and the income statement.

(AICPA adapted)

P–26–5 The Walter Corporation, a retailer, was organized during January, 1979, with the issuance of 60,000 shares of $10 par value common stock. The firm wishes to prepare constant dollar financial statements for the first time during 1981. The postclosing trial balance taken from its accounts on December 31, 1981, is as follows:

	Debit	Credit
Cash and receivables (net)	$530,000	
Marketable securities (common stock)	125,000	
Merchandise inventory	410,000	
Equipment	780,000	
Accumulated depreciation		$172,000
Accounts payable		177,000
Bonds payable		500,000
Common stock		600,000
Retained earnings		396,000

The following additional information is obtained:

a) Net monetary liabilities on January 1, 1981, were $197,000. Current liabilities on this date totaled $165,000.

b) Net income for 1981 was $300,000, whereas dividends of $50,000 were declared and paid during December, 1981. These were the only items affecting retained earnings during the period.

c) Purchases of inventory items ($920,000) exceeded the cost of goods sold by $10,000. A LIFO cost flow assumption is used. Purchases and sales occur evenly over each year. The inventory on December 31, 1981, consisted of the following layers, which were added evenly over their respective years:

1979 layer	$380,000
1980 layer	20,000
1981 layer	10,000
	$410,000

d) Depreciation is computed using the straight-line method, with a full year's depreciation taken in the year of acquisition and none in the year of sale. The depreciation rate is 10%, and no salvage value is anticipated. Acquisitions and sales have been made evenly for each year. The equipment sold during 1981 for a total of $35,000 was acquired during 1979. An analysis of the equipment account reveals the following:

Year	Beginning Balance	Acquisitions	Disposals	Ending Balance
1979	—	$500,000	—	$500,000
1980	500,000	20,000	—	520,000
1981	520,000	300,000	$40,000	780,000

e) The bonds were issued in December, 1979, at par value. The marketable securities were acquired during December, 1980, and are stated at acquisition cost, which is less than market value.

f) An index of consumer prices on various dates is as follows:

January, 1979	160
December, 1979	180
December, 1980	200
December, 1981	220
Average, 1979	170
Average, 1980	190
Average, 1981	210

Required:
1. Prepare a comparative constant dollar balance sheet on December 31, 1981 and 1980. Retained earnings should be the amount necessary to equal restated total assets and restated total equities.
2. Reconcile to the restated retained earnings amount in part 1. by (a) calculating the restated beginning balance in retained earnings, (b) calculating restated net income including the purchasing power gain or loss on monetary items, and (c) calculating restated dividends.

(AICPA adapted)

P–26–6 Valuation to reflect general price-level adjustments, as opposed to replacement cost, would yield differing amounts on a firm's financial statements.

Several transactions concerning one asset of a calendar-year company are summarized as follows:

1982 Purchased land for $40,000 cash on December 31. Replacement cost at year-end was $40,000.

1983   Held this land all year.
Replacement cost at year-end was $52,000.
1984   October 31—sold this land for $68,000.
General price-level index:
December 31, 1982   100
December 31, 1983   110
October 31, 1984   120

Required:
Duplicate the following schedules and complete the information required based upon the transactions described above.

Valuation of Land on Statement of Financial Position	General Price Level	Replacement Cost
December 31, 1982	$	$
December 31, 1983		

Gain on Earnings Statement	General Price Level	Replacement Cost
1982	$	$
1983		
1984		
Total		

(AICPA adapted)

P–26–7   The president of the Hawkens Company is concerned about the effects of inflation on the firm's reported earnings. She provides you with the following historical cost income statement and other data:

HAWKENS COMPANY
Historical Cost Income Statement
For the Year Ended December 31, 1982

Sales		$10,000,000
Cost of goods sold		
Beginning inventory	$ 2,000,000	
Purchases	13,000,000	
Goods available for sale	$15,000,000	
Less: Ending inventory	7,000,000	8,000,000
Gross margin on sales		$ 2,000,000
Operating expenses		
Selling	600,000	
General and administrative	300,000	900,000
Income before taxes		$ 1,100,000
Income taxes		440,000
Net income		$ 660,000

Other data:
a)   The firm uses FIFO basis of inventory valuation. The beginning inventory was acquired when the price index was 120, while the ending inventory was acquired when the price index was 148.

b) Depreciation expense is included in operating expenses. It is allocated 60% to selling and 40% to general and administrative expenses, respectively. Relevant data are below:

Account	Date Purchased	Cost	Price Index at Date of Purchase	Depreciation* Method	Life
Building	Jan. 2, 1978	$5,000,000	100	Straight-line	40 years
Equipment	2, 1978	50,000	100	Straight-line	5 years
Equipment	July 1, 1982	75,000	140	Straight-line	5 years

*No estimated residual value; 6 months depreciation taken in year of purchase and year of sale.

c) Dividends of $40,000 were declared on December 1, 1982. They were paid on December 31, 1982.

d) The firm began the year with a $100,000 net monetary asset position.

e) Price indexes are as follows:

January 2, 1978	100
January 2, 1982	130
July 1, 1982	140 (average for the year)
December 1, 1982	148
31, 1982	150

f) Unless otherwise indicated, all income and expense items were incurred evenly throughout the year.

Required:

Prepare a constant dollar income statement for the Hawkens Corporation. Include a schedule computing the purchasing power gain or loss.

P–26–8   The latest income statement for Ford Factory is given below (in historical dollars):

FORD FACTORY
Income Statement
For the Year Ended December 31, 1982

Sales revenue	$750,000
Less: Expenses	
Cost of goods sold	$250,000
Depreciation expenses	30,000
Selling & administrative expenses	45,000
Total expenses	$325,000
Net income	$425,000

Additional information is as follows:

a) The beginning and ending inventory remained constant at $40,000.

b) Relevant consumer price indexes are as follows:

(1) When store equipment acquired	125
(2) Average for year (assume all income and expense items were incurred evenly throughout year.)	135
(3) On January 1, 1982	130
(4) On December 31, 1982	140

c) Current replacement cost information is presented below:

Inventory at December 31, 1982	$ 90,000
Store equipment (net) at December 31, 1982	340,000
Cost of goods sold for year	290,000
Depreciation expense	42,000

d) Historical cost information:

Store equipment (net) at December 31, 1982	$270,000

Required:
1. Prepare a current cost income statement for 1982. (Assume that there were no unrealized gains or losses at the beginning of the year.)
2. Assuming the firm suffered a purchasing power loss of $2,400, prepare a constant dollar income statement for 1982.
3. Compare and contrast these two statements.

P–26–9   The Pauley Company has asked you to prepare a current cost balance sheet. You have been provided with the following information:

THE PAULEY COMPANY
Historical Cost Balance Sheet
December 31, 1982

Assets		Equities	
Cash	$ 10,000	Accounts payable	$ 15,000
Marketable equity		Wages payable	18,000
securities	12,000	Other accrued payable	10,000
Accounts and loans		Bonds payable (10%)	50,000
receivable, net of		Common stock	30,000
allowance for bad		Retained earnings	30,000
debts	16,000		
Inventory	25,000		
Property, plant			
& equipment (net)	80,000		
Other assets	10,000		
Total assets	$153,000	Total equities	$153,000

Additional information is as follows:
   a) Marketable equity securities. Your analysis indicates the following:

Security	Purchase Price	Current Market Value
JLA	$ 4,000	$ 3,500
MAD	6,000	8,200
AAC	2,000	3,300
	$12,000	$15,000

   b) Inventory. Reference to a specific index indicates that the current cost of the ending inventory is 12% more than its historical cost.
   c) Your analysis of the property, plant, and equipment account indicates the following:

Account	Historical Cost (Net)	Current Cost	Purchased	Depreciation (Straight-Line) Rate
Land	$20,000	$42,000	Jan. 2, 1980	—
Plant	50,000	(1)	2, 1980	5%
Equipment	10,000	(2)	2, 1980	10%
	$80,000			

(1) The plant has 3,000 square feet. Current building costs are $22.00 per square foot.
(2) The specific price index indicates prices have risen 10% since purchase.

d)   The other asset is a note receivable from the firm's principal stockholder. It was issued without interest on January 2, 1981, and is due on January 2, 1987. Your investigation indicates that the stockholder can borrow at 1% above prime. During 1982 the price averaged 14%.

e)   The bonds were issued at par on January 2, 1982. They mature 15 years from the date of issuance. Interest is payable semiannually. The current rate on similar bonds is 16%.

Required:

Prepare a current cost balance sheet as of December 31, 1982.

P–26–10   The E. K. Cobb Corporation is concerned about the effects of price changes on its financial condition. As a result, the company has decided to prepare financial statements based on current costs, and you have been hired to complete this task. You have obtained the following adjusted trial balance based on historical costs as of December 31, 1982:

Account	Debit	Credit
Cash	$ 2,000	
Marketable equity securities	8,000	
Accounts Receivable	15,000	
Supplies	500	
Inventory	24,000	
Land	15,500	
Building, net	60,000	
Equipment, net	3,000	
Deferred charges	2,000	
Accounts payable		$ 5,000
Short-term notes payable		10,000
Wages payable		12,000
Long-term bonds payable		40,000
Common stock		20,000
Retained earnings		15,000
Sales		100,000
Cost of goods sold	40,000	
Selling expenses	12,000	
General and administrative expenses	8,000	
Depreciation	10,000	
Income taxes	2,000	
	$202,000	$202,000

In addition, you have been able to determine the following current cost data:

Account	Current Cost
Marketable equity securities	$12,000
Inventories	26,000
Land	17,000
Building, net	88,000
Equipment, net	4,000
Cost of goods sold	45,000
Depreciation	12,000

Your examination of the income statement for the year ended December 31, 1981, indicates that unrealized gains totaled $6,500. Assume that for all other items the current cost is not materially different from the historical cost.

Required:

1. Prepare a current cost balance sheet and income statement for 1982.
2. How would a current cost/constant dollar balance sheet and income statement differ from the current cost statement. Explain your answer. However, do not prepare current cost/constant dollar statements.

P–26–11 The controller of the Sax Company believes that her company is affected by both general and specific price changes. As a result, she asks you to prepare current cost/constant dollar financial statements. She provides you with the following current cost financial statement and additional data:

THE SAX COMPANY
Comparative Current Cost Balance Sheet
December 31

	1982	1981
Assets		
Cash	$ 18,000	$ 8,500
Marketable securities	12,000	14,000
Accounts receivable, net	30,000	24,000
Inventory	50,000	38,000
Land	20,000	20,000
Building, net	60,000	78,000
	$190,000	$182,500
Equities		
Accounts payable	$ 4,500	$ 5,500
Accrued payables	3,000	6,400
Bond payable—10%	50,000	50,000
Common stock	60,000	60,000
Retained earnings	72,500	60,600
	$190,000	$182,500

THE SAX COMPANY
Current Cost Income Statement
For The Year Ended December 31, 1982

Sales		$180,000
Cost of goods sold		140,000
Gross margin		$ 40,000
Other expenses		
Selling, and general and administrative,		
including interest expense	$10,000	
Depreciation	28,000	38,000
Current cost operating income		$ 2,000
Realized holding gain		
Depreciation	5,000	
Cost of goods sold	6,000	11,000
		$ 13,000
Traditional net income		
Unrealized holding gain		
Inventory	1,500	
Depreciable assets	(2,600)	(1,100)
Current cost net income		$ 11,900

Additional data are as follows:

a) The company was formed on January 2, 1981, when the Consumer Price Index was 100. All fixed assets were purchased at that time. Bonds and common stock also were issued then.

b) Relevant price indexes are below:

December 31, 1981	110
December 31, 1982	115
Average, 1982	112

c) You're given the following constant dollar data:

Account	Amounts
Depreciation	$ 29,000
Cost of goods sold	140,000
Inventory	45,000
Building, net	46,239
Bonds payable	50,000

d) The purchasing power loss equals $17,894.

e) Unless otherwise indicated, all income and expense items were incurred evenly thoughout the year

Required:

1. Prepare comparative current cost/constant dollar balance sheets for 1982 and 1981.

2. Prepare a current cost/constant dollar income statement for the year ended December 31, 1982. Assume there are no unrealized gains or losses at the beginning of the year.

3. Prove the constant dollar income before purchasing power amount you determined in Part 2.

P–26–12   The Craig Company began operations on January 2, 1981. You have been provided with the following financial statement data:

THE CRAIG COMPANY
Comparative Historical Cost Balance Sheet
December 31

	1982	1981
Assets		
Monetary assets	$14,000	$12,000
Inventory	30,000	20,000
Property, plant, & equipment, net	45,000	50,000
Total assets	$89,000	$82,000
Equities		
Monetary liabilities	$13,000	$15,000
Common stock, no par	40,000	40,000
Retained earnings	36,000	27,000
Total equities	$89,000	$82,000

THE CRAIG COMPANY
Historical Cost Income Statement
For the Year Ended December 31, 1982

Sales		$70,000
Cost of goods sold		
Beginning inventory	$20,000	
Purchases	50,000	
Goods available for sale	$70,000	
Ending inventory	30,000	40,000
Gross margin		$30,000
Operating expenses		
Selling, and general and administrative, excluding depreciation	8,000	
Depreciation	5,000	13,000
Income before taxes		$17,000
Taxes		8,000
Net income		$ 9,000

Additional data are as follows:

a)   Price level on January 2, 1981, when the corporation was formed and common stock issued—100.

b)   Price level when 1981 beginning inventory acquired—105. This was also the average for 1981.

c)   Price level at December 31, 1981—110. This was when the property, plant, and equipment was purchased and the 1981 ending inventory acquired.

d)   Price level when ending inventory for 1982 acquired—118.

e)   Average price level for 1982—115.

f)   Price level on December 31, 1982—120.

g)   Current cost data are presented below:

Account	Dec. 31, 1982 Amount	Dec. 31, 1981 Amount
Inventory—beginning	—	$23,000
Inventory—ending	$31,000	—
Property, plant, and equipment, net	63,000	50,000

h) Assume that income and expense items were incurred evenly throughout the year.

Required:

Based on the data for the Craig Company prepare the following:

a) Comparative historical cost/constant dollar balance sheets as of Dec. 31, 1980, and Dec. 31, 1981.

b) A historical cost/constant dollar income statement for the year ended December 31, 1982. Include a schedule computing a purchasing power gain or loss.

P–26–13 Based on the data for the Craig Company presented in P–26–12 prepare the following:

a) Comparative current cost balance sheets as of Dec. 31, 1982, and Dec. 31, 1981.

b) A current cost income statement for the year ended December 31, 1982. Include a supplemental schedule of realized and unrealized gains and losses.

P–26–14 Based on the data for the Craig Company presented in P–26–12, prepare the following:

a) Comparative current cost/constant dollar balance sheets as of Dec. 31, 1982, and Dec. 31, 1981.

b) A current cost/constant dollar income statement for the year ended December 31, 1982. Include a supplemental schedule of realized and unrealized gains and losses.

P–26–15 Based on the data for the Craig Company presented in P–26–12, prepare the required FASB *Statement No. 33* disclosures. The five-year summary is not required.

27

Analysis and Disclosure of Financial Information

Accounting in the News

Financial analysts, bankers, stockholders, and others frequently use ratio analysis to analyze financial statements. Such information is important input into investor and loan decisions. A new area in which ratio analysis is being used is analysis of a company's pension plan.

> Financial statement analysts, brokers, and investors have long recognized the valuable information that can be derived from financial ratios developed by combining certain items from the income statement and the balance sheet. While there is not always complete agreement on the interpretation of these ratios, they do provide a set of easily understood measuring rods that aid readers in understanding and using financial statements.
>
> Over the past six years these same analysts, brokers, and investors have been focusing their attention on the meager information about defined benefit pension plans currently found in the financial statements of companies that sponsor such plans. . . .
>
> Ten basic ratios, or keys to understanding, will provide a succinct, easily understood explanation of:
> - The budgeting considerations associated with the plan.
> - The funded status of the plan as a going concern.
> - The funded status of benefits if the plan is terminating.
>
> While certainly not exhaustive, these ten ratios provide a starting point from which meaningful analysis of pension plan liabilities can proceed.*

This chapter presents basic financial statement analysis techniques, which include horizontal and vertical analysis as well as ratio analysis.

*Frank G. Burianek, "Using Financial Ratios to Analyze Pension Liabilities," *Financial Executive*, January 1981, p. 29.

Financial statements summarize the activities of an enterprise for a given period of time. The purpose of preparing financial statements is to communicate information to interested parties, including owners, long-term and short-term creditors, potential investors, management, and some governmental regulatory agencies.

Owners and potential owners are concerned primarily with the earnings and the stability of the earnings. Short-term creditors are concerned with the firm's liquidity position—its ability to meet currently maturing debt. Long-term creditors are much like owners in that they must take a longer range view; they must be concerned with the firm's financial structure and with the earnings prospects in the long run. Company management has a continuing need for all types of financial data, including earnings data and projections of earnings for long-range planning, and daily financial information for inventory analysis, standard cost systems, and other internal control purposes. Governmental regulatory agencies require large amounts of detailed financial information. All of these users of the accounting data look to the accountant to provide not only the information, but some analysis and interpretation of the financial data as well.

Throughout this text a great deal of emphasis has been placed on disclosure requirements because the accounting profession has adopted the principle of **full disclosure,** which means that all significant events and financial data should be reported. A significant piece of information is one that would influence the opinion of an informed person. It is important that all financial statement information, including footnote disclosures, be used when analyzing financial statements.

Many different techniques or methods are used in financial statement analysis. The primary methods fall into two categories: ratio analysis, and trend and percentage analysis.

Ratio Analysis

Ratio analysis is perhaps the tool most frequently used for financial analysis. Different ratios can be computed to satisfy the information needs of the various users of accounting data. Short-term creditors, for example, have entirely different objectives from those of long-term creditors. The short-term creditor is interested primarily in liquidity and debt-paying ability in the short run whereas a long-term creditor is interested primarily in profitability and the firm's long-run prospects. A company's internal management would be concerned with operating efficiency as well as profitability. Stockholders and prospective investors would like to be able to make comparisons of one company with another—sometimes in different industries, and over a period of several years—to obtain an idea of performance over time.

Ratio, trend, and percentage analysis are very useful for both interfirm and interperiod comparisons. Interfirm comparisons are valuable from the viewpoint of investors, creditors, and management because they indicate the performance of a particular firm in relation to an industry standard or to other individual firms. For example, Company A might be operating very happily with a 20% gross profit margin while the industry average is over 40%. This would indicate that Company A either is operating inefficiently or pricing too low. By converting financial data to ratios, users of the data can make more meaningful comparisons between firms. Interperiod comparisons are necessary to judge the progress of the specific company over time. They provide an indication of trends.

Ratios also are useful for spotting problems and changes that may occur from year to year. For example, if the gross margin percentage is decreasing from year to year, it is an indication of decreasing profitability. Or, if the current ratio suddenly drops from 2 : 1 to less than 1 : 1, this may signal short-term debt-paying ability problems. Auditors frequently will use ratios in their analytical review work to reveal potential problem areas.

Ratio analysis has become quite standardized, and ratios are computed routinely on an industry basis. These industry average ratios serve as benchmarks for comparison with individual firm ratios, for comparison of several firms with each other, or for examination of a particular firm over a period of years.

There are a wide variety of ratios that are used and discussed in the financial literature. Of all these ratios, a few have been used most frequently. These standard ratios can be grouped into four categories: (1) liquidity measures, (2) activity measures, (3) profitability measures, and (4) financial stability measures. These

---

Exhibit 27-1
JOHNSON CORPORATION
Consolidated Statement of Income
For the Years Ended December 31, 1981 and 1982

	(000)	
	1982	*1981*
Revenues		
Net sales	$2,410,000	$2,180,000
Interest income	4,000	3,000
Other income	9,000	5,000
Total revenues	$2,423,000	$2,188,000
Expenses		
Cost of goods sold	$1,790,000	$1,628,000
Selling, general, and administrative	444,000	406,000
Interest	27,000	23,000
Total expenses	$2,261,000	$2,057,000
Income before taxes	162,000	131,000
Federal, state, and foreign income tax	71,000	59,000
Net income	$ 91,000	$ 72,000
Number of common shares	14,000	14,000
Earnings per share	$ 6.50	$ 5.143
Dividends per share	$ 2.00	$ 1.50
Market price of common, 12/31	$ 58.00	$ 55.00

Exhibit 27-2
JOHNSON CORPORATION
Consolidated Balance Sheet
As of December 31, 1981 and 1982

	000	
	1982	*1981*
Assets		
Current assets		
Cash and marketable securities	$ 23,000	$ 28,000
Receivables (net)	455,000	426,000
Inventories (lower of cost or market)	481,000	421,000
Prepaid expenses	21,000	20,000
Total current assets	$ 980,000	$ 895,000
Property, plant, and equipment (cost)	$ 538,000	$ 484,000
Less: Accumulated depreciation	(258,000)	(229,000)
Net	$ 280,000	$ 255,000
Investment and advances	$ 12,000	$ 18,000
Other assets	$ 13,000	$ 12,000
Total assets	$1,285,000	$1,180,000
Liabilities		
Current liabilities		
Accounts payable	$ 119,000	$ 102,000
Notes payable	26,000	43,000
Accrued expenses	136,000	119,000
Other	88,000	71,000
Total current liabilities	$ 369,000	$ 335,000
Long-term liabilities		
Total long-term debt	346,000	338,000
Total liabilities	$ 715,000	$ 673,000
Stockholders' Equity		
Common stock ($5 par)	$ 70,000	$ 70,000
Capital in excess of par value	140,000	140,000
Retained earnings	360,000	297,000
Total stockholders' equity	$ 570,000	$ 507,000
Total liabilities and equity	$1,285,000	$1,180,000

four sets of ratios will be discussed and illustrated using the data from the John-son Corporation found in Exhibits 27-1 and 27-2. Exhibit 27-1 contains consoli-dated statements of income for Johnson for the years ending December 31, 1981, and 1982 and dividend and market value information, and Exhibit 27-2 contains the balance sheet.

Liquidity Measures

Measures of liquidity evaluate a firm's ability to pay its current debts. For example, Johnson Corporation has $369,000 in current liabilities; can these debts be paid when they are due? An analysis using the measures of liquidity will help to answer that question. The liquidity ratios used most often are the current ratio and the acid-test ratio.

Current Ratio.   The **current ratio** is calculated by dividing the total current assets by the total current liabilities. This ratio is referred to also as the **working capital ratio.** The general standard for the current ratio historically has been 2.0 to 1.0; that is, a company generally was considered to be in relatively good shape if it had twice as many current assets as current liabilities. Recently, more em-phasis has been placed on the composition of the current assets and on the indus-try practices than on an absolute ratio.

 Since the current ratio is an indicator of short-run solvency, creditors are keenly interested in the composition of the current assets. For example, a ratio that is very high because of excessive amounts of slow-moving inventory could portend debt-paying problems. The method of inventory valuation also can have a dramatic impact on the ratio; if a company used LIFO instead of FIFO, the inven-tory value may be significantly different. If the composition of the current assets is such that a large proportion of the assets is in items that will be converted readily to cash, a measure of safety will be afforded to the short-term creditors.

 The computation of the current ratio for the Johnson Corporation in 1982 is below:

$$\text{Current ratio} = \frac{\text{current assets}}{\text{current liabilities}}$$

$$= \frac{\$980,000}{\$369,000} = 2.66 \text{ times}$$

The current ratio of 2.66 would be compared to the industry average or to the rule of thumb of 2.00. A ratio of 2.66 would tend to indicate that Johnson is in a fairly liquid position. Additional analyses should be made on the inventories and receiv-ables, however, to determine whether they are very old or have been moving regularly.

Acid-Test Ratio.   The **acid-test ratio** provides better information to short-term creditors than does the current ratio because it excludes inventories and prepaid items from the current assets in the calculation of the ratio. Exclusion of the inventories and prepaid assets leaves only the current assets that are convertible readily into cash and would be available to pay short-term creditors. This ratio will indicate potential liquidity problems, as in the case of the company with a large investment in slow-moving inventories. The general rule-of-thumb for this ratio is about $1:1$. Again, prevailing industry practices usually are considered more important than the general rule. For the Johnson Corporation, the acid-test ratio would be calculated as follows:

$$\text{Acid-test ratio} = \frac{\text{current assets-(inventories + prepaid expenses)}}{\text{current liabilities}}$$

$$= \frac{\$980,000 - (\$481,000 + \$21,000)}{\$369,000} = 1.295 \text{ times}$$

Compared to the general rule of $1:1$, Johnson appears to be in a fairly safe liquidity position.

Activity Measures

Activity measures are ratios that measure efficiency; they are used to determine how quickly the inventory and receivables **turn over,** or how quickly they are converted into cash. This is an indication of the quality of the receivables and the inventory. Asset turnover is calculated to give a measure of the efficiency of utilization of the assets. Activity ratios provide management with yardsticks for measuring performance.

Receivables Turnover. The **receivables turnover ratio** provides an indication of how quickly the company collects an average trade account receivable. The ratio is calculated by dividing the net credit sales by the average trade accounts receivable outstanding during the year. The average receivables generally are calculated using the beginning and ending balance of the *net* (rather than gross) receivables. A large turnover indicates that the company is collecting receivables rather quickly; low turnover would indicate just the opposite, a long collection period. Of course, a shorter collection period is advantageous for two reasons: (1) the company receives the cash faster, and (2) a better chance of collection is indicated. As debts get older they become more difficult to collect. (A company can evaluate its credit policies and cash discount incentives by comparing the turnover ratio before and after any changes are implemented.)

For the Johnson company, if you assume that 80% of the sales are on credit, then the receivables turnover ratio would be as follows:

$$\text{Accounts receivable turnover} = \frac{\text{net credit sales}}{\text{average trade receivables (net)}}$$

$$= \frac{\$2,410,000 \times 0.80}{\dfrac{426,000 + 455,000}{2}} = 4.377 \text{ times}$$

The turnover ratio can be converted into days by dividing 365 days by the ratio.

$$\frac{365}{4.377} = 83.39 \text{ days}$$

This indicates that an average receivable is outstanding for slightly over 83 days. If the credit terms are n/90 days, a collection period of 83 days would be good, indicating early collections. However, if the credit terms were n/60 days, a collection period of 83 days would indicate many delinquent accounts and would suggest that Johnson should improve its credit and collection policies. Often 360 days is used in the calculation instead of 365, for convenience.

Inventory Turnover.   The **inventory turnover ratio** indicates how fast (or slow) the inventory is sold. A high turnover ratio would indicate that the inventory is sold very quickly, whereas a low turnover would indicate that it is sold very slowly. In general, a company is better off if its inventory is sold quickly because there is then less chance for damage or obsolescence. However, if the company finds that the turnover ratio is very high, there may be a stockout problem. **Stockout** means that the company does not have goods on hand when customers want them. Stockout problems occur if the company reduces the inventory size too much. A balance must be maintained between the cost of having the inventory and the cost, in lost sales, of being out of inventory.

The inventory turnover ratio is computed by dividing the cost of goods sold by the average inventory. For Johnson company the ratio would be as follows:

$$\text{Inventory turnover} = \frac{\text{cost of goods sold}}{\text{average inventory}}$$

$$= \frac{\$1,790,000}{\dfrac{\$421,000 + \$481,000}{2}} = 3.97 \text{ times}$$

A turnover ratio of 3.97 times indicates that Johnson Company is replacing its inventory almost four times per year. This can be converted into days as follows:

$$\frac{365}{3.97} = 91.94 \text{ days}$$

These turnover figures should be compared with the industry average figures and last year's figures to see if they need improvement.

The analysts must be aware of significant differences between industries. For example, the retail industry generally has a very high inventory turnover ratio, whereas a construction company generally has a fairly low one. The analyst also must be aware that the inventory evaluation method will affect the turnover ratio. For example, assume that Johnson company uses LIFO as its valuation method. In periods of rising prices, LIFO will reflect a smaller inventory value than other methods. A smaller value will show an increased turnover rate because the denominator in the ratio is smaller. On the other hand, the use of FIFO in periods of rising prices would reduce the turnover ratio. If an analyst is comparing two or more companies, s/he will have to restate the inventory figures to a common valuation method to be comparable. The notes to the financial statements may indicate the impact of LIFO on the inventory value.

Asset Turnover. The **asset turnover ratio** is an indicator of how efficiently the company is using its assets and is computed by dividing the net sales by the average total assets for the period. A high ratio (compared to the industry) would indicate that the company is utilizing its assets effectively to generate sales. A high utilization rate signifies that the assets are not sitting idle, but instead are being used and are generating revenues. A low ratio would indicate that the company is not utilizing its assets effectively; the assets are sitting idle instead of being in operation.

This ratio has the potential of being somewhat misleading. Because the denominator is usually the net or book value of the assets, some problems can occur. As the assets get older, the book value decreases because of accumulated depreciation charges. A manager who is concerned with improving this particular ratio may be discouraged from replacing older assets because that would increase the denominator and reduce the ratio. This is a very difficult problem for an analyst to recognize since typically the manager might be at the departmental or divisional level, and the analyst may not be able to obtain that information. Another problem may arise when comparing two companies. If Company A uses accelerated depreciation and Company B uses straight-line, the ratio for Company A will be better (assuming other things are equal), because the book value for A will be less.

For Johnson Corporation, the asset turnover ratio for 1982 would be calculated as follows:

$$\text{Asset turnover} = \frac{\text{net sales}}{\text{average total assets}}$$

$$= \frac{\$2,410,000}{\dfrac{\$1,285,000 + \$1,180,000}{2}} = \underline{\underline{1.955}}$$

The ratio of 1.955 now should be compared to the industry average ratio.

Profitability Measures

Profitability measures are ratios that have been developed to indicate whether the company has met its profit and earnings objectives. Profitability ratios that are particularly important to owners would include the earnings per share, the price/earnings ratio, and the dividend payout ratio. Profitability ratios particularly significant to management include the sales profit margin, gross profit margin, return on investment, and return on equity.

Earnings Per Share. The **earnings per share ratio** (EPS) is undoubtedly one of the numbers quoted and used most frequently in financial analysis. The primary and diluted earnings per share are required to be disclosed in the financial statements. The computations, which can be exceedingly complex, are discussed in detail in Chapter 21. The basic computation is to divide the net income less the preferred dividend requirement by the average number of shares outstanding for the period. For the Johnson Corporation, the calculations would be as follows:

$$\text{Earnings per share} = \frac{\text{net income} - \text{preferred dividends}}{\text{average common shares outstanding}}$$

$$= \frac{\$91,000 - 0}{14,000} = \underline{\underline{\$6.50}}$$

Because so much attention is focused on the earnings per share figure, it has assumed a very prominent position in financial analysis, perhaps overly so. For example, investors have interpreted an increasing trend in EPS as a very favorable trend. Companies with consistently increasing earnings per share have had their stock prices bid very high in the market. However, increases in EPS can be the result of factors other than improving operating earnings. A very obvious factor would be a simple reduction in the number of shares outstanding with no change in the income, which would increase the total ratio. As with all ratios, the investor should look at the substance of the change, and not merely at the cosmetic effect.

We must emphasize here that EPS by itself is really meaningless. Earnings per share becomes meaningful only when it is compared to prior years' earnings, and a trend is established, or when it is compared to the market price of the stock, and the price/earnings ratio is computed. For example, assume that Company A has an earnings per share of $5, and Company B has an earnings per share of $10. Does this mean that Company B is twice as profitable or is a better investment than Company A? The answer depends on additional comparisons. If Company A's stock is selling for $15 per share and Company B's stock is selling for $50 per share, A would be the better investment. The point made here is that EPS alone is rather meaningless; only through comparison does it become significant.

Price/Earnings Ratio. The **price/earnings ratio** (P/E ratio) provides a comparison of the price of the stock for a particular company relative to the earnings of the company. The P/E ratio is calculated by dividing the market price per share by the earnings per share (EPS). A very high P/E ratio would indicate that investors expect a steady trend of growth in earnings for the company. Conversely, a low ratio would indicate that investors are not optimistic about the company's prospects for future growth. General economic conditions also influence the ratio. In times of business expansion, the average P/E ratio for all firms is higher than during times of recession.

The P/E ratio could be thought of as a type of inverted return on investment measure for prospective stock purchasers. For Johnson Company the P/E ratio would be calculated as follows:

$$\text{Price earnings} = \frac{\text{market price per share}}{\text{earnings per share}}$$

$$= \frac{\$58.00}{\$6.50} = \underline{\underline{8.923 \text{ times}}}$$

The inverse of this ratio would be the income compared to the investment on a per share basis. This is calculated below:

$$E/P = \frac{\$6.50}{\$58.00} = \underline{\underline{11.2\%}}$$

The 11.2% represents a kind of return on the investment for the investor. For an individual stock this may be more meaningful than the P/E ratio.

Dividend Payout Ratio.   The **dividend payout ratio** indicates the percentage of earnings that is paid to the owners or stockholders of the firm. The ratio is calculated by dividing the dividends paid per common share by the earnings per common share (EPS). Theoretically, the company will retain and reinvest only that portion of the income that can be reinvested at a rate higher than alternative investments available to the stockholders. As a practical matter, many companies will establish a dividend rate and will try very hard to maintain or increase that rate regardless of the fluctuations in income or investment opportunity.

For Johnson Corporation the dividend payout ratio would be as follows:

$$\text{Dividend payout} = \frac{\text{dividends per share}}{\text{earnings per share}}$$
$$= \frac{\$2.00}{\$6.50} = \underline{\underline{30.77\%}}$$

Some companies adhere to a policy of a fairly high payout ratio, whereas others will have a rather low payout ratio. Typically, companies that are expanding rapidly in new markets will have small or even zero payout ratios. These companies prefer to reinvest their earnings in the business because they are growing rapidly and usually have a great need for funds. From an investor's point of view, this kind of company is one in which the investor will forego current income in exchange for long-term price appreciation in the stock and capital gains upon its sale. Investors who purchase stock in companies with high payout ratios are attempting to maximize their current income and do not expect large price increases in the future.

Sales Profit Margin.   The profit margin on sales is an indication of management's efficiency in controlling costs and expenses. Management often is evaluated on how well it has achieved profitability; the **sales profit margin ratio** is one of the evaluation measures. It is calculated by dividing the net income by the net sales. For companies that report segment data in accordance with FASB *Statement No. 14*, this ratio may be computed for the various segments of the company. The sales profit margin for Johnson Corporation would be as follows:

$$\text{Sales profit margin} = \frac{\text{net income}}{\text{net sales}}$$
$$= \frac{\$91,000}{\$2,410,000} = \underline{\underline{3.78\%}}$$

The profit margin on sales can vary greatly from industry to industry, or even from company to company within the same industry. Consider, for example, two retailers—one a specialty men's clothing store, and the other a discount outlet for men's clothes. The sales profit margin in the specialty store will be much higher than in the discount store. The total profit of the two stores may be exactly the same, but the margins will be much different. The discount store makes up the profit by selling a greater volume of the lower-priced merchandise and accepts a lower margin on each unit. The specialty shop makes a higher profit on each unit but sells fewer units.

This relationship between margin and turnover is very important to businesses when choosing their market. A high-volume business must have lower profit margins to attract a sufficient number of customers. It was this concept that allowed the supermarkets to be very successful; the large chain supermarkets were willing to accept a lower price on each unit of merchandise and sold more of them than the small corner store was able to. We are now seeing the advent of stores that provide very little in store service and sell foodstuffs by the case, but at cheaper prices than the regular supermarkets.

To stay in business a firm must earn a competitive return on its investment. The firm can choose to maximize profit margins or turnover, or fall somewhere in the middle for both. The end result, however, is that the firm must earn a competitive return to stay in business over the long run.

Return on Investment (ROI). The **return on investment** is sometimes referred to as the earning power of the business and, as mentioned above, it is a function of the margin times the turnover.

Using profit margin on sales alone does not provide information concerning the firm's profitability for a particular period of time. When the profit margin is combined with asset turnover, however, the analyst can determine the amount of profits earned on the assets during the particular time period. The combination is necessary because of the different nature of various businesses. For example, a discount store with low profit margins and high turnover can be just as profitable as a jewelry store with high profit margins and low asset turnover. The return on investment ratio (ROI) would be calculated as follows:

$$\text{Return on investment} = \frac{\text{net income}}{\text{sales}} \times \frac{\text{sales}}{\text{average total assets}}$$

This ratio can be stated also as:

$$\text{Return on investment} = \frac{\text{net income}}{\text{average total assets}}$$

This also is called the **rate of return on assets,** where assets are considered a measure of investment. For Johnson Company, the ROI would be calculated as follows:

$$\text{ROI} = \text{margin} \times \text{turnover}$$

$$ROI = \frac{\$91{,}000}{\$2{,}410{,}000} \times \frac{\$2{,}410{,}000}{\dfrac{\$1{,}180{,}000 + \$1{,}285{,}000}{2}}$$

$$ROI = \frac{\$91{,}000}{\dfrac{\$1{,}180{,}000 + \$1{,}285{,}000}{2}}$$

$$ROI = \underline{\underline{7.38\%}}$$

The 7.38% would be compared to the industry average or to other competitor companies.

In this example the net income was used in the numerator and the average total assets were used in the denominator. Many analysts contend that the numerator should be net income *excluding the interest charge but after tax* because interest represents a cost of buying more assets and thus should not be included. The return on assets for Johnson Corporation would be calculated as follows:

$$Return\ on\ assets = \frac{net\ income + interest\ expense - tax\ savings}{average\ total\ assets}$$

$$= \frac{\$91{,}000 + \$27{,}100 - 0.438*(\$27{,}000)}{\dfrac{\$1{,}180{,}000 + \$1{,}285{,}000}{2}}$$

$$= \underline{\underline{8.61\%}}$$

*$71,000 (tax) ÷ $162,000 (income before tax) = 0.438 (tax rate)

Since the net income figure is net of interest expense, the net of tax interest expense must be added back to get income before interest. The argument for removing the interest expense is that it represents a financing cost of acquisition of the assets as opposed to an operating cost, and hence should be excluded. The denominator uses the average total assets because the income was generated over the entire period using the assets available over the entire period.

Note that the *book value* of the assets is used in this ratio. Consider the impact of using the replacement cost of the assets: the return would certainly be decreased, probably significantly for most companies. This means that the real return would be much less than the stated return. The policy implication is that companies may not be earning a return sufficiently great enough to replace and modernize their productive capacity.

Return on Common Stockholders' Equity. Like the ROI ratio, the **return on equity** ratio is a measure of management efficiency. This return on equity ratio, however, provides added information about the efficiency of the company's use of financing, use of leverage, or trading on the equity. The ratio is calculated by dividing net income minus preferred dividends by the average common stockholders' equity. For the Johnson Corporation the return on equity would be as follows:

$$\text{Return on stockholder's equity} = \frac{\text{net income} - \text{preferred dividends}}{\text{average common stockholders' equity}}$$

$$= \frac{\$91,000 - 0}{\dfrac{\$507,000 + \$570,000}{2}} = \underline{16.9\%}$$

The return on common stockholders' equity is greater than the return on assets (16.9% compared to 8.61%), which indicates Johnson's use of favorable financial leverage. Unlike the return on total assets, which considers all sources of funds in the computation of the ratio, return on common equity uses only the common shareholders' equity in the denominator. When the return on equity is greater than the return on assets, it indicates that management is using creditor funds to enhance the earnings for the stockholders. If the return on equity were less than the return on assets, this would indicate unfavorable financial leverage. Unfavorable leverage means that management would pay more for creditor funds than it could earn on those funds. It is similar to borrowing money at 20% to make an investment with a return of 15%, clearly a losing proposition.

Measures of Financial Stability

Measures of financial stability provide indications of the company's long-term solvency and stability. They are of most interest to long-term creditors, who use them to gauge the safety of their investments. The measures of financial stability include total debt to total assets, times interest earned, book value per share, and cash flow per share.

Total Debt to Total Assets. The **total debt to total assets ratio** is calculated by dividing the total debt outstanding by the total assets; it gives an indication of the percentage of total assets financed by creditor funds. From the creditors' viewpoint, the smaller this ratio is, the better off the creditors are because a small percentage of assets is financed by creditor funds. As this ratio gets larger, it signifies a greater reliance on creditor funds compared to ownership investment. The ratio for any specific company should be compared to the industry average to determine if it is "high" or "low." A company with a very "high" ratio would find it increasingly difficult to borrow additional funds, or at best, the interest rates would become exorbitant.

Certain industries, however, are able to carry a much higher percentage of debt than others because of unique characteristics inherent in the industry. For example, the utility industry has long been an industry heavily financed by debt. The revenues generated by utilities are not subject to a great deal of fluctuation, but instead have been characterized by a steady growth rate. The growth and stability of revenues allow the industry to carry very large percentages of debt compared to industries with uncertain revenue trends. The Johnson Corporation would calculate its debt ratio as follows:

$$\text{Total debt to total assets} = \frac{\text{total debt}}{\text{total assets}}$$

$$= \frac{\$715,000}{\$1,285,000} = \underline{55.6\%}$$

Times Interest Earned.   The **times interest earned ratio** provides a measure of the creditors' safety or of the company's ability to meet its current interest obligations. A high ratio would indicate that the company is not in danger of defaulting on interest payments, whereas a low ratio would be cause for concern.

The numerator of the ratio is usually the income before interest charges and income taxes. Because taxes are paid after interest charges are deducted from income, they are excluded in the ratio calculation as well. The denominator used is the interest charge for the period. For the Johnson Corporation, the ratio would be as follows:

$$\text{Times interest earned} = \frac{\text{earnings before interest and taxes}}{\text{interest charges}}$$

$$= \frac{\$162,000 + \$27,000}{\$27,000} = \underline{\underline{7 \text{ times}}}$$

Book Value Per Share.   The **book value per share ratio** refers to the net assets per share of common stock and is calculated by dividing the common shareholders' equity by the shares of common stock outstanding. This figure is an indication of what the common shareholders might expect to receive in the event of the company's liquidation, if the assets were sold at the values shown on the balance sheet. That is, if the assets were sold at their net balance sheet values, if the creditors and preferred shareholders were repaid their investments, and if the remainder were divided among the common shareholders, each share of common stock would receive the book value amount.

Obviously, these assumptions are unrealistic. Balance sheet values of assets reflect unamortized historical cost values and are not at all related to the current value of the assets. If the business were liquidated, it is very unlikely that the actual amount received from the sale of the assets would be even close to the book value amount. Thus, this ratio loses much of its usefulness and relevance. However, for some reason it is still used by analysts and investors.

The book value per share for Johnson Corporation would be as follows:

$$\text{Book value} = \frac{\text{common stockholders' equity}}{\text{outstanding common shares}}$$

$$= \frac{\$570,000}{14,000} = \underline{\underline{\$40.714 \text{ per share}}}$$

Cash Flow Per Share.   The **cash flow per share ratio** is calculated by adding noncash charges back to net income and dividing by the number of shares outstanding. For Johnson Company let us assume that the depreciation charges represent the only noncash charges to income and that they total $29,000. The cash flow per share is calculated below:

$$\text{Cash flow per share} = \frac{\$91,000 + \$29,000}{14,000}$$

$$= \underline{\underline{\$8.57}}$$

What does the $8.57 per share represent? The cash flow number ($91,000 + $29,000) does not represent all of the dollars that flowed into the firm. At best, it is only an approximation of the resources (dollars) generated internally through normal operations and available for reinvestment. Dividing by the number of shares outstanding does not add any new information. Analysts, however, frequently use this ratio.

Exhibit 27-3 provides a summary of all the ratios discussed. The exhibit illustrates the computational formulas for each ratio and the computation of each ratio for the Johnson Corporation. The ratios discussed in this chapter are representative of the common ratios used for analysis. There are a number of other ratios that can be used also. Whenever ratios are used for analysis, the ratios should be compared to industry averages and other standards for the particular ratio. In this way they will be most meaningful and helpful to the analyst.

Trend and Percentage Analysis

Financial analysts often are most concerned with trends of financial data over some period of time. **Trend and percentage analysis** is considered important because it can indicate patterns and directions that a company may be taking. By examining trends, analysts can determine if the company is in a growth period, a stagnant period, or a period of decline. Most companies will present comparative financial statements in their annual reports, typically covering a five- or ten-year period. Comparing data and trends over a number of years sometimes is referred to as horizontal analysis. Comparison of data in a single year sometimes is referred to as vertical analysis.

Horizontal Analysis

Horizontal analysis provides information about trends over a period of time. Typically, two or more years' data will be presented in absolute numbers and in percentages. The percentage comparisons most often are based on the initial year presented in the analysis. The percentage change from the base year allows the analyst to detect trends and patterns of growth. Exhibit 27-4 illustrates a horizontal analysis of income for the Johnson Corporation for the years 1981 and 1982 and is based on the data from Exhibit 27-1. A horizontal analysis of balance sheet data is presented in Exhibit 27-5 and uses the data from Exhibit 27-2.

As can be seen in the exhibits, horizontal analysis provides comparative data over a period of time. Often, instead of only two years' data being presented, five or more years' data will be included in the annual report. Note that the percentage changes for each item is a reflection of the increase for 1982 compared to the 1981 base year.

The comparative income statements in Exhibit 27-4 indicate favorable trends for Johnson. Revenues increased by 10.74% while the cost of goods sold increased by only 9.95%. This indicates that Johnson was able to increase the spread between its costs and sales prices, and thus improved its gross profit. The income before tax increased by 23.66%, indicating a definite improvement in operations. The balance sheets in Exhibit 27-5 can be used to calculate ratios, such as the current ratio, acid-test ratio, debt equity ratio, and to see if they have improved or worsened over time.

Exhibit 27-3

JOHNSON CORPORATION
Summary of Ratios

	Formula	Computation
1. *Liquidity Measures*		
a) Current ratio	$\dfrac{\text{Current assets}}{\text{Current liabilities}}$	$\dfrac{\$980,000}{\$369,000} = 2.66 \text{ to } 1$
b) Acid-test	$\dfrac{\text{Current assets} - \text{inventories} - \text{prepaid expenses}}{\text{Current liabilities}}$	$\dfrac{\$980,000 - \$481,000 - \$21,000}{\$369,000} = \underline{\underline{1.295 \text{ to } 1}}$
2. *Activity Measures*		
a) Receivables turnover	$\dfrac{\text{Net credit sales}}{\text{Average trade receivables (net)}}$	$\dfrac{\$2,410,000 \times 0.8}{\dfrac{\$426,000 + \$455,000}{2}} = \underline{\underline{4.377 \text{ times}}}$
b) Inventory turnover	$\dfrac{\text{Cost of goods sold}}{\text{Average inventory}}$	$\dfrac{\$1,790,000}{\dfrac{\$421,000 + \$481,000}{2}} = \underline{\underline{3.97 \text{ times}}}$
c) Asset turnover	$\dfrac{\text{Net sales}}{\text{Average total assets}}$	$\dfrac{\$2,410,000}{\dfrac{\$1,285,000 + \$1,180,000}{2}} = \underline{\underline{1.955 \text{ times}}}$

3. *Profitability Measures*

a) Earnings per share

$$\frac{\text{Net income} - \text{preferred dividends}}{\text{Average common shares}} \quad \frac{\$91,000}{14,000} = \underline{\$6.50/\text{share}}$$
$$\text{outstanding}$$

b) Price/earnings ratio

$$\frac{\text{Market price per share}}{\text{Earnings per share}} \quad \frac{\$58.00}{\$\ 6.50} = \underline{8.923 \text{ times}}$$

c) Dividend payout ratio

$$\frac{\text{Dividends per share}}{\text{Earnings per share}} \quad \frac{\$2.00}{\$6.50} = \underline{30.77\%}$$

d) Sales profit margin

$$\frac{\text{Net income}}{\text{Net sales}} \quad \frac{\$91,000}{\$2,410,000} = \underline{3.78\%}$$

e) Return on assets

$$\frac{\text{Net income} + \text{interest expense}}{\text{Average total assets}} \quad \frac{\$91,000 + \$27,000 - \$11,826}{\dfrac{\$1,180,000 + \$1,285,000}{2}} = \underline{8.614\%}$$

f) Return on common stockholder's equity

$$\frac{\text{Net income} - \text{preferred dividends}}{\text{Average common stockholders'}} \quad \frac{\$91,000 - 0}{\dfrac{\$507,000 + \$570,000}{2}} = \underline{16.9\%}$$
$$\text{equity}$$

4. *Measures of Financial Stability*

a) Total debt to total assets

$$\frac{\text{Total debt}}{\text{Total assets}} \quad \frac{\$715,000}{\$1,285,000} = \underline{55.6\%}$$

b) Times interest earned

$$\frac{\text{Earnings before interest}}{\text{Interest charges}} \quad \frac{\$162,000 + \$27,000}{\$27,000} = \underline{7 \text{ times}}$$
$$\text{and taxes}$$

c) Book value per share

$$\frac{\text{Common stockholders' equity}}{\text{Outstanding common shares}} \quad \frac{\$570,000}{14,000} = \underline{\$40.714 \text{ per share}}$$

d) Cash flow per share

$$\frac{\text{Net income} + \text{noncash charges}}{\text{Outstanding common shares}} \quad \frac{\$91,000 + \$29,000}{14,000} = \underline{\$8.57 \text{ per share}}$$

Exhibit 27-4
JOHNSON CORPORATION
Comparative Statements of Income
(000,000)

	Year Ending 12/31		Increase (Decrease) 1982 over 1981	
	1982	1981	Amount	Percent
Total revenues	$2,423	$2,188	$ 235	10.74
Cost of goods sold	1,790	1,628	162	9.95
Gross profit	$ 633	$ 560	$ 73	13.04
Selling, general, and administrative expenses	444	406	38	9.36
Interest expense	27	23	4	17.39
Income before tax	$ 162	$ 131	$ 31	23.66
Income taxes	71	59	12	20.34
Net income	$ 91	$ 72	$ 19	26.39
Number of common shares	14	14	0	0
Earnings per share	$ 6.50	$5.143	$1.357	26.39
Dividends per share	$ 2.00	$ 1.50	$ 0.50	33.33

Vertical Analysis

Vertical analysis provides a percentage analysis of each item in the financial statements for a single year. That is, each item in the income statement is expressed as a percentage of total revenues. In the balance sheet each asset item is expressed as a percentage of total assets, while each liability and equity item are expressed as a percentage of the total liabilities and equities. Exhibit 27-6 provides a vertical analysis for Johnson Corporation income statements for 1981–82, and Exhibit 27-7 provides the balance sheet analysis.

The vertical analysis income statements in Exhibit 27-6 reflect each item as a percent of sales. This is useful in analysis because you can see how the proportions change from year to year and how they compare with the industry averages for the year. Johnson's gross profit of 26.1% in 1982 is 0.5% greater than its profit in 1981, which is favorable. If the industry average for 1981 were 29%, however, this would indicate that Johnson still is not as profitable as it should be. The balance sheet indicates that Johnson's current assets are a very high proportion of its total assets. You would now want to look at the inventory and receivables turnover to assure yourself that these assets are not old and obsolete.

A **common-size** statement is a variation of vertical analysis in which only the percentages, not the dollar amounts, are shown.

Exhibit 27-5
JOHNSON CORPORATION
Comparative Balance Sheets
(000,000)

	1982	1981	Increase (Decrease) 1982 over 1981 Amount	Percent
Current assets				
Cash and marketable securities	$ 23	$ 28	$ (5)	(17.86)
Receivables (net)	455	426	29	6.81
Inventories (LCM)	481	421	60	14.25
Prepaid expenses	21	20	1	5.00
Total current assets	$ 980	$ 895	$ 85	9.50
Property, plant, and equipment	538	484	54	11.16
Less: Accumulated depreciation	(258)	(229)	29	12.66
Net property, plant, and equipment	280	255	25	9.80
Investments and advances	$ 12	$ 18	$ (6)	(33.33)
Other assets	13	12	1	8.33
Total assets	$1,285	$1,180	$105	8.99
Current liabilities				
Accounts payable	$ 119	$ 102	$ 17	16.67
Notes payable	26	43	(17)	(39.53)
Accrued expenses	136	119	17	14.29
Other	88	71	17	23.94
Total current liabilities	$ 369	$ 335	$ 34	10.15
Long-term debt	346	338	8	2.37
Total liabilities	$ 715	$ 673	$ 42	6.24
Common stock ($5 par)	$ 70	$ 70	$-0-	-0-
Capital in excess of par	140	140	-0-	-0-
Retained earnings	360	297	63	21.21
Total stockholders' equity	$ 570	$ 507	$ 63	12.42

Exhibit 27-6
JOHNSON CORPORATION
Vertical Analysis Income Statement
(000,000)

	1982		1981	
	Amount	*%*	*Amount*	*%*
Total revenues	$2,423	100.0	$2,188	100.0
Cost of goods sold	(1,790)	(73.9)	(1,628)	(74.4)
Gross profit	$ 633	26.1	$ 560	25.6
Selling, general, and administrative expenses	(444)	(18.3)	(406)	(18.6)
Interest expense	(27)	(1.1)	(23)	(1.1)
Income before tax	$ 162	6.7	$ 131	5.9
Income tax	(71)	(2.9)	(59)	(2.7)
Net income	$ 91	3.8	$ 72	3.2

Evaluation of Financial Statement Analysis

Because ratios and trend percentages can be computed very precisely, there is often a tendency to place too much emphasis on the computation and values obtained. It is far more important to examine the underlying numbers involved in the calculations. In other words, the numbers used are frequently more important than the calculated value. Although ratios and trends are useful as analytic tools, they should be used only in conjunction with other evaluative and comparative procedures.

Analysts and investors must bear in mind that ratios and trends are based on financial data. The underlying financial data may not be comparable among companies because of the use of differing accounting policies or estimates or because the historical cost principle may distort asset values severely. Differing accounting principles, such as inventory valuation methods, depreciation methods, treatment of leases, treatment of pension costs, and many others similar to these, make it very difficult to compare companies across industries or even within the same industry. Therefore, ratio analysis should not be regarded as a panacea for decision making, but as a tool to be used with other analytical processes and information.

Consider the problem of differing accounting policies. Different accounting policies usually are most serious in the following areas: inventory valuation methods, depreciation methods, capitalization versus expensing of certain costs, and pooling as opposed to purchase for business combinations. The use of LIFO rather than FIFO or average cost can have a dramatic impact on asset values and consequently on the cost of goods sold and income. The same is true for depreciation methods. In order to make realistic comparisons between firms, the analyst

Exhibit 27-7
JOHNSON CORPORATION
Vertical Analysis Balance Sheet
(000,000)

	1982		1981	
	Amount	*%*	*Amount*	*%*
Current assets				
Cash and marketable securities	$ 23	1.8	$ 28	2.4
Receivables (net)	455	35.4	426	36.1
Inventories (LCM)	481	37.4	421	35.7
Prepaid expenses	21	1.6	20	1.7
Total current assets	$ 980	76.2	$ 895	75.9
Property, plant, and equipment	538	41.9	484	41.0
Less: Accumulated depreciation	(258)	(20.1)	(229)	(19.4)
Net property, plant, and equipment	$ 280	21.8	$ 255	21.6
Investments and advances	12	1.0	18	1.5
Other assets	13	1.0	12	1.0
Total assets	$1,285	100.0	$1,180	100.0
Current liabilities				
Accounts payable	$ 119	9.3	$ 102	8.7
Notes payable	26	2.0	43	3.6
Accrued expenses	136	10.6	119	10.1
Other	88	6.8	71	6.0
Total current liabilities	$ 369	28.7	$ 335	28.4
Long-term liabilities	346	26.9	338	28.6
Total liabilities	$ 715	55.6	$ 673	57.0
Common stock	70	5.5	70	5.9
Capital in excess of par	140	10.9	140	11.9
Retained earnings	360	28.0	297	25.2
Total stockholders' equity	$ 570	44.4	$ 507	43.0
Total liabilities and equity	$1,285	100.0	$1,180	100.0

must try to restate the financial data to a common basis within the firms being compared.

Perhaps an even more significant problem is associated with the use of historical cost for asset valuation. The analyst really has no idea what the current values of the assets are for a company that is not required to report current values. For most companies the current values of their assets are not even close to their historical cost-carrying values on the balance sheet. This distorts the ratios computed using the asset values and also distorts the ratios using income because depreciation is distorted.

Finally, there are very significant problems resulting from the differences in businesses and changes in the nature of the business. Is it really meaningful to compare companies in different industries? Even more fundamental, many companies have diversified into several industries; comparison of the diversified companies is very difficult. An uninformed person very likely will find it extremely difficult to make intelligent comparisons and evaluations between firms.

Concept Summary

TECHNIQUES OF FINANCIAL ANALYSIS

RATIO ANALYSIS

Measure	Ratio	Computation	Purpose
Liquidity	Current ratio	$\dfrac{\text{Current assets}}{\text{Current liabilities}}$	Measures short-term debt paying ability
	Acid test	$\dfrac{\text{Current assets-inventories-prepaid expenses}}{\text{Current liabilities}}$	Measures immediate debt paying ability
Activity	Receivables turnover	$\dfrac{\text{Net credit sales}}{\text{Net average trade receivables}}$	Gives an indication of how slowly (or quickly) the receivables are collected
	Inventory turnover	$\dfrac{\text{Cost of goods sold}}{\text{Average inventory}}$	Gives an indication of how fast the inventory is turned over
	Asset turnover	$\dfrac{\text{Net sales}}{\text{Average total assets}}$	Gives an indication of how well the total assets are utilized to generate sales
Profitability	Earnings per share	$\dfrac{\text{Net income-preferred dividends}}{\text{Average common shares outstanding}}$	Used by analysts to help determine the value of the stock
	Price/ earnings	$\dfrac{\text{Market price per share}}{\text{Earnings per shares}}$	A useful ratio for comparison with stock prices from other potential investments

	Dividend payout	$$\frac{\text{Dividends per share}}{\text{Earnings per share}}$$	Used by investors to determine the yield or return on their investment.
	Sales profit margin	$$\frac{\text{Net income}}{\text{Net sales}}$$	An indicator of whether expenses are too high in relation to sales generated
	Return on investment	$$\frac{\text{Net income}}{\text{Average total assets}}$$	A measure of management efficiency, whether management is using resources wisely
	Return on equity	$$\frac{\text{Net income-preferred dividends}}{\text{Average common stockholders' equity}}$$	An indicator of the owners' return on their investment
Financial Stability	Debt to assets	$$\frac{\text{Total debt}}{\text{Total assets}}$$	A measure of the financial leverage being employed by the company
	Times interest earned	$$\frac{\text{Earnings before interest \& taxes}}{\text{Interest charges}}$$	A measure of the safety of the creditors, the debt-paying ability of the company
	Book value	$$\frac{\text{Common shareholders' equity}}{\text{Outstanding common shares}}$$	The asset value (on a historical cost basis) of a common share
	Cash flow per share	$$\frac{\text{Net income + noncash charges}}{\text{Outstanding common shares}}$$	The amount of cash generated per common share

TREND OR HORIZONTAL ANALYSIS

Definition—comparison of data over a period of time.
Purpose—used by analysts and investors to note improvement or decline by individual companies.

PERCENTAGE ANALYSIS

Definition—stating all values on the financial statements as a percentage of the total.
Purpose—used by analysts and investors for comparing two or more companies.

Questions

Q–27–1   Who are some of the users of financial statements, and what kinds of information do they look for?

Q–27–2   What are some of the techniques that have been developed to facilitate financial statement analysis?

Q–27–3   How do the objectives of short-term creditors differ from the objectives of long-term creditors?

Q–27–4   How do the objectives of internal management differ from the objectives of stockholders and prospective owners with regard to the analysis of financial data?

Q–27–5   What do liquidity measures indicate? Which ratios are included as liquidity measures?

Q–27–6   Which current assets are excluded from the acid-test ratio? Why?

Q–27–7   How would the inventory valuation method used by the company affect the current ratio? How would it affect the acid-test ratio?

Q–27–8   How are activity measures used? Which ratios are included as activity measures?

Q–27–9   What information is conveyed in the receivables turnover ratio? What are the implications of a high turnover rate versus a low turnover rate?

Q–27–10   What information is conveyed by the inventory turnover ratio? What are some dangers associated with a very high turnover rate? A very low turnover rate?

Q–27–11   What information is contained in the asset turnover ratio?

Q–27–12   Indicate some problems that may exist with the asset turnover ratio.

Q–27–13   What do profitability measures indicate? Which of the profitability measures are particularly important to owners? To management?

Q–27–14   What is the purpose of the price/earnings ratio? What are the implications of a very high or very low ratio?

Q–27–15   What relationship exists between sales profit margin and asset turnover?

Q–27–16   How does the return on equity ratio differ from the return on assets ratio?

Q–27–17   What is meant by financial leverage, or trading on the equity? What is favorable as opposed to unfavorable financial leverage?

Q–27–18   What are measures of financial stability? Who uses them and why?

Q–27–19   Generally, does book value per share equal market value per share? Why or why not? What is book value?

Q–27–20   What is trend and percentage analysis? How is it useful?

Q–27–21   Indicate some of the problems related to ratio analysis.

Q–27–22   Answer the following series of multiple choice questions related to ratio analysis.

    a)   Payment of a dividend in stock
       (1)   Increases the current ratio.
       (2)   Decreases the amount of working capital.
       (3)   Increases total stockholders' equity.
       (4)   Decreases book value per share of stock outstanding.

    b)   Companies A and B begin 1972 with identical account balances, and their revenues and expenses for 1972 are identical in amount except that Company A has a higher ratio of cash to noncash expenses. If the cash balances of both companies increase as a result of operations (no financing or dividends), the ending cash balance of Company A as compared to Company B will be
       (1)   Higher.
       (2)   The same.

(3) Lower.

(4) Indeterminate from the information given.

c) Eden Company has outstanding both common stock and nonparticipating, noncumulative preferred stock. The liquidation value of the preferred stock is equal to its par value. The book value per share of the common stock is unaffected by which of the following?

(1) The declaration of a stock dividend on preferred payable in preferred stock when the market price of the preferred is equal to its par value.

(2) The declaration of a stock dividend on common payable in common stock when the market price of the common stock is equal to its par value.

(3) The payment of a previously declared cash dividend on the common stock.

(4) A two for one split of the common stock.

d) On April 15, 1971, the Rest-More Corporation accepted delivery of merchandise that it purchased on account. As of April 30 the Corporation had not recorded the transaction or included the merchandise in its inventory. What effect would this have on its balance sheet for April 30, 1971?

(1) Assets and owners' equity were overstated, but liabilities were not affected.

(2) Owners' equity was the only item affected by the omission.

(3) Assets and liabilities were understated, but owners' equity was not affected.

(4) Assets and owners' equity were understated, but liabilities were not affected.

e) If you assume stable business conditions, a decline in the number of days' sales outstanding in a company's accounts receivable at year-end from one year to the next might indicate which of the following?

(1) A stiffening of the company's credit policies.

(2) The second year's sales were made at lower prices than the first year's sales.

(3) A longer discount period and a more distant due date were extended to customers in the second period.

(4) A significant decrease in the volume of sales of the second year.

f) Trail, Inc. has a current ratio of 0.65 to 1. A cash dividend declared last month is paid this month. What is the effect of this dividend payment on the current ratio and working capital, respectively?

(1) Rise and decline.

(2) Rise and no effect.

(3) Decline and no effect.

(4) No effect on either.

(AICPA adapted)

Discussion Questions and Cases

D–27–1 Listed below are four different situations which deal with the calculations of ratios and the determination of other factors considered important in analyzing financial statements. You are to assume that prior to the occurrence of the independent events described below, the corporation had a current ratio in excess of one to one, and an acid-test (quick) ratio in excess of one to one also. Further assume that the corporation reported a net income (as opposed to a loss) for the period just ended. You may ignore the effects of income taxes. The corporation had only one class of shares of stock outstanding.

Situation 1: If the corporation records a 100% stock dividend, what would be the effect on working capital, the current ratio, book value per share, earnings per share, and the debt/equity ratio?

Situation 2: When the corporation records the payment of a cash dividend whose declaration was already recorded, what will be the effect on working capital, the current ratio, and earnings per share?

Situation 3: If the corporation purchases its own shares in the open market at a price greater than the book value per share, what would be the effect on book value per share and earnings per share?

Situation 4: What would be the most probable cause of an inventory turnover rate increase while the rate of receivables turnover decreased when compared to the prior period?

(AICPA adapted)

D–27–2 Items 1 through 4 are based on the following instructions:
Each item describes an independent situation. For each situation, one factor is denoted X and the other factor is denoted Y.

1. Delta Corporation wrote off a $100 uncollectible account receivable against the $1,200 balance in its allowance account. Compare the current ratio before the write-off (X) with the current ratio after the write-off (Y).

2. Kappa, Inc. neglected to amortize the premium on its bonds payable. Compare the company's net earnings without this premium amortization (X) and the company's net earnings with such amortization (Y).

3. Aaron, Inc. owns 80% of the outstanding stock of Belle, Inc. Compare the consolidated net earnings of Aaron and Belle (X) and Aaron's net earnings if it does not consolidate with Belle (Y).

4. Epsilon Company has a current ratio of two to one. A transaction reduces the current ratio. Compare the working capital before this transaction (X) and the working capital after this transaction (Y).

Required:
For each situation, compare the two factors to determine whether X is greater than, equal to, or less than Y.

(AICPA adapted)

D–27–3 Jones Corporation is a small, privately held, very successful company. The owners have followed the policy of reinvesting earnings in the business over the years. As a result of this policy, Jones has had steady, if unspectacular growth. The balance sheet indicates that there are no long-term liabilities outstanding; the company has avoided borrowing on a long-term basis. The only short-term debt is related to trade accounts payable and a small short-term loan from the bank which was used to purchase some equipment. The owners are considering a major expansion into a new territory. This would require a significant cash outlay which would have to be borrowed.

Required:
1. If the venture is profitable and Jones is successful at "trading on the equity," explain what the effect will be on the ratio of owners' equity to total assets and the ratio of net income to owners' equity?

2. Explain what the effect on the same ratios will be of unsuccessful trading on the equity.

D–27–4 Smith Corporation is engaged in the sales of industrial cleaning equipment to manufacturing plants. Smith has been a privately held company and the owners are ready to issue stock to the public to finance an expansion. Smith Company management is concerned with what type of reception their stock will receive in the market place. Their investment banker has advised them that potential investors will look to the underlying business, the past and future earnings potential, and at various ratios to compare Smith's performance with other companies.

Required:
Smith has asked that you indicate the major categories of ratios and what they are used for.

D–27–5   Martha Company is a retailer of specialty products for use in the kitchen. The company started with a single store and now has a total of five in a fairly compressed geographic region. Martha would like to open another territory. Expansion would require a significant amount of additional capital which would be raised by issuing either common stock or long-term bonds. At the same time, Martha is considering two significant accounting principle changes, from FIFO to LIFO for inventory valuation, and from straight-line to sum-of-the-years'-digits depreciation.

Required:

1.   What will be the impact of the inventory and depreciation changes on the liquidity and the profitability ratios?

2.   What will be the impact on the financial stability and profitability ratios of the common stock versus the long-term debt issue?

Exercises

E–27–1   The Weeks Corporation has net accounts receivable of $42,000 at December 31, 1982, and $62,000 at December 31, 1983. All sales were credit sales. If the receivables turnover was 8.8 for the year 1983, what were the sales?

E–27–2   April Corporation's net accounts receivable increased by 40% during 1983. April had total sales of 500,000, 80% of which were credit sales. If the receivables turnover ratio is 6, what was the balance of receivables at the beginning of 1983 and at the end of 1983?

E–27–3   The Crimson Corporation had net sales in 1983 of $750,000. Crimson consistently has maintained a 40% gross profit margin throughout the years (including 1983). During the year 1983, Crimson worked very hard to decrease the size of the inventory. The turnover ratio increased from 10 in 1982 to 12 in 1983, and the amount of the inventory decreased in 1983 by 10%. What were the amounts of the beginning and the ending inventories for 1983?

E–27–4   Fridays Corporation had net credit sales in 1983 of $550,000 and cash sales of $170,000. At the end of 1982 Fridays' balance sheet indicated total liabilities of $400,000 and total stockholders' equity of $300,000. At the end of 1983 the liabilities had decreased to $350,000, and the stockholders' equity had increased to $550,000. What was the asset turnover for the year 1983?

E–27–5   The following data are available at the end of the fiscal years 1982 and 1983:

	1983	1982
Income before interest and tax	$ 750,000	$ 600,000
Bonds payable outstanding (12%)	$1,000,000	$1,000,000
Preferred stock ($100 par, 6%)	10,000 shares	10,000 shares
Common shares outstanding	60,000	40,000
Total dividends paid	$ 180,000	$ 120,000

Assume a tax rate of 40%.

Required (assume the number of common shares did not change in 1982):

1.   Calculate the earnings per share for both years.

2.   Calculate the dividend payout ratio for both years.

3.   If the market price of the common stock were $95.40 at the end of 1983, what was the price/earnings ratio?

E–27–6   Refer to the information in Exercise 27–5. For both years 1982 and 1983, calculate the following:

   a)   Times interest earned.

   b)   Cash flow per share if depreciation is the only noncash charge and amounted to $42,000 each year.

E–27–7   Utica Company's net accounts receivable were $250,000 at December 31, 1978, and $300,000 at December 31, 1979. Net cash sales for 1979 were $100,000. The accounts receivable turnover for 1979 was 5.0. What were Utica's total net sales for 1979?

(AICPA adapted)

E–27–8   Selected information for Irvington Company is as follows:

	December 31,	
	1978	*1979*
Preferred stock, 8%, par value $100, nonconvertible, noncumulative	$125,000	$125,000
Common stock	300,000	400,000
Retained earnings	75,000	185,000
Dividends paid on preferred stock for year ended	10,000	10,000
Net income for year ended	60,000	120,000

Required:
What is Irvington's return on common stockholders' equity for 1979, rounded to the nearest percentage point?

(AICPA adapted)

E–27–9   Refer to the information in Exercise 27–8. Assume that the common stock is $10 par value. Calculate the book value per share in both 1978 and 1979.

E–27–10   Assume that the following data are available at the end of the fiscal year 1983:

Cost of goods sold	$ 7,500,000
Net sales (all credit)	10,000,000
Net income	800,000
Average inventory	2,500,000
Average receivables	1,666,667

Required:
1.   Calculate the sales profit margin.
2.   Calculate the gross profit margin.

E–27–11   Refer to the data for Exercise 27–10. Calculate the average number of days to collect a receivable and the number of days' sales in inventory. Assume a 360-day year.

E–27–12   The following common-size income statements are available for Sparky Corporation for the two years ended December 31, 1975, and 1974:

	1975	*1974*
Sales	100%	100%
Cost of sales	55	70
Gross profit on sales	45%	30%
Operating expenses (including income tax expense)	20	18
Net income	25%	12%

The trend percentages for sales are as follows:

1975	130%
1974	100%

Required:

What should be the trend percentage for gross profit on sales for 1975?

(AICPA adapted)

E–27–13 During 1978 Red, Incorporated purchased $2,000,000 of inventory. The cost of goods sold for 1978 was $2,200,000, and the ending inventory at December 31, 1978, was $400,000.

Required:

Calculate the inventory turnover for 1978.

(AICPA adapted)

E–27–14 Information from Lon Company's balance sheet at December 31, 1977, is as follows:

Current assets	
Cash	$ 3,000,000
Marketable securities, at cost that	
approximates market	7,000,000
Accounts receivable, net of allowance	
for doubtful accounts	100,000,000
Inventories, lower of cost or market	130,000,000
Prepaid expenses	2,000,000
Total current assets	$242,000,000
Current liabilities	
Notes payable	$ 4,000,000
Accounts payable	40,000,000
Accrued expenses	30,000,000
Income taxes payable	1,000,000
Payments due within one year on long-	
term debt	6,000,000
Total current liabilities	$ 81,000,000
Long-term debt	$180,000,000

Required:

1. What is the current ratio?
2. What is the quick (acid-test) ratio?

(AICPA adapted)

E–27–15 Selected information from the accounting records of the Vigor Company is as follows:

Net accounts receivable at December 31, 1975	$ 900,000
Net accounts receivable at December 31, 1976	1,000,000
Accounts receivable turnover	five to one
Inventories at December 31, 1975	$1,100,000
Inventories at December 31, 1976	1,200,000
Inventory turnover	four to one

Required:

1. If you assume that a business year consists of 300 days, how many days are in Vigor's operating cycle for 1976?
2. What was Vigor's gross profit for 1976?

(AICPA adapted)

E–27–16 The following data were abstracted from the financial records of the Glum Corporation for 1974:

Sales	$3,600,000
Bond interest expense	120,000
Income taxes	600,000
Net income	800,000

Required:

How many times was bond interest earned in 1974?

(AICPA adapted)

E–27–17 Maple Corporation's stockholders' equity at June 30, 1980, consisted of the following:

10% preferred stock, $50 par value; liquidating value, $55 per share; 20,000 shares issued and outstanding	$1,000,000
Common stock, $10 par value; 500,000 shares authorized; 150,000 shares issued and outstanding	1,500,000
Retained earnings	500,000

Required:

What is the book value per share of common stock?

(AICPA adapted)

E–27–18 Pine Corporation's stockholders' equity at December 31, 1980, consisted of the following:

6% cumulative preferred stock, $100 par value; 1,000 shares issued and outstanding	$100,000
Common stock, $10 par value; 300,000 shares authorized; 50,000 shares issued and outstanding	500,000
Retained earnings	90,000

Required:

Dividends have not been declared on the preferred stock for the years 1976 through 1980. What is the book value per share of common stock?

(AICPA adapted)

E–27–19 Selected information for 1979 for the Prince Company is as follows:

Cost of goods sold	$5,400,000
Average inventory	1,800,000
Net sales	7,200,000
Average receivables	960,000
Net income	720,000

Required:

If you assume that a business year consists of 360 days, what was the average number of days in the operating cycle for 1979?

(AICPA adapted)

E–27–20   The current asset section of the balance sheet for the years 1982 and 1983 follows:

	1983	1982
Cash	$ 40,000	$ 50,000
Accounts receivable	100,000	70,000
Inventories	400,000	410,000
Prepaid expenses	60,000	50,000
Total	$600,000	$580,000

Required:

1. Prepare a trend or horizontal analysis for 1983.
2. Prepare a percentage or vertical analysis for both 1982 and 1983.

Problems

P–27–1   The following financial statements relate to the Cape Construction Company for 1983:

CAPE CONSTRUCTION COMPANY
Balance Sheet (000)
December 31, 1983

Assets		*Equities*	
Cash	$ 100	Accounts payable	$ 220
A/R (net)	370	Notes payable (short-term)	300
Inventory	780	Bonds payable (12% due in 1995)	1,000
Fixed assets (net)	2,500	Preferred stock ($100 par; 8%	
Intangibles	40	cumulative)	500
Other assets	20	Common stock ($10 par; 100,000	
Total assets	$3,810	shares authorized, issued,	
		and outstanding)	1,000
		Retained earnings	790
			$3,810

CAPE CONSTRUCTION COMPANY
Income Statement
For Year Ended December 31, 1983

Net sales		$3,540,000
Beginning inventory	$ 700,000	
Purchase (net)	2,130,000	
Ending inventory	(780,000)	

Cost of sales		2,050,000
Gross profit		$1,490,000
Operating expense	$720,000	
Interest expense	120,000	840,000
Income before tax		$ 650,000
Income tax		260,000
Net income		$ 390,000

Assume $420 in A/R at the beginning of the year and a 365-day year. There are no preferred dividends in arrears, and the preferred stock has a liquidating value of $110 per share.

Required:

Calculate the following ratios:

a) Current.
b) Acid-test.
c) Receivables turnover.
d) Inventory turnover.
e) Asset turnover.
f) Days' sales in receivables.
g) Days' sales in inventory.
h) Number of days in the operating cycle.

P–27–2 Use the data from P–27–1 and calculate the following additional ratios:

a) Earnings per share.
b) Dividend payout ratio if $200,000 are paid to the common shareholders.
c) Sales profit margin.
d) Return on assets (use year-end figure).
e) Return on common equity.
f) Total debt to total assets.
g) Times interest earned.
h) Book value per share.

P–27–3 The following financial statements are from the L & S Corporation:

L & S CORPORATION
Income Statement
For Years Ended Dec. 31, 1983, and Dec. 31, 1982

(000)

	1983	1982
Sales (net)	$3,100	$2,800
Cost of goods sold	(2,500)	(2,330)
Gross profit	600	470
Operating expenses		
Selling expense	200	140
Administrative & other	50	20
Interest expense	150	150
Total expenses	400	310
Income before income tax	200	160
Income tax	(80)	(64)
Net income	$ 120	$ 96

L & S CORPORATION
Balance Sheets

(000)

	12-31-83	12-31-82
Assets		
Cash	$ 220	$ 200
Marketable securities	50	40
Accounts receivable	410	360
Inventories	830	850
Prepaid expenses	20	20
Total current assets	$1,530	$1,470
Property, plant, & equipment	2,450	2,400
Less: Accumulated depreciation	(670)	(650)
Net property, plant, & equipment	$1,780	$1,750
Intangible assets	190	200
Total assets	$3,500	$3,420
Equities		
Accounts payable	$ 450	$ 410
Note payable (short-term)	150	150
Total current liabilities	600	560
Bonds payable (10%)	1,500	1,500
Total liabilities	$2,100	$2,060
Common stock ($10 par; 100,000 shares issued and outstanding)	$1,000	$1,000
Additional paid-in capital—common	80	80
Retained earnings	320	280
Total stockholders' equity	$1,400	$1,360

Dividends of $80,000 were paid in 1983 and $60,000 in 1982 to the common shareholders.

Required:
Prepare common-sized financial statements for L & S Corporation for 1982 and 1983.

P–27–4 Use the data for the L & S Corporation in P–27–3 and prepare the following:
  a) A trend or horizontal analysis of the income statements for 1982 and 1983.
  b) A trend or horizontal analysis of the balance sheets for 1982 and 1983.
  c) A percentage or vertical analysis of the income statement and the balance sheet for 1983.

P–27–5 The Amidon Corporation provides the following selected data for the years 1982 and 1983:

	1983	1982
Inventory turnover	6	9
Earnings per share	$12	$10
Sales profit margin	10%	10%
Number of common shares	10,000	9,000
Price/earnings ratio	20	18
Gross profit margin	40%	40%
Income tax rate	40%	40%

In 1983 the beginning inventory was equal to 60% of the ending inventory.

Required:
For each year, 1982 and 1983, calculate the following items:
- **a)** Sales.
- **b)** Cost of goods sold.
- **c)** Net income.
- **d)** Gross profit.
- **e)** Operating expense.
- **f)** Income tax.
- **g)** Beginning inventory.
- **h)** Ending inventory.

P–27–6 Holmes Company has the following selected data for 1982:

Sales	$1,300,000, 80% on account
Gross profit margin	40%
Beginning inventory	$ 80,000
Ending inventory	60,000
Beginning balance, accounts receivable (net)	125,000
Ending balance, accounts receivable (net)	195,000
Net income before taxes	100,000
Income tax	26,250
Increase in retained earnings	33,750
Common shares outstanding	25,000
Price earnings ratio	12

Required:
1. Compute the inventory turnover.
2. Compute the receivables turnover.
3. Compute the dividend payout ratio.
4. Compute the market price per share.

P–27–7 Sumter Company's data for the years ended December 31, 1980, and 1981 are presented below:

SUMTER COMPANY
Comparative Balance Sheets

	1981	1980
Current Assets:		
Cash	$ 15,000	$ 30,000
Accounts receivable, net	135,000	60,000
Inventory	150,000	180,000
Total current assets	$300,000	$270,000
Plant and Equipment:		
Plant and equipment	525,000	450,000
Less: Accumulated depreciation	(105,000)	(75,000)
Net Plant & equipment	$420,000	$375,000
Intangible assets:		
patents	$ 37,500	$ 40,000
Total assets	$757,500	$685,000

Liabilities and stockholders' equity

Current liabilities

Accounts payable	$105,000	$ 60,000
Accrued liabilities	45,000	30,000
Taxes payable	10,000	18,000
Total current liabilities	$160,000	$108,000

Long-term liabilities:

Mortgage payable	50,000	60,000
Bonds payable	10,000	0
Total long-term liabilities	$ 60,000	$ 60,000
Total liabilities	$220,000	$168,000

Stockholders' equity

Common stock ($10 par)	$250,000	$250,000
Capital in excess of par	100,000	100,000
Retained earnings	187,500	167,000
Total stockholders' equity	$537,500	$517,000
Total liabilities and stockholders' equity	$757,500	$685,000

SUMTER COMPANY
Statement of Income
For the Year Ended December 31

	1981	1980
Sales	$2,430,000	$1,860,000
Cost of goods sold	1,675,000	1,085,000
Gross profit	$ 755,000	$775,000
Operating expenses	659,000	661,000
Net income before interest and taxes	$ 96,000	$114,000
Interest expense	6,000	6,000
Net income before taxes	$ 90,000	$108,000
Taxes	20,000	28,000
	$ 70,000	$80,000

Dividends are paid semiannually on June 23 and December 23. Annual dividends are $1.98. Market price per share is $54 as of December 31, 1981, and $60 as of December 31, 1980.

Required:

1. Compute the current ratio for 1980 and 1981.
2. Compute the acid-test ratio for both years.
3. Compute the inventory turnover for 1981.
4. Assuming that 80% of all sales are sold on account, compute the average collection period for 1981 using 360 days.
5. Compute the asset turnover for 1981.
6. Compute the price/earnings ratio for 1981.
7. Compute the dividend payout ratio for 1981.
8. Compute the sales profit margin for 1981.
9. Compute the return on assets for 1981.

P-27-8   Bones Corporation's 1975 partial data are presented below:

Assets	
Cash	$ 775,000
Accounts receivable	300,000
Inventory	?
Plant & equipment (net)	?
Total assets	$2,325,000

Liabilities and stockholders' equities	
Accounts payable (trade)	$ 325,000
Income taxes payable (current)	100,000
Long-term debt	?
Common stock	400,000
Retained earnings	?
	$2,325,000

Additional information is as follows:

Current ratio—3.2 to 1
Total debt to total assets—0.6
Inventory turnover based on cost of goods sold—12
Ending balance of inventory—same as beginning.
Gross profit margin—25% of sales

Required:
1. Compute the ending inventory.
2. Compute the plant & equipment balance.
3. Calculate the long-term debt.
4. Calculate retained earnings.
5. Compute sales.

P-27-9   Builders Incorporation's balance sheet for 1981 follows:

Current assets	
Cash	$ 100,000
Marketable securities	300,000
Accounts receivable	1,000,000
Inventories	6,400,000
Prepaid	400,000
Total current assets	$ 8,200,000
Property and plant, net	$ 3,900,000
Investments at equity	200,000
Goodwill and patents, net	500,000
Total assets	$12,800,000

Liabilities and stockholders' equity	
Current liabilities	
Notes payable	$ 200,000
Accounts payable	1,100,000
Accrued expenses	500,000
Income tax payable	300,000
Current portion of long-term debt	100,000

Total current liabilities	$ 2,200,000
Long-term debt	5,800,000
Total debt	$ 8,000,000
Stockholders' equity	
Capital stock, $4 par	1,000,000
Paid-in capital in excess of par	2,400,000
Retained earnings	1,400,000
Total stockholders' equity	$ 4,800,000
Total liabilities and stockholders' equity	$12,800,000

Required:

Prepare a common-sized balance sheet for 1981.

P–27–10   As the CPA responsible for an "opinion" audit engagement, you are requested by the client to organize the work to provide him at the earliest possible date with some key ratios based on the final figures appearing on the comparative financial statements. This information is to be used to convince creditors that the client business is solvent and to support the use of going-concern valuation procedures in the financial statements. The client wishes to save time by concentrating on only these key data. The data requested and the computations taken from the financial statements follow:

	Last Year	This Year
Current ratio	2.0:1	2.5:1
Quick (acid-test) ratio	1.2:1	0.7:1
Property, plant, and equipment to owners' equity	2.3:1	2.6:1
Sales to owners' equity	2.8:1	2.5:1
Net income	Down 10%	Up 30%
Earnings per common share	$2.40	$3.12
Book value per common share	Up 8%	Up 5%

Required:

1.   The client asks that you prepare a list of brief comments stating how each of these items supports the solvency and going-concern potential of his business. He wishes to use these comments to support his presentation of data to his creditors. You are to prepare the comments as requested, giving the implications and the limitations of each item separately and the collective inference one may draw from the items about the client's solvency and going-concern potential.

2.   Having done as the client requested in Part 1., prepare for this client a brief listing of additional ratio-analysis type data, which you think his creditors are going to ask for to supplement the data provided in Part 1. Explain why you think the additional data will be helpful to these creditors in evaluating this client's solvency.

3.   What warnings should you offer these creditors about the limitations of ratio analysis for the purpose stated here?

(AICPA adapted)

P–27–11   The Printing Company is listed on the New York Stock Exchange. The market value of its common stock was quoted at $10 per share at December 31, 1975, and 1974. Printing's balance sheet at December 31, 1975, and 1974, and its statement of income and retained earnings for the years then ended are presented below:

PRINTING COMPANY
Balance Sheet

	December 31,	
	1975	*1974*
Assets		
Current assets		
Cash	$ 3,500,000	$ 3,600,000
Marketable securities	13,000,000	11,000,000
Accounts receivable	105,000,000	95,000,000
Inventories	126,000,000	154,000,000
Prepaid expense	2,500,000	2,400,000
Total current assets	$250,000,000	$266,000,000
Property and plant, net	311,000,000	308,000,000
Investments, at equity	2,000,000	3,000,000
Long-term receivables	14,000,000	16,000,000
Goodwill and patents, net	6,000,000	6,500,000
Other assets	7,000,000	8,500,000
Total assets	$590,000,000	$608,000,000
Liabilities and Stockholders' Equity		
Current liabilities		
Notes payable	$ 5,000,000	$ 15,000,000
Accounts payable	38,000,000	48,000,000
Accrued expenses	24,500,000	27,000,000
Income taxes payable	1,000,000	1,000,000
Current portion of long-term debt	6,500,000	7,000,000
Total current liabilities	$ 75,000,000	$ 98,000,000
Long-term debt	$169,000,000	$180,000,000
Deferred income taxes	$ 74,000,000	$ 67,000,000
Other liabilities	$ 9,000,000	$ 8,000,000
Stockholders' equity		
Com. stock, $1 par value	$ 10,000,000	$ 10,000,000
5% cumulative preferred stock, par value		
$100 per share; $100 liquidating value	4,000,000	4,000,000
Additional paid-in capital	107,000,000	107,000,000
Retained earnings	142,000,000	134,000,000
Total stockholders' equity	$263,000,000	$255,000,000
Total liabilities and stockholders' equity	$590,000,000	$608,000,000

PRINTING COMPANY
Statement of Income
and Retained Earnings

Net sales	$600,000,000	$500,000,000
Costs and expenses		
Cost of goods sold	490,000,000	400,000,000
S, G, & A expense	66,000,000	60,000,000
Other, net	7,000,000	6,000,000

Total costs	$563,000,000	$466,000,000
Income before taxes	37,000,000	34,000,000
Income taxes	16,800,000	15,800,000
Net income	20,200,000	18,200,000
Beginning retained earnings	134,000,000	126,000,000
Common stock dividends	12,000,000	10,000,000
Preferred stock dividends	200,000	200,000
Ending retained earnings	$142,000,000	$134,000,000

Required:
Based on the information above, compute (for the year 1975 only) the following (show
supporting computations in good form):
   a) Current (working capital) ratio.
   b) Quick (acid-test) ratio.
   c) Number of days' sales in average receivables, assuming a business year consisting of 30 days and all sales on account.
   d) Inventory turnover.
   e) Book value per share of common stock.
   f) Earnings per share on common stock.
   g) Price/earnings ratio on common stock.
   h) Dividend payout ratio on common stock.

                                                          (AICPA adapted)

P–27–12 Missing Data Company has some missing data because of an inept bookkeeper.
Data salvaged include the following:

Inventory, January 1, 1981	$ 200,000
Cost of goods sold	2,325,000
Inventory turnover	15 times
Cash, December 31, 1981	$ 150,000
Average collection period for accounts receivable (based on 360 days)	25 days
Sales	$2,952,000 all credit
Interest expense	30,000
Income taxes (income tax rate 35% of net income before taxes)	45,500
Accounts receivable, January 1	110,000
Current ratio	2.4 to 1
Long-term debt	$ 500,000
Long-term investments	150,000
Marketable securities	0
Prepaid expenses	5,000
Common stock, ($40 par)	775,000

Required:
1. Compute current liabilities.
2. Compute the acid-test ratio.
3. Compute earnings per share.
4. If dividends equaled $2.00 a share, calculate the dividend payout ratio.
5. If the acid-test ratio were 1.3 for the prior year, indicate whether the ratio increased
or decreased, and give some possible reasons why.

P–27–13 The December 31, 1975, balance sheet of Ratio, Inc. is presented below. These
are the only accounts in Ratio's balance sheet. Amounts indicated by a question mark (?)

can be calculated from the additional information given.

Assets	
Cash	$ 25,000
Accounts receivable (net)	?
Inventory	?
Property, plant, and equipment (net)	294,000
	$432,000
Liabilities and stockholders' equity	
Accounts payable (trade)	?
Income taxes payable (current)	25,000
Long-term debt	?
Common stock	300,000
Retained earnings	?
	?

Additional information:

Current ratio (at year-end)	1.5 to 1
Total liabilities divided by total stockholders' equity	0.8
Inventory turnover based on sales and ending inventory	15 times
Inventory turnover based on cost of goods sold and ending inventory	10.5 times
Gross margin for 1975	$315,000

Required:
1. Determine the Dec. 31, 1975, balance in trade accounts payable.
2. Determine the Dec. 31, 1975, balance in retained earnings.
3. Determine the Dec. 31, 1975, balance in the inventory account.
4. Determine the long-term liabilities.

(AICPA adapted)

P–27–14   The following information pertains to the Brief Company:

BRIEF COMPANY
Balance Sheet
December 31, 1971

Assets	
Cash	$ 106,000
Accounts receivable	566,000
Inventories	320,000
Plant and equipment, net of depreciation	740,000
Patents	26,000
Other intangible assets	14,000
	$1,772,000
Liabilities and Equity	
Accounts payable	$ 170,000
Federal income tax payable	32,000
Miscellaneous accrued payables	38,000

Bonds payable (4%, due in 1992)	300,000
Preferred stock ($100 par; 7% cumulative, nonparticipating, and callable at $110)	200,000
Common stock (no par; 20,000 shares authorized, issued, and outstanding)	400,000
Retained earnings	720,000
Treasury stock—800 shares of preferred	(88,000)
	$1,772,000

BRIEF COMPANY
Income Statement
Year Ended December 31, 1971

Net sales	$1,500,000
Costs of goods sold	900,000
Gross margin on sales	$ 600,000
Operating expenses (including bond interest expense)	498,000
Income before federal income taxes	$ 102,000
Income tax expense	37,000
Net income	$ 65,000

Additional information is as follows:

There are no preferred dividends in arrears, and the balances in the accounts receivable and inventory accounts are unchanged from January 1, 1971. There were no changes in the bonds payable, preferred stock, or common stock accounts during 1971.

Required:

Calculate the following:

a) Current ratio.
b) Times bond interest was earned.
c) Times bond interest and preferred dividends were earned.
d) Average days sales in ending inventories (365 days).
e) Average number of days in the operating cycle (365 days).
f) Book value per share of common stock.
g) Ratio of total debt to total equity.

P–27–15 The following balance sheet and income statement are available for the Jensen Manufacturing Company.

JENSEN MANUFACTURING COMPANY
Comparative Income Statements
For Years Ended Dec. 31, 1982, and 1983

	(000)	
	1983	1982
Sales	$10,500	$9,800
Cost of goods sold	4,200	4,900
Gross profit	$ 6,300	$4,900
Operating expenses	2,400	1,700
Income before interest and tax	$ 3,900	$3,200
Interest expense	1,100	1,200

Income before tax	$ 2,800	$2,000
Income tax	1,240	800
Net income	$ 1,560	$1,200

JENSEN MANUFACTURING COMPANY
Balance Sheet

(000)

	1983	1982
Assets		
Cash	$ 1,100	$ 3,900
A/R (net)	1,500	2,800
Inventories	9,000	6,000
Fixed assets (net)	11,500	8,500
Intangible assets	1,540	800
Total assets	$24,640	$22,000
Liabilities		
Accounts and notes payable	$ 5,000	$ 3,600
Income tax payable	800	400
Bonds payable (18%)	6,000	6,000
Total liabilities	$11,800	$10,000
Stockholders' Equity		
Preferred stock ($50 par; 8%; 80,000 shares outstanding)	$ 4,000	$ 4,000
Common stock ($30 par; 150,000 shares authorized; 100,000 outstanding)	3,000	3,000
Paid-in capital on common	4,000	4,000
Retained earnings	1,840	1,000
Total stockholders' equity	$12,840	$12,000
Total liabilities and equity	$24,640	$22,000

Required:

Calculate the following ratios and other information for 1983:

    a) Current ratio.

    b) Acid-test ratio.

    c) Inventory turnover.

    d) Receivables turnover.

    e) Asset turnover

    f) Earnings per share.

    g) Dividends paid to common and to preferred.

    h) Sales profit margin.

    i) Return on investment (ROI).

    j) Return on common equity.

    k) Total debt to total assets.

    l) Times interest earned.

    m) Book value per common share.

P–27–16 Use the information from Problem 27–15.

Required:

1. Prepare a trend or horizontal analysis for the income statement data.
2. Prepare a trend or horizontal analysis for the balance sheet data.

P–27–17 Again, use the information from Problem 27–15.

Required:

1. Prepare a percentage or vertical analysis of the income statement for the years 1982 and 1983.

2. Repeat Part 1 for the balance sheet data.

P–27–18 Using the data from Problem 27–15, prepare a common-sized income statement and balance sheet for 1982 and 1983.

Glossary

Abandonment Occurs when an asset is thrown away or sold for scrap.

Accelerated Cost Recovery System A depreciation method established in the Economic-Recovery Tax Act of 1981. It is a system for depreciating assets on an accelerated basis over predetermined recovery periods.

Accounting Control The plan of organization, procedures, and records regarding the safeguarding of assets and the reliability of financial records.

Accounting Principles Board (APB) Board that established accounting principles from 1959 to 1973. The Board was part of the American Institute of Certified Public Accountants.

Accounts Payable Monies owed to the enterprise's suppliers or vendors for the purchase of goods or services.

Accrued Benefit Cost Method The actuarial cost method in which the amount assigned to the current year usually represents the present value of the increase in present employees' retirement benefits resulting from that year's service.

Accumulated Deficit (or Deficit) The amount by which net losses have exceeded net incomes; a debit balance in retained earnings.

Accumulated Depreciation The total of all prior allocations of the cost of tangible assets reported in the property, plant, and equipment category.

Acid-Test Ratio Current assets minus inventories and prepaid items, all divided by current liabilities.

Activity Measures Ratios used to measure efficiency in using the firm's assets.

Actuarial Assumptions Assumptions relating to interest rates, employee turnover, life expectancy, salary increases, and so forth, that are used to determine pension costs.

Actuarial Gain or Loss Gain or loss that results from changes in actuarial assumptions.

Additions Expansions or enlargements of existing assets.

Adjusting Journal Entries Making journal entries at financial statement preparation dates to adjust the records to reflect revenues earned and expenses incurred.

Administrative Control The decision-making processes leading to management's authorization of transactions.

Age of Receivables The length of time receivables have been outstanding.

Aggregate Cost The summation of costs of individual securities included in either the current and the noncurrent portfolios of marketable securities.

Aggregate Market The summation of fair values of individual securities included in either the current and noncurrent portfolios of marketable securities.

Aging Schedule A presentation of accounts receivables according to their length of time outstanding.

All-Inclusive Concept An approach to income measurement whereby no distinction is made between operating and nonoperating revenues and expenses. Even prior period adjustments and corrections of errors would constitute determinants of income under the purest form of this concept.

Allowance for Uncollectible Accounts (Allowance for Bad Debts) A contra-receivable account that reduces net accounts receivable by the estimated loss from bad debts.

Allowance Method A method used to account for bad debts that estimates uncollectables at each balance sheet date.

American Institute of Certified Public Accountants (AICPA) A national organization of CPAs.

Amortization The process of writing off the cost of an intangible asset to the periods benefited.

Amount of a Single Sum (Future Value of a Single Sum) The amount to which an investment today will accumulate given a specified interest rate and period of time.

Annuity A series of equal payments (receipts) at a regular interval.

Annuity Due An annuity whose payments (receipts) are made at the beginning of each period.

Articles of Incorporation (Corporate Charter) The rules and guidelines under which the corporation will transact its business.

Asserted Claims Legal claims that actually have been made against the company.

Assets All of the rights and possessions of the firm as of the balance sheet date.

Assignment with Recourse The transfer of receivables to a third party with the option that the third party may return the receivables in the event they prove uncollectable.

Average Cost An inventory valuation method in which the costs of all the merchandise on hand are valued at an average cost, and the value attached to the units sold is at the average cost figure.

Balance Sheet A statement of financial position at a particular point in time.

Banker's Rule Uses 365 days in interest computations.

Bank Reconciliation The reconciliation of bank balances and book balances for a given month.

Bargain Purchase Option An option that gives the lessee the right to purchase the leased property for an amount significantly less than the estimated fair value of the property at the date the option becomes exercisable.

Bargain Renewal Option An option that gives the lessee the right to renew the lease for a rental significantly less than the fair rental of the property at the date the option becomes exercisable.

Base Stock The normal or base amount of goods that should be maintained in inventory at all times.

Base Year The year of initial adoption of the LIFO method.

Bearer or Coupon Bonds These bonds are not registered in the name of the holder but are negotiable by whoever holds them. In order to receive an interest payment, the current holder simply clips off a coupon and redeems it at an authorized bank.

Bond A type of insurance purchased by a company as protection against losses incurred through employee theft.

Bond A written agreement between a borrower and a lender in which the borrower agrees to repay a stated sum and to make periodic interest payments at specified dates.

Bond Issue Costs Those costs related to issuing a bond, including the costs of printing and engraving and legal and accounting fees. Should be accounted for separately as a deferred charge and amortized over the life of the bond.

Bonds with Detachable Stock Warrants Bonds that have attached stock warrants that can be separated from the bond and used to purchase common stock at a specific price.

Book Value Method A method of recording bond conversions in which the capital stock issued is valued at the book value of the bonds converted.

Book Value Per Share Common stockholders' equity divided by outstanding common shares.

Branch Accounts Accounts set up for different geographic locations.

Callable Preferred Stock Preferred stock with a provision that allows the issuing corporation to call or retire the stock at a predetermined price.

Capital Expenditure An expenditure that will benefit both current and future periods.

Capital Stock Account The amount of *legal value*, usually referred to as *par value*, for the stock issued.

Capital Stock Shares The certificates representing ownership rights in an incorporated business; the term applies to common and preferred stocks.

Cash Coin and currency and unrestricted funds on deposit with a bank. Also includes negotiable instruments on hand, such as certified checks, money orders, cashiers checks, and personal checks.

Cash-Clearing Account A type of branch account for the deposit and receipt of cash.

Cash Discounts A discount offered to encourage customers to pay their obligations promptly.

Cash Dividend A distribution of cash paid out of unrestricted capital to the shareholders of a corporation.

Cash Flow Per Share Net income plus noncash charges divided by outstanding common shares.

Cash Over or Short An account that allows for the adjustment of cash on hand and the imprest amount.

Ceiling Upper bound on lower of cost or market, the net realizable value.

Certificates of Deposit A type of investment

instrument that allows for early withdrawal only by assessing a penalty.

Change in Accounting Estimate A change caused by the revision of an estimate used in accounting measurements.

Change in Accounting Principle A change that occurs any time a reporting entity changes from one generally accepted accounting principle to another generally accepted accounting principle.

Change in Reporting Entity The type of change that occurs when the reporting entity changes from one period to the next.

Classified Balance Sheet A presentation of the major groupings, assets, liabilities, and owners' equity that usually is subdivided into smaller groups for more informative presentation.

Closing the Books A process that transfers undistributed income to stockholders' equity accounts and establishes a zero balance in all nominal accounts.

Common Size Statement A statement that is a variation of vertical analysis in which only the percentages, not the dollar amounts, are shown.

Common Stock The class of stock that represents the residual claim to assets after creditors and preferred stock claims have been satisfied.

Common Stock Equivalent A security that, in substance, is equivalent to common stock, based on its terms or the circumstances under which it was issued.

Comparability Principle States that since economic decisions are nothing more than a selection of one of a number of available alternatives, financial statements must facilitate the comparison of the various alternatives.

Compensated Absences Certain accrued fringe benefits of employment, such as vacation, sick, and holiday pay.

Compensating Balances A minimum balance required to be maintained as part of a loan agreement.

Completed Contract Method A method of profit recognition for long-term construction contracts in which the gross profit recognition is delayed until the contract is completed fully.

Complex Capital Structure A corporation that has issued, in addition to common stock, securities that have a dilutive effect on earnings per share.

Composite Depreciation A depreciation method that groups together dissimilar assets and depreciates them as one unit.

Compound Interest Interest is computed on the principal plus any previously accrued unpaid interest.

Comprehensive Income Tax Allocation Under comprehensive allocation the income tax expense for the current period includes the tax effects of all transactions—recurring and non-recurring —entering into the determination of pretax accounting income for the period, even though some transactions may affect the determination of taxable income in a different period.

Conservatism Dictates that given two alternative methods of presenting an economic event, each being of equal theoretical and logical validity, the one that results in the lowest reported levels of net income and/or net assets should be selected.

Consignment of Merchandise A marketing arrangement in which goods are given to a third party to sell, and the consignor retains title until the goods are sold.

Consolidated Financial Statements A financial statement that reflects income, financial position, and changes in financial position of legally separate entities as they would appear if they were one entity.

Constant Value An assumption in accounting that disregards the changing value of money over time.

Contingent Issues Agreements to issue additional common stock based upon some future event.

Contingent Rentals The increases or decreases in lease payments that result from changes, occurring after the inception of the lease, in the factors (other than the passage of time) on which lease payments are based, except that any escalation of minimum lease payments relating to increases in construction or acquisition cost of the leased property or to increases in some measure of cost or value during the construction or preconstruction period shall be excluded from contingent rentals.

Contributed Capital Represents the total assets contributed to the firm by its owners.

Contributory Pension Plan A plan in which the employees as well as the employer make contributions.

Control Account Summarizes a substantial activity that requires segregation into smaller units (subsidiary accounts).

Controlling Interest Generally, ownership of more than 50% of the outstanding shares of another entity gives the investor the ability to control the entity (consolidated financial statements are generally appropriate).

Conversion Cost Cost of converting the raw materials and labor into finished products in the manufacturing process.

Convertible Bonds A type of bond that allows the holder to convert the debt security into common stock.

Convertible Debt Debt securities that may be converted into capital stock at a specified future date.

Convertible Preferred Stock Preferred stock with a right that allows the shareholder to exchange that stock for some other security at a specified conversion ratio.

Copyright A right granted by the federal government to creators of literary, musical, and other artistic works giving the creator the exclusive right to control the reproduction, sale, or other use of the copyrighted work.

Corporation A separate legal entity that is created under the laws of the state of incorporation.

Cost Depletion Depletion based on the cost of an asset and determined on a unit-of-production basis.

Cost Method—Investments An approach to accounting for investments in stock of another company whereby the investment is reflected at acquisition cost, and only dividends declared are considered revenue.

Cost Method—Treasury Stock The method of accounting that records treasury stock at its cost of acquisition.

Cost of Goods Manufactured Cost of merchandise transferred from work-in-process to finished goods.

Cost of Goods Sold The total cost attributed to goods sold in a particular period.

Cost/Benefit Constraint The total cost of gathering information must be compared to the benefit to be derived from its dissemination.

Credits Increases liabilities, stockholders' equity, and revenues accounts and decreases asset and expense accounts.

Cumulative Restatement Requires that the entire effect of an accounting change be reported in the current period as a separate item of gain or loss.

Cumulative Right The right of preferred stock to accumulate unpaid dividends yearly; such dividends must be paid before any dividends can be paid to common stockholders.

Current Assets Cash and noncash assets that reasonably can be expected to be converted into cash or be consumed within one year.

Current Cost The cost equal to the current replacement cost of the assets owned, adjusted for the value of any operating advantages or disadvantages of the asset owned.

Current Cost Net Income Traditional net income plus or minus unrealized holding gains or losses.

Current Cost Operating Margin Sales less operating expenses, calculated on a current cost basis.

Current Cost/Constant Dollar Financial statements that adjust for both general price-level changes and specific price-level changes.

Current Cost/Nominal Dollar Financial statements that reflect changes in the value of individual assets but are not adjusted for changes in the general price level.

Current Liabilities Obligations that are expected to be satisfied either through the use of existing current assets or by creation of other current liabilities.

Current Maturities of Long-Term Debt Those portions of long-term liabilities that are payable within one year of the balance sheet date.

Current Operating Concept An approach to income measurement whereby only ordinary, normal, and recurring operations for the period are included in income.

Current Ratio Current assets divided by current liabilities.

Date of Declaration The date on which the board of directors authorizes a dividend distribution; a liability to pay the dividend is incurred on this date.

Date of Record The date on which a person must be listed as a stockholder to receive a dividend that has been declared.

Debentures Unsecured bonds secured only by the general credit rating of the company.

Debits An increase in assets or expenses and a decrease in liability, equity, and revenue accounts.

Debt/Equity Ratio Total debt divided by total assets.

Deferral Method A method of accounting for the investment credit that treats the credit as a reduction in the cost of the asset or a reduction in income tax expense over the life of the asset purchased.

Deferred Annuity An annuity that starts after a specified time period.

Deferred Cost A cost that is incurred and paid in the current period, but in some way relates to future periods.

Deferred Method of Income Tax Allocation Under this method the tax effects of current timing differences are deferred currently and allocated to the income tax of future periods when the differences reverse. The debit or credit to the deferred tax account is determined on the basis of the tax rates in effect at the time the differences originate and is not adjusted for any subsequent tax rate changes.

Defined Benefit Plans Pension plans that have a specified formula for computing pension benefits.

Defined Contribution Plans Pension plans that have a specified formula for computing pension contributions.

Depletion The allocation of the cost of a natural resource to the periods benefited.

Depreciable Cost The cost of the asset less its salvage value.

Depreciation Allocation of the cost of an asset to the periods benefited.

Detachable Warrants Stock purchase warrants that may be separated from the debt instrument to which they are attached and exercised.

Development Activities The translation of research findings or other knowledge into a plan or design for a new product or process, or for a significant improvement of an existing product or process whether intended for sale or use.

Dilutive Debt Securities Securities that allow the holder to ultimately gain an equity position, thus diluting the ownership interest of current equity holders. Included are convertible bonds and bonds with detachable stock warrants.

Dilutive Securities Those securities that will cause income per share to decrease or loss per share to increase.

Direct Financing Lease A capital lease that does not give rise to manufacturer or dealer profit (or loss). The fair value of the property at the inception of the lease equals the cost or carrying value of the property.

Direct Labor Labor cost incurred by the person(s) working directly on a product being manufactured.

Direct Write-off Method A method used to account for bad debts that makes no adjustment until a receivable proves to be uncollectable.

Discontinued Operations A separate major line of business or a separate major class of customer that has been sold, abandoned, or otherwise segregated from entity operations.

Discount The amount received below face value when issuing a bond to yield more than the face (coupon) rate of interest.

Discounted Present Value Concept of Income Measures income as the difference between the present value of the company at the beginning and end of the year.

Discounting a Future Sum Determining the present value of a future amount given a specified interest rate.

Discount of Notes Receivable The sale of notes receivable to a third party with or without recourse.

Discount on Capital Stock The amount by which the issue price of the stock is below the par or stated value.

Discovery Value A drastic increase in the value of an asset caused by the discovery of some unknown positive characteristic of the asset.

Discussion Memorandum An outline of the fundamental issues inherent in the topic addressed by the FASB; invites input for any individual or organization interested in the topic.

Disposal Date Applicable to discontinued operations, the disposal date is the date on which operations cease if disposal is through abandonment, or the date of the sale if disposal is through sale.

Dividend Payout Ratio Dividend per share divided by earnings per share.

Dividends in Arrears Those dividends that were not declared on cumulative preferred stock. Although the accumulation is not a liability of the corporation, it must be paid before any dividends can be declared on common stock.

Dollar-Value LIFO A LIFO inventory method that uses dollars of inventory, specific price indexes, and broad inventory pools instead of physical units.

Dollar-Value Retail LIFO An inventory valuation technique that combines the dollar-value LIFO method and the retail method.

Donated Stock Reacquired shares that have all the characteristics of treasury stock, except that the corporation obtained them free of charge from the stockholder.

Double-Declining-Balance Method A method of depreciation in which an asset is depreciated by multiplying the book value of the asset by twice the straight-line write-off rate.

Early Extinguishment of Debt Early extinguishment of debt occurs when debt is retired before its maturity date. It can be the result of call provisions, repurchase on the open market, or refunding through the proceeds from a new issue.

Earned Capital Capital resulting from reinvestment of the company's prior earnings.

Earnings Per Share A financial ratio that expresses the amount of earnings available to each share of common stock outstanding.

Earnings/Price Ratio (E/P Ratio) Earnings per share divided by market price per share.

Employee Retirement Income Security Act of 1974 (ERISA) A federal act that set participation, vesting, and funding requirements.

Equity in Entity Earnings Based on the investor's percentage of ownership in the investee's stock, the equity in entity earnings represents the measure of investee earnings attributable to the investor's ownership shares (used when the investor has the ability at least to exercise significant influence over the investee).

Equity Method An approach to accounting for investments in stock of another company whereby a proportionate share of the earnings of the other company is included in the carrying value of the investment and earnings of the investor.

Estimated Economic Life of Leased Property The estimated remaining period during which the property, with normal repairs and maintenance, is expected to be economically usable by one or more users for the purpose for which it was intended at the inception of the lease, without limitation by the lease term.

Estimated Residual Value of Leased Property The estimated fair value of the property at the end of the lease term.

Exchange Transaction The transfer of value between two or more parties.

Ex-Dividend Date The date after which all subsequent holders of stock will not receive a previously declared dividend.

Executory Agreements Promises of two enterprises to perform future services for future payments.

Expense The cost of a good or service used up in the generation of revenue (an expired cost).

Exposure Draft Issued by the FASB, it is a summary of the Board's initial position on the issue in question and invites further comment with respect to this position.

Extraordinary Item A gain or loss that is unusual in nature and infrequent in occurrence given the environment in which the entity operates.

Face Value (Par Value) The denomination or the principal amount of the bond.

Factoring A process by which accounts receivable are sold to and collected by a third party for a fee.

Factory Overhead All factory costs incurred except the costs of direct material and direct labor.

Fair Market Value The normal cash selling price of an asset in an arm's-length transaction.

Fair Value of the Leased Property The price for which the leased property could be sold in an arm's-length transaction between unrelated parties.

Financial Accounting Standards Board (FASB) A seven-member body charged with supervising the development of GAAP. The board has been establishing accounting principles since 1973.

Financial Position The status of an enterprise's assets and claims to those assets at a specific point in time.

Financing Activity That aspect of a transaction that results in an inflow of financial resources.

Finished Goods Inventories Completed products of the manufacturing process that are being held for sale.

First-In, First-Out (FIFO) An inventory valuation method in which the first cost elements introduced into the system are also the first cost elements transferred out of the system.

Fixed Assets (Property, Plant, and Equipment) Tangible long-lived assets used in the operations of the business.

Fixed - Percentage - on - Declining - Balance Method A depreciation method in which an asset is depreciated by multiplying a fixed percentage times the book value of the asset.

Floor Lower bound on lower of cost or market, net realizable value less normal profit margin.

Flow-Through Method A method of accounting for the investment credit that treats the credit as a reduction in income taxes in the year in which the asset is purchased.

F.O.B. Destination Shipping term in which the title passes to the buyer when the buyer receives the goods from the common carrier.

F.O.B. Shipping Point Shipping term in which the title passes to the buyer at the time the goods are delivered to the common carrier.

Franchise An agreement in which the franchisor grants to the franchisee the right to provide certain services or sell certain products.

Full Cost Method A method of oil and gas accounting that capitalizes the cost of both successful and unsuccessful wells.

Full Disclosure Disclosing of all significant

events and financial data that could have a significant effect on decisions.

Fully Diluted Earnings Per Share Computations EPS computations that include common stock, common stock equivalents, and any other potentially dilutive securities.

Fund Retirement plan assets maintained by the funding agency.

Funded Pension Plan A plan that has a funding agency.

Funding Cash payments made by an employer into a retirement plan.

Funding Agency An organization separate from an employer that receives pension payments, invests pension assets, and disburses payments to retired employees.

Future Value of an Annuity The worth of a series of payments (receipts) taken to a future date.

Future Value of a Single Sum The worth of a current amount taken to a stated future period.

Gain Contingency An existing condition, situation, or set of circumstances, the outcome of which is uncertain, that could result in a gain to the company.

Gains Excess of revenues over expenses from a specific transaction (used most often in the context of transactions outside the normal course of business).

General Cash Account Account that ultimately handles most cash receipts and disbursements.

Generally Accepted Accounting Principles (GAAP) The fundamental body of practical accounting knowledge, procedures, and techniques.

General Price Level Changes Changes in the value of the dollar, measured in terms of its ability to purchase a variety of goods and services.

Going Concern Assumption The assumption that an entity will survive and continue to pursue its business purpose.

Goodwill The excess cost of an acquired entity over the current fair value of the entity's net assets.

Grant Date The date a stock option or stock purchase right is granted to an employee.

Gross Change Method of Computing Deferred Taxes Under this method separate computations are made for the tax effects of originating differences at current tax rates and for reversing differences at tax rates at the time of their origination.

Gross Method The method by which sales or purchases are recorded without considering cash discounts.

Gross Profit Margin Gross profit divided by net sales.

Gross Profit Method A method for estimating inventory value based on the rate of gross profit on sales.

Group Depreciation A depreciation method that groups similar assets together and depreciates them as one unit.

Group-of-Similar-Items Basis Under this basis all similar items are grouped, and deferred taxes are determined for the group.

Historical Cost Measured on the date of acquisition; includes the cash or cash equivalent price of obtaining the asset and getting it ready for its intended use.

Historical Cost Principle States that historical cost, once measured in an arms-length transaction, is the best continuing measure of the economic value derived from a given transaction.

Historical Cost/Constant Dollars Financial statements that follow the traditional approach of historical cost except that adjustments are made for general price-level changes.

Historical Cost/Nominal Dollar Characteristic of traditional financial statements; assets and liabilities are recorded and maintained at historical cost with dollar amounts combined from year to year without adjustment for changes in the purchasing power of the dollar.

Holding Gains (Losses) Increase (decreases) in the value of an asset currently owned.

Horizontal Analysis An analysis that indicates the proportionate change over a period of time in a financial statement item.

Impairment A drastic decrease in the value of an asset caused by the discovery of some previously unknown negative characteristic of the asset.

Imprest Accounts Accounts set up to handle routine transactions; accounts have fixed maximum balance.

Improvement A repair involving the substitution of a new, superior part for an old part.

Imputed Interest Rate An estimated interest rate that recognizes the cost of borrowing to the borrower.

Inadequacy Obsolescence of an asset caused by a firm's needs outgrowing the asset's capabilities.

Inception of the Lease The date of the lease agreement or commitment, if earlier.

Income Excess of revenues and gains over expenses and losses for a time period (net income).

Income Bonds Bonds with variable interest payments that depend on the issuers' operating income.

Income from Continuing Operations All revenues less all expenses except for the following: discontinued operations, extraordinary items, and the cumulative effect of accounting changes.

Income Statement A statement of operations; a representation of the results of the firm's operations over a period of time.

Incremental Method A means of allocating the proceeds from the issuance of securities in a package. They are allocated first to the securities with a known fair market value; then the residual amount is allocated to the securities with no known market value.

Individual Item Basis An income tax deferral method that treats each originating difference and its subsequent reversing differences as a distinct item from other timing differences.

Initial Direct Cost Those costs incurred by the lessor that are directly associated with negotiating and consummating completed leasing transactions.

Installment Accounting Method A method in which the revenues, costs, and profits inherent in a given transaction are recognized only as cash payments are received.

Installment Sale A sale in which payment for merchandise is spread over a long period of time. Title remains with the seller.

Intangible Assets Long-lived assets such as patents or copyrights that lack physical substance and are acquired for purposes of operations rather than investment.

Interaccount Transfers The transfer of money from one account to another in a system of multiple checking accounts.

Interest The cost for (or income from) the use of funds over time.

Interfirm Comparability The comparability of the financial statements of different entities in the same industry.

Interim Reports Financial statements issued between year-end financial statements.

Interindustry Comparability The comparability of the financial statements of firms in different industries.

Internal Control All of the measures taken to safeguard cash and other assets.

Interperiod Income Tax Allocation The process of apportioning income taxes among periods to insure the proper matching of income and expenses.

Intrafirm Comparability The comparability of a firm's financial statements from year to year.

Inventory Assets held by the business either for future sale in the ordinary course of business or for use in the production of goods or services for future sale.

Inventory Depreciation Method A depreciation method used when there is an asset made up of numerous small items. Depreciation is the asset book value at the beginning of the year less the asset's appraisal value at the end of the year.

Inventory Pool Units in inventory that have the same function and are treated the same way in LIFO valuation methods.

Inventory Turnover Cost of goods sold divided by average inventory.

Investee A company whose stock is owned by another entity.

Investing Activity That aspect of a transaction that results in an outflow of financial resources.

Investment Credit A tax credit established to stimulate investment in capital goods. The credit is based on the purchase price of qualified investments.

Investor The owner of securities of another entity.

Involuntary Conversion Disposal of an asset due to acts of God or government condemnation.

Journal A chronological record of all of the economic transactions in which the firm has engaged.

Last-In, First-Out (LIFO) An inventory valuation method in which the most recent cost elements introduced into the system are the first costs used or transferred out of the system.

Lease A contractual agreement between a lessor and a lessee that provides the lessee the right to use the property for a specified time period in return for designated cash payments to be made to the lessor over the terms of the lease.

Lease-Term The number of years the lease is in effect.

Legal Capital A portion of owner's equity, determined according to state law, that must be maintained for the protection of creditors. Generally it is the par or stated value of shares outstanding.

Lessee's Incremental Borrowing Rate The rate that, at the inception of the lease, the lessee would have incurred to borrow, over a similar term, the funds necessary to purchase the leased property.

Leverage Using equity to borrow money to be invested at a return greater than the interest rate, thereby increasing the return to the equity holders.

Leveraged Lease A three-party lease agreement involving a lessee, a lessor, and a long-term creditor.

Liabilities Obligations to transfer economic resources to another entity resulting from past transactions of the enterprise.

Liability Method of Income Tax Allocation This method measures taxes at the amount that ultimately will be paid in future periods. Therefore, the tax liability or prepaid taxes are computed at the tax rate expected to be in effect in the period they reverse.

Liquidating Dividend A dividend paid out of capital contributed by the stockholders rather than out of earnings.

Liquidation of LIFO Layer A temporary or permanent reduction of an inventory layer in a LIFO system.

Liquidity Measures Ratios that measure the firm's ability to pay its current debts.

Lockbox Service A special service performed by financial institutions for the receipt and deposit of cash.

Long-Term Asset An asset expected to benefit the operations of the company for more than one year.

Long-Term Investments Investments that are not used in the operation of the firm and are to be held longer than the current year or operating cycle.

Long-Term Liabilities Those obligations of an enterprise that are due in more than one year or the operating cycle, if longer. Examples include mortgages payable, bonds payable, and long-term notes payable.

Loss Carryback and Loss Carryforward Under current tax law, the current period's losses can be carried back three years to offset prior years' income and/or carried forward 15 years to offset future years' income.

Loss Contingency An existing condition, situation, or set of circumstances, the outcome of which is uncertain, that could result in a loss to the company.

Losses Excess of expenses over revenues from a specific transaction (used most often in the context of transactions outside the normal course of business).

Lower of Cost or Market (LCM)—Inventory An inventory valuation method in which the inventory value is written down to lower of cost or market if the market value has declined below cost.

Lower of Cost or Market Method—Investments The currently required method of accounting for stock investments in which the investor does not have at least the ability to exercise significant influence over the investee. The method results in the recognition of unrealized losses on the valuation of marketable securities in the aggregate.

Lump Sum Purchase A purchase involving more than the purchase of a single asset.

Machine-Readable Account Codes A technological innovation that has reduced bank errors by allowing deposits and withdrawals to be read by computer.

Maintenance The cost of recurring service on an asset, such as cleaning and lubrication.

Major Repairs Repairs involving significant dollar amounts that are expected to benefit more than one period.

Mandatory Redemption A restriction on preferred stock that requires that the stock be redeemed, or retired, at a specified date.

Manufacturing Costs Direct material, direct labor, and factory overhead costs that are incurred in the manufacturing process.

Markdown A decrease in the sales price below the original sales price.

Markdown Cancellation Cancellation of part or all of the markdown.

Marketable Securities Securities (stocks and bonds) of other companies owned by the entity that can be sold readily on the stock exchanges or in the over-the-counter market. The entity plans to sell these securities as cash is needed.

Market Value Income Income measured as the difference in the market value of the firm at the beginning and end of the year, adjusted for additional investments and withdrawals.

Market Value Method A method of recording bond conversions in which the capital stock issued is recorded at its market value.

Markup The amount by which the original sales price exceeds the cost. Also referred to as mark-on.

Markup Cancellation The cancellation of all or part of the additional markup.

Matching Principle States that expenses associated with the process of producing revenues should be reported in the period in which those revenues are recognized.

Materiality The concept that information is only worthy of accumulation and disclosure if this information is significant to the economic entity.

Maturity Date The date on which the principal payment is due.

Maturity Value The denomination or the principal of the bond.

Measurement Date—Discontinued Operations The date on which management adopts a formal plan to dispose of a separate major line of business or separate major class of customer.

Measurement Date—Stock Options The date under a stock option plan when the employee has been given a stock option, and both the number of shares and the option price are known.

Measures of Financial Stability Ratios that attempt to measure the long-term solvency and stability of the company.

Merchandise Inventory Inventory held for sale in a merchandising company.

Merchandise on Consignment A third party (consignee) holds merchandise for the owner (consignor) for the purpose of selling it to a buyer.

Merchant's Rule Uses 360 days in interest computations.

Minimum Lease Payments (Lessee) Payments the lessee is obligated to make or can be required to make plus the payment stipulated in any bargain purchase option.

Minimum Lease Payments (Lessor) These payments are the same as those of the lessee except that any guarantee of the residual value or of rental payments beyond the lease term by a third party unrelated to either the lessee or lessor must be added, provided the third party is financially capable of discharging the obligation that may arise as a result of the guarantee.

Modified Treasury Stock Method Similar to the treasury stock method except that under the modified method a maximum of 20% of the outstanding shares can be assumed to be repurchased. Additional proceeds from exercise are assumed to reduce debt.

Monetary Asset An asset, such as cash or receivables, whose value generally does not change.

Monetary Liabilities Those obligations payable in fixed amounts of dollars.

Mortality Tables Tables from which estimates of age at death are made.

Mortgage Bonds Bonds that are secured by

collateral or some specified assets of the borrower.

Mortgage Payable A promissory note secured by an asset whose title is pledged to the lender.

Multiple Trade Discount A type of discount in which two or more consecutive percentage discounts are given on the list price of an item.

Multiple-Step Income Statement An income statement with revenues and expenses classified in several different categories.

Net Change Method Under this method the originating and reversing differences are netted, and the current tax rate is applied to calculate the change in the deferred tax account.

Net Markdown The difference between the total markdown and the total markdown cancellations.

Net Markup The difference between the total additional markup and the total markup cancellations.

Net Method The method in which accounts receivables or accounts payable are recorded net of cash discounts.

Net-of-Tax Method of Income Tax Allocation Under this method the tax effects of timing differences are recognized in the valuation of the respective asset or liability account.

Net Realizable Value The net cash expected from the disposal of an asset or the collection of a receivable.

Neutrality Accounting information is neutral when the format of the information's presentation has no effect on the decision being made.

Nominal Interest Rate The stated rate of interest specified on the bond.

Noncontributory Plan Plan in which only the employer makes contributions.

Noncumulative Preferred Stock Stock that does not have the right to past dividends that have not been declared.

Nonmonetary Asset An asset whose price or value in terms of a monetary unit may change over time.

Nonmonetary Liabilities Those liabilities that do not represent claims against the company that are fixed as to a sum certain in cash.

Nonparticipating A restriction on the amount of dividends paid to preferred stockholders by not allowing participation in the distribution of dividends above a stated dividend amount or rate.

Nonreciprocal Transfer A transaction that involves the transfer of a donated asset.

Non-Trade Receivables Receivables that arise from transactions with employees, officers, or affiliates.

No-Par Stock Capital stock that is issued without a par value. Usually no-par stock will have a stated value that essentially establishes the minimum legal capital amount.

Normal Pension Costs The yearly costs of providing pension benefits for any year after the adoption of the plan.

Notes Receivable Distinguishable from other receivables due to a formal written promise to document the receivable.

Notes Receivable Discounted A contra account to notes receivable used for notes that have been discounted with recourse.

Obsolescence A decrease in the value of an asset caused by economic rather than use factors.

Operating Expenses The selling, general, and administrative expenses of operating a company.

Operating Revenues Revenues derived from selling goods or rendering services.

Ordinary Annuity An annuity whose payments (receipts) are made at the end of each period.

Ordinary Repairs A recurring repair expense, such as minor repairs.

Organization Costs Costs incurred in and directly associated with the formation of a business.

Originating Difference The initial difference between taxable income and financial income due to a particular timing difference.

Other Assets Assets that can't be classified into one of the other asset categories on the balance sheet.

Other Liabilities Liabilities that cannot be classified as current or long-term liabilities.

Other Revenue and Expenses Secondary or minor revenues or expenses.

Owners' Equity The residual interest in the assets of the owners after all of the liabilities and obligations have been satisfied.

Paid-in Capital (Capital in Excess of Par) Any capital contributed in excess of the legal or par value of the stock issued by the firm.

Parent Company The company owning a controlled investee company.

Partial Income Tax Allocation This method is based on the presumption that the tax expense for the period should be the same for financial accounting purposes as the taxes payable for the period. However, in order not to misstate income tax expense for the period, you should allocate nonrecurring differences between periods.

Participating Right A right granted to some preferred stocks that allows them to receive dividends in excess of their stated rate.

Partnership An association of one or more individuals united for the purpose of transacting business.

Par Value A dollar amount per share that is the minimum contribution allowed if the stock is to be sold as fully paid.

Par Value Method The method of accounting that records treasury stock at its par value.

Past Service Costs The costs of giving employees credit for pension purposes from the date of their initial employment to the date of the adoption of the pension plan.

Patent An exclusive right granted by the U.S. Patent Office that enables its holder to use, manufacture, sell, or otherwise control the product or process patented without interference or infringement by others.

Pay-As-You-Go Method Pension expense is recognized when retirement payments are made.

Peer Review A review and evaluation of one CPA firm's quality of work by another CPA firm.

Pension Plan An arrangement whereby a company undertakes to provide its retired employees with benefits that can be determined or estimated in advance from the provisions of a document or documents, or from the company's practices.

Percentage-of-Completion Method A method of revenue recognition for long-term construction projects that recognizes revenues periodically based on the percent of construction completed.

Periodic Inventory System Inventory determined by physical count at the end of the accounting period.

Permanent Differences Differences between taxable income and pretax accounting income that will not turn around or reverse in later periods. They are the result of statutory differences between GAAP and the IRC.

Perpetual Inventory System System in which the purchases and sales of merchandise all flow through the inventory account, so it always should reflect the current balance.

Petty Cash Fund A small cash fund used to pay the minor expense items that a company incurs.

Physical Flow Inventory unit flow through the company.

Pledging of Receivables A method of providing collateral in negotiating a loan. Pledged accounts are billed and collected by the borrower.

Posting A process that transfers the journalized information to the ledger.

Preemptive Right A basic right of common stockholders that allows them to maintain their proportional share of ownership by purchasing their proportional share of any new issues of stock.

Preferred Stock A class of stock that is granted certain privileges, such as priority claims to assets and dividends, not accorded to common shareholders.

Premium The amount received above the face value of a bond when issued to yield less than the face (coupon) rate of interest.

Present Realizable Value The discounted value of expected future receipts.

Present Value Method Assets and liabilities are valued at the present value of future cash inflows or outflows.

Present Value of an Annuity The value today of a future promise to pay (receive) a fixed amount at regular intervals.

Present Value of a Single Sum The value today of a future promise to pay (receive) a single amount.

Price Index A ratio of the current year's inventory costs divided by the base year's inventory costs which is applied to the LIFO layer of that year under the dollar value LIFO method.

Price/Earnings Ratio (P/E Ratio) Market price per share divided by earnings per share.

Primary Earnings per Share Earnings per share calculations in which common stock and common stock equivalents are included.

Prior Period Adjustments Corrections of prior year's errors or adjustments that result from realization of income tax benefits of preacquisition operating loss carryforwards of purchased subsidiaries.

Prior Service Costs Pension costs that provide retroactive increases to employees from a change in an ongoing pension fund.

Profitability Measures Ratios used to analyze a firm's profits from operations.

Pro Forma As related to changes in accounting principle, pro forma information tells readers what would have appeared on the financial statements if the new accounting principle had been in use in the prior period.

Projected Benefit Cost Method The actuarial cost method in which the amount assigned to the current year usually represents the level amount (or an amount based on a computed level percentage of compensation) that will provide for the estimated projected retirement benefits over the service lives of either the individual employees or the employee group, depending on the method selected.

Promulgated Extraordinary Item Income statement classification of an item, event, or transaction as extraordinary without regard to the extraordinary item criteria; for example, SFAS *No. 4* requires that gains and losses on extinguishment of debt be aggregated and, if material, classified as an extraordinary item.

Promulgated GAAP The generally accepted accounting principles that have been developed by authoritative bodies and therefore are binding upon practicing members of the accounting profession.

Proof of Cash A four-column bank reconciliation that reconciles the book balance and the bank balance for cash.

Property Dividend A dividend paid in the form of noncash assets of the corporation.

Property, Plant, and Equipment (Fixed Assets) Includes all of the entity's long-lived tangible assets that are used to maintain the firm's operations.

Proportional Method A method of allocating the proceeds from the issuance of securities in a package on the basis of fair market value of each individual security.

Proprietorship A form of business organization where an individual transacts business and assumes complete control and responsibility for its operation.

Prospective Restatement Requires that the effects of an accounting change be integrated into the current and future financial statements.

Proven Reserves Mineral reserves that engineering and geological data indicate, with reasonable certainty, can be recovered from known reservoirs under current economic and operating conditions.

Purchase Commitment Contract to buy merchandise at a firm price at a future date.

Purchase Discounts Reductions in the price for early payment, accounted for on either a gross or net basis.

Qualified Pension Plan A plan that meets IRS rules to allow tax advantages to the employer, the employees, and the pension fund.

Quasi Reorganization A procedure to eliminate an accumulated deficit of a corporation without having to go through a complete legal reorganization.

Raw Materials Inventory Goods and natural resources used in the manufacture of a final product.

Realized Gains and Losses on Marketable Securities Gains and losses on the disposition of securities. Gains and losses from transferring securities between current and noncurrent portfolios and from declines in the value of securities in the noncurrent portfolio that are deemed "other than temporary" should be accounted for as if realized.

Receivables Turnover Net credit sales divided by average accounts receivable.

Reinstallments and Rearrangements Costs that are incurred to change plant layout or move machinery and are expected to benefit future periods.

Related Parties These include a parent company and its subsidiaries, an owner company and its joint ventures and partnerships, and investor/ investees provided that the investor has the ability to exercise significant influence over the operating and financing policies of the related party.

Relevance The degree to which information constitutes significant imput into the decision-making process.

Reliability The degree to which a decision maker can place faith in the accuracy of data supplied.

Replacement A repair substituting a new part for a similar, old part.

Replacement Cost—Inventory Market value used in lower of cost or market, means the cost of replacement either by purchase or by manufacture.

Replacement Cost The amount of cash (or its equivalent) that would have to be paid to acquire currently the best asset available to undertake the function of the asset owned (less depreciation or amortization, if appropriate).

Replacement Method Depreciation based on the cost of units purchased to replace existing returned units. The cost is adjusted for the salvage value of the retired units.

Representational Faithfulness Exists when the data are free from bias; the accountant who gathered or communicated the information introduced no bias into the measurement.

Research Activities A planned search or critical investigation aimed at the discovery of new knowledge with the hope that such knowledge will be useful in developing a new product or service or a new process or technique, or in bringing about a significant improvement in an existing product or process.

Retail Average Cost An inventory valuation technique that includes the beginning inventory value in the calculation of the cost-to-retail ratio, and also includes the net markups and the net markdowns.

Retail Average Cost—LCM An inventory valuation method that includes the beginning inventory value and net markups, in the calculation of the cost-to-retail ratio, but excludes the net markdowns.

Retail FIFO An inventory valuation technique that excludes beginning inventory value from the calculation of the cost-to-retail ratio and includes the net markups and net markdowns.

Retail FIFO—LCM An inventory valuation method that excludes the beginning inventory value from the calculation of the cost-to-retail ratio, includes net markups, but excludes net markdowns.

Retail LIFO An inventory valuation technique that requires the calculation of separate cost-to-retail ratios for the beginning inventory and the current period purchases. If the size of the inventory is increased, the added layer is valued at the current cost-to-retail ratio. If the size of the inventory is decreased, the cost-to-retail ratio existing in the layer of the opening inventory is used to reduce those layers.

Retail Method A method for estimating inventory value based on the relationship between cost and retail prices.

Retained Earnings The portion of owners' equity that is the accumulated net income not distributed as dividends.

Retirement Method Depreciation based on the cost (less salvages) of assets retired from service.

Retroactive Restatement Requires that financial statements previously issued be recast to reflect the impact of an accounting change.

Return on Assets Net income plus interest expense net of tax divided by average total assets.

Return on Common Stockholders' Equity Net income minus preferred dividends divided by average common stockholders' equity.

Return on Equity A percentage measure of the profits generated by a business that go to the owners of that business.

Return on Investment Net income divided by average total assets.

Revenue Inflows or other enhancements of assets of an entity or settlements of its liabilities (or a combination of both) during a period that includes delivering or producing goods, and rendering services or other activities that constitute the entity's ongoing major or central operations.

Revenue Expenditure Expenditures that are expected to benefit only the current period.

Revenue Realization Principle Revenue should not be considered earned for financial statement purposes until the earnings process is substantially complete and an exchange has taken place.

Revenue Recognition The process of measuring and reporting revenue.

Reverse Stock Split A transaction in which the par value of the stock is *increased*, and the number of shares outstanding is proportionately *decreased*.

Reversing Difference The difference between accounting and tax income that occurs when the original timing difference begins to turn around.

Sales Profit Margin Net income divided by net sales.

Sales-Type Lease A lease that gives rise to manufacturer or dealer profit (or loss). The fair value of the property at the inception of the lease is greater (or less) than the cost or carrying value of the asset.

Salvage Value The estimated value of an asset at the end of its useful life.

Scrip Dividend A distribution that is a promise to pay a cash dividend at some future date.

Secret Reserve A condition that can occur when stock issued for noncash consideration is undervalued, thus understating the asset and the contributed capital.

Secured Liabilities Those obligations secured by a creditor's lien on specific property owned by the firm.

Securities and Exchange Commission (SEC) An arm of the federal government responsible for supervising the operation of the interstate securities market; established in 1934.

Segment of a Business A component of an entity whose activities represent a separate major line of business or major class of customer.

Separate Entity Assumption States that every economic entity is an independent unit and is separate and distinct from its owner's.

Serial Bond Bond whose principal is payable in periodic installments.

Short-Term Notes Payable Notes that generally arise from cash borrowings from banks or other financial institutions; they may be partially or fully secured by the enterprise's assets.

Short-Term Obligations Liabilities that will require liquidation within the coming year or operating cycle, if longer.

Significant Influence In the absence of evidence to the contrary, ownership of 20% or more of the outstanding voting shares of another entity gives the investor the ability to exercise significant influence over the entity (equity method of accounting generally appropriate).

Simple Capital Structure One that consists of only common stock and has no potentially dilutive securities.

Simple Interest Interest is computed only on the principal amount.

Single-Step Income Statement An income statement that makes no attempt to distinguish between different types of revenues and expenses.

Sinking Fund Cash or other assets that are set aside to be used to repurchase bonds outstanding.

Specific Identification An inventory method in which the cost of each individual unit is matched with that unit and traced through the accounting system.

Specific Price-Level Changes Changes measured by looking at the change in the current cost or value of individual assets.

Spin-Off A distribution of stock that previously was held as an investment in another corporation.

Standard Cost Carefully predetermined unit cost, usually set by engineering estimates, labor contracts, or current market conditions.

Stated Interest Rate The rate specified on the bond. Also referred to as the *nominal rate*.

Stated Value An arbitrary amount set by the board of directors that establishes the legal capital requirement for no-par stock.

Statement of Changes in Financial Position The financial statement that discloses a company's *sources* and *uses* of funds during a given year.

Statement of Financial Position (Balance Sheet) Financial statement that presents the financial position of the company at a particular date.

Statement of Retained Earnings A reconciliation of the retained earnings balances presented on the two most recent balance sheets.

Statements of Financial Accounting Standards (standards) One of four distinct types of authoritative documents produced by the FASB.

Statutory Depletion Depletion provided by tax law that allows a company depletion based on a statutory percentage of the gross revenues from a natural resource.

Stock Dividend A dividend payable in the shares of stock of the corporation distributing the dividend.

Stockholder's Equity The claims of the owners of the firm against the assets owned by the firm.

Stock Option Plan A plan that grants employees the option to purchase a fixed number of shares of capital stock at a stated price during a specified time interval.

Stock Split A transaction that results in an *increase* in the number of shares outstanding and a proportional *decrease* in the par value of those shares.

Straight-Line Depreciation A method of depreciation that depreciates an asset over time on the basis of the number of years in the asset's useful life.

Subscription Contract A legal, binding contract for the sale and purchase of stock at a set price over a definite period of time.

Subsidiary Account Individual accounts making up a control account.

Subsidiary Company An investee company that is controlled by the investor company.

Successful Efforts A method of oil and gas accounting that capitalizes only those exploration costs that relate to successful wells.

Sum-of-the-Years'-Digits Depreciation A method of depreciation that depreciates assets on the basis of a decreasing fraction (remaining useful life/sum-of-the-years'-digits) multiplied by the assets' depreciable cost.

Supplies Inventory An inventory of small items that are used in the operations of the business.

Tangible Assets Assets having physical characteristics.

Technological Obsolesence Obsolesence caused by a change in the technology related to as asset.

Temporary Investments Investments in marketable securities or money accounts that are for less than a year.

Term Bonds Bonds in which the entire principal amount is due at a single date.

Terminal Funding Method Pension expense is recognized when retirement payments are made.

Timeliness The degree to which information reaches the decision maker within the proper time frame.

Time Period Assumption States that all relevant economic data can be segregated into separate, distinct, and identifiable time periods.

Times Interest Earned Earnings before interest and taxes divided by interest charges.

Time Value of Money A dollar received today is more valuable than a dollar received in the future since it can be invested and can earn interest.

Timing Differences These result from the fact that some items affect taxable income and pretax accounting income in different periods. Timing differences originate in one period and reverse or turn around in different periods.

Total Debt to Total Asset Ratio A ratio calculated by dividing total debt by total assets.

Trade Discounts The percentage discount off the list price quoted to customers.

Trademark (Tradename) A name, symbol, or other device used to identify distinctively a given product or organization.

Trade Notes Payable Formal written obligations to the enterprise's suppliers and vendors.

Trade Receivables Receivables that arise from the sale of goods and services to customers.

Treasury Stock Stock that has the characteristics of being issued but not outstanding. It has been repurchased and is held by the issuing corporation.

Treasury Stock Method Method that assumes that all options and warrants are exercised at the beginning of the period (or at the time of issuance if later) and that the proceeds obtained from exercise are used to purchase common stock.

Trial Balance A listing of all account balances as of a specific date.

Troubled-Debt Restructuring Occurs when the creditor, for economic or legal reasons related to the debtor's financial difficulties, grants a concession to the debtor it would not otherwise consider.

Unasserted Claims The company believes it may have a liability, but the claimant currently is not aware that s/he has a claim against the company.

Uncollectible Accounts Expense (Bad Debts Expense) The amount of receivables in a period that have been determined to be uncollectible.

Understandability The quality of information that enables users to perceive its significance.

Unfunded Plan A plan in which the employer does not make payments directly to a funding agency.

Unguaranteed Residual Value The estimated residual value of the leased property exclusive of any portion guaranteed by the lessee or by a third party unrelated to the lessor.

Unit of Production Depreciation A depreciation method that charges depreciation on the basis of the ratio of current units produced to total lifetime production of an asset.

Unpromulgated GAAP Generally accepted accounting principles that have been developed by nonauthoritative bodies, or that have evolved over time.

Unrealized Gains and Losses on Marketable Securities Gains and losses resulting from the valuation of marketable securities at lower of cost or market.

Unsecured Liabilities Those obligations secured only by the general credit worthiness of the borrowing entity.

Unusual or Infrequently Occurring Item An item, event, or transaction that meets one but not both the criteria for being classified as extraordinary.

Useful Life The period of time in which an asset will be useful in an economic sense.

Usefulness Accounting information must aid the decision maker with respect to the economic decisions being made.

User Needs Assumption States that the users of financial statements are investors and creditors interested in general purpose financial information that enables them to predict the future cash flows of the entity.

Verifiability The degree to which independent parties, using essentially the same measuring technique, measure the same event and reach the same conclusion.

Vertical Analysis An analysis that provides an expression of each item in a financial statement in a given period as a percent of one specific item, referred to as the *base*.

Vested When an employee's benefits become irrevocable.

Vesting Schedule A schedule that is provided in the pension agreement and is used to determine the amount vested.

Warrants Certificates that grant the holder the right to purchase a stated number of share of stock at a specified price within a specified time period.

Watered Stock A condition that can occur when stock issued for a noncash consideration is overvalued, thus overstating the asset received and the contributed capital of the corporation.

Wealth The value of all the rights and possessions owned by the firm at a point in time, less all of the obligations that the firm is required to pay.

Working Capital Current assets less current liabilities.

Work-In-Process Inventory Items in production that are partially complete at the end of the accounting period.

Yield Rate The effective interest rate on bonds issued. Determined by market interest rates and relative risk. Also referred to as the *market rate*.

Index

Abandonment, of plant assets, 420
Accelerated Cost Recovery System
(ACRS), 452–54, 650
Accelerated methods of
depreciation, 449–54
Accounting
basic assumptions, 28–31
basic principles, 31–38
defined, 2
historical development of, 2, 3
modifying conventions, 38
primary uses of accounting
information, 3, 4
process, 75–97
See also Accounting conventions;
Accounting principles;
Accounting process
Accounting by lessees
capital lease method, 737–38
classification of leases, 735–37
disclosures required, 757–60
leveraged leases, 765–72
operating lease method, 738–41
real estate leases, 749–54
sales with leasebacks, 754–56
subleases, 748–49
Accounting by lessors
classification of leases, 735–37
direct financing lease method,
743–46
disclosures required, 757–60
initial direct costs, 746–47
leveraged leases, 765–72
operating lease method, 746
real estate leases, 749–54
sales-type lease method, 741–43
sales with leasebacks, 754–56
subleases, 748
Accounting changes
change in an accounting estimate,
934–37
change in an accounting principle,
925–34
change in a reporting entity,
939–40

combined estimate-principle
change, 937–39
disclosures required, 955–57
income statement presentation,
1004–6
methods of reporting change,
924–25
See also Accounting principles,
changes in; Accounting
estimates, changes in
Accounting conventions
conservatism, 38
materiality, 38
Accounting errors. *See* Error
correction
Accounting estimates, changes in
combined estimate-principle
changes, 937–39
described, 934–37
income statement presentation,
1005
multi-period estimate changes,
935
single-period estimate changes,
935
Accounting principles
comparability, 36–37
full disclosure, 37
historical cost, 31–32
matching, 34–36
revenue realization, 32–34
substance over form, 37–38
Accounting Principles Board. *See*
APB
Accounting principles, changes in
changes in income tax, 927–29
combined estimate-principle
change, 937–39
described, 925–34
exceptions to general rules,
932–34
general rules for changes in,
926–32
income statement presentation,
1004–5

interim financial reporting,
932
presentation of comparative
statements, 929–31
Accounting process
accounting cycle, 78
accounting model, 75–78
adjusting data, 87–94
collecting data, 78–79
closing the books, 94–97
posting data, 81–87
purpose of, 74–97
recording data, 79–80
See also Computerized accounting
systems; Financial statements
*Accounting Research and
Terminology Bulletins*, 329 n
*Accounting Research and
Terminology Bulletins*,
AICPA, 329 n
Accounting Research Bulletins
(ARBs), 6
Accounting Research Studies
(AICPA), 15
Accounting Research Study No. 2,
1089 n.4
Accounting Research Study No. 6,
1178 n.6
Accounting Research Study No. 8,
702 n.1, 704
Accounting Research Study No. 10,
500 n
Accounting Review, 7, 16
Accounting Series Releases (ASR),
13
*Accounting Terminology Bulletin
No. 1*, 6
Accounting theory
evolution of, 22–38
modifying conventions, 38
Accounts payable, 530–31
Accrual method, accounting for
warranty and guarantee costs,
545–49
Accrual method of accounting, 34

Accruals
defined, 89
kinds of, 89–90
Acid-test ratio, 1267–68
Activity ratios
asset turnover, 1270
inventory turnover, 1269
receivables turnover, 1268–69
Additions, to plant assets, 418
Adjusted trial balance, 94
Adjusting entries
need for, 88
treatment of, 92
Aging schedule, 191
AICPA (American Institute of
Certified Public Accountants)
committees of, 6, 15
continuing education programs, 16
defined, 15
development of APB, 6–7
development of Public Oversight
Board, 15
Journal of Accounting, 16
role in developing GAAP, 6,
15–16
role in sponsoring scholarly
research, 15–16
self-initiated reorganization,
14–15
AICPA Committee on Accounting
Procedure (CAP), 6, 839, 840,
883
AICPA Committee on Terminology,
6
*AICPA Professional Standards—
Auditing, Management
Advisory Services, Tax
Practice*, 173 n.2
All-inclusive approach, 57
American Accounting Association
(AAA)
Accounting Review, 16
research sponsored by, 16
American Institute of Certified
Public Accountants (AICPA).
See AICPA
Annuity due
calculation of future value of
annuity, 143–44
calculation of present value of
annuity, 146–48
defined, 143
Antidilutive securities, 890 n
APB (Accounting Principles Board)
development of, 6–7
evolution of Opinions, 7
evolution of Statements, 7
replacement by FASB, 7
role in developing GAAP, 6

*APB Interpretation of Opinion No.
15*, 888 n
APB Opinion No. 2, 462 n.2
APB Opinion No. 3, 1089 n.5
APB Opinion No. 4, 462 n.3
APB Opinion No. 5, 734–35
APB Opinion No. 6, 184 n.9, 398,
421
APB Opinion No. 7, 734–35
APB Opinion No. 8, 702 n.2, 704,
707, 709, 712, 713, 717, 718,
719
APB Opinion No. 9, 57 n.8, 59, 61,
604, 872, 884, 994
APB Opinion No. 10, 56 n.7
APB Opinion No. 11, 649, 650 n.2,
654, 655, 658, 669, 672, 675–77
APB Opinion No. 12, 421 n.16,
465, 852–53, 855
APB Opinion No. 14, 873 n, 878
APB Opinion No. 15, 872 n.1, 878,
884, 900, 903
APB Opinion No. 16, 503 n
APB Opinion No. 17, 487 n, 488,
489, 490, 505
APB Opinion No. 18, 226 n.4, 237
APB Opinion No. 19, 1088 n.3,
1089, 1096–1100, 1108–9,
1120–21, 1130, 1132
APB Opinion No. 20, 337 n, 460,
548, 925, 926, 932, 1004, 1005,
1109
APB Opinion No. 21, 184 n.7, 194,
201, 406, 529, 577, 578, 590
APB Opinion No. 22, 421 n.17, 465
APB Opinion No. 25, 880 n
APB Opinion No. 26, 603, 604
n.11, 875
APB Opinion No. 27, 734
APB Opinion No. 28, 354, 932 n.4,
1056–60, 1061
APB Opinion No. 29, 408 n, 413,
421, 837
APB Opinion No. 30, 59 n.14, 62,
419, 420, 421, 604, 612, 995,
1002, 1109
APB Opinion No. 31, 734
APB Statement No. 3, 1178 n.7
APB Statement No. 4, 528 n.2,
987, 988
ARB No. 43, 173 n.1, 201, 274,
279, 315, 487 n, 505, 533, 540,
707, 883, 992
ARB No. 45, 286 n
ARB No. 47, 704
ARB No. 49, 883–84
ARB No. 51, 226 n.2
Articulation, 75–76
ASR No. 117, 1089 n.6

ASR No. 143, 533
ASR No. 149, 678
ASR No. 158, 471 n
ASR No. 190, 14, 289, 1030,
1178–79 n.9, 1200, 1208
ASR No. 253, 471 n
ASR No. 257, 471 n
ASR No. 268, 793
Assets
balance sheet presentation,
98–100
defined, 98, 1032
See also Donated assets;
Intangible assets;
Nonmonetary assets; Property,
plant, and equipment;
Self-constructed assets
Assets, self-constructed, 401–2, 488
Asset turnover ratio, 1270
Average cost method
described, 323
retail average cost, 365, 367–68
retail average cost—LCM, 365,
369–70
under periodic inventory system,
323–24
under perpetual inventory
system, 324–25
Averaging method, treatment of
actuarial gains and losses, 718

Balance sheet
classifications in, 1031–35
described, 75, 986
early emphasis on, 50–51
limitations of, 1031
major sections of, 98–103
purpose and usefulness of, 1031
restated, 1191
Bank accounts
branch, 170
depository (cash clearing), 170
general cash, 170
imprest, 170
payroll, 170
savings, 171
Bankers Rule, 136
Bank reconciliations, 176–81. *See
also* Four-column bank
reconciliations
Bargain purchase option, 736 n.2,
749, 750, 762
Bargain renewal option, leases, 762
Base stock method, 328–29
Bearer or coupon bonds, defined,
586
Bond investment
accounting for acquisition of
bonds, 605–7

accounting for bonds by investor, 605–9
discount and premium amortization, 607–9
effective interest amortization method, 607–8
sale of bonds before maturity date, 609
straight-line amortization method, 607–8
See also Bond premium and discount; Bonds payable
Bond premium and discount
amortization by investors, 607–9
amortization, serial bonds, 629–31
bonds issued between interest dates, 596–601
determination of bond prices, 588–90
early extinguishment of debt, 602–3
effective interest amortization method, 594–96
presentation on balance sheet, 590–92
straight-line amortization method, 594
subsequent entries, 600–601
subsequent entries after bond issue date, 592–96
See also Bonds; Bonds payable; Serial bonds
Bonds, defined, 584. *See also* Bond investment; Bonds payable; Serial bonds
Bonds outstanding method, amortization of serial bond premium or discount, 629–30; 632–33
Bonds payable
accounting for bonds by borrower, 588–602
bond sinking fund provisions, 602
determination of bond prices—premium and discount, 588–91
early extinguishment of debt, 602–5
effective interest amortization method, 594–96
expenses incurred when issuing bonds, 601–2
issuance between interest dates, 599–600
nature of, 584–87
straight-line amortization method, 594
subsequent entries after bond issue date, 592–96

See also Bond premium and discount; Bond investment; Bonds
Bonus agreements, 542
Book value per share ratio, 1276
Boot, defined, 408
Buildings, cost of, 400–401

Callable bonds, 603
Callable preferred stock, 792
Capital lease method
criteria for capital lease classification, 735–36
lessee accounting and reporting for, 737–38
lessor accounting and reporting for direct financing leases, 743–46
lessor accounting and reporting for sales-type leases, 741–43
Capital leases
classification by lessees, 735–36
classification by lessors, 735–36
disclosure requirements, 757–60
types of, 737
See also Leases; Real estate leases
Capital stock
accounting for, 794–98
balance sheet presentation, 101
incremental method, 797–98
issuance of securities in a package, 796–98
items included in, 1035
nature of, 786
proportional method, 797
stock issued for cash, 795
stock issued for noncash consideration, 795–96
Cash
bank reconciliations, 176–81
control of, 173–76
imprest petty cash systems, 181–83
in bank accounts, 170–71
internal control, 173–76
nature and composition of, 170–73
on hand, 171–73
restricted, 173
using receivables to generate, 196–201
See also Bank reconciliations; Imprest petty cash systems
Cash concept of income, 62–63
Cash discounts
described, 186
gross method, 187
net method, 186–87
with asset acquisition, 405

Cash dividends, 836
Cash flow per share ratio, 1276–77
Changes. *See* Accounting changes
Closing the books, 94–97
Collections for third parties and payrolls
compensated absences, 538–39
payroll taxes and employee withholding taxes, 536–38
sales taxes, 536
Commission on Auditor's Responsibilities, 14
Committee on Accounting Procedure (CAP). *See* AICPA Committee on Accounting Procedure
Committee on Terminology (AICPA). *See* AICPA Committee on Terminology
Common stock, 786, 787–88
Common stock equivalents, 889
Comparability principle, 36–37
Comparative income statements, 992
Compensated absences, 538–39
Compensatory stock option plans, 880
Completed-contract method
defined, 56
for long-term construction contracts, 296
Complex capital structures, 884–85, 888–89
Compound interest, 136–37
Comprehensive income tax allocation, 657–58
Computerized accounting systems, 97
Conditional liabilities
bonus agreements, 542
income taxes payable, 539
other, 543
property taxes payable, 540–41
Congress
initiation of studies of accounting profession, 14
Metcalf Committee report, 14
Moss Committee report, 14
role in developing GAAP, 14–15
Conservatism principle, 38, 279
Consigned merchandise, 270
Consolidated financial statements, 77
Constant dollar accounting
advantages and disadvantages of, 1197–98
calculation of purchasing power gains or losses, 1191–95
described, 1179–80

Constant dollar accounting *(Cont.)*
  monetary and nonmonetary
    items, 1180
  purchasing power gains and
    losses on net monetary items,
    1180–81
  restatement procedures–
    comprehensive illustration,
    1183–97
  restating income statement
    items, 1182–83
  restating nonmonetary assets and
    liabilities, 1181–82
  restating nonmonetary items,
    1182
  See also Current value
    accounting
Constant dollar statements,
    1176–77, 1180, 1197
Construction-type contracts
  accounting for, 292–96
  completed-contract method, 296
  percentage-of-completion method,
    292–95
  revenue recognition methods,
    33–34, 57
  valuation of inventory, 286
Consumer Price Index, 53
Consumer Price Index for All
    Urban Consumers (CPI-U),
    1182
Contingency
  accounting for, 543–45
  defined, 543
Contingent agreements, 901–3
Contingent liabilities
  accounting for contingencies,
    543–45
  accrued, 545–50
  defined, 543
  footnote disclosure, 552
  litigation and other claims, 551
  not accrued, 550–52
  premiums, 549–50
  trading stamps, 550
  warranty and guarantee costs,
    545–49
Contingent rentals, 764
Contributed capital
  accounting for, 793–801
  accounting for capital stock,
    794–98
  balance sheet presentation, 101
  costs of issuing stock, 801
  disclosures required, 812–14
  items included in, 1035
  stock subscriptions, 798–801
  See also Stockholders' equity
Contributory pension plans, 703

Control account, 86
Controlling interest, 224–26
Conversion costs, defined, 266
Convertible bonds, defined, 586
Convertible debt
  accounting for, 873–76
  book value method, 874–76
  described, 872–76
  market value method, 874–76
Convertible preferred stock, 791,
    878–79
Convertible securities, computation
  of primary earnings per share,
    890–93
Copyrights, 492
Corporations
  advantages of corporate form,
    784–85
  common stock, 788–89
  defined, 784
  forming, 785–86
  nature of the capital stock, 786
  par and no-par stocks, 787
  See also Stockholders' equity
Cost allocation
  defined, 92–93
  how to record, 93
  types of, 93–94
Cost flow methods, inventories
  comparison of, 325–28
  cost flow, defined, 315
  described, 316–25
  disclosure requirements, 338–40
Cost method, stock investments,
    229
Cost of goods sold, income
  statement presentation, 104
Credits, defined, 77
Credit cards, accepting, 199
Cumulative restatement
  computational analysis of
    cumulative and retroactive
    restatement, 949–55
  defined, 924
  journal entry approach, 949–52
  worksheet approach, 952–55
Current assets
  balance sheet presentation, 98,
    1032–33
  items included in, 1032–33
Current cost accounting
  advantages and disadvantages of,
    1208–10
  balance sheet items, 1202–3
  complete illustration, 1202–10
  described, 1200–1202
  income statement items, 1203–8
  major components of current cost
    income statement, 1202

  See also Constant dollar
    accounting; current
    cost/constant dollar accounting
Current cost/constant dollar
  accounting
  advantages and disadvantages of,
    1215–16
  balance sheet, 1210–11
  described, 1210
  income statement, 1211–12
  realized holding gains and losses,
    1212
  unrealized gains and losses,
    1212–15
Current cost depreciation, 1233–36
Current cost method, for
  determining current value,
  1200
Current liabilities
  accounts payable, 530–31
  balance sheet presentation, 100
  classification of liabilities, 529
  collections for third parties and
    payrolls, 535–39
  contingent, 543–52
  current maturities of long-term
    debt, 532–33
  defined, 100, 529
  definition of liabilities, 528–29
  deposits and advances from
    customers, 552
  determinable in amount, 530–35
  determination and measurement
    of, 530–55
  disclosure requirements, 553–56
  dividends payable, 535
  items included in, 1034
  liabilities conditional on
    operations, 539–43
  obligations arising from executory
    agreements, 552
  short-term notes payable,
    531–32
  short-term obligations to be
    refinanced, 533–35
  trade notes payable, 531
  valuation of, 529–30
  See also Collections for third
    parties and payrolls;
    Conditional liabilities;
    Contingent liabilities;
    Liabilities
Current operating approach, 57
Current portfolio
  defined, 230
  equity securities, 231–34
  See also Lower of cost or market
    method
Current ratio, 1267

Current value accounting
    current cost, 1200
    described, 1198
    development of, 1178–79
    net realizable value, 1199
    present value of future cash
        flows, 1198–99
    replacement cost, 1199–1200
    See also Current cost accounting

Debenture bonds, defined, 586
Debits, defined, 77
Deferred annuity, 148
Deferred method of income tax
        allocation
    applications of, 661–68
    described, 658–59
    group-of-similar-items basis,
        662–66
    individual item basis, 662
    with and without method, 666–68
Deferred payment contracts
    acquisition of property, plant,
        and equipment, 405–7
    installment method, 34
Defined benefit plans
    accounting for, 706–17
    actuarial cost methods, 709
    defined, 702–3
    determining pension expense,
        707–9
    FASB Statement No. 35, 718–19
    recording pension expense,
        709–17
Defined contribution plans
    accounting for, 706
    defined, 703
Depletion, of plant assets
    calculating, 464
    cost depletion, 464
    defined, 463
    determining cost of, 463–64
    disclosures required, 464
    statutory depletion, 464
Depreciation, of plant assets
    accelerated cost recovery system,
        452–54
    accelerated methods, 449–54
    asset's salvage value, 445
    asset's useful life, 445–46
    cost of asset, 445
    double-declining balance method,
        451–52
    elements of, 445–48
    fixed-percentage-on-declining-
        balance method, 450–51
    group and composite methods,
        456–57
    inventory method, 455

methods of, 448–57
    nature of, 444–45
    partial year depreciation, 458–59
    replacement funds, 458
    retirement and replacement
        methods, 455–56
    revision of estimates, 460–61
    special depreciation methods,
        454–57
    special problems, 458–61
    straight-line method, 449
    sum-of-the-years'-digits method,
        449–50
    units of production method,
        448–49
Dilutive securities
    convertible debt, 872–76
    convertible preferred stock,
        878–79
    debt issued with stock warrants,
        876–78
    described, 610, 872
    stock option plans, 879–83
    See also Convertible debt; Stock
        option plans
Direct financing leases
    definition of, for lessors, 737
    initial direct costs, 747
    lessor recording and accounting
        for, 743–46
Discontinued operations
    defined, 62, 995
    disclosures required, 1001–2
    formal plan of disposal, defined,
        995
    income statement presentation,
        995–1001
    See also Disposal of a segment of
        a business
Discounted present value concept,
        of income, 63
Disposal of a segment of a business
    determination of gain or loss on,
        995–1001
    income statement presentation,
        995–1001
Dividend payout ratio, 1272
Dividends
    accounting for, 835–43
    availability of cash, 833–34
    contractual restrictions, 834
    cumulative and noncumulative,
        789
    dividend policy, 834
    dividend preference, preferred
        stock, 788–89
    dividends on treasury stock, 842
    factors affecting dividend
        decisions, 833–35

in arrears, 535, 789
    kinds of, 836–42
    legality of, 833
    limitations on preferred stock,
        792
    liquidating, 842–43
    payable, 535
Dollar-value LIFO
    described, 330, 334
    dollar-value retail LIFO method,
        370–83
Dollar-value retail LIFO method
    advantages of, 370–71
    computing inventory cost, 373–83
Donated assets, 413–14
Donated treasury stock, 808–9
Double-declining balance method of
        depreciation, 451–52

Early extinguishment of debt
    accounting for, 603
    described, 602–3
    nature of gain or loss, 604–5
    period in which gain or loss
        recognized, 603
Earned capital section of balance
        sheet, items included in, 1035
Earnings per share (EPS)
    APB Opinion No. 15, 885
    common stock equivalents, 889
    comprehensive illustration,
        907–10
    contingent agreements, 901–3
    convertible securities, 890–93
    defined, 872
    disclosures required, 903–5
    fully diluted earnings per share,
        889–90
    income statement presentation,
        1007–8
    primary earnings per share, 889
    simple vs. complex structures,
        884–85
    stock options and warrants,
        893–901
    weighted average common
        shares, 885–87
Earnings per share ratio, 1270–71
Economic Recovery Tax Act of
        1981, 452
Effective interest amortization
        method, of bond premium and
        discount
    bond investments, 607–8
    bonds payable, 594–96
    serial bonds, 630–32, 633
Employee Retirement Income
        Security Act. *See* ERISA
Employee withholding taxes, 536–38

Equipment, cost of, 401
Equity method
  change from, 243–44
  change to, 244–47
  described (accounting for equity
    investments), 237–47
  determining significant influence,
    226–27
  disclosure requirements, 251
  losses exceed carrying amount, 243
  purchase price greater than book
    value, 238–42
  purchase price less than book
    value, 242–43
ERISA (Employee Retirement
  Income Security Act of 1974),
  705, 709
Error correction
  computational analysis for
    cumulative and retroactive
    restatement, 949–55
  definition of accounting error, 940
  errors made and discovered in
    different periods, 942–49
  errors made and discovered in
    same period, 941–42
  errors not requiring balance
    sheet adjustment, 946–49
  errors requiring balance sheet
    adjustment, 943–46
  examples of accounting errors,
    1006
  income statement presentation,
    1006
Exchange, of assets
  acquisition through, 408–12
  disposition by, 420
  exchange of dissimilar assets,
    408–10
  exchange of similar assets—gain
    involved, 410–12
  summary of, 412
Exchange transaction, 79
Executory agreements, 552
Expenses
  APB's definition of, 987
  income statement presentation, 103
  of a period, 988
Extraordinary items
  defined, 59, 1002–3
  disclosure of, 59–61
  income statement presentation,
    106, 1002–4

Factoring trade receivables, 198–99
FASB (Financial Accounting
  Standards Board)
  defined, 3–4
  development of, 7–13

development of new disclosure
  requirements for oil and gas
  industry, 472
evolution of Concepts, 9
evolution of Interpretations, 9
evolution of Statements, 9
evolution of Technical Bulletins, 9
objectives of financial reporting,
  51
position on income statement, 51
replacement of APB, 7
role in developing GAAP, 1, 7–13
FASB Discussion Memorandum, 9
FASB Discussion Memorandum,
  "An Analysis of Issues Related
  to Employers' Accounting for
  Pensions and other
  Postemployment Benefits,"
  702 n.4
FASB Discussion Memorandum,
  "An Analysis of the Issues
  Related to Reporting
  Earnings," 58 n.9
FASB Discussion Memorandum,
  "Employers' Accounting for
  Pensions and other
  Postemployment Benefits," 705
FASB Exposure Draft, 9
FASB Exposure Draft, "Financial
  Reporting in Units of General
  Purchasing Power," 1178 n.8
FASB Interpretation No. 3, 705 n.12
FASB Interpretation No. 6, 496 n
FASB Interpretation No. 18,
  1056–57, 1061 n
FASB Interpretation No. 24,
  753 n.9
FASB Interpretation No. 28, 879 n
FASB Statement of Financial
  Accounting Concepts No. 1, 3,
  4 n.1, 22, 51, 224
FASB Statement of Financial
  Accounting Concepts No. 2,
  22 n.2
FASB Statement of Financial
  Accounting Concepts No. 3,
  50 n.1, 528, 530, 544, 601, 661
FASB Statement No. 2, 448 n.2,
  491, 492, 494, 497
FASB Statement No. 3, 932 n.5,
  1056, 1060, 1061
FASB Statement No. 4, 604 n.13,
  612, 875, 1120
FASB Statement No. 5, 188 n.11,
  543–45, 549, 550, 551, 552, 748
FASB Statement No. 6, 529 n, 533,
  610
FASB Statement No. 12, 227 n.7,
  228, 230, 247

FASB Statement No. 13, 735 n,
  747, 749, 750, 754, 762, 764
FASB Statement No. 14, 1046 n.3,
  1047, 1049, 1055
FASB Statement No. 15, 611 n.15,
  614, 616, 618, 619
FASB Statement No. 16, 62 n.16,
  1008
FASB Statement No. 17, 764 n.12
FASB Statement No 18, 1046 n.4,
  1047
FASB Statement No. 19, 471
FASB Statement No. 21, 872 n.3,
  1046, 1047
FASB Statement No. 24, 1046 n.4,
  1047, 1049
FASB Statement No. 25, 472 n
FASB Statement No. 26, 753 n.10
FASB Statement No. 27, 736 n.5
FASB Statement No. 28, 754–55 n
FASB Statement No. 29, 757, 764
  n.13
FASB Statement No. 30, 1046 n.4,
  1047, 1049
FASB Statement No. 33, 14, 289,
  465 n.6, 1172, 1179, 1182, 1198,
  1200, 1207, 1208, 1216–24
FASB Statement No. 34, 276 n.4,
  402, 405
FASB Statement No. 35, 705 n.15,
  718, 719
FASB Statement No. 36, 705 n.14,
  719
FASB Statement No. 37, 675 n.16,
  676
FASB Statement No. 43, 538 n
FASB Statement No. 45, 493 n
Federal Insurance Contributions
  Act. See FICA
Federal Unemployment Tax Act
  (F.U.T.A.), 537
FICA (Federal Insurance
  Contributions Act), 536–37
FIFO (First-in, first-out) method
  advantages and disadvantages of,
    318–19
  comparison of cost flow methods,
    325–28
  described, 317–19
  retail FIFO, 365, 367
  retail FIFO—LCM, 365,
    368–69
Financial Accounting Foundation,
  7–8
Financial Accounting Standards
  Advisory Council, 8
Financial Accounting Standards
  Board. See FASB
Financial Executive Institute, 16

Financial reporting
  concept of income, 986–88
  differences in FASB restatement
    procedures, 1217
  disclosure of financial
    information, 1036–43
  FASB disclosures, 1222–23
  FASB Statement No. 33, 1216–23
  financial statements required, 986
  income statement, 989–1008
  objectives of, 21, 51
  restatement procedures required
    by *Statement No. 33*, 1218–22
  statement of retained earnings,
    1008–10
  the future, 1223–24
  See also Constant dollar
    accounting; Current value
    accounting; Price changes
Financial stability ratios
  book value per share ratio, 1276
  cash flow per share ratio,
    1276–77
  defined, 1275
  times interest earned ratio, 1276
  total debt to total assets ratio,
    1275
Financial statement analysis
  evaluation of, 1282–84
  ratio analysis, 1264–77
  trend and percentage analysis,
    1277–82
  See also Ratio analysis; Trend
    and percentage analysis
Financial statements
  accounting assumptions, 28–31
  accounting principles, 31–38
  balance sheet, 98–103
  content and objects of (SFAC
    No. 1 and 2), 21–28
  footnotes to, 37
  full disclosure principle, 37, 1264
  income statement, 103–6
  statement of changes in financial
    position, 106–7
  statement of retained earnings, 107
  supplementary financial
    information, 108
  See also Financial statement
    analysis
Finished goods inventory, costs
  included in, 267
First-in, first-out. *See* FIFO
Fixed-percentage-on-declining-
  balance method of depreciation,
  450–51
Footnote disclosure
  comprehensive illustration of,
    1036–43

  described, 108, 1030
  for departures from GAAP, 7
Four-column bank reconciliations,
  181, 206–8
Franchises, 493
Full disclosure principle, 37, 1030,
  1264
Fully diluted earnings per share,
  889–90
Funded pension plans, defined, 703
Funds, presentation of on
  statement of changes in
  financial position, 106–7,
  1089–90
Future value of an annuity, 134,
  141–42
Future value of an annuity due,
  143–44
Future value of annuity of $1 in
  arrears table, 1429–30
Future value of an ordinary
  annuity, 142–43
Fuure value of a single sum, 134,
  137–39
Future value of $1 table, 138,
  1425–26

GAAP (Generally Accepted
    Accounting Principles)
  benefits vs. costs, 23–24
  comparability, 26
  decision maker characteristics, 23
  defined, 2, 5
  development of, 6–17
  income measurement, 27–28
  materiality, 26–27
  need for, 5–6
  position on construction
    contracts, 57
  purpose of, 5
  qualitative objectives of, 22–27
  quantitative objectives of, 27–28
  revenue recognition, 49–65
  understandable information, 24–25
  useful information, 24–25
  wealth measurement, 27
  See also Promulgated GAAP;
    Unpromulgated GAAP
Generally Accepted Accounting
    Principles. *See* GAAP
General price-level changes,
  1172–73
GNP Implicit Price Deflector, 53
Going concern assumption, 29, 32
Goodwill
  accounting for, 500–502
  components of, 500
  definition of purchased goodwill,
    488, 501

  described, 497–505
  estimating value of business,
    503–5
  negative, 502–3
Gross profit method, basis for
    estimating inventory
  application of, 356–59
  assumptions underlying, 356
  calculation of gross profit
    percentages, 356–59
  comprehensive illustration of,
    361
  described, 355–62
  evaluation of, 361–62
Group and composite methods of
  depreciation, 456–57
Group-of-similar-items basis
  described, 662–66
  gross change method, 662–63
  illustration of methods, 663–66
  net change method, 663

Historical cost, as basis for
  valuation of inventories, 273–74
Historical cost principle, 31–32,
  1176–77
Horizontal analysis, 1277–80

Implicit interest, 144
Imprest petty cash systems, 181–83
Improvements and replacements, of
  plant assets, 416–18
Income
  concept of, defined, 27, 986–88
  recognition of, 33
  See also Income measurement;
    Income reporting
Income bonds, defined, 586
Income measurement, 50–65. *See
    also* Income reporting
Income reporting
  alternative concepts of income,
    62–65
  cash concept, 62–63
  current operating vs. all-inclusive
    income, 57–58
  disclosures required, 58–62
  discontinued operations, 62
  discounted present value concept,
    63
  emphasis on income, 50–51
  estimation of, 52–54
  extraordinary items, 59–62
  market value concepts, 63–65
  nature of, 50–58
  prior period adjustments, 61–62
  realization principle, 54–57
  realization vs. recognition of
    revenues, 54

Income statement
comparative income statements, 992
comprehensive illustration of, 1010
described, 75, 103–6, 986
evolution of, 50–51
format, 989–92
four basic elements of, 986–87
multiple-step format, 990–91
restated, 1191, 1195, 1197
sections of, 992–1008
single-step format, 989–90
See also Multistep income statement; Single-step income statement
Income tax accounting
accounting for net operating losses, 668–75
differences between pretax accounting income and taxable income, 647–50
income statement presentation, 1007
interperiod income tax allocation, 650–68
permanent differences, 649–50
timing differences, 649–50
See also Interperiod income tax allocation; Net operating losses
Income taxes payable, as current liabilities, 539
Individual item basis, 662
Inflation, effects of. *See* Price changes
Initial direct costs, leasing transactions, 746–47, 764
Installment accounting method, 34, 56
Installment sales, 270
Intangible assets
abnormal write-offs, 490
accounting after acquisition, 489–90
balance sheet presentation, 99
copyrights, 492
deferred charges, 493
defined, 487
disclosures required, 505–7
disposal by sale or exchange, 490
franchises, 493
goodwill, 497–505
internally developed, specifically identifiable, 488
internally developed, unidentifiable, 488
items included in, 1034
leases, 492
normal amortization, 489–90

organization costs, 493
patents, 490–92
purchased, specifically identifiable, 488
purchased, unidentifiable, 488
research and development costs, 493–97
specifically identifiable, 490
trademarks and tradenames, 492
valuation at acquisition, 487–88
See also Goodwill; Research and development costs
Interaccount transfers, 171
Interest
compound, 136–37
defined, 133
simple, 135–36
Interest costs
asset acquisitions, 402–5
inventories, 276
Interim reporting
defined, 1056
evaluation of, 1061
problems created by, 1056
requirements and disclosure requirements of *APB Opinion No. 28*, 1057–60
requirements of *FASB Interpretation No. 18*, 1061
requirements of *FASB Statement No. 3*, 1060
Internal control
categories of, 174
described, 173
elements of, 174–76
Interperiod income tax allocation
applications of deferred method of comprehensive tax allocation in practice, 661–68
APB Opinion No. 11 disclosures, 675–77
APB's position, 658
deferred method, 658–59
defined, 647
different methods of, 658–61
disclosures required, 675–78
liability method, 659
need for, 650–54
net of tax method, 659–61
partial vs. comprehensive income tax allocation, 655–58
procedures for applying, 654–55
SEC required disclosure, 678
tax allocation in practice, 661–68
See also Deferred method of income tax allocation
Interpolation, 149
Intraperiod tax allocation, defined, 647

Inventories
accounting for long-term construction contracts, 286
average cost method, 323–25
base stock method, 328–29
basic cost flow methods, 316–25
classifications of, 266–69
comparison of cost flow methods, 325–28
cost estimation methods, 355–62
defined, 265
disclosure of cost flow assumption, 338–40
disclosures required, 287–90, 383–85
dollar-value retail LIFO method, 370–83
effects of inventory errors, 276–79
FIFO, 317–19
gross profit method, 355–62
impact on economy, 264–65
installment sales, 270
interest costs, 276
LIFO, 319–23
lower of cost or market, 279–81
merchandise in transit, 269
merchandise on consignment, 270
other valuation methods, 328–30
periodic and perpetual inventory systems, 270–73
physical composition of, 269–70
physical flow and cost flow, 315–16
purchase commitments, 287
purchase discounts, 275–76
relative sales value method, 286
restatement procedure—constant dollar, 1185–87
retail inventory method, 362–70
retail LIFO method, 373–74
specific identification, 316–17
standard cost system, 329
valuation of, exceptions to historical cost, 279–87
valuation of, historical cost, 273–79
variable or direct costing, 330
See also average cost; FIFO; Gross profit method; LIFO; Lower of cost or market; Retail inventory method
Inventory method of depreciation, 455
Inventory turnover ratio, 1269
Investment credit, 461–63
Investments, stock. *See* Stock investments
Involuntary conversion, of plant assets, 420

Journal, defined, 79
Journal entry, composition of, 79
Journal of Accountancy, 16

Land, cost of, 399
Last-in, first-out method. *See* LIFO
Leases
  accounting for initial direct costs,
    746–47
  accounting for subleases, 747–49
  advantages of, 734
  classification criteria, 735–37
  classified as intangible assets, 492
  defined, 733–34
  development of authoritative
    lease accounting literature,
    734–35
  disclosures required, 757–60
  leveraged leases, 765–72
  real estate leases, 749–54
  sales with leasebacks, 754–56
  See also Accounting by lessees;
    Accounting by lessors; Capital
    lease method; Leveraged
    leases; Operating lease method;
    Real estate leases
Ledger, defined, 83–84
Ledger entry, composition of,
    84–86
Leverage, defined, 576, 1031
Leveraged leases
  accounting for, 767–72
  advantages for lessors, 765
  described, 737, 765–67
Liabilities
  balance sheet presentation,
    100–101
  defined, 100, 528–29, 1032
  See also Current liabilities;
    Long-term liabilities
Liability method, of income tax
    allocation, 659
LIFO (Last-in, first-out) method
  comparison of cost flow methods,
    325–28
  complexities of, 330–37
  described, 319–20
  dollar-value LIFO method,
    330–34
  dollar-value retail LIFO method,
    370–83
  initial adoption of, 337
  interim reporting of, 336–37
  LIFO—periodic, 321
  LIFO—perpetual, 321–23
  LIFO valuations, 336
  measuring income vs. current
    financial position, 50–51
  other problems, 336–37

price index used, 334–35
  retail LIFO method, 372–73
LIFO retail method. *See* Retail
    LIFO method
Liquidating dividends, 842–43
Liquidity ratios
  acid-test ratio; 1267–68
  current ratio, 1267
Litigation, recording of liabilities,
    551
Lock-box service, 171
Long-term assets, defined, 398. *See
    also* Property, plant, and
    equipment
Long-term contracts
  for construction industry, 33–34
  revenue recognition methods,
    33–34
Long-term debt
  current maturities of, 532–33
  definition of noncurrent liabilities,
    529
  See also Long-term liabilities;
    Troubled debt restructurings
Long-term investments
  balance sheet presentation, 98–99
  items included in, 1033
  See also Bond investments
Long-term liabilities
  accounting for serial bonds,
    627–33
  balance sheet presentation,
    100–101
  bond investment, 605–9
  bonds payable, 584–605
  defined, 576
  deposits and advances from
    customers, 552
  dilutive debt securities, 610
  financial statement presentation,
    618–23
  items included in, 1034
  mortgages payable, 610
  notes exchanged for property,
    goods, or services, 581–84
  notes issued solely for cash,
    578–79
  notes issued with unstated rights
    or privileges, 579–81
  other forms of, 609–10
  short-term debt expected to be
    refinanced, 533–35, 610
  troubled debt restructurings,
    610–18
  valuation of, 576–84
  See also Bond investment; Bonds
    payable; Long-term debt;
    Serial bonds; Troubled debt
    restructurings

Loss carrybacks, 669–70
Loss carryforwards
  described, 670–71
  tax benefit assured beyond
    reasonable doubt, 672–73
  tax benefit not assured, 671–72
Lower of cost or market method
  definition of *market*, 280
  described, 230–37
  disclosures required, 247–51
  equity securities—current
    portfolio, 231–34
  equity securities—noncurrent
    portfolio, 234–36
  evaluation of, 285
  methods of applying, 281–82
  recording reductions of inventory
    cost to market, 282–85
  required by *FASB Statement No.
    12*, 227
  retail average cost—LCM, 365,
    369–70
  retail FIFO—LCM, 365, 368–69
  transfers between portfolios, 237
  valuation of inventories, 279–81
  See also Marketable equity
    securities
Lump Sum purchases, 412–13

Maintenance and repairs, of plant
    assets, 415–16
Markdown, 364
Markdown cancellation, 364
Marketable equity securities
  current portfolio, 231–34
  FASB definition of, 228–29
  noncurrent portfolio, 234–36
  permanent declines in value,
    236–37
  transfers between portfolios, 237
  use of to acquire property, plant,
    and equipment, 407
  See also Stock investments
Market method, stock investments,
    229–30
Market value concepts of income
  net realizable value, 64–65
  replacement cost, 64
Markup, 359–64
Markup cancellation, 364
Marshall, John (Chief Justice),
    definition of corporation, 784
Matching principle, 34–36
Materiality, 38
Medicare, 537
Merchandise in transit, passage of
    title rule, 269
Merchandise inventory, costs
    included in, 267

Merchants Rule, 136
Metcalf Committee, 14
Metcalf, Senator Lee, 14
Model Corporation Act, 802, 810
Modified treasury stock method,
    897–901
Monetary assets, constant dollar
    accounting, 1180, 1183
Monetary liabilities, constant dollar
    accounting, 1180, 1183
Mortality tables, 706
Mortgage bonds, defined, 586
Mortgages payable, 610
Moss Committee, 14
Moss, Rep. John, 14
Multi-Employer Pension Plan
    Amendments Act of 1980, 705
    n.11
Multiple-step income statement
    described, 104–6
    format, 990–91
Municipal Finance Offices
    Association, 16

National Association of Accountants
    (NAA), 16
Net of tax method of income tax
    allocation, 659–61
Net operating losses
    accounting for loss carrybacks,
        669–70
    accounting for loss
        carryforwards, 670–73
    described, 668–69
    effect of timing differences,
        673–75
Net realizable value
    advantages and disadvantages of,
        64–65
    defined, 64
    for determining current value,
        1199
Nominal dollar statements, 1176,
    1177, 1180, 1197
Noncallable bonds, 603
Noncompensatory stock option
    plans, 879–80
Noncontributory pension plans, 703
Noncurrent portfolio
    defined, 230
    equity securities, 234–36
    permanent declines in value,
        236–37
    See also Lower of cost or market
        method; Marketable equity
        securities
Nonmonetary assets
    constant dollar accounting, 1180,
        1181–82, 1185–91

defined, 408
exchanges of, 408–12
See also Intangible assets
Nonmonetary liabilities, constant
    dollar accounting, 1180, 1181–82,
    1185–91
Nontrade receivables, 183
No-par stock, defined, 787
Notes exchanged for property,
    goods, or services
    non-interest-bearing notes,
        581–84
    note payable with unreasonably
        low interest, 584
    recording of, 581
Notes issued solely for cash,
    578–79
Notes issued with unstated rights
    or privileges, 579–81
Notes receivable
    defined, 183
    disclosures required, 196
    discounting, 199–201
    pledging, 196
    valuation of, 194–96

Obsolescence of assets, 446
Oil and gas accounting
    described, 470–72
    full-cost method, 470
    successful efforts method, 470
Old Age, Survivor, and Disability
    Insurance (O.A.S.D.I.), 536–37
Operating cycle
    defined, 98
    with regard to current liabilities,
        529
Operating expenses, income
    statement
    presentation of, 104–05
Operating lease method
    criteria for capital lease
        classification, 735–36
    lessee accounting and reporting
        for, 738–41
    lessor accounting and reporting
        for, 746
Operating leases
    classification by lessees, 735
    classification by lessors, 735–36
    disclosures required, 757–60
    initial direct costs, 747
    See also Leases; Real estate
        leases
Operating revenue, income
    statement presentation of,
    104
Opinions of the Accounting
    Principles Board, 7

Ordinary Annuity
    calculation of future value of
        annuity, 142–43
    calculation of present value of
        annuity, 145–46
Originating differences, 661
Other assets section of balance
    sheet, items included in, 1034
Other liabilities section of balance
    sheet, items included in, 1034
Owners' equity, defined, 1032. See
    also Stockholders' equity

Pacioli, Luca, 2
Partial income tax allocation,
    655–57
Par value, defined, 101
Par value stock, defined, 787
Patents, 490–92
Payroll taxes, 536–38
Pension costs accounting
    accounting and reporting by
        defined benefit plans, 718–19
    accounting for defined benefit
        plans, 706–17
    accounting for defined
        contribution plans, 706
    actuarial gains and losses, 717–18
    disclosures required, 719–21
    historical development of pension
        GAAP, 704–5
    nature of pension plans, 702–4
    pension accounting, 705–17
    See also Defined benefit plans
Pension plan, defined, 702
Percentage-of-completion method,
    for long-term construction
    contracts, 33–34, 57, 292–95
Percentage of receivables method
    comparison of sales and
        receivables methods, 193–94
    described, 190–93
Percentage of sales method
    comparison of sales and
        receivables methods, 193–94
    described, 189–90
Periodic inventory system
    cost allocations, 93
    described, 270–73
    differences between periodic and
        perpetual, 270–73
    with average cost method,
    with LIFO, 321
Periodicity, 30
Permanent differences, 648–49
Perpetual inventory system
    described, 270–73
    differences between perpetual
        and periodic, 270–73

with average cost method, 324–25
with LIFO, 321–23
Physical flow, defined, 315
Plant assets. *See* Property, plant, and equipment
Pledging of receivables, 196
Posting, 82–83
Preferred stock
asset preference, 792
callable, 792
convertible, 791
cumulative and noncumulative, 789
defined, 786–88
dividend preference, 788–89
limitations of, 792–93
mandatory redemption, 793
participating or nonparticipating, 789–91
rights of, 788–92
Premium, as contingent liability, 549–50
Prepaid items, 90–92
Present value method, for determining current value, 1198–99
Present value of an annuity, 134, 144–48
Present value of an annuity due, 146–48
Present value of an annuity of $1 in arrears table, 1431–32
Present value of an ordinary annuity, 145–46
Present value of a single sum, 134, 139–41
Present value of $1 table, 141, 1427–28
Price changes
FASB Statement No. 33, 1216–23
the future, 1223–24
general prive-level vs. specific price-level changes, 1172–73
official pronouncements, accounting for, 1177–79
problems with financial statements not adjusted for, 1175–76
relationship between general and specific price changes, 1173–75
types of, 1172–75
See also Constant dollar accounting; Current cost accounting; Current cost/constant dollar accounting; Current value accounting
Price/earnings ratio, 1271–72
Price index, with dollar-value LIFO, 334–35

Primary earnings per share, 889
Prior period adjustments
classification of, 61–62
income statement presentation, 1008
items included in, 1008
reporting, 61
Producer's Price Index, 53
Profitability ratios
dividend payout ratio, 1272
earnings per share ratio, 1270–71
price/earnings ratio, 1271–72
return on common stockholders' equity ratio, 1274–75
return on investment ratio, 1273–74
sales profit margin ratio, 1272–73
Promulgated GAAP
AICPA committees, 6–7
Congress, 14–15
defined, 5
development of, 6–15
FASB, 7–13
government promulgated GAAP, 13–15
profession promulgated GAAP, 6–13
SEC, 13–14
Property dividends, 836–37
Property, plant, and equipment
abandonment, 420
acquisition for cash, 405
acquisition of, 405–14
acquisition through exchanges, 408–12
acquisition under deferred payment plans, 405–7
acquisition with equity securities, 407
additions, 418
asset impairment, 421
balance sheet presentation, 99
characteristics of, 398
cost of buildings, 400–401
cost of equipment, 401
cost of land, 399
cost of self-constructed assets, 401–2
costs incurred after acquisition, 414–19
depletion of, 463–65
depreciation of, 444–61
disclosures required, 421–23, 465–68
discovery value, 421
disposition of, 419–20
donated assets, 413–14
exchanges of, 420
improvements and replacements, 416–18

initial acquisition cost, 399–405
interest costs, 402–5
investment credit, 461–63
involuntary conversion, 420
items included in, 1033–34
lump sum purchases, 412–13
maintenance and repairs, 415–16
oil and gas accounting, 470–72
reinstallments and rearrangements, 418
sale of plant assets, 419
valuation of, 398–99
See also Depletion; Depreciation
Property taxes payable, as current liabilities, 540–41
Prospective restatement, 924–25
Public Oversight Board (AICPA), 15
Purchase commitments, 287
Purchase discounts, 275–76

Qualified pension plans, 703–4
Quasi reorganizations, 849–52

Railroads, accounting for investment in track, 443
Ratio analysis
activity ratios, 1268–70
described, 1264–67
financial stability ratios, 1275–77
kinds of ratios, 1265–67
liquidity ratios, 1267–68
profitability ratios, 1270–75
See also Activity ratios; Financial stability ratios; Liquidity ratios; Profitability ratios
Raw materials inventory, costs included in, 266
Real estate leases
leases involving equipment and real estate, 752–53
leases involving land and building, 750–52
leases involving land only, 750
leases involving part of building, 753
profit recognition of sales-type leases of real estate, 753–54
Receivables
financial statement disclosures, 201–5
nature and types of, 183–84
notes receivable, 194–96
other, 201
trade accounts receivable, 184–88
uncollectible accounts, 188–94
using receivables to generate cash, 196–201
See also Notes receivable; Trade accounts receivable

Receivables turnover ratio, 1268–69
Regulation S-X (SEC), 13
Reinstallments and
    rearrangements, of plant
    assets, 418
Relative sales value method, 286
Replacement cost
    as way of determining current
        value, 1199–1200
    defined, 64, 1199
    SEC requirements, 64
Reporting entity, change in
    described, 939–40
    examples of, 1006
    income statement presentation,
        1006
Research and development (R & D)
        costs
    contract services, 497
    costs associated with, 496–97
    costs not covered by GAAP, 497
    definition of, 494–96
    equipment and facilities, 496
    GAAP relating to, 494
    indirect costs, 497
    intangibles purchased from
        others, 496–97
    materials, 496
    personnel, 496
Reserve Recognition Accounting
    (RRA), 471
Retail inventory method
    advantages of, 363
    application of, 365–70
    assumptions of, 362
    comparison of alternative
        methods, 370
    described, 362–70
    dollar-value retail LIFO, 370–83
    retail average cost, 365, 367–68
    retail average cost—LCM, 365,
        369–70
    retail FIFO, 365, 367, 368
    retail FIFO—LCM, 365, 368–69
    retail LIFO, 365, 372–73
    terminology, 363–64
Retail LIFO method, 372–73
Retained earnings
    appropriations of, 846–49
    balance sheet presentation, 101
    contractual restriction, 846–48
    disclosures required, 852–55
    functions of, 832
    legal restriction, 846
    restriction of, for treasury stock,
        810–11
    voluntary restriction, 848–49
    See also Stockholders' equity
Retained earnings statement,
    restatement of, 1190–91, 1195

Retirement and replacement
    methods of depreciation,
    455–56
Retroactive restatement
    computational analysis of
        cumulative and retroactive
        restatement, 949–55
    defined, 924
    journal entry approach, 949–52
    worksheet approach, 952–55
Return on common stockholders'
    equity ratio, 1274–75
Return on investment ratio,
    1273–74
Revenue
    APB's definition, 986–87
    defined, 50
    income statement presentation,
        103
    measurement of, 49
    when earned, 54–55
    See also Income; Revenue
        realization; Revenue
        recognition
Revenue realization, defined, 54
Revenue realization principle,
    32–33, 54–57
Revenue recognition, defined, 54
Reversing differences, 662

Sales profit margin ratio, 1272–73
Sales taxes, as current liabilities,
    536
Sales-type (capital) leases
    definition of, for lessors, 737
    initial direct costs, 747
    lessor recording and accounting
        for, 741–43
    profit recognition of sales-type
        leases of real estate, 753–54
Sales with leaseback, 754–56
Salvage value, of plant assets, 445
Scrip dividends, 838
SEC (Securities and Exchange
        Commission)
    arguments for and against
        reserve recognition accounting,
        471
    creation of, 13
    enforcement of promulgated
        accounting principles, 13
    evolution of Accounting Series
        Releases (ASR), 13
    evolution of Regulation S-X, 13
    evolution of Staff Accounting
        Bulletins, 13
    replacement cost requirements,
        14
    requirements for replacement
        cost, 29

    role in developing GAAP, 1,
        13–14
Secured liabilities, 100–101
Securities and Exchange
    Commission. See SEC
Securities Exchange Act of 1934,
    13, 992
Segment reporting
    described, 1043–49
    disclosures required, 1055
    evaluation of, 1055–56
    identification of a reportable
        segment, 1049–54
Self-constructed assets. See Assets,
    self-constructed
Separate entity assumption, 30
Serial bonds
    accounting for issuance of,
        627–29
    bonds outstanding method,
        629–30
    defined, 586, 627
    discount or premium
        amortization, 629–31
    effective interest method, 630–32
    redemption before scheduled
        maturity, 632–33
Short-term notes payable, 531–32
Short-term obligations expected to
        be refinanced
    classification as long-term debt,
        535, 610
    classification on balance sheet,
        533–35
Simple capital structures, 884,
    887–88
Simple interest, 135–36
Single-step income statement
    described, 103–4
    format, 989–90
Sinking funds, bonds, 602
Smith, Adam, Wealth of Nations, 3
Social Security taxes, as current
    liabilities, 536–37
Specific identification method, of
    inventory validation, 316–17
Specific price-level changes,
    1172–73
Spreading method, treatment of
    actuarial gains and losses, 718
Staff Accounting Bulletins (SABs),
    SEC, 13
Standard cost system, 329
Statement of changes in financial
        position
    cash basis, 1126–30
    comparison of procedures for
        cash and working capital,
        1126–27
    computing cash flows, 1127–30

described, 106–7, 986, 1088
disclosures required, 1130–33
evolution of, 1088–89
measuring changes in financial position, 1089–91
preparing the, general model, 1091–1100
T-account approach, 1135–37
working capital basis, 1100–1118
See also Worksheet approach
Statement of financial position. See Balance sheet
Statement of retained earnings, 57, 107, 986, 1008–10. See also Retained earnings
Statements of Financial Accounting Concepts (SFAC), FASB, 9, 22
Statements of Financial Accounting Standards (FASB), 9
Statements of the Accounting Principles Board, 7
Stock dividends, 838–42
Stockholders' equity
accounting for contributed capital, 793–801
appropriations of retained earnings, 846–49
balance sheet presentation, 101–3
common stock, 787–88
defined, 75–76
disclosure requirements for contributed capital, 812–14
disclosure requirements for retained earnings, 852–55
dividends, 833–43
forms of business organization, 784–87
issuance of stock, 783–801
other retirements of stock, 811
preferred stock, 788–93
quasi reorganizations, 849–52
reacquisition of stock, 801–11
stock split, 843–46
treasury stock, 801–11
See also Capital stock; Contributed capital; Corporations; Dividends; Preferred Stock; Retained earnings; Treasury stock
Stock investments
accounting for equity investments, subsequent to acquisition, 228–47
controlling interest, 224–26
determining appropriate accounting method, 224–27
disclosures required, 247–52

lack of significant influence, 227
reasons for, 223–24
recording the investment, at date of acquisition, 227–28
significant interest, 226–27
See also Cost method; Equity method; Lower of cost or market method; Marketable equity securities; Market method
Stock option plans
characteristics of, 880
defined, 879
determination of amount of compensation cost, 880
determination of proper accounting period to which compensation cost should be allocated, 881
disclosure requirements for, 883
Stock options
inclusion in earnings per share computations, 893–901
modified treasury stock method, 897–901
treasury stock method, 895–97
Stock split
alternative form of stock split, 844–45
defined, 843
ordinary stock split, 843–44
reverse stock split, 845–46
Stock subscriptions
described, 798–801
financial statement presentation, 799
unpaid, 800–801
Stock warrants
described, 876–78
detachable, 876–78
inclusion in earnings per share computations, 893–901
modified treasury stock method, 897–901
nondetachable, 876–78
treasury stock method, 895–97
Straight-line amortization method, of bond premium and discount
bond investment, 607
bonds payable, 594
Straight-line method, of depreciation, 449
Subleases
accounting by original lessee (sublessor), 748–49
accounting by original lessor, 748
described, 747–48
Subsidiary account, 86
Substance over form principle, 37–38

Sum-of-the-years'-digits method of depreciation, 449–50
Supplies inventory, 267
Sweeney, Henry, Stabilized Accounting, 1177

T-account approach, 1135–37
T-account, defined, 86
Technical Bulletins (FASB), 9
Term bonds, defined, 585–86
Time period assumption, 30, 32, 53, 56–57
Times interest earned ratio, 1276
Time value of money, 132–35, 149–51
Timing differences
applications of deferred method of interperiod tax allocation, 661–68
described, 649–50
net operating losses, 673–75
Total debt to total assets ratio, 1275
Trade accounts receivable
assignment of, 197–98
cash discounts, 186–87
credit cards, 199
described, 183–85
factoring, 198–99
other deductions, 187
sale of, 198
trade discounts, 185–86
See also Uncollectible accounts receivable
Trade discounts, 185–86, 276
Trademarks and tradenames, 492
Trade notes payable, 531
Trading stamps, 550
Treasury stock
accounting for acquisition of, 802–8
characteristics of, 801
cost method, 802–4
dividends on, 842
donated, 808–9
par value method, 805–8
restriction of retained earnings for, 810–11
retirement of, 809–10
Treasury stock method, 895–97
Trend and percentage analysis
defined, 1277
horizontal analysis, 1277–80
vertical analysis, 1280–82
Trial balance, 87
Troubled debt restructurings
accounting for, 612–16
controversy over FASB Statement No. 15, 618
definition by FASB Statement No. 15, 611

Troubled debt restructurings *(Cont.)*
described, 610–11
full satisfaction through
asset/equity transfer, 612–14
modification of terms, 614
no gain or loss recognized,
614–16
recognition of gain or loss, 616
summary of troubled debt
transactions, 616–18

Uncollectible accounts receivable
allowance method, 188
comparison of sales and
receivables methods, 193–94
direct write-off method, 188
percentage of receivables
method, 190–93
percentage of sales method,
189–90
Unit of measure assumption, 28–29,
32
Units of production method, of
depreciation, 448–49
Unpromulgated GAAP
AICPA, 15–16
American Accounting
Association, 16

defined, 5, 15
development of, 15–17
other sources of, 16–17
Unsecured liabilities, 101
Useful life, of plant asset,
445–46
User needs assumption, 31

Variable costing, 330
Vertical analysis, 1280–82
Vested employee benefits, 703, 708
n.22, 721 n.33

Warranty and guarantee costs
cash basis method, 548–49
defined, 545
expense method, 545–48
sales method, 545–48
Wealth of Nations (Smith), 3
Weighted average, computing the,
885
With and without method, of
treating originating and
reversing differences, 666–68
Work-in-process inventory, costs
included in, 266–67
Worksheet, preparation of,
111–15

Worksheet approach-working
capital basis
amortization of discount/premium
on bond investments, 1118
amortization of discount/premium
on bonds payable, 1117–18
comparison of procedures for
cash and working capital,
1126–27
comprehensive illustration,
1119–26
cumulative effect of change in
accounting principle, 1113–14
deferred income taxes, 1116–17
discontinued operations, 1112–13
extraordinary items, 1109–11
format and procedures, 1101–8
gains (losses) on sale of current
assets, 1114–15
investments in equity method
investees, 1115–16
special gains and losses in
general, 1108–9
special problem areas, 1108–18
underlying foundation, 1100–1101

Zero-coupon or zero-interest bonds,
586–87

†